The Cook's Encyclopedia

The Cook's Encyclopedia

Ingredients and Processes

TOM STOBART

edited by Millie Owen

Illustrations by
Ruth Bornschlegel, Alice Golden,
Millie Owen, and Nina L. Williams

1817

HARPER & ROW, PUBLISHERS, New York
Cambridge, Philadelphia, San Francisco,
London, Mexico City, São Paulo, Sydney

Illustration credits

Ruth Bornschlegel: p. 357
Alice Golden: pp. 11, 18, 83, 84, 85, 105, 114, 116, 121, 126, 154, 163, 192, 215, 252, 286, 303, 313, 321, 332, 339 r., 340, 354, 376, 411, 416, 432, 437 l.,439, 454, 484, 492, 501, 505
Millie Owen: pp. 32, 36, 38, 97, 137, 151, 182, 256, 260, 275, 290, 306, 339 l., 356 r., 374, 375, 388, 389, 410, 438
Nina L. Williams: pp. 16, 37, 91, 145, 174, 230, 237, 272, 278, 307, 312, 356 l., 368, 420, 437 r., 441, 444, 471, 499

FIRST U.S. EDITION

Designer: C. Linda Dingler

Library of Congress Cataloging in Publication Data

Stobart, Tom.
 The cook's encyclopedia.

 1. Cookery—Dictionaries.   I. Owen, Millie.
II. Title.
TX349.S74   1981   641'.03'21   81-47785
ISBN 0-06-014127-1   AACR2

81   82   83   84   85   10   9   8   7   6   5   4   3   2   1

Editor's Note

As I read the British edition of this book, I got the impression that Tom Stobart has visited all the markets, restaurants, and wilds from the south pole to the north, sampling everything along the way. His knowledge of food is enormous—and you know why when you follow his experiences at making haggis while on one of his numerous expeditions, collecting marigold seeds in a Tibetan monastery garden, hearing nettle beer explode in the larder when he was a child, eating fresh whale steaks in the Antarctic, and cooking wallaby with Australian aborigines.

But Stobart's writing is not only a pleasure to read; it presents firsthand information that is hard to find elsewhere. He authoritatively explains the chemistry of culinary processes and the nutritive composition of foods along with other details on edible products you may encounter in foreign cookbooks or while traveling around the world. In addition, he provides fascinating and little-known facts on food and cooking procedures plus selected recipes.

To make this book more accessible and useful to the American reader, I have added some entries on foods that are special to our country, including native game, fish, wild vegetables, and other items that are of particular interest to the U.S. cook and the wanderer to our woods for mushrooms or to ethnic restaurants for fresh local fare. For English food regulations I have substituted the latest information from U.S. government agencies. European products have been explored further as they have become amalgamated into our cuisine, and British terms have been Americanized—all in an effort to make this an even more useful guide and reference to food and cooking throughout the world.

—Millie Owen

Northfield, Vermont
May 1981

Introduction

Ingredients are the fundamentals of cookery, and every cook who hopes to excel should know about them. Great chefs and restaurateurs are likely to pay just as much attention to choosing their ingredients as they do to choosing their recipes—the two are inseparable.

When I was making films on European cooking, I got to know a number of distinguished chefs from various countries. Many of them worked in towns with good open-air markets. As I have always been fascinated by markets (and my love for them is one of the reasons why this book came to be written), I would visit them as soon as they opened, which was well before even an early breakfast. In the beginning, I was surprised to see a certain master chef, one of that exclusive body the Maîtres Cuisiniers de France, was at the market before me. He was not young and was certainly wealthy enough to take it easy, but still he had come himself to prod the strawberries, smell the melons, and squeeze the onions. Later, I came to accept this keenness as normal, as I observed chefs doing the same in country after country.

Great chefs become marvelously choosy and dogmatic. They are likely to tell us that *coq au vin* absolutely requires a real Bresse chicken and thyme from Provence, so that any idea of making it in America or Australia is absurd. In many ways, that is the right approach, even if it is a little chauvinistic. We might equally ask if a Frenchman in France could bake a proper New England johnnycake or a Yorkshire pudding.

Of course, some ingredients—olive oil, for instance—are more critical than others, but even seemingly mundane things, like salt, are worthy of close attention. The very air can come into the equation. It is not just that local dishes do not taste right or that recipes do not work with the wrong ingredients—using the right ones is among the secrets of good cooking.

There is, of course, a no-nonsense view that holds that if a recipe calls for a Bresse chicken, the operative word is chicken and any chicken, even a broiler, will do. This is a sure route to mediocrity, since it will inevitably eliminate the subtleties that are the mark of fine cooking. The more "nonsense," then, the better. Why waste effort trying to imitate classic recipes with only substitutes for the ingredients they demand? Surely it is better to discover the virtues of what is actually available. We should remember, too, that inspired improvisation by cooks in circumstances where only a limited range of ingredients were obtainable led to the invention of some of the world's great dishes.

No book can list every ingredient that is locally available or discuss every nuance. Nor can it be totally objective about such subjective qualities as taste. Personal judgment cannot be avoided—in any case, there is no such thing as a good but impersonal cookery book. What I have tried to do is to list as wide a range of ingredients as possible, to give some of their background, and to identify their particular characteristics. They should have an individuality and an identity beyond mere appearance—a brown root or a white powder. It is the specific qualities of ingredients that give the cook something to build on.

While I hope that this book will provide entertainment for people who like to browse in cookbooks (as I do), my aim has been to offer practical advice to cooks who buy unfamiliar ingredients and try to use them. Today, shops and markets offer the most staggering variety of produce. In them, you can drool over anything from bottled insects to dried duck's feet and long for advice. "Oh, those!" the shop-keeper may well say. "Some Tibetans or Koreans from up the road come in for them, but God knows how they cook them. We just get them from the wholesaler." It is possible that, after boiling the things for several hours, you will find that they are pan scourers.

With the jet age, the world's food has entered a phase of explosive evolution, and anyone who is essentially curious is likely to have a hard time keeping up. Indeed, while writing this book, I have sometimes felt like a hunter tracking the Yeti; it became evident that the Yeti was walking faster than I was. New ingredients crop up faster than they can be tried out—which should not be a cause for despair but rather of rejoicing at the richness that is available to us. At least by mastering the usual ingredients and processes, we can have more time to devote to the unusual.

This is not a recipe book, but recipes have been included for a variety of reasons. In some cases, they have been chosen simply to illustrate the use of an ingredient, or how to prepare it in ways other than those commonly used in American or British cooking. For instance, nuts are not just for eating at Christmas but can make subtle additions to the consistency and flavor of every course. Recipes are also given so that expatriates can make basic ingredients for themselves when they are living out of reach of suitable suppliers. Others are there because showing how something is made may be the best way of defining or describing it. The rest are there just because I felt like putting them in or because one of the many people who have helped with the book wanted some particular recipe. The same freedom has been taken with the methods and the science. In general, I have put in what I remember that I once did not know myself and what I still have to look up, often in books on agricultural botany or geography or biochemistry or nutrition rather than on cookery. I have also tried to straighten out old confusions. Again, even though the book has grown far beyond its intended size, there has had to be selection, as the subject is infinite.

I am frequently asked why someone who has spent so much time traveling and "exploring" should want to write books about food instead of concentrating on such excitements as man-eating tigers. Food, though, is one of the greatest of all travel subjects—people who fly around the globe but never eat outside the international hotels are hardly to be described as travelers. Their only contact with foreign lands is through the soles of their shoes; they never become involved. Anthropologists, on the other hand, sometimes go as far as to marry a native of the country they want to study, which is hardly a practical solution for the traveler, who is unlikely to spend more than a few months in any country (it is also liable to create little problems). Visiting a place and eating the food that the people there enjoy at home or on their feast days is also a way of becoming involved in local life. Those who have smelled the aroma of garlic and Gauloises, eaten *tapas* or *meze,* or chewed grilled meat wrapped in entrails will understand why, as a traveler, I became interested in cooking. They are the kindred souls that I had particularly in mind when I was writing this book. My aim has been to provide a reference source for cooks who are adventurous in spirit, whether they are able to travel widely or must find their culinary adventures at home.

ABOUT THIS BOOK

Contents. The majority of the entries in this book deal with the ingredients and processes used in cooking. The ingredients that I have included are in general of sufficient culinary importance to be sold somewhere in the world. Very many things that grow wild can also be eaten or at least made edible and used in cooking to an extent that depends on the cook's determination and ingenuity (or sometimes eccentricity). Although there are various books about edible wild things, these can relate only to a particular country or area. A similar effort on a worldwide scale would be endless; on the whole, the wild animals and plants covered here are, at least locally, objects of commerce. Even so, I have been rather sparing in the number of entries allotted to one category of wild food that is very widely sold: fish and shellfish come in such a multitude of species, many of them rather restricted in distribution, that I have dealt only with the main edible groups. Finally among the list of intentional exclusions, I should mention that I have not gone into cuts of meat. Again, regional variation is the reason. Because not just the names but the actual cuts can differ even between different areas of the same country, any straightforward translation tables are likely to be misleadingly oversimplified. In any case, those outlines of carcasses divided up with neat lines into named areas are moderately uninformative. The best way of learning about the cuts of meat you can buy is from the butcher who actually produces them.

Arrangement. The entries are arranged alphabetically and cross-referenced. Words preceded by stars (★) can be looked up for further information relevant to the entry in which they appear. However, the absence of a star does not mean the absence of an entry for the word, merely that looking it up will not yield much that is germane to the matter in hand.

Foodstuffs often go under so many different names that it would have been easy to swamp the whole book with cross-references for every imaginable synonym. Two restrictions have been applied to save the day here. First, only the most important dialect names, archaic names, and spelling variants have been included (a particularly rich source of cross-references could have been alternative transliterations from, say, Arabic). Second, I have taken advantage of the undoubted intelligence of my readers by doing away with cross-references from the whole of a name to its second word. Thus, you will not be given a cross-reference to take you from brown sugar to sugar or from red mullet to mullet. Where the destination is not the second word of the name, a cross-reference is, of course, provided, as from butter bean to lima bean.

Units. Much of the English-speaking world is at present in an awkward stage of partial metrication. A large part of the population, especially its older members, can cope only with the traditional units, while school graduates now emerge into society thinking entirely metric. The rest of us switch uneasily back and forth between the old units and the metric ones. At present, and probably for some years to come, the only sensible course in a cookbook is to include both units.

In the American edition of this book, metric units are given in parentheses following U.S. measurements. Anyone who cares to check the conversions will quickly find that they vary considerably in their accuracy. The rule here is a very simple one: conversions have been made only as accurate as they need to be, which is to say pretty accurate for baking, where quantities are often critical, and often quite approximate elsewhere. The abbreviations that have been used for the various units are the conventional ones with the exception of liters, for which the Italian abbreviation lt has been chosen as being less confusing typographically than the more usual l. The various units are covered in some detail in the entry on weights and measures.

Scientific names. Popular names for plants or animals can often be confusing, with the same thing having a variety of names or, worse still, the same name applying to a variety of things. Scientific names are supposed to sort out the confusion by being internationally accepted. Unfortunately, though, the scientists have managed to create some muddles of their own and have had to ape the College of Heralds in unscrambling confusions in nomenclature. For example, two biologists may independently have given a name to what later turns out to be the same species; the older of the two names is the one that sticks (unless, of course, it has previously been used by someone else as a name for another species altogether). Groupings into genera, families, and so on are meant to reflect relationships and to make up a sort of genealogical table. But since there are no church registers in evolution, taxonomists have to work on the available evidence, so that generic names (the first word in the name of any species) tend to be changed. To make a biological name unambiguous, you have to add the name of the person who first described the species (and ideally the date of the description). You will then know that when you are talking about white mustard as *Sinapis alba* Linnaeus, you are referring to the same species that other authorities have called *Brassica alba* or *Brassica hirta,* which is all very clear for a scientist. For the purposes of this book, such extremes of scientific pedantry seem unnecessary and the scientific name that seems to be most commonly used has been adopted without the name of its author. For the most part, scientific names are there either for precision or just as an extra piece of information that might be useful. There are, however, some things such as edible fungi and exotic fish and shellfish that have no popular names in English. Where a number of species of the same genus have been referred to in the same entry, the convention has been adopted of abbreviating the generic name on its second and subsequent appearances, as in *Brassica napus* and *B. rapa.*

Translations. Entries for the more usual ingredients and processes give translations in French, German, Italian, and Spanish. For processes the translation is always the infinitive, i.e., the French for boiling is given as *bouillir*—literally "to boil."

Sources. Books that have been important as sources of information have been acknowledged in the particular entries for which they have been used, and the publisher has been given for the edition that was consulted. Some books, such as Alan Davidson's invaluable works on seafood, therefore receive quite a number of mentions. There are, however, a number of titles that have been consulted for a large number of entries. Five that have been at hand throughout the writing of this book are *Food Science—A Chemical Approach* by Brian A. Fox and Allan G. Cameron (University of London Press, 1970), *Success in Nutrition* by Magnus Pyke (John Murray, 1975), *Teaching Nutrition and Food Science* by Margaret Knight (Batsford, 1976), *The Oxford Book of Food Plants* by S. G. Harrison, G. B. Masefield, and Michael Wallace (Oxford University Press, 1969) and my own *Herbs, Spices and Flavourings* (Penguin Books, 1978). In addition, the following have been useful:

Rosemary Brissenden, *South East Asian Food* (Penguin, 1972).
Elizabeth David, *French Provincial Cooking* (Penguin, 1970).

————, *Italian Food* (Knopf, 1975).

Alan Davidson, *North Atlantic Seafood* (Viking, 1979).

Susan Derecskey, *The Hungarian Cookbook* (Harper & Row, 1972).

James Sholto Douglas, *Alternative Foods* (Pelham Books, 1978).

Euell Gibbons, *Stalking the Wild Asparagus* (David McKay, 1962).

Jane Grigson, *The Art of Charcuterie* (Knopf, 1968).

————, *The Mushroom Feast* (Knopf, 1975).

Alice Watson Houston, *The American Heritage Book of Fish Cookery* (American Heritage, 1980).

Evan Jones, *American Food* (Dutton, 1975).

Diana Kennedy, *The Cuisines of Mexico* (Harper & Row, 1972).

————, *Recipes from the Regional Cooks of Mexico* (Harper & Row, 1978).

Elisabeth Lambert Ortiz, *The Complete Book of Caribbean Cooking* (M. Evans, 1973).

Claudia Roden, *A Book of Middle Eastern Food* (Knopf, 1972).

Bernice K. Watt and Annabel L. Merrill, *Composition of Foods* (U.S. Department of Agriculture, 1963).

Paula Wolfert, *Couscous and Other Good Food from Morocco* (Harper & Row, 1973).

Donald Wyman, *Wyman's Gardening Encyclopedia* (Macmillan, 1971).

Acknowledgments. The information contained in this encyclopedia came from many people and many books. Indeed, it is in the very nature of an encyclopedia that it gathers together what other people have discovered. They cannot all be named, but they must not be forgotten; the agriculturists, economic botanists, food scientists, and cookery writers have all, in their various ways, contributed toward our daily bread and have often made it more enjoyable. What better work is there than that? However, many people, firms, and organizations have contributed directly to this book, and special thanks are due to them.

It requires a very special type of person to keep calm and avoid panic when faced with an office piled with scribbled-all-over paper full of an author's spelling mistakes and fantasies. Those who remain sane during the editing of an encyclopedia deserve particular praise, as I do not think that many people realize just what a shattering amount of very meticulous work is involved.

—Tom Stobart

Hassocks, Sussex
1980

A

ABALONE and **ORMER.** These flattened mollusks of the genus *Haliotis,* the sea-ears, are best known for their ornamental shells, which have a row of holes and a fine moth-er-of-pearl lining. They have almost lost their spiral shape and creep around in a lim-petlike way eating the algae on rocks below the low-tide mark. The edible part is the muscular foot which serves the creature for both anchorage and locomotion. After the animal has been taken out of its shell, the dark-colored visceral hump (the entrails) must be removed. The remaining foot should be beaten soundly to break up the muscle fibers. Otherwise it will be very tough.

Abalone is the Californian Spanish name for the species of *Haliotis* found in warm seas; they are commonly much larger and finer in flavor than ormers. The true aba-lone is the red abalone (*H. rufescens*), which is fished in southern California and tradi-tionally prepared for market by Japanese girls whose forebears would have eaten them in their own country. Other species, such as the black abalone (*H. cracherodii*), are pop-ular in Mexico. Indeed, abalone are eaten wherever they occur in sufficient numbers. In Australia, they are known as mutton fish. In Japan, they are famous as *awabi* or *turbo,* and the fishing was done traditionally by almost naked girls, called *ama,* who went down to a depth of 40 ft (12 m), wearing no more than a G-string and carrying a large stone to help them sink.

In countries where abalone is found, the foot, cleaned and pounded, is sold by weight, fresh and sliced. It can be eaten raw or cooked. Fresh or frozen slices may be cov-ered with bread crumbs and fried like cut-lets, but they must be cooked on each side for no more than a minute or they will be-come tough. Recipes can be found in Ameri-can, Japanese, and Chinese cookbooks. In China, abalone is often dried; it is then called *pao yü* and must be soaked for 4 days in fresh water before use. Canned abalone is also available. The cream-colored foot should be sliced; it may be served in a salad or as part of an hors d'oeuvre.

Ormers are small European abalones which are found as far north as Guernsey, although they have become very scarce; they are rare in Jersey (which is too far from the Gulf Stream) and are almost absent from Britain. The name is a Channel Islands cor-ruption of the French *ormeau* or *oreille de mer.* Ormers may be gathered from the rocks at spring low tides. They are out of season in the summer, when they are at their toughest. Some authorities distinguish the slightly smaller Mediterranean ormer (*H. lamellosa*) from the Atlantic ormer (*H. tuberculata*).

[*Ormer*—French: *oreille de mer, ormeau;* German: *See-ohr, Ohrmuschel;* Italian: *orec-chia marina, orecchia di San Pietro;* Spanish: *oreja de mar*]

ACETIC ACID (CH₃COOH). This, the acid of *vinegar and of spoiled wine, is an important organic acid formed when alcohol is oxidized by acetic-acid-producing bacteria. These are aerobic—they require oxygen from the air—and so cannot spoil a properly corked bottle of wine but can turn it sour after it has been opened. Natural wine vinegar will contain 5–10% acetic acid. Acetic acid is an important flavoring, and traces of it are responsible for a pleasant tang in yogurt and cheese. Since acetic acid is volatile, the strength of vinegar can be increased by distillation or conversely weakened by long boiling. Industrially, acetic acid can be made from coal and limestone. (They are heated together to make calcium carbide. This, slaked, makes acetylene gas, which in turn is converted to acetic acid.)

Pure acetic acid looks a little like a mixture of ice and water, which is why it is known as glacial acetic acid. Being a highly corrosive substance, it is not one to keep in the kitchen, but suitably diluted (to 5%), and often colored with burnt sugar, it is used in cheap pickles and as a vinegar substitute. It also is added to natural vinegar (like fortifying wine with alcohol) to make it keep better, since dilute vinegar is open to attack by bacteria which change acetic acid into carbon dioxide and water. Acetic acid is stronger than the other common kitchen acids (citric, lactic, and tartaric), and even at the same *pH is more toxic to spoilage organisms, though less so than benzoic acid (*see* preservation). Even a 1% solution strongly inhibits most bacteria, though not molds. These qualities make vinegar effective in pickling.

[*Acetic acid*—French: *acide acétique;* German: *Essigsäure;* Italian: *acido acetico;* Spanish: *ácido acético*]

ACIDS. From the Latin *acidus* (sour). All sour foods contain acids. Sourness is an important taste and is supplied by acids in many natural ingredients, such as *acetic acid in vinegar, *citric acid in lemon juice, *tartaric acid in wine and unripe fruit, *malic acid in sour apples, *lactic acid in sour milk, and *oxalic acid in sorrel and rhubarb.

Although naturally occurring sour ingredients are the ones most commonly used in cooking, there is sometimes a need for pure acids such as citric and tartaric, which may be bought as crystalline powders. Even *hydrochloric and *sulfuric acids, which are highly corrosive and dangerous, have some relevance to food.

Acids are highly active chemicals: even rather weak ones will attack iron, zinc (on galvanized articles), and, more slowly, lead and copper in the circumstances in which they may occur in the kitchen. The resulting salts of zinc, copper, and, above all, lead are poisonous. On the other hand, for practical purposes, organic acids do not attack enamel, stainless steel, tin (on cans or tinned pans of brass or copper), aluminum, silver, or gold. Wooden tubs, china, stoneware, enamel, and plastics are also resistant, but acids should not be kept in marble mortars, which they will dissolve, in earthenware vessels with low-fired glazes that are high in lead content, or in high-lead crystal glass bottles—the last two are potentially dangerous. Acids dissolve carbonates (marble, limestone, chalk, washing soda) and bicarbonates (baking soda), giving off a fizz of carbon dioxide gas. This property is used in sherbets and baking powder.

Acids are always neutralized by *alkalis, and the two cannot exist together. It is useless to mix fuming hydrochloric acid and caustic soda together to make a double-acting cleaner—one will neutralize the other with some violence. In theory, fruits can be made less sour by adding soda or lime. Home winemakers sometimes temper rhubarb by adding chalk, which is quite logical, but the salts formed can taste nasty and may be purgative. Sugar, on the other hand, does not neutralize acids but produces a pleasant sweet-sour sensation in the mouth.

Adjustment of acidity, and therefore of sourness, is a fundamental operation in cooking, which is why a last-minute squeeze of lemon juice can be so important in finishing a dish. Fruits with insufficient acidity are insipid. A wine with less than 0.2% acid will be uninteresting and, moreover, will not keep, while one with more than 1.5% will be too sour.

Acids above a certain strength are *preservatives (though some are more toxic to bacteria than others), which is why vegetables are preserved in vinegar.

Acid and alkaline solutions can be distinguished with litmus papers, which are turned red by acid and blue by alkalis. Many of the natural colors of food behave in a similar manner. Acid vinegar will turn beets or red cabbage a bright red, while cabbage boiled in acid water turns an unappetizing yellow.

Weight for weight, some acids are much stronger than others. For instance a 1% solution of hydrochloric acid is much stronger than a 1% solution of citric acid, in that it is sourer and able to neutralize a greater amount of soda, attack metals faster, and so on. In fact, it is more acid. The essential acidity of solutions, irrespective of which acids are present, can be compared by means of the *pH scale.

[*Acids*—French: *acides;* German: *Säuren;* Italian: *acidi;* Spanish: *ácidos*]

ACIDULATED WATER is water that has been made slightly acid with a teaspoon or so of vinegar or lemon juice to each pint (½ lt) of water. It is used for briefly holding cut fruit or vegetables which would otherwise darken quite quickly when their cut surfaces came in contact with the air, and is effective for fruit such as apples and pears and for vegetables such as globe and Jerusalem artichokes and salsify. It can also be used as a cooking medium—cauliflower cooked in acidulated water will be beautifully white even if the curd was rather yellow when raw.

ACITRÓN. A candied substance made in Mexico from the large cushionlike bisnaga cactus (*Echinocactus grandis*). It is shaped into bars and is used for meat stuffings. Any sweet candied fruit may be used as a substitute if it is not too strongly flavored.

ACKEE or **akee.** A tropical fruit (*Blighia sapida*) belonging to the same family as the *lychee but very different in appearance. It was introduced from West Africa to Jamaica, where it has become particularly popular. The fruit, some 3 in. (8 mm) in diameter, is bright red. When ripe, it bursts open to reveal three large shiny black seeds and a creamy aril that is well described by the name "vegetable brain." This is all that is eaten, because the pink parts of the fruit are very poisonous, as are both the unripe and overripe fruits. The flavor of ackee as a fruit is delicate, but its most famous use is cooked in the West Indian salt fish and ackee. Since canned ackees are available outside the West Indies, anyone could attempt the following recipe:

SALT COD AND ACKEE

Soak 1 lb (450 g) of salt cod for 24 hours, drain, and cook it in water for 30 minutes. Fifteen minutes before the fish is cooked, add the creamy part of 24 ackees. Drain, skin, and bone the fish, flake it, and mix with the ackee. Dice 4 oz (100 g) of salt pork and fry it until crisp and brown. Remove the pork, and in the fat fry 2 finely chopped medium onions and a chopped sweet pepper until very lightly browned. Then add 1 or 2 chopped green chilies, 4 chopped spring onions, 3 peeled and coarsely chopped tomatoes, and a sprig of thyme. Fry this gently for about 5 minutes, then add the salt cod, ackee, and fried salt pork, to warm through. Serve seasoned with pepper and garnished with crisply fried slices of bacon, a few tomato wedges, and parsley or watercress for decoration. If canned ackees are used, a 1-lb (450-g) can will suffice. They do not require cooking but should be drained and added with the fish and pork near the end of cooking. Those interested in further recipes should consult Elisabeth Lambert

Ortiz's *The Complete Book of Caribbean Cooking* (M. Evans, 1973), on which this salt fish and ackee recipe is based.

ACORN. One of the original foods of man, acorns are still used extensively in some parts of Europe and also by North American Indians. Acorns from all species of oak are edible, but those (e.g., of the English oak, *Quercus robur*) that taste very astringent should first be ground and washed or boiled in water until the water-soluble tannins, which could cause stomach upsets, are dissolved out. However, a number of oak species bear acorns that are sweet and edible without treatment. Among the best is the evergreen holm oak (or ilex or holly oak), *Quercus ilex*, which grows on the stony hillsides of Mediterranean countries and has plump brown acorns. The cultivated sweet varieties (var. *ballota*) are sold in the markets of Spain, Algeria, and Morocco in January and fetch the same price as chestnuts (which in many ways they resemble). They become sweeter with keeping, but may acquire a winy flavor.

Other sweet acorns commonly eaten in Europe are those of the valonia oak (*Q. macrolepis*) from Italy, Greece, and the eastern Mediterranean, and of the manna oak (*Q. persica*) and the kermes oak (*Q. coccifera*), also from Mediterranean hillsides. In North America, the best are from the white oak (*Q. alba*) and the live oak (*Q. virginiana*). Acorns are also eaten in China (*Q. cornea*) and in Japan (*Q. cuspidata*).

Acorns are usually eaten roasted like chestnuts, but I have also found them useful as a substitute for water chestnuts, since they do not disintegrate quickly on boiling. It is possible to make use of any acorns by shelling and boiling them until they are sweet and dark brown. Roasted acorns are sometimes used as a coffee substitute, and acorn flour can be made into bread.

[*Acorn*—French: *gland;* German: *Eichel;* Italian: *ghianda;* Spanish: *bellota*]

ADDITIVES. There was a time when there was no strawberry ice cream. Then there was a time when a manufacturer could legally peddle, under the name "strawberry ice cream," a concoction of coloring (perhaps toxic), artificial flavoring, and grass seed. Today the consumer, surveying the label on a box of strawberry ice cream with its bewildering terms for thickeners, colorings, flavorings, and other ingredients seemingly unrelated to either strawberries or cream, may wish he had the simple life of the caveman.

As broadly defined, additives—any substance that becomes part of a food product when added either directly or indirectly—are nothing new. Salt and spices, for instance, have been used to heighten the flavor of food since the beginning of history. In more recent times, additives have taken the form of adulteration: only a century ago, manufacturers used toxic metals—lead, copper, and arsenic—to color foods and stretched ground black pepper with bits of charcoal. Not until the Food and Drugs Act of 1906 did the U.S. government begin to assume authority to remove adulterated and obviously poisonous foods from the market.

According to the Food and Drug Administration, today some 2,800 substances are intentionally added to foods to achieve desired effects. Perhaps 10,000 others find their way into foods at various points. These include small amounts of drugs fed to animals, residues of pesticides used to treat crops, and chemical substances from packaging materials such as plastics.

Owing to a number of acts and amendments, the FDA strictly regulates our food. For some people, distressed by the long list of additives on food labels, the regulation is not enough. One of the problems is that the government has no power to limit the number of additives that have been approved or to judge whether a particular additive is really needed—it simply requires that the manufacturer prove the additive is safe. What "safe" means and how it is to be proved are controversial questions. Food processors maintain that the public wants their additives for several reasons:

1. To make food more appealing by enhancing flavor and color. For this purpose, the most widely used additives are sugar, salt, and corn syrup. These three, plus citric acid, baking soda, vegetable colors, mustard, and pepper, account for more than 98%, by weight, of all food additives used in the U.S.

2. To maintain or improve nutritional value by fortifying with vitamins and minerals. Breads and cereals may be enriched with B vitamins lost while processing grain; iodine may be added to table salt; milk may be fortified with vitamin D.

3. To maintain freshness by retarding spoilage and preserving natural color and flavor. Preservatives such as sodium nitrates and nitrites are added to meats, and antioxidants help prevent changes in color, flavor, and texture when foods are exposed to air.

4. To aid in processing or preparation by giving desired body and texture to foods, controlling acidity or alkalinity (pH), and retaining moisture. Thus, emulsifiers are added to mayonnaise to prevent separation, thickeners add body and smoothness to soups, and humectants keep coconut moist.

While the FDA continues to review additives used for all these purposes and consumer advocates yell halt to the proliferation of substances that are unnecessary, perhaps even harmful, in foods, the person who buys and eats the food still has the power of choice. By reading labels, learning what terms mean, and questioning the FDA or the manufacturer about what you don't understand, you can better decide what you want to ingest in your body. You can make an informed decision about which characteristics of food mean the most to you, whether storage time, color appeal, and convenience are essential. To aid you in reading labels, the USDA provides the following list of substances commonly added to foods with explanations of their purpose.

♦ **Maintain/Improve Nutritional Quality.** *Nutrients:* enrich (replace vitamins and minerals lost in processing) or fortify (add nutrients that may be lacking in the diet).

● **Maintain Product Quality.** *Preservatives (antimicrobials):* prevent food spoilage from bacteria, molds, fungi, and yeast; extend shelf life; protect natural color/flavor. *Antioxidants:* delay/prevent rancidity or enzymatic browning.

■ **Aid in Processing or Preparation.** *Emulsifiers:* help to distribute evenly tiny particles of one liquid into another; improve homogeneity, consistency, stability, texture. *Stabilizers, Thickeners, Texturizers:* impart body, improve consistency or texture; stabilize emulsions; affect feel of food in mouth. *Leavening Agents:* affect cooking results—texture and volume. *pH Control Agents:* change/maintain acidity or alkalinity. *Humectants:* cause moisture retention. *Maturing and Bleaching Agents, Dough Conditioners:* accelerate the aging process; improve baking qualities. *Anticaking Agents:* prevent caking, lumping, or clustering of a finely powdered or crystalline substance.

▲ **Affect Appeal Characteristics.** *Flavor Enhancers:* supplement, magnify, or modify the original taste and/or aroma of food without imparting a characteristic flavor of their own. *Flavors:* heighten natural flavor; restore flavors lost in processing. *Colors:* give desired, appetizing, or characteristic color to food. *Sweeteners:* make the aroma or taste of food more agreeable.

Acetic acid	■ pH control agent
Acetone peroxide	■ maturing and bleaching agent, dough conditioner
Adipic acid	■ pH control agent
Ammonium alginate	■ stabilizer-thickener-texturizer
Annatto extract	▲ color
Arabinogalactan	■ stabilizer-thickener-texturizer
Ascorbic acid	♦ nutrient
	● preservative
	● antioxidant
Azodicarbonamide	■ maturing and bleaching agent, dough conditioner

Benzoic acid — ● preservative

Benzoyl peroxide — ■ maturing and bleaching agent, dough conditioner

Beta-apo-8′ carotenal — ▲ color

Beta carotene — ◆ nutrient
▲ color

BHA (butylated hydroxyanisole) — ● antioxidant

BHT (butylated hydroxytoluene) — ● antioxidant

Butylpareben — ● preservative

Calcium alginate — ■ stabilizer-thickener-texturizer

Calcium bromate — ■ maturing and bleaching agent, dough conditioner

Calcium lactate — ● preservative

Calcium phosphate — ■ leavening agent

Calcium propionate — ● preservative

Calcium silicate — ■ anticaking agent

Calcium sorbate — ● preservative

Canthaxanthin — ▲ color

Caramel — ▲ color

Carob bean gum — ■ stabilizer-thickener-texturizer

Carrageenan — ■ emulsifier
■ stabilizer-thickener-texturizer

Carrot oil — ▲ color

Cellulose — ■ stabilizer-thickener-texturizer

Citric acid — ● preservative
● antioxidant
■ pH control agent

Citrus Red No. 2 — ▲ color

Cochineal extract — ▲ color

Corn endosperm — ▲ color

Corn syrup — ▲ sweetener

Dehydrated beets — ▲ color

Dextrose — ▲ sweetener

Diglycerides — ■ emulsifier

Dioctyl sodium sulfosuccinate — ■ emulsifier

Disodium guanylate — ▲ flavor enhancer

Disodium inosinate — ▲ flavor enhancer

Dried algae meal — ▲ color

EDTA (ethylenedi-amine-tetraacetic acid) — ● antioxidant

FD&C Colors:
Blue No. 1 — ▲ color

Red No. 3 — ▲ color

Red No. 40 — ▲ color

Yellow No. 5 — ▲ color

Fructose — ▲ sweetener

Gelatin — ■ stabilizer-thickener-texturizer

Glucose — ▲ sweetener

Glycerine — ■ humectant

Glycerol monostearate — ■ humectant

Grape skin extract — ▲ color

Guar gum — ■ stabilizer-thickener-texturizer

Gum arabic — ■ stabilizer-thickener-texturizer

Gum ghatti — ■ stabilizer-thickener-texturizer

Heptylparaben — ● preservative

Hydrogen peroxide — ■ maturing and bleaching agent, dough conditioner

Hydrolyzed vegetable protein — ▲ flavor enhancer

Invert sugar — ▲ sweetener

Iodine — ◆ nutrient

Iron — ◆ nutrient

Iron-ammonium citrate — ■ anticaking agent

Iron oxide — ▲ color

Karaya gum — ■ stabilizer-thickener-texturizer

Lactic acid — ■ pH control agent
● preservative

Larch gum — ■ stabilizer-thickener-texturizer

Lecithin — ■ emulsifier

Locust bean gum — ■ stabilizer-thickener-texturizer

Mannitol — ▲ sweetener
■ anticaking agent
■ stabilizer-thickener-texturizer

Methylparaben — ● preservative

Modified food starch — ■ stabilizer-thickener-texturizer

Monoglycerides — ■ emulsifier

MSG (monosodium glutamate) — ▲ flavor enhancer

Niacinamide — ◆ nutrient

Paprika (and oleoresin) — ▲ flavor
▲ color

Pectin — ■ stabilizer-thickener-texturizer

Phosphates — ■ pH control agent

Phosphoric acid	■ pH control agent	Titanium dioxide	▲ color
Polysorbates	■ emulsifiers	Toasted, partially	▲ color
Potassium alginate	■ stabilizer-thickener-texturizer	defatted cooked cottonseed flour	
Potassium bromate	■ maturing and bleaching agent, dough conditioner	Tocopherols (vitamin E)	♦ nutrient ● antioxidant
Potassium iodide	♦ nutrient	Tragacanth gum	■ stabilizer-thickener-texturizer
Potassium propionate	● preservative		
Potassium sorbate	● preservative	Turmeric (oleoresin)	▲ flavor
Propionic acid	● preservative		▲ color
Propyl gallate	● antioxidant	Ultramarine blue	▲ color
Propylene glycol	■ stabilizer-thickener-texturizer	Vanilla, vanillin	▲ flavor
		Vitamin A	♦ nutrient
	■ humectant	Vitamin C (ascorbic acid)	♦ nutrient
Propylparaben	● preservative		● preservative
Riboflavin	♦ nutrient		● antioxidant
	▲ color	Vitamin D (D$_2$, D$_3$)	♦ nutrient
Saccharin	▲ sweetener	Vitamin E (tocopherols)	♦ nutrient
Saffron	▲ color		
Silicon dioxide	■ anticaking agent	Yeast-malt sprout extract	▲ flavor enhancer
Sodium acetate	■ pH control agent	Yellow prussiate of soda	■ anticaking agent
Sodium alginate	■ stabilizer-thickener-texturizer		
Sodium aluminum sulfate	■ leavening		
Sodium benzoate	● preservative		
Sodium bicarbonate	■ leavening		
Sodium calcium alginate	■ stabilizer-thickener-texturizer		
Sodium citrate	■ pH control agent		
Sodium diacetate	● preservative		
Sodium erythorbate	● preservative		
Sodium nitrate	● preservative		
Sodium nitrite	● preservative		
Sodium propionate	● preservative		
Sodium sorbate	● preservative		
Sodium stearyl fumarate	■ maturing and bleaching agent, dough conditioner		
Sorbic acid	● preservative		
Sorbitan monostearate	■ emulsifier		
Sorbitol	■ humectant		
	▲ sweetener		
Sucrose (table sugar)	▲ sweetener		
Tagetes (Aztec marigold)	▲ color		
Tartaric acid	■ pH control agent		
TBHQ (tertiary butyl hydroquinone)	● antioxidant		
Thiamine	♦ nutrient		

ADZUKI or **azuki bean.** A small reddish brown bean (*Phaseolus angularis*), easily cooked and with a very pleasant, sweet flavor. Adzuki beans are much grown in China and Japan, and have now become generally available outside the Orient. In Japanese cooking, the boiled beans, mashed and sweetened, are an important base for various cakes (e.g. *yonkan*) and sweets, and in red rice. The beans are also sold powdered (*azuki-sarashien*)—a shortcut. I have found adzuki beans tender and palatable when used in place of other small beans in non-Oriental recipes.

AGAR, agar-agar, kanten, Japanese gelatin, or **vegetable gelatin.** Available as a powder, in sticks, or in shreds, agar is obtained from a number of seaweeds by boiling them in water, then filtering and drying the resultant jelly. It is a complex carbohydrate, unlike gelatin, which is a protein. Agar melts at about 194°F (90°C) and sets at about 112°F (45°C); gelatin melts at about 80°F (27°C) and sets at 68°F (20°C).

Agar can be obtained from pharmacists, because it is the usual medium for cultures of bacteria. It does not melt at blood heat and so can be incubated, a characteristic that suits the bacteriologist but makes agar unpopular in the kitchen. It does not melt in the mouth as other jellies do, and the texture is peculiarly brittle.

Agar will dissolve only in boiling water. Like gelatin, it varies in jelling power from sample to sample, but 1 teaspoon per about 1½ cups (¾ lt) of water would be a sensible point to start from. Because agar jelly sets at 104–111°F (40–44°C)—which is lukewarm—it is not too long a job to learn by experiment. Do not, however, boil agar for long with an acid, or it will change its character and fail to set at all. On the other hand, one can make fresh pineapple and papaya juice into jellies with agar, but not with gelatin, since they contain substances which attack the protein in gelatin.

As *kanten,* agar is an ingredient of Japanese cooking and is often used to make a very stiff, colored jelly from which decorative shapes—leaves or fruits—are cut. For this purpose, *kanten,* which often comes in cakes, is heated rather gently in water until it melts; then it is seasoned, colored, and set in sheets of the required thickness. *Kanten* is also an ingredient of fake birds'-nest soup, in which it provides the viscous texture.

AÏOLI. *See* mayonnaise.

AKALA. Native to the Hawaiian islands, the akala (*Rubus macraei*) is a shrub that bears raspberrylike fruit. The berries are large, juicy, and small-seeded and may be purple, red, or orange. Some akalas are slightly bitter; the most desirable ones are delicately sweet and taste like raspberries or strawberries.

AKAVIT. *See* liqueurs and cordials.

AKEE. *See* ackee.

ALBACORE. *See* tuna.

ALBUMIN. Member of a class of proteins once thought to make up almost the entire protein content of egg white, which was called albumen. In fact, the protein of egg white is about 70% ovalbumin and 9% conalbumin. Albumins are an important constituent of seeds, a stored food for the embryo to use for a start in life. They are also a constituent of milk and of meat, as well as being the main protein in blood plasma, which is why egg-white substitutes used by commercial confectioners are often made from blood. Like many proteins, albumin coagulates and hardens when heated. Ovalbumin starts to coagulate at 140°F (60°C); it is also partially coagulated if beaten into a foam (*see* whipping). Because this process is slowed down at low temperatures, it is slower work to beat the whites of eggs that have come straight out of the refrigerator than it is with them at room temperature.

[*Albumin*—French: *albumine;* German: *Albumin;* Italian: *albumina;* Spanish: *albúmina*]

ALCOHOL. Chemically, there are dozens of alcohols, several ranges of them, but popularly (and in our context) by alcohol we mean, unless otherwise qualified, only potable alcohol, silent alcohol, or neutral spirit—all names for ethyl alcohol mixed with water. Ethyl alcohol or ethanol is one of a series of alcohols of which the simplest members are:

methyl alcohol	CH_3OH	boils at	149°F	55°C
ethyl alcohol	C_2H_5OH	boils at	173°F	78°C
propyl alcohol	C_3H_7OH	boils at	208°F	98°C
butyl alcohol	C_4H_9OH	boils at	244°F	118°C

Each member of the series has one carbon and two hydrogen atoms more than its predecessor and has a higher boiling point; from this list the would-be moonshiner who wishes to distill ethyl alcohol without too many of its more poisonous relations may get some idea of his problems. Methyl alcohol, also known as wood alcohol or methanol, is the most volatile. It is the stuff that sends methylated-spirit drinkers blind. Other series of alcohols include such substances as glycerine and are well represented in the higher boiling point mixture of congenerics known as *fusel oil, which comes over toward the end of distillation. Ethyl alcohol is produced when sugars are fermented by yeasts, but the raw materials usually used for making alcoholic drinks—grapes, melted grains, potatoes, rice, fruit juices—contain much more than sugars, so that many reactions take place, and other substances—the congenerics—are formed in fermentation. Many people regard ethyl alcohol itself as a poison, but some of the other substances are far more poisonous and are largely responsible for hangover headaches (see distillation).

The Properties of Ethyl Alcohol.

At ordinary atmospheric pressure, pure alcohol boils at 173°F (78°C). Since pure water boils at 212°F (100°C), a mixture of water and alcohol will boil somewhere between these two extremes, depending on the relative amounts of each. Of course, the alcohol does not all boil away suddenly when the temperature of wine, for example, reaches the boiling point of alcohol, but the higher the temperature of hot punch or spiced wine, the more alcohol is lost until finally at 212°F (100°C) it is gone altogether.

Alcohol freezes at a much lower temperature than water (thermometers for low temperatures are sometimes filled with colored spirit for this reason). Every winter fatal accidents occur in the Arctic when thirsty travelers who swig vodka or aquavit that has been left in subzero weather get internal burns from frostbite and caustic burns because the alcohol has been strengthened as the water freezes out of the original mixture.

Pure ethyl alcohol is known as absolute alcohol; it is clear, flammable, and exceedingly caustic. The strongest alcohol normally sold is 90–95% and is found in countries where the duty is not prohibitive, such as Spain (as *alcohol para licores*) or Italy (as *alcool puro grado*). It is used in homemade

liqueurs and for preserving fruits such as grapes and cherries. This alcohol must be cut with an equal quantity of water before it is in any way comparable to ordinary spirits, such as gin and whiskey. Taken neat, it will skin the mouth and possibly have fatal consequences. When water is added to such strong alcohol, the total volume shrinks slightly and heat is generated. It is best to dilute it with ice water.

The Effects of Alcohol.

Alcohol depresses, but because it depresses first those parts of the brain which cause depression and inhibition, it appears to act as a stimulant. Later effects are impaired efficiency, slow reactions, recklessness, self-pity, bad temper, aggressiveness, and falling flat on your face. Alcohol also increases the circulation in the skin, which may make you feel warmer but will, in reality, lead to cooling. Thus, a planter's punch on a hot day is sensible, but the idea of a Saint Bernard bringing help with the brandy keg is sheer lunacy. Brandy makes the avalanche victim feel warmer but increases his heat loss and reduces his chance of survival. A man who is cold must get into a warm place before having his whiskey and hot water.

Absorption of alcohol into the bloodstream starts soon after a drink has been swallowed and is especially rapid once the drink has entered the small intestine. This happens quickly if the drink is diluted and is taken on an empty stomach. The absorption occurs more slowly if you are eating as well as drinking, especially when the food is oily. There is some sense in taking a spoonful of oil or a slice of bread thickly spread with pâté before a drinking party. Similar wisdom lies behind the Russian *zakousky*, the Spanish *tapas*, or the Levantine *meze*. Elimination of alcohol from the blood goes on much more slowly than its absorption, particularly if drinks have been taken which are rich in the higher alcohols (fusel oil). It is a scientific fact, and not an advertising gimmick, that people will sober up far more quickly after a session on highly rectified vodka than after the same quantities of brandy or whiskey. The trouble with mixing drinks is not the alcohol but the congenerics.

Germicidal effect. Tests have shown that the germicidal effect of alcohol is greatest at a 50% concentration. Stronger or weaker mixtures are less effective. At a concentration over 18%, alcohol will stop the fermenting action of yeasts and will not be turned to acetic acid by bacteria. At this sort of strength it is used to preserve fruit syrups (e.g., crème de cassis). When preserving fruit such as grapes or cherries in alcohol, you should remember that it will be diluted by the juices of the fruit. You therefore have to start with a good, strong spirit.

ITALIAN CHERRY LIQUEUR

Wash 1 lb (450 g) of ripe bitter black cherries. Put 11 oz (300 g) of sugar, 2 cloves, a 2-in. (5-cm) stick of cinnamon, and ¼ pt (150 ml) of water in a pan, bring to the boil, and cool. Mix the cooled syrup with ½ pt (300 ml) 90% alcohol. Pack the cherries into the jars without breaking them, including a couple of cracked cherry pits if you like. Fill the jars until the fruit is covered. Seal. Put the jars daily in the sun, turning and shaking them gently each day. After some weeks, the bottles are ready. The liquid may be drained off and bottled. You can eat the cherries.

[*Alcohol*—French: *alcool;* German: *Alkohol;* Italian: *alcool;* Spanish: *alcohol*]

ALE. Alcoholic drink brewed from a cereal. Now more or less synonymous with *beer, a term which used to refer to hopped ale.

[*Ale*—French: *ale, bière;* German: *englisches Bier, Ale;* Italian: *birra;* Spanish: *cerveza*]

ALECOST. *See* costmary.

ALFALFA. Probably the world's most important forage legume, alfalfa (*Medicago sativa*) is a native of the Mediterranean region. It was grown by the ancient Persians, Greeks, and Romans, and spread into China and the whole of Europe. Although it is largely grown for forage in the U.S., it is fashionable at the moment to sprout alfalfa seeds as a salad food. The flavor is mild and pleasant.

ALKALIS are, in many ways, the opposites or antagonists of *acids. The word comes from the old Arab alchemists and referred to the white ashes of wood: mostly carbonates of potassium and sodium, these were used in experiments as well as for cleaning and for making soap. Today we would use the much stronger *caustic soda. When dissolved in water, and perhaps filtered, the wood-ash solution was known as *lye. Other common alkalis are bicarbonate of soda (the one alkali commonly used in cooking), *ammonia, and *lime. Substances which neutralize acids and combine with them to form salts are known in chemistry as bases; alkalis are bases that are soluble in water. The alkalinity of a solution is measured by its *pH.

Many alkalis are dangerously caustic when strong. Even when highly diluted, they feel slimy on the fingers and often have an unpleasant soda taste, although an alkaline flavor is sometimes liked in soda bread, scones, and pancakes, or as the ash on bonfire-roasted potatoes or on the bottom of old-fashioned brick-oven bread.

Alkalis turn litmus paper blue and likewise affect beets and red cabbage, turning them purple; on the other hand, they intensify the green of green cabbage. Also, they soften the skins of seeds, which is why bicarbonate of soda is frequently added to the water in which beans or chickpeas are cooked. They can even be used to remove skins entirely. In some places, bicarbonate of soda is also used to tenderize meat. *Limewater and lye are required in some pickle recipes, and dilute caustic soda enters into quick commercial cures for green olives.

[*Alkalis*—French: *alcalis;* German: *Alkalien;* Italian: *alcali;* Spanish: *álcalis*]

ALKALOIDS. Nitrogenous organic substances which are basic (alkaline, hence the name) and often poisonous and bitter, alkaloids are found in certain plants. Many of them are used as drugs. Examples are morphine in the gum of unripe poppy capsules, belladonna (atropine) in the leaves and roots of deadly nightshade, cocaine in coca leaves, and strychnine from the seeds of the East Indian nux vomica tree. Perhaps the instinctive dislike we have of bitter tastes could be an archaic survival trait.

Quinine in very dilute form is used in the Indian tonic water of gin and tonic. In larger quantities, it is a powerful and dangerous drug, but in amounts likely to be immediately harmful, the bitterness would be intolerable. *Caffeine is a common alkaloid present in coffee, tea, and cola nuts. Another alkaloid associated with caffeine is theobromine, which does not stimulate the brain but dilates the arteries.

[*Alkaloids*—French: *alcaloides;* German: *Alkaloide;* Italian: *alcaloidi;* Spanish: *alcaloides*]

ALKANNA, anchusa, or **dyer's alkanet.** A plant of the borage family (*Alkanna tinctoria*), native to the Mediterranean and southeast Europe. It has bright blue flowers, and the roots contain a powerful red dye, soluble in oil, alcohol, and water (in the last giving a brownish color). Alkanna is used to color wine, drinks, ices, sausage skins, margarine, etc. As a coloring for meat dishes, it is frequently mentioned in 14th-century recipes.

[*Alkanna*—French: *orcanète;* German: *Alkanna;* Italian: *alcanna;* Spanish: *alcama, orcaneta*]

ALKERMES. An old-fashioned French and Italian sweet red cordial made with *kermes.

ALLIGATOR PEAR. *See* avocado.

ALLSPICE, Jamaica pepper, or **myrtle pepper.** The dried berry of a tree (*Pimenta dioica*) native to tropical America. Although it is grown in other tropical countries, the bulk comes from Jamaica. The name "allspice" describes its taste, which resembles a mixture of several Old World spices, in which cloves predominate.

ALLSPICE

Whole allspice berries look like large peppercorns and are often included in pickle-spice mixtures, in marinades, and in brines for herring and beef. In Arab countries, although allspice is not normally used in curries, it has been adopted for pilafs. Ground, preferably freshly, it is a usual spice in fruitcakes, mince pies, and plum pudding. It can be used with discretion in many places where a hint, but no more, of cloves might be nice, for instance with tomatoes and beets or, for those who like it, with cooked apples and pears. In fact, allspice is rather liked in northern Europe, but surprisingly, in view of historical connections, it is not much used in Spain.

(*Allspice*—French: *toute-épice, piment jamaïque;* German: *Allgewürz, Jamaikapfeffer, Nelkenpfeffer;* Italian: *pimento;* Spanish: *pimiento de Jamaica*)

ALMOND. From a gastronomic point of view, undoubtedly the world's most important nut. Almonds come from the kernel of a fruit closely related to the apricot and are like it in many ways, except that the fruit of the ripe almond is leathery, dusky green, and quite inedible. Only when they are very young, before the nut is formed, is it possible to enjoy the sour, hard little fruits as a rough sort of hors d'oeuvre, for which they are eaten occasionally in the places where they grow. They have the same gastric effects as sour apples.

Almond trees (*Prunus amygdalus*) are essentially Mediterranean and indeed are probably indigenous to the eastern Mediterranean (they are mentioned in the Old Testament), although it has been claimed that they came from farther east. They were spread by the Romans and later by the Arabs, but can be grown profitably only in the warm climate liked by the rather hardier lemon and olive. The almond is the first orchard tree to flower in the spring, which makes the young fruit exceedingly vulnerable to frost. The decorative blossom often seen in gardens is usually of hard-stoned, bitter varieties, which rarely get nuts, not just because of the frost but because almonds are self-sterile and need another almond of a compatible variety growing nearby.

Today almonds are grown extensively in South Africa and Australia, but do not like the tropics, where the so-called tropical almonds (which are not almonds at all) have to take their place. The bulk of the world's supply comes from Spain, Italy, and California, and almonds are also grown in Provence (especially around Aix), Languedoc, Portugal, the Canary Islands, North Africa (especially in Algeria and Morocco), Greece, Turkey, Persia, Afghanistan, and Kashmir. This distribution means that almonds are traditional in the cooking of Europe, the Middle East, and as far away as northern India, where they are commonly used in the more elaborate Mogul food.

Bitter Almonds (*Prunus amygdalus* var. *amara*), grown mainly in Sicily, Sardinia, North Africa, and southern France, are small with very hard shiny shells. The kernels are usually less oily than those of sweet almonds, but the important distinguishing characteristic is the strong taste the bitter almond develops when mixed with water (or saliva). They contain a glucoside (a nitrogenous substance related to sugar) which,

when acted on by an enzyme, reacts with water to form prussic (hydrocyanic) acid and benzaldehyde. Prussic acid is lethal in very small doses, which is why it is unsafe to eat more than one or two bitter almonds, peach stones, or other bitter-almond-flavored nuts or leaves. Fortunately, this acid is highly volatile and vanishes into the air on heating, leaving behind only the bitter-almond-flavored benzaldehyde, which is relatively harmless in small quantities. Roasting fruit kernels will also destroy the enzyme system. Those who like the taste of bitter almonds will find it in confections like *amaretti* (but not in *amaretti di Saronno,* which contain apricot kernels), macaroons, and some pastes; there is also *noyau. With more delicacy, the flavor pleases most people in plum, cherry, and apricot jam, to which it is imparted by adding a few crushed stones. An almost unrecognizable waft of it is delicious with pork, too. But almond extract, as bought in bottles, is almost always an unpleasant substance, and since it is used heavily in the average multistory wedding cake, people with discriminating palates may be encouraged to live in sin. When the flavor is wanted in emergency, then cherry laurel (*Prunus laurocerasus*) or peach leaves may be used *provided that, after maceration in water, the liquid is heated.* Ratafia, orgeat, noyau, and other almond-flavored liqueurs may also be pressed into service. Bitter almonds are illegal as a commercial ingredient in the U.S.

AMARETTI

Blanch 4 oz (100 g) each of sweet almonds and bitter almonds. Dry them in a cool oven and pound them with 8 oz (200 g) of sugar. Beat 2 egg whites until they are stiff, and gently fold in the almond mixture to form a medium-soft paste. Pipe blobs of this onto rice paper. Sprinkle them with confectioner's sugar and let them stand for a few hours. Then bake for 40 minutes in a moderate oven.

Sweet Almonds. When the type of almond is not specified in a recipe, one should use sweet almonds. They have a delicate flavor with no trace of benzaldehyde. The many varieties differ in size, shape, oil content, and shell hardness (important in dessert almonds). There are paper-shell and soft-shell types, which can be cracked with the fingers, and famous varieties like the Jordan (*jardin*) almond and the Italian *premice* with fine, large, flat, regular-shaped nuts. You should suspect round nuts, especially if they have close-textured, shiny shells: these are usually commercial types intended to be cracked by machine and may not be sweet almonds at all. For purposes other than dessert, most people will prefer to buy shelled almonds, which keep well and can be bought whole, either in the skin or blanched, in halves (for cake decoration), sliced, shaved, chopped, or ground. They are also available roasted and salted for snacks. Ground almond is easy to adulterate, and since almonds are expensive, this is frequently done (though in most countries will be indicated in the ingredients listed on the label). When buying ground almonds or almond flour, check to make sure that it has not been padded with cheaper products. If it is, avoid it — it will ruin any recipe.

The use of almonds in confectionery is well known. They are used in almost every country, in *panforte* from Siena, in *schokoladetorte mit mandeln* from Austria, and in Bakewell tart from Derbyshire. There are also sugared almonds and rich sweetmeats such as *torrone* (Italy), *turrón* (Spain), or *tourron* (France), and marzipan, marchpane, *massepain* (France), *marzapani* (Italy), or *mazapán* (Spain), which are of ancient origin. Less well known outside the almond-producing countries of the Middle East and Mediterranean are the various forms of almond milk; for instance, the popular *leche de almendras* of Spain, which, with sugar, becomes an *almendrada* or a *horchata de almendras* (and is made like *horchata de *chufas*). Spanish supermarkets sell *miel de almendras* (literally, honey of almonds) in jars.

Of the savory uses of almonds, everyone knows *truite aux amandes,* a universal restaurant dish. Oriental countries, from Turkey to India, use almonds with rice in stuffings for poultry and in pilaf. Chinese chicken or pork with almonds is widely known. Raw or toasted almonds are used in salads for nourishment or texture, as in *salade forestière* (sliced raw mushrooms, bound lightly with mayonnaise and covered with a layer of almond shavings), or the *nougada* of the Middle East (which, like *hummus,* is more of a dip than a salad: a cream of pounded almonds, garlic, parsley, and lemon juice). In the *sopa blanca* of Andalusia, an emulsion is made by pounding together a small handful of blanched almonds with an equal volume of peeled broad beans and a clove of garlic. Into this, olive oil is gradually worked; finally, the emulsion is diluted with the juice of a lemon and 4½ cups (1 lt) of cold water, salted to taste, and strained over bread cubes in a tureen.

Dishes containing toasted almonds have a rather different flavor. Such almonds are used particularly in Catalan cooking. A paste of toasted almonds (sometimes with pine nuts) pounded with garlic, fried bread cubes, parsley, and saffron is added to many dishes. One may see a bottle labeled *picada* (made by blending olive oil, saffron, almonds, parsley, and water) standing near the stove in restaurants from the Costa Brava to Tarragona. Examples of dishes using this combination are *mero à la costa brava, langosta del ampurdán* (a casserole of langouste with snails, onion, tomato, and wine), and *gallina tibidado* (chicken). Spain has many almond recipes, including those for eels and other fish in almond sauce, artichokes stuffed with almonds, and kidneys with almonds. Other countries do not so far seem to have been so prolific in this respect.

AJO BLANCO

Soak 1 or 2 crustless slices of bread in water and squeeze them dry. Pound them to a paste with 4 oz (100 g) of blanched almonds and 2 large cloves of garlic. Work the mixture to a cream, slowly adding olive oil and wine vinegar. Beat well and add salt to taste. This can be eaten, diluted, as a cold soup, as a seasoning, or as a sauce with fish, vegetables, or anything with which its smooth garlicky flavor will blend.

SALTED ALMONDS

Many recipes advise frying almonds, but this leaves them rather oily. It is better to roast them very slowly, watching all the time, until they turn pale beige and can be snapped. Cool them and, when they are almost cold, shake them first with egg white and then with very fine salt. Some people put them into saturated brine before drying.

[*Almond*—French: *amande;* German: *Mandel;* Italian: *mandorla;* Spanish: *almendra. Bitter almond*—French: *amande amère;* German: *Bittermandel;* Italian: *mandorla amara;* Spanish: *almendra amarga*]

ALTITUDE. The effects of altitude on cooking are considerable, because the higher the altitude, the greater the drop in atmospheric pressure and the lower the temperature at which water boils. For those who live at around 13,000 ft (4000 m), it is impossible to cook a potato or a cabbage properly without a pressure cooker. Such effects are felt not only in places like La Paz, Bolivia, at 11,800 ft (3490 m), but even in Johannesburg—at about half that altitude. In particular, the lowered boiling point critically affects such processes as sterilization and canning. Camping on the shores of the Dead Sea, 1,296 ft (395 m) below sea level, one can notice a slight shortening of cooking times. In canning and bottling, temperatures and pressures should be adjusted as follows.

Altitude		Water Boils		To Sterilize		
ft	m	°F	°C	Extra minutes	or	Extra pressure
Sea level		212	100		lb/in²	kg/cm²
500	150	211	99.4	2	1	
1000	305	210	98.9	4	1	0.07
2000	610	208	97.8	8	1	
3000	914	206	96.7	12	2	
4000	1219	204	95.6	16	2	0.14
5000	1524	202	94.4	20	3	
6000	1829	201	93.9	25	3	0.21
7000	2134	199	92.8	30	4	0.28

In rough terms, the boiling point of water drops about 2°F (1°C) for every 100 ft (300 m) of altitude.

[*Altitude*—French: *altitude;* German: *Höhe;* Italian: *altitudine;* Spanish: *altitud*]

ALUM. The alum which has most commonly been used in the kitchen is potash alum, potassium aluminum sulfate, $K_2SO \cdot Al_2(SO_4)_3 \cdot 2H_2O$. Like all alums, it is a double salt, and is made by mixing solutions of potassium sulfate and aluminum sulfate and crystallizing out the alum. It also occurs naturally (as in the Yorkshire alum shales, which have been worked since 1600) and in 18th-century recipes was called rock alum. It was used by the Arabs as a mordant for dyes and used to be a common household remedy: being very astringent, it was used to treat hemorrhoids, gumboils, and sore gums caused by ill-fitting false teeth; it also formed the basis of an invalid drink called alum whey.

In cooking, alum had various uses (an old recipe I have for curd cheese cakes used it) and was not thought harmful. Today, it is often banned from commercial products.

[*Alum*—French: *alun;* German: *Alaun;* Italian: *allume;* Spanish: *alumbre*]

ALUMINUM. The most abundant metal in the earth's crust, aluminum cannot be smelted from its ore by simple means, so was one of the last of our common metals to be discovered (in 1825). Even then, there was no way of making it in quantity until 1886, when the electrolytic process was invented. For many years more, it remained expensive, but in this century, with the arrival of plentiful electric power, it has become the cheap everyday metal of kitchen utensils, while the iron pots have become more costly.

Aluminum, when exposed to the air, gets a thin coating of oxide which protects it. It is dissolved by strong alkalis, such as caustic soda, but only to a small extent by fruit and kitchen acids, although these are likely to strip off the film of oxide. In any case, after extensive research, no harm has been found to come from using aluminum pans, and taste changes are much less than with iron saucepans. (The violent antipathy that some people have to aluminum utensils has no scientific basis.) Aluminum is an excellent conductor of heat, better than iron, though not as good as copper—as long as pans are fairly thick and heavy, they do not develop hot spots. Some foods have a tendency to stick to aluminum, especially when the pan bottom becomes pitted. Unlike cast iron, aluminum is not porous, so does not trap fat and develop its own nonstick surface, nor can it be coated with tin. It may be treated with a nonstick plastic, but that is all too vulnerable to scratching.

Foils made of aluminum have replaced lead foil for most purposes. They have also come into general kitchen use for wrapping meat for the oven, for pit barbecues, covering pans, sealing sandwiches, and a host of other purposes. The foil does not burn, and, being shiny, reflects radiant heat (which is why it must be removed to allow meat to brown). However, it does not absorb fat, so in that respect is inferior to parchment paper for oven wrapping. Heavy-gauge aluminum wire is easily bent and makes excellent small skewers for kebabs. To make them, nothing more is needed than a small pair of pliers.

[Aluminum—French: aluminium; German: Aluminium; Italian: alluminio; Spanish: aluminio]

AMARANTH. Plants of the family Amaranthaceae have recently acquired importance in the U.S. (where they have long been simply a weed) because of the efforts of the staff of Rodale Press, Inc., who have touted this plant as a source of nutritious food that was important to the Aztecs and should be revived in the U.S. and around the world as our planet looks for grain that is nourishing and plentiful.

The amaranth is an annual with large seed heads ranging in color from purple to white. Some people call it pigweed, but it should be distinguished from the pigweed called *lamb's-quarters—the similarities are that both weeds flourish wild, both are food appreciated by pigs (who seem to be sensitive to good foods such as truffles), and both have amazing food value: amaranths are high in protein, which is lacking in most grains.

Amaranths, of which the Rodale germplasm collection includes some 650 varieties, have many qualities that recommend them to the market: the seeds can be ground into flour and made into bread (especially such flatbreads as Indian chapaties or Mexican tortillas); they can be popped into small white kernels similar to popcorn; the greens are delicious and nutritious stir-fried; and furthermore, the plant does not wilt or turn bitter in hot weather.

AMCHUR or **amchoor.** Dried *mango powder.

AMINO ACIDS. These weak organic acids containing the nitrogenous amino group are the bricks from which proteins are made and into which they are broken down during digestion. Of about 20 amino acids required by the body only 8 cannot be made by it. They are: tryptophan, lysine, methionine, phenylalanine, threonine, valine, leucine, and isoleucine. Others—glycine, alanine, glutamic acid, proline, aspartic acid, serine, tyrosine, cysteine, cystine, asparagine, glutamine, histidine, and arginine—can all be made by the body, but children sometimes cannot produce enough histidine and arginine to meet their nutritional requirements. Protein foods that contain the full range of amino acids are egg yolk, fresh milk, liver, and kidney. There is some evidence that if all the amino acids are not present in a meal, much or all of the others consumed are wasted. Vegetarian complete sources are brewer's yeast, soybeans, and wheat germ. Other pulses, on which much of the world depends for protein, are inadequate unless eaten with good whole-wheat bread or other protein.

AMMONIA (NH₃). Sometimes called spirits of hartshorn (because it was made from the antlers of deer), ammonia is an exceedingly pungent gas with a characteristic smell. Household ammonia is a dilute solution of the gas in water. Ammonia is sometimes released by certain sorts of baking powder, but it is highly volatile and passes off during cooking. Ammoniacal smells are produced in the breakdown of amino acids (from proteins) by bacteria, and the smell—for instance, in Camembert cheese which has been wrongly handled—is a warning of decomposition.

[*Ammonia*—French: *ammoniaque;* German: *Ammoniak;* Italian: *ammoniaca;* Spanish: *amonieco*]

AMMONIUM BICARBONATE (NH₄-HCO₃). A colorless, crystalline substance with some smell of ammonia. At 140°F (60°C), it slowly decomposes into carbon dioxide, water, and ammonia, and can thus be used as a baking powder, since the ammonia is lost into the atmosphere.

AMONTILLADO. *See* sherry.

AMYLASE. *See* diastase.

ANAR DANA. *See* pomegranate.

ANCHOVY. All over the world there are species of small fish locally known as anchovies (and many are species of the same genus *Engraulis*), but they do not, when cured, de-

ANCHOVY

velop the flavor of the true anchovy (*E. encrasicholus*), which comes from the Mediterranean and the coasts of southern Europe. When the fish is bought fresh in the market (as commonly seen in Spain and Italy), it is 3–6 in. (8–16 cm) long and bright silver, except for the back, which is green when freshly caught but soon darkens toward mackerel blue and finally almost to black. This is a barometer of freshness. Anchovies move in large shoals that are attracted to fishermen's lights at night. Although caught from March to September, anchovies are most plentiful in summer, when the bulk of the catch is treated commercially. Anchovies, incidentally, can always be distinguished from sardines (which may also be in the market) because the anchovy's mouth is very large indeed, extending to the back of the head, and when opened it gives the fish spectacular gape—the Spanish call the fish *boquerón,* which one might translate as "big-mouth."

Fresh anchovies are delicious, but they have white flesh and none of the special anchovy taste. This, together with the red color, develops by fermentative changes under alkaline conditions after salting for at least a month. In many places on the European coasts where anchovies are caught, people usually cure their own.

The salting of anchovies goes back thousands of years, into antiquity. Later, in Victorian times, they were often used for larding meat. Anchovy sauce was served with beef steaks and on fish, and anchovy butter on hot toast was simple and popular. Bottled anchovy essence was a usual kitchen ingredient, and plain salted anchovies were available. Today, these are difficult to obtain because, as the Portuguese Instituto de Conservas de Peixe told me, "A long time ago we exported anchovied fish in brine, which is not done anymore because it represents the raw material for our fillets industry." In fact, anchovy fillets in oil do quite well for most cooking purposes, and anchovy paste in a tube is useful in small amounts for flavoring rémoulade sauce and making anchovy butter.

ACCIUGA IN SALAMOIA

This is the way of salting anchovies used in Italy, where special straight-sided glass jars are sold for the purpose. However, any wide-mouthed jar big enough to get your hand into will do. You also need a clean, flat stone to act as a weight in the jar. The anchovies must be quite fresh and firm.

To clean anchovies, hold them in your left hand. With your right hand, pinch them behind the head, through the backbone, and pull, in one movement, bringing out the entrails still attached to the head. Do not wash the fish, but pack them in layers in the jar, sprinkling each layer well with salt (start with salt at the bottom). When the jar is nearly full, but not filled to the top, finish with a good sprinkle of salt and put the clean stone on top. Cover to keep out dust. Shortly, the liquid extracted from the fish by the salt will come up to cover them as the weight sinks. If mold grows, remove it and sprinkle on a little more salt. After 3 months, the fish should be ready—the red color develops naturally. Before use, soak the anchovies for a short time in water to remove some of the salt.

Anchovies are often used for flavoring in Austrian cooking, and the garnish *à la viennoise* contains anchovies. They are used even more in Italy, where they are frequently mixed with garlic as a flavoring, as in the sauce used for dipping vegetable pieces in *bagna cauda* and in many sauces for pasta. In Spain, anchovies are eaten as *boquerones*.

SPAGHETTI CON ALICI E POMODORI
(SPAGHETTI WITH ANCHOVIES AND
TOMATOES)

Chop, peel, and seed about 1 lb (400 g) of tomatoes and fry them slowly for 20 minutes in 2 tablespoons of good olive oil together with 8 chopped (canned) anchovy fillets and a clove of garlic (whole). Meanwhile, put 1 lb (450 g) of spaghetti to cook in fast-boiling salted water. Heat a serving dish. Chop up a handful each of fresh basil and parsley and add them, plus plenty of freshly ground pepper, to the sauce 1½ minutes before the spaghetti is cooked. Drain the pasta. Mix it immediately with 4 tablespoons grated Parmesan cheese and 5 tablespoons olive oil. Pour the sauce over and mix again. Rush it to the table, where it will feed four people as a main course and more as a starter.

[*Anchovy*—French: *anchois;* German: *Anschovis;* Italian: *acciuga, alice;* Spanish: *anchoa, boquerón*]

ANCHUSA. *See* alkanna.

ANDOUILLE. Type of thick French sausage, originally from Normandy and Brittany, made of pig's entrails, tripe, and a little belly, salted, cut in strips, and packed into convenient lengths of large intestine. The sausages are cooked by boiling in a marinade (which often contains white wine but varies with local practice), then treated for 2 days in salt brine and finally smoked for about 3 days. *Andouille* is not a keeping sausage: it lasts about a week and is usually bought sliced and ready for eating cold as part of an hors d'oeuvre. Some small local varieties are made to be sold whole. *Andouilles* from Vire in Normandy are the most famous. Generally not a very elegant-looking sausage, the *andouille* is black or brown from the smoke and wrinkled and knobbly from the bits of tripe. When cut, it has an interesting section, with thick whitish squiggles of tripe embedded like fossils in a matrix. The taste, however, is excellent.

ANDOUILLETTE. Virtually the same in contents as an *andouille* but much smaller, being packed into the small intestine of the pig. *Andouillettes* are often not smoked and are intended for broiling, although they can be eaten cold, since they are already cooked. They are sold either glazed with fat or wrapped in paper, and have sometimes been pressed while cooling, which improves their appearance, but they may also be left in their original knobbly state. In either case, they will keep only for a couple of days. They are usually slashed and grilled or fried. There are some fancy local varieties, such as those from Nancy which contain truffles and Madeira wine. *Andouillettes* are a delicious French specialty, and easy to make, so anyone who has access to pig's tripes should possess Jane Grigson's *The Art of Charcuterie* (Knopf, 1968), which gives full directions on how to make these and other pork products at home.

ANGELFISH or **angel shark.** *See* shark.

ANGELICA. A giant umbelliferous plant standing as high as a man. A native of Scandinavia and most countries northeast of the Alps, it has white flowers, a thick, hollow stem, and a distinctive musky smell. Angelica (*Angelica archangelica*) is best known for its green, candied stems, which are used in confectionery and for decorating sweets. It is now little grown in gardens and very difficult to buy fresh. Nevertheless, the leaves and stems of angelica have many uses: as an herb for flavoring fish, in salads, with stewed rhubarb, or in marmalade. The roots are mainly used in herbal medicine. The seeds may be harvested and used as a flavoring. Angelica is sometimes said to have certain flavor similarities with juniper (although not to my palate), and it may be used in flavoring gin and liqueurs.

CANDIED ANGELICA

Cut young angelica stems, boil them in water until tender, then strip off the outer skin. Put the stems back in the water and simmer until they are green. Dry and weigh. Cover with an equal weight of sugar and leave for 2 days to make a syrup in which they should be boiled well, then taken out, and drained. Concentrate the syrup by further boiling or by adding more sugar, being careful not to let it caramelize (brush down the sides of the pan with water). Put back the angelica. Allow it to cool in the syrup, then drain and dry in a cool oven with the door ajar.

[*Angelica*—French: *angélique;* German: *Angelika;* Italian: *angelica;* Spanish: *angélica*]

ANGELWING. *See* clam.

ANGOSTURA BITTERS. Named after a Venezuelan town, now called Ciudad Bolívar, on the Orinoco River, angostura bitters were originally formulated as medicine for fever. Today (like Indian tonic water, which also contains quinine) they are used with gin and other alcoholic beverages for fun. The formula is secret, but the contents are said to be cloves, mace, cinnamon, and nutmeg, with orange and lemon peel, prunes, quinine, and rum.

HICCUP CURE

Cut a thin slice of lemon. Heap ½–1 teaspoon sugar on it. Moisten the sugar with a few drops of angostura bitters. Eat the whole thing in one mouthful.

ANISE or **aniseed.** From an umbelliferous plant (*Pimpinella anisum*) native to the Middle East and cultivated at least since the days of the pharaohs, this seed was used by

ANISE

the Romans to flavor cakes. Today its most important use is in certain Mediterranean and Aegean drinks: pastis, ouzo, arrack, and anisette.

Many people do not like its taste. Although anise blends delightfully with dried figs, I cannot approve the Spanish habit of using it to flavor bran for a breakfast cereal. In savory dishes, it gives a new dimension when traces are used in fish soup; it blends well with garlic, and its perfume suits langouste and prawns of various kinds. There are, too, specialty dishes in which it is used with chicken, partridge, and other birds.

In France, anise is usually introduced in the form of pastis, a mixture of flavors with anise predominant. In Southeast Asia, and to a lesser extent in India, the seed is ground as one of the spice ingredients in certain curries, and the seeds are often chewed as a digestive and to sweeten the breath after a meal. Anise also plays its part in Chinese cooking, but there it usually comes from *star anise. The appearance, size, and taste of aniseed vary greatly from country to country. As a flavoring for use in difficult-to-recognize amounts, anise is neglected and repays experiment.

[*Anise*—French: *anis;* German: *Anis;* Italian: *anice;* Spanish: *anis*]

ANISE PEPPER. *See* Chinese pepper.

ANNATTO. A bright, orange-yellow dye, virtually tasteless and long used for coloring butter (which is often naturally white), margarine, cheese (like Cheshire), and smoked fish. It comes from a small evergreen tree (*Bixa orellana*), locally called *urucú* by the Indians of tropical South America. The spiny pods are full of seeds surrounded by bright red arils. The arils are scraped out and made into a paste for commercial annatto. The seeds are ground whole and used as a spice in parts of Latin America.

APPLE. The apple (*Malus* genus) is the world's most important temperate-zone fruit. Apples have been cultivated for at least 3000 years. More than 20 distinct varieties were known and grown even in Roman times. Since apples are highly variable and many trees cross easily when flowers are pollinated from one variety to another, thousands of varieties are known. However, the number that are widely grown has decreased with the emergence of types, including self-fertile hybrids, which are outstanding in either commercial or gastronomic qualities.

Apples grow anywhere in the northern hemisphere south of latitude 65°N (and in similar climates in the southern hemisphere), provided they get an adequately cold resting period in winter and are not nipped by frost during flowering.

Apples were among the first items planted by the colonists in America. Some 7000 varieties have been recorded in the U.S., and apple pie is virtually the national dessert. Among the best-known apples in this country are the following:

Cortland is medium red, smooth, and shiny, with white tender flesh. Rich and tart, it is excellent for eating and can be baked, poached, or used in pies or applesauce.

Golden Delicious, available almost everywhere almost any time, accounts for one-fifth of the U.S. apple crop. It has pale to bright yellow skin. The sweet flesh is fine-grained and crisp, though some apple connoisseurs find it bland, and its texture can be mealy. It retains its shape when baked and also makes fine applesauce.

Granny Smith, native to the southern hemisphere, is increasingly available in the U.S. Many cooks prefer its tart-sweet flavor and superb cooking qualities. It has yellow-green skin and keeps very well.

Jonathan is a bright red apple with tiny white dots, rich and lively in flavor. Its juiciness causes it to cook down considerably, but it is good for pies and makes delicious pink applesauce and apple butter.

McIntosh, a favorite all-around apple, is thin-skinned, tender, and greenish, blushed with red. It requires less cooking time than other apples.

Northern Spy has skin that appears to be red-striped. It is crisp and juicy, with a spicy taste, and is a fine all-purpose apple.

Red Delicious, with its distinctive shape and five-knobbed crown, is glossy dark red and one of the favorite eating varieties. It has been described as having a "sugar-and-spice" flavor.

Rhode Island Greening has smooth, waxy skin that is green to somewhat yellow. A quite tart apple, it is excellent for baking or applesauce. Once the favorite green apple in the U.S., it is now sometimes hard to find.

Rome Beauty, with a pleasant, mild flavor and firm texture, has a reputation as a superior baking apple. It has cherry-red fruit with slight yellow stripping and is known as a "winter" apple because of its excellent keeping qualities.

Winesap, a dark-red apple with firm flesh, is a favorite for cider. It has a distinctive, subtle winy flavor and is a good keeper.

Apples store well for many months, and thus they were at one time the only fresh fruit to be had at all during the winter. Today, with the techniques of chilling and gas storage (by which apples can be kept in good condition for up to a year), we have forgotten what it was like to be dependent on the seasons. Few people still bother to lay down apples at home.

Don't bother to store early or midseason varieties—they will keep for only a short period. However, late varieties that mature only after gathering need to be stored for from 4 weeks to several months. Select apples that are not damaged or bruised in any way and then wrap them singly in newspaper or put them individually into small plastic bags, making sure that they are not sealed. Wrapping prolongs the life of an apple, helps prevent shriveling, and stops the spread of rot from one apple to another. Once wrapped, apples can be stored in boxes or metal bins and left in a cool, frost-free place such as a cellar or garden shed. Keep apples that ripen at different times in separate containers. They shouldn't be left in a loft or attic where the air tends to be too warm and dry.

The variety of apple is important in cider-making—the special *cider types provide some bitterness. (From cider we get cider *vinegar as well as applejack and Calvados brandy.) Experience will show that crab apples differ in their quality for making jelly; country people know the best trees and ignore those that make insipid crab-apple jelly.

Products made from apples include dried apples (see drying), *pectin (from cores and skins), and apple butter, which the Dutch took to America for spreading on bread. Applesauce and apple butter were laid down in large quantities in the autumn to see the American colonists through the winter. An early recipe for apple butter gives some idea of the quantities involved: "10 gallons sweet cider. 3 pecks of cored and quartered apples (do a few at a time). Cook slowly. Add 10 lb. of sugar, 5 oz. of cinnamon. Stir for 5–6 hours with a wooden paddle."

[*Apple*—French: *pomme;* German: *Apfel;* Italian: *mela;* Spanish: *manzana*]

APRICOT. The apricot (*Prunus armeniaca*) has been cultivated for so long (it has been grown in China for some 4000 years) that it is impossible to be quite certain of its natural home, which is probably somewhere in Asia. It is a staple fruit in Middle Eastern valleys—those flat parcels of alluvial soil irrigated by a river, shaded by poplars, and surrounded by barren mountains. In fact, apricots thrive in the sort of climate where the pomegranate and almond grow. They do not like the tropics, save in exceptional situations. Apricots are extensively grown in Iran, Afghanistan, the western Himalayas, China, Japan, California, South Africa, and Australia, as well as the warmer areas near the Mediterranean, notably North Africa and Spain (Murcia, Valencia, and the Balearic Islands).

There are many varieties, differing in hardness, texture, and size. Colors range from pale yellow to deep reddish orange, and some are sun-freckled with brick or carmine, even with rosy patches. Inside, the apricot flesh is usually a shade of yellow or orange, but some are white-fleshed. Apricots do not peel easily—anyway, some of the flavor lies in the skin—but they can be pulled into two halves and the stone is always free. A fresh, perfectly ripe apricot of a good variety, picked warm off the tree, has an incomparable smell and a delicious taste. Imported apricots will have been picked rather unripe—though with full color—and the flavor is never the same.

Apricots are cooked with meat in Iran and the Middle East; they go especially well with lamb, the staple meat of the area. From there, by a roundabout route, apricots have got into the sauce for *sassaties* (kebabs) in South Africa. In sweet dishes, they are much more interesting in flavor than peaches when cooked.

Usually an apricot dish should be very sweet. Syrups that apricots are poached in should be heavy. Stuffed with almonds or almond paste, apricots are Allah's gift to the Arab sweet tooth, but one of the simplest and most delicious ways of eating them is in the Austrian *marillenknödel,* an apricot dumpling of diet-shattering splendor (an apricot, stuffed with a lump of sugar, sealed in a thin coat of light dumpling mixture, poached, and finished in crispy, butter-fried bread crumbs and sugar).

Because apricots travel badly and do not keep, many are canned or dried, or are made into jam. Canned apricots are very often disappointing; they do not take on a new dimension as does the canned peach. Dried apricots are made by splitting them and leaving them out on mats to dry in the sun. To prevent browning, the halves are usually treated with burning sulfur fumes. More modern methods of treatment produce a softer, more pliable, and sweeter product—nice even to chew raw—but those who suspect the use of chemicals will prefer small whole dried apricots, which are untreated chemically.

Apricots and their kernels have recently come in for attention following the discovery that the people of Gilgit, where apricots are a staple food, do not suffer from many of our common Western diseases, and cancer is virtually unknown there. Apricots are particularly rich in vitamin A compared to both peaches and apples.

Apricots are easily made into jam, and apricot jam—with its pleasant but not assertive taste—is much used in confectionery for filling and glaze. With fresh apricots, jam is usually made with equal weights of sugar and fruit, but with dried apricots, the sugar must be 3 times the weight of the fruit.

Apricot liqueurs are produced in most countries—apricot brandy, *apry, abricota, abricotine, capricot,* etc. Some taste rather too strongly of bitter almonds, while others are very sweet. However, the Hungarian eau de vie *barack* (made by distilling a fermented apricot mash) is my favorite spirit; it may with advantage be used either before or after a meal. The flavor is nothing like apricots, being rather reminiscent of a very fine mirabelle. The kernels of apricot stones may be poisonous for the same reason that bitter *almonds are poisonous, and can equally be made safe by roasting. A delicious liqueur, *noyau, can easily be made from them, and they are the traditional ingredient of the famous *amaretti di Saronno.* Apricot kernels are exported in bulk from Australia and are important in commercial baking and confectionery, particularly in the U.S., where bitter almonds are banned.

APRICOTS IN SYRUP

Wash 2 lb (1 Kg) of very fine, ripe apricots, put them in a pan of cold water, and bring them to the boil. Immediately refresh the fruit in ice-cold water and leave it for 3 hours to cool thoroughly. Put the apricots in a cold syrup made by dissolving 2 lb (1 Kg) of sugar in 2 cups (600 ml) of water. Bring them to the boil and cook until they are tender. Cool the fruit in the syrup.

[*Apricot*—French: *abricot;* German: *Aprikose, Marille* (Austria); Italian: *albicocca:* Spanish: *albaricoque*]

APRY. *See* liqueurs and cordials.

ARBUTUS. *See* cranberry.

ARECA NUT. *See* betel nut.

ARGOL or **winestone.** The name for the hard, crusty deposit in casks or tanks of maturing wine. It is dried and exported from wine-growing areas as hard, shiny scales and is the raw material from which ★cream of tartar and ★tartaric acid are made. The semipurified form is called tartar. To remove impurities, the argol is dissolved in boiling water and mixed with absorbent clay and blood charcoal to take up color and other unwanted material. It is then filtered, and the pure cream of tartar is crystallized out.

[*Argol*—French: *tartre brut;* German: *Weinstein;* Italian: *tartaro;* Spanish: *tártaro*]

ARMADILLO. Various species of this armor-covered mammal (order Edentata, family Dasypodidae) are esteemed good eating by the inhabitants of the tropical and temperate parts of South America, where most armadillos live. A few species range farther north into the southwestern U.S., and the nine-banded armadillo (*Dasypus novemcinctus*) is hunted for food in the U.S.

As with turtles, the carapace of the armadillo is removed before cooking. The flesh has a somewhat musky taste, though its flavor has been compared to that of duck, and it is often seasoned with spices, lemon, or wine. The meat is most frequently used in soups and chili con carne.

ARMAGNAC. French brandy, second only to cognac and with its own marked, individual character. Armagnac comes from Gascony, in the vicinity of Condom, a town southeast of Bordeaux. It is made from the poor acid wine of the *picpoul* grape (a variety of the *folle blanche*), which must, by law, be grown, fermented, and distilled in the Bas-Armagnac, Haut-Armagnac, or Ténarèze districts (that from the Bas-Armagnac and Ténarèze is the best). Like cognac, armagnac is aged in oak casks for up to 40 years. It is empty to argue whether cognac or armagnac is the better, because they are different, and it is a matter of each person's taste. However, in cooking, armagnac is sometimes specified and then the recipe must be followed. For example, a *bécasse à l'armagnac* (woodcock cooked with armagnac) would be distinguished from the same bird cooked *à la fine champagne* (cognac).

ARROWROOT. This old-fashioned ingredient, a fine white powder, consists of more than 80% starch. The original arrowroot plant is from Central and South America and is named after *aru* root of the Aruac Indians, but other sources of starch have been used and given the name "arrowroot." True West Indian or Bermuda arrowroot is made from the young rhizomes of tropical species of *Maranta*, mainly *M. arundinacea*, and supplies mainly come from St. Vincent in the Caribbean. The rhizomes are dealt with in the usual way for starch preparation. They are first pulverized (originally in wooden mortars but now by machinery); the pulp is then mixed with water, the fiber removed, and the milky liquid strained into settling tanks. For further purification, the water is drained off; the white sludge is again mixed with water and again settled. It is finally drained and dried to a powder of starch grains with very little debris. Because of the small size of the grains, it is easily digestible. As a thickening, it is superior to cornstarch in clarity, appearance, and the absence of any taste of its own. West India arrowroot forms a firm, clear starch jelly when heated with syrup or water; it is particularly good for fruit glazes and for flans and puddings. Arrowroot can be made to substitute for other starch substances. Arrowroot noodles, which are made in China, differ from other pasta in being completely transparent.

Other arrowroots include Florida arrowroot (from *Zamia floridana*), East Indian arrowroot (from *Curcuma angustifolia*), and Tous-les-mois, Tulema, or Queensland arrowroot (from *Canna edulis*). Queensland arrowroot, in spite of its name, comes from a plant native to South America and there is called *achira*. Brazilian arrowroot is from the cassava, and Oswega arrowroot is an American product made from corn. Portland arrowroot is made from the poisonous cuckoopint or lords-and-ladies (*Arum maculatum*) but is acrid, despite many washings, and so is only survival food in an emergency.

[*Arrowroot*—French: *arrow-root;* German: *Pfeiwurz;* Italian: *maranta, tubero edule;* Spanish: *arrurruz*]

ARTICHOKE. A name shared by three unrelated plants, ★Chinese artichoke, ★globe artichoke, and ★Jerusalem artichoke.

ARUGULA. *See* rocket.

ASAFETIDA. A gum obtained from the root of a giant fennel-like plant, *Ferula assafoetida*, which is mainly grown in Iran, Afghanistan, and India. It is usually bought ground. Although it has a horrible, garlicky smell, it is a useful spice in small quantities, with fish for instance, and is quite essential in many Indian vegetarian dishes.

[*Asafetida*—French: *assafoetida, férule perisque;* German: *Teufelsdreck;* Italian: *assafetida;* Spanish: *asafétida*]

ASCORBIC ACID. *See* vitamin C.

ASPARAGUS is a cultivated form of the wild *Asparagus officinalis,* a member of the lily family which grows quite plentifully in some parts of Europe and Russia and is naturalized elsewhere, for instance in the eastern states of the U.S. and in irrigated parts of the American West. A subspecies, *prostratus,* is a rare native of the coasts of Dorset, Cornwall, South Wales, and Ireland. The wild asparagus often seen in spring in Spanish markets—bunches of very spindly green stalks—is a different species (*Asparagus aphyllus*), in which leaves have become strong spines. It grows in dry, rocky situations in the hotter parts of the Mediterranean region—Spain and the Balearic Islands, Sardinia (but not Corsica), Sicily,

Greece, Cyprus, and North Africa. It is much gathered as a local specialty and has a strong, rather bitter flavor which comes through when it is mixed with other vegetables. Asparagus fern is a decorative species of asparagus and not a fern.

Cultivated asparagus has been prized in Europe for more than 2000 years, although in Britain it was not much grown until Elizabethan times. We eat the only part of the plant that is not impossibly tough and woody, the young shoot just before or just after it leaves the ground. Asparagus is expensive because it takes several years to establish a good bed, and although the bed will last and improve for many years, the crop occupies the ground continually, requires a great deal of fertilizer, and does not produce a heavy yield of food. It also demands a lot of handwork, since each spear must be harvested individually with a long asparagus knife probing beneath the soil. Its merit is its deliciousness.

There is much controversy as to which type of asparagus is the best: white, green, or purple. The white is more popular in Belgium, Germany, and parts of France, the green or purple in the U.S., Britain, and most of Italy. Essentially, white asparagus consists of shoots which have never seen the light, and it is claimed that they are more tender in texture and more delicate in taste as a result. The spears are usually thick, with almost no scales, but only a short part of the length is young enough to be edible. Early varieties, too, tend to be white, as also is out-of-season asparagus obtained by forcing roots artificially.

Green and purple types, however, are cut when the shoots are well clear of the soil, and advocates say that having seen the sun they have a better flavor and more vitamins. They have a more pointed tip and are more open, sometimes loose and "scaly," usually with the tender, edible part of the spear longer. These tend to be main-crop or later varieties.

When buying asparagus, look first for freshness, since stale asparagus is bitter. Stale spears look dry or wrinkled and are often dirty-colored; also the cut ends may be soggy if the bundles have been standing in water. Spears should be of even size (not a few large ones on the outside of the bunch concealing the poor ones in the middle). Asparagus may be freshened up at home by standing the cut ends for a short time in water, but the sooner it is eaten the better. The points, which are very brittle in good asparagus, should be intact, and only the base of the stem should feel woody. Bargain asparagus must always be suspected except when the reason for the low price is that the spears are misshapen or thin. Such asparagus is, however, fine for soups or with eggs.

Many people like to peel asparagus spears—you can use a sharp potato peeler—from the base of the scaly tip down to the cut end. You can then tie them in small bunches, put them into boiling, salted water, cover the pan, and boil fast until you can easily pierce the base of the stem with a knife point. Depending on the size and freshness of the asparagus, this can take 5–15 minutes. You can also stand the bunches upright so that the tips steam clear of the water. There are special asparagus boilers, some rather like small, rectangular fish kettles, with a perforated plate on which the asparagus is laid, and others in which the spears stand upright. After draining, put the asparagus on a folded napkin or, if it is to be served cold, chill it immediately in a colander under running water. Some consider that asparagus is best eaten lukewarm.

There are dozens of sauces to go with asparagus: it is usually served hot with melted butter, but other preferences include vinaigrette, mayonnaise (especially if combined with orange juice and cooked peel, or bitter orange juice), hollandaise, mousseline, and mornay sauces. Asparagus goes very well with cheese and is often eaten combined with or sprinkled with Parmesan cheese in Italy (*asparagi alla parmigiana, risotto di asparagi, ris e spargit*). The many classic asparagus dishes range from soup and *asperges frites* to *soufflé aux pointes d'asperges*.

Asparagus is rich in vitamin A as well as in vitamins B_1, B_2, and C. The diet-conscious may gorge on it (but not on most of its accompaniments), since it offers only 15 to 18 Calories per 4 oz (100 g). Asparagus is diuretic. Canned asparagus is good when not too soft, as are frozen asparagus spears, though they are still inferior to fresh ones.

[*Asparagus*—French: *asperge;* German: *Spargel;* Italian: *asparago;* Spanish: *esparrago*]

ASPIC. A clear, light savory jelly used for embedding or glazing cold dishes of eggs, fish and meat. It may be bought as a powder (in which case follow the instructions) or made from gelatin and stock cubes. As a garnish, it is a way of serving and improving cold dishes. It may be cubed and used to surround cold meats, or even chopped finely and piped. Its main use, though, is as the basis of molded dishes, which can be a decorative part of a buffet if they include in their outer layers carefully arranged patterns made up of such colorful ingredients as pieces of red pepper. Tomato aspic is a gelatin of flavored tomato juice, usually molded and served as a salad.

[*Aspic*—French: *aspic;* German: *Aspik;* Italian: *aspic;* Spanish: *áspic*]

AUBERGINE. *See* eggplant.

AURUM. *See* liqueurs and cordials.

AUSTRALIAN BARRACUDA. *See* snoek.

AVOCADO, avocado pear, or **alligator pear**. A fruit borne on a tropical and subtropical evergreen tree (*Persea americana*) of the laurel family. Behind the strikingly different types in shops and markets are three races. The Mexican, with small fruits and anise-scented leaves, is the hardiest; the Guatemalan, from the highlands of Central America, has medium to large fruits with a thick, woody skin; the West Indian grows only in a properly tropical climate and often has very large fruits. There are plenty of crosses between these races, and varieties (now more than 500 of them) are easily propagated by layering, budding, or grafting.

The avocado was used by the Aztecs, who called it *ahuacatl*, from which the modern name is derived via the Spanish *aguacate*. Although the fruit had been noted by the Spaniards as long ago as 1519, and it was planted in the Botanical Gardens in Bangalore, India, in 1819, the general opinion used to be that it was tasteless (as poor varieties certainly are), and its value went unrecognized. It has come into its own, only rather recently, mainly through the work of American breeders; it is still not really popular in the Orient, where it could make a significant contribution to the local diet in many places. However, it is now grown in most tropical and subtropical countries, although it will not tolerate winds or too dry a climate. Avocados thrive in Central and South America, Florida and California, Hawaii and the South Pacific, Australia, South Africa, West Africa, Israel, Madeira, and the Canary Islands, as well as in the Mediterranean regions.

Avocados may be round or pear-shaped, smooth or rough-skinned, green, flecked with yellow, reddish, crimson, purple, or almost black. In size, they vary from that of a hen's egg in small Mexican varieties to huge fruits weighing several pounds each, which can be grown in the West Indies and have no doubt given rise to the name "poor man's breakfast." The avocado, which in many places is an expensive luxury, is a very cheap food in others. It has a very high protein content for fresh fruit and contains at least 25% fat as well as vitamins A and B.

In nature, avocados drop before they are ripe; because they are clipped as soon as they begin to color, they must be given time to ripen. (Until ripe, they need a warm place and must not be put in the refrigerator.) The ripe fruit yields to gentle pressure; you are aware that you could squash it. The single stone comes out cleanly in good varie-

ties. The flesh is creamy, yellowish or greenish, and, when ripe, has a smooth, buttery texture.

Avocados may be cut in half lengthwise and eaten straight out of the skin with a spoon, and the hole left by the stone will conveniently accommodate the dressing— pepper, salt, oil, and vinegar is the simplest of many—but the cavity can also be filled with shrimps or other delicacies. Chopped or cubed avocados are used in salads. There is avocado soup and even avocado ice cream, but perhaps the most famous avocado dish is guacamole, a favorite dish of the Aztecs long before the Spanish conquest. Once just a smooth purée of avocado with tomato (or tomatillo) and chili, it has, with the introduction of onions, coriander leaves, olive oil, vinegar, and other ingredients, been elaborated into many versions.

GUACAMOLE

In Mexico, where avocado trees can be grown in the backyard, the fruit is a staple food and guacamole is not an elegant party dish but everyday fare. Therefore guacamole becomes a "go-as-you-please" dish; there are dozens of recipes, which vary from one part of the country to another and can also depend on what is on hand. In the north, for instance, the tomatillo is an ingredient, whereas in the south the ordinary tomato is commoner. Other recipes do not include tomato at all. Essentially, guacamole is only mashed, ripe avocado flesh seasoned with salt and flavored with the ubiquitous hot green chili and green coriander. Outside Mexico, canned serrano, jalapeño, or other very hot chilies can be substituted for fresh ones without much alteration from the original—even hot chili sauce or cayenne will do if there is nothing else—but the substitution of parsley for green *coriander (which is used like parsley in Mexico) will remove an essential taste. (It is not much trouble to grow a pot of coriander on the window sill. Many Americans can buy it as cilantro in Spanish markets, and it is also known as Chinese parsley or dhania.) To the essentials are frequently added peeled, seeded, and chopped ripe tomato, finely chopped onion, garlic, and lemon or lime juice. A typical recipe is as follows:

Roughly mash the flesh of 2 large, ripe avocados. Add 1 peeled, seeded, and chopped ripe tomato (not too large), 2 teaspoons of very finely chopped mild onion, a trace of garlic, 2-3 finely chopped, seeded green chilies (the amount depends on their hotness), and a small handful of green coriander leaves, finely chopped. Mix and season with salt and lemon juice to taste. A layer of mayonnaise or oil across the top will keep the guacamole from turning dark.

In some parts of Mexico, avocado leaves are used either fresh or dried as a flavoring (at last, a use for plants raised from avocado pits sprouted in a jar). The leaves should be toasted lightly. When ground, they have an aroma which has been described as "mixed anise and hazel," although this will be mild if they have been grown in a cold climate.

[*Avocado*—French: *avocat, poire d'avocat;* German: *Advokatbirne;* Italian: *avocado;* Spanish: *aguacate*]

AVOIRDUPOIS. *See* weights and measures.

AWABI. *See* abalone.

AZEROLE. *See* rowan.

AZUKI. *See* adzuki.

B

BACALAO. *See* salt cod.

BACON. Although this word once referred to the fat on the back of a pig, today bacon is usually made of the meat from a pig's side or belly, between the fourth or fifth rib and the flank. After the spareribs are removed, a rectangular piece is cut to be cured and smoked. In the U.S., bacon is usually sold sliced in strips and wrapped in cellophane; slab bacon is also available, the best quality being lean, firm slabs with a mahogany color and smoky, aromatic flavor. Cured fatty pork from the belly or back is sometimes called "white bacon" but more usually referred to as salt pork or fatback.

Canadian-style bacon comes from the lean strip of pork loin after the tenderloin and bones are removed. It is cured, lightly smoked, and wrapped in plastic or canned.

In Europe, bacon usually means a Wiltshire side, the entire side of a pig with the backbone, tenderloin, breastbone, and pelvic bone removed. The remaining piece of meat and fat is then cured and smoked. Wiltshire sides are graded as leanest, lean, and prime according to fat content. The various cuts of Wiltshires include the flitch (the side of bacon minus the shoulder and ham), gammon (same word as the French *jambon,* but given a shorter, weaker cure than ham), and rashers (which are any thin slices of bacon; streaky rashers have alternating streaks of fat and lean).

The Danes have built up their large export trade of bacon through efficient production based on their bacon pig breed, the Danish Landrace, which has been bred to combine leanness and length of back to the exclusion of all else. It produces a high proportion of the best cuts and a nice balance between lean meat and fat.

Because good-quality bacon requires considerable fat for tenderness and satisfactory frying, food manufacturers have developed a variety of ersatz bacon products for consumers who wish to avoid calories, saturated fat, and nitrates. These products are often processed from soybeans and may include other meats smoked to resemble bacon flavor.

Curing a pig is not difficult, provided that you are not intimidated by the vast technology which has been built up by the bacon industry and is needed only for mass-producing a uniform product without waste. Baconmaking was a yearly task on every farm not so long ago.

Farm bacon. The carcass, after scalding and scraping to remove the bristles, is hung in a cool place to harden. It is split down the back, and the backbone (chine) is removed. The fillets are also taken out, since they do not cure well, and usually the hams and shoulders are taken for separate treatment, leaving the side (flitch) to be cured. The *dry-salting method is the most usual on farms. Here, the sides are rubbed with a mixture of salt, saltpeter, and sugar over a period of about 2 weeks. This method gives the best bacon with the highest keeping quality.

SIMPLE CURING

First clean the side well, soaking and washing it for half an hour in strong, cold brine (2 Tb salt per 4¼ cups water or 30 g per lt) with a pinch of saltpeter. Dry the side with a clean cloth and weigh it. You will need 8% of this weight in salting mixture, which should consist of coarse salt containing 3–4% saltpeter and some sugar—best is light-brown sugar—which is optional, but may be from 5% to as much as 33% of the cure. The temperature should be cool, but not icy (40–50°F or 4–10°C). To begin, carefully give all pockets a little saltpeter for safety, then rub the skin side well with the dry-salting mixture until it begins to sweat. Turn it over and rub the meat side a little. Put the side, skin down, on a bed of salt, and cover it with more salt. Add more the next day, and every day afterward (as it gets wet)—with some inspection and rubbing in any discolored or otherwise suspicious places—for the first 4–5 days. After that, leave the side until it is cured—about 14 days on average. Finally, wipe off the adhering salt with a cloth dipped in boiled water and hang the bacon to dry in a current of cold air, unless you prefer to smoke it. As it matures, bacon may need protection from flies; common coverings include pepper, paraffin, and mesh bags. Well-cured farm bacon hung in a cool dry place will keep for a year.

Factory bacon is mostly cured in brine (sometimes after an initial dry salting), because brine cures give more even results with less handwork. The carcasses can be quickly chilled by refrigeration, which makes it possible to make good bacon all the year and not just in winter.

Mild brine is pumped into the arteries or directly into the muscles by a sort of embalming process. This is so efficient that the curing solution often goes right into the bones. Pumping is an excellent technique if the manufacturer can resist the temptation of making "instant" bacon (some modern methods have produced something approximating bacon within hours). Such cures often use nitrites instead of saltpeter and load the injection fluids with monosodium glutamate and flavorings to replace the natural hammy tastes which have no time to develop. Artificial sweeteners can also replace sugar. The general use of refrigeration has made possible a very lightly cured green (unsmoked) bacon which will survive no more than a few days at room temperatures and would have been unthinkable under farm conditions. In factories, it is often customary to cure the whole ham and shoulder intact. The farm practice of detaching the legs from the flitches and curing them separately as hams is still predominant in countries that eat more ham than bacon.

European bacons include the following:

Guanciale. A specialty from southern Italy and usually translated as a bacon, although it is the cured jaw of the pig. It has a special type of fat and is the correct "bacon" to use in spaghetti *alla carbonara* and *all'amatriciana,* two well-known Italian dishes.

Lard. French for bacon, although the French often use the word *bacon* in the English sense. (*Bacon* is originally a French word meaning any sort of pork, as indeed it was in English until after Shakespeare's time.) The French for lard is *saindoux.*

Pancetta. Italian salted pig's belly. When smoked it is called *bacon.*

Poitrine fumée. Literally smoked breast, the French for bacon.

Selschcarée. Perhaps this just comes in the category of bacon. It is carefully trimmed back, cured in spiced brine for only 3 days, lightly smoked (cold) for 24 hours, and usually eaten boiled with sauerkraut.

Speck. German for bacon but covers items which would hardly come under the same heading in other countries, such as *zigeuner* *speck,* which is little more than cured and smoked fat rolled in paprika; you can eat it raw on cold days when skiing or climbing in the Alps.

Tocino. Spanish salted fat belly or other fat pork. Often covered with a layer of crystalline salt, it is not smoked and bears little resemblance to bacon. Smoked, cured belly in Spain is known as *bacon.*

[*Bacon*—French: *lard;* German: *Speck;* Italian: *lardo;* Spanish: *jamón*]

BACTERIA. These microscopic organisms are smaller than *yeasts and are found everywhere in astronomical numbers. Even though processes involving them were managed by mankind long before bacteria were discovered, some knowledge about them can be useful in the kitchen.

There are thousands of different bacteria, just as there are thousands of different animals and plants, but bacteria have to be distinguished not by their appearance (there are only a few shapes and many look alike) but by what they do. This is possible because each species operates in a specific way and in specific conditions. For instance, *Lactobacillus bulgaricus* (bacteria have no popular names, though they may be referred to by the name of the process or disease which involves them) will always turn milk sugar into lactic acid, but it cannot utilize cane sugar or produce alcohol.

Each single bacterium has an infinitesimally small effect on its surroundings, but we are normally dealing with millions of millions. Bacteria can multiply at a startling rate by simply splitting into two; they can split twice—even three times—in an hour when conditions are exactly right. This accounts for the surprising fact that a single teaspoon of starter will clabber 3½ pt (2 lt) of milk in 5 hours—it would set three times that amount if conditions were perfect, which they never are. Twelve hours later it would, in theory, have clabbered more than 175,000 pt (100,000 lt). It has been calculated that the offspring from a single bacterium

could in theory cover the entire surface of the earth in 2 or 3 days. However, bacteria rapidly use up the available food or pollute their environment with their own waste products—they overwhelm themselves with their unbridled breeding.

In nature, it is rare to find one sort of bacterium growing alone; they are always in mixtures. Indeed, some will not grow at all except in association. Certain kinds are habitually found together in a particular situation (in milk, for instance), and they work together to produce an end product in a way that none of them could do singly. They feed on each other's waste products and follow one another in logical order. It is such a chain of events (which also includes yeasts and fungi) rather than the effect of one organism that we have to deal with in the kitchen. A good example is the ripening of cheese. People were making cheese long before they knew that it was a living process they were controlling. Today, although it taxes the best dairy bacteriologists to follow the sequence of events in any detail, at least we understand why the accepted procedures must be followed exactly and why shortcuts or variations may lead to disaster. If the book says boil for 20 minutes, then the substance must boil for 20 minutes and not for 10.

Bacterial processes can be controlled first of all by temperature. Yogurt-production bacteria grow at around 104°F (40°C), but will be beaten out of the race by other organisms when the temperature is lower. Acidity, type of food, moisture, salt, light or dark, air or no air, the presence or absence of certain other types of organism, and the presence of antibiotics or antiseptics—all these are factors influencing the growth of bacteria.

Certain rod-shaped bacteria can produce spores, which create a special problem. There are only about 150 kinds of these, 100 aerobes (which need air) and 50 anaerobes (which do not need air). Unlike the spores of fungi (but like the spores of yeasts), bacterial spores are not produced for purposes of multiplication, but so that the organism can survive tough conditions. Spores usually form only when the community or culture becomes old, the environment is polluted by waste, or food is scarce. It takes 24 hours for bacteria to form spores (but only 4–6 hours to start germination again). Spores are very difficult to kill. Some can lie dormant for up to 10 years and survive hours of boiling. *See* pasteurization; poisoning.

[*Bacteria*—French: *bactérie;* German: *Bakterie;* Italian: *batteri;* Spanish: *bacteria*]

BAGACEIRA. *See* marc.

BAJRA. *See* millet.

BAKING. In English, this somewhat inexact term usually means cooking bread or cakes in an oven. The Germans have the word *backen* too, from the same source, but in French, Italian, and Spanish one has to be specific and say "cook in an oven." Baking can also mean almost any method of cooking in which the food comes into contact with dry heat or is cooked in ashes. Griddle cakes, muffins, chapaties, and similar breads are baked on an iron plate or griddle, and potatoes may be baked in the ashes of a campfire. For a clam bake, the shellfish is steamed in seaweed, but the seaweed is in contact with hot ashes and stones in a pit—a variation on the most primitive method of baking there is.

In the Orient, a traditional way of cooking is to wrap food in banana leaves and cover it in hot ashes. The modern variant is to wrap the food first in foil and then to bury it in a pit in which a fire has burned for many hours. (Sheep-stealers bake their stolen lamb *under* the fire.) The supposed gypsy way of cooking a hedgehog encased in clay is baking. So also, perhaps, is the even more basic method used by some Australian aborigines whom I have seen throw a wallaby, skin and all, into the campfire. The skin and fur char to form a protective shell of carbon inside which the meat is beautifully baked.

The most primitive form of oven for baking is no doubt the tandoor, which in its simplest form is a large pot sunk into the earth. This is a Middle Eastern device—you find it much used in Iran—and it has spilled eastward into the Punjab, where it is the common way of cooking. In more sophisticated versions, the pot is raised aboveground and built into a sort of stove, which is well insulated with plaster and mud. There may be a means of letting air in at the bottom of the pot to adjust the heat. The fire of wood or dried dung is lit some 2 hours before cooking time, and fuel is controlled so that it will have burned down to ashes by the time the tandoor is hot. Breads are slapped onto the hot sides near the top (beginners will burn their arms and drop the bread into the coals), and meat is threaded on a sword or metal spit and thrust down into the heat. (A square tandoor is easy to construct with fire bricks.)

The tandoor type of oven is limited, and an advance is the brick oven with a side opening which was once common in Britain and America and is still used in rural parts of Europe and in the Middle East. The usual form has a flat bottom, an arched or domed top, and a chimney at the back. The door is closed with an iron sheet that also provides the means of controlling the rate of burning by the amount of air let in—the oven is heated by burning brushwood *in* it, not underneath. The heat permeates the brickwork to give an oven which cools slowly as it is being used; in some ovens a bank of pebbles is heated up. The time taken to heat is several hours, depending on when the oven was last used. When the wood is reduced to ashes, these can be either drawn out or pushed to the back, and the chimney is blocked with a stone. Experts judge the heat of the oven by rubbing a piece of charred stick on the brickwork and noting the sparks formed. There are other tests, such as the time taken to char paper. To work with this type of oven, one must get used to baking on a falling heat, but because bread cooked in such an old-fashioned brick oven has an incomparable taste, it is worth the little practice (and some disasters) needed to master the technique. Flat bread, pizzas, and *nan*—or other doughs—should be put straight onto the hot, ashy brick to bake. They never stick.

The most modern way of baking involves microwaves, created when electrical energy is converted by a magnetron tube into electromagnetic energy. As microwaves contact the food, they cause the liquid molecules in it to vibrate, thus producing heat from friction. Unlike other forms of baking, in microwave cooking the food is heated from within itself, and its surroundings remain cold. Microwave ovens are advantageous for rapid cooking; for this reason, and because it is not necessary to add water to foods, more vitamins and minerals may be retained than in other forms of cooking. Microwave ovens have wide commercial use, and their manufacture has been regulated for safety by the Food and Drug Administration since 1971. However, since the microwave process does not brown food as well and tends to dry out meats and vegetables such as potatoes, it is often not a satisfactory substitute for conventional gas or electric ovens. These can now be bought with interior convection fans. Because they keep the heated air in constant motion, evenly distributed around the food, convection ovens are excellent for baking breads and sealing in the natural juices of meats.

[*Baking*—French: *cuisson au four;* German: *backen, im Ofen braten;* Italian: *cuocere al forno;* Spanish: *cocer al horno*]

BAKING POWDER is a mixture of acid and alkaline substances. When moistened and/or heated, they react together to produce carbon dioxide gas, which in baking makes cakes rise. It is a relative newcomer to cooking. Until the end of the 18th century,

*leavening was managed only with *yeast, although lightness in cakemaking could be produced by beating in air—some recipes suggested "beating for an hour or two"—or by adding spirits, which, being volatile, would expand into a gaseous state when heated.

In 1790, in America, it was found that a refined form of wood ash called pearl ash (a carbonate of potash) could be used in baking cakes to make them rise. Only 2 years later some 8000 tons were exported to Europe. However, pearl ash produces a soapy taste in baked goods, so its use was limited to highly spiced cakes such as gingerbread. Pearl ash was followed by *bicarbonate of soda, also called saleratus (aerating salt). One writer remarked that "it was said to be responsible for much of the dyspepsia common in the USA."

By the mid-19th century, baking powder had been introduced. This was a mixture of bicarbonate of soda with a mild acid, usually *cream of tartar or *tartaric acid, and rice flour. Modern baking powder still contains bicarbonate of soda as its alkaline ingredient, plus a combination of acids to provide a double action with the bicarbonate—an acid such as tartaric acid (which reacts on moistening, releasing gas to aid in the mixing), and a slower-acting acid such as acid sodium pyrophosphate (which releases very little gas until it is heated in the oven). Dried starch or flour is added to baking powder as a filler; it also absorbs any moisture in the atmosphere and thus prevents any reaction from taking place during storage.

In the absence of a bought baking powder, you may use bicarbonate of soda in a mixture containing an acid, such as *buttermilk. An alternative is to make up your own simple baking powder by mixing a tablespoon of bicarbonate of soda with 2 tablespoons of cream of tartar—both of which must be very dry. A drawback of this preparation is that it starts to fizz as soon as it is mixed with liquid; therefore the cake should be baked as soon as possible, or the powder may have exhausted its potential before the cake is heated through enough to set it.

The quantity of baking powder required varies from recipe to recipe, but a good general rule is that the plainer the cake mixture the more baking powder is required; the richer the cake the less baking powder is needed. Too much or too little baking powder upsets the balance of the ingredients, so it is always worth measuring baking powder carefully.

[*Baking powder*—French: *levure chimique;* German: *Backenpulver;* Italian: *lievito;* Spanish: *levadura*]

BAKING SODA. *See* bicarbonate of soda.

BALACHAN, balachong, or **blachan** (and various other spellings) is a very important flavoring in the cooking of Malaysia, Indonesia (where it is called *trasi*), and other Southeast Asian countries. It is made of shrimps or prawns, which are caught in huge numbers in the tropical creeks and salted, dried, pounded, and allowed to mature in a humid heat until a ripe smell and taste develops. One might describe it as gamey, but it is quite essential in the dishes of the region.

Balachan may be colored from pink to dark brick, and may be caked, powdered, or in the form of a pinkish paste. There is no real substitute, although anchovy paste has been suggested as the nearest thing outside the Orient. It keeps almost indefinitely in the refrigerator, provided it is kept dry in a closed jar. *Balachan* is never eaten raw, but is fried with the spices in a recipe, or is roasted dry, then ground and added. You would be well advised to wrap the piece to be roasted in foil; this helps to prevent the smell from pervading the house.

BALACHONG, balichow, or **balachow** is a pickle made in South India of salted shrimp, mangoes, and even fried duck eggs and eaten as a relish with curry (but see *ba-lachan*). It is hot and strongly flavored, for although fresh shrimp are used, the tropical sun has usually given them a ripe taste before the pickle is made. This relish can be bought, or you can make it as follows:

SHRIMP BALACHOW

Clean, shell, and mince 1 lb (450 g) of shrimp. Heat 2 cups (½ lt) of oil and fry in it 1⅓ cups (300 g) of minced onion, and 1½ cups (300 g) skinned, seeded, and chopped tomato. Combine 2 oz (50 g) of garlic, 2 oz (50 g) of fresh ginger, 1 teaspoon of cumin, 1 tablespoon of peppercorns, 2 tablespoons of ground turmeric, 5 oz (125 g) of hot chili, and a little vinegar, and pound them to a paste. Fry this paste and then add the minced shrimp with a small handful of curry leaves (if available). Fry for another minute or so, then add salt and vinegar up to 2 cups (½ lt) to obtain a nice taste and consistency for a relish. Simmer gently until cooked, allow to cool a little, bottle, and seal.

BALM, lemon balm, or **melissa.** A labiate plant native to southern Europe, balm (*Melissa officinalis*) was first introduced to Britain by the Romans. An easily grown peren-

BALM

nial with mintlike leaves, it has a strong lemony scent and can make a change as a flavoring where a little lemon zest might be nice; it is useful as a substitute for *lemon grass and particularly as a flavoring in liqueurs. Lemon balm also makes a pleasantly aromatic tea.

[*Balm*—French: *amélisse, eau de mélisse;* German: *Bienenkraut, Melisse, Zitronenmelisse;* Italian: *melisa, melissa;* Spanish: *balsamita mayor, toronjil, toronjiña*]

BAMBOO SHOOTS. Bamboo is a huge grass. There are many different species, some of which grow to 100 ft (30 m) with a width of 20 in. (50 cm) at the base. Bamboo is one of the characteristic plants of eastern Asia, where it has an important role in the economy. The shoots of those species used for food are dug just before they come above the ground. They can be up to 4 in. (10 cm) in diameter and 1 ft (30 cm) long, looking in that case rather like giant asparagus spears. Hungry travelers should not experiment with bamboo without guidance. Not all species of bamboo are edible, and those that are include some that have a hard outer coat or irritant hairs which must be removed; others contain the exceedingly poisonous prussic (hydrocyanic) acid, which is volatile and thus dissipated when the shoots are boiled. The season when the shoots can be dug is also variable. In northern countries, such as China and Japan, there is a definite spring and autumn, but in the monsoon tropical regions farther south the season for bamboo is dictated by the rains. There are also great differences in the way in which the various sorts of bamboo shoots must be prepared. Some need only to have the scales removed and to be boiled for 10 minutes; others need boiling for several hours.

Bamboo shoots dry and conserve very well. They retain their flavor and crispness when canned. In fact, canned bamboo shoots are often used in the Orient in preference to fresh ones, since they are already cooked and ready to use.

Canned bamboo shoots are exported from China and Japan (where they are called *takenoko*), canned either in water (usually best) or brine, in pieces or whole (best). They look like ivory-colored spinning tops. If the whole can is not to be used at once,

the shoots will keep in the refrigerator for up to 10 days if put in a jar of fresh water which is changed daily. Canned bamboo shoots are ready for use in Chinese or Japanese dishes. In most cases, they are cooked for 5 minutes—just warmed through—but they may also be eaten cold. Pickled bamboo shoots are steamed with beef or pork.

Dried bamboo shoots have been dried in the sun and are even tastier than the canned shoots, but they require more preparation. Their color varies from white to yellow and black. The thin, dark shoots are more flavorful than white ones. The white need to be boiled for 1 hour, cut up, and cooked for a further 30 minutes. The yellow must be soaked for 3 hours in water, then cooked for at least 2 hours before they become tender, but they are worth it for the taste.

[*Bamboo shoot*—French: *pousse de bambou;* German: *Bambusprosse;* Italian: *germoglio di bambu;* Spanish: *caña de bambu*]

BANANA and **plantain.** Originally from India and southern Asia, the banana (*Musa sapientum*) is now cultivated all over the world in frost-free climates. In the warm, humid, windless tropics, it is both the most important commercial fruit and a home-grown staple for subsistence-level farmers, and it is the most popular fruit in the U.S. The banana is said to be one of the first fruits to have been brought into cultivation. Documentary evidence suggests that it was being grown in Assyria more than 3000 years ago, but it must then have died out: the armies of Alexander the Great were surprised at the sight of the strange fruit growing in the Indus Valley in 327 B.C. A thousand years later, the Arabs brought bananas into Egypt and Palestine. In the 15th century, Portuguese navigators found bananas on the Guinea coast of Africa and established them in the Canary Islands, which had been discovered and colonized in 1402. They were taken to the West Indies by a Dominican friar in 1516 and within 25 years had spread throughout the West Indies and tropical America, now the world's main banana-producing area. They had also, it seems, traveled in the opposite direction from Asia across the Pacific, because they were already growing in Hawaii when Captain Cook arrived in 1778.

Bananas remained a luxury in northern Europe until the Imperial Direct Line started operations in the West Indies in 1901. Before the days of refrigeration and fast steamships, Europe had depended on the Canary Islands for bananas (and Canary bananas were the only bananas accepted by my grandmother, who despised the rest as "plantains").

The "hands" of a dozen or so fruit ("fingers") in which bananas are usually marketed are part of a larger bunch—up to a dozen hands arranged around a central stem—which grows on a plant that may be up to 30 ft (10 m) high but is botanically an herb rather than a tree.

Bananas to be transported are cut when they are fully plumped but still green, and the bunches are packed carefully in cartons. They are kept at a temperature of 53–56°F (12–13°C)—never colder, because cold turns bananas black—during shipment; when needed, the bunches are hung to ripen in warmed rooms. Good though such bananas are, they are never quite as excellent as those sun-ripened on the plant. The food value of bananas is high—from a nutritional point of view, they are better than apples in their content of potassium, vitamin A, and vitamin C.

Some species of the genus *Musa* are cultivated for fiber and not for fruit (the Manila rope used by mountaineers was made from these). There are some 400 varieties of bananas; in India and Southeast Asia, the multitude of different sorts in markets may be bewildering. Not only are there varieties grown to withstand transport or for climatic reasons (some will survive several degrees of frost), but some are grown for their fine leaves, which are used to wrap food for cooking (this gives the contents a special taste) or as throwaway plates for serving food. The leaves are used as a wrapping for food in Mexico as well as India. Passing the half leaf (with midrib removed) over a flame to warm it thoroughly will make it more flexible.

Of the bananas grown for eating, some are intended for consumption raw, while others require cooking. There are even varieties with stony black seeds on which you can break your teeth. Small bananas are often the most tasty and sweet (one of these is called lady's fingers and is not to be confused with *okra). Fat, red bananas are particularly used as offerings in Hindu ceremonies.

Cooking varieties, often referred to as plantains (*Musa paradisiaca*), are not sweet at all. They are very firm and excellent finely sliced and fried. In India, bananas are frequently curried with their skins on.

In European and North American cooking, the role of bananas is much more restricted, usually limited to sweet dishes. In the Caribbean, where bananas are used much more in cooking, a great favorite on the Spanish-speaking islands is *tostones,* slices of green plantain, partly fried, then squashed down and fried again until crisp. They are served as a vegetable and as an appetizer with cocktails. On the French-speaking islands, plantains are called *banane,* whereas the sweet, eating varieties are known as *figues* and are popular in a wide range of exotic puddings, usually flavored with rum.

Dried bananas, also known as banana figs, have been peeled, spread out to dry in the sun, and turned daily until they are desiccated. Treated in this simple way, the bananas may darken and are inclined to be attacked by insects. A more sophisticated method is to treat the peeled bananas with sulfur dioxide (from burning sulfur) for 20 minutes, or to dip them in 1% citric acid solution, before sun drying.

Cooking varieties are also dried in a similar manner and ground to make banana flour (plantain meal, *pisang* starch, banana meal, etc.), which is very digestible and sustaining

(Stanley, the famous African explorer, is reputed to have used it). Finally, part of the flower, or the heart of the flower before it opens, is used as a vegetable, as also is the central part of the stem. Banana jam, banana wine, and banana-flavored liqueurs (often reinforced with synthetics) are made, but I have yet to meet anyone who likes them.

[Banana—French: *banane;* German: *Banane;* Italian: *banana;* Spanish: *plátano. Plantain*—French: *plaintain, banane des Antilles;* German: *Wegerich;* Italian: *piantaggine, petacciuola;* Spanish: *llantén*]

BARACK. *See* fruit brandy.

BARBARY PEAR. *See* prickly pear.

BARBE. *See* chicory.

BARBECUE SAUCE. The word "barbecue" comes from the Mexican-Spanish *barbacoa (barbacua),* which originally described the grilling of meat over a fire on bars of green wood. Today it has come to mean almost any open-air cooking of food; whether on an electric spit, a hibachi, or a wood fire. This is perhaps the most primitive method of cooking, but it can be delicious. Many ready-made barbecue sauces are on sale. Homemade ones are usually based on minced onion, tomato purée or paste, or ketchup, sugar, and Worcestershire sauce. Many such sauces are apt to add a cloying flavor to the food. Barbecue sauces should complement the food being grilled, not mask its flavor. For seafood and vegetables, the simplest mixture is sea salt and lemon juice, perhaps with oil or butter to retain moisture. Beef and pork can be grilled with a heavier sauce containing appropriate herbs. Barbecue sauces containing wine or citrus juices to tenderize the meat are often used as marinades. They are then brushed on the food to baste it as it cooks.

BARBERRY (*Berberis vulgaris*) is a shrub that may be native in parts of England, as it is over much of Europe. It used to be grown for its elongated, bright-red berries. They were candied, made into pies and jellies, or pickled for use as a garnish. Barberry is much less common than it was, because the discovery that it is an intermediate host of a cereal fungus, black rust, led to its eradication in many areas. In the U.S., the Department of Agriculture has placed many restrictions on the growth of *B. vulgaris,* which was brought to America by the colonists and has become naturalized in New England. Other species of barberry, however, are immune to black rust and may be grown.

BARCELONA NUT. *See* hazelnut.

BARDING. A bard was an armored breastplate for a horse. In cooking, it is a breastplate of fat, salted fat, or bacon, a thin slice of which is tied around meat or fowl to protect and moisten it during roasting. This is particularly necessary when the meat lacks its own fat; the bard also helps to keep rolled meat neatly in place. It is usually removed when the retaining string is cut before sending to table.

BARLEY (*Hordeum vulgare*) was one of the first cereals to be cultivated by man, and it was used even before wheat in making bread. A very hardy plant, it was the staple grain in many far northern countries until recently. It was used in the form of unleavened barley cakes because it has insufficient gluten to be leavened like wheaten bread. The main culinary use of barley today is as pearl barley, which is the grain with the outside ground off. Barley with most but not all of the outside removed is known as hulled barley or pot barley.

Barley has an attractive and individual taste which goes well in soups and stews, but it is also excellent when boiled and mixed with plenty of thick cream, a taste I remember well from childhood. Most barley, however, goes for brewing, and what is important to the farmer is its malting quality, which decides the price he gets for it (see malt). A high-starch grain is superior in this respect and looks white when it is cut in half. Poor-quality malting barley looks flinty but is the more nutritious food.

Barley meal is whole-meal ground barley; it can be made into a porridge or into simple barley cakes baked on a griddle. Barley water, usually flavored with lemon zest, is made by infusing pearl barley in boiling water and allowing it to get cold before straining off the liquid. (1 part by volume of washed pearl barley needs to be boiled in 10 parts of water for 20 minutes.) It is a famous and very soothing drink for invalids. Barley sugar was originally made of lemon, barley water, and sugar; now it is simply sugar boiled to crack and acidified, a sweet for children.

[*Barley*—French: *orge;* German: *Gerste;* Italian: *orzo;* Spanish: *cebada. Pearl barley*—French: *orge perlée;* German: *Perlgraupen;* Italian: *orzo perlato;* Spanish: *cebada perlada*]

BARM. Brewer's *yeast.

BARNACLE. Although the barnacles that are common on rocks on the seashore may look like mollusks, they are actually crustaceans. They are something like lazy shrimps which have taken to lying on their backs and kicking food into their mouths with their feet. The famous *percebe,* so popular in *tapas* bars in Spain, is a type of barnacle (*Pollicipes cornucopia*) found on the Atlantic coast (but not in the Mediterranean). It has a long, flexible "stalk," the part that is eaten. *Percebes* are washed thoroughly, put into boiling brine—2 teaspoons salt per 4 cups (1 lt) of water—and cooked for 15 minutes, timed from the moment the water reboils. They are eaten cold, with or without a squeeze of lemon; the technique is to draw the stalk through your teeth and eat what squeezes out, discarding not only the hard shell but the tough skin of the stalk. They are expensive, much sought after in Spain and also eaten in South American countries. They taste a little like shrimp.

[*Barnacle*—French: *anatife;* German: *Entenmuschel;* Italian: *dattero di mare;* Spanish: *barnaclas*]

BASES. *See* alkalis.

BASIL or **sweet basil.** A very aromatic labiate annual plant (*Ocimum basilicum*), usually with white flowers and tender, light-green leaves. Basil is extremely variable; the

BASIL

leaves may be small or half the size of a hand, and an ornamental purple-leafed basil is available, but this herb is always recognizable by its smell, which is very scented and rather like sweet cloves. Basil is one of the most worthwhile herbs to grow at home, but it is a warm-country plant, a native of India, and in temperate climates is better started in a greenhouse. Even on the Italian Riviera, it is forced in greenhouses with a high humidity during summer's heat to produce the most tender, delicately scented leaves. Basil is much grown in Spain and Greece, but mainly to keep flies away. Its greatest importance is in Italy, where it is the basis of the fabulous Ligurian spaghetti sauce with pine nuts, *pesto alla genovese,* and other delicious local specialties. It is also the basis of the French *pistou* and is recommended as the best herb for tomatoes, salads, and various sauces. In this context, it is sometimes used to excess.

To preserve basil for winter use, it is best to deep-freeze it after dipping it quickly into boiling water. It may alternatively be preserved in the Italian way, packed in jars with each layer of leaves well sprinkled with salt, and covered with oil. The jar is best kept in the refrigerator. The leaves go black, but the taste remains almost unimpaired. The same cannot be said for dried basil, which acquires a currylike taste. Bush basil has much smaller leaves and an inferior taste.

[*Basil*—French: *basilic;* German: *Basilienkraut;* Italian: *basilico;* Spanish: *albahaca*]

BASS. The word "bass" has no exact meaning and is applied to different fish in different parts of the world; cookbook writers sometimes fail to specify which bass should be used. Many forms of freshwater bass are sporting anglers' rather than cooks' fish, although the largemouth bass (*Micropterus salmonides*) and the smallmouth bass (*M. dolomieui*) can be splendid table fare.

The various sea bass (Serranidae) are gastronomically more important. The black sea bass of the U.S. East Coast (*Centropristis striatus*) is an important food fish. Common from the Carolinas to New York, it has firm white flesh and can weigh up to 6 lb (3 Kg). The striped bass or rockfish (*Morone saxatilis*), also known as striper or sea bass, occurs on both seaboards and often weighs 22 lb (10 Kg) and can reach 110 lb (50 Kg). Giant sea bass (*Stereolepsis gigas*), sometimes mistakenly called jewfish or black sea bass, range from southern California to Baja and can grow to more than 500 lb (228 Kg). Their flesh is lean and white.

But the most famous of all bass to gastronomes is the common bass (*Dicentrarchus labrax*) under its French names of *bar* or *loup* (*de mer*). This is among the best of all fish, with firm, delicately flavored flesh and no trouble from bones. It is fished in the Mediterranean and on the Atlantic coast of Europe as far north as the English Channel; in France, it is sufficiently valued to be the subject of fish farming in the maritime part of the Vendée. The Mediterranean name of *loup* (wolf) does not indicate relationship with the wolffish (*Anarhichas lupus*) of northern seas, which the French call *loup du nord*—an ugly and savage relative of the blenny, excellent eating but not to be compared with the common bass.

Bass should be handled with care, since they bruise easily. Gut them through the gills and by a small incision in the belly. Do not scale them if they are to be poached. If they must be scaled, do so gently to avoid tearing the skin.

Closely related to sea bass are the groupers, of which there are many species, some of them reaching an enormous size. We used to catch 550-lb (250-Kg) monsters with shark hook and rope in the Gulf of Carpentaria in northern Australia, but only for crocodile bait, since the flesh was far too tough to be palatable. However, the Mediterranean grouper or mérou (*Epinephelus guaza*), often shot in caves by spear fishermen, is delicious.

Groupers are common along the U.S. Atlantic and Caribbean coast as warm-water reef fish; among the best-known are the red grouper (*E. morio*), the hamlet or Nassau grouper (*E. striatus*), the black grouper (*Mycteroperca bonaci*), and the gag (*M. microlepis*). The largest of the groupers is the jewfish (*Epinephelus itajara*). It can weigh 800 lb (364 Kg) or more. Groupers have sweet, lean flesh and are easily filleted. Many are used in chowders.

[*Bass*—French: *bar, loup (de mer);* German: *Wolfsbarsch;* Italian: *spigola, branzino;* Spanish: *lubina. Grouper*—French: *mérou;* Italian: *cernia;* Spanish: *mero*]

STRIPED BASS

BASSWOOD, lime tree, or **linden.** Members of the *Tilia* species, relatives of the beautiful linden trees planted in many European towns, are found in rich forests from New York to Florida and west to the Plains. (They are not related to the citrus *lime.) Basswood leaves are heart-shaped, and the tree's creamy white fragrant flowers are so filled with nectar that the basswood is a valuable source of honey. The flowers are also used as a flavoring and to make homemade liqueur. Steeped, they make a sweet and fragrant tea. The basswood was important to early American settlers, who boiled down its sap to make sugar and ground its flowers and fruit together to make a paste resembling chocolate in flavor.

BASTING. The main purpose of basting—moistening food (especially roasts) during cooking by adding pan drippings, melted butter, or liquid—is to prevent the surface of the food from drying out. It may also be a method of coating surfaces with flavoring substances or juices, as when basting foods with a marinade.

[*Basting*—French: *arroser;* German: *begiessen;* Italian: *spruzzare;* Spanish: *pringar*]

BATAVIA ENDIVE. *See* chicory.

BATH CHAP. A chap is the fleshy part of the jaw—the jowl—and a Bath chap consists of half the lower jaw meat of a pig, salt-cured, boiled, boned, and rolled into the shape of a miniature ham. Bath chaps are usually served cold, cut in slices, but sometimes are eaten hot. Being fatty, they are best when combined with other cold meats. They must be taken from a lean, long-snouted breed of pig.

BAUMÉ. Antoine Baumé (1728–1804) was a French chemist who produced scales for a hydrometer to measure brine strengths—a *brinometer—and for a saccharometer to measure the strengths of sugar syrups.

BAY, sweet bay, or **sweet laurel.** The aromatic leaves of this bush (*Lauris nobilis*) or small tree—it can grow up to 60 ft (18 m)—are an essential and absolutely basic flavor-

BAY

ing in any self-respecting kitchen. The tree originally came from Asia Minor, but became known generally around the Mediterranean at a very early date. It was not only a culinary and medicinal herb but also one of magical significance, used for the victor's crown of laurel in ancient Greece and Rome.

Bay leaves can be used fresh or dried. They have a strong balsamic scent which fades with age, so that old dried leaves are quite flavorless. Bay is always part of a *bouquet garni. It is used with fish, meat, and fowl, especially when wine is included in the recipe; it also goes into marinades, pickles, preserves, and even sweet dishes. Bay is a humble, everyday, cheap flavoring, but it can also be used grandly, as when thick veal fillets are skewered with a wreath of bay and fried in butter.

Bay should not be confused with other types of laurel, such as the mountain laurel and the cherry laurel, which has a bitter-almond flavor, or with the two important leaves of Indian cooking—which might be thought to have a very superficial resemblance—the *cassia leaf and the *curry leaf.

[*Bay*—French: *laurier;* German: *Lorbeer;* Italian: *lauro;* Spanish: *laurel*]

BAY SALT. Coarse *salt from sea water evaporated in bays.

BEAN CURD, a pressed purée of *soybeans, is a very common and nourishing ingredient of Chinese and Japanese cooking. It is available from Oriental shops, fresh, canned, or dried. If dried, it must be soaked before being added to vegetable soups, stir-fried dishes, and so on. There are also sweet bean-curd sticks, used with fish and vegetables, as well as sheets of bean-curd skin for egg rolls and vegetable dishes.

TOFU

Mix 1 cup (225 g) of soybean powder with 4 cups (900 g) of water and let it soak for half an hour, giving it an occasional stir. Then put the mixture on the heat and bring it to the boil, stirring all the time. As soon as it boils, lower the heat to simmer for 5 minutes. Then turn off the heat and add 4 tablespoons of lemon juice. Stir until the protein begins to curdle. Finally, after giving it time to separate completely, tip the curd into a clean cloth and hang it up to drain, as if you were making cottage cheese. When it has drained, the *tofu* should be a compact curd, white and with very little taste. It can be preserved under water in the refrigerator for several days.

Recipes for using *tofu* will be found in Japanese cookbooks and sometimes in vegetarian books as well as in the highly regarded *Book of Tofu* by William Shurtleff and Akiko Aoyagi (1975; distributed by Random House). Like the Indian *panir,* which is made from milk, it has almost no taste of its own, but is nice cubed, fried golden, and mixed with other things. It makes a very good curry treated in the Indian way, as for curried *panir* and peas.

BEAN-CURD CHEESE. White bean-curd cheese slightly resembles Camembert and is made from small squares of bean curd, which are salted and matured in rice wine. It is eaten raw with a little oil or sugar as an accompaniment to rice, but it is mainly used as a flavoring in Chinese pasta dishes or with chicken, pork, or fish. Red cheese, too, is made from bean curd and is fermented with salt, wine, and spices. It is more strongly flavored than the white and goes well with duck, chicken, or pork. Both are available canned or in jars.

BEAN PASTE and **BEAN SAUCE.** Pastes of red and yellow beans are important in Chinese cooking. Red bean paste is sweet and is made from *adzuki beans. The yellow variety is made from *soybeans and is salty and pungent—it can be used as a flavoring and, like the red paste, can be bought in cans. Fermented salted black beans, made from a black variety of soybeans and known as black bean sauce, are a flavoring in fish, lobster, chicken, and pork dishes. The sauce is heavily salted and, once opened, will therefore keep well in the refrigerator. Brown bean sauce is a thick paste of salted brown or yellowish beans and is also used as a flavoring with fish, fowl, vegetables, or *bean curd. It is rather like a thick soy sauce and is more or less interchangeable with black bean sauce in some dishes; it is also available in cans or jars.

BEANS. Among the thousands of species of beans and peas (Leguminosae), the Asian *soybean, the American haricot bean, and the European *broad bean are the most important. All have been domesticated for thousands of years. All are a rich source of protein and, when combined with cereals, make good meat substitutes.

The word "haricot" usually applies to the bean species *Phaseolus,* by far the most versatile of the beans. (The word "haricot" is a corruption of the Aztec *ayacotl* and has no connection with haricots of meat, whose name derives from the old French *harigoter,* to cut into bits.) But nomenclature for beans and peas is often bewildering. "Haricot" may refer to oval white beans, including the *cowpea (which is really a bean), and in England "kidney bean" may be applied to almost any haricot because the first specimens introduced there were red and kidney-shaped. At any rate, the haricot comprises bush or tall climbing beans; they may be round, oval, flat, kidney-shaped, or long; their colors range from white, red, and brown to black; they may be eaten, pod and all, while young, shelled when mature, or dried.

In addition to the beans discussed elsewhere in this book (*adzuki, *chickpea, *cowpea, *dal, *flageolet, *ful medames, *goa beans, *gram, *green bean, *jack bean, *lablab bean, *legume, *lentil, *lima bean, *mung bean, *rice bean, *runner bean, *snap pea, *sprouted seeds), the following are important.

Red kidney bean. Large, dark-red beans, kidneys are associated with chile con carne, New Orleans cooking, and many Mexican dishes. When mashed and fried they become *frijoles refritos,* and they are often used in salads.

Navy bean. These small, round, white beans are the usual choice for Boston baked beans (it is best, however, not to be dogmatic here: some Boston bean bakers are fiercely loyal to white pea beans or Dutch brown beans). Navy beans are widely used in this country and are often called "common beans."

Black bean or **Mexican black bean.** Highly distinctive, with creamy flesh and a strong, meaty flavor, these beans are used for making a thick black sauce, for black bean soup, and for some Mexican dishes (*frijoles negros*).

Pinto bean. These have pink markings (*pinto* means "painted" in Spanish). Pintos are common in Spain and all over Latin America. An ingredient in many stews, they are often mixed with rice.

Borlotti bean. The most popular bean in Italy, borlottis are striated with red, similar to the pinto bean. They are mixed with pasta to make the soup *pasta e fagioli.*

Cannellini is a generic name for Italian white beans, particularly large ones such as *bianco de Spagna.* Cannellini are especially popular in Tuscany, where they are eaten in soups or cold salads, such as *tonno e fagioli,* tuna fish and beans in garlicky vinaigrette.

Soisson. These white haricot beans are the ones usually preferred for cassoulet, the French dish of mutton, sausage, and preserved goose or duck.

Fresh shell bean. The beans are ripe and the pods have turned to parchment, usually yellowish and perhaps splashed with scarlet. According to variety, the beans may be large or small, red, white, purple, black, or yellow, either in one color or eyed (with a dark spot round the hilum, where the bean is attached in the pod), or mottled, streaked, squiggled, or splotched in brown or reds. Beans are as pretty as bird eggs, but the patterns are destroyed by cooking. Some strains have a high proportion of hard seeds; others have thick, tough seed coats. (A bean is not necessarily tender because it is small.) Fresh ripe beans cook without soaking. Put them into boiling water and cook gently until they are tender.

After boiling, beans are dressed in many ways, some of those preferred by bean lovers being very simple. In Spain, a meal may be begun with a plate of boiled beans into which each person mixes chopped parsley, chopped onion, *pimentón,* olive oil, and vinegar according to his taste. In Venice, a dressing is made by warming some parsley and anchovy in garlic-flavored oil and adjusting with a little vinegar. This sauce is mixed with the beans and left to mature for 10 minutes before serving.

Dried bean or **haricot sec.** Unless the beans are very old, the modern opinion is that they have a better flavor and are more digestible if they are not soaked, although traditionally and in old recipes they always are. Modern authorities say that beans should be soaked for only a few hours at most. The objection to soaking is that it starts enzyme changes which lead to germination; in warm weather, soaking may also start fermentation by microorganisms. This is obviated by putting the beans into boiling water, blanching them for 2 minutes—which upsets the enzymes and kills the beans and most of the organisms—and then soaking them for 1–2 hours. (Softening the skins in tough varieties can be helped with a pinch of bicarbonate of soda.) However, in most cases it is sufficient to put the beans into cold water and bring them gradually to the boil. Mature beans should always be cooked slowly—according to size and variety, they will need cooking for 3 hours or more. Many recipes leave them in a low oven overnight. One of the best ways is to do them in a pressure cooker. Wash the beans, put them in the pressure cooker without salt, and cover them with cold water. Seal, bring up to the boil, and cook for 5 minutes. Cool the cooker under the tap, open it, and drain the beans. Now put them back with suitable flavorings (onion, cloves, bouquet garni, garlic, and other seasoning if necessary), and salt. Cover them with boiling water, seal, and bring up to pressure. Cook for 40 minutes (according to size). This method produces very digestible beans.

[*Beans*—French: *haricots;* German: *Bohnen;* Italian: *Fagiuoli, fagiolini;* Spanish: *habas*]

BEARBERRY *See* cranberry.

BEARD. The beard of an oyster is its gills. Some people like to have the beard removed; others do not. The byssus of a mussel (the fibrous extrusion which attaches the mussel to the rock) is also called the beard.

BEARGRASS, squawgrass, or **elkgrass** (*Xerophyllum*). A wild, grasslike member of the lily family, beargrass is found throughout the mountains and dry hillsides of the northwestern U.S. Turkey-beard, another member of the family, grows in dry areas from New Jersey to Florida. Members of *Xerophyllum* are plants with a tall, tapering unbranched stem, long, narrow leaves around the base of the stalk, and racemes of creamy flowers. The tender stems of beargrass are eaten like asparagus, and the bulbous roots are roasted.

Some yuccas (e.g., *Yucca glauca*) are also called beargrass. Their young stalks are eaten, and the fruit, shaped somewhat like a papaya, has a sweet flavor when peeled and eaten raw. Indians of the Southwest roasted and dried it.

BEATING. *See* whipping.

BÊCHE DE MER. *See* sea cucumber.

BEECHNUT or **beechmast.** The small triangular nuts of various species of beech, such as *Fagus grandifolia,* are edible. They were important in the past, not only as food for pigs that foraged in the forest but also for humans and as a source of oil. Beechnuts vary in size: many years you will find most of the nuts empty, but sometimes you may come upon a tree bearing well-filled nuts that are worth gathering.

The nuts should be heated gently in an oven until the husk becomes brittle. It can then be broken by rubbing and winnowed off. The inner seed coat can be removed after blanching or frying. The flavor of whole beechnuts is excellent, but they were most commonly used as a source of beechnut oil (especially in France). This was extracted by grinding the nuts, preferably with the skins removed, in a little water, then pressing the slurry in stout linen bags. The oil can be drawn off because it floats on the water. After the impurities have been allowed to settle, the oil is again siphoned off and is ready for storage. It improves with keeping and is said to be best after 6 years. If you can find beechnut oil, it is excellent in salads. Beechnuts are rich in oil and protein but low in carbohydrate. The seed coat (and to a small extent the nut) contains a poisonous substance, fagin, which is harmless to us in any quantity we are likely to take but poisonous to horses.

In North America, the indigenous beech bears slightly smaller but oilier nuts than its similar European brother. In the past, the nuts were used as a coffee substitute and the young leaves as a potherb.

[*Beechnut*—French: *faîne;* German: *Buchei-chel;* Italian: *faggiuola;* Spanish: *hayuco*]

BEECHWHEAT. *See* buckwheat.

BEEF and **veal.** Beef is the meat of a cow; veal is that of a young cow, preferably one that has fed exclusively on milk. Cattle were originally domesticated for pulling carts and plows. Only in the last 200 years have they been systematically selected for either milk or beef, and since the invention of artificial insemination, there has been great change in this direction. In the last century, the preference was for large roasts or steaks, well marbled with fat and from not too young animals. Well hung, these give the most flavorful yet tender meat, yet with families getting smaller, costs going up, and dire warnings being issued against saturated fats and calories, the modern tendency has been toward leaner, smaller cuts. Farm economics are a dominant factor here: an animal that grows quickly to a reasonable size brings in more cash to the producer. It may be fattened in a stall, which saves on food but does not give the best flavor. Beef is now usually eaten fairly fresh.

Beef bought from the butcher will rarely have been hung for more than a week, since proper hanging occupies storage space and thus raises the price of the meat. Large restaurants can buy their steak in great hunks and hang it for 2–3 weeks in a cool place, but the mold that develops on the surface must be cut off and thrown away. This matters little in restaurant expenses, but does make a difference at home when the piece is small—so hanging one's own meat is scarcely practicable.

The best beef comes from steers bred for culinary purposes. Bull's meat is tough and strong. (In Spain, after bullfights, it is commonly sold to the poor and to those who think it gives them virility.) Cow meat is good if the animal is young, but it often comes from old cows that have run out of milk; the meat, which is stringy and tough, tends to go into hamburger.

Veal also varies greatly. Young, unwanted calves, which it would be unprofitable to rear, give tasteless, watery meat. The best veal, such as is produced in Holland, is from animals several months old and finished on dried milk. It is white, firm, and delicious. Older animals that have eaten some solid food are often known as "baby beef"; their meat, intermediate between beef and veal, can be made satisfactorily to do duty for either. Alpine countries like Austria and Italy made great use of veal in the past, because calves necessarily born to ensure the cow's lactation could not be fattened over winter when the mountain pastures were covered in snow. Good veal is expensive; the butchery is elaborate and involves dissecting out particular muscles. From these, slices can be cut for schnitzels, veal birds, escallops, etc.

Because meat-cutting systems vary so widely from country to country, it is useful to have some basic knowledge of a cow's anatomy when entering a butcher shop or ordering in a restaurant. Even within the U.S., a beef loin steak may be sold under some dozen different names, depending on the region of the country. Recognition of types of beef may be facilitated by studying meat charts, but the most reliable training comes from experience in preparing many different cuts of meat.

[*Beef*—French: *boeuf;* German: *Ochsen-fleisch;* Italian: *manzo;* Spanish: *carne de vaca*]

BEER. Alcoholic drinks have been made by *brewing from cereals since the very earliest times. For instance, a Babylonian inscribed clay tablet from the 6th century B.C. shows brewing. Many different types of ale were made in ancient Egypt, and the techniques were passed on by the Greeks to the Romans. The Britons were already brewing ale when the Romans invaded in 45 B.C. Indeed, brewing is not a very difficult discovery to make: if a porridge of grain and water is left standing, it will ferment into a sour, alcoholic brew which can have pleasant effects when drunk, even if its taste is rather unpleasant. Any grain may be used: barley, wheat, rice, millet, corn, etc. Primitive brews which are still made today are Zulu beer and Tibetan *chang.* Rice wine, which is important in the cooking of China and Japan, would more correctly be called rice ale.

The great advances were the malting of barley and, later, the introduction of *hops. Although ale and beer are now almost synonymous, the old word was ale, and beer referred to hopped ale.

Various herbs had long been used to flavor ale, since unflavored ales are rather insipid. The use of hops for this purpose first gained favor in Germany, and a taste for hopped ale is said to have been brought to Britain by soldiers returning from Flanders during the Hundred Years' War. By the middle of the 15th century, hops were being cultivated in Britain, and a bitter controversy was raging between those who liked hopped ale and those who considered it good only for foreigners. It seemed incredible that, in 1464, London brewers even petitioned the Lord Mayor to forbid altogether the use of hops and herbs of any kind. Real ale should be made from just malted barley, yeast, and water, they said. But in the end, hopped ale won, and today beer is universal. People liked the refreshing, bitter taste of hops, and hopped ale was cheaper because an interesting drink could be made with half the quantity of malt required to produce a passable unhopped ale. It would also keep a month, as compared with 2 weeks for the unhopped brews. The economic significance of this was vast, because in those days, and for a century to come, there was neither tea nor coffee—ale was the drink for man, woman, and child at every meal.

The various types of beer are determined mainly by the types of yeast and malt that are used. Lager and American beers use the most lightly cured malt and a yeast that works slowly on the bottom of the vat; lager (which is from the German *Lagerbier,* meaning beer kept in store) should be stored for up to 3 months, although some is kept even longer. British beers are brewed with faster-working yeasts that live mainly on the surface. Bitter is made with lightly cured malt and is thus pale in color and has a dry, rather bitter taste; bottled, fizzy versions of ordinary and best bitter are usually known respectively as light ale and pale ale. Mild is made in the same way as bitter but with darker, more highly cured malts, extra sugar or caramel, and less hops; it is less bitter in taste and usually somewhat weaker. Brown ale is bottled mild. Stout, the darkest beer, is made with black malt, which has a burnt taste.

The occasional use of ale and beer in the kitchen must be of some antiquity, although it is only in Belgium and neighboring parts of France that it has become classic—in the dishes known as *carbonnades.* Belgian cooks are insistent that the correct type of beer must be used, as well as the strong local onions. Authentic *carbonnade à la flamande* is beef cooked in the strongly hopped Belgian beer *lambic de gueuze* or simply *La Gueuze.* The same beer is used as a liquid in which to cook pike (*brochet à la gueuze*). On the other hand, in *carbonnade à la walons,* which is sweet and black with prunes, the beer used must be *diest noire.*

In Britain, people cook shin of beef in mild beer, and there are a number of recipes using Guinness stout, one of which, Mr. Guinness's cake, is a popular version of the older porter cake of Ireland and the West Country. Beer is also used in many cures for ham and as a medium in which ham is cooked. Some of the famous German sweet soups, which are served either hot or cold, are made from beer or beer and milk; a mild, sweetish beer is usually best for these.

Beer is a relatively cheap and handy ingredient with which to experiment in the kitchen, although as a cooking medium it is not greatly admired by most French chefs.

CARBONNADE À LA FLAMANDE

Trim a piece of stewing beef (3¼ lb or 1½ Kg) and cut it into 2-in. (5-cm) cubes. Thinly slice 5–6 medium onions and cook them gently in fat or oil until they become opaque but not brown. Remove them from the pan. Now heat the fat until it is almost smoking. Dredge the cubes of meat in flour seasoned with salt and pepper, and quickly brown them, a handful at a time, in the fat, adding more fat if needed. Return all the meat to the pan, put the onions back on top of the beef, and add a scant 2 cups (½ lt) each of beef broth and beer, 2–3 cloves of crushed garlic, and a bouquet garni of thyme, parsley, and bay leaves. (The more flavorful the beer, the richer the gravy will be.)

Simmer the stew for 1–1½ hours, or until the meat is tender. Remove the bouquet garni, add 2 teaspoons each of sugar and vinegar, and continue the simmering for a few minutes. If there is too much gravy at this stage, pour it, without the meat or onions, into a saucepan and reduce it until there is enough to half-cover the stew. Pour it over the meat and onions, adjust the seasoning, and serve with boiled potatoes. Serves 6–8.

MR. GUINNESS'S CAKE

Cream together 1 cup (225 g) each of butter and soft brown sugar until they are light and creamy. Gradually beat in 4 lightly beaten eggs. Sieve together 1⅓ cups (350 g) flour with 2 level teaspoons of mixed spices and fold this into the butter mixture. Stir in 1 cup (225 g) each of seedless dark raisins and yellow raisins and ½ cup (100 g) each of mixed fruit peel and chopped walnuts. Mix together well. Stir in 4 tablespoons of Guinness stout and mix all to a soft, dropping consistency. Grease and flour a 7-in. (18-cm) round cake pan and turn the batter into it. Bake it at 325°F (160°C) for 1 hour, then reduce the heat to 300°F (150°C) and bake it for another 1½ hours. When the cake is done, allow it to become cold before taking it from the pan. Prick the base of the cake with a skewer and spoon a further 4–8 tablespoons of Guinness over it. Keep the cake for a week before eating it.

[*Beer*—French: *bière;* German: *Bier;* Italian: *birra;* Spanish: *cerveza*]

BEETS belong to the family Chenopodiaceae, which includes some important edible plants, such as spinach, orach, Good King Henry, and *quinoa* (grown for its seed and a staple in Ecuador, Bolivia, and Peru). The beets are all varieties of one species, *Beta vulgaris,* of which the wild one, subspecies *maritima,* grows on seashores in many places from Britain through to Asia. This is known locally as sea spinach; its leaves, gathered from clean shores and cooked like spinach, are delicious. It is from Mediterranean, North African stock of subspecies *vulgaris* that our cultivated types seem to have been derived.

Although beets (var. *esculenta*) have been selected for their roots for over 1000 years, it is only in the last 150 that we have had the tender, uniform roots we know today. The 1633 edition of Gerard's *Herbal* illustrates some very rough specimens and says that red beets brought into England from abroad were then treated with grave suspicion, so most beets then were presumably white. It was not until the early years of the 19th century that Vilmorin, the famous French plant breeder, put beet roots properly on the gastronomic map. Even today, in Spain and other places where the seed is not always good, it is possible to experience what those old beets must have been like—anything from orange to white, with a tough, fibrous core and an unpleasant, earthy, oversweet taste like sugar beets.

Beet roots are an important vegetable in Poland and Russia. Nutritionally, they are rich in sugar, in potassium, and in betaine, a substance which the body seems to be able to use to replace choline. There are a number of different shapes—spherical, top-shaped, or cylindrical—and choice is merely a matter of preference or purpose: some are better for pickling, others for storing.

When handling and cooking beets, do everything you can to minimize their bleeding.

Tops should be twisted off, not cut, and the roots should be washed gently to avoid breaking rootlets or damaging the skin. Some prefer to bake them in a moderate oven, but they may be boiled or steamed; perhaps they are most conveniently cooked in a pressure cooker. A dash of vinegar helps keep the color red. It is best to remove the skin when the beets are hot, after dipping them in cold water to make them possible to handle. The skins will then slip off. Raw, grated beets have a pleasant nutty taste. Cooked beets are served simply with melted butter, but they are often dressed with something sour, such as vinegar or lemon juice, or mixed with apples, sour grapes, or sour cream, since sourness counteracts the rather earthy taste. Other combinations are sweet-sour (e.g., with red currant jelly). Beets go well with allspice, cloves, caraway, mustard, horseradish, celery, onion, chives, garlic, and capers. If they are simply dressed as a salad, a good olive oil with the vinegar makes all the difference. Since beets bleed, some aesthetic consideration should be given before combining them with other ingredients in salads.

The red juice can be used as a dye, even in icing for cakes. For that purpose, grate the beets raw, soak them in lemon juice, and squeeze the juice out in a cloth. If the juice is extracted in this way, then concentrated by boiling (not too long, or the color will turn brown), its earthy taste is not noticed.

The leaves of beets can also be cooked and eaten as greens.

To store beets, put them in a box, right way up, and cover them with dry sand, soil, or peat. They must be kept dry or they will sprout or become mildewed.

Spinach beet is another name for Swiss *chard.

[Beets—French: *betterave, navet;* German: *Rübe, Runkelrübe;* Italian: *bietola;* Spanish: *betarraga.* Beet roots—French: *bette rouge;* German: *rote Rübe;* Italian: *barbabietola;* Spanish: *remofacha*]

BELL PEPPER. *See* sweet pepper.

BELUGA. *See* caviar.

BENGAL GRAM. *See channa.*

BENZOIC ACID. *See* preservatives.

BERGAMOT. *See* orange.

BESAN FLOUR. In Indian cookery, fine flour made by grinding *channa.* It can be bought from shops which specialize in Indian foodstuffs or made at home by grinding chickpeas and sieving out the husks. If you are trying to do the grinding in a whirling-type coffee mill, the chickpeas must be crushed first or they may break the blades. *Besan* flour is a pale creamy yellow. It is high in protein and very nutritious. Mixed with water, it forms a batter much used in India for coating food for frying, to make such dishes as *bhajias* (or their North Indian equivalents, *pakoras*) and *bondas* (spiced potato balls coated in *besan* batter and fried). It also appears in *dahi* (sour curd or yogurt) curries as a stabilizer and thickener, in spicy snacks such as *murukas,* and in various sweetmeats. Although a stranger to non-Indian kitchens, *besan* has a number of uses, for example in thickening soups.

BHAJIAS
(DEEP-FRIED VEGETABLES)

Make a thick batter with *besan* flour (or half *besan,* half rice flour) and water, flavoring it with salt, chili powder, and a pinch of asafetida. Other mixtures contain garlic, fresh ginger, chili, cloves, and cinnamon. Into the batter dip lightly salted onion rings, whole seeded fresh green chilies, strips of sweet pepper, potato slices, salted eggplant slices, spinach leaves—and any other bits of vegetable you wish. Deep-fry them until they are crisp. Drain on absorbent paper and serve hot as an appetizer.

BETEL LEAF is the leaf of the betel vine (*Piper betel*), a very close relation of the pepper vine (*P. nigrum*) that produces black pepper. Although sometimes the cassia leaf (related to cinnamon) is chewed in the Orient, it is the betel leaf that is the usual wrapping of *pan, and the selection of the leaf is of social as well as gastronomic significance in India.

BETEL NUT or **areca nut.** The astringency in a *pan or betel chewing is provided by betel nuts, which come from tall, very slender palms (*Areca catechu*). Originally from Malaysia, this palm is common in most tropical areas today. To get the nuts, which grow in bunches of a hundred or more, a person has to climb the trees—an acrobatic feat. The nuts may be harvested when green for tender nuts (*chikni* in India) or when ripe (*chali*) and orange or scarlet. The nut is encased in a husk and is about the size and shape of a nutmeg, with ivory-white meat veined with intricate folds of brown. The tender nuts are shelled, boiled to extract the tannin, and dried in the sun. The ripe nuts are dried in the husk without boiling and then shelled. Betel nuts, whole, cracked, or as a paste, can be bought in Indian food shops. They may be chewed alone or mixed with sugar and spices in the absence of *betel leaf.

[*Betel nut*—French: *noix d'arec;* German: *Arecanuss;* Italian: *noce di areca;* Spanish: *nuez de areca*]

BEURRE MANIÉ. See binding.

BHANG. See religious food laws (Hindus).

BHARTI. See millet.

BIBLELEAF. See costmary.

BICARBONATE OF SODA, sodium bicarbonate, or **baking soda** ($NaHCO_3$). In old books, this common kitchen chemical is often called "carbonate of soda." When strongly heated to 518°F (270°C), it gives off water and carbon dioxide to change to the carbonate, but such temperatures are not usually reached in cooking. It also effervesces strongly, giving off a fizz of carbon dioxide gas, when mixed with an acid solution. This is the reaction which enables bicarbonate of soda to be used as a leavening agent, the acid being sometimes supplied by buttermilk, lemon juice, or cream of tartar (*see* baking powder).

In every case, the bicarbonate of soda should be mixed in just before baking; otherwise the gas is lost. It effervesces rather slowly with cream of tartar, but much more quickly with lemon juice or an acid like tartaric acid. As an *alkali, bicarbonate of soda can be used instead of lime in softening the skin of corn for making *masa, or added to the water in which chickpeas and other pulses are cooked or soaked in order to soften the skins and to make them more digestible. A pinch added to the water for cooking cabbage gives it an attractive green color. It does, however, neutralize and destroy vitamins B_1 and C. One less-known use of bicarbonate of soda is in the Rumanian skinless sausages called *mititei,* which are flavored also with ground caraway seed and garlic. The bicarbonate tenderizes the meat, puffs it up a little, and gives a strong, unusual, and slightly ammoniac taste to the sausage.

[*Bicarbonate of soda*—French: *bicarbonate de soude;* German: *Doppelkohlensaures Salz;* Italian: *bicarbonato;* Spanish: *bicabornato de soda*]

BIERWURST is a German slicing sausage which should be rather coarse in texture. It may be spiced with juniper berries and cardamom and sometimes flavored with garlic. A common component in selections of German cold cuts, it derives its name (literally "beer sausage") from the fact that it was once made with ham that had been marinated in beer. *Bierschinken* is similar but contains pieces of ham.

BILBERRY, blaeberry, or **whortleberry** (*Vaccinium myrtillus*) is the common blue berry of moors, mountains, and open woodlands in Britain, Europe, and northern Asia. The juicy blue-black fruits, about ⅓ in. (8mm) in diameter and with a cup-shaped depression in the top, are ripe from July to September. During this season the hands and mouths of children in the Alps are stained black with bilberry juice. Although bilberries are often neglected because of the bother of picking them, they are an excellent fruit and worthy of more attention. Their commercial possibilities are overshadowed by the American ★blueberries, which are very similar but larger and sweeter.

[*Bilberry*—French: *airelle, myrtille;* German: *Heidelbeere, Blaubeere;* Italian: *mirtillo;* Spanish: *arándano*]

BILTONG. This dried meat (from the Dutch *bil* = buttock; *tong* = tongue) is the South African equivalent of jerky, *charqui,* or jerked beef. Originally a food of the pioneers who trekked northward from the Cape, it consisted of dried strips of meat cut from game, ostriches, even failing oxen.

To make *biltong*, lean meat is cut in long strips 1 × 2 in. (2½ × 5 cm) along the grain of the muscle. It is salted, often well spiced with pepper, and hung to dry in a current of air, away from flies and in a shady place. Sometimes it is hung so that it is touched by the smoke of the campfire. It may be marinated for 3 days in a dry-salting mixture of 1 lb (450 g) of salt, ¼ cup (50 g) of sugar, and 2 tablespoons (25 g) of saltpeter before rubbing with spices and drying. The surface is often wiped with vinegar. The quality of *biltong* varies from deliciously meaty and with the consistency of good plug tobacco to a dry, fibrous material like old shoe leather. It is best cut in very thin slices and chewed with the sundowner.

BINDING. In cooking, materials are bound together by substances that set when heated, or occasionally by jellies, which set when cold. In the first category come protein substances that are coagulated by heat—egg, blood, and the gluten of flour are examples—while the second includes gelatin, agar, and starch jellies that congeal when cold.

Excessive use of binding agents results in a tough, heavy, leathery, sometimes barely edible product, and the skill of the cook lies in sailing as close to the wind as possible—too little binding and the structure disintegrates. An Austrian chef once advised me: "If your bread dumpling falls to pieces when you poach it [as a test], you can always add some flour. That is what they do in *gasthaus* kitchens where they can't cook. If they add too much flour, they make little cannon balls—to throw at the chef." Adding too much binding agent is a common error in hotel kitchens. On one occasion when I had rather foolishly undertaken to make a kofta (meatball) curry for 150 people, I expressed concern to the Spanish chef who was helping me that with such a quantity the meatballs would collapse and we would finish with a mess. He looked at me patronizingly, grabbed the flour bin, and tipped several kilos into the mixture. "Now they will remain whole," he said confidently. He was certainly right. But the most featherweight and delicious quenelles, meatballs, pâtés, and other creations that need binders are made by cooks who have the subtlety and skill to reduce binding substances to almost nothing.

The word "binding" is also used to describe the thickening of sauces, as with beurre manié (an intimate mixture of flour and butter which chefs keep at hand to bind sauces quickly), egg, blood, or cornstarch.

BIRCH. Black birch, cherry birch, and sweet birch are common names for *Betula lenta,* a tree whose fragrant bark smells and tastes like wintergreen. Found from Maine to Tennessee and west to Iowa, it is a tall slender tree with dark-colored bark. The sweet birch produces a copious flow of sap, and it is tapped just as ★maples are, only about a month later, and boiled down to make syrup. Birch tea is made from the red inner bark of the tree or from the leaves, and birch beer is concocted from the twigs and sap. Commercial wintergreen flavoring is distilled from birch twigs and bark.

BIRDS. Domestic and game birds have individual entries, as have ostrich, and pigeon. Wild birds of many other kinds were commonly eaten in the past. They were a necessity to colonists in the New World and to the poor in Europe. As food, some were nice and some were not. A few, if kept on an artificial diet for a while, would improve in flavor. Seagulls kept on bread and scraps lost their fishy taste. Others had first to be skinned. It was even claimed that certain birds—wild geese for instance—would lose their fishy taste if buried in the ground for a few hours. (Some friends advise that a cock capercaillie is much improved by this treatment, especially if you forget where you buried it.)

Today, many birds which were once eaten freely have become rare and are protected. Others are still used as food in some countries but not in others. Few will see harm in a *salmis* of moorhen served in some country restaurant in the Camargue, but it is another matter when birds are sent in thousands to town markets. If larger grain-eating, running, or swimming birds are seriously wanted for the table, then some enterprising person will start to breed them. But this does not happen with the smaller birds, especially if they eat insects. Most notable among the wild birds regarded as delicacies are thrushes, ortolans, warblers, and larks. These are birds which flock together in autumn or migrate southward to winter quarters. In either case, they are then in large groups and are easily netted or caught with bird lime. They are caught either as they come southward through France and Italy, or when they land to rest on Mediterranean islands such as Cyprus, Sardinia, Sicily, and the Balearics. Such small birds have to be consumed in quantity, since each one is little more than a mouthful.

Choosing to eat game birds—grouse, pheasant, or partridge—but not lark or thrush is not merely a question of sentiment. Game birds are controlled, encouraged, and even bred for shooting, but every adult male from Biscay to the Adriatic seems to be armed with a shotgun, and blasts away at everything that moves (including his own kind). The birds are decimated every year. It is heartbreaking to see a sack of small birds, which have been shot indiscriminately, dumped on a kitchen table. One may watch the wife sorting them through, discarding a crossbill here and a rare warbler there among the assortment of kinds she does not recognize or relish.

Garden warblers (*Sylvia borin*) and lesser whitethroats (*Sylvia curruca*) are the main warblers among the victims, but other species get caught on bird lime or nets. These little birds migrate southward in autumn and are caught particularly in the South of France, Greece, and the larger Mediterranean. They are plucked and singed, sometimes drawn and sometimes not, but the feet are usually cut off. They are then cooked in various ways and eaten whole, beak and all. In France, they are brushed with butter and wrapped in vine leaves for cooking. Elizabeth David, in *Italian Food* (Knopf, 1958), mentions them put inside *ovole* (*Amanita caesarea*), those beautiful orange mushrooms related to the death cap. In Sicily they are sometimes cooked inside hollowed-out onions, with the top put back so that they are steamed in an atmosphere of onion vapor. In northern Italy, they are generally served with polenta, usually after grilling on skewers (in the company of robins and other small birds); in Cyprus and Greece they are even pickled. One is expected to chomp the whole bird, head, beak, and all.

Skylarks (*Alauda arvensis*) flock together in autumn, when the birds are very fat. Thousands used to be netted each year and sold in markets both in Britain and in continental Europe. The flesh of larks is excellent. They are probably best known these days as the basis for the famous Pithiviers lark pâté.

Song thrushes (*Turdus philomelos*) and Mistle thrushes (*Turdus viscivorus*) are netted in huge numbers each autumn when they run the Mediterranean bird gauntlet on their way south. In Majorca, for instance, people start out before dawn with huge V-shaped clap nets to go to the tops of the mountains. At dawn, they are in position with nets spread, waiting for the flights of migrating thrushes to come in. Thrushes are still commonly sold in the market. In Spain they are stuffed with sweet white grapes, wrapped in cabbage leaves, and braised. Thrushes taste good, but not sensational, and surely only a deaf man could ever prefer a thrush on a plate or in a *pâté de grives*.

The ortolan bunting (*Emberiza hortulana*) is widely celebrated for the delicacy of its flesh, while its fat is, in the opinion of many gourmets, almost the equal of that of the green turtle. The birds were once netted annually with a decoy in many thousands, put in dark rooms (which kept them quiet), and fattened on millet and oatmeal, until, in the words of one old author, they became "mere lumps of fat weighing three ounces." At this point, they were killed. Today, they are a particular specialty of the Landes and are sometimes to be found in cages behind the restaurants that serve them. Sometimes ortolans are merely beheaded and have only the crop removed before being cooked with the insides (trail) intact; they may also be drawn and stuffed with foie gras or a delicate forcemeat, or threaded on skewers between slices of toast (to catch their fat) before being grilled. There are also very elaborate recipes in which ortolans are cooked in hollowed-out black truffles and served with a Madeira sauce. Like warblers, they are eaten beak and all if they are whole, merely cut into two by the diner "like a sausage and just as tender." They may even be boned and stuffed, a job requiring total dedication to gastronomic art.

To the disappointment of many immigrants from European countries, the taking, selling, transporting, and importing of migratory birds is strictly regulated in the U.S. This includes treaties with Canada and Mexico. Before killing any wild birds, one should check with the U.S. Fish and Wildlife Service—even wild fowl that have open seasons for hunting may be restricted by seasons or bag limits.

[*Birds*—French: *oiseaux;* German: *Vögel;* Italian: *uccelli;* Spanish: *ave*]

BIRDS' NESTS. "Among the many travellers' tales which called forth such ridicule from sceptical readers of early voyages, the accounts of the Chinese cuisine were held to be amongst the most extravagant . . . that the Chinese should make soup out of birds' nests, was an absurdity so self-evident that it destroyed all possibility of faith . . . the reader having no conception of the possibility that a bird's nest could be made of anything but sticks, moss, mud and feathers" (The Rev. J. A. Wood's *Natural History*, 1861).

The birds (of the genus *Collocalia*) that make the nests used for soup are similar to swifts. One of the species was named the edible swallow (as if it were the bird one ate). The birds nest in colonies in stupendous caverns in Southeast Asia—Java, Malaya, Thailand, the Philippines—and, like swallows, stick their nests to the rocky walls and ceilings. They make them, however, not of mud but of a gelatinous spit which they secrete for the purpose. Collecting the nests in semidarkness and the odor from the droppings is dangerous work.

Two main categories of birds' nest are eaten: black and white. Black nests are cheaper, but they are full of debris and need considerable cleaning to make them edible. The white nests are cleaner and are more expensive. Among the numerous grades, the best are the most absorbent and therefore swell more when soaked. First-grade nests are whole, almost white cups with few feathers and foreign matter. Second-grade, or dragon's teeth, are bits of broken nest, and the third grade is made of fragments pressed into cakes. Nests from different areas are also assessed on their own merits by experts and are even used for distinct purposes.

Basic preparation depends on what the nests are to be used for—soup, stuffings, or sweets—but one method is to clean them, soak them overnight, remove any feathers, boil them for 10 minutes, then rinse. To most of us, however, birds' nests are fragments of translucent material, a bit like dried seaweed, bought ready prepared in a packet from a Chinese provision shop. Exhortations such as "use half a nest per person" or "one should use nests in the year in which they were gathered" are superfluous when directions are printed on the pack. The sense of adventure has gone, but the results are probably better for it.

[*Bird's nest*—French: *nid d'oiseau;* German: *Vogelnest;* Italian: *nido di uccello;* Spanish: *nido de pájaro*]

BISCUIT. In England this is the general collective word for all sorts of flat, thin, dryish baked goods, and it causes some confusion when people try to translate it into other languages, in which it cannot be rendered by a single word. Even Americans have the words "cookie" and "cracker" to cover the field. What appear at first sight to be the equivalents in French, Italian, and Spanish are not so except in the original meaning of the word.

The word "biscuit" came from the French and meant "twice cooked," as also did the Italian *biscotto*, the Spanish *bizcocho*, and the German *zwieback*. It referred to what we might call ship's biscuits—army biscuits, hardtack, *biscuits de guerre*—the very dry, bone-hard, little slabs of cooked flour and water paste made to keep for ever and ever (unless destroyed by sea water or weevils) on voyages in old sailing ships. So hard were biscuits that they had to be soaked before use, and many an ancient mariner broke his teeth on them. Ship's biscuits have long been extinct (I used to buy them with difficulty from the Army and Navy Stores to take climbing) and would cause a mutiny on a modern ship. In French, *biscuit* is now used for several sorts of baked goods, including

some we would call sponge cake (so a cake tin is *un moulard de biscuit*). The Italian equivalent is *biscoccia*, while the word *biscotta* (and the French *biscotte*) indicates a sort of rusk, though there are biscuitlike cakes from Genoa and Sardinia that bear that name (*biscotti sardi, biscotti di san martino, biscotti del lagaccio*—or simply *lagaccio*), often covered with fennel or anise seeds and intended for long storage. In Spanish, *bizcocho* can mean a rusk or toasted bread, but is also applied to mixtures of flour, eggs, and sugar cooked in the oven which are in some cases a kind of biscuit (*bizcochos de avellanas* with hazelnuts), but equally a sort of cake (*bizcocho de chocolate*) to be served with cream, or even something like a sponge (the Cuban *bizcocho relleno al ron* filled with jam and sprinkled with rum). The German *zwieback* is a very popular kind of rusk.

In the U.S., of course, a biscuit is usually a hot bread, basically made of flour, shortening, and milk. Baking powder biscuits are tender because they contain a large amount of fat. Beaten biscuits are more like the British biscuit. A southern specialty, beaten biscuits contain no leavening and are hard and crackerlike. Buttermilk biscuits, leavened with baking soda, have a pleasantly acid flavor. Many flavorings—cheese, sour cream, honey, herbs—may be added to biscuits.

BIVALVES. The *oysters, *mussels, *cockles, *clams, *scallops, and so on—mollusks with two shells hinged together and closed by strong muscles. They may bury themselves in sand or mud and move laboriously by a foot, attach themselves to rocks with threads like the mussel, bore into rocks like the sea date, or even swim by flapping their shells like scallops. Most bivalves are edible, but they are sometimes responsible for poisoning or spreading infections: they feed by filtering out particles from the water and may pick up pathogenic bacteria from sewage or poisonous plankton. Undisturbed shells gape to allow entry of food and oxygenated water, but if a bivalve still gapes when it is disturbed, do not eat it—it is dead or dying. A healthy bivalve indeed closes tight as a clam.

[*Bivalves*—French: *bivalves;* German: *zweischalige Muscheln;* Italian: *bivalvi;* Spanish: *bivalvos*]

BLACHAN. *See* balachan.

BLACK BEAN. *See* bean.

BLACKBERRY. Blackberries belong to the genus *Rubus*. This genus, the rose family, is confusing: it includes the *raspberry (which may also be black, though usually red); the boysenberry, a cross between blackberries and raspberries developed by Rudolph Boysen in 1923; the loganberry, apparently a cross between blackberries and raspberries, discovered by J. H. Logan in 1881; the dewberry, a blackberry with a trailing rather than upright plant; the youngberry, an improved blackberry that is cultivated in Africa more than in the U.S.; and the honeyberry or arctic bramble of Scandinavia. In England and Scotland the blackberry is called the bramble. Hundreds of species of blackberry grow in the northern temperate zones of the U.S., and they are known by many local names. Although varieties have been improved by cultivation, and thornless ones are available, most blackberries are picked from wild, very prickly bushes.

Other relatives of *Rubus* do not look exactly like blackberries or raspberries—the cloudberry (*R. chamaemorus*), for example, is orange. A berry that I came on one day when hot and thirsty in the Himalayas (it has stayed in my mind as one of the most delicious fruits I have ever eaten) was beyond question a *Rubus*, but I have never discovered exactly what it was.

There is considerable natural hybridization between the species. The cultivated varieties of blackberry are large, juicy, and often seedless. However, wild ones can be so seedy as to be fit only for jelly or alcoholic drinks—for which blackberries, with their acid sweetness, are very fit indeed. They have been an important "free" food for centuries, used in pies, cobblers, wine, and jam. Euell Gibbons, in *Stalking the Wild Asparagus* (David McKay, 1962), also recommends another use: "In the spring when next year's canes are sprouting from the base of the blackberry plant, one can gather these tender sprouts before the prickles harden, peel them and slice them into a tossed salad."

A linguistic warning: the same word is used in French, Spanish, and Italian for both blackberries and black mulberries (which are of course a different fruit altogether).

[*Blackberry*—French: *mûre;* German: *Brombeer;* Italian: *mora selvatica;* Spanish: *mora, zarzamora*]

BLACK CURRANT. *See* currant.

BLACK-EYED PEA or **black-eyed bean.** *See* cowpea.

BLACK GRAM, urd, or **mash** (*Phaseolus mungo*), a pulse about half the size of a pea, usually has a black seedcoat, though this is sometimes green, which can lead to confusion with the green gram or *mung bean. However, when split for *dal*, the mung bean is yellow, whereas the flesh of the black gram is white. This is especially obvious in the expensive *dhuli urd* from which any black flecks of husk have been washed out. It is exceedingly important in Indian cooking and is grown and used all over the subcontinent, but especially in the northwest, the Punjab, where in winter it is eaten as a daily food. It is very nutritious—"heating," they say in South India—and so is more suitable for cold weather, though a bit stodgy and difficult to digest. Black gram is best cooked without prior soaking. It takes longer to soften than either *mung bean or *pigeon pea (*tur*), and it does not mix readily into its water. Usually the most costly pulse, black gram is nonetheless essential in a number of important dishes. Roasted, it goes into the mixture for flavoring vegetarian curries. Soaked and ground to a paste, it is one of the ingredients of the classic *idlis* and *dosas* of South India, and is also the usual basis for poppadoms.

BLACK PUDDING, blood pudding, or blood sausage.
Blood does not keep well, but drained and mixed with cereal, onion, fat, salt, and spices it can be made into blood sausages or black puddings.

Variations on this theme exist in every country in Europe and have emigrated to America. In Britain, commercial black puddings are often too heavily padded with cereal—barley, oatmeal, flour, and rusk; their flavoring is undistinguished, and in most places the results are deservedly not very popular. Sometimes in Scotland they are made with sheep's blood. The *boudins noirs* of France, those glossy black sausages one sees in the charcutier, which are cheap only in comparison to most of the other pork butcher's products, are made with finer ingredients: they contain a smaller proportion of cereal and usually some cream. They are correspondingly more delicious, although, as a northcountryman, I like to make blood sausages with the French materials and the distinctive English pennyroyal flavoring. Black puddings keep only a few days in the refrigerator but may be frozen. Although cooked when made, most versions are intended to be eaten sliced and fried, or cooked according to local recipes.

Boudin noir. Apart from pig's blood, these contain varying amounts of fat, cream, onion, and *quatre épices*. There are many local variants, e.g., *de Poitou* (containing spinach), *de Lyon* (with herbs and brandy), *aux pommes, aux marrons, à l'ail* (containing apple, chestnut, and garlic respectively), as well as many other additions to the basic mixture.

Blutwurst. German blood sausage is made of blood with pork and bacon fat, which show when it is cut, and flavored with marjoram and allspice. Unlike other blood sausages, it is intended for eating cold in slices, but is also good fried.

BLACKSTRAP.
A type of *molasses.

BLADDER CHERRY.
See physalis fruit.

BLANCHING.
To blanch something, put it into boiling water, or bring water with the ingredient in it to the boil for a relatively short time. In practice, the name is given to several rather different operations. Blanching can mean:

1. To whiten and harden meat and temper its flavor, as when slices of bacon are blanched before adding to a delicately flavored dish, when rabbit is blanched to whiten the meat, or when roasts are blanched to harden them before larding.

2. To set the color and partly cook vegetables in the French method: vegetables are first cooked for a short time in boiling water, then refreshed in ice-cold water to cool them quickly, drained, and finally heated again in butter or cream.

3. To dip vegetables or bundles of herbs into boiling water for various lengths of time before freezing in order to destroy and inactivate enzymes and to set color.

4. To make it easy to remove skins. Peaches and tomatoes should be dipped in boiling water for a few seconds only; oranges, for ½–1 minute. Nuts, like almonds and hazels, are usually covered with boiling water and left to soak only until the skins become soft and easy to slip off. Chickens' feet can be peeled after leaving in boiling water for 10 seconds—no more. The skin of tongue and salt pork requires much longer to loosen it, and the operation is usually begun in cold water which is brought to the boil. Onions for pickling need 12–14 seconds blanching, then cooling in cold water, before skinning.

When boiling water is poured over something, this is known as scalding, but the word also describes bringing milk or cream almost to the boil.

To a gardener, blanching means whitening vegetables (e.g., celery) by depriving them of light, for example by banking up earth over them.

[*Blanching*—French: *blanchir;* German: *abkochen;* Italian: *imbiancare;* Spanish: *emblanquecer*]

BLENDING. One dictionary definition of blending is "mixing together, especially intimately and harmoniously," and that applies in cooking. But the word has other specialized meanings—a blended, as opposed to a straight, whiskey; a blend, as in "our own blend of tea," meaning a formula. The word is also applied to operations carried out by the modern electric blender, and in that case implies reducing ingredients to a fine state of suspension in a liquid, even to an emulsion.

[*Blending*—French: *mélanger;* German: *mischen;* Italian: *mischiare;* Spanish: *mezclar*]

BLOATER. *See* herring.

BLOOD. The Masai tribe might be called the vampires of East Africa; they drink fresh blood (sometimes mixed with milk) warm from the cow, and it is partly to this diet that they owe their marvelous slender figures. It is also a humane practice that involves no killing. They take blood by tying a cord around the neck of one of their cattle, just tight enough to cause the jugular vein to swell, but not to cause distress. With a special tiny bow, they then shoot, at point-blank range, a small arrow with a blunt end armed with two pins into the vein. From the two small punctures thus made, a pint or so of blood is collected. Afterward, mud is rubbed on the puncture to stop the bleeding, and the animal is released with no more harm than is suffered by a human donor to the blood bank. One might recommend the practice to vegetarians who eat eggs and cheese or drink milk. Since blood coagulates very quickly, it must be well stirred or beaten with twigs as soon as it is drawn.

Blood is much used in traditional country cooking. Pigs' blood, not to be wasted, goes into *black pudding and related sausages. For really hearty food, it can be substituted for egg in a batter to make blood pancakes which few, other than Scandinavians, can tolerate. (The Norwegian cook on the Antarctic expedition I was with many years ago used to make excruciating pancakes out of seals' blood.) Chickens' blood is the correct medium for thickening the sauce of a *coq au vin.* It needs careful collecting in a vessel which contains a little brandy and vinegar to prevent coagulation. There is really no substitute for blood in a *coq au vin;* other thickeners do not give the proper black, ointment-like sauce of a *coq au chambertin* as made in Dijon.

Because sauces thickened with blood behave like sauces thickened with egg, they are likely to curdle if boiled. In some European countries, especially in districts where there is still a robust, old-fashioned peasant style of cooking, blood which has been coagulated by boiling or baking is sold in shallow earthenware pans in the market. Even coagulated chickens' blood is offered for sale in small pots. Although some people try to reconstitute such coagulated blood by liquidizing it in the blender, it will not thicken sauces properly because it is already coagulated. Baked blood—sold by weight—is mainly used in fried dishes, of which the Spanish *sangre con cebolla* (blood with onion) and *sangre con pimientos* (blood with peppers) are typical examples. It is also put into the well-known *fritos mallorquine.*

SANGRE CON CEBOLLA

Put some oil in a frying pan with a few crushed cloves of garlic and plenty of onion which has been sliced lengthwise so that it retains its identity. When this is cooked to your liking, add some finely chopped fennel, some small fried potatoes, and some pieces of baked blood. Mix together and continue frying until the blood and potatoes are nicely hot. Serve with grilled pork chops.

[*Blood*—French: *sang;* German: *Blut;* Italian: *sangue;* Spanish: *sangre*]

BLOOD SAUSAGE or **blood pudding.** *See* black pudding.

BLUEBERRY and **huckleberry.** The fruits of these two plants are grouped together here because they are similar and often confused by people who use the two names interchangeably. Blueberries and huckleberries do both belong to the heather family, but blueberries have been assigned to the genus *Vaccinium* (related to *cranberries) and huckleberries to *Gaylussacia*. While blueberries are now widely cultivated, huckleberries are almost always gathered from wild bushes. Blueberries have numerous small soft seeds, whereas huckleberries produce ten larger, harder ones in each berry. Although people picking wild berries drop both genuses into the same pail without distinction, and those buying blueberries in markets have little choice of species, botanists have categorized them as follows.

Blueberry. Whether wild or cultivated, blueberries are very American, and those found in Europe have been imported (partly because they are easier to pick than the *bilberry, a close relative). The many species range from above the Arctic circle to as far south as Florida. The highbush blueberry (*Vaccinium corymbosum*) is economically the most important of the blueberry clan. It grows up to 10 ft (3 m) high and fruits profusely. Owing to a USDA project of selecting wild good-fruiting plants, cloning, and hybridizing, cultivated highbush blueberries now account for more sales on the market than wild ones.

The lowbush blueberry (*V. angustifolium* or *V. pennsylvanicum*) grows wild over much of the northeastern U.S. and is also grown commercially, especially in Maine. It grows about 6 in. (15 cm) high. Rabbiteye blueberries (*V. ashei*) are native to the southeastern U.S. Some varieties bear blue fruit, others mostly black. The dryland blueberry (*V. pallidum*) has light-blue fruit and grows in dry soil. Some other so-called blueberries imported from China and Japan have reddish fruit.

Blueberries are very versatile in cooking. Delicious raw, perhaps with cream and sugar, they also make wonderful pies, jam, syrup, pancakes, ice cream, soup, muffins, cakes, and puddings. They can be canned, dried, or frozen just as they are, packed dry in containers.

The name "blueberry" is also applied to the edible fruit of two Australian plants unrelated to the U.S. blueberry, the cockatoo bush and the blueberry ash.

BLUEBERRY MUFFINS

Sift 2 cups (280 g) of plain flour with 2 tablespoons of sugar, ½ teaspoon of salt, 2 teaspoons of baking powder, and almost a teaspoon of baking soda. Wash a cup of blueberries, drain them, and, when they are still slightly wet, shake them carefully into the flour mixture and turn it gently so they are coated. Now add 1 lightly beaten egg, 2 tablespoons of melted butter and ¾ cup (175 ml) of buttermilk. Stir gently until just mixed, no more, and then half fill greased muffin tins with the thick mixture. Bake at 400°F (200°C) for 18 minutes.

Huckleberry. The common huckleberry (*Gaylussacia baccata*) is found in the same general range as wild blueberries. Also called the black huckleberry or the highbush huckleberry, it has dark, shiny, tart fruit. The blue huckleberry or tangleberry (*G. frondosa*) and the bear huckleberry or buckberry (*G. ursina*) are less tasty. All huckleberries can be prepared in the same ways as blueberries, although they are often strained to remove the hard seeds. They were used extensively, fresh and dried, by American Indians.

BLUTWURST. *See* black pudding.

BOAR. The wild hog (*Sus scrofa*) occurs in deciduous and mixed forests and in scrub in many parts of Europe and Asia, but became extinct in Britain in the 17th century. Wild hogs have been imported in the U.S., but do not occur in large numbers. European boars grow to about 5 ft (155 cm) in Europe, but in some places, such as Kashmir, they grow to weigh over 660 lb (300 Kg); at that size, one is capable of taking on a tiger. Because wild boar is not bled like pork, the meat is dark. There is little fat, and the flesh can be dry and tough unless marinated and larded, but the flavor is excellent.

The American wild pig, or peccary (*Tayassu tajacu*), is smaller than a boar. It weighs up to 65 lb (30 Kg) and ranges from Texas to Paraguay. The meat is light-colored and dry in texture.

A CLASSIC FRENCH MARINADE FOR BOAR

Take ½ cup (100 g) each of sliced onions and carrots, 2 shallots, a clove of garlic, a small stick of chopped celery, and 4 sprigs of parsley. Color all lightly in oil, then add 4 glasses of red wine, 1 glass of good wine vinegar, 1 teaspoon of salt, a few peppercorns, a large sprig of thyme, and several bay leaves. Simmer this gently for 45 minutes, then strain it over the meat. After marinating for 24 hours, the meat can be larded and roasted until tender. This marinade also suits hare and venison.

[*Boar*—French: *sanglier;* German: *wildes Schwein;* Italian: *cinghiale;* Spanish: *jabali*]

BOCKWURST. *See* frankfurter.

BOILING is an easily recognized reference point: it is the hottest water can get in an open pot. Go on heating it over the fire and the extra heat is used up in changing the water into steam. Water boils—and stays boiling—at 212°F (100°C). The only way in which the temperature of boiling water can be raised above this is by adding sugar or salt (which will push it up a few degrees), by increasing the pressure (in a pressure cooker), or perhaps by carrying the cooking pot down to the Dead Sea. Conversely, water boils at a lower temperature when pressure is reduced, e.g., at a higher *altitude. Himalayan climbers take pressure cookers with them. At about 20,000 ft (6000 m), with less atmospheric pressure, water boils at only 176°F (80°C), ideal for simmering yak but hopeless for making a decent cup of tea. The effect of pressure on boiling point is made use of when water is extracted from delicate foodstuffs by evaporating under reduced pressure.

Although boiling is a common operation in cooking because it is easily recognized without a thermometer, the temperature is often not ideal for cooking. For the proteins of fish or meat it is too high, and for vegetables not high enough. A quick blast of a higher temperature for vegetables preserves color and vitamins better. Pressure cookers would undoubtedly be used more if they allowed the cook to prod, stir, and observe the food while it cooked.

[*Boiling*—French: *bouillir;* German: *sieden;* Italian: *fare, bollire;* Spanish: *hacer hervir*]

BOLETUS. *See* cèpe.

BOLOGNA is the home of the *mortadella, but the name of the city is also used, particularly in the U.S., to mean a large sausage, usually made of finely ground pork and beef that has been smoked and sometimes also simmered. Products range from the bland, pinkish gray slices used mostly in sandwiches to the pungent Lebanon bologna sausage made of coarsely ground beef that has been aged, seasoned with sweet spices, and smoked over smoldering sawdust.

BOMBAY DUCK or **bummalo** (*Harpodon neherius*). These small, semitransparent, peculiarly shaped fishes live mainly in the Arabian Sea off the coast of India, although they migrate elsewhere in search of food, and are fished from the end of the monsoon (October) to the end of January. They are so plentiful (second only to mackerel) that only some 20% of the catch is eaten fresh.

The rest is hung on racks on the beaches to dry in the hot tropical sun. The smell (mingled with drying ribbon fish and sandy mixtures of whitebait and prawns spread on mats) is like a fish-glue factory in full spate. It blows through the fishing villages of the Bombay coast: you can smell it on the breeze among the coconut palms or across the black mud of mangrove-bordered creeks. And this picturesque smell invades the kitchens of curry addicts the world over, because dried Bombay duck is not only eaten around Bombay but is exported in flat tins or packets. It keeps for a long time, provided it is kept dry, and is usually eaten as a curry adjunct, either crisped in the oven or fried to the point where it can be crumbled over rice. Some even like it as a cocktail snack with drinks. An excellent product for the many who like a high-fish taste.

BONAVIST BEAN. *See* lablab bean.

BONDIOLA. *See coppa.*

BONE forms the skeleton of vertebrate animals, apart from some fish, such as *sharks, which have skeletons of cartilage. Over half the weight of bones consists of calcium phosphate, an insoluble substance which is not broken down by boiling. The other main component of bone is collagen, a fibrous protein which gives it tensile strength. Boiling turns collagen into soluble gelatin, which will form a jelly on cooling. *Marrow bones of mammals are tubular, with soft marrow in the middle—they are limb bones, which need to resist bending, against which a tubular structure is mechanically the most effective. Many of the bones in birds have their cavities connected to the lungs so that they are filled with air, which makes for more efficient breathing and a lighter skeleton, both important in flying.

Closely attached to bone is a tough sheath, the periosteum, to which the tendons are attached. Bones, together with their accompanying cartilage and connective tissue (gristle), are used in cooking to make *stock.

Bone is very dense, although it does contain canals connecting the cells and holes through which nerves and blood vessels pass. Extraction of soluble substances in stockmaking is therefore helped if the bones are well broken up with a hammer before boiling.

An important and often neglected use for bones is to keep food away from the bottom of the pan; this prevents sticking and at the same time makes a contribution to the flavor. For instance, chopped bones are used to cover the bottom of the pan under a pork roast in Austria and under stuffed vine leaves in Lebanon. This is a most useful practice, with many applications.

[*Bone*—French: *os;* German: *Knochen;* Italian: *osso;* Spanish: *hueso*]

BONITO. Cooks and zoologists often fail to agree on the classification of fishes. Thus, the name bonito covers a number of distinct species, of which two are of culinary importance. The bonito or Atlantic bonito (*Sarda sarda*), a larger relative of the mackerel, is up to 27 in. (70 cm) long and thus big enough to be sold cut into steaks for grilling. It has stripes along its back and is found in the Black Sea, the Mediterranean, and both sides of the Atlantic. The skipjack (*Katsuwonus pelamis*), otherwise known as the Oceanic, California, or Pacific bonito, is a smaller relative of the *tuna—up to 31 in. (80 cm) long. It has stripes along the belly and occurs in both the Atlantic and the Pacific; in the Mediterranean, it is mainly caught on the North African coast. It is cooked in the same way as other species of tuna and emanates from Pacific canneries as tuna (or more precisely as skipjack tuna). In Japan, the skipjack is called *katsuo,* and dried fillets (*katsuobushi*) are a basic necessity in the preparation of foundation stocks or *dashi.*

BOQUERONES. *Anchovies in Spanish, but usually referring to the fillets pickled in salt and vinegar—a popular Spanish snack. They are white and are commonly sold in boxes or loose by weight in markets. Anyone who likes rollmops will like *boquerones*.

BORAGE (*Borago officinalis*) is an herb that gives its name to a whole family, the Boraginaceae. It has a beautiful blue flower and is easily grown (it self-seeds) in any warm situation and often escapes and goes wild. Borage leaves have a cucumber flavor and can be used in salads or beverages—but, to be frank, borage is mainly used as decoration. The plant is very hairy, and the young leaves must be finely chopped for salads; it is considerably more trouble than cucumber. The best use for it is to boil it like spinach to make a stuffing for ravioli (as they do in Liguria) or to dip it in batter and fry it; both ways get rid of the prickly hairs. The flowers can be candied. Borage is reputed by herbalists to be very healthful—it is high in potassium and calcium—and to give one courage, which, if true, could be useful.

BORECOLE. *See* kale.

BORIC ACID. *See* preservatives.

BORLOTTI BEAN. *See* bean.

BOTARGO, botarega, botargue, or **poutarg.** *Botargo,* from the Arab *batarkhah* or *batarekh,* is the salted, pressed, dried female roe of either the tunny or the striped gray mullet. It is an old eastern Mediterranean delicacy, known even in ancient Egypt and still popular in that country; it is also a favorite in Italy; the Greek *tarama is virtually the same. In Britain, though it was popular in the 17th century, mentioned in Pepys's *Diary* (he was eating it with bread as a blotting paper during a heavy night's drinking) and served at James II's coronation, it is not well known today. In Victorian times, they called it *poutarg* (from the French). Today it is usually *botargo* and may be bought from shops which sell Levantine or Italian foods. If it is made from tuna roes, the pieces can weigh up to 16 lb (7 Kg), and they look like large, square-sec-

tioned sausages. When made from mullet roe, the pieces are much smaller, and usually each piece is squashed flat to only a few centimeters thick. The roes are in pairs, each one in its original membrane, and have usually been dipped in preservative wax. The color varies among rose pink, dirty brown, and translucent amber. *Botargo* is expensive and may be bought in the piece, by weight, sliced or packed as slices in oil. It is eaten as an hors d'oeuvre, *meze,* or snack with drinks. It can be served alone or with oil, which may be combined with a little vinegar or lemon juice plus freshly ground black pepper or a pinch of finely chopped parsley or cayenne pepper, according to taste. In Italy it is also grated over pasta or rice.

Botargo from tunny. This, as an example, is the Sicilian method. The roes are carefully removed, so as not to damage the membrane around them, and they are put on a long table, covered with salt, and left there for 2 days. Then a funnel is inserted into the duct, and the sacs containing the roes are filled and irrigated several times with saturated brine. After that the roes are put into dry salt and left for another 2 days. When the salt is changed the next time, a clean board is placed on top and lightly weighted with stones. From then on, the salt is changed every day and the weight gradually increased, the only variation being that, after the first day, the sacs are pricked with beechwood skewers to promote drainage. The daily change of salt and increase in pressure is continued until the roe is completely impregnated, a period which varies according to size. When judged ready, the roes are washed in water and hung in a current of air to dry.

Botargo from gray mullet. The species of gray mullet used for *botargo* is known in the U.S. as the striped or black mullet (*Mugil cephalus*). *Botargo* from mullet is mainly made in Corsica, Sardinia, and Tunisia, as well as in Egypt and Turkey. The following method is used in Sardinian homes. The roes are removed in pairs without breaking or puncturing the sacs. The pairs of roe are then well salted, pressed between boards, and left for 2–3 days under an 11-lb (5-Kg) weight. The roes, when pressed, are about 7 in. (18 cm) long and ¾ in. (2 cm) thick. After salting, they are hung in the shade to dry and when ready are dipped for an instant in molten wax. They must not be dried so much that they become powdery. In *A Book of Middle Eastern Food* (Knopf, 1972), Claudia Roden gives details of a *botargo* made from the frozen mullet roes which are sold out of barrels in Canada. As always, the membrane must be free from holes. The roes are rolled in fine kitchen salt and laid on absorbent paper. The salt is changed and the roes are turned whenever the papers become wet. This process continues until weeping stops altogether. Drying in air and dipping in wax is as before, or the *botargo* may be kept in the refrigerator in plastic bags.

BOTTLED SAUCES. Certain bottled sauces are commonly used as ingredients and flavorings in cooking, among them *Tabasco, *tomato, and *Worcestershire sauces. Most of the recipes for commercial bottled sauces are trade secrets and may depend on the special quality of ingredients. It is not difficult to make good bottled table sauces at home (*see* ketchup). Those based on vinegar, salt, and spices improve with maturation and keep almost indefinitely.

BOTTLING. The word covers filling bottles with liquids such as wine and preserving foodstuffs in glass jars under sterile conditions.

Filling bottles (mainly for wine). Try to get hold of the right bottles for the job. To force wine corks into bottles made without suitably strong necks is asking for trouble. Red wine should be put into dark bottles, unless it is certain to be kept in the dark. Uniform and correct bottles, properly labeled, also have aesthetic appeal. Bottles must be scrupulously clean inside. Stubborn deposits at the bottom may be removed by swishing

around lead shot, fine gravel, or sand with water, and a bottle brush deals with the neck. After cleaning, bottles must be thoroughly rinsed and inspected by holding them to the light and peering down the neck. After washing, bottles should be stacked neck down to drain and dry. This keeps out bacteria, yeasts, and dust. Bottles should be filled to leave only a small space (¾ in. or 2 cm) between the surface and the cork. New corks of good quality are best and should first be soaked in boiled water for 24 hours to soften them. If old corks have to be used, they must be in good condition—not pierced by the corkscrew—and should be boiled to sterilize them. Plastic stoppers are likely to pop out. Corks and stoppers may be tied down with string or wired. Bottles should be stored on their sides to keep the corks wet and swollen, so that they will not dry out and admit air and bacteria.

Preserving food in jars is essentially the same as *canning and depends on complete sterilization by heat and hermetic sealing. Bottling is a more expensive method than canning in tins (manufacturers prefer cans where possible), but it is the popular home method because it requires a minimum of apparatus, and the bottles can be used over again indefinitely. As a technique, it is not very old—there is little mention of bottling in cookbooks even as late as the turn of this century, when the older methods of preservation were still popular: salting, potting under fat, drying, and conserving with sugar. In fact, bottling followed on the work of Nicolas Appert (1749–1841), who was the first—under the spur of the Napoleonic wars—to patent a method of preserving foods by heating and sealing them in cans or jars. The technique was improved around 1850 by Chevalier Appert, who added heating in a water bath under pressure to the existing technique. One cannot call it sterilization, since the word was not yet invented—it was not until 1854 that Louis Pasteur began his famous work on fermentation, which demonstrated the role of *microorganisms. Thereafter, progress was rapid. Before home bottling could become popular, suitable jars with reliable seals had to be available at a reasonable price. This did not happen overnight. Today, there are several alternative methods of closure—screw tops, clip tops, wired tops—and the seal of rubber or plastic makes an airtight joint with the glass.

Packing. There are two methods used in bottling, the hot pack and the cold pack. In the hot pack, which is the older method, the foods are cooked first, then put into heated sterilized jars and sealed immediately. The jars may sometimes need heat treatment after that. Because the hot-pack method is liable to damage the form and texture of the food, the cold-pack method is generally preferred today. In foods where the form does not matter, such as purées, sauces, and creamed corn, the hot-pack method may actually be preferable. Heat travels to the center of jars of solidly packed, dense, or viscous foods rather slowly, and it may be better to do at least the cooking in an open pan where the product can be stirred. It seems silly to let purées, which have to pass through a sieve after cooking, get cold and then heat them up again for sterilization.

In the cold-pack method, the fruit or vegetables are arranged in the jar raw (or at most partly cooked if they are inclined to shrink with heat), then cooked and sterilized in one operation in the sealed jar. In practice, jars with a lid held by a screw ring—which is not flexible—must be screwed tight and loosened half a turn to allow any pressure build-up to escape. They are tightened again after being taken out of the sterilizing bath.

Liquids in bottling. Fruits are usually packed in syrup. As a general rule, a strong syrup helps preserve taste, color, and texture (obviously, also, more sugar is necessary for very sour fruit). In commercial practice, the best grades are packed in 40–60% syrups, the cheap grades in as low as 10%. A few fruits, which may be wanted sour, can be packed in plain water. Sugar syrups are prepared as a percentage of sugar to water by weight (4 oz or 100 g of sugar in 3½ cups or 1 lt of water is a 10% syrup; so also is 1 lb or 450 g of sugar in 7 qt or 4½ lt). Anyone who does a lot of bottling will find a hydrometer useful. A rough home system is to use equal volume measures (e.g., cups) of sugar and water for a heavy syrup, 1:2 of sugar to water for a medium syrup and 1:3 of sugar to water for a light one.

Vegetables, on the other hand, are commonly packed in a very light brine (2% is usual), but some are packed in water. A home method is to add a teaspoon of salt to each quart (or liter) jar before filling with water.

Preparation. Fruits and vegetables for bottling (or canning) should be in good condition—fresh, undamaged, and unbruised. They need to be cleaned, destalked, peeled, cut in bits, pitted, blanched, parboiled, or otherwise prepared. It is best to use a stainless-steel knife. Fruits which tend to discolor in the air on cut surfaces should be put into some form of antioxidant solution, such as lemon juice or 2 tablespoons each of vinegar and salt per gallon of water (30 g salt and 30 ml vinegar per 4 lt) until ready to fill the bottles. Peaches and tomatoes can be peeled easily after dunking in boiling water.

Sterilization temperatures. Boiling will rapidly kill all organisms, including the heat-resistant spores of botulism, if the foodstuff is sufficiently acid. This is the case with most fruits and tomatoes. In fact, sour fruit juices can be rendered sterile merely by *pasteurizing at 120–150°F (50–60°C). Not so vegetables, which are usually slightly alkaline. They cannot be sterilized by boiling, unless an acid such as lemon juice or vinegar is first added. To sterilize them without an acid, a higher temperature, such as can be reached in an autoclave or pressure cooker, is necessary. The usual pressure chosen is 10 lb/in.² (0.7 Kg/cm²), which gives a temperature of 240°F (115°C) at sea level, but some vegetables, such as spinach and Swiss chard, are more usually sterilized at 15 lb/in.² (1.05 Kg/cm²) (250°F or 122°C) because of the time they take at the lower pressure.

Sterilization times. The object is to raise the temperature in the middle of the jar to the point where, if it is held for an appropriate time, all organisms are killed. In the cold-pack method, the food also has to be cooked. Since it is not very practical to stick a thermometer into a sealed jar, we have to depend on times worked out by food scientists. For most cold-packed fruits, 30 minutes of processing submerged in a boiling water bath is necessary for 1-qt (1-Kg) jars. Pint jars (½ Kg) take 5 minutes less. Vegetables (with the exception of tomatoes) are much more critical in their requirements and must always be sterilized in a pressure cooker. Only if directions are followed to the letter and the bottles are in good condition with new rings is home bottling of vegetables foolproof and safe. Cutting corners is risky.

Testing and storage. When bottles are heated, the contents expand a little (in some cases, as with peas and corn, there is also swelling during cooking), and some air is driven out. On cooling, there is contraction, and if the seal is good, a partial vacuum is formed which sucks the lid on tightly. In this condition, no organisms can get in to infect the contents. Jars should be tested, because if the lid is not sucked on properly, air will continually go in and out with the changes in atmospheric pressure, and spoilage organisms may enter. Although we are always told to store bottled fruit in a dry place, anywhere will do, although preferably it should be dark (unless the jars are wrapped). Light promotes bleaching, and after a time the appearance of the product is spoiled. Naturally, the jars should be labeled with contents and date.

[*Bottling*—French: *mise en bouteille;* German: *in Flaschen konservieren;* Italian: *infiascatura;* Spanish: *embottellado*]

BOTULISM. *See* poisoning.

BOUDIN BLANC. Not like the British white pudding but a delicate, costly, smooth, creamy sausage about 6 in. (15 cm) long. It is made of finely minced white pork with chicken—and sometimes rabbit or other meat—milk or cream, eggs, sometimes a little bland cereal, and a light flavoring of salt, spice, and onion. Although poached in the making, it is best brushed with melted butter and broiled before eating. *Boudin blanc de Paris* contains chicken breasts, and *de Mans* does not, but the exact makeup is local.

BOUDIN NOIR. *See* black pudding.

BOUILLON. *See* broth.

BOUILLON CUBES are marketed as a shortcut in making a variety of stocks. The usual flavors are chicken and beef, but there are also mushroom, onion, and other bouillon cubes for particular purposes (such as pot-au-feu cubes). *Bouillon de légume* cubes are useful for adding the aromatic flavors of carrots, parsley, celery, leeks, and tomatoes to soups and sauces. Bouillon cubes are made according to each manufacturer's secret formulas and mainly consist of salt, spices, monosodium glutamate, and chicken or beef flavor (which may or may not have involved poultry or cattle), plus a binder. They vary enormously, according to price and manufacturer. Some bouillon cubes are awful, and it is easy to dismiss them all, but good ones are useful for reinforcing flavor or to cover an emergency. They are, however, only a source of flavor and not intended primarily as a source of nourishment.

BOUQUET GARNI. A bundle of herbs tied together or enclosed in a cheesecloth bag so that they can be removed at any time, either at the end of cooking or when they have given sufficient flavor to the dish. The basic bouquet consists of a bay leaf, a sprig of thyme, and three sprigs of parsley, but there are endless variants: bouquets may contain marjoram, basil, chervil, savory, tarragon, chilies, mace, cinnamon sticks, bitter orange peel, and anything else that the cook thinks will improve flavor. The bouquet garni is absolutely essential to good European cooking. It should be kept simple to begin with and elaborated by experience.

BOURGOURI. *See* burghul.

BOYSENBERRY. *See* blackberry.

BRACKEN. *See* fern.

BRAIN has a soft and creamy texture when cooked. Although the brains of all the main meat animals are eaten, calf's brain is the most used as a dish in its own right. All brains should be soaked in cold water for 1 hour (calf's brain) to 4 hours (beef brain). The surrounding membranes are then removed together with any traces of blood that are still visible. The first stage in most recipes for brain is simmering for about 20 minutes in a court bouillon that has been slightly acidified with vinegar. Brains may then, for example, be browned in butter or dipped in batter and deep fried.

[*Brain*—French: *cervelle;* German: *Gehirn;* Italian: *cervelli* (pl); Spanish: *cerebro*]

BRAISING. A combined roasting and stewing technique applied to meat, fish, or vegetables. The food is put in a pan with a closely fitting lid (which stops evaporation and keeps in the aromas) and cooked very slowly on top of the stove or in the oven. Very little liquid is added, and the meat or fish is usually laid on a mirepoix of chopped or diced vegetables, chopped bones, or blanched pork rind to protect it from the hot pan bottom. The correct utensil to use is a *braisière,* and the best are made of tinned copper or enameled ironware.

BRAN is the fibrous skin of the *wheat grain which is separated in milling. It may be fine or coarse and varies in color from yellowish to dark reddish brown. Because bran provides roughage, which is useful in alleviating constipation, it has long been sold as a health food, although not everyone will like the flavor, which in some cases seems to have been developed on the principle that what tastes nasty must do you good. Much bran is therefore toasted and made into breakfast cereals.

Bran contains a high proportion of B vitamins as well as about half of the mineral content of the grain. Most of its weight, though, is made up of cellulose, which humans cannot digest. Bran is now valued by many dietitians as a source of fiber in the diet to compensate for the general over-refinement of our food. A diet that is rich in fiber is said to have the result of reducing the cholesterol level in the blood. The idea that such an inexpensive item as bran might actually be health-giving inevitably excited the food manufacturers, with the result that proprietary brands of bread and other products are now promoted in bran-enriched versions.

During milling, bran is deliberately kept in flakes so that it can be separated easily. Where whole-wheat flour is unobtainable, you can grind up bran finely in a coffee grinder and add it to white flour. This cheating will produce something with the grittiness of *atta,* the Indian whole-meal flour which makes the best *parathas* and other unleavened breads.

[*Bran*—French: *son;* German: *Kleie;* Italian: *crusca;* Spanish: *salvado*]

BRANDY (from the Dutch *brandewijn,* burned wine) is distilled from wine (unlike *marc) and is found in every country where there are vineyards. Originally an expensive remedy sold by apothecaries, brandy is made from many types of wine (and hence from many different grapes). It is an exceedingly variable product. Every country produces its own range, and there are strong local preferences and tastes. In France, the finest brandies are *cognac and *armagnac. A good, lesser brandy is usually called a *fine,* with possibly the area of origin tacked on. If recipes specify *un verre à liqueur de fine bourgogne,* it would probably (to anyone other than a Burgundian) be permissible to use another *fine,* but never cooking brandy, and certainly not a brandy from another country which might be muscat-flavored or oversweet to French tastes.

Spain produces brandies of its own which are not imitations of French brandies; indeed, the Spanish probably learned the technique of distillation from the Arabs. Popular Spanish brands vary greatly, and there are also fine Spanish liqueur brandies long aged in the wood. In cooking Spanish dishes, such as *zarzuela* of fish, the selection of the right local brandy is necessary for the authentic dockside taste (if that is what you want), especially since cheaper brandies are often faked up with vanilla or sassafras.

Whereas Spain is addicted to brandy for both cooking and drinking, Italy is not, and brandy is not a common ingredient in Italian food. When used, it tends to be in sophisticated recipes, for which cognac is often specified.

In Germany, people often refer to *Weinbrand* as cognac, without implying that it is the genuine article from France. For a country that produces such superb wines, the brandy is usually fiery stuff, but then the Germans are schnapps drinkers and prefer it like that; otherwise they wouldn't make it that way. In German recipes containing brandy, however, nothing is to be gained by searching for a German brandy—a French one can be used. In Greece, brandy is a popular drink and has its own peculiar taste which is derived from the local grapes. It is not much used in Greek cooking.

Outside Europe, important producers are the U.S., which manufactures enormous quantities of brandy, South Africa (another country where brandy is a very popular drink), and Australia, where the home market is limited—Australians prefer beer. In the past, South African brandies were noted for their overstrong, raisiny taste, since they were made from muscat grapes. There, as in many countries, *folle blanche* and other special brandy grapes have recently been introduced from France and a great improvement has been the result. (I must say, though, that hard-boiled penguin eggs, without that raisiny brandy, will never taste quite so memorably horrible again.) South America also makes a great deal of brandy that follows the usual pattern, but *pisco,* a brandy from Peru, has a highly characteristic taste: it was originally derived from the beeswax used in pioneer days to waterproof earthenware amphorae, which had to serve instead of oak casks. Naturally, if a recipe calls for *pisco* you have to use *pisco,* but use one made in Peru; imitations made elsewhere are little like the brandy they purport to imitate.

[*Brandy*—French: *cognac, eau de vie;* German: *Weinbrand, Branntwein, Kognak, Schnaps* (colloquial); Italian: *acquavite, cognac;* Spanish: *aguardiente, coñac*]

BRANK. *See* buckwheat.

BRASS, an alloy of copper and zinc, was probably first known to the Romans at about the time of Christ. An earlier alloy (probably that referred to as brass in the Bible) was bronze, a mixture of copper and tin. In the Orient, brass is still much used for utensils, though it is, alas, fast being replaced by aluminum—aesthetically less pleasing, but cheaper. Coppersmiths in the bazaars beat brass, since it can be worked cold if it contains over 64% copper.

Naked brass is used for making those beautiful water vessels village girls in India carry on their heads. The vessels are kept scrupulously clean by scouring with ashes inside and out. Naked brass is also traditionally used for drinking mugs for water or milk. For cooking, however, brass pots are usually tinned inside; the exceptions are preserving pans and the pans used for heating jam glaze. Heavy tinned brass pans can still be bought in the Orient, and although it takes much work to keep them clean (they are not as easy to clean as copper), they are durable, beautiful, and excellent for cooking. My kitchen is full of them. However, these pans should be retinned, since the original tinning is likely to contain lead.

[*Brass*—French: *cuivre;* German: *Messing;* Italian: *ottone;* Spanish: *cobre amarillo*]

BRATWURST is a German sausage for grilling or frying. It is pale in color and made of finely ground pork or veal. There are also smoked varieties which should be cooked only for a short time.

BRAWN. *See* headcheese.

BRAZIL NUT, para nut, or **cream nut.** This nut is the seed of a giant tree (*Bertholettia excelsa*) that grows wild in the tropical South American jungle. Although domestication has begun and the tree has been tried in other tropical places, the odds are still that the nuts one buys have come from some remote tributary of the Amazon. They grow packed together like the sections of an orange inside a large, spherical woody fruit. The tree itself grows to a great height and, with its long unbranched trunk, thrusts its head far above the general green canopy of thick forest. When the nuts are ripe, the whole fruit comes crashing to the ground. Since each one weighs several pounds and falls from such a height, collecting is a dangerous occupation. It goes on from November to June. The nuts are broken open with a machete and washed in the nearest creek (bad nuts tend to float away). They are then dried on mats, taken downstream by canoe during the rainy season, and finally transported by river steamer.

Brazil nuts are graded. The largest come mainly from the higher forest of the upper Amazon. Most common are the average-size nuts. The small ones go to chocolatemakers.

Apart from the whole dessert nuts, which have become traditional at Christmas, it is usual, for cooking purposes, to buy nuts already cracked, because extracting the kernel in a whole state is difficult with ordinary nutcrackers. Commercially, they are cracked by rollers. Because Brazils become rancid fairly soon after exposure to the air, you need to be careful when buying cracked ones. They are easy to grate or grind.

Since Brazil nuts contain 60–65% oils and up to 20% protein, they are very nutritious. They are high in cobalt and even higher in Calories than almonds, which, in analysis, they rather resemble. Even the oil pressed from Brazils is like almond oil. When fresh, it is pale yellow, almost odorless, and pleasantly nutty. It is sometimes used in Brazil as an olive oil substitute.

Brazil nuts are used in modern vegetarian or health-food recipes but are otherwise neglected. When freshly cracked, they have a delicious and individual flavor, so the field is wide open for experiment.

Paradise or **Sapucaya nut** (*Lecythis sabucajo*). A near relative of the Brazil, and rather like it, but more rounded and with deep grooves running from end to end. The shell is so fragile that it can often be broken with the fingers. The creamy-white kernel is sweeter than that of the Brazil and has a more delicate flavor. Though used mainly in tropical South America, export is increasing, so we shall no doubt soon come across this nut.

[*Brazil nut*—French: *noix du Brésil;* German: *Paranuss;* Italian: *noce del Brasile, noce del Para;* Spanish: *nuez del Brasil*]

BREAD. Unleavened bread has been a staple food for many thousands of years. In Europe and Asia, it was mainly made of wheat, barley, or millet, but in America up to the time of Columbus, bread was baked from maize, the only cereal known on that side of the Atlantic. It is interesting that rice was usually boiled and not baked into a bread (although such exists), while in northern China (where wheat, not rice, is the staple), the wheat is traditionally eaten steamed as dumplings or made into pasta rather than being baked into bread.

Although leavened bread with yeast was well known in the Middle East of the Old Testament among poor people, especially nomads, this bread would usually have been baked on a flat iron plate or stone; an oven is more costly to construct and cannot be conveniently moved about. The old brick ovens were ideal for making bread: they provided a falling heat, and the fuels added flavor to the bread. Compared to modern ovens, though, they are tricky to manage. Some think that bread tastes better if the oven has been fired with wood. Modern bakeries use ovens heated by oil or electricity, and the bread is often baked on continuous belts.

Until the middle of the 19th century, bread was always leavened by yeast, but then various forms of baking powder were tried. This leavening is still used for biscuits, griddle cakes, and soda bread (as well as for cakes). The so-called aerated bread was also invented and introduced in Victorian times. This contained no yeast; the dough was artificially inflated by gas. It never became really popular because of its uncharacteristic flavor. Today, in some developed countries, much bread is made in factories, and new, shorter methods of making bread without yeast have again been introduced. One of their advantages is that they allow a higher proportion of low-gluten flour to be used. Also, partly because fermentation losses are smaller, more loaves can be made from the same quantity of flour. In one process, the gluten fibers are "developed" during a few minutes of high-power mixing. Bread made this way also contains a very high proportion of yeast to make up for the lack of maturing time. Another method relies mainly on chemicals to work on the gluten; the additives include vitamin C, potassium bromate, and the amino acid cysteine.

Many people today, brought up on the sliced, wrapped product, have never tasted an old-fashioned baker's loaf. Those who have may consider that modern technology has not made bread better, but worse. Part of the attraction of commercial, wrapped bread is its long shelf life. It can hang about in the shop for days, so there is less waste, and it is now baked in such a way as to have a soft crust, which allows it to be sliced easily at the factory. Such bread is even gaining ground in France, Italy, and Spain.

Bread is sometimes sold part-baked and refrigerated or frozen. The dough has been baked at a low temperature to set it and to make a very light soft crust. The baking is then finished in the home. Such bread is popular in the U.S. and is becoming so elsewhere.

Toast is sliced bread held in radiant heat until brown caramel and dextrins are formed on the surface. Toasting destroys some of the B vitamins and thiamine, and toast is no less caloric than the same quantity of untoasted bread.

Baked bread keeps well when frozen, especially if it has a soft crust. Hard crusts are likely to separate from loaves which have been kept frozen for more than a few weeks. To minimize staling, which occurs fastest at temperatures just above freezing point, freeze and thaw bread as quickly as possible.

Nowadays, those who like a decent loaf of bread may have to make it themselves. With home-baked bread, faults may occur, but these are usually easily corrected. Bread which has not been baked long enough will have a doughy, sticky consistency. If it has not proved (i.e., risen) thoroughly, it will have very small holes, and if it has proved too long, it may have developed an air pocket between the crust and the loaf. If it is not kneaded properly, it may have lumps of dry flour in it, a streaky crumb, and oversized air holes.

There are a bewildering number of breads, many of which show national and local variations. In addition, there are baked products which are difficult to categorize as breads, pastries, or cakes. What, for instance, are those specialties made with currants, from the Welsh *bara brith* to the Italian *panettone?* Do we consider *croissants* as bread rolls? And what about the Spanish *ensaimadas?* Brioches and *guglhupf* are other doubtful cases. Almond breads, fig breads, and spiced breads are not bread in the usual sense. And unleavened mixtures, such as chapaties, are also not considered to be bread. Scandinavian rye breads, such as *knakkebrød*, verge on crackers. The following are some basic categories of bread.

Whole-wheat bread, whole-meal bread, graham bread, pain integral, and **pan negro** should be made from the whole, ground wheat kernel, including the germ and the bran, with nothing else except yeast, salt, and a little fat and sugar added. This is the ideal bread of the health-food enthusiast and for those who like the flavor of the whole grain. It contains fibrous bran as well as more vitamins and mineral elements than white bread. It used to be thought that whole-wheat bread also contains more of the organic phosphorus compound phytic acid, which reduces the absorption of calcium, iron, and zinc (although it is partly broken down by the action of enzymes during the fermentation of the dough). This theory has been disproved, but nevertheless tests carried out in schools did not show that whole-wheat bread was superior to white in terms of the growth of the children studied.

Brown bread is intermediate between whole-wheat and white breads, since it contains some wheat bran, with the germ extracted. It may be made with white flour with a little bran and coloring added. There are also brown breads with added wheat germ which has had its enzymes inactivated by heat so that the flour will keep.

Granary bread is made with a proprietary meal containing malted flour and pieces of whole cereal or coarsely ground flour. It may have a fake, rough, country-baked appearance and is not the same as whole-wheat bread.

White bread is made from white flour which contains little bran and germ. It is significant that throughout history, when people could afford it, they have always preferred bread made from low-extraction (white) flour. Unless it is fortified, this is much less rich in B vitamins and minerals, such as iron, than whole-wheat flour. In some countries, vitamin B_1 and nicotinic acid are added as supplements, together with iron and calcium compounds.

Rye bread. Rye flour by itself makes very heavy bread (it does not have the coherence as dough to aerate properly—the dough tends to crack) and is usually mixed with wheat flour. The original rye bread, popular in Scandinavia, Germany, and through into Russia, was made by a *sourdough process, which helped to give it a special flavor. Unfortunately, the magnificent rye bread that was available before World War II has largely disappeared, and some modern rye breads contain only a small quantity of rye and are soured by added acid.

Soda bread is leavened with bicarbonate of soda or baking powder. The alkali destroys some of the vitamin value, but the bread can be made quickly, and some like the taste.

Diet bread and **starch-reduced bread.** Such breads are made by various means to have a higher percentage of protein in comparison with their starch content. They may be made by adding high-protein soy flour or extra gluten to the flour or by removing some of the starch from the flour. Ordinary bread contains about 13% protein, gluten bread 16%, high-protein bread 22%, and extra-high-protein or starch-reduced bread around 50% (all of these figures being expressed on a dry basis). As the percentage of protein is increased, the percentage of starch becomes less. Other diet breads depend on extra aeration of the loaf. Each slice or roll therefore weighs less than a slice of ordinary bread, although weight for weight the energy value would be the same.

Bread in cooking is a very versatile ingredient. It was used as a thickener for sauces in medieval recipes. Perhaps it was needed because the sauces had to be solid enough to stay on the bread trenchers that served as plates. Achieving the same thickness with flour would have turned the sauces to glue. Today, it gives flavor as well as texture to bread sauce and thickens soups such as gazpacho. Slices of bread or croutons give the eater something to get a purchase on in the thin broths of garlic soups and French onion soup.

*Crumbs or croutons on top of casseroles or gratins absorb the juices, butter, and oil from the ingredients below and form a crust. If the recipe is appropriate, herbs can be mixed with the bread crumbs to make the crust even better.

Bread is often the main ingredient in stuffings and is added to oily ingredients, such as the roe in *taramasalata,* to lighten the texture. It is also called for in many meatloaf recipes and in some for hamburgers—in such recipes, the bread is often meant to stretch the meat and make it feed more; if the bread is used to excess and underseasoned, the intention will be only too obvious.

Bread can also become a container, as when a large brioche is hollowed out and filled with pâté, or when rectangles of bread dipped in melted butter line a tin which is then filled with thickened, spiced apple purée—baked, the result is apple charlotte. Buttered bread is a main ingredient in steamed puddings (including Christmas pudding) and in baked bread-and-butter pudding. Bread crumbs appear in cake recipes, notably from North Africa, often in combination with ground nuts. The cakes are moist, puddinglike, and delicious.

[*Bread*—French: *pain;* German: *Brot;* Italian: *pane;* Spanish: *pan. Brown bread*—French: *pain noir;* German: *Weizenbrot;* Italian: *pane scuro;* Spanish: *pan moreno. Rye bread*—French: *pain de seigle;* German: *Roggenbrot;* Italian: *pane de segala;* Spanish: *pan de centeno. White bread*—French: *pain blanc;* German: *Weissbrot;* Italian: *pane bianco;* Spanish: *pan bianco*]

BREAD CRUMBS. *See* crumbs.

BREADFRUIT. Related to the *jackfruit, this belongs to the same family as mulberries and figs. The fruits are borne on a large tropical tree (*Artocarpus communis*) and are yellow-brown when ripe. The average size is about that of a small soccer ball, but there are over a hundred varieties, which vary a great deal. The original home of the breadfruit is Southeast Asia and the Pacific, where it is the staple starchy food. It was introduced to other countries (among others by Captain Bligh of the *Bounty*) but has not achieved equal importance elsewhere.

Breadfruit trees are easy to cultivate. Once established (after 8 years), they yield about 700–800 fruits annually over most of the year. These can be baked, roasted, boiled, sliced and fried, ground to a paste, dried into a sort of flour, stored, and baked into bread. Breadfruit is high in iron, thiamine, and vitamin C. Some varieties have seeds, which are also edible. The breadfruit seems to make possible that fortunate state of complete idleness for which many have longed.

[*Breadfruit*—French: *fruit à pain;* German: *Frucht des Brotbaumes;* Italian: *frutto del albero del pane;* Spanish: *fruta del árbol del pan*]

BREAM is a name given to several quite distinct types of fish. The freshwater bream (*Abramis brama*), a handsome fish of little gastronomic value, is related to the carp, while the marine Ray's bream (*Brama brama*) belongs to quite a different family. Fishmongers used sometimes to sell the very ordinary redfish (*Sebastes marinus*) and Norway haddock (*Sebastes viviparus*)—both scorpionfish related to the rascasse, which is an important item in bouillabaisse—as red bream, which they are not.

The bream of real gastronomic importance belong to yet another family, the Sparidae, which are mostly warm-water fish, plentiful in the Mediterranean but with a single member that is common around northern Europe, the genuine red bream

(*Pagellus centrodontus*). More than a dozen species of sea bream live off the coast of the U.S., where they are known as porgy (among other names). Sea bream is one of the most popular fish in Japan, raw in sashimi or cooked by grilling or poaching. The species there is *Chrysophrys major,* which is closely related to the gilthead bream, the French *daurade* (*Chrysophrys aurata*), probably the best of the breams found in European waters. The black bream or "old wife" (*Spondiliosoma cantharus*), which is caught in the Mediterranean and around British coasts as far north as the Tyne, also makes good eating. Among my own favorites in this group is the dentex (*Dentex dentex*); it will be known to tourists under its Spanish name, *dentón.*

Most fish labeled as bream are stocky-looking fish with Roman noses and one long fin right down the back. Since they usually live on shellfish, they have grinding teeth rather than the sharp teeth of hunting fish. Bream are not generally large fish, but the biggest, such as the dentex, can reach 39 in. (1 m) long and weigh 66 lb (30 Kg). In general, sea bream can be baked or grilled for excellent results.

The name "bream" is sometimes applied loosely in the U.S. to any number of small fish, including the bluegill sunfish, and unrelated saltwater fish such as the ocean perch and porgy.

[*Gilthead bream*—French: *daurade;* Italian: *orata;* Spanish: *dorada. Red bream*—French: *daurade commune;* German: *nordische Meerbrassen;* Italian: *occhialone;* Spanish: *besugo. Black bream*—French: *griset, brème (des rochers);* German: *Seekarpfen;* Italian: *tanuta;* Spanish: *chopa. Ray's bream*—French: *brème de mer;* German: *Brachsenmakrele;* Italian: *pesce castagna;* Spanish: *palometa, japuta*]

BRESAOLA. Dried beef fillet or other tender lean cuts, matured for about 2 months to a dark red color; it is somewhat similar to *bundnerfleisch and a specialty of the Valtellina in the Italian Alps. *Bresaola* is usually served finely sliced and seasoned with olive oil (it is costly, so it deserves the best), a little lemon juice, and freshly ground black pepper. It is better if left to marinate for half an hour before serving as an appetizer with drinks.

BREWING. The brewing of *ale has prehistoric origins. It would not have been a difficult discovery; if pounded grain is mixed with water and allowed to stand for a time in warm weather, it ferments and produces alcohol. Even animals sometimes get drunk from eating fruit that has fermented naturally, so we may conclude that alcoholic beverages of some sort were inevitable. Primitive ales do not please sophisticated palates, but still have their effect. *Chang* (rice beer) from Nepal, Kafir beer or Zulu beer (made with corn and millet) from Africa, and no doubt other brews which I have not personally suffered taste like sour, watery porridge but can be much improved if flavored with herbs and clarified. Even the ancient Egyptians knew a bit about brewing. They used herbs and even, some claim, *hops, which would bring their brew close to *beer.

Modern beer is brewed by fermenting a hop-flavored *wort with a suitable strain of *yeast. In home brewing, beer may be made from malt extract (powder or syrup) or directly from *malt by mashing, a process that is rather difficult to manage at home. Canned, concentrated, ready-to-use worts can also be bought, and they are simply diluted with a specified amount of warm water and put—with yeast—to ferment.

The type of ale or beer brewed depends on the type of malt, the quantity of sugar (maltose, sucrose, glucose), the quantity and quality of hops, the strain of yeast, and whether top or bottom fermentation is used, as well as on physical conditions such as temperature. There are now many excellent books on home brewing.

Beer spends, on average, 5 days fermenting, though lager takes much longer; for some beers, modern conical fermenters used commercially enable the job to be done in 2–3 days, a fact liked by the brewers, but possibly less so by consumers. As fermentation declines, the yeast tends to fall to the bottom of the vessel, a process speeded up by cooling until only a small amount is left in suspension. The newly brewed beer is generally called green beer. This can be, and once was, put straight into casks, matured for a few days, then sent to the pub. Today, the beer is put into conditioning tanks. The rising bubbles of carbon dioxide from the slow fermentation that is still continuing carry away some of the strongly flavored substances which are responsible for harshness in green beer. Most of the yeast can be removed by *fining. Once, finings (isinglass) were added to casks in pub cellars. Sometimes sugar syrup is added to promote a natural sparkle by secondary fermentation.

The best draft beer comes from casks kept in the bar, but this may be impossible, because of space limitations or an unsuitable temperature, in which case the beer has to be drawn up from the cellars, most often by pumping through pipes.

Bottled beers are almost always filtered, pasteurized, and gassed, although a few aristocrats are bottled in their natural condition with yeast still living in the bottles. They contain some sediment, so need careful pouring—like wine. The dregs should be left in the bottle.

Canned beers, essentially similar to bottled ones, have become increasingly popular for their convenience, although they are often overgassed and of poor flavor.

Keg beers have been filtered and usually pasteurized. They are flat, clear, and free of yeasts capable of initiating a secondary fermentation. They are gassed in stainless steel containers at the brewery. Keg beer is served from taps in the bar (forced out by the pressure) and is often very fizzy. Pubs with a large sale may have the same sterile beer delivered by tanker into cellar tanks. The beer is gassed with cylinders of carbon dioxide.

Again, top pressure forces the beer up to the bar, but it is not quite as fizzy as beer gassed at the brewery.

[*Brewing*—French: *brasser;* German: *brauen;* Italian: *fare la birra;* Spanish: *braceaje de cerveza*]

BRILL (*Scophthalmus rhombus*). A sinistral *flatfish of European waters, brill is similar to *turbot but smaller—6½–9 lb (3–4 Kg)—oval in shape, and lacking protuberances on its upper side. The flesh is delicate and sweet, though generally considered inferior to turbot, except in the upper Adriatic, where brill is prized.

In the U.S., one may occasionally encounter a relative of brill and turbot called the windowpane (*S. aquosus*). It has sometimes been marketed as "New York plaice."

[*Brill*—French: *barbue;* German: *Kleist, Glattbutt, Meerbutt;* Italian: *rombo liscio;* Spanish: *rémol*]

BRINE. Brines of salt dissolved in water are used for curing meat (ham, bacon, tongue, beef, and even sausages) and fish (for which the brine is formed from water extracted from the fish after dry salting), and for holding vegetables and fruits until it is possible to turn them into pickles or otherwise process them.

As a rule, bacteria cease to function in 25% salt solutions, and most spoilage organisms give up even in a 10% solution. Some, however, are exceedingly sensitive to salt, and a few are salt lovers. Practical methods of using brines for preservation have been developed over the centuries by simple trial and error.

Cleanliness. Sterility is not essential, and may be actually detrimental to the working of a cure, but all crocks, tubs, and utensils should be very clean and well rinsed before they are used for brining.

Boiling. Brines are boiled to help dissolve the salt, to extract the flavor from the spice bag, and to reduce the number of microorganisms. Some vegetables are put into brine when it is boiling, but usually (always for meat) brine should be cooled until it is stone cold before it is used.

Storage temperature can be critical, because a brine strong enough to preserve in cool conditions may not work in warm ones. Recipes for preserving vegetables through a north German winter will probably be wrong if they are tried without adaptation in a Mediterranean summer.

Scum. Various air-loving organisms form a scum on top of the brine tub. Though not harmful themselves, they should be skimmed off regularly—they create musty flavors when they die and decompose.

Immersion. Whatever is to be preserved in brine must be kept well below the surface. Otherwise, spoilage of the whole tub is certain. A slate, a board weighted by a stone, or even a plastic bag filled with salt and sealed will serve the purpose.

Injection brines. In modern curing, the brine for hams and other large pieces of meat is usually injected, like embalming fluid, with a syringe plugged into the arteries (not veins, which have valves to prevent reverse flow). Brines for this purpose can be weaker. The results are quick and certain, but there is not the same development of flavor.

Basting with brine is a technique halfway between immersion and dry salting; it is useful for home curing where space is limited. Such brines are strongly acidified with vinegar and do not give delicate cures.

Additives. *Saltpeter, *Chile saltpeter, sodium or potassium nitrite (see nitrites)—any of these may be added to brines, especially to those for meat and fish, not only for their cosmetic action of turning meat pink, but also for their preservative effect.

Sugar is added to meat cures because it counteracts the hardening effect of saltpeter and makes the meat taste sweeter and less salty. If brown sugars, molasses, or syrups

are used, they add their flavor. An important action of sugar is to encourage the growth of bacteria which create a little acidity, helping preservation and improving the flavor. Vinegar is used particularly in basting cures for meat but is also usual with vegetables. Spices used for flavor have also some preservative action. The most common in brines are black pepper, allspice, juniper berries, ginger, mace, cloves, cinnamon, and bay leaves.

Brine strength. The preservative effect of brine is related to its strength. Because fluids diffuse out of the foods being preserved, it may be necessary to fortify them with more salt, and some method of checking becomes necessary, especially if the brine is to be used more than once. The easiest way to think of brine strength is as a straight percentage by weight, because that is the way we make it up. 1 lb (450 g) of salt in 8 pt (4½ lt) of water is 10% brine. Old recipes call for brine strong enough to float an egg. It must be a fresh egg, which lies on the bottom of fresh water and not one already starting to take off. It should just rise to the surface of the brine, not float proud. Although pretty inaccurate, this method has served farmers' wives for centuries (a potato is another object they used), but any hydrometer, even a homemade one, will do a better job. *See* brinometer.

Saturated brine is the strongest brine it is possible to make. At room temperature, water will dissolve about 35% salt (3½ lb per 8 pt or 350 g per 1 lt), but since solubility increases with temperature, boiling water will dissolve 40% (4 lb per 8 pt or 400 g per 1 lt). Excess will crystallize out again on cooling. Saturated brine is too strong and crude for most purposes (the art of all salting is to use no more than is necessary and so make a delicate product), but it is used for preserving limes and lemons.

INDIAN BRINED LIMES

Wash and dry the limes, and cut them in quarters but not completely through. Boil them in saturated brine for 5 minutes. Pack the fruit in hot bottles and fill them with boiling brine. Seal immediately.

A STANDARD BUTCHERS' BRINE FOR TONGUE, BACON, AND MEAT

This is a 20% brine, which contains 40 pt (25 lt) water, 11 lb (5 Kg) salt, 3½ oz (100 g) saltpeter, and 11 oz (300 g) sugar. Boil the ingredients for 20 minutes, adding a spice bag toward the end. A good spice bag used by butchers is made of equal weights of coriander and allspice with a half weight of juniper berries. Use 1 oz per 8 pt (25 g per 4½ lt), but do not follow the formula slavishly, to allow for individual taste and the quality of the spices. Cool the brine, remove the spice bag, throw in a slice of bacon (to start the denitrifying bacteria), and sink the meat under the brine. An old rule of thumb says you should leave the meat in the pickle 1 day for every pound (½ Kg) of meat, but thin pieces obviously take less time than thick ones of the same weight.

BRINE FOR HOLDING VEGETABLES

This is a 15% brine, which contains 40 pt (25 lt) water (preferably soft water or rain water), 7½ lb (3¾ Kg) salt, and 2½ pt (1½ lt) vinegar. Boil the water with the salt for 20 minutes, then add the vinegar. Boil it for a minute or so and let it cool. The vegetables which are put into this brine must be fresh and free from blemishes. Keep them below the surface of the liquid and remove any trapped pockets of air. Later, because the brine strength will be reduced by water extracted from the vegetables, check the solution and raise it once more back to strength by adding extra salt: 4½ lb (2 kilos) of salt per 22 lb (10 Kg) of vegetables is roughly what will be required (though it is better to measure); it may be added as saturated brine or simply put on the board covering the vegetables to diffuse slowly into the pickle. (If the salt is tipped in, it sinks to the bottom, leaving the top layers understrength.) Vegetables brined this way need soaking to remove salt before they are cooked, but may be made directly into pickles. This brine is suitable for holding large pieces of vegetables such as cauliflower and for small carrots, green beans, etc.

BRINE FOR FERMENTED VEGETABLE PICKLE

This is a 5% brine, which contains 40 pt (25 lt) water, 2½ lb (1¼ Kg) salt, and 2½ pt (1½ lt) vinegar. Into this brine, made in the same way as the preceding one, put cauliflower divided into florets, French beans, small carrots, beets, cucumbers, turnip slices, or greens. Pack the vegetables tightly, remove air bubbles, and weight the contents under the surface. A lactic acid fermentation will take place and the acidity will increase. Aerobic organisms will form a flor (or white scum) on the surface which must be skimmed off daily. The pickle will be ready in about 10 days, depending on the kind of vegetables and on the temperature. Naturally the process takes less time in hot weather.

If it is not to be eaten immediately (it can be held for a few days in the refrigerator), the pickle should be packed in preserving jars, covered with the brine, and sealed (if the jars have screw caps, loosen them half a turn for safety). Immerse them in cold water, bring them to the boil, and hold them at boiling point for 30 minutes to sterilize them (screw caps then need to be tightened). This pickle does not need desalting but may be rinsed if it is too acid.

[Brine—French: *saumure;* German: *Salzwasser, Salzbrühe;* Italian: *salamoia;* Spanish: *salmuera*]

BRINJAL. Indian name for *eggplant.

BRINOMETER. A special type of hydrometer used by butchers to measure the percentage saturation of brine. On this scale, fresh water is 0° and saturated brine is 100°. The older *Baumé scale, still often used by European butchers, takes 0° for fresh water but 20° for saturated brine, so

1° on the brinometer scale is 5° Baumé. Thus we have the following set of approximate conversions:

	Salt in lb/gallon or g/lt	Hydrometer	Baumé
Fresh water	0	0°	0°
5% brine	5	14°	2.9°
10% brine	10	29°	5.7°
15% brine	15	43°	8.6°
20% brine	20	57°	11.4°
Saturated brine (at room temperature)	35	100°	20°

BRISLING. The Scandinavian name for *sprat. Brisling are often canned and treated as a substitute for sardines, to which they are inferior.

BRISTOL MILK and **Bristol cream.** *See* sherry.

BROAD BEAN, fava bean, shell bean, Windsor bean, field bean, or **horse bean** (*Vicia faba*). The field bean was the original bean and has been cultivated in Europe and Asia since the Stone Age. The modern broad bean is merely an improved variety. Field beans are still commonly grown as farm crops and, except for their size, are gastronomically indistinguishable from broad beans. It is easy to see why they were one of the first plants to be taken into cultivation by early man; they have a large seed (to dry and keep over the winter) and will grow almost anywhere, in any poor soil, as long as there is a suitable climate. You still see them in the more primitive places around the Mediterranean, *il carne del povero,* the meat of the poor.

Broad beans are the first beans for picking in spring. Very young pods can be eaten whole, though the texture is a bit slimy. Young beans, which are bright green, are delicious raw with coarse salt or *prosciutto crudo.* After a few more days, when the skin begins to turn a grayish pink (some varieties remain green and are considered superior), they are better boiled until tender (about 15 minutes) and eaten with chopped parsley and butter, or with a sauce made with plenty of parsley, since the flavors of beans and parsley seem to be complementary. The French combine broad beans with savory, as do the Germans, but this taste is not shared by everybody.

When old broad beans become tough, they are hardly worth eating, even skinned, and are better left on the plant to ripen. They can then be dried and used in winter. In Spain, dried broad beans (*habas secas*) are particularly popular and are sold both whole and peeled (often sliced) in the market. Whole beans must be soaked and the skins removed before using, but sliced beans cook quickly to a purée when simply boiled in water. The Spanish also make much use of canned broad or field beans; bean dishes are served as an "appetite stopper" (although they might not admit it) at the beginning of a meal.

HABAS CON LONGANIZAS

Longanizas or *longanizas blancas* are the long, white, low-fat pork sausages of Cataluña, but any not too fatty pork sausage will do. The beans can be fresh, shelled broad beans or canned broad beans, drained. Heat ½ cup oil until it spits and then cool it a little before putting in 2 lb (1 Kg) of beans, a bay leaf and salt. Cook on low heat until the beans are half cooked—about 5 minutes. Then add ½ cup of water and about ½ lb (250 g) of sausage. Continue to cook on slow heat until all the liquid has been absorbed and the sausages are ready.

[*Broad bean*—French: *haricot large;* German: *grosse Bohne;* Italian: *fava;* Spanish: *haba*]

BROCCOLI (*Brassica oleracea* var. *italica*) is a cauliflowerlike plant, but rather than white and compact like cauliflower, broccoli heads are green, branched, and loose. The central inflorescence develops clusters of buds that rapidly open to yellow flowers.

The cluster should be cut before the buds open, while the head is still firm. Lateral bud clusters will then develop in the leaf axils, and these side branches may be eaten in the same way as the main broccoli head.

In England, broccoli is known as *cauliflower, winter cauliflower, or heading broccoli. The plants usually grown there are very sensitive to heat, requiring a long period of cool weather and constant moisture. The sprouting or Italian broccoli generally grown in the U.S. likes similar conditions but is more cold- and heat-resistant and has a longer harvesting period. When buying broccoli, select firm heads of good color; avoid ones that are yellowish or beginning to flower.

Broccoli is very nutritious, an excellent source of vitamins A and C. In addition to the flower heads, a portion of the stems may also be peeled and eaten, and the leaves may be cooked as greens. Broccoli should be steamed or quickly cooked in fast-boiling water just until tender, and in general treated with the same respect as asparagus. It also freezes well.

[*Broccoli*—French: *chou-broccoli;* German: *Spargelkohl;* Italian: *broccoli;* Spanish: *bróculi, brécol*]

BROILING and **grilling.** The words "broiling" and "grilling" are often used synonymously in the U.S., and both involve the application of direct heat to food. However, broiling usually refers to cooking *under* an oven broiler, whereas grilling is done *over* intense heat (except in England, where the word is equivalent to U.S. broiling). Although many different foods can be broiled, it is a rapid process that is best suited to tender cuts of meat, fish, and moist vegetables. Many finished dishes are also run under the broiler to give them a brown glaze.

In barbecue grilling, it is important that the grill be really clean, something that cooks often neglect, and that the fire be really hot. Before use, the grill should be heated and rubbed with fat so that food does not stick. The grill should preferably be slightly inclined to encourage the fat to run down the bars and so to minimize dripping into the fire. Salt should be sprinkled on meat only at the last moment before it is put on the heat, since it will make the juices run.

[*Broiling*—French: *griller;* German: *rösten;* Italian: *arrostire sulla, graticula;* Spanish: *asar. Grilling*—French: *griller;* German: *auf dem Rost braten rösten;* Italian: *cuicere alla graticola;* Spanish: *asar a la parrilla*]

BROTH. The liquid in which any bones, meat, or vegetables have been boiled. It is usually concentrated, flavored, and salted to make a soup, but is always unclarified. Bouillon (French for broth) is concentrated, also usually unclarified, and likely to be made from beef or veal. Consommé is both concentrated and clarified. *Stock is also made by boiling bones, meat, fish, or vegetables in water. It is never a finished dish, but only a basic material from which soups or sauces are made.

[*Broth*—French: *bouillon;* German: *Fleischbrühe;* Italian: *brodo;* Spanish: *caldo*]

BRUSSELS SPROUTS. Sprouts are a variety of the *cabbage species (*Brassica oleracea,* var. *gemmifera*) which originated, as far as is known, in the early 13th century near Brussels. Modern varieties of Brussels sprouts produce regular and tight buds that require little trimming. The small "cabbage" at the top of the long, sprout-bearing stem is used as greens (sprout tops). It is often believed that a frost is necessary to make sprouts sweet, but certainly with modern varieties this is not necessary. Some types are naturally sweeter than others. The purple-red sprouts often taste as sweet as the chestnuts with which they are sometimes cooked. Loose, blown sprouts are cheap, but often take a lot of cleaning and are therefore wasteful. If sprouts are yellowish, they are stale, have a horrible smell and taste, and should not be bought under any circumstances. Fresh sprouts are usually a healthy dark green but recently a pale-green, very large variety has appeared. These large sprouts, looking almost like miniature cabbages, can be as big as an orange; they are excellent and very economical.

[*Brussels sprouts*—French: *chou de Bruxelles;* German: *Rosenkohl;* Italian: *cavolino di Brusselle;* Spanish: *col de Bruselas*]

BUAL. See madeira.

BUCKWHEAT, beechwheat, brank, or **Saracen corn.** Being the seed of a starch plant (*Fagopyrum esculentum*) belonging to the same family as rhubarb, sorrel, and dock (*Polygonaceae*), buckwheat is not a true cereal, although it is treated as such. The plant has pink or white flowers (good for honey), reddish stems, and long, pointed, heart-shaped leaves. It is a native of Asiatic Russia, where it is still found growing wild in its original form (which usually means that it has been taken into cultivation very late in history—it is said, under 1000 years ago); it did not reach Europe until the 15th century. It is useful because it grows very rapidly, even on poor soil, and so will smother weeds.

Buckwheat gets its name through the Dutch *boek-weit,* meaning beechwheat, because the grain is shaped like a beechnut, though smaller. It is an important staple in Russia, but is also grown extensively both for its grain and as green fodder in the U.S., Germany, France, Japan, and elsewhere. It can usually be found on sale in health-food shops.

As a food, buckwheat has a distinctive flavor. Buckwheat flour, either plain or mixed with wheat flour, is the basis for buckwheat pancakes, a well-known winter breakfast favorite in parts of the U.S. Recipes vary from a simple type of griddle cake leavened with baking powder to more elaborate versions based on yeast. The famous Russian yeast-leavened pancakes, blinis, are also often made with a mixture containing buckwheat flour, and savory crêpes can be made wholly or partly with buckwheat.

Whole, husked buckwheat is the basis for kasha in Russian cookery. It can be made into a porridge or cakes, or cooked in loose grains, when it may be compared to rice. Traditionally, buckwheat goes with borscht and with *shchi* (thick vegetable soups). It is used as a stuffing for both fish (such as carp and trout) and meat (including pork and goose). Many prefer it to rice with beef Stroganoff, goulash, or other meats cooked in a sauce.

KASHA

Measure the required amount of husked buckwheat grain (¼–½ cup per person) and pick it over to remove husks and any unhusked grains. Roast the grain with care, stirring and shaking it continually, in an ungreased frying pan until the grain begins to pop. Now turn it into an ovenproof dish with a lid, or into a double boiler, and add 1½–2 times the volume of boiling, salted water. Cook in the oven at moderate heat (350°F, 180°C), or in a double boiler for about 45 minutes, or until the grains are soft but not soggy. Add plenty of butter, fluff it with a fork, and serve.

[*Buckwheat*—French: *sarrasin, blé noir;* German: *Buchweizen;* Italian: *grano saraceno;* Spanish: *trigo negro*]

BULGAR WHEAT. See burghul.

BULLACE. A small wild variety (*Prunus domestica,* ssp. *insititia*) of the European *plum, the bullace tree looks very like the blackthorn, but the bark of the twigs is brown, not black, and the tree is less thorny. The fruits also look very like sloes, though they are a little larger; they have the same blue bloom, but there are also yellow varieties. Wild bullaces are locally common in hedgerows and at the edges of woods in England. They are also common over much of southern Europe and into Asia.

Bullaces, though less sour and astringent than sloes, are of greatest use for similar purposes—to make bullace wine and bullace gin. They can also be made into jam and even, given enough sugar, used as stewed fruit. Although gastronomically intermediate between sloes and damsons, they lack the incomparable flavor of the latter. Bullace is not often planted now, although cultivated varieties are very prolific and fairly sweet, especially if, like wild bullaces, they are left on the trees well into the autumn, after the leaves have fallen.

[*Bullace*—French: *crèque;* German: *Pflaumenschlehe;* Italian: *susino selvatico;* Spanish: *endrina grande*]

BULLOCK'S HEART. *See* custard apple.

BULLY BEEF. Canned *corned beef.

BUMMALO. *See* Bombay duck.

BUNDNERFLEISCH. Swiss cured and dried beef, similar to the *bresaola* from neighboring districts of Italy, and traditionally made in the Grisons in winter. In some other areas the beef is smoked, but not in the Grisons. An expensive delicacy, it is served in very thin slices as an appetizer.

A Swiss woman whose mother used to make *bundnerfleisch* at home says that a pickle was made with all sorts of chopped vegetables, mountain herbs, onions, chives, parsley, thyme, and so on mixed with coarse salt (*gros sel*). First the meat was dipped in white wine, then rubbed with the salt mixture (and very little saltpeter for color), and put in a barrel in a cool cellar. The juice extracted by the salt was drained off, and the meat again rubbed with the mixture, a process repeated until no more juice flowed out. After that, the pieces of meat were hung to dry in an attic "where we had a little tower, *la tournalette,* for the purpose." The windows, covered with wire mesh to keep out the flies, were left open, but if it was cold at night someone had to go up to shut them and prevent the meat from freezing. The finished *bundnerfleisch* was taken down when it was thoroughly dried.

In a more cynical modern vein, a butcher says that *bundnerfleisch* used to be made in the Grisons in winter, but that now, with air conditioning, any salami manufacturer can make it all year round, wherever his factory happens to be, "because it is a good method of getting rid of meat that is too tough to be sold in any other way. It is sometimes made out of donkey, and you can buy a version in horse-butchers' shops." He goes on to say that he doesn't like selling *bundnerfleisch,* because unless it is sold quickly, it loses so much weight that there is no profit in it.

BURGHUL, bulgar wheat, bourgouri, or **pourgouri.** Often described as cracked wheat, burghul is cracked by boiling, not mechanically. It is a staple in the Middle East, especially in Syria and in the Lebanon, and is the essential basis of tabbouleh and kibbeh. Finely ground burghul is used for kibbeh and tabbouleh, the coarse for other dishes (*kishk* and pilaf). It can be bought already cracked or made at home as follows:

BURGHUL

Take good-quality whole wheat and, if necessary, pick it over and wash it. Put the wheat in a saucepan and cover it with water. Boil it until it is somewhat soft and begins to crack open. Then drain well and dry in the sun or in a very low oven. The dried burghul must then be ground in a hand grinder (or coffee mill if only small quantities are needed) and sieved.

TABBOULEH

Soak 1 cup (225 g) finely ground burghul for about an hour in cold water, until it has softened but gives a little resistance to the bite. Drain the water from it thoroughly, then spread it on a tea towel and press further moisture out of it. Put the burghul in a bowl and add 2–3 tablespoons of olive oil.

Finely chop 1 medium onion, several sprigs of mint, and a large handful of parsley, and add them to the burghul. Stir everything together, keeping the mixture light, and season it with the juice of 1 juicy lemon, salt, and pepper. If you wish, add shredded lettuce, pieces of cucumber, and chopped tomato.

BURNET. Several plants are called burnet, but the one that is relevant to the kitchen is salad burnet (*Sanguisorba minor*). This plant, a member of the rose family, is a native of most of Europe and was taken to North America by the early colonists. It grows up to 12 in. (30 cm) high, and the insignificant flower head looks like a greenish bobble with a few purple wisps sticking out of it. The leaves, which are eaten, have small, round leaflets with regularly toothed edges. When crushed, they have a smell of cucumber, which gives a final identification, but salad burnet would not be easily confused with anything poisonous. It is grown in some herb gardens and is collected together with shoots of wild chicory in many southern European countries as a winter or spring salad. It is an ingredient of ravigote and chivry sauces as well as of various butters.

[*Burnet*—French: *grande pimprenelle, pimprenelle commune des prés;* German: *Pimpinelle, grosser Weisenkopf;* Italian: *pimpinella;* Spanish: *pimpinela, salvastrella*]

BUTTER is an ancient invention of herdsmen, one of the original, simple ways of preserving milk. If butter is rendered to a form of pure fat, it will keep for many weeks. The milk of most mammals (except that of the *camel) can be made into butter by shaking it until the fat globules come together into more or less solid butterfat. This would be done, for instance, in skins—the Bedouins' *mirjahah* and others like it are still seen among nomadic tribes in North Africa and the Middle East. An earthen pot with a whirling wooden paddle is a device that is still used in Indian villages. We are used to butter from cow's milk, but we must not forget that it is also made from buffalo milk, yak milk, and, in arid regions, from ewe milk (e.g., the Syrian yellow butter).

HOMEMADE BUTTER

Few people these days possess a wooden barrel churn or even one of those glass jars fitted with revolving paddles. Butter can, however, be made in a large screw-topped jar of any sort by anyone with the energy to shake it for long enough, or with willing children.

First, the fat must be concentrated as cream, by letting the milk stand in a refrigerator and skimming off the top (homogenized milk is obviously no use for this)—or cream may be bought. For the most flavorful butter, the cream should be ripened for 2–3 days; a temperature of 77°F (25°C) is the best. Bacterial action produces butter aroma (particularly a substance called diacetyl); butter made from unripened sweet cream is relatively tasteless, but keeps better. Churning is best done at 60°F (15–16°C). If the weather is very cold, churning can take longer.

During churning, the cream first thickens, like custard, but it soon becomes grainy with tiny flecks of butter. This is the time to add a cup of cold water, which helps the butter to separate. As churning proceeds, the flecks become larger, and finally coalesce into blobs of butter. Strain these out of the watery whey and beat them together into a lump with wooden paddles. Finally, wash the butter several times in cold water, to remove the sour *buttermilk. When clean and well compacted, add salt or leave the butter unsalted, as wished. Salted butter keeps better.

In addition to butter flavors produced by lactic bacteria in maturing cream, there are flavors derived from the milk itself. They come from the pastures on which the cows are fed. In modern farming practice, pastures are no longer natural: they lack the flowers and herbs that give the finest butters their incomparable taste. However, you can still find good butters such as those from Normandy and, even better, from cows kept on meadows in the Alps. Some recipes depend entirely on the quality of fine ingredients (for instance, *fettuccine al burro*—ribbon pasta with butter), but they do not always mention the attention that must be given to the butter. With the best cheese and butter brought down from a mountain village, a simple dish of pasta is superb, but it will be less appetizing if made with imported cooking butter (or even margarine) and any old cheese.

CLARIFIED BUTTER

For frying, clarified butter (that is, pure butter fat) is best; otherwise the small percentage of milk protein and sugars that ordinary butter contains will precipitate and burn. Traces of water also need to be removed from the fat. To clarify butter, heat it gently until the sediment comes down and frothing ceases, then cool it in the refrigerator until you can easily separate the solidified butter from the milky residue.

GHEE

Indian *ghee* is much the same as clarified butter, but has a much stronger taste. It starts with butter made perhaps from well-soured buffalo's milk (or cow's milk) and is kept on a very low heat for up to 45 minutes. By this time, the sediment will have browned slightly, and the oily *ghee* will have acquired a very special taste: some describe it as "nutty," and it makes a most delicious food.

[*Butter*—French: *beurre;* German: *Butter;* Italian: *burro;* Spanish: *mantequilla*]

BUTTER BEAN. *See* lima bean.

BUTTERFISH. These small silvery fish, *Boronotus triacanthus,* are known as pumpkin seeds in Connecticut and dollarfish in Maine. They are fished along the Atlantic Coast from Florida to Canada. Their scales are fine and easily scrubbed off. Butterfish flesh is dark but delicate and has a pleasing buttery taste. Smoked butterfish are found in many delicatessens, especially in the Eastern U.S., where fresh butterfish are available nearly year-round.

BUTTERMILK, traditionally, is the fluid remaining when milk is churned to butter. However, little buttermilk left over from butter production is available in this country. Today's buttermilk is cultured by a process of fermentation. Milk processors add salt to fresh low-fat or skim milk and pasteurize it to destroy bacteria. It may then be homogenized to distribute the fat globules. After the milk has cooled to about 70°F (21°C), selected starter cultures of bacteria, chiefly *Streptococcus lactis,* are added and the mixture is ripened for about 12 hours in vats at 60–72°F (20–22°C). During this time the bacteria convert some of the milk sugar lactose to lactic acid, causing a curd to form. The product is stirred gently and cooled to 50°F (10°C) or lower to halt fermentation.

Liquid butter that forms granules or flakes is sometimes added to cultured buttermilk to give the appearance of churned buttermilk; its tart flavor may be enhanced by adding small amounts of citric acid or sodium citrate, and it is occasionally fortified with vitamin A or other nutrients. Such added ingredients must be listed on the buttermilk carton in the U.S. In Europe buttermilk flavored with fruit or chocolate is available. The so-called Bulgarian buttermilk sold in some countries is made with *Lactobacillus bulgaricus;* it has a very tart flavor.

The caloric and nutrient content of buttermilk is similar to that of the fluid milk from which it is made. It is high in protein, riboflavin, and calcium.

Buttermilk has long been valued as a cooking ingredient as well as a thirst-quenching beverage. It is used with baking soda to make light and tender cakes, breads, and pancakes, and its acidity helps tenderize foods and offset the gaminess of meats like venison.

[*Buttermilk*—French: *petit lait, babeurre;* German: *Buttermilch;* Italian: *siero di latte;* Spanish: *leche de manteca*]

BUTTERNUT is the name commonly given to the American white walnut (*Juglans cinerea*). The nuts are longer than black walnuts and have thick shells, and the kernels are sweet and oily. The term "butternut" is also applied to the souari nut (*Caryocar nuciferum*) of South America, whose oil is used in cooking. The Nara nut or butter pit (*Acanthosicyos horrida*), also called butternut, is found growing wild in the deserts of southwest Africa. It looks like a large melon seed and is in fact the oily seed of a gourd, the fruit of a spiny shrub.

C

CABBAGE. All types of cabbage—with the exception of the various forms of ★Chinese cabbage—are probably derived from the wild species, *Brassica oleracea,* which still grows in a few places on the coasts of Britain, France, Spain, and Italy. This plant takes the prize for having produced the most weirdly different varieties: it does not just come as open and ball cabbages—red and green at that—but is the forerunner of ★kale, ★collards, ★Brussels sprouts, ★cauliflower, ★broccoli, and probably ★kohlrabi. Cabbage has a certain taste similarity to other plants of the same family (Cruciferae), to turnips and their tops, to mustard greens, and even to cress and rocket. (Perhaps this is a reason why mustard goes well with cabbage.)

Common hearted cabbage (var. *capitata*—"with a head") is very old. It was introduced into Britain by the Romans and into America by the first settlers. There are many types, of which some form exceedingly dense hearts, others only loose ones. Different varieties make hearts at different times of the year, so that fresh cabbage can be had at all seasons.

A few special cabbages should be noted by the cook. The very tight white cabbages (grown particularly in Holland and widely exported) keep for many weeks (most other types of cabbage do not), are easily shredded, and are good for salads and for ★sauerkraut, but they are not very tasty when cooked. For that, the best is undoubtedly the Savoy, a winter variety with wrinkled leaves, which was developed in Savoy during the Middle Ages. A Savoy compares with an ordinary cabbage as a sole with a whiting. On one occasion, a fussy Italian arrived at my home just as I was sitting down to a very frugal dinner—a Savoy—and had nothing more to offer. Crazy English and their cabbage! I could see it on his face. Yet, when he saw it, a lovely green on the dish, he wanted to try some. He ate two helpings.

BOILED SAVOY

Take a sparkling fresh Savoy, remove the outer leaves, and wash only if necessary. Cut out the thick stalks of the core without disturbing the shape. Plunge it into a large amount of rapidly boiling salted water over high heat. Put on a well-fitting lid with a weight on top. (This will raise the temperature slightly, a sort of primitive pressure cooker.) Watch, test, and remove the cabbage the moment it is tender enough, but slightly crisp. It is better to undercook than overcook it. Drain very thoroughly, bottom downwards, so that the water can run out, helping with light pressure. Serve immediately with good salt, freshly ground pepper, and fine butter.

Red cabbage is often pickled, but it is also very decorative raw in salads. In a sweet-sour form—sometimes with apple and caraway seeds—it is one of the best-loved vegetables in Germany, Denmark, and Holland.

RODKAAL

Shred a red cabbage. Put it in a heavy pan (not iron) with a very little water and, for each 2 lb of cabbage, a tablespoon of sugar, 2 of butter, and a little vinegar. Stew gently for 2–3 hours; when it is nearly cooked, add ½ cup (roughly) of the juice squeezed from red currants, and more vinegar and sugar to taste. This red cabbage is better made the day before and reheated.

[Cabbage—French: chou; German: Kohl; Italian: cavolo; Spanish: col. Savoy cabbage—French: chou de Milan; German: Wirsingkohl; Italian: verza; Spanish: berza rizada. Red cabbage—French: chou rouge; German: Rötkohl; Italian: cavolo rosso; Spanish: col lombada]

CABBAGE PALM. See palm cabbage.

CACAO. See chocolate.

CACTUS PEAR. See prickly pear.

CAFFEINE. The principal *alkaloid found in tea, coffee, cocoa, and cola. Its effects are to stimulate the nervous system, and thus excessive amounts can cause nervousness or insomnia. It also increases the flow of urine. The amount of caffeine necessary to have an effect varies between 100 and 300 mg. A cup of tea has 50 to 100 mg, coffee 100 to 150 mg, and cocoa 50 mg. Cola drinks may contain 35 to 55 mg per bottle. Tea leaves and coffee beans may be treated to extract caffeine without significantly altering flavor: unroasted coffee beans are soaked to swell their cells, submerged in a solvent that flushes out 97% of their caffeine, then roasted and ground.

The U.S. Food and Drug Administration has recommended that caffeine used as an additive be removed from its "safe" list until further tests determine its effect on health.

[Caffeine—French: caféine; German: Kaffeestoff; Italian: caffeina; Spanish: cafeina]

CALALOO. See callaloo.

CALAMARE. See squid.

CALAMONDIN. See orange.

CALAMUS or **sweet flag.** A common marsh plant of the northern hemisphere, native in the U.S. and Asia but introduced to Europe. The plant (Acorus calamus), which grows wild in shallow water, is aromatic, and the roots were at one time candied. Calamus is a flavoring used in liqueurs, but rarely in other contexts.

[Calamus—French: roseau, jonc odorant, lis des marais; German: gemeiner Kalmus; Italian: calamo aromatico; Spanish: calamento]

CALCIUM (Ca). A metallic element that makes up nearly 3.5% of the earth's crust yet cannot exist as a metal in nature because it reacts instantly with water. It occurs mainly as a carbonate in limestone, chalk, and marble, but also as a sulfate in gypsum and as a phosphate (apatite). Calcium chloride occurs in sea water. Calcium makes up 5% of the weight of the human body and is an element of extreme biological importance, because calcium phosphate is a main constituent of bones and is essential in smaller amounts for the health of nerves and muscles, and for the blood clotting mechanism. Adequate calcium in assimilable form is essential in the diet and must be accompanied by vitamin D, which aids in its absorption. Whole or skimmed milk, yogurt, and cheese are outstandingly rich in calcium, but not such milk products as cream, cream cheese, and butter, in which the fat is concentrated. Cauliflower, broccoli, cabbage, and other Brassica greens are good sources, as are other vegetables including beans, leeks, watercress, and lettuce. Small fish eaten complete with bones, such as whitebait and sardines in oil, are another. It is thought that an adult needs to take in 500 mg of calcium a day (others say double that or over) to be really healthy. In practice, much calcium is thrown away with the vegetable water.

[*Calcium*—French: *calcium;* German: *Kalzium;* Italian: *calcio;* Spanish: *calcio*]

CALCIUM CARBONATE. *See* chalk.

CALF'S-FOOT JELLY was once considered a wonderful restorative after sickness (I remember having it forced down my throat as a child after the 1918 influenza epidemic). Today it is treated with less enthusiasm. It is made by boiling calf's feet until a natural aspic is obtained. This is then strained, clarified, and flavored with wine, vinegar, lemon juice, or spices.

CALLALOO or **calaloo** (although there seem to be almost as many spellings as there are Caribbean islands) is a West Indian soup and also the green leaves that are the soup's main ingredient. These are the young leaves of various *yams belonging to the arum family, notably those of dasheen and yautia. Also used as (and in) callaloo are local species of amaranth *spinach; this is sold in cans in shops that sell Caribbean produce. According to Elisabeth Lambert Ortiz, who gives several callaloo recipes in *The Complete Book of Caribbean Cooking* (M. Evans, 1973), ordinary spinach or Swiss chard tastes much the same and can be used as a substitute.

CALORIES. The Calorie of biology, medicine, and diet sheets is the large calorie or kilocalorie and is often spelled with a capital C. It is 1000 times the basic calorie of the physics lab, which is too small to be of use as a measurement in matters of eating. The Calorie is the amount of heat necessary to raise the temperature of 1 lt of water by 1°C. It is necessary to think of it also as the way of expressing the quantity of heat produced when a substance is burned, i.e., as a measure of the energy a food contains. Since heat is a form of energy and energy is expended as work, we can also use Calories to measure what we use up in being alive (metabolism) and what we need to do our chores, have fun, and take exercise. This enables a balance to be struck between what we need and what we eat. If we eat more than we need, then we must either burn away the surplus food or store it as fat. Since there are many other considerations, such as whether the food is absorbed into the blood, the Calorie way of looking at diet gives us only a rather crude and basic sum. In particular, it takes no notice of the types of food, the proteins, oils, vitamins, and trace elements, necessary for health. But it does provide an indication and is something to base a weight-watching diet on.

[*Calories*—French: *calories;* German: *Kalorien;* Italian: *calorie;* Spanish: *calorías*]

CALVADOS. *See* fruit brandy.

CAMEL. There are two sorts of camel: the one-humped dromedary and the heavier, two-humped bactrian. Camels were first domesticated in deep southeastern Arabia around 1300 B.C. There are many recognized strains, some good for hauling loads, some for swift riding, and others for giving milk. Because they are precious animals and their meat is a bit coarse and beefy, the people of the deserts generally prefer to eat goat or sheep, the other livestock that survive in all but the most arid regions. However, young camels are at times killed for feast days, and camel meat is quite commonly eaten in some places during the winter, especially in November and December when the sheep are bags of bones from the shortage of grass. The camel's hump is considered the best eating, and the meat is supposed to be "warming." People who must stand temperatures up to 140°F (60°C) in the summer and well below zero in the winter need a good variety of food, as I can bear out, having myself experienced the quite ghastly extremes of Iraq.

Camel milk is commonly drunk in desert regions and in towns with a desert hinterland. Together with dates, it is the main source of food for Bedouin herdsmen. It is nourishing but inclined to be purgative. Because the fat globules are in a finely divided state (homogenized by nature, so to speak), no cream will rise, and it is profitless to try churning it to butter. It is, however, soured and churned to make *leben* (a kind of yogurt), although more commonly it is drunk plain.

[*Camel*—French: *chameau;* German: *Kamel;* Italian: *cammello;* Spanish: *camello*]

CAMOMILE or **chamomile.** Camomile tea is a well-known calming drink. It can be made from either of two herbs, both belonging to the composite family and claimed to be equally effective. They are the sweet camomile (*Anthemis nobilis*), a native of England, western Europe, and North Africa, and the wild camomile or German camomile (*Matricaria chamomilla*), which grows wild over much of Europe and has been introduced in North America and Australia. Both camomiles have escaped widely in the U.S., and both have small daisylike flowers, a strong aromatic smell, and a bitter flavor. Camomile can be bought in packets, dried and ready for making into camomile tea, which is brewed by pouring boiling water on the dried herb and infusing like any other tea.

[*Camomile*—French: *camomille;* German: *Kamille;* Italian: *camomilla;* Spanish: *camomila, manzanilla*]

CANDIED FRUIT, glacé fruit, crystallized fruit, and **preserved fruit.** Candied fruit is fruit or pieces of fruit (e.g., candied peel) impregnated with sugar (which acts as a preservative), then washed and dried on the surface. The surface is covered with crystalline sugar in crystallized fruits. A glazed surface characterizes glacé fruit (e.g., glacé cherries, and *marrons glacés*). Preserved fruit is packed in a dense syrup (e.g., preserved ginger), unless the sense suggests otherwise.

Essentially, the technique leading up to all of these products is the same. The fruits (and certain vegetables, such as carrots, and angelica stalks) are peeled, cored, scraped, cut in suitable-sized pieces, or otherwise prepared. A few items demand special techniques, such as an initial soaking of the pieces in *limewater overnight, and fruit which discolors when cut up must be kept in water which has been laced with ascorbic acid (vitamin C) or lemon juice. After preparation, the fruit must be boiled until it is just tender and, if it is in large pieces, pricked all over with a needle to aid sugar penetration.

The methods used in preserving fruit to be packed in syrup and to be candied differ in some details. In preserved fruit, some of the juices can flavor the syrup, but in candied fruit, the juices should stay in the fruit. Preserving fruit in syrup is a less critical process: the sugar concentration can be raised fairly rapidly, and the syrup can be made with pure cane sugar. Candying needs more care: the sugar concentration must be raised slowly, and (for best results) the sugar should be mixed with glucose.

Candied peel is the peel of various citrus fruit (oranges, bitter oranges, lemons, and citrons) preserved by impregnating with sugar. The fruits can be cut in half, held in brine until wanted, then soaked to remove the salt. The peel is cooked and soaked in syrups of increasing strengths. Candied peel varies enormously in quality; it may be succulent or hard. These days, it is very often chopped in the factory and sold as mixed peel. Many people who like the taste of candied peel do not like the hard bits, which are rather indigestible, and prefer to put peel through the mincer.

[*Candied fruits*—French: *fruits candis, fruits glacés;* German: *glacé Früchte;* Italian: *frutto candito;* Spanish: *fruta azucarada*]

CANDLE NUT. This tropical nut (*Aleurites moluccana*), a member of the spurge family, is so oily that it can be burned like a candle. Under the name of *kemiri* or *buah keras* (kras), it is used in Malay and Indonesian cooking, crushed in soups, or ground with other ingredients for *saté* and curry pastes. When fresh and raw, the nuts are violently purgative, indeed poisonous, but the poison dissipates after they have been kept for some time, and the nuts can be used, often first roasted, in cooking. *Macadamia nuts are recommended as a substitute, as are the less oily almonds, and are even preferred in Southeast Asia by those who can afford them.

CANDY. *See* sugar.

CANNELLINI. *See* bean.

CANNING. Before food preserved in metal cans could replace food canned in glass containers, tinplate had to be invented. Today, canning is a large industry, and since certain varieties of fruit and vegetable respond to canning in metal better than others, huge acreages of produce are grown near the canneries by farmers working under contract and often using seeds or plants developed and provided by the canners. Crops have also to be harvested at exactly the right stage, which demands close collaboration between farmer and canner.

Canning is mainly done in containers made of plain or lacquered tinplate. Although the materials used pass under human inspection, the processes of selection, grading, and cleaning in large factories are done almost entirely by machinery. So also is the filling of the cans with the food. The cans are usually sealed before sterilization, in contrast to the old methods in which the food was sealed in the container immediately after heating, to remove as much air as possible. Fruit is usually sterilized at a temperature near boiling, and vegetables at well over boiling temperature in an autoclave for 20–45 minutes, which is necessary to ensure the destruction of all bacterial spores.

There is little point in home canning in tin containers, and there are strong reasons against it. Whereas canning or bottling acid fruit may be safe, the home canning of vegetables in metal containers is not, unless the person doing it is very careful, very expert, and very well equipped. Statistics show that most outbreaks of botulism (*see* poisoning) can be traced to home canning. Since this disease is so often fatal, do-it-yourself canning is best forgotten. An expert whom I consulted advised: "Don't do it!" However, in spite of a very few highly publicized scares, food poisoning from commercially canned foods is so rare as to be negligible, because of the scientific control which has been perfected over the years by engineers and scientists in the canners' laboratories. Persons with large quantities of food that they wish to have canned should investigate whether there is a community cannery in their area; here food can be processed and sealed in metal containers in conditions similar to those of commercial canneries.

[*Canning*—French: *conserve en boite;* German: *konservieren, eindosen;* Italian: *conservare in iscatola;* Spanish: *envasado, enlatado*]

CANTALOUPE. *See* melon.

CAPE GOOSEBERRY. *See* physalis fruit.

CAPER. Capers (*Capparis spinosa,* spiny; *Capperis inermis,* spineless), which grow wild all around the Mediterranean, have been used as a condiment for thousands of years. Plants may often be seen hanging down over old walls and growing on building sites or on the rough ground at the edges of roads. They can be recognized by their flowers, which look a little like large wild roses with tassels of long purple stamens. Caper flowers have a very short life—they open in the morning and are wilted by lunch time, but if a spray is cut and put in water in the house, the unopened buds will burst into flower and last for a day or more.

CAPERS

Capers are the small, immature flower buds (the cucumberlike fruit, which has annoying small seeds inside, is sometimes pickled in country areas). Raw capers have none of the interesting goaty taste that develops only when they have been pickled.

Although capers are very easy to grow in a dry warm climate, they are expensive because of the great amount of handwork necessary in picking them. This is especially the case with the best capers, which are made from the very small hard buds. The plant has to be picked over almost every morning, just as the buds reach the proper size, and it takes a long time to gather a worthwhile quantity. Raw capers may sometimes be bought in Mediterranean country markets, or you can pick your own, as I do each year.

The capers should be washed well to remove dust and then spread out in the sun to dry and wilt for a day. They can then be put into jars of strongly salted wine vinegar. The best pickled capers (non-pareilles) can be bought packed in bottles, and their quality is shown by the price; but in the countries around the Mediterranean, where capers are an everyday ingredient, they are also sold in the markets, loose, by weight. Some are even dry-salted (but are not very pleasant). In either case, loose capers should be covered with well-salted vinegar at home if they are not to be used within a few days. Capers should always be kept covered with liquid, as otherwise they develop a nasty taste. A well-known use of capers is in the caper sauce which is eaten with boiled mutton, but they also go into tartare, rémoulade, ravigote, gribiche, and sometimes vinaigrette sauces. Grated lemon rind and garlic combine exceptionally well with capers, and I always use them together. Capers are used with fish, in salads and hors d'oeuvre, for decoration, and for special accent (as in liptauer cheese). Addicts eat them on bread and butter when nobody is looking.

Other buds and seeds that look superficially rather like capers are sometimes advocated as substitutes, particularly the caper spurge (*Euphorbia lathyrus*) and the young fruit of the nasturtium. Spurges are best avoided, since most species are poisonous. Pickled nasturtium pods have a very interesting mustard overtone and may be regarded as a condiment in their own right. They are wilted and put into salted vinegar in exactly the same way as capers.

[*Caper*—French: *câpre;* German: *Kaper;* Italian: *cappero;* Spanish: *alcaparra*]

CAPERCAILLIE. *See* grouse.

CAPOCOLLA. *See* coppa.

CAPSICUM. A genus of plants in the Solanaceae, the potato, tomato, and nightshade family, capsicums are native to tropical America and the West Indies. The two gastronomically important species are ★chili pepper (*Capsicum frutescens*), which is also sold dried and ground as red pepper or cayenne pepper, and ★sweet pepper (*Capsicum annuum*), which, dried and ground, forms the spices ★paprika and *pimentón*.

[*Capsicum*—French: *piment;* German: *spanischer Pfeffer;* Italian: *peperone;* Spanish: *pimiento*]

CARAMBOLA (*Averrhoa carambola*). A tropical fruit belonging to the Oxalidaceae, the wood-sorrel family, and native to Indonesia. The fruits, borne on a small tree, are a delicate, translucent yellow or green-yellow, and 3–5 in. (7–12 cm) long, with a characteristic lobed shape. When sweet, this can be a nice juicy fruit; it is popular in China. It is used in fruit salads, jellies, drinks, and preserves. When sour, it makes a useful souring agent and is used in South India, where it is a substitute for tamarind. The carambola prefers a hot humid climate. The Indian name is *kamrakh*.

CARAMEL. If sugar is heated through the various stages to hard crack and extra-hard crack, further heating will produce caramel. Caramelization begins when the sugar starts to turn amber; it then becomes red-brown and finally black. This occurs at around 356°F (180°C), although, in practice, sugar may begin to caramelize before that, during boiling. In the process, sugar breaks down into other substances and a characteristic flavor develops.

Caramel to be used as a flavoring or to coat molds is easily made by heating sugar with a very little water to melt it, then continuing to heat it, watching carefully, until the desired degree of caramelization is reached. Overheating results in burning and a bitter taste. The unwanted caramelization that takes place during jam making or when boiling sugar for sweets is usually due to overheating on the bottom of the pan or on the sides where sugar has splashed. It may be prevented by careful stirring to make sure that sugar never sticks to the bottom and by washing down the sides of the pan with a brush dipped in water. Caramel also tends to form when sugar is cooked too long. It is responsible for giving overcooked jam its brownish color and poor flavor. As a schoolboy, I used to work at making butterscotch for pocket money. The aim, I was told, was to get it as light-colored as possible, with no hint of a caramel taste. The quicker the temperature could be raced up without burning,

the less caramelization there would be, and the paler and more delicate the result. In the end, I became so proficient that my aunt (who kept a rather famous tea shop) was no longer able to sell it. "It doesn't look homemade," the customers complained.

[*Caramel*—French: *caramel;* German: *Karamel;* Italian: *caramella;* Spanish: *caramelo*]

CARAWAY. This spice seed comes from an umbelliferous plant (*Carum carvi*) that grows wild in many parts of Europe and Asia. The young green leaves of caraway are sometimes

CARAWAY

used as a green herb and have a flavor somewhere between parsley and dill. However, it is the ripe seeds that are important, particularly in German and Austrian cooking. Caraway lies often unrecognized in the characteristic flavor of Austrian food—with meat as well as in sweet dishes. Caraway seeds are used with cheese, with cabbage, in sauerkraut, sprinkled over roast pork, ground in sausages, with paprika in goulash, and on bread. The aromatic oil in the seeds is used to flavor liqueurs such as kümmel.

[*Caraway*—French: *carvi, cumin des prés;* German: *Kümmel;* Italian: *carvi, comino dei prati;* Spanish: *alcaravea*]

CARBOHYDRATES get their name because they contain carbon combined with hydrogen and oxygen in the same 2:1 proportion as in water. Among carbohydrates are starch, sugar, glucose, pectin, and cellulose. They are synthesized out of carbon dioxide and water by green plants, which use energy from sunlight in the process called photosynthesis. Carbohydrates are used as fuel by animals, although some people are apparently so constituted that they are unable to utilize the carbohydrate from their food and only store it as fat. Total or almost total removal of carbohydrate from the diet forces the body to mobilize and use its fat reserves to make its own carbohydrate.

[*Carbohydrates*—French: *hydrates de carbone;* German: *Kohlenhydrat;* Italian: *idrati di carbonio;* Spanish: *hidratos de carbone*]

CARBONATED WATER. *See* soda water.

CARBON DIOXIDE or **carbonic acid gas** (CO_2). The gas of soda water exists in small amounts in the air and is a necessary food for green plant life. It is formed when there is a fire—whenever organic matter is burned with adequate air (with insufficient air the very poisonous carbon monoxide, CO, is formed instead). Carbon dioxide gas is denser than air. It dissolves in water to give a weak acid—carbonic acid—which in nature slowly dissolves limestone and chalk, making the water hard and causing caverns in the rock. Carbon dioxide can be solidified by cold and high pressure; blocks of carbon dioxide snow or "dry ice" are often used in ice cream trucks—the blocks evaporating to gas at atmospheric pressure have a temperature of -108°F (-78°C). Carbon dioxide is the gas formed during the fermentation of wine and beer. If it is prevented from escaping (e.g., in a screw-top bottle), its pressure builds up. Under pressure, carbon dioxide dissolves in water to a greater extent than under normal atmospheric pressure; it comes out again as a fizz when the pressure is released. Because dissolved carbon dioxide gives a pleasant prickle in the throat, drinks

with a natural fizz, known since ancient times, were later joined by drinks whose carbon dioxide has been produced under artificial pressure. Carbon dioxide under high pressure stops fermentation, a quality used to hold fruit juices in bulk before filtration to remove yeast cells. This technique has made possible the bottling of certain nonalcoholic fruit juices without pasteurization or preservatives.

CARDAMOM. A highly aromatic spice seed, cardamom tastes vaguely like eucalyptus but is far sweeter and richer. The plant *Elettaria cardamomum* is related to ginger.

CARDAMOM

A native of the wet, tropical jungles of southern India, it is now grown in many other places in the tropics. The small dark-brown or black seeds are borne inside capsules which may, as they reach us, be creamy, brownish, pale green, or white. Much larger, dark-brown, often hairy seed capsules of another cardamom species are commonly sold as black cardamoms. They are less aromatic, but cheaper. Cardamom is an expensive spice, one good reason why it should not be bought ready-ground—adulteration is too tempting. The other reason is that ground cardamom rapidly loses its best essential oils. It is better to break open the capsules and use the fresh seeds. Cardamom is important in Indian cooking. It is also much used in Scandinavia and Germany in cakes, in meat dishes (like sauerbraten), and in pickled herrings. A seed dropped into coffee gives a strange taste (well known to anyone who has traveled in the Middle East) which most people will enjoy and which guests inquire about.

[*Cardamom*—French: *cardamome;* German: *Kardamome;* Italian: *cardamomo;* Spanish: *cardamomo*]

CARDOON. A native of the Mediterranean region, the cardoon (*Cynara cardunculus*) is a close relative of the globe artichoke. However, it is not eaten for its thistle heads, but for its leaf stalks (which are like very large sticks of celery). Cardoons are best when blanched; otherwise they are too bitter. To prepare them, scrape the tender ribs and strip off the fibers and prickles on the outside. Then cut the ribs into suitable lengths. The simplest way to cook them is in boiling salted water until they are tender (25–30 minutes). They may then be served with butter, a rich white sauce, or a cheese sauce; other methods are described in French and Italian cookbooks. Raw cardoon is eaten with the *bagna cauda* in Piedmont. The tender leaf part may also be eaten if it is treated in the same way as spinach. The flower buds can be used like artichokes. The flavor of cardoon is delicate and only vaguely like artichoke.

[*Cardoon*—French: *cardon;* German: *Kardone;* Italian: *cardone;* Spanish: *cardo silvestre*]

CAROB or **locust bean.** A leguminous tree (*Ceratonia siliqua*) which is said to have its origin in Syria, although it has been grown around the Mediterranean for so long that it is one of the commonest sights among the pines on stony, dry hillsides, where few other trees can gain a footing. The pods, which turn dark brown in the autumn, have a very sweet pulp (50% sugar) and are sometimes sold as sweets for children. But they have a peculiar taste—not very pleasant perhaps, especially after you have smelled a stack of them fermenting on the quayside of a Mediterranean island, as they wait for shipment as cattle food. They are supposed to be the locusts eaten by John the Baptist, but why should those locusts not refer to the insects which are also eaten in many countries? Carob beans have recently come into fashion as a health food, but I have never succeeded in making anything very nice out of them (I have tried, as they are going begging). In the countries where they grow, carob beans are often not gathered. In Majorca, a thick, brown, treacly apéritif called *palo* is made from them and is much prized locally for its good effect on the stomach. The leathery leaves are used to stuff into the tops of jars of olives to keep them under the brine.

[*Carob*—French: *caroube;* German: *Johannisbrot;* Italian: *carruba;* Spanish: *algarroba*]

CARP. There are hundreds of species of carp, mostly fish of fresh or brackish water, ranging from the goldfish to huge, active fish like the *mahseer,* a famous game fish of the northern hill streams of India. Surprisingly, the common carp (*Cyprinus carpio*) is not native to Europe; it was introduced from farther east during the Middle Ages and was soon widely established in rivers and fish ponds. It was taken onward to North America in the latter half of the 19th century and became naturalized, particularly in the Midwest. Carp are plentiful in the great inland seas of Russia, in the Sea of Azov and the Caspian, where they are fished along with the sturgeon. Even there, they may have been introduced, and their natural home may be the rivers of China.

The importance of the common carp is that it can so easily be farmed—as can many of its close relatives, which are often much larger. Because carp live on plankton, they live peacefully with other fish, and their food can be encouraged to proliferate by fertilizing the water with measured amounts of manure or purified sewage. They can, however, acquire a muddy taste when they live in stagnant ponds—which perhaps accounts for the poor reputation they had in Britain before the Industrial Revolution when the streams and rivers still held a profusion of fine fish. Carp are not only hardy, standing considerable variation in conditions, but can even survive for a long time—up to a week—out of water if they are packed in wet moss. They are long-lived, reaching at least 50 years and weighing as much as 44 lb (20 Kg). In parks, they become very tame, since they regard people as a source of food, not as a danger, whereas in the wild state they have become cunning and have earned the title of "fox of the waters" from anglers.

As food fish, carp are inclined to be coarse even when young; they need a good sauce. Their flavor also depends much on their food, although some of their occasional muddy taste can be removed by soaking in brine or in vinegar and water. Nevertheless, the only thing to do with a really muddy carp is throw it away. On the other hand, with its firm flesh and easy bones, the carp is highly esteemed in many countries. It is a versatile fish and can be cooked in almost any way, even *au bleu*—many national cookbooks give regional recipes. Normal sizes range from 2 lb (1 Kg) to fine specimens of 9 lb (4 Kg), above which the fish become increasingly coarse. Specimens from carp farms are normally around 2 lb (1 Kg), a weight they reach at the end of their third summer. The typical carp has large, strong scales, which can be left on if the fish is to be skinned after cooking. Otherwise, they have to be removed, an operation which is made easier by quickly dunking the fish in boiling water. The gills should generally be removed—they can be a source of the muddy taste, and the gall sac must be extracted carefully.

There are two artificially bred varieties: the mirror carp, which has a few very large scales, and the leather carp, which has a leathery skin and almost no scales at all. The soft roe is a delicacy which is often cooked separately.

Many important Chinese dishes are built around carp, and a sweet-sour sauce of some kind is also popular with this fish in Europe. In Japan, carp is one of the fishes that is eaten raw and is also the symbol of the masculine virtues; a house with a son in the family will fly a windsock representing a carp on Children's Day. In other countries, carp are eaten on festive occasions. Stuffed carp is a traditional Jewish dish, and carp is the traditional ingredient in gefüllte fish. In Poland and northern Germany carp is eaten on Christmas Eve, when everyone takes one of the big scales to keep as a good-luck charm, much as the British once had sixpences in Christmas pudding.

[*Carp*—French: *carpe;* German: *Karpfen;* Italian: *carpa;* Spanish: *carpa*]

CARRAGEEN, Irish moss, sea moss, or **pearl moss.** One of the red algae, a tufted and fanlike seaweed, carrageen (*Chondrus crispus*) is found on rocky coasts of northern Europe—notably in Ireland and Brittany—and across the Atlantic from Maine to North Carolina. This weed is collected especially in New England and commercially in Massachusetts, where it is spread out to dry and bleach on the beaches. It is moistened with sea water and allowed to dry again four or five times until the pale yellow, horny material called "moss" results. This material contains a mucilaginous substance, carrageenin, which is much used in the preparation of commercial ice cream, soups, and salad dressings. Carrageen can be gathered and sun-dried by anyone interested enough, but can be bought as well. Typically, soak the dried material—after careful washing—for 20–30 minutes, then boil it in water or milk for 15 minutes or so. Strain off the liquid, which can be sweetened with sugar or honey. Add flavorings, such as fruit juice or sherry. When the liquid begins to set, fold in cream or beaten egg white.

CARROT. One of the world's most important root vegetables, the garden carrot (*Daucus carota*) has been cultivated for 2000 or 3000 years. The shape of the root ranges from conical to almost cylindrical and even globular. Orange varieties are the most commonly cultivated. Others with dark-purple roots and usually a paler white or greenish core are cultivated mostly in the warmer countries, such as Spain, Italy, and India. Poor varieties may have a woody central core, especially when old. Carrots have an incomparable flavor when freshly pulled and cooked without scraping, since most of the flavor is in the skin. Unfortunately, they are now usually washed with high-pressure hoses to remove mud before marketing, and this ruins them. The outside quickly goes slushy and, after this has been removed, a tasteless vegetable results. Some recipes use herbs or add caramelized sugar and butter to produce a toffee flavor but such expedients should not be necessary, for carrots are an aromatic in themselves. As such, they are frequently used in marinades, court bouillons, fumets, and stocks, occasionally browned to caramelize their sugar.

Although carrots are rich in vitamins and in substances from which the body can make vitamin A, relatively little is absorbed by the human body from raw carrots—which, however, especially when lightly perfumed with lemon zest, are an excellent part of salads or crudités. Many umbelliferous herbs (e.g. chervil, parsley, anise, fennel) go well with carrots, which are also an umbellifer.

Carrots contain more sugar than any other vegetable except beets, and they are made into jam and used as a dessert by various peoples: in the classic sweet Jewish *tzimmes*, in an Irish pudding, and in the Hindu *gajar-ka-halva*, in which carrots are cooked to a homogenous mass with milk and sugar.

The familiar Queen Anne's lace of roadsides is nothing but the garden carrot gone wild. Its white roots can be eaten, although their flavor is insipid compared to the orange version, and its seeds can be used as a flavoring like the seeds of its relatives caraway, celery, and anise.

[*Carrot*—French: *carotte;* German: *Möhre;* Italian: *carota;* Spanish: *zanahoria*]

CASEIN. A heat-stable, insoluble substance containing phosphorus and calcium, casein is the main protein that can be extracted from milk. The tiny protein particles which are in colloidal suspension in milk are precipitated by dilute mineral acids—like the hydrochloric acid in the stomach—and by the lactic acid which is formed when milk sours, as in yogurt. Casein is digested by the enzymes in the stomach (pepsin) and the large intestine (pancreatin) and by similar enzymes which are produced by microorganisms, such as the bacteria in hard cheese and the molds in blue-veined cheese.

[*Casein*—French: *caséine;* German: *Kasein;* Italian: *caseina;* Spanish: *caseína*]

CASHEW. The nut of the cashew (*Anacardium occidentale*) grows out of the end of the fruit in a most peculiar and distinctive manner. The tree belongs to the same family as the mango and pistachio and comes from Brazil, where the native Indian name was *acaju.* As *cajú,* it was taken to Goa in India by the Portuguese and planted there in the 16th century; today, South India is one of the world's largest exporters of nuts, on a level with Brazil itself. The cashew is also grown around the African coasts, in Malaya, the West Indies, and elsewhere.

The tree will grow in poor sandy soil with a low rainfall, but is at its best in the tropics near the sea. The fruit turns from green to yellow or orange with reddish tints when ripe. It is edible, but somewhat tart, fibrous, and astringent from its tannin content. When this has been removed by boiling (3–4 minutes in slightly salty water) or pressure cooking for 5 minutes, it makes a very nice drink. Sugar must be added, because the malic acid in the fruit makes it sour. Both in Brazil and in India (especially in Goa), the cashew fruit, or "apple," is fermented to make a wine and is also the basis for vinegar.

Cashew nuts are green or pinkish when tender, becoming gray when fully ripe. They can be eaten green and, in South India, are considered a delicacy when fried in various dishes. However, the shell is hard and oozes a dangerously blistering oily substance containing cardol and anacardic acid, even when the nuts are fully ripe. Green nuts must therefore be removed and washed with great care, without getting this oil on the skin. Wood ashes will help neutralize the oil, which is also dissipated by heating. Commercially, nuts are roasted in the shell in a rotating kiln. If doing the job by hand, use care—they easily burn. The acrid fumes are nasty. The shells used to be cracked by hand, but machines have been recently devised to do this delicate job.

Cashew nuts have become internationally popular only in the last few decades. Previously, the kernels were too difficult to ship and store, and too often rancid or full of weevils. Now that the problem has been solved by careful drying and by packing in a vacuum or in carbon dioxide gas, this delicious nut has come into its own.

Good cashews are white, plump, and sweet. The best-quality nuts are sold whole or as halves; they are rather brittle, with a "short" texture, unlike that of other nuts. Containing 47% oils, 21% protein, and 22% carbohydrate, with considerable vitamin and mineral value, they are a good food. It is better to buy cashew nuts as required and not attempt to store them for very long at home.

For a long time, cashews have been roasted and salted to serve with drinks in the tropics. When I first went to India, I was advised that eating too many would make me sick, but I have never found this to be the case and have frequently eaten more than a reasonable amount. Cashew nuts are much used in the cooking of South India, particularly in dishes from Kerala. They may be used whole or ground and are usually added late in the cooking, sometimes just before the dish is taken off the fire.

[*Cashew nut*—French: *noix d'acajou;* German: *Elefantenlaus;* Italian: *noce d'anacardo;* Spanish: *nuez de anacardo*]

CASSAREEP. A dark, almost black, syrupy substance, essential for pepperpot, a Caribbean stew which orginated in Guyana. Cassareep is made by grating peeled bitter *cassava root, mixing it with about ½ cup (100 ml) cold water per 2 lb (1 Kg) of root, leaving it to soak for some minutes, then squeezing out the juice. To this, add about 2 teaspoons brown sugar per 2 lb (1 Kg) cassava and a pinch each of cloves and cinnamon (although these spices came from the East and must not have figured in original pre-Columbian recipes); simmer the liquid until a syrupy consistency is reached. Bottled, prepared cassareep can be bought in shops that specialize in West Indian food. It can be very good.

CASSAVA, manioc or **yuca.** The large, starchy tubers of the cassava plant (*Manihot esculenta*) are a staple in some tropical countries, notably in Central America and West Africa. The plant is easy to grow—it shoots up to some 10 ft (3 m) in nine months—and the tubers are easy to harvest. In fact, it is a good, lazy, hot-country crop.

There are some 150 varieties, which fall broadly into two classes: sweet and bitter. Cassavas belong to the spurge family (Euphorbiaceae) whose members are often poisonous, and tubers of many varieties contain a glucoside which, when acted on by enzymes, produces quantities of deadly hydrocyanic acid (*see* bitter *almonds). This is exceedingly volatile and is driven off on cooking, and bitter cassavas are poisonous unless cooked.

Cassava tubers are typically about 12 in. (25–30 cm) long and as thick as your wrist. They are covered with a scaly, rather hairy, bark which has to be peeled off (best do it under a tap). After this, the flesh can be grated, the juice squeezed out in a cloth (*cassareep can be made from that), and the pulp baked as flat cakes. It is also chipped, soaked, dried, and deep fried (exactly as for potato chips), or made into a dried meal (*farhina* or *farine de manioc*). Outside the tropics, though, most people know cassava best as *tapioca.

A correspondent from the West Indies writes: "Cassava bread is not a taste teaser. We used to pour a rough Spanish red wine over it, and call it 'wet dishrag' in Cuba and the Dominican Republic, the presumption being a wet dishrag would have tasted better, soap and all." As a food, cassava is particularly low in protein and high in starch; a diet in which it predominates can lead to malnutrition.

[*Cassava*—French: *cassave, manioc;* German: *Maniok;* Italian: *manioca;* Spanish: *mandioca*]

CASSIA. *See* cinnamon.

CASTOR OIL. Some idiot once told my small daughter that the seeds of the castor oil plant (*Ricinus communis* and allied species) were good to eat. Luckily, she did not eat many—they contain not only the well-known oil but also some very poisonous substances (one of which, ricin, has recently come to prominence as a means of political assassination). I have, however, one reference to castor oil's being used in India to grease the *tava* (the circular iron plate, rather like a griddle) with *ghee* for frying chilies for a mutton pilaf: "The castor oil will counteract the heating effect of the green chilies (its pungency disappears on cooking)."

[*Castor oil*—French: *huile de ricin;* German: *Rizinusöl;* Italian: *olio di ricino;* Spanish: *aceite de ricino*]

CATCHUP. *See* ketchup.

CATECHU or **cutch** is the gummy substance which forms when chips of wood from the Indian tree *Acacia catechu* are boiled in water and the resulting solution is evaporated by further boiling. Catechu, very astringent and rich in tannin, is used in *pan* for chewing. It is also the red-brown dye with which the sails of fishing boats were once preserved and, suitably mordant-ed, was also used to dye khaki.

CATFISH. Mark Twain was writing of a now bygone era when he described in *Huckleberry Finn* how "the first thing we done was to bait one of the big hooks with a skinned rabbit and set it and catch a cat-fish that was as big as a man, being six foot two inches long, and weighed over two hundred pounds." The catfish, which has long barbels hanging around its mouth like a cat's whiskers, did come man-sized in the nineteenth century in the U.S., and the European catfish (*Siluris glanis*) may weigh several times a man's weight, but today the U.S. freshwater catfish, of the family Ictaluridae, is usually no bigger than a large cat. Most weigh only a few pounds.

Paeans to the catfish are rare, though in the South it is rather sentimentally viewed as soul food, and some gourmets consider its fine-grained flesh superb. The catfish, with its sharp spine, is a strong fighter and a pesky creature to handle, and it must be skinned as soon as it is caught. It may have a muddy flavor, since it is a bottom feeder, and the best specimens for eating come from clear waters.

Catfish are oily, and they may be cooked in almost any way. Catfish stew, with bacon, tomatoes, potatoes, and onions, often spiced with hot pepper sauce, is an old southern favorite. Catfish are also delicious dusted with corn meal and fried in bacon fat or baked in a lemony, garlicky sauce with tomatoes, green peppers, and thyme.

Of the 2000 species of catfish, the following are most important in the U.S., where more than 10 million pounds are commercially caught each year.

Brown bullhead (*Ictalarus nebulosus*). This is the most common catfish, and it is found coast to coast. It survives in waters too warm for most fish, but the best bullheads, averaging less than a pound, come from clear, cool waters.

Channel catfish (*I. punctatus*). Some consider this catfish, with its firm white flesh and delicate flavor, the finest for the table. It averages less than 3 lb (1½ Kg) and is the species most often grown in catfish farms.

Blue catfish (*I. furcatus*). Among the larger catfish, these can weigh 25 lb (11 Kg) or

BLUE CATFISH

more. They are found in clear, swift waters in the Mississippi River system. Their white flesh is firm and sweet.

[*Catfish*—German: *Katfisch;* Spanish: *siluro, bagre, amiuro*]

CATNIP or **catmint** (*Nepeta cataria*). This typical labiate is well known as a garden plant loved by bees and cats. Catnip also grows wild over much of the U.S. and Europe. It is sometimes used as a culinary herb, but was more popular in the past and was used in Roman times. Dried, it can be used on pork roasted on a spit over an open fire. Rub on as much as will stick to the meat, and use no other seasoning. Dried catnip, intended as a medicinal tea, can be bought from health-food shops. Its flavor is minty, and it goes well with lemon.

[*Catnip*—French: *cataire;* German: *Katzenminze;* Italian: *erba dei gatti;* Spanish: *calaminta*]

CATSUP. *See* ketchup.

CATTLEY. *See* guava.

CAUL. A membranous cap that covers the heads of some babies at birth, and the name often used for the omentum, the mesenteries, and even the peritoneum of mammals. It is a strong, nearly transparent membrane with islands of fat, which give it a lacy appearance. It is strong because it has to suspend the various organs inside the abdominal cav-

ity. Butchers once used it to cover legs of mutton, to make them look attractive. By the cook, it is used as casing for sausage and a covering for *crépinettes* and *gayettes*. Before trying to use caul, put it in warm water with a little salt or vinegar to soften the fat and unstick the layers of membrane; otherwise it tears easily.

CAULIFLOWER. The original cauliflower (*cavoli a fiore* or "flower cabbage") appears to have come from the Orient, where it goes back to ancient times. Cauliflower (*Brassica oleracea* var. *botrytis*) is said to have come into Spain with the Arabs in the 12th century, into Italy in the 16th, and it was being grown in Britain by the 18th century.

Cauliflower is grown for its compact, tender white curd, or flower head. (There is also a purple-headed cauliflower that turns pale green when cooked.) Although cauliflower and *broccoli are similar except for color, cauliflower is more difficult to grow successfully. It thrives best in a moist cool climate, and most varieties are blanched by tying their long jacket leaves around the head soon after the curd appears. When the heads are full size, they must be harvested before the curd begins to discolor and resemble rice. When cauliflower heads are cut they begin to deteriorate rapidly: avoid those in the market that are brownish or have been closely trimmed to eliminate wilted leaves. Select heads that look and feel really fresh and firm. Stems and leaves are also quite edible.

Perhaps the fact that cauliflower stalks have become thickened into storage organs accounts for their nutritive richness. In addition to the usual vegetable vitamins (ascorbic acid, riboflavin, thiamine, and niacin), considerable amounts of folic acid, one of the B vitamins, are found in cauliflower. Since lack of folic acid causes certain types of anemia, cauliflower has been christened "vegetable liver" by some health-food enthusiasts. Because it also contains considerable amounts of calcium in an assimilable form, as well as useful iron, it is helpful to anyone who cannot take milk.

Tender raw cauliflorets make excellent crudités, and cooked cauliflower can be served with hot or cold sauces. Unless it is to be puréed, it should be cooked just until barely tender to preserve flavor and vitamins.

[*Cauliflower*—French: *chou-fleur;* German: *Blumenkohl;* Italian: *cavolfiore;* Spanish: *coliflor*]

CAUSTIC SODA or **sodium hydroxide** (NaOH). As the name suggests, this is highly caustic and dangerous; it should be kept in an airtight container (or it loses its strength) and well out of reach of children. Caustic soda dissolves readily in water, getting very hot in the process, to form an alkaline solution which, when strong, will dissolve paper and other vegetable matter; it reacts with fats to form soap. It must be handled with rubber gloves: it will seriously blister the skin and, even when dilute, will soften the nails. Like other alkalis, it feels slimy (the slimy feeling can be removed with an acid like vinegar). Caustic soda was once a common household ingredient, because people saved fat and made their own kitchen soap. Today it is used commercially in dilute solution for various purposes (for instance to speed the cure of green olives by removing their bitterness, and for treating the skins of peaches before canning).

CAVEACH. The word comes through the Spanish from the Arab *sakbay,* meaning meat or fish pickled in vinegar. It is usually fish that is preserved in this way, but the method is sometimes used for meat, brains, or tongue. Caveach differs from soused fish or **seviche* in being fried before pickling and having extra oil added to cover it if the fish is to be preserved. *Escabeche,* the Spanish and Provençal version, is used mainly as an hors d'oeuvre. It can be bought by weight or packed in jars at delicatessens but is very easy and rewarding to make at home and will keep for some months in a cool place.

Most fish can be caveached—cod, salmon, mackerel, smelts, whiting, red mullet, sardines, tuna, and anchovies are all recommended.

Fried fish preserved in vinegar was a Roman dish. The famous South African pickled fish, which was my favorite summer breakfast when I worked there, is really a form of caveach. Variations on the theme are also popular in northern Italy (the Veneto), Turkey, and the Balkans; the method is always the same.

ESCABECHE

Cut and clean 2 lb (1 Kg) of fish, leaving small ones whole but cutting large ones into fillets or pieces. Flour the fish and fry it a pale brown in plenty of oil. Take the fish out, and in the same oil fry 1 large sliced onion and 6 cloves of crushed garlic until they just start to color. Take off the heat, and add a bouquet garni of parsley, bay, and thyme. Stir in 1 teaspoon of paprika or *pimentón,* and immediately add 1 cup (250 ml) of vinegar, a little water, and (optional) a finely sliced lemon. Cook the mixture slowly for 15 minutes, salt to taste, then put in the fish and bring back to the boil. Arrange the fish in a suitable dish and cover with the liquid. Leave it for 2 days in a cool place. If the fried fish is fully covered with the marinade (which in turn is covered with a layer of oil) and packed in a jar with lemon slices, if wished, it will keep, refrigerated, for some months. The vinegar can be more heavily spiced.

SOUTH AFRICAN PICKLED FISH

Flour and fry fish fillets, and arrange them in a dish. Make a marinade, using for each 1 lb (450 g) of fish fillets, 1½ cups (425 ml) of vinegar, a sliced onion, a bay leaf, a good pinch of peppercorns and another of coriander seeds, plus 1 clove. Boil until the onion is soft. Then stir together about ¼ cup (25 g) of curry powder and ¼ cup (25 g) of flour and make them into a paste with a little cold vinegar. When you have a smooth liquid sauce, salt it to taste and then pour it hot over the fried fish. Cover and refrigerate it for 2 days or more before eating. It will keep at least a week in the refrigerator, or longer if covered with oil and sealed in a jar.

Original Indian versions of pickled fish are many. Naturally, they use fresh spices, not curry powder, and very often the pieces of fish are rubbed with salt and turmeric powder and left to drain for an hour or more to remove some of the water from the fish. It keeps better if you do this. The spicing in India is heavy (which helps preservation), and the pickles are also well saturated with oil in addition to the vinegar. Mustard oil in particular seems to have special preservative properties. Such Indian pickles are, however, used as a relish with curry and rice and not eaten as a separate dish as is South African pickled fish.

CAVIAR. Although we associate caviar with Russia, the word comes from the Italian *caviale* or *cavia* via the Turkish *khavyar*. The Russians call it *ikra*. Real caviar is made only from the ripe eggs of various species of sturgeon—primitive fish of rather sharklike appearance. When I first disturbed one while wading across an Iranian river and saw a shark's tail lashing out of the water, I did find myself wondering whether freshwater sharks existed. However, sturgeon are quite inoffensive and actually toothless; they feed by sucking up detritus off the bottom of the river.

The two dozen species of sturgeon are found only in the northern hemisphere. The smallest is the sterlet (*Acipenser ruthenus*) from eastern Europe; the largest is the beluga (*Huso huso*), an enormous fish which lives to be 100 years old and can then weigh up to 3500 lb (1600 Kg). This fish should not be confused with the white whale, a mammal which is also called beluga. Other well-known sturgeon species used for caviar are the common sturgeon (*Acipenser sturio*) of the Atlantic and the Mediterranean, the sevruga (*Acipenser stellatus*), and the osciotre (*Acipenser guldenstädti*), both of the Caspian Sea.

The center for sturgeon is in the area of the Black and Caspian seas. The world's largest sturgeon fisheries are in Russia and, since 1950, in Iran. The Rumanian fishery at the mouth of the Danube is of lesser importance. Some sturgeon are also fished in North America, and caviar is made from them—there are species found, for instance, in the Great Lakes, and in the St. Lawrence and Delaware rivers. There is now a problem with pollution, which the Russians have also had to face in the northern Caspian Sea and the Volga, and one of their responses has been to introduce sturgeon into new and unpolluted habitats.

Sturgeon are fished with gill nets laid off the mouths of the rivers up which they will spawn. The riper the eggs, the better the caviar, so the best comes from sturgeon caught off the mouths of short rivers, such as those arising in the Elburz Mountains of northern Iran. Here, with little distance to travel, the fish can wait until the last moment before going upstream. Only about one in every 15 fish caught contains eggs suitable for making into caviar. Beluga will produce 38–45 lb (17–20 Kg) of caviar, osciotre 9–17 lb (4–7 Kg), and sevruga only 3½–5 lb (1½– 2 Kg).

Caviar can be made only from the roes of perfectly fresh fish: once taken out of the net, they must reach the processing station within an hour or two. The stations are sited near the mouths of the rivers, sometimes on wooden artificial islands in particularly shallow areas of the Caspian. The sturgeon roes have to be removed with the greatest care so that the eggs do not get smeared with blood. If roe has to be washed, it does not make good caviar. Roes are cut in pieces the size of a fist and rubbed gently on a string sieve to free the eggs from the membranes. The mass of eggs, which has fallen through the sieve into a basin, is now drained, accurately weighed, and mixed by hand with fine salt according to the judgment of the highly skilled caviarmaker. In caviar destined for most countries of Europe, a small percentage of boric acid is also added. This preservative improves the flavor by giving a slight acidity and preventing the growth of a fishy taste; it is not legally permitted in caviar for the U.S.

The caviar is later packed in the special tins, and the lid is sealed with a rubber band. This is, therefore, not a sterile product, so it must be kept chilled (never frozen) and handled carefully until it reaches the table. Caviar is at its best 3 days after making. It is then totally devoid of any fishy taste (as I know from having spent a morning tasting with the chief Iranian caviar grader). It is unfortunate that by the time caviar reaches restaurants, its price is astronomical and it is often not worth eating. The taste is fishy, which perhaps explains why many people who have tried caviar once do not like it, and why it is so often served with lemon or onion.

The best caviar is lightly salted. Russian tins are marked *malassol* (from *malo,* "little," and *ssoleny,* "salted"). The eggs should be separate and not squashed together. They will, of course, vary in size according to the species of sturgeon from which they come. The largest, from the beluga, are usually the most expensive, but probably not the best, since beluga caviar does not travel as well as some of the others. Caviar from the sterlet (*sterlyad*) was once reserved for the czars and the emperors of Austria, just as the golden caviar from Iran was reserved for the shah. The excellence of golden caviar, however, is entirely in its appearance; the color of caviar has no bearing on flavor. Because appearance is important, caviar from different fish is not mixed—the result would be speckled. Colors vary from black through shades of gray to almost white, and from golden to orange-brown and even greenish.

Caviar should be served surrounded by crushed ice and accompanied by lightly toasted, fresh white bread and fine butter. Etceteras like chopped hard-boiled eggs are added merely to make it go further. While it is traditional outside Russia to drink champagne with caviar, you eat it with a spoon out of greaseproof paper and wash it down with vodka on a Caspian caviar station. This (the vodka, not the paper) is also the norm at Soviet diplomatic parties, but you may think the spirits kill the delicate flavor. Cav-

iar is sometimes served in small tarts, or with sour cream stuffed into blinis, but the caviar itself should never be cooked or heated.

Pressed caviar or **payousnaya** is a cheaper product made from sturgeon eggs that are not quite mature. After being separated from the membranes in the usual way, the slushy, half-formed eggs are treated with hot brine to coagulate them. The mass of eggs is then pressed into small wooden tubs. Pressed caviar has a sticky, waxy texture and is always rather salty. It is usually served spread on squares of toast, or in small tarts or *barquettes.*

Red caviar or **ketovaia** is, strictly speaking, not caviar: it is made from the eggs of the *keta* or dog salmon (*Onchorynchus keta*) found in rivers of Siberia that drain into the Pacific and on the west coast of Canada. The eggs are very large, red, and almost transparent. Red caviar is much more salty than true caviar and has a different flavor— which some people even prefer.

Imitation caviar. Salted fish eggs of other kinds are a popular delicacy in many fish-eating countries, but unfortunately there are also many such products which are artificially colored gray or black and sold at inflated prices to simulate caviar and provide snob appeal. These substitutes are heavily salted, with a hard and grainy texture. They are commonly sold in glass jars with a sealed metal lid, and have such names as "German caviar."

Salted roe of this type can be made at home if hard (female) roes are taken from fish just before spawning, cleared of fiber, washed if necessary in cold water, drained, and mixed with salt: 1 part by weight to 6 of roe. (For good caviar the proportion is only 1:20.) After being kept for 2 days in a cool place and being turned occasionally in the brine that is formed, the eggs can be drained, spread on a board 3 ft (1 m) from a fire, and dried thoroughly for 10–12 hours before being pressed into jars.

Lumpfish caviar. The lumpfish (*Cyclopterus lumpus*) is also called lump-sucker, sea-owl, or cock-paddle, because its dorsal fin is reminiscent of a cock's comb. It is fished in the North Atlantic, and the main source of supply is Iceland, but it is also found off the coasts of Scotland. Its flesh is not regarded highly, except smoked, but in spring the females are stuffed with eggs, which are used to make lumpfish caviar.

Salted roes can be made at home if ripe roes are taken from fish just before they spawn. The method is that given above for imitation caviar; before final drying, the eggs can be slightly acidified with powdered citric acid (to taste). The product, though without black grains and concomitant snob appeal, is tasty. It can be kept in the refrigerator for some days.

Synthetic caviar. It had to come. The Russians, after years of research, are making synthetic caviar for the common man. They do this by blowing little bubbles of protein, flavoring them, and adding salt. The result is said to be a bit slushy, though better than feared. Since the price is right, it is immediately snapped up, for only a small quantity is at present being made.

Egyptian caviar is a name for *botargo, while "poor man's caviar" is a dip made of puréed *eggplant.

[Caviar—French: caviar; German: Kaviar; Italian: caviale; Spanish: caviar]

CAYENNE PEPPER. See chili.

CELERIAC. See celery.

CELERY (Apium graveolens) is a strong-smelling umbellifer that grows wild through much of the temperate world. The cultivated variety (var. dulce) is grown as both an aromatic and as a vegetable. When it has thinnish green stems (usually known as Pascal celery), it is much used in soups and as a flavoring. Other varieties have thick stems and have been earthed up to make the stems white; some types are self-blanching. Green celery stems are often bitter, but others are quite sweet. Celery is eaten raw in crudités,

with cheese, or chopped in mixed salads, and it may be braised as a wonderful vegetable.

Turnip-rooted celery or celeriac (var. rapaceum) is a variety selected for its bulbous root. The skin is fibrous and covered with roots, so it needs to be peeled deeply. Celeriac can be cooked—it is excellent in a purée with potatoes—but it is more often shredded and, either raw or lightly cooked, marinated in French dressing for a few hours to make an hors d'oeuvre.

Celery seed is commonly used as a flavoring, but it is rather bitter. When combined with salt, it makes celery salt, a popular flavoring with eggs.

[Celery—French: céleri; German: Sellerie; Italian: sedano; Spanish: apio. Celeriac—French: céleri-rave; German: Knollensellerie; Italian: sedano-rapa; Spanish: apionabo]

CELERY CABBAGE. See Chinese cabbage.

CELSIUS. In 1742, Anders Celsius, a Swedish astronomer, described a scale for *temperature measurement which took the melting point of ice (or freezing point of water) as 0° and the boiling point of water as 100°. Measurements on this scale are known as degrees Celsius or centigrade (either way, °C). Apart from the convenience of having two easy-to-check reference points (although the boiling point of water varies with the atmospheric pressure), the Celsius scale became linked with the metric system in scientific definitions and, as a result, the Fahrenheit scale is gradually becoming obsolete. To convert Celsius to Fahrenheit, multiply by 9, divide by 5 and add 32. To convert Fahrenheit to centigrade, subtract 32, then multiply by 5 and divide by 9.

CENTIGRADE. See Celsius.

CÈPE or **cep** (Boletus edulis) is the most delicious member of a largely edible genus of fungi which are characterized by having tubes rather than gills under their caps. The cèpe has a brownish cap and a pale brown, usually very swollen stalk. It is found particularly in beech woods. It keeps its flavor better than any other fungus in drying or prolonged cooking, and can be used in almost any recipe instead of cultivated mushrooms. The Italians produce large quantities of sliced and dried *cèpes*, which they call *funghi porcini*. (*See* mushrooms.)

CEPHALOPODS. The most advanced mollusks, including the *squid, *cuttlefish, and *octopus. They are all marine and range over every ocean. Their common characteristic is that they have arms with suckers surrounding the mouth, a beak like a parrot (but with the larger half below), and well-developed eyes, which give them a savage, baleful glare. They all have ink sacs. A further characteristic, which has had an influence on cooks, is that their gills and internal organs are all contained in a hollow, muscular sac called the mantle (which the animals fill with water and contract to jet themselves backward). It just asks to be filled with stuffing. Although these animals are much eaten in southern Europe and were relished by the Romans, who spread so many gastronomic habits about, they have never become popular in North America or Britain, except among people of Spanish, Italian, or Greek stock. The Japanese probably eat more cephalopods than any other nation: about a fifth of their seafood consumption (including shellfish and seaweeds) is cephalopod.

CERAMIC GLAZES. Most ceramics, particularly *earthenware, are to some extent porous. Except where the porousness does not matter (as in flower pots) or is actually an advantage (as in old-fashioned milk coolers), pots are normally given an impermeable surface by firing them with a glaze. The reason that glazes are of concern to the cook is that they come into direct contact with food and drink, and they can contain such poisonous elements as selenium, chromium, cadmium, antimony, and—commonest of all—*lead.

Glazes consist of substances that fuse to-

gether during firing to form, in effect, a glass. Lead oxides are excellent fluxes which work at relatively low temperatures to produce a fine, shiny surface. Unfortunately, glazes with a high lead content, especially if they have been fired at low temperatures, may have some of their lead still in a form that is soluble in weak acids. The danger here is not immediate lead poisoning but something rather more insidious: lead is a cumulative poison. Improved techniques have made modern glazes almost entirely safe, and in many countries there are strict regulations about the soluble lead content of glazes.

It is the interesting peasant pots, notably the low-fired ones that can be used on a naked flame, that must be treated with some care. They should be reserved for braising and frying, which is what they are intended for, and for which they are perfectly safe. On the other hand, sour fruit, vinegar, wine, and cider should not be left standing in them, since the acid content will attack underfired lead glazes—brewing and storing drinks in lead-glazed vessels used to cause many cases of poisoning.

Salt glazes are highly resistant to acids and were once used for pipes to carry chemicals. They are commonly used on *stoneware, producing a semi-matt, orange-peel surface texture. Salt-glazed vessels are ideal, among other things, for brewing.

CERASELLA. *See* liqueurs and cordials.

CEREALS (from Ceres, the Roman name for the Greek goddess of grain, Demeter) include any sort of grain derived from a grass. From the Old World come *wheat, *barley, *oats, *rye, *rice, and *millets of many kinds; *buckwheat, though not from a grass, is usually included as a cereal crop. In the New World, only *corn, maize, was known to the civilizations before Columbus.

[*Cereals*—French: *céréales;* German: *Getreide;* Italian: *cereali;* Spanish: *cereales*]

CERIMAN. *See* monstera.

CERVELAS may once, from its name, have been made with brain. The English saveloy is descended from the same word in Old French. French *cervelas* is normally a rather short sausage made of pork and often flavored with garlic. It is usually slightly dried and is eaten hot after being poached in water. One variety is *saucisson* (= *cervelas*) *de Paris.*

CERVELAT is a large German sausage of minced pork and beef, usually smoked. It is a rather different item from the French *★cervelas* and is sliced and eaten cold. It can be rather like a very mild, fine-textured salame.

CEVICHE. *See* seviche.

CHALK or **calcium carbonate** ($CaCO_3$). Calcium carbonate is a white, odorless, and tasteless substance, insoluble in plain water but soluble in acids. It dissolves in water containing carbon dioxide, forming calcium bicarbonate, a reaction which is reversed by heating—hence the chalky scale which is deposited in kettles and hot-water pipes in places with hard water. Impure forms of calcium carbonate occur naturally as chalk, marble, or limestone. Pure chalk (such as precipitated chalk, drop chalk, whiting, or English whites) is sometimes used in the kitchen. Chalk can be used to neutralize acids (such as fruit acids and acids used for hydrolysis) and forms a calcium salt of the acid concerned (e.g., calcium chloride, calcium citrate).

[*Chalk*—French: *craie;* German: *Kreide;* Italian: *creta;* Spanish: *creta*]

CHAMOMILE. *See* camomile.

CHANNA, chana, Bengal gram, or **gram.** A variety of small *★chickpea* and the most common pulse food of the masses in India, where millions of tons are grown, making

up more than half of the total pulse production. The *★dal* made from it is yellow, somewhat oval, and rather larger than other *dals.* (A split pea, with which it is most easily confused, is round.) Much of the crop is roasted or parched, and some is ground into *★besan* flour. Channa is nutritious and easily digested but does not have an exceptional flavor.

CHANTERELLE or **girolle** (*Cantharellus cibarius*) is a fungus of deciduous woodlands. It is distinguished by its funnel shape and the fact that it is not merely apricot yel-

CHANTERELLE

low in color but smells of apricots as well. Fried in butter with onion or garlic and parsley, it is one of the very best of wild fungi. In *The Mushroom Feast* (Knopf, 1975), Jane Grigson points out that chanterelles are always slightly chewy; they are toughened by overcooking. They can be bought dried or canned. (*See* mushrooms.)

CHAR. *See* trout.

CHARCUTERIE. Literally and mainly the products of the pork butcher, the charcutier—hams, sausages, terrines, galantines, *crêpinettes, gayettes, boulettes,* pies, *boudins*—or the shop itself. The charcutiers in France were first formed into a unity by royal edict in 1476, a measure to protect the public from fraud and from bad meat. At that time, they were allowed to sell only cooked pork and raw pork fat, but not to slaughter the animals themselves. At the beginning of the 17th century, they gained the right to sell uncooked pork as well. From these beginnings has developed the French charcuterie of today, where sausages made of veal and terrines of game may be found in addition to the pork products. In English, the word "charcuterie" embraces all these things. Readers are referred to Jane Grigson's *The Art of Charcuterie* (Knopf, 1968) for full information and recipes.

CHARD, Swiss chard, spinach beet, or **seakale beet** (*Beta vulgaris cicla*) is a variety of beet grown for its thick stalks and midribs. Dark-green types with red stalks are called rhubarb chard. Chard is an easy plant to grow, and it is popular in Mediterranean countries, where it is often seen growing wild (as an escape) in salty soil near the sea. Chard leaves are eaten raw or cooked like spinach, a close relative; the stalks are cooked like asparagus. Chard is rich in vitamins and iron and contains much less oxalic acid than spinach—a benefit, since oxalic acid tends to lock up the iron utilized by the body.

[*Chard*—French: *carde;* German: *Mangold;* Italian: *bietola da coste;* Spanish: *acelga*]

CHARQUI. The American equivalent of *biltong: beef cut in strips and sun-dried.

CHASOBA. *See* noodles.

CHAYOTE, pepinello, choko, or **vegetable pear.** This species of squash, *Sechium edule*, came originally from tropical America and was a food of the Aztecs and the Mayas. The fruit, borne on a trailing vine, is irregularly ridged, pear-shaped, and often covered with prickly hairs. The color varies from creamy white to dark green. In Mexico, three main types are grown—the small and light-green, the cream, and the large, spiny dark-green variety—of which the last is reckoned to be superior. Chayotes have begun to gain commercial importance in recent years. They need a warm climate and grow

well in the southern states of the U.S., in Australia, and in Italy, Spain, Algeria, and other Mediterranean countries. The fruit, the size of a large pear, contains one big seed. The flesh is firm, and the taste delicate. We usually peel the fruits, slice them thinly, and fry them in batter.

This is a most useful plant because the shoots, when young, can be boiled and served like asparagus, the leaves can be eaten as greens, and the huge tuberous roots, which can weigh 22 lb (10 Kg), are similar to yams in appearance and use. The chayote is a vigorous and heavy-yielding plant, growing in all sorts of conditions when asked to; no doubt it will be increasingly popular as it becomes better known.

CHEESE was an early discovery in the Old World—the Sumerians are known to have made it 6000 years ago—but it was never discovered by the American civilizations, perhaps because they lacked sheep, cows, and horses. The story of David and Goliath begins with David's being sent by his father, Jesse, to take parched grain and bread to his brothers, who were camped with the army confronting the Philistines. At the same time, he was charged to deliver "ten cheeses to the commander of their thousand." We may speculate on what those cheeses were like. Possibly they resembled the Bedouin *igt*, which sounds like an exclamation of disgust but is actually a sort of cheese made by boiling down sour curds until they are almost dry, then mixing the paste with desert herbs.

The ancient Greeks made cheese, and Aristotle wrote about it; the Romans were also cheesemakers, and Virgil wrote about it. Indeed, the Romans were quite sophisticated about cheese and used it in cooking, perhaps starting the passion that Italians have for it to this day. Romans made a number of different types of cheese which were sold in the *velabrum*, the dairy market in Rome, and no doubt also in Britain, since the Roman soldiers carried cheese on the march whenever they were lucky enough to get it. Large Roman houses of the period had cheese rooms where the cheese was made, and other rooms for storage and maturation. Smoked cheese was also popular; larger towns had centers where the populace could take their home-made cheeses to be smoked. Some of the cheeses known today have been made for centuries. Gorgonzola, for instance, has been made since before A.D. 879. Italy remained the cheesemaking center of the world until after the Renaissance, but has now been overtaken by France, which heads the world, at least in the number of different cheeses and the interest taken in them. Italy still makes more use of cheese in cooking than any other country, and it sometimes seems that Italians put grated Parmesan, just for luck, into everything.

Cheese depends for its existence on a property of milk: that the protein in it will coagulate and form a curd of casein when it is treated with acids, rennets, certain plant extracts, or alum. It depends for its incomparable array of tastes on the combined effects of rennet and of the bacteria and (for some types of cheese) the molds which attack it and cause chemical changes of unbelievable complexity, processes not understood until recently. During the last 100 years, cheesemaking has gradually moved from the farmhouse to the factory, and a complicated technology has grown up around it. This need not intimidate the amateur cheesemaker. The technology is necessary to turn out thousands of uniform, average cheeses, without waste or failure. The amateur, filled with enthusiasm, may make some bad cheeses but, with some basic knowledge and care, has the chance of making some splendid ones.

The simplest cheese is exemplified by ordinary soft or cottage cheese, in which milk curdled by natural souring is hung in a cloth to drain. Although the curd is acid and mixed with salt, the cheese is very moist and so will not keep well. An even more elementary cheese is the Indian *panir, which is almost tasteless and has a rubbery texture but can be cut into cubes, fried, and made into curry (usually in combination with fresh peas). Similar cheeses are made in many countries (e.g., requeson in Spain); they may be eaten with quince paste (membrillo) or used in cakes.

For what we might call "real" cheese, milk is soured to develop acidity and the curd is ripened with the help of bacteria and sometimes mold. If milk is pasteurized (and usually also when it is not), the souring bacteria are added as a starter culture. This contains the correct proportions of organisms needed for the cheese being made. A cheese is like a developing community. If the rind is thick, it may be almost a closed community, but in a small cheese, such as a Camembert, the center is ripened by enzymes diffusing in from aerobic molds which need oxygen and thus grow on the surface. When first made, the young cheese is acid, but later bacteria which feed on the acid come into prominence, and the cheese becomes sweeter. At the same time, organisms attack and break down the casein. These protein-splitting organisms make the curd into a digestible substance that melts when heated. Concurrently, certain compounds are formed which give flavor. In cheese such as Emmentaler special bacteria form that cannot escape and so make "eyes."

The important thing to realize is that a cheese contains living organisms; the various operations of the cheesemaker are intended to guide its evolution. Development is influenced by temperature, since there is an optimum temperature for each type of microorganism. It is influenced in surface-mold types by the humidity of the air, which controls the drying of the rind on which the molds are growing. Some types are washed with beer or wine, or treated by scraping, oiling, and so on. Size and shape determine whether or not enzymes produced by organisms in the rind can diffuse to the middle. Major factors in the ripening are the amount of moisture in the curd and the quantity of salt. At each stage in making a cheese, there are a large number of choices, and many combinations of factors are possible, which is why there are some thousand named cheeses, with more being constantly invented.

The milk. In theory, cheese can be made from any sort of milk, but in practice, cows, goats, sheep, and water buffalo are the most usual sources, although perhaps some of the earliest "cheese" was made from ass's milk or mare's milk. The composition of the milk from different animals varies considerably in the amounts of protein, sugar, and fat. Cow's milk usually contains some 4% butterfat, but the fat level can be adjusted to anything from skimmed milk to thick cream and used as a basis for cheese. Since the cow is now the most common source of milk, it is used in many cases to make types of cheese that were once made from the milk of sheep or goats. While the cheeses are roughly the same, they lack the flavor of the original, since the fat of sheep's milk and that of goat's milk are different from cow-milk fat. A mozzarella made from buffalo's milk, as it was originally, no doubt tastes richer than a modern cow's-milk version.

The composition and flavor of milk also depend on the time of year and the sort of pasture on which the animals have grazed. An animal fed artificially in winter and one fed on grass leys or a summer Alpine pasture full of flowers cannot be expected to produce the same milk.

Pasteurization. All factory and much farmhouse cheese is now made from pasteurized milk. This ensures that any disease organisms are destroyed and enables the cheesemaker to start with a more or less clean slate, although the milk is not sterile. To sterilize milk, it would have to be heated to boiling point at least, and this would make the calcium salts insoluble. Since soluble calcium and some acidity are necessary for rennet to act, cheese cannot be made from boiled milk in the usual way. Even pasteurization destroys some of the enzymes which are present in raw milk and so influences the final result.

The starter. Carefully devised cultures or starters are now always used to introduce the right types of microorganism in the right proportion. This removes some of the chance factors. The starter is added when the milk is warm and contains special souring organisms, because the first consideration is to develop acidity. This is necessary for good curd formation by the rennet. The acidity and the rennet act together to shrink the curd, to promote drainage, to prevent the growth of putrefying organisms, to encourage the matting of the curd, and to affect its elasticity.

Curdling. In most types of cheese, the curd is set with a strong cheese rennet. There are also a few in which curdling is brought about purely by natural souring, and others in which the curd is set with certain plant juices. Variations are produced by the amount of rennet used, the point in souring at which it is added, the temperature, etc. When the rennet coagulates the milk, casein, fat globules, and most of the microorganisms are trapped; only a little drains away in the whey.

Cutting the curd. When the curd is set, it must be cut or broken up to allow the whey to drain out. This is one of the most important operations in cheesemaking, since the fineness of the curd particles and the amount of whey left in the cheese will determine its type. In the simplest, old-fashioned methods, the curd is simply broken up and stirred with the hand; the amount of heat which the hand can tolerate then limits the temperatures at which such cheeses can be made. I have watched shepherds in Sardinia making their sheep's-milk cheese (*pecorino sardo*) by this simple method, with the pot kept warm by the wood fire and the curd stirred with the bare hand and gradually kneaded into a lump which is then scooped into the mold. However, the curd is usually cut into cubes with a knife or an arrangement of knives and, if it is for heated or "scalded" curd cheese, the curd is heated further and stirred to make the granules finer and to cause them to shrink, thus ensuring that even more whey can be drained out. Because the size of grain is vital, the cutting is often done with a device of wires strung on a frame (a harp).

Cheddaring is one of the essential stages in making Cheddar cheese. Here, the curd, when firm enough to be turned without breaking, is cut in slabs, drained by stacking, and finally milled in a curd mill before being mixed with salt, allowed to drain once more, and finally pressed into hoops.

Cooking the curd. For the harder types of cheese, the curd is usually warmed to up to about 130°F (54°C), which is rather more than can be endured by the bare hand. This shrinks the curd and hardens it, making it easier to get the whey out. These cooked types of cheese, such as Emmentaler or Parmesan, are therefore harder than, say, Cheddar. Just how hard will also depend on other factors as well, but in general the higher the cooking temperature, the harder the cheese. The limit to which the curds are "cooked" is 130–132°F (54–55°C), but higher temperatures are used in making plastic curd cheese and Scandinavian sweet cheeses.

Draining the curd. Whether the curd has been cooked or not, it now has to be drained. In the soft cheeses, where quite a lot of whey will be left, the cut curd, stirred or unstirred, is ladled directly from the vat into the forms, but there are many variations. For instance, in the very simple types of cheese made in some parts of the Carpathians, the curd is simply squeezed into lumps in the hands and eventually cured in brine. In making Pont l'Evêque, the curd is first drained slightly on straw mats, gently squeezed by the cheesemaker by rolling up the mat, and then ladled into square wooden forms (careful and even packing being part of the skill), and the forms left to drain on straw mats. The curd compacts under its own weight. Other types of cheese are drained in baskets or in tall perforated molds.

Pressing the curd. For the harder types of cheese, pressure is applied to help the whey drain out. This may be no more than a matter of putting a brick on top, or it may involve a hydraulic press. For instance, in the making of Emmentaler, after cutting, cooking, and stirring in giant steam-heated kettles, the huge mass of curd is scooped into a cloth which is drawn under it and lifted with a block and tackle into an adjustable wooden form positioned under a hydraulic press. The press squeezes it into the huge cartwheel shapes. The pressure applied is an important factor in cheesemaking.

Salt in cheese is not only necessary for taste but also has a great influence on microorganisms; some are very sensitive to it. For instance, one of the heat-loving, milk-souring bacteria, *Streptococcus thermophilus* (used as a starter for Emmentaler) will not grow in as little, even, as 2% salt (which, in effect, means in most cheeses except fresh curd cheese). Some types of cheese are salted by rubbing with dry salt or washing in brine. This also discourages the growth of molds. Some cheeses, such as the Greek feta, are packed in salt in barrels, and a brine soon forms which preserves the cheese. Other additives are colors (most commonly annatto), spices (such as caraway or cloves in Leyden), pepper, wine, sage, etc.

Ripening or **maturing.** There are unripened cheeses which are eaten fresh, such as cottage cheese, *boursin* (with pepper or garlic and herbs), *petit Suisse, demi-sel, fromage blanc,* and so on. The soft-curd types are matured for a short time and are soft and perishable, because of their high whey or moisture content.

They can be broadly divided into two types: those like Camembert, Brie, and Coulommiers, in which molds are encouraged to grow on the surface, and the others, such as Maroilles and Muenster, in which surface molds are deliberately discouraged by washing and salting. Some, like Pont l'Evêque, come in between: some mold is wanted, but not too much.

Surface molds ripen cheeses by means of enzymes which diffuse inward from them; hence you may get a Camembert that is soft and ripe throughout, except for a small white layer in the center, where the enzymes have not yet reached. Cheeses ripened by molds, which grow only on the surface where they have sufficient air, are small or, if large in diameter, like a Brie, are at least thin. Other cheeses are ripened internally by green molds, among them Stilton, Gorgonzola, and Roquefort. The curd for such cheeses has to be packed loosely to leave cracks for the mold to grow in; today, however, the cheeses are stabbed to let air in. Other cheeses are ripened by the action of bacteria working within and are not limited in size, although a really soft cheese is likely to be small, if only for mechanical reasons.

The hard-pressed cheeses are made by cooking or "scalding" the curd, so more whey is taken out and the cheeses are harder. They include the Dutch Gouda and Edam, and the French Port-Salut, Cantal, and Saint Paulin; the more strongly cooked types are represented by Emmentaler, Gruyère, and Parmesan. These are large cheeses, ripened only by bacteria and enzymes. Their surfaces are often washed, scraped, salted, oiled, waxed, or covered in various compounds to stop molds from growing on the surface and create a thick, tough, impervious rind. Today, hard cheeses are often wrapped in moistureproof film so that no rind is formed.

Since ripening involves microorganisms and enzymes, the control of temperature and humidity is of the greatest importance. Cheeses may be stacked in ripening rooms or in natural caves and cellars. Most cheeses are frequently turned and inspected, and in the case of the cheeses that come in huge cartwheels, the work is so heavy that the turning is these days done by machinery.

Although the details of each type of cheese are different, maturation is characterized in general by a reduction of the acidity by bacteria which feed on the acid. At the start, the strong acidity gives elasticity to the curd. If the curd is washed to reduce its calcium content, it can be drawn out into strings, a factor made use of in making plastic curd cheeses. Cheeses like Camembert, initially very acid, become hard as they dry out. They are then softened by enzymes in the molds. Immature cheese, like fresh Cheddar, will become stringy if cooked—like a mixture of chewing gum and butter, as one author described it.

The cook needs to know about ripening cheese only to be aware of the stages of ripeness when buying it. A maturation period of a year or more, as is needed for hard Italian *grana* like Parmesan, explains to some extent why it is so expensive. Cheeses are best bought when ripe, and the ripening should not be attempted at home. At most, a Camembert should be kept until the next day; if the cheesemonger tries to foist off a leathery Camembert on the grounds that it will be ripe in a day or so, it is best not to buy it. The odds are that, because of mishandling, it will never ripen properly. In general, cheeses are best ripened in their proper environment. Thus, you can never get a perfect Gorgonzola far from the caves of northern Italy, where they are matured, for, unless removed early (like fruit), they will not stand up to travel, being large and, when ripe, rather squashy.

Buying cheese. Most cheese today is sold prepacked in plastic film. If, however, you are lucky enough to have access to a cheese merchant who still cuts pieces to order, always ask to taste a sliver before buying, and get fully ripe cheese in manageable quantities. Since it is impossible to describe tastes with any accuracy, try to build up over a period of time a working knowledge of cheeses available locally.

Keeping cheese. Ideally, cheese should not be kept long: it starts to deteriorate once cut. However, some storage is usually inevitable. One may wrap cheese in greaseproof paper or foil and put it in a cool larder (if anyone possesses such a thing these days). The cold of a refrigerator slows down the growth of ripening microorganisms but may encourage others that prefer low temperatures and so spoil the cheese. Never forget that a cheese is a living community of organisms; if you destroy the balance, then the cheese is likely never to recover. Only processed cheese, which is "dead" and designed for a long shelf life, will keep, but it is not noted for its character.

Cheese rinds. The rind and what grows on it has a profound effect on the cheese. The rind may be bathed in wine or beer to encourage microorganisms, or coated with lamp black, burnt umber, gum, even (at least in the past) varnish bitumen to discourage them. Some cheeses are smoked, others wrapped in leaves or coated with grapeskins, pepper, dried thyme, or plastics. The question sometimes asked is whether or not one should eat the rind. Added coatings should obviously not be eaten, and in general, even natural rinds are best removed. As one maker of Pont l'Evêque told me, "We spend a lot of effort making sure that the cheese is not bitter, and then some idiots go and eat the rind as if it were Camembert." I have even known people to eat the grape pips on *tôme au raisin.*

Plastic curd cheeses are characteristic of southern Italy, the best-known being the sausage-shaped provolone. To make these cheeses, the soured curd is heated in water to 137°F (57°C) until it becomes plastic and can be stretched and kneaded; it is then shaped and molded while still hot.

Classification of cheeses. Since there are at least a thousand named cheeses, it would be useful to be able to classify and group them for purposes of description. Unfortunately, this has so far defeated even the experts. According to the writers of *Cheeses of the World* (U.S. Department of Agriculture,

1969), there are probably only eighteen distinct types of cheese, which are typified as follows: Brick, Camembert, Cheddar, Cottage, Cream, Edam, Gouda, Hand, Limburger, Neufchâtel, Parmesan, Provolone, Romano, Roquefort, Sapsago, Swiss, Trappist, and whey cheeses (Mysost and Ricotta).

One basic characteristic used for description is consistency: very hard (grating), hard, semihard, semisoft, soft, or very soft and runny. These groups may be subdivided into those ripened by bacteria only, by molds (external and internal), and by organisms growing on the surface and their enzymes—or by a combination—as well as the fresh cheeses which are unripened.

Very hard	*Ripened by bacteria:* Asiago (old), Parmesan, Romano, Sapsago, Spalen
Hard	*Ripened by bacteria and with no eyes:* Cheddar, Provolone *Ripened by bacteria and with eyes:* Emmentaler, Gruyère
Semihard and semisoft	*Ripened by bacteria:* Brick, Muenster *Ripened by both bacteria and surface organisms:* Limburger, Port-Salut, Trappist *Ripened by interior blue mold:* Danblu, Gorgonzola, Roquefort, Stilton
Soft	*Ripened:* Bel Paese, Brie, Camembert, Hand, Neufchâtel *Unripened:* Cottage, Cream, Fromage Blanc, Petit Suisse, Ricotta
Very soft	Many cheeses could be described as very soft or runny when fully ripe, such as Vacherin.

It is part of the problem of classification that the texture of many cheeses changes as they ripen: some are table cheeses or grating cheeses according to their age and dryness. To the consumer, the question of whether a cheese is ripened by molds or by bacteria is largely academic, though interesting. Of more importance are the following considerations. Do you buy by weight or must you buy the whole cheese? What does it look like when ripe? How is the genuine cheese marked and packed? Is it strong or mild? Is it for eating, cooking, or grating?

Cheese in cooking. Wherever cheese is made, it figures in the local cooking. Thus, when trying traditional recipes, you must use the correct cheese if you want the dish to taste as it is meant to. When it is impossible to find the right cheese, trial and error with other cheeses may become necessary, but if you are aiming at authenticity, try to use cheese of the right type and age. Avoid using too young a cheese for melting—it is likely to become stringy when heated.

Certain types of cheese have distinctive characteristics which either make them highly suitable for some dishes or give a particular flavor to a cuisine. For British cooking, Lancashire and Cheshire cheeses melt best, although others, such as Cheddar types, melt well too. Americans have discovered that blue cheeses, in addition to giving a fine flavor to a vinaigrette or a mayonnaise, melt well on the ubiquitous hamburger. In Italy, where cheese is a basic culinary flavor, the *grana* cheeses such as Parmesan are grated into and over innumerable dishes. The elastic mozzarella melts beautifully, while the whey cheese ricotta is found in both savory and sweet dishes. French cooking frequently uses Gruyère and Emmentaler in savory dishes and soft cream cheeses in sweets such as *fromage à la crème* and *tourteau fromagé*. In Greece, feta cheese is found not only in salads but also layered between sheets of *phyllo* pastry with spinach or other ingredients.

Generally, curd and cream cheeses bake well; they are the basis of some Danish pastry fillings and of endless cheesecake recipes. Simple cottage cheeses are a very useful basic ingredient in *cuisine minceur* and for diets. For such purposes, it is often processed in a blender to make light temporary emulsions.

[*Cheese*—French: *fromage;* German: *Käse;* Italian: *formaggio;* Spanish: *queso*]

CHERIMOYA. *See* custard apple.

CHERRY. Like plums, cherries are members of the genus *Prunus.* There are well over a thousand varieties, some of them almost unchanged since Etruscan times. Most of the important ones are derived from two species, the sour cherries (pie or morello cherries) coming from *P. cerasus,* a shrub or small tree, and the sweet cherries from the mazzard or gean (*P. avium*), a larger tree. There are hybrids between the two species which go under the name of duke cherries. In addition, a number of wild cherries are indigenous to both North America and Europe.

The U.S. is the leading cherry-producing country of the world. In North America, both the sweet cherry and the sour cherry have escaped and gone wild. None of the indigenous American cherries is cultivated, but the sweet black rum cherry (*P. serotina*) was used by the early New Englanders to turn raw rum into a fine cherry liqueur and also to make "cherry bounce" (by a technique similar to that used for sloe gin, with brandy instead of gin, suitably sweetened with sugar). Then there is the common chokecherry (*P. virginiana*), whose astringent, pea-sized cherries make good jelly and wine, and the very similar *P. melanocarpa,* which is less astringent. In the U.S., the name of bird cherry or pin cherry is given to *P. pennsylvanica,* which is sour and not much utilized, but which can also make a good jelly.

In Europe, there is the bird cherry *P. padus,* a hardy northern species with small bittersweet black berries which can be fermented to make a fruit brandy, and the mahaleb or St. Lucie's cherry (*P. mahaleb*), with wood that is prized for making pipes and fruit that is sometimes used for liqueurs. Another European species, the cherry laurel (*P. laurocerasus*), smells of the *hydrocyanic acid it contains; it is very poisonous. The cornelian cherry or cornel (*Cornus mas*) of central and southern Europe has edible fruit, although it is related not to the cherry but to the dogwood (*C. sanguinea*).

The sweet cherries are rather particular about the soil and climate and are very prone to diseases—one reason why they are expensive. They are also highly perishable and have to be packed very carefully and refrigerated. Old cherries can usually be recognized by their stalks, which are dark, not crisp and green like those of freshly picked cherries. There are some 600 varieties in cultivation. At one time, they were classified into the *bigarreaux,* with firm dryish flesh, and the *guignes* or geans, with soft and juicy flesh—a distinction that no longer works because of the many intermediate forms. Their color varies from dark red to almost white or yellow, the meat from white to dark red, and the hearts white or black. Sweet cherry varieties are usually sweet, but some can be bitter, veering toward the wild mazzard. The great majority of varieties are intended for eating as dessert and are not of much interest when cooked.

The sour or morello cherry has some 300 cultivated varieties and is the one for cooking. The morello itself is dark, almost black, with colored juice, but there are red varieties with colorless juice called *amarelles.* This is the species for cherry pie, liqueurs, and cherry brandy. Few varieties are good to eat from the hand. However, the hybrid duke cherries (*royale* in France, where they originated), which may be black or red, include varieties both for eating and for cooking. Some 65 kinds are grown.

Special uses of cherries are in making fruit brandies and liqueurs. Kirsch, which comes from the area including Alsace, the Black Forest, and northeast Switzerland, is a dry, white spirit with a characteristic flavor, but tasting nothing of cherries. In cooking, it is used with fruit (e.g. with pineapple), in some cakes, and in a cheese fondue, which it also accompanies in the glass. It is a totally different drink from maraschino, which is sweet and again often used as a flavoring with fruits and sweets. Maraschino is said to have originated in Dalmatia, but it now comes equally from Italy on the other side of the Adriatic. Apart from being made from a different variety of cherry, the stones are crushed for maraschino (but not for kirsch), and honey is added to make the fermentable mash. The taste of maraschino contains a dash of bitter almond from the stones and is quite unlike that of kirsch. Cherry brandy, of which the finest is probably Grants, an old English make, has a strong taste of cherries and is made by infusion, not by fermenting and distilling the cherries. Its use in cooking would be original rather than classical. Glacé cherries (*see* candied fruit), which appear much in cakes and in cake decoration, are often faked. The cherries are pitted, hardened with chemicals, and most often dyed (sometimes green) with synthetic dyes. Occasionally they are not even made out of cherries.

[*Cherry*—French: *cerise;* German: *Kirsche;* Italian: *ciliegia;* Spanish: *cereza*]

CHERRYSTONE. American hard-shell *clam.

CHERVIL (*Anthriscus cerefolium*) is a feathery umbelliferous herb with a delicate taste that is somewhere between parsley and

CHERVIL

anise. It came originally from the Balkans and the Middle East. In Britain, where it was probably introduced by the Romans, it is widely naturalized. It has also been introduced into North America and New Zealand. Although it is not often available in markets outside France, it can easily be grown in any garden or window box where conditions are not too hot and dry. It is a standard component of fines herbes, for example in omelets, as well as being a classic ingredient of ravigote sauce. The Belgians use it as a major ingredient in soups. However it is used, though, it should not be boiled, since this will destroy its flavor; it is normally added to hot dishes just before serving.

[*Chervil*—French: *cerfeuil;* German: *Kerbel;* Italian: *cerfoglio;* Spanish: *perifollo*]

CHESTNUT, sweet chestnut, or **Spanish chestnut.** There are some 10 species of chestnut. The sweet chestnut (*Castanea sativa*) has been cultivated in southern Europe for several thousand years. Today, there are hundreds of varieties propagated by grafting. They are particularly grown in France (around the Massif Central), Italy, Spain, and Portugal, and are very important in the regional cooking of such places as Corsica (where, alas, property developments are ousting the chestnut plantations). In more northerly countries, like Britain (where chestnuts were probably introduced by—inevitably—the Romans), the crop is uncertain and quality nuts are not produced. In North America, there are good local varieties of sweet chestnut, although the nuts are not so generally familiar as in Europe. They were introduced by the early colonists, who also used the indigenous American chestnut (*C. dentata*), which has an excellent nut but has now almost been wiped out by a blight. It is often replaced by the Japanese chestnut, *C. crenata*, which has a large but inferior nut. There are other sweet chestnuts, all edible, and some are of excellent quality.

Sweet chestnuts are formed inside very prickly capsules which split open when ripe to release the nuts. In this, they are similar to the unrelated horse chestnut (*Aesculus hippocastanum*), an ornamental tree with inedible nuts (though *in extremis,* these may be made edible by grinding and washing in many changes of water to leach out the astringent substances, leaving a flour which can be dried and roasted). According to the locality, chestnuts start to ripen from September onward, but there are early, late, and midseason varieties. Chestnuts are sugary and starchy, but contain little oil. Many varieties are distinctly astringent, especially when freshly gathered, and they are rarely eaten raw. In the great chestnut forests, such as those of the Apennines, the semiwild trees produce the small rounded *castagne* used for feeding animals or for drying and grinding into flour. These normally have three nuts to a capsule. The more expensive eating varieties, the *marroni,* are produced from grafted trees, which bear nuts that are much larger, usually only one to a capsule, and often square. Although there is some variation in flavor and sweetness, the consideration of greatest practical importance to the cook is whether or not the chestnuts are easy to peel, which here means removing the brown inner skin of the nut, not the outside husk. In some small or wild nuts, the inner skin may be folded into the meat, which makes skinning almost impossible. Even with a good variety, you may have difficulty unless the correct methods are employed.

PEELING CHESTNUTS

Cut each chestnut through the outer husk along the convex face. Then (a) bake them for 7–8 minutes on the tray at the bottom of the oven, moistening them with a few spoons of water, or (b) put them in a pan of cold water, bring to the boil, and boil for 1 minute, or (c) throw the chestnuts into boiling water and boil them for 5 minutes. With any of these methods it is easy to peel off the outer husk of the chestnut.

Now to remove the brown inner skin. Put the husked chestnuts into cold water with a little cooking oil and bring them to the boil. Then turn down the heat to the lowest possible. When the skins start to come off, take out a few at a time (they must be peeled hot) and rub them with a cloth, while holding the chestnut with another cloth to avoid burning your fingers. Since there are some very stubborn varieties, an alternative method is to put the husked chestnuts into a frying pan and fry them in a little sweet oil or butter until the skins become crisp. They can then easily be rubbed off.

When buying whole nuts, examine them carefully for spoilage from insects or fungus. Because it is not easy to tell from the outside, try to cut a few open. Carry a penknife when buying them in quantity. Really fresh nuts are firm and feel solid. Nuts which give when pressed have been dried out somewhat, but may be excellent and even sweeter from the storage.

In the U.S. and Britain, chestnuts are mostly eaten roasted in the husk or used for stuffing the Christmas turkey. Roasting may be done in a hot oven, but the flavor is much better if they are roasted very quickly and "shown the fire." One can buy special pans (like a frying pan with large holes in the bottom) for roasting chestnuts over the flames. Every child knows that the husk must be pierced before roasting or the nut will explode. Some people advocate boiling the nuts before roasting, which makes them soft but does not give the best flavor. Roasted chestnuts are probably nicest eaten by the fireside—with a little salt handy—but if sent to the table they must be hot, and it is correct to serve them in a napkin.

Recipes for chestnuts abound in countries where in the past these nuts were a winter staple, taking the place of potatoes. Even forms of bread and polenta were made from them (although chestnuts, like corn, are unsuitable for making proper bread—they contain insufficient glutinous substances for binding). The everyday peasant recipes would often have been no more than rustic porridges.

Among the more sophisticated chestnut-based dishes, France offers soups like *potage de marrons dauphinois, soufflé aux marrons et potiron* (chestnut and pumpkin soufflé), and purées of chestnuts to be eaten with mutton and pork or game like boar, hare, and venison. There are also various chestnut gâteaux, and the world-famous *marrons glacés,* as well as the Lucullan *marrons au kirsch* (poached in a thick syrup and flavored with kirsch). The chestnuts which are canned either in syrup or as purée come from the Ardèche region, which is the main source of chestnuts in France. In Italy, we have the delectable *monte bianco* (cooked chestnuts riced into a mountain and given an Alpine look with fine sugar and avalanches of beaten cream) and the various forms of *castagnaccio* (a blend of chestnuts, raisins, and pine nuts, which may be flavored with fennel, rosemary, or vanilla according to locality). More modern dishes include the *dolce di castagne,* the *semifreddo di castagne,* and the *budino di castagne al savoiardi.* The Austrians have their Nesselrode pudding, a chestnut ice. Any of these rich chestnut dishes would put a delicious but firm stop to any meal. In Spain, you might eat *castañas con mantequilla* (with butter), *con jaraba* (in syrup), and *helado de castañas* (ice cream). Similarly, there are many chestnut dishes from the Balkans, Greece, and farther east. They are often flavored with anise.

Dried chestnuts are commonly on sale in all Mediterranean countries. As *secchielli,* they may be bought from Italian grocers. Chestnut flour is also available, and the best quality contains little of the red skin. Commercially made chestnut jams and spreads are all hideously suitable for children. Canned chestnut purée is useful and available in many countries.

CASTAÑAS CON MANTEQUILLA

Peel 2 lb (1 Kg) of chestnuts. Put them with a stick of celery, 2 tablespoons (25 g) of butter, and a pinch each of salt and sugar in a saucepan with hot water barely to cover. Put the lid on and simmer without stirring for about 40 minutes. Remove the celery, drain, and add another 2 tablespoons (25 g) of butter. Reheat and serve very hot.

CASTAGNE ALL' UBRIACO

A simple Italian peasant dish (literally "drunk chestnuts") for the fireside. Roast chestnuts, preferably in a chestnut roaster, and peel them. Put them in a dish by the fire, cover them with a clean cloth soaked in red wine, and leave them for 30 minutes to absorb the wine flavor, keeping them hot. You can eat these drunken wine-flavored chestnuts as they are or cover them with honey and again serve hot.

MINESTRA DI CASTAGNE SECCHE

Wash and then soak 11 oz (300 g) of dried chestnuts for 24 hours, then boil them in water to cover for 2-3 hours. Add about 1 cup (300 g) of rice, and, when it is half-cooked, 3½ cups (1 lt) of milk and 4 tablespoons (50 g) of butter. Cook until rice is tender. Salt to taste. The soup should be creamy.

CASTAGNACCIO

Pour boiling water over ¾ cup (100 g) of seedless raisins and leave them until they are cool enough to take out with the fingers. Put them to dry. Sift 1 lb (450 g) of chestnut flour with a good pinch of salt, and add water, mixing to a soft paste. Pour into a well-oiled baking tray. Sprinkle with 1 teaspoon of fennel seed, ½ cup (50 g) of pine nuts, and the raisins. Dribble a little olive oil on top and bake in the oven until a crust is formed. Eat hot or cold.

[*Chestnut*—French: *marron, châtaigne;* German: *Edelkastanie;* Italian: *castagna, marrone;* Spanish: *castaña, marrona*]

CHICKEN. The original domestication of the chicken probably took place in Southeast Asia. Among its many breeds was the great Cochin China fowl, of enormous size and ungainly form, which took England by storm in the middle of the last century. It was in such demand that, according to a contemporary, people paid huge sums of money for a bird, and talked almost about nothing else. Indeed, the prices paid would have bought three or four good cows or a reasonable flock of sheep.

If you go into the jungles of the Sundarbans, at the mouth of the Ganges and Brahmaputra rivers, you will hear the hens clucking and the cocks crowing from the treetops at dawn every morning. The jungle fowl there are small birds, almost bantam size, but there is little doubt that these are pretty much what the first chickens must have looked like. From some such ancestors are descended our modern hens, the White Leghorn and New Hampshire and Rhode Island Red—poor, egg-laying machines of the modern world—and the heavy, quick-maturing table birds, like Jersey White Giant and White Rock, which have been computer-selected to gain the most weight on the least food in the shortest time. It is these that have done for us what Henry IV of France (1553–1610) failed to do—to put a chicken in every Frenchman's Sunday pot.

Anything outside mass production will be more difficult to get and more expensive. It will also probably taste better. Top restaurants in France still insist on a Bresse or Le Mans, and a bird with black or white feet, but never yellow. If choosing a bird in a market, where you are probably not allowed to handle it, look at the legs. If they are coarse, scaly, and battered, the bird is old. Then look for bruises. Those inflicted during life show as dark red marks. In European markets, be careful that the butcher does not chop up your chicken into pieces before you can tell him not to. The British, who expect chickens with white fat, are often surprised to find that the chickens sold elsewhere, for instance in France and the U.S., often have yellow fat, and are none the worse for it. The size of a bird depends more on breed and feeding than on age.

Following are the names of various types of chicken.

Broiler, baby chicken, or **poussin.** 4–6 weeks old. ¾–1¼ lb (350–600 g). Usually broiled or grilled. Very tender but with little taste.

Coquelet (French). Very young cock. Around 2 lb (1 Kg).

Fryer, spring chicken or **poulet.** 2–4½ lb (1–2 Kg).

Fat fowl, roaster, or **poularde.** 3¼–4½ lb (1½–2 Kg) plus.

Boiling fowl or **poule.** 4½ lb (2 Kg) plus. Often with much fat. Can be roasted if less than 8 months old. Fowl over a year old should be boiled. Real barnyard fowl may be expensive, but they are full of flavor.

Cock, cockerel, or **coq.** 3¼–4½ lb (1½–2 Kg). Mature male birds. Not as good eating as hens.

Capon or **chapon.** A castrated cock, or one in which the administration of female hormones has had a similar effect. Capons are very large, 6–7½ lb (2½–3½ Kg), and can approach the size of a small turkey.

Some idea of a chicken's anatomy is a help when *drawing it, cutting it up, or boning it. Points to notice are that the foot is cut off below (and not through) the joint to prevent the drumstick from contracting during cooking. The tips of the wings are usually removed, and they join the bones for stock.

There are many ways of cutting up a chicken for cooking. The usual way is to cut off both legs, not through the joint as in carving, but by breaking and cutting off the strip of back which contains the "oyster" (the bit of meat in the front hollow) and leaving it attached to the leg. The oyster muscle, after all, is part of the leg's musculature. Then cut off each wing with a diagonal cut made from the center of the wishbone, so that a good piece of breast goes with each wing. Finally, cut away what is left of the breast on either side from the carcass. This gives five portions of more or less equal size and leaves the back and trimmings to go into the stockpot, or to be used in any other way to add flavor, although there is little meat on the bones.

A quicker and easier method, which is often used in French restaurants, is to cut off both legs, being careful to scoop out the oyster still attached as part of the leg, before severing the joint as in carving. Then find the shoulder joint, hold the wing against the body to present the joint, and cut through the tip of the joint. If you find the right spot, you do not have to cut through anything harder than cartilage. Sever the tendons around it with the knife point, put your finger inside (there is a pocket in which to put it), and rip backward. This pulls off the wing and outer breast in one piece. After doing this on both sides, cut the back of the breastbone free from the ribs and grasp the breastbone. Pull it forward to break it free and pull away together with the wishbone, which should then be removed, since it is somewhat unsightly. This gives five pieces, two legs as before, two side breasts with wing attached, and a double fillet of inner breast attached to the breastbone.

Boning a chicken requires a modicum of patience and practice but is a skill worth learning. The easiest way is to cut through the skin right down the back and to dissect the meat away on each side, cutting through the joints as you come to them. When all of the body bones are free, the bones of legs and wings can be removed with little difficulty: first free the joint and then scrape down the bone while holding the joint and gradually drawing out the bone. When you reach the knee joint, that must in turn be freed and the next bone drawn out; the leg meat will all turn inside out in the process. Finally when you reach the end point, it is easiest to snip off the rest with a pair of scissors. One takes only the first bone out of the wing, since boning the whole lot would demand more skill and patience than the results would justify. When the boned chicken is laid flat, meat side up, the stuffing can be put on top and the chicken rolled up around it and sewn with needle and thread into something which usually looks like a cross between a chicken and a sausage but when cooked can be cut into elegant slices.

The alternative method is to start from the rear with the back and gradually free and roll back the skin and meat, treating the legs and wings as already described. To do this one needs a thin, sharp knife, and a bit more patience. The finished product looks a little more like a chicken.

[*Chicken*—French: *poulet;* German: *Hühn-chen;* Italian: *pollo;* Spanish: *gallina*]

CHICKPEA, garbanzo, channa, Egyptian bean, or **ram's-head pea.** Chickpeas (*Cicer arietinum*) are one of the most important legumes. They are sometimes eaten green but are mostly dried. The plant is indigenous to the Levant and the Near East, where it has been cultivated since antiquity. Later, chickpeas, which are exceedingly nutritious, were the food of the Arab armies in their conquest of North Africa and Spain. Since they will not stand frost, growing them is confined to the belt stretching eastward from the Mediterranean countries, through Rumania, southern Russia, and the Middle East, extending to India and onward. Nowadays, they are also grown extensively in the Americas, South Africa, and Australia. The plants are a striking gray-green color and stand about 18 in. (40 cm) high. The pods are short, fat, and hairy, containing two or three large seeds. They are sticky and secrete so much oxalic acid that walking through the crop can spoil your shoes. In the countries where they grow and the seeds are frequently eaten green, the pulling must be done with gloves to protect the hands from the acid.

Legend has it that the plant was cursed by the Virgin Mary because it refused to hide the Holy Family when they were pursued by Herod's soldiers. The name "ram's-head pea" or "ram's-head chiche" comes from the fact that seeds of the larger varieties, when seen from the side, suggest a ram's head with large curly horns. Other, smaller varieties have round seeds not much bigger than a pea. Though usually cream-colored, they can also be pale green, brown, or even black. Chickpeas are especially important in Arab cooking and hence in Spanish cooking and in the countries of Spanish America. They are an essential part of many "poor-man's stews" with meat and vegetables—in couscous, for instance. Then there is that famous Arab purée of chickpeas called *hummus,* which usually contains tahini (and sometimes yogurt) and is used as a dip for bread. Farther east, in India, a smaller chickpea called *★channa* is grown.

Chickpeas must be soaked before being boiled; unlike other pulses, they are almost impossible to cook otherwise, and soaking is usually done overnight. Many cooks add a teaspoon of bicarbonate of soda per 2 lb (1 Kg) chickpeas to the soaking water to help to soften the skins, although this does not improve the flavor and is not always necessary with modern varieties. Old-fashioned ones may need to be boiled for up to 4 hours in an open pan or cooked for an hour in a pressure cooker, but new types will be tender in as little as 20 minutes in a pressure cooker. Since it is almost impossible to overcook chickpeas, it is best always to err on the generous side. If the skins have to be removed, this may be done by soaking the peas for an hour in a strong solution of bicarbonate of soda—say 2 teaspoons per ½ lb (225 g) of chickpeas—and then giving them a quick boil in the solution. After that the peas may be drained and put into cold water, rubbed hard between the hands, and the skins washed off. The skinned chickpeas should be rinsed in several waters.

In Mediterranean countries, cooked chickpeas may be found in the markets. Chickpeas are also available canned, a great saving in time and effort. *★Besan* flour can always be found in Indian shops, but if it is not available, chickpeas can be ground at home; it is, however, necessary to put them through the grinder twice, once to break them coarsely and again to grind the broken bits to a flour. The bits of husk have to be delved out. (An ordinary coffee grinder is unsuitable—chickpeas are so hard that they will break the machine.) Roasted chickpeas used to be added to coffee with chicory, not to adulterate it but because some people liked the flavor.

Chickpeas have always been common in Spanish cooking, despite criticisms of them. "As for *garbanzos,*" said Théophile Gautier, "they sounded in our bellies like pieces of lead in a Basque drum." And Alexandre Dumas, in his great *Dictionnaire Gastronomique,* claimed that they are "bullet-sized peas quite beyond the powers of digestion." But whatever these Frenchmen may say, chickpeas are an essential part of a Spanish *cocido.* For instance, a Castilian *cocido* consists of ham, stewing beef, chorizo sausage, and chickpeas, simmered for 3–4 hours in water with some olive oil, a piece of fat, and a bone. Vegetables (cabbages, leeks, onion, and garlic) are cooked separately and seasoned with a little *pimentón.* The liquid is served first as a soup with some pasta cooked in it, then the meat, chickpeas, and other vegetables are eaten with a salad of lettuce and tomato dressed with oil and lemon. Plenty of coarse salt is essential. Other versions are more elaborate.

At the simpler end of the scale are the Spanish *potajes de garbanzos,* in which, after cooking, a few• of the chickpeas are crushed to thicken the juice, and perhaps a handful of spinach or some potato is added. The soup may be seasoned with olive oil (in which several cloves of garlic have been fried and some red *pimentón* stirred in), or alternatively with a sofrito of garlic and tomato fried in oil. To this, a little chopped *raw* garlic, cumin seed, and black pepper may be added, following the common Spanish custom of combining raw and cooked garlic. For a more nourishing dish, chopped hard-boiled eggs, meatballs, minced salt fish (*bacalao*), or even a pasta may be included. These are comforting winter dishes, best not demanded by tourists in August.

[*Chickpea*—French: *pois chiche;* German: *Kichererbse;* Italian: *cece;* Spanish: *garbanzo*]

CHICORY and **endive.** There is a great deal of popular confusion between these two plants, which is not surprising: both wild and cultivated forms are very much alike, belonging to the same genus of the composite family. In any case, from the culinary point of view, it is more important to distinguish between the various types of chicory than between chicory and endive in a botanical sense.

Chicory or succory (*Cicorium intybus*) grows wild throughout much of Europe and is a common escape in the U.S. It is recognized by its pale blue flowers and does not look promising to eat. However, the very young shoots, hardly appearing above the ground, have been used as a salad since at least Roman times and are still eagerly grubbed out in Mediterranean countries and sold in winter and early spring.

Endive (*C. endivia*) comes originally from eastern Asia and has gone wild in places in Mediterranean countries. It came into Europe as a salad plant at a much later date.

Both chicory and endive are usually blanched by the grower, since they are bitter when green (and still rather bitter when blanched). Commercially, they are always blanched. Greenness is thus not a sign of freshness but of age. They are even best kept in the dark at home until eaten.

The true endives fall into two general types. First there is the frizzly form, called moss curled or stagshorn endive. Rarely is it seen perfectly white; more often, a cover has been put on the plant or the outer leaves have been tied up so that only the center is properly blanched—the rest will be somewhat bitter and the outer leaves tough. There is also a well-known form with broad, slightly curled leaves, known as Batavia endive or escarole. It looks more like a curly lettuce. In chicory also there are similar leafy forms such as the Italian *spadona*, in which the leaves are bunched, and the form with long narrow leaves, the *puntarelle* of the Roman markets (also called *cicoria asparagio* or *di Brindisi*, or *catalogna*). Again in Italy there are the exotics, the *fiori commestibile* (edible flowers), which, when blanched, are red or variegated pink, orange, or yellow, instead of white. The chicory that looks like a red-leafed brush—the root being the handle—is called *radicchio di Treviso*, while the pink, flowerlike chicory, which is sometimes almost like a vegetable rose, is *radicchio di Castelfranco Veneto* and *rosso di Verona*, *radicchio* being an alternative Italian word for chicory. These flower types have almost no bitterness and give color to winter salads.

The well-known Brussels chicory or Belgian endive is a true chicory with the tight spindle-shaped hearts (*chicons*) forced and blanched. The alternative name for this is witloof (white leaf). Like other chicories, it is slightly bitter; it can be eaten raw or cooked.

There are also varieties grown for their large taproots, of which the best-known is Magdeburg chicory. In the second half of the 18th century, the roasted root began to be used to flavor coffee—and soon to adulterate it. Cheating became so rife that in Britain the use of chicory in coffee was banned altogether in 1832, but 8 years later—because those who liked chicory in their coffee protested—it was once more allowed, provided it was marked on the label.

To make chicory for coffee, the taproots are washed, cut in bits, and dried in gentle heat. Then the dry pieces are broken into nibs, roasted brown, and ground. Chicory in coffee has a characteristic taste and is liked in France and in some of the southern states in America.

Yet more unwanted confusion about names can be caused by using *barbe* (beard) for chicory and other related salad plants and vegetables. *Barbe-de-bouc* (goatsbeard) is Brussels chicory (forced *chicons*) in Belgium. In France, *barbe-de-capucin* is the shoots of wild chicory, as also in Italy is

barba di cappuccine di campo (Capuchin-friar's-beard); Italian *barba di becco* (billy-goat's-beard) is white *salsify, and *barba di frate* or *di prete* (priest's-beard) is another relative of salsify which is used as a salad plant and vegetable in Italy. In England it is called Jack-go-to-bed-at-noon or goatsbeard (*Tragopogon pratensis*).

[*Chicory*—French: *chicorée;* German: *Zichorie;* Italian: *cicoria;* Spanish: *achicoria.* *Endive*—French: *endive;* German: *Endivie;* Italian: *indivia;* Spanish: *endibia, escarola*]

CHIHLI. *See* Chinese cabbage.

CHIKU. *See* sapodilla.

CHILE SALTPETER or **sodium nitrate** ($NaNO_3$) is used as an alternative to *saltpeter (potassium nitrate) because it is cheaper. It is roughly one-sixth stronger in its action on meat, so quantities should be scaled down accordingly.

CHILI, chilli, or even **chilly.** Chilies and *sweet peppers belong in the same genus and mostly perhaps in the same species (*Capsicum annuum*). However, the tiny, very pungent chilies at least can be referred to another species, *C. frutescens.* Two other chili species are cultivated in South America. Some long, pointed forms with the classic chili outline are sweet and mild, while certain large kinds, especially those from Peru, look as if they ought to be mild but are blistering. Even color is nothing to go by. Most chilies start green and turn red when ripe. Some may first be yellow, and then red, and others turn chocolate, brown, or even black. In size, there are varieties 12 in. (30 cm) or longer and others no bigger than a pea. To many people, a chili is merely a source of painful hotness, the raw material for cayenne pepper, but in Mexico, Spain, India, and South America, the selection of exactly the right chili for a particular purpose is a matter of gastronomic importance. Chilies vary not only in hotness but also in flavor—and in intensity of flavor. The hotness can be adjusted, with added cayenne perhaps, but the flavor cannot.

Chilies are natives of tropical America. They have been found in prehistoric Incan remains from Peru and were in common use by the Aztecs before the arrival of the Spanish in Mexico. It is difficult to imagine how Asiatic countries like India (which today is the largest producer of chilies) managed before they were introduced. Chilies are the flavoring above all used by poor people the world over, since a little goes a long way and they make almost anything palatable.

People who use chilies at every meal become used to their burning principle and need increasingly larger doses and hotter chilies to obtain any impact. It is therefore quite wrong to make Mexican or Indian food blindingly hot on the grounds that it is authentic. That is not how it tastes to the people of those countries. Very hot chili, especially if the dish contains seeds or bits of the fruit, is not very good for the insides when suddenly sprung upon them and can even cause internal blisters. You must wash your hands carefully after handling chilies— any residual capsaicin on the fingers can burn the eyes if they are rubbed by accident.

Chilies of many types are canned, and they freeze fairly well. Fresh green chilies, which cannot be replaced by dried ones, are often available in markets, especially where there are customers who enjoy Mexican food, for which they are essential.

The use of chilies is more sophisticated in Mexico than anywhere else in the world. It has been estimated that there are about 200 types of chili, half of which are used in Mexico, including those listed below. When the hottest Mexican chilies are not obtainable, fresh cayenne pepper makes an acceptable substitute.

Cascabel. Dried. A small, plum-shaped chili which has a nutty flavor after roasting. It makes the not overhot *salsa de chile cascabel.*

Chilaca. Fresh, this is a long, thin, almost black chili, very hot and well flavored. *Chilacas* are roasted and skinned before use. When dried, they are *pasillas,* which, toasted

and ground, are used particularly in sauce for seafood.

Guajillo. Dried and exceedingly hot, this average-shaped, slender, pointed chili is smooth, red-brown, and sometimes sold as the much milder and rounded *cascabel.*

Güero. Fresh, this is a pale yellow chili of variable size and typical long shape. It may be lightly grilled and used as a salad or added to sauces; it is hot and has a distinctive flavor.

Habanero. This tiny, light-green, irregular chili is possibly the hottest of them all. It is the one Mexican chili that probably belongs to a separate species, *Capsicum sinense.*

Jalapeño. A short, fat green chili that is top-shaped with a rounded end. It is also fairly well known in the U.S., where it is put into processed cheese. This is a fairly hot chili if the seeds and septa are included. It is the basis for the common sauce *chiles jalapeños en escabeche,* a Mexican table condiment also used in cooking. Jalapeños are sometimes available frozen as well as in cans. Dried, smoked jalapeño is *chipotle;* used to flavor soups and stews, it is obtainable canned in vinegar or red *adobo* sauce.

Poblano. This top-shaped, very dark-green chili is usually rather mild but has a rich flavor. It is roasted and skinned and is used particularly for stuffing. The dried ripe *poblano* is an *ancho,* the dried chili that is most used in Mexico; it is dark brown, becoming brick red when soaked. The *mulato,* another brown dried chili, is very like the *ancho* but is sweeter in flavor.

Serrano. These small green chilies have very piquant seeds and septa. They are used fresh or toasted, often in green sauces, and are among the commonest types of Mexican chili, being also available canned and in *escabeche* with other vegetables.

In the U.S., chilies are produced particularly in Florida, Louisiana, Texas, and California. Best known is the Anaheim or Californian green chili, which is about 8 in.

(20 cm) long. This fairly mild, sometimes even sweet, chili is often stuffed with cheese or other filling and fried in batter (*chiles rellenos*). The Fresno is a small, conical chili

CAYENNE

something like the jalapeño, but not so hot. Among yellow types, banana chilies are mild and sweet, while the yellow wax *caribe* and *güero* are pretty hot. (You should approach all chilies warily.) The hot cayenne peppers, dried and ground to a hot, red powder, are used as a condiment. Tabasco peppers, small and red, are grown mainly in Louisiana for sauce.

The use of chilies in parts of the U.S. is influenced by traditional Mexican dishes. The same Mexican influence has also traveled to Spain, where chilies are valued. Hot chilies, called *guindillas*, are used notably to add a kick to the dishes cooked *al ajillo* (fried with garlic), and green chilies are in the markets, but only in small quantities, from summer to autumn. (Substituting *guindillas*, as some foreign books do, for the Romesco peppers, which are mild *sweet peppers, in Romesco sauce is disastrous.)

Indians make wonderful fresh chutney, a thick purée of ground green chili, coriander leaves, salt, lemon juice, and coconut. Many varieties of chili are grown in the East, mainly chosen for yield in a given climate and soil. They are dried by the thousands of tons and used whole or ground to make chili powder, often after a mild roasting that im-

proves the flavor. Chili powder is pure chili, hot, but not as hot as cayenne. The chili powder sold in the U.S. and used for chili beans or chili con carne is usually mixed with cumin or oregano. The most famous chili condiment is *Tabasco sauce; other chili sauces are often highly flavored unsieved ketchups. Nepal pepper—not much seen these days—is merely a variety of chili, and the *harissa* of North Africa is a mixture of chili and cumin.

CHINE. The chine of a small pig consists of two undivided loins (the same cut as saddle of mutton), but from larger pigs, especially bacon pigs, the chine is the backbone with some meat between the wings of the vertebrae attached to it. The word is applied to similar parts of other animals.

Chining a loin of lamb or pork is sawing close alongside the backbone from the inner surface, cutting through the bases of the ribs and/or the wings of the vertebrae, but leaving the backbone attached to the meat. It is then easily removed when the loin is cooked, to make carving very much easier.

[*Chine*—French: *échine;* German: *Rückenstück;* Italian: *coppa;* Spanish: *espinazo*]

CHINESE ARTICHOKE or **chorogi.** These small tubers from a labiate plant, *Stachys sieboldii,* get their name from a slight resemblance in flavor to *globe and *Jerusalem artichokes. They are popular in winter in France, as well as in the Far East, whence they came. The French name, *crosnes,* is from Crosnes, where they were first grown in Europe in 1882. (They were sent to a Monsieur Pailleux by the doctor to the Russian ambassador in Peking.) It is essential that Chinese artichokes be fresh— they rapidly lose flavor when dug out of the ground. (They can safely be left in the soil and dug as required.) After washing them well, remove the skin by shaking the tubers in a cloth with coarse salt or by blanching them in boiling water and rubbing the skin. Some leave the skin on. There are many ways of cooking them, but they may simply be boiled for 15 minutes in salted water, drained, and finished in butter with chopped parsley or heated in gravy or a creamy sauce.

CHINESE CABBAGE. There is a lot of confusion about the two Chinese species of *Brassica* and their variants, partly because the original "Chinese cabbages" were much improved in the U.S. after World War I and returned to their former country in a greatly changed form. The Chinese cabbage or *pe-tsai* (*B. pekinensis*) usually sold looks a little like a cos lettuce with large white midribs, but other Chinese cabbages look almost like Swiss chard. So, too, does Chinese mustard or *pak-choi* (*B. chinensis*), which is also known as mustard greens; two other varieties of this species are known as *wong bok* and *chihli*.

The pickle often called Chinese sauerkraut is made from *pak-choi* fermented in salt; it is used in stir-fried dishes or steamed with meat and fish. Available in cans and sometimes also from the barrel in Chinese stores, it is generally rinsed in water and squeezed dry, just like ordinary sauerkraut, before use. Dried, salted cabbage, which is usually sold tied in bundles, needs to be soaked in warm water until it is soft (about 15 minutes). It can be used as a particularly interesting flavoring in soups.

CHINESE FIVE SPICES or **five-fragrance powder** consists of equal parts of star anise, cassia or cinnamon, cloves, fennel seed, and Chinese pepper or ginger. It may be bought ready ground from shops that specialize in Chinese foods or made at home, although the spices are difficult to grind finely. Since you will have to visit the Chinese suppliers for the Chinese pepper, you might as well buy the five spices. Apart from being essential in certain Chinese dishes, it is also a most useful flavoring with pork.

[*Chinese five spices*—Chinese: *heung new fun, hung-liu, ngung heung;* French: *cinq*

épices chinoises; German: *fünf Gewürze;* Italian: *cinque spezie cinese;* Spanish: *cinco especias chinas*]

CHINESE GOOSEBERRY. *See* kiwi.

CHINESE LANTERN PLANT. *See* physalis fruit.

CHINESE MUSTARD. *See* Chinese cabbage.

CHINESE PARSLEY. *See* coriander.

CHINESE PEPPER, Japanese pepper, anise pepper, or **Szechwan pepper.** This useful spice—which, despite its peppery taste, is no relation to ordinary black pepper—is the dried berry of a shrub (*Zanthoxylum piperitum*) belonging to the same family, the Rutaceae, as citruses and rue. Among its close relatives are satinwood (once commonly used for furniture) and the prickly ashes of North America, which have medicinal barks. The Chinese pepper bush can be grown in any temperate climates. In China, where it is called *hua chiao*, this spice is commonly mixed with salt and used as a table condiment. For this, it is first gently roasted until crisp, then ground and mixed with a little salt (1 teaspoon to 2 tablespoons of the powdered spice). Chinese pepper is also an ingredient of *Chinese five spices. When allowed to get stale, it develops a nasty scent.

CHITTERLINGS, the small intestines of hogs, are eaten in many countries. In the U.S., especially in the South, chitterlings (often called "chitlins") are usually fried, boiled with greens, or cooked in sauces. The name is also given to sausages made of bits of intestine, usually pig's. To butchers making sausages, chitterlings may refer to the frilly part of the large intestine of the pig.

CHIVE. An onion with pretty purple or white flowers and fine, tubular, grasslike leaves—which are the part of the plant used in the kitchen. They are chopped finely and should be added to hot dishes at the last moment. Chives (*Allium schoenoprasum*) have long been used as a flavoring in soups, om-

CHIVES

elets, and sauces, with cream cheese, and in salads. Although the flavor of chives is unmistakably onion, it is subtly different.

Anyone with green fingers but no garden should be able to have a supply of fresh chives (which are infinitely superior to the dried variety) by growing them in a window box or flower pot. Remove any flower buds as they appear.

[*Chive*—French: *ciboulette;* German: *Schnittlauch;* Italian: *erba cipollina;* Spanish: *cebolleta*]

CHLORINE (Cl). A poisonous yellow-green gas, found on earth mainly in the form of its sodium salt (sodium chloride or common salt) in sea water. Chlorine is an important element in life processes, but is chemically too active ever to be found in its uncombined state in nature. First discovered in 1774, it has long been used for bleaching and disinfecting, since it dissolves in water to form a powerful oxidizing agent, hypochlorous acid. Its smell and taste are well known in overchlorinated tap water.

[*Chlorine*—French: *chlore;* German: *Chlor;* Italian: *cloro;* Spanish: *cloro*]

CHLOROPHYLL. The green pigment of plants, the means by which they use the energy of sunlight to build complex carbohydrates from carbon dioxide and water molecules. Chlorophyll, which contains magnesium, is often mixed with other pigments—yellow, red, or brown—to produce the range of leaf colors we see in nature. Chlorophyll is used as a green food coloring, but synthetic green dyes are more often used.

[*Chlorophyll*—French: *chlorophylle;* German: *Chlorophyll;* Italian: *clorofilla;* Spanish: *clorofila*]

CHOCOLATE, from the Aztec, *chocolatl,* was used as a drink long before the Spaniards arrived in Mexico. Columbus noticed it on his fourth voyage, when it was found in an Indian trading boat in the Gulf of Honduras, but it was first brought to Spain by Cortés in 1526. The Spanish tried to keep its existence a secret, and for a good while few people north of the Pyrenees had any idea of its value or use. Dutch and English pirates, for instance, threw cocoa (or cacao) beans overboard when they captured a cargo, calling them "sheep shit." The first chocolate house opened in London in 1657, but the high customs duty imposed on cocoa kept it a rich man's beverage until as late as 1828. The tree (*Theobroma cacao*—the generic name means "food of the gods") which provides chocolate is native to tropical America, but to satisfy world demand it was soon being cultivated in other countries—notably West Africa—between 20° north and south of the equator.

The "beans" from which chocolate is made grow inside fat, spindle-shaped pods which are borne directly on the main branches and trunk of the tree. The beans are scooped out of the pod with the adhering pulp, fermented to develop their flavor, then dried in the sun. After shipping to the factory, the beans are roasted and broken into small nibs, and the shell is winnowed away. The grinding and refining of the nibs is a long and skilled process, on which the fineness of the finished chocolate depends. The pressure of the refining mills liquefies the cocoa nibs as they are ground, turning them into what is called chocolate liquor, and this emerges from the mill as a solidified block.

Drinking chocolate—as opposed to *cocoa—is chocolate with much of the fat (known as cocoa butter) pressed out, leaving a dry cake which is then pulverized. If you add extra cocoa butter to the chocolate and refine it by "conching" (rolling the chocolate liquor back and forth in a curved trough by a mechanical roller), you get fondant chocolate; it usually has sugar added to make it bittersweet or semisweet. The longer conching continues—it can last from less than a day or as long as 7 days—the finer the chocolate.

The quality of chocolate you get depends to a large extent on the price you pay. It seems obvious (but has to be said) that chocolate varies enormously in flavor and that you cannot expect to make a good chocolate dish with inferior chocolate. The problem today is finding good chocolate—for example, in the U.S., chocolate may be totally defatted, then reconstituted with inferior fat; careful inspection of the label is advisable. Perhaps it is because chocolate is usually sweetened commercially that people find it so extraordinary that it is used in savory dishes—with meat, game, octopus, and so on—but unsweetened chocolate does appear in this role in Mexico, Spain, and Italy. Bitter chocolate goes well with onion and tomato, for instance, as a base for a dish of fish or meat. In Mexico, it is added to chili powder. For sweet dishes, it combines especially well with vanilla, another Central American discovery, and also with cinnamon. There are chocolate-based liqueurs, too, which are usually unbearably sweet.

[Chocolate—French: chocolat; German: Schokolade; Italian: cioccolata; Spanish: chocolate]

CHOKO. Australian name for *chayote.

CHORIZO is the most famous Spanish sausage and comes in many regional varieties. They are all smoked and combine chopped pork with pimentón. Chorizos are made in other countries, including France and, particularly, Mexico, which took the tradition of making them from northern Spain. Mexican varieties, of which there are said to be 124, each with its own balance of chilies, herbs, and spices, are generally less tough than the Spanish ones. Chorizos are very good grilled (preferably over charcoal) until they are crisp on the outside and cooked right through. They are also an important ingredient in Spanish and Mexican cooking; for some recipes they are skinned before being added.

CHOROGI. See Chinese artichoke.

CHOWCHOW. No doubt derived from the Chinese, chowchow can refer to a mixed fruit relish preserved in syrup, often sweethot in taste. In the U.S., chowchow is usually a vegetable mixture, rich with mustard seed. The following is a typical recipe.

CHOWCHOW

Cut into small pieces 2 lb (1 Kg) of green tomatoes, 1 large bunch of celery, 1 lb (450 g) each of green beans and green peppers, 2 lb (1 Kg) of firm cucumbers, 1 small cauliflower, and 14 oz (400 g) of onions. Sprinkle well with salt. Leave overnight. Next day, bring to the boil 7 cups (2 lt) of vinegar plus 2½ oz (60 g) of mustard seed, 1 oz (25 g) of ground turmeric, and 1 tablespoon each of ground cloves, allspice, and black pepper. Drain and squeeze the vegetables to remove some of the water and throw them into the boiling vinegar. Cook gently until the vegetables are tender, then seal in glass containers.

CHROMIUM (Cr). A very shiny, silvery metal often used for plating, usually over a film of nickel. Chromium is corrosion-resistant, because of the film of its oxide which forms on the surface. It is an important constituent of stainless steel, and also a trace element present in an available form in raw vegetables and unrefined foods. Good sources are brewer's yeast, wheat germ, mushrooms, even beer and pepper, but the metal is made unavailable by temperatures over 248°F (120°C), which means that food sterilized in an autoclave or cooked in a pressure cooker—which for practical purposes means canned goods—is lacking in chromium.

[*Chromium*—French: *chrome;* German: *Chrom;* Italian: *cromo;* Spanish: *cromo*]

CHRYSANTHEMUM. This genus of the daisy family (Compositae) has about 150 species ranging from the ox-eye daisy to the enormous varieties sold by florists. Among its members are *costmary (*Chrysanthemum balsamita*), *tansy (*C. vulgare*), and pyrethrum (*C. cinerariifolium*). They may be annuals or perennials. The chrysanthemum varieties grown as flowers belong to a number of species, and since they are not poisonous—though not necessarily nice to eat— they can be safely used as decoration in food.

Although chrysanthemum greens or *shungiku,* an annual, is sometimes thought to be a separate species (*C. spatiosum*), it may well be a cultivated variety, with larger leaves, of the crown daisy (*C. coronarium*), also called garland chrysanthemum. The crown daisy, of which the wild form is so common in Mediterranean countries, has feathery leaves, which are strong in taste and less worth eating. Japanese chrysanthemum greens can easily be grown. They should be young and tender; old leaves are not worth eating. *Shungiku* is called for in Japanese recipes and may be used raw in salads.

[*Chrysanthemum*—French: *chrysanthème;* German: *Chrysanthemum;* Italian: *crisantema;* Spanish: *crisantemo*]

CHUFA, tiger nut, earthnut, earth almond, ground almond, yellow nut grass, pignut, or **rush nut.** The chufa is the small tuber of a sedge (*Cyperus esculentus*) which is native to Mediterranean Europe and Portugal. The plant is related to *C. papyrus,* from which the ancient Egyptians made a precursor of paper. Chufas have certainly been eaten for several thousand years, but though cultivated in a number of countries, it is in Spain that they are of most importance. As bought, chufas are knobbly, shriveled little objects about the size of the thumbnail and with a sweetish taste. They are better when shriveled than when fresh, since storing makes them sweeter. Although eaten as nuts and used occasionally for ice cream, their gastronomic importance is in the preparation of *horchata de chufas,* a milky drink much loved in Spain.

HORCHATA DE CHUFAS

Soak ½ lb (225 g) of chufas in water overnight and wash them very carefully. Put them in a blender with a little water and reduce to a fine state. Add a bit of cinnamon stick (bruised), a little grated lemon rind, about ¾ cup (150 g) of sugar, to taste, and 4 cups (1 lt) of water. Stir well and leave to stand for another 4–5 hours. Then strain through cheesecloth and bottle. Chill in the refrigerator. (A *horchata* of almonds is made in the same way.) *Horchata* is drunk as a cool, refreshing drink on a hot day. *Horchatas* are also made with melon seeds and with other nuts.

CHUTNEY. A chutney is a piquant Indian relish, eaten in small amounts to add an accent to a meal. There is a great difference in what is understood to be chutney in the East and the West. A chutney in India is almost invariably a mixture ground fresh on a curry stone; it consists of a paste of raw ingredients, such as fresh ginger, fresh green chili, onion, garlic, mint, coriander leaves, sour fruits, coconut—in fact, anything considered tasty, stimulating, or refreshing to the palate. Within wide limits, the cook is free to create from what happens to be available.

The sweet, bottled chutney sold elsewhere is quite different. Although it is of Indian inspiration (and quite often manufactured there), most people in India would call it a sweet pickle rather than a chutney. This chutney is always cooked and always combines sugar and vinegar with spices and fruit—usually mango, but more rarely, apples, raisins, or other fruits, such as apricots, are used.

MINT CHUTNEY

Chop and blend (with about ½ cup of water) a handful of mint leaves, a small onion, 1 teaspoon of salt, 5 fresh green chilies, and the juice of about ½ lemon. The remaining component is freshly grated or dried coconut. If you are using dried coconut and a blender, first grind the coconut dry to a powder. Finally add the coconut to the other ingredients a little at a time until you have a smooth, soft paste. Quantities are flexible.

GREEN CORIANDER CHUTNEY

Make as above with a handful of coriander leaves, 2–6 fresh green chilies, salt, lemon juice, and water.

MRS. LUCK'S BENGAL CHUTNEE

The following comes from Spellow House near Harrogate in Yorkshire. Mrs. Luck was my grandfather's cook and must have been born about 1850—a real Victorian. Her method of dealing with holes in her stockings (as reported by my father) is interesting. She would draw the stocking together around the hole, tie it with a piece of string, and cut off the surplus tuft with a pair of scissors. After which, as she forced the stocking on again, she would remark: "It's a bad foot indeed that won't shape its own stocking."

Dissolve ½ lb (225 g) of salt and 2 lb (1 Kg) of brown sugar in 6 pt (3½ lt) of cold brown vinegar. Add 3 dozen peeled and cored apples, 4 oz (100 g) of raisins, and ½ lb (225 g) of crystallized ginger of cooking quality, cut into small pieces. Slice up 5 Spanish onions and add them together with 1 oz (25 g) of mustard seed, 6 shallots, and 1½ oz (40 g) of chilies. Boil everything together until the apples are tender. Bottle.

Keep for some months before use.

SWEET MANGO CHUTNEY

This Indian recipe needs ripe, but not soft, mangoes, washed, peeled, and sliced. Heat in a very little water until they are soft. For each 2 lb (1 Kg) of mango slices, add 2 lb (1 Kg) of sugar, and 2½ oz (60 g) of salt. Pound together 1 oz (25 g) of mixed spices (equal parts of cumin, cardamom, cinnamon), ½ oz (15 g) of ground chili, 2 oz (50 g) of onion, 2–3 cloves of garlic, and 4½ oz (125 g) of green ginger, and place them in a cheesecloth bag. Add to the mangoes. Cook the whole to a jammy consistency before putting in about ½ cup (100–128 ml) of vinegar, depending on strength, per 2 lb (1 Kg) of mango slices. Then cook for 5 minutes, remove the spice bag, and bottle the chutney.

CIDER is an ancient drink, although exactly how ancient is a matter for argument. It has certainly been made for over 1000 years, and it is possible that the Romans were the first to introduce sweet apples, suitable for cider-making, into Britain. By the 17th century, when the British cider apples were classified by the first Viscount Scudamore, more than 300 varieties were being grown, with splendid names like Handsome Maud's, Slack-my-Girdle, and Skryme's Kerne. Cidermaking had become a traditional cottage industry in the west of England, and in the 19th century it was not uncommon for farm laborers to get part of their wages in cider, just as the Scottish farm workers got part of theirs in oatmeal. The West Country colonists also took their knowledge of cidermaking to America, and cider was the usual drink of the early settlers (with the applejack they learned to distill from it).

In the old days, cider varied enormously from place to place and from year to year, because of the wild yeasts which made fermentation an uncertain process. At the end of the 19th century, the isolation of good yeasts made reliable cidermaking possible on a bulk scale. Today, the best cider is made from blends of cider apples, which give a fine balance between astringency, acidity, and sugar, but cheap, run-of-the-mill ciders are sweet and uninteresting.

In making cider, the apples are milled to a pulp and the juice pressed out of them. It is fermented in barrels or, commercially, in large tanks, in the same way that grape juice is fermented in a winery. The residue is used as a source of *pectin. What remains after that goes into animal foodstuffs. Cider can vary between a fine dry drink of champagnelike quality, to a sweet, child's drink, or from something smooth to a rough farm cider, suitable for scaling a boiler. "Old Scrumpy" will still dissolve rats, as it was said to in the past (and as my father's cider used to do), although, as PR men are quick to point out, this no longer happens in the factories.

Obviously, the type and quality of cider is of great importance if one is cooking with it. Recipes for using cider come from all the American apple states, as well as from Normandy and the west of England. Northern Spain, in the main, produces sweet cider and does not seem to use it much in cooking. Opinions are sharply divided as to the merits of cider in meat and fish dishes, where it has often been advocated merely as a cheap substitute for wine. French chefs, who, like most good cooks, are apt to have definite opinions, do not look on it as a particularly notable ingredient unless they are Norman—you have to make up your own mind. The dishes in the classic cuisine which use cider are all Norman; they include *tripe à la mode de Caen* and *l'oie en daube à la Normande* (goose cooked slowly in a closed pot with onion, celery, leek, carrot, apples and cider). They usually contain Calvados (which is to Normans what applejack is to Americans). Indeed, Calvados is a more frequent cooking ingredient than cider.

PORK CHOPS IN CIDER

Score 4 pork chops on one side and ease them away from the bone. Slit the fat diagonally in several places on the outside to prevent the chop from curling up when it is cooking. Chop 2 tablespoons of fresh herbs and use them to fill the slits on top of the meat. Crush 8 juniper berries and place them in the meat, two to a chop. Marinate the chops in 1 cup (300 ml) of cider for an hour. Remove the chops and season them with salt and pepper on the side opposite from the herbs. Heat the broiler to the maximum heat and broil the chops in a pan for about 2 minutes on each side. Turn down the heat to 350°F (180°C) and, after about 10 minutes, drain off the excess fat. Add the marinade and cook for a further 5 minutes or until no pink shows in the chops. Serve the chops garnished with 1 tablespoon each of chopped capers and gherkins.

CIDER CAKE

Heat the oven to 350°F (180°C). Grease and line a 7-in. (17-cm) cake pan. Grate the peel of an orange and squeeze it. Make up the juice to 1 cup (300 ml) with sweet cider. Cream ½ cup (100 g) of butter and ¾ cup (175 g) of sugar with the orange rind until the mixture is light and fluffy. Beat in 2 eggs, one at a time. Sift 8 oz (225 g) of flour with ½ teaspoon each of powdered cinnamon and allspice; stir into the butter mixture alternately with the cider, beating until smooth after each addition. Turn the batter into the pan. Bake for about 1 hour, or until the cake feels firm to the touch and a warmed skewer inserted into the center comes out clean. Leave the cake to cool for 10 minutes, then turn it out. Serve it with apple purée and whipped cream.

[*Cider*—French: *cidre;* German: *Apfelwein;* Italian: *sidro;* Spanish: *sidra*]

CILANTRO. *See* coriander.

CINNAMON and cassia. Cinnamon, which many know only as a powdered spice, is the dried bark of a tree (*Cinnamomum zeylanicum*), a native of Ceylon and adjacent parts of South India. When cinnamon trees are 2–3 years old, cutting begins. The bark is stripped off and flattened; after the corky outside is planed away, it is ready to be dried. It rolls up into a scroll and is known as a quill. Several quills are usually packed together, one inside the other.

CINNAMON

In the related cassia (*C. cassia*), the bark is thicker; it is not usually planed clean on the outside or packed quill inside quill. Cassia is rather more pungent than true cinnamon and has a less delicate taste. In many countries, the two are sold as one, but in others this is now not allowed, although much confusion remains.

Cinnamon is one of the most important spices; it is very common in sweet dishes, for which it is best bought ground (in small quantities, since ground cinnamon quickly loses its aroma and becomes stale). In any case, it is difficult to grind to atomic fineness at home. In savory meat dishes—and there are many in which cinnamon is used, especially in mutton dishes influenced by the cooking of the Middle East—the spice can be added in whole pieces or ground in a simple coffee mill (which is kept for grinding spices). Like all spices, it keeps its flavor best when whole. However, cinnamon sticks are thin and inclined to break up into small splinters, which are a nuisance in food. This is one reason for using cassia, which breaks up less easily, in pilafs. In Indian dishes, cassia is also more correct, though cinnamon is better for sweet dishes. The powerfully antiseptic essential oils in cinnamon help to preserve food. The leaves of the cassia, under their Indian name of *tej pata*, are also used in Indian cooking.

[*Cinnamon*—French: *cannelle;* German: *Zimt;* Italian: *cannella;* Spanish: *canela.* *Cassia*—French: *casse;* German: *Kassie;* Italian: *cassia;* Spanish: *casia*]

CITRIC ACID. A fairly weak organic acid which occurs particularly in the juice of lemons and other citrus fruits as well as in many other fruits, in wine, and even in cheese. One of the few acids used in the kitchen in pure, crystalline form, it is included in recipes for homemade soft drinks and in yeast nutrients for homemade wine. It is a useful stand-by souring agent, can be made to do in place of lemon juice, and is perhaps preferable to bottled lemon juice, which sometimes has an unpleasant flavor. Commercially, it is made by a fermentation involving citric-acid-producing organisms. Citric acid has antioxidant properties and, in dilute solution, will prevent cut vegetable surfaces from browning. It is also preservative, but less so than the acetic acid of vinegar.

[*Citric acid*—French: *acide citrique;* German: *Zitronensäure;* Italian: *acido citrato;* Spanish: *ácido cítrico*]

CITRON. A citrus fruit which looks like a large, warty lemon with very thick peel. Citrons can sometimes be found on sale in Italy. The citron was the first citrus fruit to reach Europe (it probably originated in India), and the ancient Greeks found citrons growing in the land of the Medes and Persians (hence its botanical name, *Citrus medica*). It was later cultivated in the famous Hanging Gardens of Babylon and used to perfume toilet waters.

The main use for citron in the kitchen is as a candied peel. It has a resinous taste and is thicker than other candied peels. Citron is made into a liqueur in some parts of the Mediterranean—this is called *kitrinos* in the Cyclades and *cédratine* in Corsica.

[*Citron*—French: *citron;* German: *Zitron;* Italian: *cedro;* Spanish: *cidra*]

CITRUS FRUITS are a very closely related group, all coming from shrubs or small trees of the genus *Citrus,* which grows from the tropics to warm but temperate regions such as southern Europe. They are all rich in vitamin C. Their sweetness or sourness depends on the balance between the sugars and fruit acids, which together form 80–90% of the solid matter that is dissolved in the juice. The main sweet species are the sweet *orange (*C. sinensis*), and tangerine or mandarin (*C. reticulata*). The *grapefruit (*C. paradisi*), Seville *orange (*C. aurantium*), *lemon (*C. limon*), and *lime (*C. aurantifolia*) range from less sweet to definitely acid. Other species are the *citron (*C. medica*), *shaddock (*C. grandis*), and papeda (*C. hystrix*). The bergamot (*C. bergamia*) is used mainly in perfumery—its skin, like that of other citrus fruits, contains aromatic essential oils. A related genus, *Fortunella,* includes the *kumquats. There are also hybrids (such as tangelos, e.g., the ugli, which are grapefruit X tangerine), varieties and forms which are known in their own right (such as the ortanique, a flattened, thin-skinned sweet orange, which might be a hybrid), and one or two types of uncertain origin, such as the clementine (which could be either tangerine X sweet orange or a variety of tangerine).

CLABBER. Thick, sour milk which has not separated into curds and whey. Clabbering is souring milk until it reaches this point.

CLAM. A term applied to various types of bivalve mollusk. Many people tend to think of clams as American—clam chowder, clam bakes, clam juice, and canned clam broth. "A kind of cockle," says a Victorian cookbook, "to be found on the west coast of Ireland and Scotland, and in Devonshire and Cornwall, and some parts of Wales. Though they figure largely in American cookery they are not much used in England." Clam is an old English word for a fetter, clamped to arms and wrists, and then for any gripping tool. Hence clamshell, a shell that grips tight. It is a useful portmanteau word without exact definition: almost any bivalve may be called a clam if it does not have a special name of its own.

There are said to be over 20,000 species of bivalve in the world, all of them probably edible, although the number of clam species that are commonly eaten is probably no more than 50. They range in size up to the giant clams of tropical reefs, which have shells weighing 550 lb (250 Kg) and 22 lb (10 Kg) of meat inside, enough to feed a large party. Clams vary greatly in flavor and toughness. Alexis Soyer is said to have claimed that they were superior in flavor to oysters, and that clams the same size as oysters should be eaten raw, larger ones cooked. Such sweeping statements without reference to species or locality are valueless, but the *praire* of Brittany and Normandy is indeed very fine.

The recognition of unknown clams in strange markets is for shell collectors, hardly for cooks. About 10 years ago, after being bewildered by fish markets in Normandy, Italy, and Spain, all within the space of two months, I decided to start buying and identifying samples of clams in markets wherever I went. Very soon, I concluded that there are so many local differences, so many sizes, so many local names, and even so many scientific names given to the same species that clam collecting, taken seriously, would become a lifetime hobby. Nevertheless, there are certain basic facts about clams that the consumer needs to know thoroughly.

Clams very often live buried in sand or mud. Some are dug or plowed up on beaches near the low-tide mark, while others have to be dredged from under the water. Clams feed and breathe by drawing a current of water through their bodies; they filter food particles out of the stream of water. It is important to understand this, because it explains why clams that have grown in dirty places can be infected with harmful organisms—disease germs like typhoid or even poisonous plankton (*see* poisoning). It also explains why clams will clean themselves of grit if they are left in clear water. Commercially dredged or farmed clams are kept for some days in tanks of clear sea water under ultraviolet light (which kills bacteria but not plankton) and are therefore sand-free and safe to eat.

Clams bought in markets from local fishermen need to be cleaned. First they should be well scrubbed and picked over for dead or damaged specimens—dead ones will gape open. Then they should be put, not too many together, in a wide shallow basin filled with clean sea water (if you are near the sea) and kept quietly in a cool place for a couple of days *with frequent changes of sea water*—if the clams die from lack of oxygen in the water, it will be worse than not bothering to wash them. If you are not near the sea, the clams should be put into cold water in which has been dissolved about ½ cup (100 g) of salt (preferably sea salt) per 7 pt (4 lt) of water. Clams will clean themselves in this, at least partially, if left quietly for 2–3 hours. They will live up to a week when kept cool and packed in seaweed.

Clams are eaten either cooked or raw. If cooked, they can be opened by heat, like mussels. Many types may benefit by being opened by hand before cooking, which should be short or the flesh will toughen. A clam that may take some time to steam open can be cooked in a minute under the grill if it has already been opened.

Clams are often more difficult to open raw than oysters. The best implement for the purpose is a short, thin-bladed, double-edged stainless knife. Insert it between the shells, or drive the point in near the hinge, depending on the type of clam. Move the knife close to the uppermost shell, being careful not to puncture the animal's body, and cut the two muscles—one at each end—which hold the valves together. Then pull the top shell off and free the animal from the bottom shell by cutting underneath it. If the clam is held flat, the juice may be preserved—or the job can be done over a bowl. As when opening oysters, you should wear some protection on the hand holding the clam; otherwise, if the knife slips, there can be blood all over the kitchen. Some advocate putting clams in the freezer for a few hours before opening. After a short thawing, the clams are in no condition to resist the cook's designs upon them. The treatment does not alter their quality.

With canning and freezing, clams now come from all over the world. They can be put into a freezer without any preparation other than cleaning and still eaten raw for up to two months afterward. If kept longer, they are good only for cooking.

In many cases, the commercial exploitation of clam beds by mechanical methods of digging (which are overefficient) have made formerly plentiful clams come to the verge of extinction. A good example is the New Zealand *toheroa*, which makes one of the world's most delicious soups. Another now-scarce clam is the Pismo clam of California. In recent years, however, the farming of clams has gained momentum, and fine clams are now cultivated where they formerly did not exist. France is a pioneer in this business. *Palourdes* have long been tended near the estuary of the Loire, and American hard-shell clams were introduced into the mouth of the Charente at the time of World War I. Britons can feel pleased that since the 1940s the same type of clam (probably brought from America on liners using Southampton) has established itself in the Solent, in waters warmed by the coolers of the Fawley petroleum refinery. In Spain, a common snack is the *almeja*. These are much canned in northern Spain, and it is not always easy to know what kind you are eating, since *almeja* seems to cover many species. So also does the Italian word *vongola*. *Spaghetti alla vongole* must be one of the most internationally known Italian dishes. Clams of all kinds are particularly fished and eaten around Naples and Venice.

In North America, clams are a popular

food on both coasts; they are eagerly sought after both fresh and canned. In times past, they were a favorite food of the Indians, not only around the coasts but also inland, where various fresh-water clams were eaten. Notable among the many American clams are:

Hard-shell clam (*Mercenaria mercenaria*). Alternatively, round-shell clam, quahaug, or quahog (from the Narragansett Indian name), this clam is indigenous to the East Coast and is found in shallow estuarine waters. When large (about 4½ in./11 cm), these clams are known as chowder clams, when smaller (about 3 in./7½ cm) as cherrystones, and when smaller still (about 2½ in./6 cm) as littlenecks; the last two are generally eaten raw.

Soft-shell clam (*Mya arenaria*). Alternatively, long-shell clam, soft clam, oval clam, or sand gaper, this is another East Coast clam, but occurs on both sides of the Atlantic and was introduced accidentally to the West Coast in the 19th century, probably with oysters. It lives in sandy mud and has a fragile shell, from which it gets its name. This is the best clam for steaming—it is sometimes called steamer clam. It cooks in about 15 minutes.

Pismo clam (*Tivela stultorum*). The Pismo clam is a large (1 lb./450 g) species of hard-shell that lives in the surf off southern California. It was once so ruthlessly harvested that it is now becoming rare, and drastic conservation measures are enforced to protect this prized clam.

Eastern surf clam or **skimmer** (*Spisula solidissima*). A large (7 in./18 cm) clam with a smooth, tan-colored, oval shell. Found from Nova Scotia to South Carolina, this is usually used in commercial clam chowders.

Geoduck (*Panope generosa*). The largest American clam, the West Coast geoduck grows to about 5 lb (2½ Kg). Buried in the sand, it has a large siphon to the surface from which it expels water high in the air,

thus revealing its presence to clammers. It is eaten as cutlets or, with its siphon, in chowders.

Horse clam, gaper, or **otter shell** (*Schizothaerus nuttalli*). Rivaling the geoduck in size, the horse clam also has similar habits. Its range is from Alaska to San Diego. A bonus of this clam is that in its mantle are freeloading pea crabs that can be sautéed or deep-fried like soft-shell crabs.

Butter clam, Washington clam, or **money clam** (*Saxidomus giganteus*). Found from Alaska to southern California, this plump little clam is called money clam because its shells were used as a medium of exchange by California Indians. It is delicious raw.

Angelwing (*Cyrtopleura costata*). This member of the boring clam family (Pholadidae), unlike other clams that dwell in soft sand and mud, resides in very hard clay or even soft rock. It has a beautiful winglike shell and yellowish flesh that can be cooked like any other clam. It occurs from Massachusetts to Central America and is a favorite shellfish around the West Indies.

Razor shell. These clams, distributed throughout the world, are shaped like an old-fashioned cutthroat razor, either straight or slightly curved. Their shells are nearly transparent and the meat is cream-colored. On the East Coast they include the Atlantic razor clam (*Ensis directus*) and the stout razor (*Tagelus gibbus*), called the jackknife on the Pacific Coast. West Coast razors (*Siliqua patula* and *S. lucida*) are shorter and broader than the eastern razor and have rounded ends. These shellfish lie buried in sand in a vertical position with their siphons—inhalant and exhalant—at the top. In many cases, they live just at or below the low-tide mark and are best fished at low spring tides. An indication is a keyhole-shaped hole in the sand, from which occasional squirts of water are ejected. Razor clams are regarded as good eating, although I find them rather strong-tasting. Some people eat them raw—there is no problem in opening them, since they cannot close tightly—and they are also made into soup or included with other shellfish. Intrepid Italians can be observed catching and eating them raw on Adriatic beaches, notably the Lido in Venice.

In addition to the razor clam, the following are among the best-known clams in Europe.

Palourde (*Venerupis decussata*). French: *palourde;* Italian: *vongola nera* or *vongola verace;* Spanish: *almeja. Palourdes* are also often called *vongole napoletane* (Neapolitan). This is the largest of the European "gastronomic" clams, reaching 3 in. (8 cm), and one of the best. Found in both the Atlantic and the Mediterranean, it is cultivated in the sandy muds north and south of the Loire estuary and is common in Brittany. *Palourdes* are also fished off the Gulf Stream-warmed coasts of Southern Ireland (where they are called *ruacan* or *kirkeen*) and exported to France. In Britain, they are found only locally in warm waters. *Palourdes* are the classic clams for *spaghetti con vongole,* the sauce for which is made from small ones. These clams have tender meat and a fine flavor. They are eaten raw or cooked. Raw ones can have a bitter aftertaste, but they have many devotees. They are also superb stuffed with garlic butter, or with an herb butter containing shallots, tarragon, and parsley.

Clovisse (*Venerupis geographica*, gray, and *V. aurea*, yellow). French: *clovisse* and *clovisse jaune:* Italian: *vongola grigia* and *vongola gialla;* Spanish: *amarguela* and *margarita.* These two very similar species of clam are mainly from the Mediterranean (they are scarce in the Atlantic and not so tasty) and are commonly eaten in the South of France. They are fished all the year, but are best in summer and autumn when they are larger and fatter. These are common types of *vongole* used in Italy, but considered inferior to the *vongola nera,* and are usually referred to as *vongola commune.*

Praire (*Venus verrucosa*). Warty venus. French: *praire;* Italian: *tartufo di mare* (sea truffle); Spanish: *verigüeto.* This clam has a very heavy concentrically ridged shell about 2 in. (5 cm) wide. It occurs in both the Mediterranean and the Atlantic (e.g., Brittany coasts); it is common in Britain, though neglected as a food and with no popular English name. Elsewhere *praires* are regarded as delicious—usually eaten raw—and one of the more expensive bivalves; they are also cooked, with garlic butter and in other ways.

Wedge shell (*Donax trunculus*). French: *olive;* Italian: *tellina;* Spanish: *coquina.* This bivalve is small, 1¼–1½ in. (3–4 cm), and wedge-shaped. It is tender, and the taste is fine and sweet. In Italy, it ranks with the *vongola nera,* and many Italians consider it the very finest for making soup, or to go into sauces for spaghetti and risotto. It is also delicious eaten raw, but, being so small, can only be a *passa tempo,* like sunflower or melon seeds. *Telline* are available all year round in Mediterranean countries.

[*Clam*—French: *palourde;* German: *essbare Muschel;* Italian: *vongola verace;* Spanish: *almeja, telina*]

CLARIFYING and **CLEARING.** Clarifying, as applied to fats rendered from meat or chicken, consists of washing out the impurities. This can be done by boiling the fat for a few minutes with a largish volume of water, pouring it off the top into a container, letting it cool, refrigerating it until solid, then removing and cleaning the underside of the fat. If the fat is still not clear enough, repeat the operation. There are also gadgets which enable liquid fat or oil to be separated from water. Clarifying, as applied to butter or margarine, consists of heating the butter (preferably unsalted) or margarine until the solids come down as a sediment which can be strained out with cheesecloth. Indian clarified butter, *ghee,* is cooked over a low heat for longer until it gets a special nutty taste.

Clarifying is also used synonymously with

clearing when applied to things like wine and aspic. Two techniques are used. In the first, a substance is added which dissolves or changes the substance causing the cloudiness. This is done with wine when an enzyme, a pectinase, is added to remove cloudiness caused by pectin. The second, and more usual, technique is to add something which will bring down the offending cloud to the bottom of the vessel. With wine, this is known as fining. In the kitchen, we are mostly concerned with clearing *stocks.

CLARY. A labiate herb (*Salvia sclarea*), native to southern Europe and closely related to common sage. As a culinary herb, it was more used in the past than today; it is bitter and aromatic, and can be used fresh or dried in omelets, as a potherb, or for any other purpose if you like it.

CLEARING. *See* clarifying.

CLEMENTINE. *See* orange.

CLOTTED CREAM, Devonshire cream, or **Cornish cream.** This delicious thick cream, with its characteristic "boiled-milk" taste, was made from the rich milk of Devon cows on lush pastures and was at one time used on farms in southwest England as others use butter. Clotted cream is about 60% fat—the legal minimum is 55%. It was traditionally made in special, shallow, glazed earthenware pans holding about 2 gallons (9 lt) of milk. The milk was strained into these pans while still warm from the cow. Sometimes a little water was added to help separate the cream, and the pans were then put into a cool dairy, where the cream would rise. After this, the pans were moved very carefully (so as not to disturb the cream) onto the back of the stove, or put over hot water, to slowly raise the temperature to 176–185°F (80–85°C). The cream was ready when a ring the size of the base of the pan appeared on the surface. (For amateurs it is best to heat the pan over hot water; if the heating is done too quickly, the cream

becomes greasy and lacks the special, delicious taste.) The pan was then cooled quickly and the cream removed. Naturally, the yield of clotted cream would depend on the richness of the milk. Jersey milk gave more than would the now common Friesian milk. Clotted cream made from machine-separated milk lacks some of the fine flavor but is still good with raspberry jam and warm bread.

CLOVES. With black pepper, cinnamon, and nutmeg, cloves rank as one of the world's most important spices. Cloves are native to the "Spice Islands" of Southeast

CLOVE

Asia (and were traded into Europe even in Roman times), but in the 18th century, plantations were established in many other tropical countries, notably Zanzibar (now the most important producer), Madagascar, and the West Indies. The tall evergreen clove trees (*Eugenia aromatica*) flourish only near the sea. Cloves are the flower buds, picked when they are pink and spread out to dry on mats. They contain an essential oil (eugenol) which is powerfully antiseptic and has a preservative action.

Cloves are well known in pickle spice, hot bottled sauces, and chutneys, and are often stuck into an onion to flavor sauces or other dishes. They go into apple pie, mixed spice, and the caramelized brown-sugar glazing for ham and pork. A little less well known is the clove in beef stock, or in a stew, where it gives a richness without being identified. Used wrongly, clove flavor is crude—a reminder of the dentist (who may use clove oil as a penetrating antiseptic). It should be used with care (and that may mean using no more than a tiny crumble of the clove head) so that it becomes part of the background. As a flavoring, cloves are best when kept below the level of recognition.

The best cloves are large and difficult to break. When powdered cloves are needed, it is best to grind them yourself. Disposable grinders filled with whole cloves are now available for this purpose.

[Clove—French: clou de girofle; German: Nelke; Italian: chiòdo di garofano; Spanish: clavo]

COATING. Food to be fried, broiled, or roasted can be coated with egg and bread crumbs, batter, flour, oatmeal, egg white and so on. There are two important considerations whatever coating is used: that it should stick to the food being coated, and that it should not be thick and stodgy. Reasons for stodginess include having too thick a batter, pressing the bread crumbs onto the egg instead of shaking them off, or using fine toasted bread crumbs instead of coarser untoasted ones. As to adhesion, if food is wet and the least bit slimy, the egg will not make a sufficiently intimate contact for it to stick. The surface must be lightly floured first. Egg should be beaten a little and may be thinned with a little milk or water so that it does not form too thick a layer. The very lightest batter coating is made on the food, not separately in a bowl. For instance, food may be simply dipped in flour or cornstarch and then in egg diluted with milk, or in white of egg diluted with a very little water. After coating, the food should be quickly cooked and not be left to go soggy. If the coating is to keep fat from soaking into the preparation, then a quick dip into egg white is often sufficient. An interesting batter for coating is the Indian one made simply of water and *besan flour with salt and some spices. The Chinese and Japanese usually make batter of egg and cornstarch.

[Coating—French: enduire; German: bestreichen; Italian: intonacare; Spanish: cubrir]

COB. See hazelnut.

COCA. The chewing of coca leaves, which contain the alkaloid cocaine, is traditional in the Andes and nearby parts of the Amazon basin, where the plant (Erythroxylon coca and other species) grows wild. Coca chewing was common among the ancient Incas, and Pizarro found it in general use in 1553. The effect of cocaine is highly stimulating (as we know from Sherlock Holmes), and it enables its users to travel or to work for long periods without food. Habitual coca chewers can become addicts and run the risk of sickness, even death, from anorexia, since the drug destroys the appetite for food. Coca leaves are not used outside the tropical areas where the plant can be grown—after picking, the drug is rapidly lost. As a masticatory, like *betel leaves, coca leaves are chewed with lime or wood ash. Coca is mentioned here in case it might be confused with the *cola nut, which is used in soft drinks.

COCHINEAL. See kermes.

COCKLES. Heart-shaped bivalves with thickly ribbed shells. In some species, the ribs are ornamented with knobs or spines. Several species of cockle, including the common cockle, Cerastoderma edule, and Acanthocardia aculeata (spiny), A. echinata (prickly), and A. tuberculata (tuberculate), are found commonly around the coasts of Britain and Europe. In the U.S., the term "cockle" may be loosely applied to any number of clams as well as species of Cardium, "heart shells," the genus that contains the original cockle. The giant Atlantic cockle (Dinocardium robustum), one of the largest, finest cockles in the world, is found from Cape Hatteras to Mexico. It has a strong but good flavor. Among the true cockles on the West Coast is the basket cockle (*Clinococardium nuttalli*), which tastes like clams.

Cockles were an important food in the past; witness the following written over 100 years ago. "A crowd of the more youthful description of peasantry are collected every spring tide to gather Cockles on the sands by daylight when the tide overruns. The quantities of these shellfish thus procured would almost exceed belief; and I have frequently seen more than would load a donkey collected in one tide by the children of a single cabin. They form a valuable and wholesome addition to the limited variety that the Irish peasant boasts at his humble board; and afford children, too young for other tasks, a safe and useful employment." One wishes that the beaches were as clean now as in those days.

All cockles live buried in sand, usually around low-tide mark. They are therefore liable to be gritty unless allowed to clean themselves for several hours in clear sea water, or water with some salt (7 pt/4 lt per 4 oz/100 g) added. First wash them well in several waters and scrub each one with a hard brush. Throw out any that are broken or do not close tightly when handled. Cockles are often eaten raw or roasted on a stove top until they open; they are popularly seasoned with pepper and vinegar, and accompanied by buttered brown bread. They may be opened like mussels, by putting them in a saucepan with a dash of water and, with the lid on tight, heating and shaking the pan. As soon as they open, they are done. Like other shellfish, overcooking will make them tough. Cockles are sometimes covered with sauce or cooked in more elaborate ways. They are also available canned.

[*Cockle*—French: *coque;* German: *Herzmuschel;* Italian: *cuore edule, cocciola;* Spanish: *berberecho*]

COCOA. The cocoa bean, from which *★chocolate is made, naturally contains an unpalatable amount of fat. In Holland, Conrad van Houten, following his early work in pressing out part of this fat to make an improved drinking chocolate (1828), went on to treat drinking chocolate with an alkali which darkened it and destroyed part of the flavor, but saponified the fats, leaving traces of soap. This is cocoa. It blends more easily with milk but has not the fine taste of a good drinking chocolate.

[*Cocoa*—French: *cacao;* German: *Kakao;* Italian: *cacao;* Spanish: *cacao*]

COCONUT palms (*Cocos nucifera*) lean out over tropical beaches in both the Old and the New Worlds, and nobody knows whether they got there through the nuts being carried on ocean currents or by the agency of man. Indeed, it is not absolutely certain that Southeast Asia was the coconut's original home, although it probably was. Certainly it is in parts of southern Asia that it is most important in cooking. Coconuts do not only grow on the coast; in many places, there are plantations hundreds of miles inland, but the palms prefer sandy soil. There are many cultivated varieties.

Coconut juice. Unhusked green nuts are opened by cutting off the top with a sharp machete or panga, and the juice, which is always cool and pure, is drunk straight out of the nut. This is a welcome and life-saving drink for travelers in the tropics. It should not be confused with the heavy, sweet liquid (milk or cream) that is contained in ripe coconuts.

Unripe or **green nuts.** The flesh of unripe coconuts is gelatinous and may be scraped off the inside of the nut after you have drunk the juice. There are a few recipes for its use in puddings.

Toddy. The coconut palm, like several other species of palm, is often tapped for its juice. The flowering shoots are cut off and earthenware pots are hung to catch the sap, which flows copiously. In the hot tropical sun, sap caught during the day has usually fermented by the evening. That caught during the night may have only just started to turn. Unfermented juice is a pleasant drink, much liked by teetotal Hindus. During prohibition in India, it became common to put preservatives in the catching pots to prevent natural fermentation. Drinking toddy was illegal. In fact, toddy is usually a crude, sour drink and leaves a very unpleasant smell on the breath. It is used sometimes instead of brewer's yeast in Indian cooking, and gives a distinctive and unusual taste to the South Indian rice preparations leavened with it.

Palm sugar is made by boiling down the juice (*see* sugar).

Choosing coconuts. A good coconut is heavy, and you should be able to hear the juice when the nut is shaken. If the nut has dried out or leaked, it may be bad. It is also important that the eyes be dry and not smell moldy, since they are the weak point in an otherwise impervious shell and the point of entry for spoilage organisms. In particular, beware of nuts with fiber still covering the eyes. It may hide the mold.

Opening the nuts. Pierce two of the eyes with a skewer. Drain out the liquid into a glass. Now hold the nut horizontally in both hands and bang it down hard on one of its three ridges against a stone or a concrete floor. It should split into two halves. If you want to free the kernel, after draining and before splitting put the nut in a hot (400°F/ 200°C) oven for 20 minutes and then bang it all over.

Shredding the nut. In countries where coconut is much used in cooking, devices are available for scraping shreds out of the shell. For occasional needs, it is enough to remove the flesh, pare off the thin brown skin, and grate or liquidize the flesh. A medium nut gives 3–4 cups of grated coconut.

Keeping nut pieces fresh. Put the nut pieces in the liquid you drained from the nut and keep in the refrigerator. After all, it is this liquid that keeps the nut fresh until you open it.

Desiccated coconut. Modern desiccated coconut is a high-quality product made by shredding the coconut and drying it in a vacuum at 158°F (70°C) for an hour. The result has none of the slight rancidity of the sun-dried nut. It is sold in flakes of varying fineness. It can be more finely ground by giving it a whirl in a coffee grinder. Although it lacks some of the delicate flavor of the fresh nut, desiccated coconut commends itself for being cheap and easy to use (18 oz or 500 g roughly equal 3 nuts).

Coconut milk and **coconut cream.** Not to be confused with the juice of the nuts. It is necessary for many Indian and Southeast Asian dishes. Boiling water is poured over grated (or desiccated) coconut and left to cool somewhat before the milk is squeezed out with the hands or in a cloth. A thinner milk is made by pouring a second lot of boiling water over the partly spent nut shreds. For thick milk, pour 2 cups of boiling water over 1 cup of shredded nut. Half that amount of water makes thick cream (but naturally it depends on the size and quality of the nut). It is best to err in making it thick and thinning it down later with water or second-pressing thin milk. A somewhat improved yield can be obtained by using a blender. "Cream of coconut" and "coconut cream" are names given to several products, sold in cakes or frozen, which may be used to make coconut milk. Both coconut milk and coconut cream are also canned. Such products should never be used if they taste rancid.

FISH MOLEE

Molees are essentially dishes from the coconut-growing areas of India, but they are enjoyed everywhere in that country. Heat a little cooking oil in a pan and add to it in turn 1 large chopped onion, 4 cloves of chopped garlic, 3–4 chopped green chilies, and a 1-in. (2.5-cm) piece of fresh ginger, chopped. The mixture should not be allowed to brown but should cook gently until the onion is soft. Allow the pan to cool slightly to avoid burning the spices which are now added: 1 teaspoon of ground turmeric, 1 pinch of red chili powder (to taste), 4 cloves, 4 cardamoms, and a 1-in. (2.5-cm) cinnamon stick. Fry for 30 seconds, mixing the turmeric into the oil, then add, little by little, 2–3 cups of thick coconut milk (from 1 grated coconut), letting it amalgamate into a sauce. Cook this for a further 15 minutes uncovered, without letting it boil. Put in the fish fillets and shake the pan to cover them with the sauce. Continue to cook without boiling until the fish is ready. (Add some thin coconut milk if the sauce becomes too dry.) Adjust the salt and add a few drops of lemon juice if it is needed. Sprinkle with chopped coriander leaves, if you have them, and serve with rice.

Coconut oil. This is a usual cooking fat in parts of South India, Ceylon, Malaysia, and elsewhere in coconut areas, although there has been a tendency to replace it with hydrogenated vegetable cooking fats. Some people find food cooked with coconut oil difficult to digest. In South India, the oil was made at home by grating the kernel, soaking it in water, and then boiling it until the oil floated to the surface. The oil was then skimmed off and strained. This oil tastes of fresh coconut. Villages had their *chekku* or oil press.

Other coconut products. Coconut syrup is a product made by evaporating expressed coconut juices with invert sugar. Coconut honey is a thicker, darker product made in a similar way but with longer cooking. These and other coconut products are modern commercial ingredients to be judged on their individual merits.

[*Coconut*—French: *noix de coco;* German: *Kokosnuss;* Italian: *noce di cocco;* Spanish: *nuez de coco*]

COD. The codfish and its family (Gandidae) are particularly important to the countries bordering on the North Atlantic, cod having been one of the major food fishes for centuries. The survival of colonial America was much dependent on these abundant fish. First caught with lines and later with trawls, cod had great value because it could be salted and dried, and so gave significance to distant fishing grounds, such as the Grand Banks, which would not have been so valuable for perishable fish. (*See* salt cod.)

Atlantic codfish (*Gadus morhua*) are perhaps the world's greatest commercial fish. They are caught from the New England coast north to Newfoundland. They average under 10 lb (4½ Kg) but can be much larger. The Pacific cod (*G. macrocephalus*) is almost identical. Cod have tender white flesh. When young, they are marketed as scrod.

Haddock (*Melanogrammus aeglefinus*) is similar to cod but is usually smaller, 16–24 in. (40–60 cm), and has a black lateral line rather than a white one like cod. Its range is on both sides of the Atlantic, from Cape Hatteras to Newfoundland. Haddock is an important U.S. commercial fish—especially sold as frozen fillets—but the catch has been seriously depleted by heavy foreign fishing off the U.S. coast. Fresh haddock is as delicious as cod, and it is smoked to make that great delicacy *finnan haddock.

Hake (*Merluccius merluccius*), which grows up to 39 in. (1 m) long, is generally regarded as the best of the cod family in Europe, although there are others, like the silver hake, *M. bilinearis* (commonly marketed as whiting), on the northern coasts of America, which are good or better. On the Pacific coast the most plentiful hake is *M. productus*. The hake is the easiest of the cod family to bone. It is excellent poached whole or used for *seviche;* the head is good for soup.

Pollock (*Pollachius virens*) spans the Atlantic in northern waters and is known by a great many vernacular names, including saithe, coalfish, coley, Boston bluefish, and green cod. Young pollock, freshly caught, is excellent, but most people are likely to encounter it as frozen fillets. The flesh is a bit darker than a cod's when raw but quite white when cooked. The Germans and

Danes salt and smoke pollock; it resembles smoked salmon.

Whiting (*Merlangus merlangus*) is not found in U.S. waters (although silver hake is called whiting). It ranges from Norway to the Mediterranean and is very common in the North Sea. Whiting are small fish, rarely over 12 in. (30 cm) long and at most 4½ lb (2 Kg) in weight. The flesh is rather dry but is considered wholesome and digestible. The fish has a black mark on its side but no barbel, which distinguishes it from the haddock. This is the fish which always used to be served with its tail bent around in a loop and held in its mouth. Whitings are smoked, as butterfly fillets, and like small haddocks are sold as cutlets.

Other European species of the cod family that are less sought as table fare are the pollack or lythe (*Gadus pollachius*), a large, watery fish; the ling (*Molva molva*), known as lutfisk and popular in Sweden, also smoked; and the pouting or bib (*Gadus luscus*), which resembles haddock. The burbot (*Lota lota*), a freshwater member of the cod family, is found in deep, cold lakes and streams in the northern U.S., Canada, and Alaska. It is fine eating, and burbot-liver oil is one of the most valuable sources of vitamin A.

[*Cod*—French: *morue, cabillaud;* German: *Kabeljau, Dorsch;* Italian: *merluzzo;* Spanish: *bacalao, abadejo. Haddock*—French: *églefin, aiglefin;* German: *Schellfisch;* Spanish: *eglefizo. Hake*—French: *merluche, merlu;* German: *Hechtdorsch, Seehecht;* Italian: *nasello, merluzzo;* Spanish: *merluza. Pollock*—French: *lieu noir;* German: *Kohler, Seelachs;* Spanish: *gado. Whiting*—French: *merlan;* German: *Weissfisch, Wittling;* Italian: *merlano;* Spanish: *plegonero, merlan*]

COFFEE probably came first from Ethiopia, where it is still to be seen growing in a semiwild state, although it is possible that it originated in the mountains of the Yemen on the ·other side of the Red Sea. In the 16th century, it was brought up the Red Sea to Egypt, and coffeehouses began to open in London and Paris in 1650. The plants were introduced to both the East and the West Indies, and reached Brazil in 1727. Of the many different species of *Coffea,* the most important is still the original one to be cultivated, *C. arabica.* A second species, the prolific *C. canephora,* produces "robusta" coffee, which is cheaper and used for blending.

Coffee plants are small trees, but they are cultivated as bushes. Their fruits, called cherries, grow in clusters and, when ripe, are red and the size of a cherry. Each cherry normally contains two "beans," flat sides together, in a parchmentlike skin. (The few varieties with a single rounded berry give peaberry coffee, which roasts more evenly.) The flesh of the beans is sweet but without value and is removed by stacking the beans until they begin to rot (ferment is the usual word), then by washing it off with water. The seeds are separated, cleaned, dried, and graded. Fresh, unroasted beans are anything from gray-green to yellow-brown and have no trace of coffee flavor.

Coffee varies enormously in appearance and in quality. It is very much a field for experts, especially since blending is usual. Few straight coffees are used, because it is rare to find a coffee that is perfectly balanced in flavor, acidity, and strength. Some people make their own blends, but for most of us it is best to leave this to the professionals, who have made a life study of the subject, know the thousands of different types available, and have developed a palate. With the present high price of coffee, it is a costly business to start from scratch.

The roasting which gives the coffee beans their distinctive taste may be light, medium, or dark. Fine coffees rarely, if ever, are heavily roasted, because this would spoil their subtle flavor. Once roasted, coffee beans must be cooled as rapidly as possible: as long as they are hot, they are rapidly losing the most delicious and ethereal essential oils. These oils are continually dissipating, though not so fast, even when the beans are cold. Thus, the sooner the beans are used, the better—anyone who cares about coffee will always look for freshly roasted beans.

A mechanical roaster is not a common item of domestic equipment, and thus beans are generally roasted at home in a pan on the stove. Old Boer farmers in South Africa always insisted that their wives roast the coffee freshly in the mornings, but these days, few people will bother to do that except on special occasions. The coffee beans must be continually but gently turned over in a dry pan; to stop turning them for even a second burns them. Roasting will take some 15 minutes of undivided attention. At the end you may put in a little sugar to melt and coat the beans, thus helping to seal in the flavor, but I find that this gives a caramel taste—which some, I suppose, may like.

Although it may be argued that the imperfections of home roasting are likely to cancel out the advantages of freshness, there can be no question of the superiority of home-ground coffee. It repays the effort overwhelmingly, quite as much as—perhaps even more than—using freshly ground pepper from the mill. Ground coffee deteriorates in flavor noticeably in half an hour. Manufacturers minimize losses by packing ground coffee in a vacuum or an inert gas, but once the can is opened, deterioration begins just as quickly. Small electric grinders are cheap and efficient, so there is really no reason for buying ground coffee.

Each of the many methods of making coffee has its advocates. Those who like strong, bitter espresso like a strong, bitter espresso, and it is useless to argue that other coffees are better. Fine coffees are best made by putting a generous amount of the ground coffee into a warmed earthenware pot and pouring on boiling water. After stirring, then letting the coffee stand for some minutes, you may put a teaspoon of cold water gently over the top to help settle the grains, but filtration is not usually necessary. Also popular are filter methods in which the ground coffee is put in a paper filter in a funnel of some sort which rests on top of the coffee pot. Boiling water is then poured over the coffee and drips through to the pot.

Good coffees are produced in many countries. The famous mocha coffee, originally from Arabia, is very aromatic and, at best, tastes like the smell that wafts down the street from the shop with the roaster. Blue Mountain is another familiar name and is from Jamaica. Fine coffees also come from Central and South America. Coffee from other sources (Kenya, for instance) are continually improving in quality.

Turkish coffee (or Greek coffee, depending on where you are drinking it) is served throughout the Levant. To make it, coffee beans are ground to a powder in a mortar or in a special hand grinder, and the drink is made by boiling the powdered coffee with a little water and sugar in a special, long-handled pot (an *ibrik*). It is boiled up several times to get exactly the right froth on top and is offered in several degrees of sweetness. In Arab countries, coffee is part of the traditional hospitality, and its serving can be almost as much a ritual as the Japanese tea ceremony. Arab coffee pots have a peaked spout into which can be put some vegetable fiber for straining; opened cardamom seeds or even cloves can be used for added flavor.

Instant coffee is popular for its convenience. Flavor varies from brand to brand, but connoisseurs are unlikely to find it delicious, though many now use it as a flavoring in cooking.

Exhaustive medical tests have been made, and nobody has definitively shown that coffee in ordinary amounts is harmful. Excess, especially when coupled with bad eating habits, is another matter. Because coffee is expensive, it is susceptible to adulteration and imitation. *Chicory root, roasted and broken into nibs, is the most common additive, and its use has become so hallowed by tradition that some people prefer blends that contain it.

Coffee substitutes include roasted barley (sometimes malted), which is also used as a cheap additive to "stretch" coffee and produce a less expensive drink, roasted dandelion root (which is something like chicory), and roasted sugar beet. *See* caffeine.

[*Coffee*—French: *café;* German: *Kaffee;* Italian: *caffè;* Spanish: *café*]

COGNAC is a particular type of *brandy made in a legally specified area around the town of Cognac about 60 miles (100 km) north of Bordeaux, but the word is popularly used in many countries as a synonym for brandy. Cognac is distilled in old-fashioned pot stills from a thin, sourish white wine which is made traditionally from the *folle blanche* grape, but today also from other less frost-prone varieties. The wine is undrinkable, but the brandy is superb. After distillation, the cognac is matured for periods of up to 40 years in casks of local oak.

For sale, cognac is almost always blended. A *fine champagne* must contain at least 51% from the central Grande Champagne region of the Cognac area and the remainder from the adjacent Petite Champagne. (In this case, "Champagne" means countryside and has nothing to do with the sparkling wine from near Rheims.) A shorthand, not legally defined but generally accepted, is used for indicating the quality of cognac and the length of time it has been matured in the cask. One star (*) has been matured for at least 3 years, ** at least 4, *** at least 5. Older brandies are denoted by initials starting with VO, very old; then VSO, very superior old (12–17 years in cask); VSOP, very superior old pale (20 years); VVSOP, very, very superior old pale; XO, extra old (30 years). After, at most, 40 years, the quality begins to decline.

In cooking, unless otherwise specified, use a three-star cognac for "brandy" wherever the spirit is to be used cold or sprinkled in toward the end of cooking. A cheaper spirit might be used when it is to be flamed.

COINTREAU. *See* liqueurs and cordials.

COLA NUTS or **kola nuts** are used for chewing because they contain relatively large amounts of *caffeine and other stimulating alkaloids. The tree (*Cola nitida*) is native to the forests of tropical West Africa, but today is grown in many other parts of the tropics. The taste is at first bitter, then sweet, and a simple drink can be made by boiling the powdered nuts in water. Prepared drinks containing cola are today almost, if not quite, universal.

COLE or **coleseed.** *See* rape.

COLLARD (*Brassica oleracea acephala*). One of the favorite forms of cabbage in the southeastern U.S., collard greens—affectionately known as collie greens—have been eaten since Roman times. It is possible that black slaves brought collards to America, and the greens are still popular in Africa; a national dish of Ethiopia is *yegomen kitfo*, collard greens with buttermilk curds. Collards, an outstanding source of vitamins A and C, have large, blue-green, juicy leaves on a sturdy central stem. The plant withstands hot summers, but it is also becoming popular in northern areas because it withstands cold. Collards have a mild, slightly sweet, cabbagelike flavor. They are usually cooked with pork or ham, often with other greens such as *kale. Tender young collard leaves can also be eaten in salads.

COLLOP. A fairly thick slice of meat, but alternatively an egg fried with bacon.

COLORINGS. Most countries have their own lists of approved food colorings and synthetic dyes which are thought by the pundits to be harmless and therefore allowed in foods (*see* additives). Some countries are more cautious than others, and experts do not always agree. Harmful and even carcinogenic substances have, in the past, got through the net, and since nobody can be sure of long-term effects until substances have been used over a period of time, we are no doubt going to find other wolves among the lambs. Having said that, one should also say that there is no *a priori* reason for thinking that synthetic substances are more toxic than natural ones. Dyes are very often active chemicals and so likely to be harmful, but the food industry knows that the public buys by sight. Yellow butter must be rich, and the Spaniard must offer yellow paella to the tourist (and to himself), for even though there is no taste of saffron, the yellow color fools the tourists into thinking there is; such is the power of suggestion that the Spanish may even imagine the missing taste. I would always leave dyes out.

Natural food colors which have been in use for a long time are: cochineal (crimson), *kermes (purple red), *annatto (yellow), *safflower (yellow), *chlorophyll (green), *alkanna (crimson and violet), cudbear (red), and the juices of various berries and roots. Colored substances often have strong flavors which limit their application as simple coloring agents—examples are saffron and turmeric.

In cake decoration, I use: for red, the juice expressed from raw, grated beets mixed with plenty of lemon juice and concentrated by boiling (not much or it turns brown) to reduce the volume; for green, spinach, blanched and pounded and the juice squeezed out; for brown, instant coffee or chocolate. With these simple materials, it is possible to make beautiful floral decorations on cakes.

[Coloring—French: colorant; German: Farbmittel; Italian: colorito; Spanish: colorante]

COMPOSITE. Member of the plant family Compositae, which includes such common flowers as thistles, daisies, and dandelions. The common feature of composites is that what we might think of as their flowers are in fact groups of tiny flowers or florets. The composites are the largest family of flowering plants, with more than 14,000 species ranging from annuals to trees. Among them are many plants of culinary significance. The seeds of sunflower and safflower yield fine oils. The most important salad greens— lettuce, endive, and chicory—are composites, as are some root vegetables, notably salsify,

scorzonera, and Jerusalem artichoke. Other composite vegetables are the globe artichoke, of which the young flower heads are eaten, and cardoon, which is grown for its leaf stalks. Composite herbs include tarragon, tansy, camomile, and wormwood.

COMPRESSED YEAST. *See* yeast.

CONDENSED MILK. When people speak of condensed milk they usually mean sweetened condensed milk. (They refer to the unsweetened as *evaporated milk. The two have different characteristics and are preserved by different methods.)

The idea of concentrating milk by boiling is ancient. Indian *khoa* or *mawa* (often used in Indian sweets) is made by boiling and concentrating milk—originally buffalo milk—right down to a paste. Modern canned condensed milk is made after first pasteurizing the milk at just below boiling (176-194°F/80-90°C) for a minute and then adding sugar. After that, the pressure is lowered until the milk boils at 122-140°F (50-60°C). It is reduced by boiling to about a third of its original volume. This leaves the sweet sticky condensed milk; it consists of 40-45% cane sugar with 28% milk solids and the rest water. The preliminary pasteurization destroys the enzymes (which, if left, might cause undesirable changes) and kills most bacteria, but sweetened condensed milk is not sterile and, when canned and sealed, it is not sterilized by heat. Sweetened condensed milk nevertheless keeps well, even after it is opened, because, like jam, it has a high sugar content. If, as occasionally happens, one finds a blown or bad-tasting tin, the contents are harmless though unpleasant. In cooking, it is mainly used as a shortcut in making some simple puddings and salad dressings, but it is useful for making Indian sweetmeats to offer after a curry.

INDIAN COCONUT SWEETS

Grate some coconut. (If fresh coconut is not available, dried coconut can be used, though it is not quite as good.) Mix the grated coconut with condensed milk until a paste is formed of such a consistency that it can be rolled into balls. As each ball is made, roll it in more coconut and set it on a plate to dry a little.

[*Condensed milk*—French: *lait condensé;* German: *Kondensmilch;* Italian: *latte condensato;* Spanish: *leche condensada*]

CONDIMENT. Salt, pepper, mustard, vinegar, spice, pickle, or relish. The word, from the Latin *condimentum* (pickle or seasoning), has very little exact meaning, except that we understand condiments to be taken to the table rather than added in the kitchen. (Seasoning is what the cook does in the kitchen.) Condiments are also always salty, spicy, piquant, or stimulating. We would not usually call sugar a condiment, nor currant jelly, but we would include horseradish and mustard, and we may certainly copy the French and include *nuoc-nam. We also include ketchups and bottled sauces. Powdered dried lime and *sumac are other possibles, and I often feel the need for such sour powders as are used in some countries of the Middle East for sprinkling on rice; their use might well be more widely adopted.

[*Condiment*—French: *condiment;* German: *Würze;* Italian: *condimenti;* Spanish: *condimentos*]

CONGER EEL (*Conger conger*) is a marine fish which is widely distributed throughout the world. Congers grow to a very large size—monsters are 9 ft (3 m) long and weigh over 160 lb (70 Kg). They are gifted with the same tenacity of life as common *eels. Large ones are formidable creatures and give a very severe bite. Fishermen usually kill them in the boat. Congers have some superficial resemblance to the adult common eel as caught in the sea, but the eyes and gill openings are much larger, and the conger is without scales, while the common eel has scales embedded in the skin. Although the conger is a good fish and not bony, it lacks the richness and oiliness of the

common eel and is not regarded as a delicacy. Conger is much used in soups, for instance in the Genoese *burrida,* in French bouillabaisse, *cotriade,* and so on. Its flesh is firm. It is abundant off rocky coasts in the winter months from September to April.

[*Conger*—French: *congre;* German: *Seeaal, Meeraal;* Italian: *grongo;* Spanish: *congrio*]

CONSOMMÉ. *See* broth.

CONVERSIONS. Although official tables offer conversions between units that are accurate to six places of decimals, the inaccuracy of most kitchen measuring equipment will invalidate any pretensions to scientific accuracy. The conversions given below are quite accurate enough for the kitchen and are, I hope, reasonably easy to handle.

Temperature
Fahrenheit to Centigrade (Celsius): subtract 32, multiply by 5, and divide by 9.
Centigrade (Celsius) to Fahrenheit: multiply by 9, divide by 5, and subtract 32.

Weight
Pounds to Kilograms: multiply by 5 and divide by 11.
Kilograms to pounds: multiply by 11 and divide by 5.
Ounces to grams: multiply by 25 or 30 (the exact conversion is 28.3).
Grams to ounces: divide by 25 or 30.

Volume: British/Metric
Gallons to liters: multiply by 9 and divide by 2.
Liters to gallons: multiply by 2 and divide by 9.
Pints to liters: multiply by 4 and divide by 7.
Liters to pints: multiply by 7 and divide by 4.
Fluid ounces to milliliters: multiply by 25 or 30.
Milliliters to fluid ounces: divide by 25 or 30.

Volume: American/Metric
Gallons to liters: multiply by 4.

Liters to gallons: divide by 4.
Liquid pints to liters: divide by 2.
Liters to liquid pints: multiply by 2.
Fluid ounces to milliliters: multiply by 25 or 30.
Milliliters to fluid ounces: divide by 25 or 30.

Volume: British/American

There are rich possibilities for confusion here because the U.S. dry pint and the U.S. liquid pint represent different volumes. Effectively the U.S. dry pint is the same as the U.K. pint, while the U.S. liquid pint is smaller (16 fluid ounces instead of 20). Thus:
Liquid pint and gallon, U.K. to U.S.: multiply by 5 and divide by 6.
Liquid pint and gallon, U.S. to U.K.: multiply by 6 and divide by 5.
U.K. and U.S. fluid ounces are effectively the same (though the U.S. fluid ounce actually equals 1.04 U.K. fluid ounces).

Volume: U.S. Cups and Spoons/British

U.S. cups to fluid ounces: multiply by 8.
Fluid ounces to U.S. cups: divide by 8.
U.S. tablespoons (the same as U.K. dessertspoons) to fluid ounces: divide by 2.
Fluid ounces to U.S. tablespoons: multiply by 2.
U.S. teaspoons to fluid ounces: divide by 6.
Fluid ounces to U.S. teaspoons: multiply by 6.

Volume: U.S. Cups and Spoons/Metric

U.S. cups to liters: divide by 4.
Liters to U.S. cups: multiply by 4.
U.S. tablespoons to milliliters: multiply by 15.
Milliliters to U.S. tablespoons: divide by 15.
U.S. teaspoons to milliliters: multiply by 5.
Milliliters to U.S. teaspoons: divide by 5.

Length

Inches to centimeters: multiply by 10 and divide by 4.
Centimeters to inches: multiply by 4 and divide by 10.
Feet to meters: multiply by 3 and divide by 10.
Meters to feet: multiply by 10 and divide by 3.

COPPA. This is usually *coppa cruda* (raw), but there is also *coppa cotta* (cooked), which is of less gastronomic importance.

Coppa cruda consists of cured collar (neck) of pig, pressed raw—whole or in large pieces—into sausage skins (bladder or large gut) and hung to dry and mature for 2–4 months. Although a typical product of Emilia-Romagna from around Piacenza, Parma, and Langhirano, it is also made traditionally in neighboring Tuscany and Umbria—there is a version from Perugia. It may also be known as *bondiola* or *capocollo*. Thin slices of *coppa cruda* are a classic part of an Italian antipasto of cold meats.

Coppa cotta is typical of central Italy, where it is made of the cooked and pressed meat of pig's head and tongue, flavored with pepper, bay, and spices. In Rome, it is something like headcheese, though more solid, but in Venice it may be more like a mold of cooked ham and tongue. It is not usually enclosed in a skin.

COPPER (Cu) is a necessary element in the diet, and lack of it causes serious health problems. It is needed, for instance, for the formation of red blood cells. The daily intake for most people is adequate but not handsomely so.

The richest dietary sources of copper are oysters and crustaceans, which can contain as much as 400 parts per million, but ordinary fish are low in copper. Other good sources are yeast (50–100 ppm), liver (50–100 ppm), gelatin (25 ppm), cocoa, chocolate, tea, and coffee (10–20 ppm), currants (17 ppm), and nuts (10 ppm). Meat, eggs, milk, cheese, fruit, and vegetables are all low in copper. Copper salts in large quantities are poisonous to animals and plants.

Unlined copper vessels were once common, and they served well as long as they were in continual use and kept scrupulously clean. A copper water jug even had the advantage that since copper is lethal for bacteria, even in tiny quantities, it made the water safer to drink. However, when copper pots were used spasmodically and verdigris (a green coating of copper carbonate) was allowed to develop or when common kitchen acids, such as vinegar, were stored or boiled in copper pans, there were cases of poisoning. This led to the lining of copper pots with other metals, first lead or a 50:50 mixture of tin and lead, and finally tin with only a little lead. This last was used until quite recently and still is in some countries, but in the last few years pure tin with lead present only as a trace is usually specified by law. Since such pure tin is very costly, it is one of the reasons why tinned copper utensils are so expensive. Untinned copper pans are still used for bowls for beating egg whites— French chefs insist on it when they can—for sugar-boiling pans (tin would be on the verge of melting at the temperatures that may have to be reached), and for jam pans.

There are two reasons for the excellence of copper pans. One is that copper is a superb conductor of heat. Copper pans heat evenly over their whole surface and do not burn (pans of stainless steel—a bad conductor of heat—are often given copper bottoms to spread the heat). The other reason is that copper has a low specific heat, which means that copper pans heat up quickly and, conversely, quickly cool down. It is therefore easy to control the rate of cooking. Also, almost any damage done to copper pans can be repaired. They can be retinned, and hammered into shape if dented; handles can be reriveted if they become loose, and splits in the copper can be sealed. All the advantages far offset the bother of keeping copper pans clean.

In air, copper becomes dull, and when moist will develop the green coating of copper carbonate. To clean copper, rub it with a mixture of vinegar (or lemon juice) and salt, rinsing it thoroughly afterward. Never use an abrasive cleaner on the tin lining—it will wear the tin away. Above all, do not overheat the pan; it will melt the tin.

[*Copper*—French: *cuivre;* German: *Kupfer;* Italian: *rame;* Spanish: *cobre*]

CORIANDER (*Coriandrum sativum*), also called Chinese or Japanese parsley, cilantro, or dhania (India), is one of the world's most commonly used herbs in spite of the fact that

CORIANDER

the name comes from the Greek *koris*—a bug. There is a supposed similarity between the smell of the green leaves and the smell of bedbugs. A green umbelliferous herb, it takes the place of parsley, not only in China and Japan, but also in Southeast Asia, India, the Middle East, Mexico, and Spanish America. Its peculiar taste grows on one until it is difficult to do without it. It combines especially well with green chili. The seed is also an important spice seed. "And the house of Israel called the name thereof Manna: and it was like coriander seed, white; and the taste of it was like wafers made with honey" (Exodus 16:31).

Coriander is a native of southern Europe, and its use is very ancient. For Mexican or Indian cooking, it is sufficient to sow the seed you buy as a spice; provided it is fresh, it will germinate. The plants can be used chopped as soon as they are a few inches high. Not only is green coriander delicious, but it is also highly nutritious.

The seeds have a flavor somewhat reminiscent of oranges, and quite unlike that of the green leaves. They are round and easily split in two but are difficult to grind finely unless they have first been slightly dry-roasted to be crisp but not to spoil the delicate taste. The seed, unlike the green leaf, is much used in European cooking, in any-thing *à la grecque,* in pickles, and on roast meat; it is the secret of a fine steak and kidney pudding. In the Middle East, *taklia,* an Arab flavoring for spinach, chickpeas, meatballs, etc., is made by gently frying 3 cloves of garlic which have been crushed with salt together with a teaspoon of ground coriander until the mixture gives off an aromatic smell. The *taklia* is added to the dish at the end of cooking. In India, coriander is one of the foundation spices of curry. It is an essential spice to have on the shelf and has even been used in sweet dishes.

Although coriander is used both as seed and, above all, as a green herb in Southeast Asian food, it is the use of the root as a flavoring that is a unique feature of Thai cooking. In Costa Rica and Dominica, cilantro is used as the name for another herb with a rather similar flavor which has the scientific name *Geringium foetidum;* this is also used in southern Mexico.

[*Coriander*—French: *coriandre;* German: *Koriander;* Italian: *coriandolo;* Spanish: *coriandro*]

CORN, maize, or **Indian corn** (*Zea mays*), has been cultivated in both North and South America for at least 3000 years, according to radiocarbon dating of remains found in caves; it was the only cereal of the Aztec, Mayan, and Incan civilizations—the name "maize" is from the American Indian *máhis.* Maize was brought to Europe by the Spanish in the late 15th century and was later taken by the Portuguese to Asia. In the early days there seems to have been popular confusion as to where it came from, because the British, French, and Dutch called it "Turkey" corn (the Turks, "Egyptian" corn; the Egyptians, "Syrian"). Today, corn grows in every country with sufficient warmth and water, if not for human food, then at least for animal fodder. About half of the world's crop, though, is grown in the corn belt of the Mississippi basin—Illinois, Indiana, Missouri, Iowa, Kansas, and Ne-braska. No wild forms of corn exist today.

Corn is a heavy-yielding crop, but it is not very satisfactory as a staple for humans. It does not have the gluten needed for leavened bread and is also lacking in niacin, a deficiency of which causes pellagra. This problem is made worse by the fact that corn is mostly eaten by poor people who cannot make up their vitamin requirements from other sources (e.g., in central and southern Africa, where it is called "mealies"). Gerard demonstrates a sound knowledge when he writes: "Turkey wheat doth nourish far less than either wheat, rye, barley or otes. The bread made thereof is mealy white without bran: it is hard and dry as Bisket, and hath in it no clamminess at all: for which case it is hard of digestion, and yealdeth to the body little or no nourishment; it slowly descendeth and bindeth the belly as that doth which is made of Mill [millet]." And with prophetic insight he goes on: "We have no certaine proofe or experience concerning the virtues of this kind of corn, although the barbarous Indians which knoweth no better, are constrained to make a virtue of necessitie, and think it good food: whereas we may judge that it is more convenient food for swine than for men." It is true that Benjamin Franklin, writing in 1766, was stung to rise in corn's defense: "Indian corn, take it for all in all, is one of the most agreable and wholesome grains in the world—johnny and hoecake hot from the fire is better than a Yorkshire muffin." But although corn is certainly good, the verdict of history is that, given the choice, many people prefer wheat.

There are hundreds of types of corn, ranging from tiny popcorn varieties smaller than a finger to the enormous long cobs of the Jala valley in Mexico. The color ranges from yellow and white to red, blue, brown, and variegated. The main products and types are as follows:

Corn husks are sold ready-prepared for making tamales. Otherwise, the point and bottom parts of these outer coverings of the ears of corn must be cut off. If they are dry and not flexible, pour a kettle of boiling water over them and soak them for several hours until they are pliable. They must then be drained and dried on a cloth before filling, as directed in Mexican cookbooks.

Corn meal. Early American settlers adopted the Indian ways of using maize and adapted them for their own cooking. The meal they used was ground from locally grown varieties of corn. Thus, southern corn pone, ashcake, hoecake, and spoonbread were made of dent (*see below*), while Rhode Island johnnycakes and corn breads were made from the less starchy flint (*see below*). There was a general preference for white varieties of both types, although yellow meal was preferred for a few purposes, such as mixing with pork bits to make scrapple. The most primitive indigenous use was to make cakes out of meal and water, then bake them in the ashes of the campfire. When they were cooked and still hot, the ash could be quickly washed off and they would dry instantly, ready for eating. Settlers, of course, used iron sheets and ovens. Modern meal, ground in roller mills by several methods (and usually with the germ extracted to make it keep better), does not make the authentic, rough article. For this, it is necessary to find meal ground by stones in the few remaining old grist mills, which are usually powered by water.

Dent. This is the most commonly grown commercial corn, the type of the American corn belt. In this grain, the hard coat covers only the sides of the grain, so that a dent forms at the top. Dent corn may be yellow or white. It is starchier than flint corn.

Flint. The grains are entirely surrounded by a flinty, hard skin. Because flint varieties mature early, they were grown in the more northerly parts of the U.S. However, growing flint today is unprofitable, since yields are low, and thus flint varieties are less grown than formerly.

Hulled corn. *Hominy.

Mamaliga. The Rumanian equivalent of polenta, this is a corn-flour dish which no doubt descended from the gruels of other cereals made by the Romans in their colony of Dacia Felix. Although it is a simple peasant dish, there are gourmet versions dripping with butter and melted cheese.

Polenta. Corn is extensively grown in northern Italy. It is a staple food north of the River Po, in a strip south of the Alps and running through Piedmont, Lombardy, Trentino, and the Veneto. Ground corn, *farina gialla*, may be coarse or fine. To cook it, water is brought to a boil and salted before corn flour is stirred in. The proportion varies according to the dish and the quality of the flour, but 11 oz (300 g) to 1¾ pt (1 lt) of water is average. Polenta becomes very thick and should be cooked for about 40 minutes (20 is the absolute minimum), so it is quite likely to stick and burn, which is why it was traditionally cooked in a copper cauldron hung over the fire. The taste of polenta is strong, and many people do not like it. However, it can be excellent with cheese and rough red wine; it is even better if allowed to cool, then sliced and broiled.

Popcorn. The grains may be pointed or round, but are always small, hard, and flinty. When they are heated, the starchy interior swells, but it is confined at first by the hard skin. When pressure builds up, the grain suddenly bursts—pops, in fact—and turns inside out. Popcorn is nothing new; it was known to the Incas.

Soft corn, flour corn, or **squaw corn.** This has soft, mealy grains and is preferred by the Indians and by people in Bolivia, Ecuador, and Peru. It will not normally be met with by the cook elsewhere.

Sweet corn. There are over 60 varieties of sweet corn from which to choose. Sweet corn is high in sugars, which start turning to starch as soon as the ear is removed from the stalk. To be at its best, it should be picked, husked, and cooked within minutes, which means that really perfect sweet corn can never be bought in a store. Boiling should be only for a few minutes for very fresh corn (up to 10 minutes for less fresh ears): longer cooking, far from making it tender, makes it tougher and removes the flavor. Corn can also be cooked in the husk, and this method is often used for outdoor corn roasts and clam bakes. Soaking the ears in water first will help the corn steam, and when the kernels are translucent the husk and silk can easily be pulled off.

Dried sweet corn was familiar in the U.S. before the days of canning and freezing. Today it is largely a Pennsylvania Dutch specialty. Reconstituted dried corn has an incomparable nutty flavor and is a splendid accompaniment to roast fowl and pork.

As the following translations of "corn" indicate, in many countries what Americans consider corn is called "maize." The word "corn" may apply to whatever grain is most familiar: e.g., in northern Germany *Korn* means rye; in England "corn" may be wheat; in Scotland it may refer to oats.

[*Corn*—French: *maïs;* German: *Mais;* Italian: *mais;* Spanish: *maíz*]

CORNED BEEF is beef that has been cured—with salt, sugar, and often spices and saltpeter—and is so named probably because coarse grains or "corns" of salt were in the past used in the cure. Corned beef may be whole pieces of salted meat; as such, it is used in the New England boiled dinner or sliced for sandwiches. (It is what the British call salt beef.)

Pressed corned beef is another similar preparation; a piece—usually of brisket—is cured, boiled, and, while it cools, pressed or molded in a can. In Britain, canned corned beef is called bully beef (a corruption of the French *bouilli,* boiled). It was a ration for the French army in the Franco-Prussian war of 1870–71 and was used extensively in World Wars I and II.

Cures for corned beef vary a great deal. The following are examples of a dry-cure method and a brine method.

CORNED BEEF

A dry cure might be made of 2 lb (1 Kg) of salt, 1 oz (25 g) of saltpeter, 5 oz (150 g) of brown sugar, and 1 teaspoon of black pepper; the mixture should be rubbed into the piece of beef twice a day for 8 days.

To make a brine pickle, add to each 9 qt (10 lt) of water: 4½ lb (2 Kg) of salt, 2 lb (1 Kg) of sugar, and 2¼ oz (60 g) of saltpeter. The meat should remain in the brine for about 1 day per pound (2 days per Kg).

To cook the corned beef, boil it in unsalted water for about 20 minutes per lb (40 minutes per Kg).

GIMMER BULLY

Among the dozens of desperation recipes for disguising canned corned beef is this one which I invented in Langdale many years ago. After a day's climbing on Gimmer Crag (from the name it should have been made of Cumberland mutton), it tasted good, and ways of varying outdoor rations are sometimes useful.

Slice corned beef generously and make neat sandwiches, sprinkling the inside of each sandwich with some mixed herbs.

Make a white sauce with flour, good butter, and good milk. Season it well with pepper and cook until the raw taste goes. Then put it aside. Quickly fry the sandwiches on both sides in butter until the bread is crisp. Put on the plates; smother with the sauce. Eat at once while there is the contrasting texture between the crisp fried bread and the unctuous sauce. For variation the sauce can be flavored with mustard pickles, capers, mustard, or cheese, but with good ingredients the herbs and good butter are enough.

CORNISH CREAM. *See* clotted cream.

CORN SALAD. *See* lettuce.

CORNSTARCH or **corn flour.** Commercially, cornstarch is made as follows. Corn is soaked in water with a small percentage of sulfurous acid to prevent fermentation and to soften the kernels, which facilitates easy separation of the components. The soaked corn is then ground in such a way as to keep the germ intact and the bran in flakes, since these must be separated from the starch. Finally the very finely ground, starchy part of the grain is mixed with water and the milky liquid run onto inclined trays, where the starch settles and the water is run off. The starch can then be collected and dried in kilns. Cornstarch is therefore almost pure starch and in this respect differs from corn meal (*polenta*) and *masa*.

Cornstarch, unlike ordinary flour, contains no gluten. Because this decreases its tendency to form lumps, it makes a better thickener than flour. When mixed into a cream with water, then boiled, it forms a gelatinous, rather clear jelly—though not as clear as *arrowroot. Like arrowroot, cornstarch has little taste.

[*Cornstarch*—French: *farine de maïs;* German: *Maismehl;* Italian: *farina di granturco;* Spanish: *harina de maíz*]

CORN SUGAR. *See* glucose.

CORN SYRUP is a sweet *glucose syrup made commercially by heating cornstarch and water under pressure with a little sulfuric acid or hydrochloric acid to convert the starch to simple sugars. Hydrolysis may also be achieved by the use of enzymes or by a combination of enzyme and acid treatments. The acid is subsequently neutralized by adding an alkali, and the syrup is then decolorized with charcoal. (In Europe, glucose is mainly made from potato starch.) Corn syrup is much used in the U.S. for commercial purposes (brewing and confectionery) and also as a table syrup, sometimes flavored or mixed with maple syrup, brown sugar, honey, or molasses.

COSTMARY, alecost, or **bibleleaf.** A perennial, hardy herb (*Chrysanthemum balsamita*) of the daisy family, with yellow buttonlike flowers. This plant was well known to the ancients, and the name alecost was given it because it was one of the herbs used to flavor beer. It can be used as a flavoring herb in soups and in stuffings for poultry, veal, etc. Although I have come across it in recipes from northern Italy, it is not a commonly used herb these days.

[*Costmary*—French: *balsamite;* German: *Balsamkraut;* Italian: *balsamite;* Spanish: *balsamita*]

COTECHINO. A specialty of Emilia-Romagna, a *cotechino* is a large succulent sausage with a filling similar to *zampone,* which includes pork skin, mainly the soft rind of head and snout; this is what makes the sausage gelatinous after boiling. (*Cotenna*—as the French *couenne*—means pig skin, hence *cotechino*.) Normally, this sausage is flavored with salt and pepper, but there are varieties with garlic and even vanilla, moistened with white wine. *Cotechino* is eaten boiled (soak, prick, and cook very slowly for about 2 hours)—never raw—and is usually served with a purée of lentils or as part of a *bollito misto* (mixed boiled meats). The *bondiane* and *malette* are similar but of different shape. The most famous *cotechini* are made in Modena and Reggio Emilia.

COTIGNAC. *See* quince.

COTTONSEED OIL. Up to 1880, the cottonseeds from which this vegetable oil is expressed were treated as waste. Today huge amounts of cottonseed oil are made in all cotton-producing countries, particularly the U.S. Cottonseeds are hulled, crushed, heated, and pressed to obtain the oil which, when refined, is a good cooking and salad oil. Most of it goes as an important raw material for margarine and hydrogenated cooking fats, for salad dressings, as an olive oil substitute in packing sardines, and for the commercial frying of potato chips and doughnuts. Although known to cause allergies, it is wholesome to most people. Cottonseed oil is much used in Egypt as a cooking oil and, like all except highly refined cooking oils and fats, gives a regional flavor to food cooked in it.

[*Cottonseed oil*—French: *huile de graine de coton;* German: *Baumwollöl;* Italian: *olio di cotone;* Spanish: *aceite de algodon*]

COURGETTE. *See* squash.

COURT BOUILLON. Any previously prepared liquid in which something is to be boiled or poached is called a court bouillon. Its purpose is to improve the flavor, aromatize or perfume, even improve the color of the ingredient. Fish and shellfish are the items most often cooked in a court bouillon, which may be salted and acidified with lemon juice, white wine, or vinegar and aromatized with onion, garlic, carrot, herbs (such as parsley, thyme, and bay) or spices (such as peppercorns and coriander). Cooks soon arrive at their own formulas, and there is a lot of national prejudice. (For instance, Danes insist on sugar in the water when they cook lobsters.)

Meats and vegetables are less often cooked in court bouillon for an obvious reason. A court bouillon is prepared in advance by boiling the flavoring ingredients *before* the food is put in to cook. This is necessary with fish and shellfish, since they spend only a short time in the cooking liquid. But with meats and vegetables that take longer to cook, the flavoring materials can usually be boiled while the food is cooking. Court bouillon is very easily overflavored in a fit of enthusiasm; it can swamp, instead of enhance, natural flavors, and be quite unsuitable for use in a sauce. When the food is to be cooked in the liquid and marinated (as in pickled fish), one is dealing with a different dimension.

COUSCOUS is a dish of Berber origin and a staple of North African Mediterranean countries—Tunisia, Morocco, and Algeria. Now adopted in France, it is traditional also in Sicily, as an Arab introduction long ago. The dish consists of a stew spiced with red pepper and usually made of mutton with vegetables and chickpeas, over which, in a perforated bowl, is cooked a special type of semolina preparation referred to as couscous. Couscous may also be turned into a sweet dish—a versatile product. In the Sicilian version, the basis for the stew is fish.

Couscous can be bought in packets, ready to be cooked and with instructions and recipes on the packet. It is on sale everywhere in France, and "instant" forms of couscous are available for noncooks to play with. There are many ways of making the basic material, which the Italians regard as a form of pasta, as minute gnocchi—*gnocchettini di semola,* in fact. You need a 50:50 mixture of coarse and fine semolina, preferably from hard wheat, but it can be made from one grade of hard semolina.

The simplest way is to have ready a basin of water, a shallow dish of the semolina, and a clean cloth spread on the table. Touch the palm of one hand into the water to wet it slightly, then lay it on the semolina mixture so that some of it sticks to the palm and rub one palm against the other, finishing with a circular movement to roughly round the grains. Then let the grains fall on the cloth. Naturally the touch must be light or the grains will become dough. The fine particles of semolina are of course necessary to make the coarser ones stick together. The final operation is to sieve out any surplus flour or fine bits, and then to let the couscous dry. In Sicily, where it is called *cùscusu,* it is made using water with saffron—as is appropriate with a fish dish—and the mixture of fine and coarse semolina is rubbed on a special dish known as a *mafaradda.* A spoonful of the saffron water is put into the dish to wet it, and a handful of the semolina mixture put on top and then rubbed gently into a granular form with the fingers. It is essentially the same process, but for beginners the hand system is probably easier. Other forms of couscous are made by using a little mutton fat as a binder instead of water.

To cook, couscous is first moistened by sprinkling with a little water and mixing gently to allow the grains to swell. Then when the "stew," over which the couscous pan fits, is about an hour from being ready, the couscous is put into the steaming pan, sprinkled with a little more water, and put to steam. The couscous is not covered. A tip that was given to me is to pack the junction of the steamer and the pan below with a damp rag so that no steam can escape. If you do not have a *couscousière,* the special pan for making couscous, you can use a colander that fits tightly over the stew pot.

COWBERRY. *See* cranberry.

COWPEA, cow-gram, yard-long bean and **asparagus bean.** We are dealing here with three beans of the genus *Vigna* which may be regarded as different species or as varieties of the same species. From our point of view, it is easier to consider them as different species. The genus *Vigna* is mostly tropical; 40 or 50 species are known, of which only a few are cultivated.

The name cowpea originated in the U.S., where in the South it is known as the black-eyed pea. The earlier English name of cavalance was first used in the West Indies. The cowpea (*V. unguiculata*) is much used in India, where it has been cultivated since ancient times, although its original home may have been Africa, where wild varieties of the plant can still be found. The pods are about the thickness of a pencil and up to 12 in. (30 cm) long, but often less. They hang downward on the plant. The young pods are used in curries or are boiled as a vegetable, some varieties being better than others for this purpose. The seed of the ripe bean, which may be colored anything from maroon to red, blue, brown, black, pink or white, plain or speckled according to variety, is used whole, split as *dal,* or even ground to a flour. Although in India the cowpea is generally considered inferior to green *mung or *black gram, it can grow in dry areas and so is an important food, not only in India (as *lobya*), but also in Africa and parts of tropical America. The black-eyed pea has also been

important in the diet of southerners in the U.S. Fresh or dried, it has been used in many dishes, including the legendary Hoppin' John (a mixture of ham, black-eyed peas, and rice), and is valued in Creole cookery.

Catjang bean (*V. catjang*) is less often grown. It is included in case someone should be puzzled to see what looks like a cowpea but with pods about half the length and standing upright on the plant instead of drooping. Catjang beans have otherwise the same uses.

Yard-long bean, asparagus bean or **Chinese bean** (*Vigna sesquipedalis*) has pods which grow very long and thin—up to 39 in. (1 m)—hence its name. As you might guess, such long beans droop on the plant. The taste of the young pods is delicate, hence the alternative name asparagus bean, and the young beans are soft and flabby. This characteristic has been made use of in a dish called *lambchi and boonchi (boonchi* being the local name for these beans in the Dutch West Indies), which is described fully by Elisabeth Lambert Ortiz in her excellent *The Complete Book of Caribbean Cooking* (M. Evans, 1973). In this dish, the long flabby beans are wound spirally around skewers of lamb (which have been previously marinated in spices) and the whole brochette is grilled over charcoal.

CRAB. A decapod crustacean related to lobsters, crayfish, and shrimps, but distinguished from them by the large flattened body and small tail, which is kept tucked underneath, serving as a flap to hold the eggs but not much else. Even in swimming, the crab's propulsion is by the back legs, which are modified into paddles, and not by the tail. The internal anatomy of crabs is basically similar to that of lobsters, but crabs are more highly evolved creatures. Their nerve cord (which as in all crustaceans is situated underneath) is concentrated in two centers and not (as in lobsters) diffuse. Thus, it is claimed that crabs can be killed humanely by piercing through the shell from underneath with a needle to destroy the cerebral ganglion (which lies just under the shell between the base of the eyes and the mouth) and the thoracic ganglion (which lies just under the shell in the midline and opposite the base of the front legs). For the operation, the crab must be laid on its back. It is doubtful whether the job can be done efficiently without some practice.

Another method (described more fully in the section on lobsters) is to put the animal into cold salted water and gradually raise the temperature to boiling. The creature gradually loses consciousness. The time taken to cook a crab depends on its size, of course, but there is great difference between the recommendations of various authors. This suggests that, within reason, it is not very critical. French experts, for instance, may advocate a short cooking time and allow the crabs to cool in the cooking liquid. Crabs are plunged into boiling court bouillon and cooked (after being brought back to a gentle boil) for the following times: 10 minutes for up to about 1 lb (300–500 g); 12 minutes for up to 1½ lb (600 g); 18 minutes for 1½–1¾ lb (700–800 g); 25–30 minutes for about 2 lb (900 g to 1 Kg); 30–35 minutes for 3½–4½ lb (1½–2 Kg). These times apply to all large crustaceans, including lobsters and langoustes, cooled in the court bouillon.

At the opposite end of the scale, American methods may call for the immediate cooling of cooked crabs in cold water, and in that case they must be cooked for somewhat longer. If crabs are killed by the method of raising them to boiling point from cold brine, then 15 minutes for the first pound (450 g) and 10 minutes for each additional pound is recommended; the crabs are taken out and allowed to cool.

The legs and claws of a cooked crab can be twisted off and cracked, and the meat pulled or poked out. One must make sure that no bits of shell or internal septum are left in the meat. The job is fussy, and small legs are best sucked at table. The body is opened along the suture at the back, and usually the two halves can be simply forced apart by thumb pressure with the crab laid on its back. Some types of crab may need a strong knife point and some leverage. Pressure on the mouth parts will snap them inward, and the whole of the stomach and intestine—parts to be discarded—can then be lifted out still attached and in one piece. The only other parts to be discarded are the gills—called devil's fingers or dead man's fingers. In spite of their name, these are harmless, but would be impossibly chewy and indigestible if you tried to eat them. The meat in the bases of the legs can be got at most simply by breaking the lower part of the crab in two down the middle line, and then digging the meat out with a marrow scoop or other implement.

Crabs may, of course, be bought ready-boiled, and indeed that is the way they usually come nowadays, but where possible it is still better to buy a live crab and cook it yourself.

In choosing a live crab, pick one that is active and not already half dead. Look for one that is heavy for its size, and then shake it. Do not buy it if there is any suspicion of water swishing about, as this means the crab has recently molted; it will be watery and out of condition. In buying cooked crabs, you naturally buy only those that smell fresh and avoid ones in which the joints have become flaccid or floppy. A crab of decent size should yield just under half its weight of meat (about 40% in a good one). If crabs are to be served in the shell, the shells should be well cleaned, scrubbed (some even boil them in water with washing soda), and then rubbed with a little fat or oil to make them shine. The edges may need to be trimmed. When small crabs are served whole, as they often are in France for an hors d'oeuvre, finger bowls are essential.

An enormous number of different species of crab are eaten around the world. They range from the tiny pea crabs to gigantic Alaskan king crabs weighing 22 lb (10 Kg) and with legs spanning up to 11 ft (3½ m). Crabs are found in both icy and tropical seas. In North Queensland, I once subsisted for several days on Horlicks Malted Milk tablets and the giant mud crabs, a diet which is not recommended. However, they are very nutritious, and I do not know of any crabs that are poisonous to eat when they are fresh and in good health. Many species are now eaten which were formerly despised in days when there were fewer people, less overfishing, and more seafood at reasonable prices. When I was on a trawler north of the Shetlands in 1935, octopus, cuttlefish, and spider crabs that came up in the trawl were simply thrown back, and the Aberdeen fishermen laughed when I said they were good eating.

North American crabs are far from being the same as those in Europe. The most important of all, and comprising nearly three-quarters of the total crab catch in America, is the blue crab (*Callinectes sapidus*), which is confined to the East Coast, going as far south as the Gulf of Mexico. The blue crab is characterized by its color and by the shape, which might be described as pointed sideways. Even the claws are rather pointed. Blue crabs weigh 5 oz to 1 lb (150–450 g). In normal times, they may be known as eastern hard-shells, but at the molt they become soft-shells or "softies," although at various stages they may be "busters" or "shedders"—when the old shell is loose but not yet shed—and later "peelers" and "paper-shell," the latter being the state when the new shell has just begun to harden. Epicures consider "busters" the finest. Soft-shell crabs packed in ice and seaweed can live long enough in good condition to be air-freighted to any part of the U.S., but they are famous as an Atlantic coast delicacy. Unlike the Italian *moleche*, the soft-shelled blue crab must be cleaned before cooking. The front of the crab, enough to include eyes, mouth parts, and the stomach (sandbag), is snipped off with scissors. Then the tail (apron) is removed and the points on either side are lifted up and the spongy material underneath is discarded. Some also remove the gut before cooking.

On the Pacific coast of the U.S., the greenish-colored Dungeness crab (*Cancer magister*) ranges from Alaska to Baja California. State laws prohibit its use as a soft-shell. The excellent meat of the Dungeness crab is slightly pink, in contrast to that of the rock crabs from both the Atlantic (*Cancer irroratus*) and the Pacific (*C. antennarius*), which is brownish. Rock crabs are eaten locally as soft-shells. Many other local North American crabs are highly valued where they occur: the Jonah crabs (*C. borealis*) of New England, the stone crabs (*Menippe mercenaria*) of Florida, and the minute oyster or pea crabs (of the Pinnotheridae family) of New England. Oyster crabs live in mollusk shells for protection, but nevertheless get stewed in cream and fla-

OYSTER CRAB

vored with Madeira to be eaten whole as a local delicacy. The Alaskan king crab or *taraba gani* (*Paralithodes camtschatica*), which ranges across the Pacific to Japanese and Russian waters, is a monster deep-water crab with a huge claw span. Its meat is of superb quality. Much used as canned or frozen crab meat, king crabs are often processed on factory ships within a very short time of catching. As the price of king crab has escalated, some people have turned to so-called snow crab or queen crab, which is the sweet flesh of spider crabs, or red crab (*Geryon quinquedens*), which is smaller than king crab but has similar pinkish delicious meat.

In Britain, the crab most often eaten is the common edible crab (*Cancer pagurus*), a large, smooth-shelled, clean-looking creature, with pinkish brown coloring and exceedingly powerful pincers. It lives on rocky coasts, and a big one can be dangerous. The first reaction of a crab when disturbed is to close up, but very soon its response changes to attack. (Fishermen in the part of Wales where I lived as a child used to quieten crabs by spitting in their faces.) Never hold a crab where it can reach you with its claws, which it is best to tie up. Crabs are cannibals and will eat each other, so do not put two together. The spider crab (*Maia squinado*), a popular delicacy around Venice and elsewhere in the Mediterranean, is fished off the south coast of England and exported live to Spain, although it is also beginning to be accepted in Britain as well.

In France, the swimming crab (*Portunus puber*), the *étrille,* is commonly eaten. Swimming crabs are found in both the Atlantic and the Mediterranean. These crabs (of which there are many other species) are 2–4 in. (5–10 cm) across the shell and never grow very big.

The little shore crabs (*Cancer maenas*) are common in Britain, France, and the Mediterranean. In spring and autumn, when they molt, they have a particular gastronomic importance in Venice (where they abound in the lagoons on the Adriatic coast) and are known as *moleche*. In one method, *moleche ripiene* (stuffed), small soft-shell crabs are put alive into beaten egg and left there for a couple of hours, by which time they will be dead and have absorbed some of the egg (thus they are called stuffed); they are then floured and fried. In Italy, softshell crabs are traditionally eaten with polenta or a salad of finely sliced leeks. Another method is to drown them in milk, and some even claim that they taste best when raw. Traditionally, small crabs are hung up, tied in strings far enough apart to keep them out of claw range of each other. Shore crabs, being closely related to land crabs, will stay alive out of water for long periods (several weeks) in a cool damp place. In Mediterranean countries particularly, many other small crabs are eaten. They give an excellent taste to fish soup. Small swimming crabs, of which there are six species in the Mediterranean, are commonly found in markets there. The hairy *ériphie* (*Eriphia verrucosa*) is

perhaps the most treasured crab on the Côte d'Azur because of its exquisite flavor. A Mediterranean curiosity which visitors may wonder at sometimes in Spanish markets is the box crab (*Calappa granulata*), a handsome pink crab about the size and shape of a clenched fist, with red spots. It is striking because the claws are designed to fit snugly over the face, and it can box itself in (becoming like a ball) for protection. When the claws are apart, it looks out with a peculiarly bulldog expression and, once seen, is never forgotten. Box or no box, it is eaten.

Hermit crabs, although not strictly crabs, belong to the same group (Decapoda). They are often on sale in Mediterranean markets and are mainly used in soups, since they are too small for other purposes. Hermit crabs are boiled and cleaned like any other crustaceans—they are not hard to get out of their shells once they have been cooked—but gastronomically are largely neglected. Perhaps they would be good as "softies."

[*Crab*—French: *crabe, cancre;* German: *Krabbe, Krebs;* Italian: *granchio;* Spanish: *cangrejo*]

CRACKER. Few people make crackers today, although they are among the simplest of baked goods; at their most primitive, called ship biscuits, pilot biscuits, or hardtack, crackers are a mixture of flour and water baked until dry and crisp. Most recipes call for improvements: milk for richness, butter for softness, salt or sugar for flavor, and leavening (such as baking soda for soda crackers). Commercial cracker meal is available, but any unsweetened cracker may be rolled or crumbled to use as a thickener (in chowders), as an extender (in meatloaf), as a topping (for escalloped dishes), or as a coating (for foods to be fried). Graham crackers and other sweetened crackers can also be crumbled to make toppings for desserts or crusts for pies.

CRACKLINGS. In the U.S., cracklings are usually the crisp brown particles left after pork fat has been rendered (*see* rendering). They have long been eaten hot out of the pan as a snack, they add delicious flavor and texture to corn bread and white breads, and they can be used instead of croutons on salads and soups.

Cracklings may also be made from rendered goose fat or the skin of a goose. According to Susan Derecskey's *The Hungarian Cookbook* (Harper & Row, 1972), goose cracklings, *liba teperto,* are a luxury made only from the breast skin of the goose. The skin is removed with a thin layer of meat attached, cut into small squares, and placed in a pan large enough to hold the skin in one layer. This is covered by a 2-to-1 mixture of water and milk, which "brings out the fine, nutty taste of cracklings." The pan is covered and cooked until the fat starts sputtering, then the lid is removed and the heat turned up until the goose skin turns golden brown. It is sprinkled with water, drained of fat, and eaten with salt.

In Europe, crackling is also the crisp, roasted skin of a pig, preferably suckling pig. To prepare it, score the pig's skin with a very sharp knife or a razor blade, cutting just through the skin in neat strips ¼–½ in. (½–1 cm) wide, and rub salt into the cuts. During roasting the skin and fat will turn crisp and appetizing. The Danes brush the skin with water just before it is ready, which makes the crackling bubble. If the crackling refuses to crisp in the oven, it can be removed, brushed with water, and finished under the broiler.

CRANBERRY and related berries are members of the heather family (Ericaceae) which thrive in the acid soil of bogs, moorlands, and mountains. The same family includes the rhododendrons, all of which, from the lovely Alpenrose to the huge crimson-flowered tree rhododendrons of the Himalayan gorges, are very poisonous—even honey from the flowers is toxic (which certainly sets them apart from the heathers). On the other hand, the 130 or so species of the genus *Vaccinium,* including cranberries, *bil-berries, *blueberries, and cowberries, all bear edible (though not necessarily appetizing) fruits, as do some related genera, notably *Gaylussacia* (huckleberries—*see* blueberries) and *Arctostaphylos* (bearberries), as well as the similar genus *Empetrum* (crowberries), which belongs to another family. Of these, a few, such as the American cranberry and blueberries, are cultivated, but most are gathered wild. They fruit in summer and autumn and are particular favorites in mountain country where the berries are plentiful. The fruits of the heather family are of special importance in all sorts of traditional fruit dishes and pies both all over Europe and in America.

Cranberry. There are two main sorts of cranberry, the European cranberry (*Vaccinium oxycoccus*) which grows wild on moors all over northern Europe and Asia, as well as in North America, and the American or large cranberry (*V. macrocarpon*), which is naturalized locally in Europe, including parts of Britain. In America, it grows wild from Newfoundland south to North Carolina and westward to Saskatchewan. It is the American cranberry which is cultivated, because it has larger fruits, up to ¾ in. (2 cm) in diameter compared to the ⅓ in. (8 mm) of the European species. Cranberry growing is centered in Massachusetts, with Cape Cod producing 70% of the total. Two hundred years ago, there were laws in America against picking cranberries before September; and the season is from September to December, peaking in November. American cranberries used to be exported to Europe in the days of sailing ships. They were simply packed in barrels and covered with water, in which condition they would remain good for the long sea voyage. Even today, some people keep cranberries in jars covered with water; in this way the berries remain good for months in the refrigerator. They can, of course, be frozen. (In view of the fantastic keeping qualities of cranberries, it is interesting to note that they naturally contain benzoic acid, which is a preservative and is used in tomato sauce, for instance, in the form of sodium benzoate.) Cranberries can be preserved in jars by boiling them with a little water and sugar until they burst— about 10 minutes—and then sealing them in sterile jars. No heat treatment is necessary. Proportions for cranberry sauce are 2 cups of cranberries to 1 cup of water and 1 cup of sugar.

Cranberries are known as "bouncing berries" because good ones bounce. In the old days, they were tipped down steps; the bad ones remained on the steps because they did not bounce. Modern grading machines use the same principle, each berry having seven chances to bounce over a 4-in. (10-cm) barrier. Cranberries are foolproof to buy and will keep up to 8 months in a refrigerator. They have a refreshing sourness, and recipes for other uses than cranberry sauce will be found in many cookbooks.

Cowberry or **mountain cranberry** (*Vaccinium vitis-idaea*). These grow wild in the mountains of the northern hemisphere, over the whole of Europe except the Iberian Peninsula. The dark-red, globular berries are about ½ in. (1 cm) in diameter, so it might be confused with the bearberry, but not with the cranberry (which has very small leaves in relation to the size of fruit). It is popular in Scandinavian countries, and the taste is spicier than the cranberry's.

Crowberry (*Empetrum nigrum*) grows on moors, bogs, and mountains over most of Europe. It has black fruits. While not of great culinary importance, crowberries are welcome to climbers.

Bearberry (*Arctostaphylus uva-ursi*) grows on moors and mountains of Europe. Its red fruits are of little culinary interest.

Strawberry tree or **arbutus** (*Arbutus unedo*). This is a Mediterranean bush of rather dark leafed, almost rhododendronlike appearance, which also grows in Ireland. It is found among the vegetation on the rough hillsides, often in the gullies where there is a little more water. It flowers one year and the berries form the next. Though very decorative, the fruits, which are dark red, rough, and the size of a strawberry, are disappointing to eat. The outside is covered with tiny, woody warts, and the inside is soft and flavorless. The French make a liqueur out of the berries.

[*Cranberry*—French: *canneberge;* German: *Moosbeere;* Italian: *mortella di palude;* Spanish: *arándano agrio*]

CRAWFISH. A confusing name that is perhaps better avoided. Particularly in the U.S., it is a synonym for the freshwater *crayfish, while in Britain it normally refers to a marine variety of lobster, which is perhaps best called by its unambiguous French name of *langouste.

[*Crawfish*—French: *langouste;* German: *Languste;* Italian: *gambero;* Spanish: *cigala*]

CRAYFISH. These small, freshwater crustaceans, *Astacus astacus* (red-clawed) and *A. pallipes* (white-clawed), are very like tiny lobsters in both appearance and habits. They exist on every continent but Africa, and for some reason they are prized as table delicacies in most countries but rejected as repulsive in others. They are considered a great delicacy in France (which imports them from Turkey, where they are spurned). The Norwegians have a late summer festival dedicated to eating *kraftor*. But nowhere are they appreciated more than in Cajun country of south Louisiana, where farmers use dip nets or tend traplines to harvest some 20 million pounds of crayfish (locally known as crawfish) each year from December through June.

Crayfish are sometimes abundant in streams, lakes, freshwater swamps, and even roadside ditches in North America and Europe. They live in the holes in banks and can be caught in traps like small lobster pots or fished with nets stretched in hoops. These are baited in the center with meat and sunk flat on the bottom of the water. When the net is pulled up quickly, the feasting crayfish will usually be surprised before they can escape. They can be kept alive in a bucket with about 1 in. (2½ cm) of water or covered with wet grass or nettles. In winter they will live for up to a week in a cool place. Crayfish must always be alive when prepared. There are more than 300 species, but all are to be treated the same.

Female crayfish are reckoned to be better than males, and egg roe, when found, is made into crayfish butter. The threadlike gut of crayfish should be removed, since it tastes bitter, although some cooks starve the animals for 2 days instead. The classic method of removing the gut is to move the center two blades to either side, which breaks the articulation, and then pull gently. The gut should come out as a fine string. Alternatively, the job can be done by finding the anal opening at the base of the tail, sticking a sharp knife point beneath it, and pulling out the gut. The animals are then often thrown straight into boiling court bouillon or hot butter. They may be killed instantly by piercing through the top of the head, behind the beak, and on a level with the back of the eyes, where the cerebral ganglion, which does duty for a brain, is situated. Great emphasis is always placed on the necessity for crayfish to be alive when cooking begins, and they must be cooked quickly for 10 minutes, no more, in a very little liquid. They should never be cooked in red wine, which turns them black. There are dozens of ways of preparing crayfish. I give one typical recipe from the Hôtel de la Poste, Chevillot, Beaune.

ÉCREVISSES À LA CRÈME

Put about 2 dozen crayfish in a pan in a little hot butter, salt, and pepper. Sauté, then flame them with cognac. Add a mixture of chopped parsley and shallots, half a bottle of dry white wine, 2 tablespoons of skinned, seeded, and crushed tomato, and 4 tablespoons of heavy cream. Cook for 10 minutes. Take out the crayfish and reduce the sauce. Bind it with a little beurre manié. Taste and adjust the seasoning. Add a pinch of finely chopped tarragon, a few drops of cognac, and several nuts of good butter. Cover the crayfish with the sauce and serve very hot.

[*Crayfish*—French: *écrevisse;* German: *Flusskrebs;* Italian: *gamberi di fiume;* Spanish: *cangrejo de rio*]

CREAM is a concentration of the fatty part which collects on top when milk is allowed to stand. The amount depends on the breed and breeding of the cow, on when it calved, and on its food; the color depends mainly on the pastures on which the cow was fed and on the season. Cream consists of the larger fat globules which float because they are less dense than water. Such large globules and clusters are broken up by homogenization, which makes them small and evenly dispersed. In the old days, cream used to be obtained by letting milk stand for 8–10 hours, then skimming the cream off the top, leaving skimmed milk. Heavy cream came from standing the milk for 24 hours before skimming. The milk would be poured into a wide earthenware pan, then placed in a cool larder at about 52°F (11°C) in winter and 60°F (15–16°C) in summer. However, since the beginning of this century, cream has been generally removed with a separator, which spins the milk and concentrates the cream by centrifugal force. Light or heavy cream can be obtained with this machine merely by an adjustment. Such cream, unless deliberately matured to allow favorable bacteria to multiply, lacks the flavor of naturally skimmed cream.

If it has not come straight from a farm, bought cream will always be pasteurized—which takes out some flavor-producing organisms. Pasteurized cream will keep for some days in the refrigerator before going nasty—not sour, since souring organisms do not operate at low temperatures and other bacteria become predominant. They work on the fat and protein content to produce an unpleasant taste. However, when unpasteurized cream is held at room temperature, lactic bacilli become predominant and the cream develops a sour taste (*see* sour cream).

When using cream to enrich sauces, you should avoid boiling them after adding the cream, which is likely to curdle. In using well-matured cream, always add the hot liquid to it, since cream poured into hot liquid (including coffee) is also liable to curdle.

U.S. federal standards require that cream contain not less than 18% milkfat and specify the following percentages of milkfat for cream products:

half-and-half	10.5–18%
light cream	18–30%
light whipping cream	30–36%
heavy cream	at least 36%

Whipped cream. Cream whips best at about 40°F (5°C) but can be whipped at 50°F (10°C). It will not fluff as much if it is taken straight out of the refrigerator or if it is allowed to reach the temperature of a warm room—over 65°F (18°C). If beaten too hard and long, especially in summer, it is likely to start turning to butter; as soon as cream starts to stick to the whisk or beater, it is time to stop. Equal quantities of light and heavy cream form a mixture suitable for whipping.

Artificial cream. There are many versions of artificial cream on the market, as well as devices for making it by reconstituting cream from milk and unsalted butter. In the latter, milk and butter are warmed together until all the butter is melted to a yellow oil, and the two are then forced together through a small hole (a machine for the purpose can be bought). This breaks up the fat into tiny globules and forms an emulsion. At its best, reconstituted cream is very like real cream—it has the same constituents—but it is usually more oily. Artificial creams do not have the constituents of real cream but merely simulate it. They consist of an emulsified fat, which is not butterfat, with substances to improve texture and flavor. Skimmed milk, lard, and alginates (from seaweed) are the sort of things that commonly go into them, together with sugar, color, perhaps, and flavorings.

[*Cream*—French: *crème;* German: *Sahne;* Italian: *panna;* Spanish: *crema, nata*]

CREAM NUT. *See* Brazil nut.

CREAM OF TARTAR. Purified form of tartar which, in crude form, is obtained from the encrusted *argol and lees in wine. It is essentially acid potassium tartrate, a white crystalline powder with a slightly sour taste. Cream of tartar is at most sparingly soluble in water, and hardly at all when the water is cold. One of the main reasons for keeping wine cool in the cellar is to get the tartar to crystallize out and fall to the bottom of the tank. Cream of tartar is used in baking powders, but is rather an old-fashioned ingredient in the modern kitchen. Three teaspoons of cream of tartar to 1 teaspoon of *bicarbonate of soda in a cake mixture (with the two ingredients mixed in separately) can be used as a substitute for baking powder.

[*Cream of tartar*—French: *crème de tartre;* German: *gereinigter Weinstein;* Italian: *cremore di tartaro;* Spanish: *crêmor*]

CRÈME DE CACAO and **crème de cassis.** *See* liqueurs and cordials.

CRÈME FRAÎCHE. French "sweet cream" is called *fleurette;* when it thickens by the natural process of fermentation of lactic acid, very heavy cream, *crème double* with some 35% butterfat, becomes *crème fraîche.* It is similar to sour cream but only slightly acid, with a somewhat nutlike flavor. Pasteurization kills the natural ferments in cream. Unlike in the U.S., in France, after cream is pasteurized, ferments are returned to it so the characteristics of *crème fraîche* develop. Julia Child, in *From Julia Child's Kitchen* (Knopf, 1975), recommends making "a reasonable facsimile" of *crème fraîche* by mixing and gently heating 1 cup of commercially soured cream with 2 cups of heavy cream just until the chill is taken off. Set partially covered at 75°F (24°C) for 6–8 hours, until cream has thickened. Stir up, cover, and refrigerate. It will keep for 10 days. When it is nearly used up, blend in more heavy cream and repeat the process.

CRÉPINETTE in French charcuterie is any mixture of minced meat, usually pork, but also lamb, veal, chicken or liver, with fat, herbs, spices, and seasonings (sometimes with a slice of truffle), wrapped up in a piece of mesentery or caul (*crépin*), and usually given a round, slightly flattened shape. *Gayettes,* from southern France, are similar but ball-shaped and stuffed with variety meats—liver, lungs, spleen, etc. Sometimes *crépinettes* can be bought already cooked, in which case they can be eaten cold, but otherwise they should be dipped in melted butter (or butter and bread crumbs) and broiled, roasted, sautéed, fried, or even poached in gravy or sauce.

CRESS. A number of plants, mostly crucifers, are called cress if they have pungent or peppery leaves.

Watercress (*Nasturtium officinale*) is a plant of shallow water which is native to Europe and western Asia and naturalized in many other countries—it is a serious weed

WATERCRESS

of rivers in New Zealand. Commercially, it is cultivated in shallow tanks fed by natural springs or boreholes because of the danger that it may carry typhoid or other diseases if it is grown in river water (or gathered wild from streams). If you are in any doubt about the cleanliness of the source, it is best to cook the watercress as soup. The cultivated strains of watercress range from green to bronze or almost black. Watercress may be almost too pungent to eat or so mild as to be uninteresting. It should preferably be moderately free from small roots.

To keep it fresh, the bunch can be immersed in cold water right up to the base of the leaves. Freshly gathered watercress, if it is unbruised, will keep for some days in a plastic bag in the refrigerator (away from the freezer compartment); you should first pick off any roots and dead or battered leaves, wash it gently but thoroughly in several changes of water, and drain it.

Cress, garden cress, pepper cress, or **peppergrass** (*Lepidium sativum*) is native in Egypt and western Asia but naturalized as a wild plant in Europe and North America. As a garden salad plant, cress has the advantage of growing rapidly, needing little water, and not developing small roots along its stems. It has a pleasantly peppery flavor. In England it is often eaten with the young plants of white mustard.

Winter cress or **yellow rocket** (*Barbarea vulgaris*) and **land cress** or **early flowering yellow rocket** (*B. verna*) both grow wild. These and probably other species of *Barbarea* go under various names. Pungent in taste, such cresses are a useful winter or early spring salad, and they may also be eaten as boiled greens.

*Rocket (*Eruca sativa*) is another crucifer that is often grown as a salad.

Indian cress is better known as the garden flower *nasturtium (*Tropaeolum majus*).

[*Cress*—French: *cresson de ruisseau;* German: *Brunnekresse;* Italian: *crescione di fonte;* Spanish: *berro. Garden cress*—French: *cresson cultivé;* German: *Gartenkresse;* Italian: *crescione di giardino;* Spanish: *mastuerzo de jardín. Winter cress*—French: *cresson alénois;* German: *Barbarakraut*]

CRIMPING. In cooking, this means making gashes (as transversely in the sides of a fish) to allow penetration of marinade and to make for quicker cooking, with more flavor.

Crimping also means to corrugate in small pleats, and so is applied to shaping the edge of a flan or pie crust. However, a crimping iron is for hair.

CRISPBREAD. *See* flatbread.

CROSNES. *See* Chinese artichoke.

CROWBERRY. *See* cranberry.

CRUCIFER. Member of the plant family Cruciferae, which has about 1900 species, mainly in the temperate regions of the northern hemisphere. The family is characterized by the four-petaled, usually white or yellow flowers and a seed capsule that opens on two sides, starting at the stalk end (it may be short and flat or long and thin). The most important food plants in the family belong to the genus *Brassica,* which includes both leaf and root vegetables: *B. oleracea* (cabbage, cauliflower, kale, broccoli, kohlrabi, and Brussels sprouts), *B. napobrassica* (rutabaga) and *B. rapa* (turnip). Two more species, *B. nigra* and *B. juncea,* provide mustard seed, as does the white mustard (*Sinapis alba*). Both mustard and rape seeds are sources of oil. The leaves of many species, both wild and cultivated, are eaten as salad, notably watercress and other cresses as well as rocket. Horseradish root is used not as a vegetable but as a flavoring.

CRUMBS. Anyone who thinks that crumbs are not worthy of attention may well ruin a lot of food as a result, for crumbs have a taste as well as a texture. They are an important ingredient and not a way of using up bits of stale, otherwise inedible, bread.

Dried bread crumbs can be bought ready-prepared. Bakers find them a way of using up unsold bread and may or may not make them well. They can also be bought in packets from supermarkets and are often artificially colored, which may make food look equally artificial. Dried bread crumbs are easily made by drying crustless leftover bread in a cool oven until it is crisp and pale-colored. This can be reduced to crumbs with a rolling pin or in a blender. Crumbs should be sieved and stored, bone dry, in a screw-topped jar. It is best to replace them every few weeks and not expect them to keep sweet forever. Such crumbs are for sprinkling on food which has been covered with a sauce and put in the oven, or under the broiler, to be browned. With dots of butter and perhaps grated cheese, they sop up the fat to form a crust. They are also used to cover the fatty nakedness of such foods as boiled ham. They should not be used for coating food to be fried, or for stuffings. For such purposes, fresh white bread crumbs are best.

Fresh white bread crumbs will not keep (unless frozen) but can be quickly made with a fast blender. Day-old bread is sliced and the crust cut off, ideally some hours before it is used, so that it can dry a little. Then it can be roughly broken into the container and reduced to crumbs. If they are not fine enough after the first go, they can be spread out on a tray and left in a warm place to dry a little before being given another whirl. For coating fried food, such fresh bread crumbs are greatly superior to the dried, brown crumbs that are so frequently used. They do not get overfried or give a rank taste. For stuffings and bread sauce, it is better to use very finely cubed bread, not bread crumbs, since a lighter texture can be achieved that way, but if bread crumbs are used they should be coarse.

Cake crumbs, from plain cake, and cookie crumbs are used in some dishes. Crackers and cornflakes may also be crumbled and used in ways similar to dried bread crumbs.

[*Crumbs*—French: *panure;* German: *panieren;* Italian: *panare;* Spanish: *empanar*]

CRUSTACEANS. Nearly always aquatic creatures, crustaceans—the *shrimps, *lobsters, *crayfish, *crabs, and *barnacles—have a hard, jointed outside skeleton and include, among the inedible kinds, woodlice and water fleas. The meat of crustaceans is rather slowly digested, and after dining on lobster or shrimp, you will be sustained for a considerable period.

[*Crustaceans*—French: *crustacés;* German: *Krustentieren, Krebstieren;* Italian: *crostacei;* Spanish: *crustáceos*]

CRYSTALLIZED FRUIT. *See* candied fruit.

CRYSTALS. Examples of crystalline substances used in the kitchen are cane sugar and salt. The geometrical shape of a crystal is due to the regular way in which the molecules arrange themselves when it forms. Crystals may form either when a suitable molten substance cools and becomes solid or when a saturated solution is cooled or allowed to evaporate. Large crystals form when the liquid is cooled or evaporated very slowly, small crystals when the liquid is chilled rapidly. They do not have time to grow. That is why foods must be frozen quickly. Large crystals break cell walls and spoil the texture.

Crystals are sometimes grown for decoration. The sugar crystals grown on those twigs in liqueur bottles indicate that the liqueur is saturated with sugar and very sweet.

[*Crystals*—French: *cristaux;* German: *Kristall;* Italian: *crystalli;* Spanish: *cristales*]

CUCUMBER (*Cucumis sativus*). One of the oldest cultivated vegetables, cucumbers have been grown for some 4000 years. They possibly came from southern India originally, but this is not certain. It is recorded that the Emperor Tiberius demanded a continuous supply of them, so they were even forced in winter. In Britain, cucumbers were commonly grown at the time of Edward III (1327), but then went out of favor, not to be revived until the days of Henry VIII. They were introduced by Columbus to Haiti in 1494 and soon spread all over the North American mainland, since they were liked by the Indian tribes. The popularity of the cucumber depends on its refreshing taste—it is 96% water and a gift for anyone on a slimming diet.

The many varieties of cucumber may be prickly, warty, or smooth. In the U.S., a distinction is often made between eating and pickling types. Eating varieties can be pickled but are liable to go hollow, while pickling varieties can be eaten fresh but may be bitter. Varieties of cucumber which are stubby and yellow are known as lemon cucumbers. They taste fine but have a tough skin. Those from the Middle East and northern India are selected to stand some drought and are much grown in pits in the sand in half-dry river beds.

A long, very pale type, with a finely ridged and very tender skin, is the one commonly seen in markets from Turkey to the Indus valley. This I take to be similar to the variety Americans call Armenian, Turkish, or Syrian cucumber. These cucumbers have rather dry flesh, no seeds to matter when young, and a strong, excellent taste. You will see them (well sprinkled with dirty water) in a Pakistani town like Dera Ghazi Khan, where the market is thronged with wild, bearded, hook-nosed characters swathed in black turbans. It is the common cucumber of that sort of market in Muslim countries. Chinese and Japanese cucumbers are long outdoor varieties; they may be smooth, ribbed, or prickly and have recently been grown in Europe and America.

In buying cucumbers, always look for young firm ones. Older ones are likely to have large seeds and, at best, can be used only for stuffing after the seeds have been scraped out with a spoon. Commercial cucumbers have often been dipped in wax, which is unpleasant for anyone who likes to eat cucumber with the skin on. Old-fashioned varieties had to be salted to remove some of the bitter juice, a habit that has persisted. Some people still like to remove part of the water, but the long salting advocated in old books is unnecessary. Simply slice, sprinkle generously with salt, leave no more than a minute, tip the cucumbers into a clean cloth, and gently squeeze out as much of the juice as you like. Cucumber is often dressed with yogurt and a touch of vinegar; it goes particularly well with yogurt—dishes range from Indian cucumber *raïta* to the Turkish *cacik* and Greek *zaziki*. Cooked cucumbers are also excellent. Cucumber halves stuffed with meat and served with sour cream were one of my favorite dishes when I was in Rumania long ago.

[*Cucumber*—French: *concombre;* German: *Gurke;* Italian: *cetriolo;* Spanish: *pepino*]

CULATELLO. This raw ham product of Italy consists of lean meat only, cut from the backside of a pig (*culo,* vulgarly, means arse), cured as for a ham, soaked in wine, packed in a bladder, and hung to mature. It has a fine, rosy color and a delicate taste. A specialty of Zibello, Busseto, and Soragna, between Parma and Piacenza (in Emilia), *culatello* is one of the best, and so most expensive, Italian raw ham products, and quite exceptional. It is sliced thinly and served as antipasto.

CUMIN. This close relative of caraway is a vital spice in Indian and Middle Eastern cooking and important all over the world. It came originally from the Orient but was being grown in the Mediterranean regions well over 2000 years ago. The Romans used

CUMIN

cumin seeds as a substitute for pepper and even ground them to a paste for spreading on bread. Much confusion is caused in European markets by shops muddling the names of cumin and caraway. For instance, the alternative name for caraway in France is *cumin des prés*, while in Spain caraway is often known as *comino holandese* (Dutch cumin). Worse still, Indian cookbooks often translate cumin as caraway. There is very little taste resemblance.

Cumin (*Cuminum cyminum*) is little used in European cooking (except in Portugal and Spain), but it is important in North Africa and through to the Far East, in Mexico and South America, and in any place where there are sizable numbers of Indian colonists. Americans may use it in chili con carne and pickles. Its taste is both strong and assertive. Two forms are commonly used in Indian cooking—black *zeera* (*kala zeera*) and white *zeera* (*safed zeera*), *zeera* or *jeera* being the usual word for cumin. If cumin is dry-roasted in an old pan until it is just too hot to touch and has turned very slightly brown, much of its raucous flavor is turned to a more nutty one.

[*Cumin*—French: *cumin;* German: *Kreuzkümmel;* Italian: *cumino;* Spanish: *comino*]

CURDLING AGENTS. *See* rennet.

CURDS. When milk is coagulated by acids, natural souring, rennet, or crushed herbs, the solid part is known as curds, and the liquid as whey. ("Curd" is also used to describe the curdy-looking white part of a cauliflower and the soft material that forms between the flakes of really fresh salmon when it is cooked.) Milk curd is basically casein and fat.

To make curds, rennet essence is added to lukewarm milk, and the milk is kept warm until the curd is solid and the whey is clear. Lemon juice or any other acid food will hasten the process.

Curds are usually drained of the whey before being eaten (except in junket, Miss

Muffet's curds and whey) or used in cooking. A pinch of salt stirred into the curdled milk will assist the separation, and the whey is usually strained off through cheesecloth. The classic way to eat curds is with an equal amount of cream and with wine as a flavoring. Curd is used to make cheesecake, mixed with egg and fried as fritters, or used in various puddings that were more popular in the past than they are today. Curds are also, of course, the starting point in making *cheese.

[Curds—French: *lait caillé;* German: *Quark;* Italian: *giuncata;* Spanish: *cuajada*]

CURING means preserving by drying, brining, and so on. *See* brine, drying, dry salting.

CURRANT. The term originally applied to a small, black, dried grape, imported from the Levant and taking its name from Corinth in Greece. The grapes from which currants are made are of a tiny black variety which has been known for at least 2000 years. To this day, Greece is a prime producer and exporter of currants, although other countries, such as Australia, have taken a large share of the market.

Red currants (and white currants, a variety of the same thing) are bred from *Ribes rubrum,* which grows wild in Europe. The name "currant" came from a fancied resemblance to the Corinth currant, although red currants belong to the same family as gooseberries and are not related to grapes. Currants are so well known in Britain, Germany, and northern Europe generally that it is surprising to find they are almost unheard of in the Mediterranean countries. The Italians and Spanish do not even have a word for this fruit (they use the Latin). Even the French lump it with the gooseberry, although currants have long been grown in the northern part of the country. Red-currant juice was a popular drink in Paris in the mid-18th century; the fruit was formerly called *groseille d'outre mer* and thus considered foreign. Many people in Britain agree that red-currant jelly, especially if it is rath-

er tart, is an almost indispensable kitchen ingredient. It is necessary for Cumberland sauce, of course, but also in other contexts to counteract oversweetness. Red currants are, with rowan berries, the best fruity souring agent that grows in northern Europe and are the natural equivalent of sumac, pomegranate, and even tamarind if one wishes to use them as such.

Black currants (*Ribes nigrum*) are a close relative of the red currant and grow wild in northern Europe, Asia, and parts of the U.S. They have increased in importance as a commercial crop since they were found to be rich in vitamin C, but have always been in demand as a medicine for soothing sore throats. They are not very pleasant raw but make delicious jam. In France, black currants are particularly grown in Burgundy, where they are used to make the alcoholic cordial *crème de cassis;* this drink, mixed with white wine, makes one of the best of all summer apéritifs, *vin blanc cassis* or *kir,* named after its famous inventor, the Resistance hero Abbé Kir. Like red currants, black currants are rarely to be seen in any Mediterranean country.

Currants are not as important in the U.S. as in Europe, partly because they are susceptible as alternate hosts to white pine blister rust disease; they are therefore restricted in some areas.

[Currant—French: *raisin de Corinthe;* German: *Korinthe;* Italian: *uve passe, uve secche;* Spanish: *uvas, pasas de Corinto*]

CURRY LEAF, one of the most important flavorings of Indian vegetarian cooking, is also used in Malay and Indonesian foods. The plant is native to southern Asia and grows wild profusely in the forests of the Himalayan foothills. In the Corbett National Park, the smell is overpowering as your elephant bursts through thickets of this plant. The scientific name is *Murraya koenigii,* and it belongs to the citrus-rue family (Rutaceae). In fact, citrus fruits have even been grafted onto it. To make a typical seasoning for South Indian food, take a good pinch of black mustard seed, a small pinch of asafetida, and half a dozen curry leaves. Fry these briefly in oil or *ghee* in a large spoon or ladle, until the mustard seeds start to splutter, then quench the whole in the dish (*dal* for instance, or a curry of yogurt with spices). There is no substitute for curry leaves or for this seasoning—nothing else will give its very special taste. Fairly fresh curry leaves can sometimes be bought in shops that specialize in Indian foods. If the leaves offered do not smell strongly of curry, do not buy them—curry leaves quickly lose their virtue.

CURRY PASTE. Frying the spices is the most difficult part of making any curry, and when you add to that the undoubted fact that curry improves and matures with keeping, you have the raison d'être for curry pastes. In addition, it is not always possible to get fresh ginger and fresh green chilies—two items necessary for many types of curry and difficult to incorporate in a powder. Many types of curry paste are on the market, but the name of E. P. Veeraswamy is associated with this type of product, which, in the past, was necessary to introduce Indian cooking to the West. Anyone who makes curry can easily make curry pastes when fresh ingredients are handy, and, because of the preservative action of spices, it is not difficult to devise formulas that will keep for many months. Easiest, perhaps, is vindaloo paste, which contains vinegar and keeps without difficulty.

VINDALOO PASTE

Use 1 oz (20–25 g) of hot red chilies—or double, even treble, that. Vindaloo should be hot, but chilies vary, as do tastes. If they are dried, soak them in 1 cup (¼ lt) of vinegar for 3 hours or until soft. Put them in a blender with 20 cloves of garlic and 1½ oz (35 g) of fresh ginger, scraped and cut in bits. Blend until liquidized. In a coffee grinder, grind a pinch of cumin, a big pinch of black mustard seed, and 2 oz (50 g) of

coriander seed; add to it 1 teaspoon (5 g) of ground turmeric. Mix everything to a paste and fry in 1 cup (¼ lt) of oil for about 10 minutes or until the oil separates. Add a tablespoon of salt (which helps to preserve it), and bottle when cool enough.

To use the paste, fry an onion in oil, add paste (according to your taste), mix into the fat, and fry a moment; then add meat. Fry for a moment more (but do not burn), then add a little water. Cook until the meat is tender. Adjust the salt.

CURRY POWDER. Curry comes from the Tamil (South Indian) word *kari,* meaning a sauce. To many people, it covers any hot, spicy Indian stew, but in India there are hundreds of dishes that would qualify under this definition, each quite distinct and with its own name. These dishes use varying combinations from a list of two dozen spicy ingredients—thus, hoping to reduce Indian cooking to "curry powder" is like hoping for a ready-mix "cake powder" to make all cakes. Curry powder, in fact, is a convenience food, but there is no agreed mixture. Unfortunately, many recipes that call for curry powder treat it almost as if it were a natural spice or a definite substance. It is not, so when one reads "mijoter dans une bonne sauce currie" in a recipe for lobster *à la Créole,* one feels that the famous chef who wrote it was leaving much in doubt.

Books commonly say that Indians do not use curry powder. This may have been largely true in the days when even servants had servants and the *masala* of fresh ginger, garlic, onion, coconut, green chili, and spices was ground on the stone freshly for each dish. But today, a First World cost of servants has caught up with Third World households, and ready-ground convenience spice mixtures are no longer beyond the pale. However, Indians do not generally use "curry powder" but rather a variety of mixtures (which they may have formulated and have had specially ground in the bazaar), including not only the traditional *garam masalas* (hot mixtures) but also powders for particular types of curry: *sambar, kolumbu, rasam,* or *dhansak masala,* to name but a few, and the mixtures are *always* fresh.

Alerted to the fact that curry powders are not standard, cooks have a wide choice of what they will use in recipes. Trial is the only way to choose. The chef has expressed no opinion, so we are back to the cook's personal taste. When choosing a recipe for homemade curry powder (and all serious cooks make their own), keep the following points in mind. One may want to vary the hotness: use a light hand with the chili in the powder and keep a jar of pure chili powder on the shelf to add for additional hotness. Turmeric makes curries yellow but does not necessarily have to go into them. Although it is not very spicy, its taste is assertive, penetrating, and rather banal. It is best not to overdo it. Fenugreek can also very easily be overdone, and its flavor gets stronger with time. Cumin is a taste some people do not like, especially if it is rank because it has not been properly roasted. Ginger makes you perspire. Some do not like the taste of dried ginger very much, and others, often those who tolerate chili, find its peculiar hotness overpowering. In India, ginger in curries is usually fresh and thus has a kinder taste. Volatile, oily spices, such as cloves, cinnamon, cardamom, and mace, are needed, particularly in powders for very aromatic meat curries or as a flavoring for raw or lightly cooked dishes, such as stuffed eggs and sauces. For best results curry powders should be fried a little (not burned), and it is worth making up your own *curry pastes and bottling them for adding curry flavor.

The spices most commonly used in curry powders are dealt with separately in this book. They are: chili, turmeric, ginger, coriander, cumin (black and white), fenugreek, cloves, cinnamon, cardamom, mace, black pepper, mustard, asafetida, cassia leaves, curry leaves, poppy seeds, and various *dals.* Other spices, such as ajowan, pomegranate seeds, kalonji, anise, and mango powder are used for special purposes. Curries from farther south and east may include zedoary,

lemon grass, galangal, and other less-known ingredients.

Making curry powder at home. Before grinding, certain whole spices should be roasted, an operation that has to be learned by experience. Roasting partly dries the spice and helps to develop and change the flavor. It is done in a dry pan (such as an iron frying pan) on top of the stove, and the spice must be stirred and lifted constantly to prevent burning. Whole dry chilies may be roasted in a cool oven. Each spice should be roasted separately and receive individual attention. Chilies should be brittle, but not burned. Coriander seed should be heated slowly until it gives off a lovely orange scent and is just too hot to touch comfortably. If it is not roasted and dried long enough, it will be difficult to grind. Cumin is roasted until the crude smell disappears and the aroma becomes slightly nutty. The color taken is very slight. Black peppercorns are roasted a little, just until they begin to smell. Most tricky of all is fenugreek seed, which must just begin to color a brown-yellow; if it is roasted too much, so that it starts to turn red, the spice becomes impossibly bitter. The more volatile and oily spices, such as cloves, cinnamon, cardamom, and mace, are not usually roasted, but some recipes call for roasting various *dals* as well as mustard seeds and asafetida. *Dals* turn pale-colored and develop special tastes necessary to the background in vegetarian curries. Mustard seeds lose their ability to produce hot flavors with water and develop a nutty taste when roasted until they splutter (the enzymes are destroyed). Asafetida mellows slightly but should be only very lightly warmed, or it will lose its special flavor.

Spices are easily ground in a small whirling-blade electric coffee grinder. The exceptions are ginger and turmeric, which are the better for a preliminary bashing with a hammer, since they are apt to break the blades of the mill. Thus, roast and grind the whole spices separately, sieve them into a bowl (grinding the residue, if there is any, a second time), and then mix well together. Pack the powder immediately into bottles, excluding as much air as possible, and seal. Exposure to air destroys flavor, or it is lost into the atmosphere. Damp also destroys curry powder.

Curry Powder Formulas

The thirteen formulas given below are from my book *Herbs, Spices and Flavourings* (Penguin). They give some idea of the enormous variations possible in curry powder recipes. The numbers indicate parts by weight.

	A	B	C	D	E	F	G	H	I	J	K	L	M
Black pepper	1	1	4	1	1	1½	2	2	½	1	1¼	8	4
Chili	1	2	-	1	8	1	3	2	6	8	4	-	-
Cloves	1	1	4	-	-	-	-	-	-	-	½	2	2
Cinnamon	-	2	1	-	-	-	-	-	-	1	½	2	2
Cardamom	1	1	1	-	-	1	-	-	-	1	½	2	4
Coriander	8	6	-	8	6	8	8	8	8	8	8	8	8
Cumin	-	2	4	2	1	-	1	1	1½	4	2	6	4
Curry leaves	-	-	½	-	½	-	-	-	-	-	-	-	-
Fenugreek	-	½	-	2	1	-	1	-	1½	-	1	-	-
Ginger	1	-	-	1	-	2	-	1	-	-	-	-	-
Mace, Nutmeg, Allspice	-	1	1	-	-	-	-	-	-	-	-	-	-
Mustard seed	-	-	-	½	1	-	-	2	-	-	-	-	-
Poppy seed, Lentils	-	-	-	1	-	-	-	-	-	-	-	-	-
Turmeric	10	-	-	5	-	10	4	2	2	3	2½	-	-

[*Curry powder*—French: *poudre de cari;* German: *indisches Currypulver;* Italian: *curry;* Spanish: *polvo de curry*]

CUSTARD. Basically eggs and milk cooked together, custard is a kind of *pudding that may be sweetened or unsweetened, cooked over heat for soft custard or baked for custard with a jellylike consistency. Delicate, nourishing soft custards are used as dessert sauces, for blending with fruits, and as a base for ice cream. Baked custards, flavored with fruits, chocolate, or coffee, are often cooked in a pie crust or in the custard cups in which they will be served. Many custard powders are now available, but they usually contain cornstarch, dye, and artificial flavorings and cannot be compared to a custard homemade with fresh eggs and rich milk.

CUSTARD APPLE is an American tropical fruit of the family Annonaceae, which is represented in the temperate zone only by the *pawpaw from the U.S. The other edible fruits of this family are rarely seen outside the tropics; some have been cultivated in tropical Asia as well as America. They are multiple fruits made up of many divisions, each containing a seed, and vary in taste from acid to sweet. One of the most acid is the soursop (*Annona muricata*), which is also the largest—its fruits, which are green and have rows of spines, typically weigh up to 6 lb (2.7 Kg) and may reach 8 lb (3.6 Kg); they are popular in Cuba, where they are used to make drinks and ices. The sweetsop or sugar apple (*A. squamosa*) is also popular in the Caribbean and is the one which you are most likely to find being referred to simply as the custard apple. It is eaten as a fruit as well as being used as pulp in drinks and ices. Sweetsops are picked when they are firm but after the skin between the segments has turned creamy yellow; they are kept in straw for a few days until they are soft, with rather custardlike flesh. In this state, they must be handled with great care—they are difficult to transport over any distance. Bullock's-heart or ramphal (*A. reticulata*) has more solid and granular flesh and can be heart-shaped and reddish brown or buff. The cherimoya (*A. cherimola*) has a scaly surface and a flavor not unlike pineapple; it is a species of tropical highlands, while the similar ilama (*A. diversifolia*) grows in lowland areas. The soncoya (*A. purpurea*) has particularly large fruit and is restricted to Mexico and Central America.

CUTTING IN. In making pastry, it was once usual to rub the fat lightly into the flour with the fingers, an operation which needed cold hands and a sensitive touch. These days, it is more usual to cut the fat into the flour, using two knives, one knife, a pastry blender, a blending fork, or other device, according to the skill and taste of the pastrymaker, but the newer food processors do the job superlatively, even for the novice. Light pastry can thus be made by the hot- and heavy-handed.

CUTTLEFISH. Cuttles are *cephalopods with a stiffening "bone," a familiar white porous object which is washed up on beaches and used to provide grit for cage birds. The living cuttle is a free-swimming, savage animal with eight arms and two tentacles. The latter are kept retracted, ready to shoot out and grab the prey. Living cuttlefish should be handled with care—they bite if given a chance, as a rather important lady, who once picked up one I had speared, discovered to her cost. The common cuttlefish of Europe (*Sepia officinalis*) is 12–16 in. (30–40 cm) long but is best at 1 ft (25 cm). The smaller *S. elegans* is only 8 in. (20 cm) long, but only people in places like Naples will be able to tell the species apart. The very tiny *seppiola* (*Sepiola rondoleti*), only 1¼–2½ in. (3–6 cm) long, is commonly seen in Mediterranean fish markets. Very often *seppiole* are mixed with the young of the larger species, which are even better, being very tender. The *seppiole* have fins like little ears sticking out at the sides, but the tender young have fins running almost from end to end.

To prepare cuttlefish, first make a slit in one end and remove the bone through the slit. Turn the animal inside out and remove the guts (reserving the ink sac if needed). Cut off the head and remove the parrotlike beak. Skin the cuttlefish and wash well before cooking. In *seppiole*, the body is the best part; they are very often stuffed.

[*Cuttlefish*—French: *Seiche;* German: *Tintenfisch, gemeine Sepie;* Spanish: *jibia*]

CYANOCOBALAMIN. *See* vitamin B$_{12}$.

CYCLAMATE. A chemical accidentally discovered in a laboratory in 1937, cyclamate was introduced on the U.S. market as a sweetener in the early 1950s. Its advent led to the development of a host of artificially sweetened commercial products, particularly soft drinks but also canned fruits, chewing gum, ice cream, candies, and even toothpaste and mouthwash. By the 1960s, sodium and calcium cyclamate were the basis of a billion-dollar-a-year diet-product business.

Cyclamates are about thirty times as sweet as ordinary sugar, are not fattening, and do not have the unpleasant lingering sweetness and bitterness of *saccharin. At first they were judged safe for human consumption, but tests on animals began to indicate that cyclamates might not be as harmless as they first appeared. During 1969 and 1970 they were removed from the permitted lists of food additives in many countries when American tests showed that artificial sweetening mixtures of cyclamates and saccharin caused a significant increase in bladder cancer when fed to rats. Some people have said that the scare over artificial sweeteners was promoted by sugar interests, that the amount of cyclamate consumed in the normal diet was insignificant, and that in any case the cancer was provoked in laboratory animals and not in humans. Others have said that the harm was done by impurities and not by the substance itself. However, tests in animals have raised further questions about the effects of cyclamates on the cardiovascular system, and until such matters are settled to the satisfaction of the Food and Drug Administration, cyclamates are not likely to reappear in food products in the U.S.

CYMLING. *See* squash.

D

DAB (*Limanda limanda*) are small, lozenge-shaped dextral *flatfish, usually not more than 12–15 in. (30–38 cm) long. The dab has a rough skin to which its scientific name refers (Latin, *lima,* file). Dabs occur in north European waters but not in the Mediterranean or the west Atlantic. As food, they are good rather than exceptional.

A related species, the yellowtail dab or rusty flounder (*L. ferruginea*), occurs in North American waters. The American or Canadian *plaice is sometimes called a sand dab.

Dabs may be skinned and fried or broiled. Larger ones may be filleted. In Jutland and on the Belgian coast they are salted and dried, and they may also be smoked.

[*Dab*—French: *limande;* German: *Kliesche;* Italian: *pianuzza, lima;* Spanish: *lenguado, platija*]

DAIKON. *See* radish.

DAL, dhal, or **dholl** is the Indian term for a split pulse or grain of any kind. In Central and South India, the seed is soaked and re-dried before it is split, which is economical because it gives a maximum yield of clean, whole grains. In North India, Gujarat, and Maharashtra, the seed is not soaked before splitting. This method leaves more waste and makes the *dal* more expensive, but the flavor is better. Such *dal* is always smooth on the outer (curved) face, but wet-split *dal* has the face rather flattened, with a depression in the middle due to shrinkage. Good *dal* is all of one color, with few bits, husks, or shriveled grains. It should also be free from rogue seeds and stones, though for safety it is always a good idea to spread the *dal* out and pick it over. A quicker and more wasteful way is to shake the *dal* with water and then take it out with a perforated spoon, leaving the stones (and some of the *dal*) behind on the bottom. *Dal* stored for long is prone to attack by weevils.

Dal cooks best in soft water, without salt (which is added at the end) and without prior soaking. It is soaked only when it is to be ground raw to a paste, as for some Indian preparations (e.g., *dosas* and *idlis*). *Dal* is vital in Indian cooking and in the cooking of the Southeast Asian countries, not only because it is the main source of protein for many people—and almost the only one for some poor vegetarians—but also because it is the basis on which many vegetarian flavors are created (it is even the basis for sweet dishes). For this reason, it is important to use the type specified in the recipe, because the *dals* are very different, and it will frequently spoil or change the dish if you try to use substitutes without knowing what you are doing. The types of *dal* are best called by their Indian names; even when they are varieties of species well known elsewhere; they are often rather different.

*Channa. Large-textured and yellowish.

Can be made into a simple purée (*sar*) but is very often eaten parched or ground into *_be-san_ flour.

Tur or *arhar* (*tuvaram* in the south of India). This is the *pigeon pea or red gram. It is usually fairly small and pale yellow, but bits of skin may be red or brown, even cream. It is little used in dishes from North India, where it will not grow well on account of frost, but it is the type of *dal* most used in the south and west, in Gujarat and Bombay. When people from Bombay write about *dal*, they mean *tur*. *Tur* mixes easily with water when cooked, and is light and easily digested. It is the *dal* of Parsi *dhansak* and also of the *rasam* and *sambhar* of the south.

Urd, ulutham, or *mash* is *black gram and a close relative of mung. The grain is small and the color white with flecks of black, even of green skin, according to the variety. *Dhuli urd,* the expensive washed type, is dead white.

Mung or *mug*. Green *dal*. The split *mung bean is cream or yellow, not white; the flecks of seed coat in it may be black or green. It is very digestible, perhaps the most digestible of all the *dals*.

Masur or *masoor*. Lentils. This is regarded as the most humble *dal*, but it is much eaten in Bengal and by Muslims. The *masur* of India differs somewhat from the lentils of the Middle East (such as the small, orange Egyptian lentils) and European varieties, but is regarded as a variety of the same thing. Some varieties cook to a mush, and others do not.

DAMSON (*Prunus damascena*). Both the popular name and the specific name of this small *plum go back to the Latin *prunum damascenum*—Damascus plum. The Middle English name was damascene.

Damsons are small, deep-purple fruit with a rich, slightly bitter flavor. Of all plums they make the finest stewed fruit and jam. The traditional damson cheese is a solid conserve of damsons and sugar. Although damsons are not a favorite with commercial growers today, they were a popular fruit in English kitchens in the days before World War II. Some damson trees that grow more or less wild produce outstanding fruit (there was one such in a handy hedgerow when I was a child), but "improved" cultivated varieties are often disappointing.

DANDELION. Perhaps the most neglected free food in the U.S. is the common dandelion (*Taraxacum officinale*). Surely more time is spent trying to eradicate it than in preparing it for the table.

Yet all parts of the lowly dandelion are edible. Young leaves, with their tangy flavor, can be added to salads or cooked as greens. One cup of cooked dandelion greens, only 60 Calories, has 21,000 International Units of vitamin A (several times the recommended daily allowance), 252 mg of calcium, 3.2 mg of iron, .24 mg of thiamine, .29 mg of riboflavin, and 32 mg of vitamin C. Dandelion buds can be sautéed in butter for a mushroomlike flavor. The flowers are collected for homemade wine. Dandelion roots can be eaten like parsnips or be roasted and ground to use, like chicory, for a coffee substitute. And thick-textured dandelion honey is a Colorado specialty.

Cultivated, paler varieties of dandelion are available from seed companies, the leaves are sometimes sold in ethnic markets in spring, and dandelion-root "coffee" may be bought in health-food stores, but most people need wander no farther than their lawns for this food. Even in city parks the indomitable dandelion flourishes. The only caution is to wash the leaves carefully if you gather them along highways or wherever they may have been sprayed by weedkillers.

In France, where dandelions are called *pissenlits* (indicating their diuretic properties), the plants are protected from sunlight to blanch the leaves and produce a milder flavor. These are often used in *pissenlits au lard*, whole small dandelion plants in vinaigrette with hot bacon on top. The Pennsylvania Dutch prepare the greens similarly, adding sugar to the dressing and sprinkling with chopped hard-boiled egg. In the South dandelions are cooked, often along with other greens, with salt pork or a ham hock and seasoned with vinegar and pepper. Dandelion greens can also be used in any way one uses spinach—for example, they add splendid color and flavor to green noodles—and can be blended for nutrients in vegetable juices. The Algerians even make a honey cake, *yubba,* with dandelion greens.

[*Dandelion*—French: *pissenlit;* German: *Löwenzahn;* Italian: *dente di leone;* Spanish: *diente de léon, amargon*]

DASHEEN. *See* yam (dasheen).

DASHI. A basic Japanese stock, based upon dried *bonito, seaweed, monosodium glutamate, and water.

DATE. The sticky objects that reach temperate countries are dried dates; fresh ones are firm and not wrinkled. Date palms were among the earliest trees to be cultivated, having been grown in the ancient civilizations of the Middle East. Iran is still the most important date-growing country, but the fruit is grown in other suitably dry and hot climates, including parts of the U.S. The date industry there began only in the twentieth century. Today nearly all the dates grown commercially in the U.S. come from California, especially the Coachella Valley.

Male and female date flowers grow on separate trees, and one male is allotted by growers to 50–100 females. In some areas pollen from fine trees is bottled and sold to date growers to sprinkle over the flowers of their best female trees. Dates may be black, meaty, and sweet with a thin skin or golden brown with a coarse texture and larger seed. They are classified as invert-sugar dates (containing mostly dextrose and glucose) or cane-sugar dates (containing mostly cane sugar).

There are three important classes of commercial date: soft, which are usually sold in compressed blocks and are intensely sweet; semidry, such as those sold in boxes with a stalk (or a plastic replica of one) down the middle; and dry, which are hard and ideal for carrying by travelers or for storage. Containing some 54% sugar and 7% protein when fresh, and higher concentrations when dried, dates are good high-energy food, splendid for iron rations on climbs or walks.

In the days before oil transformed their lives, the Bedouin of Arabia virtually lived on dates, together with the products from their camels and flocks of sheep. It is said that the date palm has 360 different uses—even the stones can be reduced to charcoal for the fire. The fruit, in addition to being eaten fresh, is pressed for juice that is evaporated to thick syrup and used as an ingredient in fermented drinks and vinegar. The crown of the date palm can be tapped for sap that is also boiled down or fermented. India produces date sugar from sap. The foliage sprouting from the crown of an old tree is eaten as a vegetable. Date palm meal is obtained from the stem of a small species that grows in the hills of southern India.

Dates have been cooked with almost every other food imaginable. In medieval days when taste buds favored the sweet-savory combination, dates went into dishes of lamb, chicken, and numerous other meats, and today this sort of dish is found in many Middle Eastern countries. It often contains other dried fruits—raisins, figs, apricots—and nuts, especially almonds. Dates may even be used with rice as a stuffing for oily fish, and they are an excellent complement to wild game. Dates are often stuffed with a sweet mixture, marzipan, or soft cheese, but in the U.S. they are mainly used in desserts: cakes, puddings, cookies, and whips.

[*Date*—French: *datte;* German: *Dattel;* Italian: *dattero;* Spanish: *dátil*]

DATE MUSSEL or **date shell.** *See* sea date.

DECANTING. Red wines, very old wines even if they are white, and vintage port should be decanted. *Vins ordinaires* are normally served from the bottle. Decanting gets rid of sediment, which spoils a wine's appearance, and helps the wine breathe by getting air to it and so allowing it to lose any mustiness or "bottle stink."

Decanting is simple for anyone with a steady hand. The bottle should be stood upright for 12 hours or so to let any sediment sink to the bottom. Red wines should be decanted about an hour before serving. There is no rule of thumb here, since the optimum time varies with the type of wine and its year; it is a question for experts to argue about. After wiping the top of the bottle, draw the cork, taking care not to disturb the sediment. Then wipe the inside of the neck and decant the wine slowly into a scrupulously clean decanter. To make this easier, a funnel can be used and the bottle should be viewed against the light so that you can see exactly when the sediment is in danger of coming out of the bottle. Wine does not keep in the decanter, and although port can be kept for a week or more, it gradually loses its best aromas.

[*Decanting*—French: *décanter;* German: *dekantieren, abklären;* Italian: *versare, travasare;* Spanish: *decantar, trasegar*]

DEHYDRATION. *See* drying.

DEVONSHIRE CREAM. *See* clotted cream.

DEWBERRY. *See* blackberry.

DEXTROSE. *See* glucose.

DHAL or **dhol.** *See dal.*

DIASTASE or **amylase.** Class of *enzymes which break down starch to sugar (*maltose). Such enzymes occur in many microorganisms, especially in yeasts and molds, and also are formed in quantity when grain germinates as part of the mechanism by which the growing embryo gets at the stored starch. The diastase content gradually increases in sprouting barley, for instance, and this is used to produce *malt. Diastases are also the means by which we digest starch: there is one (ptyalin) in human saliva, and a more efficient one is produced by the pancreas of adults and works in the small intestine. Very little of it is produced by babies—which is why starchy gruel is not very good as baby food.

DIBS. A household syrup made in the Middle East by dissolving out the sugar from raisins, carob beans, or sweet grapes and boiling down the solution until it forms a thick syrup which can be used as a sweetener.

DILL. The dill plant (*Anethus graveolens*) looks very like fennel, with similar yellow umbelliferous flowers and feathery leaves, but it is smaller and an annual, not a peren-

DILL

nial. When crushed, dill has a quite distinctive aroma with nothing of the anise background of fennel. It is a native of Asia but has been grown in Mediterranean countries since ancient times and is now naturalized over most of Europe. As a green herb, it is very popular in Scandinavia (e.g., in *gravlax), Russia, Germany, central and southeastern Europe, Iran, and Turkey. It is not so well known farther west, in Italy and Spain, or farther east, in India—and among all the herbs of French cooking, it scarcely gets a mention.

In the U.S., dill is strongly associated with pickled cucumbers—dill pickles, which can be far superior to the commercial product if made with home-grown cucumbers and fresh dill. Dill goes well with cabbage, and is excellent with fish and veal. The leaves or the seeds flavor dill bread and potato dishes. Dill vinegar is made by steeping dill sprigs in white vinegar, and dill butter is handy for stirring into hot vegetables. In fact, this herb is used lavishly—and with great pleasure— by dill addicts, who have even been known to add it to chutney and apple pie.

Dill seed, with a flavor reminiscent of caraway, and dill leaves (dill weed) are sold on any good spice rack. Sniff them to be sure they have a strong scent. But fresh dill is so good and so easy to grow that it should be in every garden.

[*Dill*—French: *aneth;* German: *Dill;* Italian: *aneto;* Spanish: *eneldo*]

DISACCHARIDES. *See* sugar.

DISINFECTANTS, germicides, and **antiseptics** are almost synonymous; they prevent microorganisms from multiplying, may reduce their numbers by killing them, and occasionally kill their spores. Disinfection should not be confused with *sterilization, which is the total destruction of all living organisms, including spores.

In the kitchen, household disinfectants are used for cleaning. There are special disinfectants for treating bottles, casks, and jars for home preserving and winemaking. In unhygienic places, particularly in the tropics, it may be necessary to disinfect water or vegetables that are to be eaten raw. Occasionally small quantities of disinfectant are added to food. Kitchen disinfectants must be harmless in the amounts used; they must either be flavorless and odorless or have odors that are quickly dispelled by heat. Disinfectants overlap with *preservatives, as in the case of *alcohol and acids.

Formaldehyde. Formalin is a 40% solution of formaldehyde gas in water and is very active against any organisms, including growing cells and spores. Although it has a strong smell, it was formerly used in minute concentrations as a preservative in milk and cream, but it is now generally forbidden by law. It makes the eyes water and is potentially dangerous, so if used it should be handled in well-ventilated places. But it is much too unpleasant to find a place among the regular kitchen disinfectants.

Oxidizing agents. Powerful oxidizing agents are very active in killing germs, especially when they contain chlorine. Well-known substances in this category are hypochlorous acid, hypochlorites such as sodium hypochlorite (bleaching powder), chloramine, which is used in water-sterilizing tablets, and dichloramine.

Among the oxidizing disinfectants which do not contain chlorine is potassium permanganate, which gives a bright purple-red solution when dissolved in water. It is a powerful germ-killer, especially when combined with an acid (a 1% solution of permanganate containing 1.1% hydrochloric acid will kill anthrax spores in 30 seconds). In the old days, travelers in the Third World always used permanganate to rinse salads, though a quick rinse in very dilute solution was doubtfully effective. In contact with organic matter, hydrogen peroxide (H_2O_2) gives off its extra oxygen atom to become water. It is a good cleaner, because the froth of oxygen it gives off dislodges dirt and gets behind it, but it is not commonly used for kitchen disinfection.

Soap is an antiseptic as well as a cleaning agent. I was taught by the head of British Army medical services in India in World War II that a pure soap, free from perfume, can with advantage be used to wash the skins of fruit and vegetables when they are to be eaten raw. For fruit, this is probably more effective than washing in dilute permanganate because soap removes grease, a prime protector of bacteria. Naturally, after soaping, the fruit must be well rinsed in pure water.

Salt. Brine is not normally thought of as a disinfectant, but salt stops the growth of bacteria in solutions of 25% and over, and it inhibits many bacteria in considerably smaller concentration.

[*Disinfectant*—French: *désinfectant;* German: *Desinfektionsmittel;* Italian: *disinfettante;* Spanish: *desinfectante*]

DISTILLATION (from the Latin, *stilla,* a drop) is a method of separating or refining volatile substances by heating them until they vaporize and then cooling (condensing) the vapor back to the original state; the apparatus used is called a still. The ancient Greeks knew how to get fresh water by distilling sea water (that was easy, since the dry salt was left behind), but separating *alcohol from the water in wine or a fermented mash was more difficult, and the technique is probably no more than 1000 years old, if that. When introduced into Europe, spirits were first called by names such as eaux de vie and *uisge-beath* (whiskey), which mean "waters of life," because they were medicinal and sold by apothecaries, not pubs.

The separation of alcohol from water is possible because it is more volatile than water and boils at a lower temperature—172°F (78°C) as opposed to 212°F (100°C). A mixture boils at an intermediate temperature (depending on the relative proportion of water and alcohol), and the vapors contain both alcohol and water. The first run-through with a simple still will produce a distillate of 20–40% alcohol. Distilling this a second time may increase the alcohol content to 70% , depending on the spirits being made and the distiller's technique. Further distillation can get the alcohol up to 97.2% alcohol (by volume) but never more, since this mixture boils at a lower temperature than does 100% alcohol. The only uses related to cooking for alcohol of great strength are in making liqueurs and alcohol-preserved fruits. It is dangerous and potentially explosive stuff.

In spirits for drinking, such as whiskey, brandy, rum, fruit brandies, and gin, there are important considerations other than strength. Fermented mashes contain varying amounts of other volatile substances. One such is methyl alcohol, of which very little is produced in the fermentation of sugar solution (or sugar from starch), but some will be formed from woody cell walls and pectin (in stalks and pips) when fruit mashes are fermented. Methyl alcohol is poisonous, but the amount formed is usually too small to be harmful, and it will come over in the first runnings (heads or foreshots), which is why these are discarded. At the other end of the scale are the congenerics, which make up *fusel oil. This is a mixture of higher alcohols and other substances, which are less volatile and mainly come over last in distillation. Although the congenerics are removed almost entirely from vodka, some are retained for flavor in other spirits. It is the distiller's art to leave in exactly enough of these; with too little there is a poor flavor, while too much produces nasty hangovers.

In many countries, governments have made laws forbidding the citizen to distill his own liquor, an infringement of liberty which often goes unnoticed. Perhaps it is also officialdom that has perpetuated the myth that distillation is difficult, and that homemade or bathtub gin is likely to cause blindness. Oil men working in "dry" Arab countries have devised simple ways of making "silent spirits," which resemble vodka and, though lacking in flavor, give less hangover than bought brandy or whiskey. They have also demonstrated that the main danger lies not in blindness or the revenue officers but in blowing up the kitchen. Until distillation is made legal, the shops specializing in materials for home brewing and winemaking will not be able to sell properly made, safe home stills and books will not be able to offer responsible instructions. The distillation of overproof alcohol is just about as dangerous as distilling gasoline, and anyone attempting it should observe every precaution and work in a well-ventilated area. Like eating wild mushrooms or driving a car, distillation has to be done with a lot of knowledge and sense or not at all.

[*Distillation*—French: *distillation;* German: *brennen;* Italian: *distillazione;* Spanish: *destilación*]

DISTILLED WATER. Water which, after distillation, is virtually free from mineral matter and contains very little dissolved air. Although it tastes flat, it is safe to drink, but will need mineralizing if it is to be used for long periods. Water distilled from sea water is increasingly used in waterless but oil-rich regions and on ships (like nuclear submarines) which have to stay at sea for long periods. The only usual use for distilled water in the home—apart from car batteries—is in steam irons. The water from ice melted in defrosting the refrigerator can be used for both purposes.

DOGFISH. *See* shark.

DOLPHIN. *See musciame.*

DRAMBUIE. Liqueur based on *whiskey.

DRAWING. The process of extracting the entrails of birds. Make sure that the bird has been properly plucked and singed. Some Italians advocate washing the skin of chickens with plain soap and water, and they claim that this makes a significant improvement in the flavor. (It could be a sensible precaution.)

The head is retained only in very small birds. Otherwise, cut it off. Heads and combs are used in country cooking, but most people throw them away.

The feet should be cut off just below the joint. If they are cut above the joint, the thigh muscle attachments are severed and the meat shrinks, exposing the bone on cooking. Remove the claws and dip the feet into boiling water while you count to ten. (If they are kept in the water too long, the job is more difficult.) Immediately scrape the fine skin off. The cleaned feet are then ready for the stockpot.

The neck is chopped off near, but not too near, the body; remove the gullet and windpipe. The neck usually goes into the stockpot, but the neck skin can be used for stuffing, like a sausage.

The crop is joined to the gullet and is the thin bag at the base of the throat. The crop lies just under the skin; it may be freed by blunt dissection with the fingers, then severed from the rest of the gullet where it passes into the main body cavity. There is no use for the crop. Discard it.

The vent. Birds have a common vent situated beneath the tail stump or parson's (or pope's) nose. Make a slit below the vent (in fact above it, because you will have the bird breast uppermost); I always enlarge the slit by snipping right around the vent and freeing it entirely. Put two fingers inside the bird and free the viscera from the cavity walls by blunt dissection. When they are free, gently pull out all the guts—first the gizzard, then the liver, and finally the heart and remains of the gullet.

The liver. In most birds (but not, for instance, in pigeons), there is a gall bladder. This is a small green sac closely applied to the liver. Locate it and snip it out without breaking it, as the gall inside is intensely bitter. Wash the liver and set it aside.

The heart. One of the giblets. Separate and wash it.

The gizzard is a large muscular sac, part of the digestive canal, where the food is ground up with grit. Cut it free from the rest of the guts (which are discarded) and slice carefully into it until the knife feels the surface of the horny lining (there is a gristly lining to be snicked through first). If this is done properly, the gizzard can now be pulled open and the horny lining separated and discarded as a complete bag with the contents enclosed in it. Wash the gizzard, which usually goes into the stockpot.

Other internal organs include the lungs, which are spongy and closely stuck to the top of the body cavity, the testes or oviducts and ovaries (which may contain partly formed eggs, sometimes used in cooking) and the kidneys. They can be left in or not, according to preference. Rinse out the cavity (and dry it) only if necessary.

Skin. To skin a chicken, cut through the skin along the breastbone and, with a knife, free it from the muscles underneath. Using fingers as instruments for blunt dissection, free the skin at the sides of the breast and around the base of the thigh. Pull the skin inside out over the whole leg. When one leg is completely skinned, do the same for the other. Now get the fingers under the skin and push them right across the back to the other side. Run the fingers along, tearing the skin free up to the parson's nose. Cut off the nose and skin it in one stroke of the knife. Now pull the skin forward, blunt dissecting with the fingers around the base of the wings and up to the neck. Pull the skin off, inside out, over the base of the wings. It will tear, but do not bother—the skin on the wings is almost impossible to remove entirely.

[*Drawing*—French: *vider;* German: *ausnehmen;* Italian: *esstrarre;* Spanish: *destripar*]

DRAWN BUTTER. In America, this is simply clarified butter. In Britain, melted butter sauce is thickened with flour; drawn butter is melted butter to which either water or vinegar has been added and which is then beaten until it is thick.

DREDGING. Sprinkling heavily with sugar or flour—more than a light sprinkling or dusting and less than a coating.

DRIED MEAT. Many countries have ancient types of dried meat. *Drying has a preservative action because spoilage organisms cannot multiply without water. Salting,

*smoking, and even spicing are adjuncts. *Dry salting in particular works by extracting water from meat as well as through the preservative action of the salt. Equally, drying is essential for hams and sausages which are mainly preserved by salt, saltpeter, and smoke. It is difficult (and pointless) to try to draw any line between hams and dried meats except one of convenience. However, in recent years, the introduction of scientific methods of desiccation under reduced pressure, freeze drying, and so on have resulted in thoroughly dehydrated foods, which are a logical extension of the same processes, and these are a thing apart.

The primitive method of drying is hanging strips of lean meat in the sun. Such a product is the *den-dang* of Southeast Asia, made of buffalo or game. In Africa, I have often seen strips of game meat hung to dry in the smoke of the campfire (which I suspect was how smoking meat was discovered, not, as is usually claimed, through hanging it in the roofs of caves with their damp and stagnant air). The campfire smoke exerts a preservative action, but, perhaps even more important, it keeps away flies which would otherwise lay their eggs on the meat and walk about on it with their filthy, contaminated feet.

The best-known dried meats include the *biltong of South Africa, the *tassajo* or *charqui* of Spanish America (which in North America is corrupted to "jerked" beef or jerky), the more sophisticated *bundnerfleish* of the Grisons in Switzerland, and the *bresaola* from just over the border in the Adda valley region (Valtellina) of northern Italy. Beef is the meat most commonly dried, plus game in the jungle, sheep (the *chalona* of Latin America and also a horrible dried mutton in Tibet), goat, and even dolphin meat (*musciame*) in Sardinia and the Ligurian coast of Italy.

DRIPPINGS. The fat that dripped from roasting meat, in the days when meat really had fat on it, was called drippings. When cold and solidified, some brown meat jelly was usually trapped and preserved under the fat. When the fat (especially of beef drippings) was mixed with the jelly, salted, and spread on toast, it used to be a standard—and delicious—appetite stopper for farm workers and children at tea time on raw evenings in winter or after skating. Drippings were also commonly clarified and used as a cooking fat. In that case, the distinction between drippings and rendered fat is mainly one of usage. (Chicken fat, so much a part of Jewish cooking, is not called "chicken drippings.") Drippings from bacon or sausage are excellent for sautéing or for frying potatoes, and the drippings from beef roasts are used to make Yorkshire pudding.

[*Drippings*—French: *graisse de rôti;* German: *Bratenfett, Schmalz;* Italian: *grasso d'arrosto;* Spanish: *pringue*]

DRUMSTICK. Not just the lower part of the legs of chickens, turkeys, or other fowl, but also the name of a tree, *Moringa oleifera,* which is used as a vegetable. It is also called horseradish tree (because its roots taste like horseradish and are used as a flavoring) and ben tree (the seeds—ben nuts— give oil of ben, which is used commercially). It is a native of India but is planted in southern parts of the U.S. and has gone wild in the West Indies. The drumstick tree is important in Indian cooking, where the flowers, leaves, and even the twigs are cooked. The leaves are pounded with onion and sour pomegranate seeds to make a chutney. Most important of all are the unripe pods, which are long (up to 18 in or 0.5 m) and, though often rather fibrous, have a delicious taste, sometimes compared with asparagus. Particularly in Madras and Bengal, they are often used in vegetarian curries to which they give an incomparable, almost meaty flavor. Drumsticks can occasionally be found in shops that specialize in Indian foods, or may be acquired locally in Florida and southern California.

DRYING is the oldest method of preserving food, and in its modern form of dehydration is of great industrial importance. It works because dry food is not spoiled by yeasts, molds, and bacteria—or even by enzymes— as long as the amount of water left in it is not enough to support life processes. Since microorganisms are not necessarily killed by drying, dried foods which get damp spoil very quickly; kept dry, though, they will keep for long periods. Even such highly perishable items as fish and shellfish can be preserved by natural drying.

Drying depends on relative humidity, the quantity of water vapor in the air in relation to the amount it will hold. But since the amount of water the air will hold increases with temperature, warming air drops the relative humidity, not by removing water vapor but by increasing the quantity that the air can potentially hold. That is why, even on the dampest day, things will dry in a low oven or in an airing cupboard.

In deserts, the relative humidity is often naturally low, so drying is easy, even in the shade, but on humid tropical beaches the relative humidity is often very high, in spite of the heat, and the drying of shrimps, fish, or octopus must be done in the sun—which raises the temperature. In such conditions, rapid drying is necessary to forestall decomposition. Even so, the products—Bombay duck is typical—develop a gamy flavor. (In Arctic regions, fish may be laid on rocks or hung in rigging to dry slowly, as in the preparation of stockfish.) Sun drying is not the method for most foods. True, the ultraviolet rays help kill surface bacteria, but they also increase the effects of oxygen and so tend to destroy color and flavor. Drying in the shade is therefore usually preferable if low relative humidity makes it possible.

A breeze helps drying because it continually changes the air; in stagnant conditions, the air is quickly saturated with moisture from the objects that are drying. Reduced pressure also promotes drying—at high altitudes, evaporation directly from ice produces the strange pinnacled glaciers around Mount Everest. Cold, in itself, does not prevent drying.

Dried food is convenient because it is light

in weight and takes up little space. With modern high-speed techniques such as drying under reduced pressure, spray drying, and freeze drying, the end products are often almost indistinguishable from those made with fresh ingredients. However, dried foods usually need to be soaked before use, and if this is not properly done the results may be unsatisfactory. Oversoaking can lead to decomposition, and living products, such as pulses, should not be soaked if they can be cooked without it.

The simplest dried foods are grain, pulses, and nuts, all of which require very little drying. Fruit mostly dries well, although large species like apples need to be sliced. Some fruit discolors when cut and needs to be treated chemically if appearance is important. Vegetables must be blanched before drying. Drying fish, meat, eggs, and milk is normally a commercial undertaking.

Fruit, provided it is not too watery, can be dried in the sun (as tomatoes are in southern Italy). Figs need no treatment, but apricots must be split and stoned, while apples and pears have to be peeled, cored, and cut in rings or pieces about ¼ in. (.5 cm) thick. Spread them out on mats or screens to dry. The time taken will depend on the type of fruit and the amount of sun, as well as on the relative humidity. Naturally, the fruit should be taken in or covered at night or when there is a possibility of rain.

More certain results are obtained by drying in ovens or in special driers in which everything is under control. A cool oven, with the door ajar for ventilation, is difficult to regulate exactly. Driers can be bought and are not difficult to construct, the requirements being an easily controlled source of heat and a means of creating ventilation.

DRY SALTING, curing meat by salting and drying, involves rubbing the surface with mixtures of salt, sugar, and saltpeter. There is more handwork than when curing in brine, but the dry-salting cure penetrates more slowly and produces a better flavor. Ham, bacon, and other cured meats can be produced by brining (*see* brine), by dry salt-

ing, or by a mixture of both. Dry salting, however, is used for the most expensive products.

When salt is rubbed dry on meat, there can be no penetration by salt until some of it has dissolved in liquid extracted from the tissues. From then on, as water flows out of the meat, the salt solution diffuses in, a process that takes place rather slowly. Very finely ground salt (or sugar) is never recommended for curing because it sops up liquid like blotting paper, thus increasing the rate at which the meat loses water while slowing down the penetration of the salt. In dry salting, the greatest care must be taken to see that all pockets in the meat and places near the bones are in contact with salt and saltpeter, as they may otherwise become centers of putrefaction.

[*Drying*—French: *sécher;* German: *trocknen;* Italian: *seccare;* Spanish: *secar*]

DUCK. Like geese and swans, ducks belong to the family Anatidae. Wild ducks are found all over the world, and some of the many species are excellent to eat, while others are horrible. Within a species, palatability also depends on the time of year and on the duck's age and diet. Almost all the domesticated ducks have been derived from the mallard, which is widely distributed throughout the world, but ducks have been domesticated for so long that they have changed enormously from their original form. Breeding involves selection for special characteristics: for instance, some ducks are bred for laying, others for eating. Domesticating ducklings does not take much effort. They don't even need to be on water, but they appreciate a trough or bucket of water in which they can wash their beaks and heads.

Ducks have been eaten in Europe and China for many thousands of years. The Greeks and the Romans ate them (gourmets consumed only the breasts and brains), and in China the duck is highly prized. In fact, the trouble the Chinese take with ducks— removing the oil glands in the tail, inflating the bird to separate the skin from the flesh to get a better crackle, or stuffing it with mixtures of stir-fried pork, water chestnuts, ginkgo nuts, ham, shrimp, and rice wine—makes even pressed Rouen duck seem simple. The Chinese also value ducks for their beauty, especially the mandarin, which is commonplace today but was not so a little more than 100 years ago. The Chinese, according to a 19th-century naturalist, took "a singular dislike to seeing their birds pass into the hands of Europeans." Another writer in the mid-19th century reported: "A gentleman very recently wrote from Sydney to China requesting some of these birds sent to him. The reply was that from the present disturbed state of China it would be easier to send him a pair of mandarins than a pair of Mandarin ducks." Nevertheless, shortly after that, nine white Peking ducks, which had previously been bred only in the Imperial Palace, arrived in the U.S., and it is claimed that these are the ancestors of today's Long Island ducklings. With time, the number of common breeds has reduced to those regarded as best—or most profitable. In the U.S. and Europe, these include the following:

Long Island ducklings of Chinese ancestry are said to be produced in greater numbers than any other breed in the world. They are excellent and run to 5–6 lb (3 Kg) as ducks, and something under 3½–4 lb (2 Kg) as ducklings. In the U.S., applesauce is traditional with roast duckling.

Aylesbury is the most important English breed. White, with some similarity to Rouen ducks, Aylesburys put on weight rapidly and have dark, tender, and tasty flesh. They run to about 4–5 lb (2 Kg) when dressed. The British have a preference for roast duck and green peas, but there are other interesting dishes, such as the excellent boiled duck of North Wales. Many British restaurants go in for a sloppy version of the French *Caneton à l'orange,* which too often means duck with a dollop of marmalade in the gravy.

Nantes ducks, famous in France, are smaller than Rouen ducks but have a fine texture and flavor. At 4 months, they are usually a little over 3¼ lb (1.5 Kg). Nantes ducks, unlike Rouens, are always bled when they are killed. The easiest way to do this is to chop off the head and to hang the duck up by the feet to drain off the blood.

Rouen ducks, from Normandy, are large. They reach about 6 lb (3 Kg) in 4 months and are never bled when killed. Instead, they are suffocated or strangled so that they do not lose any blood. This gives a very dark meat and a special taste. Once killed, a Rouen duck must be eaten within 24 hours. The most famous dish is *Caneton à la rouennaise.* While the duck is still warm, the breast must be plucked so that the blood flows into it. In drawing the bird, care is taken to lose as little blood as possible from the duck, and any that does escape is caught in a bowl. The gall bladder is separated from the liver and the liver returned to the cavity. The bird is trussed and roasted on a spit for only 15–30 minutes, depending on its size; it is then skinned. Legs and wings are cut off for separate treatment. The thigh bone is removed from the leg, which is then marked with a hot skewer, brushed with melted butter, broiled, and, finally, sprinkled with coarse salt. The wing tips are rolled in bread crumbs and broiled. These are put on the hot serving dish with the breast, pink and sliced, and are covered with a sauce made with Bordeaux wine in which shallots have been simmered. The juices from the carcass are pressed in a special press and the liver and heart are sieved. Full details of this classic dish are given in that book of marvelous recipes, *Les recettes secrètes des meilleurs restaurants de France,* by Louisette Bertholle (an abridged version in English is *Secrets of the Great French Restaurants,* published by Macmillan, 1974).

The other domesticated species of note apart from the mallard and its descendants is the grotesque-looking Muscovy duck (*Cairina moschata*), which hails not from Muscovy (Russia) but from South America. It is the favorite table duck in Australia and is also eaten in the U.S. and Britain. The flesh is musky unless the ducks are very young. Because they are so big, their livers are sometimes used to make pâté de foie gras.

Although ducks are so valued in France, they are much less so in Spain and Italy, where recipes are relatively few. Perhaps one reason is that the French roast duck for rather a short time (as the British do with wild duck) and eat it pink, though not bloody (15 minutes per 1 lb/450 g is the rule of thumb), whereas Spanish recipes advocate roasting a duck for 2 hours. They also say that the meat is dry and inferior to chicken, which is not surprising. In Italy, the Venetians have several original recipes for stuffed duck (*anara col pien*), including in the stuffing veal, sausage, bread soaked in Marsala, bitter-almond biscuits, and the inevitable Parmesan cheese, and basting, for example, with wine and rosemary.

Choosing domestic ducks—or ducklings— is not difficult, since it is fairly obvious from the look of a duck if it is old—and, in any case, commercially produced birds are killed when quite young. It may be less easy in some remote market or with wild ducks, and the following rules will help. Ducks should be fresh, without smell, and plump (particularly on the breast, which is the important part). The bottom half of the beak should be flexible, and one should be able to bend it back easily. The webs of the feet should be soft—in old ducks they are hard—and the wing pinions should also be flexible. To carve a duck, remove the legs and carve the breast in long, thin slices fore and aft, more or less vertically, down to the bone.

In Europe, the U.S., and Asia, wild ducks of various species come in from farther north to winter, settling in large numbers in estuaries and lakes, or feeding inland in fields according to their habit. The mallard is the commonest wild duck (it is the *canard sauvage* of France) and the one most eaten everywhere, since it is abundant and of excellent table quality. It is at its best in November and December. In southern France, it is preserved in brine.

Other ducks commonly eaten in Britain are the pintail (*Anas acuta*); the teal (*A. crecca*), which is small; the scaup (*Aythya marila*); the shoveler (*Spatula clypeata*); the widgeon (*Anas penelope*), and the pochard (*Aythya ferina*). Others, like the shelduck (*Tadorna tadorna*) and the tufted duck (*Aythya fuligula*), are protected or avoided. Nature-lovers get more pleasure from flights of ducks over the water than from wild duck on the table.

In North America, the most prized wild duck is the canvasback (*Aythya valisineria*), so called for its light canvas-colored back; it is said to get its delicious flavor from the "wild celery" it gets from diving. In addition to the pintail, teal, scaup, shoveler, and widgeon, other ducks which are highly prized in North America are the redhead (*Nyroca americana*); the black duck (*Anas rubripes*), of which the Cayuga is a domesticated version; the colorful Carolina or wood duck (*Aix sponsa*); the ring-neck (*Aythya collaris*), and farther south, the Dominican masked duck (*Nomonyx dominicus*), as well as many others of less quality. There are also favorite wild ducks in Asia, Africa, Australia, and New Zealand, and some gastronomic oddities like the dried fray duck (*Anas zonorhyncha*) of China. Opinions vary as to the respective merits of ducks; some are good when young but not when old. Old ducks of edible species make good game stock, though.

Wild ducks should not be hung, though some recipes call for them to be marinated to tenderize them and rid them of any fishy flavor. Plucking out the down is tedious; one solution is dunking the bird in scalding water for a couple of minutes and then rubbing it with finely powdered resin, which brings off the down by sticking to it. After plucking, the duck needs singeing. Cut off the head and draw and wipe out the ducks in the normal manner. In the old days, wild ducks were usually trussed with the feet left on, and the feet were scalded and skinned, but people today are more squeamish and don't like to be reminded of what they are eating. Wild duck is usually served rare—the old saying was that a mallard should walk through the kitchen, a widgeon should run slowly through, and a teal should rush through. Most experts recommend about 20 minutes in a hot oven, but such short cooking might be inadvisable with frozen game or with any that might be infected with salmonella (*see* eggs).

[*Duck*—French: *canard;* German: *Ente;* Italian: *anitra;* Spanish: *pato*]

DULSE. *See* seaweed.

DURIAN or **durion** (*Durio zibethinus*), a tropical fruit, is a native of Malaysia. It looks something like a *jackfruit but is not related. The green football-shaped fruits have a hard shell with pointed warts or spines and weigh about 4½ lb (2 Kg). When they are ripe, they turn yellowish and may fall, making it inadvisable to walk underneath the trees, which may reach 100 ft (30 m). Many people find the fruit delicious, although it has a dreadful stench. Optimists say that this can be removed if the pieces of fruit are soaked in coconut milk for a day. The flesh of durian has the consistency of custard; the taste is rich, aromatic, and sweet, with a strange balsamic background.

DYES. Nearly 90% of food colorings sold are synthetic dyes and have to be certified as safe by the responsible authorities (*see* additives). The first coal-tar dye, aniline purple, was discovered by the British chemist Sir William H. Perkin in 1856, and by the beginning of this century, dye chemists had developed dozens of these synthetic colorings, any one of which could be added to food, provided there was no obvious and immediate harmful effect. At that time, nobody had registered that dyes could also have long-term ill effects. Gradually, over the years, the more obviously harmful dyes have been weeded out and banned, but it has recently become clear that the control and selection has not been done well enough. Even more alarming, authorities such as the World Health Organization, the U.S. Food and Drug Administration, and the responsible agencies of the various European governments do not agree on the dyes which should be considered safe, in spite of the pressure they are under to standardize, because differences upset international trade. Such a situation arose, for example, over the color amaranth. When this was provisionally banned, on suspicion, in the U.S., the authorities in Britain (where it is most commonly used for coloring jams and other foods that tend to be eaten by children) did nothing about it, on the grounds that the tests were inconclusive. Most parents would consider it more sensible to take the attitude that any chemical is guilty until proved innocent, rather than waiting for cast-iron proof of harmfulness before taking action. Although figures are continually varying, national attitudes are expressed in the following figures of the number of artificial colorings allowed in food: 18 in Britain, 16 in the EEC, 7 in the U.S., and none in Norway. Of course, the amount consumed must be taken into consideration, and this varies from country to country. Children, who eat most of these dyes, are also most vulnerable. Dyes can cause, among other things, cancer, allergies, and damage to unborn babies.

However, in fairness, it is a mistake to think that every natural substance is harmless and every synthetic one harmful. All cooking, all life, is chemical. Naturally charred substances used to color gravies could be carcinogenic. One concludes it is best to use food colors only on special occasions and to keep soft drinks and sweets to a minimum. Making them at home is not only more wholesome but also cheaper. Flowers, fresh or crystallized, nuts, and fruits can be used for color (*see* colorings) and decoration.

E

EARTHENWARE. This is the simplest and most primitive form of pottery. It is soft, porous, and fragile. Although easily broken by a knock, it is comparatively resistant to thermal shock—that is, it is not as easily cracked by sudden changes of temperature. Cold liquid poured into a hot, dry earthenware pot is still likely to crack it. Earthenware does not heat evenly like a metal, but good-quality earthenware cooking pots can often be put straight on the open fire or gas flame without harm, especially when the bottom of the pot is rounded.

Unglazed earthenware is the classic material for water pots. The water soaks through, evaporates, and so cools the contents. For wine, it was once more usual to use skins, gourds, or other less permeable containers, with good reason. Nobody wants to lose wine by evaporation, and glazed earthenware in the past was dangerous when used for storing an acid substance (*see* ceramic glazes).

Earthenware pots, such as the Spanish *ollas* or *graxioneras* and Italian *padellas,* are splendid to cook in, if you understand their characteristics. Some dishes, like the pot-roasted rabbit with herbs and black olives of Liguria (*coniglio alla sanremese*), taste even better when cooked in earthenware (although I have not been able to work out the reason). However, if food is allowed to burn in earthenware, it burns badly. The glaze of an earthenware pot which has been used regularly on a fierce fire or on naked gas for some months may crack or craze. The exposed earthenware can then give an unpleasant taste to the food and the pot must be replaced.

Earthenware has a high specific heat—it needs to absorb a lot of heat to raise the temperature—but it also cools slowly. Food brought to the table in the pot in which it was cooked will stay hot—and may even go on cooking. Should the instability of pots with a rounded bottom be an embarrassment, a mat of straw or wood, shaped like a ring, is the traditional rustic solution for the table; a metal flan ring will solve the problem on the stove.

[*Earthenware*—French: *terre cuite;* German: *Töpferware, Steingut;* Italian: *terraglie, stoviglie;* Spanish: *loza de barro*]

EAU DE VIE. *See* fruit brandy.

EDDO. *See* yam (dasheen).

EELS are fish which show a resemblance to snakes in shape. This makes them repugnant to some people, but they are all good eating, and the common eel has become an expensive delicacy. The large marine eels, the ★conger and ★moray, belong to different but related families.

The common eel of Europe and North Africa (*Anguilla anguilla*) used to be a most mysterious creature. Every spring, about March, baby eels (or elvers), tiny wormlike animals only 2¼–3¼ in. (6–8 cm) long and $\frac{1}{12}$–⅛ in. (2–3 mm) thick, came wriggling up

AMERICAN EEL

rivers in a massive migration known as an eel-fare. The elvers pushed on into every tiny stream and even crossed fields to reach ponds and ditches. Every autumn, large silvery eels left those ponds and ditches, reached the streams, and headed downriver to the sea. Old books carry descriptions of silver and yellow eels, of sharp and broad-nosed eels which were thought to be of different species. In the days when even mice were thought to arise from fermenting grain, there were bizarre notions about the origin of eels. In 1905, the International Council for the Study of the Sea assigned to Denmark the task of unraveling the life history of the eel, and Dr. Johannes Schmidt of the Carlsberg Laboratory in Copenhagen was chosen to head the team. It took almost twenty years and the cooperation of countless ships' captains before the mystery was unraveled. Eels were found to breed 900 ft (275 m) down in the depths of the Atlantic to the southwest of Bermuda, not far from the Sargasso Sea. The eel larvae—very small, almost transparent leaflike objects—drift about 3000 miles (5000 km) in the Gulf Stream until they reach the shores of Europe—a journey which takes three years. They then change their shape and turn into elvers, which swim up the rivers (a large proportion of males stay in the estuaries). They live in fresh water for eight to ten years, feeding voraciously and growing.

These eels are yellow. Then they change: their eyes get larger, their lips thinner, their noses more pointed, and their color goes from yellow to silvery before they start to migrate in autumn, crawling like snakes through the grass on wet nights, knowing where to go by some incredible instinct. Once back in the sea, they swim for their breeding ground, a journey which takes them six months to complete. The following spring, they are ready to lay their eggs in the place they left as minute larvae. After breeding, they die—or so it is presumed—because they never return to their rivers. The American eel (*A. rostrata*), which is closely related, breeds not far away from its European cousin and so has a shorter distance to travel. Eels in Japan (*A. japonica*), Australasia (*A. australis*), and elsewhere have similar habits and closer breeding grounds, so they do not travel the same vast distances as the European species.

In the past, elvers were a common seasonal delicacy; they were boiled and pressed into eel cakes. Today, the high price of eels means that most of the elvers caught go to stock eel farms, but they can still sometimes be obtained locally. Elvers are usually bought ready for cooking. As soon as they have been brought home, they should be well washed in salted water.

In Spain, elvers (*angulas*) are a popular and expensive spring treat. They are usually cooked *a la bilbaina,* quickly boiled in oil with chili and garlic. For 11 oz (300 g) of elvers, fry 8 cloves of garlic and a red chili in oil until the garlic begins to color. Then put in the elvers and continue to fry for a couple of minutes. The elvers are still soft and white (they look unfortunately like parasitic worms). They are usually cooked in individual earthenware dishes, to be fished out of bubbling hot oil and eaten with a wooden spoon.

Fully grown eels are another sort of delicacy. They need to be mature; when yellow they are poor eating. The best size is under 2 lb (1 Kg), although females sometimes grow to a monstrous 5 ft (1½ m) and 13–

15½ lb (6–7 Kg). Mature silver eels are caught in nets as they migrate toward the sea in autumn. They are also fattened on eel farms. Near Venice, eels from the *valli,* as the saltwater lagoons in that part of the Adriatic are called, are kept in huge, half-sunken baskets called *bolaghe* and left to fatten until they are ready for eating.

It is a shame that pollution and modern drainage have led to drastic reduction in the numbers of eels. At one time, canals were full of eels, and barge men carried a trident-like eel spear for jabbing at the muddy banks as they went past—eels disclose their presence by telltale bubbles. Even in those days, there was a pollution problem: the Dutch eel boats would not come above Gravesend for fear that the live eels, carried in perforated "wells" open to the sea, would be poisoned.

Eels should be bought live. It is best to get the fishmonger to kill and skin your eel for you (but cook it immediately). However, it is quite easy to kill eels by banging the heads against a hard object; the trouble is they go on wriggling after they are dead. To skin an eel, cut a ring in the skin round the neck with a sharp knife. Get someone to hold the head (a skewer passed through it helps the grip) and pull the skin back, inside out, like peeling off a glove. A pair of pliers helps in gripping the skin; so also do wood ashes or coarse salt.

The eel is not prized by most Americans today, though it is valued in Creole cookery and is made into delicious soup by the Pennsylvania Dutch. New Englanders bake eels in a "stifle," a casserole layered with potatoes and onions and flavored with salt pork. Eels, with their sweet, meaty flavor, are quite nutritious, high in vitamins D and A. They may be grilled, baked, or cooked in dozens of ways. In Germany, it may be eels in dill sauce; in Britain, jellied eel is famous; and eels are a traditional dish during the Italian celebration of Christmas Eve. But now, alas, price has turned eels from poor man's food into a rich man's delicacy (like salmon and oysters). Eels are popular in al-most every other European country from Norway, through Holland, to France, Spain, and Italy. Frozen eel is imported from as far away as Japan and New Zealand (but is not as good as the freshly killed article).

Smoked eel is also a great delicacy and an excellent, if expensive, start to a meal. The skin, dried by smoke, is easily peeled off and the fillets are removed from the backbone. Smoked eel is usually served with brown bread and butter and lemon wedges. The finest smoked eel comes from Holland.

[*Eel*—French: *anguille;* German: *Aal;* Italian: *anguilla;* Spanish: *anguila*]

EGGPLANT or **aubergine.** The plant (*Solanum melongena*) belongs to the nightshade family and is native to tropical Asia, probably to India, where it has been cultivated since antiquity. The eggplant is an important vegetable in all warm countries.

The first eggplant I ever saw growing was in my garden in India. It was of a poor local variety but did look exactly like an egg in size, shape, and color. Since such varieties are rarely grown today, the origin of the name "eggplant" is not usually so obvious. Modern varieties, when ripe, are mostly large and colored violet or purple. Some are streaked with white and mauve, even with green. They may be round, football-shaped, or elongated like clubs. The last are necessary for certain dishes; the footballs are preferred for others. Poor eggplants have rather many seeds and may be bitter, but modern varieties rarely need the salting and draining of juice which was once essential. The flesh of eggplants is always white and a little spongy. It discolors badly when exposed to the air and should preferably be cut with a stainless-steel knife. Experts advocate mashing cooked eggplant with a wooden fork rather than with one of metal. Eggplants are almost always eaten cooked—boiled, baked, or fried. Their spongy texture does incline them to mop up too much fat in frying, especially if they have not been salted, and they are best dipped first in a light batter. On the other hand, they take up spices and flavorings excellently. Famous eggplant dishes include *ratatouille niçoise* from Provence, *melanzane ripieni* (stuffed eggplants baked in tomato sauce) from Italy, *moussaka* from Greece, *imam bayeldi* from Turkey, and another Levantine specialty, the smoky-flavored "poor man's caviar," of which probably the best is made in Rumania. In India eggplants are called *brinjals* and are the basis for the delicious hot *brinjal kassaundi* or pickle.

POOR MAN'S CAVIAR

Cut the stems off 3 medium eggplants and broil or grill them, turning them occasionally, until the skin is black and cracking and they are soft to the touch. Let them cool a bit, then peel off the skin (or halve them lengthwise) and put the pulp, cleaned of all bits of skin, into the blender with 1–2 cloves of garlic and 3–4 tablespoons of olive oil. Blend until it is a purée, then add the juice of ½–1 lemon (or more to taste) and season it with salt. Stir in 2 tablespoons of chopped parsley and serve with hot pitta or other bread. Poor man's caviar also makes a delicious dressing for a tomato salad.

[*Eggplant*—French *aubergine;* German: *Eierfrucht;* Italian: *melanzana;* Spanish: *berenjena*]

EGGS. It is generally stated that all fresh eggs are edible, though possibly not palatable. I do not know if this bold statement is intended to cover reptile eggs—although turtle and alligator eggs are certainly good to eat; what about snake eggs? With birds' eggs, though, I feel inclined to accept the generalization. (Having climbed several times to vultures' nests, I will leave the trial of their smelly offerings to someone else.)

However, the eating of wild birds' eggs, once prevalent, has now become a matter of conscience because of our dwindling wildlife. It is also often a matter of what is allowed by law, even though, with some species, taking eggs expertly might do no harm. The nests must be found before the bird has finished laying her clutch. If only one or two eggs are now quietly taken when the bird is away feeding, she will usually go on laying to make good the loss. With management—an egg being taken every day—a continuous supply can be arranged over a period of a week or more, and yet the bird in the end can be left to hatch out a full clutch. This benefits the robber. He is following the pattern of the good parasite which does not exterminate its host. It is quite immoral to grab a whole nest of eggs or through ignorance to cause birds to desert the nest.

Eggs have superlative food value (containing about 12% fat and 12% protein). While hens' eggs in particular are excellent value for money, they are also a promoter of good health, although in recent years some medical opinion has denigrated them. Eggs contain cholesterol, the stuff that they say clogs up the arteries. But eggs also contain lecithin—which unclogs arteries—and the sulfur-rich amino acid methionine, which also helps in this.

Since eggs are also rich in iron, in vitamin B_{12}, and in vitamin A, it is not surprising that there are doctors who greatly approve of them and advise eating up to four a day; they say that excluding eggs is a disaster, especially for people with defective circulation and heart, for whom an egg-free diet is often prescribed. One day, no doubt, the truth will be known. When people are allergic to eggs, the trouble is almost always due to the white, especially if it is raw or lightly cooked. Raw white, in fact, is said to contain traces of a harmful substance, but in practice this can be ignored. For most people, who are outside the controversy, eggs for breakfast, or with oil in mayonnaise, are probably a passport to good health.

Hen eggs. "Egg," without qualification, always means the egg of the domestic fowl. It is an article of food produced yearly by the billion. There is scarcely a village in the whole world, outside the high Arctic, perhaps, where hens cannot be found. Indeed, eggs are probably the most universally known food of man.

The domestic hen is descended from a species of jungle fowl and was domesticated in India or Indonesia, where wild jungle fowl are still common in places. Domestication took place quite early in history, and the practice of keeping hens soon spread from the East over the Old World. The Romans noted them in Britain when they arrived, but they did not reach America until they were taken there by Columbus on his second voyage.

The shell of a hen's egg is usually under 1/50 in. (½ mm) thick and weighs roughly one-eighth of the total weight of the egg; it is made up largely of calcium carbonate. The strength of the shell varies with breed and with the hen's food and health. Battery hens often lay eggs with fragile shells. Color may vary from dead white through cream to brown, even speckled. Brown eggs are sometimes more expensive than white eggs, but apart from their aesthetic appeal as boiled eggs in the shell they have only one advantage to offset their greater price—they have slightly less porous shells and so may possibly keep longer. The shells of all eggs have to be porous to some extent, to allow air to enter for the developing chick (which, we sometimes forget, was what the egg was designed for). This porosity means that aromas can enter (an advantage only if you are keeping eggs in a bag with truffles), as can microorganisms. One in ten eggs contains harmless bacteria even when freshly laid, but less harmless kinds can get in subsequently, especially when the shell is dirty and wet. That is why, if an egg has to be washed, it should be used at once.

Lining the shell is a flexible double membrane, the two layers of which are virtually stuck together except at the large end of the egg where they separate to enclose an air space. This pocket grows bigger as the egg gets older, until after some days it gets big enough to cause the egg to float, or at least for the large end to lift off the bottom of a basin of water. It is on this that the tests for freshness are based.

The white of an egg is layered, the outer layer being more watery than the inner. Egg white consists of on average 9% protein and 88% water, and makes up a little over half the total weight of the egg. Egg white mixes with water when raw, but coagulates when heated to about 160°F (70°C) and becomes very hard and indigestible when heated to still higher temperatures. However, like meat protein, it becomes soft again when boiled for several hours, as in Chinese tea-leaf eggs and the *hamine* eggs of Egypt, for which see Claudia Roden's *A Book of Middle Eastern Food* (Knopf, 1972).

Tea-leaf eggs are boiled for 2–3 hours in water containing tea leaves and star anise, with various other additions—salt, monosodium glutamate, soy sauce, sugar, onion, etc.—according to the recipe. These eggs have pale brown marbling which is produced by cracking the shell after the first 20–30 minutes cooking, a smoother tender texture which comes from the long boiling, and flavor that has seeped in from the anise and other substances in the water. Tea-leaf eggs are served cold as hors d'oeuvre or with salads.

Egg white dries into a hard, shiny coat—something like varnish—and can, of course, be whipped to a firm froth (*see* whipping). In stale eggs, the white becomes watery.

The yolk is contained in a sac—the vitelline membrane—and is suspended at either end by a stringy chalaza or balancer. The chalaza is attached to the yolk so firmly that it clings to it as a tail when the egg is separated. Yolk makes up about a third of the weight of an egg and consists of 16% protein, 51% water, and 30% fat. It is the most nutritious part of the egg. The color of the yolk depends upon the food eaten by the hen.

Blemishes in commercially packed eggs are rare because they have been examined against a light (candled) at the packing station. Blood spots, unless very large, can be ignored—they merely indicate that a tiny blood vessel was ruptured while the egg was being formed. Commercially produced eggs are rarely fertile, but in fertile eggs a minute spot can be seen on the upper surface of the yolk. This is the germ from which the chick would develop if the egg were to be incubated. Some say that fertile eggs are better than infertile ones, an opinion not shared by vegetarians, who prefer unfertilized eggs because eating them does not involve taking life. Battery-produced eggs are avoided by many people because they lack flavor and possibly some of the more subtle nutrient qualities of free-range eggs, but here the question of price is also involved.

There is, however, universal agreement that an egg is best when fresh. A simple test is to put the egg in water. If it lies flat on its side on the bottom, it is fresh; if it shows a tendency to get up at the broad end, eventually standing vertical, it is stale; if it floats under water, it is 2–3 weeks old; if it floats on the surface, it may have been laid for several months and be bad. A more sensitive test is to put the egg into 12% salt solution (which can be kept in a bottle and used many times). Fresh eggs will lie flat on the bottom, but they will get up at the broad end after only 2–3 days and will eventually hang suspended in balance when they have the same specific gravity as the brine.

At only four days, the eggs will come to the surface and float vertically with the broad end peeping out; thereafter they will float higher each day. After fifteen days, the egg will topple and lie flat, floating on the surface of the brine. This test is depressing. Most of the eggs you buy in the shops are at least a week old, good but not excellent. When broken onto a flat surface, really fresh eggs stand up in a convex mound, but as they get older the convexity decreases. In really stale eggs, the white is watery and the vitelline membrane so weakened that yolk and white mix. Such eggs may still be tolerable in cakes but are not much use for anything else.

In the poorer countries, eggs are almost always smaller than the American average and allowances should be made for this when following recipes from such countries. Egg sizes are standardized by the U.S. government. Eggs specified "extra large" weigh 27 oz per dozen; "large" eggs weigh 2 oz each or 24 oz a dozen; "medium" weigh 21 oz per dozen; "small" weigh 18 oz per dozen.

Coagulation. The white of an egg coagulates at about 140–149°F (60–65°C) and the yolk at the slightly higher temperature of 144–158°F (62–70°C). When yolk and white are mixed the coagulation takes place at about 156°F (69°C). The coagulation temperature is even higher when milk, water, or sugar is added, so that custard coagulates at around 175–185°F (80–85°C). Those making custard or sauces thickened with eggs may also find it useful to know that coagulation will begin at a lower temperature—though only slightly so—when the temperature is raised slowly than it does when the temperature is raised fast, and that while the custard is thickening the temperature in it does not continue to rise because— put simply—heat is used up in the thickening process. Once the temperature starts to rise again it means that coagulation is completed. If the heating is continued, the sauce will curdle (at around 190°F/88°C). Of course, the sauce must be stirred because otherwise it will set solid, like baked custard.

Smoked eggs from China are lightly hard-boiled eggs which have been shelled, marinated, and smoked. They are served as hors d'oeuvre or as part of a cold plate. A similar result can be obtained by marinating hard-boiled eggs in soy sauce seasoned with smoked salt and slightly sweetened with sugar.

Preserving eggs. You need to use new-laid, clean eggs. Even so, you can expect one in ten to be contaminated by bacteria. This means that a few may go off, though they will not be dangerous, only unpleasant. Preserved eggs should always be broken one at a time into a separate container. There are many methods of preservation to choose from, some old-fashioned, as follows:

PRESERVING EGGS IN LIME

Make a mixture of 7–9 oz (200–250 g) slaked lime, 1–1½ oz (30–40 g) salt, and 1 teaspoon cream of tartar to each 3½ cups (1 lt) of water. Boil the mixture, but do not put the eggs in until it is stone cold. Keep in a cold cellar.

The effect of lime is to seal the pores in the eggshell. Other methods of doing this are also effective. Shells may be rubbed with clarified butter, dipped in molten wax, or painted with gum arabic; the eggs are then stored in bone-dry sawdust, bran, charcoal, or ashes. Another way is simply to pack the eggs tightly in dry salt. (They are packed thus to exclude air.) An interesting way— which relies on a thin coagulated layer—is to plunge the eggs for 20 seconds into boiling water before drying and packing them in dry bran. Some people even store eggs for shorter periods by wrapping in greaseproof paper.

Eggs will stay good for a long time if they are chilled—stored at 43°F (6°C) but not below this.

Eggs should not be frozen in the shell. To freeze eggs, first crack them, then either separate the yolks and whites or stir the two together. Mix with either salt or sugar (according to the purpose for which they will later be used) at the rate of 1 teaspoon per dozen eggs and freeze as usual in containers. Frozen white does not return to normal after unfreezing, but it can be whipped and used in cooking.

Dried egg. The idea of drying eggs was thought up in the 19th century but was first successfully undertaken by German engineers in China in the present one. China was the principal source of dried egg for the world until the 1930s, when production became viable in the U.S. and Britain. Dried-egg production reached a peak during World War II and immediately afterward dropped sharply, no doubt because of a general aversion to anything to do with rationing and wartime shortages. Since then, intensive research has improved the product, and the commercial use of dried egg has grown steadily. Eggs to be dried may be separated into yolk and white or mixed up and dried whole. They are generally spray-dried and pasteurized. Drying causes little or no loss to the nutritional value of eggs, but the flavor does alter. However, dried eggs usually taste much the same as fresh eggs in custards or scrambled. The whipping qualities which are largely lost in drying can be restored by the addition of certain chemical compounds and carbohydrates such as sugar. Dried-egg products are principally used in the baking industry and in manufacture of sweets (e.g., in the fondant filling for chocolates). Dried egg is now of little interest outside the food industry except to the nostalgia-prone who want to follow wartime recipes and to campers in remote places.

Duck eggs have a chalky white or very pale blue shell. Many people prefer them to hen eggs for flavor. They have a distinctive taste, and a somewhat gelatinous, blue-tinted white. Some varieties of duck beat all records for egg laying—almost one a day for the whole year—but the eggs are not as popular as hens', because ducks, being messy and none too disciplined, may drop their eggs in dirty and contaminated places. Occasionally, they have become infected with *Salmonella* bacteria and have caused food poisoning.

However, duck eggs are very popular in the Far East and are the basis for the famous Chinese thousand-year eggs (*trúng-den*). They are in fact ready to eat in something under two months and become solid by a maturation process—ripened as if they were cheese. The egg inside is variable in color from greenish yellow to malachite green and black, usually in concentric rings, following the pattern of the original egg layers. The texture is smooth and creamy, the flavor original and unlike anything else, although overtones of bad egg are detectable when they are first broached. Thousand-year eggs are served at the start of a meal, usually quartered and served as an appetizer, perhaps with lime and fresh ginger. They can be bought at shops that specialize in Chinese foods, but it is probably better to be introduced to them by Chinese friends who know what a good bad egg should taste like.

Salted eggs are another Chinese specialty. These duck eggs preserved in strong brine may be bought from Chinese shops and are very salty. Keep them in a refrigerator.

THOUSAND-YEAR EGGS

For a couple of dozen absolutely clean and fresh duck eggs, mix up a paste of 4¼ oz (120 g) each of salt and wood ash, and 3½ oz (100 g) slaked lime, with about 2 cups (½ lt) of water. Wash the eggs in hot water and roll each one in a handful of the "paste," coating each about ½ in. (1 cm) thick. Roll each coated egg in chaff to give it a nonstick coating. Pile the eggs in a crock and cover with a lid. After 3 days turn the pile over, eggs on top to the bottom, and do this every 3 days for 15 days. After that, seal the jar and leave it for a month. The eggs are now ready to eat. Remove paste and shell, and cut the cheesy egg into pieces for serving.

Goose eggs are something like a very large duck egg, but rather milder in flavor.

Guinea-fowl eggs look something like small hen eggs and are of excellent quality with a mild flavor.

Black-headed gull eggs have now replaced plover eggs. They have a somewhat similar appearance (brownish olive-green with dark-brown spots) and are not much larger. They are good, but not quite equal to plover eggs, like which they are usually eaten hard-boiled. The eggs of the herring gull and other seabirds (e.g., the gannet) were—and still are in places—harvested off the cliffs. I remember from my childhood the egg-gatherers arriving yearly with ropes at the great red sandstone cliffs of St. Bees Head. After gathering eggs, they boiled great buckets of them on the beach below. This was a wasteful process, since many of the eggs already had chicks half developed inside them. The eggs of herring gulls are tolerable if fresh, though stronger than those of the black-headed gull. In the past, they were an essential food to many islanders, but their collection is no longer necessary, and it is hardly worth risking your neck to get them.

Moorhen eggs. The eggs of this common bird are good and were once much taken by country people. Provided eggs are removed quietly, a few at a time, moorhens will go on laying for many weeks.

Ostrich eggs are available only in South Africa and other places where ostriches are farmed. One of these enormous eggs is equivalent to one to two dozen hen eggs. They have a rather eggy taste, but are excellent for cooking and are sometimes sold as dried egg.

Partridge and **pheasant eggs** are sometimes available where game birds are bred. They are smaller than hen eggs and are excellent.

Penguin eggs. Penguins nest in huge rookeries, so the eggs just beg to be gathered and eaten. Eggs of the Cape or jackass penguin are officially taken in modest numbers from the islands off Cape Province, in South Africa. They fetch a high price. Penguin eggs are peculiar, in that the whites remain clear even when they are hard-boiled (so they look like eyes on the plate), but since they are usually eaten well laced with Worcestershire sauce, I cannot help feeling that motives for eating them are more snobbish than gastronomic.

Pigeon eggs. Small and delicious, pinkish white eggs, most often served hard-boiled. As the author of the Time-Life publication *The Cooking of China* says, it is something of a chore to eat a hard-boiled pigeon's egg with chopsticks, and anyone who has mastered the art can justly claim to be an expert.

Plover eggs. In the past, these were considered a great delicacy, and there are recipes for them not only hard-boiled but also cooked in other ways. Unfortunately, the population of plovers has declined (mainly because of changes in agricultural methods), and it is now against the law to gather the eggs in Britain. Plovers must have been very plentiful in the past—because their nests are hard to find—and gathering was done by professionals with the care necessary to induce the birds to go on laying over a period and subsequently to hatch their normal setting.

Quail eggs. Very small eggs, usually eaten hard-boiled. They have become available in recent years as a by-product of quail farming. For a long time, they have been highly regarded as a delicacy in the Far East.

Turkey eggs. Large, brown, spotted eggs of excellent quality. The smaller eggs of young birds—paler than those of older birds—are good boiled; the others are used for cooking. They taste rather like hen eggs and make splendid omelets.

[*Egg*—French: *oeuf;* German: *Ei;* Italian: *uovo;* Spanish: *huevo*]

EGYPTIAN BEAN. *See* chickpea, lablab bean.

EGYPTIAN PEA. *See* chickpea.

ELDER and **elderberry.** The common American elderberry (*Sambucus canadensis*) is one of the most abundant of our native wild fruits. It is also one of the most healthful (far higher in vitamin C than citrus fruits) and most neglected.

The elderberry has pinnate leaves with five to eleven leaflets. During June and July it bears umbels of creamy white flowers. These are edible and may be deep-fried in a batter, stirred into fritters or muffins, or made into tea or wine. In August, if you have not eaten all the flowers, the plant is weighed down with umbels of purple-black berries. Elderberries are not very palatable as fresh fruit, but their other uses are versatile. They are delicious in jelly. However, they lack acid, so they are often mixed with other fruits or lemon juice. A good tart combination is elderberries with acid scarlet *su-mac fruit or crab apples. Elderberry wine has long been prized in the U.S., and the juice before fermentation is healthful. The berries can be made into chutney or soup. Drying elderberries removes some of the rather strong elder taste; they can then be stewed or used in pies.

[*Elder*—French: *sureau;* German: *Holunder;* Italian: *sambuco;* Spanish: *saúco*]

ELVER. Baby *eel.

EMULSIONS. An emulsion is a mixture of two liquids which are not mutually soluble, for example, oil and water. Instead, one liquid is dispersed as tiny globules in the other. The emulsions which mainly concern us in cooking are of oil and water. Milk is an emulsion, and so is mayonnaise. Emulsions can be made by forcing oil and water together through a fine nozzle, or by using emulsifying agents such as egg yolk or some mustards. Emulsions break when the globules of like substances come together and amalgamate.

[*Emulsion*—French: *émulsion;* German: *Emulsion;* Italian: *emulsione;* Spanish: *emulsión*]

ENDIVE. *See* chicory.

ENOKITAKE. *See* mushrooms.

ENZYMES, which were also called ferments, are organic catalysts fabricated by living cells. Catalysts are substances which cause or accelerate chemical changes without themselves being used up or permanently altered in the process. In nature, there are countless numbers of enzymes, each of which is responsible for its own reaction or group of reactions. Enzymes, in other words, are specific. They control and initiate most of the chemical reactions making up the life processes. Some operate only inside living cells. Others can also function outside the cell or after the organism that created them has died. Enzymes are sensitive to temperature; many will be killed by heat or strong chemicals, almost as if they were living. They may also be prevented from working by substances such as salt and vinegar. Enzymes produced by yeasts, fungi, and bacteria are responsible for many natural food processes such as fermentation, ripening of cheese, souring of milk, and vinegar production. Plant enzymes play their part in such diverse operations as producing a bitter-almond flavor in peach stones (or bitter almonds), a bite in mustard, or the spoilage of unblanched vegetables in the deep freezer. The names of enzymes end in -ase. For instance, an enzyme which oxidizes is an oxidase, and one that hydrolyzes carbohydrates is a carbohydrase. Pectinase acts on pectin. Invertase (produced by most yeasts and molds) inverts sugar. There are proteinases, phosphatases, glycerophosphatases, and polysaccharidases, even penicillinases. This is the specialist world of the biochemist, the cheese technologist, and the brewer, but we should register the simple fact that most things we handle in the kitchen are subject to alteration by enzymes and that changes, one after another in patterns of astronomical complexity, are constantly going on in foods we keep (except in those that have been treated to prolong their shelf life).

[*Enzyme*—French: *enzyme;* German: *Enzym;* Italian: *enzima;* Spanish: *enzima*]

EPAZOTE, Mexican tea, or **wormseed.** This is a strongly flavored herb (the name comes from Nahuatl *epatl* and *tzotl,* meaning an animal smelling like a skunk, some-

EPAZOTE

thing dirty), native to tropical America. It is best fresh, but can also be dried. The plant (*Chenopodium ambrosioides*) belongs to the same family as goosefoot and spinach. It grows wild in parks and backyards in such unlikely places as New York City, although

it does not have such a strong flavor there as it does farther south. It is used in soups, with beans, in tortilla dishes, and as a tea.

ERGOT. *See* molds.

ESCABECHE. *See* caveach.

ESCARGOT. *See* snail.

ESCAROLE. *See* chicory.

ESSENCES. An essence should contain the fundamental quality of a substance in a concentrated form, but in cooking the word is given many loose meanings. Flavored waters, such as orange-flower water and rosewater, are sometimes called essences because they are liquids in bottles, as are coffee essences and *sirops.* The French use of the word implies the natural, concentrated juices which run from food during cooking—the juices from roasting meat, for instance. However, with these exceptions—and a few concentrated products like essence of rennet—we are dealing with flavorings in bottles; they may be extracts, essential oils (natural or synthetic), or new chemical compounds created by the chemists. Powders, produced by drying under reduced pressure, may strictly speaking be essences but are not usually so regarded. It is best to forget definitions and to discuss the whole complex together.

Essences may be made by extracting with a solvent. If the solvent is harmless, like water or alcohol, the essential flavorings may be left in solution (a tincture), but other solvents such as hydrocarbons or ether have subsequently to be removed by evaporation. On the other hand, essential oils, which are found in aromatic herbs and spices, are usually volatile and can be obtained from the natural source by distillation (usually by steam distillation, since they are often fragile). Rose oil (attar of roses), for instance, has been made for many hundreds of years by simple distillation from a watery mash. Modern techniques can separate and purify the various essential oils. For instance, the aroma and taste of dill or sage can be extracted and split up into its various components, even though it is usual for something to be lost in the process. Manufacturers like these essential oils, and we cannot entirely blame them. The public expects a particular product always to taste the same, something that is difficult to achieve using natural (and thus highly variable) herbs and spices. It is much easier to reconstitute the components to a fixed formula.

Out of the 2000 or so flavorings currently available to the food industry, only some 500 are in any way natural; the balance are the brain children of chemists and are not known to occur in plants in nature. Artificial flavorings are imitations of natural ones, perhaps, and may contain 20 or more separate substances in carefully formulated proportion.

And how many of this bewildering range of substances are really necessary? One thing cooks can learn from the food trade is that small, unrecognizable quantities of very unlikely flavorings can be used in improbable contexts. You might be astounded to know that the oil distilled from *rue (a nasty-smelling herb) is used, for instance, in raspberry, blueberry, rum, and peach flavorings. *Asafetida (another horrid smell) goes into ice cream and candy, eucalyptus into ginger-ale flavor. All this should encourage us to experiment.

[*Essence*—French: *essence;* German: *Extrakt;* Italian: *essenza;* Spanish: *essencia*]

ESSENTIAL OIL. Volatile oil containing substances which provide flavor and aroma. Essential oils may be extracted (e.g., from the skins of *citrus fruits) and used in perfumery or as *essences.

EVAPORATED MILK is unsweetened whole milk which has been evaporated to half its original volume, homogenized, canned, and sterilized by heat (unlike *condensed milk, which has sugar added as a preservative). Diluted with an equal quantity of water, it can be a substitute for fresh milk in all recipes that do not involve the use of rennet. Undiluted, it can make a substitute for cream, although it has a boiled milk taste. It can be whipped if the unopened can is first heated in boiling water for 20 minutes and then cooled before opening or, more simply, if it is put into the refrigerator for 12 hours and then mixed with 2½ tablespoons of lemon juice before whipping.

EXTRACTS in cooking are flavorings that have been dissolved out and concentrated. They thus include natural *essences, which are extracts, for example, of spices and fruit peels, usually made with ethyl alcohol. Also classified as extracts are meat concentrates, which are effectively clarified *stocks that have been boiled down to a fraction of their initial volume and stored for use in sauces and gravies. Commercial beef extracts such as Bovril contain salt, yeast extract, and various other flavoring ingredients.

F

FAGGOT. An old English way of using the insides of the pig, very similar in concept to the French *gayette* and *crépinette*. All are made of minced meats with flavorings wrapped up in *caul. Much less time is needed to make faggots than to make sausages, at least if you are doing it from scratch. Traditionally liver, lungs, spleen, and scraps are minced with fat, usually a filler such as bread crumbs, and flavorings such as onion, sage (or other herbs), spices (mainly pepper and nutmeg or mace), and salt. The mixture is rolled in squares of caul, packed in a pan, and baked brown on top. Faggots are available locally at butchers in Britain, particularly in the midlands and north of England, and in parts of Wales. An old-fashioned convenience food, faggots can be eaten hot with gravy or cold.

FAHRENHEIT. Named after German physicist Gabriel Daniel Fahrenheit (1686–1736), this system of measuring temperature is gradually being phased out of use. Fahrenheit took as zero the temperature of an equal mixture of snow and salt and, as 100, the temperature of the human body. This put the freezing point of water at 32°F and its boiling point at 212°F—a difference of 180°. Improved instruments later showed that the temperature of the human body was not exactly 100°F. Although the Fahrenheit scale was satisfactory for all daily purposes, it was not used by science because the *Celsius scale was linked with metric definitions.

FARINA. Although this word is applied to any flour (for instance, *farina dolce* is chestnut flour in Italy), it most often refers to potato flour. This mixes easily with water and absorbs it quickly. It is a good binder, so is used commercially as a filler in cooked sausages, where a compact texture is needed. Farina made from wheat, another common type, would not produce the same result, so one cannot necessarily substitute one farina for another. Fecula is much the same as farina, but with the starch separated from the source (potato, corn, or arrowroot) by washing with water; it is then allowed to settle out and dried. *Cornstarch and *arrowroot are typical feculas.

FATS and **oils** are essentially similar substances, fats being solid and oils being liquid at ordinary room temperatures. Mutton fat can melt in Death Valley, and sunflower oil will solidify when the Fahrenheit thermometer reads zero (-18°C).

A little simple chemistry is necessary to show what is meant by words such as "saturated" and "polyunsaturated," which are much bandied about in discussions on diet and health. Fats and oils are formed by the combination of a fatty acid with an *alcohol (usually glycerin).

There are dozens of fatty acids, of which the simplest is *formic acid (HCOOH) and the next *acetic acid ($CH_3.COOH$). The fatty acids form a series of ascending complexity which goes on through butyric acid (C_3H_7COOH), which is found in rancid butter, and caproic acid ($C_5H_{11}.COOH$), the smell of billygoats, to the very much larger molecules involved in most of the fats. The molecules are composed of carbon and hydrogen atoms in chains, and when these chains contain only carbon atoms with their fullest possible complement of hydrogen atoms attached, then the fatty acid and any fat formed from it are said to be saturated—their molecules can take no more hydrogen. But in some fatty acid molecules, there are extra linkages between adjacent pairs of carbon atoms in the chain, and each of the two carbon atoms involved in such a double bond consequently has one less hydrogen atom linked to it. The fatty acid is then unsaturated—monounsaturated if it has one double bond, polyunsaturated if it has more than one.

The double bond represents a potentially active point in the chain, and unsaturated fats are thus less stable and more easily changed. For instance, it is relatively easy for the oxygen in the air to attack the double bonds. The oxidation products have an unpleasant smell and taste—we say the oil has gone rancid. But if the double bonds are replaced by extra hydrogen atoms—a process known as hydrogenation—then the slow oxidation is prevented. Hydrogenation also raises the melting point, and the unsaturated oil becomes a saturated fat—the basis of margarine production.

As an industrial process, hydrogenation involves heating oil with hydrogen under pressure, using nickel as a catalyst. Any oil can be hydrogenated—fish oil, whale oil, or vegetable oil (even mineral oils, but they are not used as food). Although saturated oils keep well, they appear to increase cholesterol in the blood and to clog up the arteries. Monounsaturated fats appear to be neutral in this respect, but polyunsaturates actually lower the blood cholesterol (though not as rapidly as saturated fats can build it up) and so are valuable diet aids—just how valuable is still a matter of controversy.

Of the vegetable oils regarded as suitable in a low-cholesterol diet, safflower, sunflower, soy, peanut, corn, and sesame are best, but wheat-germ oil has exceptional qualities when raw and fresh. Olive oil and cottonseed oil are in the middle category, as are the oils in some nuts and in avocados. Oils in fish are generally good—some, like herring oil, very good—and chicken fat is tolerable. But coconut oil or fat, ordinary commercial hydrogenated peanut butter, palm oil, cashew nuts, butter, and pork, mutton, and beef dripping are all high in saturated fats, as also are hard margarines and vegetable shortening.

A few fatty acids seem to be harmful quite irrespective of their saturation. One such is erucic acid, which in quantity can cause heart damage, at least in experiments on animals. It is found in rape and colza oils, which are put into the blends used for salad oil. The allied mustard oil is much used in Indian cooking in various areas, particularly in Bengal, and might be suspect. We should not worry unduly about this, but remember that over the centuries man has evolved a physiology to deal with a wide variety of different foods. He is likely to get into trouble only when he takes a lot of any one thing continuously, without a change.

The best oils gastronomically are cold pressed and retain some of the flavor of their origin. Most oils that come from oilseeds have tastes which are thought displeasing or interfere with the purposes for which they will be used. This is particularly so when the oils have been heat-treated or extracted with solvents. Such oils are decolorized and stripped of their flavors by heating with steam under reduced pressure. This treatment removes unpleasant (indeed almost any) tastes but is also likely to destroy the vitamins.

In normal conditions, fats and oils exposed to the air gradually become rancid because of oxidation. This can be arrested only by extreme measures, such as removing the air (as when nuts are sealed in a vacuum). Polyunsaturated oils, being more reactive than saturated fats, turn rancid more quickly. The process is encouraged by traces of metals (molybdenum, nickel, copper) which act as catalysts, by ultraviolet light (so oils are best stored in the dark), by the presence of free fatty acids (present as impurities or produced by heating), and by warmth (since it accelerates chemical reactions).

Common sense therefore dictates keeping oils in the refrigerator, decanting from large containers into small ones for use, and keeping bottles full. Many fresh, cold-pressed oils contain a fair amount—some a lot—of vitamin E, which is an antioxidant and helps to protect the oil from turning rancid. Manufacturers may add synthetic antioxidants (even vitamin E sometimes) and sequestrants. The latter are chemicals that hijack stray ions and attach themselves to metals. They render inactive the substances that encourage changes. Sequestrants are much used to maintain color, flavor and texture in commercial products, from beverages to canned crab.

Oil that has been continually heated in the deep fryer is prone to rancidity, because of the accumulation of free fatty acids; it also loses its polyunsaturated elements and vitamins. It will gain bad flavors as well, and even harmful substances, if overheated. Fats or oils which have become broken down in a deep fryer over a period should be discarded. The fat will have developed a yellowish foam. Fat lasts longer if it is kept clean by straining, never overheated, and carefully covered, cool and away from air, when not in use. The metal from which the cooking utensil is made is important. Iron pans and, worse still, untinned brass or copper pans encourage fats to break down, but stainless steel or chromium-plated pans do not have this effect.

The type of oil or fat used in the kitchen is immensely important. Fats give flavor and character, and even the most careful stripping does not render them entirely neutral. Even if tasteless, each has its own quality of "greasiness" and produces quite different results when mixed with flour in a sauce, boiled in a pudding, or used in a pastry. Recipe instructions that call simply for "oil" or "shortening" should be more specific. When a mayonnaise recipe says "oil" it is possible to use a fine olive oil or a claggy corn oil, but the difference between the results will be only too obvious.

It is common knowledge that Normandy cooks with butter, Provence with oil, eastern France with lard, and southwestern France with goose fat—not always, of course, but often enough to give a regional flavor. Pastry is usually made with butter, margarine, lard, or a mixture; or it may be made with a modern hydrogenated fat. Each gives a different result. My neighbor makes her pastry with olive oil; the result is very rich and crumbly.

There is an incredible difference between a curry made with *ghee*, coconut oil, *til* (sesame-seed oil), or Crisco (hydrogenated fat), and this comes through any amount of spice and chili. The Chinese do not generally use butter. The lard that is much used in Chinese cooking is not the tasteless steam-stripped version that comes in cans but the more flavorful rendered pork fat. Chinese cooking also uses oils such as sesame and peanut, but the sesame oil that is employed as a flavoring is a virgin one which has not been stripped of its natural taste.

These few examples are mentioned here only to show the enormous significance of the choice of oil or fat in cooking. The most important fats and oils in the alphabetical list below have their own entries elsewhere in this book.

Almond oil is sweet and is made by pressing milled sweet *almonds (the less shapely varieties) or from bitter almonds. In bitter almond oil, traces of hydrocyanic acid and benzaldehyde have to be eliminated. Almond oil is expensive. Its main use is in confectionery, both on molds to prevent boiled sugar from sticking and on the marble slabs where hot sugar is to be worked or toffee kneaded. It is valuable in the kitchen to coat molds for sweet things.

Animal fats are almost entirely saturated and so are used less than they used to be in days before cholesterol was considered to be a health factor. However, they are vital flavors in regional cooking. Many are dealt with below.

Arachide. Peanut oil (*see below*).

Avocado oil. The *avocado has a high fat content, around 30%, and is sometimes used as a source of oil. In this, 20% of the fatty acids are saturated, 50% are monounsaturated, and some 15% are polyunsaturated.

Beef fat is suitable for frying, but is rarely available in modern families which eat small, lean roasts. It contains more saturated fatty acids than any other fat in general use, but farmers in the north of England where I lived as a boy regularly ate bread and *drippings and lived long active lives. In Yorkshire, beef drippings are still used for frying potatoes, and alternatives are despised.

***Butter** consists mainly of butterfat; it has 40% saturated fatty acids and very few polyunsaturated fatty acids (4%). It remains the most delicious cooking fat, but often needs to be clarified before use.

***Candle-nut oil** is used somewhat locally in Southeast Asia, where candle nuts grow.

***Castor oil** is medicinal as well as unpleasant-tasting. I have heard of its being used to grease the iron plate used for baking in India.

Chicken fat is not very saturated for an animal fat, with 25% saturated fatty acids, 45% monounsaturated, and 20% polyunsaturated. Chicken fat is softer and nearer in consistency to oil than other animal fats. When clarified, it fries well and can be heated to 392°F (200°C) without burning. It is much used in Jewish cooking, perhaps because it is the nearest thing to butter which can be used with meat when dietary laws forbid meat and dairy products being used together.

Cocoa butter is the fat which is pressed out of cocoa beans. White or yellowish and with a chocolate smell, it is full of highly saturated fatty acids and is firm at room temperature. It is a main constituent of bar chocolate and is not usually a kitchen ingredient.

Coconut oil is one of the most saturated of vegetable fats and has an almost buttery consistency. Saturated fatty acids are 75% of the total. The taste of *coconut is necessary in much tropical cooking, although it is often added in the form of coconut milk or cream. Coconut oil itself may be needed in the cooking of India, Southeast Asia, the West Indies, and the Pacific. It is a common constituent of vegetable cooking fats and margarines and is good for frying, since it can be heated to 482°F (250°C) before it burns; it is not, however, very easily digested.

Cod-liver oil is very rich in vitamins, like other fish-liver oils. It is especially high in vitamin D (which may be lacking in parts of the less sunny northern countries) and is used as a diet supplement.

Colza oil is extracted by cold-pressing the seeds of *Brassica napus* (rape) and *B. campestris* (field mustard). It is used in salad oils and cooking oil mixtures in Europe.

Corn oil is expressed from the germ of corn (which is some 50% oil). It contains only 10% saturated fatty acids, but 35% monounsaturated and 50% polyunsaturated. From the cook's point of view, it is all right for frying, but not in the top bracket as a raw oil. You can make mayonnaise with it very easily, since it readily emulsifies, but the resulting flavor is not very pleasant. Some people also detect unpleasant flavors in corn oil.

***Cottonseed oil.** A good oil for cooking and salads. It contains 25% saturated fatty acids, 20% monounsaturated, and 50% polyunsaturated.

*Drippings usually mean beef fat (*see above*).

Fish oils are mainly polyunsaturated, but the percentage varies from type to type. The oil of herrings, for instance, has 20% saturated fatty acids, 25% monounsaturated, and 50% polyunsaturated. Oily fish may be as much as 30% fat and are likely to be high in the fat-soluble vitamins.

Frying oils. Oils that are marketed as frying oils may have a cottonseed oil base or be a mixture of vegetable oils; they will normally be cheaper than those labeled as salad oils. They are sometimes perfumed with lemon but essentially are highly stripped oils with little or no taste of their own. When they are used for deep frying, it matters little from a dietary viewpoint what oils are in the mixture.

Ghee. Indian clarified *butter.

Goose fat is a good cooking fat, with some of the characteristics of chicken fat. It is soft and can be heated to around 390°F (200°C) before it burns. It imparts a characteristic taste to any food cooked with it.

Grape-seed oil. An oil extracted from the residues of grapes.

Horse fat, claimed by a few to be the best for deep frying and used in some restaurants, may be obtained from horse butchers in many European countries.

Hydrogenated fats. Many brands of cooking fat, such as Crisco and Spry, are made by hydrogenating oils, usually vegetable oils, and look approximately like lard. Though lacking in flavor, these products can be very useful in everyday cooking.

*Lard is purified pork fat.

Linseed oil is pressed from the seed of the flax plant (*Linum usitatissimum*). It is an important ingredient in paints and varnishes, for which it is extracted with heat and pressure or with solvents. However, such oils are only for painting. Cold-pressed lin-seed oil, on the other hand, is used as a food oil, and has very healthful qualities. It is particularly rich in one of the essential fatty acids, linoleic acid.

*Margarine is made from oils by hydrogenation and was originally a substitute for butter rather than a product in its own right.

Mineral oils. In general, these are very undesirable in foods, and there are horrific stories of the effects produced when unscrupulous vendors have sold them for frying. However, highly purified mineral oil is common in food production. A little of the mineral oil used to lubricate machinery such as choppers and mincers gets into food. Mineral oil is used as a defoaming compound, to coat and give a shine to dried fruit, and, in confectionery, to seal and moisture-proof surfaces. Although it is an inert substance, its power of coating and isolating interferes with the body's absorption of vitamins A and D. Petroleum jelly (such as Vaseline) and paraffin wax are similar mineral hydrocarbons, though with larger molecules. Paraffin wax is solid at body temperature and is inert. It is used for sealing surfaces of preserves to exclude organisms and moisture, but it is slightly permeable to oxygen. It is also used in chewing gums. Vaseline is sometimes used in the kitchen for coating iron utensils to prevent rust. It should be cleaned away completely before a utensil is used on the stove.

Mowra butter, also known as bassia fat and illipe butter (Tamil: *illupai*), is a fat extracted from the *mohwa* or Indian butter tree (*Madhuca indica* and *M. longifolia*), which grows wild in the jungles in the dry, hilly regions of central India. In spring, the flowers, with their long sweet tubes, attract peacocks, bears, and other wild creatures, while the villagers sweep the ground clean under the trees and harvest the flowers, which they use to make a wine or dry for food. Later, the greenish yellow fruits, about the size of an egg, are gathered. The seeds contain 55–65% of a soft yellow oil. In India, it is used locally for cooking and also exported to be made into margarine.

Mustard oil. An important cooking oil in India, where it is a generic term covering *sarson* oil (from varieties of turnip, *Brassica rapa*, which are grown for oil seed and not for fat taproots), *toria* (from another variety of turnip), *taramira* or *tara* (from *rocket, *Eruca sativa*), and *rai* (from Indian mustard, *Brassica juncea*). In the food trade, all these are described as rape-seed oil or colza oil, except *rai,* which is known as mustard oil.

Mustard oil is much used in Indian cooking. It may have a strong mustard flavor (which vanishes on heating), and the oil is not, to my knowledge, ever used raw. Although there is some difference in taste when curries are made with mustard oil rather than other oils, the great value of mustard oil is in making Indian pickles: they never seem to go bad, even when opened. (A homemade eggplant pickle left for 3 years after opening was still in perfect condition.) Mustard oil is available in Indian shops, but is rather expensive. It is worth trying.

Mutton fat or **lamb fat.** This is the least-used common fat in Western cooking. It is hard and has a flavor which some find incompatible with many other foods. Those who fear fat for health reasons avoid it, since it is between beef and pork in saturated fatty acids with 30%; it has 50% monounsaturated and only 5% polyunsaturated. However, in the Middle East, with its hard people and hard lands, fat-tailed sheep and mutton fat are prized foods. Meat is preserved in mutton fat *(qawwrama)* and eggs are fried in it, which gives them a characteristic taste.

Niger oil. The niger plant (*Guizotia abyssinica*), a composite, is a native of tropical Africa and especially of Ethiopia. It is grown as an oil seed in many areas, although India is the largest producer. The seeds contain up to 50% oil and are sometimes ground into a chutney. The oil is pale yellow, with a nice, nutty taste. By the time it reaches the shops, it has usually been blended with other oils for cooking.

Nut oils. Oils expressed from nuts such as pecans, filberts, pistachios, Brazils, and cashews are expensive but are a way of using nuts that are too small or broken to be sold without processing. These oils are used for confectionery or cosmetics. There are also nut oils of varieties so local that they scarcely get outside their native jungles. The only oils from temperate-zone nuts that are in common kitchen use are almond oil and walnut oil.

*Olive oil. The original oil, and the word "oil" even comes from the same root as "olive." The Spanish word for oil, *aceite* (not to be confused with *aceto,* the Italian for vinegar), comes from the Arab word *az-zait,* meaning fruit of the olive. It contains 15% saturated fatty acids, 70% monounsaturated, and 10% polyunsaturated. Olive oil and seed oils are often custom-mixed, on demand, in village shops in Europe.

Palm oil comes from the fruit of the African oil palm *(Elais guineensis),* which is native to West Africa, though cultivated elsewhere in the tropics. In Honduras, it is called *dende* oil. Palm-kernel oil is a more delicate white oil expressed from just the kernels rather than from the whole pulp. It has a pleasant flavor and is much used by margarine and candy manufacturers. Many other palm oils come from Brazilian species of palm, notably *babassu, cohune, licuri, tucum,* and *murumuru* palm oils. Anyone who stays in a West African household will meet the special and rather nice oily taste of palm oil (which is characteristic of the food there) the first time there are fried eggs for breakfast. Palm oil is rich in saturated fatty acids—45%—with 40% monounsaturates and only 10% polyunsaturates.

Peanut oil. One of the most important cooking oils and preferred on salads by those who do not like olive oil. It congeals at −23°F (−5°C) and can be heated to 518°F (270°C) before it burns; it contains 15% saturated fatty acids, 50% monounsaturates, and 30% polyunsaturates. *Peanuts for oil extraction are often exported from Third World countries.

Perilla oil is an oil from the seeds of the perilla (*Perilla frutescens*), a labiate plant which is native to northern India, China, and Japan. An edible oil can be got by crushing the roasted seeds, and this has been used in Oriental food from very early times. It is a well-known oil of commerce.

Poppy-seed oil is expressed from opium *poppy seeds. The first pressing gives a fine oil which can be used as a salad oil, but the reddish oil from a second pressing with heat is inedible and used as a medium by painters. Poppy-seed oil—*huile blanche*—is well known in northern France.

Pork fat is marginally less saturated than that of mutton or beef (saturated fatty acids 28%, monounsaturated 50%, polyunsaturated 8%), but cooks use it because they like it. Purified pork fat is *lard.

Rape-seed oil. According to some authorities, rape (*Brassica napus*) is another cultivated variety of the same species as the rutabaga. It can be found growing wild over most of Europe. The green tops are poisonous to cattle, and large quantities of rapeseed oil should not be used because of the high erucic acid content. It contains 5% saturated fatty acids, 15% monounsaturated, and 15% polyunsaturated. It is used a lot in Indian cooking and may be referred to as colza or mustard oil (*see above*).

Safflower oil comes from the seed of a kind of thistle (*Carthamus tinctorius*) that is possibly native to the mountains of Abyssinia and Afghanistan but has escaped in southern Europe. It is cultivated in Egypt, Iran, India, and China as well as in the U.S. At one time, it was also grown for the yellow dye which can be extracted from the dried flower petals. The oil content of the seeds is 24–36%, and the seeds can be roasted and eaten, but more usually the cold-pressed oil, which is golden yellow, is used for cooking and to adulterate *ghee*. It is an oil high in polyunsaturated fatty acids (70%) and low in saturated ones (5%). It is a good source of vitamin E.

Salad oils. The salad oil *par excellence* is *olive oil, if it is light and delicately flavored, but heavy, fruity olive oils are not liked by most people. If good olive oil is not available, it is best to copy the French and use peanut oil, poppy-seed oil, or another delicate oil to replace it. Strongly flavored oils, like walnut oil, are favored in some parts of France, but again it is a matter of taste. Commercial salad oils are usually a mixture and are adequate but never sensational. Since oil should make up three-quarters of a French dressing, its quality is of the first importance in salads.

Sesame oil. The *sesame plant (*Sesamum indicum*) is probably native to India, which ranks first in production, but it is also grown over a wide area of the Orient. Sesame oil is much used in South Indian and Oriental cooking and is excellent for many purposes if it can be found unmixed with other oils.

Shortening. Originally this was fat which made pastry "short," or brittle, but it now often refers to fat or oil of any sort.

Soy oil. The *soybean is now one of the world's most important sources of vegetable oil. Soy is the cheapest vegetable oil in many places. It is nutritionally excellent, but often has a slightly fishy smell. Soy oil is high in polyunsaturated fatty acids—55% against 10% saturated and 25% monounsaturated. Most people would probably rate this oil lower than most of the other important ones for flavor.

***Suet** is the hard fat from around the kidneys of beef or mutton. Its very definite flavor is necessary in suet crust for steak and kidney puddings and for suet pudding.

Sunflower oil. The oil extracted from the seeds of the sunflower (*Helianthus annus*) is of ever-growing importance. The seeds contain up to 45% of a pale golden oil which has an excellent taste and very high nutritive and dietary value. The percentage of saturated fatty acid is only 5%, of the neutral monounsaturates 25%, and of the polyunsaturates as much as 65%. It is a pity to use sunflower oil for deep frying, but for all other kitchen uses, including making mayonnaise and dressing salads, it is excellent.

Sweet oil may mean a nut oil like almond oil, although oils are not actually sweet. It can also mean oils that are not rancid.

Tallow is any coarse, hard fat. In the past, tallow was used for candles. Occasionally, in old books, you are told to smear something with tallow, or to use it for other kitchen purposes.

Walnut oil. Oil expressed from *walnuts is used in parts of France as a salad oil, although it is expensive. Walnut oil from the Dordogne, but not that from Jura or the Loire, is strong-tasting and thus will not be liked by everyone.

Whale oil. I remember being taken down into the bowels of a whaling factory ship somewhere south of South Georgia and shown a clear, water-white oil that came out of a tap. It was totally odorless, surprisingly so in relation to the ghastly stink on deck. The clear oil was *whale oil destined for margarine. Despite the work of the International Whaling Commission, which is supposed to husband the world's whales, the animals are rapidly becoming scarce, and whaling from most civilized countries has stopped. At present whale oil is likely to be found in margarine only in the Soviet Union and Japan.

Wheat-germ oil. The oil expressed from the germ of wheat has outstanding medicinal qualities, but its dietary value is rapidly destroyed on heating or on exposure to air. It is also very expensive, and has at best an interesting taste which is halfway between whole-wheat bread and varnish. It might perhaps be used as a flavoring, but at present is used mainly for dietary purposes. It is high in vitamin E as well as in polyunsaturated fatty acids.

[*Cottonseed oil*—French: *huile de coton;* German: *Baumwollöl;* Italian: *olio di cotone;* Spanish: *aceite de algodón. Rape-seed oil*— French: *huile de colza;* German: *Rapsöl;* Italian: *olio di colza;* Spanish: *aceite de colza. Sunflower oil*—French: *huile de tournesol;* German: *Sonnenblumenöl;* Italian: *olio di girasole;* Spanish: *aceite de girasol. Walnut oil*—French: *huile de noix;* German: *Nussöl;* Italian: *olio di noce*]

FAVA BEAN. *See* broad bean.

FECULA. *See* farina.

FENNEL. The word may refer to an herb or a vegetable. The herb fennel (*Foeniculum vulgare*) is a tall, strong, umbelliferous perennial with yellow flowers and feathery foliage. Looking very much like a large version of dill, but quite different in taste, it is grown all over the world in suitable climates for its seed, which varies from the slightly bitter wild type to some cultivated kinds that have little bitterness and are not always easy to distinguish from anise. A very common wayside plant in Mediterranean Europe, especially near the sea, it has also gone wild in the Californian climate since it was introduced there and has become one of the most prevalent weeds.

As a green herb, fennel has been used in European cooking since ancient times. Although traditionally used with fish, it has countless other uses, especially in Mediterranean cookery, since it is so readily to hand. It is used for flavoring everything from pork to olives and snails. The dried seed makes a useful spice and appears in items ranging from the Florentine salami *finocchiona* to various types of curry. It is particularly popular in Italian cooking. Fennel is also used in cordials and liqueurs, often predominating in the *hierba* that is sometimes drunk after a meal in Spain.

Florence fennel or finocchio (*F. dulce*) has

a thick, bulbous leaf stalk that can be eaten either raw or cooked. Its foliage is similar to that of *F. vulgare,* but it is a smaller plant and is usually harvested annually, when the

FLORENCE FENNEL

globelike base forms a large cluster. Florence fennel is much grown in Italy and is becoming increasingly popular elsewhere. It has a sweetish aniselike flavor and can be served in the same ways as celery: take off the tough outer ribs and slice the fennel to eat raw with a dip, marinate thin slices in vinaigrette, braise julienne strips, or make cream soup. Like fennel seed, Florence fennel goes well with seafood.

[*Fennel*—French: *fenouil;* German: *Fenchel;* Italian: *finocchio;* Spanish: *hinojo*]

FENUGREEK. A native of Europe and Asia, related to clover. The name means "Greek hay," and the plant is grown as a fodder crop in seed mixtures, often where it is virtually unknown as a spice.

Fenugreek (*Trigonella foenum-graecum*) is used to a small extent in countries bordering the eastern Mediterranean, but it is overwhelmingly important in India, where the seed is a flavoring in curries (and many other dishes) and the leaves, usually of special varieties, are used as a vegetable. In Hindi, fenugreek is called *methi.* In recent years, many people in the West have taken to sprouting it or sowing it in boxes, for use

in the same way as mustard and cress, since the flavor is pleasantly bitter. Leaves of the fully grown plant (which are curried in India) vary from shatteringly bitter to only moderately so, depending on the type. They may have an exceedingly aromatic smell and can be bought dried in Indian and Pakistani shops. The seed is equally variable in its aromatic quality. It should be gently roasted to develop its flavor before being ground, but roasting must be done with extreme care. If fenugreek is overheated (when it turns red), the taste becomes indescribably bitter, and it has to be thrown away. Some Indian cooks roast fenugreek seed until it becomes almost black, when it loses its bitterness again. Many people do not like the taste of fenugreek, which is associated with cheap curry powders. Those who like the traditional English curry powder will find they know the taste of fenugreek very well.

[*Fenugreek*—French: *fenugrec;* German: *Bockshornklee, Griechisches Heu;* Italian: *fieno greco;* Spanish: *fenogreco, alholva*]

FERMENTATION. The origin of the word relates to boiling because of the bubbles of gas evolved during alcoholic fermentation. However, fermentation is used as a general term for any process of change induced by living organisms and their enzymes (e.g., alcoholic fermentation, lactic acid fermentation); ferment is a synonym for enzyme. The organisms producing fermentation can be bacteria and molds as well as yeasts. We use fermentative processes, for instance, in brewing and in making wine, cheese, yogurt, sauerkraut, and bread. Control depends on so adjusting the environment (food material, acidity, saltiness, temperature, etc.) that the organism or organisms whose effects are wanted grow at their best—or that unwanted organisms grow most slowly or not at all. In practice, we are rarely dealing with one type of organism by itself but with a mixture, often of interdependent types that produce an effect no one of them could do alone. Making a good fermented product therefore

FIG | 193

means achieving the correct balance of types, and this is particularly important in creating flavor. For instance, certain bacteria produce small quantities of flavoring substances, such as those giving a creamy taste in milk products. Since the balance is affected by quite slight changes in conditions, recipes for any fermented products should be followed to the letter.

[*Fermentation*—French: *fermentation;* German: *Gärungsprozess;* Italian: *fermentazione;* Spanish: *fermentación*]

FERNS. The young, half-coiled shoots of various fern species are eaten, particularly in North America and the Orient—in Japan, for instance (as *warabi*)—but rather rarely in Europe. The first ones I ate were roasted over a campfire, peeled to remove the furry outside, and sprinkled with salt.

The young shoots of brake or bracken (*Pteridium aquilinum*) are edible—and plentiful, since farm animals will not eat them. Bracken has a very wide distribution, and even the roots are edible. The ferns grow in pastures or open woods and when mature have triangular, three-branched fronds. The curled shoots are covered with a rusty-looking felt and are mucilaginous when cooked. Their flavor has been compared to okra and wild rice.

Of more gastronomic significance are the shoots of the ostrich fern, *Matteucia struthiopteris,* which are known as fiddleheads because the opening shoots look like the scroll on a violin. This fern grows in damp places and beside streams over much of the eastern side of North America and is particularly plentiful in New Brunswick. It can be identified by its dark-brown plumes of spore stalks. Young fiddleheads have a papery covering and a dry texture. They taste something like a combination of avocado and asparagus.

All fern shoots should be gathered when they are only a few inches high. Species with scaly or hairy skins have to be scraped or peeled before cooking. They can be treated in the same way as asparagus, boiled or steamed until tender. Some people steep them first in wine and herbs to counteract their woodsy flavor. Some prefer them *al dente,* while others cook them in several changes of water. In any case, they can be served hot with hollandaise, cream, or butter, or cold with mayonnaise or vinaigrette. After parboiling, they can be deep-fried as tempura, added to salads, frozen, or canned.

Since some ferns are poisonous, it is best not to experiment with unknown species.

[*Fern*—French: *fougère;* German: *Farnkraut;* Italian: *felce;* Spanish: *helecho*]

FETTUCINE. *See* pasta.

FIDDLEHEAD. *See* ferns.

FIELD MUSHROOM. *See* meadow mushroom.

FIG. A very ancient cultivated fruit, the fig (*Ficus carica*) is often mentioned in the Bible and was probably found wild somewhere in Arabia in ancient times. Figs have been growing in all Mediterranean countries long enough to go wild; they spring up wherever someone has dropped a seed between two rocks—a favorite place for figs to get a hold. They belong to the family Moraceae (together with mulberries and breadfruit), and there are dozens of wild species, such as the famous banyan and pipal trees (*Ficus religiosa*), under which the sadhus sit in India. Figs grow in the same climates as almonds, olives, and oranges.

But figs are not fruit in the usual sense—the flowers are actually inside the fruit—and they have a most complicated life history. There are several basic types—common figs, Smyrna figs, San Pedro figs, and caprifigs. Common figs need no pollination and have no seeds. There are some hundreds of different varieties, both white and black. They are propagated by cuttings, and the varieties thus tend to be regional; they form a wide spectrum of flavor, sweetness, and tenderness—not to mention size and color.

In the Mediterranean regions, fig trees bear two crops. In Italy, first-crop figs are known as *fioroni* and arrive in June and July. *Fioroni* are usually large but not as sweet as the second-crop figs. (In some varieties, only one crop ripens.) Second-crop figs, the most plentiful, are smaller in size, juicy, and full of sugar. They are produced in August, September, and even into October and November. These second-crop figs, though eaten fresh, are also dried. To my taste, they are usually too sweet—especially the black ones, which can have a strong wild taste—and they do not go with ham as well as those that ripened earlier.

Smyrna figs are varieties which need to be pollinated and thus produce seeds. This is said to give them a more nutty flavor. They are pollinated by a small wasp (*Blastophaga psenes*), which is hatched in caprifigs (otherwise useless, semiwild types), so caprifigs must be grown near Smyrna figs; otherwise there will be no crop. In fact, branches of caprifigs are actually suspended in the Smyrna fig trees to make sure of this caprification. Smyrna figs are the most important type for drying and are grown in Turkey, Greece, North Africa, and California (where the caprifigs and wasps had to be introduced). San Pedro figs are intermediate between Smyrna and common figs; they give a first crop without caprification but must be caprified for the second.

Ripe figs are highly perishable. The varieties that reach the market, the more durable figs, are usually picked rather unripe. Figs are incomparably better picked straight from the tree at the desired state of ripeness and eaten either hot from the sun or chilled in the refrigerator. In most Mediterranean countries, it is a tradition that the traveler may help himself to a fig as he passes—but not, of course, pick them into a basket. Dried figs combine especially well with the flavors of anise and fennel. The bay leaf in a box of Smyrna figs is there to keep away weevils.

[*Fig*—French: *figue;* German: *Feife;* Italian: *fico;* Spanish: *higo*]

FILBERT. *See* hazelnut.

FILÉ POWDER or **filet powder.** Young leaves of *sassafras (Sassafras albidum)* have a very mucilaginous quality and a nice, spicy taste. They are thoroughly dried, then rubbed to a powder. The result, after sieving to remove bits of stalk, is filé powder. An important ingredient in Creole cooking and essential for filé gumbo, it gives a special flavor and a smooth, mucilaginous texture to dishes in which it is used. It can also be used as a table condiment.

FILLET. From the French *filet*, a diminutive of *fil* (thread). As applied to cooking without qualification, it usually means a beef fillet, the undercut of the sirloin. Pork fillet, veal fillet, mutton fillet, and so on are generally specified. Fillets of chicken and turkey are fairly thin slices cut from the breast. Fillets of fish are slices or whole boned sides of fish, depending on size. Filet mignon is a steak taken from the small end of the beef fillet.

[*Fillet*—French: *filet;* German: *Filet, Lendenstück;* Italian: *filetto;* Spanish: *filete*]

FILLETING. *See* fish.

FILLING. *See* stuffing.

FINES HERBES. Finely chopped *fresh* herbs, a mixture which may include parsley, tarragon, chervil, chives, and so on, according to choice—or even parsley alone. The pundits say that fines herbes could once have included such things as mushrooms and shallots. Unless one grows the herbs oneself, some of the ingredients are fairly difficult to obtain except dried, and *omelettes fines herbes* are, alas, often made with ready-mixed dried herbs.

FINING means removing cloudiness and sediment, as in the clarifying of beer or wine, though the clearing of aspic is essentially the same. The usual method is the mechanical one of adding something that will stick to the minute particles causing the cloudiness. (They may be so fine that they would take months to settle naturally.) Substances used for the purpose include egg white (often with the shell to make it sink more quickly), isinglass, gelatin, alkaline alginates, blood, milk, casein, bentonite (an earth), kieselguhr (diatomaceous earth), and kaolin (china clay). Amateur winemakers can buy packaged fining agents with instructions. For home use, the simplest is egg white.

Filtration through a filter paper or a porcelain filter (commercially filtration is done in huge filter presses) is another mechanical method of fining. Chemical methods rely on altering the substances causing the cloudiness. A pectin cloud, often developed in homemade wines that have been boiled, is dispelled by the enzyme pectinase.

Home winemakers sometimes add a few drops of milk to clear white wine. If this fails, the white of one egg and a tiny pinch of salt beaten up in a small quantity of the wine (1 cup or 250 ml) will clear up to 10 gal (45 lt). Gelatin, softened and dissolved in hot water, is frequently used to clear red wine, but it reacts with tannin in the wine to form an insoluble precipitate and so to some extent changes the character of the wine. The use of asbestos pulp, advocated by some authorities, now seems a dubious practice, since asbestos is carcinogenic when inhaled as dust.

FINNAN HADDOCK or **finnan haddie.** Named after the village of Findon, near Aberdeen, this, in pre-Victorian times, was a haddock, split open, dry-salted, and heavily smoked over peat or seaweed to withstand the journey to London by stagecoach. However, the popularity of finnan haddock has been decreasing over the last 20 years, as has that of most fish with bones in.

Finnan haddocks are now prepared with beheaded, gutted, and cleaned fish. They are split open from the belly, leaving the bone on one side, put in strong brine for 5–15 minutes (depending on size), speared with stainless-steel rods, then left to drain for 2–3 hours. The longer the draining period, the higher the gloss. The haddocks are finally smoked over oak sawdust or over peat or white-wood sawdust, which imparts a color fairly quickly, so that the fish are still moist when the required shade is reached. The finished item has a golden-brown color with a good gloss and should feel dry to the touch—hence the fishmongers' expression "a dry haddock."

To produce finnan haddock at home, clean and split the fish. Dry-salt them for a few hours—overnight if you want to keep them for more than a week. Hang them to dry in the breeze and cold-smoke them (not above 80°F/27°C) over oak sawdust started with a hot iron bar. They are smoked to a "fine yellow," a process which takes at most 12 hours.

They are prepared for the table by skinning, rubbing with butter, broiling, and serving with pats of cold butter—the best method according to the late André Simon. The Scottish dish is prepared by lightly poaching the finnan haddie in water and serving it with a poached egg on top.

Glasgow pales are another type of smoked split haddock, smaller than the finnan and given less smoke to bring about a barely visible color change. Golden cutlets are double or "butterfly" fillets of either small haddock or whiting. They are lightly brined in a salt solution containing a lemon-colored dye and are either hung on hooks by the tail or laid in trays for smoking over white-wood sawdust.

Any of the smoked haddock or whiting products can be shallow-fried, or poached in water or milk with a little butter. The cooked, boned flesh of smoked haddock is the base for the English kedgeree.

FINO. *See* sherry.

FINOCCHIETTO and **finocchiona.** *See* salame.

FINOCCHIO. *See* fennel.

FISH is the only important type of food animal that is not fully domesticated. It is true that fish ponds have been maintained at least since classical times (and there are some tall stories about Romans feeding moray eels on slaves), but we still depend mainly on wild fish caught in nets. Battery-reared sole and salmon have not yet arrived, so we must eat the types of fish that are caught in the proportions in which they are available. Anyone who has the luck to watch the "cod end" being undone to let the catch of a North Sea trawler onto the deck will see a marvelous selection of seafood, although certain fish, like ling or cod, will predominate, according to the season and the area. By the time this catch is sold, the variety will have been severely reduced; many types will be skinned and beheaded or tidied up and sold as fish fingers, fish cakes, and fish balls. Many shoppers undoubtedly prefer fish fillets to be square, and others would not like to see the head of an angler fish or wolf fish in all their natural ugliness (even though they are two of the nicest of all fish to eat). Lucky people can still visit fish markets near the sea, where the fish will be locally caught and the number of species on sale will run into dozens, but where some knowledge of the quality of the local fish is necessary.

Some countries depend to a large extent on fish for their protein. Japan, the world's premier fishing nation, once ate no red meat at all (meat eating was introduced by foreign visitors). The poor of tropical Southeast Asia depend on fish, not only along their coasts, but inland where fish abound in rivers, ponds, creeks, and artificial tanks. Even the water flooding the rice fields is alive with small fish, which may be bony and taste of mud, but are still nutritious enough.

Fish markets in unfamiliar or exotic places are bewildering; you will have to depend on the dealers for identification of the fish. Not only is the number of different species in the world enormous, but identification from books is not at all easy. Books intended for sportsmen are often good, but tend to deal with the few fish that offer the finest sport rather than with those that are best to eat. Advice should also be sought on cooking and edibility; although most fish are good in all their parts, some do have poisonous organs or are purgative. Care should always be taken in handling fish: many have spines (on the back, fins, or gill covers) that at very least can inflict a nasty wound and at worst may be rankly poisonous. A fish that is not quite dead may suddenly become galvanized into thrashing the fisherman with a thorny tail, or even biting the hand about to feed on it.

Skate and sole are exceptions to the rule that fish should be eaten as fresh as possible. Perfectly fresh fish have virtually no fishy smell (though some, like pike, have an odor of their own). The eyes are bright, shiny, and transparent, never cloudy. If the mouth is gaping and the gill flaps open, then the fish has just died. Other checks, such as the color of the gills, do not always work. If scales are being shed, the fish is probably not quite fresh, but there is enormous variation in the ease with which scales are shed in different species. With many fish, skin color is an important indication. Signs of staleness are when silveriness fades, iridescent blue or green lights disappear, and black or brown fish turn gray. Sunken eyes or an unpleasant smell mean that when the fish is opened at home, the flesh will look yellow or dull, the guts will have softened, the blood will be thin and watery, and the "ribs" will have started to come loose through the wall of the body cavity. Such fish is not fit for consumption. White fish may not go bad as quickly as oily fish, but it can be equally unpleasant.

All fish, no matter how strangely shaped,

share the same basic anatomy. Knowing this can be a help when you have to deal with a fish that you have never seen before.

Skin may be smooth, soft, and scaleless, in which case it can be left as it is and cooked without problems, or it may be rough like a dogfish's or covered with scales overlapping like the tiles on a roof. Dogfish and skate (*see* shark) may be skinned or alternatively blanched in boiling water and then rubbed with a cloth to remove the roughness. Remove scales from other fish by scraping them against their grain, from tail to head, unless they are so firmly fixed that you can start only by scraping off a few at the front and gradually working backwards, taking off a strip at a time—too vigorous scraping from the tail may just tear the skin. In the stubbornest cases, quickly dunking the fish into boiling water will loosen the scales.

Head and **gills** are usually removed and are either thrown to the cat or used for soup or stock. They are sometimes left on for the sake of appearance when the whole fish is served, and discarded at table. With a few fish, the head is a delicacy, as, for instance, is that of some large species of sturgeon, which are supposed to have seven different types of meat in the head to be picked out by aficionados.

Fins. There are two paired sets, pectoral (front) and pelvic (back). These fins are anchored to structures of bones which are rarely extensive and can usually be taken out with little difficulty. In many fish, the pectoral fins and their associated bones are situated so far forward that they can be removed with the head and gills in one cut. The single fins along the back and the underside (the dorsal and ventral fins—which may sometimes be reduced to no more than spines) can often be removed by cutting down on either side to free them and then pulling them out.

Bones. In some fish, the spine and bones present few problems. The spine has "ribs" which lie in the wall of the gut cavity, but there is little else to worry about. With such fish (most catfish, for instance), the bones are easy to remove. However, other fish have a second set of bones extending from the spine at each side, above the "ribs." These are a particular nuisance, since they may be cut through in filleting and left embedded in the flesh. Many fish go even further and have intermuscular bones. Really bony fish like these are best used for soup. Another solution is to pickle them in vinegar, which will soften small bones to the point where they will not be noticed within a day or so.

Gutting. The simplest method is to put the point of kitchen scissors into the vent and to snip forward as far as the gills, opening the body cavity along the belly. With some fish it is then enough to cut through the spine behind the head and to pull the head forward and downward, which will also bring the bony pectoral girdle and the gills away together, followed by the guts. With small fish, such as anchovies, all you have to do is pinch through the spine behind the head and pull.

Among the guts can be recognized the two roes (male roe or milt is soft, and female is hard with eggs) and the liver. In a few fish, such as skate, the liver is a delicacy. However, roes and livers may be poisonous in some otherwise edible fish (deadly in the case of the puffer fish and definitely harmful in others), so these parts of unfamiliar fish should not be eaten. The swim bladder, a shiny, elongated sausage shape which lies just under the backbone, is the source of *isinglass. Sharks and rays do not have a swim bladder and sink if they stop swimming. The rest of the gut is normally thrown away, although the Chinese dry and eat the stomach of the shark.

If fish have to be washed, they are best washed quickly, just before they are cooked, and they should never be put into water unless this is necessary to soak out blood.

Filleting. It is difficult to learn how to fillet fish from a book and much better to watch someone doing it. Because fish vary enormously, the best technique for filleting one species does not necessarily work for another. Fish with many intermuscular bones should rarely be filleted—this might lead the unsuspecting diner to think that the fish is boneless when it is not. Few things are worse to eat than fillets with bones in them, especially if these are well concealed by a sauce. Short of getting your fingers into the dish and feeling, like a surgeon, there is no possible remedy.

In the absence of precise instructions, use the following general method for filleting. First cut diagonally behind the head and gills, and then down the back beside the dorsal fins. Then, following the dorsal spines of the backbone, with the knife always cutting and scraping along the direction of the bones, dissect the flesh away until you reach the vertebral column itself. Still moving the flesh away from the bones, separate the flesh from the rib cage and ventral spines until the fillet comes free. After that, the fish is turned over and the method repeated on the other side. In some fish, two fillets are taken from each side; a cut made down to the backbone on each side before filleting is started will simplify the operation. Filleting many fish is quite easy if it is done with a sharp, flexible knife, such as the sort made for the purpose. On fishing trips, we used to fillet perch with a penknife in the boat, and drop the fillets into vinegar and water, so that they were ready to cook for breakfast the moment we landed.

If fish is to be flaked, it is best to cook it first on the bone, since this produces better fish and easier boning.

Cooking. The simplest way to serve fish is raw, as is done in Holland and Indonesia as well as in Japan. It may be "cooked" without heat by salting (as with anchovies), by salting and marinating (as with Scandinavian salt herring), or by simply marinating in lemon juice or lime juice (*seviche) or vinegar until the protein coagulates. Fish may be simmered or poached in a *court bouillon, then eaten hot or cold, or they may

be steamed, baked, planked, or roasted beside the heat of a wood fire (especially trout), or cooked in hot smoke. What is important is that fish should be just cooked and no more. Although there are rough rules for timing, the factors involved vary so much that one cannot rely on formulas, and it is best to test the fish frequently as it approaches doneness. You can then snatch it away from the heat at the exact moment that it is ready. When the fish is just coming away from the bone or has become flaky right through, it is done. In general, fish cooked with skin and bones still intact loses less moisture and is therefore more succulent. It is difficult to cook a very large fish to perfection without getting the outside overdone by the time the inside is just right.

Frozen fish. I once attended a lunch organized by some fish freezers in which fish bought from a fishmonger by an independent expert and as fresh as possible was matched against the highest quality frozen fish of the same species. Dishes using both were cooked in identical ways, so that one could be compared with the other. While, ideally, there should have been virtually no difference between fresh and frozen, the general opinion of the guests was that the fresh fish had the better texture, but the frozen fish had the better flavor. Neither would compare with fish landed straight out of the water, but nobody claimed that. Frozen fish is at present only the best possible solution for handling a commodity that is so very perishable. On the old trawlers, the fish, though immediately gutted, were packed down on ice. But even on ice, a week or more's storage on trawlers fishing in far northern waters left the fish far from fresh when they were landed. Today, most fish is deep-frozen on board ship very shortly after netting.

Frozen fish may need to be thawed if it is to be fried, broiled, filleted, rolled, or stuffed, but not if it is to be baked, simmered, or poached. Thaw it in the refrigerator. This may take 24 hours.

[*Fish*—French: *poisson;* German: *Fisch;* Italian: *pesce;* Spanish: *pez*]

FIVE-FRAGRANCE POWDER. *See* Chinese five spices.

FLAGEOLET. The flageolet is a rather special and expensive French variety of haricot bean, with a pale-green, tender skin and fine flavor. Flageolets are not soaked before cooking and are often cooked in fancier ways than those applied to the average bean, for instance with fresh cream.

[*Flageolet*—French: *flageolet;* German: *Flageolett;* Italian: *fagiolino;* Spanish: *judía verde*]

FLAMING. Spirits, unlike wine, can be set alight and used for flaming (although only the very strongest will burn without prior warming). The massive use of spirits in cooking is a modern innovation, and in recipes from the last century, the use of brandy, even as a flavoring, was limited. Cooks relied more on wine, port, or madeira, and rum was the most important kitchen spirit. When brandy was added to cakes and batters, it was largely to promote lightness of texture; the volatile alcohol turned to gas and acted as a leavening when heated. In older French cookbooks, it is rare to find the word *flambé* (and the verb *flamber* usually referred to singeing the fluff off chickens before roasting).

The question of whether spirits should or should not be ignited is calculated to start an argument. It is claimed that flaming will burn off excess fat or take the raw taste off the spirits. However, the heat generated is mainly above the flame and not under it. Expert opinions vary. In Burgundy, one famous *maître cuisinier de France* does not flame his *coq au vin* but sprinkles it with a *fine champagne* cognac just before the dish is ready, and he does this himself in the kitchen. On the other hand, another Burgundy chef I talked to (a local traditionalist) was quite belligerent in his insistence that spirits must be ignited. Raymond Oliver says that burning spirits is risky because it can make the food bitter.

FLATBREAD. The Anglicized version of the Norwegian word *flatbrød,* also called crispbread (*knakkebrød*). Many forms of these crackerlike breads are made in Scandinavia, not necessarily the elegant rectangles we get in packets but also great rough sheets, usually based on rye flour but sometimes mixed with up to three times the weight of wheat flour or potato. One wonders why this type of bread and its many commercial variants should be so popular in slimming diets. Perhaps it is for the same reason that toast is also hopefully used instead of bread—you may eat less of it.

A FLATBREAD

Mix 18 oz (500 g) rye flour with 3¼ lb (1500 g) mashed potatoes or 18 oz (500 g) rye flour with 26 oz (750 g) plain flour and knead into a dough with water. It is usual to incorporate a little fat, salt, or sugar, and often some baking powder (or allow a day to stand in a warm place for some fermentation). The dough is rolled out thin and baked to crispness in a slow oven.

FLATFISH. Among the flatfish, the best-known are the *brill, *dab, *flounder, *halibut, *lemon sole, *plaice, *sole, *turbot, and *witch. All members of this zoological order have one outstanding common denominator: back in their evolutionary past, they elected to lie lazily on their side on the bottom of the sea and wait for their prey to come within range. The heads of the adults have become twisted around so that both eyes are now on the side which is on top, while the side on which they lie has become white. They rely on camouflage and have developed a capacity to change color to match the seabed on which they lurk. Some flatfish lie on their right side and look left, while others lie on their left side and look right. Although mirror-image fish do turn up very occasionally, the distinction between dextral species, with the eye on the right, and sinistral, or left-looking, species is important in identifying flatfish.

Skates and rays are also white underneath and adapted to lie on the seabed, but they lie on their belly, not on their side, and are cartilaginous fish related to *sharks. Narrow fish of various sorts, such as the pomfret, swim around upright but sometimes get called flatfish and are treated as such by the cook.

With the exception of the huge halibut, which is a powerful swimmer and often pursues its prey, the flatfish do not move around very much. Perhaps that is why some, like soles, tend to develop local variations, even in quite a small distance. The French say of the soles that they differ between Boulogne, Dover, and Ostend. From the cook's point of view, the species vary greatly in quality from Dover sole, which is a gastronomic prince of fishes, to the megrim, which is not. But they all have one feature that makes them acceptable: an easily removed set of bones. And because they are thin-bodied, they cook evenly and quickly.

To fillet a flatfish, you merely make a cut along the length of the spine, cutting down to the bone, then, with sweeping strokes of the knife, lift the two fillets. The fish can then be turned over and the other two fillets removed. Flatfish have soft skins and do not need to be scaled, but some, in particular the sole, are usually skinned. If you make a transverse cut through the skin, just short of the tail, and loosen a large enough flap to get a grip on, the skin can be pulled off toward the head. An alternative is to lay the fillets on a board, skin side down, and slice the skin off with a very sharp knife.

FLAVORINGS. Apart from natural herbs, vegetables, spices, and condiments, there are a number of flavorings which cooks find useful in the kitchen. True, many commercial *essences (particularly bitter almond and synthetic vanilla) can be horrid, but I suppose everyone would allow oil of peppermint (which has a taste that is difficult to get from the fresh or dried herb). A whole range of chemicals are also supposed to simulate anything from bananas to cherries. Such flavorings are to be avoided where possible.

Other substances, like maple syrup flavoring (because real maple syrup is difficult to come by), must be kept out of sight of purists, but every cook is entitled to some secret ingredients; a box of tricks with which to tart up the tasteless and disguise the failures is fine so long as you do not depend on it too much.

[*Flavoring*—French: *saveur artificielle;* German: *künstliches Schmackmittel;* Italian: *artificiale aroma;* Spanish: *artificial sabor*]

FLIES. Among the thousands of different kinds of flies, the ones that mainly bother the cook are blowflies and houseflies.

Houseflies, filthy creatures that breed in refuse and excreta, not only bring possibly pathogenic bacteria to food on their feet but actually vomit part of their last meal onto it. The famous old French naturalist Henri Fabre once put the body of a bird in a paper bag and hung it up. It did not go bad but became dry and mummified. Had flies walked on it, the result would have been putrefaction. Moral: food should always be kept covered and not left lying exposed for flies to walk on.

Blowflies, bluebottles, and greenbottles all lay their eggs on meat, and the eggs hatch to maggots, which feed and grow before turning into pupae and eventually adult flies. Some species do not "lay" eggs but tiny maggots which have already hatched in the mother, and some are able to shoot their maggots or eggs sideways, so that meat can be reached.

[*Flies*—French: *mouches;* German: *Fliegen;* Italian: *mosca;* Spanish: *moscas*]

FLORENCE FENNEL. *See* fennel.

FLOTØST. *See* whey.

FLOUNDER. The name "flounder," like that of *sole, has been applied to so many different *flatfish in the U.S. that it is sometimes difficult to be certain precisely what one is buying or eating. It may be any one of the abundant members of the flounder family, the dab, gray sole, yellowtail, or fluke. Even the two following flounders go under various local names.

Winter flounder (*Pseudopleuronectes americanus*) is also known as the common flounder, blackback, or lemon sole (not to be confused with the European *lemon sole). It is often reddish brown on the eyed side and is therefore called *plie rouge* in French Canada. The most abundant and popular flatfish on the East Coast, winter flounder occur from Labrador to Georgia and are especially abundant in New England waters. They average 2 lb (1 Kg) and have white, fine-textured flesh and delicious roe.

Summer flounder (*Paralichthys dentatus*) is also sold under the name fluke. Its range is from Maine to the Carolinas. It averages 3 lb (1½ Kg), and its back is usually brown or gray with a number of black spots. A smaller species, the four-spotted flounder (*P. oblongus*), is also common in New England waters. Its flavor is excellent, similar to that of winter flounder, and it may be fried, grilled, or baked.

In Europe, the flounder (*Platichthys flesus*) is a species of small dextral flatfish. The eyed side is brown, grayish, or dull green. This flounder is found in the English Channel, the Mediterranean and Black seas, and on the muddy bottoms of estuaries and creeks. The flavor of its flesh is also about bottom, as European flatfish go.

[*Flounder*—French: *flet;* German: *Flunder;* Italian: *passera pianuzza;* Spanish: *platija*]

FLOUR means wheat flour, unless otherwise qualified as rice flour, corn flour, barley flour, *besan* flour, pea flour, and so on.

White flour is usually ground in roller mills (*see* milling), during which almost all the *bran and *wheat germ are separated out, leaving mainly the starchy endosperm, the inside of the wheat (which makes up 85% of the grain). This endosperm is ground

to the required fineness and separated by sieving through woven wire, silk, or nylon screens in Plansifters (vertical nests of horizontal sieves which gyrate in a horizontal plane). Stone-ground flour, which has been ground between old-fashioned millstones, contains much more of the bran and germ than does white flour.

Flour improves both in breadmaking quality and in whiteness if it is stored for several months. These improvements, which develop more rapidly if the flour is exposed to the air, are caused by the oxidization of the flour pigments and the components of the protein, respectively. It was found that certain substances would bleach and "improve" flour very quickly. This made storage for long periods unnecessary and reduced the risk of spoilage; the public demand for white flour and bread could thus more easily be satisfied. Chlorine gas was patented as a flour bleach as long ago as 1879, although its use for this purpose seems not to have been commercially exploited until much later. In the early 1900s, nitrogen peroxide was introduced; by 1920, other oxidizing agents, including benzoyl peroxide, potassium bromate, and nitrogen trichloride were in use as bleaching and/or improving agents. Nitrogen trichloride continued to be widely used until it was shown that heavily treated flour caused hysteria in dogs. It was replaced by another bleacher/improver, chlorine dioxide. White flour is often fortified with certain nutrients lost during milling (thiamine, nicotinic acid, iron).

Extraction rate is the percentage of the whole grain that is produced as flour during milling. Whole-wheat flour has a 100% extraction rate, but what are known as brown or wheat-meal flours contain 80–90% of the wheat grain (thus have an 80–90% extraction rate). Flour of 85% extraction rate still contains the germ, but the bulk of the bran has been removed. White flours contain mainly the endosperm and have a 70–75% extraction rate because, although the endosperm makes up 85% of the grain, some of it always remains attached to the bran and the germ. Even white flours will contain a trace of bran, since separation is never perfect. Patent flours, which are the whitest of all, have an extraction rate of about 40–50% and are used only for special purposes, because they are expensive.

Flour varies in granularity. Some special flours for making the finest pastries are ground and sieved to an exceedingly fine powder. Flour also varies in strength. Strong flours are often from *wheat with a high *gluten content and are best for bread and other yeast-raised goods; softer flours are good for cakes and biscuits. Coarsely ground flours, especially if they are whole wheat, do not rise as much as fine flour and bake to a closer texture. Flour for crackers may even have *rice flour or *cornstarch—ingredients with no gluten and much starch—added.

Self-rising flour contains chemical leaveners, usually added at the mill. The mechanical mixing methods used are more efficient than the blending done by hand in the kitchen. The rising agents are formulated in such a way that doughs and batters made from self-rising flour can be left standing for short periods in a cool place with little loss of performance.

Cake flours are specially treated flours that are snow-white, low in gluten, starchy, soft, and finely ground. When combined with specially emulsified fat, they take up high quantities of liquid and sugar. Cake batters made with this flour have a pouring consistency; the cakes are of a melting quality—sweet, rich, and moist.

Supersifted flours. Modified methods of grinding and sifting have enabled millers to produce a flour which is free-flowing. Particles do not cling together into lumps, and they mix smoothly with liquids. This makes the flour easier to use and is a convenience for the cook.

Proprietary flours and meals. In addition to the usual grades of white, brown, and whole-wheat flour, some flours are available for special purposes. They may contain ingredients such as wheat germ, bran, soy flour, malt flour, rye, and barley. They are for making special types of bread and are available mainly to professional bakers, but also in health-food shops. In the more famous patent wheat-germ flours, the germ has been toasted and much of its value has thus been destroyed.

Storing and keeping. Experts recommend keeping flour in its bag on a cool, dry, airy shelf, but if the kitchen is damp or steamy the bag should be put into an airtight container. Fresh flour should not be added to old, and containers should always be carefully cleaned and washed, then thoroughly dried before refilling. Plain flour can keep for 4–6 months (white flour much longer than that) and self-rising flour for 2–3 months, but whole-wheat flour, which contains the germ, should be kept for only 2 months in ordinary circumstances, because the oil in the germ tends to become rancid.

[*Flour*—French: *farine;* German: *Mehl;* Italian: *farina;* Spanish: *harina*]

FLUORINE (F). This element, which does not exist in an uncombined state in nature, is a yellow gas, very similar to chlorine but even more active and toxic. It is used industrially in making PTFE (polytetrafluoroethylene) nonstick plastic, and the fluoro-and chlorofluoro-carbons such as freon for refrigerators and propellants for aerosols. Fluorine has become noticed in recent years as a trace element because of its effect in preventing tooth decay, although the whole subject is still extremely controversial, and feelings run very high over the merits and demerits of fluoridating water supplies. Nevertheless, many water supplies are now fluoridated with fluorine salts (e.g., sodium fluoride or sodium fluorosilicate) to a level of 1 part per million. Too much fluorine, however, is definitely bad and will produce mottled teeth. Sea fish contain 5 to 10 parts per million and tea some 80 (China tea even 100), but you would have to eat a lot of fish and drink a lot of tea to make up for tap water that is deficient in the element.

[*Fluorine*—French: *fluor;* German: *Fluor;* Italian: *fluorina;* Spanish: *flúor*]

FOIE GRAS is goose-liver pâté, one of the great French delicacies. Large breeds of geese (Toulouse or Strasbourg) are fattened on a rich diet, which includes hard-boiled eggs and skimmed milk as well as the usual barley and potatoes. They are finished by being force-fed boiled corn through a funnel. Geese are naturally greedy, but this force feeding, combined with total lack of exercise (they are kept in tiny cages), causes the livers to become huge (reaching 3¼ lb/1.5 Kg) and bloated with fat. In France, such livers are mainly produced in Alsace, in the Périgord region, and in the southwest. The livers are fat from mid-November until January. Most convenient for the amateur are medium-size livers of 1–1½ lb (500–750 g), which should be pink, without hard nodules or spots. Most people will prefer to buy their foie gras ready-made, but serious French cookbooks offer recipes.

For a start, any parts stained yellow with gall will have to be cut off. Livers may be soaked overnight in anything from cold water to spices and port, or simply salted and peppered and allowed to rest. The livers are often kneaded first, any threads of connective tissue are removed, then the livers are perhaps placed overnight in a marinade of Armagnac, kirsch, pepper, and allspice, but the treatment varies with the chef. Finally, the livers are slit, pieces of black truffle are put in, and some salt is sprinkled on. This done, the livers are squashed into terrines, and the lids are sealed on with flour-and-water paste. They are cooked in an oven in a bain-marie for periods of 30–80 minutes for a 1-lb (500-g) liver, according to the type of terrine and the ideas of the chef. Certainly the water in the bain-marie must never come to the boil. When cooked, the fois gras is chilled, although a version from the Landes is served hot. Alsatian foie gras is pinker than the foie gras of Périgord, but opinions differ as to which is better. Those who are rich enough can spend many happy hours trying to decide. Outside France, you are usually limited to the foie gras from a can. It may be in one piece or sliced. The black bits are the truffle.

Cans labeled pâté de foie gras must, by law, contain 80% goose liver. Mousse de foie gras, which must contain over 55%, is only slightly inferior and is difficult to tell from the real thing, but it cannot be used as a garnish on hot dishes (like *tournedos Rossini*) because it will melt. However, mousse and purée are excellent for sauces. *Foie gras en croûte,* in which the liver is cooked in a pastry case, is sometimes to be found but is a very expensive delicacy.

Although foie gras is usually served at the start of a meal, it can also be a second course, as it sometimes is in France. Because it is very rich, not much is required for a serving. It should be well chilled (but not frozen) and should be cut in slices or served in curls scooped with a spoon. (Dip the spoon or knife in hot water to prevent it from sticking.) Foie gras deserves a good wine. Dry champagne, Alsatian Riesling, dry or sweet white Bordeaux, even a light red Bordeaux, all have their advocates.

Foie gras de canard, made from duck liver, has devotees who think that it is even better than the more usual goose version. It comes from the Landes and the Dordogne.

FORCEMEAT. *See* stuffing.

FORMALDEHYDE (HCHO). A simple organic gas made by the partial oxidation of methyl alcohol. Formaldehyde is best known as formalin, a 40% solution in water. Even when greatly diluted, it has a strong and distinctive smell. Because of its powerful action against bacteria, yeasts, and fungi, it is used as a *disinfectant for barrels and in other situations when sterilization by heat is impossible. Formalin is poisonous. It damages the eyes and lungs and will harden the skin of the hands, so needs to be used with care in well-ventilated places or in the open air. Once dissipated, however, it leaves no harmful residues.

FORMIC ACID (HCOOH). The acid of ants and the simplest organic acid, formed when the simplest alcohol, methyl alcohol, is oxidized. A sharp, blistering acid and very toxic to microorganisms, it is used sometimes for disinfecting wine barrels, but is too unpleasant for general use in the household. A strong solution (55%) in water is sold under proprietary names for removing hard-water scale from kettles.

FOULE MEDAMES. *See ful medames.*

FRAISE. *See* fruit brandy.

FRAMBOISE. *See* fruit brandy.

FRANKFURTER. Smoked sausage of German origin, the frankfurter in its original form was made of very finely ground lean pork with a small amount of salted bacon fat. Other versions contain varying proportions of beef and other meat, while some American frankfurters (and all kosher ones) contain no meat other than beef or chicken.

The American-style hot dog served in a split roll with various condiments supposedly originated at the St. Louis World's Fair of 1904. Like the hamburger, it has undergone quite a change from the original German version. Hot dogs vary in nutritional content, methods of processing, and size, and they are served in many ways: small ones as a cocktail snack; larger ones used in casseroles, grilled over open fire, or coated with batter and deep-fried to make corn dogs or pig-in-a-blanket; foot-long hot dogs broiled by vendors at sports events—and many more, since the hot dog has become an American tradition influenced by local cultures and fast-food chains.

Knackwurst or knockwurst look like fat frankfurters and are similarly smoked. They usually contain finely ground pork, beef, and pork fat and are often seasoned with cumin, garlic, and salt. Bockwurst, at least in Frankfurt, look like large frankfurters. They are traditionally made in the spring, when winter-made bock beer is ready to drink.

FREEZING. All spoilage organisms and enzyme processes are slowed and finally brought to a standstill if the temperature is lowered sufficiently. A few specialized microorganisms can grow in Arctic cold, and some molds can carry on when yeasts and bacteria have given up, but as a general rule, 14°F (−10°C) brings biological and biochemical processes to a halt—the basis of deep-freeze storage. Snow, ice, and natural freezing have always been taken advantage of in northern countries and in areas with snow on the mountains, but modern freezing techniques were impossible until after the invention of mechanical freezers, and were first tried out only in the middle of the last century.

The American Clarence Birdseye, who is regarded as the father of deep freezing, thought up his revolutionary ideas between 1912 and 1916 when he was living in Labrador, where in winter the fish froze as soon as it was caught in temperatures that hovered around −50°F (−43°C). He experimented with fish, seal, and caribou meat, and had a special shipment of cabbages sent him—probably the first-ever deliberately frozen vegetables. In 1924, Birdseye built his first automatic quick-freezing machine, but the general introduction of frozen foods depended on convenient packaging of the foods and the installment of display freezers in the stores. In the U.S., this innovation began in the late 1930s, but in Britain packaged frozen food was not generally sold until after World War II.

Now, however, the frozen-food business is vast, and even the home freezer is becoming standard equipment. A freezer, though rarely a means of saving money, at least enables people to live better on the same money. It is a boon to the cook, who can now have many items that were previously unobtainable out of season, at least in passable condition if not quite as good as they would be if fresh. In comparison with commercial quick-freezing methods, the slower action of the home freezer is relatively inefficient. However, this should not deter you. If all the proper steps are taken in preparing it, frozen food at least has the same nutritive value as fresh food.

The storage temperature in a freezer should be 0°F (-18°C). Frozen food does not improve in quality with keeping; the time for which it can be held in a freezer depends on the kind of food. It varies from a week or so to a year, but there is no rule of thumb. Correct preparation and packing are essential when freezing food; anyone who wants to do it should have one of the many books on the subject.

Vegetables. Use only very fresh, young vegetables. On the whole, vegetables that are normally cooked freeze well, while salad vegetables with a high water content, such as lettuces, radishes, green and red peppers, and celery, lose their crispness when frozen.

To prepare vegetables, wash, trim, and slice them as for cooking, then blanch them. *Blanching is a very important step: it inactivates the enzymes which are likely to cause deterioration and checks the natural loss of flavor and color. It also helps to retain vitamins. Blanching times vary from 1½ minutes for peas to 10 minutes for large corn on the cob, but most vegetables need 2–4 minutes. There are two methods of blanching:

Immersion in boiling water. Place a small quantity of the vegetables in a wire basket and immerse them in a pan of boiling water. Bring back to the boil and count the blanching time from the moment the water returns to the boil. Shake the basket to ensure that all the vegetables are blanched. Remove the basket and plunge it into iced water for 1–2 minutes. Drain well, dry the vegetables on towels, and pack.

Steam blanching. This is especially good for French green beans, diced turnip, and cut kernel corn. The method conserves vitamins and minerals better than immersion in boiling water. Bring 1 in. (2.5 cm) of water to the boil in a pan, place the vegetables in a wire basket above water level, and cover the

pan tightly. Dry the vegetables and pack them in rigid containers or plastic bags, sealing so that they are completely airtight. Always remove the air from plastic bags before sealing.

Frozen vegetables require about half the normal cooking time because they have already been blanched. Most are best cooked, still frozen, in a minimum of lightly salted, boiling water. However, corn on the cob should be completely thawed before cooking. Vegetables will keep for 9–12 months, except onions, which keep for only 2–3 months.

Fruit. Nearly all fruits, except bananas and pineapple, freeze well. Use fresh and ripe, though not overripe, fruit. Do not wash it (especially soft fruit, such as strawberries, raspberries, currants, blackberries)—this tends to make it mushy.

Three ways of freezing fruit are as follows:

Open freezing is generally best for soft fruit. Spread the fruit on trays and freeze at the lowest possible temperature until it is solid (30–60 minutes). Then place it in rigid containers and seal them for storage in the freezer.

With sugar. This is suitable for harder fruit, such as gooseberries, rhubarb, and citrus fruit. Pack in rigid containers, alternating a layer of fruit with a layer of sugar. Allow ½ in. (1 cm) headspace for expansion, seal, and freeze.

With sugar syrup. This is good for such fruit as pears and peaches, which discolor when peeled, and for fruit salads (do not include pineapple or banana). An average syrup contains 10 oz (275 g) of sugar to 1 pt (500 ml) of water. Place the sugar and water in a pan, and add 1 tablespoon of lemon juice or ¼ teaspoon of ascorbic acid (*vitamin C). Bring the syrup to a boil, stirring occasionally, then simmer for 5 minutes. Cool it before adding the peeled, chopped, or sliced fruit. Pack in a rigid container, allowing ½ in. (1 cm) headspace. Seal, label, and freeze.

Cooked and puréed fruit may be prepared in the usual way, packed in cartons, and frozen.

Frozen fruit should be allowed to thaw at room temperature for 3–4 hours, but should not be allowed to become too warm. It will keep in the freezer for 9–12 months.

Dairy products. Butter, margarine, lard, and cheese all freeze very well. You should overwrap the packets in plastic bags before storing them in the freezer. These products can keep for up to 6 months, except soft cheese, which will keep for 4 months. Heavy, clotted, and whipped cream can be frozen, but light cream does not freeze well. Adding a tablespoon of sugar per 1 pt (500 ml) of cream helps to increase its storage life. Cream can be frozen in its original container, wrapped in plastic, and will keep for up to 3 months. Frozen yogurt can be bought. The homemade variety does not freeze very well.

Fish. Prepare fish as for cooking. The fresher it is, the longer will be its storage life. Wrap each fish, fillet, or steak in wax paper or foil and pack in plastic bags. Once frozen, white fish will store for 6–9 months; oily fish, such as mackerel and trout, will keep for 4 months.

Shellfish. If possible, buy lobster, crab, and crayfish live and cook them by plunging them into boiling water for 10–15 minutes. Let them cool, then remove the meat, pack it into rigid containers, seal and freeze. Shrimp should preferably be frozen uncooked in their shells but with the heads and tails removed. Wash them in cold salted water before freezing them.

Oysters, clams, and scallops are best frozen uncooked. Remove them from their shells, taking care to keep any natural juices. Discard any that have already opened. Pack them in rigid containers with their juices. Fill any headspace with crumpled foil, seal, and freeze.

Shellfish does not have the storage life of other fish and will keep for only about 2 months. Shellfish and whole fish should be allowed to thaw in the refrigerator for about 14 hours before cooking. Small fish, fillets, and steaks may be cooked while still frozen, allowing extra cooking time.

Poultry and game. Game should be hung before freezing. Game birds and poultry should be plucked and gutted, the head and tail removed, and the insides washed out with cold water. They may be frozen whole or in pieces; either way, they should be wrapped in airtight plastic bags. It is not advisable to stuff birds before freezing—the stuffing will keep for only a month, while the bird can be frozen for up to a year. The liver and giblets may be washed, packed separately, and frozen in plastic bags. Birds must be thoroughly thawed overnight in the refrigerator before cooking. Venison should be hung for 5–8 days and then frozen as you would other meat.

Hare may be hung for 5–6 days, then skinned and gutted. Freeze it whole or jointed, packed in airtight plastic bags. The blood, which is required in recipes such as jugged hare, can be frozen in ice-cube molds. Rabbit, which does not need to be hung, can otherwise be treated in the same way as hare.

Meat. Before freezing meat, remove as much bone as possible, since it wastes freezer space. Care should be taken when packing meat for freezing, because it is particularly susceptible to "freezer burn." This is unsightly, but not harmful. Wipe meat clean, prepare as for cooking, wrap in plastic, seal, and freeze.

Prepare stews and casseroles as for cooking and pack in plastic bags.

Steak, chops, and cutlets should be trimmed, separated with pieces of foil, and packed in plastic bags for freezing. Sausages and sausage meat should also be packed in plastic bags.

Meat is best thawed overnight in the refrigerator; it then cooks more evenly.

Bread and cakes. Bread, buns, and cakes freeze very successfully and can be stored for up to 6 months. Cakes are better frozen before they are iced, since the frosting tends to smudge when it is packed. Pack bread and cakes in plastic bags. Wrap sandwiches in foil or plastic film and then in plastic bags.

Pastry. Uncooked pastry freezes very well indeed and will keep for up to 6 months. Shape the pastry into a block, wrap it in plastic film, and put into a plastic bag. Cooked pastry, such as flan cases, is very fragile and should be packed carefully in rigid containers.

General tips. The quicker food is frozen the better. If it is frozen slowly, large crystals of ice form in it and rupture the cells. On the other hand, the more slowly most food is thawed the better. Hot or warm food should never be put into a freezer—this will raise the temperature in the freezer and may cause damage to its other contents. It is generally sensible to freeze food in small quantities; you thus avoid the temptation to refreeze it, which is inadvisable. When labeling packages, always give the date of freezing so that you can be sure that the food has not outlived its freezer life. It is also a good idea to note how many people a packet will serve. When preparing dishes for the freezer, take care not to overcook them, since they will continue to cook when you heat them for use. It is best to leave most of the seasoning until then, because tastes change during freezing. For example, cloves, garlic, pepper, and sage become much more pronounced, while salt and onions lose their flavor.

Foods that do not freeze well or should be avoided are hard-boiled eggs (they quickly become tough and rubbery), light and sour cream, mayonnaise and custard (which separate if frozen), and cooked potatoes (which turn hard and discolor).

If you know in advance that there is going to be a power cut, fill any space in the freezer with crumpled newspaper (to help keep the food cold for longer). Do not on any account open the freezer again. Cover the top of the freezer with heavy blankets to provide extra insulation. After power is restored, keep the door firmly shut for at least 6 hours. If you are taken by surprise and have no time to make these preparations, remember that the food will keep for 24 hours if you do not open the freezer.

If worse comes to worst and your food thaws, there are a few points to bear in mind. All uncooked vegetables, meat, poultry, and fish must be cooked before refreezing. All ice cream and puddings made with fresh cream should be eaten immediately or thrown away, as should all precooked dishes. Most fruit can be refrozen, but it will probably lose some of its flavor and color. Bread and cakes may safely be refrozen.

FROG. All frogs are probably wholesome to eat, although many are too small to bother with, and some no doubt taste better than others. The European edible frog (*Rana esculenta*), found in ponds and streams from southern Sweden to northern Italy and eastward through Hungary and Rumania, is rather larger than the common frog and usually greenish with black markings. However, frogs vary greatly in color, so it is useful to know that green frogs such as the European edible frog do not have the conspicuous black mark behind each eye which is characteristic of brown frogs. The edible frog is closely related to other species and may be a hybrid between them; they are the larger marsh frog (*R. ridibunda*) and the pool frog (*R. lessonae*), both of which are edible. European edible frogs grow to 5 in. (12 cm) for a really big female (they are larger than the males), but American bullfrogs (*R. catesbeiana*) grow to 16 in. (40 cm), and in the U.S. there are few inhibitions about eating frog's legs. There are frog farms, particularly in Florida and Louisiana, and frozen frog's legs are also imported from Japan.

It is common to compare frogs with chicken: one writer says they taste like "smelt with breast of chicken," while in the Caribbean, the large hill frogs are called "mountain chicken." Dr. David Livingstone wrote that when cooked the African bullfrog looked "exactly like chicken."

Frogs are eaten all over the world—they can be seen in markets in the Orient—although throughout history the fashion for them has been spasmodic. It seems that they were not favored by the Romans, but at other periods they have been an expensive luxury.

Frogs are at their best in spring. It is usual to eat only the back legs; there is little meat on the rest of the body, although there are recipes for whole frogs, which are, for example, stuffed with spinach in Italy. Unfortunately, the back legs are often chopped off living frogs and the animals thrown into a waste tub to bleed slowly to death. Most people will buy frog's legs already prepared—they are often sold skewered together for cooking *en brochette*—but if they are fresh, they must be skinned and have the feet cut off.

Frog's legs are usually soaked in cold water or milk for an hour to plump the meat before cooking. (Frogs dry out very quickly even when alive, but equally quickly absorb water through the skin when put in damp surroundings.) With frozen frog's legs, follow the packager's instructions. The simplest way to cook frog's legs is to fry them gently in butter for 5 minutes; they may also be poached and served hot with a sauce or cold in vinaigrette.

[*Frog*—French: *grenouille;* German: *Frosch;* Italian: *rana;* Spanish: *rana*]

FROMAGE DE TÊTE. *See* headcheese.

FRUCTOSE, fruit sugar, or **levulose** is a monosaccharide *sugar that is found in fruit juices, honey, and the nectar of flowers, usually with *glucose and *sucrose. When sucrose (cane or beet sugar) is hydrolyzed (inverted), the resulting invert sugar contains equal quantities of fructose and glucose; fructose alone is formed by the hydrolysis of another sugar, inulin, found in the roots of composite plants such as chicory and dahlia. Fructose is more soluble in water than glucose and has a much sweeter taste. Like glucose, it is fermented by yeasts to form alcohol and carbon dioxide. Unlike glucose, it can be utilized by diabetics.

FRUIT BRANDY or **eau de vie.** As the name suggests, fruit brandies are distilled from fruit wines. They are usually drunk as apéritifs or schnapps but sometimes also as liqueurs. Undoubtedly the most important fruit brandies used in cooking are Calvados (from apples) and kirsch (from cherries). However, because some of the others may be found in regional recipes, they are listed here.

Barack. A Hungarian eau de vie made of apricots, usually clear and at most a pale straw color. Often very strong and, when matured, an excellent spirit with a flavor something between apricots and slivovitz, but distinctive.

Calvados. Distilled, fermented apple juice from Calvados, Normandy. Pot stills are used, and the Calvados is aged for varying periods. As a drink, a bad Calvados (or applejack for that matter) is one of the most excruciating spirits known to man, but an aged Calvados can be superb. In cooking, Calvados is often used in Norman dishes, with fish (as in *truite à la normande*), with pork, veal, or chicken, and of course in the classic version of *tripes à la mode de Caen*. In some recipes, the Calvados is ignited and in others not. Calvados gives a special taste to dishes; if it is not available, whiskey is suggested as the best substitute.

Fraise and **framboise.** Made respectively from strawberries and raspberries in Alsace, correctly from wild fruit. Expensive eaux de vie, they are clear and colorless.

Kirsch or **kirschwasser.** Distilled from fermented crushed *cherries of types which vary from place to place, kirsch is a spirit of the area including Alsace, the Vosges Mountains, the part of Switzerland south of Zurich and Basel, and the Black Forest in Germany across the Rhine. In some brands of kirsch, a proportion of the kernels are crushed with the fruit, which gives a trace of bitter-almond flavor. To be good, kirsch has to be distilled in pot stills and aged. It is much used in cooking with fruit (e.g., with apricots, or with pineapple in *ananas au kirsch*) and in creams and cakes. Kirsch is also considered indispensable for cheese fondue—both in the fondue and to drink—and adds great distinction to Alsatian sauerkraut.

Maraschino. Made from Dalmatian *marasco* *cherries and usually very sweet, this liqueur is slightly redolent of the bitter-almond taste from crushed stones. It is much used as a flavoring in sweet dishes and with fruit compotes.

Mirabelle. Distilled from the small yellow mirabelle plums, which are sweet and strongly flavored, this Alsatian eau de vie has similarities to quetsch and slivovitz. It is colorless and clear, and is matured in the bottle.

Quetsch. Distilled from the quetsch plum, like mirabelle it is an Alsatian eau de vie, clear, colorless, and matured in the bottle.

Slivovitz. Distilled from plums in Yugoslavia, Hungary, and Bulgaria. A clear, colorless spirit, rather similar to mirabelle and quetsch, it may or may not have a bitter-almond taste from crushed plum stones.

FRUIT SUGAR. *See* fructose.

FRYING is cooking in fat or oil which is at a temperature well above 212°F (100°C), the boiling point of water. Fats and oils can be made very hot without vaporizing, although they do eventually burn or decompose. The temperature is different for each particular fat or oil, but most vegetable oils stand temperatures well over 392°F (200°C), far above the 374°F (165°C) usually needed for frying.

The effect of putting food (which contains water even if it looks dry) into hot fat is to cause the water on the surface, and progressively inward, to be converted in a flash into steam. There is a violent bubbling and a coagulation of protein, and fat cannot enter the food through the pores that are left because of the rush of steam coming out. Very shortly, as the temperature rises (having dropped when the food was put in), starches and su-

gars in the outside layers become dried and caramelized. The food acquires a brown and crisp coating. The coating is important, and great attention is given to it by competent cooks. Those who cannot judge when the fat is at the correct temperature should use a thermometer. If the fat is heated too much, it burns (and never heat it to smoking, as some books advise, because when it smokes, it is burning) and its temperature is such that the food may well carbonize before the center is cooked. On the other hand, if food is put into fat that is not hot enough, then the instantaneous coagulation and outflow of steam does not take place; the fat gets into the food and makes it soggy. A similar effect is produced when too much food is put into the fat; the food causes the temperature to drop and may lower it too much.

Egg is a very good coating for things to be fried because it coagulates quickly and forms a more or less impenetrable skin. Egg batters also have a sealing effect, but dusting the food with flour or cornstarch alone, though it absorbs surface moisture, will not make surfaces impervious, although it may help crisp them. For shallow frying, fat should come halfway up the food; otherwise, when the food is turned over, a strip all around it will be either uncooked or twice cooked. For deep frying, there must be enough fat for the food to be totally immersed. When frying is done properly, the fat should not pick up tastes from the foods fried in it. Fat used for deep frying should be strained frequently through a fine cloth to remove any crumbs or bits; otherwise they will burn and spoil the flavor of the next food cooked in the fat. Because oils tend to turn rancid more easily after they have been heated, it is ideal to keep fat or oil for deep frying in the refrigerator between uses. It is also healthful to avoid using the same fat for too long. Although it can be refreshened some by heating it with slices of raw potato, it should be discarded when it turns dark from residues or develops a rancid odor.

FUL MEDAMES or **foule medames.** A brown broad bean which is the basic ingredient of the Egyptian dish of the same name. For this, the dried beans are soaked overnight, then cooked until tender (or they can be bought canned) and mixed with garlic. *Hamine* eggs, which have been simmered with onion skins for some hours until they have stopped being hard and have become creamy, are the usual accompaniment to *ful medames,* together with seasoning of parsley, olive oil, lemon juice, and black pepper.

FUMET. *See* stock.

FUNGHI PORCINI. *See cèpe.*

FUNGI. *See* mushrooms; truffles; molds.

FUSEL OIL. Toward the end of alcoholic distillation, an oily, high boiling-point fraction comes over; this is fusel oil. It consists largely of *d*-amyl and isoamyl alcohols plus other alcohols such as glycerine and aromatic ethers. In all naturally flavored spirits—such as brandy, whiskey, and rum—some of these substances are necessary to give the drink its character. This is unfortunate, because it is the fusel oil which is the prime cause of hangover headaches, and it also delays the sobering-up process (thus, there is less hangover and quicker recovery from vodka, which contains very little fusel oil). Good distillers, such as those making cognac, manage to keep the maximum flavor and yet lose the worst of the fusel-oil components. Bad distillers do not. One glass of bad moonshine whiskey can make you feel as if you had been hit on the head with a steamhammer.

Home distillers should know that the quantity of fusel oil formed during fermentation depends both on the type of yeast and on whether it has sufficient nitrogen for its needs without having to depend on the amino acids isoleucine and leucine in the dead yeast cells. The less the amino acids are broken down, the less amyl alcohols are formed.

G

GALACTOSE ($C_6H_{12}O_6$) is a white, crystalline monosaccharide sugar, which, with *glucose, is obtained by the hydrolysis of *lactose (milk sugar). During the digestion of milk, lactose is split down into these two component sugars, both of which are absorbed through the intestines and handled by the liver.

Some babies with defective metabolisms are unable to handle galactose and therefore ordinary milk. They have a hereditary disease called galactosemia and must be fed on lactose-free milks if they are to survive. Even later in life, they must avoid all milk products, such as cheese and yogurt, as well as foods containing milk. *Agar, *carrageen moss, beets, and molasses must also be avoided, since they contain a sugar, raffinose, which is broken down by bacteria, giving a mixture of glucose, fructose, and galactose. Unlike glucose and fructose, galactose is not fermented by baker's yeast, although it is by some other yeasts.

GALANGAL. There are two galangals, both members of the ginger family. Greater galangal (*Alpinia galanga*) is a native of Indonesia. Its knobbly roots are gingery and are used for flavoring the curries of the region. Lesser galangal (*Alpinia officinarum*) is native to South China and is mentioned in ancient Chinese and Indian manuscripts. The roots are small, red-brown on the outside and pale inside. The flavor is something between ginger and pepper. It is known as *laos* or *leuqkuas* in Malay and Indonesian cooking and is used in Russian cooking for flavoring vinegar and the liqueur *nastoika*. Galangal is used fresh in Southeast Asia, but is also sold dried.

[*Galangal*—French: *souchet long, souchet odorant;* German: *Galangawurzel, Galantwurzel;* Italian: *galanga;* Spanish: *galanga*]

GAME originally meant any animal killed for game or sport. Today, the term generally refers to edible undomesticated mammals killed by hunters—it may mean any vertebrate animal, but in the U.S. it generally applies to bear, fox, squirrel, rabbit, deer, bison, and wild sheep and goats. These and many more wild animals were abundant in America when the colonists arrived. Today wildlife is threatened by human population, and many regulations have been passed to prevent extinction of game animals. You should check with a local game department to determine license fees and other details.

If you go hunting for big game, especially in foreign countries, it is worth noting some further items: consult local people about edibility of the beast, and always cook the game thoroughly (whether you bag hippopotamus, bear, deer, elephant, ibex, or lion, the animal can suffer from parasites communicable to human beings). Most big game should be cooked while it is still warm or be hung well before eating.

[*Game*—French: *gibier;* German: *Wildbret, Hochwild, Federwild;* Italian: *selvaggina;* Spanish: *caza*]

GARAM MASALA, a mixture of ground spices used as seasoning in Indian food and usually added at the end of cooking or even sprinkled on food when served, is neither the same as curry powder nor a complete spicing. There are hundreds of formulas, and some commercial ones are elaborate, although the basic ingredients are similar. In the table below, the figures represent quantities by weight, but if you are using ground spices, for a start you can take the figures as teaspoons and work from there until you reach the proportions you like.

Black peppercorns	2	4	4
Coriander seeds	4	4	4
Cumin seeds	4	3½	3
Cloves	1	1½	2
Cinnamon	2	1	2

If you are making *garam masala* at home from whole spices, as is best, the spices should be finely ground in a coffee mill and sieved. You can, if you wish, gently roast the cumin, coriander, and black pepper before grinding them.

GARBANZO. *See* chickpea.

GARLIC (*Allium sativum*) is a member of the same genus as leeks and onions and is probably a native of Central Asia. There are dozens of varieties, differing in size of bulb, pungency, and skin color. In the U.S., garlic is grown commercially in California, Louisiana, and Texas, but it is also imported from Mexico, Italy, France, and elsewhere.

There are three common types: the white-skinned American or Creole has a strong taste, the Mexican or Italian has a pink or purple skin, and the large Tahitian has enormous bulbs. The types of garlic with very small cloves are the ones for the timid, who use only a little in the cooking. Other types have large cloves, some quite enormous cloves, and are the ones for people who use a lot or who have to peel it by the pound to make chutney. There is at least a twentyfold difference in size between a small and a large clove.

Garlic has a strong flavor from its oil, which is excreted through the lungs and so perfumes the breath. This is an irritant—though harmless and even healthful in the quantities used in food—but it will cause severe blisters on fingers if a lot of garlic—say a pound or so—has to be peeled. This process is made easier if the bulbs of garlic are split into cloves and then put in the sun for an hour or so to dry. The skin comes free. On the other hand, skinning of garlic is often an unnecessary chore; the cloves can be crushed with the skin on (it is removed in due course), or the whole can be liquidized in a blender, depending on what the garlic is to be used for. Cloves can be crushed by putting them under the flat of a kitchen knife and banging it with your fist; or by putting the clove, concave side down, on a plate and leaning on it with the ball of your thumb. A little is best got by rubbing the clove against the prongs of a fork pressed flat on a plate. In some places, garlic is fried to "temper" the oil, and the cloves, after being fried brown, are thrown out. Garlic salt is easily made by pounding a few cloves of garlic with bone-dry salt—previously dried in the oven—and can be kept in a closed jar for quick use. However, garlic salt and garlicked foods that have been stored for any length of time can smell horrid and taste worse.

The quantity of garlic in cooking is a highly personal matter, though it should never be allowed to overwhelm delicate food. The cautious will interpret "a clove" as a small one, aficionados will add more than is called for, and addicts will need still more to satisfy their palates. Generally, though, if the garlic flavoring is to be light, just rub the inside of the mixing bowl or salad bowl with a peeled clove of garlic or rub the clove over the surface of a piece of meat; the flavor can be strengthened by pressing the clove harder to release the juices. Chopping, pounding, or pressing the garlic clove will give an even stronger result. Some dishes call for roasted garlic; it is roasted in a dry pan or on the stove before peeling. This treatment gives it a rich flavor.

Cooked whole garlic cloves are quite a different vegetable. When care is taken not to bruise the whole cloves, their volatile oils condense and are transformed within the clove to yield a subtle, sweet, nutlike, buttery flavor with none of the odor or taste characteristic of raw garlic. One of the best ways to do this is to stuff a chicken with all the whole peeled garlic cloves that will fit. After roasting, the garlic can be removed and mashed to a purée to serve with the chicken.

[*Garlic*—French: *ail;* German: *Knoblauch;* Italian: *aglio;* Spanish: *ajo*]

GASTROPODS. One of the three main classes of mollusks, the gastropods include the *snails and slugs, the marine shellfish that look like them (such as *whelks and *winkles), the large and extravagant variations on this theme that are found in tropical seas and coral reefs, the conch shells, cowries, and spider shells, as well as the *limpets and *abalones, which have shells with the spiral form lost (or obscured) in the course of evolution.

Small gastropods such as snails and winkles are eaten whole (after removal from the shell), but the larger ones—from the Burgundy snail upward—should first have the visceral spiral (the dark-colored part deep in the shell) removed. This consists of the liver and digestive organs; it may taste bitter or contain partly digested poisonous food as well as grit. Gastropods in general tend to be edible though tough.

Unlike the bivalves, which include oysters, clams, and mussels, there are no great gastronomic treats among the gastropods; even snails and abalones are hardly in the same class. However, a large number are eaten. Apart from the commonplace whelks and periwinkles, other marine gastropods that are eaten include the horn shells, of which the common Mediterranean species is called *torricella* (*Cerithium vulgatum*). In Italy it is used in soups. The top shells (notably *Monodonta turbinata*) occupy the place of the periwinkle in the Mediterranean world. Above all, there are the various species of *Murex,* sea snails, which were the source of the dye Tyrian purple. The animals are tough, but the beauty of their shells ensures them a place in many a collection of seafood, and lovers of Mediterranean seafood restaurants are bound to come on them. The local people like them (but some will eat almost anything that comes from the sea). Others think that the best place for sea snails is in a soup.

GAUR or **cluster bean.** Until recently, *gaur* (*Cyamopsis psoraloides*) was little known outside India, whence the name comes and where *gaur* has been cultivated for countless years. The long, pencil-like green pods with pointed ends are commonly seen in the markets of Bombay and the south of the subcontinent, less so in the north. While some varieties are for green manure or forage, others are eaten as green beans and make an excellent hot-country vegetable. They are cut in bits and mixed with potato or included in vegetable curries of various kinds. *Gaur* is not usually used as a dried pulse. Commercially, it is the source of a gum which is used to stabilize or give viscosity to ice creams, processed cheese, salad dressings, and canned fruit.

GAYETTE. See crépinette.

GELATIN or **gelatine.** From the Latin *gelare,* to freeze. A protein substance obtained commercially from cattle bones (though skin, tendons, gristle, and connective tissue can all be used) by digesting them in hot water. It is basically the same as old-fashioned glue, and in the last century, when it was first made commercially, gelatin apparently often tasted gluey. Today, it is highly refined and virtually tasteless. It may be made by either an acid or an alkaline process; the product of the latter is the stronger and more expensive, but is also less clear. The cook is mainly concerned with finding a reliable brand and sticking to it. Gelatin may be bought as a powder, cubed, diced, or in transparent sheets. It should be clear, not yellowish, and with almost no taste of its own. Quality is also related to the amount needed to make a good gel and the firmness with which it sets. Gelatin is a variable product, and recipes cannot therefore be dogmatic about the proportion of gelatin and liquid to use. In any case, jellies of different stiffnesses are needed for different purposes. Stiff jellies are easy to turn out and handle, but light jellies are more pleasant to eat.

Gelatin is used to make fruit jellies; it is also put into ice cream, since it helps to prevent the growth of ice crystals. Commercially, it is added to soups and syrups to give them a thicker consistency. It is used in glazes to protect meat products and for fake *aspic. Gelatin was once thought to be a useful food, but it has little nutritive value compared with many other proteins, since it lacks tryptophan, one of the essential *amino acids.

Alternatives to gelatin in various circumstances include *agar, *carrageen, and *isinglass.

[*Gelatin*—French: *gélatine;* German: *Gallert;* Italian: *gelatina;* Spanish: *gelatina*]

GENTIAN. The excruciatingly bitter root of the yellow gentian (*Gentiana lutea*), which is native to the mountains of Europe, is used in apéritifs such as the French *suze* and the Austrian *enzian,* but rarely in the kitchen.

[*Gentian*—French: *gentiane;* German: *Enzian;* Italian: *genziana;* Spanish: *genciana*]

GERANIUM. Garden geraniums, which are natives of South Africa and more correctly called pelargoniums (*Pelargonium ca-*

pitatum and *P. odoratissimum*), are much grown for the perfume of their leaves—rose, orange, lemon, apple, nutmeg, according to variety. Like most herbs, the plants reach maximum fragrance just before flowering, and the leaves can be used to perfume jams and jellies or to make tea.

[*Geranium*—French: *géranium, pélargonium;* German: *Storchschnabel, Geranie;* Italian: *geranio, pelargonio;* Spanish: *geranio*]

GHEE. *See* butter.

GHERKIN. True gherkins are not very small cucumbers, or even a special dwarf variety of cucumber, but a separate plant, *Cucumis anguria,* a native of the Caribbean and much grown in America. However, small varieties of cucumber are also grown for making pickles. Good varieties must remain firm yet have a tender skin. Sour pickled gherkins, cornichons, are a classic garnish and accompaniment to cold meats and pork pâtés.

[*Gherkin*—French: *cornichon;* German: *Pfeffergurke, Essiggurke;* Italian: *cetriolino;* Spanish: *pepinillo, cohombrillo*]

GIBLETS. The neck, ends of wings (pinions), liver, heart, and gizzard of chickens and other birds. The feet, which, when trimmed and peeled, make an excellent stock, are for some reason usually not included in the definition. Giblets are generally used for stock and gravy, but they can be used, in combination or singly (especially in the case of liver), in many dishes.

[*Giblets*—French: *abatis;* German: *Gänseklein, Innereien;* Italian: *rigaglie, frattaglie;* Spanish: *menudillos*]

GIN is occasionally used as an ingredient in the cooking, though more frequently in the cook. The name is a corruption of *jenever* from *genièvre,* meaning juniper, and it was first distilled as a medicine by the doctors at Leyden University in Holland toward the end of the 18th century. Shortly afterward, it was being distilled in London, Bristol, and Plymouth. To begin with, gin was generally sweet, but as time went on, different places evolved their own style. In spite of its popularity, until well into this century gin remained rather naughty: "mother's ruin," the rotgut of the poor. (However, I am amazed at the number of recipes for sloe gin collected by my aunts around the turn of this century.)

The flavor of gin is based on juniper berries. Cheap gin may be made with alcohol flavored by having the "botanicals" (the berries and other flavoring plants) steeped in it, while the better gins are redistilled so that essential oils and other volatile substances are refined in the process. Gin is usually a rather unsatisfactory spirit for use in cooking and for flaming, but there are some good modern recipes that use it (such as *rognons à la liégoise*).

[*Gin*—French: *gin;* German: *Genever, Wachholderschnaps;* Italian: *gin, liquore di ginepro;* Spanish: *ginebra*]

GINGER *(Zingiber officinale)*, used in China for thousands of years, came along the trade route into Europe long before Roman times. A few years ago, many people

GINGER

knew it only dried, powdered, or crystallized, or as Chinese ginger preserved in syr-

up. Today, it is fairly easy to buy fresh ginger and it is grown all over the world in suitably warm climates, including Florida. Farther north, if sprouting rhizomes are planted in good, humus-rich soil, they will grow into a plant, but even in a Mediterranean climate the yield of ginger root at the end of the growing period will be negligible. Fresh ginger rhizomes bought in the autumn, when they are resting, keep well for a long time in a dry place. I used to keep them in sherry in the refrigerator, but they are then less good than fresh ginger, so there is no point in preserving ginger this way except in summertime when it has sprouted and will not keep. You can also wrap the rhizome in foil, keep it in the freezer, and take it out to grate off what you want.

Dried ginger comes in two varieties: black, also known as green, which is simply dried; and white, which is parboiled, bleached, and skinned. The flavor depends more on where the ginger has originated, but dried ginger has a markedly different taste from fresh ginger and cannot accurately replace it in Asian dishes.

[*Ginger*—French: *gingembre;* German: *Ingwer;* Italian: *zenzero;* Spanish: *jengibre*]

GINGER BEER. A drink made by fermenting a solution of sugar in water with added lemon juice, ground ginger, and sometimes other flavorings. The so-called ginger beer plant is a mixture of yeasts fed with ginger and sugar. Real ginger beer is alcoholic; how alcoholic depends on the strain of yeast used, the amount of sugar, and the length of fermentation. Ginger beer is sometimes used as the liquid in which to cook ham.

GINGERBREAD, as sold in Paris as early as the 14th century, was a highly spiced hard cake sweetened with honey and very elaborately decorated, even gilded with gold leaf, since it was used as a gift. It may have been made in Britain in medieval times, and its ingredients sometimes included honey and almonds. After 1660, treacle, which is now accepted as a traditional component of gingerbread, became available. The French version, *pain d'épice,* is made with honey and rye flour instead of treacle and wheat flour as in the British version; it is an ingredient in *carpe à la polonaise,* in which, with onion, shallots, caramel, and wine, it goes to make up the sauce.

In the U.S., gingerbread may be a moist spicy cake sweetened with molasses; gingerbread also refers to ginger-flavored cookies, which are often cut into fanciful shapes and frosted.

[Gingerbread—French: *pain d'épices;* German: *Pfefferkuchen, Lebkuchen;* Italian: *panforte, pane pepato;* Spanish: *bizcocho melado*]

GINKGO or **maidenhair tree.** The ginkgo tree (*Ginkgo biloba*) is probably native to western China, although it has been grown for many centuries in Japan. Called the maidenhair tree because the leaves are shaped like those of the maidenhair fern, it is the last representative of a plant order which was very important in prehistoric times, a sort of living fossil. There are separate male and female trees. Ginkgo trees were first planted in Europe in 1780. They fruit well in Mediterranean countries such as Italy. The fruit resembles a small greenish yellow plum 1–1½ in. (2.5–4 cm) long. The flesh smells dreadful, but the nut inside is an important ingredient in Japanese cooking, and it is also eaten roasted. Ginkgo nuts will keep in a covered can for some weeks, if refrigerated.

GIROLLE. *See* chanterelle.

GLACÉ FRUIT. *See* candied fruit.

GLASSWORT. *See* samphire.

GLAYVA. Liqueur based on *whiskey.

GLAZING is covering with a thin film of anything that looks like glass, so includes *ceramic glazing. Food glazing has several meanings. For instance, to brown a dish quickly under the broiler is to glaze it, especially when the dish is sprinkled with fine sugar that caramelizes to make a shiny topping. Egg white, milk, or *dextrin brushed on buns glazes them. In other contexts, glazing can mean brushing with melted jelly or jam.

Cold meat dishes are often glazed with a jelly that is traditionally made by boiling down the more cartilaginous parts of animals—knuckle of veal, shin of beef, mutton shank—to produce a clear, fat-free stock, and then reducing it by further boiling until a strong jelly forms. However, most people these days use gelatin as a basis for glaze, and make a very firm jelly (9–14% gelatin). Since the gelatin itself is tasteless, it is salted and flavored with meat extract or, better, the jelly that has formed under roasted meat. Vinegar, lemon juice, or other flavorings may be added as well, and the glaze can be colored with caramel, whitened with a little cornstarch, or left clear. It is always melted in a bain-marie (like an old-fashioned glue pot), never on an open flame, and lightly brushed on the meat when it is almost cool enough to set. Once it has set, a second or even third coat can be given. While glaze is usually applied for the sake of appearance, it is also used commercially to protect meat products and in that case may contain sodium benzoate as a preservative.

GLOBE ARTICHOKE. The original artichoke, a thistle (*Cynara scolymus*), is related to the *cardoon (*Cynara cardunculus*). Both come from the Mediterranean region, where the cardoon can still be seen growing wild, unlike the artichoke, which has been in cultivation for thousands of years.

The part of the globe artichoke eaten is the young flower bud, most of which is tough unless the artichoke is very young. Only the bases of the scales are usually tender enough to eat; also, the spiny filaments of the center choke (which will eventually become the purple part of the flower) must be discarded. The meatiest parts are the flower base or *fond* and the top of the stalk. The latter only needs peeling to remove the fibrous outer part. Blanched shoots and tender leaf midribs are also sometimes eaten in the same way as the cardoon. They must be carefully peeled to remove the stringy parts before cooking.

In Mediterranean regions, globe artichokes are a common and cheap winter and spring vegetable. There are a number of distinct varieties propagated by suckers, since seed does not run true. The plant is perennial, and each year the flower buds are cut when they are young and tender. Italy has many varieties, including ones with purplish leaves and very small ones that are packed in oil and exported all over the world. France grows small, purplish russet, spindle-shaped artichokes and the *verts de Florence,* both of which can be eaten in their entirety. The artichoke was introduced into the U.S. at the beginning of the 19th century, and by the end of the century French and Italian immigrants were cultivating it commercially in Louisiana and California. Today virtually the entire crop of globe artichokes in the U.S. comes from six coastal counties in California.

Globe artichokes are most commonly prepared simply by boiling them in plenty of salted water (a pinch of bicarbonate of soda will keep them green) and then serving, hot or cold, with melted butter, vinaigrette, mayonnaise, or other appropriate sauces. They have to be eaten with the fingers: the scales are pulled off one at a time, the base of each dipped in the sauce, and the flesh scraped off between the teeth. The spiky choke must be scooped out and discarded before the base is eaten. Tender stems, after trimming, are delicious boiled in salted water and served with a béchamel or Mornay sauce. Very young and tender artichokes are excellent raw and are commonly eaten this way in Spain and Italy. Globe artichokes are also the basis of the apéritif Cynar.

For more elaborate dishes, the tough parts of the scales are pared away and the unpleasant choke removed, so that everything that remains is edible. Experience shows how much must be cut away—to begin with it is best to bite a piece to test it. It is a serious mistake to be stingy and leave fibrous bits—better to throw away too much than too little. To prevent the artichokes from turning black on cut surfaces, rub them with a slice of lemon or keep them submerged in acidulated water until they are ready to cook. Once cooked, artichokes should not be kept for more than a day, as toxins develop which can be upsetting.

ALCACHOFAS A LA ROMANA

A delicious way to eat young artichokes. After paring them, slice them vertically. Dip the slices in flour and egg to coat them lightly, then fry them in deep oil. Eat them with a squeeze of lemon juice.

[*Globe artichoke*—French: *artichaut;* German: *Artischocke;* Italian: *carciofo;* Spanish: *alcachofa*]

GLUCOSE ($C_6H_{12}O_6$) is the best-known of the monosaccharide *sugars and is often referred to as dextrose, which is, more specifically, the name given to the naturally occurring form of glucose. It can be said to be the most abundant organic compound in nature, since cellulose, starch, and the carbohydrate storage material of animals, glycogen, are all built up from it (and can be broken down into it). It occurs in its own right, along with *fructose, in sweet fruits and honey.

What we know as glucose in the kitchen is not usually a pure sugar but a mixture of dextrose with *maltose and *dextrins made by the hydrolysis of starch with dilute mineral acids. It is usually sold as a pale-colored, heavy syrup (*corn syrup in the U.S.). Pure glucose, which is sold by pharmacists, is a fine white powder.

Glucose will not crystallize and is used to prevent graining during sugar boiling. Commercial glucose is used largely in confectionery and jam manufacture, in canning, and sometimes to supplement the natural sugars of the grapes in winemaking. Although glucose is sometimes advertised as a source of "instant energy" in glucose drinks, it is worth noting that cane sugar is converted to glucose in the body and absorbed almost as quickly.

[*Glucose*—French: *glucose;* German: *Glukose, Glykose;* Italian: *glucosio;* Spanish: *glucosa*]

GLUTEN is a mixture of proteins which occurs especially in wheat and to a lesser extent in some other cereals. Its two main constituents are proteins called gliadin and glutenin, which absorb water and form elastic strands when flour is kneaded with water. If a small ball of dough is soaked in water for half an hour, the starch can be washed out of it by kneading under a running tap. The sticky material, something like chewing gum, which is left behind, is the gluten. This is the constituent of flour that makes possible the light structure of leavened bread. The proportion of gluten varies with the type of wheat from which the flour is made, as well as with its variety and where it was grown.

When a dough is leavened with yeast or baking powder, tiny bubbles of carbon dioxide gas are trapped in the gluten. These bubbles expand when the dough is baked to give a light, open texture. Gluten with a tough quality is hard to blow up, but soft gluten, although it blows up easily, also collapses easily. It should thus be sufficiently elastic to blow up into bubbles of the right size, but should also hold its shape until set by baking. Gluten is toughened by kneading and mixing, by salt (dough without salt becomes sticky), or by acid (sour milk in scones or lemon juice in puff pastry), but it is made softer by fat, sugar, yeast enzymes, malt enzymes, bran, and germ (as in whole-wheat flours).

Gluten absorbs water—the greater the gluten content of a flour, the more water it will hold and the larger the mass of dough that can be made from a given quantity. A strong flour with a high gluten content usually has a high-rising, high water-absorbing quality; it can make a large volume of dough with a light, open texture, such as is needed in bread. A low-gluten, soft, starchy flour usually makes the best cakes. Variation in gluten content and in other water-absorbing constituents often makes it impossible for cookery writers to specify exactly the quantity of liquid required in a mixture.

Low-density, highly aerated starch-reduced rolls are made from flour from which almost all the starch has been taken, leaving mainly gluten. It is marketed as gluten flour.

[*Gluten*—French: *gluten;* German: *Gluten;* Italian: *glutine;* Spanish: *gluten*]

GOA BEAN. Used as a green bean in tropical Asia and West Africa, this *legume is characterized by its four-angled pods. These are cooked whole. The roots are also edible.

GOAT and **kid.** The goat is closely related to sheep. It is sometimes quite difficult to tell them apart when faced by goatlike sheep or sheeplike goats among the many breeds, especially in the Middle East. Goats have horns which are more or less flattened or rounded behind and with a keel in front, although the keel may only be represented by knobs. Some goats, though, are hornless. Billygoats have beards and a strong smell, but rams do not. The meat of old goats is tough and worse, if possible, than old mutton. I was once forced to subsist for a week on the meat of an elderly ibex—a species that is so close a relative of the goat that they freely interbreed—and do not recommend its tough, goaty-flavored meat. However, young kid is excellent, although it tends to be bland, and is regarded in Mediterranean countries as the equal of young lamb. It is especially popular in Italy, where *capretto* or better still the *capretto di latte* (milk-fed kid) is a delicacy, roasted in a number of ways, often with garlic and rosemary.

Because goats, when they are allowed to

roam, destroy trees and eventually cause erosion, they are now less plentiful than they were, although they are making a comeback in the U.S.: they are useful to smallholders as a source of *milk, which also makes wonderful cheese. The majority of goat cheeses are simply described as "chèvres," and they may be eaten fresh, matured and velvety, or well aged until soft and creamy or very hard. Some are flavored with garlic or herbs. Whether strong or mild, they should have a nutty, sweet flavor.

In Greece a whole suckling kid is traditional for Easter dinner, and goat and kid are esteemed as food in Arab countries. In Saudi Arabia, for instance, they may be rubbed with coriander, ginger, and onion juice and stuffed with rice, dried fruits, and nuts. Goat's meat dried in the high, fresh mountain air of the Grisons is called *bindenfleisch*.

[*Goat*—French: *chèvre;* German: *Ziege;* Italian, *capra, capro;* Spanish: *cabra, cabrón*]

GOFIO. A flour made of toasted cereal—wheat, corn, or barley—and a specialty of the Canary Islands. It is sold as a health food throughout Spain. The flavor is nutty, and in many ways it is very similar to *tsampa* and *satu* of the Himalayas and Tibet. In the Canaries it is commonly eaten as a gruel, or fried in cakes and used as a substitute for bread.

GOLDENBERRY. Synonym for Cape gooseberry. *See* physalis fruit.

GOLDEN SYRUP is a thick syrup or pale, golden treacle, famous as the accompaniment to British suet pudding and, in its way, as important to Britons as maple syrup is to Americans. This syrup is a trade secret of Tate & Lyle and was devised by Abram Lyle, a sugar refiner from Scotland, in the 1880s.

GOLDWASSER. *See* liqueurs and cordials.

GOOD KING HENRY. *See* spinach.

GOOSE. The goose is the adult female, the gander the adult male, and the young up to six months are goslings. The graylag goose (*Anser anser*), from which present-day breeds are descended, was reared in numbers by the ancient Greeks, who even force-fed them to fatten the livers, as is done today for *foie gras. The goose has never become domesticated and tamed to the extent of the duck or the domestic hen. Geese do not adapt to modern intensive rearing and do not produce eggs endlessly. Even the best-laying Chinese geese produce no more than 100 eggs a year, while most table breeds lay no more than 30 or 40. Geese like to forage for themselves on green grass in fields—another problem, since they make a nasty mess, and other animals do not like to graze with them.

Farmyards used always to have a few geese, but today they are less commonly kept. You can still see them *en masse* in the parts of France where pâté de foie gras is made, in parts of Germany where they still like goose for Christmas, and in Yugoslavia, Hungary, and Rumania. There can be few more picturesque sights than children minding a flock of geese, something that takes you straight back to the old fairy-story books.

Apart from its bloody-minded attitude to being mechanized, the goose, for modern tastes, is considered rather fat. That surely is the whole joy of it, but to enjoy it demands a healthy appetite and a cold winter's day. Goose fat is the preferred and traditional cooking medium of the Landes and other parts of southwestern France, but even so, the goose does not have great dishes based on it (to complement those based on its liver). *Confit d'oie* is, however, an excellent way to preserve it in its fat, and is essential to a perfect *cassoulet de Toulouse*.

In the U.S., goose may be stuffed with sauerkraut, rice, or potatoes; in Britain, it is customarily roasted with a sage and onion stuffing; in France, the stuffing is of apples or chestnuts; in Germany, the Christmas goose is traditionally stuffed with apples and prunes, with an accompaniment of red cabbage. However, Germany has many stuffings for goose, and some include a sprig of mugwort or wormwood, a medieval custom. A sausage is made in Germany and France (where it is called *cou d'oie farcé*) from the goose's liver enclosed in the skin of the neck.

Wild goose. Many species of wild goose migrate to warmer climates in winter. Over a million geese are shot every year in the U.S., mainly blue, Brant, Canada, snow, and white-fronted geese. The meat is dark and lean (unlike the domesticated goose). Only those that are less than a year old are said to be good to eat. They may be stuffed with chestnuts or wild rice and are usually larded or braised to counteract the dryness of the meat.

[*Goose*—French: *oie;* German: *Gans;* Italian: *oca;* Spanish: *ganso*]

GOOSEBERRY. Gooseberries belong to the same genus, *Ribes*, as red currants. They are native to Europe, and their natural habitat is woods and valleys. Although they have been cultivated for a long time, they are essentially plants of the north, thriving in cold damp climates.

Gooseberries are not very popular in the U.S., since the plants do not thrive particularly well because of pests, especially the gooseberry mildew. Like the currant, gooseberries are also hosts to pine blister rust, and the USDA has prohibited the growing of *Ribes* species in areas where the white pine grows. American gooseberry varieties are usually crosses of European gooseberries with local species, notably the currant gooseberry (*R. hirtellus*) with small purple fruits and the Worcesterberry (*R. divaricatus*), and they are not as large as the English gooseberry (*R. uva-crispa*).

Varieties of gooseberry range when ripe from green through white to yellow and red. The old rule that green varieties taste better than red and hairy ones better than smooth is not always correct. Dessert varieties are larger and sweeter than cookers; they are fine to eat raw, but when cooked do not have the same "gooseberry" flavor as the cookers. Gooseberries are popular in Britain, Scandinavia, and Germany, but in France they are mainly used in the northwest—Normandy and Brittany—and then largely in a sauce for mackerel (hence the French name, *groseilles à maquereau*).

In addition to being used in fools, tarts, and jam, gooseberries can be made into jelly, wine, and vinegar.

There are old recipes for crystallized gooseberries and a dried sweet gooseberry paste on the lines of quince paste. In Germany, gooseberries have been dried as a raisin substitute.

Cape gooseberries are *physalis fruits. Chinese gooseberries are *kiwi fruit.

[*Gooseberry*—French: *groseille à maquereau;* German: *Stachelbeere;* Italian: *uva spina, ribes;* Spanish: *grosella blanca o verde*]

GOOSEFOOT. See spinach.

GOURD. See squash.

GRAHAM FLOUR. An American name for whole-wheat flour, the name "graham" indicates that the food (for instance, graham crackers) is made from whole-wheat flour—at least in theory. Rev. Sylvester Graham (1794–1851), a Connecticut parson and an early health-food advocate, preached "brown bread and the Bible" and said that spices caused insanity and meat inflamed the baser passions. Products made from graham flour do contain all the constituents of wheat in their natural proportions, and, considering some of the substances that pass for bread on the market today, one might well agree with Rev. Graham's doctrine that the more "natural" a thing is, the more virtuous.

GRAINS OF PARADISE, guinea grains, or **Melegueta pepper.** The plant from which these come, *Aframomum melegueta*, is a relative of the cardamom. It is found only on the coast and islands of tropical West Africa. The grains, which are used as a spice and as a substitute for pepper, are its seeds. With ginger and cinnamon, they went in the past into the spiced wine called hippocras. Today, they are very little used but just might be found in specialist shops.

GRAM. From the Latin *granum* (a grain), via the Portuguese *grao* to become, in India, the general term for small pulses other than those now called peas and beans. "Gram," in Indian cooking, always means *★channa*, a variety of chickpea, unless otherwise indicated as in *★black gram.

GRANA. *See* Parmesan.

GRANADILLA. *See* passionfruit.

GRAND MARNIER. *See* liqueurs and cordials.

GRANOLA. This cereal mixture, basically composed of grains, is available in many forms in the U.S. today, since it has been popularized by vegetarians and other people equally concerned with substituting healthful snacks for the junk food so readily available on the market.

Granola can be quite inexpensive or costly, depending on what is used to provide basic nutrition: if you use expensive nuts, dried fruits, and honey, you may get the tastiest combination, but you can also use what is readiest at hand in order to achieve the foundation of grain-oil-liquid-fruit. Grains can be flaked oats, wheat, rye, triticale, or soy. Oil can be any kind you like, but preferably plant oil. Liquid in the form of cider may be used to add moisture and sweetness when you mix dry ingredients. Fruits include dried apricots, coconut, raisins, sunflower seeds, sesame seed, and any other sort of dried fruit or nuts. The combination, mixed well with your hands, should be spread out on a tray and baked in the oven at a low temperature until the cereal is crispy.

GRAPE. The majority of grapes are varieties of the European grape (*Vitis vinifera*), which is one of the oldest cultivated plants. However, there are plenty of other species—little-known ones grow wild in the Himalayas, for instance, while those of North America are important because famous cultivated varieties like Concord, Catawba, and Niagara are descended from them, notably from the northern fox grape (*V. labrusca*), but also from the muscadine grape (*V. rotundifolia*). Grapes descended from American native vines tend to be large and watery in comparison with those from the European vines, and often have a foxy tang to them, but do have thin skins that slip off easily. European vines were taken to America by the early colonists (for example in 1616 by Lord Baltimore), but none did well: the East Coast climate is rather unsuitable for them, and the vines could not stand the local pests. Indeed, one of these, the root louse *Phylloxera,* when introduced into Europe accidentally in the last century, almost completely wiped out the European grapes. They were saved only by grafting them on to resistant American root stocks. However, European grape varieties do thrive west of the Rockies and are grown in huge quantities in California. Of the myriad numbers of grape varieties, a rough division is made between wine grapes and dessert grapes. In general, wine grapes are small, often tough-skinned, and very sweet. They may be black, red, or white, and they strongly influence the character of the wine made from them. In the newer wine-producing countries, which have few if any traditional names for their wines, the wines may be called after the grape—Cabernet, Sauvignon, or Riesling—and the practice, which is also usual in Alsace and Germany, is being adopted increasingly elsewhere, for example, in northern Italy. Because the grape is a *Pinot noir,* it does not, of course, follow that a wine made from it will be Burgundy. It also takes the soil and climate of the Côte d'Or and generations of experience.

Dessert grapes also come in hundreds of

varieties, ranging over a wide spectrum of color and quality, from the meaty muscat-flavored Hanepoot grapes of South Africa to the wild-flavored black Concords from the eastern U.S. Most grapes have seeds, but seedless grapes are becoming more popular, even though the number of varieties available is limited. In California, half the grape acreage is devoted to Thompson seedless, a type of raisin grape. Seedless grapes are the most convenient to use in cooking (as in *sole veronique*); varieties with seeds must be halved and seeded, a process that is worth the trouble in the case of muscats, which give a rich flavor. Unripe sour grapes are an excellent souring agent and the classic source of *verjuice, although that used in mustards today is often synthetic. The juice of sweet grapes is sterilized and bottled.

Grapes are made into jam and jelly, which can be good but often lack flavor and acidity. Sweet grape juice can with advantage replace sugar in certain dishes, and it is in some countries boiled down to a sweet syrup, *dibs.

Dessert grapes should be bought with care. Grapes are best when they have ripened on the vine; bunches that have ripened in transit may improve a bit if they are hung in the sun. The fruit is perishable and should be refrigerated if it is not to be eaten immediately. For full flavor, a grape should be sun-warm and not icy, although on a hot day cold grapes can be delicious.

In Europe, most people wash grapes by dunking them at table. They know that the fruit has been sprayed and the spray has possibly not been cleaned off by rain. But wet grapes are of doubtful gastronomic value, and it is better to wash the grapes and let them dry beforehand. A pair of scissors or clippers should accompany grapes which are served as dessert so that small bunches can be clipped off, or the division into manageable bunches can be handled less elegantly in the kitchen. Bunches of grapes are often offered for sale enclosed in bags to prevent dropping and damage in handling. They are among the few fruits that may benefit from such packaging, since grapes tend to drop badly when they have been fully ripened on the vine. Grapes for export are picked when barely ripe, packed carefully into boxes, and refrigerated, which is why northern countries can enjoy grapes grown in the southern hemisphere. Dried grapes are *raisins and *currants.

From the culinary point of view, sometimes the most important part of the vine is not the grape but the *vine leaves. Even the prunings of vine are used to make a flavorful fire for a barbecue, or for grilling spring onions. Grape-seed oil is used for frying.

[*Grape*—French: *raisin;* German: *Traube;* Italian: *uva;* Spanish: *uva*]

GRAPEFRUIT. After oranges, grapefruit (*Citrus paradisi*) are the most grown citrus fruit in the world today. Their origin is still in doubt, but it is thought that they arose as a mutation from the *shaddock in the West Indies. The first mention was in the 18th century, when they were referred to as the "Forbidden Fruit of Barbados," and it was not until 1814 that the word "grapefruit" first appeared (in John Lunan's *Hortus Jamaicensis*). Grapefruit traveled from the West Indies to Florida in 1809, and the trees were grown there by one Odet Philippe, a surgeon who had served with Napoleon and whose name is remembered by growers to this day. Florida is now by far the world's largest producer of grapefruit, although many are grown in Texas, California, and Arizona. The U.S. produces 90% of the world's grapefruit. The West Indies, South Africa, and South America are also producers. Grapefruit also grow well in Mediterranean countries—Cyprus produces a lot, for instance—and in parts of India.

The tree is large for a citrus, and the fruits vary in size, sweetness, and flesh color. Some varieties have pink flesh and some are seedless. Skins are yellow, sometimes flushed, and may be smooth or slightly rough. They are often waxed and polished for sale. Grapefruit did not come into commercial production until 1885 and were not generally known except in Florida until well into this century. Cookbooks written at the end of Victorian times may mention the shaddock orange but not the grapefruit. Today, the fresh fruit is available all year round, the sections are canned, and the juice is canned, frozen, and condensed. The fruits are not very perishable and can be kept for some time in the refrigerator. They can remain on the tree for months like lemons, gradually getting sweeter.

It is unwise to mix grapefruit with other fruits in salads—it is too assertive—and most of the appetizers in which grapefruit segments are mixed with shrimps, mayonnaise, and almost anything the magazine cookery writer can think of are better forgotten. Grapefruit does not go with wine, which hardly matters at breakfast. It freshens a furred palate, it is high in vitamin C, and it contains few Calories.

When buying grapefruit, look for dense, heavy fruit that is likely to be juicy and not to be dried out or to have a thick and pithy skin.

[*Grapefruit*—French: *pamplemousse;* German: *Pampelmuse;* Italian: *pompelmo;* Spanish: *pomelo, toronja*]

GRAPPA, the Italian equivalent of *marc, is distilled from the refuse left after pressing out the wine grapes. It is the great specialty of Bassano in the province of Treviso. Grappa has a strong, individual flavor, a taste for which one could say is acquired rather than bestowed by Providence. *Con ruta* on the bottle and a leafy sprig inside means that the grappa is flavored with rue. Some Italian recipes, mainly from the northern provinces, call for grappa. For instance, *faraona al vino rosso* (guinea fowl in red wine) from the Veneto uses it, as do such sweets and cakes as the *zelten* of Trentino and *fave dei morti* of Lombardy, and the small cheese fritters known as *sciatt* from the Valtellina.

GRAS DOUBLE. The fatter outer layer of the stomach of cattle, usually sold cooked in France; otherwise simmer it for 5 hours in slightly salted water. In England, it is not distinguished from other forms of *tripe.

GRAVLAX, gravad lax, or **gravlaks.** Literally "grave salmon," this treated salmon is one of the world's great food specialties. Methods of making it vary from one country to another, but basically the salmon is boned into two fillets, rubbed on the cut faces with a mixture of salt, saltpeter, sugar, ground black pepper, and finely chopped dill, put back together, and pressed under a weight for 24–36 hours. Gravlax is usually eaten raw—it has been "cured" by the salt—with a sauce. Occasionally, it is broiled or lightly baked in foil with dill. Gravlax is expensive but well worth trying for a treat.

Each April 30 (Walpurgis Night), Sweden celebrates the end of winter and the arrival of spring. The main dish is usually gravlax, with the following mustard sauce:

MUSTARD SAUCE FOR GRAVLAX

Mix together in a bowl 2 tablespoons of dry mustard and 1 tablespoon each of vinegar and sugar. Then add 6 tablespoons of oil, a little at a time, until well blended. The sauce will thicken rapidly and must be stirred vigorously. Finally, add 6 tablespoons of sour cream and plenty of finely chopped dill.

GREEN ALMOND. *See* pistachio nut.

GREEN BEAN, string bean, snap bean, or **haricot vert.** There are dozens of varieties of these beans, which are generally eaten young, pods and all. Their pods may be large or small, flat or cylindrical, green, yellow, or purple. The plants may be climbing (pole beans) or dwarf (bush beans).

Green beans are usually stringless. Some people believe climbing beans have better flavor than bush varieties, though most are similar except for the vines. Many pole beans are good eaten either young as snap beans or mature as shell beans. The Italian pole bean, with wide pods and meaty beans, is also available now in bush form. Yellow wax beans also grow on bushes or vines, and their seeds may be white, brown, or mottled. Purple-podded beans turn dark green when cooked.

The vegetable most people grow or buy as green beans is bright green when fresh, with slender, brittle, meaty, stringless pods and small tender seeds. Wilted or tough-looking pods should be avoided. The beans should be topped and tailed (few now need destringing), then plunged into rapidly boiling water and cooked just until tender. It is best to test doneness by tasting a bean, since cooking time depends on their size, freshness, and how crisp you like them. They may then be tossed with butter or cream, salt, and pepper, seasoned with garlic or shallot butter, bathed in an herby tomato sauce, or served cold with vinaigrette. They may also be pickled in any way you would cucumbers. *Savory is known as the bean herb because it complements the flavor of so many beans, and it is excellent either cooked with green beans or chopped into dressings for cold beans.

Green beans were once preserved by salting. Today they are available year round in the U.S. (though their flavor and texture, like that of corn, suffers from shipping). Canned beans are acceptable in salads or for long cooking with a ham hock, but they have none of the character of young fresh green beans. Frozen green beans are a fair substitute for fresh ones.

GREENGAGE. *See* plum.

GREEN GRAM. *See* mung bean.

GREEN LAVER. *See* seaweed.

GREENS. *See* collards; dandelion; kale; mustard greens.

GRENADINE. A French fruit syrup made from pomegranates and sugar, grenadine is used to flavor a number of beverages. It is manufactured in France under a secret formula.

GRILLING. *See* broiling.

GRILSE. *See* salmon.

GRINDING. Sometimes it is useful to be able to grind things in the kitchen. Those who wish to grind their own wheat or chickpeas can buy small hand grinders. With chickpeas, it will be necessary to put them through twice. Grinding spices is often best done in a small whirling-blade coffee grinder kept for this purpose. Very hard, large pieces, such as dried ginger and whole turmeric, need to be cracked with a hammer first or they may break the blades. In making spice mixtures, oily materials like cloves and mace are best ground with nonoily spices such as ginger, turmeric, or chili if possible. The difference between freshly ground spices, coffee, and even flours and the commercially milled, bought versions is immense—more than you will imagine until you have tried. Some people even prefer freshly ground salt, and salt grinders are available for this purpose. A good peppermill should hold several tablespoons of peppercorns and have an adjustable grinding mechanism. It is now possible to buy so-called disposable spice grinders, and they are ideal for freshly grinding small amounts of such spices as nutmeg, cloves, and fennel and crushing dried herbs.

[*Grinding*—French: *moudre, émoudre;* German: *mahlen;* Italian: *macinare;* Spanish: *moler*]

GRISSINI. Finger-thick, crisp bread sticks, a specialty of Piedmont, especially Turin, but now made commercially and distributed throughout the world. The excellence of *grissini* was noted in writings in the 17th century. Napoleon was partial to the *petits bâtons de Turin,* and an attempt was made to make them in Paris, with two Torinese experts brought in for the purpose. The result was a disaster: tough sticks of pale bread instead of the crisp, light, and beautiful *grissini* of Italy. *Grissini* are extremely difficult to make by hand and require great dexterity. They are formed by taking strips of dough about ⅓ in. (1 cm) thick and 3 in. (7 cm) long and pulling it out into a thin filament about 3 ft (almost 1 m) long, then swinging it to shape it and laying it out on a sheet sprinkled with rice flour. In Piedmont, Lombardy, and a few other places in Italy, it is still possible to get the authentic *grissino stirato torinese,* which is preferred by some to factory-made *grissini*. However, commercial *grissini* are often excellent and, properly packaged, have the advantage of keeping crisp and good for 2 weeks, while the handmade article keeps at most for a day. *Grissini* are very digestible, very dry—they contain only 12% moisture compared to 25–40% in bread—and are baked at a high temperature, usually 480°F (250°C).

GRITS, often known as *hominy grits in the U.S., are made of dried corn. Yellow grits are ground from the husk of the grain. More frequently eaten are the delicate, finely ground white grits from the inner white corn. Grits are boiled and eaten as a cereal with butter, as a vegetable, like rice, with gravy, or as a dessert with fruit or preserves. They may also be baked with cheese, made into pudding, or added to pancakes, muffins, or spoon bread. Fried grits or mush, a southern favorite, is made by pressing hot grits into a loaf pan and chilling; the grits are then sliced, fried in bacon drippings, and eaten with syrup. Grits are also loved with another southern favorite, red-eye gravy, which is made with the drippings from fried country ham.

In England, grits are a coarse meal of oats. Oat grits (or other grits) may be called *groats.

GROATS usually means cracked wheat, which is appreciated as food in Scotland and the Middle East (where it is called *burghul). Groats may also be the name given to other hulled and cracked grains— oats, buckwheat, and barley—and it may refer to *grits.

GROS SEL. *See* salt.

GROUND CHERRY. *See* physalis fruit.

GROUNDHOG. *See* woodchuck.

GROUNDNUT or **Indian potato** (*Apios americana*), not to be confused with the *peanut, is a native American legume with lemon-size tubers. Esteemed by Indians, who shared it with the Pilgrims, the groundnut is credited with helping save the Plymouth colony from starvation. Groundnuts grow wild along rivers and lakes throughout much of eastern North America. The "nuts" are strung along on the roots of a trailing plant whose blossoms resemble wisteria. Groundnuts taste much like potatoes, especially when mashed with butter, but they contain 13 percent protein—almost three times the amount found in potatoes.

GROUPER. *See* bass.

GROUSE, ptarmigan, and **capercaillie.** The grouse family, game birds of the cold North and mountain regions, is characterized by feathered legs and feet. Its members include the ptarmigan (*Lagopus mutus*) from Europe and North America; the capercaillie (*Tetrao urogallus*) of Scandinavia, northern Russia, the Alps, and the Carpathians, which clings to the north of Scotland (after having become extinct there and been reintroduced); the hazel grouse (*Tetrastes bonasia*) of Scandinavia and eastern Europe; and the black grouse (*Lyrurus tetrix*), which is also called the blackcock (male) and grayhen (female). One of the many American species, the sage grouse (*Centrocercus urophasianus*), feeds on sage buds; its crop must be removed as soon as it is shot, but even then the bird does not have a very pleasing flavor on account of its diet.

None of these relatives approaches the red or Scottish grouse (*Lagopus lagopus scoticus*)—usually just known as grouse—for quality. Indeed, many gastronomes have said that grouse is the finest game bird in the world. The red grouse is a subspecies of the willow grouse (*Lagopus lagopus*) of Scandinavia and north Russia, a bird which, like a ptarmigan, has a lot of white on it and goes almost completely white in winter. The red grouse is ruddy brown and does not turn white in winter. Probably because of its diet of heather buds and berries on the moors, it has an incomparable flavor. Such is the cult of the grouse that experts claim to distinguish between the flavor of birds from one part of Britain and another, and say it also varies from year to year, like a wine vintage. Red grouse are found only in the north and west of Britain and in Ireland; they live only on moors. The shooting season starts on August 12 and lasts until December 10. Visitors to Britain at that time may have a unique experience. The best grouse are those born the same year and eaten before mid-October. Young grouse have clean, fresh-looking claws and a flexible tip to the breastbone—like other young birds. They are hung as long as possible—a week in warm weather and considerably longer in cold (unless they have been badly shot)—and are then plucked, wiped (never washed), drawn, trussed neatly either without the head or with the head tucked under the wing, and roasted. They are best done very simply, perhaps stuffed with a spoonful of butter mixed with a few rowan berries. Older grouse may be made into pies or pâtés, but grouse recipes are never elaborate, since the bird needs little added flavor.

[*Grouse*—French: *tétras;* German: *Birkhuhn, schotisches Moorhuhn;* Italian: *starna di montagna;* Spanish: *gallo de bosque, lagópodo escocés, ortega. Ptarmigan*—French: *lagopède;* German: *Alpen Schneehuhn;* Italian: *pernice di montagna;* Spanish: *perdiz blanca*]

GUANCIALE. *See* bacon.

GUAVA. The guava (*Psidium guajava*) is a tropical and subtropical fruit, originally from central America but now grown all over the world in warm climates, though not greatly in the Mediterranean region or in the U.S. It is important in India, Southeast Asia, Hawaii, and Cuba. In many places, it is a poor man's fruit, since it runs wild, even becoming a pest and producing poor-quality fruit. It is nonetheless useful because it contains about ten times as much vitamin C as an orange, and vitamin C is a frequent deficiency in tropical diets.

The name "guava" comes from the Spanish-American *guayaba*. The plant is a small tree of the myrtle family, which includes such important plants as eucalyptus and the spices allspice and cloves. The fruit looks superficially something like a quince (though no relation), being greenish, yellowish, or creamy in color, round or pear-shaped, with a smooth or rough thin skin according to variety. The whole fruit is edible. Inside, it is divided into two zones, an outer seedless one and an inner pulp that usually contains minute gritty seeds (although there are seedless varieties). Good guavas are acid-sweet, with a strange exotic flavor. The smell is very strong, especially when the fruit is overripe, and it drowns all others in Asian fruit markets during the guava season.

Unripe fruits are so astringent that they are inedible. The best fruit are plucked perfectly ripe, but commercially they are picked when the color is just turning from green to yellow, so that they will be ready about 24 hours later. Guavas spoil rapidly. Although they can be kept in cold storage for up to a week, the results are not really satisfactory. Guavas are therefore rarely available outside the warm countries unless they have been flown in as a luxury. They make excellent jelly and guava paste (a stiff fruit butter). They are also canned, and the better brands are worth eating, although the flavor is not quite the same as in the fresh fruit.

The related cattley or strawberry guava

(*Psidium cattleianum*) is native to Brazil and is sometimes cultivated. It is reddish purple, smaller than the guava, and good to eat.

[*Guava*—French: *goyave;* Italian: *guaiva;* Spanish: *guayaba*]

GUINEA FOWL. A number of species of guinea fowl make up the small family Numididae. They come from Africa, where they are plentiful in some places. I once stayed for a month with a Kenya farmer whose wife served guinea fowl for lunch and dinner every day, and never any other meat. After a while, I became interested and made inquiries. From other guests I discovered that guinea fowl were so plentiful in the area that the farmer had probably eaten no other meat for at least 8 years. Since guinea fowl run and rarely take to the wing, the technique was to go out in the evening with a pack of assorted dogs who compelled the birds to retreat to the trees, where they could be picked off with a .22 rifle. Getting the day's supply took no more than a few minutes.

The handsome speckled bird we know was domesticated from West Africa long ago. It was known to the Romans as Carthage or Numidian hen. Until after Shakespeare's time what we now call guinea fowl were known as turkeys in English—people thought they had come from Turkey (the place everything from foreign parts seem to have been ascribed to in the old days). It was only later that the name was transferred to the American turkey. Presumably the early colonists called their new-found birds after the smaller, but in some respects similar, bird they knew at home. To confuse things further, the old French name for guinea fowl was *poule d'Inde.* Guinea fowls are smaller than chickens and were often hung and used as substitutes for pheasants in Victorian times to cover the months when real pheasant was out of season.

The flesh of young guinea fowl is excellent, though rather dry. As domestic birds, guinea fowl have the snag that they are inveterate wanderers, almost always trying to hide their nests and never quite liking captivity. The eggs, smaller than hen's, are slightly speckled, with very thick shells, so that when boiled they take some cracking— they are excellent when hard-boiled. Roasted guinea fowl tends to be rather dry, so the bird needs to be larded, or at least barded. There are also some excellent casserole recipes in British, French, and Italian cookbooks, and guinea fowl, under the guise of Bohemian pheasants, have even had a place at banquets, although they are in general neglected.

[*Guinea fowl*—French: *pintade;* German: *Perlhuhn;* Italian: *faraona, gallina di Faraone;* Spanish: *gallina de Guinea*]

GUM is used more by industry or by professional cooks and sweetmakers than in the home. British gum is another name for *dextrin. Of the true gums, gum arabic and gum tragacanth are the best-known. These, like most other gums, are chemically closely related to *pectin. Gums are colloids, which usually dissolve completely in water but not in alcohol, and they can be obtained by wounding various plants, mainly trees, and collecting the sticky stuff that exudes. In this, gums may seem similar to resins, such as *mastic, but in other respects they are quite different (resins contain essential oils and do not dissolve in water). Both gum arabic and gum tragacanth were known in pre-Christian times. In ancient Egypt, for instance, gum arabic was used in paint as long ago as 2000 B.C. It is still largely produced and shipped from Egypt, although nowadays Senegal, India, and other parts of the world, including the southern U.S., have an important production. Gum tragacanth comes mainly from Iran, Turkey, and Syria. Both these gums are exuded from small leguminous trees, gum arabic from a small acacia, *Acacia senegal,* and tragacanth from *Astragalus gummifer* of the milk-vetch genus. Acacias are well known to flower lovers and include the "mimosas" which flower so profusely in Mediterranean countries in January, although they are Australian trees more correctly called "wattles" (the flowers are candied for cake decoration). Another acacia, *Acacia farnesiana,* is abundant in the Jordan Valley; it produces a gum as fine as gum arabic.

Gum arabic. Strips of bark are removed from the acacia in spring (February to May). After about 3 weeks, the tears of gum can be removed, dried, bleached in the sun, and cleaned. Gum arabic is colorless and without taste or smell. Although some people are allergic to it, it is generally considered harmless. In food manufacturing, it is a stabilizer used in the soft drink and brewing industries, in chewing gums, jellies, marshmallows, and various food mixtures. In ices, it retards the crystallization of sugar. Gum arabic can usually be bought from drugstores (it was used in making pills). When melted in a little hot water, it makes a gum useful for sticking and varnishing in cake decoration. It can be colored and used as a paint on marzipan.

Gum tragacanth. Collected in the same way as gum arabic, it can be bought in tears or flakes. Gum tragacanth has a faintly gluey taste but is harmless. Allergies to it are very rare, and it is one of the oldest known emulsifiers. Commercially, it is used in water ices, salad dressings, jellies, and candies. Gum tragacanth can be used to make small cake ornaments if it is soaked in water, then mixed into a paste with confectioner's sugar; the mixture can be colored and molded into shapes.

[*Gum*—French: *gomme;* German: *Gummi;* Italian: *gomma;* Spanish: *goma. Gum arabic*—French: *gomme arabique;* German: *Gummiarabikum;* Italian: *gomma arabica;* Spanish: *goma arábiga*]

GUMBO. *See* okra.

GUR. *See* jaggery.

GUTTING. *See* drawing (for birds), fish.

GYPSUM, calcium sulfate ($CaSO_4$), is a common mineral. It is to some extent soluble in water and in tap water causes the "permanent" hardness which is not removed as a precipitate by boiling. Plaster of Paris is gypsum that has been heated in a furnace.

Adding gypsum to wine is known as plastering, an ancient technique for increasing acidity that was already known—and complained about—by the Romans. Hot-country grapes (unless picked early so that a percentage of them are unripe) are liable to lack the acidity necessary for the preservation and flavor of good wine. If gypsum is added, it reacts with the *cream of tartar that is naturally present to produce tartaric acid plus calcium tartrate and potassium sulfate. Calcium tartrate is not soluble in water, so is precipitated as a sludge, which settles out. Unfortunately, the potassium sulfate remains in the wine, and this is unwelcome. Plastering is always done in making sherry because the palomino grape is short on acid. Apart from that, in most wine-producing countries the use of gypsum has been discontinued. The modern alternative is to add tartaric acid instead of gypsum.

[*Gypsum*—French: *gypse;* German: *Gips;* Italian: *gesso;* Spanish: *yeso*]

H

HADDOCK. *See* cod.

HAGGIS. A type of sausage consisting of minced sheep's liver, heart, and lungs, mixed with toasted or plain oatmeal, onion and fat (usually suet), seasoned with salt, pepper, and nutmeg, packed in the stomach of a sheep, and simmered for about 4 hours. (Haggamuggie is an analogous preparation made from the liver of a fish.) There is much argument as to the origin of this, the Scottish national dish, some saying it was introduced by the Romans, others that it came from France. Why shouldn't it have come from Scotland? On a farm north of the Cairngorms, where I worked one winter, two things were plentiful besides the snow: oatmeal—the farm workers had part of their wages paid in it—and sheep. Given those two ingredients, and the bleak cold to keep out, it is difficult to see how the invention of haggis could have been avoided. Ever since then, whenever I have killed a sheep on expeditions, I have made haggis (with wild onions and porridge oats). Apart from being tasty and filling, sheep's innards dealt with in this way keep good for up to 2 weeks, even when carried about from place to place. Haggis, indeed, is an economical, basic food of hard-living people. A variation of haggis is the Pennsylvania Dutch *metzelsuppe*, a hog's stomach stuffed with meat scraps left from butchering.

Carefully wash a sheep's stomach, soak it for an hour, turn it inside out, and scrape it, then scald it. Meanwhile boil the sheep's liver and heart (and the lungs, if you like) to harden the meat before mincing it with a knife. Add 2 cups oatmeal (which has been lightly toasted in a dry pan), some chopped fat or suet—2-3 handfuls—plenty of salt, pepper, and nutmeg, and a couple of chopped onions. Mix all together with some water to make a paste. Stuff it into the cleaned stomach—not too full or the oatmeal will burst the bag when it swells. Sew up the openings and any weak places, and secure in loops of string for easy handling. Pop the haggis into boiling, salted water and cook it slowly for 4 hours. Hang it up to dry. When you are ready to eat it, cook it again in salt water until it is thoroughly hot. Slash through the stomach wall and spoon out the savory contents. Drink whiskey with it.

HAKE. *See* cod.

HALAL. *See* religious food laws (Muslim).

HALIBUT. The largest of the *flatfish, halibuts live in cold waters. In appearance and habit, they exist on the fringes of their lazy, shifty-eyed, flat-bodied cousins. They rise to attack other fish rather than passively gliding along the ocean floor, and they are proportionately longer and plumper than the flounder, sole, and other flatfish. The flesh of the halibut is very white, firm, and of good flavor, is inclined to be dry, and is usually bought in steaks, cutlets, or fillets. Delicate halibut cheeks are also sometimes available, and small halibuts are called chicken halibut.

Atlantic halibut (*Hippoglossus hippoglossus*) can weigh up to 1320 lb (600 Kg). These are deepwater fish, ranging north from New Jersey and Scotland to Iceland and Greenland.

Pacific halibut (*H. stenolepis*) is almost identical to Atlantic halibut. It ranges from California to Alaska.

PACIFIC HALIBUT

Greenland halibut (*Reinhardtius hippoglossoides*), sometimes called little halibut, is a much smaller fish, 39 in. (1 m) long. It is fished through holes in the ice by Greenlanders, who call it *kalleraglik* and marinate its fins in vinegar and spices. Greenland halibut, with its high fat content, is smoked in Denmark.

[*Halibut*—French: *flétan;* German: *Heilbutt;* Italian: *grosso rombo, ippoglosso;* Spanish: *hipoglose, halibut*]

HAM. From the Old English word *hamm,* a thigh, ham is usually the salted and aged back leg of the pig. Commercially cured and pressed pork shoulder is also referred to as "ham," which strictly speaking it is not.

It is probable that ham curing was originally perfected by the Gauls, who exported hams to Rome more than 2000 years ago. Their products cannot have been very different from the best hams of today, since they raised pigs of the semiwild ridgeback type in the forests that then covered most of France. They salted the hams for 2–3 days, smoked them, and finally rubbed them with oil and vinegar before hanging them up to dry. Lean, rangy, forest-fed hogs make the best-flavored ham to this day.

Ham, like cheese, comes in a host of different types according to the way in which it is made and matured. Of first importance is the breed of pig, its age, and the food it has eaten. It also matters whether the pig has been living a sedentary or energetic life, and whether it was killed without exhaustion or fear. Pigs that have been chased around and frightened are thought everywhere to make bad ham and bacon. Experts can tell by the smell of the meat if the pig has been tired or disturbed. (For once, humanity and commercial practice are in agreement.) Curing may be done with many mixtures, although almost all are based on salt. Usually *saltpeter is in the mixture, and often sugar. For the rest, there is a choice of molasses, vinegar, herbs, spices, and no doubt secret ingredients. The curing may be done with dry salt or brine, or a combination of the two, with varying strengths and times. Commercial hams are now usually "pumped"; that is, brine is forced directly into the meat through the femoral artery before the more traditional curing processes begin. Hams may be dried off in fresh air or smoked with oak, beech, pine, juniper berries, hickory, apple, sage, bay, heather, peat, and even seaweed. Combinations of these will give quite different smoky tastes.

Finally there is variation in the aging and maturation—in the length of time, the conditions, and the temperature involved. During this period, which may be from a few months to 2 years, the ham develops its hammy taste by complicated and incompletely understood processes. At best, the subtlety is like that of winemaking, and some districts excel in making superb hams just as some produce superb wines: it is most likely that the tradition of expert knowledge, love, and care produces the best product.

Some hams are intended to be eaten raw; others, cooked. There are also dual-purpose hams. Any ham is safe to eat raw after it has hung for several months (if not, it will also be unfit to eat cooked), but most dual-purpose hams are better cooked. The finest raw ham can equally be cooked, though it is a crime to do so except where small amounts are used as a flavoring (for instance, *prosciutto crudo* goes into some of the best stuffings for tortellini).

To keep whole hams at home, simply hang them in free air in a cool, dry place. The temperature should be between 32°F (0°C) and 60°F (15°C). Whole hams for long aging are best hung where an eye can be kept on them. Cracks may be filled with a mixture of salt fat and pepper (pepper helps to keep away flies). A white powdering of mold is part of the normal ripening process—like the rind of a cheese—but if the ham grows long whiskers or green mold, it is too damp. Ham that has been bought sliced should be kept well wrapped in the refrigerator. It does not improve with keeping.

Before cooking, all hams—except ready-to-bake commercial hams and very lightly salted hams like *jambon blanc*—need to be soaked in cool fresh water to remove some of the salt. The soaking time varies with the saltiness of the ham and its size. There may be manufacturer's recommendations to follow, or the shopkeeper may offer good advice. If you have to guess, you should taste the water after 15 minutes of cooking: if it is too salty for comfort, start again with fresh cold water. Although some correction is possible, a bad error, oversaltiness, especially with a big ham, may be beyond recall. Home-cured hams, farm hams, Smithfield and Virginia hams—hams made by old methods—are usually soaked overnight. It is easier to bone ham after soaking than before.

Before cooking, most hams should be trimmed, which, in practice, means cutting off any bits you would not like to eat. Good hams are always started in cold water and brought slowly up to temperature, which should ideally be 171°F (77°C), at which there is least shrinkage; *they must never boil.* Average cooking time is around 25 minutes per lb (50 minutes per Kg), but it may be more or less according to the size and type of ham. You should cook the ham until you get a meat thermometer reading of around 150°F (65°C) in the center of the thickest part. Ham should be allowed to cool in its liquid until it is easy to handle; the skin should then be pulled off. To finish, the fatty surface may be covered with bread crumbs or glazed, according to preference, though ham is widely thought to taste better without a covering. Part of the fat is sometimes pared away, but some people like the fat and prefer to leave it on.

Some 20% of the weight of a ham consists of inedible bone and trimmings, while 20% is often lost in cooking. Since a further 20% is sometimes lost by evaporation during long aging, the amount of cooked ham you finish with might be only 40% of the weight of the original leg—one reason why ham can be an expensive food. Even the pumped, under-aged hams of ordinary commerce usually yield only 60–70% of their original weight in cooked meat.

The most renowned U.S. ham comes from peanut-fed pigs in Smithfield, Virginia, although you will find advocates for the hams of Kentucky, Georgia, Tennessee, and North Carolina—and they can well be praised for their individual characteristics. Lean Smithfield hams are not very lovely to look at—they are very heavily smoked and aged to a dark color—and a little of their rich, salty, dry taste goes a long way. Smithfield ham corresponds to the lean Chinese ham called for in some Oriental recipes. It is eaten baked or boiled (rarely if ever raw), served hot or cold, and often glazed with jam, brown sugar, or honey. Unless otherwise instructed, soak the ham overnight and cook 20–30 minutes per lb (450 g). Virginia hams are traditionally made from razorback hogs. Every week, Queen Victoria used to have six hams from Smithfield sent to her—or were they for Albert?

Kentucky hams, made from Hampshire hogs, are range-fed on acorns, beans, and clover and finished on grain. They are dry-salted and smoked over apple and hickory for 30 days, after which they are aged for 10–12 months. Run-of-the-mill American hams, produced by the quick-cure injection method, are not noteworthy.

Ham, especially raw ham, is very popular in Italy, and the best Parma ham, *prosciutto crudo,* is probably the finest of all raw hams, unless you prefer a smoky flavor. We must thank the Italians for creating perhaps the world's finest summer hors d'oeuvre: raw ham with green figs. In addition, Italy produces cooked ham (*prosciutto cotto*), often boned and pressed into shape, as well as the redder and less tasty pressed shoulder (*spalla*), which is forced into a rectangular mold. Other Italian ham products include *coppa and *culatello.

Germany makes some delicious hams and is especially renowned for types that are subtly, yet strongly, smoked. The most famous is Westphalian ham, which has a lovely dark chestnut color and a strong, but subtle, smoky taste. It is smoked at very low temperatures over beechwood sawdust mixed with juniper twigs. Westphalian ham is eaten raw in thin slices, either alone or, at most, with brown bread and butter and fresh black pepper. *Lachsschinken,* literally "salmon ham," is so called from its salmon-pink color. An expensive German smoked-pork product, it is not strictly a ham, since it is made by lightly curing and smoking a loin of pork cut and rolled in sheets of bacon fat to conserve moisture and flavor. It is always eaten raw, cut in thin slices and accompanied by horseradish sauce. In French charcuterie, it is called *filet de saxe.* A similar product is made in Poland and widely exported.

There are many traditional cures for British and Irish hams, ranging from Cumberland hams, which are simply dry-salted for 3 weeks and hung in the kitchen rafters to mature, to hams with sweet Suffolk and Devonshire treacle cures, in which vinegar or beer is used. Many county hams are only locally available. Irish hams are usually peat-smoked, which gives them a characteristic flavor. Bradenham ham, made at Chippenham, Wiltshire, can be recognized by its coal-black outside with the name branded on it. It has a sweet, unusual taste derived from curing in molasses, juniper berries, and spices. York ham has a dry-salt cure; mild and pale pink, it is regarded as the finest type of cooked ham.

France produces excellent hams with many regional types of *jambons de campagne* (country hams), both unsmoked and smoked, and many are eaten raw as well as cooked. *Jambon de Bayonne* is smoked to a golden brown color and has a smoky flavor, though not aggressively so; it is eaten raw, though sometimes used as a flavoring in cooked dishes. *Jambon de Toulouse,* a fine, unsmoked ham, is eaten raw or cooked.

Of great importance in Spain is the *jamón serrano* (mountain ham), which is eaten raw in sandwiches or as an hors d'oeuvre. At its best, it is made from Iberian pigs which have been allowed to run free in the forests, getting plenty of exercise and staying lean. Spanish raw ham is liable to be tough, but its flavor is very fine. Other Spanish hams of quality may be labeled *jamón de York, jamón cocido* (cooked ham), or *jamón en dulce* (sweet).

Other hams worthy of note include Belgian hams, which are excellent; *jambon d'Ardennes* has an international reputation. *Pragerschinken,* which despite its German name comes from Czechoslovakia, is salted and brined before being smoked over beech sawdust; it is considered by many to be the finest ham for serving hot. China produces some of the best hams in the world; those from Che-Kiang and Yunnan provinces are particularly desirable.

[*Ham*—French: *jambon;* German: *Schinken;* Italian: *prosciutto;* Spanish: *jamón*]

HANGING. When an animal is freshly killed, the muscles are soft and relaxed, but after an hour or so (as every reader of detective stories knows) rigor mortis sets in and the muscles become hard. Animals eaten completely fresh are usually tender, but are likely to be tasteless. With rigor, the flesh becomes tough; later, after a variable time (depending on temperature and other factors), the rigor passes off. The flesh starts once more to become tender. This tenderizing process is due to autolysis by enzymes in the meat, not to bacterial decomposition, although that will later play a part. At the same time, as the meat becomes more tender, it gains in flavor and eventually becomes "gamy." The cycle is very obvious in a fish, which passes through the changes quickly. A mackerel, to take an example, is flexible when landed but soon becomes stiff. Pick one up by the tail in the fish market. If it sticks out horizontally and is nice and stiff, then it is fresh enough and good to eat. But if it flops, rigor mortis has already passed off, and the mackerel when opened will be found to have started deteriorating. Fish is usually eaten fresh, although skate may be better slightly hung. The length of time a mammal or bird should be hung for best tenderness and taste is very variable—getting it right is a matter of judgment and experience.

Only a few definite instructions can be given. Meat should always be hung in a dry, cool, airy place, away from a wall, and kept entirely clear of *flies. In many cases, butcher's meat has not been hung long enough when you buy it, but it would be inadvisable, if only for economic reasons, to hang small cuts of, say, *beef after you have bought them. The length of time that game is hung is discussed under individual entries. Long-hung meat very often gets a mold growing on it, but this is harmless and is cut off before the piece is prepared. Indeed, meat can be stinking high and full of maggots, as long as it is to be cooked. The main problem over really high game is not that it is bad to eat when cooked but that it is likely to be very unpleasant for the cook who has to prepare it. The danger of food *poisoning lies in meats that have been left lying around after they have been cooked. Certain peoples, like the Turkana tribe in northern Kenya, are used to eating really rotten meat. They will eat it when it smells so bad that other people feel sick; they even eat vultures on occasion. Because the Turkana have iron constitutions which have adapted over the centuries to their diet, they can even eat putrid meat raw without apparent harm— which would not be wise for the rest of us.

HARE. *See* rabbit and hare.

HARENG SAUR. *See* herring.

HARICOT. *See* bean.

HARISSA. A very hot chili-based mixture of spices used in North African cooking, especially with couscous. It can contain up to 20 spices and might be likened to a curry powder or *garam masala,* though it tastes nothing like either. *Harissa* can be bought in specialist shops, and formulas are often secret. It is also available as a paste in small cans. You can use a pinch of cayenne or some chili if *harissa* is not available. Paula Wolfert, in her *Couscous and Other Good Food from Morocco* (Harper & Row, 1973), suggests another chili-based preparation, Indonesian *sambal oelek,* as a substitute. Her recipe for *harissa* is adapted below:

HARISSA

Cover 1 oz (30 g) dried red chilies with hot water. Soak for 1 hour, then drain and cut into small pieces. Make into a purée by pounding in a mortar or grinding in an electric spice mill with 1 clove garlic and 2 teaspoons caraway seeds (or 1 teaspoon caraway seeds plus ½ teaspoon each ground cumin and coriander seeds). Sprinkle with a little salt before spooning the purée into a clean jar and covering it with a layer of olive oil. Covered tightly and refrigerated, this *harissa* keeps for 2–3 months.

HARUSAME. *See* noodles.

HASLET or **harslet** is the edible innards usually of a pig, or these parts—heart, liver, etc.—prepared and spiced in the caul and cooked as a sort of jumbo *faggot which can be sliced and eaten cold. More refined (which does not mean better) versions replace the innards with pork meat.

HAWTHORN. *See* rowan.

HAZELNUT, filbert, cobnut, or **Barcelona nut.** A dozen species of wild hazel are found in the temperate woods of America, Europe, and Asia. The trees bear nuts of varying sizes and excellence which were no doubt eaten by our ancestors even before *Homo sapiens* became human. Apart from the familiar hazelnuts, there are good species of local importance in China and Japan, as well as hazels in Tibet and the Himalayas that bear nuts in strange prickly clusters.

The cultivated nuts we know are derived from *Corylus avellana* (the cob, which grows wild in Britain), *C. maxima* (the filbert, a larger nut from warmer southern Europe and countries bordering the Mediterranean), and *C. colurna* (the Turkish hazel, which overlaps the filbert in the Middle East, especially in Turkey). It need not bother us that the first two are sometimes claimed to be mere varieties of the same species. You can tell the difference between cobs and filberts when the nuts are growing (in the filbert the husk completely covers the nut and extends beyond it, while in the cob it does not—you can usually see the nut peeping out), but it is almost impossible to tell them apart when they are shelled or even in the shell.

The most important producers of hazelnuts are Italy, Spain, Turkey, and France. Spain makes the most original use of nuts in its regional cooking. Turkish nuts tend to be cheaper and smaller than the good Italian and Spanish nuts but are excellent nonetheless. Portugal, Greece, Tunisia, Algeria, and Morocco also grow hazels in quantity. Other countries tend to produce them only for local consumption. In North America, little use is made of varieties of the largest indigenous hazel (*C. americana*), but European varieties are grown in Washington and Oregon. The beaked hazel (*C. cornuta*), a shrub bearing small, sweet nuts, grows in northern states and western Canada.

In Germany, immature hazelnuts are sometimes preserved in brine or used in salads. Very young fresh hazels are delicious and are local specialties. Ripe nuts in the shell for dessert purposes keep well and are usually of the larger varieties. Hazels with very dark, almost mahogany-colored shells have been kiln-dried. For most cooking, nuts can be bought already shelled or even ground into a flour because shelled hazels, like almonds, keep better than most nuts and do not turn rancid so rapidly.

Although hazels have been in use for so long (they were certainly collected and stored in the Bronze Age), in most countries they seem primarily to have been eaten as fresh nuts and not used in cooking. When they are, it is usually in cakes and sweet dishes. They are especially popular in the confectioners' creations of Switzerland and Austria (in which they are often mixed with almonds), less so in France. In Italy they appear in many versions of *torrone* (Italian nougat), in *gianduia* (a hazelnut spread from Turin), and in *torta alle nocciole*. Indeed, many people seem to prefer hazelnuts to almonds in cakes, since they are more easily digested and have a lovely texture and flavor.

Although the French have *beurre de noisette* (lightly roasted hazelnuts pounded with butter used as a garnish for hors d'oeuvre), it is only in Spain that the full possibilities of the hazelnut in savory dishes have been realized, as in the Castilian *higado a la molinera* (liver cooked with onion, white wine, and pounded hazelnuts) or the famous *salsa romesco* from Tarragona, which is used with fish or vegetables, or especially in a *calçotada* (a feast of spring onions grilled over vine clippings).

To remove the husk from freshly picked hazelnuts, leave them in a layer about 10 in.

(25 cm) deep for a day or so until the nuts separate from the husk. Dry the nuts in a cool oven or in the sun for better keeping, and store them in sawdust or sand.

To blanch and remove the inner skins, pour boiling water over the shelled nuts. Let them stand for 6 minutes and remove the skins with a knife.

HIGADO A LA MOLINERA

Cut 1 lb (500 g) liver, preferably calf's, in pieces and coat it in flour. Fry the pieces in hot oil until they are just cooked and put them aside to keep warm. Bruise 2 cloves of garlic, put them in the hot oil, add a chopped onion, and cook until they are golden. Return the cooked liver. Add a little flour to thicken the juice (plus a dash of water if needed), a handful of chopped, roasted hazelnuts, and a handful of chopped parsley. Adjust the seasoning with pepper, salt, and a squeeze of lemon juice, if you like, before serving.

[*Hazelnuts*—French: *noisette;* German: *Haselnuss;* Italian: *nocciuola;* Spanish: *avellana*]

HEADCHEESE, souse, or **brawn.** Usually pig's head (sometimes with the addition of feet and heart), salted and cured very briefly, boiled with seasonings, boned and chopped, then molded with some of the gelatinous broth formed during boiling. In this form, it is equivalent to the French *fromage de tête* or *fromage de cochon.* Sheep and cow heads may also be used, and brawn was even made from baby rabbits by the hard-hearted farmers' wives where I lived as a child.

Although most modern recipes call for the head to be chopped and the headcheese set in a mold, other directions specify leaving the outside of the head, the skin, and the cheeks intact to serve as a covering. After removal of the bones, and arrangement of tongue and other bits, the whole is rolled and tied in a cloth in a sausage shape before being given a final boiling. In France, this form of headcheese might be called *hûre* (head, as in *hûre de sanglier,* boar's head). Refined versions of headcheese, in which the broth is clarified and used to coat a mold (often with cut-out vegetable decorations), merge with galantine, although this was usually made from chicken or veal. Headcheese is eaten cold (otherwise the jelly would melt) and needs mustard and pickles or, better, Dijon mustard with it.

HEADCHEESE

Headcheese (in my opinion) is best when made from a young pig, the head lightly dry-cured, and cooked very simply without flavorings. The following is based on a recipe from Sussex, England.

For half a head, well cleaned and washed in cold water, you will need 1 cup (225 g) salt, 2 tablespoons (25 g) saltpeter, and ½ cup (100 g) sugar, with 1 cup (¼ lt) of vinegar. Have the brains removed by the butcher and possibly also the tongue; but traditionally the latter is included in the brawn.

Cut off the ears, cut them open, and clean them well. Scald the head and scrape off any bristles à careless butcher may have left. Dry the meat and ears well and rub all over with half of the salt. Leave it overnight. Next day, throw out the accumulated liquid and rub the meat with a mixture of the saltpeter, sugar, and remaining salt. Make quite sure that this mixture is poked into every hole and cranny. Leave until next day. Then pour on the vinegar and turn all the bits around in the brine that has been formed until they are well wetted. Turn the meat (I always drain off the brine and pour it back over again) daily for at least another 2 days (you can continue for up to a week). Then wash the head, tongue, and ears, and put them to soak in plain water for 2 hours to remove some of the salt. Put them into a pan of cold water, bring to the boil, skim, and simmer until the tongue can be skinned and the bones removed. Do this as soon as the meat is cool enough to handle. Check that everything is tender and sufficiently cooked (the tongue or ear gristle occasionally needs a little longer than the rest). When they are ready, cut the cheek (the main piece of meat) into 3 slices, parallel to the skin. Line a basin with 2 of these slices, and fill the center with the bits of muscle, ears, and cut-up tongue. Cover with the third slice of cheek. Press down. (I like to use a basin which is just overflowing and press the meat down into it with a weighted board, but others wrap the meat in a cloth, or bandage it, and then press it down under a board.) When cold, unmold the headcheese and, if possible, keep it in the refrigerator to mature for 2 days before use. Headcheese may be flavored with onion, pepper, nutmeg, bouquet garni, or lemon juice, but if it is well made, the meat can stand on its own. Some headcheese is made by cutting the meat into small bits and incorporating it into the jelly. The choice is open, and the results range from a delicately flavored, pale pink, tender headcheese to a tough, grayish jelly with bits of chopped gristle embedded in it.

[*Headcheese*—French: *fromage de tête, galantine de porc, pâté de cochon;* German: *Schweinesülze;* Italian: *salame di porco, sminuzzato;* Spanish: *carne en gelatine*]

HEART, unlike most other offal, is made up largely of muscle, and very hard-working muscle at that, since it has spent the animal's entire life pumping away, circulating the blood around the body. Not surprisingly, it is inclined to be tough. The most tender (and tasteless) is calf's heart, which it is possible to broil or fry gently, but heart in general benefits from long, slow, moist cooking. Small lambs' hearts are usually stuffed and served whole, while large, tough beef heart is best cut in slices and stewed. All heart needs to be prepared for cooking by washing in water and removing fat, arteries, veins, and any remaining clots of blood.

[*Heart*—French: *coeur;* German: *Herz;* Italian: *cuore;* Spanish: *corazón*]

HEMLOCK. *See* spruce.

HERBS. Essentially, in the context of cooking, an herb is a plant with aromatic leaves used as a flavoring. In the past, when the range of foodstuffs was narrow and the quality probably poor, herbs were of enormous importance in the kitchen; they were also the basis of medicine. Indeed, many of the herbs used as flavorings were originally brought into use medicinally—some even for magical reasons.

In Elizabethan times, the herb garden was a most elaborate affair. Numerous wild herbs were known to North American Indians and early settlers. At the opposite end of the scale, in this century herbs became reduced in some areas to dried sage, mint, and thyme. Fresh parsley was used only for decoration, and an occasional bay leaf would be seen in more advanced kitchens. Cookbooks continued to mention chervil and tarragon, but who could get them? For years, virtually no one.

But the use of herbs is coming back, partly because of greatly improved modern methods of drying (and even of freeze-drying), partly because people have hybridized a greater interest in international cooking, and partly because of increased awareness of nutrition (many fresh herbs contain valuable vitamins and minerals). People have learned that herbs—even garlic—are a part of delicious and economical country cooking as well as *haute cuisine.* And they have found that even when the grocery store produce manager cannot manage to produce a variety of fresh herbs, there is always the possibility of a small herb garden or a box of earth under plant lights in the kitchen. So once more herbs are becoming familiar to cooks, and it is common to hear discussions about where to buy tarragon plants, what markets have coriander leaves, how to identify wild epazote to use in Mexican dishes, how much basil is needed for pesto, and which herbs are useful as salt substitutes.

There are no rules laying down which herb must be used with what dish, but certain herbs or combinations of herbs are used in particular national or local styles of cooking. For instance, French cooking uses bay, thyme, and parsley in the bouquet garni, and chervil and tarragon are popular. In Italy, rosemary, sage, oregano, and basil occur alone or in various combinations. Chives and dill are more commonly used in northern or eastern European cooking. To cook in regional style, you must select the right palate of flavorings. The many individual entries for herbs in this book suggest some of the possibilities.

[*Herbs*—French: *fines herbes;* German: *Kräuter;* Italian: *erbe;* Spanish: *hierbas*]

HERRING *(Clupea harengus)* is one of the group (including the sprat, sardine, and pilchard) which has been possibly the most important of all fish both for human consump-

HERRING

tion and, dried, for animal feed and oil. Fresh herrings are delicious, full of flavor, oily, and rich. They are perhaps best cooked in simple, traditional ways, either slashed and broiled, or rolled in oatmeal and fried. A fresh herring can be boned by removing the head and gut, then massaging the flesh for a couple of minutes. Then grip the exposed top of the vertebrae and pull. The herring will be turned inside out. Break off the bone near the tail end and turn the herring back, skin side out. The open cavity is ready for stuffing, and the fish is practically bone-free, apart from the very fine floating rib bones which are left in. The *roes are often packed and sold separately as a by-product of the kipper industry.

Before refrigeration came along, herrings were caught in glut quantity when the shoals arrived; this led to the many preserving methods, such as salting, smoking, and pickling—products that have become a part of tradition and are now made for their own sake rather than from necessity.

Whenever possible, use fresh herrings the day you buy them. Otherwise, store them in a closed container in the refrigerator for as short a time as possible. Kippers—dried,

smoked herrings—will keep for several days after purchase, but the sooner they are eaten the better they taste. If they are to be stored, keep them in an airy place in a container lined with greaseproof paper.

Baltic herring. There are herrings in the Baltic, a small species (*Opisthonema oglinum*). In France, the name Bismarck herring was changed to Baltic after the Franco-Prussian war of 1870, when Bismarck was naturally not very popular.

Bismarck herring. Boned herring fillets, marinated in vinegar (or vinegar and white wine), with onion and spices ranging from red peppers to juniper berries. To make them, soak fresh herring fillets in vinegar for 6 hours, then pack them into jars in layers between each of which is a sprinkle of salt, sliced onion, a pinch of chili and a few juniper berries. Leave 24 hours and they are ready for eating.

Bloater. A specialty of Great Yarmouth in Norfolk, this type of smoked herring has been made for about 300 years. The herrings are sprinkled with dry salt and left overnight. The surplus salt is washed off and the fish is dried for several hours, then lightly smoked. Bloaters are not gutted and so develop a somewhat gamy flavor. They do not keep for much more than a day unless refrigerated. To prepare bloaters, open them down the back, bone them, butter the inside, refold them, and broil. Bloater paste is a famous English delicacy, a favorite for tea sandwiches. The soft roes of bloaters, dusted with cayenne pepper and fried in butter, were served on toast as a well-known Victorian savory.

Bratheringe. A German delicacy of boned herrings, floured and fried, then marinated in vinegar with onion slices, bay, peppercorns and mustard seed.

Buckling. Originally a German specialty from the Baltic (the alternative French name is *Bornholmere*), this type of smoked herring is now produced in Holland and Britain. At one time, the Jewish population in London would accept these only if the box felt hot, so that the fish were still warm from the kiln. After a light salting, the fish are hot-smoked. The skin is toughened and should easily lift off to disclose the moist flesh underneath. In this respect, buckling are rather like smoked trout. They are usually eaten without further preparation, accompanied by buttered brown bread, lemon, red pepper, and sometimes horseradish. Skinned, filleted, and cut in pieces, they may be used in salads.

Hareng saur. The French equivalent of a red herring, *saur* referring to the color and derived from the same old French as our word "sorrel," which is still used to describe the red-brown color of horses. The fish, at least originally, were salted on board the fishing boats and later cold-smoked. Before being eaten, *hareng saur* are desalted by soaking in milk, tea, or white wine for a couple of hours and then cooked—usually filleted, buttered, and broiled. The French also marinate the fillets in oil and use them as part of an hors d'oeuvre. The smoked hard and soft roes are sold separately, often packed in wooden boxes, and used for the same purposes.

Kipper is, classically, a herring which has been split down the back, gutted, salted in brine for about 10–15 minutes, and then cold-smoked over oak sawdust for 6–18 hours. However, since oak sawdust is now practically impossible to obtain, mixed hardwoods are used instead. A kipper was originally a male salmon after spawning, or a smoked salmon, and not a smoked herring. The method was then applied to herring. Splitting before smoking made possible a less salty product which compared favorably with red herring (*see below*). Kippers should not have a gamy smell and should be fat and pale. Excellent kippers, such as those from Loch Fyne and Craster (Northumberland), can be bought outside their areas, and the difference between them and the ordinary run-of-the-mill, commercial kipper is enormous. Fine kippers should be put, head down, in a container which is then filled with boiling water. After leaving them for

10 minutes, they are cooked. They may also be broiled. My uncle's method is good for the more usual quality: butter the kippers, refold them, wrap them in greaseproof paper, and bake the packets in the oven. Modern methods of selling kippers include packing fillets with butter in a plastic wrapper and also canning them. As with canned salmon, the bones are softened and the kippers can be broken up with a fork, spread on toast, and lightly broiled.

Marinated herring of various kinds are especially popular in all the Scandinavian countries, where they are used in open sandwiches and, it often seems, as a starter for every meal. Great inventiveness has resulted in dozens of recipes, often secret, for herring fillets, which may be dark red, gray, or pink, and in sauces that range from cream to mustard and wine. Denmark makes dozens of kinds of marinated salt herring, and many excellent ones are canned or packed in plastic and available as an export. Versions come in sauces including sweet-sour, tarragon, cherry, mustard, sherry, and curry. These preparations are ready to eat without cooking and usually need to be kept cool or in the refrigerator.

SWEDISH MARINATED SALT HERRING

The herrings recommended (by a housekeeper in Degafors) are the fat, wet, salted herrings that are exported from Iceland in barrels, but any good salted herrings will do. They are filleted and the fillets soaked in water overnight to remove most of the salt.

A marinade is prepared by boiling ½ pt (300 ml) water with a cup (or more to taste) of sugar, a good pinch of peppercorns and allspice, and a few bay leaves. When this is cold, add 1 cup of vinegar with some sliced onion and carrot. Marinate the herring fillets in this for 2 days. Although the recipe is simple, the result is excellent.

MARINATED FRESH HERRING

Skin and fillet the herrings, sprinkle them with salt, pack them in a dish, and leave them 2–3 hours, then drain and dry. Pack them into a wide-mouthed jar and cover with the following marinade:

To ½ pt (300 ml) each of white wine and vinegar add 4 onions cut in rings, 1 teaspoon of peppercorns, 1 teaspoon of coriander seeds, 6 cloves, and 2 tablespoons of salt. (The spices are an individual matter. You can use allspice berries, juniper berries, bay leaves, or what you will.) Leave at least 24 hours. This product will keep some 10 days in the refrigerator. The ideal quantities will vary with the ingredients used. A simple mixture of vinegar and water, when salted and softened with a little sugar, gives excellent results if it is formulated by taste before pouring over the fish.

Matjes herring. *Matje* means "virgin" in Dutch, and *matje* herrings are the first of the season's herring, very lightly cured in a brine of salt, saltpeter, and sugar. They are eaten raw with chopped onion and boiled green beans and are available in May. They are also salted in the normal way and are often used to make red herrings with a rather cheesy flavor. This is a German specialty which is also eaten in Belgium and Holland (where they are called *groene haring*—green herring—and where, by tradition, the first barrel is offered to the queen). Elsewhere, *matjes* are a rather expensive import.

Matjessill is a sweet pickled herring and is the traditional lunch for Midsummer's Day in Sweden.

Red herring. In the Middle Ages, red herring became an important product. After gutting, herrings were heavily salted and heavily smoked. This produced an article that would keep for some time; it was tough, dry, and easily transported inland. Red herrings were common until the beginning of this century, but were replaced by the kipper, which is less salty and needs no soaking. They are still produced in England and are exported—Greeks eat them raw with bread and wine for lunch. Red herrings need several hours in lukewarm water or milk before they are ready for cooking. They can then be slashed—the simplest method—or split

down the back, boned, buttered, and refolded before being broiled.

Rollmop. Butterfly fillets of herring, rolled around a stuffing of onion, gherkin, and spices, held with a wooden splinter, and marinated in a vinegar and salt solution. The fish is not cooked and is hardened instead by the salt and the acetic acid of the vinegar. Commercial rollmops can be bought loose or in jars.

ROLLMOPS

Soak 4 salted herrings for 12–24 hours in water—the time depends on the saltiness. Fillet them and strip off the skin. Place skin side down and spread with German mustard. Put on top a teaspoon of mixed sliced onion, pickled gherkin, and capers. Roll up and skewer with a toothpick. Pack the rolls in a glass jar.

Make a marinade of 1 cup of white vinegar diluted with ½ cup of water (taste to get the right sourness, since the exact quantities depend on the strength of the vinegar). Add 2 sliced carrots, 2 sliced onions, 1 teaspoon of peppercorns, 8 juniper berries, 1 teaspoon of white mustard seed, and 2 bay leaves. Bring this to the boil, allow it to cool, then pour it to cover the rolls of fish and fill the jars. Leave for a week before using. Some recipes use a mixture of vinegar and white wine, and some stuff the rollmops with other mixtures which may include sliced peppers and even chilies. In others, the prepared mustard is omitted.

Salt herring. Before the days of refrigeration, herrings had to be salted down in barrels, on board ship or ashore, and formed the starting point for all the herring products. In some cases, the fish rested temporarily in the salt or in brine and were then smoked; in others, they were heavily salted and packed for shipment in sealed casks. Scandinavians argue about which is the best salt herring, but for most people the argument is academic—they have to use whatever salted herring they can get. If salt herrings are not available, they can be made at home.

Scale and gut the fish, leaving the roes in.

Then soak them in brine (strong enough just to float an egg) for 14–16 hours; drain them well and pack them into jars with a layer of salt between each herring layer. Keep them tightly covered and below the surface of the liquid that forms; otherwise they will develop rancid flavors. Herrings may also be salted with the addition of spices such as pepper, allspice, and bay.

[*Herring*—French: *hareng;* German: *Hering;* Italian: *aringa;* Spanish: *arenque*]

HICKORY is closely related to the walnut. Most species are indigenous to North America; the most famous is the *pecan. Other species have been neglected by breeders, in spite of their excellent nuts, because the relatively thick shells make the nuts difficult to crack. So, in general, hickory nuts have been collected from wild trees in the forest and sold in local markets. They have rarely been exported and in general are known only by name outside America. However, with improved commercial varieties and hybrids, this situation may alter. Hickory nuts keep well, and many have an excellent flavor.

Shagbark hickory (*Carya ovata*) is the best of the hickories and is found particularly around the Great Lakes and in the Ohio River Valley. Its nuts were an important food of the North American Indians, who pounded them (apparently not bothering to shell them) with water to make a nut milk. This was added to corn cakes, soup, and sweet potatoes. It was also evaporated to a thick cream for storage in jars or fermented to make a drink called *pawcohickora.* Hickory-nut oil was also important to the early settlers.

Big shellbark hickory (*C. laciniosa*) has a slightly coarser flavor than the shagbark, but runs it a close second for quality. It is common in bottom lands of the Ohio and Mississippi river basins. The nut is rather large and has a thick, spongy husk.

The pignut or switchbred hickory (*C. glabra*) and mockernut or common hickory (*C. tomentosa*) both produce good nuts, though much inferior to those mentioned before.

Other hickories may be eaten locally, but they are mainly too small or too hard to be worth cracking. Some, like the small-fruited hickory (*C. microcarpa*) are sweet, but others like the bitternut (*C. cordiformis*) are full of tannin. Hickory wood chips are important in the U.S. for smoking hams.

[*Hickory*—French: *hickory;* German: *Hickorynuss;* Italian: *noce bianco americano;* Spanish: *nuez americano*]

HOMINY. Hulled corn, one of the staples of the South and North American Indians, was adopted from them by the pioneers. Taking its name from the Algonquin, *rockahominy,* hominy was originally made by soaking and boiling corn in wood lye (ashes and water) until the outer skin of the grain could be rubbed off. Boiled whole, it is used as a starchy food instead of potatoes. When dried, and left in fairly large pieces, it is called samp or pearl hominy; or it can be ground into coarse grits—hominy *grits.

Hominy is particularly a food of the southern states. Although available canned, it is not difficult to make from corn, but all varieties are by no means equally good. American seedsmen sell hominy corn with a white kernel for those who like to start even earlier in the process and grow their own.

HOMINY

Prepare a solution of bicarbonate of soda, 1 teaspoon to a quart or liter of water, and soak dried corn kernels in it overnight. Next morning, boil it rapidly for about an hour until the hulls start to loosen and slough off. Rinse the corn in cold water, rubbing it to free the skins. Wash the skins away in clean water (which will also remove any remaining soda), put the hominy in fresh water, and boil it until it is tender. The hominy may be dried in the sun or a very cool oven. When thoroughly dry, it will keep like any other grain. It may be ground into grits in a mill and may also be frozen.

HOMOGENIZING. A process often applied to milk, which makes all the fat globules roughly the same size and so prevents the cream from rising to the top. It is done by forcing the milk through small nozzles. (A similar technique is used to make emulsions like fake mayonnaise and reconstituted cream.) Homogenized milk is claimed to be more digestible than the plain, crude, old-fashioned variety, with cream rising to the top, but cooks would usually like to have the practice stopped, disliking the dead quality of the liquid and missing the useful creamy top.

HONEY is the most ancient sweetening substance and, in the past, was the basis of the confectioner's art. A complete Roman confectioner's shop excavated at Herculaneum together with all its molds, pans, and implements proved very similar to those used to this day. In those days, honey was boiled, but unlike cane sugar (which came much later), it contains large amounts of glucose and fructose, formed when the sucrose, the sugar in nectar of flowers, is broken down by the saliva of the bees. An average honey contains 38% fructose, 31% glucose, and 7% maltose with other substances as well. Honey will granulate easily if the percentage of glucose in it is high (as in alfalfa, clover, or buckwheat honeys), and almost always if kept long enough. The crystals are mainly glucose and the liquid fructose. It will become runny again (and will not easily re-granulate) if kept for half an hour at 140–150°F (60–65°C), because the tiny glucose crystals dissolve and do not easily form again. On the other hand, stirring honey encourages it to granulate. (Granulation is not due to added sugar, as some suspect.)

Honeys vary a great deal, according to the flowers from which they come. A beekeeper can take out what is gathered from each honey flow, thus getting honey with a preponderance of flavor from a single flower. Several hundred different honeys are available in the U.S. alone, and they vary in color from white or cream, to brown, purple, or even black. A few are red or green. The flavors also vary greatly. Some are even poisonous (if, for instance, the bees have been tak-

ing the nectar from a lot of oleander trees). A very special honey is heather honey from the ling (*Calluna vulgaris*). It is gelatinous in texture, full of air bubbles, and does not flow when the comb is cut. (Honey from other heathers flows normally.) Heather honey contains a lot of protein and so granulation is slow—it takes 2 years even to start. If honey is heated in cooking, the heat drives off its special aromatics and the sugars begin to caramelize, so delicate honey is spoiled. (Heather honey also stiffens.)

Fine honeys should always be kept for eating raw and for sweets that do not need to be cooked. A delicious one which will be acceptable to the most dedicated health-food fan is thick creamy yogurt, honey, and wheat germ. Honey is the basis for several liqueurs, including those made from Scotch whisky, and, of course, the famous Atholl Brose. A turn-of-the-century cookbook gives the following recipe: "Upon virgin honeycomb pour the oldest procurable French Brandy and the best old Scotch whisky in equal proportions. Allow this mixture to stand for five or six days in a large earthen pipkin in a cool place, strain it, and it is ready for drinking." Other recipes also incorporate oatmeal and cream.

[*Honey*—French: *miel;* German: *Honig;* Italian: *miele;* Spanish: *miel*]

HOPS. The hop plant (*Humulus lupulus*) belongs to the same family as hemp (cannabis) and is a perennial climber native to both Europe (including Britain) and North America. It can sometimes be seen growing wild in its natural state, sprawling over hedges and bushes. The use of wild hops for flavoring and preserving *beer seems to have started in Germany some thousand years ago; records show that they were being cultivated on a small scale at least as early as 1079. Hopped ale gradually increased in popularity in Europe, and by the middle of the 14th century it was being brewed commercially in Holland. Hops not only give a refreshing, bitter taste to ale, but they are also a preservative; a hopped ale keeps about twice as long as an ale brewed without them. Substances in the hop also have a calming and sleep-promoting effect on the human system, according to the herbalists.

Under cultivation, the hop plants are encouraged to grow up strings or wires in hop yards or gardens. The hop has separate male and female plants; it is the cone-shaped female flower that is dried and used in brewing. Like all dried herbs, hops tend to lose flavor with storage, especially if they have been exposed to the light. When freshly dried, hops have a pale-yellow color; rubbing them between the palms of the hand makes them emit a bright, intensely aromatic smell, and particles of a waxy substance, lupulin (which gives the flavor), should stick to the fingers. Hop extracts and hop oils are used by some brewers. Such essences reduce the skill the brewer needs to the minimum but do not make the finest beers.

In hop-growing areas, young shoots are used in spring as a vegetable, but they can rarely be found in markets. Hop shoots are popular in Belgium and northern France, where they are known as *jets* or *pointes de houblon*. Basic preparation is to scrape the tender, young shoots lightly, rinse them, and plunge them into fast boiling, salted, and slightly acidulated water. After being cooked until just tender, they are drained, heated in cream or butter, or used in the many recipes *à l'anversoise* (with eggs and so on). Wild hop shoots are eaten in Italy, particularly in a Venetian risotto, but they may be misleadingly described as wild asparagus. If the shoots are to be eaten cold as salad—as in Germany—they are best cooked tied in bundles like asparagus.

[*Hops*—French: *houblon;* German: *Hopfen;* Italian: *luppolo;* Spanish: *lúpulo*]

HORSE. There are few recipes for horse meat in American or British cookbooks. Most European countries admit it, although only in Belgium and northern France with any enthusiasm, but there are certainly restaurants in Italy (e.g., in Modena) where

horse appears on the menu alongside the more usual meats. In Italy, horse meat is prescribed raw for invalids. Since the horse is so far removed from the usual human food cycle, there are few parasites or diseases which man and horse have in common—horse is one of the safest of all raw meats. Horse meat is rather sweet—which one does not notice in *cheval bourguignon* but would in other dishes.

In the U.S., horse meat was eaten by prehistoric Indians and, much later, by cowboys, but it is found on few menus today. The British love horses to the extent that they would rather eat the rider than eat the horse. In Britain, horse butchers are synonymous with knackers and the meat they are selling is for dogs. In France, Italy, and Spain horse-meat stalls and shops offer respectable horse meat at about the same price as beef. The Swedes eat thin slices of smoked horse meat.

The word "horse," applied to any foodstuff, means strong, big, or coarse. Horse mackerel, for instance, are a large, inferior species of mackerel; horse mushrooms, a large, tough species of mushroom (*Agaricus arvensis*); horseradish is large, tough, and exceedingly pungent in comparison to the ordinary salad radish.

[*Horse*—French: *cheval;* German: *Pferd;* Italian: *cavallo;* Spanish: *caballo*]

HORSE BEAN. Alternative name for *broad bean and *jack bean.

HORSE GRAM, Madras gram, or **kulthi bean.** Much grown as a pulse and eaten especially in southern India. Its scientific name, *Dolichos biflorus*, shows it as a close relative of the *lablab bean. It is eaten both green and as a pulse. The seeds are red, white, mottled, or black, but most frequently reddish brown. The bean is smaller and flatter than a pea. Horse gram is rarely if ever split, but is used whole. It may be soaked overnight, but the flavor is better if it is cooked without a prior soaking, although this takes longer—3 hours or more.

HORSERADISH (*Armoracia rusticana*) is a cruciferous plant with large, usually wavy-edged leaves. A native of southeastern Europe and western Asia which now grows wild in North America, Britain, Europe, and New Zealand, it is cultivated for its pungently flavored taproot. For use, this is scrubbed clean and any discolored bits are cut out before the outer part, which has the strongest taste, is finely grated or scraped off; the core is discarded. Horseradish is used as a cold garnish or flavoring and is added to mayonnaise to go with fish or salads. Horseradish sauces, which are usually uncooked or at most cooked or warmed very gently, tend to contain cream and vinegar or (in France) lemon juice. The flavor of horseradish depends entirely on volatile essential oils, which quickly disappear in cooking. Grated horeradish does not retain its pungency for very long, but sliced horseradish can be dried in an oven at the lowest temperature setting—commercially dried horseradish has a much better flavor than the bottled horseradish sauces. Although its main use these days is as sauce with beef and smoked fish, horseradish used to be more popular and goes well with other things, notably chicken and hard-boiled eggs.

[*Horseradish*—French: *raifort;* German: *Meerrettich;* Italian: *rafano;* Spanish: *rábano picante*]

HOT DOG. *See* frankfurter.

HUCKLEBERRY. *See* blueberry.

HUITLACOCHE is the Mexican term for a fungus (*Ustilago maydis*) which grows on the ears of sweet corn and makes the kernels swell and become deformed. The skin of the kernels turns silver-gray; the inside is black. In cooking, a black juice with a delicious fungus flavor is given out. There is no substitute for the fungus, which to U.S. farmers is known as corn smut.

HULLED CORN. *See* hominy.

HYACINTH BEAN. *See* lablab bean.

HYDROCHLORIC ACID (HCl). A strong mineral acid that is found in a very dilute form in human stomach juices. Strong fuming hydrochloric acid is highly dangerous and no kitchen product. A few drops of the dilute acid shaken up in a cane sugar syrup and allowed to stand in a warm place for several days will convert the cane sugar to glucose and fructose. The acid can be neutralized with a pinch of chalk or bicarbonate of soda.

[*Hydrochloric acid*—French: *acide chlorhydrique;* German: *Chlorwasserstoff;* Italian: *acido idroclorico;* Spanish: *ácido hidroclórico*]

HYDROGEN PEROXIDE. *See* disinfectants.

HYDROLYSIS. The breaking down of complex substances into simpler ones by the addition of hydrogen and oxygen atoms in the proportion in which they occur in water—2:1. Hydrolysis may be achieved by warming with dilute acids, as when starch is hydrolyzed to maltose and dextrose, cane sugar to glucose, or proteins to amino acids. It often happens as a result of the activity of enzymes (e.g., in *malt) and also with alkalis.

[*Hydrolysis*—French: *hydrolyse;* German: *Hydrolyse;* Spanish: *hidrólisis*]

HYDROLYZED PROTEIN has been broken down by acid hydrolysis and is used as a flavoring by the food industry. Hydrolyzed vegetable protein (from corn, wheat, or soybeans) has a rather meaty taste and is the basis of flavoring sauces as well as a component of various meat cubes, stock cubes, and meat extracts.

HYGIENE is a system of principles evolved to maintain good health and is not synonymous with cleanliness. Indeed, many convenience foods of impeccable sterilization but doubtful content are unhygienic, and most country kitchens full of ash and soil from fresh vegetables are quite as hygienic as the soulless palaces of stainless steel and white enamel. The latter have the advantage that if they are dirty they look it, and so are more work to maintain, but rarely does the best food come from them. Hygiene begins with government inspectors who are supposed to see that food, milk, and water are fresh, wholesome, and free from disease when they come to us. They are also supposed to see that what is sold as food *is* food, and not just an exercise in advertising, consumer research, and shelf life.

In the kitchen, few rules are necessarily observed, but the following are important. Always wash your hands before starting to cook. Surfaces used for cutting or chopping need to be kept clean, especially if they are made of wood, which is porous. A good scrub with soap and a rinse in really hot water are all that is needed. Knives and surfaces used for cutting raw meat must be washed before cutting cooked meat. In general, raw and cooked foods should be kept apart. Pans, plates, bowls, and cutlery must be well washed and properly rinsed. (The long-term effect of synthetic detergents on the intestines has not yet been determined.) If the washing water is really hot, then no disease organisms will be passed from one person to another on glasses, cups, or forks, the key points for cross-infection. Crockery and cutlery are better left to drain dry than to be dried with a towel. Foods should not be left lying about in the kitchen or kept for long periods forgotten at the back of the refrigerator. *Copper pans should be properly tinned, or at least used and emptied immediately, and any earthenware covered with lead glaze should be kept for foods that are not acid. *Flies are public enemy number one; they are filthy and should not come in contact with food—all food should be kept covered if it is not in the refrigerator.

Finally it is worth looking at the question of washing fruits and salads. In the developed countries, the main reason for this is to remove insecticidal or fungicidal sprays, and preservatives, the bad effects, if any, of which are long-term and sometimes cumulative. In developing countries, where sewage disposal is often dubious, the skins of fruit and tomatoes to be eaten raw should be washed carefully with water containing unscented soap as *disinfectant. Alternatively, you can dip the fruit in boiling water, count to 15, take it out and skin it. *Citrus fruits are effectively protected by their skins but in some areas might need scrubbing if you are going to use the peel and not just the contents. Green salads in such areas can never be certainly safe if they have been bought in the market and are best replaced by home-sprouted seed—mustard and cress or sprouted fenugreek. Anything cooked or pasteurized is safe if it is not recontaminated.

[*Hygiene*—French: *hygiène;* German: *Hygiene;* Italian: *igiene;* Spanish: *higiene*]

HYSSOP (*Hyssopus officinalis*). A beautiful, decorative labiate herb of the thyme family which grows wild in Mediterranean Europe from the Alps across to Russia (but not in Greece or Turkey). Hyssop has long been used for its warm, aromatic smell, but it has no firm place in cooking, although it is sometimes used as a flavoring. More commonly, it is an ingredient of liqueurs (e.g., chartreuse), because it is soothing to the stomach; the taste is slightly minty but bitter. It is recommended for the herb garden.

[*Hyssop*—French: *hysope;* German: *Ysop, Eisop;* Italian: *issopo;* Spanish: *hisopo*]

I

ICE. The freezing point of water and the melting point of ice are at the same temperature, 32°F or 0°C. This does not mean that if you cool water to 0°C it will suddenly solidify or that if you raise the temperature of ice to 0°C it will suddenly melt. To freeze water at zero, it is necessary to go on taking out heat, or to melt ice at zero it is necessary to go on supplying heat. In fact, it is necessary to put in or take out heat in order to cause a change of state (just as it is to change water to steam), and during this period the temperature remains the same. Thirsty Himalayan climbers must sit for hours melting snow, and all the snow has to melt before the water can be heated to make a hot drink. A drink with ice floating in it (once it has settled down) will be at roughly 0°C, with both the ice and the water at the same temperature. The temperature of ice can, of course, be reduced below zero. It becomes crisp and the cubes do not stick together, but they do stick to the fingers.

Before the invention of refrigerators, winter snow was stored in pits or icehouses insulated with straw for use later in the year. There is even a huge icehouse in the middle of the great Persian salt desert, a building the size (and rather the shape) of a tennis stadium, where snow was once packed to help people survive the summer's awful heat.

When water freezes to ice, it expands—which is why bottles of beer will crack in the freezer and why, being less dense than water, ice floats. It will melt under pressure, as anyone who has left a bottle standing on a block of ice will have noticed—the bottle sinks in. Ice also melts when salt is put on it, but the heat consumption in the change of state from solid to liquid makes the temperature drop. This is the basis for the use of ice and salt in old-fashioned methods of freezing ice cream.

[Ice—French: glace; German: Eis; Italian: ghiaccio; Spanish: hielo]

ICE CREAM, water ice, and sorbet. Ice creams were probably invented in China, or at least somewhere in the East. At any rate, ices spread to the rest of Europe from northern Italy; it was one of the cooks who went to France with Catherine de Medici in 1533 who introduced ices to the French court. Some hundred years later, another Italian chef brought them to the court of Charles I. In that same century, Italians opened cafés to sell ices in Paris (the first in 1670), at first selling sorbets and later ice creams. It was Italians once more who introduced ice cream into the U.S. early in the 19th century. At that time ice cream was a real luxury, and nobody could have foreseen the enormous profits which would be made in the 20th century from selling frozen froth. True, the machines that make the drums of colored mixture into ices are rather expensive, but the product can then be sold at a remarkable profit margin. If ices were cheaper and more certainly harmless, they would have to be praised, since (*pace* the dental profession) they are undoubtedly fun, especially for children. However, as a vehicle for synthetic dyes, sugar, synthetic flavorings, emulsifiers, stabilizers, and lard they are not above suspicion. Ices are very easily made at home. The primitive method (and still the best to use) is an ice-cream churn, consisting of a metal drum with a lid. Into this are put the materials to be frozen; the drum is surrounded with a freezing mixture of ice and salt, and is fitted with spring-loaded paddles which keep the ice-cream mixture continually stirred and pressed against the sides. Such a machine can be laboriously worked by hand or can have an electric motor. There are also electric *sorbétières* with stirring paddles, which make ice cream in the freezer or freezing compartment of the refrigerator. Many people use recipes containing gelatin or egg white which need little stirring. There are two basic types of ice: water ice (sorbet, *granita*, or *frappé*) and cream ices. In the former, fruit juices or purées are sweetened with sugar. This family of ices is expected to be granular, and so is suitably made in the freezer compartment of the refrigerator. Water ices should be stirred four or five times, or beaten with egg white while freezing to keep them from being too solid. Gelatin is another substance which helps to minimize the formation of ice crystals. Total freezing time is 4–6 hours, depending on the circumstances. Sorbets and water ices should be light and refreshing. Cream ices, on the other hand, are rich and delicious. The cream and egg yolks have also a decided effect in preventing the growth of ice crystals. Again, there are many successful recipes for making ices in the freezer, with no more than an occasional stir while freezing, although the best texture and exactly the right temperature results from using an ice-cream churn.

[*Ice cream*—French: *glace, crème glacée, sorbet;* German: *Eis, Speiseeis;* Italian: *gelato;* Spanish: *helado*]

ICELAND MOSS (*Cetraria islandica*) is not a moss but a lichen, almost the only one that is used as a food (although the genus *Roccella,* which grows on coastal cliffs, yields dyes such as cudbear and litmus). It is a moorland and mountain plant with a bitter taste which needs to be removed by thorough soaking in numerous changes of water. It can then be boiled to produce an edible jelly or dried and ground to a flour which is used in the Arctic to make bread.

ILAMA. *See* custard apple.

INDIAN CORN. *See* corn.

INDIAN CRESS. *See* nasturtium.

INDIAN DATE. *See* tamarind.

INDIAN FIG or **Indian pear.** *See* prickly pear.

INDIAN RICE. *See* wild rice.

INKY CAP. *See* shaggy mane.

INSECTS. Marine crustaceans like shrimps, crabs, and lobsters are forbidden to Orthodox Jews, so it is interesting to read in the Bible (*Leviticus 11:21–22*) that Moses allowed four different kinds of insect as food, while the Islamic food laws, which have a common origin, allow the eating of locusts, though not of grasshoppers. Insects are a traditional food in many countries: in Africa, in parts of Southeast Asia (where spiders and scorpions are also sometimes put in the pot), in China (where silkworms are eaten), and in parts of Australia. Locusts were also liked in ancient Greece, but the tradition of eating them was never carried on into European and American cooking.

Indeed, the very idea of eating insects is repulsive to most people, even though they eat honey (which we forget has been swallowed and regurgitated by insects) and put cochineal into cake icing. If the comb containing bee larvae is blanched and the grubs are removed, dried, and then dry-fried in a little salt, the result is an excellent appetizer. In fact, insects generally have a good taste. The witchity grub I once ate in North Queensland tasted like fish cooked in cream, while fried locusts have been described as tasting like roasted chestnuts. Many people I know like fried termites, and there are various combinations of insects and chocolate on the market. The insects used for food are much cleaner feeders than shrimps, but of course the reader should not rush off in a burst of enthusiasm and eat any sort of insect. Some probably taste horrible, and others, like the Spanish fly, a beetle used in the past as an aphrodisiac, are dangerously poisonous.

A great many, though, are known locally as good food and a valuable source of protein when the insects swarm or can be collected in sufficient numbers. The red or carmine locust (*Nomadacris septemfasciata*) is the one most commonly eaten in Arabia. Only the females are eaten. They are boiled for about 5 minutes, the legs and wings are removed, and the locusts are then fried in butter. Termites, species of *Macrotermes,* are often eaten in Africa when they swarm at the beginning of the rainy season. They are dry-fried, dried in the sun, have the wings winnowed away, and are then refried with a little salt and fat. Crickets, grasshoppers, shield bugs, flying ants, and even some caterpillars are eaten. They may need to have the intestines removed before they are cooked, just like some crustaceans, and it is necessary to follow local practice. One of the most interesting insect foods is provided by the lake fly (*Chaobora edulis*), which swarms at new moon over Lake Nyasa. Though this is a tiny insect, it occurs in such numbers that the black clouds of countless millions can be seen for a considerable distance. The insects, when caught and dried in cakes, are a useful food. The cake is broken into bits, boiled in a little salt water until soft, and then incorporated with tomato, onion, and pounded fried peanuts to make a sauce to go with rice or corn-meal porridge. I have no doubt that as the problem of feeding the world grows, the question of insects as a source of food will receive increasing attention.

[*Insects*—French: *insectes;* German: *Insekten;* Italian: *insetti;* Spanish: *insectos*]

INVERT SUGAR. A mixture of simple *sugars, *glucose, and *fructose which occurs naturally in many fruits, but is also made when cane sugar is warmed with a dilute acid ("inverted").

[*Invert sugar*—French: *sucre inverti;* German: *Invertzucker;* Italian: *zucchero inverso;* Spanish: *azúcar inverto*]

IODINE (I). An element that belongs to the same group as fluorine and chlorine. Small quantities in a combined form are essential in the human body, and shortage of iodine causes goiter, a condition that used to be very prevalent in countries far from the sea. Sea water is the major source of the element in nature. The iodine content of foods varies widely from place to place, but most people get enough in a balanced diet. Good sources of iodine are seafish, shellfish, kelp, agar, laver, and other seaweed products or iodized salt, which is common salt to which 25 parts per million of potassium iodide have been added. In some seaweeds, as much as .2% of the living plant is iodine.

[*Iodine*—French: *iode;* German: *Jod;* Italian: *iodio;* Spanish: *yodo*]

IRISH MOSS. See carrageen.

IRON (Fe). A metal that makes up 4.7% of the earth's crust (and almost certainly is one of the main constituents of its molten core), yet some soils are deficient in it. Iron is an essential element for human nutrition: it is vital for the formation of the hemoglobin of red blood cells and also, for instance, of myoglobin, the respiratory pigment in muscles. We need to assimilate about 10 mg of iron per day. Although iron is available in many unrefined foods—liver, whole wheat, fruits, and vegetables—it is often not properly absorbed, particularly when oxalic acid is present, and it is absent, or inadequate, in milk, white bread, and sugar. In the U.S. "enriched" bread flour has 2.9 mg iron per 100 g. It is better to get iron from food than by taking supplements, and ferrous sulfate and chloride are best avoided.

The Iron Age is the most recent archaeological age. As far as is known, iron was first worked in the Middle East about 2500 B.C., but it was not until about 1200 B.C. that iron smelting became common. It is a very suitable metal for pots, grills, knives, and other cooking utensils, being harmless (though not ideal for sour fruits or other acids). Early vessels were of beaten iron; much later came cast iron, which was cheap, brittle, and porous. Cast-iron frying pans actually benefit from being porous—they become saturated with fat and so get a good, nonstick surface. Iron surfaces are best "cured" with fat and then rubbed with paper to remove excess fat. Griddles, *thoas* for making chapaties, and iron plates for cooking *à la plancha* may be so cleaned and treated.

Steel is iron with a little carbon and often other metals such as nickel or vanadium added. Mild steel is easily bent and makes excellent kebab skewers. Stainless steel contains chromium and other metals in alloy; the chromium protects the surface, but knives made with it do not take a good edge, whereas carbon steel knives, although they also rust and stain, take an excellent edge. Some modern steels are stainless and sharpen reasonably well.

[*Iron*—French: *fer;* German: *Eisen;* Italian: *ferro;* Spanish: *hierro*]

ISINGLASS. Originally, an equivalent of *gelatin made from the swim bladders of sturgeon (Dutch: *huysenblas,* from *huso,* the beluga), although more recently the swim bladders of cod, ling, carp, and other fish have been used. The swim bladders were removed from the sturgeon, washed in fresh water, and hung to dry for a couple of days until it was possible to peel away the outer membrane. The bladders were then cut into strips. The best isinglass was in long staples, dull and hard. You may still sometimes see these dried strips, but in general the crude isinglass has been replaced by refined forms or by *gelatin. To use isinglass, it must be boiled until dissolved in an appropriate amount of water. The best will take about 30 minutes to dissolve completely. It is said to set 100 times its weight of liquid, but isinglass varies in quality, and ordinarily you should allow a proportion by weight of 1 in 30—however, this depends on the stiffness of jelly that is required. Isinglass is also used for clarifying vinegar, wine, and particularly beer.

[*Isinglass*—French: *colle de poisson;* German: *Hausenblase, Fischleim;* Italian: *colla di pesce;* Spanish: *colapez, cola de pescado*]

J

JACK BEAN or **horse bean** (*Canavalia ensiformis*) is a native of tropical America. A related species of large bean is the sword bean or saber bean (*C. gladiata*) from tropical areas of Asia. The two species are sufficiently similar to be confused, although the sword bean has red, pink, or brown seeds and the jack has white ones. The pod of the sword bean is curved like a saber. Both beans are used green as vegetables. The sword bean at least is also eaten ripe as a pulse, but ripe jack beans may possibly be slightly poisonous.

In India, both beans are known as *bara sem*. The plant is a perennial, and there is a dwarf variety for small gardens. Jack beans, under the name of horse beans, are grown to a considerable extent in the southern parts of the U.S.

JACKFRUIT or **jak** (*Artocarpus integrifolia*). You are not likely to see this fruit unless you go to the tropics where it grows, since it is among the world's largest fruits—weighing sometimes 90 lb (40 Kg)—and not the sort of thing grocery stores like to handle. It is, however, available canned in syrup. Because the immature fruit (as well as the flowers and seeds) is used in curries, some may occasionally be exported from the growing areas. The tree belongs to the mulberry family (Moraceae) and is of the same genus as the breadfruit. The jack tree, a native of the Western Ghats in India, is today grown in most tropical countries, particularly in Southeast Asia, Brazil, and parts of Africa.

The enormous fruits are green and carried on short stems hanging strangely from the main trunk and large branches. There are two types of fruit, one with a firm, sweet meat and the other softer and more acid. There are also some wild relatives. The fruit should not be confused with the *durian.

JAGGERY or **gur.** Crude, dark sugar from India. The name is often used for palm sugar, but is also applicable to cane sugar. Jaggery has an aromatic, winy smell overlying the molasses smell of unrefined sugar. Shaped into large, sticky balls the size of a coconut and sometimes wrapped in leaves, it may be sold very unhygienically in Indian bazaars. It looks unappetizing, but has a delicious taste and is an extremely important part of the flavoring of vegetarian curries. It also sweetens the hot milk that may be offered in hospitality when a traveler visits an Indian village.

JAK. *See* jackfruit.

JAMAICA FLOWER. The acid flower of a hibiscus (*Hibiscus sabdariffa*) is popular in Mexico as a basis for a refreshing drink, and in the form of a syrup for making punches. The flower is available dried, as dark-red petals, and tastes rather like *sumac water.

The flower petals should be put into a saucepan, boiled for 3 minutes, and then left in a china container for some hours, preferably overnight. The syrup is then sugared to taste.

JAMAICA PEPPER. *See* allspice.

JAMBERRY. *See* physalis fruit.

JAM, jelly, marmalade, and **preserves.** Jam is a conserve of fruit boiled with sugar; a jelly is the juice only, boiled with sugar; the term "marmalade" is normally reserved for jams made from citrus fruits—orange, lemon, grapefruit, lime—and preserves contain fruit or pieces of fruit in a thick transparent syrup. A thick paste of boiled-down quinces was an early sweetmeat all around the Mediterranean, and the term "marmalade" comes via French from the Portuguese *marmelada,* which in turn comes from the word for quince, *marmela.* Quince and other fruit marmalades long preceded orange marmalade in English parlance; 16th- and 17th-century recipe books abound in recipes for marmalades, particularly guava.

There are three basic problems in making jams or other preserves. The first is making sure that it contains sufficient sugar to preserve it. Organisms cannot grow when the sugar percentage is over 50–55%. In early days, honey or the natural sugars in the fruits themselves were used, but today sugar is added to bring the content up to 50%. You can then add acid juice if the jam is too sweet, or more sugar if the jam is too sour. However, because cane sugar crystallizes, there is an upper limit to the amount that can be added. The fact that the boiling point of water is raised by adding sugar makes it possible to roughly determine the sugar concentration by taking the temperature at any time. Jams are usually cooked until they reach roughly 235°F (113°C). The old rule for jelly—1 lb of sugar to 1 pt of juice (or 475 g of sugar to 600 ml of juice)—will, when the evaporation that takes place during boiling is allowed for, give a jelly that will keep.

The second problem is whether the jam or jelly will set. Setting depends on the formation of a *pectin jelly, for which there must be sufficient pectin, sugar, and acidity. Fruits lacking in pectin may be made to set by adding pectin extracted from citrus peel (one of the richest sources) or apples, and a similar result can be obtained by mixing in a pectin-rich fruit to make a compound jelly.

The third problem is flavor. Many fruits lose flavor when they are boiled for a long time, and others—like strawberries and raspberries—can hardly be boiled at all. Moreover, long boiling causes sugars to caramelize, which spoils the jam's color, and gives an underlying bitter caramel taste. To reduce the time jam is on the heat, the sugar is made hot before it is added to the fruit, or it is added as a syrup boiled to soft-ball stage 240°F (116°C)—while added liquid is kept to a minimum. Because efficient heating of jam is so important, it is necessary to use pans of aluminum or untinned brass and copper. Iron pans cannot be used because of the acids in the fruit, and enamel pans do not conduct heat fast enough and burn easily.

Although we may be used to jam as something to be used in tarts or spread on bread, in the Middle East and the Balkans, as well as at times in France, it is something to be eaten as a sweetmeat with a spoon. In houses from Bulgaria to Egypt, and from Greece to Iran, you can experience those awful social arrivals when you sit stiffly in the best room and accept the offered token of hospitality, a glass of water and a spoon of incredibly sweet jam. That is the minimum. A cup of Turkish coffee usually goes with it. It is the equivalent of the British biscuit and cup of tea, the brandy or sweet liqueur, the madeira and piece of cake. Nowadays the ritual is often replaced by a Coke.

Jams are made of many things which would be unfamiliar at a vicarage tea party. So we can have rose petal and orange flower jam, fig and date jam, jams made of whole green oranges and jam of chestnuts. One of the oddest is *cabellas de ángel* (angel's hair), a specialty of parts of Spain, a tasteless jam made from the "stringy bits" surrounding the seeds of a special type of squash bred to be almost all stringy bits (it is grown and sold in the U.S. as "spaghetti squash"). The jam is much prized and is used in cakes.

In the past in the U.S., jams, jellies, and preserves (or conserves) were made of ingredients not commonly used for such purposes today: green tomatoes, geraniums, ground cherries, and such wild foods as scuppernong grapes, sassafras, mints, and elderberries. With the discovery of the high vitamin C content of rose hips has come their use in jams and jellies; violet flowers can also be made into a lovely jam that is high in vitamins A and C.

[*Jam*—French: *confiture;* German: *Marmelade, Eingemachte;* Italian: *marmellata, conserva di frutta;* Spanish: *mermelada*]

JAPANESE MEDLAR. *See* loquat.

JAPANESE PEPPER. *See* Chinese pepper.

JELLY. *See* jam; gelatin.

JERKED BEEF or **jerky.** A North American corruption of the word *charqui* (*see biltong;* dried meat).

JERUSALEM ARTICHOKE (*Helianthus tuberosus*) is related to the sunflower, not to the thistle (like the *globe artichoke). It is said that the name Jerusalem is a corruption of the Spanish *girasol* (turning with the sun), i.e., sunflower. Both plants are said to have originated in North America, although some authorities say the sunflower originated in Peru. John Goodyer, who revised Gerard's *Herbal,* wrote in 1621 that he did not know whether Jerusalem artichokes originated in Peru, Brazil, or Canada, but placed them next to the sunflower (which he called "marigold of Peru"), so the kinship had been observed.

The name "artichoke," of course, was given because of some fancied likeness in taste to the globe artichoke. The similarity is not strong. The original varieties were irreg-

ular and difficult to peel (although the skin slips off easily if they are first parboiled), but modern varieties are more potatolike in shape. Jerusalem artichokes can be eaten raw—they have a sweet nutty taste and crisp texture—but are more usually boiled. They are cooked when they can be easily pierced with a knife point. In France, they are often boiled in milk flavored with an onion stuck with a clove, then drained, dipped in batter, and fried.

[*Jerusalem artichoke*—French: *topinambour;* German: *Erdartischocke;* Italian: *topinambur, carciofo di Giudea;* Spanish: *cotufa, pataca, aguaturma*]

JET. *See* hop.

JEW'S EAR. *See* mushrooms.

JICANA. *See* water chestnut.

JOB'S TEARS. *See* millet.

JOULES and **kilojoules.** The joule, named after British physicist James Prescott Joule (1818–1889), is a unit of energy and is therefore considered by scientists more apt than the calorie (which is a unit of *heat*) as a means of comparing the crude fuel values of foods. At any rate, it has been adopted internationally, and the slogan is now: "Watch your kilojoules!" It is kilojoule and not joule because, like the ordinary calorie, the joule itself is too small a unit to be practical in measuring what we eat. So just as we used to use 1000 ordinary calories, i.e., a Calorie with a capital C (or a kilocalorie), as our unit, now we are taking 1000 joules and using the kilojoule. You multiply Calories by 4.2 to get them into the new terms.

JOWAR. *See* millet.

JUJUBE is the name given to small trees and shrubs of the genus *Zizyphus* which are found in hot, dry areas around the world. Their fruits are generally candied or preserved in sugar or honey. Some, such as the

North African and Middle Eastern Christ's-thorn or crown of thorns (*Z. spina-Christi*), are eaten dried. The fruits of the Mauritanian jujube (*Z. mauritiana*) are known as Chinese dates or *tsa*. The berries of an Andean species, the mistol or Argentinian jujube (*Z. mistol*), form the basis of a Bolivian drink, *chicha*. Perhaps the most important species is the common jujube or Chinese jujube (*Z. jujuba*), a native of eastern India and Malaysia that has been introduced elsewhere in Asia and around the Mediterranean; its ovoid fruits are about the size of an olive. According to James Sholto Douglas in *Alternative Foods* (Pelham Books), "they may be eaten fresh or dried like dates, cooked with rice or millet or in honey or syrup, stewed, boiled or baked, made into glacé fruit or jujube bread." The fruits of the lotus jujube (*Z. lotus*) of North Africa were what were consumed by the lotus eaters mentioned by Homer.

JUNEBERRY. *See* rowan.

JUNGLE TREE. *See* ngapi.

JUNIPER. There are 40–50 species of juniper; *Juniperus communis*, the species used for flavoring, is distributed over much of the northern hemisphere. The ripe berries, fresh or dried, are used for culinary purposes. Because the berries take 3 years to develop, several stages are found on one bush. There are separate male and female bushes. Since the juniper is exceedingly prickly, it is best to wear gloves when gathering the berries; a

JUNIPER

fork can be used for stripping them from the bush. Apart from flavoring gin, juniper berries are much used in brines for pickling meat, in marinades for game, and in stuffings for various birds. They go well with most herbs, and a jar of dried juniper berries should be in every well-stocked kitchen.

[*Juniper*—French: *genièvre;* German: *Wacholder;* Italian: *ginepro;* Spanish: *enebro, junípero*]

JUNKET. *See* rennet.

K

KAFFIR CORN. *See* millet.

KAHLÚA. *See* liqueurs and cordials.

KAKI. *See* persimmon.

KALE, kail, or **borecole.** "Kale" is a form of "cole," an old name for cabbage. "Borecole" comes from the Dutch *boerenkool* (farmer's cabbage). Kales, *cabbages that do not have a heart, include a specific variety of cabbage (*Brassica oleracea,* var. *acephala*) and often rape kale (*B. napus*), a variety of turnip greens. The purpose of kales is suggested by one variety name—Hungry Gap. Because kale is high in vitamins, it played an important part in the old domestic European economy, keeping cottagers alive at the end of winter. In the U.S., kale, *collards, *mustard greens, and turnip tops have performed a similar function, especially in the South.

Curly kale, when young, is good (cooked for at most 20 minutes in fast-boiling water), but the flavor is strong; it is often cooked with milder greens. It may be creamed, puréed, or boiled gently with salt pork or bacon.

[*Kale*—French: *chou frisé;* German: *Krauskohl, Winterkohl;* Italian: *cavolo riccio;* Spanish: *col rizada*]

KALONJI. *See* nigella.

KANTEN. *See* agar.

KASHA. *See* buckwheat.

KATSUOBUSHI. Dried, boned *bonito. With *kombu,* one of the main ingredients of *dashi,* the foundation broth of Japanese cooking.

KÉFIR. A sour-milk product originating in the Caucasus, it is made from cow's milk, using *kéfir* grains, a special starter. They are yellow and may vary from the size of small seeds to that of almonds. For use, they are soaked in water at 68–86°F (20–30°C) for a day, then washed, and soaked in water at the same temperature for another day, until they have swollen to three or four times their original volume. They are then taken out of the water and put into pasteurized milk at about 68°F (20°C) and kept there for a day.

If they are washed after use, the grains can be kept and reused half a dozen times. *Kéfir* is slightly alcoholic and has a creamy texture.

KENTJOER or **kentjur.** *See* zodoary.

KERMES. An ancient red dye, made from the dried bodies of a female scale insect, *Coccus ilicis,* which lives on the kermes oak (also called holly oak or grain tree). Chaucer refers to it as "the grain of Portugal." There is also a similar dye-producing bug, *Coccus polonicus,* the Polish scarlet grain. The best-known today of these insect dyes is cochineal, which has the finest color.

Kermes was used as a food coloring and gave its name to the old-fashioned French cordial alkermes. The *al-* is presumably Arab, and *kermes* comes from the Arabic *qirmiz.* Alkermes is crimson red and very sweet. It contains distilled extracts of nutmeg, cinnamon, cloves, and bay leaves, sugared and colored.

[*Kermes*—French: *kermès;* German: *Kermes;* Spanish: *quermes*]

KETCHUP, catchup, or **catsup.** A ketchup is a kind of sauce—the word came into English from the Orient, perhaps from Malay or Chinese. In fact, it is still used there to describe various salty sauces, often of fish, products which vary from country to country. If *katjap* is called for in a recipe from Indonesia, or *kēchap* in a Malay one, then it must be the right sort. Javanese *katjap,* for example, is a very sweet *soy sauce. In the West, ketchup, without qualification, has come to mean tomato ketchup, although the word originally referred to a host of salty, spiced condiment liquids made from fish, shellfish, fruit, vegetables, mushrooms, etc. Cookbooks of the last century abound with recipes—oyster ketchup (oysters with white wine, brandy, sherry, shallots, and spices), mussel ketchup (mussels and cider), pontac or pontack ketchup (elderberries), Windermere ketchup (mushrooms and horseradish), wolfram ketchup (beer, anchovies, and mushrooms), and ketchups based on walnuts, cucumbers, and all manner of other items that caught the cook's imagination.

MUSHROOM KETCHUP

In the days when transport depended on horses, when there were permanent pastures and no artificial fertilizers, mushrooms used to whiten the fields in August and September. Since the glut of mushrooms could not be preserved easily by primitive methods, mushroom ketchup was a way in which their flavor could be kept for use year-round.

Use large, open mushrooms if possible. Clean, but do not wash them. Chop or crush them in your hands and fill a container (such as a plastic bucket or aluminum pan) with layers of the mushrooms sprinkled with salt. Leave the salt to extract the juice overnight (or longer) and then put the mixture in a pan and bring slowly to the boil. Boil the mixture for about 5 minutes and stand it aside to cool. Strain out the debris, squeezing out any remaining juice in a cloth, and bring the liquid to the boil again. You may now add a spice bag—allspice, cloves, mace, and ginger in various combinations can be used as you wish—with black peppercorns and cayenne. Brandy is often added as well. If the mushroom ketchup is to be used for flavoring, it is best to keep the spices to a minimum so that they do not mask the mushroom taste (I use only black pepper and a trace of garlic). Mushroom ketchup contains no acid, so it must depend on the salt for preservation or needs a half-hour in a pressure cooker before bottling hot in sterile bottles. Long boiling destroys the flavor, and can produce a ketchup that makes dishes become oversalted before enough has been added to enhance their taste.

TOMATO KETCHUP

Make up a spice bag containing (for each 9 lb or 4 Kg of tomatoes): 1 teaspoon of bruised celery seed, 1 teaspoon of cloves, a 2-in. (5-cm) piece of cinnamon stick broken in pieces, a 1¼-in. (3-cm) piece of bruised ginger, ½ teaspoon of allspice berries, and 1 teaspoon of peppercorns. Put it in 1 cup (250 ml) of boiling vinegar and allow to cool.

Take well-flavored ripe tomatoes—the quality matters—peel them, and squeeze out the seeds into a strainer. Discard the seeds (which make the ketchup bitter), but save the juice. Put the tomato and any juice on a low heat with ¼ clove of garlic and a little olive oil. Cook slowly for 30 minutes or until soft, then strain. Return to the pan and add 4 oz (100 g) of sugar and a pinch of cayenne. Simmer uncovered until the volume is reduced by about half (it will take about 1¼ hours). Gradually add the spiced vinegar and about 4 teaspoons of salt, tasting as you go to get the balance right. It may be necessary to add more or less vinegar—according to the sourness or sweetness of the tomatoes—and more or less salt. Continue the boiling until the right consistency is reached. Pour the ketchup immediately into hot sterile bottles and seal at once. Store in the dark or wrap each bottle in brown paper to exclude light and so preserve the color.

[*Ketchup*—French: *sauce relevée;* German: *kalte pikante Sosse;* Italian: *salsa;* Spanish: *salsa*]

KETJAP. *See* soy sauce.

KETOVAIA. *See* caviar.

KEWRA or **screwpine** (*Pandanus tectorius* and other species) is a tree which forms umbrellas of aerial roots in humid, swampy areas of tropical Asia. Its male flowers have an exquisite perfume and are used as a flavoring with *betel. Outside the tropics, it is possible to obtain *kewra* flavor in the form of *kewra* water and in syrups and cordials. *Kewra* is used in sweet dishes and is often included in *birianis.* Pieces of dried *kewra* may be put into curries, notably in Sri Lanka. The soft, sweet fruit, which is said to taste like pineapple, is also eaten.

KHAS-KHAS or **vetiver** (*Vetiveria zizanioides*) is an Indian aromatic grass also grown in the tropics and in Louisiana. It is used in Indian cooking as a flavoring and its roots yield vetiver oil, which is used in perfumes. *Khas* syrup and *khas* water may be bought from shops specializing in Indian products.

KID. *See* goat.

KIDNEY. Although the kidneys of different mammals vary in shape, they all have roughly the same structure: a soft outside part and a tough central core surrounding a cavity from which runs a tube that drains the urine into the bladder. This central core is tough and gristly; it should be cut out and discarded. Kidneys should also be examined to make sure that they do not contain "gravel" (sharp kidney stones)—man is not the only mammal to suffer from this complaint.

Lamb kidneys are the sort cooked for the traditional Englishman's breakfast, while veal (calf's) kidneys are used for more elegant dishes and beef kidneys for homelier ones.

[*Kidney*—French: *rognon;* German: *Niere;* Italian: *rognone;* Spanish: *riñón*]

KIMCHI. This staple Korean relish, served at every meal, is highly characteristic of Korean food. There are dozens of different types, but essentially *kimchi* is made from sliced or shredded vegetables—cabbage, cucumbers, onions, radishes, garlic, chilies—and sometimes fruit, all fermented in brine by lactic-acid-producing organisms and often with added spices and fresh ginger. This method of preserving food for the winter is an ancient one and is still an annual task for which all the family must be mobilized each autumn. In warm weather, the fermentation takes little more than a day, but in the cold it takes longer. The jar of *kimchi* for the winter is buried under the ground and taken out as necessary; it usually has a very bad smell. "Civilized" *kimchi,* sterilized in jars, is sometimes found in specialist shops.

KIMCHI

Cut 1 lb (450 g) of white cabbage into 1-in. (2½-cm) squares, and salt them for 15 minutes, using about 2 tablespoons of salt. Wash the salt off the wilted cabbage with fresh water, drain, and mix with 4 shredded spring onions—the green part included—2–3 chopped cloves of garlic, and a small, chopped fresh chili. Add a small piece of fresh ginger, finely sliced, and a tablespoon of salt. Put the mixture into a jar and cover with cold water. Shake the jar to dissolve the salt and stand it in the sun for a day. If the weather is warm, fermentation may be completed in 24 hours but in cold weather it will take considerably longer, perhaps 5 days. When the fermentation is completed, the jar of *kimchi* may be kept in a refrigerator for several weeks.

KIPPER. *See* herring.

KIRSCH or **kirschwasser.** *See* cherries; fruit brandy.

KIRSEBOER. *See* liqueurs and cordials.

KISHK, a Lebanese and Syrian staple food, is made in autumn after the harvest has been gathered for use in the winter. Milk, yogurt, and *burghul are mixed and allowed to ferment. Each day, for a period of 9 days, the mass is kneaded, after which the fermentation is complete and the product is spread out to dry, usually on clean cloths on the flat roofs. When it is completely dry, the *kishk* is rubbed to a powder between the palms of the hands and stored in a dry place. Its usual use is as a porridge, made by frying several cloves of garlic in a tablespoon of *qawwrama (preserved sheep fat) and then adding 2 tablespoons of the *kishk*. Frying is continued for several minutes. Finally, a cup of water is put in with some salt and the whole is boiled to the consistency of a porridge.

KIWI or **Chinese gooseberry.** The kiwi (*Actinidia sinensis*) was first grown commercially in New Zealand and is now being cultivated in California. The egg-shaped fruit is covered with a furry brown skin, inside which are pleasant, firm, lime-green pulp and edible black seeds. The taste is slightly acid, and the texture is more like honeydew melon than gooseberry. The fruit is supposed to have a tenderizing effect when it is rubbed on meat, and it contains more vitamin C than the lemon. Opinions vary as

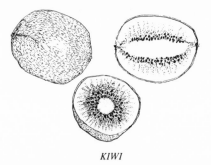

KIWI

to its gastronomic merit—some find the fruit delicious and some rather insipid—but most find the kiwi to be visually pleasing in cross section, an attractive addition to a platter of sliced fruits.

KNACKWURST. *See* frankfurter.

KNEADING. A process known and carried out ever since man learned to make bread. Flour, mixed with water, has to be worked hard to turn it into a dough, whether the dough contains yeast or is intended for such simple unleavened breads as the chapati. Kneading not only mixes the ingredients but develops the elasticity of the *gluten in the flour, the quality that is responsible for the structure of the bread, particularly when the loaf is expected to rise and stand up. It is difficult to describe the point to which kneading should be taken—words often used to describe the dough are "springy" and "silky." Average times for kneading are 5–10 minutes, depending on the energy and weight that are put into it.

[*Kneading*—French: *pétrir;* German: *kneten;* Italian: *impastare;* Spanish: *amasar*]

KNOCKWURST. *See* frankfurter.

KNOL-KOHL. *See* kohlrabi.

KNOTTED MARJORAM. *See* sweet marjoram.

KNUCKLE. In veal and pork butchery, the knuckle is the lower part of the back leg.

[Knuckle—French: *jarret;* German: *Knies-*

tück (veal), *Eisenbein* (pork); Italian: *garretto;* Spanish: *jarrete*]

KOHLRABI, turnip cabbage, or ***knolkohl.*** One of the many forms of cabbage, *Brassica oleracea,* var. *gongylodes,* kohlrabi is sometimes elevated to a separate species, *B. caulorapa.* Its stem is swollen into a bulb from which the leaf stalks arise. There are greenish white and purple varieties. An excellent vegetable, something like a turnip but blander and sweeter, with its own individuality, it is popular in Europe and the Orient. Kohlrabi should be eaten when the globes are less than 3 in. (11 cm) in diameter. They are best steamed until tender, then peeled and seasoned with herbs, lemon juice, and butter to serve hot or julienned and marinated to serve chilled. Kohlrabi is also good boiled until tender and served with sour cream and dill or placed in a casserole, topped with buttered crumbs and grated cheese, and baked until browned on top.

[*Kohlrabi*—French: *chou-rave;* German: *Kohlrabi;* Italian: *cavolrapa*]

KOKUM. The kokum of Indian cooking comes from a tree (*Garcinia indica*) that grows wild in the western Ghats and is closely related to the *mangosteen (G. mangostana).* It bears deep-purple fruits, with 4–5 large seeds (from which kokum butter is extracted). The pulp of the fruit, though much inferior to the mangosteen, has a pleasant, sour taste. It is dried—sometimes the fruit is sliced and dried, but sometimes only the skin with attached pulp—and used as a souring agent in South Indian cooking. It is slightly laxative (like tamarind, which it resembles, though tamarind is much sourer). Thoroughly dried samples can be ground to a powder and used as a condiment.

KOLA NUT. *See* cola nut.

KOMBU *seaweed is an essential ingredient, with *katsuobushi* (dried bonito), of the Japanese basic stock *dashi.*

KOSHER. From the Hebrew *kāshēr,* meaning "right," kosher food has been prepared (or, with meat, killed) by Jews or approved by the rabbi for consumption by Orthodox Jews in accordance with their *religious food laws.

KOUMISS. *See* kumiss.

KRUPEK or **krupuk.** A large crisp wafer made from dried prawns, a favorite Indonesian accompaniment to a meal. These wafers are bought ready-made even in Indonesia and need only to be fried in deep oil and well drained. If they are not available, the smaller Chinese prawn crisps are an acceptable substitute.

KULTHI BEAN. *See* horse gram.

KUMISS or **koumiss.** A sour-milk drink originally made from mare's milk by tribes in the eastern part of Russia and containing as much as 2–2½% alcohol, the strength of very weak beer. According to Marco Polo, it was drunk by Genghis Khan. Because mare's milk contains less *casein than cow's milk, it forms a much finer and weaker curd particle and so is exceedingly digestible. Although originally made in skins, it is now prepared in wooden pails as follows: mare's milk is added to sour cow's milk, and the two well stirred together. After half an hour, the milk is stirred for 20 minutes, then left again for half an hour, then stirred again for 20 minutes—the stirring takes place 3 or 4 times until kumiss of the preferred quality is ready. After that, it is put in corked bottles in a refrigerator to be kept for further fermentation and the production of gas and alcohol.

KÜMMEL. The German word for "caraway" and also for the caraway-flavored liqueur, said to have originated in Riga in Latvia, now part of the USSR, but which has for long been made in Germany, Denmark, and Holland. Different makes vary in sweetness, aroma, and strength.

KUMQUAT, a native of China, is smaller than the citrus fruits to which it is closely related, only 1–1⅔ in. (2–4 cm) in diameter. Kumquats are juicy and acid, with few seeds and a sweet, edible rind. Although often grown for ornament, they are also candied or canned whole. Two species, the oval kumquat (*Fortunella margarita*) and the round kumquat (*F. japonica*), are the most important.

KYRYNGA. A Central Asian sour-milk product, *kyrynga* is made from cow's milk and is slightly alcoholic. The method of preparation is very like that used for *kumiss and involves wooden vessels that have become impregnated with the necessary organisms and so provide a natural starter, as long as they are not cleaned out.

L

LABIATES are members of the plant family Labiatae, which includes lavender and dead-nettles. They have stems that are square in cross section and characteristic flowers with the petals joined to form a tube, usually with two lips. The fruit is a cluster of four nutlets. The labiates often have aromatic leaves and are the most important family of herbs, since they include, among others, basil, marjoram, mint, oregano, pennyroyal, rosemary, sage, savory, and thyme. A labiate vegetable is the Chinese artichoke.

LABLAB BEAN, hyacinth bean, bonavist bean, or **Egyptian bean.** This small bean (*Dolichos lablab*) is much cultivated in warm countries—South and Central America, the West Indies, China, Africa, and Southeast Asia. A native of India, the lablab is a twining, ornamental bean which is used dried or green. Even the leaves are edible, and the green pods are often pickled in India, where it is called *wal* or *val*. The dried beans are usually brown with a white central hilum.

LACTIC ACID ($CH_3 \cdot CHOH \cdot COOH$) is the acid of sour milk. As a chemical, it is used in the laboratory but never in the kitchen. Nevertheless, it is an important preservative and is commonly found in foods, in particular where lactic-acid-producing bacteria have been at work on sugars. The formation of lactic acid goes on not only in the souring of milk but also in the making of *sauerkraut, dill pickles, and *kimchi*—in fact, in all pickles that depend on acid fermentation (rather than on the addition of vinegar). The lactic acid formed when milk sours stops putrefactive organisms; if these are allowed to multiply they not only produce nasty tastes and bad smells but also may be dangerous. This is why lactic-acid bacteria are always included in cheese starters (curd that isn't soured goes bad very quickly) and why yogurt can be kept for many days in the refrigerator. Preparations in which fish is fermented with sour cream or milk also depend on lactic-acid fermentation for their preservation. With time, the lactic acid is itself attacked by a different set of bacteria and is broken down, so that cheeses that are sharply acid when young become sweet when matured. Lactic acid is formed in the working muscles of living animals. In animals that have been killed, it appears in muscles when meat first hardens and plays an important part, with enzymes, in the maturation and tenderization process during *hanging.

[*Lactic acid*—French: *acide lactique;* German: *Milchsäure;* Italian: *acido lattico;* Spanish: *ácido láctico*]

LACTOSE or **milk sugar** is the natural *sugar of milk. Like sucrose (cane sugar), it is a disaccharide which forms hard crystals, but it is much the least sweet of naturally occurring sugars and is not normally used in a pure form. It is present in the whey of coagulated milk and is the food of the bacteria which sour milk by making lactic acid. During digestion, lactose is broken down into *glucose and *galactose.

[*Lactose*—French: *lactose;* German: *Milchzuchker;* Italian: *lattosio;* Spanish: *lactosa*]

LAMB. *See* mutton.

LAMB'S LETTUCE. *See* lettuce.

LAMB'S-QUARTERS or **Pigweed** (*Chenopodium album*). This plant is known locally by many different names, but perhaps wild spinach is the most apt appellation, for

LAMB'S-QUARTERS

the leaves of lamb's-quarters are mild and the flavor is so like spinach that when they are used in, e.g., florentine dishes the taste is indistinguishable.

Since lamb's-quarters grows wild almost everywhere in the U.S. from city lots to country gardens, many people have passed it without realizing it is edible, much less that it is a highly nutritious vegetable. The plant may be only a few inches high or tall as corn in rich soil. The most useful characteristic in identifying it is the whitish mealiness on the underside of its oval or triangular, toothed leaves. The tastiest parts of lamb's-quarters are the growing tips and young leaves, though older ones can be used if they are cooked and puréed.

Native Americans were more aware of the food value of lamb's-quarters than most people are today. It was cultivated by many Indians, who ground a nutritious flour from the plant's numerous seeds. A mere half-cup of cooked lamb's-quarters provides more than the recommended daily allowance of vitamins A and C. Like spinach, lamb's-quarters cook down considerably, and the greens can be used in any way one would prepare spinach: in salads, steam-cooked, puréed into soups, added to quiche or frittata, or used in making green pasta.

LANGOSTINO. *See* shrimp.

LANGOUSTE, spiny lobster, or **southern lobster.** Langouste is the French name for the spiny lobster (*Palinurus elephas* and other species), which is also confusingly referred to as the crawfish (in contrast to *crayfish, an artificial distinction, since the two are alternative spellings of the same thing). Its habits are not identical with those of the lobster. It is confined to the warmer waters of the southern and west coasts of Britain, but is better known on the coasts of France and in the Mediterranean, where it is avidly sought. There are similar creatures on the other side of the Atlantic and other oceans—those of South Africa's Cape Province are particularly well known. Langoustes are essentially like lobsters, but without the big claws. It would be best to steal the French word *langouste*—as we have stolen and exchanged so many others (especially since they are called *langosta* in Spanish and *Languste* in German). The langouste grows to about 20 in. (50 cm) maximum in length; there are other larger species, variously colored but not much different in other respects. Preparation is generally as for lobster. Commercially available frozen crayfish tails are the abdomens of marine langoustes.

LANGOUSTINE. *See* scampi.

LAOS. *See* galangal.

LAPWING. *See* plover.

LARD is purified pig fat (but *lard* is also French for *bacon). The commercial product is white, with only the slightest porky taste. It is the usual cooking fat in some districts, for instance in parts of southwestern France. A combination of circumstances, including the introduction of vegetable cooking fats and the saturated-fatty-acid scare, have reduced its popularity, but lard still gives a wonderful texture in pastry, and a 50:50 mixture of lard and butter (for flavor) is traditional for flaky pastry. It is used in lardy cakes and delicious, though rich, sweet specialties, such as the famous *ensaimadas* (*saim* = lard) of Majorca (which are eaten fresh, with hot chocolate, at midnight on Christmas Eve).

Where pigs are home-cured, lard is usually made of the flair fat (that surrounding the kidney), since this has the highest proportion of fat to tissue in the pig. (Back fat is sometimes used too.) After washing and if necessary soaking to remove all traces of blood, the fat is minced to break up the cells; it is then rendered at a very low temperature, preferably no more than 122°F (50°C). This really needs to be done in a double boiler or bain-marie (though some mix the fat with water); with direct rendering, even over low heat, the lard is easily colored. The liquid fat is tipped off from time to time, filtered to remove any bits, and poured straight into the warmed glass jars in which it is to be kept. The whole process is likely to take 1-2 hours. The lard keeps for a month or more if properly sealed and stored in a cool place.

[*Lard*—French: *saindoux, graisse de porc, panne;* German: *Schweinefett, Schmalz;* Italian: *strutto, sugna;* Spanish: *manteca de cerdo*]

LARDING is the process of introducing ribbons of pork fat (lardoons) into meat that lacks fat and would otherwise cook dry (e.g., venison, veal, and pigeons). "This operation is great fun to do, and most soothing . . . and looks sensational," says Jane Grigson. In French cookbooks of the last century, almost every picture of a roast looks like a hedgehog. Fat, usually back fat, is cut in strips, pinched into the clip of the larding needle, and gently inserted in the meat. A modern gadget, rather on the lines of a surgeon's trocar (a tube cut diagonally and sharpened at one end), enables you to lard with frozen butter (or herb butter). Slaves to polyunsaturated oils can do a somewhat similar job with a hypodermic syringe, although one large enough for a horse is best.

[*Larding*—French: *larder;* German: *spicken;* Italian: *lardellare;* Spanish: *mechar*]

LASAGNA. *See* pasta.

LAUREL. *See* bay.

LAVER, laver-weed, red laver, or **tande** is a rosette-shaped *seaweed, pinkish purple (sometimes turning greenish brown), that grows near low-tide mark on rocky coasts of northern Europe. As a food, it is particularly famous in South Wales—it grows plentifully on the Gower coast—and similar species are used and even cultivated in Japan. In Scotland, laver (*Porphyra umbilicales*) is called sloke, slouk, or slokum; in Ireland, stoke. A very similar species, pink laver (*P. lacinata*), is also known as tangle and (in Orkney) redware. It is mainly a winter food, although it is in season from June to March. The weed must be thoroughly washed to free it of sand, soaked to remove the salt, then boiled until it is quite soft. The water is then drained off and the laver may be sieved. This thick purée, which is usually mixed with oatmeal, is now called laver bread (Welsh: *bara lawr, bara* being bread), and it is the classic Welsh accompaniment to mutton. Ready-prepared laver bread is sold in markets in South Wales out of wooden tubs lined with white cloths or in small cakes. It should be used as soon as possible—it does not keep.

LEAD is an exceedingly poisonous element and a cumulative poison, which means that apparently harmless amounts tend to remain in the body until they eventually reach a dangerous level. Tolerance to lead varies from person to person, so that levels of lead which may not affect one may cause serious symptoms of poisoning in another.

In the past, lead poisoning was much more common than it is today. Paints were very often based on lead oxides, and painters suffered from "painter's colic." Lead pipes were, however, the commonest danger, for lead got into soft water, aerated water, beer, and cider in pubs. Tea shipped in chests lined with lead foil and milk bottles topped with lead foil caps were other sources of contamination. Nowadays lead foil is rare; aluminum foil is used instead. And plastic and stainless-steel pipes have replaced lead pipes in pubs.

Pewter is a mixture of tin and lead, as also is solder. The tin used to line copper pans may sometimes have been fluxed with the addition of lead, but in modern pans, the tin is very pure. Crystal glass, in which lead replaced lime, was developed in the 17th century because of its high refractive index and brilliance for cut glass, and this lead could contaminate the contents of decanters. Because lead oxides are highly efficient fluxes, they make *ceramic glazes run at low temperatures, and so were used for old-fashioned traditional earthenware. Although glazes for earthenware no longer contain potentially dangerous amounts of lead, it is better not to use such pots for acid substances at all. Never use earthenware vessels for marinating—use stoneware, glass, enamel, or plastic.

[*Lead*—French: *plomb;* German: *Blei;* Italian: *piombo;* Spanish: *plomo*]

LEAVENING. To leaven is to lighten, in this case to lighten a bread or cake by introducing bubbles of gas which expand during cooking. This requires a means of supplying the gas bubbles and also an elastic substance which can first be blown up and then set (like egg white or gluten). Undoubtedly the first breads were unleavened and probably flat, like matzos, chapaties, or tortillas. If dough is left for a time in warm weather, the organisms that are naturally present, including yeasts, will cause fermentation. This sort of simple, natural leavening is still used in India, for instance, when batters are left overnight to ferment (as when making *idlis* and *dosas*). Such methods depend on the chance that suitable organisms are in the dough, and it became the practice to make sure by keeping back a piece of one batch of dough in order to inoculate the next. Such a starter was known as leaven; as the dough became sour (from the activity of *lactic-acid organisms) the product was called sourdough bread. Today yeast is usually added as a separate ingredient. Because it is not always convenient to use yeast—it requires warmth and time to produce sufficient gas—chemicals to do a similar job (*baking powders) were immediately popular when introduced to the public. Direct aeration by blowing in gas is a method used in industrial breadmaking; others are using cold soda water to mix, adding bubbles in the form of beaten egg, or even putting in volatile spirits like brandy.

[*Leavening*—French: *faire lever;* German: *säuern;* Italian: *lievitare;* Spanish: *leudar*]

LEBERWURST. German for *liver sausage.

LEEK. Cultivated leeks (*Allium porrum*) are possibly derived from the wild leek (*A. ampeloprasum*), which grows in Mediterranean and southeastern Europe; yet we cannot be certain, because leeks have been cultivated for so long that their origins have become clouded. In Britain, leeks tend to be regarded as only a vegetable (and there are Freudian competitions to see who can grow the largest specimen), while in the U.S., although vichyssoise is popular, leeks are rather neglected. Not so in France, or in Spain and Italy, where leeks of small and tender types, quite unlike those monstrous competition specimens, are a necessary and all-year-round ingredient. They are the sweetest of the onion tribe, which is perhaps why Nero thought that eating them improved his oratory.

Before using leeks, it is important to clean them properly because, especially after rain, mud splashes onto leeks (which are earthed up to make them white) and gets down between the leaf sheaths. After cutting off the roots and most of the green tops, and removing the outer, tough sheaths, the leek should be washed under running water—it must be held head down (it may or may not be necessary to slit the top to open up the sheath) so that any grit is washed outward. Each layer of leaf should be examined and rubbed clean of any mud. After that, the leeks can be stood upside down in clean water until they are put to cook.

When buying leeks, look for fresh-looking, young specimens, devoid of a central hard core, untrimmed, unwilted, and with a large proportion of white. Do not buy large, coarse-looking specimens. Fresh, young leeks are magnificent: old or stale leeks are bitter and horrid.

Leeks are boiled in salted water for about 30 minutes (best tied in bunches to help them keep shape), or parboiled and braised in butter or fried in batter; they can be served with various sauces. As an hors d'oeuvre, either *à la grecque* in a vinaigrette or served in the Rumanian way with olives in a sweet-sour, oily, tomato sauce, they are excellent. They go into soups of all sorts as a flavoring and are sometimes included in the bouquet garni. Young and tender leeks can be shredded raw into salads—a use that goes back to the Romans.

[*Leek*—French: *poireau;* German: *Lauch;* Italian: *porro;* Spanish: *puerro*]

LEGUME. Member of the botanical group Leguminosae, a plant that bears seeds in a pod which splits open down both seams when ripe. Among the legumes are peas, beans, lentils, clovers, vetches, alfalfa, lucerne, tamarind, acacia, mimosa, and wattle.

This very large group includes about 12,000 known species. Legumes are found in all types of climate and soil. They may be herbs, shrubs, trees, climbers, desert plants, or water plants. They are of crucial importance because many have root nodules containing bacteria that fix nitrogen from the air, and because they provide the bulk of the world's protein both for people and for livestock. Some, such as soybeans and peanuts, also provide important oils. Others—tamarind, fenugreek, and carobs—are sources of flavor, sourness, or sweetness, while gum arabic and gum tragacanth are also from legumes. Dried legume seeds are called *pulses.

Because legumes play such a widespread and important part in man's food, many of them have acquired a baffling collection of alternative names, some of which are dealt with in cross-references in this book. The main types of legume with entries of their own are adzuki bean, alfalfa, black gram, broad bean, carob, *channa*, chickpea, cowpea, fenugreek, *ful medames, gaur,* goa bean, green bean, gum, horse gram, jack bean, lablab bean, lentil, licorice, lima bean, moth bean, mung bean, pea, peanut, pigeon pea, rice bean, runner bean, soybean, tamarind, tepary bean. The legumes dealt with here are only the ones which are widely eaten; a multitude of other legumes are eaten locally around the world. Not all legume seeds are edible, however, and poisonous ones include laburnum and some vetches.

[*Legume*—French: *légume;* German: *Hülse, Hülsenfrucht;* Italian: *legume;* Spanish: *legumbre*]

LEMON *(Citrus limon)* is, with orange, the most important citrus fruit. However, it did not come into Europe from the East until at least the 1st century A.D., and possibly not until the 10th century—if it was there at the earlier date, it was probably not at all common. Nobody is sure of the lemon's country of origin; some experts say it is India, but others point out that lemons are much less common there than limes. It is unfortunate that in early writings citrons (the earliest citrus to reach Europe) and limes and lemons are confused.

Today, lemons are grown in all the countries of the Mediterranean basin—and Portugal—but not farther north, because they stand no frost and need a warm climate to thrive. In the U.S. (which now produces a gigantic quantity), lemons are mainly grown commercially in California and Arizona, for even Florida was found to have too much frost. Lemon trees are thorny, but their pale leaves and yellow fruit make them the most beautiful of the citrus trees. So that they will travel well, lemons are picked slightly green and not allowed to ripen on the tree, which is a pity, because they then never develop their full scent. In some cases, bought lemons have been treated with sprays, dyes, or wax, which can make the skin unappetizing. Growers forget that from lemons we get two separate items, the sourness of the juice and the lemon-oil taste from the zest, or skin.

Lemon juice is rich in *citric acid and is the most commonly used *souring agent in Western cooking. Lemons can be kept for up to a month in the vegetable tray of the fridge, so there is no excuse for being without "a squeeze of lemon." The lemon juice sold in bottles (or in plastic lemons) is a pale imitation of the real thing.

Lemon zest, much used in cakes and sweets, is neglected as a flavoring in many other dishes. Yet grated lemon rind can sometimes make a huge difference not only to stuffings but also to sauces flavored with herbs, and particularly to those containing capers, with which lemon seems to have a special affinity. The Italian *gremolata,* made of finely chopped lemon peel, garlic, and parsley, is an effective foil for *osso buco,* veal dishes and fish.

Lemon leaves are occasionally used, but do not have a very strong flavor. Lemon flavors also come from lemon *balm, lemon-scented *verbena, and *lemon grass, as well, of course, as lemon oil and lemon extract.

The bioflavinoid citrin (once called vitamin P), which is present in lemon pith, does not seem to have the effect on the common cold it was once credited with, but I am still convinced that lemon and honey is an excellent home treatment.

Aside from its use as a marinade for "cooking" fish (*see* seviche) and for tenderizing meat (especially lamb for shish kebab), lemon juice may be used sparingly as a seasoning or generously as a flavor in its own right. Fresh lemon juice is an excellent salt substitute, providing vitamin C as well. A few drops heighten the basic flavor of sauces and intensify the natural taste of fish. Used forthrightly, lemon juice is made into Greek *avgolemono,* which may be a soup or a sauce for fish, lamb, chicken, or vegetables. The piquant Italian *salsa verde* is a lemony green sauce that is excellent with beef, seafood, and asparagus or artichokes. And of course lemon juice and zest are used in many desserts, including the American lemon meringue pie, and beverages from lemonade to the twist of lemon in cocktails.

[*Lemon*—French: *citron;* German: *Zitrone;* Italian: *limone;* Spanish: *limón*]

LEMON BALM. *See* balm.

LEMON GRASS, sereh, or **serei.** A grass, *Cymbopogon citratus* and *Cymbopogon flexuesus,* with a bulbous base, smelling rankly of lemon (it contains *citral,* as does the zest of lemon). It is much used in the cooking of Ceylon and Southeast Asia and is available dried as *sereh* powder. It is not difficult to grow lemon grass where it can be provided with warmth. Lemon *balm or lemon-scented *verbena is usually considered a better substitute than zest of lemon. The oil extracted from lemon grass is poisonous.

[*Lemon grass*—French: *jonc odorant;* Italian: *cimbopogone*]

LEMON SOLE (*Pleuronectes microcephalus*) is not a true *sole, nor does it taste of lemon. It gets its name from the French *li-mande,* which comes, like the biological name of the *dab, from *lima,* Latin for file. A dextral *flatfish, lemon sole is distinguished by its small head, oval shape, and slimy smooth skin. It is found from the Bay of Biscay to the North Sea, Iceland, and the White and Arctic seas and averages some 16 in. (40 cm) in length. Lemon sole has a fresh, pleasant, salt-and-iodine taste that is often despised because it is compared to Dover sole. On the Belgian coast, where lemon sole is known as *Schotse schol* (Scottish sole), it is sold as a delicacy salted and dried.

The American winter *flounder, often called lemon sole, is not the same fish. Two flatfish similar to lemon sole (but both sinistral) are the scaldfish (*Arnoglossus laterna*) and the megrim or whiff (*Lepidorhombus whiffiagonis*). Neither is quite as good as lemon sole, but they are worth trying if you encounter them in European markets or restaurants.

[*Lemon sole*—French: *sole limande;* German: *Rotzunge;* Italian: *sogliola;* Spanish: *mendo limón. Scaldfish*—French: *fausse limande;* German: *Lammzunge, Schorrfisch;* Italian: *suacia;* Spanish: *serrandell. Megrim or whiff*—French: *cardine;* Italian: *rombo giallo;* Spanish: *lliseria*]

LENTIL (*Lens culinaris*) is a *pulse that came originally from the Middle East. The plant is small, 16–20 in. (40–50 cm) high, something like a vetch, with short, broad pods. There are many cultivated varieties, some with large and some with quite small seeds; colors are also variable, but the seeds are most often brown or green when whole. Inside, they are yellow, cream, orange, or red. Lentils are much grown in Egypt and North Africa, over the whole of southern Europe, and in many other warm countries. In the U.S., they are grown in the Pacific Northwest, but most lentils eaten in the States are imported. In India, *masoor* or *masur* is a variety of lentil that is popular with

the Muslim community but is otherwise regarded as a poor man's pulse, except in Bihar and Bengal. In France, the tiny, green expensive *lentilles vert du Puy* are a delicacy used for salads and hors d'oeuvre. The food value of lentils is high: they are rich in iron, protein, and vitamin B.

Lentils taste best when they are not soaked before cooking; if soaking is felt to be necessary, it should be for a short time and certainly not overnight. As a preliminary, all lentils should be washed. Seeds that float may contain grubs. Whole lentils should be examined to see if there are stones among them: these are common in samples of whole lentils badly cleaned by machine. Stones that are actually bits of dried earth will be removed by washing in several waters, but if the stones are real (and tiny like the lentils), the lentils must be shaken in water in a tilted pan until the stones (which are denser than the lentils) have slid down into the bottom corner. They can be left behind when the clean lentils are scooped out.

In the Orient, lentils and other dried seeds bought in the bazaars are often very dirty and cooks become expert at removing stones and rogue seeds by tossing them in baskets or mats. Whole lentils take ¾–1½ hours to cook, depending on age and variety. They should be watched, since they absorb a surprising amount of water. The water in which lentils are cooked makes good stock, so save the remaining water. In a pressure cooker, all except the toughest lentils can be cooked in 15–20 minutes.

Lentils are mainly a winter dish, popular in Germany as *linsensuppe* (lentil soup) or *saures linsengemüse* (savory lentil purée), which is served with *Rotwurst* (red sausage from Thuringia), *Schweinerippchen* (pork ribs), and *Blutwurst.* In northern Italy, *lenticchie un umido* (boiled) are eaten with *zampone or *cotechino; zuppa di lenticchie* (lentil soup) may be flavored with sage or mixed with chestnuts and flavored with thyme, basil, and marjoram as in the Abruzzi. In France, there are also substantial lentil dishes, *lentilles au lard, à la Dijonnaise,* or *à la Picarde,* but also more refined treats such as:

LES LENTILLES DU PUY À LA CRÈME

Put 11 oz (300 g) *lentilles de Puy* (washed but not soaked) in 2¾ pt (1½ lt) cold water on the lowest possible flame. They should take at least 45 minutes to come to the boil, during which time they soak and swell. When they come to the boil, turn up the heat slightly, and cook until they are tender—another 45 minutes. Add a little salt just before the water is all absorbed (as it should be). When the lentils are ready, add a large knob of butter and plenty of cream (keeping the pan hot but not letting it boil). Season with freshly ground black pepper.

In Spain, we have *lentejas* with potato, raw ham, and smoked bacon, flavored with tomato, bay, thyme, and parsley, and *lentejas con arroz* (lentils with rice) flavored with onion, garlic, bay, parsley, *pimentón,* and vinegar. In this connection, it is interesting to note that *masoor dal* is the correct pulse to use in a *kichri,* the Indian dish which gave rise to kedgeree, because the lentils retain their shape and do not turn into purée. If they did, lentil and rice dishes would be very stodgy indeed.

[*Lentil*—French: *lentille;* German: *Linse;* Italian: *lenticchia;* Spanish: *lenteja*]

LETTUCE (*Lactuca sativa*) has been cultivated for so long that its wild origin is uncertain, although there are a number of wild relatives. The pale yellow flowers of plants that have bolted show that they are composites—members of the daisy family. If the smell of lettuce is rather like opium, it is due to certain alkaloids. Indeed, the milky latex from another species of lettuce (*L. virosa*) is dried like opium and used as a raw material for drug manufacture, and all the species of lettuce are narcotic to a greater or lesser extent. The stems of bolted garden lettuces, if eaten in quantity, have been known to make people drowsy, even unconscious. In normal amounts, lettuce is only calming and sedative. A concoction made with lettuce is a country way of relieving coughs and soothing painful skin.

Garden lettuces are grown by the million in almost every country. Because lettuces are rather sensitive to soil type and climate, the varieties grown anywhere are likely to be determined by their success in the particular place. Different varieties come into season at different times of the year. Selecting lettuce for salad requires attention to variety as well as to freshness. Very thin-leafed types, for example, need a light dressing: they collapse when mixed with a heavy one or crowded with other vegetables in mixed salads. On the other hand, many of the thick, juicy lettuce types have a strong "opium" flavor which may go well with a stronger dressing, and is good just with salt in a sandwich. Cooks should in general be alert to texture in salads—then perhaps we would be spared those mixtures of tasteless lettuce and insipid chunks of tomato. For mixed green salad, choose from the following varieties those lettuces that combine to give complementary textures and flavors.

Boston and **Bibb lettuces,** sometimes called butterhead lettuces, resemble small, gently opened cabbage heads with glossy, dark-green leaves on the outside and inner ones blanched butter yellow. Their flavor is smooth, soft, mild, and sweet. You can use whole small heads for individual salads or tear the leaves for salade Niçoise.

Corn salad or **mâche** or **lamb's lettuce** has a rosette of smooth dark-green leaves with mild flavor. It can be eaten in salads or cooked like spinach, which it resembles.

Iceberg or **head lettuce** has, for good reason, fallen into disfavor with lettuce lovers. It is frequently etiolated, watery, and tasteless because it has been grown for weight, shelf life, and least waste. Home-grown iceberg can be fine, with more color and flavor, but otherwise it's a last resort for a good salad.

Loose-leaf lettuces that never form a tight head are numerous, and especially delicious picked fresh from the garden. They may be the familiar delicate black-seeded Simpson; oakleaf, with large rosettes of oaklike dark-green leaves; ruby lettuce, whose frilled leaves are shaded with dark red; Green Ice, a splendid loosehead lettuce with glossy green color and crisp texture.

Romaine or **cos** forms an elongated V-shaped head, with dark-green outer leaves and crunchy, juicy midribs. It is the most common lettuce in hot countries and increasingly a favorite in the U.S., where it is indispensable for Caesar salad. In Egypt people commonly tear off the tough leaf part and eat only the midrib. Living in Spain, I find it necessary to tear the leaf part into pieces, then chop the midrib. Mixed together again, they give in effect two vegetables in one salad.

Lettuce need not be the only green ingredient in salad. To cultivated lettuces you can add *dandelion leaves, *beet greens, *spinach, or other greens with more color and vitamins. Most lettuces have minimal food value, since they are composed largely of water. In general, the darker their leaves the more vitamins and minerals they contain.

Lettuce can be kept briefly in the refrigerator, though no amount of "crisping" will revive a tired lettuce. Optimistic restaurants tend to keep it until it turns transparent and tastes of nothing but the often heavy dressing intended to camouflage it. Lettuce for salads must be dry so it does not dilute the dressing.

There are many recipes for lettuce boiled, stewed, braised, puréed, stuffed, or cooked with peas. Large outer leaves of romaine are useful to lay over fish in the oven and are better than foil to prevent overbrowning. The stems of bolted lettuce are sometimes preserved in a ginger-flavored syrup, and some people even eat lettuce with sugar.

[*Lettuce*—French: *laitue;* German: *Lattich, Gartensalat, Kopfsalat;* Italian: *lattuga;* Spanish: *lechuga*]

LEVULOSE. *See* fructose.

LICORICE (*Glycyrrhiza glabra* and other species), a legume, looks something like a purple-flowered bean. It grows wild in southern Europe and was once cultivated in Yorkshire, near Pontefract, which is still the center for making licorice confectionery (e.g., Pontefract cakes) in Britain, although its raw material is now imported. Black licorice is made by extracting the root with water and concentrating the sweet liquid by boiling. It is occasionally used by home brewers. In the 16th and 17th centuries, it was an important ingredient of gingerbread and was used mainly to darken it.

[*Licorice*—French: *réglisse;* German: *Süssholz;* Italian: *liquirizia;* Spanish: *orozuz, regaliz*]

LIGHTS are lungs. They go into various meat preparations such as some pâtés and into traditional *faggots. *Larousse Gastronomique* offers half a dozen recipes for dealing with pig's lights. Most cooks, however, are likely to buy lights only for feeding the dog—if the dog will eat them.

LIMA BEAN, butter bean, or **Madagascar bean** (*Phaseolus limensus*). A native of tropical America (opinions range from Guatemala to Brazil), whose wild ancestors have disappeared—the bean has been in cultivation for thousands of years (remains were found in prehistoric Peruvian graves). Some botanists regard the sieva bean (*P. lunatus*) as a smaller variety of the same species.

The plants require a warm, moist climate and will not grow in northern countries, where they are known only as dried beans rather than as fresh lima beans. However, in the U.S. and other countries where they are grown, they are eaten fresh as shell beans—and are also available frozen or canned.

There are many varieties, some with large fat beans (known as potato types), some bushy and some of climbing habit, and in a range of sizes and colors, usually white or pale green. Some types contain a significant amount of hydrocyanic acid and so are poisonous until they are cooked. Dried lima beans are usually covered with cold water and soaked until they are plump, the time depending on the age and variety of bean. The cooking time is roughly 45 minutes. Lima beans are one of the best-flavored of all beans and are excellent hot with butter or cold as an hors d'oeuvre. In some places, mature shelled wax-pod beans are known locally as butter beans, and small butter beans are often called baby limas.

LIME (*Citrus aurantifolia*), a small, sour, citrus fruit, has much in common with the *lemon. Limes are used in the same way and for similar purposes. Like lemons, they can stand no frost; in fact, they are even fussier about climate. Like lemon trees, lime trees are very prickly, but are typically smaller and bushier. Limes probably originated somewhere in Southeast Asia, and were brought west, eventually reaching southern Spain with the Arabs. Columbus took them to America on his second voyage, in 1493. In Europe, limes are little known—they have a foothold in places like southern Italy and Sicily—and lemons are dominant. However, in very hot and tropical countries lemons do not do so well (they have a tender skin) and limes take over.

There are a number of types. The common lime in India and southern Asia, for instance, is more yellow than green, rounded, oval, and rarely with a nipple. It is also quite small: the maximum diameter is about 2 in. (5 cm) and the average is not much bigger than a table tennis ball. The skin is thin, and the flesh very sour and juicy. The flavor is characteristic, with nothing of the citron taste of lime cordial.

On the other hand, in Europe and America, limes are mainly of the type of the Tahiti lime, which originated by chance, although it has been claimed to be a hybrid. It is a markedly larger fruit than the Indian variety, green rather than yellow, and with a more citrony flavor. In Britain, both Indian and Caribbean limes turn up as imports; in the U.S., the Tahiti type are grown in Florida and California, as well as being imported. In Florida, the so-called Persian variety is much grown. It has large, oval fruits with a few seeds and is very acid. Maximum production is in thirsty August—in that respect it beats the lemon, which gets scarcer as summer advances. California comes a little later than Florida, mainly with the Bearss variety, which is smaller and seedless. There is considerable difference in the flavor of limes. A caveach of raw fish as made in Peru requires the juice of Persian limes to have the authentic taste: it is very inferior when made with the juice of lemons. Indian lime pickle does not have the authentic flavor when it is made with Caribbean limes, and is quite a different substance when it is made with lemons. In some parts of the Middle East, limes are dried and ground as a condiment. The acid powder is delicious sprinkled, for instance, on rice.

Sweet limes (*Citrus limettioides*) were once much planted in India because they are heavy bearers and hardy. The fruit looks like a greenish orange; the skin is thin, but the juice is very insipid. However, sweet limes arrive toward the end of the monsoon when other and better citruses are not available. Limes, like other citruses, hybridize easily to such creations as the limequat (lime × kumquat). The citrus lime should not be confused with the *basswood, lime, or linden tree.

[*Lime*—French: *lime, limette;* German: *süsse limone;* Italian: *cedro, lima;* Spanish: *lima*]

LIMEWATER can be made by stirring slaked lime (calcium hydroxide) in hot water, leaving it to get cold, and then filtering it (although for most purposes filtering is not really necessary). In Belgium, Holland, and Germany, dried fish (*stockfish) is soaked in it. Some people crisp watermelon rind by soaking it in limewater before pickling. Limewater is also the liquid in which corn is traditionally boiled to remove the horny yellow skin in making Mexican *nixtamal,* the first stage in producing **masa* for tortillas, tamales, etc. The limewater softens the seed coat to the point where it can be rubbed off. Limewater, being alkaline, will neutralize an acid.

[*Limewater*—French: *eau de chaux;* German: *Kalkwasser;* Italian: *acqua di calce;* Spanish: *agua de cal*]

LIMPET (species of *Acmaea*). The conical shells (sometimes called "Chinaman's hats") that stick to surf-swept rocks between tide marks contain meat that is tough but tasty. The Pacific coast of the U.S. has quite an assortment of limpets, among which the owl limpet (*Lottia gigantea*) is considered the finest for eating. Some people consume limpets raw on the spot, but usually they are pounded to tenderize them, then sautéed or coated with bread crumbs and deep-fried. Smaller ones may be used in chowder. A traditional luau in Hawaii always included the small, sweet native limpets called *opihis.* Limpets are also esteemed by the Mexicans of Lower California.

[*Limpet*—French: *patelle;* German: *Napfschnecke;* Italian: *patella;* Spanish: *lapa*]

LINDEN. *See* basswood.

LING. *See* cod; chestnut.

LIQUEURS and **cordials**—the distinction is blurred—are often made by infusing flavoring substances (which may be fruits, herbs, spices, and other aromatics) in alcohol. Such straight infusions are called ratafias. In some cases, there is subsequent distillation, and, for the sake of uniformity, the modern tendency is to use essential oils and extracts. In cheaper liqueurs, synthetics provide the flavor. Ratafias and cordials differ from *fruit brandies (eaux de vie), which are distillations of fermented fruit mashes and may also be called liqueurs.

Nobody knows exactly what goes into most of the famous liqueurs or the methods by which they are made, because these are closely guarded trade secrets. Indeed, there is such secrecy that, to take an extreme case like the making of Chartreuse, no one monk (it is made by the Carthusians) knows all the formula. It is entrusted only in parts to brothers who specialize in its manufacture.

Originally, liqueurs were medicines. Even today many are looked on as digestives. They are still often made to family formulas in countries such as Spain and Italy. These liqueurs are ratafias, made by simple infusion. As with commercial liqueurs, the alcoholic base can be a highly rectified spirit of any origin or a brandy, rum, or whiskey. Some are mixtures. There is nothing particularly difficult about making your own liqueurs, which can, for instance, contain both rum and brandy (or *gin—as in the case of sloe gin).

Liqueurs are very useful flavorings in the kitchen, and a range of miniatures can be kept for the purpose. Modern cookbooks and magazines abound with recipes, and practically every liqueur ever heard of is favored by someone. No liqueur represents the pure taste of the main flavoring ingredient. Cointreau, Grand Marnier, and Curaçao all taste more or less of orange, but are different. Other liqueurs, such as Van der Hum and Unicum, have an orangy ingredient, which is masked with spices. Cooks feel that they are safe putting like with like—say an orange liqueur with oranges, a cherry liqueur with cherries, and so on—expecting a natural unity to result. Fair enough, but from there the adventurous can depart to try complementary flavors, like the tradition-hallowed pineapple and kirsch. And liqueurs do not have to be used singly; they can be combined and mixed like cocktails.

In addition to the flavorings listed below, there are fruit cordials made from blackberries, raspberries, and strawberries, with some unusual ones from northern Europe.

Apricot flavors Apry and other apricot brandies. These are sweet liqueurs, tasting of apricots, but often also of bitter almonds (from the apricot stones). Hungarian barack, however, has a totally different flavor and is dealt with under fruit brandies.

Banana is the predominant flavor of *crème de banane* and other such liqueurs. Most are very sweet and have a ripe banana flavor.

Bitter almond. A number of ratafias, made from *Prunus* fruit kernels (apricot, peach, plum, etc.), as well as from bitter almonds, are on the market, and the name for such preparations is *noyau. They are more kindly than the synthetic almond essence of commerce, and I regularly make my own from apricot stones.

Black currant. There is black-currant rum, but the best known is *crème de cassis*, with only 18% alcohol—just enough to preserve it. It has a strong, clear flavor of black currants and is excellent with creams or as a topping for ices.

Cherry. Grant's Morello Cherry Brandy has a bite from the morello cherry, while other cherry brandies, such as Kirseboer or Cherry Heering, are sweeter. There are cherry whiskeys such as Chesky, and Cerasella is an Italian cherry liqueur with herbs from the Abruzzi mountains. Maraschino, important in cooking, is a sweet white fruit brandy made from maraschino cherries and their crushed kernels. Traditionally in a square, straw-covered bottle, it has been made for several centuries.

Chocolate. Chocolate-flavored liqueurs are very sweet, with a taste of vanilla. *Crème de cacao* is one.

Coffee. Tia Maria is the best known and is based on rum, as is Kahlúa.

Flowers. *Crème de rose* and the Bulgarian rose liqueur taste something like roses smell, but are very sweet. There are violet-flavored liqueurs, and Parfait Amour is supposed to taste of violets and vanilla. Mille Fiore is equally meant to taste of a thousand Alpine flowers; the bottles contain a sprig of a bush covered with sugar crystals. All these liqueurs are sweet and scented.

Herbs. A combination of herbs goes into many of the classic liqueurs; single-herb liqueurs are rare. Mint or peppermint is one of these, though, with most liqueur houses producing some form of crème de menthe, as well as mixtures like Royal Mint Chocolate Liqueur. There is also an angelica liqueur.

Herb seeds. As a flavoring, caraway is well represented in kümmel, aquavit, and Goldwasser. Very often, it is combined with anise. The flavor of anise can be clear, sweet, and strong, as in Anis del Mono of Spain, and the anisette, anisetta, and stellata of Italy. It may also be introduced into cooking through dry pastis drinks, such as Ricard and Pernod, which can be used, for instance, with fish. The flavor of licorice is often confused with anise; the Italian Sambuca is made with licorice and elder.

Honey is used with whiskey in Scottish liqueurs, and its taste is recognizable in Glen Mist.

Orange, from the cook's point of view, is the most important of the fruit flavors in liqueurs. Orange Curaçao, Triple Sec, Cointreau, and Grand Marnier are the ones most usually found in the kitchen. Other liqueurs with orange connections are the spicy Aurum from Italy, Unicum from Hungary, and Van der Hum from South Africa. The American Forbidden Fruit is based on shaddock or grapefruit. Grand Marnier is a good liqueur for the beginner, being slightly sweeter than Cointreau and not quite so strong.

Pineapple. Rum and pineapple liqueurs often have a somewhat synthetic flavor.

Plum, sloe, and **damson.** Best-known in this group are sloe gin and prunelle. There is also damson gin. Quite different are the flavors of quetsch, mirabelle, and slivovitz (which are all fruit brandies).

Spices, herbs, and **mixtures.** Into this category must come the great monastic liqueurs, Benedictine and Chartreuse (green and yellow), as well as Izarra, Trapestine, Drambuie, Raspail, Cuaranta-y-tres, Glayva, Bronte, Strega, Vieille Cure, Escorial, Calisaya, Galliano, Mentuccio, Herbias, Élixir d'Anvers, and even Chu Yeh Ching Chien, the green bamboo-leaf liqueur from China.

Walnut is the flavoring for a liqueur made in France and Italy, but it is mostly homemade.

Wine-based liqueurs include Cordial Médoc (sweetish and highly aromatized) and Ponche Soto, with sherry and spices.

[*Liqueur*—French: *liqueur;* German: *Likör;* Italian: *liquore;* Spanish: *licor*]

LIQUORICE. *See* licorice.

LITCHI. *See* lychee.

LITTLENECK. An American *clam.

LIVER. School meals of thick gravy containing dry-textured lumps that grew in size with chewing have done more than their share to create a widespread dislike of liver. Properly cooked, though, liver—particularly calf's liver—is moist and tender, almost melting. It is also more adaptable than the habits of broiling or frying calf's and lamb's liver and of stewing beef liver would suggest. Liver is delicious not only with fried onions or bacon but also flavored with sherry, marsala, Worcestershire sauce, or other piquant sauce. In Tuscany, for example, cubes of pig's liver are seasoned with salt, pepper, and herbs, wrapped in caul fat, and broiled or fried. Chicken livers may be sautéed in butter and served on toast, but they may also be used in risotto and are one of the correct ingredients for *ragù* or Bolognese sauce, as well as being an important ingredient in Jewish cooking. Livers may be major or minor ingredients in pâté de *foie gras. Although the main use of fish livers is for their oil content, the livers of turbot and of some rays are eaten. They may be poached in a good broth, sliced, and served on buttered toast. Some fish livers, though, are poisonous.

When buying calf's liver, look for paleness. Avoid liver of any sort that has a greenish tinge. Make sure, too, that it is cut in even slices—variation in thickness will matter most if the liver is to be broiled or fried. It is best to remove the thin membrane that covers the liver. With chicken liver, cut out any greenish yellow spots of bile before cooking; otherwise the bitterness will permeate the entire dish. Beef liver is best soaked in milk for an hour before cooking to remove any undesirable flavors.

[*Liver*—French: *foie;* German: *Leber;* Italian: *fegato;* Spanish: *hígado*]

LIVER SAUSAGE comes in a plethora of forms and textures. Pig liver is the usual basis for liver sausages, but there are kosher versions, and goose liver is used, sometimes with truffles, in the German *Gänsleberwurst.* Other parts of the pig may be added, and flavorings include various herbs and spices, onion, and anchovy. Liver sausage may or may not be smoked but is always cooked and is ready to serve cold. Some varieties are coarsely chopped and may contain flecks or lumps of fat, but the most widely marketed sorts are fine and even in texture and may be more suitable for spreading than for slicing, in which case they are effectively pâtés.

In the U.S., true liverwurst is made of pork meat and pork liver, although some manufacturers use beef, and some use a liver other than hog's. The best liverwurst is highly seasoned with pepper, salt, cardamom, and other spices, then hickory-smoked. German liver sausages are usually creamy and smoked. *Leberkäse,* a skinless sausage, is a mixture of pork and liver baked in a loaf pan. Although liver sausages can be eaten as they are, some are the basis of cooked dishes; e.g., the Swedish *gasleverkorv* is essential to Swedish black soup, and liverwurst may be cooked with cabbage.

LOBSTER (*Homarus gammarus*). A decapod, 10-legged crustacean, like *shrimps, *crayfish, *langoustes, and *crabs. The lobster has 8 legs plus 2 pincers which are modified legs. Lobsters are frequently confused with spiny lobsters, the southern lob-

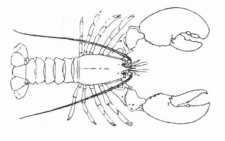

LOBSTER

sters of the U.S., the langoustes of France. The langouste has 10 legs, but no pincers; when alive, it is speckled pink or brown—in some species greenish—but the lobster is rarely greenish and almost always dark-blue to nearly black. It turns red when cooked. Lobsters have smoothish shells, at most knobbly, while langoustes are well armed with blunt spines. Lobsters mainly inhabit the colder waters of the northern hemisphere, although they are found as far south as the Mediterranean and North African coasts. Langoustes, on the other hand, prefer warmer waters, and various species are found all over the world in tropical and subtropical seas. In North America, lobsters are found as far south as North Carolina. From Florida and southern California southward, the southern lobsters are langoustes. There is a huge worldwide business in frozen tails of many species of langouste, which are generally called "crawfish tails." They come from many countries, including South Africa, Brazil, Australia, and New Zealand. This trade does not exist with lobsters, which are much rarer beasts.

Lobsters can grow to an enormous size, and the claws then become disproportionately vast. Record specimens have been over 3 ft (almost 1 m) long and have weighed 33 lb (15 Kg). Some huge ones may be 40–50

years old and are reputedly very tough.

Like other crustaceans, lobsters must molt their hard shell in order to grow. They do this some 7 times in the first growing season, but less often after that and, after 4 years, molting normally happens only once a year. It takes about 6 years to produce a 1-lb (500-g) lobster. Very small lobsters are delicious, but many countries now have conservation laws regulating the minimum size allowed to be sold.

Lobsters are caught in creels or pots—traps that allow the lobster to enter but impede its exit. The pots are baited with fish or meat, which can be bad and stinking for lobsters (crabs will eat only fresh bait). Lobsters are very belligerent, and when two or more get into a pot they fight. A damaged lobster can bleed to death; the remedy is to break off the whole limb, since lobsters regenerate lost limbs and have a mechanism for sealing off injury at the joint. Damaged lobsters are no problem if they are to be cut up and then cooked, but if they are to be poached, they should be uninjured, or any holes should be plugged with kneaded bread or dough.

When handling live lobsters, never hold them around the middle: they can close up suddenly and wound your hand. Large lobsters can be quite dangerous—so always grasp the creatures from above, just behind the head, with fingers and thumb on either side of the body, where the pincers cannot reach.

To choose a live lobster, which is essential for many dishes, look for specimens around 1 lb (500 g) in weight. Although the large lobsters are cheaper, weight for weight they are not as good. Lobsters should not be half dead but full of life, with the tail tucked under the body and plenty of movement in the legs. When picked up, a lobster should feel heavy for its size and the carapace should feel hard between the fingers and thumb, with no give. Softness shows that the lobster has recently molted and will be out of condition, because crustaceans hide and do not emerge to feed during this danger period in their lives. Hen (female) lobsters are reckoned by some to be slightly superior to the cocks (males). They have a slightly wider body, though smaller claws, and may have eggs (coral) under the tail. Other experts like big claws, and think the claw meat is the best, but there is really no significant difference between the cock and hen. At home, lobsters can be kept alive for some time in damp seaweed, but if several are together, their claws should be tied up or taped shut to prevent fights (and for safety, if curious children are about).

To choose a cooked lobster. Although it is preferable to buy living lobsters, you may not want to face killing them. If you are buying a cooked lobster, see that it smells fresh and that the tail springs back when it is opened out. If it stays open or the lobster feels floppy, then it is not fresh.

Anatomy. Lobsters are not vertebrates, and their main nerve cord runs down the underside and not the back, so exhortations to kill a lobster by severing its spinal cord are way off. The cerebral ganglion—which is probably not comparable to a brain—lies more or less between the eyes and is connected with the main cord by two branches running on either side of the stomach. This stomach, which is in the head, is full of grit and is sometimes called the grit sac. It is easily removed and discarded when the lobster is cleaned. From this, the gut runs straight between the muscles to open underneath the tail. The gut looks like a black cord or thread and is discarded. The digestive gland, liver or tomalley, is a feathery organ situated just behind the stomach and on either side of the gut. It is one of the tastiest parts and is usually scraped out separately for use in the sauce. The gills, equivalent to the "dead man's fingers" in crabs, are situated in cavities on either side of the body and can be ignored. When a lobster is split from head to tail, it is easy to pick out the gut and stomach. Another method of preparation is to remove the tail by cutting it off the body, then to cut off the fan. This makes it easy to poke the meat out in one piece; the gut must also be removed.

Killing. The old way was to plunge the lobster head first into boiling brine and then to clap on the lid to prevent it from jumping out. This seems cruel, and others advocate putting the animal into cold water and gradually raising the temperature. By the time around 100°F (40°C) or human body heat is reached, the lobster has lost consciousness. However, experimental evidence indicates that lobsters plunged into boiling water remain alive for at most 15 seconds, and thus this method is the most humane. Since some people claim that lobsters lose flavor when brought slowly to the boil, it would seem that plunging into boiling water is "the method of choice," as the surgeons would say.

When lobster meat is used for more elaborate dishes, it is needed raw, not cooked. The lobster is a very primitive creature, more so than the crab, for instance, and it has no brain, only a long nerve cord with various swellings (ganglia) along its course, and it cannot be killed instantly by a knife thrust. Only those who can split a lobster into two down the middle line in one blow can claim to kill it instantly. Others say you should stun it with a blow on the head, and that seems at least to immobilize the creature. After that, as Pellaprat advises, "Les découper sans hésitation ni attendrissement en morceaux" (Cut them in pieces without hesitation or compassion), and this boldness surely kills a lobster quicker and more humanely than any other way.

Cooking. A lobster should preferably be cooked in sea water strengthened with salt to the point where the brine will float an egg. If you are using fresh water, 4–5 oz (100–150 g) of salt per 1¾ pt (1 lt) is correct. Cook lobsters for 11 minutes per lb (12 minutes per 500 g), although small ones of 1 lb

(450 g) may need a little longer. As soon as the lobster is cooked, plunge it into ice water if it is wanted cold.

[*Lobster*—French: *homard;* German: *Hummer;* Italian: *aragosta, gambero di mare;* Spanish: *langosta, bogavante*]

LOCUST. *See* insects.

LOCUST BEAN. *See* carob.

LOGANBERRY. *See* blackberry.

LONGAN. *See* lychee.

LOQUAT or **Japanese medlar.** From the moth-eaten examples in Mediterranean markets in early spring, you would hardly realize that the loquat is a delicious subtropical fruit. The loquat (*Eriobotrya japanica*) came originally from central China but has also been cultivated in Japan for many centuries. It has considerable importance in both countries, which have developed many superior varieties. The loquat is a relative of the Europan *medlar, but the quality of their fruit is totally different. The tree is evergreen, decorative, tropical-looking and about 25 ft (7½ m) high. It is grown in the U.S., South America, Australia, South Africa, India, and wherever the climate is warm enough. Introduced into the Mediterranean by the French in 1874, it is the only fruit in the rose family (which includes most of our temperate fruits) which can stand both considerable frost and intense heat. Unfortunately, the fruit does not travel well, because the loquat must be ripened on the tree, the duration of the harvest is short, and the fruits must be picked daily. Commercially, it has everything against it.

The ripe fruit is yellow or apricot-colored, with a thin, slightly downy skin, a pleasant, slightly crunchy texture, and exceedingly juicy yellow pulp, which tastes both acid and sweet. The large, black shiny stones come free easily. It is worth looking for good varieties, because poor loquats are good only for making jelly, chutney, or jam, for which they have ample pectin. Best of all is to steal a few fruits off the trees while taking a springtime Riviera walk.

LOTUS. There are only about 100 species in the lotus family, and they are popularly known as water lilies. The common white water lily of Europe (*Nymphaea alba*) has edible underwater rhizomes. They are eaten in some places, as are most species of water lily, including the giant Victoria water lily (*Victoria regia*), which has leaves big enough to float a baby. Its seeds are eaten roasted in its native Brazil. Egyptian lotuses (*Nymphaea lotus*) and others related to it are called *chota kamal* ("little lotus") in India and are important in hungry times. Their beautiful flowers grace the tanks around temples and palaces in many places. Water lilies are worldwide and, if it were a matter of survival, it would be a fair bet to risk eating any of them.

The true lotus (*Nelumbium nuciferum*), which appears in stylized form in Hindu and Buddish sculpture, belongs to a different genus in the family. It is another beautiful flower, differing from the water lily in that the leaves stand up and do not float on the water. The plant has been cultivated since antiquity, and was grown in ancient Egypt but is no longer wild there. The rhizomes and seeds, even the leaves, are important in the cooking of the whole of Asia, particularly in Japan and China.

As a cultivated vegetable, the lotus looks like a succession of 2-in. (5-cm) thick turnips stuck top to bottom like a string of sausages. When cut in two, it has a concentric pattern of air spaces which give a lacelike impression. It can sometimes be bought fresh from Chinese shops, and canned lotus is readily available. The seeds, harvested from boats with large nets, are eaten cooked or raw. The leaves are used as wrappers. Recipes for using lotus roots will be found in most Chinese and Japanese cookbooks. After peeling, the roots can be sliced, scalded and used in salads, or grated and eaten raw. In

Japanese cooking, the lacy form of the lotus root is used to cut decorative shapes. Since lotus root turns brown when cut, it should be put straight into acidulated water. Slices of lotus root, boiled until just tender in acidulated water, may be marinated in a dressing of 4 tablespoons vinegar to 1 tablespoon sugar with a pinch of MSG and a pinch of salt to give a Japanese hors d'oeuvre. In India (called *bhain*), they are boiled, mashed, and used in vegetarian *koftas* (vegetarian meat balls) or mixed with lentils and curried.

Dried lotus roots can be bought in Chinese supermarkets and need soaking before use. Dried lotus leaves, also after soaking, are used as an aromatic wrapping in which fish or pieces of pork are steamed. These are also sold in Chinese markets.

The seeds are oblong, black, and about ¾ in. (2 cm) long. If gathered before they are fully ripe, they have a nice nutty taste, but when mature they need to be roasted or boiled, and the bitter germ should be removed. In Chinese cooking, they are used, for example, in soups.

[*Lotus*—French: *lotus, lotos;* German: *Lotos, Lotusblume;* Italian: *Loto;* Spanish: *loto, ninfea*]

LOVAGE. An umbelliferous plant *(Levisticum officinale)* rather like large celery, with strong-smelling leaves and a taste like lemony celery, but with distinctive musky

LOVAGE

overtones. It grows wild all over Europe and on America's North Atlantic coast. This is one of the most rewarding of all herbs, though neglected these days. It is particularly useful in soups, but should be added sparingly—the flavor is strong. In small amounts it can be used as an aromatic as one would use celery. Scottish lovage *(L. scoticum)*—which is, of course, just known as lovage in Scotland—grows wild on rocky coasts there; its aromatic leaves can be added to salads and are sometimes used as a potherb.

[*Lovage*—French: *livèche;* German: *Liebstückel;* Italian: *levistico;* Spanish: *ligústico*]

LUMPFISH. *See* caviar.

LYCHEE, litchi, or other spellings. The lychee *(Litchi chinensis)* is native to subtropical areas of southern China and Thailand. The fruit is borne in clusters on small trees. Typically—but varying from type to type—ripe lychees are about the size of a plum, with a beautiful red, leathery, knobbly, or spiny skin. Very shortly, the skin turns brown and becomes rather brittle. Lychees are gathered at once in whole bunches—they keep better that way. If they are for shipment, this is done when they just begin to turn red and are not fully ripe. The skin is very thin and easily separates, and inside is a juicy fruit, looking like a jumbo peeled grape. It even tastes something like a grape, though it is much more scented. There is a single, large, dark (and bitter) pip. Lychees will keep for up to 3 months in the refrigerator at around 40°F (5°C) and are best eaten chilled. The fruit cans well, and canned lychees taste remarkably like fresh ones. Dried lychees—Chinese nuts—have been either dried in the sun or kiln dried, and rattle when shaken. They are a common product and taste like raisins. Lychees also freeze well and will no doubt become more available in the future.

The lychee was certainly being cultivated in China 2000 years ago, and there is a possible reference 1500 years before that. It was tried in Europe in the 19th century, but the climate is not right, for though it seems possible to grow lychees in some Mediterranean areas, the fruit needs heat and high humidity to come to perfection; in the dry conditions of a southern European summer they crack open and go bad while ripening. In fact, the lychee is choosy. However, it thrives in parts of South Africa and has been tried in southern Florida and California.

Closely related to the lychee is the longan (*Euphoria longana*), commonly grown along with it in China. Though a smaller and inferior fruit, it has the virtue of ripening later, when the lychees are over. Tropical fruits of the same family are the rambutan (*Nephelium lappaceum*), native to Southeast Asia and something like a lychee but with dense tendrils instead of warts covering the fruits, and the pulasan (*Nephelium mutabile*), with red or yellow tubercles. In both the tropical species, the edible flesh adheres to the seed. All these fruits belong to the soapberry family (Sapindaceae), which also includes the *ackee but few other edible fruits.

LYE. Originally an alkaline solution made by boiling white, calcined wood ashes in water, then filtering and concentrating by further boiling. It consisted largely of carbonates of potassium and sodium. Soap was originally made by boiling lye with fat, lye and lime being the only alkalis available until fairly late in history. Almost any task now performed by *caustic soda was performed in the past by lye. One such process is the accelerated removal of bitterness from green olives.

[*Lye*—French: *lessive;* German: *Lauge;* Italian: *liscivia;* Spanish: *lejía*]

M

MABOLO. A close relative of the *persimmon.

MACADAMIA NUT or **Queensland nut.** *Macadamia ternifolia* (hard shell) and *M. integrifolia* (easier to crack) are native to the coastal forests of Queensland and New South Wales, where they grow wild along the edges of rivers and creeks. The value of the nuts was known to the aborigines, and it was noticed some 100 years ago by Dr. John MacAdam, for whom the nut was eventually named. Today the trees are cultivated in many areas, including California, Kenya, and South America. Even Australia has belatedly recognized the value of its native nut and is growing it commercially. The most important production center is Hawaii, which exports macadamias and many macadamia products: candy, jam (with passionfruit, poha, and guava), cakes, nut meal, even soups.

The macadamia nut is rounded, with a kernel shaped something like a hazel, but with no skin. It is white and very oily. In fact, a salad oil is expressed from macadamias, and they make an excellent nut butter. Before cracking, they are dehydrated for several days to shrink the kernel away from the tan husk. After shelling (in Honokaa, Hawaii, this is done in modern machines whose technology is a secret), the kernels are usually again dehydrated and roasted until the moisture content is less than 2%. Macadamias are recommended as a substitute for the *candle nut in Indonesian cooking, and they are a delicious dessert nut, with a creamy-crunchy sweetness. They are finding other uses as their popularity grows—at present demand exceeds supply, and thus they are quite expensive—and as they become increasingly available.

MACARONI. *See* pasta.

MACE is the dried aril—a sort of cage—surrounding the seed of the nutmeg (*Myristica fragrans*). It is bright red when fresh but is pressed flat and dried until it looks like creamy-brown seaweed. It has a fragrance and taste something like nutmeg, but subtly different, and is more expensive. Mace is difficult to grind, because it is very oily, but *grinding is easier to deal with if you are able to mix less oily spices, a little raw rice, or even flour with the mace. It is widely used in baking and can also add flavor to chocolate dishes, oyster stew, stuffings, and jellies.

[*Mace*—French: *macis, fleur de muscade;* German: *Muskatblüte;* Italian: *macis;* Spanish: *macia, macis*]

MACERATION is soaking materials in liquid, usually water or watery solutions, to soften them. The effect can be mechanical or physical—as when dried tissues reabsorb water and swell, or when gummy substances cementing cells together are leached out. The softening can also be brought about by chemical changes (owing, for instance, to acids or alkalis) or to the action of microorganisms or enzymes, which have been encouraged by water. *See* soaking.

[*Maceration*—French: *macération;* German: *Einweichung;* Italian: *macerazione;* Spanish: *maceración*]

MÂCHE. *See* lettuce.

MACKEREL. The Atlantic mackerel (*Scomber scombrus*), a small relative of the Atlantic bonito, is found on both sides of the Atlantic, in the Mediterranean, and in the

KING MACKEREL

Black Sea. These mackerel, which come in shoals, are caught in large numbers and are an important food fish. They average about a pound and have a strong, distinctive flavor. Kingfish or king mackerel (*Scomberomorus cavalla*) range from the Gulf of Mexico to New England. Their firm white flesh is stronger and oilier than most mackerels; it is enhanced by marinating in lime juice for an hour before cooking. Spanish mackerel (*S. maculatus*) and cero (*S. regalis*) are more delicately flavored.

In eastern Mediterranean countries, mackerels are salted in brine and dried. Hot-smoked mackerel is a delicacy in its own right. In Britain, mackerel is soused, like herring, in vinegar and water, but there are superior French methods of pickling in white wine. Like most oily fish, mackerel is best when eaten absolutely fresh. It is excellent broiled and has bones which are easily dealt with. It is complemented by lemon juice or a sour sauce, which in France is often made with gooseberries.

[*Mackerel*—French: *maquereau;* German: *Makrele;* Italian: *sgombro;* Spanish: *caballa*]

MADAGASCAR BEAN. *See* lima bean.

MADEIRA. The Portuguese introduced vines into Madeira in the early 15th century, and by Tudor times sweet madeira wines had become popular in Britain; *malvoisie* or malmsey wine was particularly famous. Madeiras are blended wines fortified with cane spirit and are distinguished from other fortified wines by the heating they undergo during maturation, which is said to duplicate the temperature changes of a voyage around the world in the hold of a ship. Madeira is heated very gradually—either in the cask or in large tanks—taking a month to reach a temperature which may be as high as 122°F (50°C); it is then kept hot for 4–6 months and cooled equally slowly afterward. Madeiras are shipped in four main types:

Sercial. The driest and lightest blend, with a unique flavor often described as nutty. Sercial is an apéritif wine and, as the driest madeira, is the one best used in cooking as a flavoring.

Verdelho, darker and rather sweeter than sercial, is the madeira to be drunk with cake. It is also excellent with soup.

Bual or **boal.** Rather sweet, with a delicate taste, this is the lighter of the two dessert madeiras.

Malmsey, dark, sweet, fruity, and very fragrant, is a fine dessert wine with almost the qualities of a liqueur. Its use in cooking is limited by its sweetness. Possibly confusing are wines called *malvasia* in Italy and elsewhere. The name comes from Monemvasia, the port in southern Greece through which the sweet wines of the Aegean Islands were shipped in ancient times, and from the *malvasia* grape brought from there and introduced to Italy, Madeira, and elsewhere. A *malvasia*, whether from Frascati near Rome, from Sardinia, from Stromboli or Salina (the

Lipari Islands), or elsewhere, is a strong, golden-yellow dessert wine, which is sweet and usually best served cold. It has not been given the *estufa* heat treatment of a Madeira malmsey.

Madeira is internationally used as a flavoring in many dishes; in soup (particularly turtle), in aspic, in sauces for meat and ham (e.g., *jamon asado al vino de madera*), for *sauce au madère*, and in cakes and jellies. It is also sometimes used with carrots and gives a strong, rather characteristic vinous flavor. Madeira is an excellent item for the kitchen shelf—if it is recorked after opening, it keeps almost indefinitely. As a drink, it is rather neglected these days except in Scandinavian countries.

[*Madeira*—French: *madère;* German: *Maderawein;* Italian: *vino di Madera;* Spanish: *vino de Madera*]

MAGNESIUM (Mg) is a silvery metal which burns, giving a brilliant light and leaving white magnesium oxide. It occurs naturally in dolomite, magnesite, and sea water; its sulfate is Epsom salts. Magnesium is an essential element in chlorophyll, and so is present in all green plants. It is also one of the important elements in the human body, and a deficiency can be a cause of ill health.

Among the rich sources of magnesium are almonds and Brazil nuts, soybeans, wholegrain oats and wheat (and therefore wholemeal bread), cocoa, and shrimps. The diet of people living on convenience foods, refined sugar, fats, and soft drinks (as is sometimes the case in the "civilized" world) is likely to be deficient in magnesium.

[*Magnesium*—French: *magnésium;* German: *Magnesium;* Italian: *magnesio;* Spanish: *magnesio*]

MAIDENHAIR FERN. This feathery fern (*Adiantum capillus-veneris*) can be found growing wild in shady, damp places in America and Europe. It was used as a decoration on wedding cakes in the preplastic era, and it can be boiled to make a mucilaginous liquid, even a jelly. This has little taste of its own but often has flavor added, and commercial syrups, known by their French name as *capillaire,* can taste like scented soap. According to Boswell, Doctor Johnson liked to add *capillaire* to his port.

[*Maidenhair fern*—French: *capillaire commun, cheveux de Vénus adranthe;* German: *Frauenhaar, Venushaar;* Italian: *capelvenere, adianto;* Spanish: *culantrillo*]

MAIDENHAIR TREE. *See* ginkgo.

MAIZE. *See* corn.

MALAGA. Wines from the mountain hinterland of Malaga in southern Spain are handled through that port and bear its name. Malagas are sweet wines, made mainly from the Pedro Ximénez sherry grape. In the making, malagas have similarities to *marsala in that they are sweetened with evaporated grape juice (in Spain, called *arrope;* in Italy, *mosto cotto*). They usually also contain *color* or *pantomina,* similar to *arrope* but evaporated down still further to a very dark, thick, pasty mass. Sugar is further increased in the wine by drying muscatel grapes on mats in the sun for 1–2 days (wine from these is called *vino tierno*) and by stopping fermentation before it is complete by adding alcohol (*calebre* or *vino maestro*). Varying the proportions of these elements before maturing them in casks for 2 years or more produces a great variety of malagas: *seco,* dry; *palido,* pale; *dulce,* sweet; *semi-dulce,* semisweet; *oscuro,* dark; *negro,* black (very dark).

Malagas are drunk as dessert wines and may be of great age (I once was allowed a sip of one that was nearly 200 years old). Malaga may be used as a flavoring in cooking—there are some dishes such as *jamon dulce con vino de malaga* (sweet ham with malaga wine) which demand it. The effect is somewhat similar to port, but *jamon dulce al porto* is rather different. Since there are some quite horrible "malagas" on the market (although the name is now controlled), do not go for the cheapest on the grounds that it is only for cooking.

[*Malaga*—French: *vin de Malaga;* German: *Malagawein;* Italian: *vino di Malaga;* Spanish: *vino de Malaga*]

MALDIVE FISH. Dried fish of several species, crumbled, pounded, or powdered, is much used in the cooking of Sri Lanka. There is no substitute, although Bombay duck is often given as one. The importance of dried fish is one of several ways in which Sri Lankan cooking shows its connections with Southeast Asia.

MALIC ACID. A sharply sour organic acid which takes its name from the apple (*Malus*). Besides being present in sour apples, malic acid is an important acid in grapes, especially in those produced in the cooler and less sunny wine regions. The change from malic to the less sour lactic acid, which takes place in wine, is brought about by bacteria and is known as the malo-lactic fermentation. Malic acid can be bought as a white, crystalline powder and is occasionally used by those who make fruit wines.

MALLOW. Many members of the mallow family, even hollyhocks in a pinch, are edible. The leaves of various species of wild mallows are commonly eaten. In the Jordan valley, for instance, where they are popular with Arab farmers, I had some, but they were not very enjoyable. The *abelmusk* (*Hibiscus abelmoschus*) is a musklike flavoring seed. The roselle or red sorrel (*Hibiscus subdariffa*) is another interesting plant. It has fleshy calices with a sharp, fruity flavor which are used in tarts and jams, and for refreshing drinks. The green leaves are also edible. Another mallow, abutilon (*Abutilon esculentum* and other species), has leaves that are used as a spinach; it is cultivated for this purpose in countries from India (*ranghi*) to Brazil.

Melokhia or *molokhia,* a soup that is an Egyptian national dish, is made from the leaves of a mallow, *Corchorus olitorius;* dried *melokhia* leaves, which are obtainable from Greek shops, are very acceptable in place of fresh ones. Other mallows are *marsh mallow, *okra, and cotton, which is significant in cooking as the source of *cottonseed oil.

[*Mallow*—French: *mauve;* German: *Malve, Pappelkraut;* Italian: *malva;* Spanish *morado*]

MALMSEY. *See* madeira.

MALT. Any cereal can be malted, but by "malt" we understand malted barley unless otherwise specified. Malt is the raw material from which *beer and malt *whiskey are made.

In fresh grain, the food on which the tiny sprout will have to subsist when it starts life is stored in the form of starch. Once sprouting begins, enzymes (known generically as diastase) start to break down the starch into, mainly, *maltose (a sugar) and *dextrins (gums). To make malt, *barley (preferably a variety rich in starch) is first soaked in water for 2 days and then spread out to sprout, being kept moist and turned occasionally to prevent heating. After about a week—the time varies with the temperature, the variety of barley, and its age—when the tiny first shoot is nearly, but not quite, as long as the grain, the barley is very gradually heated and dried, with the temperature rising over a period of several days. The final temperature is critical, determining the type of malt that is produced. After the rootlets have been rubbed off, the malted grain is stored for a week or so to mature and is then ready to be milled or crushed to grist for use.

The palest malt (lager malt) is heated to about 200°F (93°C), which leaves the enzymes intact. Higher temperatures will produce (in ascending order) pale malt, amber malt, crystal malt, brown malt, black malt, and patent black malt, the last being a substance in which the sugars are charred—it was originally used only for coloring. Naturally, the flavor changes as the malt is heated and more and more of the enzymes are put out of action. Black malts have a burnt taste and are used for stouts. Crystal malt is toffee-colored, has a strong flavor, and contains quite a proportion of sweet, unfermentable dextrins which make it a popular addition to brown ales, since these need to be smooth and slightly sweet.

Before they can be used in fermentation, malts must be mashed to develop the sugars and extract them in solution. The grist of milled malt is mixed with warm water and kept at a suitable temperature. At 130°F (54°C) and a pH of 4.7, a maximum amount of malt sugar is formed, but if the temperature is increased to 149°F (65°C) and the acidity reduced to pH 5.7, the conditions favor maximum production of dextrins for the sweeter, more full-bodied beers. The temperature must be maintained for at least 2 hours, but longer times are usual in brewing.

The liquid which is filtered off is known as wort. This has to be boiled to sterilize it and to destroy the enzymes before the yeast is added for brewing beer. If wort is evaporated to a thick syrup by boiling under reduced pressure, the mixture of malt sugar, gums, and flavor compounds is known as malt extract. The extract may also be dried. Extracts of the various types of malt can be bought from shops which specialize in materials for homemade beers and wines.

In cooking, malt was once added to various porridges and simple puddings for children and invalids. It was supposed to be especially effective in building up people with tuberculosis and other wasting diseases. Malt bread is a sticky, sweet, dark bread, often with currants and raisins. Malt extract is sweet and has a pleasant, distinctive taste.

Proprietary granary flour for breadmaking contains malted wheat kernels. Malted wheat-meal flour is sometimes to be found in health-food stores. Malt is highly regarded in the bakery trade to improve the volume, bloom, and crust of dough.

[Malt—French: malt; German: Malz; Italian: malto; Spanish: malta]

MALTOSE or **malt sugar** ($C_{12}H_{22}O_{11}$) is a crystalline disaccharide *sugar which is the main sugar in *malt. It is also formed in digestion by the action of enzymes produced by the salivary glands and, more important, the pancreas. Although it is not used in its pure form in the kitchen, it is of immense importance, since it is keenly fermented by yeasts to produce alcohol (the basis of brewing) and carbon dioxide (which makes bread rise).

MALVASIA. See madeira.

MANDARIN. See orange.

MANGANESE (Mn) is an unattractive gray metal which is an essential trace element in food but is toxic in any larger amount. Tea is particularly rich in manganese, containing 150–1000 parts per million, depending on where it comes from. Cloves contain 450 ppm. Bran, whole-meal flour, and liver are also common and good sources.

[Manganese—French: manganèse; German: Mangan; Italian: manganese; Spanish: manganeso]

MANGO (Mangifera indica). At their best, mangoes can claim to be the world's most delicious fruit, although another school of thought awards *mangosteens that place. A fine eating mango, such as the famous Alphonso variety, will have fine-textured, orange flesh surrounding a flattened central stone and enclosed in a leathery skin. The taste is acid-sweet and perfectly balanced, and the aroma is that of a pine wood in spring—if it is possible to describe at all the unique mango taste.

Such eating varieties are best chilled (they keep some days in the refrigerator). To eat a mango, cut off both sides of the fruit, on either side of the stone, and scoop the flesh out of the skin with a spoon. Afterward, strip the skin off the remaining central part and suck the stone clean. (This is messy, but mangoes are so delicious that even the most fastidious will not mind being smeared with juice. After eating a good mango, you may need a bath.)

At the other end of the scale, there are semiwild varieties with small, fibrous fruits that taste strongly of turpentine. Intermediate types make especially delicious pickle or chutney. There is also a tremendous range of stringy but juicy mangoes which are supposed to be sucked; these are often very sweet. People who say that mangoes are overrated have almost always got hold of a poor variety or of one grown in unsuitable soil or climate—many such inferior mangoes are produced.

The mango is a tree of the Indian region and has certainly been in cultivation there for more than 4000 years. Alexander the Great's men saw trees growing in the Indus Valley in 327 B.C. In the last few hundred years, mangoes have been introduced to suitably warm climates all around the world: Florida, California, Queensland, the Azores, the Canary Islands during the 19th century, for instance, and southern Italy early in this century. Countries which now grow and export them include Egypt, Israel, and Kenya. In fact, mango trees can exist in a wide variety of conditions as long as they have sun and no frost during the flowering season, but those fruiting in any but perfect climates will rarely give good table fruits.

Commercially, mangoes are picked just before they are ripe; if wrapped carefully and chilled at 41–50°F (5–10°C), they can be shipped by air. Mangoes are best placed carefully in straw to ripen. Once ripe, they will keep for up to 10 days at room temperature and up to 2 weeks in the refrigerator. Unfortunately, mangoes are expensive; good ones are expensive even where they are grown.

The mango belongs to the same family (Anocardiaceae) as cashew and pistachio nuts. Mango trees grow to an enormous size, often covering 100 ft (30 m) with the dense shade of their elongated, dark-green, shiny leaves. The tree is evergreen and characteristic of the landscape over large parts of India, where it is of great economic importance.

Mango *chutney, in India, may be made fresh from raw ground mango, herbs, and spices, but sweet cooked mango chutney is a common commercial item elsewhere. In Britain, it is often eaten with cold meat and goes with cheese in pub sandwiches. A typical commercial recipe is as follows:

SWEET MANGO CHUTNEY

Wash, peel, and slice ripe but firm mangoes. For 2¼ lb (1 Kg) of sliced mango, add an equal amount of sugar, 2 oz (50 g) of salt, and a very little water; boil for a short time, until the mangoes are just tender. Put 1 oz (25 g) of mixed spice (equal weights of black pepper, cumin, cloves, cinnamon, and cardamon), ½ oz (15 g) of ground chili, 4 oz (100 g) of bruised ginger, 2 oz (50 g) of chopped onion, and ½ oz (15 g) of crushed garlic in a cheesecloth bag and add to the boiling mango. Add ½ cup (150 ml) vinegar—the quantity needed to achieve a good balance will depend on the sweetness of the mangoes and the strength of the vinegar. Adjust the salt if necessary. Cook for 5 minutes or until the desired consistency is reached. Bottle and seal.

Dried mango powder is known in India as *amchur* or *amchoor* (*am* means mango in North India). It is an ingredient needed for certain Indian dishes and can be bought at most shops that specialize in Indian products.

Mango leather is made in India when there is a glut of mangoes. The juice is squeezed onto trays or plates and put in the hot sun to dry. As the juice dries, more is squeezed on until a leathery material about ½ in. (1 cm) thick has been made. This is usually rolled and cut into strips. It makes a nourishing sweet. Commercially, mango leather is made by adding a trace of potassium metabisulfite to the juice and then drying it at 140–150°F (60–65°C) on oiled wooden trays.

Mango pickle, of varying degrees of hotness, is a popular accompaniment to curries in India. It is quite a different article from the mango chutney used in the West, being salty, sour, spicy, and not at all sweet.

It is claimed that some varieties of mango are excellent when canned, but most people who have enjoyed mangoes where they grow will probably agree that canned ones are a very poor substitute. They do not change and take on a new dimension as do peaches, but rather acquire an oversweet aspect. Canned mango pulp may be used to make mango fool, and canned mango juice is also available.

[*Mango*—French: *mangue;* German: *Mango;* Italian: *mango;* Spanish: *mango, manguey*]

MANGOSTEEN. Tropical berry from a tree, *Garcinia mangostana,* that is native to Malaysia. It has a tough brownish rind around white flesh, which is divided into segments. It is eaten raw, but the related **kokum* is used in Indian cooking.

MANIOC. *See* cassava.

MANTIS SHRIMP (*Squilla mantis*) is a curious crustacean with front legs superficially like those of a praying mantis and a general shape like a shrimp or lobster with a rather large abdomen. Mantis shrimps, which reach 10 in. (25 cm) long and lurk in mud or sand below low-tide mark, are a good ingredient for fish soup. They can also be boiled and dealt with much in the same way as prawns (the tails may be served cold with the upper part of the shell removed to expose the flesh). They are popular in Italy, particularly in Romagna and the Veneto, and elsewhere around the Mediterranean. A related species, *S. empusa,* is found on the East Coast of the U.S.

[*Mantis shrimp*—French: *squille;* Italian: *pannocchia, cannocchia;* Spanish: *galera*]

MANZANILLA. *See* sherry.

MAPLE SYRUP and **maple sugar** are the boiled-down sap of the rock maple or sugar maple (*Acer saccharum*) and of the black maple (*A. nigrum*). These grow in south-eastern Canada and the northeastern U.S., from Pennsylvania north and west to Wisconsin.

The early colonists were taught by the Indians to tap the maples and evaporate the sap to syrup or sugar. Wooden spiles (spouts) were carved from sumac branches, whose soft centers could easily be burned out by hot metal rods. Sap buckets were usually made by itinerant "wet" coopers who specialized in containers for liquids, using durable woods that would not impart unwanted flavors to the sap. Horse- or oxen-drawn sleds made the rounds of the maple trees.

Today the "sugaring-off" ritual is relatively unchanged, although spiles are now metal, buckets are galvanized tin or plastic, and a snowmobile or small tractor may be used to collect the sap buckets. Many larger producers run pipe from the trees to collecting areas or the sugar house.

The 28°–40°F (-2°–5°C) range in temperatures is critical to sap flow. Such freeze-and-thaw periods occur anywhere from mid-February to mid-April. The farmer then bores holes ½ in. (1 cm) wide and some 2 in. (5 cm) deep into the sapwood, that segment of the tree's trunk up which the sap rises, inserts a spile, and hangs from it a loosely covered pail. Suitable maples must be at least 10 in. (25 cm) in diameter. Each may produce 12 gallons of sap per season, which boils down to 1¼ qt of maple syrup or 3 lb of sugar. But all this varies, depending on the quality of the sap: at best, 20 gallons of sap may be sufficient to make a gallon of syrup; at worst, it may take 80.

The liquid that flows from the spiles is almost all water, with only the faintest hint of sweetness. The buckets of sap are emptied into a large flat container located under the opening in the roof of the sugaring shack. Intense oil or wood fires evaporate the sap into syrup. A system of dividers channels the thickening liquid toward the front of the evaporator. When it reaches the proper temperature and specific gravity it is drawn off, filtered, reheated to 190°F (80.8°C), and poured into tins. Further evaporation by 25% produces maple sugar.

Such a labor-intensive process obviously results in an expensive product, and it is not likely to become cheaper as the number of trees and producers decreases. Maple syrup prices are usually pegged to grades determined by producing states. Fancy grade is the lightest in color and most delicate in flavor. Most syrup retailed is grade A, an amber liquid with more distinct maple flavor. Grade B is dark and strong-flavored, used mostly for cooking. (A liking for the best pure maple syrup is usually coupled with a dislike of any of the commercially available combinations of it with such ingredients as corn syrup, honey, or artificial flavors and colors.) Other maple products include maple butter or maple "honey," with the consistency of peanut butter, maple vinegar, and maple beer. Maple sugar is usually sold as molded candy, but it can be granulated as "Indian sugar." In colonial days it was so widely used and in demand as a sweetener that it was accepted in part payment of wages.

Sugaring-off season is a time for celebration in Vermont, the center of U.S. maple sugar production, and Quebec, where a traditional full sweet meal is served, with maple syrup dumped over everything from ham steaks to baked beans to hard-boiled eggs. Part of the festivities is the *tire de neige*, or sugar-on-the-snow. The sap is reduced to caramel, and this hot golden treacle is poured into fresh snow, where it congeals into chewy ribbons of delicately flavored taffy. To make it, boil pure maple syrup until it reaches 230°F (110°C) for waxy-textured candy, 232°F (111°C) for a crisp, lacy taffy texture. Pour it in swirls on packed clean snow. In some areas, snow is kept frozen in pans for sugar-on-the-snow on a hot summer day.

Besides the incomparable flavor of maple syrup on pancakes or waffles, it can be used with a light hand in cooking. Use it to glaze carrots; mix it with vinegar and mustard to coat baked ham; place a tablespoon in each cavity of baked acorn squash. It can flavor all sorts of desserts—ice cream, chiffon or pecan pies, puddings, gingerbread, or baked bananas.

[*Maple syrup*—French: *sirop d'érable;* German: *Ahornsaft;* Italian: *sciroppo d'acero;* Spanish: *amilbar de acre*]

MARASCHINO. *See* cherry; fruit brandy; liqueurs.

MARC or **eau de vie de marc.** This is not strictly speaking a *brandy, although they are often confused. For instance, *dop* brandy (Cape smoke) is a South African marc. Brandy is, or should be, made from wine, but marc is made by fermenting the mess of sludge, skins, pips, and stalks left over after the juice for winemaking has been pressed out. The marc must therefore always be highly rectified to get rid of the methyl alcohol and other hangover-promoting congenerics. It is less delicate and less expensive than brandy and varies greatly from region to region. Some marcs are excellent and are much drunk in France; others are firewater. In local recipes, *eau de vie de marc* is sometimes specified, and it should really, if one is sufficiently fussy, be a marc from the region of the recipe. Other countries distill marc. In Italy, the equivalent is *grappa;* in Portugal, *bagaceira;* and in Germany, *Tresterbrantwein.*

MARGARINE. Margarine was invented in France during the 1860s by Mège-Mouriés, a chemist, who patented it toward the end of the decade. At first, it was made largely of beef suet and skimmed milk and was nothing like the sophisticated product of the present day. It was variously called "oleo," "oleo margarine," or "butterine." Today, margarine is almost universally regarded not as a cheap butter substitute but as a product in its own right.

The main ingredient of margarine today is a blend of edible oils. A proportion of the oils may have to be hardened to produce a fat suitable for spreading on bread. The hardening method commonly used is hydrogenation. Oils which are liquid at room temperature contain a higher proportion of unsaturated fatty acids than fats which are solid at room temperature. Hydrogenation is the addition of hydrogen to unsaturated fatty acids in the oil with the aid of a nickel catalyst (which is recovered later). The unsaturated fatty acids become saturated, raising the melting point of the oil so that it becomes a solid fat at room temperature. The proportions of saturated and unsaturated fat vary according to the type of margarine. The ones containing most unsaturated fat are marked "high in polyunsaturates." This kind, which is recommended by doctors for lowering serum cholesterol levels, contains an oil blend of which normally less than 20% is saturated and the level of polyunsaturates is of the order of 50% or more. Other soft margarines which "spread straight from the fridge" contain less unsaturated fat and more saturated fat. However, they are still soft enough in texture to require packing in tubs. The hard margarines can be packed in foil or greaseproof paper.

Other ingredients that can go into margarine include salt, skimmed milk or whey, emulsifiers, lecithin, synthetic flavors such as lactones, color such as *annatto, and vitamins A and D. Today, the consumer has a wide range of margarines to choose from. All can be used for spreading, cooking, and baking, but some diet margarines, which may have half the fat content of other margarines, are not effective in certain recipes.

Margarines can be clarified to produce a cooking fat resembling *ghee*, but the fat does not have the same flavor. However, it would be suitable for vegetarians, and such vegetarian *ghee* is now canned.

MARIGOLD. It is the pot marigold (*Calendula officinalis*), the common plant in gardens almost all over the world, which can be used in the kitchen. (Seeds of plants used in Tibetan monastery gardens which I collected and sent to Kew Gardens in England turned out to be nothing more exciting than marigolds.) The petals were used as long

ago as Roman times as an edible yellow coloring (when extracted in milk) and are still sometimes passed off as saffron. But the flavor is no more than slightly bitter and the color is weak. The petals were much used in 17th-century English cooking, in salads and stuffings, as a pot herb, and later to color cheese and butter. Marigold leaves are said to be good in salads, but they must be very young or they are rather tough and rough fare.

Buds of the marsh marigold or kingcup (*Caltha palustris*) were once pickled and used as capers.

[*Marigold*—French: *souci;* German: *Ringelblume;* Italian: *fiorrancio, calendula;* Spanish: *caléndula, maravilla*]

MARINATING. Marinades, pickles, and brines are aromatized liquids into which food is put for various purposes. A *brine always has salt as its most important ingredient and is almost always intended to preserve, although of course in the process it alters flavor. A *pickle may be a brine or it may be based on vinegar, lemon juice, or any other sour fruit juice, or verjuice, and it is also preservative. A marinade, however, is intended primarily to change the ingredient (meat, fish, vegetable, or fruit) in some way and is only incidentally a short-term preservative. It may be intended to allow flavors to soak in, to aromatize, to impregnate meats with juice and oil if they would otherwise be dry, or to create less usual effects, such as to coagulate the protein in fish which is to be eaten raw—a sort of chemical cooking. Above all, perhaps, marinades are intended to tenderize, but one function cannot be isolated from the others. Meats like wild boar, hare, and venison are so tough as to be almost inedible unless the animals are very young. They also tend to be dry, since animals that rush madly about the countryside never have much fat on them. Even long, slow, overnight cooking on a dying fire will hardly tenderize a boar. *Hanging, that other tenderizing process, may not be possible, especially in hot weather. Turning the food in wine, vinegar, or yogurt checks immediate decomposition and allows the acids to begin breaking down the muscle fibers into less tough proteins. The inclusion of aromatics—spices, bay leaves, garlic, onion, and herbs like thyme—perfumes the meat being marinated. If oil is used, it soaks into meat and so adds fat to keep it soft during cooking—a sort of liquid larding.

[*Marinating*—French: *mariner;* German: *marinieren;* Italian: *marinare;* Spanish: *marinar*]

MARJORAM, sweet marjoram, or knotted marjoram (*Origanum majorana*) is a perennial labiate herb, a native of Africa that is cultivated in southern climates. Far-

MARJORAM

ther north, it is grown as an annual. It is beautifully sweet-smelling and one of the most important culinary herbs. When dried it is more assertive and can be effectively used in tomato sauces, stuffings, stews, and dishes with lamb and mutton. Like savory, it is excellent with all sorts of beans. Because the flavor is weakened by prolonged heat, fresh marjoram is best added shortly before the dish is ready or used in dishes (such as omelets) that are briefly cooked.

A closely related herb is *oregano, which does not have the same sweetness and is much stronger. Pot marjoram (*O. onites*) is a much hardier herb that is useful in strongly

flavored dishes in which the more delicate taste of sweet marjoram would be wasted.

[*Marjoram*—French: *marjolaine, origan;* German: *Marienkraut, Marjoran*; Italian: *maggiorana;* Spanish: *majorana*]

MARLIN. *See* swordfish.

MARMALADE. *See* jam.

MARMITE. *See* yeast extract.

MARROW. *See* squash.

MARROW BONE. Some bones are strengthened inside with a cross-lattice, but others—the long bones of the limbs—are hollow and are a good source of bone marrow. Marrow, especially marrow from beef bones, is fatty and tasty, and marrow bones have long been a delicacy. Even bones found in people's prehistoric caves have often been cracked so that the marrow could be sucked out. More elegantly, it can be extracted with the aid of long, narrow marrow scoops. In Victorian times, marrow on toast was a common savory. Marrow is used in sauces, such as *sauce bordelaise* (wine, demi-glace sauce, and marrow) or *sauce à la moelle,* and as a garnish. It is also used to enrich dishes, including risotto. As a preliminary, marrow bones, sawn in suitable lengths, are usually sealed at the ends with a flour paste, tied in a cloth for safety, and poached for an hour, but they may be treated much more simply.

MARROW ON TOAST

This is the very quick recipe that I use. Take the marrow out of the bones and poach it briefly—a minute or so is enough—in salted water. Drain well and put it on hot toast. Sprinkle it with salt, pepper, plenty of lemon juice, and chopped parsley. I often rub the toast with garlic, and some people like cayenne pepper to season the marrow.

[*Marrow bone*—French: *os à moelle;* German: *Knochenmark;* Italian: *ossobuco;* Spanish: *caña medular, hueso medular*]

MARSALA. In the second half of the 18th century, an Englishman, John Woodhouse, who was in Sicily on business, noticed that there was a large production of sweet wine in the western part of the island, behind the port of Marsala. He thought that it would be possible to introduce to Sicily the methods used to make the dessert wines of Spain and Portugal, which were at that time so popular in Britain. He opened his business in 1773 and flourished to such an extent that a second Englishman, a Mr. Ingham, founded a rival business in 1813. This was followed in 1832 by the Italian house of Florio, which swallowed the two English firms in 1929 and is to this day the most famous producer of Marsala.

Marsala is made by a process similar to that used for making *malaga. The white wine which forms the basis of marsala is made from local Sicilian grapes from a delimited area and is very strong, running to 15–17° of alcohol. With this is mixed *sifone,* sweet grape juice that has been prevented from fermenting by the addition of 20% alcohol (to prevent the yeasts from working), as well as *cotto,* a liquid made by boiling down grape juice to a syrup. (Incidentally, a syrup made from boiled grape juice—*mosto cotto,* cooked must—or boiled ripe figs is still made as a sweetener in southern Italy and, with honey, must have been the basis of all sweet dishes in the days before sugar from sugar cane was introduced from the Orient.)

Sifone gives marsala sweetness and softness, while the slightly caramelized *cotto* gives color, bitterness, and a trace of almond flavor. The ingredients are mixed in various proportions to produce different types of marsala, reinforced with more alcohol if necessary, cleared—usually with ox blood—and put to mature in the cask for several years. After that, they may be blended to produce the finished product. Marsalas can be *fini* (fine), *superiori* (superior), dry or *virgini,* or very sweet. There are also special ones such as *marsala all'ouvo* (with egg), *marsala-crema* (cream), and *marsala-mandorla* (almond). The alcoholic strength varies between 17° and 21°, the stronger being mainly for export to northern Europe. The sugar content is 5–12%. This was the wine that was drunk in Italy by *mamma, nonna,* and *zia* when they got together to gossip over a piece of cake, but today marsala has lost most of its popularity there. However, it is an important wine in the battery of kitchen flavorings and has the advantage that it will keep indefinitely as long as the bottle is recorked. A dry marsala is preferable, since it has more uses. Marsala is particularly used in the more sophisticated dishes of northern Italy: with veal, e.g., *scaloppine di vitello alla bolognese* (veal scallops as done in Bologna), *costolette alla modenese* (the marsala flavor combined with truffles), *ossibuchi alla reggiana* (veal knuckle as cooked in Reggia); with chicken (*pollo alla cacciatora*); with game, *pernici in salmi* (partridges cooked with butter, carrot, celery, onion, olive oil, rosemary, bay, dry marsala, and white truffles) from Piedmont; and *salmi alla toscana* (hare, rabbit, or chicken cooked with chicken livers, butter, olive oil, carrot, onion, celery, bay, tomato purée, and dry marsala) from Tuscany. It is rarely, if ever, traditionally used with fish, although I have found one recipe from Liguria in which marsala is used with brandy and white wine in the stuffing for squid (*totani ripieni*). The only vegetables with which it is commonly used are carrots (in Sicily itself) and truffles. Marsala is the classic wine for *zabaglione* or *zabaione* (although in some parts of Italy they use it mixed with sweet wine, and in Sardinia they prefer a sweet vernaccia wine), but the many other Italian sweet dishes and cakes in which it is used are unknown in other countries.

MARSHMALLOW. The original marshmallow sweet, or *pâte de guimauve,* was a thick decoction of the roots of the marshmallow plant, sweetened with sugar and flavored with orange flower water. The marsh mallow (*Althaea officinalis*), which is native to most of Europe and was used as a vegetable in Roman times, is a downy-looking, grayish-white plant with pink flowers, a member of the *mallow family. It was boiled and eaten as a vegetable in the eastern counties of Britain until fairly recent times; a syrup made from it was a remedy for coughs. The modern marshmallow no longer contains the mucilage from the mallow root. It is a spongy sweet made from gum arabic, egg white, sugar, orange flower water, and pure water. Other recipes replace the orange flower water by vanilla or fruit flavor.

MARSHMALLOWS

Dissolve 2 oz (50 g) of gum arabic in ¼ pt (150 ml) of water; strain it and put into a clean pan with 1½ teaspoons of sugar. Heat, stirring continuously until the sugar has dissolved, then boil until it reaches the firm-ball stage (when a bit dropped into cold water forms a sturdy but pliable ball). Have ready the stiffly beaten whites of 2 small eggs. Flavor the sugar and gum mixture with orange flower water and work in the egg whites. Spread in a layer—as thick as the marshmallows are to be—on a bed of cornstarch, cover the layer with a coating of cornstarch, and leave to set until the next day. Disinter and cut the layer into pieces. If they are to be used in recipes, marshmallows are most easily cut up with wet scissors.

[*Marshmallow*—French: *guimauve, bonbon à la guimauve;* German: *Lederzucker;* Italian: *altea, bismalva;* Spanish: *malvavisco*]

MARZIPAN or **marchpane** might have got its name from *panis martius* (March bread), a confection of almonds made even in Roman times as an offering to the gods, but the derivation is dubious. There are many recipes. Essentially, marzipan consists of pounded blanched almonds and sugar, but egg white, whole egg, and gum arabic are often added, together with various flavorings. Decorative flowers and fruits may be modeled from it, and sometimes it is lightly baked. Here is a simple recipe from Italy:

MARZIPAN

Pound 18 oz (500 g) of blanched almonds to a paste with 2 eggs and 1 lb (450 g) of sugar. Work in a little vanilla and the grated zest of 2 tangerines. Roll into small fruit shapes, sugar the outsides, and bake at a low temperature for 20 minutes on a floured baking sheet.

[*Marzipan*—French: *massepain;* German: *Marzipan;* Italian: *marzapane;* Spanish: *mazapán*]

MASA. A Spanish word for dough, especially the hulled-corn dough used in Mexico for making tortillas, tamales, and enchiladas. A modern dried version is sold in America as *masa harina,* instant masa, tortilla, or tamale flour. It is made by first simmering corn in *limewater until the skin begins to flake off—for each 2¼ lb (1 Kg) of corn, use 3½ pt (2 lt) of water and about 2 oz (60 g) of slaked lime. The skins are rubbed off and what remains is washed white in fresh water. This is called *nixtamal,* which is pounded to a flour in a stone mortar (*metate*), slapped into a paste from which the tortillas are shaped, and baked on a terra-cotta griddle called a *comal.* Though *nixtamal* is not identical to *hominy, it makes a good substitute.

MASH. *See* black gram.

MASOOR or **masur.** *See* lentil.

MASTIC is a resin from various bushes of the genus *Pistacia* (to which the pistachio nut belongs). The best-known is the lentisk (*Pistacia lentiscus*), a straggly bush with red berries, one of the most common plants of dry Mediterranean hillsides. When slashed, it produces a clear, gummy substance, sticky like pure resin and with a strange aromatic smell. This, and the gum from other species, is used for flavoring some dishes in Greece and the islands of the eastern Mediterranean, in Turkish delight—*rahat lokum*—

and for the Greek liqueur *mastika*.

[*Mastic*—French: *mastic*; German: *Mastix*; Italian: *mastice, lentischio*; Spanish: *almáciga, mastice, lentisco*]

MATÉ, Paraguay tea, yerba maté, or yerba. Maté is, after tea and coffee, the most important hot, stimulating drink, with the possible exception of cocoa. Although not much used in other parts of the world, it is the most common drink over much of South America, having been adopted by the colonists from the Indians who used it in pre-Columbian times. The plant is a species of holly (*Ilex paraguayensis*), and other species (*I. gongonha* and *I. theezans*) are also used in parts of South America for the same purpose. People have even used the leaves of holly (*I. aquifolium*) in Europe during wartime, and roasted the berries, which are emetic when raw, for coffee.

Maté leaves are oval or lance-shaped, with rather toothed edges. The branches are first dried over a fire. The leaves are then beaten off with sticks, dried in ovens, and finally powdered. Maté makes a greenish-colored tea, slightly bitter and refreshing, when boiling water is poured over it. (There are darker double-baked versions for export.)

Methods of making and serving vary, but the traditional vessel is a gourd (the *maté*), which is passed around, and the tea is sucked through a hollow tube, or *bombilla*, which has a perforated bulb at the end to act as a strainer and may be made of silver, brass, or straw, according to the wealth of the person. Maté is often drunk with lemon and sugar, sometimes with burnt sugar. Although it is a universal drink in South America, it is not popular in North America and is hardly known in Europe, although some drink it in the mistaken belief that it is caffeine or theine free, which it is not. Maté is a stimulant, but has less tannin than tea.

MATJES. *See* herring.

MATSUTAKE. *See* mushrooms.

MATZO. A thin, unleavened Jewish bread made of flour and water only. Although used by Orthodox Jews, especially during Passover, it has become popular as a cracker. It is also available ground as the matzo meal of Jewish cooking. This meal comes in two degrees of fineness: medium, which has about the consistency of burghul and is used, for example, for breading foods to be fried and in matzo balls (*knaidlach*); and fine, which is called for in potato dishes, to bind gefüllte fish, and in Passover cakes. It can also be used to thicken soups, as it sometimes is in southern Spain.

MAYONNAISE is an emulsion of oil and vinegar stabilized with egg yolk. There are many theories about the origin of its name: (1) It originated in Mahon (in Minorca and in sailing days regarded as the finest port in the Mediterranean) or may have been given the name by the Duc de Richelieu after he defeated the British there in 1756. (2) It was named after Napoleon's Irish general MacMahon by the General's chef. (3) It was derived from the French *magnonaise* (*manier*, to stir). (4) It came from the old French *moyeu* (yolk). (5) It was named after the town of Bayonne in the Basses-Pyrenees— i.e., it was originally *bayonnaise*.

Whatever the origin of the French name, it is not likely that the sauce itself was created suddenly by an 18th-century chef, and if you see crowds of Catalans making *ali-oli* at a communal picnic (using the special glazed earthenware or china mortars they have for the purpose), you get the feeling that mayonnaise was invented south of the Pyrenees and worked northward into France. Some old people in Spain say that *ali-oli* is correctly made with oil and garlic alone, without any egg yolk at all, and although it is rather difficult to make an emulsion hold without the egg, *ali-oli* means "garlic and oil," as also does *aïoli*. It seems most likely that mayonnaise was invented by peasants near the Mediterranean where the olive grows.

For some reason, mayonnaise has a reputation for being difficult to make. I remember asking a young chef, who was on his way to work at La Réserve, the famous restaurant at Beaulieu-sur-Mer on the Côte d'Azur, what job a beginner was given and was surprised when he said, "Making the mayonnaise." When I asked, "Isn't that supposed to be difficult?" he answered, "Yes, but it's easy when you start with 20 egg yolks." He had put his finger on the point. With 20 yolks, a beginner could afford to be careless in adding and working in the first few drops of oil, but with one or two yolks one cannot. (I do not know why it is that once the mayonnaise emulsion is started one can afford to be progressively generous with the additions of oil, but it is so.) Mayonnaise may also be difficult to make in very cold winter weather, and certainly neither eggs nor oil should have come straight out of the refrigerator. They should preferably both be at room temperature. A little vinegar or lemon juice should also be added to acidify the yolks before any oil is added. Powdered mustard contains an emulsifying agent and is also a help, though not everyone approves of its use. There are many opinions as to the type of oil and the type of souring agent that should be used in mayonnaise—lemon juice, vinegar, and so on. Some oils emulsify more easily than others, but poor olive oil and corn oil give an unpleasant taste.

An old lady in Majorca, known to my family as "Madame at the shop," showed me how to make mayonnaise in the local way. It involved beating with a rotary whisk until I dropped. This makes a fluffy mayonnaise. Those who use mayonnaise regularly become opinionated and with practice become so adept that ... well, I used to make mayonnaise in 60 seconds with a perforated plunger in a cylinder. The oil floated on top and it required a delicate hand to mix in the first few drops, but when the mayonnaise began to thicken—one could feel it—the stroke could be increased. However, if anyone spoke while I was making it, the mayonnaise would curdle, so now I use an electric gadget which is foolproof but takes more washing up. To make aïoli quickly, first liquidize the garlic with oil in the blender. Since (with practice) making mayonnaise is so easy, it horrifies me that many families prefer the sort bought in jars from the supermarket. The chefs employed by the manufacturers are experts at the art of flavoring, and add essential oils—such as rue—in minute and unrecognizable amounts to beguile the palate. Other permitted additives include spices, sugar, milk and milk products, mustard, edible gums, and edible starch. The creaminess of commercial products may be obtained at home by beating a teaspoon of water into each ½ pint (300 ml) of mayonnaise.

MEADOW MUSHROOM or **field mushroom** (*Agaricus campestris*). This mushroom is so similar in appearance to the commercial cultivated mushroom (*A. bisporus*)

MEADOW MUSHROOM

that they were once thought to be the same species. Meadow mushrooms are abundant on lawns and meadows—never in woods—in spring and fall or during periods of cool moist weather. The cap, which may be button size up to several inches across, is at first convex with gills enclosed, then flattened with gills gradually exposed as it enlarges.

Meadow mushrooms are sometimes called "pink bottoms" because the gills are a clear pink before they turn brown from the maturing spores. They should not be gathered, especially in the button stage, by people who cannot easily distinguish them from the poisonous *Amanita* species (*see* mushrooms).

Meadow mushrooms, which have more flavor than the commercial *Agaricus,* can be used in any way you would the ones you buy at the store.

MEAT is not an essential part of the human diet; the Japanese used to get along very well on fish. But for human beings, complete vegetarianism, in the sense of eating no animal product at all, is risky. A diet without even milk or eggs results in a likelihood of vitamin B_{12} deficiency and consequently of anemia or of nervous disorders. Especially in the rich countries of the West, far more meat is eaten than is necessary for health, because once people have acquired the meat habit, they find a diet containing little meat rather boring.

The ox and the ass were the first animals to be domesticated, but not for food; they were the beasts of burden for ancient Middle Eastern civilizations. Sheep and goats provided the milk and clothing, and were sometimes eaten, although usually in connection with a sacrifice or festival. Day-to-day meat consisted of game, when it could be hunted. Later, the horse came down into the Mediterranean from Central Asia, and it was after this that the camel was domesticated. These animals were for the work of plowing, pulling carts and carrying loads, and for riding—during several periods it was a serious matter, punishable even by death, to kill an ox or a horse for food.

Meat now effectively means the flesh of cows, sheep, and pigs, while camels, reindeer, horses, goats, and even llamas are local foods; other animals are categorized as game, even if they are kept by man and no longer wild.

To begin with, methods of butchering were no doubt primitive. I am not talking about cutting the animal's throat with a prayer, but about chopping it into joints. Even 25 years ago, village butchers in Spain more or less hacked sheep to pieces with an ax. It paid to reach the market early, because the butcher sold all the lumps, whether bone or meat, at the same price. Rather more knowledge was displayed in cutting up pigs at the autumn slaughter, when the hams, sausages, and bacon were prepared for winter. There were professional pork butchers in ancient Rome, using equipment and cuts strikingly similar to modern ones. The way in which animals are cut up has evolved gradually, and is different in each country and even from area to area. And it is still constantly changing, because public demand does. Stock breeders produce smaller or leaner animals to satisfy fashion, but ultimately it falls on the butcher to market the meat in forms that suit his public. At the same time, he must cut with economy to make a living. With all the variations, simple translation from one language or country to another is impossible; cuts are rarely equivalent.

I suppose that many people have some idea of the cuts of meat in their own country; it is when they try to reproduce foreign dishes, as is the fashion now, that they are in trouble. If they happen to be within range of a butcher who caters to French or Italian clients, then there is no problem. Some of the great food stores employ butchers who can cut in the styles of several countries. But without such resources, cooks must turn to those puzzle pages where British, American and French cuts are compared. Here, the impression is given that butchers cut the carcass up in straight lines with a band-saw (as they do these days in freezer centers). These diagrams should not be taken too literally. They show only the general area from which the cuts are made and are more to make the names meaningful than to be taken as serious indications.

Butchery depends on anatomy, and the

cuts can be defined in anatomical terms. Travelers do best, I think, to forget what they did at home and to accept the local cuts at face value. Only a few dishes, such as *ossobuco,* owe their existence to a special cut and cannot be made with an approximation. While some parts of an animal are generally accepted to be better than others, a bad cut from a good animal is better than a good cut from a bad one. As for the quality of meat, whatever you may read, you finally have to rely on finding a good butcher. He alone knows the history of the animal. Butchers vary in the trouble they take to prepare the meat properly, and in the neatness with which they do it. (In France, bad butchers scarcely make a living.) Although it may cost a little more to buy meat in which the fascia and gristle have been carefully trimmed off, it is worth it.

The cook needs a good general concept of the anatomy of meat animals, and of the different types of tissue. You can get an idea of mammalian anatomy by looking in the bathroom mirror. The human and meat animal general plans are similar. The neck, the shoulder blades, and the ribs, which are attached to the back at one end and the breastbone at the other, are obvious. Below the ribs and down to the pelvic girdle is the loin (with the fillet lying underneath it), while in front is the belly, which is thin-walled and—in the bathroom mirror view—preferably not too obvious. Finally, there is the pelvic bone and the hips, with the legs (the hind legs of a meat animal) and the large muscles of the thigh and buttocks.

Meat, red meat or butcher's meat, is muscle. All red muscles have a fibrous structure, with the fibers running lengthwise. The more work the muscle has to do, the tougher and more fibrous it has to become. Muscles are often spindle-shaped, fatter in the middle and with the ends attached by tendons to the bones they move. These splay out into the ends of the muscles and are built into them to take the strain. Therefore, the middle of a muscle is usually the tenderest part.

In general, the muscles of the forepart of the animal are coarser and tougher than those of the hindpart. The tenderest muscle is the fillet, but it is not the one with the best flavor.

Muscles are enclosed in fascia, tough elastic bags or sheaths which hold them in shape and allow one muscle to move on another. Fascia, tendons and connective tissue form the gristle, which is rich in jellying substances but needs long cooking to make it tender. The cartilage, which lines the bone joints, and the fibrous bursas and capsules, which hold the joints together, are also full of jellying substances. So are the skin and hooves. Pork rind gives *zampone its lusciousness. Knuckles and feet are used for aspics and jellies. Bones contain marrow, a fatty and tasty soft substance, and are either hollow types, like the thigh bone, or are filled with spongy bone for strengthening purposes, like the pelvic girdle or hip bone. The glandular organs—liver, kidneys, sweetbreads, etc.—have no fibrous structure, but may be enclosed in tough, protective sacs and have mesenteries from which they hang in the body cavity and ducts or tubes of tough material which may have to be removed by dissection. Stomach (tripe) and intestines are glandular, muscular, and tough. They need long cooking. The heart, muscle tissue of a special sort, is tough, because hearts work hard; they contain valves which need cutting out. Lungs, which tend to disappear from sight in the U.S., are tough, elastic, and full of air; they need special cooking. Nerve tissue, like the brain and spinal cord, is soft, even when coagulated by strong heat that would toughen other tissues. Fat, which is deposited particularly around the internal organs (e.g., *suet), varies in quality from one part of the body to another and is much influenced by the animal's feeding.

Meat has two kinds of connective tissue—collagen, which is white, and elastin, which is yellow. Meat from old animals and muscles that have had hard exercise contain a lot of elastin, which is not softened by cooking but can be broken up only by bashing. But collagen can be changed to gelatin by the combined action of heat and water; the process is hastened by acids, which is why marinating is effective.

[*Meat*—French: *viande;* German: *Fleisch;* Italian: *carne;* Spanish: *carne*]

MEAT EXTENDERS. *See* textured plant protein.

MEDLAR. The medlar (*Mespilus germanica*), which originated in southern central Europe and the Caucasus, has the merit of being exceedingly hardy; it grows wild over much of Europe and has been introduced into North America. The wild trees are thorny, but the cultivated ones are usually not. Although they were doubtless useful when the only winter fruit was stored apples, medlars are now among the least popular fruit. Even when ripe, medlars look like young apples, with russet-brown skin and a large calyx surrounding a cup-shaped depression in which the five seed vessels can be seen, and they are so hard and astringent as to be inedible. They are picked from the end of October onward, when they are ripe, but must then be kept on straw until they are "bletted"—soft, brown, and acidly aromatic. Fermentation has taken place, and you could be forgiven for saying they were rotten. At this point, they are ready to eat. There are people who love them, and dons at the ancient universities are likely to enjoy eating them as they sip the college port. In Victorian times, it was usual to keep medlars in a silver dish of moist sawdust on the sideboard.

Many authors say that the medlar ripens in Italy and is eaten there as a fresh fruit, but they confuse the common medlar with the *loquat. In fact, medlars are grown in Italy and are found wild in much of southern Europe, but the fruits there are also allowed to rot until they are bletted. They are little-loved fruit in a country rich in fruit,

but they are liked in Piedmont, where they are called *puciu*. They are also unpopular in the U.S. However, they do make a delicious jelly.

[*Medlar*—French: *nèfle;* German: *Mispel;* Italian: *nespola;* Spanish: *níspola*]

MEGRIM. *See* lemon sole.

MELEGUETA PEPPER. *See* grains of paradise.

MELILOT. Leguminous plant, sometimes grown as a fodder crop. The melilots (*Melilotus*) have the strong aromatic smell of new-mown hay because they contain coumarin. The leaves of the common melilot (*M. officinalis*), which has yellow flowers, are sometimes used for stuffing, wrapping, or marinating rabbits to give them a sweet flavor. A paste of melilot is often an ingredient of sapsago cheese, made in Glarus, at the eastern end of Lake Zurich, where it is known as schabzieger. Melilots abound in Swiss pastures, but today the blue melilot (*M. coeruleus*), introduced from Turkey, is the one used to grind and mix with the curd. Sapsago cheese, which is hard and pale green, is grated and pounded with butter for spreading or used as a flavoring and sprinkled in soups and salads. The melilot gives it a taste that is unique.

[*Melilot*—French: *mélilot;* German: *Honigklee, Steinklee;* Italian: *meliloto;* Spanish: *mililoto, trébol dulce*]

MELOKHIA. *See* mallow.

MELON (*Cucumis melo*) and **watermelon** (*Citrullus vulgaris*) were grown by the ancients, and today they are important commercial fruits, vital in the summer in the hot, dry countries of the Mediterranean and the Middle East (where the best melons, if not the best watermelons, are grown). In more northern climates, both have to be grown in greenhouses. Melons are difficult fruit, because dozens of varieties and types span a wide range in quality, and to be really good, any melon must be exactly ripe, a difficult moment to judge.

Melon seeds, which are largely wasted, are very oily and contain some 35–40% of fats. They are dried and are eaten as snacks or are used in cooking in China, Greece, Central and South America, and in other places where people cannot afford waste. Watermelon seeds are highly valued by the tribes of Nigeria.

Cantaloupe melon. The real cantaloupe is usually rather small and rounded, and the name should be reserved for melons of a certain group grown in Europe, although it is loosely applied to muskmelons grown in the U. S. Many cantaloupe varieties have a heavily netted skin and broad ribs, which seem to show where the melon might be sliced into portions. The most famous variety is probably the French *charentais,* which is small, very highly scented, and orange-fleshed, as is the tiger melon. There are also smooth-skinned, greenish-yellow-fleshed cantaloupe hybrids, like the Ogen melon from Israel, and even ones with bright scarlet flesh. Cantaloupes are considered to be ready when gentle pressure at the stalk end shows some give. There will also be a fine scent. They need a day in the refrigerator to cool properly for eating. Good cantaloupes should not be gilded with ginger or pepper and, at most, benefit from a slight squeeze of lemon if they are not acid enough.

Casaba melon, generally larger than cantaloupes and muskmelons, is mainly green, which, in a muskmelon, would suggest unripeness. Casabas, with honeydew melons, are sometimes classed as winter melon because they have a long growing season, are ready at the end of summer, keep to some extent, and ripen a bit off the vine. They are ripe when there is a little give at the opposite end from the stem. The flesh is creamy or golden yellow, orange, green, or white, according to variety, and has little aroma but sweet flavor.

Honeydew melon. These, in general, are shaped like a football and have either a smooth skin or a very slight and irregular net on a tough, heavily wrinkled outside. They are often dusky green, but may be also white and yellow. The flesh is greenish white. Honeydew melons appear at the end of the season and are available well into winter because they store well and ripen in storage. Although not comparable to the cantaloupe, they are very good when properly ripe.

Muskmelon, netted melon, nutmeg melon, or **sweet melon.** It is recorded that the first melons in the Americas were planted by Columbus's men on March 29, 1494. Muskmelons are popular summer melons in the U. S., where they are often referred to as cantaloupes, but there are so many hybrids that the cook—and presumably also the gardener—is lost. However, these melons are usually covered with a creamy netting and have orange flesh. They may or may not be segmented very clearly. They are ripe when there is a slight give at the stem end. Persian melons are of the same type, but are larger and have a finer netting. Cranshaw melons are hybrids between the Persian and the casaba; they have no net.

Snap melon. In Asia, melons are often grown in the sand along riverbeds. Because pathogenic organisms can live inside melons, especially if they are injected with dirty water, melons often cost the traveler a bellyache. The snap melon or *phooti* (var. *momordica*) of India bursts open when ripe and is used unripe as a vegetable, as also is the long melon or *kakri.*

Watermelon belongs to a different genus of the cucumber family. It is thought to have originated in Africa, but since there is a Sanskrit name for it, the fruit must have been cultivated thousands of years ago in India. Today there are many varieties, differing in shape and size: some monstrous blimp-shaped ones are so heavy that only a strong man can lift them. Watermelons contain valuable minerals and trace elements.

The skin is smooth and glossy; it may be, for example, dark green with paler green stripes and blotches or pale green with dark-green netted marks. There is even a golden-skinned variety. Most watermelons have black seeds, but some have almost white ones, even when ripe, and there are seedless hybrids. Although the flesh is usually red to purplish, there are watermelons with creamy yellow flesh.

It is not easy to judge when a watermelon is ripe, and some experts say that cutting into it is the only sure way. Since the fruit is apt to be too large for the average household, and in particular for chilling in the refrigerator, watermelons are often sold in halves or slices, which enables you to judge ripeness and to avoid any with white streaks or core, immature seeds, or a granular, pale look in the middle. When buying a whole watermelon, look for one with a matt surface; it is usually better than a shiny one. Thumping it should produce a dull, muffled sound, not a hollow ring. The standard way to tell if a watermelon is ripe is to hold it near the ear and to press the ends together sharply. If it cracks, it is ripe. If it is too ripe, it will be soft and springy to the touch.

Watermelons are harvested when ripe—after picking, they never become sweeter, just softer—but they travel well because of their tough skin. They will keep uncut for at least a week in the refrigerator. Large ones may need to be kept in the cold for up to 24 hours before they are ready to eat. Watermelon experts like to separate large melons into core and outer part along the line of the seeds by cutting in just so far but not right through. Some people prefer the outer part and others the core, and these sections are offered separately at table. The white rind underlying the skin is often made into pickle. There are dozens of recipes in American cookbooks; special varieties of watermelon for pickle are grown (with all or nearly all white part), and they are sometimes eaten immature as a vegetable in the Orient.

Although the finest ripe melons need no embellishment, their cavities do make inviting containers for melon sherbet or fruits and berries. A hollowed-out watermelon half can be a bowl for a beautiful and refreshing summer salad of melon balls or cubes of different colors and flavors. They may be chilled in white wine or sprinkled with sugar.

[*Melon*—French: *melon, cantaloup;* German: *Melone, Beutelemone;* Italian: *mellone, popone;* Spanish: *Melón. Watermelon*—French: *pastèque;* German: *Wassermelone;* Italian: *cocomero;* Spanish: *sandia*]

MERSINE. Smoked *swordfish.

METAL. Common metals and alloys such as iron, copper, aluminum, brass, tin, lead, zinc, silver, and gold have sections to themselves. As pans, other utensils, and pipes, they can all come into contact with our food and drink. Metals themselves are not soluble in water, but their various salts often are and may be poisonous in any quantity. On the other hand, many metals are necessary for health as *trace elements, even when poisonous in larger quantities. Apart from this aspect, the conductivity of metals is of importance. Food cooks well in a copper pan because copper is an excellent conductor of heat, but that same quality makes it impossible to drink hot liquids from a copper mug without burning your mouth. Food does not cook well in stainless steel, which is a poor conductor of heat (unless the bottom of the pan is copper-coated), but you can drink with reasonable comfort from a stainless-steel mug.

[*Metal*—French: *métal;* German: *Metall;* Italian: *metallo;* Spanish: *metálico*]

METRIC SYSTEM. The metric system was first introduced into France at the end of the 18th century as one of the changes of the revolution, although comprehensive decimal systems of measurement had been devised by scientists over a century earlier. The basic unit is the meter, which is a ten-millionth part of the distance between the pole and the equator, measured along the meridian running through Paris. In practice, it is the length of a platinum bar kept near Paris. The unit of volume derived from this is the liter, which is the volume of a cube with 10-centimeter sides, i.e. 10 × 10 × 10 = 1000 cubic centimeters. The unit of weight is the gram, which was originally the weight of a cubic centimeter of pure water (at 4°C) but is now based on a standard Kilogram (1000 grams), which is also kept near Paris. *See* weights and measures, conversions.

Five hundred grams is known in France as a *livre* (pound). In the mind's eye, a gram can be pictured as 15 grains of wheat. Metric shoppers think in terms of a kilo or in hundreds of grams, sometimes in a half or a quarter of a kilo. Small items like spices would be bought in 25, 50, or 100 grams. Household scales do not measure accurately under 10 grams and rarely under 25 grams, so spoons are used. In nutrition, the daily requirements of minerals and vitamins are measured in milligrams. The mind's eye picture of 10 milligrams is a large grain of wheat.

MEXICAN TEA. *See* epazote.

MICROORGANISMS or **microbes.** Readers of old cookbooks should remember that it was not until about the middle of the last century that Louis Pasteur (1822–1895) recognized that fermentation, the souring of milk, putrefaction, and, of course, diseases were caused by tiny living organisms. Their effects are felt because of their vast numbers. It is a sobering thought that in 1 oz (28 g) of grubby hamburger, the number of microorganisms is greater than that of the entire human population of the world, and in warm weather this could double inside half an hour. Microbiology is now an advanced science—in the sphere of food, it is involved in the making of such products as bread, beer, wine, vinegar, cheese, butter, yogurt, sauerkraut, pickles, ham, sausages, anchovies, and soy sauce as well as in processes like canning, bottling, freezing, and drying. Since microorganisms are everywhere and cause food spoilage, it is useful to know something about them, even for those who only buy "convenience" foods in the supermarket.

Five important groups of microorganisms can affect food: *bacteria, *molds, *yeasts, *protozoa, and *viruses. Methods of preventing their activity are dealt with under preservation, pasteurization, sterilization, freezing, and drying.

All organisms require water or moisture, which is why drying is preservative. Bacteria and yeasts need more water than molds, which can often manage on a small quantity of condensation. Organisms cannot grab water from strong solutions of salt or sugar which are therefore preservative in effect. A 60–70% sugar solution effectively stops organisms from growing, and 25% of salt stops all but special, salt-loving organisms.

Some sorts of organisms, described as aerobic, need air to live. All molds are aerobic, which is why they grow only on the surface of jam and not at the bottom of the jar, although some can manage with very little air and are microaerobic (e.g., the blue molds in cheeses). Other organisms are anaerobic and refuse to grow except in the total absence of oxygen. In between, there are all sorts of intermediate preferences, and many organisms can grow equally well both with oxygen and without it. These can be important considerations. For instance, anaerobes can thrive in canned food. Sometimes oxygen may get used up by aerobic organisms and in the resulting conditions anaerobes can operate, as happens inside large, hard-rinded, maturing cheeses.

Some organisms are very sensitive to temperature and others less so, but they all have a temperature range within which they will grow, as well as an optimum. For convenience, they are divided into three categories:

1. Cold-loving (psychrophilic) organisms do not grow well in a warm kitchen but will grow when food passes through their favored range of temperature. They do not multiply in the freezer; their temperature range for

multiplication is: lowest, 12°F (−11°C); optimum, 50°F (10°C); highest, 86°F (30°C).

2. Medium-range (mesophilic) organisms grow best at normal summer's-day temperatures, more slowly in winter, and hardly at all in a refrigerator. The majority of organisms fall into this category, including the disease producers, which prefer the precise temperature of the human body, and the yeasts, which like it comfortably warm but not very hot or very cold. Temperature range: lowest, 32°F (0°C); optimum, 77–95°F (25–35°C); highest, 104–122°F (40–50°C).

3. Heat-loving (thermophilic) organisms are hot-weather microbes. In nature, they like hot springs, compost heaps, and the temperatures of blazing deserts. This group also includes the organisms responsible for *yogurt. Temperature range: lowest, 86°F (30°C); optimum, 122–149°F (50–65°C); highest, 158–176°F (70–80°C).

Most organisms are killed by boiling for 1 minute (but see pasteurization and sterilization). Naturally, the thermophilic organisms tend to withstand more heat than the others, but there are certain bacteria which can form resistant spores. One, perhaps the world's most common organism, is the hay bacillus (*Bacillus subtilis*), which has spores that can stand fast boiling for 3 hours. Those of the deadly botulism organism (*see* poisoning) can endure 6 hours. Spores have also been known to remain alive for as long as 10 years. They form when food starts to run out and waste products accumulate (i.e., in old cultures). They take about 24 hours to form, but are killed by boiling for 5 minutes during that vulnerable period. When conditions improve, the spores germinate much more quickly—usually in 5–6 hours.

On the other hand, the effect of extreme cold is merely to prevent the multiplication of organisms rather than to kill them. For instance, the typhoid germ can live up to a week in ice cream, and some organisms have been known to survive the shattering cold of liquid hydrogen at −421°F (−252°C). Deep-freezing does not sterilize food.

For many microorganisms, the *pH is critical. Yeasts prefer acid conditions (pH 3.0–6.0), and so do molds, although some can be found to thrive at almost anything from pH 1.0 to pH 11.0. On the other hand, most bacteria prefer more or less neutral conditions (pH 6.5–8.0), and very few (and certainly not the harmful ones) will grow or even survive for long in acidity below pH 4.0 (or in really alkaline conditions over pH 9.0). You can get an idea of what this means from the fact that lemon juice is about pH 2.3. Even sour milk, which is pH 4.4, is inimical to many bacteria.

However, the activity of acids in stopping bacteria from growing is not entirely dependent on the pH. Some acids are more toxic to microorganisms than others and, therefore, more preservative. If we gave sulfuric acid an effectiveness of 1, then the relative effectiveness of the other commonly used *preservatives would be as follows: tartaric acid, 3; hydrochloric acid, 6; sulfurous acid (sulfur dioxide in water), 9; citric acid, 13; formic acid, 16; benzoic acid, 21, and salicylic acid, 33. Chemicals which either stop microorganisms from multiplying or kill them are *disinfectants.

Ultraviolet light will kill microorganisms, although some are more susceptible than others. There is ultraviolet in sunlight, and ultraviolet lamps are sometimes installed in operating rooms, factories, and food stores. If they are switched on when the rooms are not being used, they serve to reduce the number of organisms in the air.

MICROWAVE OVEN. *See* baking.

MILK has been a source of food and drink since early herdsmen first learned to take milk from their animals. However, milk and milk products (such as butter and cheese) are less common in China (though butter is popular in Tibet), and they were quite unknown to the ancient civilizations of America. Milk today is normally cow's milk, but in ancient times there were no dairy cows, and oxen were beasts of burden. Milk mainly came from sheep, goats, asses, and horses. Camels were domesticated much later—their milk is purgative but is used by Bedouin tribes. (Pigs cannot be induced to give milk, although in the Middle Ages babies sometimes suckled sows.)

Milk, a complete diet for suckling mammals, is also excellent food for people (though some doubt that it is necessary for adults). It contains good-quality protein, digestible fat, and a sugar, as well as minerals and vitamins; composition varies enormously from species to species. The main constituent of milk is water (87% by weight), in which are dissolved lactose (milk sugar), an albumin, citrates and chlorides of sodium and potassium, and vitamins B_1, B_2, and C. Partly in solution and partly in suspension are phosphates of calcium and magnesium, while caseinogen, the chief protein, is in colloidal suspension. The minute fat droplets contain the fat-soluble vitamins A and D. The yellow color of the fat in summer milk in some breeds is caused by carotene, a precursor of vitamin A that comes from the grass and herbs the animal eats. The *pH value of fresh cow's milk lies between 6.5 and 6.8 (i.e., it is very slightly acid) but is most commonly about 6.6.

Milk is an ideal food for many bacteria. Many of them can convert the lactose into lactic acid, making the milk gradually go sour. Souring can first be detected by taste at around pH 6.2; milk that is slightly more sour may curdle when heated. You should note that it is particularly liable to do so when given a sudden heat shock, for example, by being poured into hot tea; when it is treated more gently (and the tea is gradually poured into the milk), it may not curdle. When milk curdles, the main protein, which has been held in colloidal suspension, is precipitated as casein. Heat encourages curdling, as also does salt. This explains why some soups and sauces need careful handling to avoid curdling, and why they may need stabilizers such as the starch used in white sauces. Milk may curdle either with or without setting to a clabber. Bacterial action, mild acids, and rennet will cause milk to clabber, but strong acidity and salts like alum will curdle milk without producing a clabber. Acid curdling takes place when the pH reaches about 4.8 but happens at higher pH values (i.e., lower acidities) when the milk is heated. Raw milk usually turns sour if it is kept at room temperature, but pasteurized milk and boiled milk, in which the acid-forming bacteria have been destroyed, usually develop a bitter taste and unpleasant flavors.

The composition of milk varies appreciably not just between species but between different breeds of the same species, between animals in the same breed, and even in each individual animal around the year. The figures given in the table are average ones.

Composition of Milks of Various Mammals

Average % of	Fat	Protein	Lactose	Minerals	Water
Cow	3.80	3.30	4.80	0.72	87.40
Zebu (Eastern Humped Cattle)	4.92	3.21	4.58	0.75	86.56
Water Buffalo	7.16	3.77	4.81	0.76	83.56
Goat	4.10	3.60	4.60	0.85	86.85
Sheep	6.70	5.80	4.60	0.82	82.08
Camel	4.50	3.50	4.90	0.70	86.40
Mare	1.00	2.00	6.70	0.30	90.00
Human	3.50	1.70	6.70	0.20	87.00

Several interesting points emerge from these figures. Cow's milk is richer in protein and contains less sugar than human milk; some adjustment is advisable when cow's milk is used to feed babies. Mare's milk is high in milk sugar; in Asia, it is fermented to make alcoholic drinks such as *kumiss. Buffalo's milk is very rich in fat and protein, and so makes splendid cheese and butter.

Pasteurized milk has been heated to 160°F (71°C) for 15 seconds and quickly cooled to 50°F (10°C). It keeps for several days in the refrigerator. Pasteurization, while killing harmful bacteria, also destroys vitamin C and thiamine. Pasteurized milk will not naturally sour and separate into curds and whey—it will only spoil.

In the U.S., rigid controls are placed on the sales of milk. The PMO (Grade A Pasteurized Milk Ordinance), a complicated set of recommendations, regulates milk production from the cow to the grocery shelf and affects all segments of the dairy industry (producers, processors, equipment manufacturers), regulatory officials at all levels of government, and educational and research associations. Proper pasteurization of milk is only one aspect of the PMO, but it is an important part, and as the family cow has once more become familiar in the U.S., the rigid chemical, bacteriological, and temperature standards of the PMO have run against the wishes of people to drink whole raw milk. Most states have certification programs for the retail sale of raw milk, although many health authorities do not advocate its consumption, and raw milk should ideally be purchased from certified or otherwise approved dairies.

Homogenized milk has been mechanically treated so that the cream no longer rises when the milk is left to stand. *See* homogenizing.

Ultrapasteurized or **long-life milk.** This is a relatively new method of sterilizing milk at a temperature midway between *pasteurization (which does not produce sterility) and conventional sterilization by autoclave. By definition, it involves thermal processing at or above 280°F (130°C) for at least 2 seconds before packaging. The treatment kills all organisms without greatly altering the taste, but it does not inactivate all the enzymes the microorganisms have produced. Thus, although ultrapasteurized milk will keep without souring for up to 6 months even at ordinary room temperature (providing it has been bottled or packaged in perfectly aseptic conditions), it will eventually gel because of the enzymes.

Ultrapasteurized milk is useful in countries with an inadequate dairy industry—such as those in the Middle East—or where there is an overwhelming tourist influx at certain seasons. It is more expensive than pasteurized milk and so, for ordinary purposes, has not yet replaced it. However, in some countries it is increasingly to be seen in small shops, which can thus avoid the problems of dealing with fresh, perishable milk. In the U.S., ultrapasteurization is seldom applied to milk, partly because milk is so plentiful and partly because ultrapasteurized milk has a cooked flavor. Ultrapasteurized cream, however, is becoming familiar. Although it has a longer shelf life and its nutritive values are not significantly changed, its whipping properties are reduced and some people think its flavor is diminished.

Sterilized milk is about as dead as milk can be. It is homogenized and sterilized in bottles at 226–239°F (108–115°C) for 20–30 minutes. Sterilized milk requires no refrigeration. Although it is marketed extensively in Europe and may be the only fluid milk product available to some consumers in countries where refrigeration is uncommon, it has very poor flavor and its nutritive value has been decreased.

Low-fat milk contains 0.5–2% milkfat and usually has vitamin A added. A check of the label in the U.S. will reveal what else has been added—milk-derived ingredients are often added to increase viscosity, opacity, and palatability.

*Skim milk** has had practically all the fat removed by separation.

Low-sodium milk. Whole milk generally contains about 49 mg of sodium per 100 g. By ion exchange, sodium can be reduced to about 2.5 mg per 100 g. The sodium is replaced with potassium, making milk more acceptable for people on sodium-restricted diets.

Dried milk, powdered milk, or **dehydrated milk.** Spray-dried milk is made by spraying whole or skim milk into a large chamber of hot dry air; the powder which is formed falls to the bottom of the chamber. It is almost 100% soluble in water. Roller-dried milk is made by putting a film of concentrated milk on a heated steel roller and scraping it off when it has dried. Reconstituted rolled-dried milk contains small insoluble particles, which fall to the bottom. Milk powder, whether whole or skimmed, contains about 4% moisture. Because of changes which take place on heating and exposure to the air, it is nutritionally slightly inferior to fresh milk. The fat—26% in full-cream powdered milk—becomes partly oxidized in drying: this produces the characteristic, not very nice, flavor of dried milk. Skim-milk powder, with very little fat (about 1%), tastes better. At a pinch, melted butter, even oil or margarine, can be emulsified in a blender with water and skim-milk powder, and the result is better flavored than that of reconstituted whole-milk powder. Most nonfat dry milk is fortified with vitamins A and D.

Frozen milk. If milk is frozen slowly, it will keep but does not return to normal when thawed, because of protein destabilization and the settling of some milk solids. It should be used only for cooking. If milk is held just above freezing, its life is lengthened, but after a week it can begin to putrefy without souring, and poisons can accumulate, making it dangerous.

Milk products include *cream, *crème fraîche, *evaporated milk, *condensed milk, *buttermilk, *yogurt, and *sour-milk products.

Milk substitutes are the filled milks and nondairy creamers which are made with skim-milk solids, fats or oils (such as lard or hydrogenated vegetable oils), emulsifiers, and antioxidants. Those made with vegetable oils may have a higher unsaturated fatty acid content than ordinary milk and no cholesterol. Imitation fluid milks do not contain dairy products per se, but they may contain derivatives of milk, such as casein, whey, and lactose; in general, they are nutritionally inferior to milk.

Vegetable milk can be the milky sap of plants such as that of *Galactodendron,* which is used in Colombia as a drink and in cooking, or it can be an emulsion made with oil-rich nuts, such as milk of almonds or the coconut milk and cream which are used in Indian cooking. It can also be made from soybeans—soy milk.

[*Milk*—French: *lait;* German: *Milch;* Italian: *latte;* Spanish: *leche*]

MILK SUGAR. *See* lactose.

MILKWEED (*Asclepias syriaca*). One of the most versatile of wild plants, milkweed can be eaten at almost every stage of growth. It grows in fields and along roadsides and gets its name from the milky fluid it exudes from its fat stems when the plant is broken. Most people know it for its exploding pods, practically the only part of the plant that is not edible. The young shoots (which resemble asparagus), the leaves (cooked like greens), the fragrant pink flowers (similar to broccoli before they open), and the tender green seed pods (with a texture like okra) can all be cooked as palatable free food. Unfortunately, milkweed requires boiling in several changes of water to remove its bitterness, and this results in loss of nutrients and a somewhat bland flavor, but milkweed dressed with garlic butter, sour cream, or vinaigrette can be a most pleasant vegetable.

MILLE FIORE. *See* liqueurs and cordials.

MILLET and **sorghum.** Various grasses, with small edible grains, are known as millets, a word derived from the Latin *milium,* the common millet grown by the Romans. Millets vary greatly in the quality of their grain, and none is as good as wheat, but they are grown because they produce a crop, often a good crop, even in the poorest soils, both waterlogged and in drought. Some, like the bullrush millet, make it just possible for people to exist in areas of extreme aridity and heat.

Most people in Britain see millet only as bird seed—sometimes the whole ears are hung up in cages. The seeds will often sprout and grow on waste dumps—and even ripen in a good year. In the U.S., millets are grown extensively as animal feed, and the sweet variety is used for sorghum syrup. Otherwise, millets are foods of the world's poor—they are rough, but healthful. The common millet contains about 10–13% protein and about 4% oil, although millets are considered as carbohydrate cereals. Millets are quite commonly fermented and made into beers, both the crude "native beers" and more sophisticated brews in which the grain is malted. Millets do not make gourmet foods; they are mostly ground and boiled into porridges or made into unleavened bread. Recipes for other millet dishes are few, but one for *ragi* (finger millet) *dosas* is offered as an example.

RAGI DOSAS

Dosas might be described as South Indian pancakes, usually made of a fermented batter of soaked and pounded black *dal and rice (though modern shortcuts use rice flour). *Dosas* are often rolled and stuffed with vegetable curry as a breakfast dish. *Ragi dosas* are not very good to look at but are still delicious.

Take 2½ cups of ground finger millet, add a teaspoon of salt, and mix with water into a stiff paste. Soak 7½ tablespoons of black gram *dal* for an hour, then put it in the blender and grind it to a thin, frothy paste. Mix the two pastes together into a batter of thick pouring consistency. Cook by putting a large spoonful onto a hot iron griddle which has been smeared with a little oil and spreading it quickly into a thin, round plate-sized pancake with the back of a spoon. When the underside is golden brown, turn it over and cook the other side rather more lightly. Put a spoon of curried meat or vegetable filling on it and roll it up, or eat it with butter and honey (and some fresh coriander–green chili chutney for perfection).

Barnyard millet or **bharti** (*Echinochloa crusgalli*), a naturalized weed in the U.S. and Britain, is grown as a crop in the Orient, but mainly for fodder. The Japanese millet or *sanwa* (*E. frumentacea*) and the smaller *shama* millet (*E. colona*) are eaten as a porridge or with rice.

Bullrush millet, bajra, cattail, or **reedmace** (*Pennisetum typhoideum*) is a tropical millet that is important in India, Nigeria, and the Sudan; it grows quickly and stands drought. Under the name of *bajra*, it is one of the most important Indian millets (although it is native to Africa) and is used to make flour and unleavened bread.

Common millet, broom-corn proso, Indian millet, or **hog millet** (*Panicum miliaceum*) is a temperate millet. It is grown in Russia, China, Japan, North America, and southern Europe. In the U.S. and southern Europe, it is rarely used today as human food—for long it has been grown only for chickens and other livestock—but its use as human food is prehistoric, and it makes good unleavened bread. The grain of common millet is oval and varies from white to straw-colored, red, or brown. It is often used as a bird seed.

Finger millet or **ragi** (*Eleusine coracana*) is of Indian origin. Although it grows in many forms, it gets its name from a common type in which the head looks like five stubby, outwardly curved fingers. It is a staple in India, not only because it can grow in poor soils but also because it gives a heavy yield and the grain stores particularly well. In Africa, it is grown from Rhodesia to the Sudan. Coarse when compared to wheat, it has a good taste and is made into breads and other cereal preparations. It is also fermented into beers and is even malted.

Foxtail millet, German millet, Hungarian millet, Italian millet, or **Siberian millet** (*Setaria italica*) is a warm-temperate millet that came originally from the Orient. It was used in China in 2700 B.C., and also by the Lake Dwellers in prehistoric Europe. It is still reaped in Russia to a considerable extent for beer. The grain may be white, yellow, red, brown, or even black. It is grown in southern Europe and the U.S. for chicken food and fodder. It can be used boiled or parched as human food but is not particularly tasty.

Hungry rice (*Digitaria exilis*) is a grain that is locally important in dry West Africa.

Job's tears (*Coix lachryma-jobi*) is not really a millet, since the seeds are large. A tropical and subtropical crop, native to India, it can also be found growing in the U.S. and southern Europe as an ornamental plant. The pearly fruits are used for necklaces, and it is claimed that the seeds contain more protein than any other cereal. This is eaten mostly in Southeast Asia and the Philippines (where it is called *adley*). It is sometimes used medicinally, as well as for sustenance.

Little millet (*Panicum miliare*) is like the common millet but smaller. It gives a moderate yield on very poor soils. In India, it is known as the poor-man's crop (which there means *really* poor).

Sorghum (*Sorghum vulgare*) is often a tropical crop, and in India and Africa is a staple for the poor. Varieties differ considerably and may be grouped into categories based on their uses as well as on their characteristics.

Sweet sorghum or sugar sorghum (var. *saccharatum*) has a stem rich in sugars and is crushed to obtain the juice, which is boiled down and evaporated in shallow pans to make sorghum syrup (which is a thinner and sourer equivalent of molasses). Millions of gallons of this are used in cooking in the U.S. every year, but elsewhere sorghum syrup is less known.

Durra or great millet is called *jowar* in India. It is a staple food for millions around the world and is one of the world's most vital crops. There are two main types: white-grained sorghum, which is favored for bread, and red-grained, which is bitter and mainly used for brewing beer. In India, *jowar* is ground daily in most poor homes; used to make flat unleavened bread, it is not as refined as the chapaties or *rotis* made from wheat flour (*atta*), but it makes a satisfying meal. This, not wheat or rice, is the main food in the dry areas of the subcontinent.

Kaffir corn (var. *caffrorum*) and milo (var. *subglabrescens*) are of African origin and are essentially the same from the gastronomic, if not the cultivator's, point of view, as is the Chinese kaoliang.

Teff (*Eragrostis abyssinica*) is the most widely grown cereal in Ethiopia. It is ground to form the basis of the fermented flat bread called *injura*, which is eaten with the hot currylike stew called *wot*. *Injura* is full of bubbles and has the texture of tripe. The taste is sour. It is rather nice, once you are used to it.

[*Millet*—French: *millet*; German: *Hirse*; Italian: *miglio*; Spanish: *mijo*]

MILLING is reducing to a powder or paste. The most primitive method is pounding, and since such creatures as different as otters and vultures have learned to use stones as tools, it is probable that man learned to pound grain even before he could grow it. Today, in the more basic tropical countries, you can still see grain being pounded in large mortars hollowed out of stones or tree trunks. Primitive grinding with stones, the precursor of milling, is done daily by countless Indians when they grind their fresh curry spices with a roller on a stone slab.

A more sophisticated grinder is the quern, which is typically constructed of two round stones, the top one revolving on a peg set in the lower. The peg must be shaped to allow grain to fall around it down between the stones. The top stone is rotated by hand. Portable querns are still used today—for instance, by the nomadic tribes in Baluchistan—and were common everywhere in the past (there were even special mini-querns for mustard).

It is only a step from the hand quern to some sort of mechanization. The simplest powered mills are still to be seen in remote mountain regions, such as the Himalayas (where people have even harnessed water power to say their prayers for them). Almost every village has at least one diminutive water mill housed in a stone hut that is little bigger than a dog kennel and is built across a side stream of the river. The stones are 3¼ feet (less than 1 meter) across; the bottom one is driven, without any gears, by an arrangement of inclined wooden paddles. More complicated and bigger arrangements, such as those found in windmills or the old water-powered grist mills, require gears, which usually turn the top stone.

The stones used in old-fashioned mills had to be abrasive, long-wearing, and sharp. Various types of rock were used; some were highly prized, such as buhrstones, which were finely pitted quartzite stones. These were even shipped to the U.S. from France. Stones were dressed so that the ridges in them both ground the flour and moved it outward from the center. Heat is generated by the friction of grinding, but skilled millers managed to keep the flour from getting too hot.

Progress in milling was aimed mainly toward obtaining a whiter, finer flour. Special bolting cloth was woven for fine sifting, but that only separated the large particles from the small. However, a machine called a purifier, invented in the early years of the 19th century, enabled particles of the same size but different weights to be separated, as was possible by winnowing; it depended, like winnowing, on currents of air. It allowed a greater proportion of the husk (bran) to be taken out of flour in large-scale milling.

Another radical development was roller milling, which was widely adopted in the latter years of the 19th century and is still in use today. Passing the wheat between fluted rollers revolving at slightly different speeds and with diminishing clearance literally scrapes the white starchy inside of the grain (the endosperm) off the skin, leaving the flakes of almost pure bran, which can then be removed by sifting. The particles of endosperm are then reduced in size by smooth reduction rollers. This process, perfected over the years, enables the modern miller to separate endosperm, bran, and germ fairly

completely. The white flours that result are preferred by the public. They undoubtedly make better cakes and fine white bread, but there is increasing evidence that a long-term shortage of bran in the diet may contribute to some diseases that are prevalent in modern societies.

Milling or grinding at home can be easily done in a hand mill, and several types are on the market. Mills that grind between two cutters or grooved plates will easily reduce even hard seeds, such as corn or chickpeas, to a flour (though it is hard work and there are now electric grain mills on the market for domestic use). Flour will have to be sifted and the coarser particles returned to the mill for further grinding.

A whirling-blade electric coffee grinder can deal only with small quantities of grain but is useful for spices, although the hardest seeds and spices (such as turmeric and ginger) need to be cracked first by hammering.

[*Milling*—French: *moudre;* German: *mahlen;* Italian: *macinare;* Spanish: *moler*]

MILT. Male *roe.

MINT. Mints (species of *Mentha*) are among the most important culinary herbs. They are mostly native to the temperate regions of the Old World, and the ease with

MINT

which the 25 or so species cross, even in the wild, has resulted in a baffling range of hybrids. Peppermint (*M.* ✕ *piperita*) is not a separate species but a hybrid between water mint (*M. aquatica*) and spearmint (*M. spicata*). Mints produce a wide range of flavors—some, like eau-de-cologne mint (*M. citrata*), have very scented overtones. Spearmint is the type that is normally cultivated for use in cooking, but cooks must decide for themselves what mint they prefer and will doubtless be influenced by the choice available locally or easily grown in their garden. The juicy leaves of apple mint (*M. rotundifolia*) are ideal for mint sauce, which was used by the Romans and is delicious when properly made. Mint is a common flavoring in Mideastern cooking. Fresh mint *chutney is a very Indian taste that is worth trying. Peppermint is rarely used as an herb in cooking, but its oil is important in confectionery. Another species of the genus is *pennyroyal.

[*Mint*—French: *menthe;* German: *Minze;* Italian: *menta;* Spanish: *hierbabuena, menta*]

MIRABELLE. *See* fruit brandy.

MIRIN. *See* sake.

MISO. *See* soybean.

MOCHA. Variety of *coffee.

MOLASSES is the liquid residue in sugar-making which is separated from the crystals of crude brown sugar. It is usually made from sugar cane, though sugar beets and sweet potatoes will also yield molasses. Molasses, added to foods instead of sugar and used like syrup or jam, was the principal sweetener in 18th-century America. With improvements in sugar refining and an abundant supply of sugar cane the popularity of molasses declined, and today it is rarely homemade. In factories, the sugar cane is crushed, and the juice is concentrated, usually by boiling. The natural sugar crystallizes and the molasses is drawn off. The finest grade of molasses for table use is from the first boiling, in which only part of the sugar is removed. Second-boil molasses is darker and less sweet; much of it is used in baking and in candymaking. Blackstrap molasses comes from the third boiling; most of it goes for the manufacture of alcohol and cattle feed, but it is used at the table and in cooking by people who like its rich, pungent flavor. A tablespoon of blackstrap provides about a third of the daily minimum adult requirement of iron.

Molasses, less sweet than honey, is used in gingerbread, Boston baked beans, Indian pudding, shoo-fly pie, and fruit cakes. In baking, bicarbonate of soda neutralizes the acid in molasses, providing a leavening gas in an action similar to that of baking soda with buttermilk. *See also* treacle.

MOLDS are small fungi which can just be seen as downy, cottony, or powdery plants, growing on stale bread, jam, and rotten fruit. There are thousands of different kinds. Molds reproduce and spread by means of minute spores which blow everywhere in the air. Some species of mold will attack almost anything, even glass and chemicals.

Molds need air to varying degrees. Some, like *Penicillium camembertii*, which grows on the rind of Camembert and other similar *cheeses, need a lot. Others, like *P. roquefortii*, which makes blue veins inside cheese, can manage with little air.

Molds also require moisture. The spores need it to germinate, and the threads to grow. However, they do not need as much moisture as most other organisms and can often manage on what is condensed on surfaces from damp air. Although molds will not grow on jams that contain plenty of sugar, the dilution at the surface produced by condensation may be enough to let them get hold. That is why dry, airy places are always advocated for storage.

Usually molds prefer somewhat acid conditions (pH 3 to 6), but some are able to stand extremes (anything from pH 1 to pH 11), so pickles may be attacked on occasion.

Molds also like warm but not hot surroundings and are slowed down by cold. Although poisonous molds do exist, most merely spoil food with musty or bitter tastes. They are rarely harmful in any quantity that is likely to be eaten. An exception is the parasitic mold *Claviceps purpurea*, which affects cereals, especially rye. The black ears attacked by this parasite, which is called ergot, are virulently poisonous, causing delirium and often death. The illness was common in the Middle Ages; although it is rare today, its existence should be noted by grow-it-yourself survival enthusiasts.

[*Mold*—French: *moisissure;* German: *Schimmel;* Italian: *muffa;* Spanish: *moho*]

MOLLUSKS include gastropods (such as slugs and *snails, *limpets, and *abalone), bivalves (such as *mussels, *clams, *oysters, and *cockles), and cephalopods (*octopuses, *cuttlefish, and *squids). The word comes from the Latin *mollis* (soft) or *molluscus* (softish), perhaps.

[*Mollusk*—French: *molusque;* German: *Molluske, Weichtier;* Italian: *mollusco;* Spanish: *molusco*]

MOLOKHIA. *See* mallow.

MONKFISH. *See* shark.

MONOSACCHARIDES. *See* sugars.

MONOSODIUM GLUTAMATE, MSG, taste powder, p'sst, or **ve-tsin.** This is the sodium salt of glutamic acid, one of the amino acids, and can be bought as a white, crystalline substance. It occurs naturally in soy sauce and can be made from wheat (as it was originally) or, as now, from glutamic acid recovered from sugar beet molasses or by bacterial fermentation of solutions of glucose and simple nitrogen compounds. Although MSG has very little taste of its own, it has the property of bringing out the natural flavor of other ingredients, particularly of meat but also of vegetables and mush-

rooms. It is not, as commonly believed, a preservative or tenderizer. MSG is commonly used in commercial products, canned goods, and bouillon cubes and in Chinese and Japanese cooking. If it is used in a food in the U.S., it must be listed on the product label.

In some people monosodium glutamate can cause the so-called Chinese restaurant syndrome, which is accompanied by a temporary burning sensation in the neck and forearms, tightness in the chest, and headaches. One puzzle about the additive is why the Chinese do not seem to be sensitive to it. The U.S. Food and Drug Administration is continuing its investigation of MSG, and in 1969 U.S. baby food manufacturers discontinued its use in their products because of safety concerns.

[*Monosodium glutamate*—French: *glutamate de soude;* German: *Mononstriumglutamat;* Italian: *glutiminato di soda;* Spanish: *glutamato de sodio*]

MONSTERA, ceriman, or **Mexican breadfruit** (*Monstera deliciosa*) has a fruit that looks like an elongated green pine cone. The plant, a favorite of the indoor horticulturist, has natural slashes in the leaves; it is an epiphyte from tropical America which belongs to the Arum lily family. It is ripe when the cone begins to break up; you can then take off the outer segments with the green surface attached. Inside are white, creamy segments reminiscent of a custard apple, with black flakes and a central core. The flavor is acid-sweet and refreshing, vaguely like a pineapple. It is liable to make the mouth sore, especially if it is not quite ripe.

MONTILLA. *See* sherry.

MORAY EEL (*Muraena helena*) is a sinister-looking creature that is common in warm seas but rare farther north. Morays used to be plentiful in the Mediterranean until pollution took charge. Their heads, teeth bared, were a familiar sight to skin divers who probed under rocks. The moray is brown or purple-brown, mottled with yellow spots, up to 5 ft (150 cm) long and exceedingly aggressive. Its bite, though not venomous, is very painful. It is said that the moray can also live in fresh water—though it prefers the sea. The taste of the moray is excellent—it reminds me of sole—but it is full of bones. There is supposed to be a local way of removing the bones by rubbing the fish with ashes and pulling it through a noose, but I have never found anyone who can demonstrate this. Moray eel is excellent cut in pieces and used with other fish as the basis for fish soup.

MOREL. This fungus, of which the most usual species in the kitchen are *Morchella esculenta* and *M. vulgaris,* does not have the parasol shape of most mushrooms. Its cone-

MOREL

shaped cap is covered with a honeycomb of pits which give a spongelike appearance. Unlike most edible fungi, morels appear in the spring, from April to May, in orchards, open woods, and pastures. (They should not be confused with the toxic false morel, which has a convoluted rather than a pitted cap.)

Morels are usually sliced lengthwise, then washed in salted water to remove earth and insects. Some fungus books suggest that they should be blanched in boiling water before being prepared for the table or incorporated in sauces, but this is not necessary. They can be simply sautéed, served with a cream sauce, stuffed, or pickled. Morels are excellent in *coq au vin* and other poultry dishes.

If you cannot get them fresh—morels are so prized that people will do anything to keep their source secret—they can be bought dried or canned. (*See* mushrooms.)

[Morel—French: *morille;* German: *Morchel;* Italian: *morchella;* Spanish: *colmenilla*]

MORELLO. *See* cherry.

MORTADELLA is a large, often balloon-shaped sausage that originated in Bologna, which still produces the best examples, although mortadella is now also made in other towns and other countries. It is a finely textured sausage, usually containing large flecks of fat, and has been cooked by steaming so that it is ready to eat cold and finely sliced. The best mortadella is made with pure pork, but the possible ingredients listed by Elizabeth David in *Italian Food* (Knopf, 1958) for cheap mortadella include not just soy flour but also donkey meat. Mortadella is used in cooking in the stuffing for some sorts of pasta and in the croquettes called *supplì* together with mozzarella cheese.

MOTH BEAN or **mat bean** (*Phaseolus aconitifolius*) grows wild in India and has been taken into cultivation fairly recently.

It is useful because it is exceedingly drought-resistant and so will grow where other pulses will not, even in the desert regions of Rajastan. It is used whole or as a split *dal,* but is of small importance outside its locality. The seeds are green or black.

MOUNTAIN ASH. *See* rowan.

MOWRA BUTTER. *See* fats.

MSG. *See* monosodium glutamate.

MULBERRY (species of *Morus*). The black mulberry (*M. nigra*) is common in Europe. Its fruit has been grown since ancient times, and it was probably introduced from western Asia. The tree has clusters of small flowers which together form one multiple fruit (unlike the blackberry, which is formed from a single flower). The red mulberry (*M. rubra*) is similar to *M. nigra* and native to the eastern U.S. In Asia, the leaves of the white mulberry or silk mulberry (*M. alba*) are used as the food of the silkworm. This mulberry was imported to the U.S. in an attempt to found a silk industry, and it now grows wild over much of the country.

Mulberries should not be picked until they are completely ripe; they are then very perishable and very juicy and will stain everything in sight. They can be eaten raw or made into pies, jelly, beverages, puddings, or sherbet. In parts of Afghanistan, dried mulberries, often mixed with ground almonds, are a staple food.

[*Mulberry*—French: *mure;* German: *Maulbeere;* Italian: *mora;* Spanish: *mora*]

MULLET. The two sorts of mullet, gray and red, belong to quite different groups of fish. Both are important as food.

Gray mullet. There are about a hundred species of gray mullet (family Mugilidae), mainly in the warm seas. They are long, slender fish, usually in some shade of silver

STRIPED MULLET

or gray and with large scales, but occasionally they are brightly colored, like the rainbow mullet from the Far East. They feed on weeds, and some species, nicknamed *cochons de mer* (sea pigs) in France, swim far up estuaries with the tide. Species that frequent harbors are best avoided: they can taste very nasty and at worst have their guts full of oil. Because of their vegetarian diet and ability to live in water of varying salinity, species of

mullet are farmed in ponds and tanks; among them is the largest (up to 30 in./75 cm) and most widely distributed species, the common gray mullet (*Mugil cephalus*), which in the U.S. is called the striped mullet (black mullet in Florida). The white mullet (*M. curema*) is found in Florida bayous and in the Caribbean. Particularly in the eastern Mediterranean area, mullets are plentiful, and the female roes are salted and pressed to make *★botargo*.

Good species of gray mullet, which are in general the ones that avoid ports, have firm, white flesh and a good taste. Among the best are the gray mullet itself and the golden gray mullet (*M. auratus*), which has golden spots on its gill covers. Most people will find difficulty in telling one species of gray mullet from another, since the distinguishing features tend to be subtle. Mullets should be scaled carefully. They bruise very easily, and preferably should be gutted through the gills, the roes being left inside. Some say that it is best to keep them for 24 hours before eating, but this service has usually been performed by the fishmonger. Others wash them in brine or vinegared water. Gray mullet is a good fish, but not sensational, and some prefer it smoked.

Red mullet is actually two very similar species, *Mullus surmuletus* and *M. barbatus,* which respectively reach 16 in. (40 cm) and 10 in. (25 cm) in length. The family Mullidae, to which they belong, has some 50 species, including various goatfish. The red mullet is found in the Mediterranean and from the Canary Islands to Norway, although it is rarely caught in northern waters. The red mullet is a great delicacy, and was much sought after by the Romans. The French sometimes call it *becasse de mer* (sea woodcock) because it can be cooked without gutting, like woodcock; it is usually hung for 24 hours to increase the gamy flavor. If the fish is gutted, the liver, which is a great delicacy, should be left in it or incorporated in the sauce.

Because of its red color, people sometimes

confuse the red mullet with the unrelated red gurnard (*Trigla pini*), which has a more angular shape and does not have long barbels hanging from the underside of its mouth; the red gurnard is not of the same quality.

The season for fresh red mullet varies according to locality, but is generally during the summer months; fish imported from North Africa are available at other seasons and may be frozen. Red mullet are very often sold already scaled. If they are to be gutted, this is best done through the gill opening. Recipes can be found in any book on Mediterranean cookery and also in English cookbooks, since *M. surmuletus* is caught off the southwestern coasts of the British Isles. It does not reach North America.

[Red mullet—French: *rouget;* German: *gestreifte Meerbarbe;* Italian: *triglia;* Spanish: *salmonete. Gray mullet*—French: *mulet gris;* German: *grossköpfige Meeräsche;* Italian: *cefalo;* Spanish: *pardete*]

MUNG BEAN or **green gram** (*Phaseolus aureus*) is a tiny bean that is usually green. Some varieties are yellow or black, and these can be confused from the outside with *black gram (which, to make matters worse, sometimes has green seeds). The difference is that the flesh of the seeds is yellow in mung and white in black gram.

Mung beans cook quickly without prior soaking. In total contrast to black gram, they are light and easily digested. In India, they are frequently given to invalids. They are eaten more as a whole grain or sprouted than split as a *dal. They are used particularly in recipes from Central and South India, although they are not a daily food. In China, too, mung beans are often used as bean sprouts. The usual procedure is to soak them overnight and then to hang them up loose in a wet sack and occasionally dunk it when it seems to be getting dry. The seed coats mostly come off when the sprouted gram is washed. Like all *sprouted seeds, mung sprouts should be very lightly cooked.

MUSCIAME is dried dolphin meat, a specialty from the Ligurian and Tuscan coasts of Italy (Genoa, Camogli, Viareggio). Fishermen hate dolphins, which follow the fish and often break up the nets. The flesh of dolphins harpooned in the course of fishing (they are rarely deliberately hunted) is cut in strips, salted a few days, and hung in the rigging whenever the weather is sunny and there is a drying breeze. The finished product is hard as leather, black, and usually covered in green mold. When this is wiped off with a cloth dampened in vinegar, the *musciame* is finely sliced, marinated for half an hour in olive oil, and often sprinkled with lemon juice like *bresaola. Slices are chewed with a slice of fresh garlic. It is an acceptable *zakouski* with vodka—the Polish painter Romain Balinski used to serve it thus—but is perhaps only for the strong.

MUSHROOMS and other fungi provide some of the most delicious items in our diet. Most types, from *truffles downward, are gathered in the wild. Continental Europeans are often fanatical about bringing in the yearly crop of wild fungi, which provides healthful exercise and the excitement of the chase. Pressure on some sorts of fungi is so great that they must be treated like game, with closed seasons and laws to prevent their becoming extinct. As a friend wrote to me from Switzerland, "Everyone knows his mushrooms to such an extent that if you come on one still standing after 4 a.m., you can be quite sure that it is no good." European countries have popular names for all the common or delicious sorts; to make sure that the boxes of wild fungi on sale in the markets are good, they have professional fungus inspectors and regulations defining what may be sold (usually species that are not easily confused with poisonous ones).

Contrast this with the Anglo-Saxon approach, which is to regard all fungi as poisonous except perhaps the meadow mushroom, although most fungi are not poisonous. Few people are poisoned by mushrooms in the U. S., but this is probably because there is such widespread fear of wild fungi. This phobia denies people thousands of tons of good free food every day. However, a healthy caution is advisable: **You should eat only mushroom species that you know to be edible and avoid all others.** A good illustrated mushroom guidebook, such as *The Mushrkom Hunter's Field Guide,* by Alexander H. Smith (University of Michigan Press: 3rd edition, 1981), should be studied by any beginner. It is ideal if one can go mushrooming with an experienced hunter, and joining a mycology society may give you access to knowledgeable members and experts who will help you avoid mistakes. Ignore any folklore about determining toxicity of mushrooms by such tests as whether they blacken silver or peel easily: **There is no simple rule or test to distinguish edible and poisonous mushrooms.** Spore prints, explained in mushroom guides, can be useful in identifying dubious species. When collecting specimens for identification, keep the different kinds in different bags to avoid possible contamination. Even when collecting different species that you know well, it is better to keep each kind separate, since they may require different treatment in cooking.

Poisonous fungi. What complicates the fungus hunter's life is that the poisonous species are not restricted to a few easily recognizable groups but are scattered among the various sorts of fungi. Thus even the relatively safe and easily recognizable genus *Boletus,* which includes the delicious *cèpe (B. edulis),* also embraces several unpleasantly bitter species and at least one poisonous but not deadly one, *B. satanas.* Anyone who wishes to eat wild fungi will not be content with the negative approach of merely recognizing the killers but will want to go after as many of the good ones as possible. For this, a good book on fungi is essential.

The star performers among killer fungi belong to the genus *Amanita,* as do one or two quite delectable species such as the

oronge (A. caesarea) and the tawny grisette *(A. fulva).* The species of *Amanita* have a ring around the stalk (as do many mushrooms) and a volva, an outer membrane that at first encloses the entire fungus but is ruptured as the cap expands; usually it leaves a cup around the base of the stalk (so always dig doubtful specimens out of the ground) and often bits of broken volva on the cap. Unfortunately, the cup may have disintegrated or been eaten by snails and the bits washed off the cap by rain. A single specimen of anything may be misleading or atypical, which is why, at least to begin with, identification of fungi to eat should be made from several specimens.

A. muscaria, which has a red cap with white dots and is much favored by gnomes and pixies, is far from being the most poisonous of the genus, although it used to be ground up in milk and used to kill flies— hence its name, fly agaric. It is hallucinogenic and seriously poisonous in quantity, especially when raw, but is eaten in small amounts by people who want to take a dangerous "trip." After treatment, it can be used as food, but it is not advisable to experiment with it. A similar but brown-capped species, *A. pantherina,* is more poisonous and causes serious nervous disorders; it can be confused with the blusher (*A. rubescens*), which is eaten in some places but is best avoided for risk of mistakes. It is advisable to reject all species of *Amanita* that, like these, have white gills, since they include the really deadly ones: the death cap (*A. phalloides*) and its even more dangerous sisters, *A. virosa, A. verna,* and *A. bisporigera*—more dangerous because they are more easily confused with the field mushroom (but edible mushrooms all have no volva and gills that start pink or gray and get darker). Even a taste can cause serious illness, and as little as ¾ oz (20 g) will kill.

Other deadly species include a tiny parasol mushroom, *Lepiota helveola,* and the small *Cortinarius orellanus,* which is brownish red with a paler stem. This is so unlikely to be gathered that it has only recently been recognized as the runner-up to *Amanita phalloides* in the toxicity stakes; its symptoms are similar but may not develop for 15 days after eating. Various other species may cause vomiting or more serious digestive or nervous disorders, but are usually fatal only to the elderly or infirm. Many of them belong to genera that include edible species, such as *Cortinarius* (again), *Clitocybe, Tricholoma, Ramaria, Russula,* and *Agaricus.* Since this last genus includes the edible mushrooms, it is worth mentioning here that the two species which can be poisonous, *A. xanthoderma* and *A. placomyces,* can be detected because the flesh at the base of the stalk in both species turns bright yellow immediately after it is cut.

Many fungi which are excellent to eat when cooked, salted, dried, or otherwise treated are poisonous when raw. For this reason, never go into a market and buy unknown fungi without asking how they should be prepared. Other fungi may be good if fresh, but dangerous stale. In this caregory is *Gyromitra esculenta,* an odd-looking fungus that resembles a tangled coil of rope on a stem, rather than having the conventional toadstool shape. The knobbly cap is brownish, and the stem whitish. In spite of its name, *esculenta,* and the fact that it is sold in many Continental markets, it is poisonous when raw but safe when dried—and then only if the specimens were fresh and not rotted. Because some people are allergic to it anyway, care is especially necessary.

The unpleasant effects of fungi are not always straightforward. There is the case of *Coprinus atramentarius,* a small species of shaggy manes, which grows commonly in clumps in grassy places, especially on manure. It is mentioned here not because it is very poisonous, but because it causes alarming symptoms to people who are drinking or are allergic to it. The substance that causes the symptoms is the same as a drug called Antabuse, which is produced from another source and is used in the treatment of alcoholism.

Cultivated fungi. Attempts to cultivate edible fungi have been made with some success from the earliest times. *Agrocybe aegerita* was grown by the ancient Greeks and Romans on disks of poplar, and goodness knows how long the Chinese and the Japanese have been growing other species on logs of oak, pine or chestnut—for instance, the *shiitake (Lentinus edodes)* and *matsutake (Tricholoma matsutake),* the cultivation of which is documented in Japan as far back as A.D. 199. The mushroom *Agaricus bisporus,* a species that grows on dung rather than among grass, was first cultivated in Paris at the turn of the 18th century, and for this reason is still called *champignon de Paris* in many countries. Mushrooms were grown on composted horse manure at first outdoors, but later in cellars. They vary from white to russet brown and may be scaly; some are very dense and hard, others soft and more like the field mushroom. No cultivated mushrooms have the flavor of wild mushrooms, especially as buttons, and devices such as sweating them in vine leaves or cooking them with a fine sliver of garlic are attempts to improve matters. The inclusion of a few dried and soaked *Boletus* is another method. In the past, button mushrooms or larger ones with slightly open caps were sold; the stalks were separated for soups and flavoring. The stage at which mushrooms are picked depends on market preference and on growers' considerations. For one thing, once caps are open and the spores ripe (the gills have turned brown), it is easier for disease to spread around the production unit if it happens to be introduced. At one time, large open mushrooms were sold cheaply, but they are now common, since they have a better flavor.

In warmer countries which have come under Chinese influence and where the temperature is not below 70°F (21°C), the paddy straw fungus (*Volvariella volvacea*) is commonly cultivated on rotting rice straw. It is best gathered as a button, with the volva still intact. These are excellent edible fungi, whether fresh or dried.

Enokitake mushrooms, with tiny, rounded caps borne on clumps of fragile yellowish white stems, have a slightly crunchy texture and a mild flavor. They are the first fresh Asian mushrooms to become widely available abroad, since they can easily be commercially cultivated. Sold in plastic 3-oz (85-g) packages, they are perfect in salads as well as soups and with charcoal-grilled foil-wrapped fish or poultry. Shizuo Tsuji's *Japanese Cooking* (Kodansha, 1980) has splendid recipes for preparing and presenting *enokitake* and other Oriental mushrooms.

Other species can be cultivated, such as the shaggy mane or inky cap (*Coprinus comatus*), which has too short a life to be a commercial proposition, and various wood fungi, such as Chinese wood ears (Auricularia polylrichia) and even horns of plenty (*Craterellus cornucopioides*). Unfortunately, most of the best will not thrive on dead wood or rotting vegetation alone, but need to be in a symbiotic relationship with the roots of growing plants or trees. Some success has attended the cultivation of morels and even truffles, but it may be limited to planting the necessary trees and introducing the fungus into the place rather than the intensive production used for mushrooms.

Dried fungi. Huge quantities of fungi are dried and can be bought in shops. They vary from the sliced and dried *cèpes* (*Boletus edulis*), which have a meaty flavor and are much used in Italian cooking (as *funghi porcini*), to the Chinese wood ear. The paddy straw fungus from China is dried over charcoal for 12 hours. If these dried mushrooms get damp, they acquire a bad smell which disappears when they are cooked. The Japanese *shiitake* and *matsutake* are mainly dried in the sun or over charcoal fires, but they are also available canned or pickled. These fungi must be used or preserved when young and just beginning to produce white spore powder. After that, they become tough.

Dried fungi are very useful in the kitchen, and should be kept handy as a flavoring. *Funghi porcini* need to be rinsed in warm water before use, and other species may have to be soaked for up to 24 hours. The easiest fungus to dry at home is the fairy ring mushroom (*Morasmium oreades*), which is common in fields and is easily recognized. It is necessary only to string the caps on cotton thread and to hang them in a warm, dry place. Once bone-dry, they can be put into jars, and they keep indefinitely.

Pickled fungi, salted fungi, and **fungi under oil.** Some countries with extensive forests, such as Russia, produce a glut of wild fungi, and pickling or salting is of great importance. Indeed, some of the species which are not so good when fresh (e.g., the Russian or Polish *gruzd, Lactarius scrobiculatus*), and are perhaps too acrid or even poisonous, become sought after and expensive once treated. In Britain, the only use made of the huge quantities of mushrooms that once existed before pastures were plowed up was to extract the juices with salt and make mushroom *ketchup. Ordinary bottling must be done with care to avoid botulism, and a pressure cooker should be used. There are many methods of preserving fungi with salt, vinegar, or oil.

Wild fungi are gathered all over the world. Some of them are large enough to make a meal for several people (I have a photograph of one from Zaïre which is big enough to use as an umbrella); others are tiny. I would recommend particularly the *Boletus* species (*cèpes*), which it is almost impossible to go wrong with, since the "sponge" (where the gills are normally) keeps them entirely separate from any lethal species. Inedible species of *Boletus* either taste horrid or are only mildly poisonous.

When gathering fungi, it is best to lay the specimens down carefully, after inspecting them and cutting off the dirty stalk. Put the stalk downward, so that grit cannot fall into the sponge or gills. Do not eat soft, old, or maggoty specimens: some species then become harmful. Expose mushrooms to as little water as possible when cleaning them; rinse them quickly under the tap if necessary, or carefully wipe them with a clean damp cloth. Wild mushrooms often exude more liquid when cooked than cultivated ones, so you may need to allow for more when substituting them for cultivated mushrooms in a recipe. Dried mushrooms often have a more concentrated flavor, and fewer may be needed to add richness to a dish.

In a peasant economy, people gather everything edible, and keen fungus amateurs may do the same just for fun. However, the cook, especially to begin with, had best limit the search to the very best fungi from a gastronomic viewpoint and to the sorts which are plentiful locally. In the U.S. these may be *morels, *puffballs, *shaggy manes, *meadow or field mushrooms, and *chanterelles. For further information on cooking all sorts of fungi, see Jane Grigson, *The Mushroom Feast* (Knopf, 1975).

[*Mushroom*—French: *champignon;* German: *Pilz;* Italian *fungo;* Spanish: *hongo*]

MUSKRAT (*Ondatra zibethica*). Menus in Maryland may offer "marsh rabbit," and in Louisiana the "marsh hare" is eaten. Both are likely to be euphemisms for the aquatic rodent the muskrat (although there is a true marsh rabbit, *Sylvilagus palustris,* an edible cottontail). Evan Jones, in *American Food* (Dutton, 1975), describes muskrat as "a fine flavored meat which, after marinating overnight, is coated with flour and fried, then served up with currant jelly and beaten biscuits so hot they burn the fingers." The small, plump, furry animals, which live just offshore in ponds, lakes, and quiet streams, are also roasted, baked, stewed, and made into pies in the South, and some fancy butcher shops sell "marsh rabbits."

MUSSEL. Familiar bivalves, mussels of various species are found in most seas and are usually dark blue to almost black but may be yellowish brown, and one New Zealand species is bright green. The blue mussel (*Mytilus edulis*) is both delicious and abundant. It occurs on shores from the Arctic to North Carolina and the Mediterranean. Edible mussels on the U.S. West Coast include *M. edulis* and *M. californianus,* but mussels

there should be eaten only from November through April, when they are not feeding on plankton that make them slightly poisonous to human beings. Mussels are probably the greatest unused seafood resource found on U.S. coasts, and they are quite inexpensive, for Americans do not eat many mussels, except locally on the coast or among particular ethnic groups. In Britain, the current neglect of the mussel is not traditional: in the middle of the 19th century, mussels were "farmed" in Britain to the extent that people complained of harbors being blocked. Today, there are mussel farms, *bouchots,* around the coasts of France and of many other European countries where mussels are keenly eaten. They will no doubt be cultivated even more in the future on account of the tremendous bulk of protein per acre that they make (10,000 lb or 4,535 Kg of mussel meat per acre). Mussels take 3 years to grow to some 2 in. (5 cm) long. They prefer slightly brackish water and tend to grow best near estuaries or in harbors. In these days, such locations also offer sewage and pollution—if you gather your own, bear this in mind and make sure that your catch has come from a clean place.

Although other members of the mussel family lie buried upright in mud or bore into rocks, the mussels of the genus *Mytilus* attach themselves to rocks or harbor piles, or to the hurdles and ropes of the mussel farms, with a bunch of horny hairs called the byssus. In the more civilized (and so usually more polluted) countries, mussels spend some time in purifying tanks before being sold. Although a few people are allergic to mussels, most people can eat them regularly all their lives without experiencing anything but benefit, since mussels are rich in *trace elements. Unless you are certain that mussels have been cleansed, place them in clean

BLUE MUSSEL

water with a little salt dissolved in it (some people put in a little flour or oatmeal) for a couple of hours—but no more, or they will asphyxiate. Mussels must always be scraped to remove barnacles and weed, then scrubbed and well washed to get rid of sand. The byssus should be gently pulled out. Any shells that gape should be thrown out, as should any that feel very heavy—they are likely to be full of mud. Use only fresh, live mussels that pull their shells together strongly when disturbed.

The clean mussels are opened by putting them wet into a pan—not a deep layer—and cooking on high heat with the pan lid on tight. It may be necessary to add a few spoons of water or a dash of white wine (according to the recipe), but they should not be swamped with liquid. The moment the mussels are all open (it takes only a couple of minutes), they must be removed. Strain the juice through a cloth to remove the sand, and use the liquid for sauce. To overcook mussels is to shrink and toughen them. Cold mussels can be served on the half-shell with mayonnaise. If sprinkled with lemon juice, covered with garlic butter, and heated briefly in the oven, they make a delicious hors d'oeuvre. The recipes for mussels range from the relatively straightforward *moules marinière* (white wine and shallots) and *moules à la crème* (in cream) of Normandy to *mitili ripieni alla spezzina* (mussels stuffed with a mixture of spinach, minced meat, ham, and Parmesan cheese, bound with egg and cooked in a light tomato sauce), a specialty of the Italian Riviera.

Smoked mussels can mainly be bought preserved in oil. They are made as follows. Cooked mussels are removed from their shells and soaked for 5 minutes in a brine of 40 oz of salt per gallon of water (250 g salt per liter). They are then dipped in oil and smoked on mesh trays, in Britain for 30 minutes at 180°F (82°C)—elsewhere they are sometimes dried for 25 minutes, then smoked for a further 25 minutes at 160°F (71°C)—before being packed into jars, covered with oil, and heat-processed in water at

250°F (121°C) or 15 lb per sq in. pressure in a pressure cooker. An 8-oz (225-g) jar requires some 15 minutes. Smoked mussels are rather sweet. Although they are sometimes served as an hors d'oeuvre or as a cocktail snack, smoked mussels are perhaps better in combination than alone.

[*Mussel*—French: *moule;* German: *Muschel;* Italian: *dattero di mare;* Spanish: *mejillón*]

MUSTARD. The three species of mustard plant are all crucifers related to the cabbage, but they have quite different characteristics.

The exceedingly pungent black mustard

MUSTARD

(*Brassica nigra*) is probably a native of Europe and grows wild as an escape in North America. The plant is very big—it can grow up to 6 ft (2 m) high—and since it drops its seeds very easily, it is not suitable for mechanical farming. It is thus grown less today than it was in the past, although it is the traditional seed to use in making condiment mustard.

White mustard (*Sinapis alba*) is also probably a native of Mediterranean Europe. The seed is large, pale yellow, and much milder in flavor than black mustard. It has a characteristic taste which you can recognize quickly as being typical of American mustards. A little white mustard is used in English mustard, but it is forbidden in Dijon mustard.

Brown mustard, sometimes also called Indian mustard (*Brassica juncea*), has seed which looks rather like that of black mustard but is a lighter brown or reddish. Although it is not as hot as black mustard, brown mustard has tended to replace it in condiment mustards in recent years because it can be harvested mechanically. Varieties of *B. juncea* from India have a rather rough taste if they are used for making European mustards, but their use is correct in Indian cooking, and after frying their flavor is merely nutty. Mustard oil (*see* fats and oils) is important in Indian cooking.

The pungency of mustard comes from an essential oil which forms through enzyme action when ground mustard seed is mixed with water. (Hence if the enzymes are destroyed by heat no hotness is produced.) When mustard powder is mixed, it must be left for 10–15 minutes before it develops its full strength. Mixing mustard powder with vinegar, salt, or boiling water is inadvisable, since the treatment destroys part of the enzymes and may leave bitter unconverted glucosides, though vinegar and salt may be added after the taste has developed. White mustard seed, though not so well flavored as black, can be useful because it contains enzymes that are less easily inactivated than those of black mustard. White mustard is also strongly preservative, which is why it is often included in the spices for pickle.

Mustard has been used as a spice for thousands of years. In Shakespeare's day, the mustard used in England was in the form of a thick sauce; it was later sold as a powder. A particularly fine quality was developed by Jeremiah Colman in Norwich during the 19th century, so much so that today English powdered mustard is virtually synonymous with the name of Colman. It contains wheat flour and turmeric as well as powdered huskless mustard seed. Mustard powder is the mustard to use in English recipes, for fish sauces, and sauces for vegetables—particularly vegetables of the cabbage family—for Welsh rarebit, and so on. A little powdered mustard in mayonnaise helps to stabilize the emulsion, as well as adding its flavor, but the practice is not universally approved by cooking experts. An English prepared mustard, Savora, is sweetish and very popular in South America and France.

French prepared mustards include Bordeaux, which is rather dark because the whole seed, including the seed coat, is ground up to make it. It contains fermented Bordeaux wine or vinegar, sugar, tarragon, and other herbs and spices. Bordeaux mustard, acid, earthy, and aromatic, is suitable for eating with foods that need a picklelike complement, such as sliced sausages. Dijon mustard, on the other hand, is pale grayish yellow in color (the seed coat is removed), with a cleaner taste of mustard. It may be subtle or sharp in flavor. The famous Dijon house of Poupon makes dozens of blends. Dijon is the mustard to eat with foods when it has to bring out and not mask their natural flavor. It is also the type of mustard to be used in French recipes unless otherwise specified. Moutarde de Meaux is a grainy mustard made of ground and half-ground seeds. Somewhat hot, with a pleasantly musty taste, it is excellent with cold cuts and sausages. This is the mustard sold by Pommery in wide-mouthed stoneware jars. Other French mustards may be flavored with herbs, tomato purée, or green peppercorns (*moutarde au poivre verte*).

German mustards are usually made from a blend of strong mustard powder and vinegar. They may be very hot, to eat with highly seasoned sausages, or milder to accompany blander sausages such as the *weisswurst* of South Germany. Germans are very fond of mustards, and they produce many blends, including herbed mixtures.

American mustard may be plain or spiced, but generally it is very mild and consists mostly of ground white mustard and turmeric. It is considered too sweet and characterless by mustard connoisseurs.

Mostarda di frutta is a sort of relish made in Italy from fruits—cherries, figs, peaches, lemons, pears—preserved in a syrup containing mustard oil. It is eaten like jam or with cold cuts.

To experiment with homemade mustard

blends, pound or grind black and/or white mustard seeds and moisten them with water. Let stand, then add vinegar, salt, and sugar (or honey, as the Welsh do) to taste. Additional flavorings may be chosen from a wide selection of herbs—e.g., tarragon, dill, horseradish—and spices. Let the mixture stand for a few days so flavors can blend, then taste and adjust further if necessary, adding a little oil if the mustard is too hot. Such mustards should be stored in the refrigerator and used within a few months.

[*Mustard*—French: *moutarde;* German: *Senf;* Italian: *senape, mostarda;* Spanish: *mostaza*]

MUSTARD GREENS (*Brassica* species). The leaves of many members of the *Cruciferae,* or mustard family, are called mustard greens because of their pungency and slight bitterness. The most abundant and widespread mustard is *B. nigra,* black mustard, which is cultivated for both its leaves and its seeds. It has become a weed in many areas in the U.S. The seeds of *B. alba,* white mustard, are also used to make prepared mustard, and its broad leaves are cooked as greens. Japanese mustard (*B. japonica*) is grown in the South for its large, plumelike leaves.

Many varieties of mustard are available from seed companies, and one can usually choose between mustard greens with fringed and deeply curled leaves and those with large, broad, thick leaves. Cultivated varieties are considerably milder than the wild mustards that can be found growing in vacant lots in New York City as well as in fields of grain crops. While the leaves of cultivated mustards can be eaten until the plant is full grown, only the young leaves of wild mustard are very good. Mustard greens should be cooked until tender (longer than one would cook spinach), then seasoned with butter, bacon drippings, vinegar, or chopped onion. They are often cooked with a ham hock and other greens—*kale, *dandelions, *collards, and *turnip greens. Small mustard leaves add tang to salads and sandwiches. Like broccoli, a relative, mustard is also good to eat at the bud stage: the flower heads, cooked for only a few minutes, taste like mustardy broccoli.

Few vegetables surpass mustard greens as a source of vitamins A and C; they also contain B vitamins and trace minerals.

MUTTON and **LAMB.** Sheep and *goats have been domesticated for many thousands of years. They are very closely related, and indeed, as travelers will know, it is not always easy to tell them apart. Sheep, however, are of very much greater importance as a source of meat and much less important as a source of milk; the most celebrated use of ewe's milk is in Roquefort cheese.

Among the many breeds of sheep, there are the goatlike sheep of the deserts, the fattailed sheep, and even the fat-bottomed steatopygic sheep. The small sheep with orange spots in Islamic countries are not naturally spotted. The spots are painted on them with henna, and they are awaiting sacrifice for some feast.

Since the beginning of this century, there has been a great change of opinion over the relative merits of mutton and lamb. In Victorian times young sheep were considered tasteless, and mutton 3–6 years old was preferred. "Mutton two years old is flabby, pale and savourless" is hardly an opinion one would hear today. "To suit the palate of an epicure, a sheep should never be killed earlier than its third or later than its fifth year, at which age the mutton will be firm and succulent, dark coloured and full of the richest gravy." In these days, people are so afraid of mutton's being tough that in some places mutton is inaccurately labeled lamb. Technically, a lamb is under a year—modern breeds put on weight very quickly. Indeed it is not economical for farmers to sell mutton anymore, because of the extra feed required, unless they can charge much more for it than for lamb. But the public expects to pay less for mutton than for lamb, and the mutton offered is mostly from old breeding ewes, which are killed at 3-4 years, before they need false teeth. Ewe mutton can be lovely boiled with herbs and eaten with onion, soubise, or caper sauce, or pressure-cooked and minced or curried. Chinese mutton stew may be flavored with ginger, candied orange peel, and soy sauce. Fine mutton, reared to eat, is an expensive luxury and difficult to get. It is usually killed at 15-18 months. Most Americans have not eaten it and are not likely to.

Another specialty is milk-fed baby lamb, 3-4 weeks old and weighing 9-11 lb (4-5 Kg), the ovine equivalent of suckling pig. It is usually a lamb born in winter, raised in shelter, and fed on milk. In France, such a lamb is the *agnelet* or Pauillac lamb. In Italy, roasted *abbacchio* or *agnello di latte* is a famous Roman dish (some find kid, *capretto di latte,* even better). These very young animals may be rather tasteless and lacking in fat for some palates.

Milk lamb should be eaten fresh, without hanging. Mutton is usually hung for about a week. When a "high" taste was generally liked, cooks went further and used mutton to imitate venison by making a gravy of woodcocks or other game birds that had gone too far to be roasted for table.

Grass-fed lambs do not have much flavor at 2 months, when they weigh 15-18 lb (7-8 Kg), and the ideal lamb is 3-4 months old and weighs at least 22 lb (10 Kg). The traditional season for lamb once started at Easter and went on through the summer, with lambs coming from farther and farther north. Nowadays, the old seasons do not have the same meaning, because of freezing and the evolution of breeds that lamb twice a year. However, autumn-born lambs do not have the flavor of spring-born ones, since they have not been fed on fresh spring flowers and grass. Frozen lamb, which began to come from Australia and New Zealand during the 19th century, can now be so good as to be preferable to home-grown lamb during the off-season in winter.

Mountain breeds of sheep are in general rather active creatures, and even the lambs can be tougher than those of lowland breeds, but they have a fine flavor. French mutton from southern sheep that graze on aromatic herbs on the high plateaus is considered superior. On the other hand, yearlings raised on salt meadows near the sea have a very special flavor and are famous in gastronomy as *pré-salé,* a term that, strictly speaking, applies only to sheep that graze in the Mont-Saint-Michel area. The hardy little sheep from the Scottish islands are gaining a reputation for excellence of flavor. In the U.S. the best mutton is said to come from the Downs breeds of sheep. Although mutton is eaten very little in the U.S., in Kentucky barbecued mutton is a specialty.

There is disagreement over the best cuts, just as there is over the best age of sheep. Although it is difficult to carve (and less meaty), the shoulder is nearly always better than the leg, while the often-despised breast is the tastiest part of all. Today, lamb, like most other meat, is bred to have little fat—too little for the best taste. In the U.S., mint jelly is the traditional accompaniment, and in Britain, mint sauce, but mutton and lamb combine with many herbs and spices. Garlic and rosemary have been known as compatible seasonings for many years, but another method is to rub the meat with powdered ginger before roasting it. Welsh mountain lamb—one of the best—is traditionally served with *laver. Other possibilities are cranberry, red currant, and rowan jellies. Boiled lamb is often eaten with onion or caper sauce. Ground lamb can be prepared in any way one would hamburger. Other countries offer a whole gamut of lamb and mutton recipes, particularly in the Middle East, where they often contain cinnamon, which goes well with mutton. (*See also* qawwrama.)

Mutton hams are produced in many places. In Britain, they are traditionally made in the Border country between England and Scotland, and they are also made in several Muslim countries where eating pork is forbidden. There is even mutton bacon.

As always with meat, differences in cuts between countries can cause confusion. Essentially, the body apart from the limbs and their attachments can be divided into the back to the rear of the ribs and the back over the ribs, leading to the neck. The division is marked by the diaphragm, which separates the abdominal cavity from the chest. The back to the rear of the ribs is the loin. Since the middle neck chops lie under the shoulder blade, the chops from under the ribs are called "uncovered" (*découvertes*). Each side of the back over the ribs is a *carré,* and two of them put together inside out in a circle make the crown roast. In France, the long bony rib bit of the chops is removed as a flat, ribby piece, the *haute de côtelettes.* A not very attractive square of bone, periosteum, and intercostal muscle, it nevertheless is excellent for a tasty ragout.

The neck of mutton or lamb may include the entire length of the rib cage as well as what the layman might think of as neck. This latter is very bony, the least valued cut, used mainly for stews, *blanquettes,* and the like. Shoulder contains a large shoulder blade and, even in lean animals, quite a bit of fat. Because it is awkward to carve, it is frequently boned and stuffed for roasting. It can also be turned into fancy cuts, such as the American mock duck. Shoulder, well trimmed, is the cut most often ground to use for stuffing peppers and grape leaves. In the Middle East, it is pounded to a paste to make *kibbeh,* little patties that are eaten raw with onions.

The breast of mutton and lamb is fatty but the best-flavored piece. The breastbone, where it is chopped through in the middle, gives an indication of the age of the animal. In a lamb (up to a year), it is red all through. At 1–2 years, the upper and lower bones change gradually to white, but the middle part remains red. At 3, a small streak of white appears in the middle of the four middle bones, and at 4 all the breastbone will be white.

Breast, freed from bone and gristle, is often stuffed and rolled. One stuffing (which can also be used for shoulder) is made by mixing together a cup of bread crumbs, chopped parsley, 2 chopped anchovies, and the yolks of 3–4 hard-boiled eggs; it is seasoned with nutmeg or mace, a pinch of ground cloves, the zest of half a lemon, pepper, and salt. Cover the meat with this mixture, roll it, and tie it. Either put it into boiling water and simmer it for 2 hours or roast it in a medium oven for 20 minutes per lb (450 g). Breast, well roasted with just garlic and rosemary, will lose much of the fat and is delicious.

The loin, the back between the pelvic girdle and the beginning of the ribs, includes the fillet (which lies below the backbone on each side); the word "fillet" is sometimes used for the whole cut, which is also called the saddle, a term usually reserved for both sides of the loin cut as a single piece. None of these terms is very exact, when translated from one language to another, because butchers cut differently even between one part of a country and another.

Leg or gigot is often divided into two pieces, the fillet end and the shank end. When boned and left flat it is a butterfly leg of lamb. Although it is the most meaty part of the sheep, I do not find the leg to be the best-flavored. The shank is the bottom part of the leg, above the foot.

Among variety meats, sheep's feet are eaten in France—*Larousse Gastronomique* offers ten recipes—and can sometimes be bought already blanched. Head (especially brains) and ears are regarded in some countries as a delicacy, as also are sheep's tongues. Everyone knows the tale that when dining with a desert sheik you are likely to be given the sheep's eyes, picked carefully from the stew and offered as the choicest piece. Many people who are not desert Arabs also enjoy their taste and texture, but they are not for the squeamish. Lamb kidneys are often left attached to the loin, and they are included in English lamb chops—the meat is wrapped around the kidney. Lamb sweetbreads compare with those from veal in quality.

The tails of most sheep are docked when they are lambs, because in long-wool breeds the tail gets clogged with manure and encourages flies. The shepherd fills his basket with lamb's tails and testicles as he goes through the flock; this collection was the basis for a tasty shepherd's pie in times past. However, fat-tailed sheep are bred for their enormously fat tails. Tails can weigh as much as 80 lb (35 Kg). Since the sheep have to drag their tails, the shepherds tie boards under them to protect them from the stony ground; they sometimes even use wheels. Fat-tailed sheep are commonly reared in many countries of the Middle East. In the fat-bottomed sheep, the tail is reduced to a mere stump sticking out of an enlarged backside. In fact, both peculiarities are adaptations of nature to store food in hard, desert conditions and are equivalent to the camel's hump—Bushmen living in the Kalahari desert also grew enormous fat bottoms at certain seasons. The meat of fat-tailed sheep usually has a strong but delicious taste, perhaps given it by the desert herbs.

[*Mutton*—French: *mouton;* German: *Hammelfleisch;* Italian: *montone;* Spanish: *carnero*. *Lamb*—French: *agneau;* German: *junges Hammelfleisch;* Italian: *agnello;* Spanish: *cordero*]

MYRTLE (*Myrtus communis*). The edible myrtle (not related to three other plants also called myrtle: laurel, bog myrtle, and periwinkle), a plant with fragrant white flowers and leaves, grows wild in Mediterranean countries. Its leaves are used for wrapping pork or stuffing small birds to impart a myrtle aroma after roasting and while the food is waiting to come to table. The black berries are edible and can be eaten on a walk or dried and used in the same way as juniper, although they are milder. Sardinians make oil from the ripe berries and claim that it is superior to olive oil for frying fish.

[*Myrtle*—French: *myrte;* German: *Mryte;* Italian: *mirto, mortella;* Spanish: *arrayán, mirto*]

MYRTLE PEPPER. *See* allspice.

N

NAM PLA. The salty, matured fish sauce of Thailand, the equivalent of other "rotten fish" sauces from Southeast Asian countries, such as *ngapi. It is used both in cooking and as a condiment.

NARA NUT. *See* butternut.

NASEBERRY. *See* sapodilla.

NASTOIKA. *See* galangal.

NASTURTIUM or Indian cress (*Tropaeolum majus*). This well-known garden plant, a native of Peru, has leaves with a cresslike flavor and high vitamin C content. Small tender leaves can be added to salads, used in sandwiches, or chopped fine to sprinkle over food as a salt and pepper substitute. The flowers are also good to eat and for making nasturtium vinegar. The large fruits, when still green and tender, can be pickled by putting them in well-salted vinegar, and they make a very nice, slightly pungent pickle, which can be used in a similar way to capers, although the taste is not identical.

[*Nasturtium*—French: *capucine, cresson d' Inde;* German: *Kapuzinerkresse;* Italian: *naturzio;* Spanish: *capuchina, nasturcia*]

NAVY BEAN. *See* bean.

NECTARINE. *See* peach.

NEPAL PEPPER. *See* chili.

NETTLE. There are many species of nettle (*Urtica*), some of which have a savage sting. Of the three general species, the stinging nettle (*Urtica diocia*), which is distributed in temperate regions throughout the world, has been used since ancient times as a source of fiber—nettle cloth is excellent—and in spring the tops are often eaten before other vegetables come in. The stinging hairs are destroyed by boiling, but nettle tops must be gathered with gloves. Cooked in the water that is left on them from washing, plus a little butter, they make a tasty green vegetable. Nettles were sometimes blanched by earthing them up, but that destroys part of their nutritional value, and they are sweet enough without. My grandmother, who came from Lancashire, where nettle beer used to be sold on stalls, made it every year for the men working in the hayfield. At that season, great stone flagons frequently exploded in the larder during the night, or so it seemed to me as a child. Nettle beer is an excellent drink, more delicious and refreshing than ginger beer.

NETTLE BEER

A bucket full of nettle tops and 4 handfuls of dandelion leaves make 16 pt (9 lt) of nettle beer. Some people also add a few handfuls of goose grass (or cleavers—*Galium apar-*

ine—a common plant that sticks to clothing) and other herbs. Boil the lot in 16 pt (9 lt) of boiling water with 2 oz (50 g) of bruised ginger. After 40 minutes strain off the liquid and add to it about 2 cups of brown sugar plus the juice of a lemon for acidity. When the liquid is almost cool, float 1 oz (25 g) of yeast on top and leave it to ferment for 6–7 hours. Skim, stir in a tablespoon of cream of tartar, and bottle, leaving room for expanding gas. The beer is ready as soon as it is judged gassy enough.

[*Nettles*—French: *ortie;* German: *Nessel;* Italian: *ortica;* Spanish: *ortiga*]

NGAPI. From Burmese *nga* (fish) and *pi* (rotten, decayed), this is a dark-gray paste of decomposed fish used in Burma as a relish and flavoring; without it Burmese food would be incomplete. The best quality is said to come from Moulmein, and the beauty of the local girls is attributed to its body-building qualities. The liquid drained from *ngapi* is similar to the Malaysian *balachan,* the Vietnamese *nuoc-nam,* the Thai *nam pla,* and is used in much the same manner. In Burma, the seed of the jungle tree (*Pithecolobium lobatum*) is also used, raw or cooked, under the name *ngapi* nut; it has a strong smell, reminiscent of *ngapi* itself.

NIACIN. *See* vitamins.

NICOTINIC ACID. *See* vitamins (niacin).

NIGELLA (*Nigella sativa*) is a plain-looking species of love-in-a-mist with creamy flowers; it is grown for its black seed, which has a spicy taste and is sometimes known as *quatre épices* in France. As *kalonji,* this is a moderately important spice in Indian cooking and often is confused with onion seed and with black *cumin. It is sometimes mixed with sesame seed and sprinkled on bread before baking.

[*Nigella*—French: *nigelle;* German: *Schwarzkümmel;* Italian: *nigella;* Spanish: *neguilla, pasionara*]

NITRATES and **nitrites.** Nitrites are formed from nitrates—potassium nitrate or *saltpeter and sodium nitrate or *Chile saltpeter—by heating or by the action of bacteria during the brining of food. Nitrates are far less toxic than nitrites and occur naturally in very small amounts in vegetables and water. Nitrites turn meat pink and, even in small quantities, are lethal against many sorts of bacteria, in particular those that cause botulism (*see* poisoning). The color, flavor, and texture of many meat, fish, and poultry products depend on nitrates and nitrites. Without nitrites, ham is salty roast pork and bacon is simply salt pork.

As with other additives, the Food and Drug Administration regulates the amounts of nitrates and nitrites that can be used in curing meat and fish products. It is still investigating the role of nitrosamines in the human diet. Under certain conditions, nitrites and amines (the natural breakdown products of proteins) can combine to form nitrosamines, chemicals shown to cause cancer in animals. The question still remains whether many processed meat, poultry, and fish products could retain their characteristics and remain microbiologically safe to eat if the use of nitrates and nitrites in their processing were prohibited. In the meantime, products which use nitrates and nitrites as perservatives must show this information on the label.

NIXTAMAL. *See* masa.

NOODLES. In the U.S., the term "noodles" usually refers to ribbon-shaped pasta made with eggs (*see* pasta). In Oriental cooking, noodles may be made from wheat flour, with or without eggs, much in the manner of U.S. or Italian pasta. However, many other types are called for in Chinese recipes. Noodles made of rice flour, which have a flavor of their own, are sometimes fried until they puff up, or soaked briefly and stir-fried, or used in dishes with anything from pork to lily buds. Noodles made with a basis of mung bean are as shiny as nylon and need soaking before they are cooked. They are mainly mixed with other ingredients; although they are rather tasteless, they have a special gelatinous texture when cooked. Noodles can be made from all manner of starchy substances, such as arrowroot.

Japanese noodles include *udon,* which is similar to macaroni, and *somen,* which is like vermicelli. *Soba* is thin buckwheat noodles, while *chasoba* (tea *soba*) is made of buckwheat and green tea. *Harusame* is made with soybeans. *Shirataki* is a very fine vermicelli which is made from a glutinous, yamlike tuber, devil's tongue (*Amorphophallus kanjac*).

[*Noodle*—French: *nouille, pâte alimentaire;* German: *Nudel;* Italian: *pasta;* Spanish: *tallarin*]

NOPALES. *See* prickly pear.

NORI. *See* seaweed.

NORWAY LOBSTER. *See* scampi.

NOYAU. To good peasants who do not like to waste anything, the kernels of apricots, peaches, plums, and cherries present a challenge. Like bitter *almonds, they contain a glucoside which, when mixed with water (or the saliva in the mouth), is converted by enzymes into a mixture of benzaldehyde and deadly poisonous hydrocyanic acid. Noyau (from the French *noyau,* a fruit stone), a *liqueur, cordial, and useful flavoring, consists essentially of a sugar syrup, usually with alcohol, and flavored with macerated kernels or sometimes with peach leaves or bitter almonds, which contain similar principles. Noyau had a reputation for being "unwholesome"—naturally so, if there were cyanide in it. However, a quick boil will drive off the volatile poison, leaving only a delicate taste of benzaldehyde behind.

NOYAU

Collect apricot stones, peach stones, and plum stones. Wash them and dry them in the sun. When you have sufficient to produce a cup of kernels, crack them by hitting on the edge with a hammer, and extract the nuts. Put them through the blender with water and leave them to macerate overnight. Strain the liquid, squeezing the last drops out with a cloth. Add enough sugar to make a syrup and boil for a minute. Cool. Add a little lemon juice gradually, tasting, adding more sugar (or honey if you like) until you get the balance to your liking. The acid lemon will have made a cloudy precipitate form. Let it settle, then decant the clear liquid and mix it with an equal quantity of brandy—a rather sweet Spanish brand is excellent for this—or any grape or other spirits will do, provided the flavor is not too pronounced. The noyau can be drunk immediately and usually is.

NUOC-NAM is the best-known of the salty, matured fish sauces and is very important in the cooking of Vietnam and adjacent Laos and Cambodia. It is available in specialist shops, and quite generally in France, where the old colonial connection is still evident.

NUTMEG is the seed of a tree (*Myristica fragrans*) that is native to the Molucca Islands of Indonesia, but now grown in other tropical countries, notably in Granada. Nut-

NUTMEG

megs should be bought whole (if they are white, they have been treated with lime), since ground nutmeg quickly loses its fragrance. A small grater kept in the jar with the nutmegs is a convenience. In quantity, nutmeg is a narcotic, but in ordinary amounts it is a most useful flavoring for meat, fish, vegetables (especially onions and spinach), sweets, and cakes. The aril around the nutmeg seed is *mace.

[*Nutmeg*—French: *muscade;* German: *Muskat;* Italian: *moscata;* Spanish: *moscada*]

NUTS. Any large, dry fruit or seed with a hard shell and edible kernel is called a nut. There are hundreds of different kinds, most of them unknown outside the areas in which they grow, and the definition also covers sunflower seeds, melon seeds, and other kernels which many people would perhaps not regard as nuts.

When thoroughly dry, most nuts may be stored in their shells for varying periods, depending on the kind, and can be held for longer periods in cold storage provided they are left in the shell.

Commercially, nuts are graded and, if they are for dessert use, the shells may be bleached or dyed to improve the appearance. However, the bulk of the nuts produced for sale are cracked and shelled in the factory, since the public prefers the convenience, even though nuts keep better in the shell, which protects them from the oxygen of the air and from microorganisms. Many kinds go rancid rather easily once they have been shelled, unless they are packed in gas or in a vacuum. Rancid nuts are not only unpleasant but actually harmful.

Nuts are generally rich in oil. Very oily nuts like walnuts, pecans, and Brazils contain around 65% fat, and even the less oily peanut has 50%. The oils are released from the cells by pounding. Some nuts, however, like chestnuts and acorns, are mainly carbohydrate. Because many nuts are also rich in calcium and iron (e.g., almonds and Brazils), as well as being high in potassium and low in sodium, they have important possibilities in the diet. A few (e.g., peanuts) are also high in protein.

Nut butters can be made from any of the oily nuts. The best-known, of course, is peanut butter, but butters can also be made from almonds, cashew nuts, Brazil nuts, and even walnuts and pine nuts, although the product tends to be too oily. Nut butters can easily be made at home using the special nut butter attachment of a nut mill or even a meat mincer.

The most important nuts are *almonds, *peanuts, *Brazil nuts, *hazelnuts, *walnuts, *chestnuts, *coconuts, and *pistachio nuts. These are always generally available and are most used in cooking. A few other nuts, such as the *macadamia and the *cashew, have recently become popular or, like *candle nuts, feature in important regional cooking styles. There are many other nuts, especially from the tropics, which are of local importance and will be met with by travelers or as an occasional curiosity, but are not regularly exported.

[*Nut*—French: *noix;* German: *Nuss;* Italian: *noce;* Spanish: *nuez*]

O

OATS and **oatmeal.** Oats (*Avena sativa*) have been cultivated at least since the Bronze Age and in Britain since the Iron Age, but their origin is uncertain. They are essentially a cereal of cold, wet places and so did not play a part in the economy of the early Mediterranean civilizations. Oats and rye grow farther north than other cereals, and so are important in the less hospitable regions, such as Alaska and Norway. (Another species, the black oat or bristle oat, *A. strigosa,* is grown in hilly areas that are unsuitable for *A. sativa.*) In Scotland, oats used to be a staple food, and part of a farm laborer's wages were paid in oatmeal.

However, oats are now mainly grown as an animal foodstuff. They do not contain a gluten that will stand up to make leavened bread, and the dominant flavor is slightly bitter, and very characteristic. However, oatmeal is valuable from a nutritional viewpoint, since it has much the analysis of wheat but with more fat and biotin. Simple oatmeals are made by stone-grinding the grain, and fine, medium, and coarse grades are available. Fine oatmeal is used for oatcakes; coarse oatmeal for porridge, haggis, and white puddings. For many purposes, oatmeal is better after being parched, that is, slightly roasted. Rolled oats, for breakfast cereal, are made from carefully dried, cleaned, and graded oats, which have been pearled: they have the husk ground off and are then steam-softened and rolled flat.

Rolled oats keep because heating destroys the enzymes which would act on the fats in the germ of crude meal to produce free fatty acids. These quickly oxidize and make the meal go rancid; straight oatmeal is a bad keeper, which is why the Scots like coarse oatmeal for porridge to be freshly ground.

Oatmeal porridge (there are porridges made from other cereals, and during the Depression it was often made of stale bread, sugar, and water) used to be the ubiquitous British breakfast starter. The technique of making porridge is similar to that used for polenta—the grain is sprinkled into boiling water with one hand while the other hand stirs it with a spoon or fork to prevent it from getting lumpy. Porridge should be sufficiently salted and may then be eaten with no more than the addition of fresh milk. With plenty of ice-cold thick cream, the combination of hot and cold is fabulous, but then even dry-parched oatmeal and cream (crowdie) is splendid. Porridge has regrettably been largely ousted by relatively valueless breakfast cereals.

Oatmeal, though, is more than a breakfast food: there are few things more delicious than small brown trout straight from the brook, rolled in salt oatmeal, and fried over the campfire; a similar treatment is excellent for herrings. Oatmeal has an affinity with onions, as in onion and oatmeal soup and in white puddings, all hearty food for the winter mountains. For really heroic Scots winter fare a *kale brose (bone stock, kale, and oatmeal) would take some beating, though you could well prefer the famous Atholl Brose, which consists of oatmeal with Scotch whisky and heather honey.

WHITE PUDDING

Take ½ lb (225 g) of good coarse oatmeal parched to a light brown in a dry pan, ½ lb (225 g) or more of finely chopped beef suet, a small onion, very finely chopped, and a good seasoning of salt and freshly ground black pepper or allspice. Mix together—no water—and tie in a cloth into a sausage shape. Plunge the pudding straight into boiling water to cover, weight it under with a plate if necessary to begin with, and simmer it for 1½–2 hours. (More sophisticated versions are made by including minced pork or chicken and eggs in the mixture, and by cooking in sausage skin rather than cloth.) When the pudding is cool, remove the cloth. Slices of pudding can be fried or broiled.

OATCAKES

The simplest way of making oatcakes is to mix fine or medium oatmeal into a dough with salt and water, then to knead it for a couple of minutes. Sprinkle the pastry board with oatmeal, and roll out the cake as thinly as possible. Sprinkle the top with a little oatmeal, and put the cake straight onto a hot, ungreased griddle. Bake on both sides without allowing the cake to color, and then put to dry by the fire or in a very cool oven.

However, a little fat or butter is usually rubbed in before the water is added, and some people add a pinch of baking soda. Making neat oatcakes is not easy. It is best to knead enough for one cake at a time; since the dough must be slack, it gets very sticky. When the dough is rolled out, the edges crack (pinch them between thumb and finger). Round oatcakes are cut with a plate and then quartered to make the shape in which they are sold in packets. Use plenty of oatmeal for dusting, but keep the griddle brushed clean.

[Oats—French: *avoine;* German: *Hafer;* Italian: *avena;* Spanish: *avena*]

OCCA or **oca.** *See* yam (oka).

OCTOPUS is a creature that is widely regarded with revulsion. It is true that octopuses are very strong and divers have occasionally been attacked by large specimens which they have disturbed, but skin divers usually find them to be rather shy and to have a certain nobility. The salivary glands of a few species, notably the little blue octopus of the Pacific and Indian oceans, secrete a poison, and their bites can be rapidly fatal. European and American species, though, are harmless, and, unlike cuttlefish, octopuses rarely bite. Octopuses are highly regarded as food on most warm seacoasts, although in America and Britain no *cephalopods are traditionally eaten. An Aberdeen trawler skipper I once sailed with was horrified when I suggested that there were people who would be glad to have the octopuses he caught in his nets and threw away.

Octopuses are mollusks, so have no backbone and during evolution have lost the stiffening they once had. Unlike squids and cuttlefish, they prefer to crawl rather than swim and hide in holes. The lairs of octopuses are usually surrounded by the shells they have eaten and by stones, which they gather together and, when disturbed, pull over their door.

There are hundreds of different species, of variable quality as food. Some are too big or too small, some very tough, and others have a strong and musky taste. The best have been compared to lobster. Most European octopus recipes come from the Mediterranean and Portugal. The best-known species is the common octopus (*Octopus vulgaris*); the rather similar *O. macropus* has longer, thinner tentacles and is called *polpessa* by the Italians. These octopuses will be distinguished by shoppers in Mediterranean fishing ports, but most people elsewhere will not acquire that degree of expertise. Smaller octopuses of the genus *Eledone* can even be bought canned. There are two kinds. The red (*E. moschata*) is the more tender, but has a strong musky flavor, while the white (*E. cirrosa*), which has a pale color, lacks the musky taste but is tougher. The main problem with octopuses lies not in recognizing the kinds, which will become clear only with trial and error (and now that we have frozen octopus, it can come from anywhere), but in cooking them so that they look presentable and are not tough.

There are many ways of cooking octopus—it may be boiled or broiled—and the techniques for making it tender vary almost as much as those for cooking rice. The following method comes from Spain, where very good octopus is to be had.

When caught, the animal is quickly turned inside out, which kills it, then soundly beaten against the rocks. The red color turns to gray. (Greeks say that the octopus should be beaten 40 times, but such exertion is hardly necessary.) Octopus bought fresh or frozen from the market must be beaten well with a bottle or a rolling pin. The insides are taken out (keep only the ink sac if the recipe calls for it) and the beak and eyes cut away. In the octopus, unlike cuttlefish and squid, the tentacles and not the body are the best part. Put a wine cork in the head (a Spanish trick to float the animal and ensure even cooking). Drop it into boiling water, no salt, with a potato—a big one for a big octopus and a small one for a small. Cook gently. When the potato is cooked, the octopus is cooked. Take it out of the water, cool it, remove the skin, and peel off the horny suckers. Cooked this way, octopus is white, tender, and appetizing. Cut into convenient pieces, it may be simply dressed with chopped parsley, oil, and lemon juice for a seafood salad. Other recipes cook octopus with wine, onion, garlic, tomato, peppers, herbs, and oil. There are even recipes that include bitter chocolate. Dried octopus is good made into a soup, or it can be broiled. The Japanese are reputed to consider that the eyes are the best part.

[*Octopus*—French: *poulpe, pieuvre;* German: *Seepolyp, Krake, achtfüssiger Tintenfisch;* Italian: *polpo;* Spanish: *pulpo*]

OFFAL in its general sense means garbage. In butchery, it is the bits of the carcass that are not straightforward meat, fat, and bone. Thus it includes the head and all the main internal organs, notably *liver, *kidney, *sweetbreads (thymus), *tripe (stomach), *heart, and *lights (lungs).

OILS. *See* fats.

OKA. *See* yam.

OKRA, okro, lady's-fingers, or **gumbo** (*Hibiscus esculentus*) belongs to the mallow family. It has edible rocket-shaped pods, sometimes with 5–7 prominent ridges or with slight spines, colored deep or light green, and of various lengths up to 8 in. (20 cm). In buying, it is safer to choose small pods, since the long-podded varieties should be picked every 2–3 days; old ones are tough and fibrous—these plants belong to the same family as cotton, Deccan hemp, and Cuba bast—all fiber plants—and are themselves used to make paper.

Okra has yellow flowers rather like cotton, grows 3–6 ft (1–2 m) high, and needs a frost-free warm climate. It is native to Africa and came via Egypt to Mediterranean Europe in the 13th century. It was probably taken by slaves to the Caribbean (where it is still very popular) and to the U.S., where it is an essential ingredient of Creole gumbo. Okra is grown in huge quantities in the southern states for the canning industry—it is very mucilaginous and therefore useful for thickening canned soups and sauces. It is used differently in Greek, Balkan, Turkish, Middle Eastern, and Indian cooking. Even the canned okra from the countries of the eastern Mediterranean is different from the canned okra of America.

Okra has a delicious flavor, but the mucilage gives it a slimy texture many people dislike. In gumbo, this is necessary and is even added to with *filé powder, but in the Levant, where okra is a very important food, attempts are made to reduce the mucilaginous quality. The fresh pods are soaked for half an hour to an hour—even more—in vinegar, lemon juice, or mixed vinegar and water before being cooked. Alternatively they may be sprinkled with salt and left in the sun for an hour to dry. (Dried okras, small ones threaded on strings, are a common sight hanging in the shops in Turkey, and are kept in this way for use in winter. They are soaked before use and often stewed with mutton.)

In the U.S. okra is usually sliced, but in the Levant great care is taken to pare off the stalk without cutting into the pod. Cutting the pod lets the mucilage come out. Okra is usually fried before cooking it with meat, onion, tomato, or whatever the recipe calls for. Frying also reduces the glutinosity. If you are using canned okras, American ones are best for American recipes and European ones (from Greece, Cyprus, or Turkey) for Levantine recipes. Rinse canned okras before using them. Since they are already cooked, they should be added late in the cooking and not treated as if fresh. However, fresh okras are usually available in Greek or Indian shops.

BAMIEH BI ZAYT

This is a very well-known hors d'oeuvre in Lebanon. It seems to show off okra to perfection. Pare the tops of 3 cups of small okras, and, after washing, dry them well. Make a paste by pounding together a good handful of green coriander leaves, 8 cloves of garlic, and ½ teaspoon of salt. Also peel 10 small or pickling onions.

Fry the okras in plenty of olive oil until they are tender but still firm and green. Take them out, then fry the onions until they are golden. Pour off most of the oil and fry the pounded herb mixture a little. Slice 3 tomatoes into the bottom of a pressure cooker. Cover with the okras neatly arranged on top. Put the onions on top of that, and sprinkle with about ½ cup of lemon juice. Add the fried herb mixture and a little water, only just enough to prevent the contents from burning. Close the cooker. Cook for 12 minutes, open, and simmer until the juice is almost all evaporated. Season with more salt if necessary, plus a pinch of sugar and pepper to taste. Place in a serving dish, arrange the vegetables, cool, and chill.

OLIVE (*Olea europaea*) is almost certainly a Mediterranean native and may be descended from the oleaster, the wild olive which grows in many places around the Mediterranean. (The oleaster has tiny olives which are nearly all stone, and the bushes are very prickly.) Olive trees are very long-lived and perhaps span a thousand years—some gnarled old relics are supposed to have been planted around the time of Christ. The very old trees still bear fruit. In the past, the olive was one of the mainstays of life in the Mediterranean basin, growing a little way inland around most of the coasts and penetrating a few miles into the mountain valleys. It also grows over a large area of Spain (the world's largest producer) and in a few inland places south of the Alps, where it has been planted. It was taken to America by the Spaniards. Today, it is also grown in California, South Africa, Australia, and many other areas where there is a suitable climate. Some of the many varieties are more suitable for pressing, others for preserving.

Olive oil. For oil, the olives must be ripe. In the primitive method, the olives are crushed in a trough under a huge rolling stone like a millstone, and the liquid is squeezed out. This is purified by floating it on water—streams can run red with the washings. These old methods are still used in some mountain villages. The modern method is to squeeze the pulp under hydraulic presses and separate the oil with a centrifuge. Oil which is made by pressing, without any other treatment, is called virgin oil. However, there are considerable differences in the virgin oil from country to country. In Spain, for instance, virgin oil is often very rank—

only Spaniards brought up on it would like it. In Italy, the *olii vergini* are divided into various grades: *olio extra vergine* with 1.0% acidity, *olio sopraffino vergine* with 1.0–1.5%, *olio fino vergine* with 1.5–3.0%, and *olio vergine* with 3–4% acidity. Acidity, in fact, is the criterion by which oils are judged, but the buyer, visiting some village in the mountains to find an excellent salad oil, will pour a little into the palm of a hand, rub his hands together briskly to heat the oil, and then cup them to smell it. Poor oil, with an acidity too high for eating, was in the past known as *lampante* (lamp oil, more or less), and it was used for burning. Even 25 years ago, olive oil was still being burned in lamps in remote places. The dross (*sansa*) left over from pressing still contains some oil, and this is extracted with solvents, which also extract other resinous substances. Poor olive oil, like seed oils, can be treated, first with an alkali to neutralize the acids, then by heating and filtration through earths or charcoal to remove the color, and finally by steam-stripping in a vacuum to remove the flavor. *Lampante* oil that has been stripped is called *olio rettificato* in Italy; oil from the extracted residues is *olio di sansa rettificato*. Ordinary olive oil (*olio di oliva*) consists of stripped oils with 5–15% virgin oil added for flavor, but if it is made by extraction from the *sansa*, it should be so labeled (*olio di sansa e di oliva*).

Italy is usually associated with the production of the finest olive oils. But whether the finest comes from the Italian or the French Riviera is a matter of opinion and taste. Italy exports fine oils, but does not produce enough for her own requirements and has to import oil from elsewhere. Turkey, Tunisia, and Morocco are other important producers. Some of the oil produced in Spain is excellent, but Spanish themselves often have a love for very rank olive oil called *aruja* (which once upset the stomachs of tourists), which is at its worst if the olives have been allowed to get overripe and to lie on the ground, or if the trees were infested with insect pests. To this day, I have friends who find food quite tasteless without a good slosh of semirancid olive oil, and a bottle of virgin olive oil would remain unused forever by them.

All olive oil is costly, and good olive oil is very costly and hard to find—but it is worth looking for. Because light affects oils adversely, the best you can buy—short of visiting the farm—will be in cans and not in clear glass bottles. Once the can is opened, what is not for immediate use should be kept in small, full bottles in the refrigerator. There is much to be said for the custom in many Italian households of using oil-seed oils for cooking and olive oil as a condiment, which is always on the table for dressing vegetables and salads.

Pickled olives. To most of the world outside the olive-growing regions, there are three sorts of olives: green ones with stones, stuffed green ones (usually stuffed with pieces of sweet red pepper or anchovies but also with almonds, tunny, or even hot green chilies), and black ones. The counter in a market in Spain, Italy, or Greece will confront the newcomer with a bewildering number of types for sale. So taste them before buying.

Black olives are ripe olives. Commercially, they are usually black, but home-cured ones may be brown or sometimes mottled; some may be wrinkled and others plump.

Green olives are unripe. As soon as the olives are properly formed, in September, some are picked as broken or squashed olives. They are split by hitting them gently with a mallet before putting them into pure water, which is changed every day for up to 2 weeks. At the end of this time, most of the bitterness will have leached out (but some should remain). Then a brine should be prepared, at about 10% strength, which can have fennel, bay, chili, savory, or garlic boiled in it to taste. When it is cold, this pickle is poured over the olives. A slight lactic fermentation and the natural acidity of the olives makes them keep. After 2–3 months (by Christmas), these olives are ready to eat. Again, always ask to taste broken olives before buying—vendors in Mediterranean markets expect it; to ask is polite. Broken olives bought loose can be kept in a plastic bag in the refrigerator for a few days but should be allowed to warm to room temperature before serving. Firm, bitter broken olives are excellent with bread as a simple opening to a meal.

After the September-October olives come the more familiar green olives. By this time, the olives are more oily. The original method of removing the bitterness was to soak the olives in *lye, but it is now more usual to employ caustic soda solution, in which the olives are soaked for 6 hours. You can observe the penetration of the caustic soda by cutting into an olive; when the color change has reached almost to the stone, the olives are ready. They have then to be soaked in frequent changes of water for 3 days to remove all the caustic soda. For pickling, the same 10% brine with flavorings is used as for black olives, and herbs can also be packed in with the olives, which are ready to eat in a few days. In Spain, not everyone likes this quick method, and the bitterness of the olives is removed by soaking in changes of water over a 15-day period.

When the olives are just starting to color, it is time to make what the French call the *olives d'été*, to be used the following summer. These olives are simply put straight into the 10% brine (perfumed as usual) and sealed in bottles. These olives are bitter (*olives amères* is an alternative name); the salt, the fermentation that takes place, and perhaps substances in the olives make them keep quite safely.

When the olives are violet, just before they are quite ripe, they are also pickled in 10% herbed brine, usually after some knife cuts have been made in each one. These *olives taillées*, laid down around Christmas, are ready by April. They replace the early *piccolines*, which by this time have begun to soften or take on the taste of leather which is so characteristic of poor commercial olives. Shriveled olives, which are to be pressed for oil, are also pricked, allowed to bleed, and treated for a day or so with salt and herbs (they are *olives piquées* or pricked olives).

The nature of pickled olives depends not only on the method that has been used but also on the variety of olive. In Spain, for instance, many are named with simple, descriptive country names. There is the *aceituna zorzaleña,* a small round olive which gets its name from being a favorite food of certain birds (*zorzales*). Varieties named by the shape include the *picudilla* (pointed) and the *tetuda* (breast-shaped); a common type is known as *aceituna corval* (long). Olives may be called after a place (e.g., *Sevillanas*). A very small olive is the *manzanilla,* and the one reckoned to be the best of all is the *aceituna de la reina* (olive of the queen), which is very large. However, size is the last criterion by which to judge eating olives. Californian olives are often enormous but taste of nothing, while the tiny olives from Liguria taste excellent.

The olives used in cooking are usually black, but green olives are sometimes called for. It is a great mistake to add either indiscriminately to dishes, because olives, especially green ones, do not marry well with all flavors. Because olives stuffed with red pepper look decorative when sliced across, they are often used to decorate snacks in which their taste or texture is unsuitable—caviar or scrambled eggs, for instance. And black olives will not do as imitation bits of truffle.

[*Olive*—French: *olive;* German: *Olive;* Italian: *oliva, uliva;* Spanish: *olivo, oliva, aceituna*]

OLOROSO. *See* sherry.

ONION (*Allium cepa*) is certainly the most commonly used flavoring vegetable in the world and has been in cultivation for so long that the wild ancestors are unknown. In China and Japan, another onion species, *A. fistulosum,* has been cultivated since time immemorial. The onions are variously classified by botanists with daffodils in the family Amaryllidaceae, with the lilies with Liliaceae, or in their own family, the Alliaceae. The genus *Allium* includes *garlic, *leeks, *chives, and *shallots as well as onions. From the cook's point of view, onions are recognized by taste. There are dozens of species, and many grow wild. Tests carried out during World War II showed them all to be edible, although not necessarily delicious. Most onions are cultivated varieties of *A. cepa,* which is the important species over most of the world. The enormous number of varieties have a wide variation in texture and flavor, as well as in season, size, flesh color, and keeping quality. Onions of a particular variety can be milder at the beginning of the season that they are at the end of it. Some Continental chefs say that you cannot make certain regional dishes properly without the correct variety of onion. For example, an authentic Flemish *carbonnade* cannot be made without strong Flemish onions (and the right beer), but the same onions would be a disaster if used in a salad, which calls for the mild, sweet Valencia onions.

Cooks who are well alerted to the quantity of garlic required in a dish are not always so sensitive about onion, perhaps because it is such a basic ingredient. Onions vary not only in quality and intensity of flavor but also in their usefulness for cooking. Some onions are naturally tough or remain tough when baked, boiled, or fried. Others are watery and difficult to fry crisp.

The yellow or white globe onion is the popular all-purpose onion in the U. S., accounting for some 75% of the onions grown here. The moderate-size globe onion has a strong aroma and taste, a firm, crisp texture, and an ability to survive long cooking without losing flavor. It is therefore excellent for making the onion sauce *soubise,* in which a large quantity of onions are braised with rice and butter, as well as for use in stews. The other widely available onion in the U. S. is the large yellow Spanish or Bermuda onion, which is often preferred for onion soup because it contains more sugar than other types and can be sautéed until caramelized to give soup a rich color and faintly sweet flavor. These large mild onions are also the best for stuffing and for deep-fried onion rings, and they are thinly sliced for eating raw with hamburgers or sandwiches. Red Italian or Creole onions are mild and sweet, a favorite in salads and excellent chopped raw into bean dishes; they are not strong enough to add much flavor to stewed dishes. Little white onions can be a delicacy if braised in stock just until tender to accompany a main course, served in a cream sauce, or added at the last moment to any stew. They are also ideal for pickling. (To peel them easily, drop them in boiling water, count to 10, cool them under running water, and slip the skins off.)

For keeping, onions with thick, dry outer skins and a neck dried off to a mere whisp are best. Often they are not the ones with the best flavor, and they may be hard and tough. Onions that have sprouted, have a woody core, feel soft when squeezed, or are wet should be avoided, as should any that smell musty or are rotted around the neck. Even if part of a bad onion can be salvaged, it always has a bad flavor. Cut onion or chopped onion, if allowed to stand, soon gets an unpleasant smell (which is tolerable only in the kebabs of an Eastern bazaar when it is a part of the local color). If chopped onion has to be kept handy, it should be lightly fried in butter (a chef's trick) and stored in the refrigerator. Since onions are available all year round, there is little need to preserve them. Dried onion flakes can be useful in an emergency, but some people use them too often, and such products as onion salt are to be avoided—they distort flavors because of their preservatives, and they have none of the character of fresh onions.

Spring onions, green onions, or scallions can be derived from several species, harvested young for use in salads. If the leaf in cross section is flattened (with a convex outer surface and concave inner one), then it is a *cepa* onion, and a real "spring onion." If the leaf is circular in section, then it will probably be a so-called Welsh onion, a variety of *A. fistulosum,* which is also called the Japanese bouncing onion and is much cultivated in the Orient. Both these species have hollow leaves.

Another Oriental onion, the Chinese chive, Cuchay, or Cantonese onion (*A. tuberosum*), grows wild in China. It is a bigger plant than the European chive and has flat, solid leaves. The flowers taste of a mixture of onion and honey and can be used in salads. The chive proper (*A. schoenoprasum*) is very widely distributed around the world and has a thin, grasslike, round-sectioned, and hollow leaf, like the Welsh onion but much smaller. The sand leek, *A. scorodoprasum,* grows wild in sandy soils from Scotland to the Caucasus and over most of Europe. The flavor is like mild garlic, and it is cultivated occasionally. This species is sometimes called the rocambole, a name which is also used for some forms of garlic.

[*Onion*—French: *onion;* German: *Zweibel;* Italian: *cipolla;* Spanish: *cebolla*]

ORACHE. *See* spinach.

OPOSSUM (*Didelphis marsupialis*). The only marsupial in North America, the opossum (or possum) is as eagerly eaten by some people as it is shunned by others. Its original range was mostly in the U. S. South, where "possum and sweet taters" are famed, but it has been introduced into the West Coast and north into Canada. The opossum's tasty meat has been compared to pork; its liver is considered especially good. It is usually roasted or stewed. In one Ozark method, an opossum is caught live and fattened for a week on mashed persimmons. It is then killed, skinned, stuffed with persimmons, sweet potatoes, bread crumbs, and herbs, and basted with cream as it roasts.

ORANGE is a word derived from the Arabic *nāranj.* Oranges came originally from the Orient, but their history has not been established with certainty. Bitter oranges, brought by the Arabs, may have been the

first to be introduced to Europe. The first sweet oranges may have been those brought back by Vasco da Gama when he returned from his first voyage around the Cape of Good Hope in 1498. After that, they quickly spread to the West Indies and the warmer parts of America. Oranges were grown under glass in orangeries in more northern countries such as Britain, but could grow well in the ideal climate of the Mediterranean. The loose-skinned oranges, such as the tangerine, were not introduced to Europe until the early 19th century and to America not until later still, although they had been popular in Japan and China for centuries.

Oranges belong to the *citrus group of the rue family (Rutaceae), and all require warmth. Oranges grown in the tropics often remain green when ripe, but the same varieties from climates like that of the Mediterranean normally turn orange. Cold storage or treatment with gas will also turn them orange. For sales purposes, oranges may be dyed to make them more orange (in the U.S. this must be indicated with a color-added stamp). The practices of dyeing oranges and waxing the skins are not a good thing if you want to use the peel for grating. Except in the tropics, oranges usually are ripe during the winter months. In Spain, which has a typical orange-producing climate, the orange season begins with the small loose-skinned oranges (mandarins, satsumas, and clementines), which reach a peak at around Christmas—hence the association of tangerines with Christmas stockings. By January, the big navel oranges are ripe, while the supply of loose-skinned oranges declines, and the bitter Seville oranges for marmalade are also coming in. The season ends with blood oranges. This pattern is more or less repeated in the U.S. (which is now the world's largest producer of oranges), and the rest of the year is covered by imports.

Tight-skinned sweet oranges (*Citrus sinensis*) include the most popular oranges for eating and for juice. Among them is the Washington navel, a fine, usually seedless, dessert orange with the characteristic navel at the flower end. Navels were introduced to the U.S. from Brazil in the 19th century, and got the name Washington because that is where they were first grown. (They are also called Riverside, where they became established in California, and Bahia, where they came from in Brazil.) The Shamouti variety, which is large and seedless, originally came from Israel (Jaffa oranges), but is now also grown in Cyprus and elsewhere. The other predominant sweet orange variety is the Valencia, a late one with a long season. Blood oranges usually have thin skins and are difficult to peel but have plenty of sweet reddish juice. In general, sweet oranges tend to be uninteresting if used in cooking. Perhaps these oranges should never be cooked: they usually acquire a taste like weak marmalade. Mixed into fruit salads, put with nuts and cheese, or into everything-but-the-kitchen-sink salads, orange sections are more often than not a mistake, since they tend to obtrude. They do not marry well with wine.

Loose-skinned oranges (*Citrus reticulata*) include mandarins, tangerines, and satsumas, but perhaps not clementines, which may be a tangerine × sweet orange cross. In any case the names have become confused. Mandarin denotes a Chinese origin, and tangerine should refer to a variety that was originally shipped from North Africa through Tangiers. The satsuma was originally Japanese, very small; it is hardy, standing quite a bit of cold compared to other citruses, and has very few, if any, seeds. Clementines, hybrid or not, are between a tangerine and an orange in character and are commonly grown in North Africa and Spain. King oranges may also be a cross. The variety was introduced into the U.S. in 1882 as a heavy bearer, resistant to cold, but is not popular. The West Indian ortanique, with a thin, tough skin and flattened fruits, is probably a tangerine × orange cross; it is juicy and stores well. Tangerine × orange crosses are called tangors and include the temple orange, which makes excellent eating. Tangelos, which are easily confused with tangors, are tangerine × grapefruit hybrids. Among them are the ugli, which is a bit like a sweet, loose-skinned grapefruit and may be very large, and the Minneola tangelo, which is smooth, dark orange, and has a nipple at the stem end. As in all citrus fruits, the skin of oranges is the packaging. You should reject fruit in which the skin is bruised—and loose-skinned oranges are more perishable than the tight-skinned kinds—but you should not allow yourself to be beguiled too much by the packaging. E.g., the honey tangerine is very sweet but may not look good from the outside.

Tangerine peel is very different in scent from orange peel (just as the fruit has a different taste); it is used dried as a flavoring in Chinese cooking. The peel can easily be dried by threading it on a string and hanging it in a warm place, but home-dried tangerine peel is likely to have a weaker flavor than that imported from China. The peel of fresh tangerines can be grated and used as a change in dishes that are normally flavored with orange peel. Tangerine peel is also excellent in sweet dishes. (Even as a child, I asked for it in icing for Christmas cakes because I detested the taste of bitter almond.)

Bitter oranges, Seville oranges, or **sour oranges** (*Citrus aurantium*) are the most important in cooking. A typical bitter orange has a rough, tough, dark-orange skin; it is very aromatic, but the pulp is sour, astringent, and full of seeds, indeed virtually inedible. Although the juice is excellent when properly sweetened and is used in drinks, the important part of a bitter orange is its skin. Some varieties provide the basic flavoring for Curaçao and orange-flavored liqueurs such as Aurum, Grand Marnier, and Cointreau. Dried bitter orange peel is a standard ingredient in the bouquet garni used in the south of France. It is very easily dried, keeps up to 2 years, and will be treasured as a flavoring by anyone who discovers it.

The passion for orange marmalade is particularly British; large quantities of bitter Seville oranges are imported every year for marmalade. Given a good recipe, the goodness of marmalade depends entirely on the quality of the bitter oranges—something which cannot be judged by eye because as usual the best are often not the best-looking. Oddly enough, it is difficult to buy Seville oranges in Spain, and one's supply has often to be stolen from the park. Bitter orange trees, which are to be seen on roadsides in Mediterranean towns, may be recognized because they are large, thorny, and have broadly winged leaf stalks. They are also grown for the large flowers, which are used in the perfumery business. They are the basis of oil of neroli or bigarde oil (named after Anne Maria de la Tremoille, Princess of Nerole, who is supposed to have discovered it around 1670), which smells like eau de Cologne. The flowers can also be made into a sweet aromatic jam by those who like shatteringly sweet things. Oil of petitgrain is produced by steam distillation of the leaves (other types come from the leaves of lemon and tangerine) and is used commercially as a flavoring in many foods, just as the leaves of oranges and lemons can be used as a flavoring in home cooking.

Bergamot (*Citrus bergamia*) is used mainly in perfumery as a source of an aromatic essential oil. It is a smaller tree than the lemon or orange and grown particularly in Sicily and Calabria. The fruits are preserved and candied. In this respect its uses are similar to the citron.

Calamondin may be a hybrid between a kumquat and a mandarin. A separate species (*Citrus mitis*), it originated in the Philippines. Calamondins are frequently grown for ornament and have small orangelike fruits which can be candied.

OREGANO (*Origanum vulgare*) is an herb that is closely related to sweet *marjoram but is more pungent. It grows on calcareous soils in most countries in Europe, but there is a great difference between the flavors of leaves gathered in southern Italy, of those from, say, the South Downs of Britain, and

OREGANO

of the *rigani* sold in Greece (where the name covers a number of *Origanum* species). In regional dishes, the authentic flavor can depend on obtaining the herb from the correct source.

Oregano is perhaps best-known for its use in Italian cooking, but nowadays it is used all over the world in regions influenced by Mediterranean cooking. Fortunately it dries well, so fresh oregano is rarely necessary. Dried *rigani* from Greece includes flower buds as well as leaves.

[*Oregano*—French: *origan;* German: *Oregano;* Italian: *origano;* Spanish: *oregano*]

ORRIS. The dried aromatic roots of a species of iris (*Iris pallida*) that is a native of Dalmatia. The smell is reminiscent of violets, but the taste is bitter. Though it was much used as a flavoring in the past, orris will rarely if ever be called for these days. It is still used commercially as the basis for "violet" scents and flavors.

[*Orris*—French: *racine d'iris;* German: *Veilchenwürzel;* Italian: *radice di giaggiolo;* Spanish: *raiz de iris florentina, raiz de lirio*]

ORTANIQUE. *See* orange.

ORTOLAN. *See* birds.

OSMOSIS. I gained a rudimentary idea of osmosis at an early age from a French reader full of stories in which a know-all father imparted his encyclopedic knowledge to his boys. In this case, he filled a bladder with sugar solution and suspended it in fresh water. The sugar could not pass out of the bladder, but the water could pass in, and did so until the bladder burst—a case of nature trying, as usual, to iron out differences and make everything equal. The force that bursts the bladder is osmotic pressure, the bladder is a semipermeable membrane (it lets the water through but not the sugar), and the whole phenomenon is known as osmosis. The walls of living cells are semipermeable membranes. If cucumber slices are sprinkled with salt or put in brine, osmosis makes them wilt and water comes out of their cells. Osmosis in the other direction happens when wilted plants that are put into water regain their turgidity.

[Osmosis—French: osmose; German: Osmose; Italian: osmosi; Spanish: osmosis]

OSTRICH (Struthio camelus) was originally domesticated, selected, and farmed for its feathers, mainly in South Africa. At one time, ostriches were hunted almost to extinction, but huge fortunes were made by rearing them. The feathers are no longer fashionable for stoles or furs and are not even needed by nude dancers these days, but ostrich farms still exist. The skin makes a fashionable leather and the meat is dried to make *biltong. The eggs, which are equivalent to at least a dozen hen eggs, are good, though strongly eggy in flavor.

[Ostrich—French: autruche; German: Strauss; Italian: struzzo; Spanish: avestruz]

OVENS. See baking.

OXALIC ACID (COOH)$_2$ occurs in many plants, usually in the form of its potassium, sodium, or calcium salts (oxalates). The acid and its salts are poisonous in any quantity. Some people are allergic or particularly susceptible to oxalic acid poisoning and should avoid spinach, sorrel, wood sorrel, and rhubarb. Rhubarb leaves contain a much higher concentration of oxalic acid salts than the stems and have caused fatal poisonings. The poison is more active when the leaves are cooked in soft water. Oxalic acid inhibits absorption by the body of calcium and iron, which have insoluble oxalates. For this reason, spinach, which contains 10 times as much iron and 20 times as much calcium as cabbage does, is not as good a source of these elements as it might appear to be.

[Oxalic acid—French: acide oxalique; German: Oxalsäure; Italian: acido ossalico; Spanish: ácido oxálico]

OYSTER. While the term may refer to a cut of *bacon or the morsel of meat in the back of poultry, an oyster usually means a bivalve *mollusk. The many species of oyster are distributed in all except polar seas: the museum at Arcachon, an oyster-growing center in southwestern France, exhibits a collection of more than 300 types from around the world. They vary in form from the neat and flat European oysters through rough, misshapen oysters which have to be broken off rocks with chisel and hammer to strange oysters such as the zigzag-shaped purple-shelled cock's-comb oyster (Lopha cristagalli) of the Indian and Pacific oceans. Oysters also vary considerably in flavor and texture, not only with the species but also with the place in which they are fattened. Because oysters are rather vulnerable to enemies, such as the slipper limpets, and to severe winters, oyster beds get killed out from time to time and have to be relaid. Oysters introduced from elsewhere very often take on much of the flavor that is characteristic of their new home.

For commercial purposes oysters are cleaned by a sophisticated process which involves placing them in tanks of clean sea water under ultraviolet light for about a day and a half. Oysters, like other bivalves, feed on small organisms and other material that they filter out of the water, but they can equally pick up the organisms of typhoid and salmonella from polluted water or the poisonous diatoms such as those that create the red tides. In clean water, they will gradually sweep harmful organisms out with the currents they create, and any such organisms will not infect the water but in treatment will be killed by the ultraviolet light.

You can eat oysters directly from the sea—this was the norm in the past and still is in many countries—but only with suitable care. They are safer in primitive countries where there are less sewers emptying into the sea. Oysters for eating raw should be alive and fresh. Opening oysters can be risky; even the skilled sometimes knife themselves in the hand. The usual method—but not the only one—is to hold the oyster in one hand with the round side down (you do not want to lose the juices); it is best to use a cloth to protect the hand in case the knife slips. Wiggle a knife point between the two halves of the shell close to the hinge, and twist to crack it. (In species with beaks, the projections may have to be broken off with pliers first.) Push the knife in and sweep the blade carefully across, keeping the point tight against the upper shell—the object is to cut the muscle attachment as close to the upper shell as possible and not to damage any other part of the animal. Take off the flat shell, and either lay the oyster as it is on the dish or slip the knife under the oyster to cut it free from the bottom shell without spilling the juices and turn the oyster over, top side down and ready to eat. Some types with large beards need to have them cut off, but usually this is hardly necessary. When oyster are eaten raw on the half shell, a squeeze of lemon, cayenne pepper, Tabasco sauce, and brown bread and butter are some of the common accompaniments. Many oyster fanciers prefer them with no additions at all.

Cooking oysters is tricky, since heat makes them tough. They should only just curl. Long cooking will make oysters disintegrate, as they do in a steak, kidney, and oyster pudding. For this, frozen oysters can well be used, but the slightly fishy taste they give can be a mistake. The adding of oysters to this dish stems from the days when oysters were cheap, not the luxury which they usually are now, but the oysters used may well have been pickled.

The quality of oysters is reflected in their price. Names are locally important, but the oysters will probably have been brought from somewhere else and laid in the fattening grounds from which they take their taste and their name, often in an estuary where the slightly brackish water makes the oysters fat (if it is too fresh, they get bloated and soft; they die if the salt concentration is under 3%). They are graded by size.

Oysters are also sold shucked—removed from their shells. In this form they can be packed in cardboard or plastic boxes and kept on ice (they last 7–9 days) for use mainly in cooking. Shucked oysters are also sold frozen, canned, or smoked. Frozen oysters in cartons are exported from Japan; they are often considered excellent for cooking but are perhaps rather fishy. Frozen oysters will keep in the freezer for a month. Dried oysters are a Chinese ingredient.

American oysters. The Atlantic coast of North America is very rich in oysters. The main species is *Crassostrea virginica,* which is known by such local names as bluepoints, Cape Cods, Cotuits, Chincoteagues, Fire Island salts, Rappahannocks, and many more. These oysters are the best for eating on the half shell. Small coon oysters (*Ostrea frons*), so called because raccoons feast on them at low tide, are found from the Carolinas southward.

On the Pacific coast of America is found the indigenous Olympia oyster (*Ostrea lurida*), which some consider the finest-flavored of all. Although it is only a few inches long, and it takes some 200 oysters to make a pint shucked, it is so appreciated that it is profitable for tidewater oyster farmers to cultivate it commercially. As soon as the first railway to the Pacific coast was completed, the Virginia oyster was brought across and introduced to northern California. (There was no difficulty in doing so, since oysters live well for a number of days if they are packed in seaweed and kept moist.) The Pacific or Japanese oyster (*Crassostrea gigas*) is a larger species that is rarely eaten raw.

Despite folklore, American oysters are safe to eat in any month, including those whose names do not contain the letter *R*. However, months without an *R* roughly represent the oyster's spawning season, when their quality is generally lower than it is in the cooler months.

Portuguese oysters or **Ports** (*Crassostrea angulata*) are much more irregular in shape than the flat oyster and much more like the American Virginia oyster. They are less prized than the flat oyster and best cooked, though mostly eaten raw. Ports are in season all the year. They prefer warmer waters but were introduced into the Bay of Arcachon on the Atlantic coast of France by accident when a ship with live oysters aboard sank there. They have recently been relaid in British waters as well.

French oysters are usually known by their place of origin. Thus *Arcachonnaises* are very white Portuguese oysters (*Portugaises*) from the basin of Arcachon. *Belons* are rather pink oysters named after the Belon River in Finistère. *Bouziques* are *Portugaises* from near Sète, Herault—on the Mediterranean. *Marennes,* from the Vendée near Rochefort, may be green or white. The greens (*vertes*) are particularly famous for their color and the special taste they develop (whether they are locally bred or brought in at 2–3 years from elsewhere) when they are fattened in deep pits or *claires* connected by channels to the sea. In these *claires* grows a particular type of green alga, and the oysters become full of it. Brittany oysters or Bretons are flat oysters and are not in season in the summer. Bretons, excellent oysters, are usually cultivated on limed tiles. They are often used for

relaying elsewhere, after which they cease to be Bretons and adopt the local flavor.

British oysters. The native British species is the common European oyster or flat oyster (*Ostrea edulis*), which retains its eggs within the shell until fertilization. This makes them unpleasant to eat in the breeding season, which is in summer when there is not an *R* in the month. Natives is the name given in Britain to oysters from the Essex and Kentish beds; correctly, they come from between the North Foreland and Orford Ness. This includes Colchester and Whitstable oysters, but often other dud or illegitimate flat oysters steal into the act. Royal Whitstables or Royals are from the Whitstable Oyster Company (to which the word Royal—in the context of oysters—is exclusive) and are true natives although mostly relaid from France. Pearly and with a small beard, they have a reputation for sweetness of taste (to some of us, any oyster is sweet). Colchester Pyefleets are from Pyefleet Creek in the Colnes estuary in Essex, one of the finest fattening grounds. Colne oysters have been famous since Roman times. The borough of Colchester has a charter from Richard I confirming its rights over Colchester Pyefleets, which are defined as coming from an area between North Bridge and West Ness. Dutchy oysters are Helford River oysters from the Duchy of Cornwall.

Mediterranean oysters are more expensive and less good than those of the Atlantic. Offbeat oysters, like the spiny oyster (*Spondylus gaderopus,* a member of another family), which skin divers can break off the rocks in many places, are considered good eating if they are taken from places (if they still exist) where pollution is not a problem. Their flavor is apt to be strongly of iodine and takes some getting used to. Still, I know people who greedily gobble up any shellfish.

Australian and New Zealand oysters. The rock oysters of New South Wales were relaid from New Zealand and have taken on a local character from the water in which they rest. The warm-water oyster which lives on the northern part of North Island of New Zealand is *Ostrea crassostrea,* a rock oyster rather like the American and Portuguese ones. It lives high enough up to be exposed by the tides; as a result, it will keep fresh and alive for long periods. The oyster of colder Pacific waters is *O. sinuata,* a deep-water oyster that is fished off the South Island of New Zealand.

[*Oyster*—French: *huître;* German: *Auster;* Italian: *ostrica;* Spanish: *ostra*]

OYSTER PLANT. *See* salsify.

P

PAK-CHOI. *See* Chinese cabbage.

PALM. A member of the family Palmae, and there are at least 4000 species, mostly in tropical and subtropical countries. Only one, the dwarf fan palm (*Chamaerops humilis*), a very spiny denizen of Mediterranean hillsides, is a native of Europe, although many species are grown ornamentally in the warmer areas. Palms are typically tall, unbranched trees, with a crown of leaves at the top. Some are smaller branched types, and there are even a few climbers, of which the most famous is the rattan palm (*Calamus rotang*), which has edible shoots and seeds but is important as the source of cane for making chair seats and baskets; local ropes made from it are used for tying wild elephants after capture. To palms we owe *dates, *coconuts, *betel nuts, palm oil (*see* fats) *sago, and palm *sugar.

Toddy is the fermented juice of various palms, tapped by cutting off a flowering shoot and suspending a pot under it to catch the drips. After a day in the tropical heat, it is already fermented. Palm juice concentrated by boiling gives palm sugar.

The hearts, that is the terminal buds, of many species of palm are edible. Their flavor is usually mild and not very definite, but the texture is firm and delicious. One well-known species is the cabbage palm, or palmetto (*Sabal palmetto*), which grows, among other places, on the coast in the southeastern parts of the U.S. and in Mexico. This palm is used for brushes, especially those required to remain stiff in hot water, but the cabbages—i.e., hearts—are also eaten, hence the name. Palm hearts are usually boiled until they are just tender and eaten as a vegetable or cold as a salad with mayonnaise or vinaigrette. Some kinds are eaten raw, and then only the tender center is used.

Palm hearts of various kinds are eaten in the tropical countries where they grow. In the Caribbean, hearts of *palmito* or *chou palmiste* (depending on whether the place is Spanish- or French-speaking) are cooked in many ways, e.g., stuffed, fried in fritters, or served in a cream sauce. In India and Bangladesh, the men working in the mangrove forests cut the hearts out of the exceedingly prickly *hetal* palm and eat its refreshing center, raw or curried. Cutting out the terminal buds of palms in many cases destroys the plant—one reason why palm hearts are a luxury. People living outside the tropics have to be content with canned palm hearts, which are very satisfactory. Any hearts that are not for immediate use when the can is opened can be kept for about 10 days in the refrigerator, providing they are in the canning liquid in a glass jar.

[*Palm*—French: *palme;* German: *Palme;* Italian: *palma;* Spanish: *palma*]

PALO CORTADO. *See* sherry.

PAN or **betel.** Chewing betel is an ancient habit in the East. The red spit marks that greet the European traveler on street corners in India and Pakistan are symptomatic of betel chewing and not of tuberculosis.

Basic essentials for a *pan* are *betel leaf, which is filled and folded into a parcel, usually held together with a clove. The filling consists of *betel nut, *catechu* (which gives the red color), and lime—the chemical, not the fruit—as a digestive. However, the contents are highly variable, and street *pan* sellers make up the packet to the customer's requirements. In North India, for instance, the taste is for something sharp or bitter, and the *pan* contains nothing more than a paste of the basic ingredients. But in South India, it is preferred sweet, with the betel nut (which is very hard) in bits and grated coconut, colored sugar crystals, and other things added. Such *pans* can be swallowed, but if they contain tobacco, even *bhang* (marijuana) or opium, the *pan* is spat. Exceptionally, a *pan* may contain gold leaf—for rather grand people.

PANCETTA. *See* bacon.

PANELA. *See* sugar.

PANIR or **channa.** A milk curd that hardly warrants the name of cheese. It is much used in India for making sweetmeats such as *rassagullas* and *sandesh,* or for frying and currying, often mixed with peas (*matar panir*).

To make *panir,* bring milk to the boil, then add some lemon juice, sour yogurt, citric acid, or other acid. As soon as the milk curdles, pour it into a clean cloth and hang it up to drain overnight. If you are in a hurry, take down the cloth after 10 minutes and immerse it in ice water. When the curd is cold, squeeze out the water by pressing the bag. To ensure that the curd does not have an acid taste, use as little of the acid as possible—just enough to cause coagulation—and do not leave the mixture hanging long enough for the milk to go sour. After drain-ing it, press the *panir* between boards or plates to consolidate it and to remove the last liquid. Let it dry, then cut it in squares or knead it according to the use to which it is to be put. Always use *panir* fresh.

PAO YÜ. *See* abalone.

PAPAIN is an enzyme, a vegetable *pepsin extracted from the *papaya. Although similar to pepsin in breaking down protein, it acts best in an alkaline or neutral medium, whereas pepsin prefers an acid one. It is presented in the form of a cream-colored powder, often used as a meat tenderizer, and usually has a rather pungent smell. The best grade will tenderize (partly digest) up to 300 times its weight of lean meat, ordinary grades as little as 35 times. Papain is also used for clearing liquids that are hazy with protein—80% of the beer made in the U.S. is cleared with it.

Papain is obtained by making several cuts with a stainless-steel knife or wooden spike in the unripe papaya fruit and collecting the latex which drips out in glass, porcelain, or plastic containers. Tapping is usually limited to five times, since the yield decreases each time. The juice is then dried either in the sun or in a dryer, but the temperature must remain below 122°–140°F (50–60°C), above which the papain is damaged. The best drying temperature is 86–104°F (30–40°C). Commercial papain is often preserved with salt.

PAPAW (*Asimina triloba*) is a small tree of temperate North America (from New York to Florida and as far west as Nebraska), locally known as the Michigan banana or the custard apple. Indeed, it is the only member of the custard apple family, the Anonaceae, that grows outside the tropics. The fruit is kidney-shaped with a smooth yellowish skin; it contains large brown seeds surrounded by a sweet, yellowish pulp. Ripening papaws have a heavy, cloying scent and a taste that has been described as a mixture of bananas and pears. They are often gathered after they have fallen to the ground. Sometimes they are roasted or made into a purée and used in pies. (*Papayas are also called pawpaws, which leads to unnecessary confusion.)

PAPAYA or **pawpaw** (*Carica papaya*) is among the most important tropical fruits, and one that you miss when returning to colder climates. The papaya is a native of

PAPAYA

tropical America, but had already been introduced to India by 1600. It is now one of the commonest fruits in all tropical countries. The plant grows to 25 ft (7½ m) high, with the papayas clustered like giant Brussels sprouts around the main stem. There are separate male and female trees, as well as trees which are hermaphrodite or change sex from male to female.

As a crop, the papaya has a number of advantages: the tree begins bearing in a year; it gives both the highest production of fruit per acre and an income next only to the banana in tropical climates. It is very sensitive to frost. Papayas look, at first sight, like smooth, green melons with more pointed ends; the similarity continues when the fruit is cut, except that the seeds are black or gray, lying free in a hollow center. They are semi-transparent, like caviar in appearance but like mustard and cress in taste; they are sometimes used as a condiment.

Unripe papayas are sometimes cooked as a vegetable or made into pickles. Ripe ones are much more important and are eaten raw as a fruit. The flesh is much finer in texture than that of a melon and ranges from orange

to yellow in color. The flavor is sweet, delicately perfumed, and sometimes faintly sickly. The lack of acidity that is common in tropical fruits can be corrected with a squeeze of lime juice. At the beginning of a hot day, a papaya makes the best possible breakfast. The plant is also the source of the tenderizer *papain, and so the juice and leaves are used locally for tenderizing in cookery.

[*Papaya*—French: *papaye;* German: *Papaija, Melonenfrucht;* Italian: *papaia;* Spanish: *papaya*]

PAPRIKA is an orange-red powder made by drying and grinding special varieties of *sweet pepper that are said to have been taken to Hungary by the Turks. Although

PAPRIKA

these peppers are pointed in shape, they do not have the pungency of chilies. The core and seeds of the pepper are usually removed before they are dried. Paprika is now produced in many countries apart from its native Hungary—Spanish *pimentón* is essentially the same spice, though the flavor is perceptibly different. Many non-Hungarian paprikas are of poor quality, but at least they will not be adulterated with red lead, as they were said to have been on occasion in the past. Paprika is the essential flavoring of many Hungarian dishes, including goulash and chicken *paprikás;* it is meant to be used in generous quantities rather than those that would usually be appropriate for black pepper or cayenne. It is a mild, sweet spice that in Hungary comes in varying grades—noble sweet, semisweet, rose, strong, and commercial, in descending order of quality. Paprika, like most ground spices, does not keep forever—if it is a dirty brown color, it is probably stale.

PARAGUAY TEA. *See* maté.

PARA NUT and **paradise nut.** *See* Brazil nut.

PARBOILING. A stage further than *blanching, parboiling is half-cooking food in water before finishing in another way, usually by baking or frying. Food is parboiled either because the higher temperature of fat would dry it out or brown it too much before it was cooked through or because it prepares the surface for the penetration of fat and flavor, as, for instance, when potatoes are roasted in meat juices.

[*Parboiling*—French: *faire bouillir ou frire à demi;* German: *halb kochen;* Italian: *far bollire a metà;* Spanish: *sancochar*]

PARFAIT AMOUR. *See* liqueurs and cordials.

PARMESAN. This name is used outside Italy for the group of cheeses the Italians call *grana,* of which the archetype is parmigiano. These cheeses, which are hard and old, have a special strong taste and are mainly grated for flavoring. *Grana* and other grated cheeses are indispensable in Italian cooking, in which they are one of the most common flavorings. Authentic cheeses from the region around Parma have "Parmigiano-Reggiano" stamped on them. The cheeses are very large—50–80 lb (25–35 Kg) is normal—and, being expensive, are bought in pieces. For cooking, the cheeses should be at least 3 years old, and they get better up to 4 years. If kept longer than that, the cheese

starts to turn powdery. Today, a large amount of this cheese type is sold relatively fresh. It is cheaper, sweeter, and softer, intended for eating, not cooking. The Bolognese find fresh *grana* goes particularly well with pears. Parmesan is often sold grated, but this does not compare with cheese that has been freshly grated.

PARSLEY (*Petroselium crispum*) is an umbellifer of Mediterranean origin. It is the most commonly used herb in American and European cooking and second only to green

PARSLEY

coriander in the rest of the world. There are four main varieties of parsley, two of which are only locally common.

The least-known is Neapolitan parsley, from southern Italy, which is grown for its leaf stalks rather in the same way as celery. The rather better-known Hamburg parsley is grown for its root and is also called turnip-rooted or parsnip-rooted celery. It was once popular in England and is still grown in Germany and Switzerland as one of the root vegetables for flavoring soups.

The usual type grown in northern countries as an herb is curly or moss-curled parsley, which has dense, crinkly leaves. Mediterranean countries more often use the single-leafed, plain, or Italian parsley, which is not as decorative but stands sun, and indeed rain and snow, much better. I do not accept claims that the single-leafed type has a superior flavor, and when I give Spanish friends curly parsley they always agree that it is better.

Parsley is not difficult to grow in window boxes of good soil (though it is slow to germinate). It can be kept going right through the winter outdoors with suitable protection. It is a biennial which develops stronger-flavored leaves, then seeds, the second year. If you shake the dry seed heads and lightly rake soil over them, they will produce new seedlings the next spring.

Parsley can be frozen in bunches after being quickly dipped in boiling water to blanch it. Some forms of freeze-dried parsley are quite acceptable as an emergency substitute; commercial preservation of parsley has been greatly improved in recent years. Home-dried parsley usually has a haylike flavor. A bunch of parsley and a means of chopping it quickly is a necessity in every kitchen.

Parsley oil, which is extracted by the steam distillation of parsley seed, is used as a flavoring in a variety of commercial products from ice cream to condiments, and the oleoresin, which is extracted with solvents, is also used in condiments.

[*Parsley*—French: *persil;* German: *Petersilie;* Italian: *prezzemolo;* Spanish: *perejil*]

PARSNIP (*Pastinaca sativa*), like the carrot, is an umbellifer. The thin acrid roots of the wild parsnip, which is native to Europe, are inedible, but cultivated parsnips have been known for at least 2000 years—what unknown genius chose them for development or found the original mutation? Perhaps the roots were first used as a flavoring in soups, as they still are in Europe. They were an important ingredient of medieval English and European cookery, in which they were used as a sweetmeat (e.g., preserved in honey or made into fritters) and for medicinal purposes, for instance in syrups and as a cough remedy. Parsnips reached the West Indies in 1564 and Virginia in 1609. A century later, they were being grown by the

North American Indians. The plant has now gone wild in the U.S. and reverted to its original inedible state. Apparently, though, these escapes, when given the benefit of horticulture, gradually resume the cultivated form.

Parsnips are winter vegetables—at one time, it was believed they had to be frosted to be edible. Up to a point, the later they are harvested the sweeter they are, but left too long, they may grow to a huge size and develop a woody core. Young parsnips need only be scraped; old ones have to be peeled and cut in pieces. When buying, look out for brown, rotten patches which may mean that most of the root is spoiled. Parsnips are usually boiled before they are dressed in a variety of ways (for example, roasted). They cook more quickly than carrots. Parsnips are sweet—they contain enough sugar to be used for winemaking. While parsnips are usually to be found among the winter roots in grocery stores, they are not very popular in the U.S. or Britain. They are eaten in the countries of northern Europe to some extent, but hardly at all farther south, or only as a flavoring in soups and occasionally as a garnish.

[*Parsnip*—French: *panais;* German: *Pastinak, Pastinake, Pastinakwurzel;* Italian: *pastinaca;* Spanish: *chirivía*]

PARTRIDGE. There are no true partridges indigenous to North America, where the word is often incorrectly applied to other birds like *quail or *grouse. However, European partridges were introduced into the U.S. from Hungary, and so are often known as "Huns." They are naturalized in a number of states, as is the rather larger chukar or chukoor (*Alectoris chukar*), a bird of southern Asia, especially of India, which in Europe is found only in Thrace and southern Bulgaria. The common European partridge is the gray partridge (*Perdix perdix*), which is distinguished by its gray legs. It is the most widespread species in Britain and is found from Italy and Greece up to southern Scandinavia and eastward into Persia and the Altai Mountains in Siberia. It is also the best of the European partridges and well entrenched in the gastronomy of every European country.

The red-legged partridge (*Alectoris rufa*), known to sportsmen as the "Frenchman," was introduced into Britain in the 17th century. It is not quite as good as the gray and is locally common southward and eastward from Midlands. It is the main species in southwest France and in the Iberian peninsula. Partridges are in season from September 1 to the beginning of February, after which they start to breed, the young being hatched (in Britain) in June. In young birds, the legs are yellowish, the beaks sharp, and the underfeathers of the wings pointed. In older birds, the legs have turned gray. Young ones need hanging for not more than 4 days, but older ones can use a week, depending on the weather and personal preference. Because the partridge is a small bird, one per person is needed.

[*Partridge*—French: *perdrix;* German: *Rebhuhn;* Italian: *pernice;* Spanish: *perdiz*]

PASSIONFRUIT or **purple granadilla** (*Passiflora edulis*), a native of Brazil, is now grown in warm countries everywhere, including the Mediterranean region, where the fruits are rather inferior. The plant is a perennial climber that is often grown for its beautiful flowers. The fruit is about the size of an egg and is definitely purple when ripe, smooth to begin with and then becoming wrinkled. The pulp tastes delicious but is full of tiny black seeds, which discourage many people from eating it except rubbed through a sieve. In some countries, it is best to pick passionfruit with caution, since the vines may harbor snakes. The giant granadilla (*P. quadrangularis*) is purely tropical and has greenish yellow fruit. It does not have such a good taste as the passionfruit, and immature ones may sometimes be boiled and used as a vegetable. The same genus also includes the water lemon or yellow

granadilla (*P. laurifolia*) and the curuba (*P. maliformis*), which are not seen much outside tropical America.

PASTA. The word comes from the Italian and is the generic name for all forms of spaghetti, macaroni, vermicelli, ravioli, and so on; it is a more appropriate term than *noodles, which comes from the German, *Nudeln,* although Oriental forms of pasta are usually called noodles, and in the U.S. ribbon-shaped pasta, usually made of egg dough, is referred to as noodles. Italy is the undisputed world leader in pasta. Italians eat far more of it than anyone else. Although the Chinese have eaten pasta for many centuries, it is not true that it was introduced into Europe when Marco Polo came back from his journeys in the Orient in 1293. Gadgets which look as if they were for making pasta have been found in Pompeii; in any case, macaroni is mentioned in writings from as early as 1200—almost a century before Marco Polo returned. The Italians have developed the hundreds of different pasta forms and spread a liking for spaghetti around the world, although Thomas Jefferson brought a spaghetti die back to the U.S. from a trip to Italy in 1786 and used it to make quantities for himself and friends. No doubt other less famous people did so too, but it was not until the 19th century, with Italian immigration, that pasta was much eaten in the U.S. At the beginning of this century, durum wheat was introduced as a crop into the U.S., and pasta manufacture began on a large scale when supplies from Italy were cut off in World War I. Americans have their own names for several shapes. There is an old established tradition of pasta making in Spain, and it is made in many other countries, including Greece and Israel.

Italian-type pasta is correctly made from high-protein, durum *wheat, which likes a hot, dry climate and is much grown in low-rainfall areas around the Mediterranean, for instance in southern Italy and in Spain. In the U.S., it is grown in the arid lands of the

Great Plains. The varieties grown are mostly Russian in origin. Much pasta is made from unsuitable wheat, but in Italy the best is labeled *pasta di semola di grano duro* (pasta of hard wheat flour), which is what you should aim to buy. Unlike pasta made from inferior materials, it will not cook to a gluey mass unless it is grossly overdone. The color varies from translucent cream to pale brown (there are now excellent whole-wheat pastas available). Good pasta has a strong, delicious wheaty flavor. The simplest pasta, and the most popular, is made only from durum wheat flour and water; green pasta contains spinach (*con spinaci*), pink contains tomato (*con pomodoro*), and others contain extra wheat germ, bran, or gluten (*con glutine*), even malt (*con malto*). According to recent Italian law, pasta labeled *all'uovo* (with eggs) must contain at least 4 eggs per 2¼ lb (1 kilo) of flour, a modest amount compared to the classic homemade pasta of Bologna, which uses 10 eggs per kilo.

The simplicity of pasta made from flour and water contrasts with the incredible variety of shapes that have been invented. The present score is around 200, and more are continually being devised. Some of these forms are merely commercial or decorative fantasies, but many are functional, and the right pasta needs to be selected for each dish. Apart from tradition, which should be respected unless there is good reason to depart from it, considerations are as follows:

1. Pasta for broth should be small. Large pasta would be out of place, and long strings would mean eating broth with a fork as well as a spoon, a ludicrous performance.

2. Pasta for soups, like minestrone, which contain whole beans, pieces of vegetable, peas, and so on, should be of a size comparable to the bits of vegetable. Tiny pasta would fill the spaces in between and make the soup stodgy.

3. Thin tubular pasta tends to get squashed flat, while thicker pasta stands up and keeps its shape. Tubes or shells are mechanically better able to resist squashing and so give a more open texture than leaves,

strips, or butterflies. So also does frilled pasta. Hollow pasta gets filled with sauce and holds it, and certain large tubular forms like cannelloni and *bombardoni* are designed for stuffing. Other stuffed pastas are packets, square, semicircular, circular, or twisted, of which ravioli, *anolini*, and *tortellini* are examples.

Perhaps of even more importance is the surface-to-volume ratio, a stuffy way of stating the obvious fact that it takes less sauce to cover a piece of dough shaped into a ball than to cover the same piece rolled out into a large sheet, which has the same volume but a bigger surface area. Even more sauce would be necessary if the sheet were cut into strips. Ribbed forms of pasta (*rigati*) trap more sauce than smooth ones (*lisci*). Nevertheless, too much importance should not be given to the wonderful variety of shapes produced by the manufacturers in spite of the inventiveness that has gone into them. Most are named after the objects they resemble—butterflies, stars, seeds, wheels, clover leaves, elder flowers, and so on. Some manufacturers grade their pasta by numbers in sizes like shoes and hats, but Italians also make free use of suffixes and diminutives which convey size, so that from *farfalle* come *farfallette* (small), *farfallini* (very small), and *farfalloni* (large). But there are other variations which confuse all but the most determined linguists.

The word *pasta* literally means "dough." *Pasta asciutta*, dry pasta, refers to dishes in which the pasta is in a sauce as opposed to *pasta in brodo*—pasta in a broth. There is often confusion over the word *minestre,* which may just mean soups but may also include rice dishes and pasta in broth. Italians do not make fussily clear distinctions.

Cooking spaghetti. Make sure that you have a good brand. The fact that it comes from Naples and is wrapped in blue paper with an old-fashioned label is no guarantee. If your spaghetti is turning out badly, either it is being overcooked or the brand is no good, more likely the latter. Allow 5 pt (2½ lt) of water for 1 lb (½ Kg) of spaghetti, and salt it generously. When it is boiling briskly, put in the spaghetti, which should be stirred with a fork to prevent the strands from sticking together (a little oil or butter added to the water also helps). Check frequently during cooking, because the pasta must not be overcooked; caught and drained immediately it is *al dente*—cooked but still springy rather than soft when bitten. The time cannot be given because it depends on how long the spaghetti has been dried, on its thickness, and even on such things as altitude and weather. Dried pasta might take about 15 minutes, whereas similar freshly made pasta would take about 5 minutes. After draining the spaghetti, return it to the still-warm pan and mix it carefully with the other ingredients, according to the recipe. Serve it immediately from a hot dish onto hot plates. Spaghetti should always be freshly cooked and never be kept waiting or allowed to get lukewarm and glutinous. Most of these remarks also apply to other forms of pasta.

CLASSIC BOLOGNESE PASTA

This pasta is made fresh, contains eggs, and is for making any rich pasta dish, for stuffing as for *tortellini* or ravioli, or for cutting into strips (*tagliatelli*). It is made fresh every day in countless Bolognese restaurants and homes, and helped to earn the town the description "Bologna the fat."

Use 2¼ lb (1 Kg) bread flour and 10 eggs. Nothing more—no water and no salt. Pile the flour on a large pastry board or plastic tabletop. Make a well in the flour and break the eggs into it. Mix and knead energetically for at least 7 minutes (some say 15), pressing with all your weight on the dough with the ball of your hand. (Since eggs vary in size, it may be necessary to use a little extra flour.) At the end of kneading, small blisters should appear on the surface of the dough. Roll it out carefully into a sheet thin enough to see through. If it is required for *tagliatelli*, roll it loosely, cut it in strips, plump it up into nests, and allow it to dry. If it is for ravioli or *tortellini*, stuff the pieces immediately. They may be laid out on a surface that has been sprinkled with flour until you are ready to cook them.

If the quantity of eggs is reduced, an eggshell of water may be necessary, but this is frowned on by Bolognese chefs and is inclined to make the pasta sticky. Correctly made pasta can be rolled out without the board needing to be floured. In Italy, a long narrow rolling pin, rather like a broomstick, is used, and the large sheets of pasta are handled dexterously by rolling them up around the pin.

When pasta is made in hot weather (like a Bolognese summer), it may be difficult to work before it dries out and starts cracking. The only solution is to work in a closed kitchen with no drafts and the humidity pushed as high as possible. If the ball of pasta has to be kept before rolling out, the surface may be rubbed with a little oil or the ball can be wrapped in plastic. These days, nearly everyone who makes pasta at home uses an electric pasta machine.

Some forms of pasta follow. The list is mainly restricted to the more important and traditional shapes and some regional ones; there is little point in attempting an exhaustive catalog of the silly ones.

Agnolini (Lombardy). Very like *tortellini*, stuffed.

Agnollotti, agnellotti, or **agnolotti,** according to region, are from Piedmont, Tuscany, and Liguria. Like ravioli, but may be round.

Anolini (Emilia-Romagna). Stuffed, usually semicircular.

Bavette and **bavettine.** Thin oval spaghetti.

Bigoli. Spaghetti from the Veneto.

Bows. American name for *farfalle* or *cravatte*.

Bucati and **bucatini.** From *bucare,* to pierce. Forms that resemble macaroni.

Calzone (Naples). Stuffed form like a folded pizza.

Cannelle—pipes. *Cannellini* and *cannolicchi* (small), *cannelloni, canneroni* (large).

Cappelletti—little hats. Reggio Emilia and Romagna have different forms.

Cavatieddi. Small dished pasta of Puglia.

Conchiglie—conch shells. Also *conchigliette*.

Cravatte—ties or bow ties. Also *cravattine*. Similar to *farfalle*.

Elbow macaroni. Many variations of short, curved tubes.

Farfalle—butterflies. Also *farfalloni, farfallini, farfalette*.

Fedelini. Very fine form of vermicelli.

Fettuccine. *Fettuccia* is a ribbon. The name used in Rome for strip pasta, like *tagliatelli* but usually a bit narrower. Also *fetucce*, which are wider, and *fetuccelle*, which are narrower.

Fiori di sambuco—elder flowers. Small stars for soup.

Fusilli. Squiggly or spiral form of spaghetti. *Fusilli bucati* are a squiggly form of macaroni. Used especially in Campania.

Gemelli—twins. Two short bits of spaghetti twisted together like cord. Often called twists Napolitani.

Giant shells. American equivalent of *conchiglie*.

Gnocchi. Small dumplings or lumps of pasta, usually shaped with a fork and ridged. They are often made at home from potato or semolina flour. Bought forms resemble the elongated rippled shells called *cavatelli* or rippled ribbon pasta in short bits. Any short form of pasta of roughly the size of small *gnocchi* is liable to be called *gnocchetti*.

Lasagne. Wide strips or squares of pasta, very often homemade. *Lasagne verde,* green with spinach, are also common. Usually boiled and then baked with minced meat, cheese, sauce, etc. between the sheets of pasta.

Linguine. Long and flat, narrow, and slightly tapered at the edges.

Lisci—smooth, as opposed to *rigati* (striated) or *trinati* (with frilled or lacy edges).

Macaroni. English spelling of *maccheroni*.

Maccheroni. Tubes of pasta in all sizes from something as thin as spaghetti to *cannelle*. There are variations such as *maccheroncelli* and many alternative names, even *spaghetti bucati* (pierced spaghetti).

Malfatti—badly made. Homemade and shaped into balls.

Malfattini—finely chopped. Romagna.

Maltagliati—badly cut. Rough, elongated diamonds.

Manicotti—muffs. Something like cannelloni. Large tubes, usually stuffed.

Nidi—nests. Tangles of pasta, a form in which it is made at home and sometimes sold.

*Noodles. The German name for pasta is *Nudeln*. In Germany, these would include *Makkaroni* and *Spaghetti, Hausmachernudeln* (homemade), and the famous *Spätzle*. U.S. noodles are ribbonlike, varying from very thin to several inches wide, and are usually made with eggs.

Ofelle. Like ravioli. Stuffed pasta from Trieste.

Orecchiette—little ears. Also called by other local names in the Bari, Brindisi, and Taranto regions. Homemade by slicing a tiny roll of pasta and denting each slice with the point of a knife.

Pansotti. Local, usually triangular, stuffed pasta from Liguria.

Pappardelle. Broad ribbons cut in short pieces, one of the types that is often homemade.

Pastina. Small pasta of any shape for broth.

Penne—quill or pen. Macaroni in shortish lengths cut diagonally like a nib at the ends. Also *pennette* (tiny), *pennine* (small), *pennone* (large). Very common in Italy.

Perline—little pearls. *Microperline* or *perline microscopici* are even smaller. Used in soup.

Puntine—little points (the smallest). *Puntette* are larger and the same as *semini* (little seeds).

Ravioli. Very popular stuffed pasta, usually rectangular and cut with a crenellated edge. *Raviolini* are smaller. Usually freshly made but also available dried.

Riccio—curly, as in *fetucce riccie* (curly ribbons) or *lasagne riccie*.

Rigati—striped (from *rigare*, to rule). Many forms of pasta are made both smooth (*lisci*) and striated.

Rigatoni. Very large grooved tubes. A common and popular form.

Ruote—wheels. Also *ruotelline* (very small) and *ruotini* (small).

Sedani. Like celery (*sedano*)—ridged types of macaroni, usually in short bits for soup. *Sedani corti* (short) are the classic form to use in minestrone.

Spaghetti. Often sold in numbered thicknesses. Also *spaghettini* (thin) and *spaghettoni* (thick).

Stelle—stars. Also *microstelle* (smallest), *stellini, stellettine, stellette* (largest). Common types used in soup.

Tagliatelle. From *tagliare*, to cut. Ribbon pasta with eggs as made in Bologna, and a little wider than the Roman *fettuccine*. Also *tagliarini, tagliolette, tagliolini*.

Tondo—round, e.g., *farfalle tonde*, round-winged butterflies as opposed to those which look more like bow ties.

Tortelli. Like ravioli, rectangular or triangular. Mainly from Italy.

Tortellini. Twists of stuffed egg pasta well described by an alternative name in Italian—Venus's navel. Those made in Bologna rank among the world's greatest pasta dishes.

Tortelloni. Large versions of *tortellini*, but heavier and thus suffering by comparison.

Trenette. Like flattened spaghetti—the correct pasta with *pesto alla genovese*.

Trinati. A descriptive word meaning frilled, as in *tripolini trinati*, a small member of the bow and butterfly family used in soup.

Trofie. Little twisted bits of pasta used in Liguria with *pesto*.

Vermicelli—little worms. Very fine spaghetti.

Ziti. Large macaroni cut in lengths. *Zitoni* are the large version and *mezze zite* the average.

PASTEURIZATION is a process particularly applied to milk, since *sterilization of milk by boiling produces a cooked flavor, decreases the vitamin content, and causes undesirable changes in the proteins. Pasteurization—heating to a lower temperature—will kill the disease germs without these undesirable effects but also without complete sterilization. The method now usual consists of heating milk to 161°F (71°C) and holding it at that temperature for 15 seconds (after which it is cooled very rapidly). Milk being pasteurized must be continually stirred to prevent a skin from forming. If the milk is already going sour, it will curdle when heated.

Pasteurization usually kills about 99% of the microorganisms, including those of all the diseases which can be transmitted through milk: undulant fever, foot-and-mouth disease, typhoid, tuberculosis, scarlet fever, diphtheria, septic sore throat, polio, dysentery, and diarrhea.

Pasteurization is also used in winemaking to improve the keeping qualities of the wine (particularly wine with a low alcohol content) and as a remedy for various maladies that wine can develop.

[*Pasteurization*—French: *pasteuriser;* German: *pasteurisieren;* Italian: *pastorizzare;* Spanish: *pasterizar*]

PASTIS. *See* liqueurs and cordials.

PÂTE without the final accent (thus not to be confused with *pâté) means a paste and in general is the French term for doughs, pastries, and batters. *Pâte feuilletée* is puff paste, the delicate source of croissants and other flaky pastries; *pâte à crêpes* is pancake batter. Pâte literally means paste in *pâte d'amandes* (almond paste), *pâte de coigne* (quince paste), *pâte d'anchois* (anchovy paste), etc. *Les pâtes alimentaires* are pasta. But pâtée is a dog's dinner in France, or a mash for cramming into geese or chickens.

PÂTÉ, literally a pie: an apple pie in French is a *pâté de pommes*. The word has also come to mean what you might call a meat pie without a crust (although it is often enclosed in bards of bacon or pork fat), for which an alternative name is *terrine*. The French names have a certain refinement not possessed by the Anglo-Saxon equivalent, meatloaf. The borderline between pâté and some sausages, potted meats, and meat pastes is ill-defined. For instance, the Danish *leverpostej*, liver paste, used in smorgasbord, is a pâté. However, it is the French who produce by far the greatest range of pâtés. There are many regional specialties and much variation from charcutier to charcutier, with products ranging from simple *pâté de foie de porc* of pig's liver, which is among the cheapest meat dishes, through chicken, rabbit, and duck to highly truffled delicacies and the legendary pâtés of larks. The most renowned of all is pâté de foie gras. Essentially pâtés consist of minced, chopped, or slivered meat with roughly an equal amount of fat, plus flavorings (onion, garlic, truffle, salt, pepper, nutmeg, and/or any spice mixture, wine or brandy) and often natural meat jelly. Eggs, flour, and white sauces are used as binders. Most pâtés need to be given 1–2 days to mature after making. If they are sealed while hot with a layer of fat, they will keep, like potted meat, for some weeks in the refrigerator.

PAUNCHING. *See* rabbit.

PAWPAW. *See* papaya.

PAYOUSNAYA. *See* caviar.

PEA. Probably native to the Near East, peas have been cultivated as food since at least the Bronze Age and occur in the excavations of Swiss lake dwellings. They were an important pulse and a good source of protein. The name "garden peas" is not an advertising gimmick, but distinguishes the modern sweet varieties (*Pisum sativum*) from the old field peas (*P. arvense,* which are sometimes considered merely a variety of *P. sativum*), commonly eaten up to the Middle Ages. These were not grown as a green vegetable, but were dried, perhaps split, and kept for winter. After soaking, they were lengthily cooked to make puddings or soups. They were a necessary staple.

Garden peas are eaten immature. There are now hundreds of varieties, and vast quantities are grown for freezing and canning. The gardener's distinction between dwarf and climbing varieties does not affect the peas themselves or therefore the cook. Seed coats may be wrinkled or smooth; wrinkled ones are reckoned sweeter. Garden peas should be young and fresh—choose firm pods that rustle when scooped up. When a trial pod is opened, the peas should taste fresh and tender. The very best frozen peas, because they are picked at exactly the right moment, are often better than stale peas bought in the market. Nobody would claim, though, that they were as good as peas straight from the garden.

Pea pods are edible when the fibrous part is removed, but a special type of pea, known variously as the sugar pea, snow pea, or *mange-tout* (var. *saccaratum*), is grown in many countries; the pods are eaten whole when they are young and still flat. Because these are popular with Chinese cooks, they are sometimes called Chinese peas. *See also* snap pea.

Dried peas may be whole or split, bright green or yellow. They need to be soaked, usually overnight, before being cooked, although they can be reduced to a pureé in a pressure cooker.

Other legumes to which the term "pea" is applied include *chickpea, *cowpea, and *pigeon pea.

[*Pea*—French: *pois;* German: *Erbse;* Italian: *pisello;* Spanish: *guisanto*]

PEA BEAN. *See* bean.

PEACH. Originally cultivated in China (where peach blossom symbolizes long life), the peach came to Europe thousands of years ago via Persia (hence the scientific name, *Prunus persica*) and was grown by the Romans. Trees from ancient stocks have often gone wild. Conquistadors brought the peach to Florida, and it spread rapidly because the Indians were so fond of it. By the 19th century, orchards blossomed all over the eastern countryside, and varieties were being developed to ripen at different seasons.

There are many varieties of peach, thousands it is reckoned, which may be simply classified into those with yellow and those with white flesh (of which the white-fleshed are usually the better for eating, but they are less frequently found in markets because they bruise so easily), into freestone, in which the flesh is separate from the stone, and clingstone, in which it is attached. The semiclingstones come in between. Finally, there are special varieties of peach such as nectarines (var. *nectarina*) which have a smooth, rather than downy, skin and a very rich flavor. Grocers are often not aware of the variety they are selling, and there is great variation in the quality of the same variety grown in different areas. In North America, where the peach is the third most important fruit, after the orange and the apple, peaches are put through a machine which removes their down at the same time as it washes them.

Elberta, a freestone peach with red-gold skin and yellow flesh, is one of the most widely grown varieties in the U.S. Georgia Belle is a favorite white-flesh freestone. Hale and Haven peaches and hybrids from them are gold-fleshed peaches likely to be found in markets.

Among the best peaches I ever ate were in a peach orchard in Ontario during a strike of pickers. Told to help myself to the fruits which were already past the moment for commercial picking, I sat down on the grass in the drowsy, hot afternoon and listened to the plop, plop, plop of perfectly ripe peaches falling. Occasionally, I marked one that had just dropped and ate it while it was still warm from the sun. Such perfectly ripe peaches would not stand shipment; for that, they have to be picked when just mature but still firm. Bought peaches, although they get softer, do not get sweeter, and if they are greenish when bought they will never ripen at home. A peach with a pretty red blush may have an underlying green tinge and be unripe. You should look more for an underlying cream to yellow color. When peaches are ripe, they may be put into the refrigerator, and if they are unwashed and perfect, they may keep for up to a fortnight. Many people like their peaches chilled (although that is not the best way to taste them), since a chilled peach is very refreshing. Some peaches peel easily, while others do not, depending partly on the variety. A knife rubbed gently along the skin helps to free it. For cooking, peaches can also be peeled like tomatoes, after a quick dunk into boiling water.

In addition to being eaten fresh off the tree, when their flavor is incomparable, peaches are usually peeled and sliced, and often served with cream. They add a delicate flavor to ice cream and are excellent with fresh berries, especially raspberries. Perhaps the most famous peach dessert is peaches Melba, ripe peaches poached gently in syrup and served with vanilla ice cream, whipped cream, and crushed raspberries. Canned peaches, quite different in texture and flavor from fresh ones, can be cloying if their syrup is too sweet. Peaches are also frozen and dried, and dead-ripe ones are made into peach brandy and cordial. Spiced or pickled peaches are enjoyed by some people with ham, pork, and game.

[*Peach*—French: *pêche;* German: *Pfirsich;* Italian: *pesca;* Spanish: *melocotón*]

PEACOCK or **peafowl.** Peacocks were once much prized for the table in Europe. The breast is as big as that of the turkey, to which the meat is similar. In India, when turkeys were unobtainable, I twice ate peacock for Christmas and found it an excellent substitute (don't, however, try to take the peacocks that are seen wild around the villages in India: they are considered holy birds). Peacocks may have an unpleasant taste and smell if they have been feeding on certain buds, and their flesh can be tough. If you have the choice, it is better to select a peachick, which is tender and agreeable in flavor.

[*Peacock*—French: *paon;* German: *Pfau;* Italian: *pavone;* Spanish: *pavo real, pavón*]

PEANUT, groundnut, or **monkey nut** (*Arachis hypogaea*). The peanut is well named: it is a legume, and the nuts are the peas in the pod. It gets the name of groundnut because the plant pushes its pods into the earth, which must be loose enough for the "peg" to push into it; otherwise there will be no nuts. Ripe peanuts have to be dug out like potatoes.

Peanuts are unknown in the wild, but are thought to have originated and first been cultivated in South America (from evidence in Inca tombs). Portuguese slave traders carried the nuts—a convenient ration for the voyage—from Brazil to West Africa in the early 16th century, and from there peanuts were introduced to the U.S. During the 18th century, they were grown in the Carolinas and other states. Today, peanuts are an important world crop; they are rich both in oil (40–50%) and in protein (about 30%).

The many varieties differ in size, number of nuts, pod, and color (which can vary from white or cream to brown, red, or even variegated red and white). The small varieties usually go for oil and the larger, less oily ones for eating. Supplies come notably from China, Java, Nigeria and other African countries, Spain, and the U.S.

Although India claims the largest production, which is mostly needed for home consumption, there are few Indian recipes based on peanuts, which are of greater importance in West African cooking—for instance, in the form of roasted meal they are a key ingredient of peanut chop. The Egyptians make a soup, *foul sudani,* from peanuts. In Indonesian and Malay cooking, roasted peanuts, pounded to a paste, are the basis for *saté* (skewers of grilled cubes of meat in a peanut sauce), as well as for a salad dressing (*gado-gado*) and other dishes. In the U.S., dozens of recipes use peanuts, mainly for sweet dishes, candy, cakes, and cookies. Peanuts are also important to the flavor of hams from peanut-fed hogs.

In virtually all recipes, peanuts are first roasted (although the green immature pods can also be eaten boiled, and in Java they are made into a fermented paste called *onchom,* which is subsequently fried). Commercially an oil is expressed from the nuts (peanut, groundnut, or arachide oil). The residue may be converted into crackers. Peanuts are used as a basis for vegetarian nut meats, sauces, and even an artificial milk. They are suitable for adulterating coffee, cocoa, and ground spices.

Peanuts may be roasted in a very cool oven, only 240°F (115°C), until the nuts are dry, the flesh a pale brown color, and the skin brittle. A cruder way is to dry-fry the nuts in a pan over a very low heat. They must be stirred continuously. Over-roasting or burning spoils the flavor. On the other hand, roasting must be taken far enough to remove the raw flavor. Insufficiently roasted nuts do not keep.

When the roasted nuts have cooled enough to handle, rub them with your fingers to remove the brittle skins. They can then be winnowed off by dropping the nuts in front of an electric fan (or outdoors in the wind) to blow away the chaff. Salt the nuts to taste.

Once the skins have been removed, it is simple to make peanut butter, using the special nut-butter plate of a nut mill. Salt and a little vegetable oil, if necessary, are added to get the right flavor and consistency. Some varieties are oilier than others. In the absence of a nut mill, results can be obtained by quickly grinding the nuts in a whirling coffee mill, then pounding them in a mortar or even in a meat-mincing machine. Peanuts, like many other nuts, will "oil" when pounded.

In theory, the most delicious results, for instance in Indonesian food, would be obtained from freshly shelled nuts, roasted and ground at home. This is a long job, especially if you have no children to husk the nuts and you do the roasting in a pan on the fire in the unsophisticated way. I do not think that the taste is worth the trouble—you can make delicious dishes with commercial peanut butter or crunchy peanut butter of a good brand—but in commercial peanut butter, the germ is usually removed to give better shelf life (otherwise it goes rancid) and that reduces the nutritional value.

SATÉ SAUCE

The following tasty recipe was fabricated by the Indonesian wife of a Dutch friend, a restaurateur, who had been unable to get the correct type of *ketjap* in Europe. It is easy to make and is a close approximation to the real thing.

Melt 1 oz (25 g) of butter in a saucepan, then add 2 tablespoons of vinegar and 4 bouillon cubes (preferably French *poule-au-pot* cubes, or 3 chicken bouillon cubes and 1 beef bouillon cube). Mix well over a low heat until all is melted and then add up to 1 tablespoon of dark-brown sugar little by little, stirring and tasting until the sauce is no longer sour. But do not add so much sugar that the salty taste is destroyed. This is important: since sugar and salt tend to cancel each other, the operation requires some judgment in balancing the sweet-sour-salty

taste. We have now made an artificial substitute for an Indonesian *ketjap* of a particular type.

Now add 1 finely minced large onion, 2 chopped cloves of garlic, a strip of lemon peel, a bay leaf, a small pinch of thyme, and a good pinch each of ginger and chili pepper. The thyme must on no account dominate. Continue to cook the mixture slowly until the onion is soft. Then remove the pan from the heat, add about a cup of peanut butter, blend well, and pour in the juice from the meat (if any) with which you are serving the sauce. Heat gently, stirring all the time, and pour over grilled kebabs. Serve with boiled rice.

[*Peanut*—French: *cacaouette, arachide;* German: *Erdnuss;* Italian: *arachide;* Spanish: *cacahué, cacahuete*]

PEAR. The common pear (*Pyrus communis*) is a native of eastern Europe and the Middle East. Although there are about 20 species of pear in Europe and Asia—and some have been hybridized with the common pear—most of the good eating pears are derived from the one species. There are at least 5000 named varieties, of which 20–30 are cultivated on a large scale. In Europe, France is generally regarded as the leading country for pears and many are grown in Belgium and West Germany. Though pear trees do not stand quite the same range of climate as apples, they have deep roots and can endure stony, dry conditions which would not be tolerated by apples. Characteristic of pears, and unpleasant in some varieties, are the tiny hard grains (stone cells with woody cell walls) that make pears gritty. The best eating varieties are more or less grit-free.

Unlike the French, who are pear connoisseurs and even have names for the different shapes of pear, Americans have never regarded them as highly as, say, the apple or the peach. However, a number of varieties of pear are available in this country, the most familiar being the following.

Anjou, with a yellowish green skin that is often russeted, is succulent with a subtle winy flavor. It is fine for baking, broiling, poaching, and canning.

Bartlett (or Williams) is the commonest pear in the U.S. and the one most frequently canned. It has smooth yellow skin. The Barlett has juicy, fine-grained flesh that can lose its shape when poached or baked.

Bosc pears, with dark yellow to russet skins, are of Belgian origin. With firm flesh and slightly acid flavor, Boscs are ideal for poaching, broiling, or baking.

Comice is the standard by which other pears are judged. It is considered too exquisite to be cooked, and its fine buttery texture and aroma are incomparable. It has pale green to yellow skin with a red blush.

Seckel pears originated near Philadelphia in the 18th century. With bronze-colored skin when ripe and a sweet and spicy flavor, they are a favorite for pickles and preserves but are often too hard for other uses.

Pears for sale are picked before they are quite ripe. They will ripen off the tree if they are kept in an even, nicely warm temperature, but then deteriorate very quickly. It is therefore best to buy them not quite ripe and keep them to the perfect moment, which lasts at most a day. When they are ripe, they should be put in the refrigerator until eaten. Pears are ripe when pressing the neck gently shows they are *just* yielding. Some pears pass their peak within a matter of hours, and vigilance is necessary in obtaining perfect dessert pears. So is careful handling—pears bruise easily. While bruised pears should not be bought, appearance, as with most fruit, is a poor guide to quality. Some lovely-looking pears are dry and tasteless. Others, which look a bit rough, may taste wonderful. Some pears are only for cooking or bottling and not for eating. Others are for perry (the pear equivalent of cider). Many are multipurpose. The pear for any particular use depends on sea-son and the kinds that are available locally.

Of the many recipes for cooking pears, the best-known are for poaching in syrups flavored with red wine, vanilla, rum, almonds, and so on. Cooked pears do not seem to stand up on their own but always seem to need other flavors to complement them. In general, they also lack acidity, are not even sour when unripe, and tend to lose aroma on cooking.

Pears may be stored in the same way as *apples. Because they ripen better at a higher temperature than apples, they can be kept in a cool room or cellar before being brought into a warm room to finish ripening.

[*Pear*—French: *poire;* German: *Birne;* Italian: *pera;* Spanish: *pera*]

PEARL BARLEY. *See* barley.

PEARL MOSS. *See* carrageen.

PECAN (*Carya illinoensis*) is the finest of the *hickory nuts, an American native indigenous to the Mississippi Valley and neighboring states as far south as northern and central Mexico. The word "pecan" comes from American Indian languages, and all the tribes that shared the pecan's habitat have varied forms of the word. Indians pressed oil from the nuts, ground them into meal, and roasted them for rations on hunting trips. Today pecans are much grown commercially in Georgia, Texas, Oklahoma, and Florida. In general, they like climates suitable for cotton. In the U.S., the pecan does not thrive much north of the 40th parallel, although the hican, a tasty hybrid of the hickory nut and the pecan, will produce farther north. Pecans have been introduced into other countries, such as South Africa, where the climate is suitable, but they are somewhat finicky trees whose different varieties require specific soil and weather conditions.

The pecan tree can grow to almost 200 ft (61 m) in height when conditions are favorable. The best nut-producing varieties are propagated by grafting. Nuts of different types vary in size, quality, and flavor. Pecans have a smooth, elongated, usually rather thin shell. The flavor is somewhat like a walnut, but the pecan is oilier: in fact, it is the oiliest nut in common use, with 70% oil content being quite usual.

Nuts are harvested by knocking them off the tree with poles, and most of the crop is shelled by machinery after drying and treatment with ethylene gas to loosen the kernels. The proportion of meat to shell in the pecan is very high. The shells of nuts for dessert are sometimes polished and dyed red-brown with a particularly hideous combination of dyestuffs that goes ill with the lovely natural colors of other nuts on the table.

Shelled pecans go rancid rather quickly unless they are sealed under gas or in a vacuum. The use of pecans in cakes, pies, and candies is very much an American habit. Pecan pie, with loads of cream, will be part of the American-built heaven. Pecans are also used in stuffing for turkey. The nut is now beginning to be used in Europe.

MAPLE PECAN SAUCE

Gently heat ½ pt (¼ lt) of maple syrup in a heavy saucepan until it begins to thicken, within 10 minutes. Cool it slightly and add 7 oz (200 g) of chopped pecans (or to taste). Use this sauce warm on ice cream for a totally American flavor.

PECCARY. *See* boar.

PECTIN is the name of a class of jellying substances which occur naturally in many fruits, especially in cores, pips, and skins, as well as in some vegetables such as split peas and lentils. The cell walls of unripe fruit contain pectose, an insoluble substance which changes to soluble pectin as the fruit ripens. However, when the fruit is fully ripe, the pectin in turn changes to pectic acid and methyl alcohol, which is why barely ripe fruit is generally the best for jelly. Pectins are chemically derived from carbohydrates, not, like gelatin, from protein, but likewise consist of the long-chain molecules, the typical structure for forming a jelly.

For a pectin jelly, it is necessary to have not only enough pectin but also enough acid and sugar in roughly the correct proportion. The effectiveness of the acid is related to the *pH (the sourness) of the juice; of the common fruit acids, tartaric is more effective than malic, which is more effective than citric.

The minimum acidity at which a pectin jelly will form at all is pH 3.46. A good-quality homemade jelly forms at pH 3.3 (slightly more acid), and at 3.2 the jelly becomes stiffer. If the acidity is increased still further, to pH 3.1, the liquid begins to seep out of the jelly—it weeps. Boiling for long periods with acid tends to destroy pectin, as also does pressure cooking, and again the jelly becomes weak.

The third element in the balance is sugar. In fruit jellies, the necessary level will usually be somewhere near saturation (69–72%). If the percentage of sugar is more than this, a syrup may be formed and the jelly may not set at all, but the sugar may crystallize on cooling. Although setting can sometimes take place with as little as 40% sugar, such low-sugar jelly is stiff and, unless sterile, will not keep. A useful fact to know is that high acid content makes the exact sugar balance less critical, so that with the sourer fruit a larger quantity of sugar can be used.

Fruits that contain sufficient acid and pectin to set easily to jelly with the simple addition of sugar are: sour and crab apples, quinces, most plums but especially damsons, gooseberries, currants, cranberries, oranges, lemons, and grapes. Blackberries, loganberries, raspberries, and apricots are borderline cases. Sweet apples, pears, peaches, strawberries, cherries, huckleberries, guavas, and figs—and nonfruit jam materials—lack either acid or pectin, or both. Recipes for making jams or jellies from these involve adding lemon juice, prepared pectin, or other fruits rich in the missing components.

Pectin may be bought either as a liquid or as a powder. It is usually made either from apple pulp or from the white part of citrus fruit skins (the albedo) and is a by-product of the juice industry. The pectin is extracted from the albedo with water acidified usually with a mineral acid. It can also be made at home.

PECTIN

Shred 1 lb (450 g) of the white part of the peel of oranges or lemons, and let it stand in about 3½ pt (2 lt) of water with a scant ¼ pt (125 ml) of lemon juice, for 2–3 hours. Then add the same quantity of water again and bring the pan slowly to the boil. Boil 10 minutes with the lid on and stand it aside until the next day. Then boil the mixture once more for some 15 minutes and bottle or use immediately.

Because the amount of pectin in fruits is so variable, as is also its quality, a simple test is necessary to find out whether there is enough of it in a fruit juice to form a jelly. The acidity can usually be guessed at by tasting.

To test the pectin content, take a teaspoon of the juice, cool it, and drop it into a little methylated spirit (about a tablespoon). Shake the mixture very gently and let it stand for a minute. If a jellylike mass has formed, there is plenty of pectin. If there are a few blobs, and not very firm ones, then the pectin is probably just adequate. If there are only a number of small bits, then there is not enough pectin to make a jelly.

Jam is usually made with equal weights of sugar and fruit unless otherwise stated in a recipe. If there is plenty of pectin, then three-quarters the weight of the juice is a reasonable amount of sugar, but if the pectin is barely adequate this must be reduced to about 21 oz (600 g) of sugar per qt (1 lt).

Once sugar has been added to juice with adequate pectin and acidity, boiling for no more than 10 minutes will produce a jelly that will set properly on cooling. The tem-perature of boiling is the most reliable test: it should be 220°F (104.5°C), but may have to reach 222°F (105.5°C). The usual tests for setting are:

1. The flake test. Dip a spoon into the hot jelly. Take it out and twirl it until the jelly on it has cooled a little. Let some of the cooled jelly drop off the edge of the spoon. If it forms a sheet and drops off cleanly as a flake, then the jelly will set when cold.

2. The cold plate test. Put a small blob of the juice on a cold plate and let it cool. Push the blob sideways with a fingernail. If it wrinkles, it will set when cold.

[*Pectin*—French: *pectine;* German: *Pektin;* Italian: *pectina;* Spanish: *pectina*]

PELARGONIUM *See* geranium.

PEMMICAN. Originally used by North American Indians when they were hunting, traveling, or at war, pemmican was made of dried meat—buffalo or deer—pounded with rendered fat and preserved in skins. Cranberries were also supposed to have been mixed in, and perhaps dried blueberries. The purpose of pemmican was to be sustaining rather than gourmet food. Under 2 lb (1 Kg) a day would suffice to keep a man doing hard manual work. This food was adopted by polar explorers for rations on sledging trips. Sir John Richardson, an Arctic explorer in the 1820s, used a pemmican of lean meat dried on a malting kiln, ground in the malt mill, and mixed with an equal quantity of melted suet, currants, and sugar added to taste. This was sealed in canisters instead of skins. Later versions of pemmican were more gourmet-oriented. The pemmican brought back from the 1922 Spitzbergen expedition was good (at least, I thought so as a child), and later versions even better. With modern freeze-dried meat and vegetables, vitamins, and a better understanding of nutrition, there is no longer need for such heroic foods.

PENNYROYAL (*Mentha pulegium*) is a small creeping relative of mint with a strong and rather peculiar minty aroma. In England, dried pennyroyal is responsible for the special flavor of North Country black puddings.

American pennyroyal or squaw mint (*Hedeoma pulegiordes*) is a sweet-smelling herb that grows wild from New England to the Dakotas and southward to Texas and Florida. A small, branched annual, it is a member of the mint family and bears pale-violet flowers. Pennyroyal was used by American Indians as a medicine (and even a contraceptive), and it makes a very pleasant, slightly bitter tea. The crushed fresh leaves, rubbed on exposed skin, are a natural insect repellent.

[*Pennyroyal*—French: *pouliot;* German: *Flohkraut, Poleiminze;* Italian: *puleggio;* Spanish: *poleo*]

PEPINELLO. *See* chayote.

PEPPER originally meant vine pepper from a plant of the genus *Piper*. The *chili peppers and *sweet peppers, which came in later from tropical America, stole the same

PEPPER

name because they are more or less pungent.

Black pepper and white pepper both come from the same plant, *Piper nigrum,* a climbing vine native to the tropical forests of mon-

soon Asia. The vine produces hanging strings of dark-green berries, which turn bright red when ripe. If the green berries are picked and dried, they darken to form black pepper. Ripe berries are made into white pepper by the removal of the red skin and pulp. The ripe berries are stacked in piles to promote fermentation, which softens the outside. When this is washed off, the white inner seeds are left and are dried in the sun. Although there is some difference in the flavor between black pepper and white pepper, it is better experienced than described. White pepper is more expensive and less aromatic; it is used in white sauces or in any dish where black pepper would give a speckled appearance. Pepper should always be freshly ground in a mill, partly because its flavor is volatile and lost very quickly, and partly because you can then be sure that it has not been adulterated. *Mignonette* pepper (also called shot pepper), which is used in French cookery, is coarsely ground pepper made by roughly grinding and sifting peppercorns. A coarsely set pepper mill produces an approximate equivalent.

Green peppercorns are the berries of *P. nigrum* which have been canned rather than dried. Their flavor is fresh and pungent, without being excessively hot; it particularly suits meats, poultry, and fish. Once the can has been opened, green peppercorns will keep for up to 6 weeks in a well-stoppered glass or stoneware jar in the coldest part of the refrigerator.

Long pepper (*P. longum*) from India and *P. retrofractum* from Java are occasionally called for in Oriental recipes. Their flavor is rather similar to that of black pepper but slightly sweeter, and black pepper will usually do as a substitute. *Betel leaves come from a species of pepper (*P. betel*). Other plants which are popularly known as pepper are listed below.

Cubeb pepper (*Piper cubeb*) is an aromatic, pungent, and acrid spice. Originally from the East Indian "Spice Islands," it is now also grown in the West Indies and Ceylon.

A collector's piece today, used mostly as a source of medicinal cubeb camphor, cubeb pepper was important in the past and was one of the spices used in preparing the spiced apéritif wine called hippocras.

Jamaica pepper or **myrtle pepper.** Although the aromatic berries of the myrtle were used once as a substitute for pepper, myrtle pepper (*Pimenta dioica*) is not from myrtle but is *allspice, which is a member of the myrtle family.

Kava pepper (*Piper methysticum*), although related to black pepper, is not a spice but is the basis of *kava* or *kava-kava*, a drink from Samoa and other South Pacific islands. The women chew the fiber of the plant, mixing it well with their saliva and spitting the mush into a pot. The intoxicating nature of this drink is not due to alcohol, nor to the women's spit, but to alkaloids released by the salivary enzymes.

Peppergrass describes various plants with pungent fruits that are sometimes used as spices and are gathered wild in rural areas. They belong to the cabbage family (Cruciferae) and are close relatives of garden *cress (*Lepidium sativum*). The wild peppergrass (*L. virginicum*) of North America is naturalized in Europe, and roadside peppergrass (*L. ruderale*), a native of Europe, is naturalized in North America and Australia.

Pepper-root. Pungent roots of *Dentaria.*

Pepper tree. Name given to various trees, notably the common ornamental *Schinus molle,* oil from which is used commercially as a food flavoring.

[*Pepper*—French: *poivre;* German: *Pfeffer;* Italian: *pepe;* Spanish: *pimienta*]

PEPSIN is an enzyme that digests protein. It is usually prepared from fresh pig's stomachs and presented as a creamy-white, slightly acid powder. In contrast to *papain (which is often called vegetable pepsin), pepsin performs best in an acid mixture containing hydrochloric acid, which is not surprising, since those are the conditions which exist in the animal's stomach. It works best at 125°F (52°C), which is a bit hotter than it is asked to perform at in nature. In solution, it is destroyed by temperatures over 158°F (70°C). Pepsin works like *rennet in coagulating milk and is used in cheesemaking.

PERCEBE. *See* barnacle.

PERCH. Members of the perch family Percidae are generally long and slender, with heavy scales and two distinctly separate dorsal fins. Among the most flavorful of these freshwater fish are the yellow perch, walleye, and sauger. The name "perch" is also given to several ocean fish of the families Percichthyidae and Scorpaenidae. The confusion about nomenclature begins at this point. When you buy frozen fillets labeled "ocean perch" you may be purchasing rosefish, redfish, red perch, or sea perch. Together these fish—with bland flavor and firm texture—account for a large proportion of the seafood eaten in the U.S. To the angler in this country, however, the perch is one of the following more delectable fish and is usually sought in lakes.

Yellow perch (*Perca flavescens*). With firm, sweet flesh, the handsome yellow perch ranks high among America's best panfish. These perch, which are almost identical to the European *P. fluviatilis,* are found in cold northern lakes as well as slow, warmish water from the eastern U.S. and Canada to Kansas. They weigh up to 3 lb (1½ Kg), though larger ones have been caught.

Walleye (*Stizostedion vitreum*). The largest member of the Percidae, walleyes weigh up to 10 lb (4½ Kg) or more. Their range is cold waters across the U.S. and Canada and as far south as Alabama. They are often marketed under the misnomers walleyed pike, yellow pike, or pike perch.

Sauger (*Stizostedion canadense*). Saugers, also miscalled sandpike, resemble walleyes but are smaller. They live in lakes and slow rivers from central to eastern Canada, west to Minnesota and south to the Mississippi Valley. Saugers are among the best-flavored of freshwater fish.

"White perch" is a name applied to some half-dozen fish that may or may not be perch, and the appellation "sea perch" applies to at least half a dozen more. Names for perch, *bass, and *pike are often used interchangeably, perhaps because the largest order of fishes has been given the name Perciformes—perch-shaped fish. Among the saltwater fish more or less correctly called perch are the following.

White perch or **sea perch** (*Morone americanus*). A member of the bass family, this 50–60 in. (20–25-cm) fish resembles its larger relation the striped bass, but it is almost

WHITE PERCH

always called a perch. It ranges from Nova Scotia to South Carolina and is found in fresh and brackish water as well as the sea. It is often pan-fried, and larger specimens are filleted.

Redfish or **ocean perch** (*Sebastes marinus*). This bright red or orange-red fish is sometimes sold as rockfish, rosefish, red perch, or even white perch. It lives in cold, northerly waters on both sides of the Atlantic and is found at great depths. It is 12–20 in. (30–50 cm) long. Redfish is an important commercial fish in several countries.

Whatever country you visit, you are likely to find some fish called perch, from the African walking perch (which can also climb trees) to the snakehead perch of southern Asia to the so-called tropical perch of Australia. All are worth a try, including the de-

licious European pike perch, *Sander lucioperca,* and its large cousin *S. wolgensis,* found in Russia and Hungary.

[*Perch*—French: *perche;* German: *Barsch;* Italian: *pesce persico;* Spanish: *perca*]

PERI-PERI. *See* piri-piri.

PERIWINKLE. *See* winkle.

PERMANGANATE OF POTASH. *See* disinfectants.

PERRIER. *See* water.

PERSIMMON or **kaki,** a tree of the same family as ebony, is a native of China. It has been introduced all over the world and is grown in suitably warm parts of North America as well as in Mediterranean Europe. It is easily noticed, since the fruit does not ripen until well into winter when the leaves have fallen and the orange or scarlet persimmons stand out against the winter landscape like lights on the tree.

The native wild American persimmon (*Diospyros virginiana*) is only an inch or so in diameter and very astringent when green because of the large amount of tannin it contains. When ripe the fruits are a dull-orange color with a rich, sweet flavor and a gooey texture. They are best when dead-ripe—falling from the trees—and thus you rarely

PERSIMMON

find good wild persimmons in markets. The pulp of wild persimmons is delicious in nut bread, puddings, and chiffon pie, and it has been made into vinegar, molasses, and beer by enterprising country folk. The leaves of the persimmon are exceptionally high in vitamin C, and tea made from the dried leaves has a pleasant flavor comparable to sassafras.

The so-called Japanese persimmon (*D. kaki*) is the one most commonly found in stores in the U.S. It is yellow-orange and about the size of an apple. It is grown commercially in California and becomes sweet earlier than the wild persimmon. Its flavor and texture have been compared to that of apricots. The Japanese add sake to the fruit, and some like to squeeze lemon or lime juice over it. To serve it whole, score the skin in quarters and peel it back. The pulp can be used in pies, ice cream, jelly, and custards. Puréed, it makes a piquant sauce or sherbet.

There are many other varieties of persimmons, especially in China and Japan, some with yellow fruits. In these countries the tannin is sometimes removed by soaking in *limewater, and persimmons may be ripened with ethylene gas. Sometimes the Chinese allow them to freeze on the tree, and they are also dried.

The mabolo or velvet apple (*D. discolor*) is a tropical fruit of fair quality which is closely related to the persimmon. It is grown in the Philippines, Malaya, Ceylon, and Florida.

PE-TSAI. *See* Chinese cabbage.

PEWTER is 1 part lead to 4 to 6 parts tin, although sometimes brass or copper replaces lead in the alloy. Pewter was known in ancient China and used by the Romans. Today it is not much made, since anything containing lead is out of fashion when it comes into contact with food and drink, but many people like drinking beer from pewter mugs. It should be kept clean by rubbing with fine sand.

[*Pewter*—French: *étain;* German: *Hartzinn;* Italian: *peltro;* Spanish: *peltre*]

pH, a measure of acidity or alkalinity, was devised by the Norwegian biochemist Sören Sörensen in 1909. Its basis need not greatly concern us here; in fact, the pH is the loga-

rithm of the reciprocal of the hydrogen ion concentration. What matters is that the pH scale provides a measure of the effective acidity or alkalinity of a solution which works irrespective of the actual acids or alkalis present and uncomplicated by the fact that weight for weight, some acids and alkalis are stronger than others. In short, a solution of sulfuric acid and a solution of citric acid of the same pH taste equally sour.

The pH scale runs from 0 (the most acid) to 14 (the most alkaline), with a neutral point at pH 7.0. Examples measured on this scale are: lemon juice, pH 2.3; orange juice, pH 3.3; sour milk, pH 4.4; fresh milk, pH 6.6; distilled water, pH 7.0; limewater, pH 8.0; 1% bicarbonate of soda solution, pH 8.0; 1% caustic soda solution pH 13.0.

The pH of a substance is easily measured with indicator papers which change color according to the acidity or alkalinity of the liquid into which they are dipped. Litmus paper is a crude indicator: it turns red for acid and blue for alkali—but the distinction is not sharp. More sophisticated papers can be bought which allow the pH to be read with certainty.

PHEASANT (*Phasianus colchicus*). The most widespread of all game birds, the pheasant was introduced into Europe from farther east many centuries ago and is now

PHEASANT

completely naturalized and resident over most of Europe. In North America, pheasants were introduced at various times during the 18th and 19th centuries. The ring-necked pheasant is now acclimatized in many areas, especially in farm country, though less so in the southern parts of the U.S., which is almost outside its favored climate. Everywhere in their distribution, pheasants are shot for sport and also bred for the table. The season varies slightly from country to country. Among the species of pheasant that come from the Himalayas and southwest China are some of the most beautiful of all birds.

A brace of pheasants traditionally consists of a hen and a cock; the hen, which lacks the enormous tail and bright colors of the cock, is regarded as the better eating. In a young cock, the spurs are short and rounded, the beak more pliable than in older birds, and the feet are soft and smooth, while in old birds they are rough and scaly.

The birds should not be plucked before being hung. How long pheasants should be hung must obviously depend in part on the weather; a bird badly holed with shot cannot be hung for as long as a well-shot bird or one reared especially for the table, and the degree of highness is a matter of taste. Pheasants can be said to be ready when they get a slightly "off" smell. They are sometimes hung by the neck, but usually by the feet, in which case some blood beginning to drip from the beak is a sign that the birds are just about ready. The bird is also said to be ready when the long tail feathers can be easily pulled out. However, it should be noted that today many people oppose the hanging of pheasant, preferring its fresh flavor.

Because the meat is very lean and inclined to be dry, pheasants are best barded (but never larded). In France, a couple of Petit Suisse cream cheeses are sometimes put inside pheasants before roasting to provide necessary moistening. The pheasant was once so revered that it was considered food only for nobles, and as Elizabeth David writes, it is a bird which "inspires fantasies in the kitchen." In the Middle Ages, pheasants were served with gilded beaks and legs, their brains were considered a delicacy, and elaborate sauces were devised for them. Today pheasant is appreciated more in simple dishes that do not smother its subtle flavor. Roast pheasant may be basted with lemon juice or Seville orange juice. A plump pheasant poached with aromatics is often served with braised celery or endive, and sauerkraut traditionally accompanies pheasant in parts of Europe. Since wild foods are appropriate to wild fowl, many pheasant recipes include cranberries, juniper berries, watercress, chestnuts, and wild rice.

[*Pheasant*—French: *faisan;* German: *Fasan;* Italian: *fagiano;* Spanish: *faisán*]

PHOSPHORIC ACID (H_3PO_4) is colorless, syrupy, and odorless. It is used by industry to provide acidity in soft drinks and is regarded as harmless in the very small concentrations used for this purpose.

[*Phosphoric acid*—French: *acide phosphorique;* German: *Phosphorsäure;* Italian: *acido fosforico;* Spanish: *ácido fosfórico*]

PHYSALIS FRUIT. The genus *Physalis,* with about 100 species, belongs to the tomato family, and some half a dozen are cultivated, mainly in warm countries, since they are sensitive to frost.

Chinese lantern plant or **bladder cherry** (*P. alkengii*) is grown for the decorative effect of its red papery calyx, the husk which looks, as the name suggests, rather like a papery lantern. This lantern surrounds a berry which is edible when ripe. The members of the genus that are cultivated for their fruit have the same general appearance, but the lantern is light brown and not decorative.

Cape gooseberry (*P. peruviana*), in spite of its name, is a native of South America, but early in the last century had become an important crop in South Africa. The plant is also produced to some extent in southern Europe. The flavor is rather like a gooseberry, though with less character. They can be bought, canned, as goldenberries. Cape gooseberries make good jam. Allow equal weights of sugar and fruit, and bottle the jam the moment it will set.

Ground cherry, strawberry tomato, or **dwarf Cape gooseberry** (*P. fruticosa*) is native to parts of central and eastern North America, from New York to Florida and

GROUND CHERRY

west to Iowa and Minnesota. Used for jam and pies, the fruits may be stored for a month or more, during which time they become sweeter. Ground cherries are also a popular wild fruit in Hawaii, where they are called *poha* and are used particularly to make a syrupy preserve.

Tomatillo, jamberry, or **tomate verde.** Native to Mexico, the tomatillo (*P. ixocarpa*) was used by the Aztecs. The berry is larger than the other *Physalis* fruits and completely fills the lantern, so that it seems to be in a husk. When ripe, the fruits are variously colored, depending on the variety, but they generally look like small green tomatoes. In fact, *tomatillo* means "small tomato" in Spanish. The tomatillo is rather flavorless unless boiled for a few minutes. Its particular culinary importance—though it is used for jams, and for chutneys in India—lies in its being an essential ingredient in guacamole (a purée of avocados with chili and other seasonings) as made in the north of Mexico, where the fruit is often called *tomate con cascar* (with husk). Canned tomatillos are available, as well as the canned *salsa de tomatillo*. The canned fruits, when used in guacamole, require no further cooking.

PICCALILLI. *See* pickles.

PICKEREL. *See* pike.

PICKLED FISH. *See* caveach; seviche.

PICKLES and **pickling.** Pickling is an old method of preserving food by immersing it in brine or vinegar. Preservation depends on the sensitivity of putrefactive organisms to salt and acetic acid, and occasionally to other acids and spices. Although meat curers call the brines they use "pickle," popular usage restricts pickles to foods, usually vegetables and fruit (but sometimes meat and fish) preserved in various ways and used as a relish. Pickles are made by traditional methods all over the world, from Korean and Chinese pickled cabbage to British pickled walnuts. Pickles also include what Americans call relishes and the English call *chutneys. The word covers a vast number of preparations and different techniques for making them; some basic varieties and considerations are dealt with below. In general, vegetables to be pickled must be firm and as fresh as possible. Acid or salt must be sufficiently concentrated to ensure that the pickle keeps. Pickles may or may not need the addition of garlic, herbs, and spices, but of overriding importance to their flavor is the critical balance between sourness, saltiness, and sweetness.

Air, since it contains oxygen, is the enemy of pickles. It causes discoloration and encourages the growth of mold and the degrading of vinegar by bacteria. It should be kept at bay by filling jars to the brim, dislodging bubbles, and covering carefully. Pickles should always be held under the surface of the pickling liquid.

Alum is sometimes used in pickles to harden the vegetables. A piece the size of a bean will do for 4 qt (4½ lt) of vinegar; the amount is not critical and is usually given in the recipe. Although alum is harmful in large doses and is not favored by many authorities, it has a low toxicity, so is all right in the small quantities needed in pickles. It has been used in food for hundreds of years.

*Brine.** A 10% brine strength is commonly used for discouraging unwanted bacteria and for holding vegetables before pickling. This is particularly necessary when vegetables that crop at different seasons are eventually to be put together in a mixed pickle, such as piccalilli.

Color. Pickles should look attractive, so color is important. Reasons why pickles discolor include: (a) leaving cut surfaces exposed to the air instead of dropping the vegetables into water and lemon juice as soon as they are cut; (b) using hard water for brine; (c) using brown vinegar; (d) using ground spices. But it is more important that pickles should taste good than look good, and if you find it hard to make white pickles, the alternative is to color them red with a beet slice, as is often done in the Middle East. Turmeric turns pickles yellow, and also adds its flavor.

Covering. Pickles must always be covered with liquid and the jar sealed to prevent evaporation. Pickles containing oil should remain under it, and a layer of oil can sometimes be used on top of pickles to help seal them. Jars with bare metal lids should be avoided: a vinegar-salt mixture is very corrosive to metal.

Drying. Some ingredients are very watery; others, like capers, can gain in strength of flavor by being wilted in the sun before being pickled. When there is no sun, water may have to be removed by salting and squeezing. Watery pickles do not keep well, because the vinegar may become diluted by the juices below the critical level of acidity. Failing all else, it may be necessary to use extra salt or strong distilled vinegar.

Dill pickles. Cucumbers preserved by fermentation and flavored with dill (or its oil) and usually some garlic are called dill pickles. This is one of the most popular types of pickle, especially (with ethnic variations) in the U.S. and Central and Eastern Europe. Kosher dill pickles are usually made from unwaxed Kirby cucumbers which are packed into a wide-mouthed crock. Garlic, coriander seeds, mustard seeds, hot peppers,

peppercorns, and bay leaves may be added, plus plenty of sprigs of fresh dill with seed heads. The cucumbers are covered with brine, and a crust of sour rye bread may be added to aid natural fermentation, which continues until the pickles reach desired sourness. Small green tomatoes and green beans may be similarly pickled. Simpler dill pickles may be made with vinegar and perhaps alum for preservation, and some recipes call for dried dill or seeds, but the delicious pungency of good dill pickles is best achieved with fresh dill.

Fermentation. Alcoholic fermentation can occasionally occur in sweet pickles or chutneys left open in hot weather, but is unimportant in this context compared to *lactic acid fermentation, which occurs in the making of dill pickles and sauerkraut. It is the reaction that takes place in silage, and is analogous to the souring of milk. The lactic acid acts as a preservative.

Most of these pickles were originally devised in cool countries for keeping during cold winters, and they will not stand safely in hot climates, where they need to be packed in jars and sterilized. They should, in any case, always be kept in a cool place.

*Garlic is pickled whole in Middle Eastern countries and has a rather startling flavor, but a clove or two is quite a normal part of pickling spices, and often improves the pickles.

*Gherkins.** Tiny relatives of the cucumber.

Hardening. Vinegar tends to harden vegetables, and will delay softening when fruits, such as apples, are cooked in it when making chutney. If a pickle seems to be too soft, the next year try adding alum (see above). Tannin is another hardener, which is one reason why oak leaves or black-currant leaves are used in dill pickles in Poland and elsewhere.

Herbs and **spices.** The flavoring of many pickles may be traditional, but it is also often an individual matter. In commercial picklemaking, this is an area of closely guarded secrets, and mixtures of extracts and essential oils are used for greater control and a standard product. At home, you use the raw ingredients, which should (unless otherwise instructed) be put into a cheese-cloth bag, boiled or infused in the vinegar, and removed before pickling. Whole spices are also put into the jar, for slow diffusion. Common flavorings are black or white pep-percorns, garlic, shallots, onion, whole bruised ginger, tamarind, bay, cloves, cinna-mon or cassia sticks, chilies, cumin, corian-der, fenugreek, turmeric, white mustard seeds, horseradish, dill, fennel, sage, savory, and other items like rue and asafetida in tiny quantities. Although pickle-spice mixtures can be bought, the more interested cooks (such as the readers of this book) will make their own formulas to suit individual pickles. A standard mixture might be 6 black pep-percorns, 2 allspice, a large blade of mace, a clove or a chili, with a pinch of coriander and white mustard seeds, and a few white peppercorns. Too much clove is overwhelm-ing.

Maturation. Pickles and chutneys vary in the time they need to be kept before they can be eaten. Some are designed to be ready very quickly, even the same day, while others need 6 months. With highly spiced thick chutneys, the longer the better, up to a year.

Molds are likely to grow on anything, in-cluding the top of pickles, and are not too discouraged by acidity, especially if there is air around. The white scum that forms on vats of fermenting cucumbers and sauer-kraut should be skimmed off every 10 days. It is a natural growth and quite harmless, but invites secondary organisms which will turn the pickle musty.

Lemon and lime juice, being very acid, are preservative and in some cases replace vin-egar in pickles. Because the citric acid in them is not as good a preservative as acetic acid, it is necessary to follow recipes and not simply to swap lemon juice for vinegar on grounds of health or availability.

Oils are preservative only because they coat the ingredients and tend to exclude air. Mustard oil may also have some special pre-servative action. There are many oily pickles of Asian inspiration, including pickled fish and pickled chicken and pork. These are all cooked pickles. If I use other oils instead of mustard oil, I always include white mustard seed with it.

Onions. Pickled onions are so popular in Britain that they deserve special mention. Although many onions are grown locally, they also come into the country from places as far apart as Holland, Poland, Bulgaria, Hungary, and Egypt. In the trade, they are classified into three types: the large Ware onions, which are used sliced; the Baby Ware onions, which are small specimens of large onions; and the Silverskins, which come from Holland and are a different type altogether. The smallest are used as cocktail onions.

Commercially, onions are peeled by ma-chine. After the onions have been topped and tailed, either the skin is burned off (the "flash" method), or the onions are put into a machine which slits the outside skin lightly, and blows it off with a high-pressure blast of air. For ease of peeling at home, dunk them, a few at a time, into boiling water for 30 seconds (or even up to 2 minutes) and re-fresh them in cold water. The skins then come off easily. Onions are always brined for 24 hours before being pickled in vinegar. In some quarters, shallots are thought to make better pickled onions than onions do.

*pH. The degree of acidity needed to make a pickle keep depends on storage tempera-ture, type of pickle, and the spices present. A pH below 4 is safe; if a pickle tastes nicely sharp, it is pretty sure to keep.

Piccalilli. A pickle of unknown origin, and a very different commodity in America and Britain. In Britain, it is a mixed pickle in a thick, opaque, vinegary sauce full of ground white mustard and turmeric—in the U.S. it would probably be called mustard pickle. American piccalilli would in Britain be called a sweet mustard pickle.

Salt used for pickling should be pure (iodized salt will turn cucumbers dark). Special coarser salts are sold for pickling, and coarse kosher salt is fine, but a bit more is needed because it is bulkier. Reduced-sodium salt mixtures are unsafe for preserving pickles.

Scum. *See above,* molds.

Sun. Sunlight is antiseptic. It kills microorganisms, bleaches, and encourages various chemical changes, some of which (*see* fats and oils) are not beneficial, whereas others may be. In India, a country with plenty of hot sun and a love of pickles, jars of pickles are very often matured by sunlight. The heat speeds the reactions, but the light keeps fermentation in check. Sun is also used to wilt and dry vegetables to reduce their moisture content before pickling. Pickles exposed to sunlight out of doors should be only lightly covered and brought in every night.

Vessels. Since vinegar and salt together are corrosive (the mixture is recommended for cleaning copper), metal vessels should preferably not be used. Stainless steel is an exception and, in a pinch, aluminum pans can be used just for boiling, but brass or copper preserving pans never. Enamel pans are better, and glass is good. For the jars, glass is usual, but good stoneware is all right. Beware of lead-glazed *earthenware jars, which could be lethal.

Vinegar. For good color in pickles, many people use either white wine vinegar or white (uncolored) malt vinegar. But otherwise, the color of vinegar used is immaterial. It is important to use genuine vinegar and not the synthetic stuff that so often spoils commercial pickles. Living in a wine-vinegar country, I often think that English pickles are best made with malt vinegar, but the choice is of little consequence, since in nearly every case the vinegar containing the spices and herbs is brought to the boil. The congenerics of a fine vinegar and even the distinction between wine and malt vinegar therefore tend to be lost; the basic tastes are also overlaid by the spices. Strong spirit vinegar may be necessary for pickling very watery materials, like plums and tomatoes, unless they are slightly dried out before pickling.

*Water. If hard water is used for the brining of vegetables, they are liable to have a bad color. If there are problems with the water, use rainwater or even distilled water.

INDIAN ONION PICKLE

Peel 5½ lb (2½ Kg) of onions and cut them almost through in the form of a cross but without separating the parts. Add 4 oz (100 g) of salt, 2 oz (50 g) of powdered mustard, ½ teaspoon of turmeric, and up to ½ oz (15 g) of chili powder (depending on the strength of the chili and the toughness of your mouth). Mix all together in a bowl with ¼ cup of oil and a little water to moisten the spices and salt and get the onion coated. Then put the whole lot into a jar and just cover them with water. Keep the jar loosely covered in the sun for 4–5 days to ferment. Cool overnight and the pickle is ready to eat.

QUICK PICKLE

Thinly slice equal quantities of sour apples, cucumbers or celery, and young onions— sufficient to fill a qt (1-lt) jar. Put them into a bowl and mix in 2 teaspoons of salt, 1 teaspoon of chili (or more to taste), and 4 tablespoons each of soy sauce and sherry. Pack into the jar and cover with vinegar. This pickle can be used the same day.

[*Pickles*—French: *conserves au vinaigre;* German: *Eingepökelte;* Italian: *sottaceti;* Spanish: *encurtidos*]

PIG. *See* pork; ham; bacon.

PIGEON. To many city dwellers, the pigeon is a messy, disease-ridden nuisance. Even country-reared pigeons may be viewed with the suspicion that they have eaten seed poisoned with insecticides. However, those who have tasted the delicate flesh of a squab—a pigeon less than a month old—will gladly pay an extravagant price for these birds. Pigeons, once a popular food (witness the extinction of the passenger pigeon), were the mainstay of many people in the Depression, and because they are so easy to raise, there is now an upsurge in pigeon breeding for food. Some attribute the renewed interest in pigeons to the increasing tastelessness of factory-produced chickens. Even domesticated young pigeons, whose meat is less gamy than that of wild birds, have flavorful, moist flesh.

The wood pigeon (*Columba palumbus*) and the rock dove (*C. livia*), which is claimed to be the ancestor of the domestic breeds and feral town pigeons, both have their supporters as the best wild pigeon. Among U.S. species, mourning doves (*Zenaidura macroura*) are eaten in some states, while white-winged doves (*Zenaida asiatica*) occur in the South and Southeast, and the western band-tailed pigeon (*Columba fasciata*) is eaten in the West. There are some 475 different species of pigeon and dove in the world, many of which provide very good eating, such as the Australian wonga-wonga and the beautiful fruit pigeons of Africa and India, considered among the most tasty. Others have strange habits, such as the pigeons that feed on nutmegs. All are edible to a greater or lesser degree, but some are best skinned rather than plucked. In China, hard-boiled pigeon eggs are a delicacy; if they are taken carefully from the nest, one at a time, the birds will continue to lay.

Properly fattened little birds of table breed are widely available in the U.S. and Europe, though they may have to be ordered from a fancy butcher. Squabs should be about 4 weeks old, and the best have never eaten whole grain. Pigeons are best starved for 24 hours before being killed (or so the experts say) and, when dead, should be hung up by the legs and bled. If not, the meat may be dark. They should also be plucked when still warm—never scalded to loosen the feathers—and drawn while fresh. Domestic pigeons are best eaten fresh; the longer they are kept the less flavor they have. Wild pigeons may need hanging for a day or two.

Young pigeons are excellent for any cooking method, but older ones are fit only for stewing, game stock, or pies. In the Italian province of Umbria, hunters catch wild pigeons on the wooded hills, stuff them with juniper butter and black and green olives, and steam them in tarragon-flavored red wine. Tuscans make a pasta sauce from squabs, chicken livers, mushrooms, aromatics, red wine, and tomatoes. Squabs may also be braised with cabbage or lentils, stuffed with wild rice, or potted.

[*Pigeon*—French: *pigeon;* German: *Taube;* Italian: *piccione;* Spanish: *paloma*]

PIGEON PEA or **red gram.** An important pulse (*Cajanus cajan*) which originated in Africa, pigeon peas are a crop of warm countries—they stand no frost. They are important for food in the Caribbean (as gunga peas or gungo peas), tropical America, Africa, and the Orient—they had already reached Asia in prehistoric times. In India (where they are *arhar, tur* or *toor*, or *tuvaram*), they are second only to chickpeas in importance. The color of pigeon peas ranges from red to white, brown, mottled, or black. They are split and husked as ★*dal.* The green pods can be used as a vegetable. Pigeon peas are said to be slightly narcotic and can be blamed for the nap after a large curry meal.

PIGNOLIA. *See* pine nut.

PIGNUT. Alternative name for ★chufa nut.

PIGWEED. *See* lamb's-quarters; amaranth.

PIKE might well be described as the barracuda of fresh water; it is a long, fast, very savage fish which will not only clear a pond of other fish but also grab young water birds swimming on the surface. The northern or European pike (*Esox lucius*) is also found in Asia and is fished commercially in the Caspian Sea. Northern pike are found throughout lakes and streams of the U.S. and in most forest lakes in Canada, which ships millions of pounds to Europe. Possibly because the pike is improperly cooked, it is not considered as delicious in the U.S. as it is in Europe. Other pike species in North America include the small chain pickerel (*E. niger*), the even smaller grass pickerel (*E. americanus*), and the large muskellunges (*E. masquinongy*), called "muskies" in the U.S. and "lunges" in Canada, which have fine-flavored flesh.

The French count the pike among the finest of food fishes, but I have known people in Ireland who treat the pike with nothing short of revulsion because of the peculiar smell it has when caught and the slime it exudes, not to mention its murderous habits and unpleasant bones. The temptation to wash off the slime as soon as the fish is caught should be resisted: the slime contributes to the quality and tenderness. Some people think that pike is improved by hanging overnight with the mouth and throat stuffed with salt. Alternatively, the fish may be rubbed with salt and left for 8 hours or so. A good pike for the fisherman weighs around 9 lb (4 Kg); for the cook 4½–5½ lb (2–2½ Kg) is a better size unless the flesh is intended for *quenelles,* since large pike are tough.

Pike may be scaled with a grater, but if the fish is to be skinned after cooking, this will be easier if the scales are left intact. The roes are considered slightly poisonous and are sometimes (but not always) rejected. The liver, though, is a delicacy and can be used in the sauce. Pike taken from good, clean waters should not taste muddy; others may benefit from a soak in vinegared water. The fish may be cooked in a number of ways— *quenelles de brochet,* light fish dumplings, are a famous French creation. A small pike of 3¼ lb (1½ Kg) will take about 25 minutes to poach in a court bouillon. Many different

sauces have been concocted for pike, which some consider to have an undistinguished flavor. It is often served with *beurre blanc,* a mixture of butter, shallots, and vinegar. In Scandinavia, pike is boiled and eaten with horseradish. In the U.S., it may be curried or stuffed.

[*Pike*—French: *brochet;* German: *Hecht;* Italian: *luccio;* Spanish: *lucio*]

PILCHARD. The name given to the adult *sardine when it is fished around British coasts.

PILLI-PILLI. *See* piri-piri.

PIMENTO or **pimiento.** *See* sweet pepper.

PIMENTÓN. *See* sweet pepper.

PIMIENTA. Spanish for *pepper.

PINEAPPLE (*Ananas comosus*), on a world basis, is the most important tropical fruit. It originated in South America—varieties still grow wild in Brazil—and it was cultivated in the West Indies before the arrival of Columbus, whose men relished it. Very soon it spread to tropical areas around the world, although its cultivation was at first haphazard. Because of its appearance, the Spanish called it *piña* (pine cone). Today, the Hawaiian Islands are the largest pineapple producers. The plant was introduced there by a Spaniard, Don Francisco de Paula y Marin, in 1790, and scientific growing was started by an English captain, John Kidwell, toward the end of the 19th century. The canning of pineapple began in 1900; today the tonnage canned is immense.

Pineapple plants are perennial and continue bearing for a long time if allowed to, but commercial growers renew the plants every few years. The fruit is the result of the fruits of the whole inflorescence fusing into one. Most varieties are seedless.

To be really good, a pineapple must ripen on the plant, because the stem is full of starch, which is converted to sugar and rushed up into the fruit at the last minute. In the moment of ripening, the pineapple receives enough sugar to double its content almost overnight, but this sugar never reaches the fruit if it is cut immature. Thus, pineapples imported into temperate regions by ship never ripen properly, and people who have eaten pineapples in the tropics rarely buy them back home. Pineapples that have been shipped by air are another matter.

Pineapples should always be bought ripe. Unripe ones are tasteless—don't believe the produce manager who says, "It'll ripen in a warm place." It won't. Overripe pineapple is also nasty. Avoid fruit with discolored patches or bruises, dried-up or shriveled ones, and any with wilting leaves. There should be a nice pineapple smell, and you should be able to pull out a leaf of the crown. Pineapples will keep for 2–3 days in a plastic bag in the refrigerator.

Europe gets pineapples from a number of places, including Africa, the West Indies, the Azores, and the Canary Islands. In the U.S., pineapples are grown in Florida, and some come from Mexico and Puerto Rico. But the classic is the smooth cayenne pineapple from Hawaii, weighing up to 7–9 lb (3–4 Kg) and used for both canning and eating fresh.

Apart from sugar, acid, and the lovely taste, pineapple contains a digestive enzyme, bromelin, which digests proteins such as egg white, gelatin and the protein in meat. Hence, raw pineapple cannot be made into gelatin jelly, although *agar will do the trick. Recipes calling for pineapple and gelatin specify canned or cooked pineapple, since heat puts the bromelin out of action.

Pineapple is used in many sweets and in fruit salads, as well as for preserves. It is cooked with ham and pork. Savory dishes containing it often incorporate Hawaii in their name. In the U.S., pineapple often is flavored with a dash of vodka or white wine; in Europe, with kirsch.

Pineapples were already common in Europe in the 19th century, when they were grown in heated glasshouses; there are dozens of recipes in Victorian cookbooks. The skin and parings were boiled with sugar to make flavoring for creams. In canning factories now, the parings are used for juice—nothing is wasted.

[*Pineapple*—French: *ananas;* German: *Ananas;* Italian: *ananas;* Spanish: *piña*]

PINE NUT. Although the seeds of pine trees are in general edible, many are too small to be of value, and others have a strong taste of turpentine which cannot be sufficiently reduced by roasting. There remain a good number of species producing excellent nuts, which have been used as food from time immemorial. Some kinds were of more than local importance; husks have been found in the rubbish tips from Roman camps in Britain. In North America, the nuts were a favorite food of the Indians, and even today it is the Indians who collect the cones of the two-leafed nut pine commercially in Colorado, Arizona, and New Mexico.

The Mediterranean stone pine (*Pinus pinea*) provided the original nut used in European and Mideastern cooking. The stone pine is the romantic umbrella-shaped tree of Italian landscape paintings. It grows wild in coastal districts from Portugal to the Black Sea and has been planted on the North African coast. In places, the forests of stone pine are beautiful and extensive. Particularly famous is that at Ravenna on the Adriatic coast of Italy, but other notable Italian localities are Viareggio, San Rossore, Fallonica, and Castelfusano. In Spain, the best nuts come from Huelva, and the second best are from Tarragona.

The large, shiny cones of the stone pine are gathered between November and March and are stored until summer, when they are spread out in the hot sun to open. The nuts can be then shaken out of the cones. Cracking and extraction of the kernels is nowadays done by machinery. The kernels keep well in cool dry places (or, if necessary, in a jar in the refrigerator) but are always expensive.

Pine nuts are white or cream, soft in texture, with a slight piny flavor. They may be eaten raw but are better fried or roasted (they burn very easily), when they taste more nutty. They can be chocolate-coated or made into a nut butter, but their main interest lies in their use in Mediterranean cooking.

In France, stone pines grow in Provence and to some extent in the pine forests of the Landes (in *omelette landaise,* pine nuts are fried gently in butter before turning in the eggs in the usual way), but you could not say that *pignons* were an important ingredient in French cooking. In Spain it is another matter. One finds *piñones* in every shop, and uses range from sweet preparations such as *piñonate* (a paste of pine nuts and sugar) or *bandullo gallego* (a type of pudding or cake with pine nuts on top) to *bacalao* with raisins and pine nuts, and *escaldums* (a chicken dish from Majorca with onion and tomato, butter, and marjoram).

At the other end of the Mediterranean, in Turkey, Greece, and the Lebanon (where are some fine stone pines to be seen from the airplane as you land in Beirut), pine nuts come in a variety of sweetmeats, in jam, pilaf, rice pudding, and stuffings for chicken, turkey, vine leaves, and vegetables. In Italy, sweet things containing pine nuts include *zelten* and *strudel* from the Trentino Alto Adige (with a strong Austrian influence) or *pan giallo* or *pizza di plenta* from Lazio, even the *fave dei morti* or *charlotte alla milanese* of Lombardy and the *pinoccate* of Umbria. Pine nuts are also a usual ingredient in the extraordinary *sanguinaccio,* which, with many regional variations, consists of pig's blood with candied citron peel, sometimes raisins, sugar, and even chocolate. They are used with spinach (*spinaci alla romana*), pasta, and cauliflower (*pasta coi cavolfiori*), peppers or eggplant (*capunatina di melanzane*), and *sardele in saor* from Venice (in which sardines are marinated in vinegar), sardines (*pasta con le sarde*), and with swordfish (*agghiotta di pesce spada*) from Sicily. Also, as in Spain, there are pine nut–dried grape combinations in many regional recipes for *bacalao* and stockfish (as in *stoccafisso in agro-dolce*) and for hare (*lepre alla*

trentina). These combinations are a survival from an ancient style of cooking.

But the most sophisticated recipes using pine nuts come from around Genoa, where pine nuts go whole into a variety of dishes and are pounded to form the basic thickener of sauces. Best-known of these is the famous *pesto alla genovese,* a superlative sauce for pasta made from pounded pine nuts, garlic, cheese, and basil. From the region come such specialties as *salsa al funghi* (soaked dried Italian fungi pounded with garlic, anchovy, pine nuts, and tomato), *salsa alla genovese* (in which pine nuts are pounded with capers, anchovy, parsley, and olives with a dash of garlic and vinegar), and *salsa verde alla genovese* (pine nuts pounded with basil, garlic, anchovy, salt, and oil) to go with the boiled meats known as *bollito misto,* and *salsa piccante.* From the U.S. come *piñon* cookies.

It is rarely necessary to peel pine nuts, since you buy them ready to use, but the Spanish soak the nuts in tepid water for half an hour as a preliminary.

[*Pine nut*—French: *pomme de pin;* German: *Piniennuss;* Italian: *pignolo;* Spanish: *piñon*]

PINTO. *See* bean.

PIRI-PIRI, peri-peri, or **pilli-pilli** dishes are meat or fish served with a special hot-pepper sauce. They are Portuguese African, particularly from Mozambique, but the hot sauce has been taken into Portuguese and South African cooking generally and has its addicts. Although every cook in Mozambique has his own particular way of preparing piri-piri, a typical recipe might start by straining lemon juice, then simmering it with freshly picked hot peppers for a few minutes. The mixture is taken from the stove and the peppers are strained out and pressed into a fine paste with salt until no lumps are left. This pulp is returned to the pan with the original lemon juice, further simmered while being constantly stirred, then eaten with meat, fowl, or seafood with rice to soften the blow of the hot sauce.

In some recipes, the stem ends of small red chilies are put in olive oil and stored for a few months before being used in piri-piri. Other cooks let the peppers and other spices infuse in the oil in a slow oven or on top of the stove or by standing the seasoned oil in the hot noon sun. Piri-piri is also available in a powdered form.

PISCO. *See* brandy.

PISTACHIO NUT or **green almond.** The nuts are borne on a small deciduous tree (*Pistacia vera*), native to Asia and still found growing wild in the mysterious ranges around the headwaters of the Oxus. It was brought into the Mediterranean many thousands of years ago and reached Italy from Syria during the reign of the Emperor Tiberius. The tree can withstand very poor conditions. It will grow on dry, rocky hillsides as long as it gets hot summers. In Europe, it is grown in southern Italy and Sicily as well as in Greece and to a small extent in France and Spain. In the U.S., it has of late been grown in California, Texas, and Arizona. However, most travelers would associate pistachio nuts with Islamic countries of the Middle East and North Africa—Persia and Afghanistan, Tunisia, and Algeria. They go with the salted melon and sunflower seeds sold on street corners; the salted nuts are sold in the bazaars in their horny shells, open-lipped like cream-colored bivalves.

The growing nuts look like clusters of small olives. The flesh may be an intense green or sometimes paler, according to variety. The skin adhering to the nut is papery and red-brown to creamy. The nuts are gathered when the outside begins to shrivel and to turn yellow. They are spread out in the shade to dry for a week or more. Since the shell gapes to expose the kernel, there is no need for cracking. Once dried, pistachios keep well.

The flavor of the pistachio is mild, but in some varieties there is a resinous taste which is a reminder of the mastic and terebinth bushes to which the pistachio is closely related (both of them can be used as root stocks for grafting). The resinous taste is particularly strong in wild nuts and is said to be preferred by the inhabitants of Turkestan. The cultivated varieties vary considerably. They are propagated by grafting, although nuts are often planted. Since there are male and female trees, a single pistachio tree is useless; and male trees have to be included in every orchard for pollination. It takes 15–20 years for the trees to come into anything like full production, but some nuts are produced 4 years after grafting. Trees yield between 20 lb (9 Kg) and 60 lb (27 Kg) of nuts, which are always expensive.

Apart from being salted to eat by the handful, pistachios are mainly used in cooking for their decorative effect. They appear in various sweetmeats and are also included in stuffings, pâtés, and stuffed meats (like the Genovese *cima* and the *coppa romana*), where they look like green islands in the slices. There is also the famous pistachio ice cream, particularly of Italy and the U.S. If this is not expensive, it is certain to be faked with other nuts and green coloring. Other uses of the nuts as a main ingredient are limited, but include the cakelike *mazaresi al pistacchio* of Sicily. Pistachio nuts are sometimes added to expensive Indian pilaf dishes. They are grown to some extent in Kashmir but are mostly imported from Afghanistan.

To remove the skins from pistachio nuts and leave the nuts with a fine green color, blanch them in salted water, then treat them as you would *almonds. A beautiful green oil can be pressed from pistachio nuts, but it is too expensive for use in the kitchen (although it is used in perfumery), and it also goes rancid very quickly. The nuts contain about 54% oil and 22% protein, so they have good food value.

[*Pistachio nut*—French: *pistache;* German: *Pistazie;* Italian: *pistachio;* Spanish: *pistacho, alfóncigo*]

PI-TSI. *See* water chestnut.

PLAICE (*Pleuronectes platessa*). The most important *flatfish of European fisheries, plaice ranges from the western Mediterranean to Iceland and Norway. It is dextral,

AMERICAN PLAICE

usually about 16 in. (40 cm) long, and has mild, lean, soft flesh. Plaice is loved by Danes and Swedes, and it is the mainstay of English fish-and-chip shops.

The American or Canadian plaice or sand dab (*Hippoglossoides platessoides*) occurs in both North American and European waters. It is abundant in Iceland, Norway, and Scotland and from Canada to Rhode Island. As Alan Davidson writes in *North Atlantic Seafood* (Viking, 1979), "The confusion which pervades the English nomenclature of flatfish is almost total for this species. It is not only called a plaice and a dab, but also a flounder and a sole. It only remains for someone to take the hint offered by the scientific name and dub it some sort of halibut." It may be cooked like flounder—or dab or sole or halibut.

[*Plaice*—French: *carrelet;* German: *Glattbutte, Scholle, Plattfisch;* Italian: *passerino;* Spanish: *platija*]

PLANTAIN. *See* banana.

PLOVER. Plovers are small waders of the family Charadriidae. Most of these birds, including the rare dotterel, were formerly shot and netted for food in Britain and elsewhere in northern Europe. Now the British plovers are sadly reduced in numbers, and, as with any wild bird, it is important to check the status of a species before using it as food. Although there are a number of different plovers, including the familiar killdeer, in the U.S., it is illegal to kill them. Gastronomically, the golden plover (*Pluvialis apricaria*) is reckoned the best, followed by the gray plover (*P. squatarola*) and finally the lapwing or green plover (*Vanellus vanellus*), which is less nice to eat but whose *eggs were once collected. Plovers are usually hung for a day or so before cooking.

[*Plover*—French: *pluvier;* German: *Regenpfeifer;* Italian: *piviere;* Spanish: *chorlito*]

PLUCK. The heart, liver, and lungs of animals, often hung up and offered for sale as one unit in some countries.

PLUCKING. Pulling out the feathers of birds. Commercial plucking of chickens is done by machines, the simplest of which is a revolving drum with rubber spikes or pieces of hose pipe sticking out, against which the birds are held. Before plucking, the birds are immersed in hot water at about 122°F (50°C) to loosen the feathers. Plucking by hand is a tiresome business and must be done with patience, since it is easy to tear the skin of the bird. The large wing feathers may have to be pulled out with pincers. After plucking, the fine underfeathers need to be singed off. In the Orient, chickens are very often skinned, a much simpler operation which also allows spices to enter and is correct for curries.

PLUM (*Prunus domestica*) is a hybrid between the *sloe (*P. spinosa*) and the cherry plum (*P. cerasifera*), which originated naturally in western Asia, where the two species grow wild together and hybridize freely. The sloe looks like a tiny blue-bloomed plum and the cherry plum resembles a red or yellow cherry. The gage or greengage, which grows wild in Asia Minor, is sometimes treated as a separate species (*P. italica*) but is usually held to be a subspecies of *P. domestica*. Another plum species, the Japanese plum (*P. triflora*), which is actually a native of China, is the ancestor of some warm-country plums. Now of lesser importance are the *bullace (*P. domestica* ssp. *insititia*), which is sometimes considered to be a separate species, and the *damson (*P. damascema*). There are also numerous indigenous American wild plums such as the Chickasaw (*P. angustifolia*), Oregon plum (*P. subcordata*), Texan plum (*P. orthosepala*), and others, including the *P. americana, P. nigra,* and *P. hortulana,* which have been domesticated. The fruit of the last two is small and used for jam. The beach plum (*P. maritima*) of the East Coast is usually used for jelly, but Cape Codders, who like to think they have a monopoly on both quality and quantity of beach plums, use them in pies, breads, cakes, and sauces.

Plums have been cultivated seriously since classical times. Many of the best plums have been first found growing in woods and from there taken into cultivation. Plums show enormous variation in color, size, taste, and fruiting season. Of the plums proper, as opposed to greengages, some are red, some yellow, and some purple or almost black. The flesh may be greenish, yellow, red, or purple. There are clingstone and freestone varieties, cookers and dessert plums. Some varieties always remain sour, even when ripe, and some become exceedingly sweet. And the number of varieties is huge—over 1000 in Europe. In California, where 90% of American plums are produced, about 40 varieties are under commercial cultivation, although no more than a dozen are grown in great quantity. As with other fruit, the number of important commercial types is gradually becoming less.

Plums will grow in any warmish temperate climate but do best with a hot summer and cold winter. However, some can even be grown at elevations in the tropics, especially those derived from Japanese plums. Out-of-season plums for the northern hemisphere come from South Africa or South America, but plums are best when picked only just before they are ripe. In buying, you should naturally avoid overripe or damaged fruit, but slightly underripe fruit will ripen in any warm room. Plums need to be put into the refrigerator when ripe and can be held there for a day or so.

In the U.S., the Santa Rosa makes up 35% of the California crop and is of Japanese descent, having been bred by Luther Burbank (who brought Japanese plums to the U.S. a century ago) and named after the town in northern California where he lived. In Britain, the Victoria, with red-over-yellow rather translucent skin and nice, but not outstanding, taste is well known. The greengage is named after Sir Thomas Gage, who reintroduced the fruit from France (where it is called Reine Claude) into Britain in about 1725. English greengages are often not good to look at but have a superb flavor. French varieties, grown in a climate that suits them better, are twice the size, and perhaps the most delicious of all the plums to eat for dessert.

Of the other greenish yellow plums, one ought to notice the Pershore egg, grown in huge amounts for jam in western England, and the mirabelle, a small yellow-green gage much grown in Alsace. Mirabelles are sweet and are used both for preserves and for the eau de vie called after it—mirabelle. The other famous plum eau de vie is called quetsch, after the quetsch plum, which is ripe in August and is also excellent for cooking. Quetsch plums, stoned and baked flat on dough, make the well-known *Quetschenkuchen*. A cut made inside the halves of each plum prevents them from curling up in the heat of the oven and is one of the secrets of those neat confections and of tarts containing tidy rows of halved plums.

Prunes. Although any plum can be dried, varieties especially suitable for the purpose have been developed. Of these the prune d'Agen and Fellemberg are two of the best-known. Prunes used to be produced mainly in southern France, where the weather makes it possible to dry fruit out of doors. Some sorts of prune (*pistoles*) are peeled, pitted, and flattened, others are pricked or blanched, and some are dried in ovens. In the old days, French prunes were sent from Agen down the Garonne and shipped from Bordeaux, usually packed in osier baskets. Today prunes are produced on a large scale in California and elsewhere. Modern commercial prunes have sometimes been treated with lye to soften the skins; they are big, black, and beautiful after being glossed by heating in steam or boiling brine and perhaps coated with glycerine. Carlsbad prunes, known also as Carlsbad plums, are large dessert prunes meant to be eaten with dried fruits at the end of a meal. If prunes are soaked, cooked, and puréed, then mixed with cream, they make wonderful ices. Prunes pitted and stuffed, or wrapped in bacon and broiled, can be included in meat dishes; they also figure in some stuffings for turkey and goose, and they go especially well with pork. In Germany, plums go with potato, beans, and smoked sausage (*mettwurst*) into a stew or *Eintopf*. The Chinese make hot sauces containing plums as well as chili and garlic.

[*Plum*—French: *prune;* German: *Pflaume;* Italian: *susina, prugna;* Spanish: *ciruela*]

POACHING comes from the same source as the French word for pocket and was originally applied only to eggs. If they are put into almost boiling water, they soon become surrounded by a coating of coagulated white and so are in a pocket. But the word now covers cooking almost anything gently in hot, but by no means boiling, liquid. The word "simmer," at least by its sound, denotes some slight movement of the liquid and a slightly higher temperature.

POI. *See* yam (dasheen).

POISONING. We are talking here about accidents rather than felonies. Food poisoning is usually understood to mean food contaminated by harmful organisms (or the poisons they generate) rather than poisoning from eating poisonous animals, plants or poisoning from chemical poisons which somehow have got into the food. Even poi-sonings from the long-term effects of additives and colorings are excluded, as are personal allergies. However, from the point of view of the sufferer (and the poisoner), the definition may be academic.

At one time food poisoning was thought to be due to ptomaines (from *ptoma,* the Greek for a corpse), protein breakdown substances with delightfully evocative names like putrecine and cadaverine formed in decomposing food. The ptomaine theory of food poisoning has long since been abandoned, and so the word becomes meaningless, but in popular parlance ptomaine poisoning persists. It usually describes poisoning caused by Staphylococcus, the least serious of the three main categories of food poisoning, which are dealt with below in descending order of nastiness.

Botulism. A type of food poisoning (fortunately rare), from which more people die than recover—the mortality is 65%. It is caused by a deadly poison (of the "test tube in a reservoir will kill a whole city" category), made by a soil organism, *Clostridium botulinum.* This is entirely anaerobic and will not grow when any oxygen is present, so it finds ideal conditions in canned foods. Beans, spinach, sweet corn, meat, fish, milk, and cheese have all been culprits, and canned salmon was involved in a recent, well-publicized case. Occasionally the organism can find a place to grow even in the depths of hams, sausages, and salted, dried, or smoked fish. The problem is that *C. botulinum* is a spore-forming organism and, except in acid conditions, its spores are almost impossible to kill by boiling. They can withstand several hours at 212°F (100°C). Only when the temperature is pushed up higher in a pressure cooker or an autoclave (as it is commercially) can we make canned or bottled vegetables, meat, or fish really safe. Although the spores of the botulism organism can stand so much heat, the poison it produces can be made harmless even by boiling for as little as a minute. This means, of course, that you cannot get botulism from thoroughly cooked, hot food. Botulism poisoning has features in common with another killer, the mushroom *Amanita phalloides,* in that there are no immediate symptoms after eating, and no warning before the poison has been thoroughly ingested into the system. With botulism, there are rarely signs for at least hours, and often a day or more goes by before there are even stomach upsets. The real damage, however, is done to the nervous system, and early symptoms are double vision, difficulty in swallowing and speaking, giddiness, and labored breathing, finally leading to respiratory paralysis and death. As with *A. phalloides,* the merest taste can be fatal.

Cans of food—it is cans of vegetables, especially home-canned ones, that are mostly likely to cause trouble—may sometimes have an off-smell and taste, but bent, broken, or bulging cans should always be discarded without tasting. Home bottlers and canners of anything other than acid fruits should follow instructions scrupulously. Botulism organisms will not develop in conditions of high acidity or where there are plenty of spices and salt. They also dislike saltpeter and nitrites.

Salmonella. There are some 200 organisms in this genus of bacteria, and some cause the typhoidlike illness paratyphoid (though not typhoid itself), while others bring about severe or mild gastroenteritis. They get into the system through contaminated food and water and can be carried by pets, including birds and fish. There is no unusual smell or taste by which contaminated food can be recognized. Symptoms begin possibly the same day (within 7 hours), but that is a minimum and they may not start for up to 3 days. They are stomach pains, diarrhea, thirst, and perhaps vomiting (which you might expect from any digestive upset), but also high temperature, chills, and headaches. This is an infection and can be cured with antibiotics. The bacteria in the contaminated food and drink can be destroyed by boiling.

Staphylococcus belong to a genus of organisms including those that cause boils, pimples, and suppurating cuts and abrasions. The genus also contains organisms that commonly cause food poisoning. These can stand concentrations of sugar and salt that would kill other microorganisms (like those of typhoid, for instance). They find suitable nutrients in sausages and meat pies, milk, cheese, cream cakes, and sandwiches. Unlike *Salmonella* poisoning (but like botulism), staphylococcus poisoning is due to the accumulation of toxins which the organisms have made (although the upsets may, to the layman at least, be rather similar) and there is neither infection nor fever. In staphylococcus toxin poisoning, the symptoms come on almost immediately after the food has been eaten—in an hour or so—depending on susceptibility, circumstances, and how much poison was taken. Antibiotics will not fix this illness (since there is no infection), but recovery is usual after a few days on a light diet. The symptoms can be severe while they last. Food containing *staphylococcus* toxins cannot be detected by taste or smell. The toxins cannot be destroyed by ordinary cooking; they can stand up to 30 minutes' boiling without being made harmless. However, *staphylococcus* poisoning is usually the result of carelessness. If foods which might be contaminated and might provide favorable conditions for the organisms are kept in the refrigerator, there are unlikely to be any problems. But if the foods are kept lying about in the kitchen (which, even in winter, will be of a sufficiently high temperature), then poisoning is always possible. And it happens quickly. On hot summer days, with temperatures around 86°F (30°C), sufficient toxin can develop in food in as little as 5 hours—between lunch and dinner—to cause illness.

Chemical contamination. One source of chemical contamination which is easily avoided is the action of the food on the surface of the container. This can be obviated by never leaving acid foods or drinks in lead-glazed earthenware containers, or metal ones.

Poisonous chemicals are likely to get into food only as a result of carelessness. Medicines, weed-killers, and sprays for the garden, ant and cockroach powder, and other toxic substances should be kept out of the kitchen and, where there are children about, locked up. Cleaning solutions—which may include strong bleach, ammonia, caustic soda, and hydrochloric acid—should be treated with respect and rinsed away thoroughly with water after use. Substances such as saltpeter, which can be poisonous if used in quantity instead of common salt, should be clearly labeled. If poisoning occurs, immediately call a doctor or poison center.

Corrosive poisons, such as acids or caustic soda, which burn the mouth and lips demand special treatment. If the poison is acid, give bicarbonate of soda mixed with water. If it is carbolic acid, give 1–2 tablespoons of Epsom salts in water. If the poison is an alkali, give vinegar and water, or lemon or even orange juice diluted with water. If the caustic poison is unknown, give large quantities of water or some milk. *With corrosive poisoning of any kind, never try to make the patient vomit.*

However, irritant poisons, which do not cause burning of the tissues, can be treated with an emetic and plenty of water to drink. Poisoning by alkaloids and narcotics (which affect the nervous system) should also be treated by making the patient vomit, unless he is unconscious. Strong black coffee combats drowsiness.

Good emetics are 2 tablespoons of salt in a glass of warm water, or a tablespoon of dry mustard in a glass of warm water. Best of all, since it does not irritate, let the patient drink large quantities of tepid water, and then press down at the far back of his tongue (or tickle his throat) until you find the place that makes him gag. Continuing to press or tickle will make him regurgitate. The patient should then take more water and repeat the process until his stomach is washed out.

Poisonous animals. Some fish are poisonous occasionally just in certain seasons, and it is better to follow local advice unless you are absolutely certain the locals are wrong. Also remember that it is possible for a fish to be edible in one place and harmful in another because of its food. Sometimes fish are claimed to be good when small but harmful when large. Some barracudas come into this class. In fact, in Malaysia they say that barracudas become poisonous at certain times of the year because they eat poisonous sea snakes (a rather unlikely explanation) and it is commonly agreed in the Caribbean that the large barracudas there (around 3 ft/1 m and over) have poisonous flesh which, when eaten, causes pain in the joints, trembling, and vomiting. Perhaps the most famous poisonous fish is the pufferfish, which is eaten under the name of *fugu* in Japan, but only after preparation by experts officially licensed in the art. The blood and liver of this fish is very poisonous indeed, and even eating the prepared flesh causes numb mouth and lips. Another dangerously poisonous fish is the oil fish (*Ruvettus pretiosus*), which also causes numbness of the tongue, hands, and feet as well as pains in the chest and stomach. Unfortunately, there are no rule-of-thumb methods of telling the good from the poisonous fish; indeed some excellent fish, such as the garfishes with their green bones, look as if they might be poisonous when they are not. However, the U.S. Air Force's survival instructions advise against eating the fish of shallow waters and reefs if the fish are round or boxlike and have hard skins and bony plates or spines, small parrotlike mouths, small gill openings, or belly fins small or absent. These are the pufferfish, file fish, globe fish, trigger fish, and trunk fish of tropical seas. In particular, never eat the livers or roes of any tropical fish without knowing that they are safe. Some northern fish have livers overloaded with vitamin A which, like the polar bear liver, can also be poisonous. Cooking does not destroy the poison of such fish. (It is worth mentioning that many fish have poisonous spines—some lethal, like the stonefish, which has 13 unlucky spines causing agony and death.)

In general, fresh mollusks and crustaceans, whether from land (like snails) or water, are not poisonous. However, bivalves, which feed by sieving small organisms and other food particles out of the water, are easily contaminated, possibly by pathogenic bacteria (including those causing typhoid, paratyphoid and *Salmonella* poisoning in general, cholera, and hepatitis) from untreated sewage that has been spewed into the sea or rivers. Snails may have eaten poisonous plants (which is why they are starved or fed on lettuce for several days before being cooked). Once they are dead, mollusks and crustaceans provide excellent conditions in which bacteria can multiply, especially when the whole organism, including the intestines, is involved. Shellfish should therefore always be fresh, and damaged or dead specimens thrown away; it is best to buy live crabs and scallops in preference to one the fishmonger may have had on ice for several days. In certain areas of the eastern Pacific, for instance around the coasts of California, there are occasional plagues of a highly lethal form of plankton, the dinoflagellate *Goniaulax catenella*, which causes red tides. In hugh numbers, this tiny animal with its red dot makes the sea look red. It secretes a virulent poison that attacks the central nervous system and causes death to anyone eating contaminated shellfish. Anyone gathering shellfish on tropical rocks or reefs should handle cone shells with great care: some of them can shoot out a poisonous, even lethal, dart from the narrow end.

Poisonous plants. Contrary to popular belief, most fungi are not poisonous. However, one or two are often fatal, even if taken in the least amount (*see* mushrooms). The *molds, which are also fungi, are usually not harmful in the quantity that is likely to be eaten, but the black fungus, ergot, that attacks cereal heads and especially rye, is very poisonous. It is not at all common in these days.

There are a number of plants which cooks should be alert to, especially when children are around. Rhubarb leaves, which contain large amounts of oxalic acid, should never be eaten either raw or cooked. Many berries, including those of the asparagus and mistletoe, are toxic, and no wild berries, however attractive, should be eaten without positive identification. The bulbs of a number of spring-flowering plants—crocus, daffodils, hyacinths—can cause severe illness if ingested.

Sometimes people have been poisoned by oleander, which is highly poisonous when the wood is used to make meat skewers. Anything smelling strongly of bitter *almonds should be avoided, since this often indicates the presence of cyanide (prussic acid). Cherry and peach leaves, twigs, and seeds contain a compound that releases cyanide when eaten. Everyone knows that you should avoid belladonna or deadly nightshade (*Atropa belladonna*), whose black berries look tempting but are toxic. For something really poisonous, we have to go to the legendary ordeal tree of Madagascar (*Taughinia venenifera*), a seed of which, no larger than an almond, will reputedly kill 20 people.

Allergies. It is possible to have an allergy, either inherited or developed, to certain foods, and to react to them as if they were poison. An example of an inherited allergy is favism, sufferers from which get headaches, vertigo, vomiting, fever, and enlargement of the spleen and liver as a result of eating broad beans. This allergy is common in people who have Levantine blood, with ancestors who came from Greece or Armenia. It is relatively common in Sardinia, Sicily, and Southern Italy, as well as in certain ethnic groups in North America. Some sufferers from favism will be made ill by just the pollen of the broad bean plant. Many people, perhaps more than suspect it, are adversely affected by wheat *gluten, others by cheese, and so on. An example of a developed allergy: some of those who have been made ill by shellfish seem to have to give them up permanently. I remember being told many years ago by a Spanish fisherman that if I ate the flying fish I had caught I would become allergic to shellfish at least for several years. I did not risk putting this piece of local folklore to the test. Allergies to components of the diet are only beginning to be understood; they are an aspect of eating that should not be forgotten.

It is a wise precaution to keep the number of the closest Poison Control Center near the telephone. The staff at these centers are most helpful in identifying poisonous plants and other substances and giving rapid advice on treating poisoning. On request, they will send literature on poisoning and warning labels to put on containers of substances that could be harmful to children. The Food and Drug Administration publishes considerable information about food safety which you can receive by writing to them at HFG-20, 5600 Fishers Lane, Rockville, Maryland 20852.

POITRINE FUMÉE. French for *bacon.

POKE or **pokeweed** (*Phytolacca americana*). The common American folknames of this plant are derived from the languages of native American peoples, who used it as a

POKE

medicinal plant, potherb, and dye source. Although pokeweed contains toxic substances in its roots, mature leaves, stems, and berries, the young shoots are edible and much relished by country people. In the spring, pokeweed is sold in markets in the South (where it is called poke salad) and by the Pennsylvania Dutch.

Poke is a treelike perennial shrub with stout hollow stems. The leaves are light green and shaped like a lance head. The dainty flowers, growing in long clusters, are followed by purple-black berries. In spring fat young sprouts shoot up from the large root. These should be gathered while they are still small and boiled for 10 minutes. The water should be poured off and fresh water added; the poke is then cooked at least 5 minutes more, drained, and served with butter or a cream sauce. Its flavor resembles that of asparagus. In some areas poke is peeled, rolled in corn meal, and fried. Poke sprouts are also excellent pickled.

Once a widely used folk remedy, pokeweed is currently being studied by scientists as a possible treatment for a number of diseases. Meanwhile, like many other wild greens, it is both delicious and very nutritious, high in vitamins A and C.

POLE BEAN. *See* green bean.

POLENTA. *See* corn.

POLLACK or **pollock.** *See* cod.

POLONY may come from *Polonia,* the medieval Latin for Poland, or from Bologna. Either way, it now means a sausage of partly cooked, finely ground pork which has been colored with dye. It may contain a proportion of beef and is likely to have been hot-smoked. Polonies can be fried or grilled.

POLYSACCHARIDES. *See* sugar.

POLYUNSATURATES. *See* fats.

POMEGRANATE (*Punica granatum*) is neglected in most of Europe. The fruit is a large, thick-skinned berry with a mass of seeds, each surrounded by juicy jewellike pulp; the whole fruit is divided internally by tough membranes into irregular compartments. A good pomegranate is large, very juicy, and has a good balance of sugar and acids. The color of the inside varies from colorless to dark purple-red, which looks

POMEGRANATE

prettier but does not necessarily have a better taste. Poor pomegranates range through sour, astringent types with a high proportion of membranes, to those that are completely inedible.

Pomegranates originated in southern or western Asia. They were spread by the Phoenicians, and the Romans got theirs from Carthage—hence the name *Punica.* Pomegranates require a very hot, dry summer to reach perfection—they resist drought, but need irrigation—and they will stand considerable frost in winter, so they are a typical fruit of Middle Eastern gardens. They are grown in California and in all Mediterranean countries; Puglia in Italy, Spain, and Cyprus export the fruit.

The tree is small—evergreen or deciduous according to climate—and is covered with sharp spines. The fruits are painful to pick. The typical flower is vivid vermilion, but there are white-flowered kinds (usually with poor fruit) and even double-flowered varieties which are purely for decoration. The wild pomegranate or *daru,* which grows profusely in parts of the lower Himalayas, is not edible, but the seeds are dried and become an important condiment, the *anar dana* of Indian cooking. Dried pomegranate seeds of sour varieties are sprinkled on meat dishes in Middle Eastern cooking.

Good eating varieties have a superb flavor and make a fine dessert fruit if time is taken to remove the masses of glassy red or pink seeds and to separate them from the yellowish membranes. The whole mass, ice cold and rather like a pile of red crystals, looks wonderful served in a silver dish. Although seedless pomegranates are grown in some places, these are not preferred by pomegranate fanciers, who like to crunch and swallow the pleasant-textured seeds. The juicy flesh surrounding the seeds is aromatic and refreshing, and skilled diners can suck it off and discard the seeds if they prefer. The juice of pomegranates is used in meat and chicken dishes in Persian cooking, for instance in the magnificent dish called *fesenjan* or *faisinjan,* which is duck or chicken with walnuts and pomegranate juice. The juice is the basis of the sweet syrup grenadine or grenatine, which is used in drinks. A drink made of freshly squeezed pomegranate juice, chilled and mixed with gin, is fantastic for anyone looking for something bracing and new, but the problem with squeezing the juice from pomegranates is that too much tannin exudes from the membranes and makes the juice astringent. To remove some tannin, a little dissolved gelatin can be stirred in. The gelatin reacts with the tannin to form an insoluble compound—a cloud which can be settled, filtered, or removed by fining. If the fruit is allowed to shrivel before being crushed, the tannin is less.

The pomegranate season is from the end of summer, reaching a peak in October and going on to Christmas. Pomegranates are sometimes associated with Halloween. In a plastic bag in the refrigerator, pomegranates will keep for several weeks.

[*Pomegranate*—French: *grenade;* German: *Granatapfel;* Italian: *melagrana;* Spanish: *granada*]

POMELO. *See* shaddock.

POPCORN. *See* corn.

POPPY SEED used in cooking comes from the opium poppy (*Papaver somniferum*), which is probably a native of Central Europe. Used as a drug in classical times, poppy seeds were already being cultivated in India and China by A.D. 800. The drug is obtained from the latex which oozes out if the green seed pod is slashed, but when the seeds are ripe all traces of the opium alkaloids, such as morphine and codeine, are gone, and poppy seeds become a good food—an edible oil can be expressed from them.

Poppy seed varies enormously from the

POPPY

relatively large, gray-blue type commonly seen sprinkled on German and Jewish breads and cakes to the much smaller pale-cream seed used in India to thicken curries. Botanists insist that the two come from the same species. The taste of baked poppy seed is pleasantly nutty, a little like sesame seed, and perhaps rather nicer. It is a frequent constituent in curry powders and in the masala to be ground for curries, but unless it is roasted it has little flavor. Indians never use flour to thicken curries, and poppy seed makes a nice sauce, but in many recipes the quantities used are insignificant and the poppy seed may have been included only from tradition or perhaps for medicinal reasons.

PORK, from the French, refers to the meat, and pig, from Middle English, refers to the animal. Swine comes from the Old English *swin* (Latin *suinus*). Hog (a usual word for a pig in the U.S.) in Britain usually implies a castrated male reared for slaughter. A boar is an uncastrated male pig; a sow, a female; a gilt (from the old Norse), a young sow.

Perhaps no other animal has been as important as the pig to man's survival in Europe as well as in China and Southeast Asia. The highly evolved and custom-built pigs of today are the result of crossing the European

pig, which was a ridge-backed animal, not far removed from the wild pig (*Sus scrofa*), and the plumper Chinese pig. This cross is attributed to Robert Bakewell, who bred stock in the English Midlands in the middle of the 18th century. Today, very intensive upgrading and inbreeding helped by artificial insemination (which has come in generally since World War II) has produced pigs tailor-made for the bacon industry, with long bodies and a small amount of fat, and the old fat pigs (going under such delightful names as Birmingham Cutter) are either hard or impossible to get, even if you should want them. Pigs are a lot leaner than they used to be, and European butchers tend to trim off most of the fat to make the meat leaner still.

The flavor of pork and the hardness of the fat depend on the food with which the animal has been fed, so that pork for special purposes may come from animals that have been fed, for example, on peaches or acorns. Pigs are fastidious and have a very lively gastronomic sense, in spite of their greed. Following the tastes of man, they will readily eat truffles (and would no doubt get stoned on a good château bottled wine if their masters could spare it). Pigs are clean by nature, and the mud on wild pig is more correctly regarded as a mud pack for beauty treatment than a sign of slovenliness. In peasant societies, pigs are kept in atrocious conditions, but that is not the fault of the pigs. Neither are they to blame for the long and close association with man, which has meant that they share with humans a number of unpleasant parasites and diseases. Both Jews and Muslims regard pigs as unclean from a religious point of view, and it is said that this shows a practical approach to hygiene. But why? It was only necessary to cook the meat thoroughly to be safe. However, religious food laws have meant that a large area of the world, stretching from Turkey to Pakistan and southward over northern Africa, has been denied the pig's many advantages. Here man must depend on the goat and sheep, animals which may be more suited to the arid regions that make up much of this part of the world, but do not have the pig's versatility. As for the diseases, which undoubtedly exist, the danger is greatly reduced with animals kept under clean modern conditions, though it is still inadvisable to eat pork which has not been cooked to a high enough temperature throughout or which alternatively has not been salted for long enough to kill harmful parasites.

Most of the important culinary products of the pig have been covered elsewhere in this book, e.g., *ham, *bacon, *sausages, *lard—more food products are derived from the pig than from any other animal. The pig is, for instance, the only mammal whose skin we eat. We tend to take this for granted, or perhaps think we do so because of its relative hairlessness compared with the cow or the sheep. However, pigs in cold countries, such as northern China, may have quite hairy coats; in any case, even the baldest pig has to be scalded and have its bristles scraped off during preparation by the butcher. In peasant economies, the family pig is still killed in the autumn, usually in November, at well under a year old. The occasion is one for both work and feasting. In the Spanish *matanza,* the pig is caught and dragged squealing to a wooden table on which it is held while a knife is plunged into one of its arteries. This, it is claimed, with dubious justification, makes the animal instantly unconscious. It is necessary for the heart to go on beating for a while so that the blood is pumped out. (Modern methods are more humane because the pig is first knocked out with an electric shock to the head.) After the killing, the carcass is scalded and scraped free of bristles, the entrails are removed, and the carcass hung up to cool. The insides are sorted out, but the gall bladder is almost the only part of the pig that is thrown away. The intestines are opened out, washed in a stream, turned inside out, scraped, salted, and soaked to cleanse them for use as sausage skins.

It is a day's work for most families to turn a pig into the hams, bacon, and sausages that will subsequently be cured, dried, and smoked to provide food over the winter. The variety of products made from the pig is a wonderful tribute to a man's invention, since virtually nothing is wasted. Cooks who have not experimented are recommended to try trotters, head, ears, and all the other parts that are neglected in countries where people can afford to live on pork chops.

In most European countries, the skin is usually cut off the joints and used separately. It is very gelatinous and a most useful addition to the consistency of an assortment of dishes. In Britain, Denmark, and other northern countries, the skin is usually scored and crackled when pork is roasted. For good crackling the skin should never be basted with fat, which turns it to leather, but may be brushed or basted with water, which produces bubbly-looking crackling. If skin is roasted without scoring, it is inclined to turn into a hard sheet (where I live in Spain, suckling pigs are not properly scored for roasting), and scoring needs to be done neatly and carefully. It is something that butchers rarely have time to do properly, and you should do it yourself. As with other meats, the way pork is cut up is subject to great local variation. In some countries a leg of pork is very difficult to obtain, since legs all go for ham. On the other hand, the fillet, which does not cure well and is removed from bacon sides, may sometimes be relatively cheap. Spareribs, much in demand in America and China, may be inexpensive if there is not a demand for them. Pig's liver is always cheap, often ridiculously so; though inferior for cooking in its own right, it is the best liver for *pâté maison.*

Salt pork. A light brining often improves pork. The heavily salted pork used on ships in the past and known to sailors as salt junk was nothing like the salt meat we are used to, which is pinkish and served with fresh vegetables. It is said to have had something of the appearance and hardness of old mahogany, and was so salty that it could blister the tongue. Of course, at sea in sailing ships, with limited fresh water, it was not even soaked properly before being used. This unappetizing stuff was commonly believed to be the cause of scurvy and so any fresh meat or fish, even of unpalatable sorts, was eaten by sailors, but in vain, since it was fresh fruit and vegetables, even sprouted beans and grains, that contained the vitamin C that they needed. Nowadays there are better things to eat during the winter or on long sea voyages. When we complain about the additives introduced by the food technologists, as indeed we should, we ought also to remember salt junk as an example of the crude expedients once used in preserving food.

[Pork—French: porc; German: Schweinefleisch; Italian: carne di maiale; Spanish; carne de cerdo]

PORT. Portuguese *oyster.

PORT WINE technically comes from a particular region in the valley of the Douro River in northern Portugal. The hillsides where the vines grow are very steep, and holes for vines often have to be blasted in the rock.

The port that was originally shipped to Britain was just a full-bodied red wine, often fortified with brandy to make it travel better. From about 1830, however, brandy began to be added before fermentation was complete. At an alcohol concentration of 20%, the yeasts die, and further fermentation cannot take place. It is the remaining unfermented grape sugar that makes port sweet.

Until fairly recently, port was made by old methods in very picturesque surroundings, and the grape crushing was done by foot. There are now destalking machines and cleverly devised methods that remove much of the hand work without altering the quality of the wine. Crushed pips and stalks would ruin the taste, since port, unlike sherry, is fermented with the skins. When the

moment is judged right, the fermenting juice is run off straight into huge casks which already contain brandy. Fermentation then stops.

The proportion is about 40 pt (22 lt) of brandy to 176 pt (100 lt) of half-fermented must. This brings the alcohol strength to about 20%. Some 2 months later, the new wine is run off the lees and shipped down to Oporto. There, in the shippers' lodges (which are like cellars except that they are not underground), the various wines are blended in the shippers' various styles.

Ruby port, a youngish wine which has not lost its color, is blended sometimes with a tawny. Tawny is older and has mellowed and become orange-red. White port is made from white grapes. Vintage port is made only in years when the shippers consider the vintage to be exceptional, and it gets special treatment. After the best blend has been determined, the chosen wines are mixed in huge wooden vats and left there for 2 years before they are shipped to the wine merchants. There the port is rested for a couple of months and then bottled. (In my grandmother's house, a pipe—56 dozen bottles—was bought and bottled for each son and put in bins in the cellars.) Bottles are ideally black, but usually they are just dark. Very good, long corks must be used to make a tight seal against the air while the port matures. After the bottles have been filled and corked, they are stood for several days before the corks are sealed by dipping the neck of each bottle in a mixture of paraffin wax and tallow. They are then laid on their sides in bins, where they should remain undisturbed for at least 15 years. Certainly vintage port must never be moved before it has lain for 7 years or before the deposited crust has hardened. As the bottles are put down, they are marked with a streak of whitewash to indicate the upper side. Vintage port should not be drunk before it is 15 and preferably 20 years old. It usually goes on improving for up to 40 years, but after that may deteriorate.

Old port must be decanted with great

care. The whitewash mark must be kept uppermost and the bottle kept steady when the cork is removed. With exceedingly old vintages—40-50 years old—the cork may have started to crumble; the neck of the bottle then has to be removed. Before tackling this tricky job, stand the bottle upright for a day or so. Then heat the claws of a bottle tong until they are red and clamp them around the bottle neck beneath the flange. Hold them there until the redness has disappeared, then remove them. Place a cold wet cloth against the neck which, because of the contrast in temperature, will break off.

At table it is traditional to pass the port decanter to the left, but this is only a matter of convenience. It is an old custom, and practical because each person fills his glass and then places the decanter next to his neighbor's glass on the latter's right.

Port is not very popular in the hotter countries. It is a drink for the winter or for damp days, which is why it is still popular in Britain, though it is drunk to some extent in other countries of the Commonwealth, particularly Canada, as well as in Scandinavia and Switzerland. Perhaps surprisingly, France is the largest importer of port, which is drunk there as an apéritif. In cooking, its use is virtually limited to English dishes—jugged hare, Cumberland sauce, and a few sweet dishes. Port-type wines are made in South Africa, Australia, California, and elsewhere, with varying success, but as yet without great distinction.

[*Port*—French: *porto;* German: *Portowein;* Italian: *vino di Oporto;* Spanish: *vino de Oporto*]

PORTULACA. *See* purslane.

POSSUM. *See* opossum.

POTASSIUM PERMANGANATE. *See* disinfectants.

POTATO. There is hardly anywhere except the lowland tropics and the polar ice regions (excluding part of Greenland) where potatoes are not grown. They are the world's best-known vegetable.

The potato (*Solanum tuberosum*) belongs to the nightshade family and is a native of the Andes, particularly of the region around Lake Titicaca. It was an important staple for the Incas. First mentioned in Pedro de Leon's *Chronica del Peru* in 1553, potatoes were brought back to Spain by the conquistadors without arousing much interest there. Since potato, from the native word *batata,* originally referred to the *sweet potato (a hot-country plant of quite a different family), early references were confused. Even today, in Spanish, *patatas* are potatoes and *batatas* are sweet potatoes.

Tubers brought to Britain by Sir John Hawkins in 1563 were probably sweet potatoes, which do not thrive in the British climate. It is possible that the forerunner of today's potato was brought back from Chile by Thomas Heriot, a botanist, when he returned on one of Sir Francis Drake's ships in 1586. Either they were given to Sir Walter Raleigh or he brought them back himself. What is certain is that he got tubers from somewhere and had them planted on his Irish estate at Youghal, County Cork. They were not a very choice kind, long and knobbly, with deep eyes (these were not bred out until the late 18th century). However, by 1633, when the first illustration appears of a potato in the second edition of Gerard's *Herbal,* we find it listed there as the "potato of Virginia." "The Indians do call this plant pappus, meaning roots: by which name also the common potato [did Gerard mean sweet potato?] are called in most Indian countries. The temperature and virtues be referred unto the common potatoes, being likewise food, as also a meat for pleasure, equal in goodness and wholesomeness unto the same, being either roasted in embers or boiled and eaten with oil, vinegar and pepper, or dressed any other way by the hand of some cunning in cookery."

But parsons and politicians showed less enthusiasm. "*Bauhine* saith that he heard that the use of these roots was forbidden in Burgundy (where they call them Indian artichokes) for that they were persuaded the too frequent use of them caused the leprosy." Gaspar Baulion had encouraged farmers near Lyons to start growing potatoes in 1593, but they were stopped by the authorities in Besançon because of that superstition. Scottish preachers considered potatoes unfit food because they were not mentioned in the Bible.

Potatoes were accepted gradually in Ireland, and by 1739 they were being extensively grown in Scotland and were becoming known in Holland, Germany, and Italy. In France, the potato was popularized in the eighteenth century by the enthusiasm of Antoine-Auguste Parmentier, with the help of Louis XVI, who even used a potato flower as a buttonhole on one occasion. Hence, in culinary French, *parmentier* signifies that a dish contains potato.

Potatoes returned to America in 1719, with Irish immigrants to New England: in Ireland, the population had begun to depend on them. Potatoes were a crop that gave a heavy yield and suited the climate of Ireland. But first a leaf-curl virus spoiled the breeders' efforts; then, in 1845, came the potato blight after a warm, damp summer. Blight is caused by a fungus; potatoes go black and turn to a mass of rotten slime. The result of the potato blight was famine, with far-reaching political and human consequences. Today, with seed potatoes grown in cold, blight-free areas, such as Scotland, blight is less of a problem. Scientific breeding has produced disease-resistant varieties, but the dangers which would go with dependence on one crop are still sometimes demonstrated.

Potatoes have excellent nutritive value when fresh, being rich in vitamin C and potassium (0.6%) when these are not allowed to leach out into cooking water. Frying, steaming, and pressure cooking are good from this point of view, but when potatoes are peeled, left to soak in cold water, and boiled, most of the soluble nutrients are re-

moved. Although potatoes contain 18% carbohydrate, mainly as starch, they also have 2% of good protein, and since the rest is almost all water, they are not very high in calories—unless, of course, they are fried or eaten with tons of butter, but that is hardly the fault of the potato.

It is often said that the best part of the potato is in the skin. If you hold a thin slice of potato up to the light, you will see that just inside the skin there are several denser layers, and that the middle part of the potato is more transparent. This middle part contains less starch and nutrients and more water than the outer layers. Since peeling removes a good part of the outer layers, peeling is a wasteful practice. Cooking potatoes in their skins gives them a special taste which is not universally liked. It also restricts the use of potatoes as a "neutral" vegetable. If potatoes are young and freshly dug (depending to some extent on variety), the skins can be scraped off easily or rubbed off with a coarse pan cleaner. The skins are not loosened by dunking them in boiling water. While some potatoes can be scraped after being in boiling water for 2 minutes, there is no certainty that one variety will behave like another. It is important at least to use a peeler that removes only the finest sliver of skin, and to cook potatoes immediately after they have been peeled.

Only a few of the many potato varieties are grown commercially. Recognizing even these few is difficult; most cooks do little more than distinguish between the white and the red ones. It is fundamental to the cook to determine whether a potato is waxy or floury. Floury ones have more starch in their surface layers; this swells when they are heated and bursts the skin. Waxy potatoes are best for potato salad but make a gummy mess when mashed. Other differences are less fundamental. For instance, some potatoes have white flesh (which is preferred in the U.S.) and others have the yellower flesh opted for in parts of Europe. Sizes and shapes also vary greatly.

Varieties are chosen by farmers to be disease-free and give heavy crops in the potato-growing localities. Some may be grown because they are good keepers, and market preferences are also considered. What is valued in one place is not in another, and although reds tend to be more in demand and therefore more expensive in Britain, this is not the case elsewhere.

It is rare for potato varieties to be chosen and grown for their outstanding flavor, but early varieties are grown for use as "new potatoes." Main-crop potatoes lifted too soon and sold as new potatoes are inclined to be soapy and to blacken after they are cooked. New potatoes of quality come only from earlies grown for the purpose.

Potatoes are usually bought in larger quantities than other vegetables, and it is worth knowing a little about storage and the blemishes from which they are likely to suffer. Potatoes with rotten patches, holes, or cuts made during lifting should clearly be rejected. Scabs, caused by limy soil, are not of great consequence. Dark patches may indicate blight, but may result from the improper use of chemical fertilizers, a condition whose causes are not yet fully understood. Green potatoes have been exposed to the light; they taste bitter and contain mildly poisonous alkaloids called solanines, which can cause an upset stomach. Withered potatoes are old and have lost their vitamins. Potatoes that have been allowed to get too cold taste sweet (which is why potatoes should never be stored in the refrigerator). Sometimes but by no means always, the sweetness retreats if the potatoes are kept for a week in a very warm kitchen.

Potatoes that are very irregular in shape or have big eyes are wasteful. Good-sized, regular, and smooth-skinned potatoes are easier to peel. (Buying cheap potatoes may not be economical.) The washed potatoes, which are sold in bags in many supermarkets, go green quickly and will not keep well because the skins have been damaged by the high-pressure hoses used to clean them. When potatoes are mature and have been lifted at the right moment, they keep well in cool, dry, dark conditions. Eventually, they will start to sprout though, and antisprouting agents are often used to inhibit sprouting. In sprouted potatoes, the starch has been partly converted to dextrin and the food value is reduced. In some countries, ready-peeled and sliced potatoes are sold in bags. Because they have to be treated chemically with antioxidants and preservatives to keep them white, they are not allowed everywhere. Hollow potatoes can usually be blamed on a drought followed by a very wet spell.

Potato flour, potato starch, and **instant potatoes.** Potatoes are steamed, dried, and ground, or the starch is extracted by pulverizing and washing, to make various products for use in the kitchen. Potato starch or flour is of special importance to people on a gluten-free diet. It can be used for thickening but tends to have a taste of its own. Also, it is called for in various cakes and crackers in which a tender starch is needed. Instant potatoes or powdered potatoes are typical of the cooked and dried product. Some brands are a poor substitute if you are in a hurry, others are unacceptable, and none resembles the flavor and texture of a newly dug potato.

[*Potato*—French: *pomme de terre;* German: *Kartoffel;* Italian: *patata;* Spanish: *patata*]

POTTING. "By potting is generally meant the operation of preserving edible substances in a state for immediate use in small pots or jars," says *Cassell's New Dictionary of Cookery,* published at the turn of the century. "Potted meats, fish etc., are commonly sold in shops. They are all intended for relishes, and are spread on bread like butter."

The method of preserving perishable foods in pots is far, far older than preservation in sealed, sterile glass jars. As a means of preserving meat, fish, and shellfish, it depends essentially on sealing with fat. The contents of a pot, unlike the contents of a terrine, for instance, offer a small surface to the air in relation to their bulk (unless the pot is very shallow). When things are cooked with plenty of fat and little water, the temperatures are high enough to kill most organisms, and what few might be left are sealed in, unable to spread or infect their surroundings because they are isolated by solidified fat. The hard fatty surface prevents contamination from the air, especially if it is covered with a bladder, as used to be the practice in the past. When refrigeration came along, such methods of preservation became unnecessary, but the tradition of tasty potted meats remained. Potted food—as opposed to food in a pot—implies some degree of preservation combined with readiness for immediate use. In this category come the French *confits* of goose, duck, turkey, rabbit, and pork as well as *rillettes, rillons, rillots,* and *rillauds,* because spreading like butter is not a necessary part of the scenario, although potted products in England were nearly always pounded to a paste. I would also include the Arab *qawwrama, a confit* of fat-tailed sheep preserved in fat and designed to keep all through the winter.

The extent to which potting was done in the past is not realized today. Since the deep freezer makes the long-term conservation of potted foods easy, we might pay them more attention and revive old recipes. In the *Cassell's,* which is typical of its period, there are dozens of recipes for potting, which mention among fish—herring, char, trout, salmon, eel, lamprey, and sprats; among shellfish—lobster, crab, crayfish, shrimps, and prawns; among game—hare, rabbit, pheasant, partridge, larks; among meats—beef, mutton, veal, fowl, ham, tongue, and mixtures such as ham and fowl, veal, and tongue. In general, all were made the same way by cooking the meat or fish, pounding it with salt, cayenne, mace or nutmeg, and butter, baking in a moderate oven, and pouring an extra layer of clarified butter on top.

From a safety point of view, there are objections to some of the old recipes for pounding or repotting the pastes when they are cold, then sealing them without resterilizing by heat. Some of these recipes could have caused botulism. However, there will be no problem if potted meats are eaten within a few days or kept in the freezer.

Potted cheese is in a different category because the cheese was not cooked, merely pounded to a paste with butter and flavorings before being put into pots. It was then covered with a layer of clarified butter to prevent its drying out (though it would have continued to mature like any other cheese). No doubt potting cheese was often regarded as a way of using up the bits and keeping them for a day or so, but there are some distinguished recipes, such as Boulestin's for Roquefort pounded with butter and a dash of Armagnac, which Elizabeth David recommends. As she remarks, "the old recipes are coming back into use as methods of giving flavour, character and improved texture to factory cheeses which have so little personality of their own." Recently, a number of commercially made potted cheeses have also come on the market. In them, cheese is mixed with wine, beer, garlic, and herbs in various ways. Many are nice, but their claim to be potted would rest only on their being sold in pots (and many of them are sold by weight in cut pieces), since they are not sealed with clarified butter or sterilized and are not meant to be kept.

POURGOURI. *See* burghul.

POUTARG. *See* botargo.

PRALINE. A mixture of caramelized sugar and roasted nuts used in confectionery and on ice cream. The simplest way to make it is to put nuts and sugar (in equal quantities or more nuts than sugar) in a copper pan and to stir the mixture over heat until the sugar starts to caramelize, by which time, if the heating is done slowly, the nuts should also be sufficiently roasted. Turn the praline out (correctly, on a marble slab) and let it cool. Grind it in a mill or crush it in a mortar, and store it in an airtight container. Some recipes involve roasting the nuts and caramelizing the sugar separately.

[*Praline*—French: *praline;* German: *gebrannte Mandel;* Italian: *mandorla tosta;* Spanish: *almendra garapiñada*]

PRAWN. *See* shrimp.

PRÉ-SALÉ. *See* mutton.

PRESERVATION. All foods deteriorate when kept beyond their natural life, which may be anything from a few hours to a year or more. Storing food is not a human innovation—various mammals store the food necessary for their survival over the winter, using things which have dried naturally, or nuts, grains, and pulses, which are dormant but alive. Insects also store food—bees were making a good job of refining and sealing up honey long before the appearance of man.

Foods are open to attack by *microorganisms and even by their own enzymes. Storage methods are all designed to minimize spoilage, if not to remove it entirely. Until the middle of the 19th century, the methods in use had all been discovered by chance, and the reason that they worked was not understood. It was not until Pasteur showed the causal role played by microorganisms in fermentation and decomposition that progress could become systematic and rapid. Today, many of the old methods, like *smoking, are now retained only for the flavor they impart to the food, and a revolution has taken place in our eating habits.

Not all methods of preservation actually kill the microorganisms—the low temperatures of *freezing immobilize them, as does the absence of water produced by *drying. Other methods, though, do involve killing all the microorganisms in the food—*sterilization—and preventing other organisms from getting in. The most important method of sterilization is heating, but there are others, mainly involving chemical *preservatives. Microorganisms are also killed by ultraviolet light (even that in sunlight), but much more effective are other rays and radiation, which kill all living tissue. It is even possible to sterilize food in the can by radiation which will go through the metal. However, this treatment, promising though it may be at first sight, appears to cause changes in the food which lead to bad flavor, and work on the irradiation of food is still largely experimental.

Unless the sterilized food can be sealed (or unless preservatives are added), it is open to immediate reinfection. Early methods depended on a capping of fat or clarified butter. *Potting is not suitable for very long-term preserving, since fats eventually turn rancid. So do oils, which are used similarly: *mushrooms, *basil, *sardines, and *anchovies are commonly preserved under olive oil in Mediterranean countries, and mustard oil preserves pickles in India. The main methods of sealing, though, are *bottling and *canning.

The other traditional method of preserving was salting, which involved applying common salt, often mixed with saltpeter, either as a *brine or by *dry salting. It works mainly by osmosis—preventing the organisms from getting water; it is toxic to some organisms but tolerated by others. In sufficient strength, it will stop virtually all organisms as well as inhibiting the action of enzymes. Sugar in sufficient concentration also stops microorganisms from getting water; it is a preservative, for example, in jam.

*Smoking is usually an adjunct to salting and drying. It covers the surface of meat or fish with a layer of chemicals that have antiseptic properties. Today, its importance as a method of preservation is minimal.

A few modern methods are important industrially but not possible in the home—for example, the removal of microorganisms from liquids by filtration which, if done effectively, will make them keep. The shelf life of *flour is much increased by the removal of the germ from the grain—nutritionally a harmful practice. In some cases, the enzymes in the germ are inactivated by heating before it is returned "dead" to the flour.

PRESERVATIVES are substances that are added to foods to make them keep; they destroy or at least discourage microorganisms or slow down natural processes that cause spoilage. Into the last category come anti-sprouting agents, which are sprayed over vegetables, mainly potatoes, to prevent them from sprouting in storage. For their safeness, we can only trust to the vigilance of the governmental agencies which monitor our food.

Although the term "preservatives" conjures up thoughts of sinister *additives produced by the petrochemical industry, the description covers many things that food manufacturers would consider old-fashioned or downright folksy. Herbs and spices contain essential oils which can be antiseptic, often quite strongly so: thymol, which is found in thyme, is used in mouthwashes. Cloves, cinnamon, white mustard, and even pepper have similar properties. The preservative action of spices is important in sausages and pickles, while curries will keep sweet for several days in the hot Indian summer. White mustard seed is particularly effective in chutneys. A clove in stock will help keep it sweet as well as adding background flavor.

The most important traditional preservatives are salt (in *brines and *dry salting), sugar (in *jams), vinegar (in *pickles), and *lactic acid (which is produced in sauerkraut and fermented pickles). Various unpleasant substances, including *disinfectants such as formaldehyde, which were used in the past as preservatives, are now generally forbidden. Some preservatives which are purely industrial in application are outside the scope of this book. For example, carbon dioxide under great pressures stops yeasts from growing and is used to hold fruit juices, such as crude apple juice, in bulk before filtration, sterilization, and bottling.

Most preservatives are acids—in sufficient strength, and given sufficient time to operate, any acid will prevent putrefactive bacteria from growing and will kill disease organisms. The hydrochloric acid in the stomach kills most of the bacteria that we eat. Certain acids, though, have antiseptic properties over and above those that result from their acidity. They thus come into the category of chemical preservatives.

Apart from germ killing, the other important preservative function is preventing oxidation. The effect that oxygen can have on food is demonstrated by the way that cut surfaces of apples or potatoes turn brown when exposed to the air. Oxygen is a prime destroyer, which attacks many foods, helped by enzymes and the ultraviolet rays in sunlight. Oxidation destroys such vitamins as vitamin E very quickly and turns fats rancid. In the kitchen, discoloration of vegetables and fruit is prevented by using lemon juice. Commercial antioxidants include sulfurous acid and its derivatives.

*Acetic acid is the acid of vinegar, for which it is used as a substitute in some cheap pickles.

Benzoic acid and sodium benzoate. Benzoic acid was discovered in gum benzoin in 1608 and prepared from urine toward the end of the 18th century. It can be bought from pharmacists in the form of white, shiny needles. More commonly used as a preservative is the sodium salt, a crystalline powder with a sweetish, astringent taste. Sodium benzoate is slightly alkaline (pH 8), but must be used in slightly acid conditions if it is to be effective as a preservative (in an alkaline medium, such as milk, it has almost no preservative effect). In the countries—including the U.K. and U.S.—where sodium benzoate is allowed, 1 part per 1000 is considered safe. It is used particularly in fruit juices and tomato sauces (which are acid) to prevent spoilage after opening. Cranberries, which have remarkable keeping qualities, contain natural benzoic acid.

Boric acid, a mild antiseptic, used to be a standard item in medicine cupboards. It was once a common preservative for margarine, butter, cream, caviar, ham, etc. Most foods are preserved by 0.5% of boric acid, but it is now banned for commercial products in the U.K. and U.S., although many other countries allow it. There is probably no harm in its occasional home use, provided the dosage is properly measured, but few recipes specify it.

*Citric acid is an antioxidant and a weak preservative. However, bottled lemon juice has to be treated with sulfur dioxide, which has the same properties much more strongly.

*Lactic acid is unusual in being a preservative that is normally formed in foods by fermentation rather than added to them.

*Salicylic acid and its sodium salt, sodium salicylate, have been used as a commercial food preservative in some countries but are forbidden in others. Salicylic acid is chemically related to aspirin—acetylsalicylic acid—and is medically used in rheumatic liniments and for treating corns (it loosens, swells, and softens the surface cells of the skin). It is poisonous if used too freely over a long period, and some people are allergic to it, as others are to aspirin. However, recipes from Italy use salicylic acid as a preservative in homemade tomato concentrates at the rate of 1 gram per 2¼ lb (1 Kg) and no more. At this rate, and for home use, when you know how much you are using in the preserved food, it must be relatively harmless, but like any chemical it is not something to throw in by the handful. The advantage of such chemical preservatives over complete sterilization by heat is that they do not alter the flavor.

Sorbic acid is used to stop the growth of molds on cheese and bread.

Sulfur dioxide (SO$_2$), sulfurous acid (H$_2$SO$_3$), and sulfites. Sulfurous acid is not known in a pure state, but, at least in theory, is formed when sulfur dioxide (for instance, from burning sulfur) is dissolved in water. Sulfurous acid and sulfites are toxic to all microorganisms, but especially so to wild yeasts. Metabisulfites are the most convenient source of sulfur dioxide on a domestic scale. In this form, they are invaluable to home makers of wine, beer, and cider. Sulfur dioxide is also used in fruit juices and in the drying of fruit. There are limits in most countries on the concentration of sulfur dioxide and its derivatives permitted in foods. Sulfurous acid is also an antioxidant and a bleach.

[Preservative—French: préservatif; German: Schutzmittel; Italian: preservativo; Spanish: preservativo]

PRESERVED FRUIT. See candied fruit.

PRESERVES. See jam.

PRESSURE sometimes has to be applied with a weight—for example, to cheese, gravlax, tongue, and terrine—or even with a special press, as used with duck to squeeze out the juices. Most serious cooks have their own favorite weights: old kitchen weights, stones, bricks wrapped in plastic bags, and so on. The use of weights bears thinking about, since the right pressure for any job has some importance. Pressure of this type is used to squeeze out juices, to firm, to remove air pockets, to shape, or to make food stay in contact with the heat, as in frying a chicken (for recipes such as pollo alla davola).

The main significance of pressure to the cook, though, is its effect on the boiling point of water, both with variations of *altitude and in *pressure cooking.

PRESSURE COOKING. The higher the pressure, the higher is the temperature at which water boils. Thus, increasing the pressure allows a vessel containing water to reach a higher temperature than the 212°F (100°C) at which it would stay at normal atmospheric pressure until all the water had boiled away. The principle is used in the pressure cooker and autoclave (the large-scale equivalent of the pressure cooker used in commercial canning and for sterilizing in the operating room).

The first pressure cooker, known as the digesteur d'aliments, was invented in 1675 by a Frenchman, Denis Papin. In this, the top was held down by a huge clamp, and the valve—where the steam escaped when the set pressure was reached—was held down and adjusted by a long arm with a weight sliding on it. (Papin subsequently settled in England and worked with Robert Boyle on the steam engine.)

The modern pressure cooker is much simpler, but the principle is the same: sealing in the steam to cause an increase in the pressure and therefore in the temperature. The higher temperature, together with the steam forcing its way through the food, results in more rapid cooking; it cuts times by at least two-thirds.

Household pressure cookers are made of aluminum or stainless steel; they should last for many years if looked after carefully. The basic components of a pressure cooker are: a body and cover made of a gauge of metal that will withstand at least six times the maximum cooking pressure, a trivet or rack which fits into the base, a pressure control, a safety plug, a gasket or sealing ring, and a locking device to keep the cover firmly attached to the base. Separators allow more than one food to be cooked at a time—perforated separators are for small or cut fruit and vegetables; solid ones are for rice and for canned and frozen foods. Most versions have three levels of pressure.

High pressure (15 lb/sq. in. or 1.05 Kg/sq. cm) is for everyday boiling, stewing, braising, and pot-roasting meat, poultry, fish, and vegetables.

Medium pressure (10 lb/sq. in. or 0.7 Kg/sq. cm) is for softening fruit for jams, jellies, and marmalade, cooking vegetables for chutneys and sauces, and for blanching vegetables for freezing.

Low pressure (5 lb/sq. in. or 0.35 Kg/sq. cm) is for steaming puddings and preparing fruit for *bottling.

The liquid used for pressure cooking—never less than ½ pt (500 ml)—should always be put in first, so that you don't forget it. A pressure cooker can work only if it has liquid inside to produce steam. Leaving out the liquid will cause disaster. The amount of liquid used depends on the length of cooking

time and not on the quantity of food being cooked. The liquid itself must be one that produces steam when it boils—such as water, stock, soup, gravy, wine, beer, milk—and not fat or oil alone. Don't fill a pressure cooker more than two-thirds full with solid foods: the steam must circulate freely. With liquids such as soup or fruit, do not fill the cooker more than half full to allow room for them to rise when they come to the boil. The manufacturer will supply a book of instructions with the pressure cooker; to start with, you should accurately follow the timings quoted for cooking.

[*Pressure*—French: *pression;* German: *Druck;* Italian: *pressione;* Spanish: *presión*]

PRICKLY PEAR, cactus pear, Indian fig, Indian pear, Barbary pear, or **tuna fig** is not related to the pear or the fig but is the fruit of *Opuntia,* the familiar cactus with large platelike pads. The best fruit is said to come from *O. magacantha,* a native of Mexico, but the prickly pear that grows in Europe is *O. ficus-indica,* which is well established in the Mediterranean and North African areas but also came from Mexico.

The fruits, which have very nasty spines, are borne along the edges of the green pads and, when ripe, are yellow-green, rosy-red, purple or almost black. Although some sorts are small, the largest reach 5 in. (12 cm) long. Some plants produce two sets of fruit; those of the second crop—ripe in October and going on to December—are larger and better to eat. Prickly pears can be fairly tasteless, like slightly sweet, overripe cucumbers, with lots of small seeds embedded in the flesh, but some varieties can be good. In the U.S., the best are large and rose-colored, but in Europe—especially in Sicily—the nicest ones have whitish or yellowish fruits. In Sicily, those are called *bastardi* or *bastardoni.* They keep through to January and are often cut with a small piece of the pad attached to keep them fresh.

To gather the fruits, you need to have your hands well protected: the spines are tiny, irritating, and difficult to get out of your skin. When the fruits have been cut, the spines must be rubbed off them and rinsed away. Even so, it is safest to extract the pulp while holding the fruit with a thick cloth, tongs, or leather gloves. Cut off both ends of the fruit, and slit the skin from end to end, so that the pulp can be loosened and removed. This can be chilled and eaten raw, but may need a squeeze of lime or lemon, since it tends to lack acidity.

The pads of the prickly pear are eaten in Mexico, where they are called *nopales* (the fruits are called *nopalitas* or *tunas*). Very young pads are best and should have the spines but not the skin removed before cooking. They are then cut into small pieces (½ in. thick or about 1 cm) and cooked in well-salted water until they are tender. They are then drained and washed under cold water until they are no longer slimy. They are used in soups, cooked as a vegetable, or added to the vegetables for a Spanish-type omelet. They may also be slivered and eaten raw with scrambled eggs.

Nopales are available canned *en escabeche,* in vinegar, in brine, and in water (*nopalitos tiernos al natural,* the best to use). Fresh ones appear in U.S. markets that sell Mexican ingredients, but they are not used in Europe, although they could well be in the Mediterranean countries.

[*Prickly pear*—French: *figue de Barbarie;* Italian: *fico d'India;* Spanish: *higo chumbo*]

PROSCIUTTO. *See* ham (Italian).

PROTEINS, exceedingly complex, organic nitrogen compounds, form part of all living cells and are in a sense the basic stuff of life itself. Enzymes, for instance, are proteins. They are particularly concentrated in meat and fish, in cheese and eggs, in nuts and legumes—especially soybeans. Proteins differ widely in their characteristics. Some are soluble or easily mixed with water (such as egg white), whereas others (such as the casein from milk) are insoluble. Proteins start to coagulate at 122–140°F (50–60°C) and are completely coagulated around 149–158°F (65–70°C), but some need higher temperatures (e.g., milk protein, 212°F or 100°C). Proteins may harden to horny substances when strongly heated. Thus, egg white, when heated, at first becomes solid and insoluble, but, when fried in very hot fat, it becomes downright hard and brittle. However, coagulated proteins can be hydrolyzed by acids and enzymes into their constituent building bricks, the *amino acids, and most are broken down by the digestive enzymes in our bodies. The breaking down can also be achieved by long, slow cooking, but dry heat can destroy amino acids, particularly lysine.

The daily requirement of protein for an adult would be satisfied by about ½ lb (225 g) of meat or chicken per day with no protein coming from any other source, but most people in Europe and America get their requirements from a mixed diet, and 4–5½ oz (100–150 g) of meat a day is enough.

[*Protein*—French: *protéine;* German: *Protein;* Italian: *proteina;* Spanish: *proteina*]

PROTOZOA are microscopic, single-celled (or noncellular) animals. The parasitic forms have complicated life cycles and cause such tropical diseases as malaria, sleeping sickness, amebic dysentery, and bilharziasis. The most effective precaution against water-borne protozoans in the tropics is boiling; covering food and water helps protect against protozoans carried on flies. Marine protozoans are an important element in plankton and form part of the food of many shellfish. Some are poisonous and may be dangerous when they are present in exceptionally large numbers, as in the notorious "red tides" (*see* poisoning).

PRUNE. *See* plum.

PTARMIGAN. *See* grouse.

PTOMAINE. *See* poisoning.

PUDDING. Most people would be hard put to say what blood sausage and chocolate custard have in common. Both, along with an enormous variety of other dishes, are puddings. The word, derived from the Old English word for swelling, presumably relates to the action and appearance of puddings as they were once made. Food was enclosed in a casing (as with sausage) or a cloth or hand-knit pudding bag (as with mixtures of fruit, sweetener, and thickener) and boiled or steamed, expanding in the process to produce a swollen appearance. Puddings may still be cooked this way, and the method might well be recommended as a way of saving energy—the pudding can utilize the steam from another dish that is being prepared—but puddings bags have generally been retired in favor of molds and oven-baked puddings, and puddings of any sort are not as popular in the U.S. as they were in colonial America.

Puddings are still widely served in Europe. In England so-called savory puddings are made of beefsteak, kidney, mutton, game, or chicken; they usually include suet. Bread puddings are almost universal, though not necessarily universally loved, and rich steamed plum pudding, flamed with spirits and served with hard sauce, is a traditional Christmas dessert. Puddings are almost always thickened with something—flour, eggs, tapioca, gelatin, rice, bread crumbs—and they are often molded. They may be sturdy like Indian corn pudding, delicate like Bavarian cream, or nearly solid with fruits and nuts.

PUFFBALLS (genus *Calvatia*). Puffballs are considered one of the easiest mushrooms to identify and among the most appetizing. They are thus a good place for the beginning mushroomer to start experimenting. Puffballs may be small as a marble or large as a basketball in species like *C. gigantea,* and their shape may be rounded, pearlike, or pestle-shaped. They should be eaten while young and firm—when mature the interior turns into a powdery mass of spores. All puffballs are safe and good to eat as long as their flesh is white, dry, and compact. They are usually found in the fall, growing in

PUFFBALLS

fields, open woods, and pastures.

One of the best ways to eat puffballs is simply to slice them rather thin and sauté them. They may be breaded first and fried in butter or deep fat. Or they may be chopped and prepared in the same ways one uses any other mushrooms. (*See* mushrooms.)

PULSES. The general term for all ripe, dried, edible seeds of *legumes: peas, beans, grams, and lentils. They are the main source of protein for poor people, but their use is particularly developed in vegetarian India.

Pulses are generally soaked before cooking; the drier they are, the longer soaking is needed. However, in warm weather, an unpleasant fermented taste may result from the activity of microorganisms or from the onset of changes leading up to germination. It is probably better to cook pulses without soaking whenever possible. Exceptions are very old, dry beans or very large beans which have to be kept looking nice, with their skins on, to be used, for example, in an hors d'oeuvre. For such purposes, large beans are best given a very full soaking in the refrigerator, so they look thoroughly plump, not wrinkled, before they are cooked. Bicarbonate of soda in the water helps to soften the skins.

Pulses should be very well cooked—pressure cookers are useful for this. Pulses may be found indigestible and cause flatulence, but these effects may be lessened by a preliminary short cooking (with a pinch of bicarbonate of soda) and a thorough rinsing, followed by a new start with fresh water. Certain spices, notably cumin, may be used in pulse dishes to counteract indigestibility. Salt should never be added until the beans are cooked. Whether they are finished can usually be determined by blowing on a few of them; if they are cooked, the skins wrinkle. Peeled lentils and *dals* are more digestible than unpeeled ones.

[*Pulse*—French: *plantes légumineuses;* German: *Gemüsepflanzen, Hülsenfrucht;* Italian: *plante leguminose;* Spanish: *legumbres*]

PUMMELO. *See* shaddock.

PUMPKIN. *See* squash.

PURPLE GRANADILLA. *See* passionfruit.

PURSLANE, pussley, or **portulaca** (*Portulaca oleracea*), a spreading annual with fleshy leaves, is a common weed in the U.S., although it is said to have originated in In-

PURSLANE

dia, where it is known as *kulfa*. It is also popular in Arab countries, as *bagli*. It grows wild over most of southern Europe and in Asia.

If you have seen the garden flower portulaca, whose rainbow colors open to the sun, you will recognize the similar fleshy leaves of purslane: they are shiny green, turning reddish, and the plant has pale flowers that quickly pop open and self-seed until they form a succulent carpet over any tilled ground into which they can insert their tenacious roots.

Wash purslane thoroughly: it can be gritty. Tender shoots or young leaves can be dressed with oil and vinegar to be eaten raw as a salad, as purslane was hundreds of years ago. The taste is mild, slightly sour, and the texture is mucilaginous, something like okra, which is why it can be used to thicken soups and stews. The seed pods can be dried and powdered into flour. Purslane is a traditional ingredient in chivry butter, which is delicious with leg of lamb. To make it, chop purslane, chervil, parsley, tarragon, and chives into soft butter. The fleshy stems of purslane also make a crisp pickle (use your favorite pickle recipe and substitute by weight).

Because purslane is 90% water, it is not fattening, and it is astonishingly high in calcium, iron, and vitamins C and A—overall it contains more nutrients than carrots, which is why health-conscious people are increasingly eating purslane instead of throwing it on the compost heap or plowing it under.

FATTOUSH (AN ARAB SALAD)

Break a few handfuls of pitta (Arab bread) into a bowl. Sprinkle it with sumac water (made by infusing some *sumac seeds in water for 15 minutes or so and squeezing out the red juice) or some lemon juice. Add 2 minced cloves of garlic, 3 chopped small cucumbers (preferably Kirby or home-grown ones) or a cos lettuce torn to bits, a chopped green pepper, a chopped tomato, a small handful each of chopped parsley and mint, and several cups of purslane leaves. Add some chopped onion, a good sprinkling of salt, and toss with ½ cup good olive oil.

[*Purslane*—French: *pourpier;* German: *Portulak;* Italian: *portulaca, procellana;* Spanish: *verdolaga*]

PYROLIGNEOUS ACID, sometimes called liquid smoke, is made by the destructive distillation of wood. Sawdust is heated in an iron retort, and the vapors are caught and condensed. It consists of 6% acetic acid and small amounts of creosote, methyl alcohol, and acetone (a solvent which is used in nail-polish remover). The yellowish liquid was used at one time as a pickling liquid, but today it appears mainly as an artificial smoke flavoring and also, in tiny amounts, in a wide range of unlikely products from butter and caramels to rum and ice cream. It is corrosive and poisonous except in dilute form.

Q

QAWWRAMA. This is mutton preserved in its fat, much used in Lebanese cooking and interesting because it echoes products made in France with pig and goose. For *qawwrama*, sheep are fattened for killing at the end of November; in the last weeks, the women stuff food individually and by hand into the mouth of each sheep. The animals become so fat that they can scarcely move. After slaughter, the fat is cut from the carcass and rendered down in a large brass pan. Meanwhile, the lean meat is cut in pieces, pressed to remove much of the liquid (it would not keep with too much water in it), and finally fried in the mutton fat. It is seasoned with pepper and salt. Meat and fat are packed, scalding, into earthenware crocks and are sealed in with clay. These jars of *qawwrama* keep all winter.

Qawwrama is used in stews, for stuffing vegetables, for frying eggs, and for many other purposes. A Lebanese idea of a good breakfast is *kishk* (a soured mixture of wheat and milk which has been dried to a powder for storage—another local staple) mixed into a porridge with water and laced with onions and garlic fried in *qawwrama*. A good healthful dish to start the day.

QUAHOG or **quahaug.** Hard-shell *clam.

QUAIL. The "true" quail (*Coturnix coturnix*) a small European game bird, breeds in much of Europe and into Asia as far as China and migrates southward in winter. There is more confusion about the "quail" in the U.S. When Europeans discovered a New World bird that had variegated brown plumage with whitish stripes over its upper parts, they named it for the bird in the Old World they thought it resembled. Thus the bobwhite (*Colinus virginianus*) was called a partridge in the South and a quail in New England, and it goes by any one of these three names today. It does not migrate, and it prefers walking to flying. Also found on the U.S. west coast are a mountain quail, or plumed partridge, and a valley quail that is the state bird of California. Both native American and imported varieties of quail are domesticated for their meat and their eggs (*see* eggs)—increasingly so, since wild birds are becoming scarce and are protected while the quail gains popularity among U.S. cooks.

Quails are eaten fresh, although they may be hung for a few days. In the past, cooks sometimes left the *trail in, but today quails are drawn. They may be plucked or skinned. Some claim that wild quails are more succulent than domesticated ones—perhaps because the wild birds have such a delicious diet of ripe grain, wild grapes, and partridgeberries—but quail meat generally tastes like slightly gamy dark chicken meat (although quail flesh is pale-colored). Quails are so small that at least 2 per person should be served. They are delicious simply brushed with butter and roasted, with a sauce made from the drippings, a little Madeira, and some cream. They may also be roasted wrapped in bacon and vine leaves, or cooked in a casserole with shallots or garlic or grapes, and are good accompanied with wild rice. The English make jugged quail, and the French have scores of recipes, serving quails stuffed with truffles, deviled, curried, chilled in aspic or mousses, baked in pastry shells, and made into pâté.

[Quail—French: caille; German: Wachtel; Italian: quaglia; Spanish: codorniz]

QUASSIA is a bitter-tasting wood, originally from a small tropical South American tree (*Quassia amara*), but since the early 19th century more usually from a larger Caribbean tree, the bitter ash (*Pacrasma excelsa*). Both are used as a source of bitters for tonic wines and apéritifs.

[Quassia—French: quassia; German: Quassia; Italian: quassia; Spanish: cuasia]

QUATRE ÉPICES. A mixture of four spices used as a flavoring, particularly in French charcuterie. There is no standard mixture, and the name is sometimes applied to *allspice, as well as to *nigella. *Quatre épices* can even be a mixture of more than four spices. There are many formulas for such mixtures, a few of which follow.

	Percentages by weight		
Pepper	51.5 (white)	70 (black)	62.5 (white)
Nutmeg	29	10	17.5
Ginger	13	-	15
Cinnamon	-	10	-
Cloves	6.5	10	5
	100	100	100

QUETSCH. *See* fruit brandy; plum.

QUIN. *See* scallop.

QUINCE (*Cydonia vulgaris*) is related to pears and apples. The fruit may be pear-shaped or apple-shaped, according to variety, and its color is golden when ripe—possibly this is the original "golden apple" of classic legend. If so, when Paris judged the beauty contest between Aphrodite, Athena, and Hera, the prize must have been presented as a joke, because a bite of a raw quince would surely have given even Aphrodite a sour expression. Or was she expected only to smell it? A ripe quince has a wonderful perfume. The quince comes from western Asia, from that exciting corner between the Black and Caspian seas where until recently there were virgin tracts of primeval forest. Wild quinces in Europe have probably escaped from cultivation, and there are a number of cultivated varieties—though comparatively few beside pears and apples. Aroma and quality depend upon the type, and this is reflected in the quince jams made in different places. The fruit contains much pectin and sets to a good jelly; the astringency is destroyed by cooking. A thick paste of quince purée boiled down with sugar until it can be set into a tough slab is a confection made in many places from the Middle East through Spain and Portugal to France, which has a famous version called *cotignac*. Quince paste may be good, but is often oversweet and insipid, especially when filled out with cheaper apple pulp. In Spain, it is called *carne de membrillo* (quince meat) and is generally eaten with cheese, a habit that has spread to Latin America where the quince forests of Uruguay are famous. The word "marmalade" comes from the Portuguese for quince—*marmelo*. Quinces may have been introduced to Britain in the mid-10th century; during the 16th and 17th centuries hundreds of recipes for quince marmalade appeared in cookbooks. Most of these were for pastes and jellies which were equivalents of the Italian *cotognata*.

Quinces are cooked with meat in many countries; the custom possibly originated in Persia. There are even Persian dishes in which quinces are stuffed with meat mixtures. In Rumania, quinces are cooked with beef, veal, or chicken and onion—the meat and quinces are usually first fried and then combined in a sort of stew, thickened a little with flour and made slightly sweet-sour with brown sugar or caramel and a dash of vinegar. In North Africa, especially in Morocco, stews (*tagine*) of lamb or chicken often contain quinces. Recipes for stuffed quinces, *tagine,* and quince paste will be found in Claudia Roden's *A Book of Middle Eastern Food* (Knopf, 1972), which includes also a fabulous way of preparing compote of quinces. The following is an adaptation.

QUINCE COMPOTE

Peel and core 2 lb (1 Kg) of quinces. Cook the peel and cores with the juice of half a lemon, 9 oz (250 g) of sugar and ¾ pint (400 ml) of water for 30 minutes. Meanwhile, slice the quinces and put them into a bowl (if you want them pale, cover them temporarily with lemon juice and water, since they quickly discolor in air). Strain the syrup from the pan, squeezing out all the juices, over the quinces and cook the quince slices in this flavored syrup until they are tender. Check for sweetness and acidity. Chill and eat with heavy cream, whipped cream, or yogurt.

[*Quince*—French: *coing;* German: *Quitte;* Italian: *cotogna;* Spanish: *membrillo*]

QUININE. Most famous as an early antimalarial drug, this exceedingly bitter *alkaloid is extracted from various species of the South American *Cinchona* bush. It is used, very dilute, in Indian tonic water. Liquids containing quinine, as opposed to other bitter substances, may be recognized by their pale-blue fluorescence.

[*Quinine*—French: *quinine;* German: *Chinin;* Italian: *china, chinina, chinino;* Spanish: *quinina*]

R

RABBIT and **hare** belong to the same family, Leporidae. A strong distinction is made in Britain between hares and rabbits: hares have red meat and rabbits have white. But when the English names are used in other countries, the original distinction becomes blurred. For instance, the American jackrabbit is actually a hare. The important point is whether the flesh is dark or light, and hares and rabbits anywhere can be judged by this criterion and recipes selected accordingly.

Hares are easily distinguished from rabbits by their darker color and longer, more powerful back legs. Further, hares are generally larger than rabbits; they build nests on the ground, whereas some rabbits dig burrows; and while rabbit young are born blind and furless, newborn hares are fully furred with eyes wide open.

The varying hare, also called the snowshoe rabbit (*Lepus americanus*) is camouflaged to suit the seasons. It is found in treed areas from Alaska and Canada south through New England and, in the Appalachians, to Tennessee, in the Rocky Mountains, and to central California in the Sierras. Two species of Arctic hare (*L. arcticus* and *L. othus*) inhabit the far northern regions of North America, and their meat is highly regarded.

Jackrabbits are either blacktailed (*L. californicus*) or whitetailed (*L. townsendii*). Blacktailed jacks inhabit open grasslands and deserts of the western U.S.; whitetails live in grasslands and sagebrush country from Alberta to New Mexico and from the Sierras east to Lake Michigan. Younger jacks are more palatable than adults, and whitetails are considered better than blacktails.

The European common or brown hare (*L. europaeus*) is distributed across Europe and through to eastern Asia. The varying, blue, Scottish, or Alpine hare (*L. timidus*)—not the same species as the varying hare of North America—is found in the Alps, Scotland, Ireland, and Scandinavia; in snowy places, it turns white in winter. The Mediterranean hare (*L. capensis*), which is found in Spain, the Balearic Islands, Sardinia, and Crete, is strongly colored and a little smaller than the brown hare, of which it might be a variety.

Young hares can be told from old ones because they do not have a widely spread cleft in their harelip and they have sharp claws and tender ears. Up to a year old, they are called leverets. Old hares should never be roasted, but must be jugged or stewed. Unless hares have been badly shot and therefore have to be eaten immediately before they stiffen, they need hanging by the hind legs for at least 3 days—5 to 8 days if the hare is large and the weather is cool—*without drawing*. When the hare is drawn just before cooking, the blood, especially that trapped in the chest cavity, should be saved if it is to be used for thickening the sauce (this may give rather too strong a flavor for some tastes). The best part of a hare is the back; the hind legs come second. Shoulders and forelegs are usually stewed or used for soup. Hare is very often marinated in a mixture of olive oil and wine, flavored with crushed juniper berries, thyme, or mixed herbs. If it is to be roasted, it is usually larded to prevent the flesh from drying out.

In French regional cooking, there are many marvelous hare dishes ranging from the simple ragout *civet de lièvre* to more luxurious creations such as *râble de lièvre à la crème* (saddle of hare baked in cream). Germany has a version of jugged hare (*Tippenhaas*) and saddle of hare sauced with horseradish and red currant jelly (*Hasenrücken mit Meerettich*) or with cream (*mit Sahne*); the liver is sometimes cooked as a separate dish. Italy has many excellent hare dishes, including several unusual ones, such as the fantastic *lepre in dolce e forte* from Tuscany. This contains among its ingredients pine nuts, the candied peel of orange and citron, raisins, chocolate, *cavallucci* (a sweetmeat from Siena which includes walnuts and aniseed), wine, sugar, garlic, rosemary, basil, celery, tomato, parsley, onion, carrot, sage, bay leaves, oil, and vinegar. It is one of the Italian sweet-sour (*agrodolce*) dishes of ancient origin.

The most famous British hare dish is jugged hare, which is traditionally cooked in a pot that stands in water (but today more usually in the oven) and is lengthily simmered with port or Burgundy and gravy.

JUGGED HARE

Cut the hare into pieces and brown them lightly in butter or bacon fat. Put them into a stoneware jar and pour in a large glass of red wine—port or Burgundy. Turn the pieces and leave them while making a forcemeat of 6 heaping tablespoons of fresh bread crumbs, the grated rind of a lemon, a small handful of parsley finely chopped, ½ teaspoon mixed thyme and marjoram, plus seasoning of salt, pepper, and nutmeg. To this,

add a tablespoon of butter or some suet and 1–2 egg yolks for binding.

When the forcemeat has been made, cut 1 lb (450 g) of steak into thin slices and spread each with a little of the forcemeat, reserving the rest. Roll and tie these steak olives, brown them in butter, and add to the container of hare along with a very finely chopped onion and some gravy if you have it. Cover the jar closely and stand it up to the neck in boiling water. Keep the water boiling for 1½–2 hours, depending on the age of the hare. Ten minutes before serving, make the rest of the forcemeat into balls, fry them, and add them to the jar. Adjust the seasoning, remove the string from the steak olives, and serve the dish garnished with triangles of bread fried in butter and accompanied by red currant jelly. The gravy should be naturally thick, but if it needs thickening, do so with the blood or a little arrowroot mixed with butter. The steak can be omitted, but it is a usual part of jugged hare, at least in northern England.

Rabbits. There are four species of rabbit called cottontails (*Sylvilagus*) in the U.S., and several others that are in the same group, but some of them can be distinguished only by the specialist. Since these little rabbits, named for the white undersides of their tails, are widely distributed across the continent and produce so rapidly that they are rarely in short supply, they are familiar to most Americans and the source of much folklore. And because the meat of the cottontail is light in color, fine in texture, and delicious in flavor, there are hundreds of recipes for preparing it for the table.

The European rabbit (*Oryctolagus cuniculus*) is a native of southwest Europe which has been introduced into many parts of the world, including the U.S., where it is called the San Juan rabbit after the islands off the coast of Washington where it was first introduced; it is more often found in captivity than in the wild in America and is kept as a pet and for food. Before myxomatosis, a viral disease of rabbits, was let loose in Europe, rabbits there were so plentiful that they could hardly be given away. Now rabbit has become more costly than chicken.

Wild rabbits are not found in the coldest parts of Europe, but they are regularly eaten everywhere else. They have become widely domesticated, and in the U.S. alone, more than 75 varieties, bred for particular traits, have been registered. Frozen domestic rabbit meat, which is all-white, is available in most supermarkets and is often imported. The weight of a fully grown rabbit undressed may reach 4½ lb (2 Kg) but is normally less. Rabbits can live up to 13 years, though 5–6 is more usual. In young rabbits, the claws are sharp and smooth, the coat soft, and the ears easily torn. In old rabbits, the claws are long and rough, the ears are tough, and the coat may be turning gray. Unlike hares, rabbits are not hung—they ought not to have been killed more than a couple of days and are best when still stiff. If kept too long, rabbit meat smells, and the flesh turns slimy and slightly blue.

To paunch a rabbit or hare—to remove its guts—hold it with one hand by the back legs. Insert the point of a sharp knife in the underside between the back legs and slit forward as far as the rib cage, cutting through skin and belly wall only—make sure you do not cut into the intestine or stomach by mistake. Put a finger and thumb into the front end of the slit and grasp the pipe (esophagus) that runs forward from the stomach. Pull it free, and the rest of the guts will fall out cleanly. Rabbits should be paunched as soon as possible after the animal is killed, but hares are usually hung before being paunched and skinned.

To skin a rabbit, cut around the first joint of each hind leg (or chop off). Make an incision in the skin of each hind leg and slit back as far as the tail, then insert your hand between the skin and flesh and free the skin right over the back. The skin can be pulled off each leg, like turning a glove inside out, the skin pulled forward, and the front legs freed in the same way. With a little help from a knife, the skin can be pulled forward over the head, but lazy people just chop the head off, since it contains little meat. Finally, the green gall bladder must be carefully cut from the liver, and the liver and heart saved. Wash the rabbit and giblets well and dry them. Rabbit is sometimes soaked for an hour in slightly salted water before cooking.

Table breeds of domestic rabbit can grow to a huge size but remain tender and white. Young rabbits of the giant breeds weigh 4½ lb (2 Kg)—as much as a large wild rabbit—when only 8 weeks old and reach 9 lb (4 Kg) at 6 months. A dressed rabbit is not much over 60% of its live weight (a hare 75%).

Because rabbits used to be so cheap and common, there are innumerable simple recipes for cooking them, but they seem not to have merited very royal treatment. Rabbits with champagne, truffles, and cream will no doubt appear now that they are expensive. Meanwhile there are fine recipes of peasant origin, including the Italian *coneglio alla sanremese* (rabbit "roasted" brown in an earthenware pan with wine, onion, thyme, rosemary, bay, pounded walnuts, and tiny Ligurian black olives) or the Spanish *conejo a la ampurdanesa*.

CONEJO A LA AMPURDANESA

Fry a rabbit cut in pieces to a golden brown color. Take it out of the pan and fry one sliced onion and two chopped cloves of garlic. Add a skinned, deseeded, and chopped tomato, fry it a little, then put back the rabbit. Then add one glass of wine (which should be *rancio*—the word is the same as rancid—an aged Spanish wine which is almost amber in color; it is off but not vinegary) and a bouquet garni of bay, thyme, and parsley. Cook gently for 15 minutes, then add several mushrooms (which should correctly be the orange *Lactarius,* in Catalan country known as *robellones*) in pieces and a good handful of chopped mixed pine nuts, hazel nuts, and almonds. Cook on gently for 30 to 40 minutes until the meat is tender.

The wild rabbits of Provence already have an herby flavor from eating the tender shoots of wild rosemary and thyme, but rabbits reared on backyard forage can profit from a variety of herbs and spices in cooking; mustard and wine are also good flavorings. English recipes include rabbit pie flavored with salt pork or bacon, grated lemon rind, and nutmeg. Southerners in the U.S. barbecue rabbit or hare, and in Pennsylvania Dutch country one may encounter *Hasenpfeffer,* in which rabbit or hare is marinated for 2 days in acidulated water, onion, and other seasonings, simmered until tender, flavored with sour cream, and served with stewed prunes. In fact, rabbit or hare is an interesting dish to order when one is traveling, since local cuisines have so many different and good recipes for preparing it.

[*Hare*—French: *lièvre;* German: *Hase;* Italian: *lepre;* Spanish: *liebre. Rabbit*—French: *lapin;* German: *Kaninchen;* Italian: *coniglio;* Spanish: *conejo*]

RACCOON [*Procyon lotor*). Although raccoons roam wild over much of the U.S., they are not usually found on the table (unless they are scavenging picnic tables) in areas other than the South. They have long been considered a delicacy by those who have tried them; usually roasted, they may also be prepared in any of the ways one would cook rabbit. The flesh of full-grown raccoons can be rank and tough, and young ones are preferred. Great care should be taken to remove all of the unpleasant-tasting fat from the body before cooking.

RADISH (*Raphanus sativus*) is eaten for its roots, although the top is also edible. The plant has been cultivated for so long that its wild ancestor is unknown, but occasionally a radish that has gone woody suggests what the original radish might have been like once. Radishes are annual or biennial. They are unfamiliar as adult plants because the small varieties are in the ground for no more than a month before being pulled and eaten. The enormous number of varieties differ in pungency; in color from white, through pink to red, to two-colored—red on top and white below—and even black; in size, from mar-bles to huge winter radishes a foot and more long; in shape from ball to cylinder and spinning-top. The small varieties must be lifted young: they tend to become hollow when left in the soil for even a few days too long. Commercially grown radishes are now lifted and topped by machines which handle 6 rows at a time; by big American producers, they are also sorted, washed, cooled in ice-cold chlorinated water, bagged, weighed, and sealed, all by machinery, before being delivered to supermarkets in refrigerated trucks. Peering through the bag, you have to decide if the green bit looks fresh, because if it is not, the radish will also be hardly fresh; a surreptitious squeeze will show if the larger ones are hollow. If they are sold in bunches without wrapping, radishes should look bright and fresh (not just doused with water). Radishes can be kept for a couple of days if they are stood root end down in a bowl of water; they can even be revived a little if wilted, but they will never taste as they do when pulled fresh from the garden. For keeping, there are huge winter radishes, that are as big as a slicing sausage. These large winter radishes are peeled and cut into pieces—chips, slices, or grated—and are excellent. A large white variety is the Japanese *daikon.*

The *daikon* type will keep for 2 weeks in the refrigerator. *Daikon* is used in many ways in Japan—for example, grated with red caviar, or shredded and used in garnish for soups. *Daikon* is also the basis for pickles.

The small radishes are usually eaten fresh in salads, whole, sliced, or sometimes used for decoration, cut nearly through to the top in segments and dropped into ice water, so that they open like flowers. In France and Italy, radishes are eaten as part of an hors d'oeuvre with butter, although I prefer them with salty sheep's-milk cheese as eaten in southeastern Europe. It is a pity that so many radishes now seem to taste of little more than stagnant water—perhaps they are grown by hydroponics. Radishes are sometimes cooked like turnips, but are not very interesting.

[*Radish*—French: *radis;* German: *Radies-chen;* Italian: *rafano;* Spanish: *rábano*]

RAGI. *See* millet.

RAISIN is a general term for dried grapes of whatever variety, including the *currant made from very small black grapes. At one time (and in some European countries today), however, raisin was the term reserved for the dried fruit of a large seeded grape, the Muscat of Alexandria, called Malagas in general world commerce and muscats in California. Sultanas referred to small seedless raisins made from the Sultanina grape, called Thompson seedless in California. Today most Americans expect all raisins to be seedless and distinguish them only as dark or golden.

Traditionally, dark raisins are made of muscatel grape varieties. Some of the very best come from Malaga in Spain, and the very finest dessert raisins, "raisins of the sun," are at least partially dried on the vine, still attached to the stalk in a bunch. The stalk is almost, but not quite, cut through to prevent the sap from getting to the bunch, and the leaves are removed to let the hot sun bathe it. Slightly less expensive bunches are dried by laying the grapes out on mats. Seedless raisins may be raisins stoned by machine—the best—or dried seedless grapes, which lack the full muscat flavor.

Sultana-type raisins originally came as an export from Turkey, mostly through Izmir (then Smyrna), and were known as Smyrna or sultana raisins to distinguish them from currants from Corinth. Sultanas still come from Turkey and Greece, but the bulk of the world's production now comes from California and Australia, where the seedless grape varieties that are used lack the sultana flavor and are mainly sweet. In some countries, sultanas are dressed with mineral oil to prevent their overdrying and to give them a gloss. Those grown in Smyrna and Australia are usually dipped in soda or lye to hasten the curing process and produce a golden col-

or and translucent skin. California sultana-type raisins are exclusively sun-dried without additives except for a portion intended for export.

Other miscellaneous varieties of grapes are dried in some countries, and one may, of course, dry any grapes one has on hand, but these are generally inferior as raisins and are usually termed "dried grapes." All raisins are rich in fruit sugar, which acts as a natural preservative of the product, and raisin producers can with validity term them "nature's candy" and urge them upon Americans as a sweet product rich in iron and potassium that is much to be preferred to refined sugar products.

[*Raisin*—French: *raisin sec;* German: *Rosine;* Italian: *uva secca;* Spanish: *pasa de uva.* *Sultana*—French: *raisin de Smyrne;* German: *Sultanine;* Italian: *sultanina;* Spanish: *pasa de Corinto*]

RAMBUTAN. *See* lychee.

RAMPHAL. *See* custard apple.

RAM'S-HEAD PEA. *See* chickpea.

RANCIDITY. Rancid butter has a characteristic taste caused by the formation of butyric acid through a process of hydrolysis. Most rancid tastes, however, are produced by the oxidation of fats and oils exposed to the air. Commercially, this is prevented in freeze-dried meat products and in sausages by the addition of antioxidants; at home, rancidity can be very much delayed by storing fats and oils in full containers in the refrigerator. Because cold very much slows down the chemical process, keeping salad dressings, mayonnaise, margarine, drippings, and butter in the refrigerator is also sound practice, while the pan of oil or pot of old drippings kept for deep frying is not good sense for either the flavor of the food or good health. Rancid flavors that develop in crude vegetable oils, particularly in olive oil made from olives that have been damaged by flies or that were half-rotted on the ground, are removed by "stripping" (extracting the flavor), although some Spaniards who have been used to semirancid oil since childhood ~~tually come to like it.

RAPE (*Brassica napus*) is an outstandingly versatile and valuable species of food plant. It probably originated by hybridization between cabbage (*B. oleracea*) and turnip (*B. rapa*), but its history is uncertain; some varieties are of relatively recent origin, while others have been in cultivation since ancient times. Rape may be annual or biennial and may or may not have a tuberous root. The varieties grown for their roots are the swede (var. *napobrassica*) and the rutabaga (var. *rutabaga*), which can be distinguished from turnips by their conspicuous ring of concentric leaf-base scars around the neck of the vegetable.

The nontuberous varieties, such as the biennial var. *arvensis,* are known as rape, cole, or coleseed. These are grown very widely as feed for cattle (to the distress of beekeepers who find that honey produced from the yellow rape flowers has an unpleasing crystalline texture). The seeds are the source of rape-seed or colza oil (*see* oils and fats); after this has been expressed, the residue is still oily enough to be worth making into rape-seed cake for feeding to cattle.

[*Rape*—French: *colza;* German: *Raps;* Italian: *colza;* Spanish: *colza*]

RASPBERRY. The many species of raspberry belong to the same genus (*Rubus*) as the blackberry. They occur in the cooler parts of the northern hemisphere. However, there is a vast difference in taste between a raspberry and a blackberry.

In the horticultural varieties of raspberry, flavor has to be balanced against disease resistance and cropping. Although red is the usual color, there are white, yellow, and golden raspberries (which are soft and richly flavored), as well as black-fruited raspberries developed from the American species *R.*

occidentalis. A small proportion of wild raspberries, particularly in Scotland, are pale yellow.

Since raspberries, like most fruit, are best when fully ripened on the cane and are highly perishable, those bought in shops are often suspect, doubly so if they are cheap. Damp stains on the bottom of the container will indicate that the fruit underneath is rotting, but however careful you are, it is still likely that a few raspberries will be mildewed, and they may have already given a musty taste to the rest. The bad ones should be picked out with a toothpick to avoid more squashing and further contamination. Frozen raspberries are in perfect condition and may be a better buy than dubiously fresh ones.

Good raspberries have a very delicate taste which is easily destroyed by cooking. To get the most of their flavor, it is better to squash them against the roof of the mouth with the tongue than to bite them. They are best eaten raw or "cooked" by pouring boiling sugar syrup over them. Sweet, beautifully flavored raspberries may be seedy (their only fault), and are then best put through a fine nonmetal sieve. Raspberry sorbet and the figs in raspberry syrup of French *haute cuisine* are delectable but expensive; most of us, though, can manage very nicely with fruit from the garden eaten with heavy cream and a sprinkle of fine sugar. The best raspberries I ever tasted came from a single wild bush in a gorge in the South Tirol. I wish I had marked it.

Raspberries contain 1.75–2% pectin, plus sufficient citric and malic acids to set into a jelly or jam. When in good condition, raspberries will keep for a couple of days in the refrigerator, but washing, if needed, should never be done until the last minute.

Although the European raspberry varieties come mainly from *R. idaeus,* there are also cultivated varieties of the American *P. strigosa.* Other "raspberries," such as the *hinsar* and the dark, pointed *kailka,* are so refreshing in spring to the thirsty Himalayan traveler that they might one day be cultivated, as is the golden-orange wineberry (*R. phoenicolasius*) of northern China and Japan.

For crosses between raspberries and blackberries (loganberries, youngberries, and boysenberries), *see* blackberry.

[*Raspberry*—French: *framboise;* German: *Himbeere;* Italian: *lampone;* Spanish: *frambuesa*]

RATAFIA. Victorian cookbooks are full of recipes for ratafias, now largely forgotten. There were apricot, blackberry, black currant, cherry, angelica, gooseberry, orange-flower, quince, raspberry, and rose ratafias, as well as cakes, creams, cheese cakes, ice creams, and puddings, flavored with ratafia. The common factor, regardless of what else ratafias contained (mainly the juice of the fruit concerned and strong brandy) was bitter *almonds, or the flavor of bitter almonds derived from the kernels of apricots, peaches, plums, and cherries, or from the leaves of peaches and apricots gathered in spring. *Noyau is a ratafia. Books generally advise that ratafias be used with moderation as flavorings, not only because too much bitter almond taste is unpleasant but because it is poisonous in quantity, although heating will drive off the very poisonous hydrocyanic acid and leave only the benzaldehyde, which is lethal in large doses.

Ratafia today often refers to ratafia macaroons with a strong bitter almond flavor. In Italy they are called *amaretti* and are sometimes used as a flavoring.

RAVIOLI. *See* pasta.

RAY. *See* shark.

RAZOR SHELL. *See* clam.

RED GRAM. *See* pigeon pea.

REDUCING is concentrating a liquid by boiling to evaporate some of the water. Reducing increases the flavor of nonvolatile constituents, but it may reduce the flavor of volatile ones, such as essential oils of herbs and spices or the acetic acid in vinegar. It may also concentrate salt to unpleasant proportion; final salting should be done after and not before reduction.

REFRESHING is cooling hot food quickly by putting it under running tap water or by plunging it into ice water. This stops further cooking and firms up the tissues. Refreshing is part of the usual French method of cooking vegetables that are boiled, drained when not quite done, refreshed, and later heated and finished in cream or butter. Other foods that would suffer from overcooking, like shellfish, may be refreshed when they are removed from the cooking water.

REFRIGERATION. Since earliest times, food has been kept cool in iceboxes or ice chambers wherever there was winter snow. The snow or ice was stored in deep pits or special icehouses and was usually covered with straw to provide insulation. A large body of snow, if well protected, would last all through the hottest summer. In Tabas, a most remote town in the middle of the Dasht-i-lut, one of the great deserts of eastern Persia, I saw a huge domed pavilion, which I was told was an icehouse that had fallen into disuse. Even such a hot area would have had enough snow in winter to justify the building of such a structure.

It is known by observation, of course, that food keeps longer in cold weather. It has also long been understood that when salt is mixed with ice it lowers the temperature, so that other things in contact with the mixture can be frozen. In 1876, meat was shipped across the Atlantic from America to Britain using ice and salt as the freezer, and before the turn of the century meat was regularly being shipped in refrigerator ships through the tropics from Australia and New Zealand. It was not, however, until after World War I that household refrigerators began to be common and to replace the cool cellars and larders which were once as essential in a house as a kitchen or a bedroom. Today, when houses are built without cool larders, we are compelled to keep many foods colder than they should be because we have nowhere else but the refrigerator.

This invention depends on the fact that when liquids boil they absorb heat, but that if the vapor is compressed, it gives off the heat it has absorbed and returns to a liquid. A refrigerator uses a substance, such as ammonia or freon, which is a gas even at the low temperature inside a refrigerator but will become a liquid under pressure. This substance circulates continually, vaporizing and extracting heat as it passes in pipes inside the refrigerator and being compressed back to a liquid—giving off the heat it has absorbed—outside, at the back of the refrigerator.

You could say it was pumping the heat out. By this means the modern refrigerator will freeze water and ice cream in the freezing compartment or will keep frozen food frozen. Cold air, being denser than warm air, falls, but the proximity of the freezing compartment means that in practice the top part of the refrigerator is cooler than the bottom.

[*Refrigeration*—French: *réfrigération;* German: *Abkühlung;* Italian: *refrigerazione;* Spanish: *refrigeración*]

RELIGIOUS FOOD LAWS. Christians are not subjected to religious dietary laws or expressly forbidden to eat certain foods or instructed to have their meat killed in specified ways. Even "fish on Fridays" is no longer observed by most denominations, although in Catholic countries, in spite of official abolition by the Vatican Council, the old custom is still widely observed through force of habit. Muslims, Jews, Hindus, Jains, and other religious groups do, however, have dietary rules. Very orthodox followers of these religions are unlikely to accept an invitation to eat in the homes of people of different faiths. However, cooks ought to know in broad outline what the religious food laws specify, if

only because it may sometimes prevent social embarrassment to be able to provide a meal which is acceptable to people with another religion. These laws also explain many of the characteristics of ethnic cooking—why, for instance, the Middle East is not full of delectable pork recipes and why Arabs may, but Jews may not, cook meat with yogurt. The popularity in Jewish cooking of stuffed dishes in which a little meat can be made to stretch a long way goes back to the days of the ghettos, where kosher meat was a scarce commodity. This scarcity and the large number of ingredients that were forbidden led to a cuisine which produced the maximum variety from a rather limited range of raw materials. Hindus, who were to a large extent vegetarian, developed varied and elaborate vegetable dishes. A humble ingredient such as *dal can be turned into literally hundreds of very different dishes.

Dietary laws can be seen as a way of transforming the preparation and consumption of food into an act of worship or merely as the expression of principles of health and hygiene that were once essential in the hot countries of the Orient. Either way, the laws were used both to protect and to proclaim the identity of the religious group. For Jews and Hindus, who until quite recently neither encouraged nor recognized converts, the laws created a barrier between their communities and an impure world, breeding a sense of exclusiveness, of a special relation with the deity, which helped them survive in the face of hostility or persecution.

Islam, on the other hand, was fiercely proselytic and saw in the convert's abstinence from pork and alcohol a tangible sign of allegiance to his new religion. The food laws and customs bind all Muslims together, irrespective of origins or social position. In a traditional Muslim household, the sexes do not mix at meals and all the men sit around a large communal dish of food and eat from it. Any newcomer, provided he is a Muslim, will also be invited to partake of the meal, a practice that indicates a sense of equality in the eyes of God.

Christianity and Buddhism, which started as movements of reform or revolt among, respectively, Jews and Hindus, reacted against the rigid concept of food laws. These were relaxed by the Buddhists and largely abandoned by the Christians, and both religions substituted simple, plain diets which they sought to combine with a rather austere way of living. Although Christianity has no religious food laws in the sense that no food is forbidden or considered impure, abstinence from meat and rich foods during Lent is a tradition of some denominations, and in many countries there are special dishes associated with Lent. Shrove Tuesday or Mardi Gras, before Lent, also has its own dishes, of which pancakes are the most famous, many of them designed to empty the larder of rich ingredients in a final pre-Lenten eating binge.

Jews. The Jewish dietary laws (*kashruth*) are very ancient, many of them from the Bible. To be fit for eating, animals must have cloven hoofs and chew the cud. This allows beef, mutton, goat, and venison, but rules out horse (which doesn't have a cloven hoof or chew the cud) and pork (because the pig, though it has a cloven hoof, does not chew the cud and is also regarded as unclean). Most birds are allowed (except birds of prey), but seafood must have obvious fins and scales (which rules out eels and shellfish, both crustaceans and mollusks). The eggs and milk of prohibited animals are also not allowed, which rules out mare's milk and the roe of some fish. Hen eggs must be perfect, and a blood spot means that the egg should be discarded.

To be kosher, which is to say suitable for consumption by Orthodox Jews, meat must be slaughtered in the prescribed way by the *shohet*, who is licensed by the rabbi. The Jewish butcher must not only be able to slaughter by cutting the throat of the animal so that trachea, esophagus, jugular vein, and carotid artery are quickly severed (the animal almost instantly loses consciousness), but must also be fully conversant with the

law of *shehitah* and be able to examine the animal outside and inside for any disease, malformation, or impurity (such as a foreign body embedded in the gizzard of a chicken) which would make the animal *terefah*—unfit to eat. The care taken over the slaughtering of animals is to ensure the ritual purity of Jewish food and to avoid unnecessary suffering to the animal, but is also a sign of respect for the life that is being taken. In fact, the consumption of meat has constantly posed a problem to Judaism, since the Torah says: "I would prefer that you abstain from eating meat altogether." But it goes on to say that "since your desires cannot be stopped nor your nutritional requirements altered . . . since you will eat meat and perhaps need to eat meat, you may . . . but with one restriction—that you have reverence for the life you take." Meat must be eaten within a day or so of slaughter, and it must be soaked in a vessel kept for the purpose and salted for an hour in a perforated container which will allow the blood to flow away. Then, after rinsing, it is pure, or kosher. It is worth noting that kosher meat is acceptable to Muslims in places where true *halal* meat is unavailable.

The sharpest distinction between Jewish and Muslim food laws is the question of eating meat and dairy products together. The Bible says: "Thou shalt not seethe a kid in his mother's milk" (Deuteronomy 14:21). Orthodox Jews go to extreme lengths to avoid any possible mixing of dairy products and meat at the same meal. Tea or coffee with milk cannot be taken until 6 hours after meat has been eaten. Separate pots and dishes have to be kept for dairy products and meat; even tablecloths and bread that has been on the table when meat has been served must be set aside before a meal containing milk products may follow. This law makes it impossible to cook meat dishes with butter (the basis of so much French cooking) and is the reason why Jews use chicken fat, the nearest animal fat to butter in texture and character. While there are plenty of Jews who eat ham and enjoy French cooking, it should not be taken for granted that all Jewish acquaintances will do so.

Muslims, like Jews, may not eat pork, and thus not bacon or ham or pork—the hams of the Middle East are mutton hams. The meat they do eat must have been killed deliberately and in the correct way; in practice, Muslim butchers (even those in meat factories) are licensed by a mullah and the meat is known as *halal* meat. The animal must have been killed by having its throat cut while the slaughterer says, "In the name of Allah, Allah is most great." Muslims are not allowed to eat blood and may not eat the meat of animals that have died by accident, except in dire necessity. Muslims are also forbidden to drink alcohol (although many do) or even to put wine or spirits in their food. The use of gold or silver plates is also forbidden, so put them away when entertaining the local oil sheik. In general, the laws governing Muslim food are very like those governing Jewish food but with one major difference— lamb cooked in milk or yogurt is one of the great Arab dishes.

Hindus have religious food laws that vary according to caste and region. Many high-caste Hindus, particularly women, are vegetarians. Some eat eggs, some not; some fish but no meat, and so on. Prohibitions even extend into the vegetable world. Very orthodox Brahmins (the priestly caste) abstain from onion and garlic. The really strict Brahmin will eat only food cooked by himself or someone of his own caste in his own kitchen, and there are rituals to be observed (such as the cook taking a bath before preparing the dishes) which are hardly followed outside India. Hindus who are willing to visit European households for dinner will evidently accept food prepared in a European manner, but it is necessary to ask if they are vegetarians or if they eat meat. Never serve beef when you have Hindu visitors; the cow has for long been considered sacred, although a thousand or more years ago, even the Brahmins ate beef. Many Hindus regard alcoholic drinks with horror. However,

bhang, a paste prepared from the cannabis plant, is legally available in India and is frequently added to drinks and sweetmeats at festival time.

Buddhists base their religion on the teachings of Prince Siddhartha Gautama, the Buddha, who was born in northern India in the 6th century B.C. Although the Buddha did not forbid his disciples to eat animals, he advised them not to kill for food, nor to allow anyone else to kill for their special benefit. According to legend, the Buddha himself died as a result of eating bad pork (which had been offered by a poor man whose feelings would have been hurt if he had refused it), but today many Buddhists are vegetarians (particularly in Japan), so some vegetarian dishes should be offered as well as meat when Buddhists come to dinner.

Jains have a religion that is a branch of Buddhism characterized by an extreme respect for life. So Jain priests brush the ground where they walk and wear a pad over their mouths to prevent not only the accidental inhalation of small creatures but even their hot breath from distressing the very air. Jains will not eat meat, fish, or eggs but will usually take butter and milk. Some will not eat onions, garlic, or red-colored vegetables. A Jain priest is not even allowed to beg for his food, since that might cause someone to kill the vegetable on his behalf. He may eat food only if it is unsolicited and offered freely to him. In that case, it is already dead.

Parsis are followers of the prophet Zoroaster, who first came to India to escape persecution by the Muslims in Iran around A.D. 750. Parsis eat meat and drink alcoholic drinks freely, but many do not approve of smoking because fire is sacred to them.

Sikhs. The Sikh religion was founded by Guru Nanak in the late 15th century. Sikhs eat meat, even beef, but will not eat meat killed in the Muslim manner (by cutting the throat of the animal), since they regard this as a cruel practice. Sikhs in India tend to avoid beef, but only out of respect for the Hindus among whom they live.

RENDERING is melting chunks of animal fat down to a liquid. Put the fat in a pan on top of the stove or in the oven at low heat and cook it gently until the fat is liquid and the remaining solids are crisp. These bits, drained and cooled, are delicious (*see* cracklings), and the fat, transferred to a covered container and kept in the refrigerator, is an excellent frying medium.

RENNET is the stomach lining (abomasum) of an unweaned calf or any similar substance for curdling milk. Rennet is mainly used to set the curd for cheese, but also for making curds and whey, junket, and similar preparations. The action is produced by rennin, an enzyme which coagulates milk proteins and is present in quantity in the stomachs of unweaned baby mammals, as well as in other animals' digestive tracts. Calves' stomachs are the classic source of rennet, but the stomach linings of young pigs, kids, lambs, and even hares and rabbits were sometimes used.

In the past, pieces of salted and dried calf's stomach were sold by butchers. There were many recipes for preparing rennet from scratch; the simplest was to wash the abomasum carefully, rub it well with salt, and pack it, with plenty more salt, in a jar. After a month, it was taken out, drained, and stretched on sticks to dry. Once dry, it would keep for weeks. A piece about 2 in. (5 cm) square, soaked in ½ cup of hot water for 4–5 hours, would yield a liquid, 2 tablespoons of which would curdle 8 pt (4½ lt) of warmed milk. However, the strength of action was very variable. Today, it is more usual to buy rennet essence. In emergency, though, the cook can easily make rennet by washing the lining of a chicken or turkey gizzard well, rubbing it with salt, stretching it, and drying it. For a start try using the same quantity as for calf rennet. Vegetarians must use plant rennet, which can be made by infusing the flowers of the herb lady's bedstraw in water.

[*Rennet*—French: *présure, caillette;* German: *Renette;* Italian: *caglio, presame;* Spanish: *cuajo*]

REPTILES represent an evolutionary stage between amphibians such as frogs—whose young have gills and live in water—and the birds and mammals. They are cold-blooded, lay eggs, and have a general structure similar to our own but much more primitive. Most Europeans treat the thought of reptilian food, apart from *turtle, with horror. Less so Americans, who have a large number of small turtles in their lakes, rivers, and marshes, as well as on the coast, and who, on occasion, will eat alligator and rattlesnake. Having tried grilled snake with the Australian aborigines and boiled *gorpad* lizard with some Indian aborigines, I must confess to a certain revulsion which prevents me from giving an unbiased judgment, just as I would find difficulty in judging rat, dog, or boiled scorpion, all of which get eaten by someone. Some of these foods, like the *gorpad* I ate by the roadside in South India, are supposed to have magical or medicinal significance. The *gorpad* is said to make a man impotent if it happens to hit him with its tail while being captured, but it confers exceptional sexual stamina on those who eat it. However, this is a book on gastronomy. Reptile eggs are also eaten, and turtle eggs are regarded as a delicacy, but the eating of wild crocodile and turtle eggs is to be avoided where, as in most places, they are endangered species.

RESIN, when not prepared in the laboratory, is obtained from the exudations of various plants, especially pine trees. Various resins and gums are used for flavoring. Particularly worthy of notice is the Greek wine retsina, which is often made with no more effort than putting a few bruised pine cones into a barrel of white wine. Resin is a preservative, but an acquired taste.

[*Resin*—French: *résine;* German: *Hartz;* Italian: *resina;* Spanish: *resina*]

RHUBARB (*Rheum rhaponticum*) is often considered a fruit, although it is actually a leaf stem. The word "rhubarb" is possibly coined from *rha* (Greek for Volga) and *barbarium* (Latin for barbarian), the plant having first, it seems, been introduced from Russia to Britain in 1578. In the U.S. it was first grown for its round pouch of unopened flowers, which was cooked as a delicacy (in northern Asia, one rhubarb species is still raised for this purpose).

It was not until the start of the 19th century that rhubarb began to be prepared as a fruit rather than a medicinal plant. Rhubarb's popularity rested on its being the first fruit of spring, and it was commonly forced with straw and bottomless buckets to produce tender pink stems. It does not seem to have caught on in Mediterranean climates, because it needs a cold spell in winter to grow properly and because oranges and other spring and winter fruits are available when rhubarb would come in. Best flavored is the early pink-stemmed spring or champagne rhubarb, which has been forced. Older outdoor rhubarb has bright red or greenish stems and large dark-green leaves. In the U.S., both field and hothouse varieties are grown, the latter being available throughout the year. It is grown outdoors in the more northern states, where it is a very hardy perennial.

The acidity of rhubarb stalks, which is greater in plants grown in the open than in forced ones, is due to malic and oxalic acids. Oxalic acid is poisonous in quantity, but for ill effects you would have to eat a lot. The leaves, however, can be poisonous and should never be eaten. Boiling rhubarb leaves is an effective way of cleaning pans (even stewing the stalks makes the pan shine).

Rhubarb, when young and pink, is excellent. It is eaten raw by Eskimos in Alaska. It mixes well with other fruits, especially strawberries, and flavors such as ginger. *Angelica has also been much praised as a partner for rhubarb. One of its popular names, pie plant, indicates rhubarb's favorite use in the U.S. Forced rhubarb stems need only brief cooking, tougher field varieties take longer to become tender, and both need considerable sweetening to counteract the tart flavor if they are used as a dessert. To bake rhubarb, cut it in small pieces, sprinkle with sugar—½ cup (100 g) per 1 lb (450 g) rhubarb—and bake, covered, at 350°F (180°C) for about 25 minutes.

Resourceful American cooks, particularly the Pennsylvania Dutch, have found many other ways to utilize this easy-to-grow, heavy-producing plant: it is made into puddings, jelled molds, sherbet, marmalade, whips, and soufflés. In France rhubarb may be puréed to serve with fish, and rhubarb *khoresh*, a Persian stewlike sauce for rice, is made with beef cubes, chopped rhubarb, cinnamon, and lemon juice. A refreshing cold soup (or beverage) is made by cooking rhubarb in orange juice, sweetening with honey, then puréeing and chilling it. Before serving, add sauterne to taste and garnish with cantaloupe balls and sweet cherries or strawberries.

[*Rhubarb*—French: *rhubarbe;* German: *Rhabarber*; Italian: *rabarbaro;* Spanish: *ruibarbo*]

RHUBARB CHARD. *See* chard.

RIBOFLAVIN. *See* vitamin B$_2$.

RICE (*Oryza sativa*) is the staple grain of over half the world's population, although the tonnage of wheat produced each year is actually greater. Another species, red rice (*O. glaberrima*), which has a red bran layer, is grown in parts of West Africa. *Wild rice, however, is not closely related to rice.

Rice was taken into cultivation somewhere in southern Asia a very long time ago; it has certainly been in use in India and China for over 5000 years. However, it is a comparative newcomer to Mediterranean civilizations; it got to Egypt between 400 and 300 B.C. It gradually became established in the Middle East, and the Arabs took it with them to their colonies in Sicily, southern Italy, and Spain, but not until about A.D.

1000. Half a millennium later, in Elizabethan times, rice was being imported into England from Spain. It was made into porridges, puddings, and as Gerard wrote in his *Herbal,* "many other kindes of food is made with this graine as those that are skillful in cookerie can tell." In fact, he tried growing rice in his own garden in the year 1596, but not surprisingly it did not set seed "in that unseasonable year" (it was one of the worst in the 16th century), which suggested both that rice cannot be cultivated so far north and that the British climate has not altered much.

Today, Europe's most important rice-growing area is the Po Valley in northern Italy, where rice was first introduced in the mid-15th century by the Venetians, who were then powerful and wealthy from trading with the East. Rice is also grown in Portugal and Spain. More recently, cultivation has been pushed north into Hungary and to the Camargue in France. This, at present, is its limit; no variety can profitably be grown nearer the pole than 45°N.

In the U.S. rice was first successfully cultivated near Charleston, South Carolina, in 1694. American rice is still known as Carolina rice, although it now comes mainly from Texas, Louisiana, California, and Arkansas. Americans eat so little rice that despite producing only 1 percent of the world's crop, the U.S. is the leading rice exporter; over half the rice eaten in Britain is Carolina rice—an all-purpose rice distinguished for nothing. Some 90% of the world's rice is still grown and consumed in the monsoon regions of Asia.

It is not surprising that the natives of northern Europe and North America are comparatively ignorant about rice. Cookery writers often fail to specify the kind of rice for a dish and the result is likely to be pilaf coming out like pudding. In India alone, there are between 300 and 400 major rice varieties in cultivation, and over 1000 all told are grown there. The world total is said by some experts to be over 10,000 varieties. Anyone from the south of India should be able to recognize at least 20 sorts in the bazaar, rices which differ not only in such obvious characters as whether they are long- or short-grain, polished or unpolished, raw or parboiled, but also in color, translucency, smell, age, cooking quality, and, of course, price. If the shopper in India does not know a particular type and quality, then the stall-keeper certainly will. The same rice expertise exists in Southeast Asia, China, and Japan, and to some extent extends into the Middle East and even to Italy, where rice is preferred to pasta in the parts north of the Po. Selection of rice elsewhere is a hit-or-miss business when neither the buyer not the seller is expert. In general all one can say is that what the shops call "long-grained rice" is intended to cook with grains separate, although length of grain is not an infallible criterion. Some very long-grained varieties cook mushy and some of the finest pilaf rices have small, round grains.

Varieties. Rice in its natural state, after the husks have been removed, has a brown or reddish brown skin and is usually known as unpolished, unpearled, or brown rice. It has a stronger taste and is more easily digested than white, pearled rice, but it also takes longer to cook. Unpolished rice can be nice, at least as a change.

However, most people prefer white rice, even though brown rice is greatly superior in food value. Even Confucius liked his rice white. In his time, as it still is in many places, this was produced by hand-pounding until most but not quite all of the skin was removed from the grain. When machines took over to "pearl" rice, they did a much more thorough job, and rice eaters began to suffer from beriberi. This disease was subsequently shown to be due to a deficiency of thiamine (vitamin B_1), which had been lost with the rice skin. Pearled rice also loses protein and oil; it is usually known as polished rice, although real polished rice is actually polished with talc or chalk and glucose after pearling. This makes the grains shine but reduces the nutritional value even more.

Parboiled rice is a newer development designed to improve nutritional quality and yet give a product less coarse than brown rice. It will be met with in countries where rice is the staple food (and FAO nutrition experts abound). Parboiled rice has been steamed in the husk in impregnate the grain with some of the nutrients. This makes the taste rather peculiar, and parboiled rice is likely to have a characteristic smell which many people do not like. It is important only to those who subsist mainly on rice.

Genetic variation, breeding, and selection have produced thousands of rice varieties, but plant breeders are mainly concerned with heavy-cropping varieties geared to particular soils and conditions. Unfortunately, high yield does not often go with fine quality. In any case, opinions vary in different parts of the world as to what is good rice, and dishes may need a certain rice with special qualities. Most people want a rice which, with a modicum of care, cooks so that the grains do not stick together. However, a few dishes need an absorbent, tender, or even sticky grain for success.

The way a rice cooks depends on the relative amounts of various forms of starch in the grain and especially on the percentage of amylose. A rice with at least 25% amylose is preferred in most countries, though not in Indonesia or in the Philippines. If there is less than 20% amylose, the rice cooks sticky—some of the best flinty pilaf rices have 30% amylose or more.

Rices vary in temperature at which the starch grains swell irreversibly; it will be somewhere between 156°F (69°C) and 167°F (75°C)—well below boiling. They also vary in the quantity of water they absorb. Dogmatic recipes are misleading, since no two rices cook in an identical way. In general, rice absorbs between its own volume—cup for cup—and twice its volume of water, but I once bought a very costly Saudi Arabian variety of rice from a Bedouin trader and found to my amazement that it absorbed no less than nine times its volume of water and would not cook properly with any less.

Not only the variety but the age of a rice has much influence on the way it cooks. The grains of freshly harvested rice cook more quickly, absorb less water, and stick rather more easily than those of older rice of the same variety. In India, it is claimed that new rice is not easily digested, and fine pilaf rice is sometimes matured for many years. On the other hand, in Japan new rice is eagerly sought for special dishes. There, November rice, freshly harvested, tastes best. Country people living in towns send home for sacks of early rice from their district. The very word for a meal is *gohan,* meaning rice, and Japanese don't feel they have eaten without a bowl of rice. Moist new rice—*shin-mai*—needs less water, and as the year goes on, more water is required in cooking.

Washing. It is sometimes said that rice should not be washed before cooking unless it is very dirty and that even then it should be washed only with a damp cloth. True, washing has been proved to result in a slight loss of nutrients. Even so, logic and consensus say that rice should be washed to remove milling and polishing dust, which tends to cook to a glue and sticks the grains together. This is disastrous when cooking is by the total-absorption method (*see below*).

Soaking. Some authorities advocate soaking rice in water for from 30 minutes to several hours; others are equally adamant that soaking spoils the flavor. I hesitate to be dogmatic here—some varieties possibly need soaking, but it is not generally advised except for pilaf. Soaked rice cooks more quickly, which helps keep the grains separate. Naturally, soaked rice absorbs less water in cooking.

Oiling. Some cooks rub rice with oil to coat the grains in the hope that this will prevent them from sticking together. Others put butter in the cooking water. Oiling may make a marginal difference to poor rice, but it is surely better to buy one of good quality; such tricks then become unnecessary.

Frying. For pilaf, paella, and similar dishes, dry rice is fried in oil or butter until it becomes translucent before liquid is added. The oil impregnates the outer layers of the grains and helps keep them separate.

Steaming and fluffing. In many countries, when cooking is completed (or almost completed), the rice is left on a low heat to "steam" or "fluff" until it looks like blossoms. Not all varieties of rice will blossom in this way. Julia Child recommends the following system for producing fluffy rice: sprinkle rice into a large kettle of boiling water, stir, and boil uncovered until rice is just tender but not quite fully cooked; fluff under running hot water, then wrap the rice in a damp cheesecloth, place in a colander over boiling water, cover, and steam until tender. This is an effective method for most U.S. rices, and its advantage is that the rice can be parboiled ahead of time, then steamed before serving.

Drying. Allied to steaming is the drying and resting of rice, which is especially necessary after cooking by the excess-water method (*see below*). This is done, with the lid on, over a very low heat. A cloth tied around the lid, or a special cushion to act as a lid (as is used in Turkey), will absorb steam and avoid wet drips from condensation. Or turn the lid upside down and put a few glowing pieces of charcoal in the top as they do in India. The pan may also be put in a low oven.

General principles. Arguments over the best way to cook rice can be vitriolic, since half the cooks in the world are preparing it daily in their own kitchens. For instance, most Orientals put no salt in the water—they say it ruins the rice—but elsewhere rice cooked with no salt is considered insipid. One school of thought says that once the pan boils, it is ruinous to lift the lid even to see if the rice is done, but rice is often cooked with no lid on. Some cooks start rice in cold water; others say the water must be boiling. Many, but not all, agree that once the water comes to the boil the heat must be lowered. Cooked rice may be rinsed with cold water, hot water, or not at all. How are we to judge who is right when even the hardness or softness of the water affects the outcome? For beginners, here is some practical advice:

Buy the correct rice for the dish you wish to prepare, although you may have to locate a shop of the right ethnic variety in order to find it.

Always measure rice by the cup (not by weight) before washing it if you are going to cook it by the total-absorption method. Allow ½–1 cup per person (1 cup is safer if you are making curry).

Do not soak the rice unless you are quite sure that it is an exceptional variety or the recipe needs it, as does a pilaf made in the classical manner.

Whichever the method of cooking, always use a big pan to allow the rice to expand and to lie as shallow as possible. Otherwise the bottom layers will be compacted by the weight of rice on top; the lower layers will also cook faster than the top ones and will become soggy.

Excess-Water Method

Put the washed rice into plenty of boiling water, salted for most dishes, but not if it is intended to accompany curry. Turn down the heat when the pan comes to the boil and watch carefully, squeezing a grain between the fingers—or tasting it—every few minutes to begin with, but almost continuously as soon as it seems to be nearly ready. Poor rice is particularly prone to going from just right to a sticky mass in a few seconds. The moment the last trace of hard center has gone—too soon is better than too late—drain quickly, preferably in a wide, flat sieve and using a light hand. To dump it heavily in a conical strainer would lump it together. Immediately run it for a few seconds under the cold tap (hot water is sometimes used for rinsing cooked rice, but cold water immediately stops its cooking). While the rice is draining, rinse and dry the pan, put some butter or oil in the bottom, and put the pan on the heat. Return the rice gently to the pan. Wrap a clean cloth around the lid and cover. Turn down the heat to the lowest possible level and let the rice steam and dry for

10 minutes. Alternatively put the pan in a low oven. When serving, turn the rice out and fluff it gently with a fork.

Total-Absorption Method

If the rice is wet from washing, allow a cup of cold water for each cup of rice, although the precise quantity required depends on the variety and age of the rice. Put the pan on high heat. The moment the water comes to the boil, turn the flame down to a gentle boil and, as the water is absorbed, turn it even lower. You can transfer it to a low oven. Leave it until all the water has been absorbed and the rice has expanded. Then fluff the rice up with a fork and serve. This is by far the better method to use with good rice, but it is risky with sticky, poor rice—after the first minute of boiling, the grains are always in contact with each other and have a good chance of sticking together.

Besides being boiled as a basic food to be served alone or with meat and vegetables, rice is an ingredient of soups and casseroles. In Asia it is made into sweet dishes, noodles, wine, and vinegar. Rice flour is used in pasta, pastries, and sweet cakes, or combined with other flours to make bread.

Indian unpolished rice, *ukad,* is reddish and is soaked and ground to make batter for *dosas, idlis, conjee,* or other dishes in which the rice does not have to retain separate grains when cooked. For pilafs and *birianis* the best long-grain rice—sold as, e.g., Basmati or Dehra Dun rice—is a must.

A great deal of rice is eaten in the Middle East, but nowhere does it reach the perfection it does in Iran, where rice is sold in many grades and is cooked by the absorption method, often with butter added: this fries a layer next to the pan so that skillful cooks can turn out rice in a molded pile, golden brown on the outside but with the rice inside so perfect that it drops to pieces in snow-white grains the moment the golden skin is broken.

Italy's rice is graded for different cooking purposes: *superfino,* with large, long grains, includes *arborio* (for top-quality risotto) and *carnaroli; fino,* long and tapering, is used for risotta and Italian dishes of rice mixed with seafood and vegetables; *semifino,* with oval grains, is used for minestrone and is sticky enough to hold together molds and timbales; *commune,* the cheapest rice, has a small, tender, round grain that cooks to mush and is used for soups and puddings.

Spanish rice, *arroz,* is generally poor-quality, short-grained pudding rice; only recently has fairly good *arroz de grano largo* (long-grain rice) been available in shops. In Spain, rice is usually flavored and colored with saffron or cooked with fried onions and tomato (soffritto). Often it is fried and cooked with other ingredients as in that most Spanish dish, paella.

[*Rice*—French: *riz;* German: *Reis;* Italian: *riso;* Spanish: *arroz*]

RICE BEAN (*Phaseolus calceratus*). A small bean of Indian origin, rather similar to the *mung but distinguished from it by a prominent white hilum (scar) raised above the surface and crinkled at the edges. The beans may be yellow, brown, maroon and black, or mottled. This bean is particularly grown in Nepal and Assam. The Indian name is *sutari* or *meth* (*shiltong* in Nepal). It is regarded as inferior to mung, but it contains more calcium than any other bean.

RICING is forcing starchy and mealy foods, such as potatoes and chestnuts, through a perforated device, from which the food falls in a light mound slightly resembling a heap of rice.

RIGATONI. *See* pasta.

ROASTING. Meat was originally roasted by turning it in front of a glowing fire. In other words, it was cooked by radiant heat in free air. The meat was either turned on a spit or suspended, and there was a drip pan underneath so that the juices were caught and used for basting. Grilled or broiled meat was cooked on a gridiron over glowing coals.

Charring could occur when some of the drippings were wasted, and the meat took the smell of fire (and in most cases of burning fat). Meat cooked in an oven was baked meat. Meat baked in an old-fashioned oven was not subjected to intense radiant heat, and since the ovens were not ventilated, the meat was cooked by hot, moist heat. This moister heat means that oven-cooked meat requires very little basting, while truly roasted meat must be basted almost continuously to prevent it from drying up.

Roasted meats now have to be divided into two classes—those cooked before an open fire and those cooked in an oven. There are not many kitchens, except in country places, where the old-fashioned open fire is now in use. Nor can we wonder at this, for the disadvantages of this way of cooking are many: the great cost of fuel due to the large fire that is necessary; the discomfort of those in charge, since incessant basting is required; and the loss of weight caused by the melting of the fat and the evaporation of the juices. Yet it must be said that there is no other way of cooking meat quite equal to roasting it before the fire. Surrounded by air and exposed to the direct heat of the fire, it has a flavor distinctly its own, which can only be described as "tasting of the fire."

Much that is called roast meat today is in fact baked. The electric roasting spits that are now becoming common do a good job of roasting food in the correct manner.

[*Roasting* —French: *rôtir;* German: *Braten;* Italian: *arrostive;* Spanish: *asarse*]

ROBALO. *See* snook.

ROCAMBOLE. *See* onion.

ROCK CANDY. *See* sugar.

ROCKET, roquette, arugula, rugula, or rocket cress (*Eruca sativa*) is a salad plant that is sometimes neglected but is commonly used in Italy. It grows wild in much of Eu-rope, but cultivated varieties are less violently flavored, with larger, more tender leaves and excellent potential. Rocket has a peculiar, pungent flavor, unmistakably a cruci-

ROCKET

fer—a member of the cabbage family—but very original. It grows easily from seed and is an excellent addition to green salads.

[*Rocket*—French: *roquette;* German: *Rauke, Raukenkohl, Senfkohl;* Italian: *ruchetta;* Spanish: *oruga*]

ROCK LOBSTER. *See langouste.*

ROCK SALMON or **rock eel.** *See* shark.

ROE is the ovary (hard roe) or testis (soft roe or milt) of a fish. Roes are very often a delicacy, as for instance are those of herring. Some expensive products are made with roes, including *caviar, *tarama, *botargo, and *smoked cod roe. Milt herring is preserved in a sauce containing the soft roe. However, roes from unknown fish are to be avoided: a few from Arctic and tropical waters are poisonous.

Roes from cod, haddock, and other white fish are usually prepared by first parboiling in salted water, then either broiling or sautéing in butter. Or they may be poached and chilled to serve with cold fish or in salads.

[*Roe*—French: *oeufs de poisson, laitance;* German: *Rogen, Fischlaich;* Italian: *nova latte di pesce;* Spanish: *hueva*]

ROLLMOP. *See* herring.

ROSE (species of *Rosa*) is not of great culinary importance, except in the Middle East, where rose water as a flavoring appears in many sweet dishes and rose petals are made into jam (which is sickly sweet). All rose petals are edible if no poison sprays have been used on them, but they are not always very aromatic. Rose-flavored liqueurs are made, notably in Bulgaria, but most of these concoctions are too sweet for Western palates. However, the list of uses goes all the way from rose vinegar (flavored by having the petals macerated in it) through crystallized rose petals for decoration and rose-flavored candy and butter.

The method of making rose-flavored butter is a good example of enfleurage, a process used in the perfume industry for capturing delicate scents. A pat of butter loosely wrapped in paper is embedded in a pot of fragrant fresh rose petals and kept in a cool place overnight. The butter traps the rose scent just as surely as it would trap the scent of kippers if it were left uncovered near them in the refrigerator. Rose petals are also put into cherry pie, and rose brandy is made by infusing them.

Rose hips, especially those of the wild rose (*R. canina*), were in the past used to make preserves and even eaten as a cooked fruit. A wine can also be made by fermenting rose hips. The hairs surrounding the seeds inside the fruit are irritating to the intestines and should be carefully washed or strained away. Hip jelly is good, and so is rose-hip syrup, which came into prominence during World War II, when it was realized that rose hips were a valuable and neglected source of vitamin C.

[*Rose*—French: *rose;* German: *Rose;* Italian: *rosa;* Spanish: *rosa*]

ROSE FAMILY. The family Rosaceae, which includes more than 2000 species, is of enormous gastronomic importance. Apart from the *rose itself, which contributes its petals as well as its hips, and the *burnet, of which the leaves are used, the family is notable for its fruit—it is incomparably the most important group in this respect, at least in temperate zones. Some of the fruit are drupes, with a single hard-cased seed (the stone) and a fleshy outer layer; they may be valued for their stones, as in the *almond, or for their flesh, as in the *apricot, *peach, *cherry, and *plum. Others are pomes with a group of small seeds, as in the *apple, *pear, *quince, *medlar, and the smaller but similar fruit of the *rowan. The genus *Rubus,* which includes the *blackberry and *raspberry, has compound fruits made of a cluster of small drupes or drupelets. The *strawberry is very different in structure: it is not the outer layer that swells but the inside or receptacle to which the seeds are attached—hence the position of the seeds studding the outside of the fruit.

ROSEMARY. One of the commonest wild plants of dry Mediterranean hillsides, rosemary (*Rosmarinus officinalis*) is very strongly aromatic with a camphor overtone. It is a

ROSEMARY

perennial herb that must be treated as an annual in cold climates, though it grows well indoors year round. Many varieties are available, including prostrate rosemary (*R. prostratus*), with a sprawling habit that makes it an attractive houseplant, and Corsican rosemary (*R. corsicus*), with narrower leaves and deep-blue flowers.

As a culinary herb, rosemary is much used in Italy and has in recent years become fashionable for flavoring lamb (an Italian custom), but it can be used with discretion in many dishes. Whether fresh or dried, rosemary has an assertive flavor. Fresh rosemary sprigs may be laid on top of roasts or vegetables to impart their flavor as they cook. The rather piny taste and fragrance of rosemary make it ideal for seasoning game, especially venison, and it also goes well with pork and veal. Slits can be made in meat to hold garlic and rosemary sprigs as it roasts. Pungent rosemary vinegar for robust salads of dandelions and other greens is easily made by steeping sprigs of the herb in red wine or cider vinegar. When grilling meat or strong-flavored fish outdoors, you can throw rosemary branches on the hot coals to add their fragrance and flavor to the food as it cooks.

[*Rosemary*—French: *romarin;* German: *Rosmarin, Rosmarein;* Italian: *rosmarino, ramerino;* Spanish: *romero, romario*]

ROWAN and **sorb.** The rowan or mountain ash (*Sorbus acuparia*) is a common tree all over Europe except in dry, limy soils, and in North America two related species, *S. americana* and *S. scopulina*, which has larger fruit, are known as mountain ash. Because a number of garden varieties are grown for decoration, the berries are available in both town and country. Although too tart and bitter to eat, they make a fine jelly—either alone or with an equal quantity of apples. Rowan jelly is a splendid and traditional accompaniment to venison.

ROWAN JELLY

Wash the berries and put them in a pan with enough water to cover them. Simmer gently until the water is red and bitter.

Strain the juice through a jelly bag without squeezing (squeezing, which is sometimes recommended, makes a cloudy jelly). For every pt (600 ml) of juice add 1 lb (450 g) of sugar and boil until it jells. Put in jars. This is sometimes left to mature for 2 years before use.

Rowan berries were also a popular ingredient in country wines, and Samuel Pepys mentions in his diary that he had found ale brewed with rowan berries the best he had ever tasted. Today, with the new vogue for home winemaking, rowan berries are even being dried for use by winemakers and home brewers who are not able to pick their own.

The sorb apple or service tree (*Sorbus domestica*) is a close relative. The sorb is a native of southern Europe but is naturalized farther north and, unlike the rowan, is cultivated for its fruit, which looks like small green apples or pears. When unripe, it is exceptionally acid. A number of named varieties with either round or pear-shaped fruit are grown, especially in Liguria and Sicily. Good varieties can be eaten as fruit, but they are also used for making a drink, which is not very alcoholic and is similar to cider. They are also dried in the sun and threaded on strings. In countries farther north they are "bletted" like *medlars.

In North America, what are called serviceberries (*Amelanchier florida*) belong to another related genus of the same family, *Amelanchier*, which has some 20 species including juneberry or shadberry (*A. canadensis*) and swamp sugar pear (*A. intermedia*). Serviceberries have excellent fruit, which was once much used in North America by the Indians and is still gathered and made into pies, muffins, and sauce by knowledgeable country people.

Another cultivated small, almost berrylike rose family fruit of Europe is the *azerole* or Naples medlar (*Crataegus azarolus*), a native of the Mediterranean and western Asia, which has also been introduced into North America. It is, in almost all respects, just like a large version of the hawthorn (*C. monogyna*), with fruit about the size of a crab apple that is yellow, white, or red, according to the cultivated variety. The flesh is crisp, yellowish, tasty, and perfumed, with 3–4 hard seeds. The Naples medlar is eaten as a fresh fruit or is made into jam.

[*Rowan*—French: *sorbier des oiseaux;* German: *Eberesche;* Italian: *frassino di montagna;* Spanish: *serbal*]

RUE. This old medicinal herb, a member of the same botanical family as oranges and lemons, is common over most of southern Europe. There are three species—common rue (*Ruta graveolens*), fringed rue (*R. chalepensis*), and mountain rue (*R. montana*)—with slight flower differences and varying degrees of woodiness. There are also a number of garden varieties. All have the rather nasty rue smell, but wild plants from dry Mediterranean hillsides are particularly strong and repulsive. Rue is sometimes used in very discreet amounts as a culinary herb. It has been recommended for use with eggs and cream cheese, and in vegetable juice cocktails and tea. It is also put as a flavoring into *grappa* and is the herb you see in the bottles labeled *con ruta* (with rue). Medicinal effects are varied and stimulating, but rue is poisonous in quantity, and some people even get skin rashes from touching its leaves.

[*Rue*—French: *nie odorante;* German: *Raute, Gartenraute, Weinkraut;* Italian: *ruta;* Spanish: *ruda*]

RUGULA. *See* rocket.

RUM is a spirit distilled from the fermented leavings of the cane sugar industry: the molasses, the scum which rises after liming, and other residues. The product varies between white cane spirit—a firewater that does not merit the description "rum"—to the rich, dark flavorful rums containing large amounts of fruity esters. All the best rum starts as a West Indian product, although it is made in many other places—in fact, anywhere that sugar cane grows. Many of the rums, such as those of Mexico, are light and without character. Others, like that distilled in Madeira, are used to fortify wine. The rums of importance are as follows:

Jamaica produces the most highly flavored rums, with the exception of those from Martinique, although they are lighter than they were in the last century. Jamaican rums are made to high standards under very strict control and are probably the best to use in sweet dishes.

Martinique makes excellent, highly flavored rums much used in France.

The U.S. produces more rum than any other country. New England rum was made in colonial days from molasses shipped up from the West Indies, and taxes on it were resented in Boston just as much as the tax on tea. Though excellent, the flavor of American rum is less refined than that of good Jamaican.

Barbados makes a medium rum with many additions other than those natural to a cane-sugar product. They may include wine, raisins, and bitter almond.

Demerara. Named, like the sugar, from a district near Georgetown, Guyana, this is a very fruity rum with many additions, such as plums, raisins, caramel, and spices.

Cuba is famous particularly for daiquiris, and produces light-colored rums, with natural "rum" flavors removed by filtration and a light new flavoring of fruit, bay, sugar, and secret ingredients added. The colorless Bacardi rum (the sort usually made into daiquiris) originated in Cuba but is now made in Brazil.

Rum was a common kitchen ingredient in the last century, when fruity rums were particularly in fashion. It is still used in confectionery all over Europe and is a better flavoring than brandy in most cases. Less commonly, rum is used with meat, fowl, and fish. It goes excellently with shellfish, as fishermen in Spain have discovered, and it is used in one of the six courses of the famous *langostinara* of San Carlos de la Rapita at the mouth of the Ebro River. (In this fabulous specialty, the diner is served in succession with dishes of the superb local *langostinos,* possibly the world's best giant prawn, each cooked in a different way.)

LANGOSTINOS AL RON

Cook the *langostinos* on the *plancha* (i.e., the hot top of the stove or in a dry frying pan) until they are just dry. Then fry in olive oil, salt to taste, and flame in rum.

[*Rum*—French: *rhum;* German: *Rum;* Italian: *rum;* Spanish: *ron*]

RUNNER BEAN (*Phaseolus coccineus*) originated in South America and was brought to Europe as a decorative plant—there are varieties with vermilion, scarlet, and white flowers—but it has for long been the most popular green bean grown in British vegetable gardens. Runners are perennials which are grown as annuals in cold climates where they are killed by winter frost. They are nearly always eaten as green beans. Runners are climbers (pole beans) and are not usually grown commercially for dried seed, but if left on the plant until they are ripe, the beans are excellent. The flavor of runners is somewhat stronger than that of French beans.

RUSH NUT. *See* chufa nut.

RUTABAGA. *See* turnip.

RYE (*Secale cereale*) is a recent cereal compared to wheat or barley. It is thought to have been first noticed as a weed in corn fields in the arid areas around Mount Ararat, that snowy cone you pass on the road going east from Erzerum into Iran, where Noah's ark is supposed to have been grounded after the flood. The usefulness of rye rests on its ability to tolerate cold conditions in which wheat would be uncertain. It also has a better breadmaking quality than barley, since it contains a sufficiency of gluten. Up to the mid-19th century, it was the staple bread grain in much of northern Europe—in Germany, Poland, and particularly Russia—and was much used by the early settlers in North America. In those days, people considered rye bread inferior to any sort of wheat, and it is only in recent years that it has come to be valued. Perhaps one reason why it was denigrated in the past was that with rye there was always danger of poisoning from the *mold ergot, which is now very unlikely.

Rye flour is a dirty gray color, although it is frequently lightened by mixing with wheat flour, sometimes with barley flour, and with corn flour in America. It is the flour of black bread (*Schwartzbrod*), pumpernickel, and some crisp bread. The texture of rye bread is close and the taste is characteristic and usually slightly sour, partly because of the sourdough method of rising it, which takes longer than is necessary with wheat bread. Unfortunately, good rye bread is now difficult to find, since tastes have changed. The market in Innsbruck, where I used to buy beautiful, round polished rye loaves to take to the mountains (rye bread keeps better than wheat bread), now sells a very inferior product. Rye bread is an essential in making Scandinavian open sandwiches, and it goes best with German and eastern European sausage. The grain is the basis for rye *whiskey (although it is cut with other grain) and is used for making beer in Russia as well as gin in Holland and some sorts of vodka.

[*Rye*—French: *seigle;* German *Roggen;* Italian: *segala;* Spanish: *centeno*]

S

SACCHARIN ($C_6H_4COSO_2NH$) was discovered by accident in 1879 by chemists at Johns Hopkins University who were doing research on the derivatives of toluene, a constituent of coal tar. One of them found that his food tasted sweet and also found that sweetness on his hands, although he had washed them before eating. Tracing the cause back to the experiments led the scientists to identify saccharin. It is insoluble in water, and saccharin tablets are made either of its soluble sodium salt or of a mixture of saccharin and bicarbonate of soda which react together when moistened. Either way, it is sodium saccharin that sweetens your cup of tea. Although estimates of its sweetness vary, it is around 500 times as sweet as cane sugar and more than 10 times as sweet as *cyclamates.

Saccharin (along with cyclamates) has been suspected of being linked with bladder cancer and thus banned in some countries. The U.S. Food and Drug Administration is continuing its studies on saccharin while requiring manufacturers that use it to declare so on a warning label. The main disadvantage of saccharin is its unpleasant lingering aftertaste, which is said to be caused largely by impurities that can be avoided in newer methods of synthesis. Saccharin is a substitute only for the sweetness of sugar and has none of its nutritional or preservative qualities. It passes unchanged through the body, being excreted in the urine.

[*Saccharin*—French: *saccharine;* German: *Saccharin;* Italian: *saccarina;* Spanish: *sacarino*]

SAFFLOWER or saffron thistle (*Carthamus tinctorius*) comes from India but is unknown as a wild plant. It can be grown quite well in temperate areas. The orangered flowers contain a dye (carthamin) which may be used to color food and as a substitute for saffron, although this false saffron does not have the proper flavor. The seeds have greater commercial importance as a source of safflower oil, a good kitchen oil. It is often mixed with other oils in proprietary brands but can also be bought separately. The seeds and even the leaves of the plant are edible.

[*Safflower*—French: *carthame;* German: *Saflor;* Italian: *cartamo;* Spanish: *cartamo*]

SAFFRON consists of the stigmas of the saffron crocus (*Crocus sativus*). It is an ancient spice, with a peculiar, unique flavor and a strong yellow color. Nowadays, it is enormously expensive, because of the hard work involved in extracting it from the flowers. Luckily, only a pinch is needed to flavor any dish; the dried stigmas are first soaked in a little milk or water for 15 minutes or so to loosen the dye.

Powdered saffron is almost always a dye (such as carthamin from *safflower), a cosmetic with no flavor that is best avoided.

Cheap saffron does not exist, and anything masquerading as such is almost certainly the stamens of some other yellow flower, such as marigold. Where saffron is needed, as in

SAFFRON

Mediterranean fish soups and some Kashmiri dishes, there is no substitute for it. There are versions of Spanish paella which use no saffron; Spanish restaurant paellas frequently use dye.

[*Saffron*—French: *safran;* German: *Safrangewürz;* Italian: *zafferano;* Spanish: *azafrán*]

SAFFRON THISTLE. *See* safflower.

SAGE. Garden sage (*Salvia officinalis*), a perennial, is a native of southern Europe.

SAGE

There are many culinary varieties: pineapple sage (*S. rutilans*) is good in punch; clary sage (*S. sclarea*), a biennial, has fragrant flowers that make a good tea—and all that can be said about the numerous sages is that they are pungent. Their flavor is powerful, with overtones of camphor.

Sage dries well, and it is frequently used in stuffings, especially with pork.

[*Sage*—French: *sauge;* German: *Salbei;* Italian: *salvia;* Spanish: *salvia*]

SAGO is virtually pure starch extracted from the sago palm (*Metroxylon sagu*) and to a lesser extent from other plants (palms and cycads) which develop a similar starchy pith. The sago palm grows in swampy places in southern Asia. It looks like a typical palm but has the peculiarity that just before it flowers (at about 15 years old) it builds up a large reserve of starch to be drawn on for the reproductive effort. At this point, man intervenes, cuts down the palm, extracts the pith from the stem, grinds it up, washes out the starch with water, and allows it to settle. After the clear top water has been poured off, the wet starchy paste can be dried into a flour or sieved to give the well-known pearl sago. Sago is sometimes used in place of pasta in broths, and various sweets are made from it. In parts of the Orient, it has more uses, although mainly in its floury form, which cooks to a glassy starch paste, very like *arrowroot. In South India, it is used in various sun-dried wafers and deep-fried vegetarian patties, such as *vattala, pakoras, vadas,* and *chakli.* Sago is also used throughout Southeast Asia.

[*Sago*—French: *sagou;* German: *Sago;* Italian: *sagù;* Spanish: *sagú*]

SAKE is Japanese rice wine. It usually has an alcohol content of about 15% (like a very strong European wine) and is served warm. Sake is a necessary ingredient in Japanese cooking. A sweet, less strong rice wine known as *mirin* is used only for cooking (except in a New Year ritual) and is often mixed in equal quantity with soy sauce. A substitute for sake in cooking is a dry sherry slightly diluted with water.

SALAD. By far the most popular of the salad vegetables is *lettuce, but there are many others, notably the various types of *chicory and *cress. One of the most useful, and a popular winter salad in European countries, is lamb's lettuce or corn salad (*see* lettuce).

A plant I particularly like in salads is *rocket, and others are fond of tender leaves of raw *spinach, acid-tasting *sorrel, *dandelion leaves, and *lamb's-quarters. A garden flower with peppery-tasting leaves that can be good in salad is *nasturtium.

Dozens of wild herbs with pungent, peppery flavors can be used in salads, especially crucifers such as the cresses. Milder flavors come from the salad *burnet and the small new buds of hawthorn in spring.

Some people like to mix their lettuce with wet tomato or purple-staining beets, but neither is very aesthetic. A careful admixture of other leaves and herbs will make something beautiful as well as refreshing and interesting—salads repay a little experiment.

The most primitive salads are not dressed at all—they rely only on the flavors of the salad materials. A meal in an Iranian village stands out in my mind. Rice and kebabs were served with a bowl of onion tops and branches of tarragon.

The word "salad" is derived from the Latin *sal* (salt), and the simplest salad dressing is salt. A dressing of olive oil, salt, and vinegar is also an ancient one. The vinegar to go with olive should be wine vinegar. Lemon juice, which some prefer as the souring agent, is much used in the Middle East, especially where wine is frowned on for religious reasons.

From simple beginnings, both salads and the dressings have increased in complexity, and by the beginning of this century cookery writers were mildly deploring the growing use of ready-made dressings bought from the grocer. Some of these dressings are quite good, but most dedicated cooks will want to make their own. The dressing of the salad at table can be part of the gastronomic ceremonial. The type of dressing to be used must depend on the ingredients in the salad. It is a subject that gives rise to strong prejudices. For instance, I dislike salads that are a bewildering mélange of ingredients dressed with a thick, heavy dressing, and I cannot understand anyone's finding such creamy treasure hunts stimulating.

OIL AND VINEGAR, VINAIGRETTE, OR FRENCH
DRESSING

The classic directions are to use 1 part wine vinegar to 3 parts olive oil. Salt is left to the salad mixer's discretion. The amount—according to the old Spanish saying—needs a wise man to determine. The oil should preferably be a good, light olive oil with a delicate flavor. Strong-tasting olive oils, such as the Spanish oil with the very respectable label *virgin*, are overwhelming. If you can't get good olive oil, it is best to turn to light seed or nut oils, which have little flavor (most of which is stripped out during refining). Avoid thick oils that tend to make salads greasy. The vinegar should preferably be a good wine vinegar, and should be chosen with some thought. Tarragon or other flavored vinegars are sometimes used. Cider vinegar has a distinctive taste which some people like better than that of wine vinegar. There are even said to be those who prefer malt vinegar, which in general is frowned upon.

For a simple lettuce salad, using a good olive oil, the usually recommended proportion of 3 parts oil to 1 part vinegar seems wrong, and something like 4 to 1 is better. Those who mix a salad with a flourish, by eye, with lots of splashing about, will usually find this is what they arrive at by instinct if they pour the oil with some generosity. Mixing the salad with the dressing may need to be done some time before the meal for vegetables that need to absorb the dressing—beets, celery, and celeriac, for instance—but a green salad should always be mixed at the last minute, very thoroughly.

This can be done with the hands, which is best for a large party, but then the process has to be done in the kitchen. Salad bowls are often too small and badly designed for mixing at the table. Sloping sides tend to make the leaves slide up over the edge. They discourage efficient mixing and encourage the spread of salad over the table. A fairly deep, straight-sided container is better: you can mix any salad thoroughly in it. Garlic is best introduced by rubbing it on a slice of bread and laying it on the bottom of the bowl under the salad, but you will then need a little more dressing—the bread absorbs some of it.

SOULIE

One of the simplest dressings I know was always made by an old Irish friend who did not know where the name came from but said it was traditional in his family. It is useful for anyone who does not like oil. My friend heated vinegar in a large spoon with some sugar, and when the sugar had dissolved poured the hot sweet-sour soulie over the salad.

BACON FAT DRESSING

Dice about 4 oz (100 g) of lean bacon (according to the size of the salad) and fry it gently until it browns and the fat runs out of it. Then deglaze the pan with a tablespoon of vinegar, pour the mixture hot over the salad, and mix. This is particularly good for salads of slightly bitter ingredients, like chicory, dandelion, and spinach.

There are dozens of salad dressings on the market, mostly based on oil-water-vinegar emulsions with flavorings and stabilizers, and sometimes with starch and thickeners. Homemade creamy dressings can be based on *mayonnaise, fresh (or sour) cream, yogurt, or, as with boiled dressings, a cooked "custard" of egg, flour, and milk. With a modern blender, it is also easy to make creamy dressings (which will hold for a day) by emulsifying oil, water, and vinegar, using no more than mustard or garlic or both as a stabilizer, in the same way that egg yolk is used as a stabilizer in mayonnaise. For example, mix a heaped teaspoon of mustard with water and leave it to brew for 10 minutes. Meanwhile, temper some vinegar with sugar to taste, add salt, and put with the mustard in a blender. Blend in the oil, beginning with a few drops at a time, with the blender at full speed. Flavor with herbs if desired.

SALAME (plural *salami*). To many people, salame is one thing—a toughish, dry sausage which, when sliced, is dark red speckled with bits of white—but in Italy there are dozens of different types. Salame is made all over the world: fine types come from Hungary, Germany, and Denmark. Plenty of bad salame is also made, even in Italy, where there are scandals over plastic salame from time to time. However, when salame is good, it is very good and worth taking trouble to investigate.

First of all, it is worth mentioning cooked salame (*salame cotto*), which is an inferior product made from pork, or a mixture of meats not suitable for making raw salame. *Salame cotto* is relatively cheap and depends almost entirely on spices for its flavor. It is often dyed red to improve the color. The more familiar raw salame (*salame crudo*) is made generally of lean and fat pork, in which case the Italians indicate this with a metal tag bearing the letter S, but sometimes with the addition of beef or other meats (marked SB on the tag). Since salame is eaten raw, its safety depends on the action of the salt, and thus requires maturation for a long enough time to kill undesirable microorganisms.

Almost every district in Italy has its own variety, and there is great variation in flavor and quality—in the toughness of the meat, the size of grain, the texture, color, and taste. Even within a local idiom, there is variation. For instance, salame labeled *nostrani* (meaning locally made) is often coarser in texture than the usual type for the district. In general, the salame of southern Italy is likely to be more highly spiced than that from northern parts of the country and to contain red pepper. Some sort of classification is possible into lightly and strongly flavored types.

The lightly flavored types are those that most of us are familiar with: the Milanese salami (*crespone* and *bindone*), and the Hungarian, Tuscan and Alpine varieties. The expensive salame from Felino, near Parma, is made from the same quality meat as Parma hams and contains no spices except a very little pepper. It is not even matured for very long (2–3 months) and has a beautiful sweet taste. Another famous salame in this category comes from around Varzi, a town in the province of Pavia.

Strongly flavored types of salame include the Genoese (of pork, veal, and pork fat), Piedmontese, Neapolitan, Sicilian, and Sardinian, as well as *salame d'aglio* (garlic salame) and *salametto*. There are excellent strong types from Yugoslavia, which also produces mild types similar to those from Hungary. Among the more off-beat salami are the *finocchiona* and its smaller cousin, the *finocchietto*, of Florence, which are flavored with wild fennel seed. The *salame di cinghiale* of wild boar is very finely minced and usually contains sugar as well as salt and spices. *Salame di fegato* is made of liver with salt, spices, and white wine. Many other flavorings for salame are used in Italy and elsewhere. Some of these, such as crushed black peppercorns, are applied externally, while others are added to the contents (as in the orange-colored Hungarian paprika salame.).

American salame comes in German and kosher as well as Italian varieties. Milano has a fine texture, while Genoa, which is characteristically corded for hanging, is coarser. Salame should be sliced fine for an hors d'oeuvre, and it is thoughtful to remove the threads of skin, especially if the slices are being put into buttered rolls to make a sandwich.

SALICYLIC ACID occurs naturally in some plants, notably in birch bark and in the leaves of wintergreen, where it is in the form of methyl salicylate (the main component of oil of wintergreen). However, it is normally synthesized. It is used as a *preservative, but it is illegal in food in many countries, including the U.S.

[*Salicylic acid*—French: *acide salicylique;* German: *Salizylsauer;* Italian: *acido salicilico;* Spanish: *salicilico*]

SALMON originally meant only *Salmo salar,* a species which spawns and is caught in the rivers of Europe, from Norway to Spain, in Iceland, in one river in Greenland, and in Canada and the East Coast of the U.S. The name is also given to many closely related fish from other parts of the world, some of which are commonly frozen or canned, and to a few that are unrelated such as the Indian salmon, the *rawas* (*Eleutheronema tetradactylus*). These, like the salmon, are oily fish.

The true salmon is a splendid fish that normally weighs 9–26 lb (4–12 Kg) or more. North American and western European salmon live their sea lives somewhere off the coast of Greenland but ascend the rivers to spawn, each salmon returning to the river where it was born. Some salmon come upriver in the spring (spring fish) and may be caught in January (for example, rod fishing on the River Tay in Scotland opens on January 15 and netting some 3 weeks later), but other salmon do not run upriver until the summer or early autumn. None, however, spawn until the autumn. The closed season varies from river to river. Although regulations vary, salmon may not usually be sold (even if it has been caught legally on rod and line) during the season when commercial netting is not permitted. At such times only frozen or imported salmon will be available. Some salmon migrate to the sea at the end of their first year, but others remain for 2 or even 3 years. Before going to sea, the young salmon become silvery and are then known as smolts. Some fish remain in the sea for only a year before returning to their river to spawn; these are excellent small salmon of 3¼–6½ lb (1½–3 Kg), known as grilse. Only when a fish has lived for 2–3 years in the sea does it return as a fully grown salmon. After salmon have spawned they are known as kelts. They are thin and useless, since they have starved themselves during their time of breeding in the river. Some kelts make it back to the sea in December and return for a second and, more rarely, a third time to breed, but many die after only one spawning.

If you can afford it, you may eat fresh salmon happily from February through the summer to the end of August, the best fish being by repute the first spring fish. For the rest of the year, though, salmon will come chilled or deep-frozen from Canada, Norway, or Japan. Fresh salmon should indeed be as fresh as possible, because after a few hours the creamy "curd" disappears and the delicate flavor begins to go. Like other fresh fish, it is stiff, shiny, and bright. The best fish are said to have large "shoulders" and a small head. Most buyers, though, will be thinking of just a cut from a fish, in which case the middle part is the best.

Salmon is scaled and cleaned in the normal manner before cooking. It may be poached for roughly 10 minutes per lb (20 minutes per Kg) plus 20 minutes extra in a court bouillon, but the water must never boil—a trick to make certain of this is to take out some of the hot liquid and substitute cold, thus lowering the temperature. An adaptation of the Chinese method of crystal cooking, used for chicken, also works well for salmon. The court bouillon in which the salmon rests is kept just on the boil for 3 minutes, then the heat is turned off and the lid is kept on tight. The salmon will be cooked when the liquid is cold. Salmon is excellent broiled, steamed, or cooked in many other ways. *Smoked salmon is a delicacy in its own right.

In the past, salmon was abundant in European rivers—there is a much-quoted servant's contract which stipulated that salmon

should not be served more than twice a week. By the beginning of the 19th century, however, the pollution of rivers was well under way, and overefficient netting depleted the fish population still further. In North America, salmon was also superabundant, and the Indians once made pemmican from dried salmon. Later, salmon was canned in huge amounts, and in this form it could be called a poor man's food up to World War II.

Pacific and North American salmon. In North American rivers, *Salmo salar* averages only 10 lb (4.5 Kg) in weight. It is much less important commercially than the Pacific species of salmon, which belong to the related genus *Onchorhynchus*. These are the basis of a huge canning and fishing industry that deals with a million tons of salmon a year.

Of the Pacific salmon, one, the cherry salmon (*O. masu*), is found in the sea off Japan. The other five are found in North American rivers that feed into the Pacific (and in some cases on the Asian side of the ocean as well). In ascending order of size, these salmon are the pink or humpback (*O. gorbuscha*), the sockeye or red (*O. nerka*),

SOCKEYE SALMON

the coho or silver (*O. kisutch*), the chum or dog (*O. keta*), and the chinook, king, or spring (*O. tschawytscha*), which averages 23 lb (10.5 Kg) but not uncommonly reaches 50–80 lb (23–36 Kg). The pink salmon and the coho salmon are also found in the Atlantic. In general, the life cycle of Pacific salmon is similar to that of *Salmo salar,* although the time spans vary—according to species, the salmon may be 2–8 years old when it makes its spawning run up the river. Pacific salmon normally die after spawning, which takes king salmon and chum salmon as much as 2000 miles from the sea to the headwaters of the Yukon River.

In commercial terms, the pink salmon is the most important, making up half the catch, with the chum salmon accounting for a third and the sockeye salmon for almost all the rest. Chinook salmon and coho salmon are much sought by the sporting fisherman. In Russia, the roe of the chum salmon is made into red *caviar.

[*Salmon*—French: *saumon;* German: *Lachs;* Italian: *salmone;* Spanish: *salmon*]

SALMONELLA. *See* poisoning.

SAL PRUNELLA. *See* saltpeter.

SALSICCIA is a general term in Italy for any smallish sausage, whether fresh or dried. Such sausages are made in many regional types all over Italy. The ordinary *salsiccia fresca* (fresh) or *luganega* is usually thin and continuous, not pinched or twisted into individual sausages. The *salsiccia salamella* is thicker and is divided into sausages by looped string. Its varieties include the *salamella milanese* (Milan) and the *salamella vaniglia* (flavored with vanilla). Then there are the *salsiccia toscana* (with garlic, pepper, and anise), *salamella di cinghiale* (wild boar), *salsiccia da riso* and *salsiccia da patata* (containing rice and potato), *salsiccia bolognese* (from Bologna, containing minced heart and lungs), *salsiccia napoletana* (from Naples, a pork and beef sausage strongly spiced with red pepper), *salsiccia matta* (made of giblets and spleen), and *salsiccia di fegato* (liver flavored with pepper and fennel seeds). These sausages are usually to be eaten cooked, but some of them are smoked, including *salsiccia di Palermo* and *salsiccia milanese affumicata* (smoked sausages from Milan), and some are hung to dry for a couple of months before eating—*salsiccia secca* or *salsiccia asciutta*.

SALSIFY, oyster plant, or **vegetable oyster** (*Tragopogon porrifolium*) is a purple-flavored composite related to lettuce. Its long, white taproots, which look something like very slender parsnips, make an excellent winter vegetable. Salsify is popular in France and Italy but is out of fashion in the U.S. and Britain. Often confused with salsify, and often preferred to it by those who know the difference, is the closely related scorzonera or black salsify (*Scorzonera hispanica*), which has black-skinned roots and yellow flowers. Like salsify, it is a native of southern Europe. In the Middle Ages, scorzonera was valued as a medicine rather than as a vegetable; later, it was strongly recommended as a vegetable by the head of Louis XIV's kitchen. In Britain, the roots were not just eaten as a vegetable but were also candied.

The eclipse of scorzonera as a vegetable has been attributed to the custom of peeling root vegetables, which appears to have become prevalent in the Victorian period. Scorzonera suffers more than other roots from peeling, since it bleeds profusely. Both salsify and scorzonera are best dealt with by washing off the earth and cooking them whole in boiling salted water for 30–45 minutes or by steaming for perhaps an hour until they are tender. The skins will then rub or scrape off quite easily, and the roots can be cut into short lengths ready for further treatment (it is in this form that salsify is canned). Salsify and scorzonera may be served cold with vinaigrette and hot au gratin or fried in butter. The young leaves of both plants can be used in salad, and Boulestin recommends putting the young flowers of scorzonera in omelets.

Another member of the same genus as salsify is goatsbeard (*Tragopogon pratensis*). A common roadside plant in Europe, it is cultivated in Italy under the name *barba di frate* or *barba di prete* (monk's or priest's beard). Its tuft of grasslike leaves is eaten, cooked like spinach, but it does not break up and is considered a delicacy. In Britain, where a small form is found, the taproots of goatsbeard were once eaten like those of salsify.

[*Salsify*—French: *salsifis;* German: *Bocksbart;* Italian: *sassefrica;* Spanish: *salsifi*]

SALT or, more precisely, common salt is sodium chloride ($NaCl$). An essential item in the diet of humans and other animals, it is also a basic taste which is detected on the tongue; food without it often tastes insipid. Salt has been extracted and used since Neolithic times. It became an important article of trade in the Bronze Age.

Most of us today get too much salt in our diet—we like it, partly as a result of becoming accustomed to it at a very early age, and so we wolf such things as salted peanuts, salty meat, and olives. Too much salt is a contributory factor in heart disease and perhaps also in other diseases as well. The only time we are likely to need supplementary salt is when we are sweating profusely, whether crossing a desert or laboring in a steelworks. The natural reaction then is to drink large amounts of fluid, but sweat contains salt as well as water, and both need to be replaced—lack of salt can cause heat exhaustion.

The global reservoir of salt is the sea. It has been calculated that there is enough salt in the sea to cover the world's land masses to a depth of 115 ft (35 m). The average concentration of salt in sea water is about ¾ oz per pt (35 g per lt), but the Red Sea is about 15% saltier, while the Dead Sea contains a staggering 4 oz per pt (200 g per lt). On the other hand, the Black Sea is less than averagely salty and the Caspian Sea is only brackish—cows come down to it to drink.

Sodium chloride is only the most important of many salts in sea water. The next, in descending order of concentration, are magnesium chloride, magnesium sulfate (Epsom salts), potassium sulfate, calcium carbonate, and potassium and sodium bromides. Salts of many other elements are also found, some of them in infinitesimally small quantities.

Sea salt does not contain all these things in the same proportions unless it is completely unpurified, made by drying out sea water completely. Often, only part of the mineral content is crystallized out from sea water, and sea salt may also have been partially purified by recrystallization.

Sea salt is evaporated naturally in bays or enclosures and is also called bay salt or *gros sel* in older books. Salt may be produced in a similar way from salt marshes. The bays may be dried out completely or the salt crystals raked out of a saturated solution. Sea salt may also be made by evaporating the water over a fire; it was once made in quantity by this means, in wide earthenware pans—a method that dates back to the Iron Age, if not earlier.

Rock salt is found in deposits derived from the drying of ancient seas. It may be mined as a crystalline mineral, but a more modern and prosaic method is to pump water down into the salt, remove the brine which is formed, and evaporate it. The flavor of rock salt depends on the impurities present—ancient seas did not necessarily have the same composition as those of today—and some deposits may contain poisonous substances, such as arsenic. They may be stained red with iron or gray with other minerals. Edible rock salts in a roughly crushed form are sold for use in the salt mills that some people use at the table.

The old-fashioned block salt was made with crystalline salt poured into molds when it was still hot from the evaporating pans. It contained just enough dampness to stick the crystals loosely together in the block. In the kitchen, it had to be grated. Dairy salt and cheese salt were varieties of block salt that had been crushed mechanically and were sold in sacks. This crushed salt is basically the ordinary type of kitchen salt used today. Salt produced by the open-pan method is 98.5% pure sodium chloride, the rest being mainly gypsum (calcium sulfate). When open-pan salt is used in *brine for meat, the calcium sulfate reacts with the phosphates in the meat to form insoluble calcium phosphate, which makes the brine cloudy. Vacuum salt, evaporated and purified in vacuum pans, does not cause this problem: it is 99.9% pure and contains virtually no gypsum. It is free-running and is the basis of table salt, which is very finely ground and has had magnesium carbonate added to prevent caking. Sometimes starch and other carbonates and bicarbonates are also included. Dendritic salt, a new form of salt with star-shaped crystals, has a fine, soft, and floury texture. It is particularly used in manufactured seasonings and for mixing with spices. It is made from purified brine in vacuum pans and is 99.64% pure. Pickling salt is a very pure salt, since impurities can darken pickles.

Iodized salt, with iodine salts added, supplies dietary iodine, a health precaution that is essential in areas with a natural iodine deficiency (sea salt will not supply an adequate quantity). There are also salt substitutes for people on low-salt diets—usually depending on potassium salts which may be beneficial in many cases but should be used only after medical consultation. Cooks use salt freely for flavor and preservation. Salt seems to sharpen our awareness of other flavors. A normally salted food will contain about 0.9% salt, about the same content as that of the body. Water for cooking potatoes and greens should obviously be much more highly salted, since we are not usually going to drink it.

Ordinary impure salt will absorb water from the atmosphere unless it is stored at a relative humidity of under 75%. Damp salt may be dried in a slightly warm oven with the door ajar, but it will cake and will need to be crushed and sifted. Spiced and herbed salts are made by mixing dried salt with ground aromatic seeds, spices, or herbs. Garlic or onion can be pounded into bone-dry salt, the moisture being absorbed and the substance preserved by the salt, but the mixture should be kept sealed, since the flavor is destroyed by oxygen.

The selection of the right salt is important in cooking. Good sea salt is the best. Also the crystal size of salt matters. Fine salt dissolves quickly but is not recommended for *dry salting. Diana Kennedy, in *The Cuisines of Mexico* (Harper & Row, 1972), insists on "ground rock salt, sold in any supermarket or hardware store under the name of melting crystals." She notes that "the grayish appearance may put some people off, but once you have used that or sea salt you cannot return to the kosher or the normal commercially packed salt." Of course, most people will continue to use free-running table salt for everything because of its convenience, but perhaps it will eventually become gastronomically or even socially unacceptable, like factory-ground pepper.

[*Salt*—French: *sel;* German: *Salz;* Italian: *sale;* Spanish: *sal*]

SALT COD or **bacalao.** Cod live in huge numbers in the North Atlantic and have always been an important food for the U.S. and the maritime countries of northern Europe. Fishing boats ranged far into stormy seas—the Shetlands, Lofoten, Bear Island, and the White Sea were familiar names to cod fishers, who were always finding new grounds. In the middle of the 19th century, Rockall was where the cod were "as big as donkeys and as common as blackberries." Much earlier, the boats had favored the Newfoundland Grand Banks on the other side of the Atlantic. With enormous numbers of fish being caught at certain seasons, it was fortunate that cod did not have oily flesh and so could be salted and dried without difficulty. The fish were gutted, salted, and packed in flats at sea, then later washed and put out on the rocks to dry, which was why they were called klipfish or simply rockfish (not to be confused with dried, unsalted *stockfish). This simple process justified voyages to productive fishing grounds far from the markets. There was a ready sale for dried fish in southern Europe. As long ago as the 15th century, British merchants began shipping *bacalhau* into the Minho in Portugal and bringing back wine.

Soon the whole of Catholic Europe came to depend on salt cod for Friday and Lenten dishes. It was inexpensive and easy to transport. America, too, began producing it in quantity. Thoreau (writing in the first half of the 19th century, when cod was still caught on long sea-lines) described it as "stacked up like cordwood" around the wharves of Provincetown on Cape Cod. Less than 40 years after the discovery of that arm-shaped peninsula by the English explorer Bartholomew Gosnold in 1602, New Englanders were drying well over a quarter of a million codfish annually. Cod, which has always been associated with Boston, had quickly become a New England staple. Today, with large trawlers and refrigeration, dried salt cod is of less importance. In any case, northern countries never made a virtue of necessity or did anything very much with salt cod gastronomically. "Salt cod," says the Reverend J. G. Wood in his famous *Natural History* (1863), "is to many persons a great dainty, but to others, among whom I must be reckoned, it is insufferably offensive, and even with all the additions of sauce and condiment is barely eatable."

Yes! Not many people could be sinful on salt cod and parsnips, all boiled and served with an egg sauce. On the other hand, in the Mediterranean regions, from Spain through Provence, Italy, and Greece to Yugoslavia and the Middle East, methods were devised for making this unpromising material as palatable as possible. As a result, Lent could no doubt be endured on a diet of *brandade de morue* with cream and truffles. Now there are at least 200 delicious ways of preparing what was originally just a very basic fodder. Because salt cod has become a part of traditional cooking, it can be obtained easily anywhere in southern Europe, though it is no longer very cheap. It is hung or stacked up in grocers or in markets, or on sale ready-soaked every Friday. It is even available in plastic packets.

Buying and choosing. *Bacalao* (which may be ling as well as cod) should have white flesh and black skin. Yellowish-looking pieces are supposed to be old. In Mediterranean countries, you can usually judge the quality by the price, unless a dishonest merchant has seen you coming. Experts distinguish the thin sides and belly from the thick back and tail. For many dishes, the sides and belly part, which is not so good-looking, is better, being more gelatinous and of finer texture. Some cooks go so far as to say that the two parts should be soaked and cooked separately.

Soaking in running water or in water changed frequently (every 3 hours) is necessary before cooking. Depending on the quality of the fish, 24–48 hours of soaking at room temperature is needed. A modern method from Spain leaves the salt cod soaking undisturbed in a bowl (on a rack so the water can circulate underneath) in the refrigerator for 2 days. The water is not even skimmed. After that, a final soaking for 6 hours, with a couple of changes of water, will make the fish ready to cook.

Scalding. Some people, notably the Basques, scald the salt cod after it has been soaked. They put it in a pot of cold water, skin side up, and put it on the heat until the water is not quite boiling. After this, the fish is taken out or left to cool in the liquid, according to the requirements of the subsequent preparation. After scalding, the fish can be boned.

Poaching is the more usual preliminary to cooking. Use an earthenware or enamel pan, since metal can cause discoloration. It is also best to use rain water. Poaching time is 16–18 minutes. Because salt cod must never boil (it will then become stringy), bring it almost to boiling, then throw in a glass of cold water and finish the poaching on the lowest possible heat. Allow 5–7 oz (150–200g) per person.

BACALAO A LA VIZCAIN´

One of the great classical dishes of northern Spain. The fish is cooked in a spicy, but not too spicy, red pepper sauce made with *ñoras*—globular red *sweet peppers which visitors to Spain have certainly seen dried and hanging in chains in the shops.

Soak 2¼ lb (1 Kg) *bacalao* and 12 *ñoras* (deseeded, skinned if possible, and chopped) for 24 hours. Cut the fish in bits and scald (as described above), leaving it to cool in the broth. Reserve about 1 cup (¼ lt) of broth. Bone the fish. Flour it lightly and fry without browning it in a little oil. Arrange in a casserole, skin side down. Add 1 cup (250 ml) of oil to the frying pan. Fry 2 oz (50 g) of cubed bread until it is brown, then add 2 oz (50 g) of scraps of raw ham or unsmoked bacon, 2 cloves of garlic, 1 lb (450 g) of chopped onions, a bay leaf, and the *ñoras*. When the onion is cooked, add 1 heaped teaspoon *pimentón* and moisten with some of the reserved stock in which the *bacalao* was scalded. Cook the flavorings for a further 10 minutes, then put them through a blender or Mouli to make a sauce. Adjust the salt and sugar. Add more broth if necessary. Cover the *bacalao* with the sauce and cook in a 375°F (190°C) oven, shaking the casserole from time to time for 15 minutes or until everything is hot.

SALTPETER takes its name from the Latin *sal petrae* (salt of stone); chemically, it is potassium nitrate (KNO_3). Together with *Chile saltpeter (which is sodium nitrate), it is used in *brines and in *dry salting for bacon, salt beef, tongues, hams, and sausages. It is sold as a white, moist, crystalline powder with a salty, slightly bitter taste. It is not very soluble in cold water.

It is popularly supposed that it is the saltpeter in the cure which turns meat an attractive pink or red, but this is actually caused by small quantities of potassium *nitrate (KNO_2) formed by denitrifying bacteria. Although a pure nitrate will not redden meat, it does have a preservative effect, since it is particularly active against the lethal anaerobic *Clostridium botulinus* (*see* poisoning). When nitrates are put directly (in tiny amounts) into commercial cures, some saltpeter is also added. Because saltpeter hardens meat, it should not be used to excess. Saltpeter is a powerful oxidizing agent (which is why it is used in gunpowder and fuses), so butchers often mix a proportion of it with the sawdust used in smokehouses. It starts the sawdust burning and ensures that it smolders steadily.

Sal prunella, which is mentioned in old recipes, is crude saltpeter in the form of cakes. It was used for curing ham and bacon in the past, but now it is mostly used in country curing. Because it is impure and contains potassium nitrate as well as nitrate when heated, it is best to avoid it.

[*Saltpeter*—French: *salpetre;* German: *Salpeter;* Italian: *salnitro;* Spanish: *salitre*]

SAMBAL. Southeast Asian term covering both dishes of meat or fish fried with chilies and condiments in which chilies are an important constituent. The latter are equivalent to the Middle Eastern *harissa* but contain a wider variety of ingredients, such as *trasi* (*see balachan*). A number of these *sambals* are sold in jars and should be used with great caution—they can be extremely fiery. Recipes for both sorts of *sambal* are in Rosemary Brissenden's *South East Asian Food* (Penguin, 1972).

SAMBUCA. *See* liqueurs and cordials.

SAMPHIRE or **rock samphire** (*Crithmum maritimum*) is an umbelliferous plant with thick fleshy leaves which grows wild on cliffs over much of Europe and locally in Britain. It has a very strong, pungently aromatic smell and taste. Pickled samphire, though nowadays almost unknown commercially, is still commonly sold in Spanish markets. It may also be eaten as a vegetable (cooked in butter) or put into salads, although it is rather strong for that purpose.

In the U.S., the plants that are often described as samphire are not rock samphire but marsh samphire, usually known in Britain as glasswort. These peculiar plants, members of the genus *Salicomia,* belong to the same family as beets and spinach but have fleshy leaves surrounding the stem, so that the plants look as if they have fleshy stems and no leaves. They are very common in salt marshes.

[*Samphire*—French: *fenouil de mer, bacile;* German: *Meerfenchel;* Italian: *critmo, finocchio marino;* Spanish: *hinojo marino*]

SAPODILLA, sapodilla plum, tree potato, sapota, zapote, naseberry, or **chiku** (and various spellings of the last two). The sapodilla (*Achras sapota*) grows wild in the forests of southern Mexico and the northern part of Central America. As a cultivated fruit, it has now spread all over the tropics and is commonly seen in the markets of India, Southeast Asia, the West Indies, and tropical America. It is also grown in Florida and in Israel. However, it is at its best when grown in a strictly tropical climate. Since it will keep at least 5–6 weeks, if picked immature and shipped in cold storage, it can easily be exported to the colder countries, where it has not yet become popular.

The tree is small, slow-growing, and evergreen, with glossy light-green leaves and a wood that is famous for its durability—carvings over 1000 years old have withstood the tropical climate in Mayan ruins. It therefore seems likely that the fruit was eaten in the days of this ancient civilization.

The sapodilla looks like a rounded or oval potato with a rough brown skin covered in scurf which begins to be lost as the fruit ripens. At the same time, it becomes more orange and less brown. Since the fruit is quite inedible before it is ripe and is usually picked immature, it is as well to know that an unripe fruit shows green when it is scratched with the thumbnail; in ripe fruit, the scratch shows yellow. Since unripe fruit will ripen if left in a basket in a warm room, it is not necessary to anger the fruiterer by scratching his fruit. The ripe fruit can be stored for some time in the refrigerator.

Sapodillas are usually eaten as an uncooked dessert fruit. They must be peeled.

Inside is an orange-brown or yellow-brown, slightly grainy, translucent flesh. There is a core with a few large shiny black seeds which are easily removed. Poor varieties have a hard flesh and a gritty texture; good ones are soft and smooth. The taste may best be described as "vegetable brown sugar." You may find sapodillas delicious, but equally you may think them oversweet and lacking in acidity. They may be an interesting addition to a fruit bowl which is intended to be a decorative feature of the table.

Sapodillas may be made into a jam, preferably with citrus or other more tasty fruits. They contain 8–12% sugar and, in the West Indies, are boiled down into a fine syrup.

The names of this fruit are exceedingly confused. Sapodilla is the name used in Florida, derived from the Spanish *zapotillo*, meaning "little *zapote*." The name sapota or sapote really belongs to the unrelated marmalade plum (*Calocarpum sapota*) and the green sapote (*C. viride*), so is better avoided. All these names come from the native *tzicozapotl* or *tzapotl*, as does also chiku, which is a good name to use. The name naseberry is a corruption of the Spanish for *medlar, a fruit from the quite unrelated rose family. The French also use the term *néfle d'Amérique*, which also means American medlar. The white sapote (*Casimiroa edulis*) is not a relative and belongs to the same family as rue and citrus fruits.

The most important use of the sapodilla is as a source of chicle, the white latex from the tree. It is the basis for chewing gum and in exported in quantity from Central America.

[*Sapodilla*—French: *sapotille* or *néfle d'Amérique;* Italian: *sapota, sapotiglia;* Spanish: *chicozapote*]

SAPSAGO or **Schabzieger.** Hard Swiss cheese containing *melilot from the Glarus region near Zurich. An important flavoring, sapsago is grated into soups, salads, and sauces.

SAPUCAYA NUT. *See* Brazil nut.

SARACEN CORN. *See* buckwheat.

SARDINE (*Sardina pilchardus*) is a young pilchard, a fact that was not known 100 years ago when sardines were thought to be different fish. Since ancient times, the sardine has been fished in the Mediterranean with lights on calm, moonless nights, at first with torches, then with acetylene lamps, and today with bigger boats and electricity. Sardines swim in shoals and are caught in huge quantities, far exceeding immediate demand. In the past, they were salted and dried. They are used today in this form mainly in Mediterranean countries. In Spain, these sardines are often used to garnish local types of *coca* or pizza.

Sardines were the first fish to be canned (in 1834). The canning business is now enormous, particularly in Portugal. The method was evolved of canning sardines in olive oil (which in the early days took care of any imperfect sterilization), but since olive oil has gradually become expensive, the cheaper grades are now more usually canned in other edible oils. Sardines are also canned for example in tomato sauce, in *escabeche,* or with chilies, and quality has suffered as a result. In Edwardian times, the best grocers sold only sardines they had matured and turned regularly for several years, but French sardine canners considered that such practices are foolish and that 2 years is the maximum time that sardines should be kept—and French sardines are reputedly the best. Famous names are Philippe et Canaud, Saupiquet, Cassegrain, and Amieux, but the Rolls-Royce of the sardine world is canned in Bordeaux by Rodel, whose sardines are broiled and then matured for a year in vats of olive oil before canning. They are expensive and scarce. Connoisseurs claim that fine sardines should be served without seasoning on slices of hot buttered toast (although the French opt simply for bread and butter), but cheap sardines are improved by black pepper and lemon juice.

Fully grown sardines are fished off the coast of Cornwall as pilchards or gypsy herrings. The catch was originally simply salted, or salted and smoked for export; smoked pilchards were known as "fair maids," which was said to be a corruption from the Spanish. Pilchards today are canned, but those in tomato sauce are often small herrings. In the fresh fish, pilchards can be distinguished from small herrings by the raised lines that run backward from the eyes. On the other hand, sprats have a line of spiny scales which form a keel to the belly. Their young, canned in oil like sardines, are sold as brisling.

Fresh sardines are popular near coasts where they are caught. They were not thought to travel well, but are now exported frozen in some quantity. On their native shores, they are cheap, oily, and delicious. Completely fresh sardines are possibly at their best cooked in the simple Spanish style, just thrown on top of a hot stove, cooked on both sides, and served with parsley and lemon juice.

In the U.S., almost all real sardines are imported. Although the Pacific sardine (*Sardinops sagax*) was once abundant, it has been overfished almost to extinction. For local canning, young herrings are used, and in the marketplace they are called sardines.

Similar species of fish are found all over the world. Examples include the oil sardine (*Sardinella longiceps*) and the rainbow sardine *(Dussumieria acuta)*, which is fished and canned off the southwest coast of Kerala in India.

[*Sardine*—French: *sardine;* German: *Sardine;* Italian: *sardina;* Spanish: *sardina*]

SASSAFRAS (*Sassafras albidum*) is a North American tree of the laurel family; it yields an essential oil that is present throughout the plant but is most concentrated in the root bark. It lends its flavor to root beer and to sassafras tea, an infusion of the bark, leaves, or buds that was popular in parts of the U.S. as a tea substitute in the early 19th century and enjoyed by people today for its unique flavor—it is comforting as a hot tea in winter and refreshing as iced tea in summer, especially when combined with mint. The dried leaves are used to make *filé powder.

[Sassafras—French: sassafras; German: Sassafras; Italian: sassafrasso; Spanish: sasafrás]

SATÉ. See peanut.

SATSUMA. See orange.

SATURATED SOLUTION. A solution containing the maximum amount of salt, sugar, soda, or any other substance that can be dissolved in a volume of water. If more of the substance is added, it will lie undissolved on the bottom of the vessel. However, the quantity that will dissolve increases with temperature. Sometimes there is only a small rise in solubility, as with salt, but at other times the increase is spectacular, as with saltpeter.

SAUCISSE. A small French or Swiss sausage (as opposed to the large *saucisson). Saucisses are usually 1–1½ in. (2.5–4 cm) in diameter and fresh rather than cured, so that they are for cooking and eating hot. They include French equivalents of chorizos (saucisses d'Espagne) and frankfurters (saucisses de Francfort and saucisses de Strasbourg). Saucisses de campagne, country sausages, are made of mixed lean pork and fat bacon. They are dried for up to a week and contain seasonings that vary widely according to charcutier and locality. Poached gently for 20 minutes rather than fried, they are used in heavy soups and stews for the winter. Sausages of greater refinement include saucisses de Périgord, with black truffles and white wine, and saucisses au champagne, lightly spiced and flavored with champagne and black truffles. Saucisses de Toulon, which contain meat that is coarsely chopped rather than minced, are the correct sausages to use in the regional cassoulet. Saucisse en brioche is sausage baked in a brioche paste. Something like a very large and delicate sausage roll, it is sold by the slice and is warmed and eaten as a first course.

SAUCISSON. Large or very large sausages from France or Switzerland; saucissons are often supported in nets or bound. They are salted, dried, and usually smoked but not cooked. Before they are ready to eat, they are kept for 4 or, better still, 6 months. Like cheese, they are now mainly a factory product and are matured, sometimes with the help of molds growing on the skin. They are sliced and sold by weight, usually for eating cold as an hors d'oeuvre or in sandwiches. The numerous types have minor variations in texture and content. Many are named after their places of origin. The exception is *cervelas, a boiling sausage that is intermediate between saucisses and saucissons in size.

SAUERKRAUT is shredded, lightly salted cabbage which has fermented and is preserved by the *lactic acid from the fermentation. It seems probable that it was discovered by the Gauls, who were in the habit of salting food for winter, but the Romans knew the rudiments of making silage (animal fodder preserved for the winter by lactic acid fermentation). At any rate, sauerkraut was in use in the Middle Ages. Cabbages and pigs were staples that allowed survival in a hard winter. *"Chi semena le verze e un porco ingrassa par l'inverno al se la passa"* (roughly: He who sows cabbages and fattens a pig will get by the winter) is the Italian version of a proverb that was relevant for much of Europe. Sauerkraut was important, though, in central and eastern Europe, where the ground was often snowed under. Until the arrival of the potato in the 18th century, the other main standby was the beet. Sauerkraut had the then unrecognized virtue of containing vitamin C. Captain Cook credited the good health of his crews to it long before vitamins were ever heard of.

Western European languages all derive

their names for this food from the German (e.g., the French *choucroute*), and Germany and Austria are the center of the sauerkraut tradition, although it goes west into Alsace and Lorraine, east into Poland and Russia, and south into Hungary, Italy, and the Balkans. As a dish of any refinement, sauerkraut doubtless had to wait for the development of fine and suitable cabbage varieties. In the past, it was widely made on farms, but some areas and villages were especially famous for the high quality which they produced. Sauerkraut needs space and cool cellars; making it at home is inclined to be smelly. It can be bought in cans, in plastic bags, or loose from the tub in some delicatessens. There are many variations: most commonly, it is flavored with juniper berries or caraway seed, but sauerkraut may contain fennel seed or other ingredients such as beets to color it red. (In Russia, it is also quite common to salt and ferment grated beets.)

Sauerkraut is usually made in a straight-sided tub with a loose top and a false lid that fits down inside it. The cabbages are first weighed and 1½% of their weight of salt is measured out (some recipes advocate up to 4% salt). The cabbages are cleaned, washed, and finely shredded. The barrel and its lids are scalded, and a white cotton cloth large enough to cover the false lid is sterilized, together with a large nonporous stone to act as a weight. The bottom of the tub is usually first covered with a few whole cabbage leaves, and then the shredded cabbage is firmly packed down in layers, each sprinkled with salt and with salt on top. The tub ought to be about two-thirds full. It is covered with the cloth, topped with the wooden false lid, and weighted down with the stone. In a day, the false lid should be immersed in liquid extracted from the cabbage. Fermentation begins when the sugars in the cabbage are turned to lactic acid. Depending on the temperature, the sauerkraut should be ready in about 3 weeks or a little more. The surface of the liquid will become covered with a scum of yeasts or fungi, which should be skimmed off. A sample of the sauerkraut

may be taken with a wooden fork for testing. When the cabbage is ready to eat, the liquid on top is taken off with a wooden bowl (and makes a good soup), the required amount of sauerkraut is taken, and the cloth is rinsed in boiling water, then put back with the false lid and weight on top. The liquid may be topped up with plain cold water, salt water, or white wine. Wine, of course, adds to the flavor. Once fermented, the tub of sauerkraut has to be kept in a cool cellar or refrigerated.

There are many ways of cooking sauerkraut. First, it should be tasted and washed briefly in a strainer held under the cold tap if it seems too acid. (In Austria they like it sour, in Germany less so.) Flavorings which can be added include apple, garlic, onion, bay, juniper berries, caraway seed, white wine, fried bacon, and bacon rind. A typical way is to fry diced bacon crisp with a little chopped onion, then to add about half the weight of water that you have sauerkraut, a large piece of smoked bacon rind, a small clove of garlic (unpeeled but crushed), a bay leaf, a few juniper berries, a pinch of caraway seeds, and a few peppercorns. Cook slowly for 30–60 minutes, in which time the water should be absorbed—how long it takes depends on the sauerkraut; do not cook it to a mush. If a lot of liquid is left, thicken it with a little cornstarch, but not too much. Water in which bacon has been boiled can be used if it is handy (as it often is in restaurants). Serve sauerkraut with boiled bacon, frankfurters or other smoked sausage, bread dumplings, and potatoes. The Chinese also make forms of pickled cabbage, as do the Koreans with *kimchi.

[*Sauerkraut*—French: *choucroute;* German: *Sauerkraut;* Italian: *salcrautte;* Spanish: *chucruta*]

SAUSAGE. The word comes from the Latin *salsus*—salted. Originally, sausages were a means of organizing and preserving the blood and the odd bits of pig left over after the hams and bacon sides had been removed.

These bits were mixed with salt, saltpeter, herbs, and spices, enclosed in sections of carefully cleaned gut, dried, smoked, and hung in a cool place. As sausages, the scraps would keep good for months. An added bonus was that the sausages would age and mature like many cheeses; they actually improved with keeping. Sausages inevitably came to be made not just for survival but also for gastronomic delight (apparently becoming so popular in ancient Rome that at one point they were banned). Over the ages they have attracted much culinary attention, and the finest spices and the best cuts of meat have been put into them.

Many sausages have long since lost their original peasant functions: they are often for eating fresh, and some are even skinless. In Britain, fresh sausages are usual, but then the British culinary heritage (unlike that of the U.S., which has a wide range of sausages imported with its immigrants) lacks variety in its sausages. There are the university variations on the standard British sausage or banger—the Oxford and Cambridge sausages—as well as sausages of beef, mutton, and even turkey, but they all have to be eaten fresh and cooked, never raw. The British have no tradition of matured, well-hung sausages. Rare recipes for dried sausages prove the rule because they are clearly of foreign origin (e.g., Yorkshire polony). Some British sausages are called "puddings"— black puddings and white puddings, not to mention the "great chieftain of the pudding race," *haggis, which can certainly be claimed as a sausage.

Sausages intended to be eaten fresh should not be kept for more than a few days in the refrigerator (although they may be frozen). Commercial sausages often contain preservatives, because their contents offer ideal growing conditions for microorganisms, including botulism. Sausages made of raw and uncured pork should always be thoroughly cooked. On the other hand, sausages that are bought already cooked, even if they are intended to be eaten fresh (e.g., frankfurters and black puddings), can be eaten safely

cold. A few cooked sausages (e.g., mortadella) will keep for a time if they remain uncut. Rather strangely, in the really long keepers (e.g., *salame, *chorizo) the meat is uncooked. Sausages made of raw pork are perfectly safe (like raw ham) if they have been properly hung to mature. Any harmful organisms, such as those of trichinosis, have had time to be destroyed by the salt. One might say the meat has been cooked by the salt and saltpeter it contains.

Types of sausage for keeping should be hung in a cool, dry place, so that air can circulate all around them—never against a wall. Any cut surface is best protected by a piece of oiled paper. Once sliced, sausage should be kept in the least cold part of the refrigerator and must be well wrapped to prevent its drying out. The flavor does not improve in these conditions—it is best to buy only what you need for immediate use. Sliced sausage bought in packets from the supermarket is usually a convenience food for those who value convenience more than food.

Every European country can offer a range of sausages, some of which are national and local specialties, whereas others are home-produced versions of sausages that originated abroad (a large number of Scandinavian sausages fall into this category). Some types like frankfurters and salami seem to be made in some form almost everywhere in Europe; less international sausages may spread from their homeland to neighboring countries and change a little on the way, as in the case of the Spanish *chorizo, which becomes the *chorizo Basquais* and the *saucisse d'Espagne* in France and the *chouriço* in Portugal. There are also Chinese sausages: made of cured pork, they tend to contain sugar as well as salt and spices.

Sausages are an important part of French charcuterie. Although the basic number of types is not great, there are hosts of local varieties, often distinguished by the name of the town or locality where they originated, and some with names that are quite unknown except where they are made. The differences between local types is usually small; the excellence of a sausage will depend mainly on the charcutier who makes it. French sausages that need cooking are two made with intestines, *andouilles and *andouillettes, the chubby *boudin blanc and boudin noir (the equivalent of *black pudding), *crêpinettes and gayettes (which could be said to approximate the English faggots), merquez (a short, spicy sausage for grilling that is Algerian in origin), *cervelas, and a variety of *saucisses. Matured and usually large sausages are *saucissons.

The most famous matured sausages of all come from Italy and are plurally known as *salami; they vary from the slick, factory-produced versions from Milan to rough, gnarled-looking peasant varieties. Also for eating cold and finely sliced, often as part of a mixed antipasto, are sausages in which the ingredients are not chopped or minced but made with pieces of cured meat—notable examples are *bresaola, *coppa, and *culatello. The most famous cooked sausage for eating as a cold cut is *mortadella from Bologna. Small fresh sausages for cooking and eating hot are mainly known as *salsiccie. There is also the Italian equivalent of *black pudding, sanquinaccio. Two specialties of Modena and the surrounding area are boiling sausages with a filling that includes pork skin from the head and snout to produce a gelatinous texture. They are *cotechino, which comes in a sausage skin, and *zampone, which is a boned and stuffed pig's foot. Italian sausages may bear official tags made of metal to indicate the meat content: S for pork (carne suino) only, SB for pork and beef (suino and bovino), O for mutton (ovino), and E for horse meat (equino).

Although Italy is credited with having the finest sausages, Germany can claim to be the sausage-eating center of the world, and neighboring countries in all directions share much of the German passion for sausages. There is no good meal that is more easily prepared than a selection of sliced German sausages with black bread, German mustard, pickled cucumbers, and German beer. Sausages for eating cold (either sliced or, in the case of the softer varieties, spread) include *bierwurst, blutwurst (*black pudding), and its Thuringian variant rotwurst (which contains black pepper and large lumps of meat), *cervelat, and finely ground extrawurst; leberwurst (*liver sausage), mettwurst, and teewurst are often soft and spreadable. Landjäger are unusual in being pressed into a square shape; they are cured, smoked, and dried sausages for eating raw. Raw sausages for broiling are *bratwurst, but the hot sausages most foreigners associate with Germany are smoked, poached sausages eaten with sauerkraut, although this is equally a dish from eastern France—surprisingly, more sauerkraut is consumed in France than in Germany. The internationally famous names are the *frankfurter in the U.S. and the Austrian *wienerwurst. German sausages, like those from France and Italy, have a plethora of regional and local names.

In any type of sausages, there is always great variation from maker to maker. Governments may define sausage types and may legislate to specify the permitted constituents (e.g., how much horse can go into a beef sausage before it becomes a horse sausage), but wide differences in texture and taste are allowed. You can learn about sausages, as about any food, only by trying and tasting boldly.

[Sausage—French: saucisse; German: Wurst; Italian: salsiccia; Spanish: salchicha]

SAUSAGE skin is traditionally made from the cleaned intestines of pigs, sheep, or cattle, but because of the continual battle for standardization and mechanization fought by the big manufacturers, there are now skins which do not vary in size and are made of reconstituted collagen (a sort of dried jelly), cellulose, and even plastic. Small quantities of skins suitable for home use can usually be ordered through the local butcher. They range in diameter from narrow sheep casings for little *chipolatas* to wide beef bungs for mortadella or other large sausages. Real skins are preserved in salt—usually dry but sometimes in brine—and will keep indefinitely. When needed, skins should be soaked in fresh water for 12 hours or so, then washed out with running water.

Preparing your own sausage skins is a fiddly job (commercially, they are cleaned by machine), and is hardly something to tackle except on the farm, since it involves washing out the intestines, cutting them in suitable lengths, dissecting away the mesentery and fat, turning the guts inside out over a stick, and scraping off the slimy inner lining. This comes away easier if the skins are first soaked in frequent changes of clean water for a couple of days: it allows the glandular lining to soften. However, in Spain, where the annual *matanza* (pig killing) is still a lingering custom, the cleaning is done with salt and lemon juice, all on the same day, because meat from a pig killed in the morning has to be minced, salted, spiced, and packed into sausages before night. Indeed, in primitive conditions, the job had always to be done without delay. However, skins made in the old way look somewhat heavy and opaque. The commercial skins of today are more elegant and are even often bleached for the sake of appearance.

SAUTÉING. From the French *sauter* (to jump), this is cooking food in hot fat while shaking or tossing the ingredients. The correct pan is a *sautoir*, which looks like a frying pan with upright, slightly higher than normal sides, to prevent the food from falling out when it is being shaken.

SAVORY is a labiate herb that is traditionally important for flavoring beans. Two species are commonly grown: summer savory (*Satureja hortensis*), an annual plant; and the perennial winter savory (*S. montana*). The taste is vaguely like thyme in summer savory but stronger and more biting in winter savory. Savory is a distinctive herb, to be used with discretion—you can easily add too

much of it—but in general, summer savory complements fresh summer vegetables, such as tiny green beans, and delicate fish, whereas winter savory is good with such cold-

SAVORY

weather dishes as baked beans, stews, and braised meats. In Provence (as *poivre d'âne*) and in the Basses Alpes in France, savory is the traditional covering for the small white St. Marcellin cheeses (although some are now covered with rosemary).

[*Savory*—French: *sarriette;* German: *Bohnenkraut, Kölle, Winter Bergminze;* Italian: *savore, santoreggia;* Spanish: *sabroso*]

SAVOY. *See* cabbage.

SCALD. *See* lemon sole.

SCALDING is in most cases the same as *blanching. It also refers to pouring boiling water over a freshly killed pig to loosen the bristles, which can then be scraped off with a knife.

[*Scalding*—French: *blanchir;* German: *abkochen; abbrühen;* Italian: *scottare,* Spanish: *limpiar con agua muy caliente*]

SCALLION. *See* onion.

SCALLOP or **scollop** has a fan-shaped shell. There are many species in all seas. Unlike the majority of bivalves, scallops can swim by flapping their shells together, though many can also attach themselves like mussels to weeds or rocks by a byssus of threads. They are usually obtained by dredging or trawling. Scallops are often opened and cleaned by the fishmonger (or processed at sea, with only the muscle being brought ashore, usually frozen); otherwise they should be well scrubbed and then opened with a knife, as are other bivalves. The white muscle, which is eaten, is most easily cut out with scissors. In Europe—but not in America—the red "tongue" or "coral" is included with the white muscle. The rest is discarded, although the beard can go into soup.

Scallops are most often cooked in a sauce and served in the shell—there are many fine recipes, particularly from France. A typically Norman example is *coquilles St.-Jacques havraise,* scallops sautéed in a shallot butter, mixed with prawns, and heated in the shell with a sauce made of thick cream, flavored with white wine, dry vermouth, and black pepper.

The species that is found around the coasts of northern and western (Atlantic) Europe is the great scallop (*Pecten maximus*). The usual Mediterranean species, the pilgrim scallop (*P. jacobaeus*), is a little smaller but is also prized; it is best in autumn and winter. Another large North Atlantic species that is commercially fished from America is the Atlantic deep-sea scallop (*Placopecten magellanicus*). A smaller, northern species is the Iceland scallop (*Chlamys islandica*). Other small species may be eaten raw as well as cooked; among them are the queen scallop or quin (*C. opercularis*) and the variegated scallop (*C. varia*), known in France respectively as *vanneau* and *pétoncle,* and the bay scallop (*C. irradians*), which is the usual commercial scallop of eastern North America. All species can be cooked in the same ways.

The white muscle meat of the fan shell (*Pinna nobilis*) is eaten like the scallop, either cooked or raw, in Mediterranean countries. The shell has a narrow wedge shape and is commonly 20 in. (50 cm) long, whereas the scallops mentioned above are not usually more than 6 in. (16 cm) long in the case of the great scallop, and the small species normally reach only about 3 in. (8 cm).

[*Scallop*—French: *coquille St.-Jacques;* German: *Kammuschel;* Italian: *pettine, ventaglio;* Spanish: *concha de peregrino*]

SCAMPI is the plural of the Italian name (*scampo* is the singular) for the Norway lobster or Dublin Bay prawn (*Nephrops norvegicus*). Because the demand for scampi is so great, other imported crustaceans are often substituted (when the tails alone are sold, only experts can tell, and the name has rather lost its original meaning). Even the Dublin Bay prawns fished around Britain are not as tasty as scampi from the muddy sand bottom of the Adriatic, and the substitutes are often very inferior. The *scampo* is a fairly close relative of the lobster, with claws and the same general anatomy, but is much smaller—no more than 10 in. (25 cm) long at the very most. The meat is in the abdomen or tail. While perfectly fresh scampi tails may be poached for around 10 minutes in salted water and served with no more than melted butter, the average Italian recipe is much fiercer. For instance, the tails might be threaded on skewers alternately with sage leaves, marinated for an hour in oil and cognac, then grilled briefly (basted with the marinade) over hot coals. Although they are such a popular commodity today, scampi were almost unheard of outside Italy until after World War II. Indeed the very name Dublin Bay prawn was almost a term of contempt, describing the part of the catch that could be sold only by being hawked through the streets of the city. In the U.S., scampi can be the tails of any large shrimps.

SCARLET RUNNER. *See* runner bean.

SCHABZIEGER. *See* sapsago.

SCOLLOP. *See* scallop.

SCORZONERA. *See* salsify.

SCREW PINE. *See* kewra.

SCROD or **schrod,** baby codfish or any other young or small non-oily fish (e.g., haddock), is highly regarded along the New England coast. The word, which may be spelled scrod or schrod on menus in Boston, comes from the Dutch *schroode,* meaning to strip a shred from a larger piece—the same kind of action that is used to fillet a fish. It won't hurt to ask what you're getting when you order scrod or schrod, but in any case the flavor should be delicate, and it is best cooked simply.

SEA ANEMONE is a polyp, a primitive animal related to corals and jellyfish. Polyps consist essentially of a digestive sac and a ring of tentacles surrounding the mouth (which doubles as the anus). The tentacles are armed with special cells that shoot out poison darts to paralyze their prey.

These often beautiful, flowerlike creatures are not commonly used as food, but two European species are eaten in France. They are the beadlet (*Actinia equina*) and the oplet or snakelocks anemone (*Anemonia sulcata*), a species with longer tentacles. Both vary in color from brown to green, but the beadlet, as its French name, *tomate de mer* (sea tomato), suggests, may also be red. To prepare them, remove the tentacles, turn the rest inside out, and wash the body cavity clean. Remove any sand and rock adhering to the foot. Use them in soup or fry them in batter.

[*Sea anemone*—French: *anémone de mer, ortie de mer;* German: *Seeanemone;* Italian: *anemone di mare;* Spanish: *anémona de mar*]

SEA CUCUMBER is a holothurian, a roughly sausage-shaped relative of sea anemones and sea urchins. Dried holothurian, known as *bêche de mer* or trepang, is used in Chinese cooking. To prepare these unpromising objects, which are bought whole, first wash and clean them, then soak them overnight. Next day, blanch them for 5 minutes in boiling water, cut them open, and gut them. Simmer them for 4 hours, and they will swell and become gelatinous.

[*Sea cucumber*—French: *cornichon de mer, concombre de mer;* German: *Seewalze, Seegurke, Meergurke;* Italian: *cocomero di mare;* Spanish: *cohombro de mar*]

SEA DATE or **date mussel** (*Lithophaga lithophaga*). A bivalve, the size, shape, and color of a date, which lives in holes which it bores in marine rocks. Sea dates are much appreciated in Mediterranean countries for their delicately sweet taste. Though usually eaten raw, they are also excellent when cooked.

[*Sea date*—French: *datte de mer;* Italian: *cetriolo di mare*]

SEA EAR. *See* abalone.

SEAKALE (*Crambe maritima*) is a cruciferous plant with tough, thick leaves. It grows wild in many places on the seacoasts of northern Europe. In the past, it was much cultivated for its blanched shoots which, when cooked like asparagus, were considered a delicacy. Today, it has to be classed as a rare vegetable.

[*Seakale*—French: *chou marin, chou de mer;* German: *Strandkohl;* Italian: *cavolo marino;* Spanish: *berza marina*]

SEA LETTUCE. *See* seaweed.

SEA MOSS. *See* carrageen.

SEARING is sealing the surface of meat at the start of cooking by briefly exposing it to very strong heat.

SEA URCHIN. A spiny, more or less spherical creature related to starfish and sea cucumbers. Many species are eaten around the world. In Europe, the species known as the edible sea urchin is *Echinus esculentus,* which is 5 in. (12 cm) across and occurs from Scandinavia to Portugal, but this is less delicate in flavor than two smaller species of 3 in. (7–8 cm) across. One of these is the northerly green sea urchin (*Strongylocentrus droebachiensis*), which occurs on both sides of the Atlantic. It is found on the U.S. Atlantic coast from Greenland to New Jersey, and on the Pacific from the Arctic to Oregon. The more southerly *Paracentrotus lividus,* is dark purplish brown, almost black in fact; it is the sea urchin commonly eaten in Mediterranean regions. In the past, sea urchins were sometimes called sea eggs, because they were dipped for a very short time in boiling sea water, then opened and eaten like eggs. All the contents except the intestines are edible, but more often only the roes (five equally spaced vertical strips of orange stuff) are scooped up with bread and eaten raw with at most a squeeze of lemon. Sea urchins can be opened simply with a pair of scissors: poke a blade through the shell and cut around the equator (there are fancier ways and a special cutter called a *coupe-oursin*). Be careful not to get spines in your fingers. Remove the digestive tract and wash the rest in sea water. Sea urchins are at their best when the roes are ripe, just before breeding. They may be gathered easily by skin divers, but it is a job that requires gloves. The urchins should be alive until you are ready to eat them; once they are dead, they do not keep.

There are recipes for cooking the roe with scrambled eggs, and it makes a wonderful sauce if it is scooped out with a spoon and mixed with a little mayonnaise in a blender or food processor. The flavor is vaguely like crab. A paste of sea urchins (*umi*) can be bought in shops that specialize in Japanese food.

[*Sea urchin*—French: *oursin;* German: *Seeigel;* Italian: *riccio di mare;* Spanish: *erizo de mar*]

SEA WATER is used sometimes as a cooking liquid for fish or shellfish, especially in fishermen's recipes. Because of the many substances dissolved in it, sea water has a certain bitterness which is not found in a brine of pure *salt.

[*Sea water*—French: *eau de mer;* German: *Seewasser, Meerwasser;* Italian: *acqua di mare;* Spanish: *agua de mar*]

SEAWEED belongs to the group of primitive plants called algae. These can be divided into three main groups—green, red, and brown—of which the brown are the most plentiful, especially in northern seas, but the least interesting to the cook. Commercially, however, they have become very important in recent years as a source of alginates, the jellylike mucilaginous substances that are used as stabilizers and general goo-producers in the food industry. For example, in commercial ice cream, they keep the emulsified pig's fat in suspension and prevent the growth of ice crystals.

Of the green algae, the only one of any importance in Europe is the sea lettuce (*Ulva lactuca*), which actually looks rather like lettuce leaves that have become wilted and transparent with age. It is also known as green laver, lettuce laver, or ulva; it is cooked like red laver, but is less interesting. True *laver, which has gastronomic importance and an entry to itself, belongs to the red algae along with dulse, *carrageen, and the seaweeds from which *agar is obtained.

Dulse (*Rhodymenia palmata*), in theory, is supposed to be raw in salads—and must have its devotees. There are mentions of dramatic Scottish methods, which include wrapping it around red-hot tongs, but it is also referred to as a masticatory and they can say that again. I chewed some long ago, when on a marine biological course at Port Erin, Isle of Man, and it seemed like rubber sheeting laced with iodized salt. However, André Simon says that the great Alexis Soyer included it in his St. Patrick's Day Soup. Dried dulse remains pliable, and the Irish used to chew it like tobacco, just as Icelanders today chew another red alga, pepper dulse (*Laurencia pinnatifida*), which has a pungent flavor and was used in Scotland as a condiment rather than a food.

The subject of edible seaweeds is a happy hunting ground for those interested in what the half-starving Irish or Hebridean crofters managed to live on in the past (they were hard and healthy people when they survived), but is worthy of only a brief mention here.

Kelp, the general name for any of the brown seaweeds, is a source of iodine (as extracts or tablets) in health diets. Murlins (also called dabberlochs, henware, or honeyware) is *Alaria esculenta*. It is a brown alga but, as its specific name suggests, is edible if less palatable than the red algae. Tangle and redware (*ware* and *ore* mean seaweeed) are words used in Scotland and New England but do not have exact meanings except locally.

Seaweeds are eaten in many other parts of the world. For instance, there is the *Durvillea antarctica*, the *alga mar* (seaweed) of Chile, which is exported to the U.S. However, it is in Japan that the use of seaweed is of vital gastronomic importance, so much so that many species are cultivated. (Seaweeds are also cultivated in other parts of the Pacific, for instance in Hawaii, where 70 varieties are eaten.) *Kombu is the seaweed ingredient of the ubiquitous Japanese stock *dashi*, for which black sheets of the dried weed are cut into small bits; it can also be made into a tea, or soaked and cut in strips for tying up *sushi*. *Nori*, from a red seaweed related to laver, is also dried in black sheets and is used for wrapping *sushi*; after crisping over heat, which makes it turn purplish, it can be crumbled over foods as a flavoring and garnish. *Wakame*, which comes in long curly strands, is soaked, the leaves are opened out, and the midrib is removed; this seaweed may be used as a decoration.

Less use is made of seaweed in China than in Japan, but various kinds can be bought in Chinese markets. Purple laver is dried for use in vegetable soups. There is also a hairlike seaweed used in vegetable dishes. All dried seaweeds need to be soaked before use.

[*Seaweed*—French: *algue;* German: *Alge;* Italian: *alga;* Spanish: *alga*]

SELTZER. *See* water (mineral water).

SEMOLINA. The word comes from the Italian and refers to the large particles of endosperm which are sifted out in the milling of cereals. Although it was originally applied to durum wheat, it may now mean any very coarse flour (e.g., rice semolina, corn semolina). Unqualified, though, it always means semolina from wheat.

Semolina differs from flour, which is much finer, in that when cooked it has a texture more like porridge than a paste. This makes for lightness in many dishes. For instance, *gnocchi* made with fine flour are stodgy unless they are lightened by the addition of other substances such as semolina or mashed potato. Cooked semolina is an excellent binding agent for croquettes, and wonderful sweets in which semolina is used are made in the Middle East and in India. When fried in butter to a pale golden color and then sweetened, the taste of semolina is delicious. Some of these confections are dry, with the semolina grains remaining separate—almost like a *couscous.

[*Semolina*—French: *semoule*; German: *Griessmehl*; Italian: *semolino*; Spanish: *semolino*]

SERCIAL. *See* madeira.

SEREH or **serei**. *See* lemon grass.

SERVICE TREE and **serviceberry.** *See* rowan.

SESAME. A few years ago, the word "sesame" had only one association for many people: Ali Baba and the Forty Thieves. Now people know about *tahini and even about the use of sesame oil in Oriental cooking.

Sesame seed is popular in vegetarian diets for its high content of protein and polyunsaturates. The sesame plant (*Sesamum indicum*) probably originated in Africa but has

SESAME

been cultivated in India and China since ancient times. Today it is grown all over the world in tropical and subtropical climates, even in Mediterranean countries, but it will stand no frost. The plant is a strong, erect annual which reaches 6½ ft (2 m) high. When the seeds are ripe, the plants are cut, bundled, and stacked upright to dry; they can then be turned upside down and the seeds shaken out.

Sesame seeds are small, usually white and of a flattish pear shape, but they can be cream to brown, red, or black. They contain around 50% oil, which can be extracted by cold pressing. Good sesame oil, almost tasteless and colorless, can be used for salads and cooking. Under the name of gingelly oil, it is one of the most important cooking oils in South India and in Mexico, although the sesame plant does not give such a high yield of oil per acre as some other oil seeds. When raw, the seed itself is rather tasteless, but gentle roasting makes it take on a most deliciously nutty flavor. It is used sprinkled like poppy seed over bread and cakes in baking. Mixed with a pinch of kalonji (*nigella) seed, it is often sprinkled on *nan*, the North Indian leavened bread, or simply fried and mixed with sugar. Added to rice, it is used in Indian versions of stuffed peppers. In sweet dishes, sesame seed makes one of the finest *halvas*.

[*Sesame*—French: *sésame*; German; *Sesam*; Italian: *sesamo*; Spanish: *sésamo*]

SEVICHE or **ceviche** is a South American way of preparing white fish by marinating in lime or lemon juice (or a mixture of both); the action of the acid in the juices "cooks" the fish. The juice is poured over thin, raw pieces of very fresh white fish and is seasoned with a little salt and rather more pepper (or chilies), according to how hot it is to be. Thinly sliced onions and finely chopped garlic are added, and the fish marinates in the juices for several hours; it will become opaque, like ordinary cooked fish. Seviche is served with slices of tomato, sweet peppers, sections of hard-boiled egg, sweet corn, etc. *See* caveach.

SEVRUGA. *See* caviar.

SHAD. Members of the herring family, shad were once abundant in the U.S., but their population has declined as their spawning rivers have become polluted, and

AMERICAN SHAD

they are no longer cheap fish. Young shad are born in rivers in the summer. They move out to sea in the autumn, remain there for five years, then reenter the rivers to spawn in the spring. Just before spawning is when they are caught and prized as much for their delicate flesh as for their delicious roes.

Among the many shads, *Alosa sapidissima* is the commonest in the U.S. It averages 3 lb (1½ Kg) but can grow up to 12 lb (5½ Kg). The Chesapeake Bay blueback, or glut herring, is also a shad, *A. aestivalis*. The so-called false shad, *A. fallax,* is actually a true shad, known in England as the twaite shad and in France as *alose feinte,* but fish known as Indian and Chinese shads as well as those called shad in West Africa and the Caspian Sea belong to other families.

Although many countries have shad available, the fish is nowhere valued as much as it is in the U.S. and France. It was the French who invented a method of dealing with the shad's numerous fine bones by stuffing it with ★sorrel, whose oxalic acid practically dissolves the bones. The bones can also be softened by long, slow cooking methods. In the U.S., shad are often planked for shad bakes in the North, and in the South shad roes are stuffed with crabmeat.

[*Shad*—French: *alose;* German: *Alse, Maifisch;* Spanish: *sábalo, saboga*]

SHADBERRY. *See* rowan.

SHADDOCK (*Citrus grandis*) originated in Southeast Asia, where it is still planted commercially. It is called the shaddock in the Caribbean because it was first brought there by a Captain Shaddock; *pomelo* or *pummelo* is the usual name in Asia. It is the largest of the citrus fruits, sometimes weighing as much as 22 lb (10 Kg), and looks something like a huge grapefruit with a coarse, thick rind. Inside, shaddocks are often rather dry, with a hollow core, and segments enclosed in thick, tough, and leathery membranes, which easily peel away from the flesh beneath. The juice capsules of the flesh are enormous and usually pink. The taste is described as "aromatic, spicy, and bitter"—to me, it is vaguely like the taste of grapefruit with a dash of angostura. Although the whole fruit is coarse and dry, it can be a very welcome thirst quencher to the traveler who finds it on a hot day. However, the chief distinction of the shaddock is that it is probably the ancestor of the ★grapefruit.

[*Shaddock*—French: *pamplemousse;* German: *Pampelmuse;* Italian: *pampelimosa;* Spanish: *pamplemusa, citrus decumana*]

SHAGGY MANE or **inky cap** (*Coprinus comatus*). This is one of the best-known mushrooms in the U.S. and one of the most delightful to look at and eat. It may be found

SHAGGY MANE

in autumn on lawns, fields, or dumps. Narrowly cylindrical, it expands to a bell shape covered with flattened scales, then begins to resemble a folded umbrella as it autodigests or deliquesces and dissolves into inky fluid. Its stem is hollow, with a delicate white cord suspended in the cavity. Young specimens should be picked before the gills start to dissolve, and if they are not eaten soon after picking they will turn into a black mess. Most *Coprinus* species are edible, though some should not be eaten while one is drinking alcohol (*see* mushrooms) and most are not as desirable as *C. comatus.*

At their best, shaggy manes have white flesh that is thin, soft, and fragile. Their delicate flavor and texture make them a lovely complement to fish. They can be sliced and sautéed in butter, then served on toast, baked with eggs, or eaten with such fresh vegetables as asparagus, tiny peas, and new potatoes. Shaggy manes are also delicious stewed in cream.

SHALLOT. Long essential to French cooking, the *échalote,* or shallot, is now widely available in the U.S. In some areas, shallots are synonymous with scallions, but the true shallot is not a spring onion—like garlic, it is grown until mature. Although some books give the shallot as a separate species, *Allium ascalonium,* it is often regarded as a variety of onion (*Allium cepa* var. *ascalonium*). Shallots and types known as potato onions

SHALLOT

and multiplier onions have bulbs that multiply to produce clusters joined at the root end. Shallots may be round with red-brown skins, like onions, or elongated and with skins tending toward gray-blue (in forms which are usually grown farther south and have a slight garlic overtone in their flavor).

Sauce Béarnaise requires shallots, and they are delicious in potato salad, minced over raw oysters, or used to flavor braised meat. They make the best pickled onions. Shallots are more expensive to buy than ordinary onions and are small to peel, but in addition to their special flavor—delicate yet aromatic, sweet yet bity—they also are exellent keepers.

[*Shallot*—French: *échalote;* German: *Schalotte;* Italian: *scalogno;* Spanish: *chalote, cebolleta*]

SHANK. The lower part of the front leg in mutton and lamb.

SHARK, dogfish, ray, and **skate** are grouped together because they have skeletons of hard cartilage and not of true bone. In some ways they are a rather primitive group—the first sharks appeared on earth some 300 million years ago, and they seem to have changed little since then. Their skin is covered with toothlike scales (which may be large on some rays) and is rough, like sandpaper. All the cartilaginous fish are carnivorous (although some, such as the whale sharks, feed by straining small crustaceans out of the water). They are entirely marine, despite the fact that some sharks may venture some distance up large rivers, such as the Amazon and the Ganges.

I think that no cartilaginous fish reaches the highest gastronomic pinnacle (except in *shark's-fin soup), but many make good food. In general, they can stand a little overcooking—one reason for the popularity of dogfish and skate in fish-and-chip shops—and there is no problem with bones. All cartilaginous fish are likely to smell of ammonia, because of the presence of urea in the tissues, since they have a physiology somewhat different from that of other fish—the concentration of urea counteracts the osmotic effect of sea water, which would otherwise be constantly taking water out of their bodies; bony fish cope with the problem by having large and efficient kidneys. The ammonia smell is neutralized by cooking them in black butter or by deep-fat frying, or, if the smell is not strong, by poaching them in acidulated water.

Sharks are not generally thought of as good food in the U.S. and Britain. However, the flesh of many sharks is commonly eaten, and some is quite good. Sharks have the distinction of being the world's largest fish. Whale sharks, which fortunately are inoffensive, are sometimes 70 ft (21 m) in length. On the other hand, the smallest shark is only 7 in. (17 cm) when fully grown and weighs no more than about 3 oz (70 g). In general, sharks are not benign creatures, and some are famed for their ferocity, among them the great white shark (*Carcharodon carcharias*), which can grow to a maximum of 36 ft (11 m).

The porbeagle shark or mackerel shark (*Lamna nasus*) is found throughout the world and is seasonally common in American and British waters. It has a stout appearance and gets its name from a fancied likeness to a porpoise. Porbeagles grow to up to 13 ft (4 m) long; although voracious eaters of fish, they are regarded as harmless to man. I have heard of one springing at a fisherman and tearing his clothes, but it is more usual for them to rip the nets. In the past, they were considered inedible by the British, but the French value them as *veau de mer* —the flesh is said to be rather like veal and is dry unless larded. It can be grilled in steaks, like swordfish, and the flavor is delicate and good.

The blue shark (*Prionace glauce*), also common in European waters, is sometimes passed off as tuna. The hammerhead shark (*Sphyrna zygaena*) can be found in the Mediterranean and is common on the Atlantic coast of North America; it is quite palatable when young.

The tope (*Galeorhinus galeus*), a small shark which visits British waters in spring and summer, has become a popular sporting fish in recent years. Large topes run to over 67 lb (30 Kg) and can be 10 ft (3 m) long. They are liable to smell strongly of ammonia, which has given rise to the nickname Sweet William, but as with other sharks, the smell tends to vanish on cooking.

Dogfish are small species of shark, so called, perhaps, because they sometimes hunt in packs. There are many kinds, varying in size, appearance, and the quality of their flesh (which is marketed in Britain as rock salmon or rock eel). They are found in seas almost everywhere. Of the well-known European species, the best may be the spiny dogfish or spur dog (*Squalus acanthias*), which has a spine in front of its dorsal fin and reaches a maximum length of 45 in. (115 cm). The smoothhound (*Mustelus mustelus*) is slightly bigger at 63 in. (160 cm) and is also considered fairly good eating. The most common British dogfish, though, is the larger spotted dogfish or nurse hound (*Scyliorhinus stellaris*); it can reach 47 in. (120 cm) and is a bit coarse and tasteless. The lesser spotted dogfish (*Scyliorhinus caniculus*), 29 in. (75 cm) long, is also common

in British waters and is slightly better. The U.S. has the same or similar species of dogfish, which may be used for all European recipes. There are few serious recipes for dogfish, although the Italians will take trouble to get the belly of the spiny dogfish rather than the back. In Germany, the belly flaps of the dogfish, hot-smoked, are a delicacy.

The angelfish, angel shark, or monkfish (*Squatina squatina* and other species) is a flattened, bottom-dwelling shark whose pectoral fins form "wings." It is in many ways intermediate between sharks and rays. Some angelfish grow up to 10 ft (3 m) long. Although they were once despised as food, their flesh is good and there are few bones.

Rays and **skates** cannot be distinguished scientifically, since both names are given to members of the same group of flattened cartilaginous fish. However, the name "skate" is very often given to the members of the group that are eaten, while "ray" describes the vast creatures like the manta ray or devilfish, which are caught for sport, the stingrays, which have a spike and associated poison glands in the tail and can inflict a terrible wound (they are quite good to eat), and the torpedo ray or electric ray, of which there are some 35 species, all capable of delivering a powerful electric shock.

Rays and skates are kite-shaped fish with pectoral fins that have been modified into "wings" in the course of evolution. They swim with undulating, wavelike motions of the wings, and the tail is used mainly as a rudder, although it can also be a weapon. Skates are lazy and slow-swimming, in spite of their supersonic shape. They spend a great deal of their time lying on the bottom, usually on sand or mud, waiting for their prey, which they surprise rather than chase. Species of skate range from less than 39 in. (1 m) long to good-sized fish like the common skate, which can grow to 8 ft (2.5 m). Skates are found in all oceans, but not all the many species are equally excellent. They are often sold skinned and jointed—the wings are the most valuable part.

The common skate or tinker of Europe (*Raja batis*) has a long, pointed snout and smooth skin. It is considered good eating, as is the thornback ray (*R. clavata*), another species common in British waters—it also occurs in the Mediterranean, but not on the west side of the Atlantic. Although it grows to only 39 in. (1 m) long, it can give a nasty wound with its thorny tail. Common skates on the American East Coast are the barn-

BARN-DOOR SKATE

door skate (*R. laevis*) and *R. erinacea*, while on the West Coast, *R. binoculata* is found. Skates are not easy to identify, especially the young, which are called "maids."

The taste of skate improves with a couple of days' hanging—no more, or the ammonia smell will become too strong. The liver is esteemed. It is poached, pounded, and made into a sauce, or slivers of it are put inside skate fillets, which are then rolled up, tied with thread, and poached. Because the bones are very gelatinous, they give an unctuousness to the flesh when the wings are fried and make a jelly which sets when poached skate cools. In large skates, the thick part of the wing is the best buy, since there is more meat in proportion to skeleton. After hanging, skates are always skinned on both sides.

The guitar fish (*Rhinobatus rhinobatus*), from the southern Mediterranean, looks a little like the angel shark but is a true ray. It grows to 39 in. (1 m) in length and is moderately good to eat. Similar species from warm seas grows to 8 ft (2.5 m) and are used for liver oil as well as for eating. Also fished as a source of liver oil are the sawfish

(species of *Pristis*), large tropical relations of the rays which have a long, toothed "saw" on the front of the head; they are not usually eaten, as far as I know, although doubtless someone loves them.

SHARK'S FIN and **shark's stomach** are much prized in Chinese cooking and are available dried from Chinese shops. The dried stomachs, after soaking, are sautéed or made into soup; the fins are made into soup or cooked in other ways. Both are expensive. Top-quality fin is in long filament; the lowest quality in odd pieces.

Shark's-fin threads, which have been bought ready-prepared, should be soaked in water for about 20 minutes before use. Of the cruder dried fins, yellow ones need boiling for about an hour and black ones for considerably longer (boil for 2 hours, take off the black skin, and boil the flesh again for 1–2 hours in new water, then drain and shred it). The prepared shark's fins (sold in packets) are equivalent to double their weight of yellow and treble their weight of black. Fresh shark's fins need to be cleaned of all skin, meat, and cartilage other than the fin. They can be trimmed, boiled for 5 minutes, and left to soak for 4 hours, after which the skin and bones can be separated from the fins. These are then boiled for 6–7 hours, with the water being changed every 2 hours, before they are dried in the sun. Most people will prefer to use a packet of prepared fins.

SOUPE AUX ESTOMACS DE REQUIN
(CANH BONG-CÁ)

Soak 4 oz (100 g) dried shark's stomach (*bong-cá*) for 1 hour, then drain and cook it in hot oil. The stomach softens and swells; after some 20 minutes, it becomes crisp. Put it into 1¾ pt (1 lt) of stock made with chicken and lean pork and add 1 oz (25 g) each of Chinese mushrooms and dried lily flowers (soaked). Season the soup with salt, pepper, monosodium glutamate, and powdered ginger, then cover and simmer it for 30 minutes. Make an omelet with 2 eggs, slice it, and add it to the soup before serving. Sprinkle with some chopped chervil, chives, and tarragon.

SHELL BEAN. *See* beans.

SHELLFISH is a collective term for aquatic, usually marine, animals that are not fish. The main components in this delicious ragbag of biologically diverse types are *crustaceans and *mollusks.

[*Shellfish*—French: *coquilles, coquillages;* German: *Schalentieren, Muscheln;* Italian: *crostaceo;* Spanish: *crustaceo*]

SHERRY comes from the province of Cádiz in the southwestern corner of Spain. The main variety of grape is the white Palomino, which makes the finest wine when it has been grown on the white *albariza* soil. Other grape varieties, notably Pedro Ximenez and Moscatel, are used to make sweetening wines. When the bunches are picked, they are first spread out on esparto grass mats for a day or more to dry, which increases the percentage of sugar in them. Until after World War II, the grapes were, whenever possible, trodden in wooden troughs by men wearing specially nailed boots. (French wine presses were found to given an inferior sherry.) More recently, German presses, which squeeze the grapes more kindly, have been installed. These have replaced the old methods without loss of quality.

Spanish sherry comes from three towns and their areas. Jerez de la Frontera and Puerto de Santa Maria produce similar wines, but Sanlúcar de Barrameda has very different wines and is the source of all the manzanilla—the main types of sherry are listed below. A special characteristic of sherrymaking is the *flor,* a white mat of microorganisms which forms on the top of some butts several months after the vintage and causes the wine in the butt to develop into a fino. Another characteristic is the *solera* system, which was introduced around 1800, in which any wine drawn off from the oldest butt is replaced by an equal quantity from the next oldest, which in turn is replaced from the third oldest and so on until finally the youngest wine enters the chain. Sherries are fortified by adding pure alcohol, not necessarily produced from grapes, which prevents the development of unsuitable organisms. Sherry is usually also blended and sweetened. There are a few straight sherries, but these entirely natural finos and olorosos are bone dry, since the sugar has been fermented out, and would not please the majority of drinkers.

When a bottle of sherry is opened, it should not be kept hanging about until the next anniversary. In spite of its high alcohol content, most sherry will deteriorate. Indeed a fino, even when unopened, will deteriorate in the bottle and will be noticeably less good after 3 months. True sweet sherries deteriorate more slowly—some even improve with keeping, but it takes 10 years for the difference to show, and then it may not happen. The general rule is to buy sherry as you want it. Dry sherries should be served cold, down to 38°F (3–4°C) for a dry fino; 40–50°F (5–10°C) is more usual. A sweeter sherry can be a little warmer, and a sweet dessert sherry can be at room temperature. There is no law about this—it depends on personal preference. Since cold interferes with the sensation of sweetness, the colder a sherry is served the dryer it tastes.

Sherry is one of the wines most used in cooking, and a dry sherry is most adaptable for this purpose; sweetness can always be added. When a sherry is called for in a recipe, it does not mean that any old cooking sherry will do; indeed, the very idea of cooking sherry is an abomination. Equally, however, the special qualities of very rare sherry would get lost in cooking.

Amontillado is considered to have something of the taste of a montilla—hence the name. A certain number of finos will develop into amontillados if they are kept in the butt for 8 years or more, but it will not always happen, the result is unpredictable, and thus real amontillados are rare and costly. What is often sold as amontillado is a blend which tries to imitate the flavor and is more correctly an amontillado-type sherry.

Bristol milk and Bristol cream. Bristol milk, the older type, is a sweetened oloroso. Bristol Cream is the most popular sherry in the U.S. It is a sweetened blend of oloroso and amontillado sherries made to a secret recipe that belongs to Harvey's of Bristol. Although it is formulated there, the sherries are from Spain.

Cream sherry is sweetened and blended; it is for the end of a meal, to be drunk with sweet dishes, but is better perhaps with strong cheeses such as Gorgonzola or Roquefort.

Fino. When a *flor* develops on a young sherry (except in Sanlúcar), it turns into a fino. This is the lightest type of sherry (except for manzanilla) and is pale in color. A fino that is aged in the butt may perhaps turn into an amontillado or remain as an aged fino; if kept in the bottle, it will deteriorate. Fino is the most popular type of dry sherry and a good one to steal for use in the kitchen. It can be used in Japanese and Chinese cooking when genuine rice wines are not handy. Fino is served cold with shrimp, olives, and other *tapas, meze,* or hors d'oeuvre.

Manzanilla. Wine from Jerez de la Frontera must be taken to Sanlúcar to become manzanilla, and Sanlúcar wine to Jerez to turn into fino. This is because a rather different *flor* develops in each microclimate, one of the subtleties of winemaking. Manzanilla is usually very dry, too dry and severe for most people, and has a slightly medicinal taste. It is normally served cold with seafood and is often drunk with *tapas* at bars in Spain. It is good in cooking, especially in sauces, less so for sweet dishes.

Montilla is not strictly a sherry, for legal reasons, but it is a very similar wine grown on similar white soil a little north of the sherry districts, toward Córdoba. Because the wines of Montilla are naturally rather stronger than sherry, they are not fortified. They have very much the same sherry fla-

vor, and a taster will know immediately that they are from the same stable. Montillas are fine apéritif wines, less known and often a little cheaper than real sherries. They are excellent for cooking and as an apéritif are served cold like a manzanilla.

Oloroso means odorous in the nicest sense. It is the basic wine of the sherry district, which has not been changed by a *flor*. It may be sweetened and fortified with alcohol. An oloroso in Spain is dry, but elsewhere it will almost always be sweetened to make it medium. It is the archetypal sherry.

Palo cortado. A rare type of sherry for connoisseurs. It is a separate type, rather dark, but dryish and unusual. It would only be for a special occasion.

Sherry-type wines come from South Africa, Australia, California, and Cyprus. There is even British sherry, which has been made from dried fruit since the beginning of the century. South African sherries will not be distinguished from run-of-the-mill Spanish sherries except by experts, and even then not in blindfold tests. Others vary in quality from good to awful. You have to rely on your own palate and judgment.

[*Sherry*—French: *vin de Xérès;* German: *Sherry, Jerezwein;* Italian: *vino di Xeres;* Spanish: *jerez*]

SHIITAKE. *See* mushrooms.

SHIN. In beef butchery, the shin is the lower part of the front leg and is equivalent to the *shank in mutton or lamb.

SHIRATAKI. *See* noodles.

SHORTENING. Any kind of fat or oil used to make pastry brittle and crisp—i.e., short, an adjective that also crops up in shortbread and shortcake. Shortening is the normal U.S. term for fat, especially that used in baking.

SHRIMP and **prawn.** Both names indicate small crustaceans related to lobster, though much smaller, except for a few giant forms. Prawns and shrimps are not easy to identify, even for a zoologist, and the scientific nomenclature is littered with confusing syn-

SHRIMP

onyms. In England, for instance, a shrimp is small, at least in common parlance (it usually means anything more than 2–3 in./5–7 cm long), and a prawn is larger, but in the U.S. all sizes are now usually called shrimp, with modifiers such as jumbo, small, and baby. To add to the confusion, in Scotland the word "prawn" is used to describe the Norway lobster, alias *scampi; and the *mantis shrimp (*Squilla empusa*), common from Cape Cod to Florida and found in varying species in Hawaii, is not a true shrimp (but is just as delicious). The best that the layman can hope to do is to recognize the types that are in the local market by their appearance and popular name and by experience to get some idea of their quality.

There are thousand of species of prawn and shrimp in the world, and the high prices they fetch have made it commercially worthwhile for them to be flown refrigerated from the most remote places. In the jungle waterways of Asia, you can nowadays find fishermen netting with primitive gear and filling bamboo cages with huge live prawns for eventual shipment halfway around the world.

Because shrimps are very perishable when fresh, they are usually quick-frozen on shrimping boats or cooked in seawater by the fishermen on board the boats. They are seldom caught by hand in shrimp nets; usually boats drag a fine-meshed net along the seabed. They may also be caught in nets drawn over estuary flats at low tides or by horses or, now more often, by tractors.

Americans eat more shrimp than any other seafood. At least a dozen different species of edible shrimps are found in North American waters, and many more are sold in markets throughout the U.S. Except for rock shrimp (*Sicyonia brevirostris*), a large species with firm meat similar to lobsterettes, the flesh of most U.S. shrimps has the same texture and taste. Except for size, the species are not usually distinguishable to the layman and can differ in different locations— e.g., pink shrimp (*Penaeus duorarum*) and brown shrimp (*Penae aztecus*) are sometimes the same color. Northern shrimp, the American name for *Pandalus borealis,* is found in northern offshore waters of both the Atlantic and the Pacific. Southern shrimp, from southeastern and Gulf State waters, is of roughly the same size as the northern shrimp. The North Pacific shrimp, which is caught from California to Alaska, is much smaller. However, huge quantities of shrimp are imported into the U.S. from all over the world. The largest come from Pakistan and Ecuador, some of them over 2 oz (60 g) each, and there are small shrimps from Denmark and Holland. New methods of flash-freezing shrimps individually have greatly improved quality, but the best seafood in America, as elsewhere, is found on the coasts, where local shrimps, with local names, are cooked in traditional ways.

The two commonest shallow-water species of the English Channel, North Sea, and British coasts are the brown shrimp (*Crangon crangon*) and the pink shrimp or Aesop prawn (*Prandalus maontagui*); the pink shrimp looks prettier, but the brown tastes better. Famous places for shrimps in Britain are the Lancashire coast, the Wash, and Thames estuary. They are also much fished in shallow water off Holland and the French coast, as well as in Denmark, where tiny pink shrimps are used to cover an expensive but delicious open sandwich (*rejemad*). In Britain, shrimps potted in butter and flavored with mace are a famous delicacy which can be bought ready prepared. Frozen shrimps are a poor second; although frozen when fresh, they seem to lose flavor.

"Prawn" is a word that might beneficially disappear from the English cook's vocabulary. The creature to which it properly refers is the common prawn (*Palemon serratus*), a coastal species that is actually not at all common around the coasts of Britain and is scarcely fished on a commercial basis. Its place in the fish shops is usually taken by the species that the Department of Trade thinks should be called the deepwater shrimp (*Pandalus borealis*); a second, as yet unexploited, species, *P. bonnieri*, is found off the west coast of Scotland. The deepwater shrimp, which is unofficially referred to as the deepwater prawn or northern prawn, has been fished for some years by the Danes and Norwegians.

Prawns take about 5–7 minutes to cook, and large ones may be peeled before cooking, split down the back, and opened flat. At least since Victorian times, prawns prepared in this way have been sautéed as prawn cutlets (butterfly shrimp in the U.S.). King prawns, which usually make this dish today, are imported (e.g., from Malaya). Other old British prawn dishes include prawn and lobster soup, prawn pie, and curried prawns in the Anglo-Indian manner.

A few of the many other prawns found in European Altantic and Mediterranean waters need special mention. They are, for instance, the very large and striking blood-red species, *Aristeomorpha foliacea* and Edwards's red shrimp (*Plesiopenaeus edwardsianus*), which can go up to 1 ft (30 cm) long, although 8 in. (20 cm) is more usual; they live at a depth of some 822 ft (250 m). The red prawn (*Parapenaeus longirostris*) is not quite so large, rarely exceeding 6 in. (16 cm). It lives at great depths and frequently gets squashed when it is hauled up with the other creatures in the trawl. Perhaps this is why it is usually cold cooked in Italian markets, where it is called not only *gambero rosa* (pink prawn) but also *gambero bianco* (white prawn). This and another species,

Aristeus antennatus (which is red), are known as *gamba* in Spanish restaurants.

In Spain, both species are commonly sold raw in the markets. They are frequently rather soft, with an off-smell, but many people acquire a liking for a "bad prawn" taste (*see* balachan), which blends well with garlic. The aristocrat of the European prawns, and possibly a claimant to the title of best crustacean in the world (its perfumed and delicate flesh is superior to that of any crayfish or lobster), is *Paenus kerathurus*, which the Spanish call *langostino* and the Italians *mazzancolla* or *gambero imperiale*. Large— around 8 in. (20 cm) long—and pale garnet-red striped with dark garnet on the tail, it lives on the muddy bottom off the estuaries of rivers, usually buried with just its head sticking out. To eat this fabulous prawn to perfection, you have to go to the Mediterranean, best of all to San Carlos de la Rapita at the mouth of the Ebro River in Spain, where they make a feature of serving them absolutely fresh. The town's badge is a golden prawn. A *langostinara* (prawn feast), which is costly but worth every penny as a gastronomic experience of almost Chinese sophistication, is a meal composed entirely of *langostinos* cooked in different ways.

Shrimps and their relatives are very popular in most regions of the world. For example, in Japan, prawns are eaten in dozens of ways, as you might expect in a country that makes so much use of food from the sea. Famous species are the large *Penaeus japonicus* (8 in. or 20 cm long), the common Japanese prawn, and the equally large *P. nipponensis,* the Japanese red prawn. The strangest way the Japanese eat prawns is alive—as Americans do oysters. In a ritual called *odori* (dance), the living prawn is beheaded, shelled, and gutted so rapidly that the diner can pop it still moving into his mouth. At the other end of the freshness scale, there are preparations of pounded and dried rotten prawns and shrimps used particularly in the cooking of Southeast Asia.

To clean raw shrimp, a sharp knife is useful but not essential. Hold the shrimp tail belly side up, slit along the curve of the body, and use the thumbs of both hands to pry the shell apart and away from the body, removing the legs in the same motion. Deveining—removing the black intestinal tract—is a matter of aesthetics, not safety or flavor; it is advisable to improve the appearance of such dishes as butterflied shrimp, and it is easy to do under running water if the shrimp's back has been properly slit. Save the shells to make court bouillon: for a well-flavored bouillon, cook the shells with a few fish heads and aromatics such as chopped celery, parsley, a bay leaf, peppercorns, and whatever other seasonings are appropriate to the dish you plan to serve. This broth, strained, can be used to cook the shrimps and, reduced, make a sauce.

According to James Beard, the American authority on seafood cooking, "the unpardonable fault in preparing shrimp is overcooking," and it cannot be overemphasized that shrimp should be cooked only long enough to give them firmness and color—3–5 minutes—just until opaque, and they should be simmered, not violently boiled. If shrimp are to be added to a sauce and heated, they will be overcooked if you cooked them before adding them to the sauce. If they are to be added to a salad, they should be cooled under cold running water or plunged into ice water the minute they are cooked.

Recipes for shrimp are numerous, since the shrimp is a food that is delicate in flavor yet sturdy enough in texture to accommodate tomato sauces, garlic, and other seasonings that might overwhelm more fragile seafoods—although, as Beard points out, small sweet shrimp sold with heads on in certain localities in the U.S. South and West are what the French call *bouquet,* suggesting their delicacy, and should be served very simply as an hors d'oeuvre in the shell without sauces. Large shrimps, served cold, may be accompanied by various sauces—rémoulade, vinaigrette, green mayonnaise, or mayonnaise flavored with mustard. They go well as a filling for cucumbers and avocados,

topped with Russian dressing or dilled mayonnaise, and they are delicious marinaded with mushrooms. The Japanese cook shrimps to perfection in tempura, the Italians broil them with herbs, and many Americans have found shrimps excellent skewered with mushrooms and barbecued. In New Orleans, shrimp Creole and jambalaya reveal how well shrimps can be enhanced with tomatoes and herbs—some Chinese dishes resemble Creole cooking in their use of seasonings, and it is hard to say who invented sweet-and-sour shrimps, or fried rice with shrimps (which incorporates ham, green scallions, eggs, and lots of parsley), or shrimp polenta (perhaps a European adaptation of an original American dish with a Mexican background). And then there are shrimp curries, shrimp Florentine, shrimp loaf, and dried shrimps, which are eaten like French fries in some areas.

The shrimp has been with us for a long time, and it may be with us in the future in even less palatable forms than we find it today as the canned or often badly frozen item in the supermarket: krill, the tiny shrimp that once provided sustenance for whales, is now being investigated as a food for human consumption, now that the whale is disappearing and leaving its diet to those humans who have always thought wales were useful only for killing off for the benefit of *Homo sapiens.*

[*Shrimp*—French: *crevette;* German: *Garnele, Krabbe;* Italian: *gamberetto grigio;* Spanish: *quisquilla gris. Prawn*—French: *crevette rose;* German: *Sagegarnele;* Italian: *gamberello;* Spanish: *camerón, gamba*]

SHUNGIKU. *See* chrysanthemum.

SIFTING. Putting through a sieve to take out lumps or coarse particles, but also a method of mixing (sifting together) and of getting air into flour for lightness.

[*Sifting*—French: *tamiser, passer au crible, sasser;* German: *durchsieben;* Italian: *stacciare;* Spanish: *cerner*]

SILVER (Ag) is not generally regarded as an essential trace metal in the diet. Like most metallic salts, those of silver are poisonous in any quantity. Silver is also very poisonous to microorganisms; drinking water used to be kept for preference in silver jugs (which helped to purify it, although the reason was unknown). Modern filters of porous material used for purifying water are often impregnated with colloidal silver, which eliminates the need for periodic heat sterilization—otherwise the bacteria live in the pores of the filter and gradually get pushed through, but the silver kills them.

Silver is the best of all conductors of electricity—better than copper—and is a good conductor of heat, but it is soft unless mixed in alloy with other metals. It stands up well to ordinary kitchen acids but is easily tarnished by anything containing sulfur; silver spoons turn brown if they touch egg, and silver-lined pans should not be used for omelets. However, silver looks beautiful on an elegant table, and silver-covered copper (Sheffield plate) serving dishes and chafing dishes are the best of all, combining beauty with conductivity. Silver-lined copper pans for making crêpes and for flambés can also be bought. Tinners will sometimes line pans with silver. The result is not much more expensive but is a lot longer-lasting than tin.

[*Silver*—French: *argent;* German: *Silber;* Italian: *argento;* Spanish: *plata*]

SIMMERING is cooking just below boiling point, with the liquid barely trembling. In the old days, this meant pushing the pan to the side of the stove; with gas and electricity, it is often more difficult. The usual simmering temperature is 205–209°F (96–98°C), but for meat a somewhat lower temperature of 180–189°F (82–87°C) is often recommended. However, the temperatures used in simmering are not precise—that of boiling water is easily recognizable and simmering is just below it. The temperatures are not directly related to those needed to coagulate proteins, kill harmful organisms, or soften tissues. It is likely that cooks who use thermometers can make considerable improvements in their cooking by using lower simmering temperatures than they would otherwise do.

[*Simmering*—French: *bouillir lentement;* German: *langsam kochen;* Italian: *sobbollire;* Spanish: *hacer hervir a fuego lento*]

SKATE. *See* shark.

SKIM MILK or **nonfat milk** is *milk after the cream has been skimmed off, but today is more often milk in which as much fat as is technologically possible has been removed in a separator. The milkfat content is less than 0.5% (low-fat milk may contain as much as 2%). It can be bought in most countries and is much used by people on low-calorie or low-cholesterol diets.

[*Skim milk*—French: *lait écrémé;* German: *entrahmte Milch;* Italian: *latte scremato;* Spanish: *leche desnatada*]

SKIMMING is removing scum, fat, or froth from the surface of a liquid. Scum is usually most easily removed with a perforated spoon; solid fat can be taken off when the liquid is cold (but there are also gadgets—separating spoons—to help separate liquid fat and water). The last vestiges of fat may be removed by applying paper towels or blotting paper to the surface.

[*Skimming*—French: *écumer, écrémer;* German: *abschäumen;* Italian: *schiumare;* Spanish: *desnatar*]

SKINNING. *See* drawing.

SKIPJACK. *See* bonito.

SLIVOVITZ. *See* fruit brandy.

SLOE is the fruit of the blackthorn (*Prunus spinosa*), a relative of the plum that grows wild all over Europe. Its equivalent in the

U.S. is the wild plum (*P. americana*). Sloes look like tiny, spherical plums and have a heavy bloom, which makes them appear blue, although the skin is purple to black when this is rubbed off. The pulp of the fruit is greenish. Even if the sloes are left on the tree until late in the autumn, they never get sweet and are always astringent. Sloes are sometimes used in apple jelly and in dishes with apples to which the sloes add a punch, but their most important use is in sloe gin.

For this, sloes should be gathered in late autumn, pricked or crushed (together with a few of the stones), and put into bottles, which are then filled up with gin. After corking and leaving for a few months, decant the liquid and sweeten it to taste. Sloe gin, a particularly English drink, was very popular in Victorian times. Recipes abound—several of my aunts kept recipe books which seemed to have contained recipes for little else—but all are essentially the same. Made with 95% pure grape spirit (as I used to in Italy), it is even better and becomes very bracing indeed—it might perhaps be called sloe vodka. The lovely dark red color comes from the skins of the sloes. The French liqueur *prunelle* is also flavored with sloes.

[*Sloe*—French: *prunelle;* German: *Schlehe;* Italian: *prugnola, pruna selvatica;* Spanish: *endrino*]

SMOKED SALMON. The word "kipper" probably comes from the Dutch *küpper,* meaning "to spawn," and was first applied to out-of-season salmon, emaciated objects that were usually split and smoked to make them more palatable. From as early as the 14th century, there are references to the "kipper times" in the Thames salmon fishery.

Smoked salmon is now an expensive delicacy. To ensure a continuity of supply, it is prepared mainly with frozen salmon from Canada, Norway, Ireland, and Britain. The color of the flesh can vary from the very pale Polish Delta to the rich red of Canadian.

The fat content can also vary from 3% to 20%.

To prepare a whole salmon for smoking, gut it and clean the belly cavity, the thick core of blood next to the backbone should be scooped out with a teaspoon. The head is cut off, and the fish is split into two filleted sides leaving the lug bones on the fish. Because a filleted side is rather soft to handle, a loop of string is passed through the lug flaps under the fin on the lug bone. This facilitates handling and is also used to hang up the side, which is then ready to be brined or dry-salted.

Brining gives a much better appearance to the finished side but makes the drying take much longer. More often, vacuum-dried salt is used. The fillets are laid, skin down, on a thick bed of salt. The cut surface is sprinkled with salt, thickly on the thickest part of the fish, tapering to very little on the thin tail. After salting, which can take 4–5 hours for grilse (young salmon) and up to 24 hours for larger sides, the surface salt is washed off and the fillets are hung to drain. In traditional kilns, the fish can be left to drain overnight before being smoked in a dense smoke for several hours. The smoke is produced from smoldering white wood sawdust, but hardwoods, peat, or juniper can be used to impart different flavors.

The finished side should have a pleasant smoky aroma and feel firm when pressed with the fingertips at the thickest part. In a good cure, the weight loss is about one-third from the whole fish.

The sides can be vacuum-packed in plastic, or sliced, interleaved with cellophane, and laid back on the skin before vacuum packing (this has the appearance of a whole side). Smoked salmon can also be purchased frozen or canned, but it does not compare to the justifiably expensive fresh smoked product, which should be cut to order. Presliced fish may be dry, and if it is packed in oil it is best to forget it. Brine-cured salmon, known as lox in Jewish cuisine, is usually eaten with bagels and cream cheese, whereas smoked Nova Scotia salmon is more elegantly served as an hors d'oeuvre, sliced transparently thin, with lemon, brown bread and butter, and perhaps capers. *Royktlaks*—Norwegian smoked salmon—is much used in smorgasbords. Smoked salmon "trimmings"—scraps of fresh smoked salmon with bits of skin and bone attached—are a good buy if you are making dishes such as salmon mousse or scrambled eggs with salmon.

SMOKING was originally used, in conjunction with salting and drying, to preserve fish and meat. It may possibly have been done by prehistoric man; certainly it was by the Egyptians and the Chinese, and primitive methods are still used in many parts of the world. For example, East African *bonga* is made on large oil drums covered at the open end with wire mesh. The fish are laid on the mesh and cooked over a charcoal fire and then wet wood shavings (or sawdust) are scattered over the embers to produce a dense smoke.

Traditionally, smoked foods were preserved by the combined effects of drying, of bacteria-killing chemicals in the smoke, and of the high salt concentrations. Present-day smoke-cured foods, both fish and meat, contain much less smoke and salt and are thus more dependent on refrigeration to keep them in an edible condition. That is to say, smoking as a method of preservation has been made redundant by the modern technologies of canning, freezing, and drying, but it is now valued for the flavor it gives, and for that reason is handled with more subtlety.

Smoking of fish, meat, poultry, and game is preceded by treatment with salt—either *dry salting or immersion in *brine, which may contain spices and flavorings and perhaps sugar to help tenderize the tougher lumps of meat. Books on smoking may well quote brine strengths as a percentage of the strength of a saturated solution—the usual strength is about 80% of saturation, 5½ oz per pt (270 g per lt)—and the brining time is often much less than it would be if the brining were the only method of preservation: a matter of hours or even minutes rather than days. For large pieces of meat such as hams and haunches of venison, brine can be introduced into the middle, where it might not otherwise penetrate, by means of a brine pump, which is something like a large hypodermic syringe and requires much the same degree of cleanliness to avoid introducing bacteria along with the brine. After brining, most products are hung up to dry before they are smoked.

Books on smoking offer all manner of designs for smokers, ranging from sophisticated constructions down to improvisations around such items as empty oil drums, dead refrigerators, and disused outdoor privies. What all these things have in common is a smoke chamber with ventilation holes at the top and a device to feed the smoke in evenly at the bottom—the simplest is a smoke spreader made of a perforated metal sheet covering the bottom of the chamber. The chamber is fitted with bars from which the food can be suspended in the smoke. Beneath the chamber (or away from it if a smoke duct is built between) is the source of the smoke, a heap of smoldering sawdust. Sometimes there is also a source of additional heat such as a gas ring.

The sawdust used for smoking must not be wet, or it may give a moldy flavor to the food. That apart, there is no absolute consensus about the sawdust that should be used. The most favored are hardwoods such as oak, beech, birch, and hickory, which burn slowly and steadily. Softwoods, such as fir or pine, are resinous and are said to produce a bitter taste in the smoked food. Because they also give a good color, a proportion is sometimes added to the hardwood sawdust. Aromatic woods such as juniper and rosemary may also be burned in the final stages of smoking to add their own special flavor.

The basic smoke-curing process is cold smoking, in which the food is smoked at 50–85°F (10–29°C), and ideally at 75–80°F (24–27°C). This means that the food is smoked without being cooked, although it is partly dried—the weight loss that results can be used as an indication of how the smoking is progressing (smoking is completed when the weight loss compared with the untreated product is 17–18% for salmon, 25% for cod roe, and 12–14% for finnan haddock). A few cold-smoked foods are eaten raw, among them *smoked salmon, smoked cod roe, and smoked fillet of beef, but the majority, including *finnan haddock, kippers, and smoked *bacon, are cooked before they are eaten.

Cold smoking is also a stage in the preparation of hot smoked foods. After the product has been given its smoky flavor and slightly dried by cold smoking, the temperature is raised to about 180°F (82°C) for fish, which is likely to disintegrate at higher temperatures, but anything up to 240°F (115°C) for meat, game, and poultry. From its cooking in hot smoke, as long as this has not been too long or at too high a temperature, the result will be delicately flavored and ready to be eaten cold after it has been left to mature in a cool place for 24 hours. Hot smoked products include smoked mackerel and trout, buckling, and a variety of smoked game and poultry.

The small smokers that are sold in kitchen shops produce hot smoked trout and other small items by a rather different method. These smokers are closed boxes heated from below to ignite the sawdust on the floor of the box; the food rests on a rack with a drip tray to prevent the juices from falling on the sawdust. The whole apparatus gets rather hot—hotter than in other hot smoking processes—and the food is cooked in about 20 minutes to give a product that is probably acceptable rather than exquisite.

The success of smoked foods is almost as dependent on the quality of the raw materials as it is on the expertise of the smoker. Fish must be very fresh (or it can be frozen and freshly thawed), and the blood that lies along the backbone must be scooped out. Game birds should not be hung for more than 3 days before they are brined, while beef and venison need to be aged for at least a week. Brine should be made up freshly for each batch of food to be smoked, and vacuum-dried salt, which does not have added magnesium carbonate, should be used in making it (or for dry salting).

Cold smoking without prior salting can be applied to a small variety of other foods—a curious assortment, including nuts, bilberries, hard-boiled eggs, and cheese. Mild hard or semihard cheeses are suitable for smoking. For Austrian smoked cheese, though, it is not the cheese itself but the milk that goes into it that is smoked.

Smoke roasting is cooking meat such as steak or spareribs in hot smoke at 200–225°F (93–107°C) without salting or cool smoking—the meat is simply seasoned and given a coating of oil. Unlike hot-smoked meat it is eaten hot.

In the main, smoke curing is now in the hands of large food manufacturing companies which use modern technology to give a standardized product. Various lines of research have evolved processes for applying smoke in liquid form. The first such technique emerged some 40 years ago, when the Japanese used pure *pyroligneous acid from the destructive distillation of wood. This tasted and smelled like strong vinegar. More modern liquid smokes, some from natural sources and others produced chemically, are still in the experimental stage. Applying the theory of electrostatic precipitation, which is used for painting cars, smoke can be deposited on fish and colors it in a matter of minutes. However, it fails to penetrate the surface and is not always pleasant to taste. But sooner or later the scientists will conquer these little problems and come up with a product sufficiently standardized—and characterless—to suit the food industry.

[*Smoking*—French: *fumer;* German: *räuchern;* Italian: *affumicare;* Spanish: *ahumar*]

SNAILS. Many kinds of snail are eaten. Even in Britain, snails were traditionally eaten in a few districts; they were thought to be good for the lungs. Glass blowers, for instance, thought that eating snails gave them plenty of breath, and recipes for snail water and snail broth appear in 17th-century and earlier recipe books as a remedy for consumption. However, snails were not regarded as a delicious food, but were usually looked on with some disgust, perhaps because of the slime which the snail pours out as a carpet to walk on.

The Romans had no squeamishness and regarded the snail as a luxury. They went in for snail culture, building special houses called *cochlearia,* in which snails were fattened on a mixture of meal and wine. The scholar Marcus Terentius Varro *(*116–28 B.C.) even wrote on the subject in his *De re rustica,* and the tradition of snail farming continued in Europe. Today, once more, snaileries are on the increase, although wild snails gathered after rain still form the majority of those eaten. Indeed, so avidly are snails gathered that laws have had to be passed in some countries making closed seasons for snails in order to prevent their near-extinction. Snails are increasingly expensive. In France, where the annual consumption of snails is reckoned in hundreds of millions, you will have trouble finding even a single snail in the Burgundy vineyards—I know as I have hunted them there. To satisfy demand, snails have to be imported from Yugoslavia and elsewhere.

Snails are traditionally prepared when alive; canned snails sold with a bag of shells attached are a fairly recent innovation. The best-known species of snail for eating is the large Roman snail (*Helix pomata*), which is called the Burgundy snail by gourmets and is found over much of Europe. It has been introduced into Britain (some say by the Romans, but that is doubtful) and it can sometimes be found, but only in chalk or limestone country, since it needs a lot of lime to make its shell. Contrary to popular belief, the common garden snail (*H. aspera*) is excellent to eat and, with two other species (*H. vermiculata* and *H. nemoralis*), is regarded,

for instance, by the people of Liguria, as better than the large "Burgundy."

Small snails are fried with onions, cooked with garlic, rosemary, parsley, tomato, dried fungi, olive oil, and white wine; they are also cooked with oil, butter, raisins, and pine nuts—even with mint. The Spanish offer snails roasted on rocks and seasoned with salt and oil, snails in paella, and particularly snails poached in a court bouillon containing wild fennel and eaten with the strong garlic mayonnaise which the Catalans call *alioli.*

Snails are most easily gathered after rain; a good strategy is to go at night with a torch. You will need to get a dozen large Roman snails or about 20 of the smaller species (*petits gris*) per person. When the catch is brought home, put the snails in a box—a tin with holes punched in it for air is good—and keep them for a week while they clean themselves of any plants they may have eaten that are poisonous to humans. (If the snails have been taken from a garden, they may have been contaminated with poison sprays and may die.)

During this period, some people starve them completely; others fatten them on lettuce leaves, herbs (like fennel), bran or flour. At the end of the week the snails should be washed and inspected. Any dead ones must be thrown away.

The next step is to remove the slime. Put the snails in a bowl, mix them with salt—preferably coarse salt—and stir them about gently for 10–15 minutes, until they foam. Some cooks add a little vinegar. Then wash the snails in cold water and repeat the desliming process if necessary until all the snails' slime glands are emptied. (It is not a critical process, since the slime is not harmful—peasants preparing small snails often do not bother.) After giving them a final wash, plunge the snails into boiling water for from 3–5 minutes, until it is possible to extract the animals with a fork. Screw each snail out of its shell (this is not done for small species in the snail-eating countries, but I always do it even for large garden snails) and pull off and discard the black "visceral spiral"—which is in the top of the shell. It is not poisonous, but it contains the liver and, in large snails, is bitter. Now wash the snails, put them into boiling water again for 10 minutes, and drain them. Finally, cook them until they are tender (which will take 3 hours for Roman snails, but less for garden snails) in a court bouillon of salted water flavored with an onion stuck with a clove, salt and pepper, bay, thyme, and parsley. A glass of white wine or a dash of vinegar is usually added. Meanwhile, clean the shells by boiling them for 30 minutes in water with added soda; rinse them well and dry them.

When the snails are cooked, let them cool in the court bouillon, and then put them back into their shells with garlic butter. When the snails are required, put them into a hot oven (you can keep the shells upright by pressing them into a bed of salt) for 5 minutes to heat and to melt the butter.

[*Snail*—French: *escargot;* German: *Schnecke;* Italian: *chiocciola, lumaca;* Spanish: *caracol*]

SNAP BEAN. *See* green bean.

SNAP PEA. This recently developed vegetable grows on a tall vine like that of the sugar *pea but has edible pods that are thick and fleshy like *green beans. When the peas are mature and the pods full size, snap peas are picked to serve raw—in salads or with dips—or to steam, stir-fry, or boil quickly. They also freeze well. Their edible yield is higher than that of regular peas, they are crisp and juicy, and their flavor is sweeter than that of green beans. Snap peas have quickly become popular since their introduction in 1979, and they are increasingly available in markets.

SNIPE. *See* woodcock.

SNOEK or **Australian barracuda** (*Thyrsites atun*) is a relative of the tuna and the mackerel. It is found in the southern hemisphere only and is eaten in southwestern Australia, New Zealand, and parts of South Africa and South America (in Chile, it is known as *sierra*). Fresh or smoked, snoek is delicate and delicious.

SNOOK or **robalo** is the name of several pikelike fish from the tropical Atlantic and Pacific oceans. The common snook (*Centropomus undecimales*) may weight 30 lb (14 Kg), though 3–5 lb (1½–2 Kg) is the average. The white flesh has a fine flavor and is often found in local markets where the fish is caught. It is a popular game fish in Florida; and it is occasionally marketed as red snapper. Snook should be skinned before cooking.

SNOWY MESPILUS. *See* rowan.

SOAKING. In cooking, foods are often soaked to remove salt, to soften them, or to reconstitute dried products. Important considerations are to make sure that the soaking liquid gets to all parts, and to maintain the correct temperature, remembering that chemical and physical actions are in general speeded up by warmth, but the same warmth also increases the activity of microorganisms that cause spoilage. Soaking does not necessarily imply the softening of tissues; that is *maceration.

For the health-conscious cook, soaking should also be considered in the context of those minerals and vitamins that are necessary to the metabolism of the human body. Soaking foods in water leaches out minerals and water-soluble vitamins—vitamin C and the B-complex group—and foods high in these vitamins, especially leafy green vegetables, should be quickly washed if necessary, then shaken to remove water (e.g., with lettuce or other raw salad ingredients) or steamed (as with spinach or other greens) in the least amount of water. Any liquid left over after cooking will contain nutrients, so it can be put into soup, added to vegetable juice as a beverage, or used as a sauce.

SOBA. *See* noodles.

SODA may mean *caustic soda or *bicarbonate of soda (baking soda).

SODA WATER was originally a medicinal alkaline water made by dissolving small amounts of *bicarbonate of soda in water. Today, it is water containing dissolved *carbon dioxide, which has been forced in under pressure and consequently comes out again in bubbles when the pressure is released. Some brands are made slightly alkaline with soda. Soda water can also be made at home with one of the various gadgets on the market that use small capsules or cylinders of compressed carbon dioxide.

[*Soda water*—French: *eau de Seltz, soda;* German: *Sodawasser, Selterswasser;* Italian: *acqua di seltz, acqua gassosa;* Spanish: *agua de seltz, agua de soda*]

SODIUM BICARBONATE. *See* bicarbonate of soda.

SODIUM HYDROXIDE. *See* caustic soda.

SODIUM NITRATE. *See* saltpeter.

SOFT WATER. *Water with little dissolved mineral content, which in hard water is made up of calcium salts; it is sometimes slightly acid. Water from moorland and boggy mountain areas is usually soft.

SOJA. *See* soybean.

SOLE. There are many species of sole, and perhaps almost as many other fish that have at one time or another been incorrectly given this name. First, true sole should be distinguished from *lemon sole. For this reason it is often called Dover sole, and even the French admit that the best ones are caught near Dover and not on the French coast—an admission that has to be true, since torture would otherwise be needed to wring such an opinion from French chefs. The common

European sole (*Solea solea*) is a dextral *flatfish, 16–28 in. (40–70 cm) long, with firm, white, delicate flesh. It has a rounded snout and well-developed pectoral fins. This sole is not fished in U.S. waters and is available only if shipped from Europe. Most fish sold here as sole—e.g., butter sole, rex sole, petrale sole—is some member of the flounder family, including some fine-flavored Pacific flounder. Although a few species of sole (the hogchoker and tongue sole) do exist off the coast of the U.S., they are small and inferior and are not fished commercially.

Other true soles that one may encounter in Europe include the French or sand sole (*S. lascaria*), found on sandy bottoms in inshore waters from the Mediterranean to the English Channel, and the thickback sole (*S. variegata*), a smaller, thicker-bodied sole with a similar range. Both are considered somewhat inferior to the real thing.

Sole may be cooked by almost any method and lends itself to myriad sauces, but if one is fortunate enough to encounter a true fresh sole it should be savored at its finest, simply cooked on the bone and served with butter, lemon juice, and parsley.

[*Sole*—French: *sole;* German: *Seezunge;* Italian: *sogliola;* Spanish: *lenguado*]

SOLUBILITY. *See* saturated solution.

SOMEN. *See* noodles.

SONCOYA. *See* custard apple.

SORB. *See* rowan.

SORBIC ACID. *See* preservatives.

SORGHUM. *See* millet and sorghum.

SORREL. There are several species of sorrel, which belongs to the same genus as dock plants. When cultivated, sorrel looks something like large, pale-green spinach. The cultivated, or French, forms (*Rumex scutatus* and others) are derived mainly from *R.*

acetosa and *R. acetosella,* which are native to the U.S. and commonly found as weeds in acid soils. Wild sorrels, which are quite edible, are easily recognized by their habit of

SORREL

creeping along on roots that send up bursts of lance-shaped leaves, then reddish brown flower spikes.

Because its acid-tasting leaves contain oxalic acid, it is not advisable to eat sorrel in large quantities, particularly in salads, to which it can nevertheless be a delicious addition. As a sour and refreshing basis for soups, purées, and sauces, as a flavoring herb in omelets, and as a stuffing ingredient for fish, sorrel is unbeatable. It is surprising that it is now relatively little known in America and Britain. However, this was not always so. Greensauce, made with pounded sorrel, vinegar (or lemon juice), and sugar, was a popular accompaniment to meat and poultry at least until the 18th century. Indeed, greensauce was the dialect name for sorrel in many parts of England; other names were sourdock and sourgrass. An allied plant, herb patience (*R. patientia*), is eaten like spinach.

[*Sorrel*—French: *oscille;* German: *Sauerampfer;* Italian: *sauro;* Spanish: *acedera*]

SOUR CREAM is a delicious ingredient of Russian, Polish, Hungarian, Rumanian, and German cooking, and consequently it has become popular in the U.S., where it can now be bought in several slightly different forms. Commercial sour cream is produced by natural lactic acid fermentation of cream, although rennet may be added to thicken the product. Cultured sour cream is made by adding *Streptococcus lactis* to pasteurized, homogenized cream and incubating at 72°F (22°C) until acidity reaches 0.5%. Acidified sour cream results from the souring of pasteurized cream with various acidifiers, with or without the addition of bacteria that produce lactic acid. Commercial sour cream, according to federal standards, must contain not less than 18% milkfat. If nutritive sweeteners or bulky flavoring ingredients are added, the product must contain at least 14.4% milkfat. Sour, cultured, and acidified half-and-half are also available and naturally contain less milkfat. In socalled sour cream dressing, other dairy ingredients such as butter are substituted for cream. The dressing is similar to sour cream, but flavorings and other ingredients may be added.

Yogurt cannot be used in place of sour cream, since it is less rich in fat and different in taste. If sour cream is not available, cream may be soured by adding a squeeze of lemon juice and a drop or two of vinegar and then stirring; it will thicken rapidly. The sourness will, of course, be due to citric and not lactic acid. The drop of vinegar (and it must really be very little) is not essential, but soured cream does naturally contain a tiny amount of acetic acid.

Pasteurized cream that is past its prime merely goes bad and tastes very unpleasant. Fresh pasteurized cream can be made into sour cream by adding 2 tablespoons of buttermilk to each pint of cream; shake it in a sterile glass jar and let stand in a warm place 24–48 hours or until cream is thick and sour-tasting. However, unless you have your own cows, sour cream made this way will be more expensive than the commercial product.

For a low-calorie, high-protein product that has a flavor similar to sour cream and tastes as good on baked potatoes (especially with plenty of chives snipped into it), place ½ cup of buttermilk, 1 cup of whole-curd (uncreamed) cottage cheese, and ½ teaspoon of lemon juice in a blender container; blend at high speed until very smooth, and refrigerate until thick as sour cream.

Smetana in Russia is a mixture of sour and sweet cream. *Crème fraîche* is a bit like sour cream but less acid, and it has a higher milkfat content.

[*Sour cream*—French: *crème aigre;* German: *sauere Sahne;* Italian: *panna fermentata;* Spanish: *jocoque*]

SOURDOUGH is a natural leavener used as a "starter" for bread—the result is sourdough bread. Originally, sourdough was indeed just sour dough. It was a country technique of breadmaking (it was also used in cakes) that was very widely used in the days when yeast could not be so easily bought. A piece of a previous batch of bread dough was kept moistened with water as a starter—it contained yeasts as well as bacteria-producing acids that prevented the dough from going bad. It could also be mixed with water and fed with sugar and more flour to keep it going. Prospectors in the Alaska Gold Rush got the name sourdoughs because they kept a pot of the starter going and took it with them. Exactly the same thing happens today in Australia where the cattle drovers and remote farms use "hops."

Starting sourdough from scratch is, as James Beard says, a "fickle process," and he recommends using yeast as well as starter for a good loaf, but in *Beard on Bread* (Knopf, 1973), he offers a recipe: heat 1 cup of milk, add 1 cup of water, and cool to lukewarm. Stir in 1 tablespoon of sugar, 1 teaspoon of salt, and 2 cups of flour, beat, place in a large crock, cover with a cloth, and let stand in a warm place for 3–5 days, until it bubbles and has a sour aroma. ("If it really takes, it can drive you right out of the room.") Dissolve 1 package of active dry yeast in ½ cup of warm water, beat it into the starter, cover with a damp cloth, and let stand at room temperature for a week, stirring down each day. The starter is now ready to use in any recipe calling for sourdough. It should be noted that the quality of homemade starter is dependent on such factors as the weather and the presence of microorganisms in the air, and the product can vary from one region to another.

Today, with dried yeasts, it is not necessary to use sourdough anymore, but many people like the taste, especially in rye breads. In the U.S., it is possible to buy ready-made sourdough starters, which make quite good sourdough bread. San Francisco is renowned for its sourdough French bread, which owes its particular taste to a strain of bacterium that is unique to the city. The bread is at its best when made just with sourdough starter and no added yeast.

[*Sourdough*—French: *levain;* German: *Sauerteig;* Italian: *lievito naturale;* Spanish: *levadura*]

SOURING AGENTS are acid substances and are very important in cooking. Today, the usual ones used in Europe and America are lemon juice and vinegar, both of which are easily added and usually ready to hand. Yogurt, sour milk, and buttermilk are other useful sour products. Sour and unripe fruits (such as sour apples or sour grapes), and the *verjuice which can be squeezed from them, are other possibilities. So also are sour *pomegranate seeds, dried *mango powder (*amchur*), *tamarind, roselle (which is a *mallow), *sorrel, and *rhubarb. The use of different souring agents, because of their flavor overtones, can make very interesting and subtle changes in salads and other dishes.

SOUR MILK and **sour-milk products.** Sour milk has many uses providing it has gone properly sour and is not bitter, as will be the case if milk has been pasteurized, which prevents the preservative lactic acid from developing. Since virtually all milk is now pasteurized, it is safer to use cultured buttermilk wherever sour milk is called for in recipes. Unpasteurized milk can be soured by adding a little yogurt or cottage cheese and holding it at 77–86°F (25–30°C). Or for a sour milk taste, add a teaspoon of vinegar or lemon juice to a cup of milk and let it stand in a warm place for 30 minutes. Sour milk can with advantage be used in mashed potatoes, soups, and gravies or be allowed to curdle thoroughly for making cottage cheese.

Milk of all kinds contains *lactose, which can be fermented by many species of bacteria with the formation of lactic acid (sometimes yeasts also ferment it to alcohol). During the souring, other substances are produced in the milk—creamy flavors, buttery flavors, fruity and vinegary flavors (acetic acid)—and these are important. They dictate the type and quality of the finished product. The bacterial activity also causes the coagulation of the milk—the formation of curd. This may be firm or watery, ropy or slimy. Some bacteria attack fats and proteins; they may result in bitter, rancid, fishy, and putrid flavors. (Prolonged action of microorganisms has other effects, which lie more in the sphere of *cheesemaking.)

In making sour-milk products, it is important to keep a few general principles in mind. Everything should be clean—possibly sterilized by boiling—and nothing should be left uncovered for long; you do not want the milk to be contaminated with lots of the extraneous organisms that are always in the air. The culture you use to start your sour-milk product may be bought specially, or it may be a pot of yogurt, sour cream, or buttermilk from the supermarket (as long as it is not an ultrapasteurized or sterilized product), or it may be part of the last brew kept back specifically as a starter. Remember that in all cases it will be a mixture of organisms, not a pure culture, and that the control you have over it is exercised via the temperature at which you incubate it, which is critical. It is best to use a thermometer. The quantity of starter you use is important. For several reasons it affects the relative number of or-

ganisms, and so the end product. Too much starter often causes oversourness. Electric yogurt makers are convenient but not necessary; people made sour-milk products long before electricity was heard of. A saucepan, a suitably sized stoneware jar, and a means of keeping the jar warm (a Styrofoam box, an insulated picnic basket, or even a blanket) are all that you really need.

Milk can be from cow, goat, sheep, buffalo, reindeer, camel, or mare. Some milks, like mare's, contain more sugar than others and are suitable for alcoholic fermentation. There are dozens of different variants on the theme of sour milk or cream, but they seem all to have originated with the ancient tribes of Central Asia. Yogurt, for instance, reached the Middle East via Persia. It was known as "Persian milk" in 13th-century Arabia. Sour-milk products are now well known in northern Europe (the Lapps use reindeer milk); there are local sour milks such as the Finnish *piima* or *viili* and Scandinavian ropy sour milk, called *rångmjolk* or *täte,* which is slightly alcoholic and may be clabbered and flavored with butterwort (*Pinguicula vulgris*), that insectivorous plant of northern bogs. North Russian sour milk, *prostokvash,* is soured at 85°F (30°C). A hot day will do it, and the same temperature is used to make *sour cream in Russia, Hungary, and Central Europe generally.

*Yogurt is by repute the sour-milk product of Bulgaria and Turkey, but it is made in local ways in the Middle East and through Iran to India. In Persian, it is called *mast,* and from it comes *mazoon* in Armenia and *matsoni* in Georgia in the U.S.S.R., as well as *masturad* in Sicily. It is *leben* in Egypt and the rest of North Africa, and *laban* in Syria and Lebanon. Almost the same product is called *dahi* in India, where the best is made from buffalo's milk. In the Balkans, the most delicious yogurt is made from sheep's milk, sometimes from goat's milk; cow's milk yogurt, which is the commonest farther west, is considered inferior. Yogurt is a hot-country product and and uses thermophilic (heat-loving) bacteria. It plays an important role in the cooking of the Middle East and India, and is mixed with well-salted cold water to make a wonderful hot-weather drink (*doogh, ayran,* or *lassi*).

Of the more exotic products, acidophilus milk has become a health fad and is readily available. This is a culture of *Lactobacillus acidophilus,* a common inhabitant of the human intestines, which unlike the yogurt bacterium (*L. bulgaricus*) can survive inside the human digestive tract but will continue to grow only if it is given milk or milk sugar to feed on. Acidophilus milk, which has soft curds, is much used in Russia, but its flavor is not as good as that of yogurt. Its acceptance has been limited in the U.S. because of its cooked and acid taste. In recent years a new form of acidophilus milk has been developed in which the natural flavor and consistency of milk are unchanged, and its distribution is increasing as studies indicate that *L. acidophilus* has a beneficial effect on the digestive tract.

The Russians also have *kefir* made from cow's milk and *kumiss* from mare's milk, which are both alcoholic, as is *kyrynga,* which is made in Central Asia. Another Asian sour-milk product, *chal,* is made from camel's milk.

[*Sour milk*—French: *lait caillé, lait aigre;* German: *Sauermilch;* Italian: *latte acido;* Spanish: *angola*]

SOURSOP. *See* custard apple.

SOUTHERN LOBSTER. *See* langouste.

SOYBEAN, soya bean, or **soja bean.** Surely one of the most depressing statements ever made is that the world could support a population of 16,000 million people if everyone ate soybeans instead of meat. An acre of these beans can keep a moderately active man alive (but not necessarily contented) for 2200 days, while the same acre could keep him for only 75 days if he lived on beef. The soybean is the richest natural vegetable food known to man—and one of the dullest, a

typical example of the perverse sense of humor of the Creator, who never seems to make anything without snags. Why should the soybean not have been delicious as well as full of oil (18–22% in the dried beans) and protein (35%), not to mention carbohydrate? We read of special varieties of soybean with a delectable taste—there are over a thousand known varieties—and seeds that are black, chocolate, brown, reddish, greenish, or yellow, but they never seem to reach the shops. No wonder, then, that they were not taken seriously outside the Orient until research was able to show their outstanding food value.

The plant (*Glycine max*) is a legume from eastern Asia and has been in cultivation in China for thousands of years, the first written mention being in *The Heavenly Farmer* by Emperor Sheng-Nung in 2838 B.C. Confucius fans will like to know that he called it *shu*. The first news of the soybean came to Europe when the German botanist Engelbert Kaenfer came back from a visit to Japan in 1692. The beans were grown in Kew Gardens, in England, in 1790. Later still, the American expedition to Japan led by Commodore N. C. Perry in 1854 brought back two varieties (Japan pea and Japan bean), but nobody, it seems, liked them.

It was not until the 20th century that scientific research revealed the great nutritive wealth hidden in the seed. Today, the U.S. produces more even than China, indeed a third of the total world soy output—one of the most important changes in agricultural economy that have occurred this century. It is not grown in more northern latitudes, where the climate is too cold for it. It looks like a typical bean, but it has not been much eaten in Europe and America because it can have a peculiarly gelatinous texture which some people do not like. It is also very inferior in flavor when compared, for instance, to lima or green beans. Perhaps it is its oiliness which prevents it from marrying well with other flavors, such as tomato sauce. More often it is used in the form of a flour (sometimes treated to remove any bitterness) to pad other foods; most people who were around in Britain during World War II will remember with as much horror as gratitude those traumatic "pork soya links." Unlike most other flours, soy flour is high in protein and low in carbohydrate. It is often used by breadmakers as a dough improver. Soybeans can be sprouted and used in the same way as mung bean sprouts, but they have a much more beany flavor and are not pleasant raw—they need steaming to make them palatable.

Soy oil, possibly the world's most important vegetable oil and the basis for margarine, is used as a cooking oil and is cheap, but it is one of the least attractive of all the vegetable oils. However, from soybeans come a whole range of other products. The beans can be mixed with cereal and fermented to make *soy sauce. They can be made into a milk which, with certain additives, can be used to make approximations to vegetable yogurt and vegetable cheese, as well as *tempeh and the *bean curd that is known as tofu in Japan. The Chinese even dry the curd skin, and it is commonly sold in Chinese shops. Finally, of the Oriental products there is miso from Japan, an ingredient made of soybeans and cereal grains fermented with water and salt for use in soups and sauces; its residue tamari, the liquid that rises to the top during fermentation, is probably the inspiration for *soy sauce. There are various types of miso, which will be specified in Japanese recipes. Miso dissolves in water; if it is used in soups, they should boil after it has been added.

With modern Western technology, we enter a new field, the field of the soy-protein isolate. The simple form is sold as granules or grits and is used—as was the earlier soy flour—for adding to manufactured foods, sausages, hamburger, etc. (In most countries, it has to be mentioned on the label.) More sophisticated food technology has produced *textured plant protein, a fibrous substance which can be formed into fake chicken, steak, ham, and bacon. It has been forecast that textured plant protein will become to

meat what margarine has become to butter. Textured and flavored soy is also used in sweets, where it stands in for coconut.

[Soy—French: soya, soja; German: Sojabohne; Italian: soia; Spanish: soja]

SOY SAUCE or **shoyu.** This condiment, with its slightly sweet, salty, and meaty taste, is an ancient and important ingredient in the cooking of China and Japan, but it has also been popular in Britain for over 300 years and is said to be one of the ingredients of Worcestershire sauce. There were even silver soy labels to hang on bottles long before the bean itself had registered as more than a curiosity in the West. Since soy sauce is used as much in China and Japan as Westerners use vinegar, its making is a huge commercial undertaking today, but the basis of the sauce—although there are many ways of making it and many different types of it—is best understood by reference to an old description for the Japanese version.

Soybeans are first boiled until tender, then they are pounded in a mortar with an equal weight of coarsely ground barley or roasted and cracked wheat. The mixture is then covered and left in a warm place to ferment. When the mass is sufficiently fermented, a weight of salt equal to the original weight of beans is added and well mixed in. It is all covered again and left to do its worst for as much as 3 years, during which time it is well stirred or beaten every day. At the end of this time, the brown juice is pressed out through cloth, put into a tub, and left to settle. When it is clear, the sauce is ready for use.

There was a time when soy sauce was difficult to get, but now it is easy to buy the dark, light, and other varieties that are necessary in Chinese, Japanese, and Southeast Asian recipes. The very heavy Indonesian ketjap (ketjap manis or ketjap benteng), which is a type of soy sauce, can be made, if it is not available, from any dark soy sauce by adding half its volume of molasses and sweetening with brown sugar (almost 3 parts to every 8 of molasses). Another *ketjap* substitute is *saté* sauce, which is made with *peanuts.

[*Soy sauce*—French: *sauce piquante (de soya);* German: *Sosse von Soja;* Italian: *salsa di soia*]

SPAGHETTI is the most popular of all forms of *pasta. It can be bought in an assortment of grades of different diameters and lengths. It should not be broken into short lengths, since this makes it difficult for the eater to twist it around the fork. Many people eat spaghetti with a fork and spoon, using the spoon as a hollow in which to twist the fork, but purists eat with a fork alone, twisting the forkful against the plate. The latter is more refined and demonstrates your expertise but is slower.

[*Spaghetti*—French: *spaghetti;* German: *Spaghetti;* Italian: *spaghetti;* Spanish: *espaguetis*]

SPAGHETTI SQUASH. *See* squash.

SPECIFIC HEAT. It takes more heat, and therefore longer, to heat up some substances than others, and these also hold more heat than the others. They therefore cool down more slowly. Specific heat is the scientific measurement of this: it compares the amount of heat necessary to raise the temperature of a substance one degree with that necessary to raise the same mass of water by one degree. Copper has a very low specific heat; a copper pan heats and cools quickly. Because it is also a good conductor, it responds rapidly to the cook's adjustment of the flame and is therefore ideal for pans. Earthenware has a very high specific heat; it heats slowly but retains its heat and cools slowly. Its temperature cannot be made to fluctuate quickly; it is ideal for containers for hot food on the table, which copper is not. Other types of kitchenware fall somewhere in between.

SPECK. *See* bacon.

SPICE. The word comes from the same root as "species" and meant a kind of merchandise. It originally applied to aromatics shipped in from the Orient and, therefore, excluded *herbs (and their seeds) grown in Europe. Today, it is more conveniently used to include all dried aromatic seeds as well as the original Oriental spices, and it can also cover dried chilies and allspice from America.

[*Spice*—French: *épice;* German: *Gewürz;* Italian: *spezie;* Spanish: *especia*]

SPINACH. The common spinach (*Spinacea oleracea*) is thought to be of Persian origin; it was not known to the Romans, but was probably introduced to Europe by the Arabs and was being grown in Britain by the middle of the 16th century. Like most unusual foods at that time, it was regarded as medicinal—it is mildly laxative. Spinach might also seem to be a valuable source of minerals, since it contains a lot of iron and more calcium than any other common vegetable. However, its high oxalic acid content combines with the calcium and iron to form insoluble oxalates, making the minerals effectively unavailable. So spinach is valuable mainly because it is delicious, both cooked and, when young and tender, raw in salads. It is best cooked by the conservation method in the moisture it retains from washing. If spinach is gritty, it should be rinsed in several changes of water. Always take the spinach out of the water (rather than pour the water off it) so that the dirt is left behind.

Good King Henry (*Chenopodium bonus-henricus*), also known as all-good or mercury, is called *bon-Henri* in France and is a perennial relative of spinach. Its flavor is good, but it needs to have water changed during cooking. The tender young flower buds are the best part to eat.

New Zealand spinach (*Tetragonia expansa*) belongs to another family, Aizoaceae. It thrives in dry regions, and so it is the spinach grown in the warm, drier countries, but it also grows well in northern regions. The plant has characteristic fleshy, triangular leaves. It is rather lacking in flavor compared to regular spinach, but is so mild that it is good in salads.

Orache or **mountain spinach** (*Atriplex hortensis*) is a member of the same family as spinach and is called *bonne-dame* in France. It is an annual which grows up to about 6½ ft (2 m) high. It has large, arrow-shaped leaves, often with toothed or crinkly edges, and is a good spinach substitute. Varieties with red or yellow leaves are sometimes grown for ornamental rather than culinary reasons but are no less edible than green varieties.

Swiss *chard or **spinach beet** is a form of beet that is grown for its leaves and its thickened leaf stalks. Sea spinach is the wild form of the same species.

Among other leaf vegetables, *lamb's-quarters or pigweed is excellent as a free "spinach." Young stinging *nettle tops make a good "spinach," with a very good flavor but a slightly dry texture. They are useful to mix with other foods and in stuffings. The other members of the goosefoot genus, even stinking goosefoot (*Chenopodium olidum*), which has an unpleasant smell that is said to be like stale salt fish and is caused by a substance called trimethylamine, is perfectly good to eat when boiled. Another family with green leaves that are eaten like spinach is the *mallow family, various species of which are quite good. Dead-nettles, which are not nettles but labiates related to sage, also have leaves which can be boiled, notably those of the white dead-nettle (*Lamium album*), which is also good in soups and stuffings. Then there is the *amaranth; several species are used as greens in countries from Italy to India. *Fenugreek (*methi*) is much used as a green in Indian cooking, but it can be excruciatingly bitter. Indian spinach is also called Malabar nightshade. There are two species: *Basella alba*, from India, and *B. rubra*, from China. They are sometimes grown in France and can be treated just like spinach.

[*Spinach*—French: *épinard;* German: *Spinat;* Italian: *spinacio;* Spanish: *espinaca*]

SPINY LOBSTER. *See* langouste.

SPORES of molds and other fungi are analogous to seeds of higher plants—they are a means by which the plants multiply and spread. Spores form the powdery cloud given out when molds are disturbed and the smoky-looking dust that comes out of ripe puffball mushrooms. Mold spores are a nuisance to the cook, because they are usually in the air and will settle on the surface of jam, indeed on any food, that is left uncovered even for a few moments. Mold spores are killed by a short boiling.

The spores of bacteria are very different. They are formed by a relatively few rod-shaped species (about 150), and their purpose is not to multiply the numbers but to enable the organism to survive conditions which would kill it in its normal, actively proliferating state. Bacterial spores cause problems, since they survive a long time (up to 10 years on occasion) and are exceedingly hard to kill.

Spores, however, can be regarded as only potentially troublesome, because they will not cause food spoilage or poisoning as long as they do not germinate. To germinate, the food, temperature, and *pH must be right as well as the amount of air (or lack of it) and other critical conditions. Making sure that these conditions do not occur in food is one of the crucial factors in *preservation.

[*Spore*—French: *spore;* German: *Spore;* Italian: *spora;* Spanish: *espora*]

SPRAT (*Sprattus sprattus*) is a small fish, about 6 in. (15 cm) long, found around the coasts of Europe from the Black Sea to Norway. It is an oily fish, closely related to the sardine and the herring; it can be distinguished from both by its characteristically serrated belly (it has a row of spiny scales running along it). Also, the front of its ventral fin lies directly below the front, rather than the middle, of the dorsal fin. Fresh sprats are best broiled, since they are very oily, and served sprinkled with lemon juice. They are also salted, smoked, and potted. Small ones are canned in oil or tomato sauce under their Norwegian name, brisling, but are less good than sardines.

[*Sprat*—French: *esprot, sprat;* German: *Sprotte;* Italian: *spratto;* Spanish: *sardineta*]

SPROUTED SEEDS. When seeds sprout, many enzymes concerned with mobilizing the food reserves become active (an important stage in the production of *malt). At the same time, vitamins, particularly vitamin C, which were not present in significant amounts in the dormant seed are produced. Sprouted beans would have protected sailors from scurvy had the reason for the disease been known and not attributed to "salt junk," the mahogany-colored dried salt pork. Today, sprouted seeds enjoy increasing popularity, particularly among health-food enthusiasts, because they are quickly and easily grown at home.

The most widely known sprouted seeds are bean sprouts, which have been used in China for some 3000 years. The most usually and easily sprouted bean is the *mung bean. After sprouting, which takes 3–4 days or until the sprouts are 2 in. (5 cm) long, the taste is mild. Mung bean sprouts can be eaten steamed or raw as a salad. However, bean or pea sprouts which are to be eaten in any quantity should be cooked (though they need only be simmered or steamed for 3 minutes). Raw legume sprouts and seeds contain a substance that inhibits trypsin, one of the enzymes with which we digest protein. The trypsin inhibitor is quickly destroyed by heat.

Mustard and cress may be sprouted in soil and are commercially grown in peat. Other seeds may be grown on flannel, tied in a cloth, or put in a commercial sprouter, but a fairly foolproof and very popular way is the jar method. Because beans and seeds increase in volume up to 10 times the original size as they sprout, use a jar large enough to allow for this expansion. Put the seeds into a clean jar. Cover the opening with a piece of loosely woven cloth, such as cheesecloth or, better still, nylon net, and fasten the cloth securely around the jar neck with string. Fill the jar with tepid water, shake the water around, and then let it drain out through the cloth. Repeat this 2–4 times a day, or often enough to keep the seeds moist. If they are too wet, the seeds will rot; if they are too dry, they will die. Remove any seeds that do not sprout when the others have, and continue wetting and draining the sprouts until they are ready to eat. Nylon net should be rinsed between uses; cheesecloth needs to be sterilized. Sprouts can be kept for a month in an open plastic bag in the vegetable tray of the refrigerator.

Buy untreated seeds that are specifically for sprouting rather than seeds intended for planting, which may have been treated with retardants, fungicides, or insecticides. Some instructions suggest soaking the seeds for several hours before putting them into the jar.

Mung beans should be put in plenty of water and soaked for 12–24 hours, until they just start to burst their skins. Drain off the water and follow the instructions above for the jar method. When the sprouts are ready, they will taste of freshly shelled peas. Tip them into a large bowl of water and swish them around gently to loosen the husks. With a bit of jugglery, the husks can be tipped away, leaving unbroken, mostly husk-free, shoots. Any lingering husks can be removed by hand if you object to them. If the beans turn moldy before they sprout, try next time using boiled and cooled water, since the water could be the source of the mold spores.

Soybeans are the most nourishing of all but not very easy to sprout. They need to be soaked for 8–10 hours and then put into the sprouting container and kept in the dark. The best temperature for sprouting soybeans is 68–77°F (20–25°C), and they should be dunked in tepid water several times a day; otherwise they will turn moldy. It is best to tip the beans out on a tray, very gently, every day and look for any that seem to be going bad or refusing to sprout, because bad beans can give a rank flavor to the entire batch. In 3–4 days, the sprouts will be up to 2 in. (5 cm) long and ready to eat. Rinse them well in cold water and steam them quickly in very little water. Their raw taste is more "beany" than that of mung sprouts.

Lentils are delicious sprouted and are ready when the sprout is about 1 in. (2 cm) long. Their flavor is sweet and delicate.

Peas. Whole dried peas produce sprouts with a fresh pea flavor and are ready when the sprout is about 2 in. (5 cm) long.

Wheat sprouts taste of newly picked corn and are best at about ½ in. (1 cm) long, while they are tender and before they become thready.

Alfalfa gives very fine shoots of about 1 in. (2 cm) in 2 days, with a delicate, pealike flavor. It is easy to sprout and keeps green if grown in the light.

Most sprouts are eaten at an early stage of development, but it is also common to grow seeds on to the cotyledon stage, when they are a stalk with the two first false leaves. Other commonly sprouted seeds include *adzuki beans, *fenugreek, and *chickpeas.

SPRUCE is a coniferous tree of the genus *Picea.* Essence of spruce is used to flavor spruce beer. It is made by boiling the green tips of black spruce (*P. mariana*) in water and then concentrating the liquor, without the spruce tops, by boiling it down. Other species of spruce are also used. For instance, the Norway spruce (*P. abies*) was traditionally used in northern Europe to make "black beer," the most famous variety of which came from Danzig. The antiscorbutic beer of the czarist Russian army was made of spruce tops, horseradish, and beer flavored with ginger and calamus. After fermentation, a little cream of tartar was added for acidity, plus tincture of mustard and strong

spirits for a kick, as if it did not have enough already. In the more prosaic modern world, spruce oil—also called hemlock oil—is used as a flavoring in root beer, ice cream, and chewing gum. The hemlock from which it is extracted is an American conifer of the genus *Tsuga* and not the poisonous umbellifer (as taken by Socrates) to which the name is given in Britain. As a flavoring, it is more popular in North America than in Europe.

[*Spruce*—French: *sapin;* German: *Fichte;* Italian: *abete rosso;* Spanish: *pinabete*]

SQUAB. *See* pigeon.

SQUASH, pumpkin, gourd, and **marrow** are overlapping terms for members of the family Cucurbitaceae, which also includes *cucumbers, *gherkins, *melons, and *chayote. They all have a fruit which, however variable, is built on the same general plan. They like a fairly warm climate and will withstand little if any frost. The fruits are watery and mild. Squash—which comes from the Narragansett Indian *askooot-asquash*—is a word not usually understood in Britain, where summer squash is called vegetable marrow. Dwarf varieties—courgettes from France or zucchini from Italy—have been adopted on both sides of the Atlantic. Crookneck, pattypan, acorn squashes, and others are so called from their shapes. Squashes are often stuffed. They can be hollowed out to act as vessels in which to serve soup, and even carved with patterns, a nice party decoration made in China.

Warm-country gourds are cultivated in the southern states of the U.S. and can often be bought in Indian shops. Many of these are essential for Italian vegetarian cooking, some are needed for Chinese dishes, and they are often worth trying cooked in European styles. Sometimes there is a huge difference between varieties of the same species, just as much as there is between cabbages or cauliflowers. Who would suspect on first sight that a pumpkin, a zucchini, and an ornamental gourd were blood brothers? Although, from a cook's point of view, the species to which a plant belongs is mainly of academic interest, it makes sense here to use the biological names as a way of sorting out the mass of popular names.

Cucurbita pepo includes the pumpkins, summer squashes, marrows, courgettes, custard marrows, scalloped summer squashes, pattypans, cymlings, and ornamental gourds. Trailing and bush varieties are used in different conditions. *Pepo* forms are distinguished from *maxima* forms *(see below)* by their roughly bristled stems and leaves, their short, deeply grooved and slightly swollen fruit stalks, and their deeply lobed leaves. This is a North American species cultivated by the Indians before the arrival of Columbus but not known in Europe until later. In fact, even 100 years ago the vegetable marrow was thought to be a sort of pumpkin which had originated in Persia. While the British marrow, swimming in its water and thin white sauce, is no doubt selected as food for the damned in the place where the devil rewards his followers, a dish like *courgettes à l'angoumise* (slices cooked slowly with garlic, oil, and butter) is worthy of heaven to garlic lovers. Such summer squashes as crooknecks and pattypans should be eaten very young and never overcooked; they are too old for eating when a fingernail does not easily go through the skin without pressure. When buying, look always for fruit that is firm and turgid, without any sign of shriveling at the end of the stalk.

Pumpkins also belong to this species. They are often cut and sold by weight. The earthy taste is valued in America, where pumpkins provide pumpkin-pie filling and the basis for the Halloween jack-o'-lantern. If hung in a net or rested on straw, pumpkins will keep over most of the winter. The seeds, which contain a good percentage of oil, are washed, dried, and salted for eating. (Heat them in a pan with a little oil until they swell—a matter of seconds—dry them on absorbent paper, and salt them.) There are even special varieties developed for their seeds that lack a hull and can be eaten whole and unshelled.

Another squash, with very long strings inside, is called vegetable spaghetti. In Spain, these soft fibers are boiled in sugar to make a sort of tasteless jam called *cabellos de ángel* (angel's hair), but in the U.S., where they are increasingly available in markets, spaghetti squashes are used for a pasta substitute and served with any sauces—tomato, clam, pesto, etc.—that are used for spaghetti. The spaghetti squash must be boiled until the skin is tender. Then the squash is cut open and the "spaghetti" fiber is forked out until it is fluffy. It does not have quite the texture of pasta, but it makes a fine substitute that is low in calories, and it has a delicate flavor of its own—it is excellent served simply with butter and a lot of pepper.

Cucurbita maxima includes the winter squashes. Best-known among them are the Hubbard, turban, butternut, and mammoth squashes. The species is of American origin, and the plants can be distinguished from summer squashes because the hairs are soft, the stalk of the fruit is not strongly ribbed but is swollen, and the leaves are not deeply lobed. Winter squashes take longer to mature than summer squashes and make hard shells; they are allowed to mature and are stored for use in winter, although they are also excellent, usually with a sweetish flavor, when immature: sliced and grilled with chicken or spareribs over coals, they can be brushed with garlic butter or the marinade for the meat. For keeping, they need to be picked when fully mature, leaving some stalk attached. Color can be from yellow or orange to green or blue-gray, and shapes vary from club to acorn, often heavily ribbed.

Cucurbita moschata includes the cushaw and the winter crookneck or Canada crookneck, all little-known outside America, where this species originated.

Citrullus vulgaris var. *fistulosus*. The round gourd or *tinda* is a tiny variety of the watermelon, and is sometimes also called the squash melon. (Large watermelons, which are eaten as fruit, are dealt with in the melon entry.) This variety is thought to have originated in India, where it is one of the most important summer vegetables, especially in the north. It is also found where there are Indian communities abroad. There are two types, light and dark green, of which the light is reckoned the better. The first flush of fruit is removed by growers to make way for the larger second flush. The slightly hairy fruit is harvested before the seeds become hard.

Tricosanthes cucumerina. The snake gourd appears to be a native of India, where it is called *chichinda*. It is important in South India and Southeast Asia, and is useful in vegetarian cookery; it has a firm, smooth texture as well as a fine taste. The snake gourd, although subtropical, grows very well in a Mediterranean climate. It is a quick-growing climber with white, lacy-petaled flowers. The gourds are long and thin, up to 4 ft (120 cm) long, around 2 in. (5 cm) thick, and usually slightly curved (although Indian gardeners sometimes hang weights on them to make them grow straight). The greenish gourds turn a brilliant orange when mature but are eaten young. They have a strange, foxy smell and are covered with a powdery white down which is removed before cooking by rubbing with salt. It is not necessary to peel snake gourds. Both ends of snake gourds are pointed, which distinguishes them from snakelike varieties of the bottle gourd, with which they are sometimes confused. This vegetable can be seen in Indian shops and is very good indeed, either in vegetable curries or as a vegetable dressed in Western ways.

Trichosanthes dioica is a close relative of the snake gourd, called the *parwal* in India. It is much grown in Assam (where it is probably native) and in Bengal and Bihar, as well as throughout Southeast Asia. This needs a hotter, more humid climate than the snake gourd. The fruits are rather like small cucumbers and are eaten young and immature. There are light-green and dark-green varieties, and some are striped. Likely to be imported and found in Indian shops, it is regarded as one of the best Indian vegetables and is very digestible.

Momordica charantia. The bitter gourd or balsam pear and its close relative, the balsam apple (*Momordica muricata*) or *ucche,* are important vegetables in the Orient, occurring in both Indian and Chinese cooking. They are available canned and sometimes also fresh from Chinese or Indian stores. The bitter gourd is harvested when fully grown but still green, the balsam apple when young, small, and with immature seeds. In China, these gourds are used in soup or in stir-fried vegetable dishes. Usually the pulp is removed and the flesh sliced. The slices are then boiled for 3 minutes to remove some of the bitterness. In India, the gourds are often cut up and salted for 30 minutes so that some of the bitter juice can be squeezed out, but this is not always done. They are often cut in pieces and fried with spices or put into curries, and are also stuffed. In India, the bitter gourd is called *karela.*

Benincasa hispida. The ash gourd or wax gourd is important in tropical countries. In India, it is known as *petha.* It is harvested when immature and is largely used for sweet dishes. It is a round or oblong gourd sometimes reaching 22 lb (10 Kg). Said to have originated in Japan, it has been used since ancient times in China and is now eaten widely in Asia.

Luffa cylindrica. The sponge gourd, when ripe, develops a tough skeleton which makes the well-known bath luffa; it is also a good vegetable when unripe. The plant, a spreading climber, is often grown up trees. It has probably been taken into cultivation in Asia fairly recently in history, since it does not vary much (as do plants that have been cultivated for a long time), and it has no Sanskrit name. It is commonly used in South Indian vegetable curries, called *kali, tori,* or *nenna.*

Luffa acutangula. Closely related to the sponge gourd is the ridged gourd or club gourd, an important warm-country vegetable that has long green fruits with sharp ribs. Varieties range in size from 1-2 in. (a few centimeters) to 3¼ ft (1 m) long. It is known as *kali, tori,* or *jhingli* in India and *ketoloa* in Malaya. This vegetable is very important in South Indian vegetarian cooking. It has to be harvested before it becomes spongy.

Lagenania siceraria. The bottle gourd, when mature, develops a very hard, woody shell that is used to make bottles, spoons, bowls, and musical instruments. The shape is often modified by binding during growth. The plant has been used since ancient times—there is evidence from Egyptian tombs dated around 3500 B.C. and from Mexican caves as long ago as 7000 B.C. Perhaps it originated in Africa and the seeds drifted on the sea to America. Immature bottle gourds make an excellent vegetable, with firm and tender flesh, and a nice taste. Indeed the snakelike form, *L. longissima* (sometimes confused with the snake gourd), which grows in Italy and can be seen in Riviera markets, is possibly the best of all gourds and is superior to courgettes when young. When old, they become bitter, purgative, and, indeed, poisonous. Bottle gourds are much used as food in India, where they are called *kaddu, lauki,* or *ghia.*

SQUID are the most numerous of the *cephalopods and the most important as a food, particularly in Japan. There are about 350 different species, ranging from tiny creatures a few inches long to giant squids which reach over 60 ft (18 m) in length and are among the most formidable marine predators. Octopuses are bulbous, and cuttlefish are shield-shaped, but squids are more like torpedoes, with a fin on either side. They have 8 arms and 2 tentacles, like cuttlefish; the tentacles are normally kept retracted,

ready to be shot out to grab the prey. The common inshore species of the North Atlantic and Mediterranean are members of the genus *Loligo,* but various oceanic species can also be eaten.

Freshly caught squids are among the most beautiful of marine animals, firm and with iridescent colors, looking as if they were embedded in crystal glass. Within minutes of being landed, they assume the unappetizing, flabby appearance they have on the market slab. Squid is available frozen, dried (a staple food in China), or canned. Because of pollution and overfishing in the Mediterranean, the use of frozen squid has greatly increased over the last 2 decades; fortunately, they keep their flavor and are even tenderized by freezing.

Squid are fished commercially at night with lights; the hope is to attract a shoal to the surface.

There are dozens of recipes for squid in Mediterranean cooking, and the body is often stuffed. Almost everyone seems to like the fried rings of squid called *calamares a la Romana* in Spain.

CALAMARES A LA ROMANA

Clean the squid and cut the body across into ¼-in. (½-cm) rings. Dry them and salt them lightly; dip the rings in flour and then in beaten egg. Alternatively, use a batter made with 2 eggs, a heaping tablespoon of flour, and enough water to make it fairly thin. Fry the rings until they are golden, but be warned that they may explode with some violence in the early stages of frying. Eat the rings as they are with a squeeze of lemon, with mayonnaise, or with the Romesco sauce which the Spanish make with *sweet peppers.

[*Squid*—French: *calmar;* German: *Tintenfisch;* Italian: *calamaro;* Spanish: *calamar, chipiron*]

SQUIRREL. There are many different species of squirrel. Chief among them is the gray squirrel (*Sciurus carolinensis*), which is common in hardwood forests from southern Canada to the Gulf states. It has been introduced into Britain, where it is now a pest, as it sometimes is in the U.S.

The meat of young squirrels may be white or pink; it is tender and can be broiled. Older squirrels need to be stewed for 1½–2 hours. Authentic Brunswick stew includes squirrel meat, and squirrel is used in pies or is fried like chicken.

Cleaned, jointed squirrels should be soaked in salted water for a few hours, then drained and rolled in bread crumbs before frying in bacon fat. For Brunswick stew, layer salt pork, potatoes, onion slices, corn, lima beans, and squirrel parts in a heavy pot, sprinkling each layer with black pepper and a little Tabasco. Cover the layers with water and simmer for 3 hours. Remove the squirrel pieces, discard the bones, and return the meat to the pot, adding several chopped tomatoes. Simmer for another hour, then thicken the broth and serve in soup bowls. Other recipes call for adding okra, celery, and other meats, such as chicken, beef, or veal.

[*Squirrel*—French: *écureuil;* German: *Eichhörnchen;* Italian: *scoiattolo;* Spanish: *ardilla*]

STAPHYLOCOCCUS. *See* poisoning.

STAR ANISE is a component of *Chinese five spices and of some sorts of mixed spice. Its flavor, which is rather more bitter than that of European *anise, depends on the same essential oil, anethole. It is star anise from which this is mainly extracted for use as a flavoring in drinks and confectionery. In its own right, star anise is important as a spice in Chinese cooking. The star-shaped fruits, which are dried before they have ripened, grow on a small evergreen tree (*Illicium verum*), a member of the magnolia family native to China.

STARCH is built up in plants as an end product of photosynthesis. It is made up of many molecules of the simple *sugar glucose and constitutes the plant's reserve energy store as granules that are virtually insoluble in water. Although there is some starch in many plant tissues, it tends to be deposited in seeds and special storage organs such as tubers, and so is part of the human diet in potatoes, cassavas, and cereal grains. When starch grains are heated in water, they swell and then burst open, forming a transparent or translucent gel. (When starch is heated dry, but not burned, it is converted to *dextrin.) Fairly pure forms of starch such as *cornstarch, *tapioca, and *arrowroot, and somewhat less pure ones including white flour and potato flour, are used in the kitchen mainly as thickeners and stabilizers for sauces, gravies, and sweet dishes. The food industry uses starch which has been modified in various ways, by cooking and drying (pregelatinized starch), by acid or enzyme hydrolysis to make invert sugar (*corn syrup), and by treating with chemicals (modified starches). These modified starches are used as stabilizers in some food products. Starch in the kitchen should always be mixed to a cream with cold water before being cooked; it is otherwise likely to become lumpy.

[*Starch*—French: *fécule;* German: *Kohlehydrate;* Italian: *amido;* Spanish: *fécula*]

STARCH SUGAR and **starch syrup.** *See* glucose.

STEAMING. At normal atmospheric pressure, a pan of water produces steam when it boils at 212°F (100°C); although the pan is still being heated, the steam is also at that temperature. It is no hotter than the water is, but it contains the extra heat that it absorbs when it vaporizes. It will give up this extra heat when it condenses back to water. Most vegetables should be steamed over rapidly boiling water. They receive their heat from the steam that condenses on them and hardly reach boiling point themselves. However, the water that condenses and drips back dissolves out less of their soluble salts, vitamins, and natural flavors than they would lose in boiling water. Steaming above the liquid in a *pressure cooker is a particularly good method for vegetables such as potatoes and beets. Steaming covers a wide range of techniques from the heating of *couscous over the stew in a *couscousière* to cooking *puddings over heat and steaming bean sprouts in a very little water in the bottom of the pan.

[*Steam*—French: *cuire à la vapeur;* German: *dünsten;* Italian: *cuocere a vapore;* Spanish: *cocer al vapor*]

STEEL. See iron.

STEEPING is the soaking, usually prolonged, of a solid food in a liquid. It therefore includes processes for introducing preservatives or flavorings, such as brining and marinating, but also soaking for the reverse effect: making extracts of soluble substances like essential oils and colorings.

STERILIZATION means the total destruction of all living organisms, including their spores. Most microorganisms in their vegetative stages are killed in 5 minutes at 176°F (80°C) or in 30 minutes at only 144°F (62°C), as in pasteurization, but heat-loving bacteria, like those in the compost heap, can stand 176-194°F (80°-90°C) for 10 minutes. A few minutes of fast boiling will kill even these, but it will not kill spores. This is why temperatures above 212°F (100°C) generated in a pressure cooker or autoclave are used in *preservation in the canning or bottling of foods in which dangerous spores can germinate.

A temperature of 252°F (122°C) for 30 minutes will kill all spores and give complete sterilization. Instructions are given by the makers of pressure cookers and should be followed exactly. Proteinous and albuminous substances take longer to sterilize than do fruits and vegetables.

Dry sterilization in the oven needs a high-er temperature for a longer time, since organisms are more susceptible to wet heat than to dry. It takes baking at 356°F (180°C) for 1½ hours to sterilize glass jars.

Finally, there is the method known as discontinuous heating. This consists of killing the vegetative bacteria by boiling, and waiting (preferably incubating) for long enough to allow the spores to germinate, then heating again to kill them. The process will need to be repeated several times to ensure complete sterilization. Discontinuous heating is not a method usually used in the kitchen.

[*Sterilization*—French: *stérilisation;* German: *Sterilisation;* Italian: *sterilizzazione;* Spanish: *esterilización*]

STERLET. See sturgeon.

STEWING has been defined as "boiling slowly or simmering"; but it should not be *boiling,* slowly or at any other speed. Stewing is done in a pot with a firmly fitting lid and at a temperature below boiling point—it is in effect the same as *simmering. The proteins in meat are coagulated at a temperature considerably below the 194°F (90°C) of simmering, while the mechanical effects of rapid boiling will spoil the texture of any stew. In most cases, as little liquid as possible should be used so that the gravy becomes thick.

[*Stewing*—French: *cuire a l'étuvée;* German: *schmoren;* Italian: *cuocere in umido;* Spanish: *estofar*]

STINGING NETTLES. See nettle.

STOCK or **fumet** is an extract of meat, bones, fish, fowl, game, or vegetables, usually made by simmering the ingredients for a long time in water to extract their essence. Stocks are not served in their own right but are the basis for other things, not only for soups but, most important of all, for sauces. Ideally, a good stock should always be available. Fortunately, it is not necessary to make stock every week, because it can be concentrated and kept in the freezer. In Victorian Britain, the accepted rule of thumb for making stock was a pound of meat to a pint of water (almost 800 g per lt). But even before World War I such proportions began to be considered extravagant, and now most of the classic recipes are strictly for millionaires. For instance, Urbain-Dubois, writing in 1869, indicates taking a whole shoulder of veal to make stock. Chefs these days make their stock from bones, and even beef bones do well, though not, of course, for delicate white sauces. One thing is sure: while excellent stocks can be made from beef bones, veal bones, chicken carcasses and feet, tough old hares, and fish heads, the stockpot should never be treated as a rubbish bin.

A BASIC STOCK

Take a pile of veal bones or beef bones, wash them, break them into bits, and put them in a hot oven until they are dark, almost black—keep turning them until they reach this point, then cover them with cold water and bring them slowly to simmering point, but never boil them. Skim the stock frequently, especially at the start. Keep it simmering for 6–8 hours. Strain it and remove as much fat as possible from the surface. Now mix together some raw, completely lean hamburger with finely chopped carrot and celery and one egg white. Stir this mixture into the stock. Bring it back to simmering point and simmer for 15 minutes. A thick scum will form on top. Strain the stock through cheesecloth. The purpose of the meat and vegetables is not only to help the egg white in the clearing process, but to give extra fresh flavor. Fat can be removed by cooling the stock and then picking it off when it has solidified.

For a very white stock, use veal bones and blanch them. Stock should be salted very lightly, if at all, or it will get too salty when reduced. If stock is to be used for opaque sauces, such as *demi-glace* or *sauce espagnole*, then it is not necessary to clear it at all.

Once made, the stock may be reduced by boiling to a brown jelly which sets on the bottom of the pan when cold. This jelly can be cut into squares and put into the freezer. It will keep for a year and is always ready as a basis for French sauces, such as the foundation sauces, *demi-glace* and *sauce espagnole* (which lead to Bordelaise, Bourguignonne, Chateaubriand, Financière, Lyonnaise, Poivrade, and Périgueux sauces), or the white foundation sauces, such as velouté and allemande, which open up other culinary vistas.

There is little point in making fish stock in advance because it must cook for only 30 minutes at most—it will acquire a nasty taste if it is much overcooked. Game stock can be made by anyone with access to tough old hares and old birds. *Larousse Gastronomique,* which is authoritative on sauces, says that to cook "in the grand manner" you should have at hand: clear soup, veal stock, brown thin stock, brown thick stock, juice of braised meat, poultry stock, game stock, fish stock, and various jellies. Those who cook Chinese food might well add "high broth" (chicken and pork) and maybe beef and shrimp broth; a mutton broth flavored with onion, cinnamon, and cloves is useful for Indian cooking, though not traditional, since it would go bad without refrigeration. The trick is not to have every sort of stock in the freezer, but to have a few to suit the dishes you are likely to cook. For details on how to make great sauces in the French tradition, see Raymond Sokolov's *The Saucier's Apprentice* (Knopf, 1976).

[*Stock*—French: *consommé;* German: *(Suppen) brühe;* Italian: *brodo;* Spanish: *caldo*]

STOCKFISH is cod, hake, ling, or similar white fish, gutted, beheaded, and split, then washed and dried in the air without salt. It is often confused with *bacalao*, which is dried, salted cod and has a somewhat different flavor. Stockfish has to be very dry to keep in warm climates. It is popular, for instance, in parts of northern and central Italy, where it may be cooked with white wine, onions, herbs, black olives, and potatoes, or eaten with polenta. Basic preparation in Italy is to beat the fish to break the fibers and then to soak it for a week in many changes of water. However, in other parts of Europe, the treatment is very different, though it may be equally heroic. In Holland, Belgium, and Germany, where stockfish is also popular, it is soaked in *limewater. In Norway, for *lutefisk* (lye fish), a traditional Christmas dish, the stockfish is soaked in fresh water with frequent changes for 2–3 days, then in *lye for another 2–3 days, and finally returned for 2–3 days to many more changes of fresh water. After its chemical battering, the fish is cut in large pieces and simmered for a minute in unsalted water. Then salt is added at the rate of 2 oz (50 g) to 1¾ pt (1 lt) of water and the fish is simmered for a further 5 minutes. After that, it is ready to be drained and served with boiled potatoes, yellow split peas, and melted pork drippings or butter. *God yul.*

[*Stockfish*—French: *stockfisch;* German: *Stockfisch;* Italian: *baccalà, stoccafisso;* Spanish: *bacalao seco*]

STONEWARE is hard and mechanically strong pottery which has been fired at temperatures in excess of 2200°F (1200°C) and unlike *earthenware is not usually porous or particularly resistant to thermal shock. Modern glazes used on stoneware have low lead solubility, and salt-glazed stoneware is especially good for storing acid substances. Much ovenware is stoneware with a greater porosity and higher resistance to thermal shock than average. Although it is not easily broken, ovenware can rarely be put on top of the naked flame of a gas stove.

[*Stoneware*—French: *grès, poterie de grès;* German: *Steingut;* Italian: *lareggio;* Spanish: *gres*]

STRAWBERRY is unique among fruit in having the seeds dotted around on the outside rather than embedded within. Although strawberries are canned and frozen (neither with any great success) and are made into jam, they are above all a fruit for eating fresh: strawberries and cream are one of the great treats of summer. Because they are both easily damaged and highly perishable, strawberries used not to be sent great distances to market. Nowadays, however, out-of-season strawberries are for the luxury market (which too often has to be satisfied by the visual experience rather than the flavor, which can be anything but luxurious).

To avoid damage in picking and to ensure that the fruit appears in perfect condition when it gets to market, the fruit farmers gather their strawberries before they are perfectly ripe, even if they have only to travel for a matter of hours. As always, though, fruit ripened on the plant has incomparably the best flavor. Now that increasing labor costs have persuaded farmers to invite people to pick their own fruit, strawberries are the ones that most repay the effort, as the farmers let the public go to work on fields of fully ripe fruit which may have gone too far to survive commercial distribution but are at their best for immediate consumption. It makes a fantastic difference if every strawberry in a bowl has been picked at its peak.

Strawberries are members of the rose family, low plants that spread by sending out runners which root at the end and thus form new plants—this makes them very easy to propagate vegetatively. The wild strawberry, *Fragaria vesca*, has small fruit with a fine flavor that is also found in the rather larger cultivated varieties which are known as Alpine strawberries or *fraises de bois* (at least one sort of which is white rather than red). A second species, the hautboy or hautbois strawberry (*F. moschata*) from central and eastern Europe, is now rarely grown; it has fruit with a musky flavor and without seeds at the stalk end. Both these species went out of favor because they were not susceptible to much "improvement" by the plant breeders, which meant above all that they could not be persuaded to produce large fruit. Alpine strawberries are still grown commercially in Europe, for example in

France, where flavor can still be as important as size, and they are now available in the U.S. for home gardeners. The two species have the advantage that they can be raised from seed and that for some reason their fruit is not taken by birds.

Modern strawberry varieties are all derived from North and South American species with seeds sunk in the surface of the fruit rather than sticking out from it. The first American species to arrive in Europe, in the early 17th century, was the scarlet woodland strawberry (*F. virginiana*) from the eastern U.S. A variety of it, Little Scarlet, is still grown for jam making. The pine strawberry (*F. chiloensis*) from the West Coast of South and North America was brought to Europe in the 18th century; its fruit, which is pink or whitish, is said to taste distinctly of pineapple. The garden strawberry (*F.* × *ananassa*) is a hybrid of these two species, which in nature were separated geographically; it first appeared in France in the early 19th century but was quickly taken up elsewhere. There is now a plethora of varieties in all sizes from medium to gigantic to fit particular local conditions. How good any of them are can be determined only by tasting; appearance seems even less of a guide with strawberries than with any other fruit.

[*Strawberry*—French: *fraise;* German: *Erdbeere;* Italian: *fragola;* Spanish: *fresa, fresón*]

STRAWBERRY TOMATO. *See* physalis fruit.

STRAWBERRY TREE. *See* cranberry.

STRING BEAN. *See* green bean.

STUFFING, dressing, forcemeat, and **filling.** It is unnecessary to try distinguishing exactly between these inexact words. They are all preparations that are put inside something, although forcemeats are occasionally rolled into balls and fried or cooked alongside the main ingredients, and dressing may be flavored with but cooked separately from the meat it accompanies: e.g., when you make a broth from giblets and use it to moisten bread crumbs that are roasted in a packet. Stuffings must be suitable; you should not stuff something that has a delicate flavor with a strong stuffing that would overwhelm it, and it is sensible to stuff a fat goose with something absorbent and a dry guinea fowl with something juicy. Some stuffings are intended to flavor and are not expected to be eaten, like the handful of tarragon in the chicken or an orange in a duck, whereas other stuffings are intended to absorb the flavor and juices from whatever they are inside. When foods are stuffed, especially with a raw stuffing, they take longer to cook, which can sometimes be a disadvantage.

Some dishes—ravioli, cannelloni, or *crépinettes,* for instance—are stuffing done up in parcels. Other stuffings are there because the article concerned was clearly created to be stuffed—squid and sweet peppers are examples. Some stuffed dishes, like cucumbers stuffed with ground beef and sauced with sour cream, make an economical meal from ingredients which would otherwise be formless, but there are also stuffed foods which are no more than a fantasy or a gimmick. Stuffings are worth some thought and trouble. They are not leftovers or things to be bought ready-made in a packet.

The general rule for the quantity of stuffing is 1 cup per lb (450 g) for birds and about half that amount for fish. A simple stuffing for birds is made from 4 cups of bread crumbs, ½ cup of butter, and an egg if binding is necessary. Flavorings to be included are onion (parboiled), thyme and grated lemon zest, or fruit, nuts, herbs of many kinds, and celery, but not all together. Always adjust the salt and sourness (with lemon juice) and check carefully by tasting.

STUFFING FOR TORTELLONI

Mix together 9 oz (250 g) of ricotta cheese, 2 oz (50 g) of cooked spinach, a good grate of nutmeg, 2 eggs, 5 oz (150 g) of Parmesan cheese, salt, and a finely pounded clove of garlic, at your discretion. Taste and adjust the seasoning if necessary. Roll *pasta out thin, cut it in 2–2½-in. (5–6-cm) diameter circles or squares, put filling on each piece, fold it over, seal the edge, and press the ends together. Boil it for 4–5 minutes in salted water and serve with butter, tomato sauce, and grated Parmesan cheese.

RICE STUFFING FOR TOMATOES

Take 4 beautiful large ripe tomatoes. Cut off a lid, scoop out the middle (keeping the flesh and juice), and sprinkle the insides with salt, pepper, and a little olive oil. Put 3 tablespoons of cooked rice in a bowl and add some chopped parsley and chopped basil, a crushed clove of garlic, a pinch of oregano, several spoons of olive oil, and the juice and flesh of the tomato. Mix well and then remove the garlic, which is there to give only a taste. Divide the stuffing among the tomatoes, and replace their tops. Put them in a fireproof dish, standing each tomato on a thin slice of potato. Sprinkle with oil and cook in a hot oven for 45 minutes. Serve hot or cold as an hors d'oeuvre.

STUFFINGS FOR FISH

1: a cup of chopped parsley, a pinch of chopped fresh thyme, and 2 or 3 crushed juniper berries mixed with 3 tablespoons of olive oil. Or 2: a cup of chopped sorrel and ½ cup chopped spinach, both raw, a little garlic, ¼ cup of bread crumbs, 4 finely chopped mushrooms, salt, and pepper; mix together and bind with an egg and a couple of tablespoons of cream.

[*Stuffing*—French: *farce;* German: *Füllsel, Füllung;* Italian: *ripieno;* Spanish: *relleno*]

STURGEON. There are over two dozen species of sturgeon, all found in the northern hemisphere. They live in the sea or in very large lakes, but, like salmon, they swim up the rivers to spawn. Many species are armored with plates and have a sharklike tail. Their weird, prehistoric appearance is not entirely misleading—they have many ancient characters and zoologically are classified somewhere between cartilaginous fishes and bony fishes. They are bottom feeders,

ATLANTIC STURGEON

with no teeth, and are quite harmless.

Sturgeon are known mainly for the *caviar they provide, but their swim bladders make the finest isinglass, and dried sturgeon spine is *viziga,* which is used in the legendary Russian fish pie *coulibiac.* The head of the sturgeon is especially valued in some countries because of the variety of different types of flesh in it, but most species are not much prized for their flesh in the countries where they are common. Sturgeon is a meaty pink-fleshed fish, very suitable for broiling, but the ones I have eaten have a peculiar taste, perhaps because they have been slurping mud at the bottom of the Caspian. The exception is the small sterlet (*Acipenser ruthenus*) of the Black and Caspian seas, which goes up the Danube to spawn (or did) and which I have eaten in Budapest and Belgrad. Other species are better after heavy marinating in vinegar or wine to kill the taste of sturgeon.

The Atlantic sturgeon (*A. oxyrhynchus*), which reaches fish shops on occasion, is found in the North Atlantic and the Mediterranean, but not in the Black Sea. The sevruga (*A. stellatus*), the osciotre (*A. guldenstädtii*), and the giant beluga (*Huso huso*) are found from the Black Sea through the Caspian to the Sea of Azov—the osciotre as far as Lake Baikal.

Sturgeon were once important commercial fish in the U.S., and fish weighing more than a thousand pounds were sometimes caught. Caviar produced from sturgeon was exported to Germany, and the flesh, which resembles veal in taste, was known as "Albany beef" in New York State. Today their numbers are greatly reduced by overfishing, dams, and pollution, but lake sturgeon (*A. fulvescens*) range from the Mississippi River system through all the Great Lakes. Most weigh under 50 lb (23 Kg), and they have several freshwater relatives, including the pallid sturgeon and the shovelnose.

Smoked sturgeon, as made in Turkey, is considered a great delicacy which, with smoked swordfish, is sometimes held to be the equal of smoked salmon (but I feel that no one understands smoking as do northern Europeans). Like smoked salmon, it should be cut thin and along the side.

[*Sturgeon*—French: *esturgeon;* German: *Stör;* Italian: *storione;* Spanish: *esturión*]

SUCCORY. *See* chicory.

SUCROSE. *See* sugar.

SUET is the hard fat from around the kidneys of beef or mutton, beef being better flavored and more usually used in cooking. Suet was formerly more important as an ingredient than it is today, especially in the U.S. and Britain. Such famous old fare as suet pudding, steak and kidney pudding, and suet dumplings all depend on it. Today, most people buy ready-prepared suet in packets (often to feed their birds) and would not know how to start from scratch if they suddenly needed it in a country where the packets are not available (which, in fact, is most countries). But fresh suet has the best taste.

Take the fat from around beef kidneys and with the fingers free it from as much connective tissue as possible. Dust the suet liberally with part of the flour that has been measured to be used in the pastry and chop it with a sharp knife, dusting on more flour to prevent the knife from sticking to the suet when it seems necessary. Continue chopping until you judge it fine enough to make pastry. Once freed from the membranes, suet will keep for weeks in the refrigerator.

[*Suet*—French: *graisse de rognon* (*de boeuf ou de mouton*); German: *Nierenfett;* Italian: *grasso di bue;* Spanish: *sebo, sain*]

SUGAR normally means sucrose ($C_{12}H_{22}O_{11}$), the sugar of sugar cane and sugar beet. More generally, sugars are carbohydrates made by green plants from carbon dioxide and water, using the energy of sunlight. In the process, carbon dioxide is removed from the air and oxygen returned to it. When we use sugars in our bodies, we reverse the process, turning carbohydrate to carbon dioxide and water, and using the energy that is released. We take in oxygen and put out carbon dioxide. There are three main grades of carbohydrate—in ascending order of complexity:

1. the simple sugars, the monosaccharides, such as *glucose, *fructose, and *galactose.
2. the more complex sugars, the disaccharides, like sucrose (cane or beet sugar), *maltose (malt sugar), and *lactose (milk sugar), with molecules that are two molecules of simple sugars joined together.
3. the most complex carbohydrates, the polysaccharides, like *starch, cellulose (of plant cell walls), and glycogen (animal starch as stored in the liver), which are many molecules of simpler sugars joined together.

Plants commonly store food in the form of starch grains, which are virtually insoluble in the watery cell fluid, but some store it as sugar. They also produce quantities of sugars (but not of starch) in ripe fruits, and sugar flavors the nectar of flowers. Both nectar in flowers and the sweetness of ripe fruits are means by which plants bribe animals to assist them, respectively, in reproducing and spreading their seeds.

Sugars are all sweet but not equally so. They may be compared by giving sucrose a mark of 100, when others on the scale are as follows:

fructose	173
sucrose	100
glucose	74
maltose	32
lactose	16

Looking at these, one may well wonder if the making up of babies' bottle milk formulas from dried cow's milk with the sugar content increased with cane sugar instead of lactose is not training modern man to a fattening sweet tooth.

The earliest sweeteners were honey, sweet fruit, and syrups concentrated from fruit—the *dibs made in the Lebanon is an example. *Maple syrup and maple sugar were being made by the American Indians long before settlers arrived from Europe, and probably palm sugar, which is also made by boiling down sap, was made before cane sugar, since this involved squeezing out the juice, a slightly more advanced technology. Today, highly purified sucrose extracted from either sugar cane or sugar beet is the almost universal sweetener.

Sugar cane (*Saccharum officinarum*) is a huge grass which grows higher than a man's head and has a thick, solid stem that contains as much as 10–15% sugar. There are varieties for chewing, but their taste is a flat sweetness that is not relieved by any balancing acidity. The plant is a native of tropical Asia and needs a hot climate. Legend suggests that the Polynesians were the first to use sugar cane as a source of sweetness. However, it was certainly known in India at a very early date, since the word "sugar" derives from Sanskrit. In 510 B.C., the Persians noted sugar in use in the Indus Valley, and during Alexander the Great's invasion, the Greeks also learned about it. It was still crude brown sugar, of the type of *jaggery, and nothing at all like the refined white sugar of today. Later, sugar cane was taken to Persia, where the first refineries were set up in the 7th century A.D. by the Arabs, who, being chemists, made technological improvements, such as the addition of alkali. Sugar was by then used in medicine to preserve it and to disguise the taste of drugs. It was also the Arabs who first introduced sugar to Europe, and sugar cane was grown in some warm areas, including Cyprus, Sicily, and Andalusia, but it does not really thrive in a Mediterranean climate. It was taken to Madeira around 1420. However, by the end of

the 15th century, Venice had become the sugar-trading center of Europe; most of the sugar was brought from the Orient, and it was vastly expensive.

Columbus took canes to America from the Canary Islands during his second voyage in 1493. They were first planted at his headquarters on the island of Hispaniola in the Caribbean, where he reported that the canes grew faster than anywhere else in the world. Soon they were taken to other Caribbean islands and to the mainland, for example to Brazil. The planters who grew the "white gold" became vastly rich. By the early 18th century, the West Indies was the main source of supply, and it was a prime reason for the slave trade. The first refinery in England had been built in 1544, but sugar was still very costly. In the 18th century, when coffee and tea drinking became the vogue, the demand for sugar increased sharply.

Sugar from sugar beet (*Beta vulgaris* var. *cicla*) came as a direct result of the British blockade of Europe during the Napoleonic wars. In 1747 a German chemist, Andreas Marggraf, found up to 6.2% sugar in certain varieties of beet, but early efforts to exploit the discovery were a commercial failure. It was not until 1811, when Napoleon ordered an investment to be made in the process, that much progress was made. Later, the new crop was officially encouraged in Europe and North America. By 1880, beet had replaced cane as a source of sugar in a number of countries. Britain, however, still obtained most of its sugar from the West Indian colonies. Two world wars, though, encouraged even the British to be as self-sufficient in sugar as possible. Today, the growing of beets, which have been improved to contain 15–20% sugar, is still spreading; beets are even being grown in the north of India, a country associated with the origins of sugar cane production. At the moment, 40% of the world's sugar comes from beet. Refined sugar is 99% sucrose; it is not possible to tell by taste whether it is from beets or cane, but sugar beet molasses is not as pleasantly edible as cane molasses. It is a raw material for industry (e.g., in the making of *monosodium glutamate) and an animal foodstuff. There is thus no brown sugar from beets, unless it has been made artificially.

Primitive methods of sugar production are still to be seen in sugar-producing countries. In India, for instance, the lovely smell of sugar in the making still pervades villages in the cold weather. The cane is passed between two large cog wheels turned by oxen and the juice is boiled down in wide, open pans over a fire composed of the dross from the cane crushing. Lime is thrown in to neutralize the acids, and the surface is skimmed. Later, the dark-brown, richly smelling, sticky jaggery is scraped from the pans. (Boiled with butter, jaggery makes just about the best toffee in the world.)

In the large factories, the extraction process, though sophisticated, is similar. A boiled mass of sugar crystals and sticky molasses is obtained which is called *massecuite* and is essentially the same as jaggery. But then the mixture is put into a centrifuge and the molasses is spun out. The residue is crude brown sugar, which is sticky, but less so than jaggery. Raw sugar sounds delicious, but, as imported in bulk, it will likely be full of trash, soil, dirt, bacteria, molds, and even creatures called sugar lice (*Carpoglyphus anonymus* or *Acarus sacchari*). In the refineries, it is softened with warm syrup, centrifuged, strained, treated with lime and carbon dioxide, and decolorized with bone charcoal. Finally, the clear syrup is boiled under reduced pressure until the introduction of a small number of "seed" crystals causes crystallization. Though refined, it is still a mixture of crystals and syrup and has to be centrifuged again and dried in granulators before it is ready to be graded by sieving.

Beets have to be shredded and the sugar dissolved out with warm water to produce a sugary solution which is treated with lime, carbon dioxide, sulfur dioxide, and so on in successive processes until it can be evaporated, crystallized, and centrifuged in the same way as cane sugar. The largest producers of cane sugar are Cuba, Brazil, and India; the U.S.S.R., Europe, and the U.S. are the big beet sugar areas.

Caster sugar is drawn from the evaporating pan at the correct crystal size. Confectioner's sugar is made by powdering the crystals in a mill. Lump or cube sugar is made by compressing moist sugar in molds and then drying it. In the old days, the moist refined sugar was poured into a mold shaped like a volcano (a Venetian innovation) to produce loaf sugar, which had to be broken up with special tongs.

Sucrose from cane or beets will dissolve completely in about a third of its weight of water at room temperature. More will dissolve in hot water but will crystallize out again on cooling. Sucrose syrups boil at a higher temperature than pure water, but if the sugar is heated dry, it will melt at about 320°F (160°C) and will then cool to a straw-colored, glassy substance called barley sugar.

Confectioners make good use of the different physical states in which sugar can exist when it is heated to various temperatures. It is tricky to melt sugar by itself, since it is apt to overheat in spots and then caramelize. Thus it is usual to add a little water to the sugar. Even so, heat must be applied gently until the sugar has completely melted, after which the temperature is best raised as fast as possible without causing it to burn—in general, the longer sugar is heated, the greater the degree of caramelization or darkening.

Once the added water has boiled away, the sugar begins to lose the water of crystallization, which is an integral part of the sugar crystal. To prevent unwanted caramelization, never let the sides of the pan overheat, and keep them free of sugar by brushing or sponging them down with cold water. Professional confectioners may boil the sugar with the lid on the pan—called "steaming down"—so that the sugar on the sides get wet with steam.

Sugar heated above 250°F (120°C) will almost certainly grain or candy unless steps are taken to stop it. With graining, the sugar turns into an opaque hard lump when it cools. To prevent this, a lowering agent must be added. For homemade toffees, this is often a dash of vinegar or lemon juice, but serious sweetmakers mostly use thick glucose syrup at the rate of 2¼ lb (1 Kg) of glucose to 9 lb (4 Kg) of sugar. However, in hot countries it is better to use cream of tartar— 1½ level tablespoons (10 g) of cream of tartar to 9 lb (4 Kg) of sugar. Dirty pans also cause graining, as does inadequate skimming when the sugar boils.

To test the various stages of sugar boiling, professionals will dip their fingers into cold water, then quickly into the sugar and back again into the cold water. Anyone lacking speed or confidence (which means almost everyone) should use the handle of a spoon instead of fingers. For large quantities, it is best to use a sugar thermometer, which will be graduated up to about 400°F or 200°C. Keep it handy in a jug of very hot water; clipping it to the side of the pan (which the design suggests) will get in the way of the brushing down.

As sugar is heated, it changes constantly, and the stage it has reached is related to the temperature. The stages have been given names by the confectioners, but there is much variation (at least from 5 to 13) in the number of stages identified by different authorities, and there is not absolute agreement on the temperatures at which the stages are reached, not surprisingly, since another factor affects the stage of sugar—the speed of heating. The following list represents the stages that might be recognized by cooks in old-fashioned kitchens.

1. Thread—215°F (102°C). If a little of the liquid sugar is taken out, it can be pulled into brittle threads between the thumb and the forefinger. This and the next stage are used for candying fruit, for liqueurmaking, and for icing.

2. Pearl—222°F (106°C). The thread formed between thumb and finger can be stretched. The name of the stage comes from the fact that the sugar is boiling and forms small pearllike balls.

3. Blow or soufflé—230°F (110°C). The bubbles in the boiling sugar look like snowflakes, and if you dip in a perforated skimmer and then blow through the holes, bubbles or flakes will form. This is the temperature for making sugar candy.

4. Soft ball—240°F (116°C). The sugar clinging to the skimmer will now, when shaken, produce a feathery, downy effect. The syrup is now beginning to thicken and will form a soft ball if a little of it is dropped into cold water. This is the temperature for fondants, fudges, peppermint creams, and the final stages of fruit candying.

5. Hard ball—250°F (121°C). If some of the syrup is dropped into cold water, it will make a hard ball. This is the temperature for caramels, nougats, and soft toffees.

6. Light crack (or crackling)—264°F (129°C). If a spoon handle or wetted finger is dipped in the sugar, then quickly plunged into cold water, the sugar forms a hard layer. If you put it in your mouth, it will stick to your teeth. It is used for toffee icings for cakes, and slightly higher temperatures are used for most toffees. At the light-crack stage, the sugar begins to turn pale yellow in color.

7. Hard crack—289°F (143°C). The cooked sugar becomes harder and more glassy. A coating on a spoon handle (or a daring wetted finger) will, when plunged into cold water, come off in thin films that crack like glass. At somewhat higher temperatures, around 302°F (150°C), the sugar reaches a suitable state for making barley sugar, butterscotch, boiled sweets, fruit drops, and brittles. Slightly higher still, and caramel is just starting to form—this is the temperature for spun sugar and for dipping fresh fruit such as peaches, apricots, and grapes to give them a crackle covering.

8. *Caramel—356°F (180°C). There is now very little water left in the sugar. It darkens and progressively loses its sweetness, eventually *browning. At higher temperatures still, it finally burns to carbon.

Sucrose warmed with a dilute acid, such as sulfuric acid, is split by *hydrolysis into two simpler monosaccharide sugars—glucose and fructose. Enzymes in our bodies and in the saliva of bees also break down sucrose into these two simpler sugars.

Sugar has other important effects, apart from sweetening in cookery. In high concentrations it acts as a *preservative; in bottling and canning, it helps to maintain both texture and flavor in fruit; in *freezing, fruit is best if it is first coated with sugar or frozen in a 40% sugar syrup; in baking, the effect of sugar is to maintain the elasticity in the gluten so that it stays flexible for longer and so allows the cake to rise better—it does not get rigid too soon. It has a similar effect on the protein of egg in cakes and custards; it combines with the pectin in fruit (in the presence of fruit acids) to form a jelly; it forms both bulk and texture in cakes and ice creams; by encouraging peptization in marinades, it helps meat to become more tender; and it counteracts the hardening effect of saltpeter in cures for ham and bacon. On the debit side, sugar undoubtedly contributes to dental caries by encouraging decay bacteria in the mouth, and overconsumption has been blamed for a number of modern illnesses, but evidence here is so far inconclusive. Too much of most things is harmful; exactly how much is too much is difficult to decide.

Types of Sugar

Barbados sugar. Sugar-cane cultivation was introduced into Barbados in the 17th century, and the sugar from there had a high reputation. Many sugars were once labeled with the name of the place of origin, and some names have stuck. Barbados is a dark-brown, moist sugar with a fine "rummy" taste and not too coarse a grain for cakes. It is similar to dark-brown sugar in the U.S.

Bee sugar. Rough sugar is used by beekeepers to maintain hives over winter, or at any time when there is no honey flow, which may be the hot dry season in some countries. If they were not fed sugar, the bees would eat the honey that the beekeeper wants from

them, or would starve if it were taken. The saliva of bees converts sucrose to glucose and fructose, and the result is stored in the comb. The cells look white and are easily recognized; they should not be sold as honey.

Brown sugar. In the past, brown sugar was sugar partly purified and containing residual molasses to give it flavor. Today, most brown sugar is a reconstituted product made by adding calculated amounts of suitable cane molasses to purified white sugar.

Superfine, caster sugar or **castor sugar.** A very fine but crystalline sugar, this is the best for many purposes. It blends beautifully in cake mixtures, gives a sparkle finish when sifted over anything for decoration, and is the one to use in meringues.

Colored sugar. Some sugar is dyed brown to simulate brown sugar. Coarsely crystalline sugar candy is sometimes dyed for decoration. Sometimes mixed colors turn up on the coffee table. Colored crystals are also used in cake decoration. They may be made by putting colors on the palms of the hands, rubbing the crystals between them, and then drying the colored sugar. Traditionally, colors used were cochineal for pink sugar, spinach juice for green, saffron solution for yellow, chocolate syrup for brown, and indigo for blue. Nowadays the colors would probably be synthetic.

Confectioner's sugar, also called powdered sugar or icing sugar, is a fine, very white powdered sugar made by grinding it in a mill to the required consistency. It is likely to contain a harmless anticaking agent such as starch or calcium phosphate and is used for decorating cakes and for dusting, as on Turkish delight and other sweets. It dissolves instantly, is very sweet to the taste, and is used in whipped cream and in uncooked sweets (such as chocolate truffles and fondants), where there should not be a grainy texture. It is also used in meringues.

Cube sugar. Hard, small-grained crystalline

sugar pressed moist into blocks, dried, and cut into cubes of various sizes; some are wrapped in paper. Cube sugar, though more expensive than loose sugar, is preferred by cafés and restaurants where portion control is important. On the table it is less easily spilled and looks more elegant. It is also more elegant in champagne cocktails. In the kitchen, it is sometimes useful. It can be rubbed on lemons or oranges to remove flavoring oils without the bits of zest you would get if the peel were grated. Lump sugar tends to vanish in households where there are children (who have been known to stuff a lump into a hole in an orange, then suck it).

Demerara sugar. A brown sugar with large crystals and fine flavor named after the Demerara district in Guyana. It is less moist than dark-brown sugar, varies considerably in quality, and is less widely available than it used to be. The large crystals make Demerara-type sugars ideal for use on cereals and porridge. They are traditional sweeteners for coffee and are also used in meat dishes, for example on ham.

★Golden syrup, a uniquely British product, is pale yellow and has a thick, honeylike consistency. Its taste is unique, delicate, and quite unlike molasses.

Granulated sugar. Ordinary, refined crystalline sugar as used in the kitchen.

★Jaggery. Indian crude sugar or *gur*.

Lump sugar. Cube sugar.

Maple sugar is made by reduction of ★maple syrup.

★Molasses. A dark, treacly mass of sugars and other substances left over from sugar refining.

Palm sugar. Sugar made by boiling down the sap of various ★palms.

Panela. Hard, dark Colombian sugar formed into loaves.

Piloncillo. Crude brown sugar from Mexico. Very dark and shaped in the form of small corks, sometimes wrapped in raffia and also called *panocha*.

Powdered sugar. *See* confectioner's sugar (above).

Preserving sugar. Pure refined sugar in large white crystals or irregular small lumps used for making jams, jellies, and marmalades. Although ordinary granulated sugar can be used for this purpose, preserving sugar is more convenient: it does not form a compact mass and thus needs less stirring. In the initial stages of jam making, there is less likelihood of caramelization and burning.

Raw sugar. Crude brown sugar as it is shipped to the refinery.

Sorghum. Syrup or sugar from sweet sorghum (*see* millet).

Sugar candy, called rock candy in the U.S. Large sugar crystals are sometimes attached to strings or twigs in bottles of liqueurs (*fior d'Alpi*). They have to be grown by putting crystals into a saturated sugar solution and allowing the water to evaporate slowly. Smaller sugar candy crystals are used as coffee sugar.

★Treacle is a rather vague term that has been used to cover everything from golden syrup to molasses.

Turbinado sugar has been cleaned more than raw sugar, but up to 15% molasses remains, giving it a blond color and distinct flavor. It contains about the same amount of sucrose as refined white sugar.

Unrefined sugar is raw sugar, ★*jaggery,* or *gur.*

White sugar includes all the highly refined sugars that are 99% sucrose.

[*Sugar*—French: *sucre;* German: *Zucker;* Italian: *zucchero;* Spanish: *azúcar*]

SUGAR APPLE. *See* custard apple.

SULFUR DIOXIDE, sulfurous acid, and **sulfites.** *See* preservatives.

SULFURIC ACID (H_2SO_4), when concentrated, is known as oil of vitriol and is a most dangerous corrosive substance. Sulfuric acid in a dilute form is used in car batteries, but even at that strength it is very corrosive. It is much used in the chemical industry, sometimes in processes that relate to food (e.g., the synthesis of saccharin). In a very dilute form, it has been used in soft drinks and at such extremely low strengths is probably harmless.

[*Sulfuric acid*—French: *acide sulfurique;* German: *Schwefelsäure;* Italian: *acido solforico;* Spanish: *ácido sulfúrico*]

SULTANA. *See* raisin.

SUMAC is a shrub or tree which belongs to the genus *Rhus*. This includes poison ivy (*R. toxicodendron*) and other poisonous plants, some decorative species well known to gardeners, and a number of useful plants that provide Japanese lacquer, copal varnish, and tannin for leather. The sumac of Mediterranean Europe (*R. coriaria*), also known as the elm-leafed sumac or Sicilian sumac, has hairy fruits, which are dark-red to purple when ripe. The hairs are rich in *malic acid, and the berries have a sour and pleasantly astringent taste. They are an important souring agent in the cooking of some areas of the Middle East, notably Lebanon, and are also used to make a sour drink: the dried berries are infused in cold water for 20 minutes and then the juice is squeezed out. Lebanese homes traditionally kept a supply of the dried berries, which had preferably been gathered in the mountains where the quality is best. I have only once managed to buy dried sumac berries in London and the quality was disappointing. However, since sumac grows in gardens, there is nothing to prevent experiment. The berries should be ripe and of the correct species.

In North America, there are a number of sumacs. The scarlet sumac (*R. glabra*), a familiar wayside tree, has large, dense clusters of red berries that are covered in acid hairs like the European equivalent; they are wholesome and can be used to make a refreshing drink, as well as being a satisfactory substitute in Lebanese cooking. One poisonous sumac, which could possibly confuse, has white berries in strings. Sumacs with smooth, hairless fruits should be avoided: they are likely to be poisonous.

[*Sumac*—French: *sumac;* German: *Färberbaum, Sumach;* Italian: *sommacco;* Spanish: *zumaque*]

SUNFLOWER. The annual sunflower (*Helianthus annus*) has long been grown as a crop, particularly in Russia, Rumania, Hungary, and Bulgaria, but increasingly so in other countries, and today sunflowers can be seen in fields and gardens almost anywhere that there are suitably warm summers—in the U.S., they are a common plant in gardens, and because sunflower seeds are often used as birdseed, one can find sunflowers growing wild wherever bird droppings have found a likely spot to germinate. In countries where people are in the habit of nibbling to pass the time, salted sunflower seeds are popular. (In Spain, my children are always nibbling *pipes,* salted sunflower seeds that are sold in packets.)

However, the main use of sunflower seeds is as a source of oil, which makes up about half their weight. Sunflower oil is light and has a high percentage of polyunsaturated fatty acids and a low percentage of saturated fatty acids. With safflower oil, it is one of the best oils for use in cholesterol-lowering diets. Because of these qualities, it has become available quite widely (though the supermarket product may be so highly refined that it is nondescript in flavor). The cold-pressed oil, which is taken off without heat, is inclined to be expensive but is an excellent oil for salads. The second pressings, made after heating the residues, are good for most other cooking purposes.

Sunflowers probably originated in the Americas, but exactly where is in some doubt. They have been cultivated in Europe since the mid-16th century. Young buds of sunflowers are edible and can at a pinch be used in salads; they are best boiled. Recently, machine-shelled sunflower seeds have come on the market and opened up new possibilities for those who like to experiment, since they are a healthful and nutritious food. They are used in *granola and made into high-protein flour.

[Sunflower—French: girasol, tournesol; German: Sonnenblume; Italian: girasole; Spanish: girasol, mirasol]

SWAMP SUGAR PEAR. See rowan.

SWEATING in cookery means heating gently for a short time in butter (or other oil or fat) without any liquid so that the substance being cooked does not fry or brown. It is a process generally applied to green vegetables or to onions, and it is usually maintained until the vegetable becomes soft.

SWEDE. See turnip.

SWEETBREADS, soft, white, and in themselves rather flavorless, are regarded as a delicacy. They are, or should be, the thymus glands of young animals—usually calves or lambs. The thymus is large in young animals, but in older animals it virtually disappears. The glands are situated in the chest, and their function is concerned with the immunity of the young animal and the production of white blood cells. Sweetbreads are also taken from the pancreas, and other glands, including the testes, are sometimes passed off as thymus. These are all good, but are not true sweetbreads.

To prepare sweetbreads, soak them for an hour or so in cold water to remove any blood. Then trim them and poach them in stock or court bouillon for about 10 minutes. After that, cook them in one of the many ways that are particularly to be found in books on French cooking.

[Sweetbreads—French: ris de veau ou d'agneau; German: Bröschen, Kalbsbries, Kalbsmilch; Italian: animella; Spanish: lechecillas, mollejas]

SWEET CORN. See corn.

SWEET FLAG. See calamus.

SWEET LAUREL. See bay.

SWEET MARJORAM. See marjoram.

SWEET PEPPER or bell pepper. Both sweet peppers (Capsicum annuum) and *chili peppers came from tropical America and have been cultivated for so long that their origins are muddled. Opinions differ as to whether they should be regarded as one or more species, and the traveling cook will be further confused to come on large horn-shaped peppers which are mild and sweet as well as others, identical in shape, that almost blister your fingers when you touch them. Some long, chili-shaped varieties, like the American sweet banana pepper, are actually sweet peppers. The squarish and tomato-shaped varieties, commonly called bell peppers, are usually sweet, but some have quite a nip to them. The color range is from green (there are pale- and dark-green types) ripening through yellow and orange streaks to red; other varieties may be yellow when ripe, or variegated, or even almost black, and there are parchment-colored varieties used for pickling, which might be called either hot-sweet or cool-chili. Sweet peppers also vary in flavor—some modern greenhouse varieties are almost tasteless, while others have a superb capsicum flavor that develops especially when they are roasted. Thickness of flesh is another factor to be noticed—some are thin-fleshed and others juicy—and the skin of some (especially commercial varieties for export) is often thick and leathery.

Peppers are indigenous to Mexico and played an important part in the cuisine long before the Spaniards arrived. They have long been established in the cooking of the countries around the Mediterranean, in Portugal, the Balkans, and Rumania. However, they are latecomers to most European cooking because the first varieties of sweet peppers to be introduced were rather fiery and unreliable. In the 19th century, British and even French cookbooks scarcely mention sweet peppers—and, oddly, they were cultivated in Europe before they became popular in the U.S. In any case, they were grown only in very hot climates until the development of new varieties enabled them to spread farther north. In very hot countries like India there now tends to be a greater love of hot chilies (sweet peppers are called *Kashmire mirch*—Kashmir peppers—in Hindi), leaving the sweet peppers for areas that like less spicy food.

Sweet peppers are now a routine food in the U.S., at least raw in salads. It is unfortunate that so many of the varieties sold commercially taste more of pea pods than of fine sweet peppers; others are bitter and overwhelming unless used only in small quantity. Finding a good—and suitable—variety makes an enormous difference to the dishes in which peppers are used.

Both sweet and hot peppers have notable content of vitamin C, but their main gastronomic role is to provide flavor. So widely used are peppers these days that it is difficult to think what Spanish, Italian, Chinese, and many other national cuisines could have been like without them. Dried sweet peppers, *paprika from Hungary and *pimentón from Spain, are crucial to their respective national cuisines.

Cooks often like flat-bottomed, boxy peppers for stuffing, since they will stand upright; the stem end is cut off and the seeds and septa (which can be bitter) are removed before stuffing. Peppers that have to lie on their sides are best slit down the side, cleaned, stuffed, and left with the stalk end intact. Peppers to be marinated in vinaigrette or olive oil should be grilled (either by throwing them onto hot charcoal or by spearing them with a fork and turning them over a flame until charred), peeled, and put to marinate whole, with the seeds intact, since this gives them the very best flavor. If they are to be preserved under oil, the seeds can be removed later.

Some dishes require particular types of sweet pepper. In Spain, for example, Romesco sauce is authentic only if it is made with the elongated, top-shaped Romesco peppers that are grown around Tarragona. Among other Spanish peppers, *ñoras,* which are round and (like Romesco) only slightly piquant, may be found in their dried form in every Spanish market; they are the flavoring of dishes *a la vizcaina* and are also called *pimientos choriceros*—the peppers in chorizo sausages (in which *pimentón* is also used).

STUFFED SWEET PEPPERS (INDIA)

Boil and mash 4 potatoes. Slice and fry an onion in a tablespoon of fat—ideally Indian clarified butter (*ghee*)—until it is soft. Add the potatoes and 1 teaspoon of *garam masala,* ½ teaspoon of turmeric, 1 tablespoon of mango powder (*amchur*), plus salt to taste. Slit 6 smallish sweet peppers and remove the seeds, perferably through the sides. Stuff them with the potato mixture. Heat another tablespoon of fat in a frying pan. Put in the stuffed peppers with a little water. Sprinkle with salt and cover with a lid. Cook slowly until the peppers are soft.

If *amchur* is not available, use lemon juice to sour the stuffing, but the flavor will not be the same. *Amchur* is used in many other Indian dishes as a souring and flavoring agent, especially when green mangoes are not in season.

[Sweet pepper—French: *pimeton doux;* German: *Ziegenpfeffer;* Italian: *peperone;* Spanish: *pimiento*]

SWEET POTATO (*Ipomoea batatas*) is a tuber formed on a plant of the Convolvulus family. It is native to tropical America but has spread all over the tropics, where, with yam, cassava, and taro, it forms the basic starchy staple of many people. Sweet potatoes also have some importance in the Mediterranean countries. There are two main types, the dry, yellow-fleshed, and mealy varieties, and the softer, more watery, and generally sweeter white-fleshed varieties, which are more favored in the tropics. The skin may be white, red, or purple.

In the U.S., sweet potatoes are grown mainly in Louisiana, North Carolina, and Georgia. There are many ways in which they are prepared, and sometimes they are even used mashed in cakes and sweet dishes. Perhaps the simplest and best way to treat them is to peel them and cook them (for about an hour) in the pan with roasting meat, having first sprinkled them well with brown sugar, butter, and a pinch of cinnamon. They are also delicious baked in their jackets. They do not store as well as ordinary potatoes but can be kept for a week or more in a cool place.

[*Sweet potato*—French: *patate;* German: *Batate;* Italian: *patata;* Spanish: *batata*]

SWEET SOP. *See* custard apple.

SWEET WOODRUFF. *See* woodruff.

SWISS CHARD. *See* chard.

SWORD BEAN. *See* jack bean.

SWORDFISH (*Xiphias gladius*) is among the largest of the bony fishes and is found in all oceans. It may weigh 155–225 lb (70–100 Kg), and it is possibly the fastest of all fish, being able to do over 60 miles (100 Km) per hour. Its head is extended forward into a long point, or sword. When angered, it is formidable because it uses its sword as a ram, although normally the sword is used sideways to stun or maim the fish or cephalopods which are its prey. The swordfish has excellent, rather firm white flesh and is eaten everywhere it is caught, often broiled in steaks or *en brochette*. However, there are a particular number of recipes from Sicily and Calabria because the swordfish migrate along those coasts in the breeding season and have been caught there since ancient times. (Normally this fish is a loner, keeping to itself in deep water.) As with the tuna, Mediterranean people regard the belly as the best part. Swordfish are also caught in Turkey, netted in season in the Bosphorus, and it is from here that the delicacy of smoked *kiliç* (swordfish) has become known; it has been claimed as the equal of smoked salmon when at its best, although the ordinary smoked swordfish packaged in oil that is found in some supermarkets is not more than very nice. It has also been likened to smoked *★sturgeon. Before smoking, the pieces of boned swordfish are first salted in barrels, pressed down under a wooden disk, and weighted with a stone. The salting is short—12–18 hours—after which the pieces are washed in strong brine and hung in a current of air in a shady place to dry for 2–3 days. Finally, the pieces are smoked for 10–12 hours and are then ready for use. The product may be known as *mersine*. Blue marlin (*Makaira migricans*) and white marlin (*M. albida*) are similar large fish that are found in the Caribbean and off the East Coast of the U.S.; they are less good to eat than the swordfish.

[*Swordfish*—French: *espadon;* German: *Schwertfisch;* Italian: *pesca spada;* Spanish: *pez espada*]

SYRUP. *See* corn syrup; golden syrup; maple syrup.

SZECHWAN PEPPER. *See* Chinese pepper.

T

TABASCO SAUCE. A hot chili sauce, with a very characteristic flavor, made from the tabasco variety of chili pepper, which is said to have been brought to Louisiana from Mexico in 1868. Tabasco, which contains chilies, vinegar, and salt, is one of the world's most famous bottled sauces. It is found on every cocktail bar for use in a Bloody Mary, and many like it on shellfish, particularly oysters. Imitations are inferior.

TAGLIATELLE. *See* pasta.

TAHINI has emerged from its ethnic origins and become internationally known in recent years. It is an oily paste made of *sesame seeds, which have usually been roasted first to give a strong nutty taste, and is a staple in most of the countries around the eastern end of the Mediterranean. Sesame is difficult to grind or pound at home to the required fine oily state, but tahini is generally available in Greek or Lebanese shops. Typical uses for tahini are in *hummus bi tahini,* a dip to use with Arab bread, and for *taratour bi tahini,* a mayonnaiselike sauce in which lemon juice and tahini are emulsified and flavored with salt and garlic—a sort of Middle East aïoli, which is excellent for salads and fish. There is even a variant of the *eggplant purée that is sometimes called poor-man's caviar, in which tahini plays a role.

A point to notice is that when lemon juice is added, tahini first turns to a sticky, crumbly paste, but if you continue to stir in drops of lemon juice (or water if it gets too sour), it gradually turns to a beautifully smooth cream. Tahini is something with which to experiment. It keeps almost indefinitely in a glass jar in the refrigerator.

HUMMUS BI TAHINI

Soak and cook 1 cup of chickpeas, or use canned ones, drained. Put the juice of a lemon into the blender, add a little water if necessary to cover the blades, and add 4 tablespoons of tahini, a little at a time. Now add 1–2 cloves of chopped garlic, and blend. Finally add 5–6 tablespoons of chickpeas and some salt. Blend again and gradually add the remaining chickpeas. Adjust the taste by adding more tahini, garlic, salt, or lemon. When the *hummus* is to your liking, pour it into a serving bowl and sprinkle it with a little chopped parsley or decorate with a sprig of mint. Dribble good olive oil on top in a circle for an authentic decoration. Authentic, too, is to dip bits of *pitta* bread in the *hummus.*

TALLOW. *See* fats.

TAMALE FLOUR. *See masa.*

TAMARI. *See* soybean.

TAMARIND or **Indian date.** The beautiful tamarind tree (*Tamarindus indica*) is probably a native of tropical East Africa but it has been cultivated in India since time immemorial and today is grown throughout the world in suitably warm climates, even to some extent in the Mediterranean countries. It is a legume with large pods that are brown when ripe and look rather like carob pods. The pulp around the seeds is the part used. It has a fruity sour taste because it contains a lot of tartaric acid, and can be made into refreshing drinks. Tamarind sold in shops is a brown sticky mass of pods, containing fiber and a number of seeds. It is an excellent souring agent and is much used in Indian cooking.

To prepare it, pour a small amount of boiling water on a knob of tamarind, wait for it to cool, then rub and squash it with the fingers until a purée is formed. Fiber and seed can now be sieved out. Tamarind purée is mildly laxative. Sometimes recipes say that it can be replaced by lemon juice, but the result is never quite the same. Sweetened tamarind syrup can also be bought and is used as a basis for fruit drinks.

TAMARIND SAUCE

Soak 1 lb (450 g) tamarind in enough vinegar to cover it. When it is soft, rub it to a purée with the fingers. Pass the purée through a sieve and throw away the seeds and fiber. Now scrape 4 oz (100 g) of fresh ginger and cut it into small pieces. Peel the same weight of garlic and clean the same weight of hot red chilies. Put all in the blender (adding more vinegar to cover if necessary) and churn to a pulp. Add 4 oz (100 g) of kitchen salt and ½ lb (25 g) of sugar. Boil the mixture. To balance the sweet-sour-salt relationship, add more sugar or more vinegar. Usually about 1 pt (½ lt) of vinegar in all is required, but the quantity depends on the sourness of the tamarind.

[*Tamarind*—French: *tamarin;* German: *Tamarinde;* Italian: *tamarindo;* Spanish: *tamarindo*]

TANDOOR. *See* baking.

TANGERINE, tangelo, and **tangor.** *See* orange.

TANNIA. *See* yam (yautia).

TANNIN. The tannins, which include tannic acid, are strongly astringent substances that occur in many plants. Their original use was in tanning leather, since they have the ability to coagulate and toughen proteins, especially those in skin. Similar effects can be produced in human bodies if we consume many bitter acorns, horse chestnuts, or oak leaves or even drink too much old, stewed tea. "Tea drinker's dyspepsia" is not unknown among habitual drinkers of strong tea. Milk helps to counteract the tannins by reacting with some of them before they hit the stomach. In cooking, substances that contain tannin may be used in pickling to help firm up the vegetables—oak leaves are commonly used for this in Poland. Soaking salted fish in tea rather than water to remove the salt—a method that is sometimes used in France—perhaps has a firming action. Tannin is also mentioned in wine literature, because it occurs in the skins, pips, and stalks of grapes (and also comes from oak casks); it is an important element in red wines, particularly in clarification. Young wines with prospects are rough with tannin, but with maturation the tannin decreases and is involved in the formation of crust inside the bottles.

[*Tannin*—French: *tanin, tannin;* German: *Gerbsäure;* Italian: *tannino;* Spanish: *tanino*]

TANSY (*Tanacetum vulgare*) is an herb of the composite family, a common wayside and lawn plant in the U.S. and Europe. It has waxy, buttonlike yellow flowers, and the whole plant is highly scented with a slightly resinous, sharp-smelling odor that resembles the daisy—or perhaps the chrysanthemum (an alternate name for tansy is *Chrysanthemum vulgare*). Tansy was once an important medicinal herb, perhaps because of the belief that what tastes nasty must do you good (or kill you—it was reported in early American history that many deaths were caused by tansy). Nevertheless, tansy is much referred to as a flavoring in 16th- and 17th-century recipes, especially in puddings. Today few people bother with it, and many people who try it dislike it, but as herbal teas regain popularity, tansy returns to the teapot, whence it is appreciated for its distinctive flavor. It is best brewed with spearmint leaves to temper its slight bitterness.

[*Tansy*—French: *tanaisie, barbotine;* German: *Rainfarn, Wurmkraut;* Italian: *tanaceto;* Spanish: *tanaceto*]

TAPIOCA is a starchy food made by peeling and grating *cassava root, expressing the juice, and soaking the residue in water. The pulp is then kneaded to release the starch grains, strained to remove the fiber, and dried to a paste. Finally the paste is heated on an iron plate until it forms into the typical balls, flakes, or pearls of tapioca. It may also be ground into a flour. Tapioca has an international reputation for digestibility, and so, as one Spanish book says, *"Es aconsejable para los niños."* (Children do not always find it so advisable, and many adults will remember tapioca pudding with horror.) It can be used in soups in the same way as pasta or pearl barley, and it is useful for thickening stews and pie fillings. A classic Brazilian pudding is made in the same way as English tapioca pudding but with red wine or grape juice substituted for milk. The result is served cold with vanilla cream.

[*Tapioca*—French: *tapioca;* German: *Tapioka;* Italian: *tapioca;* Spanish: *tapioca*]

TARAMA. Dried and cured female roes of gray mullet, pressed and sold from the barrel in Greece. Virtually the same as *botargo. As Elizabeth David said as far back as 1950 in her *Mediterranean Food* (Penguin), the taste is not unlike that of English smoked cod's roe. In fact in Greece, where

taramasalata is a popular part of the *meze,* cod's roe, imported in barrels, is commonly used as a substitute for the roe of mullet.

TARAMASALATA

Put tarama in water and soak it for 5 minutes or so to remove part of the salt. Squeeze to remove some of the water. Pound the roe in a mortar, adding olive oil and lemon juice alternately, as if making mayonnaise, and tasting as you go. Finally mix in a little finely chopped onion and some chopped dill. Serve with good bread, toast, brown bread, or *pitta.*

TARO. *See* yam (dasheen).

TARRAGON is one of the great culinary herbs. There are two kinds, French tarragon (*Artemesia dracunculus*), which is very aromatic but rarely if ever sets seed, and Rus-

TARRAGON

sian tarragon (*A. dracunculoides*), which can be grown from seed but is virtually tasteless and odorless. Although small plants of both tarragons are similar, true tarragon grows into a bush with slender, thin leaves, whereas bastard tarragon becomes coarse-looking, with fleshier, paler-green leaves. There is no mistaking the scent of true tarragon if you crush a leaf. The safest way to start your own tarragon is to find someone with a fine-tasting plant and to steal a cutting or root division. Plants can also be ordered from reliable nurseries, but never buy tarragon seed—it is surely Russian. Once established, tarragon seems to stand any amount of butchery and go on forever, although it is choosy about where it likes to grow and needs good drainage, sun, and shelter in very cold winters.

Tarragon has a strong but subtle flavor, quite unlike any other herb, and is particularly famous for its use with chicken, although it can be used in many other ways: in sauces (it is essential for Béarnaise), with eggs, with fish (especially sautéed brook trout and cold salmon), with ham, and in all sorts of salads—mixed green salads, potato salad, and pasta salads. It is essential in many French dishes and also, of course, as the flavoring herb for tarragon vinegar (which is labeled *à l'estragon*)—you can make this for yourself simply by picking tarragon just before it flowers and pushing the sprigs into a bottle, which is then filled with white wine vinegar, stoppered, and left for a month or so before use.

Those who have eaten fresh summer foods seasoned with fresh tarragon, whose flavor has been compared to a combination of aniseed and vanilla, are often dissatisfied with dried tarragon, but well-dried tarragon that has not gone stale can be good with heartier winter dishes such as chicken stews and beans. Frozen tarragon has considerable fresh flavor, and a useful way of preserving it is to freeze tarragon butter, made by combining about ½ cup of tarragon leaves with a pound of butter in the blender.

[*Tarragon*—French: *estragon;* German: *Estragon;* Italian: *targone;* Spanish: *estragón*]

TARTAR. *See* argol.

TARTARIC ACID is an organic acid common in plants, especially in sour fruits, such as tamarind. It is the main source of acidity in wine, in which 0.2–0.6% is present. The acid can be made by treating *argol with sulfuric acid and is available as a white crystalline substance from pharmacists. It is very

sour—much sourer, weight for weight, than *cream of tartar. It can be used in homemade soft drinks and makes a passable substitute for lemon juice.

[*Tartaric acid*—French: *acide tartrique;* German: *Weinsteinsäure;* Italian: *acido tartarico;* Spanish: *ácido tartárico*]

TEA. The word probably comes from *tay* in the Cantonese Amoy dialect, and that is how it was pronounced by our ancestors. Tea is native to southwest China (and Assam) and has been drunk by the Chinese for many centuries. It was not until the 1640s that tea began to come into Britain and France in any noticeable amount. During the years of Cromwell's power, there were great advances in the use of tea, at first mainly as a medicinal brew. In 1660, Samuel Pepys recorded tasting his first sup. By the time that Charles II returned from exile two years later, tea had become a meal. Fine cups and saucers, bowls, teapots, spoons, trays, and caddies for keeping the precious tea were soon introduced, and the presiding host or hostess brewed and poured the tea—an echo of the Japanese tea ceremony, perhaps. The social history of tea had begun. Colonists in America had begun to drink tea, too, and the British government's refusal to remove the hated tax on it, along with the grant of a monopoly to the British East India Company for supplying tea to the colonies, led to the colonists' burning tea-laden vessels in Annapolis, Maryland, and to tipping tea cargoes into Boston Harbor in the famous Boston Tea Party late in 1773.

During the 18th century the imports of tea to Britain had increased sharply, but it was still highly taxed and thus expensive. At the end of the century, Sir Joseph Banks suggested growing tea in India and even visited China to collect seeds, so that some 50 years later, when Major Robert Bruce found tea growing wild in Assam, there were also tea plants from China in the botanical gardens in Calcutta. With the spread of plantations in India, tea gradually became the drink not only of every Briton but indeed of every Indian. Tea is best when fresh, and in the reign of Queen Victoria it came by fast-sailing ships. The British still drink some 5 times as much tea as coffee, unlike the Americans, who drink 25 times as much coffee as tea.

Tea is much drunk in Russia and Iran (where the samovars keep the water, not the tea, hot). In Syria you may get a cup of cardamom-flavored coffee from the police at some remote border (if you are not there under arrest), but in Iran, it will be a glass of hot, sweet, milkless tea. In India (except in the south, where the preference tends to be for coffee), tea will be thick with milk and sugar, and sometimes strongly flavored with mint as well. It is made by boiling milk, sugar, and water with tea for 2–3 minutes, then straining it.

Tea is the leaf of a tree, *Camellia sinensis*. Left alone, it will grow 25 ft (7.5 m) high, but it is pruned to form a low bush for ease of gathering. The leaves look something like bay leaves, and the flowers are beautiful, white, and sweet-smelling. Because the plant likes heavy rainfall, the typical tea garden is as often as not seen as terraces of neat bushes on mist-shrouded hills. Most beautiful are the tea gardens in Ceylon, with waterfalls, swirling clouds, and orchids in the trees. Most dramatic, though, are the gardens in northern Iran, which you come on when you cross the Elburz Mountains, leaving the desert and, within the space of a few miles, plunging into dense rain forest along the Caspian Sea.

The flavor and quality of tea depend on the variety and on the soil and climate where it is grown. Fresh tea leaves are mildly astringent and stimulating to chew. They are processed in three ways. For green tea, the fresh leaves are dried immediately after picking to inactivate enzymes and prevent oxidation. For oolong tea, the leaves are half-fermented, producing tea a stage between green and black. For black tea, the leaves are wilted, bruised by rolling, and allowed to ferment in contact with air, so that they are oxidized (like a browning apple) before they are dried. The leaves of all types are still picked by hand, usually every 7–10 days, in part because the grade of tea depends on the size of leaf—it is the labor-intensive nature of the crop that prevents tea's being grown on any scale in the U.S.

For ordinary black tea, the plucked leaves are taken to the factory and spread on racks at a temperature of 77–86°F (25–30°C) to wilt. By gentle drying, the moisture content is reduced somewhat, and the leaves become flexible. At this stage, they are rolled in machines that break up the cells (this was once done by hand) and expose the juices to the air. The rolled leaves are once more spread on trays and allowed to ferment. As the juices are oxidized, the leaves turn red-brown, after which hot air is blown through the trays until the rolled leaves are dry and the enzymes have been killed. In the case of smoky China teas, the rolled leaves are dried over a wood fire to give the characteristic tarry taste.

Teas are named after their type and leaf size, and the place of origin. Some teas are flavored with flowers or with essential oils, and many are blended, a practice that began at the tea table when hostesses, realizing that mixtures were often better than single teas, made their own combinations. Today, this is done by expert blenders who have access to a huge range of teas. Blending allows the deficiencies of particular teas to be balanced out. Price is another factor in blending—a mixture of the best teas with cheaper ones will offer some of the fine flavor without being too costly.

Hard water makes poor tea, and if naturally soft water or rain water is not available, distilled water might be used. Tea is best made by putting the leaves into a hot teapot of suitable size at the rate of 1 heaped teaspoon per person, with an extra one for the pot. The water must be fresh and have only recently come to the boil, and the pot must be taken to the kettle—not the kettle to the pot. Pour the boiling water over the leaves and let it brew for 3–5 minutes, according to the type of tea, stirring it after 2 minutes to open the leaves. If tea is to be kept hot for long, reheated, or used cold, it should be strained off the leaves after 5 minutes so that excess tannin is not infused.

Following are some of the many types and brands of tea.

Assam. The extreme northeastern corner of India, stretching between Darjeeling and Kohima, is an area with some of the highest rainfall in the world. Assam teas are usually full-bodied and provide the strength in many blends. For quantity, this is the most important tea area in the world.

Black teas are fully fermented teas that are used in all the standard English blends. Most of the teas from India, Ceylon, and Africa are black, and there are also black teas from China.

Broken grades, such as broken orange pekoe, are generally of good quality. Better grades contain tip. Flowery broken orange pekoe is fine-quality tea with tip and is much sought after by connoisseurs.

Ceylon (now Sri Lanka) started to produce tea in 1868 and gave its name to teas of a type totally different from the original China teas. The tea grown at 6000 ft (1800 m) or above is of great quality. Political and economic upheavals in Sri Lanka meant for a time that the quality of the tea was not of its previous high standards, but the quality is now returning. The teas from Indonesia are very similar in character. Many of the planters in Sri Lanka (mostly Scottish by birth) who were forced out for political reasons moved to Africa, where there is a thriving and expanding tea industry that produces excellent-quality teas.

Darjeeling teas from the Himalayan foothills in northern India are noted for their fine flavor and are very expensive. They are grown up to 7000 ft (2100 m), and production is limited. The best Darjeelings are usually blended with teas of similar character but lesser quality from the lower slopes in

order to make them commercially attractive.

Earl Grey is the name given to a blend originally formulated by the second Earl Grey. It was given to his grocer, who was a partner in the firm of Robert Jackson. The name was never registered, and the blend has been copied by other tea companies. Earl Grey has become a generic term for tea scented with oil of *bergamot.

Green teas are much used in China and Japan, and the term may be used for almost any tea served in Oriental restaurants.

Gunpowder is one of the Chinese green teas. In appearance, it is grainy, rolled into balls, as suggested by its alternative names of pearl or pinhead tea. The liquor is pale, with a sharp, distinctive taste. This tea is popular in North Africa, especially in Morocco, where it is frequently flavored with mint.

Hyson. A Chinese green tea, as is Young Hyson. It is of very good quality, expensive and full of flavor.

Ichang. A China tea from Hupeh, grown high in the mountains. It is rare and costly, with an exquisite and mellow flavor.

Jasmine. A China green tea that is mixed with jasmine flowers and then steam-heated for 5 minutes before being dried in a spin dryer.

Keemun. A black China tea from Keemun County in the beautiful Huangshan Mountains in southern Anhwei Province, south of the Yangtse.

Kenyan teas have a quality of their own, between the thick heavy teas from North India and the light flavory teas of Sri Lanka.

Lapsang souchong. A large-leafed black China tea with a distinctive tarry taste and smell derived from the smoke of the fires over which it is dried. It comes from Fukien on the Chinese mainland and from Formosa. The tarry flavor is so strong that it has to be stored separately in warehouses to prevent the standard teas from picking up the flavors.

Lung Ching or **dragon's well.** An exotic China tea with a flat, green leaf and a distinctive taste. It is produced only in small quantities.

Oolong. The leaves are allowed to ferment, but fermentation is then stopped by heat. These teas are produced in China and Formosa. The best early-crop tea has a peach-like flavor, with a large, ragged leaf. The finest have a very good show of white tip.

Orange pekoe is a name familiar to buyers of the widely available teas sold in the U.S. It indicates a black tea with a large, twisted leaf and has no bearing on quality—orange pekoe can be excellent or very poor.

Russian tea comes from the wet strip along the foothills of the Caucasus Mountains in Georgia. The Russians produce all sizes of tea, but they do not generally have the quality of the best China teas.

Souchong (from the Chinese *siao-chung,* meaning larger leaves). Very large leaf size from China.

Yunan. Teas from this province of China have a distinctive flavor and are frequently used in blends.

There are dozens of tea substitutes and tianes, of which the most important is *mate. Some of the infusions, such as the Cape or Boer bush tea (*Cyclopia vogeli*) of South Africa, were serious tea substitutes, as also was New Jersey tea (*Caenothus americanus*), a member of the heather family which, like orange tea, was used by the early American colonists as a protest at the time of the Boston Tea Party.

Many of these teas have a medicinal purpose, although some, like lime tea from the flowers of the *basswood, are very nice as a drink. Strawberry tea from Germany is made from the dried young leaves of wild strawberry plants; Algerian tea or *thé Arabe* (*Paronychia nivea*) is used medicinally in France; Swiss tea is made with relatives of yarrow such as *Achillea mosdiata* and *A. nobilis;* Japanese tea (*ama tsja,* tea of heaven) is the leaves of species of Hydrangea, such as *H. serrata.* Others are Mexican tea (*Chenopodium ambrosioides*); Réunion or Faham tea (*Angrecum fragrans* and other species); a tea made from the garden bush *Chimonanthus fragrans* (which is claimed to be so good that it may be cultivated for the purpose); *camomile tea (*Matricaria recutita*); Oswego tea, from red bergamot (*Monarda didyma*); Malay tea (*Eugenia variabilis*); mountain tea (*Gaultheria procumbens*); Barbary tea (*Lycium barbarum*); Steckel tea (*Borbonia parviflora*), and even tea from the dried leaves of the *sloe—the list could go on forever. Aromatic teas are also made of the flowers of rosemary and lavender, and from gorse, dittany, and willow herb (*Kaporie* tea in Russia). With a wide range of other aromatic herbs available to try, there are exciting possibilities for experiment, and health-food stores are a good place to start sampling.

[*Tea*—French: *thé;* German: *Tee;* Italian: *tè;* Spanish: *té*]

TEMPEH. An Indonesian food made from fermented *soybeans (though other beans may be used), tempeh is now known around the world as an inexpensive, tasty, and versatile source of protein. Tempeh shops can be found in a number of U.S. cities, and tempeh starter is readily available. Tempeh is made into countless dishes—burgers, sandwiches, creamy sauces, casseroles, fried "cutlets," cookies, and everything else the imaginative vegetarian can devise. Its flavor has been described as nutty, cheesy, mushroomy, meaty, and yeasty. To make tempeh, soybeans are simmered, soaked, and hulled, mixed with spore culture starter containing *Rhizopus oligosporus,* and incubated at about 88°F (31°C) for 24–30 hours. During the fermentation, new flavors and aromas develop, the texture changes, and nutritional value and digestibility are enhanced. Tempeh has no cholesterol and has a protein content that approaches that of beef. For a book with all the details about tempeh—processing, nutrition, scientific and cultural information, and fascinating recipes—see William Shurtleff and Akiko Aoyagi, *The Book of Tempeh* (Harper & Row, 1979).

TEMPERATURES are given in this book in both *Fahrenheit and *Celsius (Centigrade). For the kitchen, thermometers are much to be recommended: they take the guesswork out of many operations, such as frying, jam making, sugar boiling, making yogurt and cheese, and roasting. If you are doing something very frequently, perhaps professionally you can learn to judge by eye and experience, but most of us are not in that position. Tests like the time taken for bread cubes to turn brown are a nuisance. A thermometer gives certain and accurate results and materially helps toward better cooking. Thermometers reading 40–440°F (4–225°C) will handle all normal kitchen requirements. They are filled with mercury. For subzero temperatures, thermometers are usually filled with colored alcohol which, unlike mercury, will not freeze in any temperature the cook is likely to deal with but cannot be used for hot things. When taking the temperature of a liquid, first stir it to make sure that it is evenly heated and, if possible, leave the bulb in the liquid while taking the reading.

An oven thermometer may sometimes be necessary if you have an old-fashioned stove, and a roasting thermometer—one that pushes into the center of the meat—can be exceedingly useful.

Some Temperatures

Conversions in this list are approximate and are as accurate as the various circumstances demand.

32°F	0°C	Ice melts or water freezes, depending on whether heat is being added or taken away.
120°F	49°C	Add starter and put yogurt to bed.
140°F	60°C	Internal temperature for rare beef.
145°F	63°C	Internal temperature of underdone beef and lamb.
150°F	65°C	Egg begins to thicken and coagulate.
150–160°F	65–70°C	Pasteurization temperature.
160°F	71°C	Internal temperature of medium roast beef.
165°F	74°C	Internal temperature of roast lamb.
175°F	80°C	Internal temperature of well-done beef. Proteins have curdled. Mutton is well done. The correct internal temperature for veal.
180°–185°F	82–85°C	Internal temperature for roast pork.
185°–195°F	85–90°C	Simmer.
200°F	93°C	Low oven. Temperature for meringues, baked custards, etc.
230°F	110°C	Thread stage for sugar.
240°F	116°C	Soft-ball stage for sugar. About right for fondant icing.
250°F	120°C	Firm-ball stage for sugar.
278°F	137°C	Temperature for shallow frying in butter.
289°F	143°C	Hard-crack stage for sugar.
300°F	150°C	Temperature for baking fruitcake.
320°F	160°C	Moderately slow oven. Slow roast for most meats.
350°F	180°C	Moderate oven. Slow roast for pork. Middle of frying range and usual for doughnuts, tempura, French fries, etc. Caramelization of sugar.
375°F	190°C	Moderately hot oven. Usual roasting temperature for meats.
400°F	200°C	Hot oven. Pastry, sponge cake, muffins, browning meats.
450°F	230°C	For puff pastry, soufflés, some bread, croissants.
475°F	240°C	Very hot oven.
500°F	260°C	Maximum heat—too hot for baking at home but used by bakers for some bread.

[*Temperature*—French: *température*; German: *Temperatur*; Italian: *temperatura*; Spanish: *temperatura*]

TENDERIZING. Simple, old-fashioned methods of tenderizing are mechanical—beating or pounding to break up the fibers. The Greeks batter an octopus on the rocks at least 40 times to make it tender, Italians beat stockfish, and some optimists beat tough steaks in the hope it will improve them. Another simple method of tenderizing is *hanging and aging, in which the tenderizing process is done by enzymes in the meat which break down the protein. If hanging is done in the right cold conditions, it will not be accompanied by bacterial putrefaction.

Tenderizing is also achieved by heat, if it is properly applied over the correct period, but equally heat can toughen. The first reaction of protein to heat is to coagulate—as is well illustrated by the white of a boiled egg. Overcook the white and it becomes like rubber, taking an hour or more of boiling to become soft again. On the other hand, if an egg is lightly poached or coddled at below boiling point, the white is very tender. Sugar on meat is a tenderizer because it encourages the enzyme processes. Acids, such as vinegar and lemon juice, in marinades slowly tenderize by hydrolyzing proteins to amino acids, although their immediate action is to coagulate and harden, especially if heated.

Commercial tenderizers rely on *papain, an enzyme which digests protein. Usual commercial tenderizer will digest about 35 times its weight of protein, but will of course tenderize only the tissues with which it comes in contact, which is why treating meat (except minced or ground meat) with tenderizer is a poor substitute for proper hanging. Papain is deactivated by the heat of cooking. A few people are allergic to it.

TEPARY BEAN (*Phaseolus acutifolius*) is a drought-resistant and heat-adapted species that thrives in the parched U.S. Southwest. A mild-tasting bean traditionally cultivated by American Indians, it is grown today on the Papago Indian Reservation in Arizona and is being touted as a useful food crop for dry areas. Tepary beans are higher in protein than most legumes, and the plants bear heavily. They are likely to become familiar to many people other than the Indians in the future.

TERRAPIN. *See* turtle.

TEXTURED PLANT PROTEIN is a high-protein foodstuff manufactured from plants (*soybeans, peanuts, wheat, cottonseed, etc.). When processed, it resembles meat in texture and is intended as a meat substitute or extender. Originally it was aimed at the vegetarian market, but in re-cent years, with the rising cost of animal protein and the tightening world food supply, it has found its way into an assortment of processed foods. Since the U.S. Department of Agriculture in 1971 approved the limited use of textured vegetable products in the school lunch program, millions of schoolchildren have eaten meatloaf, chili, and other dishes "extended" with some form of vegetable protein. Such meat analogues are formed to resemble bacon, sausage, ham, chicken, and even fruits and nuts.

Three basic methods produce different textures of the product. The simplest is merely a matter of flavoring and coloring the concentrated protein, which is marketed and used in the form of granules. When they are reconstituted, these look like ground meat. The second method uses mainly soy proteins, which are dissolved in alkali to form a gel and then coagulated in acid. The protein is extruded like synthetic fibers and emerges in a variety of textures, from tough to tender. The result can be used in stews and casseroles.

The most expensive method involves spinning high-protein soy preparations into fibers. These are stretched on reels, and excess salt and acids are washed away. The fibers, blended with flavors, colors, extra nutrients, and binders, are heat-processed and formed into steaks, cubes, or whatever. A proportion of meat may be added for flavor and color.

It is important to read the labels on plant protein products to learn just what is in them, the nutritional content (many contain fewer calories than the food they simulate), and the suggested methods of cooking (for some products the amount of heat used in cooking is critical).

Food technologists are continually working at developing nonmeat sources of protein, and in the future the plant protein products on supermarket shelves are likely to be joined by many others fabricated from other plants, algae, and fish concentrate.

THERMOMETER. *See* temperature.

THIAMINE. *See* vitamin B₁.

THICKENING is closely related to *binding. Liquids may be thickened naturally, without addition, by reduction by boiling, but it is usually necessary to add something, and whatever is added has to be right for the dish, not only in flavor and texture but also in color. Satisfying all these demands makes it difficult to substitute one thickener for another. Dishes do not retain the same character. If a *coq au vin* is thickened with *beurre manié* (*see below*), it will not have the same dark, rich color of one thickened in the traditional way with the bird's blood. Equally, if you do as French chefs often do in India and thicken a curry with cream, you completely alter the character of the dish (although it will still be delicious).

Some of the thickeners used by food manufacturers, such as alginates and carob-bean gum, are not generally available in the shops. Others, such as the gums, are little used except for specialized purposes, partly because they are not much known in these days, although some, like *gum arabic, were much used in the past. Thickeners are also stabilizers, helping to prevent emulsions from breaking, suspensions from settling, and mixtures from separating into layers.

Starchy thickeners. Flour is the most commonly used of all thickeners and is easily incorporated into liquids in the form of *beurre manié*, flour worked to a paste with an equal weight of butter, which prevents the formation of lumps. *Beurre manié* is especially convenient because it can be added bit by bit until the required thickness is reached. Starchy thickeners depend on the capacity of starch grains to burst and form a soluble starch jelly when heated to around 167°F (75°C). Another is *cornstarch, which forms a more glassy jelly. It can also be mixed with butter or made into a cream with cold water before being stirred into the hot dish to be thickened. *Arrowroot is even purer starch and gives an almost transparent jelly. *Tapioca flour and potato flour are among other forms of *starch that can be used. Starchy thickeners must in most cases be properly cooked or they may retain a starchy taste.

Egg yolk, an excellent thickener, gives a rich, smooth texture. It should be added when the sauce is cool enough for you to dip a finger in without screaming, and the yolks are best smoothed with a very little water as a preliminary. After they have been stirred in, the sauce should be heated over water in a bain-marie or double boiler—not on a direct flame unless you have a fine thick copper pan and some skill. If the egg gets too hot anywhere on the bottom of the pan, it will form lumps of scrambled egg. Stirring with a wooden spoon should be continuous until the sauce thickens correctly, and then it must not be allowed to get any hotter. A sauce thickened with egg will curdle if it becomes too hot, and it can never be boiled.

Blood is a good thickener and can even be simmered in certain conditions, although it is better not to try it. Otherwise, blood behaves rather like egg yolk. It is used particularly in thickening jugged hare and classic Burgundian *coq au vin,* for which the bird's blood is collected when it is killed and immediately stirred with a little vinegar and brandy—just enough to prevent coagulation. Solid coagulated and cooked blood of various kinds is sold in my local market in Spain. I know of people who have tried blending this with water—a sort of reconstituted blood—but because the brew is merely watered-down coagulated blood, it cannot be expected to coagulate again and work as a thickening.

Creamy thickeners. Stirring thick or sour creams into juices at the last minute and off the fire is a delicious and simple way of giving body to many sauces. Creamy mixtures of nuts, coconut cream, tahini, ground poppy seed, and even peanut butter can also be used to give body in appropriate dishes. The important thing is always to avoid breaking the emulsion or to allow curdling. To lessen the shock on incorporating the mixtures, some of the liquid to be thickened should be stirred into the creamy thickener before it is added. A German chef, famous for his soups, advised me to think of adding mayonnaise to appropriate soups, and *aïoli* is essential in the Provençal *bourride* and in several other French fish soups, where its function is also to add a strong flavor of garlic.

Jellylike substances. A thick consistency, something like bird's-nest soup, can be obtained by thickening with gelatin, or, as would be preferred in some dishes, with a strong meat jelly or aspic. Another variation on the same theme comes from using *agar (from which fake bird's-nest soup is made in France) and even *seaweeds such as *carrageen moss. In the food trade, *pectin is sometimes used; it sets when fruit acids and sugars are present.

[*Thickening*—French: *roux;* German: *Eindickmittel;* Italian: *sostanza usata per condensare;* Spanish: *espesativo*]

THRUSH. *See* birds.

THYME, one of the great herbs of the European kitchen, belongs to the family of the labiates, which contains so many of our best culinary herbs—notably mint, sage, oregano,

THYME

and basil. The species most often used in cookery is the garden thyme (*Thymus vulgaris*). So-called French thyme has purplish, narrow leaves; English thyme is broader-leafed and gray-green. There are many other species of thyme, both garden and wild, mostly hardy plants that like dry, stony limestone soil. They all have a basic taste pattern, in which thymol predominates, but among the many variations some may be better or worse from the culinary point of view. As I write I have before me a beautifully flowering wild thyme that has a strongly acid smell and is quite unsuitable for cooking. Thyme needs to be chosen very carefully, though I have no doubt that the best grows wild on the hillsides of Provence and Liguria; even there, you have to know from experience what to gather. (The worst to look at often tastes the best.)

Thyme, bay, and parsley are the brothers in the bouquet garni. A very small amount of thyme can make all the difference to a dish. There is no herb to equal it in dishes that involve long, slow cooking in a casserole, and it is found in many West Indian dishes. Most people must be content with dried thyme, which can be as good as fresh thyme but should be bought in small quantities and continually renewed. Thyme goes with beef (though rarely with veal), with lamb, with pork, with all sorts of birds and game but especially chicken, with fish, with eggs—almost anything that can benefit from the aromatic flavoring.

[*Thyme*—French: *thym:* German: *Thymian;* Italian: *timo;* Spanish: *tomillo*]

TIA MARIA. *See* liqueurs and cordials.

TIGER NUT. *See* chufa nut.

TIN (Sn) is a metallic element, which forms the coating of tin cans and copper pans. It is probably, but not certainly, a trace element needed by man, as it is for animals. Tin has been very much used since the middle of the 19th century for coating iron, primarily to prevent its rusting in what we know as tin-plate—or simply tin. In this form it is used to manufacture tin cans for food. With some cans, small quantities of tin dissolve into the contents and have a bleaching effect on fruit like pears, peaches, and golden plums. In fact, a tin compound, stannous choloride, is an antioxidant, which is used in some countries for whitening canned asparagus. Lacquered cans are used for fruit such as strawberries in which the color content is important. Tests so far made seem to indicate that tin has a low toxicity and in the amount that usually gets into food is quite safe. However, if food is kept in opened cans, the presence of the oxygen in the air means that the tin will be rapidly dissolved. That is why food should not be left in cans that have been opened.

[*Tin*—French: *etain;* German: *Zinn;* Italian: *latta, stagno;* Spanish: *estaño, lata*]

TOCINO. *See* bacon.

TOFU. *See* bean curd.

TOHEROA (Maori for "long tongue") is a large bivalve (*Amphidesma ventricosum*) found in the sand of certain beaches in New Zealand. It is the basis for the fabled toheroa soup. Mechanical means of collecting the shellfish almost resulted in its extermination, and now its taking is strictly regulated. Although it is canned, it is not an easy luxury to find even in New Zealand.

TOMATE DE MER. *See* sea anemone.

TOMATE VERDE. *See* physalis fruit.

TOMATILLO. *See* physalis fruit.

TOMATO. Tomatoes are now one of the world's most important foods, and it is amazing that they were for so long regarded with suspicion and grown only for decoration. "Cold and unhealthy" was how one Elizabethan herbalist described them. Per-haps it was because, like potatoes, they were rather obviously related to the deadly nightshade. Tomatoes (*Lycopersicon esculentum*) may have originated in Peru and Ecuador, but they had been domesticated and had moved up into Mexico long before the Spanish arrived in America. The name "tomato," in fact, is derived (through Spanish *tomate*) from the Aztec *tomatl*. The Spanish brought the plant to Europe in the 16th century, and Gerard's *Herbal* says that they ate it with oil and vinegar as a salad, but it did not become popular. In Britain and France, it was known as the "love apple" (*pomme d'a-mour*), which perhaps came from the Italian *pomodoro*—golden apple—because the first varieties in Europe were yellow. Not until the 18th century, after two Italian Jesuit priests had brought a red variety back with them, did tomatoes begin to be taken seriously for eating. It was in southern Italy that tomatoes first became popular, and for some time they remained peasant food. In his *Cuoco galante*, published in 1778, the Neapolitan abbot Vincenzo Corrado gives a recipe for a tomato sauce—but he recommends it for fish and meat, not for pasta or rice. He also offers recipes for stuffed tomatoes of various kinds. A chef to Catherine II of Russia, a Roman named Francesco Leonardi, author of *Apicio moderno* (1790), seems to have been the first to write about tomato sauce with spaghetti, but such a dish was a poor man's, not a court chef's, invention. It was not until 1835 that tomatoes began to be adopted in the U.S., where millions of tons are grown today.

Among the bewildering number of tomato varieties are the gigantic ones that run to almost 2 lb (1 Kg) per fruit, down to cherry and cocktail tomatoes as small as marbles. However, apart from such fancy tomatoes, which also include the yellow, orange, and pink varieties, there are numerous more normal types, each with its own purpose.

Salad tomatoes are for cutting raw, for use in mixed salads and hors d'oeuvre. A salad variety should have a good acid-sweet balance and certainly, when fresh off the vine, the proper tomato taste. This is often lacking in commercial tomatoes, especially those produced out of season or with too little sunshine.

Cooking tomatoes are not just salad tomatoes that are past their prime. For stuffing, tomatoes must be of the right size, and it is noticeable that some varieties cook particularly well, while others are better canned. For example, the very old Italian variety San Marzano, one that is often peeled and canned, lends a special quality to Italian canned tomatoes.

Sauce tomatoes are usually the plum tomatoes, which make the best concentrates and sauces. Varieties include Roma, which, despite its name, is an American tomato. Plum tomatoes have more meat than juice and seeds and are often rather tasteless raw.

Juice tomatoes are different again. For salads, too much juice in a tomato is undesirable—people even let tomatoes drain. For cooking and making a dry paste, it is a nuisance, but for tomato juice, the really juicy varieties perform best in the home juicer.

Growers tend to select mainly for commercial considerations, such as suitability to climatic conditions, soil, disease resistance, yield, storage, and shipping qualities (which means a good thick skin). Regular form and attractive color are commercially more important than taste, because most people buy by appearance. However, in farmers' markets, you will often do best by looking for the smallest, roughest tomatoes because these usually have the finest taste, and they are likely to be cheaper. The canning companies organize the cultivation of huge areas of tomatoes under contract with the varieties they find best for their purpose. In general, canned tomato products are excellent and a great help to the cook. Sometimes tomatoes even acquire tastes in canning which may be preferred for certain dishes. However, brands vary in flavor, so look around and experiment before making a recipe standard. Tomatoes mix particularly well with basil and garlic, as has long been known, but also with bay, thyme, and oregano. They also go

well with cheese, with peppers, and with meaty flavors. Ripe and well-flavored tomatoes can even be eaten as a fruit with sugar and cream. (For this, they should be dunked in boiling water for a moment to loosen the skin, peeled, cut in quarters, and deseeded.)

Tomatoes have a range of tastes depending on the length of time they are cooked. For instance, chopped and very lightly cooked, as in the sauce for *spaghetti all'amatriciana* (*see below*), they have a delicious, fresh flavor—this dish should never be overcooked or contain onion or chili peppers: it is the unalloyed taste of fine tomatoes that is important. Tomatoes baked soft have yet another taste. They are best done in an old-fashioned wood-fired baker's brick oven so that they get a slightly smoky taste from the ashes. Green tomatoes are used to make pickles and preserves.

PA AMB OLLI—BREAD AND OIL (CATALAN SPAIN)

This is a popular snack everywhere and loved even by children who do not usually like tomatoes. Take a thick slice of good bread, cut a juicy tomato in two, and press the cut face onto the bread to impregnate the surface with juice. Dribble good oil (preferably olive) all over it and add salt. As with every simple dish, the quality of each of the ingredients is of the utmost importance.

PANZANELLA (TUSCANY)

Soak 8 slices of stale, good bread in water until they are soft, squeeze them out gently, and crumble them roughly into a bowl. Thinly slice a cucumber, a large mild onion, and 4 ripe tomatoes into the bowl. Add some chopped basil leaves, good olive oil, a little wine vinegar, and salt and pepper. Mix and put in a cool place until lunchtime.

SPAGHETTI ALL'AMATRICIANA

This dish is named after Amatrice, a small town between Rome and the Abruzzi. For 14 oz (400 g) of spaghetti, to be boiled in the usual way, take 11 oz (300 g) of ripe tomatoes of a sweet, fleshy variety suitable for sauce, dip them in boiling water, peel and deseed them, and break them into small pieces. Fry 4 oz (100 g) of diced, fat bacon (preferably *guanciale*) gently in some good olive oil and, when it starts to color, add the tomato and turn up the heat. When the tomato has become soft, but not overcooked, add salt and pepper to taste, mix it with the cooked spaghetti, and sprinkle with 2 oz (50 g) of grated Pecorino cheese.

TOMATO SAUCE FOR SPAGHETTI

Commercially bottled tomato sauces are intended for table use and are more or less synonymous with tomato ketchup. Tomato sauce for spaghetti is not the same thing.

Peel and remove seeds from 2 lb (1 Kg) plum tomatoes (or use canned, peeled tomatoes). Put a small finely chopped onion, 1 crushed clove of garlic, 5 tablespoons of olive oil, and 1 oz (25 g) of butter in a pan and fry gently. When the onion is soft, add the tomato, several leaves of basil, salt, and pepper. Cover and simmer slowly for about an hour, stirring occasionally to prevent the tomato from sticking. Put the sauce through a sieve or food mill. Add a pinch of sugar and another oz (25 g) of butter. Adjust the seasoning. Serve with spaghetti. This quantity of sauce will do for 14 oz (400 g) of pasta. Grated Parmesan cheese should be sprinkled generously on each serving.

[*Tomato*—French: *tomate*; Italian: *pomodoro*; Spanish: *tomate*]

TOPE. *See* shark.

TORTELLINI. *See* pasta.

TORTILLA FLOUR. *See masa.*

TRACE ELEMENTS are essential for health but required in such small amounts that it is only in recent years that the quantities have begun to be measured, although the presence of such elements has long been known. Many of the trace elements are harmful in larger amounts, even if these are still microscopically small, so ill health could result from too much as well as too little. Trace elements known to be needed in the human body are chromium, cobalt, copper, iodine, manganese, molybdenum, selenium, and vanadium. Those probably essential are fluorine, nickel, silicon, and tin. Because trace elements are naturally present in vegetables and fruit, a person eating a healthful diet need not be concerned about a deficiency of these nutrients. Iodine is added in small amounts to table salt to combat iodine deficiency in areas where the diet has little natural supply of iodine from seafood, the richest dietary source available.

TRAIL is the collective term for the entrails of such animals as snipe, woodcock, plover, and red mullet. In these cases, the trail is not removed before cooking and is considered a delicacy.

TRASI. *See balachan.*

TREACLE. Originally medicines were often mixed with honey, but later, thick, sticky sugar syrup was used. This original function remained in that devilish school medicine "brimstone and treacle" (flowers of sulfur and molasses) with which, I remember, our German matron tried to purify the blood of the school. But treacle pudding, treacle tart, treacle parkin, and treacle toffee were all another matter.

Treacle is a variable substance. Black treacle is molasses; a slightly lighter version is West India treacle, which still has the authentic molasses taste. A much lighter, medium-brown syrup made by refining molasses is also known as treacle but has a much less strong molasses taste. Finally *golden syrup is often loosely called treacle.

The expression "treacle" is not normally used in the U.S., where the niche is filled by corn syrups (light or dark), molasses (light or dark), caramel or brown-sugar syrups made at home, and maple syrup. Indeed, the world of treacles and syrups is one where there is almost total confusion in older books, although writers of recipes are now becoming more specific.

[*Treacle*—French: *mélasse;* German: *Sirup, Melasse;* Italian: *melassa, sciroppo di zucchero;* Spanish: *melaza*]

TREE POTATO. *See* sapodilla.

TREPANG. *See* sea cucumber.

TRESTERBRANTWEIN. *See* marc.

TRICHINOSIS or **trichiniasis.** One of the most terrible parasites to infect man is a tiny nematode worm, *Trichinella spiralis.* Trichinosis is usually contracted by eating undercooked pork, but the worms can be ingested from eating the meat of many other animals, including whales and game such as bear. When meat infected by *Trichinella* is digested in the human body, larvae encysted in the muscle mate, produce young, and are carried to the bloodstream and lymphatics. The worms then attack skeletal muscle fibers throughout the body, producing acute muscle inflammation.

Prevalence of trichinosis varies from country to country. Although meat which is sold today has been subjected to rigid inspection, risk of this disease is the main reason why sensible people avoid rare pork and fry samples of pâté and sausage meat before testing them for seasoning. Cooked or smoke-cooked sausages such as mortadella and frankfurters are safe because worms are killed at temperatures as low as 140°F (70°C) maintained for a specific length of time. They are also killed in meat that is kept frozen at 5°F (15°C) for 3 weeks. Raw pork products such as raw ham, bacon, salame, and chorizo sold in shops are safe, since they have been hung long enough for any trichinella worms to have been killed by the salt, saltpeter, and spices.

[*Trichinosis*—French: *trichinose;* German: *Trichinose;* Italian: *trichinosi;* Spanish: *triquinosis*]

TRIPE is usually the stomach of the cow, but the stomachs of sheep and pigs are also used for food.

If you are starting from scratch, the stomachs have to be cut open, separated into manageable pieces and cleaned carefully. After washing in several changes of water and cutting away any bits and pieces, the tripe is scalded and scraped inside to remove any slime. Kettles of boiling water are poured liberally over it. The tripe must then be soaked for 3–4 hours in water which contains a little salt and vinegar. After a final scrape and wash, the tripe is dropped into boiling, salted water, cooked for about 30 minutes, and then drained. It is now ready for basic cooking. This may be done in a pan or pressure cooker with flavoring herbs and vegetables. Ordinarily, tripe needs many hours of cooking—16 hours of simmering was recommended in the past, but then it was easy to leave a pan at the back of the kitchen range. Today, in Western countries, tripe is usually sold only after it has been cleaned and cooked, i.e., dressed. (This is the only way in which tripe is allowed to be sold in some countries.) Even so, it may need some hours of further cooking to become tender.

The most delicious tripe is veal tripe, and the best part is the honeycomb; thick and white is better than thin and brownish. The British method of cooking tripe, tripe and onions (a famous dish in the north of England), is for tripe addicts only: it has a strong visceral flavor. The most famous tripe dish is *tripes à la mode de Caen,* from Normandy, in which tripe is cooked in a sealed pot for at least 10 hours with calf's foot, onions, carrots, leeks, a bouquet garni, and cider. For good measure, it gets a lacing of Calvados. Best of all, for those who do not relish tripe, is the spicy Spanish *callos a la madrileña,* in which tripe is cooked with calf's foot, sausages, onion, garlic, white wine, brandy, sweet and chili peppers, bouquet garni, seasonings, and a squeeze of lemon juice. In Italy, tripe is cooked with white beans, with tomatoes, and with cheese; these dishes are also delicious.

[*Tripe*—French: *tripes;* German: *Kaldaunen, Flecke, Kutteln;* Italian: *trippa;* Spanish: *callos*]

TRIPLE SEC. *See* liqueurs and cordials.

TRITICALE (a hybrid word derived from *Triticum,* wheat, and *Secale,* rye) is a new cereal, a cross between wheat and rye. It has a higher protein content than wheat and a much higher amount of the essential amino acid lysine (which is already used to fortify some breads). Bread made from triticale is known as triti bread; it is quite heavy and is oftened lightened by other flavors. Triticale is also used as a *sprouted seed.

TROUT and **char** belong to the same family as the salmon. They have always been important freshwater fish to people who lived within reach of lakes and fast-flowing streams, but now they are extensively farmed, even in places where there is no permanently running water.

There is much argument over which is the best trout. The answer depends on the water in which the trout has lived, the food it has eaten, the time of year (female trout are lean after spawning), and, perhaps equally, on its birthplace; local loyalties play a major part in any gastronomic argument, and sportsmen the world over will find their local trout best. All agree that the same trout living in lakes, although they grow large, are less tasty, and that goes for trout raised on trout farms; although their flavor depends on their food in the last weeks before they are killed, their flesh is softer and often insipid compared to that of trout living in the wild state.

The chars are very similar to trout, belonging to the same genera; actually the nomenclature of trouts and chars is quite confusing—from the cook's point of view the distinctions are not important, except that

chars have smaller scales. Of the 20 or so species of trout and char found in North American waters, the following are important.

Arctic char or **omble chevalier** (*Salvelinus alpinus*), considered by some to be the most delicious fish in the world, has delicate pink flesh that is usually baked and eaten with melted butter. Silver in the sea, Arctic char turn dark with red banding when they return to cold mountain rivers in the fall. There are also some landlocked populations.

Brook trout (*Salvelinus fontinalis*), called speckled trout in Canada, are beautiful fish with blue spots and scarlet sides. Most weigh less than a pound, and they are usually cooked whole. Their firm delicate flesh is white or pinkish.

Brown trout (*Salmo trutta*) have brown backs with large spots. Hardy browns thrive in streams that are too polluted for brook trout, but their flavor is inferior unless they come from cold, clean waters. When this trout goes to sea, it gets a delicious flavor and pink flesh, perhaps from the crustaceans it eats there, and becomes one of the finest of all fish. But those who have caught the brown trout in a mountain brook and cooked it over a campfire minutes after landing it will also no doubt think it the best they have ever tasted.

Dolly Varden trout (*Salvelinus malma*) are usually found in fast, cold rivers from Alaska to northern California. They are colorfully spotted and excellent table fare.

Lake trout (*Salvelinus namaycush*) live in deep, cold lakes. Once an important commercial fish in the Great Lakes and Canada, lake trout have been reduced by the predation of invading sea lampreys. Although lake trout can reach a hundred pounds, the most delicate and tasty flesh is found in the smaller, younger fish.

Rainbow trout (*Salmo gairdneri*), native to North America, are spectacular fish now available all over the world, even in the southern hemisphere where there were no trout before. Many of the rainbow trout frozen in other countries, especially Japan, are exported to the U.S.

Because trout are so delicious, there are hundreds of trout recipes. It is best to kill large trout by stunning them, or to insert a finger in the fish's mouth and quickly snap its head back to break the neck if it is small. The fish may be gutted neatly through the gill opening or by a small ventral incision or (if for stuffing) by cutting down the back, removing the backbone and intestines, but leaving the ventral skin intact.

Smoked trout is a well-known delicacy, and it may be made at home by lightly brining the fish and then hot-smoking it in a home smoker. Potted trout or char is made by boning the fish and rubbing it well with ground mixed spices (pepper, allspice, mace, cloves, and nutmeg), then baking it, covered with butter, in a slow oven for 5 hours. Drain off the butter and press the fish firmly into pots, then cover it with some of the melted butter. (This method also works for eels, sprats, or shrimp.)

[*Trout*—French: *truite;* German: *Forelle;* Italian: *trota;* Spanish: *trucha. Char*— French: *ombre chevalier;* German: *Rotforelle, Siebling;* Italian: *ombrina;* Spanish: *umbra*]

TRUFFLES are very important in *haute cuisine.* They are fungi which most people know only as something expensive bought in a tin (even the peelings are canned, though canned truffles are not, on the whole, worthwhile), or as the black specks in the pâté. A number of species of truffle are something like underground puffballs, although they are not closely related. Some, like the *terfezias* of the Middle East and North Africa, are good, but not sensational. Two—the black or Périgord truffle (*Tuber melanosporum*) and the white or Italian truffle (*T. magnatum*)—are outstanding delicacies.

Best-known is the black truffle, which is irrevocably associated with French cooking. The best are found locally in hilly country around the edge of the Massif Central. In the west, they go southward from Périgord. In the East, they can be found on either side of the Rhône Valley as far north as Burgundy. Their season is from November to March. Because black truffles are so expensive and so much in demand, inferior species which look something like them are often substituted. With peeled truffles, a microscopic examination is needed for the fraud to be detected. Truffle bargains must always be suspected. Black truffles are very black and are covered with warts which trap the earth between them and make them difficult to clean. They have a strong perfume and are usually eaten cooked, chopped up and put into dishes as a flavoring.

The white truffle is found particularly in the foothills of the Apennines on the south side of the Lombardy plain in North Italy. It is smooth, irregularly shaped, and of a creamy color outside. It can be found in all sizes, occasionally almost as large as a football. White truffles are even more expensive than black truffles and have an even stronger smell. However, they have very little taste and are mostly eaten raw, sliced very fine over the food with a special cutter (which includes razor blades) to give a mouth-watering, though indescribable perfume. The center for white truffles is the Italian gastronomic mecca of Alba, southeast of Turin. The season is from October until snow stops play before Christmas.

Truffles of both kinds grow only in association with certain plants and trees. As yet, they cannot be cultivated like mushrooms, and several fortunes await anyone who can learn how to do it. Truffles of the kind we are talking about usually grow about 1 ft (30 cm) underground, and their presence is detected by dogs or by pigs (but they try to eat the truffles). Although there are several dozen varieties of truffles in the U.S., none is particularly palatable or numerous. Fresh truffles can be kept for some days in the refrigerator and can be sent by mail from centers like Alba.

[*Truffles*—French: *truffe;* German: *Trüffel;* Italian: *tartufo;* Spanish: *trufa, criadilla de tierra*]

TRUSSING is tying up meat into a tidy form for cooking. The term is usually applied to birds. There are many opinions as to the "correct" way to truss this or that, but at best these ways are only traditions or means which have been found most practical or convenient. Trussing was more important when birds and meat were roasted on spits and turned before the fire. Trussing is also important to butchers and poulterers, who wish to make a bird look fatter (by pushing legs up under the skin of the breast) and a roast neater. In fact, it is a form of presentation.

For trussing which looks professional, you can use a trussing needle to pass the string right through the body of the bird. Alternatively, you can stick a skewer through for anchorage. Both methods puncture the skin and let out some of the juices. The easiest method is to put a hitch in the middle of the trussing string and tie this around the tailpiece, which gives the necessary anchorage. The ends of the legs can then be tied down to this, and the string passed forward to encircle the body around the wings, thus holding them in the position required. Soft, plain white cotton string is the best to use for trussing, being wholesome and tasteless. Sewing up after stuffing should be done with heavy cotton thread.

[*Trussing*—French: *trousser, brider;* German: *dressieren;* Italian: *preparare un pollo;* Spanish: *espétar*]

TUNA or **tunny**. There are a number of species, the best-known being the bluefin tuna (*Thunnus thynnus*), the yellowfin tuna (*T. albacares*), and the albacore or longfin tuna (*T. alalunga*). The bluefin is usually up to 6 ft (2 m) long and averages about 330 lb (150 Kg), though it may be considerably larger. It may summer in the cold waters off Nova Scotia and winter in Florida waters. It

CALIFORNIA BLUEFIN TUNA

also occurs in the Mediterranean and the Black Sea. Bluefins have dark, strongly flavored meat. Yellowfin tuna are important to the U.S. West Coast fishing industry. Their firm, rich flesh is canned as "light meat" tuna. Albacore tuna are sold as "white meat" tuna. They migrate between Japan and North America.

Fresh tuna has been likened to veal and is perhaps the only fish to have had "cuts" like cuts of meat. The glut of fish each year when they migrated inshore to breeding waters meant that it had to be preserved. In early times, tuna was salted and preserved in oil, but for a long time canning it has been an important industry, and canned tuna is used in important Mediterranean specialties, such as *salade niçoise* and *vitello tonnato*.

During the first run, which in Sicily is in May and June, the fish are in prime condition and ready for spawning, and *botargo is made from the female roes. Later in the summer, when the fish are spent, they return thin and empty. At that time—up to the end of September—the flesh is inferior and blackish in color. Before canning, tuna are beheaded and hung from the tail to drain out the blood. The flesh is then washed, soaked to make it as white as possible, cooked in herbed brine, and finally canned under oil or water. Good canned tuna, which still retains its firm, meaty texture, is a relatively expensive item. The best part is the *ventresca*, the lower part and belly wall.

A relation of the tunas, the Pacific *bonito or skipjack, is canned as skipjack tuna.

[*Tuna*—French: *thon;* German: *Thunfisch;* Italian: *tonno;* Spanish: *atún*]

TUNA PEAR. *See* prickly pear.

TUNNY. *See* tuna.

TUR. *See* pigeon pea.

TURBO. *See* abalone.

TURBOT (*Scophthalmus maximus*). The firm, lean, and delicious flesh of the turbot is so prized that a special rhomboid fish kettle, a *turbotière,* was created in its honor. Turbot are found in waters from the Mediterranean to Iceland and Norway, though not on the western side of the Atlantic. They are sinistral *flatfish, closely related to *brill, and are distinguished by the bony knobs on their top side. They can weigh up to 25 lb (12 Kg) but are frequently sold as chicken turbot weighing 2¼–4½ lb (1–2 Kg). Turbot are imported to the U.S. Whole ones may be poached, pieces broiled.

[*Turbot*—French: *turbot;* German: *Steinbutt;* Italian: *rombo chiodato;* Spanish: *rodaballo*]

TURKEY (*Meleagris gallopavo*), indigenous to America, had already to an extent been domesticated in Mexico by Aztecs before the arrival of the Spanish. Turkeys were established in Spain by 1530 and in England by 1540. The Mexican stock was then taken back to America, to New England, by the colonists, and these turkeys are probably the ancestors of present-day domestic breeds.

Wild turkeys can still be found from Pennsylvania to Florida and westward to Colorado and Arizona, as well as in Mexico. They are smaller birds than the huge modern table breeds which are scarcely capable of getting off the ground, and they are lean, not fat. Even so, a big tom can weigh up to 20 lb (9 Kg), although they are more usually about 13 lb (6 Kg), with the females 10 lb (4½ Kg) and less. If the birds have been shot, their meat will be dark; they need a lot of basting or they will be dry, but they are very meaty.

There are now a great number of turkey breeds in assorted colors and offering a range of sizes at maturity; they have also been bred for commercial considerations such as hardiness, disease resistance, and efficient utilization of foodstuffs. The breeding of huge-breasted, ungainly turkeys can be managed only by artificial insemination. In a year, hen turkeys will lay 70–80 eggs, which are very large and have an excellent flavor and a nice speckled brown color, but the low rate of production is not interesting to egg producers. The eggs hatch in 28 days. It takes about 9 months to produce topweight birds, but they may be killed at anything over 4 months; old turkeys are tough and useless. Modern turkey production is highly organized—turkeys are no longer generally driven into town in flocks for Christmas, as they once were (and still are in some towns in Europe). They were even equipped with boots to keep their feet in condition. Although mainly eaten at Christmas and Thanksgiving, turkeys are now becoming a popular year-round food, thanks to small breeds and improved freezing methods.

When buying fresh turkeys, look for the maximum amount of breast and small legs. Hens are reckoned a better buy than toms; although the tom may be bigger, his bones weigh heavier, and hens are generally more tender. However, with modern commercially raised birds, there is not all that much difference. After killing, turkeys are normally hung for 5–7 days, depending on the weather. (An old method was to hang the bird suspended by a cord tied around four large tail feathers. As soon as the bird dropped onto a cloth hung below to receive it, it was ready to be cooked immediately.)

Turkeys are stuffed in various ways and, being so large, can accommodate two stuffings, one mild and the other stronger. Commonly used are sausage meat, veal force-meat, chestnut, celery, celery and dried apricot, apple and prune, and oyster stuffings. A practical one (where veal is not available) is made from minced cooked chicken mixed with bread crumbs and butter, flavored with lemon rind and juice, or mixed with smoky ham.

When buying turkey, allow at least 1 lb (450 g) per person and preferably more to allow for eating cold later. Cordon Bleu today advises about a 13–14-lb (6-Kg) bird, weighed plucked but not dressed, for 8–10 people, but in my grandmother's family it was ten aunts to a 25-lb (11-Kg) turkey at Christmas, which allowed for friends, cold turkey, and the kitchen. If calculating for a frozen bird (which has lost head, neck, and feet), you can drop the weight requirement by about a quarter—and do not forget that the bird takes some time to thaw out. With slow roasting at 325°F (160°C), 22 minutes per pound (weight including stuffing) is about right. A turkey that is ready early can rest for 30 minutes outside the oven; if it is late, you will have to go on drinking.

In recent years, turkey has replaced chicken in many preparations of fine quality, such as in the classic stuffing for tortellini, into which it goes with raw ham and Parmesan cheese. Filleted turkey slices are also now widely available to be cooked as a veal substitute. The flavor is surprisingly similar when pounded turkey fillets are cooked as veal scaloppine. In fact, turkey—being relatively inexpensive, free of much fat, and rather neutral in flavor—can be substituted satisfactorily in many recipes that call for more expensive and fatty meats such as pork or even oily fish.

[*Turkey*—French: *dinde, dindon;* German: *Puter, Truthan;* Italian: *tacchino;* Spanish: *pavo, pava*]

TURMERIC (*Curcuma longa*) is a spice of the same family as ginger, but without any of ginger's hot flavor. It is the rhizome of a plant indigenous to humid, hilly districts of South and Southeast Asia. The spice is prepared by boiling the rhizomes, peeling them, and drying them in the hot sun for several weeks. Because whole pieces of turmeric are

TURMERIC

very hard, it is one of the few spices it is better to buy ground—it will certainly break the blades of an ordinary coffee grinder. The taste is slightly bitter and musty. The color is bright yellow; alcoholic extracts of turmeric are used as a food coloring. Turmeric is the spice that colors curry yellow, and it is used in quantity in piccalilli and to give color to mustards—it is usually detectable as a taste in American mustards. It has been known to be mistranslated as "saffron" in Indian cookbooks.

[*Turmeric*—French: *curcuma, safran d'Inde;* German: *Gelbwurz Turmerikwurzel;* Italian: *curcuma;* Spanish: *cúrcuma*]

TURNIP, rutabaga, and **swede** are related vegetables grown for their roots. Because of their similarity, especially as new varieties are developed, there is much confusion over nomenclature: to many people, the swede and the rutabaga are synonymous, to some the "turnip" is just another name for swede; but in general swedes will be found in England, turnips in the U.S. and Scotland, and rutabagas wherever yellow-skinned root vegetables that look like turnips are grown. In general, whatever they are called, they can be used interchangeably in recipes.

The turnip (*Brassica rapa*) has been cultivated and used as food in Europe since very early times. Turnips are grown for both their roots and their green tops. Some varieties are large and grown for animal feed on farms; others are small and grown in market gardens as human food. Both are good to eat. Turnips may be globular or long, and white, green, or purplish according to type. They usually have white flesh. Some varieties grow very fast and will produce succulent white turnips, a little bigger than a radish, in not much over a month from planting. Such small turnips have a delicate taste, delicious raw, but some stalwart fanciers prefer the stronger taste of a large farm turnip. There are many French ways of cooking small turnips, a vegetable more popular in France than elsewhere. Turnips play a part as a flavoring vegetable in stews and soups. Grated raw turnip is an excellent salad flavoring ingredient and is often included in coleslaw.

Turnip tops or turnip greens, which will sprout in the spring if turnips are left in the ground, are excellent and make a very nice, sweet-tasting green when boiled as cabbage or broccoli would be and served with butter. They can also be a part of a dish of mixed greens, as enjoyed in the southern U.S. and in Spain. Some turnip varieties developed for their leafy tops have insignificant roots.

Rutabagas (*B. napus* var. *rutabaga*) are sometimes called big yellow turnips or Canadian turnips. To confuse things, they are also known as swede turnips. They have sweet, fine-grained yellow flesh that is bright orange when cooked. In the Scottish dish called mashed neeps that is served with haggis, rutabagas are mashed with potatoes and butter. Rutabaga greens are not usually eaten.

Swedes (*B. napus* var. *napobrassica*) are larger than turnips and have yellow flesh, although there are sorts in which the flesh is white. The skins may be purple or white. Whatever its color, a swede or rutabaga can always be distinguished from a turnip, which is smooth right up to the base of the leaves instead of having a number of concentric ridges or scars at the top.

More recent in origin than turnips, swedes, in spite of their name (which is shortened from Swedish turnip), probably originated in Bohemia in the 17th century. Although they are similar to turnips in flavor, opinions as to their culinary merit are sharply divided between those who claim that swedes are best as food for cattle and those who find them delicious and indeed superior to turnips because sweeter and with a dryer texture.

[*Turnip*—French: *navet;* German: *Rube;* Italian: *rapa;* Spanish: *nabo. Swede* or *rutabaga*—French: *rutabaga, chou navet;* German: *Streckrube;* Italian: *rapa svedese;* Spanish: *rabo sueco*]

TURNIP CABBAGE. *See* kohlrabi.

TURTLE and **terrapin.** In common usage, a turtle is a tortoise that lives in water. Many are eaten (although not the Ganges turtles, which live on dead bodies), and in particular the huge marine green turtle (*Chelonia mydas*), the species most used for turtle soup. Also famous are certain terrapins of North America, small turtles which live in salt marshes, lakes, and rivers, especially in the Gulf States and eastern coastal swamps of the U.S. Books from the 19th century are full of chicken tortoises, salt-water terrapins, alligator terrapins, and so on, since these were sold in thousands in the markets. Today the most usual is the diamondback (the best claimed to come from Chesapeake Bay), which is also available canned.

Terrapins are killed either by chopping off their heads or by plunging them alive into boiling water. After scalding for about 5 minutes, the outer skin can be removed by rubbing with a rough cloth. There are many ways of cooking them, but a usual one is to simmer the whole animal in salted water for 1–1½ hours, until the shell begins to crack and the feet to fall off. The shell can now be cut open around the under edge, the two halves separated, and the stomach, gall bladder, and large intestine removed. The small intestine is often left in (like the trail of a woodcock) and, with liver and eggs, is served with the rest of the meat. The claws are pulled out and discarded before serving. Terrapin is often seasoned with sherry or madeira, and an average terrapin serves two people. American cookbooks have many recipes, but although live terrapins used to be imported occasionally into Britain, people in Europe, where there are no suitable small turtles, must usually be content with canned terrapin.

Green turtles are taken sometimes in the Mediterranean and on the warmer Atlantic coasts of Europe, but they are becoming rare. Beaches are occupied by sunbathing humans, and too many eggs have been taken.

If ever faced with a live turtle, you have to chop off its head and hang it up by the hind flippers overnight to drain off blood. Next day, the flippers are cut off at the joints, and the two halves of the shell are separated by cutting around about 2 in. (5 cm) from the edge. (The upper shell is known as the calipash and the lower the calipee.) After any water has been drained out and the stomach and intestines and, above all, the gall bladder removed with care, the meat can be treated as veal (which it resembles), or the creature can be made into soup. For this, the flesh and green fat are reserved, and the two halves of the shell with the flippers put into boiling water. After a few minutes' boiling, the flippers can be taken out and skinned, but the shells need somewhat longer cooking until the bones can be easily removed. A stock is made from the liver, heart, kidneys, and bones; in it are then boiled the meat, flippers, and head. Also needed, though, are ham and veal plus thyme, marjoram, and basil (the turtle-soup herbs), parsley, bay, cloves, mace, etc. Soup can also be made from dried turtle meat, which requires soaking for 3 days before cooking. (It is easier to buy a can.)

Since an outcry by conservationists several years ago against the excessive killing of turtles for food, efforts have been made to breed turtles especially to fill the demands of the kitchen. Such projects are still very much in the developmental stage; while some turtle farms are having success, the supply of farmed turtles has not yet begun to fill the manufacturers' needs.

[*Turtle*—French: *tortue de mer;* German: *Meerschildkröte;* Italian: *tartaruga, testugine di mare;* Spanish: *tortuga (de mar)*. *Terrapin*—French: *terrapène;* German: *Desenschildkröte;* Italian: *tarataruga aquatica;* Spanish: *tortuga de agua dolce*]

TUSCARORA RICE. *See* wild rice.

U

UDDER has somewhat fatty white meat, which is not generally valued. It can be cooked in a number of ways—braised, stewed and served with onion sauce, or lightly salted, boiled, and served cold with vinaigrette sauce. Udder is rarely seen in butchers' shops or even in European markets but seems to have been popular enough in the past. Udder is (or was) much used in Italian cooking in the contents of stuffed pasta such as ravioli.

[*Udder*—French: *tétine, mamelle;* German: *Euter;* Italian: *poppa, mammella;* Spanish: *ubre*]

UDON. *See* noodles.

UGLI. *See* orange.

ULLUCO. *See* yam (ulluco).

UMBELLIFER. Plant belonging to the family Umbelliferae, which has small white, yellow, or pink flowers usually arranged in large, flat-topped bunches called umbels. Among the 2700 species mainly from temperate areas of the northern hemisphere are quite a number of culinary importance either as vegetables or as flavorings. *Carrot, *parsnip, celeriac (*see* celery), and Hamburg parsley are all umbellifer taproots. The family is second only to the labiates for its herbs: *chervil and *parsley are used for their leaves, while the seeds of other species are important as flavorings—*anise, *caraway, and *cumin. Some are valued for both leaves and seeds: *coriander, *dill, and *lovage; so are *celery and *fennel, which are best known for varieties with leaf stalks that are used as vegetables. *Asafetida is solidified from the juice of an umbellifer. Another umbelliferous herb, *angelica, appears in the kitchen mainly as candied stems.

UNICUM. *See* liqueurs and cordials.

V

VACUUM. Space without anything in it, not even air, is a vacuum. However, we talk loosely of a vacuum when we mean a partial vacuum, with most of the air removed from a container. Cooks come across vacuum flasks, which have double walls; the air between has been pumped out so that heat cannot pass either way between the two walls by ordinary conduction or convection (air currents). Radiant heat is stopped by silvering the glass so that heat rays are reflected back from where they came, and the flask thus insulates its contents against changes in temperature.

Reduced pressure lowers the temperature at which liquids boil, as it does at a high *altitude. In a partial vacuum, water will boil even at room temperature (and astronauts' blood would boil in space if they were not in pressure suits). This is made use of commercially in drying foodstuffs that are easily spoiled by heat. You can think of it as reduction boiling at low temperatures. Even ice will evaporate straight into water vapor at reduced pressure; freezing in a partial vacuum is the modern technique of freeze-drying.

[*Vacuum*—French: *vide;* German: *leerer Raum, Vakuum;* Italian: *vuoto;* Spanish: *vacio*]

VAN DER HUM. *See* liqueurs and cordials.

VANILLA. Real vanilla comes from the pod of a climbing orchid (*Vanilla planifolia*) native to tropical American forests. Before the Spanish arrived in America, it was already

VANILLA

being used by the Aztecs as a flavoring for chocolate. The pods are picked unripe—they are yellow, with no vanilla taste. Flavor develops through the activity of enzymes when the pods are packed tight and allowed to sweat in boxes. They turn black and acquire a white frosting of strongly aromatic vanillin crystals, which are what to look for when buying (although they can be faked).

Good vanilla pods are expensive but last a long time. Pods kept in a jar of sugar will impregnate the sugar with their flavor. For stronger vanilla flavor, the pod can be heated in the liquid to be flavored, then rinsed and dried so that it can be used again.

The best vanilla essence is made by extracting the flavor from real vanilla pods with alcohol, but a vanilla flavor may also come from synthetic vanillin made from eugenol, which occurs naturally in clove oil. Being much cheaper, vanillin is much used as a flavoring in butter, margarine, ice cream, chocolate, drinks, and liqueurs. In large doses, it is poisonous, but it is such a powerfully aromatic substance that only a minute amount is necessary for effect. As usual with virtually pure synthetic flavors, it lacks the complementary aromas of natural vanilla and is crude in comparison.

Vanilla needs to be used with great discretion, but is then a most useful flavor both in a dominant role and below the level of recognition. The violent vanilla flavor of many commercial products can be duplicated in the kitchen by anyone with a heavy hand.

[*Vanilla*—French: *vanille;* German: *Vanille;* Italian: *vaniglia;* Spanish: *vainilla*]

VEAL. *See* beef.

VEGETABLE GELATIN. *See* agar.

VEGETABLE OYSTER. *See* salsify.

VEGETABLE PEAR. *See* chayote.

VEGETABLE SPAGHETTI. *See* squash (*Cucurbita pepo*).

VELVET APPLE or **mabolo.** A close relative of the *persimmon.

VENISON is the meat of deer. Deer are native to North America, where the whitetail deer (*Odocoileus virginianus*) is the most plentiful big-game animal. The mule deer (*O. hemionus*) is also an important meat animal. In Europe, the smallest species, the roe deer (*Capreolus capreolus*), is thought to make the finest venison, followed by the fallow deer (*Dama dama*), the species which is partly domesticated in deer parks. The reindeer (*Rangifer tarandus*) is found among all the northern inhabitants of the world; it is easily domesticated and kept in large herds in Arctic Scandinavia. Reindeer venison can be delicious braised, and smoked reindeer tongue is a delicacy.

Very young deer are considered to lack taste, and older animals must be well hung and marinated to make the meat flavorful and tender. Dozens of marinades are used, of which the following is typical and gives the meat a slightly sour taste. A haunch of venison should remain in it for 4–5 days, depending on the weather. Because it is inclined to be dry, venison is best larded with strips of fat.

MARINADE FOR VENISON

Chop 10 carrots and 12 onions. Cook them gently until they are soft but not brown in 2 oz (50 g) of butter, with 3 cloves, 2 allspice berries, 10 bay leaves, a large pinch of thyme, 10 juniper berries, salt, and peppercorns. Then add 1 pt (½ lt) each of wine vinegar and stock. Boil for 2 minutes, then cool and strain the marinade over the haunch. Turn the haunch in the marinade from time to time. The mixture can also be used for *boar.

[*Venison*—French: *venaison;* German: *Wildbret;* Italian: *selvaggina, carne di cervo o capriolo cacciagione;* Spanish: *carne de venado*]

VERBENA or **lemon-scented verbena** (*Verbena tryphilla*) has a place in many gardens. It is a native of South America and requires a warm corner or sunny window. The flavor is rather rankly lemon, and the long leaves are often used in liqueurs, such as the Spanish *hierbas,* which are often homemade and digestive. It is also a passable substitute for *lemon grass in Southeast Asian dishes. Although it is inclined to be reminiscent of old-fashioned soaps, it can be used with caution in sweet dishes, fruit salads, and cups to give a lemon-peel touch, but the peel of a fresh lemon is usually nicer.

[*Verbena* —French: *verveine;* German: *Verbena, Zitronenstrauch;* Italian: *verbena;* Spanish: *verbena*]

VERDELHO. *See* madeira.

VERJUICE, from the French *vert* (green) *jus* (juice), is the sour juice of unripe fruit and was more used in the past as a souring agent than it is today. In France it was the juice of unripe grapes, and in Britain the juice of unripe apples or crab apples fermented for a day or so to remove any small amounts of sugar. After skimming and salting, the verjuice would keep well. It was sometimes concentrated by boiling. The main use for verjuice today is in prepared mustards. In recipes, the usual modern substitute is lemon juice. However, with a modern centrifugal juice extractor, the way is wide open for experiment.

[*Verjuice*—French: *verjus;* German: *Obst-Traubensaft* (*bes. von unreifen Früchten*); Italian: *agresto;* Spanish: *argraz*]

VERMICELLI. *See* pasta.

VERMOUTH is named after the German for wormwood (*wermut*). Wine has been aromatized with herbs and spices since ancient times, and such brews became particularly popular in northern Italy during the Middle Ages, when homemade versions were used as apéritifs. In 1786, a Turin cellar owner called A. B. Carpano started making vermouth on a large scale and thus not only founded the house of Carpano but also began a business which has been centered in Turin ever since. Vermouth is essentially a mixture of wines from various parts of Italy, blended with infusions of many herbs, flowers, barks, and spices, and slightly fortified with alcohol to bring it up to a strength of 16–18 proof. It may be sweet or dry, white, or colored brownish red with added caramel. Vermouth is now made all over the world in the wine-producing countries. Recipes for vermouths are the manufacturers' secrets and are occasionally changed to suit changes in taste. Vermouths were originally intended to be taken neat before a meal (and can be drunk with the first course), but today huge quantities go into cocktails. Indeed, it was cocktails such as martinis that made vermouths internationally famous. Because vermouths are fortified, they keep fairly well once opened, particularly the heavy, sweet ones; the lighter, white vermouths begin to deteriorate after 3 weeks, even when the bottle is closed, though they spoil less rapidly in the refrigerator, which for other reasons is the best place to keep the bottle.

Flavoring ingredients known to go into vermouths include angelica root, anise, calamus, cinnamon, cloves, coriander, camomile, bitter orange peel, peppermint, orris, quassia, quinine, gentian, nutmeg, and, of course, wormwood. With so much variation, the instruction to use vermouth in a sauce for fish, for instance, is not very meaningful, but specific vermouths are used as flavorings in sauces and can be excellent.

[*Vermouth*—French: *vermouth, vermout;* German: *Wermut;* Italian: *vermut;* Spanish: *vermut*]

VESIGA. *See* sturgeon.

VETIVER. *See khas-khas.*

VE-TSIN. *See* monosodium glutamate.

VINEGAR was originally sour wine (*vin aigre*), as opposed to alegar (sour ale), but today only the one word is used. Any alcoholic liquid which does not contain more than about 18% alcohol will sour if exposed to the air. Souring is caused by bacteria that attack alcohol and oxidize it to acetic acid. Because they require oxygen, the bacteria grow on the surface and stick together to form a skin, usually known as vinegar plant or mother of vinegar. It may be used as a starter.

Since vinegar comes from natural processes, it has been known for as long as wine or ale. In fact, vinegar is one of the oldest ingredients in cooking and was used in Europe for thousands of years before lemon juice was even heard of. Vinegars normally contain 4–6% *acetic acid, but the strength can be increased by distillation, and "essence of vinegar" can be up to about 14%. Vinegar is commonly made by souring wine, ale (malt vinegar), or cider (cider vinegar), but vinegars are produced locally from perry, mead, rice wine, and from fruit wines brewed with anything from currants to cashew apples.

Wine vinegar is usual in countries like France, Spain, and Italy where wine is produced in quantity, but it is not necessarily very good because it happens to be made of wine. It may be made of wine that is scarcely fit to drink, and it will be made by the quick process, in which wine is sprinkled over a container of wood shavings (to provide a large surface) with a revolving "sparger," a miniature version of a sewage works sprinkler. As the wine dribbles down over the shavings, it is violently attacked by the organisms that cover them, and everything is kept well oxygenated by air blown in at the bottom. In the process, quite a lot of heat is generated—the tank is maintained at 95–100°F (35–38°C), which is hot enough to drive off any of the more volatile flavors.

This is why the best vinegar is still made by the old Orléans process, in which barrels are filled with a mixture of 3 parts wine to 2 parts vinegar, inoculated with mother of vinegar, and left open to allow air to enter. Establishing the vat with vinegar prevents the growth of unwanted organisms and encourages vinegar organisms, which grow best in acid conditions. In the Orléans process, the organisms slowly turn the alcohol in the wine to acid without getting hot and without losing the finer flavors of the wine. At intervals, vinegar is drawn off and more wine is added. Since this is a slow process, Orléans process vinegar is expensive, especially since the finest vinegar starts with good wine. However, the amount of vinegar used in

dressing a salad ought to be small, and it is worth finding a fine wine vinegar to keep just for this purpose. The difference it makes to a salad is enormous.

The town of Modena in northern Italy produces fine wine vinegar, *aceto balsamico,* which is matured for years—it is said that it is usable after ten years, better after thirty, better still after fifty, and at its best after a hundred or more. It is too good to use for anything except salads.

Special types of vinegar come from particular wines, for example sherry vinegar. Malt vinegar is essentially beer vinegar (except that the beer is not hopped) and is usually colored brown with caramel. It is less sour than the run-of-the-mill wine vinegar, but nice flavors do not come from the fermented malt, although some aromatics may be generated by bacteria. Cider vinegar has long been popular in the northeastern U.S. and in recent years has also become better known elsewhere. It is supposed to be more healthful and is a basis for a few American folk medicines. However, cider vinegar has an apple juice taste which a few people, including myself, do not find particularly attractive. White vinegar is as colorless as water (white-wine vinegar has some color) and is used in pickles for cosmetic reasons. It can be made by decoloring ordinary vinegar with animal charcoal or can be faked (as it usually is) with acetic acid and water.

Very strong vinegars, such as essence of vinegar, spirit vinegar, and distilled vinegar, are used to preserve very watery vegetables or in any other situation in which ordinary vinegar will become overdiluted. They are made by concentrating vinegars by distillation or by diluting strong synthetic acid with water.

Vinegar is very easily made at home by putting wine (including homemade wine) or any other alcoholic liquid into a container, preferably one with a tap at the bottom, and adding a piece of mother of vinegar as a starter—or at least putting some vinegar in to increase acidity. Without this, the wine may go bad before it has developed its own acid. The container should be kept in a warm kitchen. A skin of mother of vinegar will shortly form over the wine. If this latter becomes too white and thick, the top layer should be removed because it may block air getting to the underlying bacteria; the underlying pink skin should be left. When it is ready, some of the vinegar can be run off (or siphoned off from the bottom if it is in a vessel with no tap) and more wine added. Vinegar exposed to the air will lose strength, because of bacteria which attack the acetic acid, so vinegar bottles should be well filled and corked.

In the past, it was quite usual for cooks to make sugar vinegar, something which can be done quite simply as follows: boil a suitable volume of water and add sugar at the rate of 5 oz (150 g) per 1¾ pt (1 lt); within reason, quantity is not critical. You can use brown sugar or add molasses for flavor. Traditionally, the liquid, when cool, was put in a not quite full cask and a piece of toast covered in yeast was floated on top. A piece of brown paper was pasted over the bung hole and well pricked with a skewer to let in air. A barrel of sugar and water, if put down in April, would be vinegar ready for bottling by September. It would develop more quickly if mother of vinegar was added.

Old directions for making mother of vinegar are to put 4 oz (100 g) of sugar and 8 oz (225 g) of treacle in 6 pt (3½ lt) of water, bring them to the boil and cool it, then cover it and leave it in a warm place for 6 weeks. If all goes well, the mother of vinegar will form on top and can be used as a starter. Homemade vinegar is best pasteurized or brought almost to the boil before bottling.

Vinegar is often flavored with various herbs and aromatics, the best-known varieties being tarragon, chili, and garlic vinegars, but cucumber, basil, rose, violet, celery (with celery seed), cress or mustard (also with seed), and shallot vinegars are also made. To make any of these, it is necessary only to infuse the flavorings in a bottle of vinegar for some days. Some vinegars were made with quite complicated mixtures of herbs, garlic, onion, and spices. They then verged on bottled sauces. Sweet fruit vinegars (such as raspberry, currant, and gooseberry) were made to be diluted and used as refreshing summer drinks, but most have gone out of fashion.

Vinegar is preservative, because of its acetic acid content, which is why it is used in pickles and chutneys. Since vinegars vary, it may be best to dilute them with a little water and not to slavishly follow recipes with full-strength products. Tiny amounts of vinegar can improve some surprising things (yogurt and strawberries are examples).

A Japanese sweet vinegar, which is used for seasoning rice, is called *yamabukuzu;* a substitute can be made by adding 3 tablespoons of sugar, 3 teaspoons of salt, and a pinch of monosodium glutamate to a cup of vinegar.

[*Vinegar*—French: *vinaigre;* German: *Essig;* Italian: *aceto;* Spanish: *vinagre*]

VINE LEAVES. The principal use for grapevine leaves is for stuffing to make the Levantine specialties known loosely as *dolmades* (Greek), *dolmas* (Turkey), or *mashi* (Lebanon). Young vine leaves are used—the third and fourth from the tip are said to be best—as older ones are tough. (If gathering them yourself, be careful that the leaves have not been sprayed with chemicals.) Some vine leaves have a ragged heart shape, but others are deeply indented and do not therefore make a good wrapping. The leaves of wild grapes can be used in the U.S. Vine leaves can be bought fresh throughout the summer in the markets of eastern Mediterranean countries. For winter, they are salted in barrels and sold loose. They may also be bought canned—a 15-oz (425-g) can holds 40–50 leaves.

Before vine leaves can be stuffed, they must have the stalks removed and be blanched for a few minutes in boiling water until they are pliable. It is best to blanch a few at a time, since a large number of leaves dumped into the pot will stick together and the outer ones will be done before the heat reaches the inner ones. However, since stuffed vine leaves take 45–60 minutes to cook, overblanching is merely an inconvenience. Canned vine leaves and salted leaves from the barrel need to be rinsed in warm water to remove salt before they are used.

There are many stuffings for *dolmas*—mixtures of meat, rice, and vegetables, which often contain pine nuts. They may be flavored with herbs such as parsley and mint. Some recipes are intended for eating hot; others cold. They are stuffed by laying them out with the veiny underside upward and placing a small amount of stuffing near the stalk end, which is then folded over the stuffing. The side lobes of the leaf are folded inward, and the package is then rolled up so that the tip of the leaf is on the outside. Once you become hooked on *dolmas*, especially for parties, it is difficult to do without them.

Vine leaves have a characteristic though mild taste and cannot be properly replaced by other leaves. Apart from being stuffed, they are sometimes fried in batter, cut up in salads, or used for wrapping small birds and lining pans in which other foods (such as mushrooms) are gently cooked.

[*Vine leaf*—French: *feuille de vigne;* German: *Rebenblatt;* Italian: *foglia di vite;* Spanish: *pámpano*]

VIOLET. The French name for a gray-brown saclike tunicate (*Microcosmus sulcatus*), an animal that lives fastened to rocks at a depth of 100–300 ft (30–100 m) in the Mediterranean. The soft, yellow insides are eagerly eaten raw by aficionados in France, Spain, and Italy. The taste is strong, sour, marine, and iodinelike. I spat mine out.

[*Violet*—French: *violet, figue de mer;* Italian: *limone di mare, uovo di mare;* Spanish: *probecho*]

VIOLET. The sweet violet (*Viola odorata*) is edible, as are other species, including the familiar common blue violet (*V. papiliona-*

cea). The flowers, usually bought preserved in sugar, are mostly used as cake decorations and produce the main flavoring in the very sweet violet-colored liqueur known as *parfait amour*. Violet leaves and buds have a slightly peppery flavor and may be used in spring salads. They contain enormous amounts of vitamins A and C. Cooked violet leaves are much like astringent spinach, and they are good boiled with other greens. Violets were used a lot more in the 17th century, and recipes for violet syrups and sweetmeats abound in cookbooks of the period. *Orris may be used to provide imitation violet flavorings, e.g., in chocolate cream.

[*Violet*—French: *violette;* German: *Veilchen;* Italian: *viola mammola;* Spanish: *buglosa*]

VITAMINS are not ingredients we buy and stuff into the food—as yet—but they need to be watched, because cooks are responsible for the health of the people they feed and because, in cooking, vitamins can easily be destroyed, thrown away, or lost. It was discovered long ago that scurvy on long voyages could be prevented by taking lime juice, and housewives accumulated a lot of know-how about keeping their families healthy on fresh food, but it was not until 1912 that the biochemist Sir Frederick Gowland Hopkins put vitamins firmly on the map.

Vitamins are organic substances of various sorts that the body cannot manufacture for itself but needs in small amounts in order to function properly. Originally, vitamins could not be identified by chemical names (although one, niacin, had actually been synthesized in the 19th century), and so they were known by the letters of the alphabet. Later some were found not to be one vitamin but several—in particular, vitamin B was split into B_1, B_2, B_3, and B_{12}. The whole series was called the B vitamin complex, because the vitamins did not work in isolation from one another but were interrelated. As techniques improved, the chemical structure of the vitamins began to be worked out, and during the 1930s many were synthesized (vitamin C, 1933; vitamin B$_2$, 1934; vitamin D$_2$, 1935; vitamin B$_1$, 1936). All the vitamins were eventually given chemical names, and some that had earlier been called vitamins were found to be inessential and so dropped. This accounts for the untidiness of the list today. Vitamins are now big business for pharmaceutical companies, which like us to swallow a lot of pills. Although a few people may need more than average amounts of certain vitamins, a balanced diet generally provides enough to maintain good health without vitamin supplements. Any extra is usually eliminated from the body and is a waste of cash. Cooks should be concerned to retain vitamins in everyday dishes, but it is not always easy to know if cooking is damaging the vitamins. Only a few of the more important vitamins are dealt with below.

Vitamin A or **retinol.** Deficiency causes night blindness and later flaky "toad skin," even wrinkles on the cornea of the eye, but risk of deficiency is slight in the U.S. and Europe. In cooking, retinol is fairly resistant to heat and, being fat-soluble, is not dissolved out into the cooking water. It is, however, easily destroyed by light and by rancid fats.

The normal daily requirement for most people is satisfied by as little as ⅓ oz (10 g) of liver, 1½ oz (40 g) old carrots or 3 oz (75 g) new carrots, 3 oz (75 g) spinach, margarine, or butter, or 4 eggs. Cheese, milk, cream, and apricots are also useful sources. Fish-liver oils contain a lot of vitamin A, particularly halibut-liver oil, which contains 150 times as much as cod-liver oil.

Because vitamin A is stored in the body, one serving of liver, 4 oz (100 g), would cover a week's requirement. Retinol is not excreted in the urine, and too much is toxic. The livers of sharks, whales, and polar bears are considered dangerous because of their retinol content. Polar-bear liver is fantastically rich in retinol—but is nevertheless the first part eaten by Eskimos who take it raw, and warm, from the kill. Carrots are not rich in retinol itself, but contain its precursor carotene.

Vitamin B$_1$ or **thiamine.** Deficiency causes beriberi and nervous disorders; but the risk is slight in those who eat a reasonable diet since it occurs in most fresh foods. However, alcoholics can suffer; they tend to eat badly and have an increased demand for this vitamin. Mild deficiency sometimes contributes to mental confusion in old people.

The normal daily requirement varies with the individual's carbohydrate metabolism, because thiamine is concerned with the release of energy from glucose. Men usually require more than women, and the physically active more than those who lead sedentary lives. Thiamine requirement cannot be supplied by a single serving of any one food (except perhaps a massive amount of cod's roe) but from a variety of sources. Rich ones are wheat germ, Brazil nuts, unroasted peanuts and roasted pork, while oatmeal, bacon, eggs, kidney, liver, and bread (both brown and white) all make their contribution. Synthetic thiamine hydrochloride is often added to breakfast cereals, peanut butter, and breads to replace that lost in the manufacture. It may sometimes be added to such items as skimmed milk and bottled drinks. Thiamine is not stored (although there is some reserve in the body cells); since any in excess of immediate requirements is lost in the urine, it is not toxic in excess. Thiamine is easily destroyed by heat in cooking, especially in the presence of an alkali, such as bicarbonate of soda. Also, being water-soluble, it is easily dissolved out by cooking water. Even toasting a slice of bread destroys up to a third of the vitamin and reheating or keeping food warm is exceedingly destructive.

Vitamin B$_2$, of which **riboflavin** is an important component. Deficiency in adults is not marked by an obvious disease but causes vague symptoms like sore tongue, cracks at the corners of the mouth, and itching eyes, and it stunts growth in children. Riboflavin is necessary for proper functioning of the muscles, so people doing hard physical work need it, athletes need it, and men usually need it more than women (they usually have bigger muscles), but as with all vitamins—B complex ones in particular—it is of little use on its own without the others. The risk of deficiency is negligible on an average good diet. The normal daily requirement could come from one large serving of liver or kidneys, but cheese, milk, eggs, and yeast extracts are also good sources.

In cooking, riboflavin is relatively stable to heat but will be destroyed by an alkali like bicarbonate of soda. It is also soluble in water and will be leached out when food is boiled, so use the cooking water to make gravy and stock. Ultraviolet light rapidly destroys riboflavin, and milk in a bottle left in the sun or even under fluorescent light will lose its riboflavin content in a few hours.

Niacin or **nicotinic acid** has for long had no B number, but it is an important member of the B-vitamin complex. Deficiency causes pellagra, but the risk is small in people living on normally adequate diets; it may occur in alcoholics. Our normal daily requirement would be contained in one helping of liver. Other good sources are kidneys, sardines and other oily fish, peanuts, cheese, eggs, mushrooms, milk, and pulses. Best of all are meat extracts, yeast extracts, and wheat bran. Niacin is supplied to a significant extent by coffee and beer. Niacin is little affected by the heat of cooking, but is water-soluble and some 40% may be lost from vegetables that are boiled in a lot of water. People got pellagra from a corn diet because they were unable to afford meat, eggs, or milk. Corn, unlike other cereals, lacks the amino acid tryptophan, which can be turned into niacin by the liver if vitamins B_1, B_2, and B_6 are present.

Vitamin B_{12} or **cyanocobalamin** is used as a control for pernicious anemia, because the vitamin is concerned in the formation of red cells in the blood, although the disease is not caused by vitamin deficiency. The risk of a deficiency in the diet is more or less zero, except among vegetarians who eat no food of animal origin, no milk, cheese, or eggs.

Vitamin C or **ascorbic acid.** Serious deficiency causes scurvy, the breakdown of connective tissue proteins. First symptoms are easy bruising, bleeding and spongy gums, followed by loss of teeth, weak bones, and internal hemorrhages. It is still uncertain what harm a slight deficiency might do. As early as 1601 it was discovered that lime juice prevented scurvy, although it took almost 200 years, until 1795, for lime juice to become a compulsory issue in the British navy, which caused Americans to give the British the name "lime juicers" and then "limeys" (although it seems to have been lemon juice rather than lime juice that was actually issued).

The normal daily requirement is uncertain, but most people eating plenty of fresh fruit and vegetables get enough. Common foods particularly rich in vitamin C are black currants, strawberries, watercress, green peppers, cabbage, cauliflower, tomatoes and Brussels sprouts. Oranges and lemons are all right but not sensational; apples, carrots, pears, bananas, plums, celery, and beets are less good. The risk of deficiency is small, except among those who perhaps for dietary reasons eat almost exclusively fish, fats, eggs, and meat—they will need supplementary vitamin C.

Vitamin C is very easily destroyed in cooking. Before you even start to cook them, vegetables that are not fresh, are wilted, or have been stored for long in the refrigerator will have lost much of their C vitamin content. Air also destroys vitamin C, and so do enzymes in cut-up fruit and vegetables that are exposed to the air. Heat destroys the vitamin—the longer food is kept hot, the more is lost. Vitamin C is dissolved out by water and destroyed by alkalis like bicarbonate of soda. Effectively, then, we have to rely on fresh uncooked fruit and vegetables for our main supply.

Vitamin C is not stored in the body beyond a certain saturation point, and excess is then excreted. Its use in a large dose (1 teaspoon of ascorbic acid) taken at the start of a cold has been advocated in the last few years, but the case for it is still very much in doubt. So is the value of saturating the body with it to ward off colds. Synthetic ascorbic acid is used in manufactured food as an antioxidant and by the bread industry to accelerate the proving and maturing of bread dough—this does not increase the vitamin content of the bread, since baking does away with the vitamin C.

Vitamin D is a complex of substances including calciferol (D_2) and cholecalciferol (D_3). It is found mainly in oily fish, margarine (into which it is put), and eggs. It also forms when the skin is exposed to the sun. Deficiency prevents calcium from being properly absorbed and so leads to rickets. The risk of deficiency is greater in winter and for people who spend their lives indoors, especially young children in cloudy climates. Most adults get enough to supply their needs.

The normal daily requirement would be easily supplied by a serving of herrings, kippers, mackerel, or eels, but most people probably get their supply from the sun, and from margarine and eggs. Cod-liver oil is exceedingly rich in vitamin D, and 1 teaspoon of it a day will provide all anyone could wish for. In cooking, vitamin D is not destroyed by heat and, being fat-soluble, does not dissolve out in cooking water.

Too much vitamin D is toxic and may cause calcium to be deposited in the circulatory system. (It can also harm the unborn child if an expectant mother goes on a cod-liver oil spree.) The worry at the moment is that because manufacturers enrich milk, flour, cereals, and baby foods, some people may be getting too much vitamin D in their diets.

[*Vitamin*—French: *vitamine;* German: *Vitamin;* Italian: *vitamina;* Spanish: *vitamina*]

VIZIGA. *See* sturgeon.

VODKA means "little water" and is derived from the early Russian *shizenennya voda,* meaning "water of life." It is not certain whether vodka was first produced in Poland or Russia. Unlike the other great spirits, it does not aim to be flavored by congenerics coming over in the still. It is the purest of all spirits and consequently may be distilled from grain, potatoes, wine, or any fermentable mash. Color and lingering flavor may be removed by animal charcoal or by distillation to a high degree of purity. Flavoring can be added afterward by both the maker and the cook.

Before World War II, vodka was little drunk outside eastern Europe, but now its popularity rivals gin, and it is distilled in the U.S., Britain, and almost everywhere else where people like to drink. One of its attractions is that since it contains virtually no congenerics, you can sober up quicker and with less hangover from it than from any other drink.

A Polish friend of mine let me into the secret of his own homemade vodka. He took the best pure grape spirit distilled in Italy— some 95% pure—and cut it with an equal volume of water, adding to each bottle a level teaspoon of sugar, which soon dissolved in the water. He told me with some glee how some Polish visitors, vodka connoisseurs, had complained that the vodka he offered, the best brand obtainable and bought specially for them, was not fit to drink. Rather upset, he had gone into the kitchen, unearthed a very old empty bottle of some prewar brand from a cupboard, rinsed it, and filled it with his homemade brew. "Fabulous," they said. "That's the real stuff." I don't think anyone could have pulled the trick with whiskey, brandy, rum, or even gin.

Vodka can be flavored. A coil of lemon zest or a sprig of wormwood put into the bottle and left a few days will give it taste and a most potent effect. Flavored and fruit vodkas are sold. Vodka is much used instead of gin in cocktails and is used for its own sake in a Bloody Mary. Because vodka is more or less flavorless, it is rarely used for flaming, but it is the best thing to use when an alcoholic solvent is required (unless you are in a country where you can buy strong potable alcohol). With it, you can make your own essences by infusion, and you can use it as a spirit for preserving fruit provided that the vodka is strong and the fruit not too watery.

[*Vodka*—French: *vodka;* German: *Wodka;* Italian: *vodka;* Spanish: *vodka*]

VYAZIGA. *See* sturgeon.

W

WAFER. A thin, crisp cracker, in many respects similar to a waffle (which comes essentially from the same word via the Dutch) but thinner and crisper. Wafers really need to be baked in wafer irons which are made especially for the purpose. They are heated on both sides, rubbed with a little butter, and then filled with a teaspoon of batter. The iron is closed almost immediately and put back on the heat. When it is cooked on both sides, the wafer is immediately removed and sometimes curled around a wooden spoon handle while it is still flexible, but often it is left flat. After being trimmed and allowed to cool and dry, wafers must be stored in a dry tin. The simplest wafer batter consists of only flour and water, but most contain sugar, egg, and cream. Nowadays, most people buy wafers that have been made by machinery. There are recipes for making wafers in the oven, but these are more nearly crackers or cookies.

[*Wafer*—French: *pain à cacheter;* German: *Waffel;* Italian: *cialda;* Spanish: *barquillo*]

WAKAME. *See* seaweed.

WALNUT (*Juglans regia*) is misleadingly named the English walnut in the U.S. to distinguish it from native American species. The walnut tree is a native of southeastern Europe, and its range extends across west and central Asia into China. Although walnuts were important to the ancient Greeks and Romans, they are said not to have been established in Britain until the 15th century. The early colonists took them to plant in North America. Walnuts have also been introduced into Australia, New Zealand, South Africa, and South America. They are an important crop in China, where the papershell varieties are mainly grown. The leading walnut country, however, is France, although it is fast being overtaken by the U.S. In the past, walnuts were an essential food in some French districts, not only as nuts but also for their oil, which was once as important as olive oil in French kitchens, but today it is too expensive for general use. Italy is another important producer, with nuts grown in small areas over the whole country. The bulk for export comes from the south—around Naples, Sorrento, and Benevento. Strangely, in Italian cooking, walnuts are more used in the North. In the U.S., there are huge orchards in California and Oregon.

Every country has its favored varieties, which are propagated by grafting and have been selected for such qualities as size, ratio of meat to shell, texture, flavor, and absence of astringency. Some varieties are very hard and difficult to crack, while others have thin, papery shells, but all need to have a tight seal between the halves for good keeping. There are also freaks such as the French *noix noisette,* with nuts no bigger than a hazel, delicately flavored and full of oil, and the gigantic *bijou,* which was once polished and mounted in metal to make elegant cases for jewels or, more humbly, cradles for little dolls.

Walnut trees are self-fertile, and the fruit is borne on the outer branches. Toward the end of September, or in early October, the husks split open and the fresh, ripe nuts fall to the ground. The nuts must be picked up almost daily, since any left lying on the ground quickly become discolored and moldy. In some unfavorable years there are many stick-tight nuts which cause problems by being separable from the husk only with difficulty. Walnuts are usually washed and then dried outdoors, but they must not be left in the hot sun for more than 2 hours at a time—the heat may make them split open, and they will then not keep. Commercially walnuts are often bleached and dried artificially in a stream of warm air at a maximum of 110°F (43°C).

Green walnuts are made use of at all stages of ripeness. For pickling, the fruit is taken green and the shells not yet formed. They usually reach this stage in late June—the traditional start of walnut picking was St. George's Day—and the nuts are tested by pushing a skewer right through them in several directions (the shell begins to form near the end away from the stalk). Nuts for pickle should not be too young, since they tend to disintegrate or go mushy, but of course they are no use once the shell has turned hard. In between, there is a short period when the walnuts are just right. Where the recipe calls for the husk to be skinned this may be done by scalding and rubbing the skin off with a rough cloth. Products made from the green nuts in Britain are walnut pickle, walnut ketchup, and walnut jam—in fact, the bulk of home-grown walnuts go for pickle and are not allowed to mature. In France, a cordial, *brou de noix,* is made from green walnuts. In Italy the equivalent is *nocino;* it is especially popular in Lombardy and is also used to flavor ice creams. When the

husk is still green, but the kernels are properly formed, the nut can be extracted, peeled, and preserved in syrup—as they are in the Middle East—or used to make *cerneaux au verjus,* the skinned immature kernel marinated in *verjuice for an hour or so, then seasoned with pepper, chopped shallots, and sometimes vinegar.

NOCINO

Cut about 30 green walnuts into quarters and put them in a large screw-top jar with a good sliver of lemon peel, a couple of small bits of cinnamon stick, and 6 cloves. Cover with 90% alcohol (or as strong as you can get it), put the lid on, and leave in the sun for a month, shaking it every day. At the end of this time, add 1 lb (500 g) of sugar and leave for another 2 weeks in the sun, shaking the jar every day as before. Filter and bottle the *nocino,* which should be left for a year before using.

Pickled walnuts. Pickled unripe walnuts are well known in England, but not at all, or rarely, in the countries farther south where the nuts are mainly produced. The fruit is often prepared for pickling by scalding and skinning, but Mrs. Beeton suggests pricking the skins well with a silver fork. Such treatment allows the vinegar to penetrate and accelerates pickling. The walnuts must now be put in brine strong enough to float a fresh egg, which means 2-3 oz per pt (100–150 g per lt) of salt. They are left submerged, weighted down under a board, for 6 days and are stirred at least once a day; then the brine is changed and the walnuts are left for a further week. A total of 12–13 days of salting is usual. After this, the fruit is drained, spread out in a single layer, and put in the sun. The nuts are left exposed and turned occasionally until they turn black all over, a process which may take up to 2 days, depending on the conditions. Now the black fruits are packed into jars, covered with spiced vinegar, sealed, and left for at least a month, but preferably several months, before using.

There are many formulas for making the spiced vinegar, one of which is as follows. For each 2 pt (1 lt) of vinegar add 1 small onion, 1 crushed clove of garlic, and ¾ oz (20 g) each of bruised ginger, black peppercorns, cloves, allspice, cinnamon stick, and mustard seed, plus a large blade of mace and 2 bay leaves. Bring to the boil, simmer for 5 minutes, and allow to cool, preferably overnight. Strain the vinegar and cover walnuts with it. If hot vinegar is poured over the walnuts, they will take less time to mature but the results are marginally less good.

Ripe walnuts are sold whole or shelled and as ground or broken nutmeat. When buying walnuts in the shell, look carefully to make sure that the seal between the halves of the shell is good—you should certainly not be able to pull the two halves of the shell apart. Without actually opening some nuts, it is impossible to tell if kernels have been overdried. New walnuts, on the other hand, have sometimes been soaked in water to make them heavy and moist. They are good for immediate use but will not keep. Shelled nuts quickly go rancid—dark, bitter, stale kernels are an abomination and will spoil any dish they are put in.

New walnuts are very digestible, but the skin of the kernels is bitter and should be removed. In some varieties, it will easily peel off after a short soaking in cold water, but others may first have to be scalded for a few seconds in boiling water and then dropped into ice water. Skinned, fresh walnuts are a great delicacy in the Middle East.

With time, after drying and maturing, walnuts become more oily and less easily digested, but the skin loses much of its bitterness. Even so, the skins should be removed for any delicate walnut dish. You can pour a kettle of boiling water over the kernels and take off the skins with your fingers as soon as the nuts are cool enough to handle. Alternatively, they may be put into a gentle oven until the skin becomes brittle and can be rubbed off with a cloth.

The best-known use of walnuts is in sweets, cakes, and ice cream. Whole or chopped walnuts are now also commonly used in salads, as part of a garnish for stews, and even as the main ingredient in walnut soup. They are excellent both for their flavor and to give texture when they are pounded or minced. From France there is *sauce raifort aux noix, l'aillade toulousaine* (walnuts pounded with garlic and stirred into an emulsion with olive oil), and sometimes they are used to make the traditional *raïto* of Provence. In Italy, walnuts are pounded with pine nuts for *pesto alla genovese* and form the nut base of a *pesto* variant, the *pasta alla fornaia* of Tuscany. Skinned walnuts pounded with soaked bread, a lot of parsley, salt, oil, and a trace of garlic, diluted with cream or curdled milk, form the *salsa di noci* of Liguria. It is used on a local type of ravioli, which is stuffed with a cooked mixture of herbs such as Swiss chard, borage, and wild chicory. A sauce from Piedmont uses pounded walnuts moistened with broth and mixed with mustard and honey as an accompaniment for a *bollito misto* (mixed boiled meats). In all cases, the walnuts are first peeled after blanching in boiling water.

Walnuts are grown in the Balkans, especially in Albania and Rumania. Bulgaria has a sauce very similar to the Italian *salsa di noci*. Greece has a walnut sauce to use with hare. From Iran comes the superlative *fesenjan,* in which lamb, duck, or chicken has a sauce of pounded walnuts and sour fruit juice. Rather similar combinations are found in Kashmir.

KHORESH FESENJAN

Khoreshtha (the plural of *khoresh*) are Iranian dishes that are eaten with rice. They are something between a stew and a sauce and usually combine meat, nuts, and fruit.

Chop a large onion and fry it gently in 1 tablespoon butter until just soft, then add 1 lb (500 g) of walnuts, skinned and ground fine. Mix them and continue frying gently for 2 minutes, then add 1 pt (500 ml) of water and simmer gently for about 30 minutes.

Meanwhile finely chop a small onion and add it to 1 lb (500 g) of finely minced lamb. Fry the mixture in as little fat as possible until the meat browns. Add it to the simmering walnut mixture, adding more water if necessary. Season with salt and pepper, and continue simmering for an hour. Now add ½ pt (250 ml) of pomegranate juice and 7–9 oz (200–250 g) of sugar (depending on the sourness of the juice) and continue to cook gently until the oil separates and comes to the surface. Make a final adjustment of seasoning with sugar or lemon juice, and serve with rice. As a substitute for pomegranate, the juice of sour cherries or even plums could be used, but the taste would not be quite the same.

ÇERKES TAVUĞU (CIRCASSIAN CHICKEN)

There are many variations on this famous dish. It may be served hot or more usually cold and is highly recommended for a cold buffet. The quantity of sauce in the following recipe is sufficient to go with 4½ lb (2 Kg) of chicken, which has been cooked by being carefully simmered with flavoring vegetables in its stock and cut in suitable pieces, or boned and diced. Finely grind 5 oz (150 g) of peeled walnuts and mix with 1 tablespoon of paprika or *pimentón*. Pound or press a little to bring out some of the oil from the nuts. Use a cloth to squeeze out some of the red oil, which is kept aside for decoration. (Additional oil can be used for this, but it makes the dish a little too oily.) To the walnuts add about 5 oz (150 g) of bread soaked in chicken stock. Pound together (or liquidize), adding more chicken stock to make a thick sauce. Season to taste. Mix half the sauce with the chicken, and spread the other half on top. Dribble red oil over the dish in a decorative pattern.

Walnut oil, which was once important in France, Switzerland, and North Italy (Piedmont) for salads and cooking, is now becoming scarce, since it is even more expensive than olive oil. It has a very individual taste and goes rancid rather easily.

American walnuts. A number of species of walnut grow wild in North American forests, two of which have some gastronomic and commercial importance and are also cultivated. Members of the walnut family and similar in many respects are the *hickories, including *pecan. The black walnut (*Juglans nigra*) has a large nut, but the shell is very hard and special crackers are necessary. The flavor is strong and is not lost in cooking. The white walnut or *butternut (*J. cinerea*) has a shell that is very difficult to crack. The flavor is excellent.

[*Walnut*—French: *noix;* German: *Walnuss;* Italian: *noce;* Spanish: *nuez, negal*]

WARBLER. *See* birds.

WATER (H_2O). From the point of view of the hydrologist, there are various sources of water. Surface water, which runs off without sinking down into the ground, is unlikely to contain much in the way of minerals but probably contains silt. It comes from lakes and rivers. Mountain water can be very pure but can also contain powdered rock, especially if it comes from melting glaciers. Such water looks milky and should be stood to allow the particles to settle, since drinking it can irritate the intestine. Bog water, a practical rather than a scientific classification, usually comes from moorland areas where the rocks are impervious. It is sometimes brown with peat and may tend to be acid but contains very little dissolved mineral—it is very soft water.

Water from underground has soaked down through porous rocks and become part of the water table. It comes from wells, artesian wells, and springs. Unless it has come from a limestone cave (when it may be a river that has flowed through tunnels from a pothole in the hills above) or has flowed through fissures, it is likely to be bacteriologically pure, but will contain dissolved minerals. The nature and quantity of these minerals depend on the rocks through which the water has passed. Soft water is very good for washing and cooking, for making tea and whiskey—it is good with whiskey too—but may not be quite as healthful as hard water, which contains dissolved minerals. Statistical studies have shown heart disease to be more prevalent in areas with soft water than in those with hard water. The reason is not understood at the moment and may have no direct causal connection with the water itself but might, for instance, possibly be due to the fact that soft water dissolves lead from lead pipes, which should not be used for it.

Distilled water is the ultimate in soft water, since it has nothing at all dissolved in it. Apart from its flat taste, one Italian *professoressa* has written that it is damaging, a "true poison," because in the long term it dissolves and removes essential minerals from the body. The point is purely academic, because most people meet distilled water only as something to put into car batteries and steam irons. (For such purposes, the water distilled in the refrigerator when moisture condenses to ice around the freezer compartment can be saved when the refrigerator is defrosted. Distilled water makes very good tea, especially cold tea which never goes cloudy on standing.

Hard water is particularly found in chalk, limestone, or dolomite areas, and the chemicals responsible for hardness are mainly bicarbonates, sulfates, and chlorides of calcium, magnesium, sodium, and potassium. There may also be small amounts of nitrate from mineral sources, but more than 30 parts per million is almost certainly a sign of contamination. When water containing bicarbonates of calcium and magnesium is boiled, the bicarbonates are changed to insoluble carbonates. This produces deposits on pans and furring of kettles. The bicarbonates that can be removed by heating are a source of temporary hardness, as opposed to the permanent hardness caused by the sulfates and chlorides of calcium and magnesium, most commonly by gypsum (calcium sulfate), that stay in solution when the water is boiled. Hard water is not good for making coffee or tea or for cooking. Good drinking water should not have more than 500 parts per million of dissolved solids. However, the calcium bicarbonate in hard water is thought to be a source of calcium used by the body.

Safety. It is possible to have water so rich in poisonous elements that it is not safe to drink. You would not happily drink water in old lead or copper mines. Some natural waters contain arsenic and other poisons, are radioactive, or are just downright nasty because they contain salt or alkali. Usually, however, the possible problem is sewage contamination. Rivers usually have water that is contaminated with sewage but may be used to feed reservoirs; even in the 19th century, London water was described as "very dilute sewage." Today at least it is purified and chlorinated sewage, but the ingredients can be detected in the taste. In the countries where the banks of streams are used as lavatories or the separation between water mains and sewers is not impeccable, the result can be epidemics of cholera, typhoid, and dysentery. Water containing ammonia, nitrites, phosphates, or hydrogen sulfide (which gives a smell of rotten eggs) is probably contaminated with organic waste but is not necessarily harmful. Most bacteria in water are harmless saprophytes that live on the organic matter it contains. It is only when a carrier has added pathogenic organisms (not only bacteria but amoebae and schistosomes as in parts of Africa) that there is trouble. Boiled water is safe, and any tap water that smells of chlorine is drinkable, though it may taste unpleasant. The taste of chlorine can be removed by adding a small pinch of powdered sodium thiosulfate, which is well known to photographers as "hypo" and is easily bought at a drugstore. Water-sterilizing tablets containing a chlorine-releasing compound, such as sodium hypochlorite, can be bought also at pharmacies; they work well as long as instructions are followed to the letter, which is mostly a question of waiting half an hour before drinking the water. If all else fails, water from the hot tap (if it is really hot) can be used, since most pathogenic organisms are fragile and cannot withstand water at temperatures that are too hot to dip your hand in. The best solution of all for travelers who don't want to go to the American Embassy whenever they would like a drink of water is to buy a water-sterilizing filter pump that makes use of a filter candle. The pores of the filter candle are too small to let bacteria pass, but water can be forced through. In old models, the candles had to be boiled regularly because bacteria were eventually forced through like fat men pushed down a narrow passage, but modern filter candles are impregnated with colloidal silver which kills trapped bacteria. Parasites which might be in water are even larger. Only viruses can get through a filter candle.

Drinking water. Water makes up 60 to 70% of the human body, mostly in the cells; there is far less in the blood and other body fluids. Under average conditions, we lose some 3½ pt (2 lt) a day, mainly in urine, in sweat, and through the lungs in breathing. This has to be made good by eating moist foods and by drinking liquids. Although it is possible to fast for weeks and still recover, someone from whom all sources of water have been withdrawn will last 60–70 hours (more in cool moist conditions, less in a dry, hot, windy desert) and will die after the loss of some 20% of body water. And thirst is awful. Anyone who has traveled in deserts knows that there does not seem to be enough water in the whole wide world to stop the craving.

Good table water is clear, colorless, and almost tasteless. Unlike boiled water or distilled water, it is not flat because it contains some dissolved air, as can be seen by the bubbles that come out when water stands for long in a glass. Water should always be on the table at mealtimes, especially for weight watchers, since it helps to fill the stomach. It might be served in a glass pitcher, which looks clean and attractive, in a silver pitcher (silver helps to destroy bacteria and is tradi-

tional in some places), or in an unglazed earthenware pitcher, which keeps the water cool by evaporation. How many people (besides the Turks, who are great connoisseurs of water) bother over water the way they do wine? The temperature of water for the table should ideally be 48–54°F (9–12°C) for European tastes. Americans prefer water much colder—at about 42°F (5.5°C) or even lower. This might be called ice water; swigged in long drafts it is not very good for the stomach. However, whatever you do, bad-tasting water is not going to taste good just because it is served in a nice pitcher at the right temperature.

Mineral water and **bottled water.** My grandmother was as keen as any European on visiting spas and hydros to have baths and drink the waters everywhere from Harrogate to Bad Homburg. She believed that the French drank mineral water simply because French tap water was full of typhoid. It did not occur to her, or to others of her generation, that they also drank it because it was nice. The mineral waters she drank were medicinal and nasty, while her tap water from the millstone grit of the Peak District in Derbyshire was excellent (water from there is now carbonated and bottled).

The French have 1200 registered springs, of which 50 produce water that is bottled for general consumption. A bottle of mineral water is also a normal part of a meal for many people in Italy, Spain, Germany, and other European countries. There are now signs that even Americans are beginning to realize that good water, whether still or gassed, can be delicious. The bottle of San Pellegrino water with dinner on a hot evening in Rome is something to look forward to.

Bottled waters are often divided into table waters, mineral waters (which are slightly medicinal), and medicinal waters, but it will be a matter of opinion where the line will be drawn. Some, such as the waters containing arsenic (La Bourboule and Royat), will never be drunk except on doctor's advice, and nobody drinks the sulfurous waters of Harrogate and Bath for fun.

At the opposite end of the scale are the very pure waters such as Evian, the largest-selling water in France, which is still and comes from springs in the French Alps (Haute Savoie), and Perrier, full of natural gas, from Vergèze in the South of France. Malvern water, from Worcestershire in the West of England, is still, pure, and very slightly alkaline. San Pellegrino, which comes from springs near Milan, is artificially gassed but is an excellent table water with a very refreshing taste. Solares from near Madrid is a good table water from Spain.

Slightly more mineralized waters are drunk because people like the taste or because of a diet, but are scarcely medicinal in the usual sense. Among them is Cichy Célestins, (Célestins, because there are other, openly medicinal Vichy springs) from the Allier valley near Vichy, Central France; it contains a relatively large amount of bicarbonate of soda and enough common salt to give it a salty taste. Others from France are Badoit, which is moderately alkaline and lightly gassed, and Contrexéville (Contrex), which is still and also slightly alkaline; it is mildly laxative, since it contains some magnesium sulfate (Epson salts), and is popular with French girls as a diet drink. In Germany, the most famous table water is Apollinaris, a strongly effervescent, very slightly alkaline water, from a spring in the valley of the Ahr in the Rhineland. Seltzer water from Oberselters in Westerwald, also in the Rhineland, is much imitated artificially all over the world, as is Vichy water. Other alkaline German waters are Johannis and Krontal, and optimists take them for hangovers. Dozens of varieties are reputedly good for "flushing out the kidneys," while others are purgative. Homburg, Marienbad, and Vittel contain iron.

In the past few years, scores of bottled waters have appeared on the U.S. market, including some mineral waters from former American health spas. Many of them are considered as fine as imported European bottled waters. The U.S. Food and Drug Administration has established standards of quality for bottled drinking water, which include: water must be from a pollution-free source, must be bottled under sanitary conditions, and must be free from coliform microorganisms; it must not be labeled with false or misleading therapeutic claims; additives such as salts and carbon dioxide must be declared on the label; artificially prepared waters may not be labeled "mineral water."

Undoubtedly the water you drink has a bearing on your health and may account for variations in medical statistics from area to area. The value of bottled table waters tend to be overstated by the advertising copy that goes with them—the good effect of taking the waters at spas was probably as much due to drinking some water instead of just wine as to anything else.

Water in cooking. Soft water is best for cooking, for making tea, for brines to make pickles, and for boiling vegetables. Hard or alkaline water may make cabbage greener, but it destroys vitamins. The cloudiness, due to chalk thrown out on boiling, is unsightly in cold tea; it may be dispelled by acidifying with lemon juice. Certain fountains in Rome have reputations for producing good cooking water, and several chefs I know regard the use of mineral water as one of their "secrets," especially in pastry and pasta. A water softener is helpful in kitchens where there is very hard water.

[*Water*—French: *eau;* German: *Wasser;* Italian: *acqua;* Spanish: *agua*]

WATER CHESTNUT. The common water chestnut (*Trapa natans*) is a floating water plant with sharply angled, diamond-shaped, serrated leaves that can be seen in streams in the eastern U.S. and in ponds and lakes in southern Europe. The fruits have four woody horns. The meat of the nut inside is floury and has a pleasant taste. It is sometimes eaten, usually after the nut has been boiled or roasted. Alternative names are water caltrops or Jesuits' bread. A closely allied species, Singhara nut (*T. bispinosa*), is an important local food in Kashmir, where it is grown in the lakes, while the other species of the genus, the Chinese *ling* (*T. bicornis*), has horns like a water buffalo and a similar chestnutlike kernel. It is much eaten in China, and a flour is made from it. In European cooking, water chestnuts are sliced and added to meats and stews; they are the main ingredient of a risotto made in the Loire region of France.

Gastronomically more important is Chinese water chestnut or *pi-tsi*, which is quite another thing, the tuber of a sedge (*Eleocharis tuberosa*) and not a nut at all. It is comparable to the *chufa nut (which also is not a nut but the tuber of a sedge). These water chestnuts are a common ingredient in Chinese food and can be bought canned in water. Like bamboo shoots, they retain their crispness when cooked. Their name comes from the appearance of the fresh tuber, which is chestnut-colored though otherwise only vaguely like a chestnut in appearance. The South American tuber *jicama*, which is sometimes substituted, is available in the U.S.

[*Water chestnut*—French: *saligot, macre, chataigne d'eau, corniolle;* German: *Wassernuss;* Italian: *frutto della castagno d'acqua*]

WATERCRESS. *See* cress.

WATER LEMON. *See* passionfruit.

WATERMELON. *See* melon.

WAX BEAN. Waxy-looking variety of *green bean.

WEATHER. Daily changes in barometric pressure make slight differences in the boiling point of water, but not large enough to cause trouble in the way that *altitude can. Temperature is of much greater importance (unless the kitchen is air-conditioned). For instance, a humid hot atmosphere is bad for pastrymaking, and good puff pastry is almost impossible to make and work with in a hot kitchen. In summer in Italy, when the weather is hot and dry, cooks have great difficulty in making shaped pasta like tortellini, because the paste dries and cracks before the dozens of little squares can be filled and twisted. In hot weather, you may have to make use of the refrigerator, even in such normally simple operations as making butter icing, but with operations too large for the household refrigerator to handle, you may well face disaster unless you do the work at night or very early in the morning. On the other hand, some preparations go better in warm weather; it is marginally more trouble to make mayonnaise and yogurt in winter than in summer.

[*Weather*—French: *temps;* German: *Wetter;* Italian: *tempo;* Spanish: *tiempo*]

WEIGHTS and measures. Ingredients are most easily measured out by volume, since this can be done with the simplest and least expensive equipment. The disadvantage is that it is inaccurate, particularly for measuring powdered or granular solids, because it does not take into account the size, shape, and evenness of the particles, or of the way they are packed into the measure.

However accurate measurement is mainly unnecessary in cooking (the exception is some baking). It is anyway silly to bother with fine fractions when the substances being measured are so variable in themselves. A rough measure is also good enough if it takes a fairly large variation to give a different result. We are not manufacturers called on to produce a standard article. People who painstakingly level off a quarter-teaspoon are rarely good cooks. They are usually trying to dodge the responsibility of making a judgment on the evidence provided by the eyes, tongue, and nose. But it can be equally disastrous to abandon measuring altogether. I am impressed by professional chefs who can usually recite the quantities of a recipe by heart, but who, when cooking, are continually making slight adjustments. They are using both measures and their senses in the very best way.

We have now entered an era of increasing standardization to metric measures, but this does not mean that we should throw away our old cookbooks. To do *conversions of weights to metric is only a matter of multiplying or using tables. It is also very simple to mark old spring-balance scales with the metric weights so that you have both (printed metric scales are sold for some old scales of standard makes). For volumes, it is best to keep sets of metric and American standard cups and spoons, and to work the recipe from the original. The cost of plastic measures is small, and the time saved soon pays for them. To avoid mistakes, have each set in a different color.

All systems of weights and measures start with something arbitrary. The grain was an average grain of wheat, the carat was a carob bean, and the Indian *masha* was the seed of the black gram. The innovation in the metric system was not in its basic unit, which in its way was as arbitrary as any, but because the various units were linked and made dependent one on the other. The other difference, of course, was the division of units into 10 parts. Very shortly, the old measures may be a matter of history, but we will still have our old cookbooks and it is another matter whether the old habits will completely die.

American and British volumes	Metric equivalents	
	British	American
1 gill	142 ml	118 ml
1 pint (pt) = 4 gills	568 ml	473 ml
2 pints = 1 quart (qt)	1136 ml	946 ml
4 quarts = 1 gallon (gal)	4.54 lt	3.79 lt

From the conversion table, you will see that while the Imperial pint is more than half a liter the U.S. pint is less. Up to the mid-19th century, British and American measures were the same, but on the other hand, a gallon of wine was 231 cubic inches although there was another gallon of 282 cubic inches for beer. On this basis, a gallon of water weighed roughly 8⅓ pounds; a pint did not weigh exactly a pound, nor did a fluid ounce, of which there were 16 to the pint, weigh exactly 1 ounce. In other words, the system was a mess. (You must remember in all this that a fluid ounce is a measure of volume, not of weight, and that the weight of a fluid ounce will vary according to the density of the substance being measured.)

In the 19th century, the British made an attempt to rationalize things by making a new gallon, an Imperial gallon, which was a measure of water weighing 10 lb (instead of 8⅓ as previously) and equaling 277 cubic inches. In 1864, the apothecaries' fluid ounce was changed to be exactly an ounce of water, which gave 20 instead of 16 fluid ounces to the pint. American measures stayed put. This has had British and American cooks, publishers, and food manufacturers swearing ever since.

For small quantities in the kitchen, the difference between American and British fluid ounces can be ignored. In fact, the British fluid ounce is 28.4 ml and the American is 29.6 ml. This means that the conversion rate between British 20 fl oz pints and American 16 fl oz ones is not, as you might expect, 20:16 but 6:5.

With weights, the situation is a little simpler, since the smaller measures are the same on both sides of the Atlantic. The

Avoirdupois (British)		
	1 dram or drachm (dr)	(1.77 g)
16 drams	= 1 ounce (oz)	(28.35 g)
16 ounces	= 1 pound (lb)	(453.6 g)
14 pounds	= 1 stone (st)	(6.34 Kg)
28 pounds	= 1 quarter	
4 quarters or 112 pounds	= 1 hundredweight (cwt)	(50.8 Kg)
20 hundredweights	= 1 ton	(1016 Kg)

American avoirdupois system is basically the same except that the stone has been dropped and the large commercial weights have been rounded off.

100 pounds	= 1 hundredweight	(45.4 Kg)
20 hundredweights	= 1 ton	(907 Kg)

The British ton of 2240 lbs is known as a long ton and the American ton of 2000 lbs is called a short ton. The British ton is closer to the metric ton or tonne, which is 1000 Kg (2205 lb).

Kitchen measures. In Britain and Europe, most kitchens have scales, but in the U.S., standard cups and spoons are usually used to measure both liquids and solids. This system is less accurate and sometimes means that the textures of solids must be specified—for example, a cup of coarse salt does not weigh the same as a cup of fine salt. There is actually a British standard measuring cup, but it has never been very popular, and British households tend to rely on ordinary cups and spoons or to use a graduated measure. Although crockery is not standardized, the approximate sizes of cups are as follows: breakfast cup, 7–8 fl oz (200–225 ml); teacup, 5 fl oz (140–145 ml); coffee cup, 3 fl oz (80–85 ml). The British standard cup in Imperial measures is ½ pt or 10 fl oz, and 4 British cups are thus roughly the same as 5 U.S. cups (which are 8 U.S. fl oz each). The British but not the Americans use the dessertspoon, which is 2 teaspoons (10 ml), but the teaspoon and the tablespoon are the same on both sides of the Atlantic. For measuring solid ingredients, all spoons are level ones unless otherwise stated in the recipe.

American Cups and Spoons

		1 teaspoon	5 ml
3 teaspoons	= 1 tablespoon	½ U.S. fl oz	15 ml
2 tablespoons	=	1 U.S. fl oz	30 ml
16 tablespoons	= 1 cup	8 U.S. fl oz	236 ml
2 cups	= 1 U.S. pint	16 U.S. fl oz	473 ml

Can sizes. Most cans these days are well labeled to show how much they contain. However, American recipes may confuse non-American readers by specifying quantities of canned ingredients in U.S. can sizes, which are as follows:

8 oz	= 1 cup (U.S.)
Buffet	= 1 cup
Picnic	= 1¼ cups

No. 300	= 1¾ cups
No. 1 tall	= 2 cups
No. 303	= 2 cups
No. 2	= 2½ cups
No. 2½	= 3½ cups
No. 3 cylinder	= 5¾ cups
No. 10	= 12–13 cups

Shop and market measures. In the past, many solid foods were sold by volume measure. The measure itself is cheap and portable, while the measuring itself is easy and quick. Things bought by the measure included not only seeds like grains of wheat, which will pour, but less manageable things like mussels and shrimps. As long as the commodity was reasonably cheap, the inaccuracies inherent in the system did not matter and were more than offset by the pleasure of being able to buy a measure of absolutely fresh shrimps straight from the boat. The larger measures on both sides of the Atlantic are:

4 quarts	= 1 gallon
2 gallons	= 1 peck
4 pecks	= 1 bushel
8 bushels	= 1 quarter
36 bushels	= 1 chaldron

However, it is easy to cheat in filling a measure, and therefore many of the traditional volumes were defined legally in terms of weights of particular commodities. The following list contains some of these and some other old measures.

Bushel	Wheat	60 lb (U.K. and U.S.)
	Barley	56 lb (U.K.)
		48 lb (U.S., but 32–50 lb in various states)
	Oats	39 lb (U.K.)
		32 lb (U.S.)
	Rye	60 lb (U.K.)
		56 lb (U.S.)
	Corn	56 lb (U.S., but 52–56 lb in various states)
	Potatoes	60 lb (U.S., but 56 lb in North Carolina and West Virginia)
Quarter	Wheat	480 lb (U.K.)
Peck	Flour	14 lb
Bag	Cocoa	112 lb
	Coffee	140–148 lb
	Sugar	112–196 lb

	Rice	168 lb
	Black Pepper	316 lb
	White pepper	168 lb
	Hops	280 lb
	Sago	112 lb
Sack	Flour	280 lb
	Potatoes	168 lb
Chest	Tea	84 lb
	Cloves	200 lb
Matt	Cloves	80 lb
Pocket	Hops	168–224 lb
Hogshead	Sugar	13–16 cwt
Barrel	Anchovies	30 lb
	Butter	224 lb (or 4 firkins)
	Raisins	256 lb
	Beef	200 lb
	Flour	196 lb (U.S.)

Some commodities had their own elaborate vocabulary of measures. For example, a cran of herrings in Scotland was 37½ gallons; a maze of herrings in Ireland and the Isle of Man was 615 fish; a warp was 4 herrings; a long hundred was 33 warps or 132 herrings; ten hundred was 1320 herrings.

Other weights and measures. European cookbooks and most early-American ones rarely devote space to defining exactly what they mean by a glass, a cup, or a spoon. On the occasions when greater accuracy is needed, a measure may be qualified by an exact metric weight. More often, spoons are used as a measure, and the pinch, the knife point, and the drop seem adequate to convey small amounts. Self-confident cooks, however schooled, are familiar with their own cooking traditions and do not feel the need for hair-splitting measures. As one Italian chef put it, "Cooking is a living art and so recipes should not become fixed." After all, different conductors give markedly different renderings of Beethoven, even though they may be using the same score. In cooking, we must avoid the soulless metronome beat of fussy weighing.

There are a few terms that may require explanation. In France, a *bonne livre* (i.e., a good pound) means 500 g. (The *livre* was one of the old measures in use up to the French Revolution; it weighed 489.5 g and was 16 *onces*, so that an *once* was 30.6 g—

the system was like avoirdupois although the quantities were not identical.) For small quantities, a pinch (*pincé*) or drop (*goutte*) are common descriptions. A *cuillerée* is a spoonful, and a *cuiller* or *cuillère* (spoon) can be taken to be a tablespoon but may be more accurately defined as *une cuillère à bouche* (a tablespoon), as opposed to *une cuillère à café* (a teaspoon). Other rough measures are *une tasse* (a cup), *une tasse à thé* (a teacup), *un verre* (a glass), and *un verre à liqueur* (a liqueur glass).

Italians use the metric system, and recipes are in *grammi, kilogrammi, litri,* and *decilitri.* An *etto* or *ettogrammo* is a hectogram (100 g), a common measure, as are half (*mezzo*) and quarter (*quarto*) of the metric measures (e.g., *un quarto di litro di vino bianco*—a quarter of a liter of white wine). *Una cucchiaiata* is a spoonful, *un cucchiaio* being a spoon, normally a tablespoon (*cucchiaio da tavola*). A *cucchiaino* is a teaspoon. Equally, Italian recipes use glasses (*un bicchiere di vino bianco*—a glass of white wine); you are expected to have some idea of how much wine to use in spite of the fact that this varies with the acidity of the wine, but as a basis you can take a wineglass as being a bit less than an American cup (8 fl oz). Problems come with the many Italian variants. *Un bicchierino di cognac* (a little glass), *un pizzico* or *una pizzicata* (a pinch), and *un pezzetto* (a small piece) are straightforward, but then there are *una manciata* (a handful) and *una manciatona* (a big handful). Herbs, which are much used fresh in Italian cooking, are usually given in terms such as *una foglia di lauro* (a leaf of bay), *un gambo di sedano* (a stalk of celery), *un spicchio d'aglio* (a clove of garlic), *un rametto di rosmarino* (a sprig of rosemary). Other useful Italian quantity words are *una puntina* (a point—very small amount), *un noce* (a walnut), *una scatola* (a tin), *una bustina* (a small envelope—e.g. of yeast), or *una fetta* (a slice).

The Spanish also give their recipes in metric weights and measures, *kilos, grammos, litros,* and *decilitros,* but also in *cucha-*

radas (spoonfuls) and *cucharaditas* (teaspoonfuls) as well as *vasos* (glasses), *tazas* (cups), *tacitas* (little cups), and *copas* (small glasses). Spoons may be *colmada* (heaped), or *escasa* (scant), even *muy colmada* (very heaped). *Hojas* are leaves (*un hoja de laurel* is a bay leaf). For garlic, a *cabeza* is a head and a *diente* is a clove. *Un trozo de cebolla* is a slice of onion. *Un rodaja de chorizo* is a round of chorizo (sausage). A *ramita* is a sprig, as in a *ramita de perejil* (a sprig of parsley). A *papelillo* is a little paper or envelope, as in *papelillo de azafrán* (a small packet of saffron). Spanish recipes often go in for fractions of a liter, as in ⅛ *litro de leche* (⅛ liter of milk). Who would say 12.5 deciliters outside a laboratory?

As acceptance of the metric system spread across the globe, national systems of measures were progressively eliminated. The Greeks, for example, had the *oke,* which was 1.27 Kg (2.8 lb); the Arabs had the *okieh,* which was 213 g (7½ oz) and the *rotl* of 2.5 Kg (5½ lb). In Malaysia, the basic measure of weight was the *tahil* of 38 g (1⅓ oz), 16 of which made a *katty* or *kati* of 605 g (7⅓ lb); volumes were the *chupak* and the *quantang,* respectively about a quart and about a gallon (Imperial). In India, the *tola* was 11 g (0.4 oz), the weight of a rupee coin, and was divided into 12 *mashas.* Larger units were the *chattak* or *chitak* (5 *tolas*), the *powa, pau,* or *pav* (4 *chattaks*), the *seer* (4 *powas,* 2 lb, or 930 g), and the *maund* (40 *seers*). Perhaps the most amazing of all measures was an Indian measure of volume, the *tin,* based on the cylindrical tin which was the export pack of 50 Player's Navy Cut cigarettes; it held 8 fl oz and was thus the same as an American cup.

Compared to all this confusion, the delight of the metric system lies in its simplicity. Although we have a plethora of metric units, the kitchen basics of weight and volume are taken care of by just four. Volume need be thought of only in cubic centimeters or milliliters (same thing) and in liters, which are 1000 ml. Weights will be expressed in grams or Kilograms (1000 g). For all practical purposes, the gram and Kilogram are the weights of respectively a milliliter and a liter of water. Life will be much simpler when we are all thinking metric, but for the moment it is useful to have simple formulas for rough *conversions.

WHALE. In the first edition of Thomas Pennant's *Natural History,* published in the 18th century, whales are classified with fishes. We now know that they are not only mammals but highly evolved and sensitive ones that suffer greatly from the explosive harpoons fired into their bellies. Because many of the species of whale have been almost hunted to extinction, where previously they were found by the thousand, the commercial hunting of whales has been banned by most, but unfortunately not all, countries.

Whale oil, which is obtained by rendering the blubber, was until recently an important ingredient in margarine (it is still used in Japan and Russia). After refining, it is a clear, flavorless oil and suitable for cooking. Whale meat at its best is good—like rather coarse and porous beef. On the *Norsel* in the Antarctic, we used to eat steaks cut from the back of a young cachalot (reputedly one of the best), but it had first been hung up for several weeks to drain, since fresh whale meat is watery. The taste was good, provided that every bit of the brown inside— where the air had caused oxidation—was removed. If any of this was left, even a tiny amount, the taste became fishy or tinny. Just after World War II, whale meat was often sold in Britain, but it was cut in square steaks and exposed to the air, the surest way to give it that unpleasant overtone. It was, I am sure, this ignorant handling that got whale meat its bad reputation. So if for any reason you are faced with eating whale, keep the meat in large chunks—44 lb (20 Kg) is not too much—hang them in cold conditions to drain, and cut steaks only as you need them. Be very careful to trim off all brown or discolored meat (for the dog) right down to the red meat inside, then cook immediately. Whale meat is good treated as steak and onions, and I have no doubt that some Burgundy would help it.

[*Whale*—French: *baleine;* German: *Wal;* Italian: *balena;* Spanish: *ballena*]

WHEAT has been cultivated in Eurasia for at least 6000 years. It was unknown in America until after 1529, when it was taken to Mexico by the Spaniards. It is a staple grain of most of the world—wheat, rather than rice, is eaten in northern India and northern China. As is usual with plants that have been cultivated for thousands of years, the exact origin of wheat is uncertain. There are several species involved, and many hybrids. Some ancient wheats, with romantic names such as spelt and einkorn, are mainly of interest to the plant breeder, although they are still occasionally cultivated in primitive conditions or used as fodder mixed with other grasses, as are emmer (*Triticum dicoccum*) and English wheat (*T. turgidum*). By far the most important wheat is the common wheat or bread wheat (*T. aestivum*), which may be red or white in color, hard or soft in texture, winter or spring grown. Also of importance are the amber or durum wheats (*T. durum*), which have long flinty grains and high protein; they are of little use for cakes or bread, but they make the finest pasta. They are grown around the Mediterranean and in other parts of the world where there are similar dry conditions.

A farmer has to choose wheats that are suitable for his land and climate. He may choose winter wheat (which will stand over winter) or spring wheat (which is sown in the spring and harvested later the same year), but from the cook's point of view the difference is not very significant. In cooking, it is the distinctions between hard and soft wheat that are important. Hard wheat consists of flinty, rather translucent grains which are relatively rich in protein and have good milling characteristics, whereas soft wheat grains are opaque and rather starchy; they produce fluffy, amorphous particles when milled. Although there are exceptions,

flours from hard wheats tend to be strong (which is to say that they make loaves of good volume and texture). In contrast, soft wheats yield flours that are usually weak and of poorer breadmaking quality, although they are best for making biscuits, cakes, and pastries.

Wheat, like most other cereals, is a grass, and the grains are arranged in a tightly packed inflorescence called the ear, from which they are separated during threshing. Nowadays threshing is usually one of the processes that is done in a combine harvester. The outside of the grain consists of several different layers, five of which are removed as *bran during *milling. At one end of the grain there is a tuft of fine hairs known as the beard, and at the other end, somewhat to the side, is the germ or embryo. The inside of the wheat grain is known as the endosperm and is the food reserve, to be used by the seed when it first sprouts. The endosperm makes up about 85% of the grain, the bran 13%, and the germ only 2%. There is a crease in the wheat grain which is a nuisance to millers because it interferes with the clean removal of the bran.

Although wheat is mainly ground to a flour, it may also be boiled whole (but hulled) in milk when fresh to make into frumenty, a pudding flavored with cinnamon, or it may be boiled and crushed to make *burghul, or even sprouted to make a type of malt for brewing.

[*Wheat*—French: *blé;* German: *Weizen;* Italian: *grumento, grano;* Spanish: *trigo*]

WHEAT GERM is the embryo plant, which is removed and separated from the wheat germ during the milling of white flour and is sold as a separate product. Wheat germ is rich in proteins, fats, minerals, and vitamins B_1, B_2, B_6, and E. However, health considerations apart, fresh wheat germ has a delicious flavor. It may be mixed with white flour to give its taste to bread. I like to eat it raw with fresh cream.

Once a container of wheat germ has been

opened, it should be kept in the refrigerator, since the oil it contains quickly goes rancid—the reason why whole-meal flour does not keep well. Wheat-germ oil, extracted by pressing, has a powerful flavor; it is too costly to use in the kitchen, but may be beneficial as a diet supplement. It rapidly deteriorates on exposure to air, and, once opened, a bottle should be kept in the refrigerator, well closed and quickly used.

WHELK (*Buccinum undatum*) is a carnivorous gastropod, a large marine snail, which is credited in some folklore with gargantuan aphrodisiac powers. The waved whelk is almost unknown to most Americans, although it is plentiful on this side of the Atlantic from Newfoundland to Cape Hatteras. On the other side of the ocean it is much appreciated, and it is usually discriminating immigrants from those countries who seek out whelks in the U.S.

Whelks have beautiful spired and whorled shells. Most people think the creatures are best when they are small. An old English method for small ones is to allow them to cleanse themselves for an hour or so in water and to boil them for 45 minutes in salt water or sea water before eating with vinegar like *winkles. Large ones, according to this method, are boiled for as long as an hour and a half, taken from their shells, coated with bread crumbs, and fried. Some whelks are so large they are eaten as steaks. The French, who realize that boiling any shellfish, except for a long period, makes them tough, poach whelks for only 15 minutes. In Quebec, whelks are canned in a marinade of sugar and spiced vinegar.

Other species, apart from *Buccinum undatum*, are sold as whelks. All these gastropods vary in toughness, but none of them is exactly tender, and none is usually described as a delicacy, although their flesh can be sweet and succulent.

[*Whelk*—French: *buccin;* German: *Wellhorschnecke;* Italian: *buccino, bollicina;* Spanish: *buccino*]

WHEY. When milk is curdled, either by rennet or by souring, the liquid that runs from the curd is called whey. It is regarded as healthful, since it contains all the ingredients of milk except the casein and fat, but is often thrown away. It can form the basis for soup—I always make gazpacho with the sour whey drained from yogurt cheese. In Scandinavian countries, the whey drained off when other cheeses are made is turned into the popular whey cheese *mysost*. To make this, the slightly sour whey is boiled until it is reduced to a brown, sticky mass consisting mainly of partly caramelized lactose. During the boiling, any coagulated albuminous material that forms a scum is skimmed off and kept aside to be mixed back into the cheese later. Sometimes brown sugar is added, or spices, such as caraway, cumin, and even cloves, are used as flavoring. When the boiling is finished, after 5–6 hours, the volume is reduced to about a quarter of the original. Now the skimmings are returned and stirred in well; stirring continues throughout the time that the mass is cooling to prevent the formation of sugar crystals which would make the cheese grainy. When it is set, the *mysost* is allowed to set, cut in blocks, waxed, and wrapped.

There are many variants of this cheese. *Gjetost* is made from the whey of goat's milk, *primost* or *flotøst* is softer and contains more fat, and *gomost* is made by the same technique but from whole milk. The flavor of whey cheese is sweet and, to most people not brought up on it, is an acquired taste. (For instance, it was endlessly on the table during the voyage south with the Norwegian-British-Swedish Antarctic expedition of which I was once a member, but I always disliked the sweetness and longed for a piece of really cheesy cheese.)

Some 40 billion lb (18 billion Kg) of whey are annually produced in the U.S. as a by product of the cheese industry, and cheesemakers are ever alert to ways to use it profitably, especially since environmental laws now forbid dumping it in rivers. The most recent discovery is wine made from whey, which reportedly is clear, yellow, dry, and tart. Baking is supposed to turn it into an amber sherry, and it can be aged to become brandy.

[*Whey*—French: *petit lait;* German: *Molke;* Italian: *siero di latta;* Spanish: *suero* (*de la leche*)]

WHIFF. *See* lemon sole.

WHIPPING is also called whisking (which usually applies only to egg white) and beating (which may apply to many things and implies heavier work). It is a texture-producing operation and involves frothing up and the introduction of air bubbles into whatever is being whipped—nearly always either cream or egg white. Although it seems to be a very simple operation, there are a number of points to be considered. For instance, the size of the air bubbles: with a given amount of egg white, we can obviously get a greater bulk of beaten egg if the bubbles are large than if they are small, but the froth will not be so strong mechanically and will collapse more easily. This means that we are not only concerned with the length of time and degree of whipping (because the longer the whipping, the smaller are the bubbles), but also with the implements we use.

Implements and utensils. Chefs use balloon whisks and copper bowls—one of the few places where unlined copper is normal—but such apparatus, though it is undoubtedly the best, is expensive. Smaller wire whisks and any glass or china bowl will do almost as good a job, and wire coil whisks are as good or better for whisking egg white. With electric beaters, it is easy to overdo the whipping—they are so quick that things can be spoiled in a second. Hand-held electric whisks are better than the fixed models, since they can be used more flexibly. The old hand-turned type of whisk is—or should be—obsolete. It needs two hands, is hard work, and does not do as good a job as a simple, inexpensive coil whisk.

Whipping cream. In some places, whipping *cream is sold. It is a grade in between light and heavy cream, or a mixture of the two. Heavy cream but not light cream can also be whipped. Cream should be whipped only to the point where it will hold a peak. If whipping is carried on after that, the cream will turn to butter. Sour cream very rapidly thickens but will not whip properly because it turns too easily to butter.

Whipping egg white. Egg white has a very special capacity for holding air bubbles when it is beaten. The eggs should be very fresh—really stale egg white can hardly be beaten at all. The white of egg contains several proteins, but the most important from the point of view of beating are the *albumins, particularly ovalbumin, which foams best in acid conditions. Acid also tenderizes protein and makes it stretch more easily. Therefore a pinch of cream of tartar is often added to egg white to be beaten (but for meringues is likely to make the result rather sticky). Salt also helps foaming, and sugar helps in two ways: it gives the foam stability and helps mechanically to get air into the mass. Fat, on the other hand, is the enemy of foaming—not even a speck of egg yolk must be allowed to get into the white when eggs are separated, and the bowl must be free from grease and from any traces of detergent. In practice, chefs add the acid and salt at the beginning and the sugar when the eggs are nearly whipped. However, fresh eggs at room temperature in a clean bowl should whisk up without difficulty.

The degree to which egg white is beaten is very important in cooking. The more the eggs are beaten, the more the egg white is stretched, and it can be beaten (overbeaten) to the point where it can stretch no more. The bubbles cannot then be inflated further when the air inside expands in baking. The stages are as follows: 1. Large bubbles. The white is still runny and it is little more than mixed well. It is used for blending with liquids, for coating, and for clearing stock. 2. Smaller, but still fair-sized bubbles. The peaks are rounded and will not stand up. Used for sponge cakes, soufflés, and foamy omelets. 3. Small air bubbles. The stiff foam stands in peaks; it is smooth, with no fluidity. For meringues, cake icing, and some cakes. 4. Dry and brittle. It can be cut or pulled into bits. The proteins will not stretch any more and so are no good for most purposes.

[*Whipping*—French: *battre* (eggs), *fouetter* (cream); German: *schlagen;* Italian: *sbattere;* Spanish: *batidor*]

WHISKEY or **whisky.** The spelling is whisky for Scotch and Canadian, whiskey for Irish and American. The word is a corruption of the Gaelic *uisge* (water) *beatha* (life)—*usquebaugh* in Ireland—a translation of the Latin *aqua vitae* (water of life), since spirits were originally medicinal. The art of *distillation was brought over from the Continent by monks. Although the first known written reference to the drink is as late as 1494, whiskey must have been made long before that. Distilling whiskey soon became usual kitchen work on many Scottish farms. Since it was distilled only twice, there was no danger of explosion, and the work was well within the capability of even the servant lasses, let alone the farmers' wives. In those halcyon days, there was no excise duty—Parliament borrowed that idea from the Dutch to raise money to fight Charles I, and it has stayed ever since.

Barley grown on the farm was wetted and sprouted, dried over a peat fire (which gave a smoky taste), ground to a grist, mixed with water, and set in a warm place for enzymes to work. The sugary result was mashed with yeast and left to ferment (very much as in *brewing). The alcoholic result was distilled, always in pot stills of much the same sort as are used to make malt whiskey to this day. Blended Scotch, which we know best (the world now drinks more than 100 million gallons of it every year), was then unknown.

By law, all whiskey must today be at least 3 years old before it may be sold for consumption in Britain, and similar laws apply in other countries, although the minimum time may be up to 5 years. In practice, however, whiskey is usually matured for much longer than is required by law.

The newly distilled spirit is placed for maturing in casks made of oak, which is permeable and allows the air to pass into the whiskey and evaporation to occur. During this process, certain undesirable secondary constituents are removed, producing a mellow and mature whiskey. The period of maturation is affected by the size of the casks, the strength at which the spirit is stored, and the temperature and humidity of the warehouse. The lighter grain whiskeys require less time to mature than the fuller, more mellow malt whiskeys, which are often left in the casks for 15 years or more.

Malt whiskey is made from malted barley and is distilled in pot stills. There are 117 distilleries making malt whiskey in Scotland. The whiskey from each has its own characteristic aroma and flavor, just as wines from different vineyards have theirs. Exactly why this should be so is not fully understood, in spite of enormous efforts to find out. Some of the difference comes from the water and some from the peat used to dry the malt— the air and climate may even play a part. However, if peat and water, together with Scottish distillers, are taken from Scotland to other parts of the world, the whiskey never turns out as well as it does in Scotland.

Even the lowliest malt whiskeys are more expensive than the everyday brands of blended whiskey, which contain grain spirit. Some are in limited supply and are mostly exported, while others are used mainly by the blenders. In addition to straight malts from single distilleries, there are also blended ones in which malt whiskeys only are mixed. If the age of blended whiskey is specified, it must by law be the age of the youngest used in the mixture and not an average. Malts should be drunk neat or with a little good cool water. Ice and soda water both destroy the flavor.

Grain whiskey is made largely from unmalted grain. The starch in the grist is converted to sugars by mixing it with malt which has an excess enzyme capacity. The sugary liquid can now be fermented. Distillation is carried out in continuous patent stills. Grain whiskey is very light, with almost no taste of its own. Most of the huge output from modern plants goes for blending with malts.

Blended whiskey has been made since about 1860. It uses the highly rectified spirit that is produced by the patent stills. Such spirit contains little of the congenerics which give malt whiskey its taste, and incidentally its power to produce hangovers, but blending with tasty malts results in a light product with good flavor. It is also more consistent, a great commercial asset, since the expert blender could add varying quantities of different malts to the basic grain whiskey and obtain an almost constant result. Coloring could be done with caramel. The ever growing popularity of blended Scotch as a drink has led many people to try to make it elsewhere, notably in Japan, but it has never been reproduced exactly.

Irish whiskey is made in much smaller quantity than Scotch. It is made only in pot stills—but in very large ones—and from a mixture of malt and unmalted grain, the excess diastase in the malt being able to convert the starch in the grain to sugars. Irish whiskey is distilled three times (not twice like Scotch) and thus is relatively tasteless to begin with. It acquires its flavor during maturation in casks. Casks are vital to Irish whiskey and one of the main skills in its making lies in deciding the proportions of whiskey to be mixed from different sorts of cask. Sherry casks (for a full flavor), new casks, American casks, and sometimes rum and brandy casks are used.

American whiskey. Corn whiskeys, as made in the early days, were often pretty rough, as names like Old Tomahawk, Busthead, and Red Eye attest. The tradition of fearsome home brews in the U.S. continued when their evolution was temporarily slowed down by the Volstead Act. During Prohibition, people drank what they could get. Commercial distillation is now carried out almost exclusively in huge continuous stills; the old pot stills have long since been replaced. The most famous American corn whiskey is bourbon, named after Bourbon County in Kentucky. It is said to have been discovered accidentally in 1789, when a Reverend Elijah Craig, who was a farmer as well as a preacher, put his whiskey (already good because of the local water) into charred barrels of white oak to mature. The resulting whiskey was exceptional, and to this day Kentucky bourbon is famous. The law, however, recognizes bourbon as whiskey made with a particular technique, and so bourbons are produced in other states and even in Canada. They are still legally bourbon if they are distilled from a mash of at least 55% corn and matured for at least 2 years in new, charred white oak casks in unheated warehouses. Bourbon must also be not less than 80 U.S. proof. Unblended bourbons are called "straight," and those "bottled in bond" have been stored under government supervision for 4–8 years as well as being "straight" and 100 proof. The more ordinary blended bourbons are usually around 87 proof. They have less taste and less congenerics.

Other corn whiskeys abound, and one of the great pleasures of a visit to the U.S. is organizing a tasting session; this can be easily arranged in any bar. The term "sour mash"—as opposed to "sweet mash"—means that the wort (called beer in America) is fermented with sour residues, while sweet mash is fermented only with fresh yeast. There is a considerable difference in taste.

Rye whiskey, as the name suggests, is made with a high proportion of rye (which is sometimes also used in other whiskeys) as well as barley. The method of making rye is not much different, but it is matured in heated warehouses to achieve its individual flavor. Rice spirit is in essence a whiskey.

*Liqueurs based on whiskey include

Drambuie and Glayva. In recent years, following the worldwide upsurge of the popularity of whiskey as a drink, it has also come to be used as an ingredient in cooking. Dishes such as *fagiano* (pheasant) *al whisky, scampi al whisky,* and *langouste au whisky* now appear in Mediterranean restaurants, where whiskey hardly penetrated before. In fact, whiskey is a good spirit for flaming and, according to Elizabeth David in *French Provincial Cooking* (Penguin, 1970), can substitute for Calvados if the real thing is not to hand.

[*Whiskey*—French: *whiskey;* German: *Whisky;* Italian: *whisky;* Spanish: *whisky*

WHISKING. *See* whipping.

WHITEBAIT are small fish, no more than 2 in. (5 cm) long, which are caught in quantity in shoals in the estuaries of some British rivers, notably the Thames. In Victorian times, whitebait were given a specific scientific name, *Clupea alba,* but they are now known to be the fry of sprats and herrings in Britain.

In other parts of the world, young fish of different species are highly regarded and are eaten in season. In the U.S., whitebait may be the young of such fish as herring, anchovies, and what are known as grunion on the California coast, where the fish swarm to spawn in white sand and are caught by fishermen with flashlights. The French catch baby fish called *blanchaille,* and in most Mediterranean countries tiny sardines, along with a few anchovies, are eaten.

Whitebait, whatever their scientific name, are usually not gutted but merely coated with flour and fried in hot oil. Flouring needs to be done with some care—if freshly rinsed fish are dumped into a bag of flour, the result is heavy lumps of dough with fish tails sticking out of it. The fish must be almost dry before they are shaken in seasoned flour.

Notably in Liguria and in Mediterranean Spain, very tiny fry are also sold. They are so small that they look like a mass of jelly with thousands of pinpoint eyes in it. This mass, known as *gianchetti* or *bianchetti* in Italy (and *poutine* in France) is mixed with egg and made into omelets or can form the basis for a fish soup. It is rather expensive and very nutritious. Any other such small fish can be treated in the same manner.

[*Whitebait*—French: *blanchaille;* German: *Sprotte;* Italian: *pesciolini;* Spanish: *chanquetes*]

WHITING. *See* cod.

WHORTLEBERRY. *See* bilberry.

WIENERWURST is the rival to the *frankfurter for the honor of having been the original hot dog sausage. It contains pork plus beef or veal, lightly cured and chopped. The sausages are smoked, poached in water, and hung up to dry. How far wienies differ from franks is another matter. In some cases, the meat may be less finely ground; in others, the only difference is in the name and hence the city to which their origin is ascribed.

WILD RICE, Indian rice, or **Tuscarora rice** is a large, handsome grass (*Zizania aquatica*) native to the eastern and central parts of North America; it also grows in Formosa, China, and Japan. Wild rice, which is not in any way a variety of rice, grows in shallow lakes and ponds; at a distance, the plants look like any other reed bed. The species has spread outside its original area and over much of the U.S., since it has been planted as food for waterfowl as well as for commercial harvesting. Originally it was an important wild food used by Americans Indians—Sioux and Chippewas often fought over it—and Indians still harvest much of the crop today.

The ripe grain is harvested by shaking the plumelike heads of the grass directly over a boat. The wild rice, which is purplish black, is spread out to dry, and must then be husked. In the traditional Indian method, this is done by first parching it (stirring it over a low fire for an hour in an iron or earthenware pot), lightly pounding it, rubbing it between the hands, then treading on it. When the husk is loosened, the grain is tossed in a light breeze to winnow off the chaff. Machines can do much of this work today.

Before being used, wild rice should be washed to take away the smoky taste. It can then be boiled, like rice, in lightly salted water until the rice grains puff open. It takes about 45 minutes, maybe more, to cook, but should not become mushy. Then it should be drained and left to steam over boiling water for 10 minutes. You should get 5 cups of cooked wild rice from each cup of raw rice. Wild rice, nowadays an expensive delicacy, is sold in packets ready to cook. It goes well with chicken and turkey, with pheasant and quail, and with any delicately flavored food, such as oysters and mushrooms. Turkey stuffed with it is a traditional Thanksgiving dish in Minnesota, and it also makes a good stuffing for baked fish. Wild rice can be ground to a flour and mixed (25%) into ordinary flour to make batter for pancakes and muffins.

WINE. Wine is the natural partner of most great European cooking, in which relatively few dishes call for beer or stronger spirits, and most of the world's wine is produced in Europe or places that have been colonized by Europeans. So close is the partnership between wine and food that many European dishes are considerably diminished without accompanying spirits from the vine, but wine is now so ubiquitous that few cuisines have been unaffected by it.

A small number of rich connoisseurs can buy wines so good that it becomes legitimate for them to choose the food to go with their wines and not vice versa. Anything that might spoil their delicate appreciation by an intrusive food flavor must be avoided. Vinegar or orange juice will drive them crazy—in spite of the tourists' depraved love of sangría, orange and wine do not go well together. Tons of garlic, handfuls of herbs, or Indian spicing will not be welcomed either, though they will not spoil the wine.

The occasions when food must give way to wine are rare. Usually wine is chosen to complement the food, to make it taste better, and for this reason (if for no other), cooks must take an interest in it. In a sense, wine is as much a cook's business as the sauces or the garnish. Every cook should therefore possess at least one of the many books on wine and know something about it—since many excellent paperbacks are available, no one can plead poverty. On the other hand, avoid becoming a wine snob. Wines are like paintings—it is easy to recognize the great masters, but few can afford to buy them. As for the rest, your opinion is as good as anyone else's. It is best to buy what you like, can afford, and can live with. It is significant that people in wine-drinking countries like to drink their wine, not sniff it. Any real wine lover who is invited to dinner will not swirl the wine in his glass, hold it up to the light, or take a large slurp and chew it. Neither will he groan audibly. He will only ask that the wine be properly married to the food, however humble. Some dishes indeed need rough wine. (But it is a mistake to think that any dish, even a curry, can be so highly spiced that you cannot distinguish good wine from bad through it.) To buy wines of better quality than are suitable for the food is extravagant and silly.

Cooking with wine. In wine-drinking countries—which means the Mediterranean countries, Portugal, and parts of Spanish America—wine, like Everest, is simply there. In some drier places, it may be easier to get than water and is always at hand to slosh into the food without a second thought. For this reason, wine in food was seized upon by more northern people as a symbol of nostalgic Mediterranean sunshine. The error in this is that you can have too much of it, as of all good things. Whole books are devoted to cooking with wine as if it were some magic ingredient synonymous with

French cooking or gastronomic ecstasy, not just another ingredient like, say, water. Wine is supposed to be great, a big deal—a dash of wine will "gourmetize" anything from Irish stew to hamburgers. It will not. Wine is something to be used appropriately and is no more the hallmark of great cooking than are lashings of cream or butter. It is true that in some parts of the European continent up to a third of the meat dishes, particularly chicken or game, contain wine, and wine may also be in a number of fish dishes. (It is rare to find wine in vegetable dishes.) But they are not necessarily the best dishes. And what wine! A number of books seem to suggest that food can be improved by using wine dregs collected from a number of bottles, and many are not discriminating about the wine to be used. Nobody would suggest saving ends of bottles for cooking except in countries blighted by a Protestant tax ideology (or in lucky houses where the supply is so liberal that ends of bottles are left over). Apart from the fact that anyone who does much Italian cooking will need a bottle of Marsala in the cupboard (as well as the more usual bottles of dry sherry and port), there are a certain number of rules about wine in food to be formulated:

Be selective about the dishes to which you add wine. A serious cook who is not too impoverished does *not* save dregs or use vinegar. (If you are too impoverished, it is better to move to a Mediterranean country.)

Cooks should be conscious of the effects of different wines and register that any old bottle will not improve a dish simply because it has wine on the label. The wine used in a dish is critical. It should ideally be a wine from the district where the dish comes from (until you have learned to improve on it) and should be something you would drink. In a wine country who would keep bad wine in the house just to use in the cooking?

It is perfectly easy for any cook to choose wines for the kitchen. It needs only some experimentation (and drinking the balance, a pleasurable enterprise). Then the wines selected on price and quality should be rebottled in *small* bottles. The best way is to use small, wine-glass-sized plastic bottles, fill them, squeeze them so that the wine just reaches the top, and seal them with no air inside. The wine will keep good for months. An alternative is to use one of those modern devices with a plastic bag and a spiggot, which means that the wine never gets exposed to air.

Anyone who cares should be able to keep a supply of good wine on tap in the kitchen. As for choosing the wine, even at the lowest level, be careful to avoid wine that is "chemical." Frankly, what is "chemical" is difficult to discover. Everyone in the wine countries talks about it, but nobody will answer honest questions. For many years I bought my house wine from a small winery. It was cheap and good. Later it became less good, and my neighbor, a local man, told me it was now chemical. It seemed to me unlikely, but when I try to cook with this wine, it breaks—becomes thin and acid. Experienced cooks will know immediately what I mean. Bad wine does break when used in cooking. Wine merchants might take the trouble to study and advise on the inexpensive but good wines for cooking. Cookery writers do not often state that you should use, for instance, a Burgundy or a rough Barbera or even, less specifically, a full-bodied red wine or a dry white wine.

[*Wine*—French: *vin;* German: *Wein;* Italian: *vino;* Spanish: *vino*]

WINEBERRY. *See* raspberry.

WINKLE or **periwinkle** (*Littorina littorea*) is a small, blackish brown or olive sea snail, rounded in shape and with a circular opening. It is found on rocky coasts around Britain and elsewhere in Europe. The true periwinkle is found at about low-tide mark, where it can be easily gathered in quantity. Unlike the much larger *whelks, winkles are herbivores. To prepare them, wash them well in several changes of water, then leave them in plenty of fresh water for 30 minutes before washing them again. This helps to get rid of the sand. Meanwhile, let some sea water stand to drop its sediment. Decant it into a pan and bring it to the boil. Alternatively use salted water, but sea water is traditional. Now, strain the winkles, shake them to make them withdraw into their shells, and drop them into the boiling water; boil them for 15 minutes. Extract them with a pin (they can be eaten hot or cold) and sprinkle them with malt vinegar. Winkles are not for gourmets but are, as the old books always say, the food of the poorer classes. So, once, were salmon, eels, and oysters. A visit to Southend with a pretty girl, a turn on the pier, and a feed of winkles sprinkled with vinegar (preferably with buttered brown bread), used to be something to remember. But a saucer of commercially shelled winkles full of sand and grit is not to be recommended.

[*Winkle*—French: *bigorneau;* German: *Uferschnecke;* Italian: *chiocciole;* Spanish: *bigaro*]

WITCH FLOUNDER, witch sole, Torbay sole, or **pole dab** (*Glyptocephalus cynoglossus*) is a small (12–20 in./30–50 cm) elongated *flatfish. When I was on a trawler, witches were the fish the cook picked out and flung, still flipping, into the frying pan to feed the crew, since they had less commercial value than the other fish in the trawls. However, they are well flavored. The witch, which resembles the winter *flounder, except for deep pits on the blind side of its head, occurs on both sides of the Atlantic. In Canada it is called plie grise or flet.

WONG BOK. *See* Chinese cabbage.

WOOD comes into contact with food as spoons, pestles, bowls, boards, planks, skewers, and assorted utensils and containers. It is always to some extent porous and will pick up flavors even if it is itself tasteless. Oils and fats, like bacon fat, will impregnate wood. It is best to keep wooden articles, par-

ticularly bowls and spoons, for certain specific purposes; otherwise wrong flavors can be introduced. It is possible for a bowl to make chocolate cream taste of bacon fat or garlic.

On picnics and when camping, be careful that sticks used as spits for meat or for stirring are not poisonous. People have died from using woods like oleander. Wood from oak, beech, hazel, blackthorn, cherry, and olive—from any tree with fruit you would eat—is safe.

Wood is a very good heat insulator. In the Himalayas, I always carried a wooden bowl for my cocoa. A deep wooden plate—the sort they make in Czechoslovakia with burned pattern is nice—makes a wonderful dish for the morning bacon. Wooden platters for steak are kind to knives and also help keep the steak warm.

Wooden molds and shapers for butter should be made of boxwood. The very best salad bowls are made from olive wood, which has the right taste and a beautiful pattern. Tubs and barrels are most usually of oak, which is good for sauerkraut and pickles. Birch is often used for culinary objects from Scandinavia. Utensils from tropical countries are likely to be made of unknown hardwoods and sometimes have a taste which—as with most woods—will disappear with usage. Most wooden spoons are made of beech, as are chopping boards, but hornbeam is favored for butchers' blocks.

[*Wood*—French: *bois;* German: *Holz;* Italian: *legno;* Spanish: *leña*]

WOODCHUCK or **groundhog** (*Marmota monax*). The preponderance of woodchuck bones found in midden heaps of old Indian villages testifies that woodchuck was probably the most important meat staple in the diet of the Indians who once controlled eastern North America. Today woodchucks, like raccoons, are mostly killed to prevent their ravaging gardens, but there are still many people who find them good eating. They are best when young and fattened for hibernation in the fall. In *Stalking the Wild Asparagus* (David McKay, 1962), Euell Gibbons suggests roasting wild animals such as woodchucks, opossums, and raccoons with a stuffing of wild plants: cooked and mashed wild Jerusalem artichokes, diced wild apples, hickory nuts, and maple syrup. He also recommends woodchuck boiled until tender, then chopped into a sauce of sour cream, mustard, and diced hard-boiled eggs. "There is always good hunting and good eating," Gibbons maintained, "for the true neoprimitive who has a strong stomach and weak prejudices."

WOODCOCK and **snipe** belong to the same family of waders. The woodcock (*Scolopax rusticola*), which is rather a fat, squat bird, is common in damp woods and on boggy ground, although it is not exactly a marsh bird like the snipe. It occurs at some time of the year over nearly all Europe, but moves southward in winter, being partially migrant. It is very widely distributed and occurs right through Asia to Japan. The woodcock of North America (*Scolopax minor*) is a close relative, but slightly smaller.

Woodcocks are usually hung only for a day or so before being plucked completely (including head and neck) very carefully, since the skin is tender. After that, the body is singed and the nails are cut off the claws, but the birds are not drawn in Europe, although they may be in the U.S. They are trussed by folding the legs up and tucking the head under one wing before these and the legs are tied close to the body. Another way is to twist the neck over the legs and hold them in place by pushing the beak into a leg like a skewer. Cooking should be short (7 minutes each side under the broiler is recommended). Woodcocks are served on a piece of toast to catch the trail, which comes out during cooking and is considered a great delicacy.

The snipe, of which there are many kinds (the common snipe is *Gallinago gallinago*), is a slightly smaller bird than the woodcock. Though delicious, it is inferior by compari-

son. Snipe are best when fat in winter. They are eaten fresh, not hung, and are sometimes skinned if they smell fishy; this removes the strong flavor, which the snipe can acquire from the marshes where they live. Young snipe are best and can be told by their feet (which are soft and tender), by their pointed flight feathers, and by the downy ones under the wings. Snipe roast in 15 minutes; the trail is left in them, but the gizzard is often removed before roasting.

[*Woodcock*—French: *bécasse;* German: *Waldschnepfe;* Italian: *beccacia;* Spanish: *becado. Snipe*—French: *bécassin;* German: *Bekassine;* Italian: *beccacino;* Spanish: *agachadiza*]

WOOD EAR. *See* mushrooms.

WOODRUFF or **sweet woodruff** (*Asperula odoratum*) is a woodland herb, with white flowers, which grows on chalky soil over most of Europe and in Britain. When crushed, the plant gives off an aromatic smell of new-mown hay (caused by a substance called coumarin) which is intensified when it is dried. Sweet woodruff is an essential ingredient in the German *Maitrank* (May drink), which is made by infusing the herb in Rhine wine, and it is used for similar purposes in other countries, including the U.S. (May-wine punch), where woodruff is a garden plant or ground cover.

[*Woodruff*—French: *glycérie;* German: *Waldmeister;* Italian: *asperula, stellina odorosa;* Spanish: *aspérula olorosa*]

WORCESTERBERRY. *See* gooseberry.

WORCESTERSHIRE SAUCE came into existence at the beginning of the reign of Queen Victoria, when a barrel of vinegar and spices made up for a customer according to an Indian recipe was left forgotten for some years in a chemist's cellar in Worcester. The shop's name was Lea & Perrins. During a subsequent spring cleaning, the mixture was about to be thrown out—when prudence suggested that it should first be tasted. Thus was born what is probably the world's best-known and most ubiquitous bottled sauce, one which has become a standard ingredient. It is used in many dishes ranging from soups and sauces to salad dressings, and small quantities are a "chef's secret" in many recipes. Worcestershire sauce is made by a maturation process; the exact formula is secret. Although it is much imitated, nobody seems to be able to get quite the taste of the original.

WORMSEED. *See* epazote.

WORMWOOD (*Artemisia absinthium*) is a relative of *tarragon that is a native of Britain and most of Europe. It was used in the past for medicinal purposes as well as to flavor herb and wines and apéritifs—its name comes from the same root as that of vermouth. In such drinks it is usually only one of a number of flavorings. The essential oil that can be extracted from wormwood is a narcotic poison, and readers of Emile Zola will know about the appalling results that came from the use of wormwood in absinthe.

The importation of absinthe and any other alcoholic beverages that contain an excess of wormwood is prohibited in the U.S.

[*Wormwood*—French: *absinthe, armoise amère, génépi;* German: *Absinth, Hilligbitter, Wermut, Wurmkraut;* Italian: *assenzio;* Spanish: *ajenjo*]

WORT is the sweet, watery solution which is fermented to make ale or beer. It can be made naturally from malt by mashing or produced with malt extracts and sugars. In commercial brewing, the wort may contain, among other additives, malt extract, partly caramelized or burnt malt, and substances to give a frothy head. (Some countries, such as Germany, have strict laws which forbid the use of additives in beer.) The solid residue from mashing in breweries is washed with a spray of water—a process called sparging—at 170°F (77°C), a temperature which destroys the enzymes but dissolves out any remaining sugars. The wort is in any case boiled to kill all the enzymes before fermentation.

For making beer, the wort is boiled with *hops to give it a bitter flavor. The stronger and heavier the beer is to be, the more bitterness it normally needs. As a rough guide, the following quantities have been recommended as giving an average taste. For 36 pt (20 lt) of wort:

Light beer	(3–4% alcohol)	2–3 oz (60–65 g) hops
Medium beer	(4–6% alcohol)	3–4 oz (85–170 g) hops
Strong beer	(6–8% alcohol)	4–6 oz (170–227 g) hops

For homemade worts, reduce the amount of hops if the sugar exceeds the malt extract; increase it if malt extract exceeds sugar. The hops should be boiled in the wort for 1–2 hours to extract the flavor. In home brewing, the acidity of the wort may be adjusted with citric acid or lemon juice.

[*Wort*—French: *moût;* German: *Bierwürze;* Italian: *mosto;* Spanish: *jugo de lupolo*]

WURST. German for *sausage.

Y

YAM and lesser-known tubers. Faced with a variety of yams, *cassava roots, *sweet potatoes, and other tubers in an unfamiliar tropical market, even moderately expert people are likely to become confused. The only solution is to try them. Further confusion is caused because almost any starchy root, from sweet potato to *yautia,* is likely to be called a yam. Strictly speaking, yams are only species of *Dioscorea,* but such a succinct definition has reached neither the market nor the kitchen. With few exceptions, yams in the widest sense are tropical or subtropical plants, some of which are exceedingly important staples, mainly in the poorer areas of the world. Some are grown, often as animal feed, in the southern parts of the U.S., while in Britain a whole range appears in shops patronized by Caribbean, Pakistani, or Indian immigrants. Virtually all these tubers are starchy, tasteless, and without personality, but anyone who is exploring particular areas of ethnic cooking may need them for authentic dishes. Other yams will be met with only on distant travels. Most are usually boiled and mashed, roasted, or fried. Never eat an unknown yam raw; some kinds are acrid, even poisonous, until cooked.

Tria yams belong to the genus *Dioscorea,* which has some 250 species, all climbing vines with large storage roots, mainly with one large tuber, although a few produce a number of small ones. Yams are mostly tropical and subtropical plants originating in the Old World—the cush-cush yam or yampee (*D. trifida*) is the only one from America.

Yams from Japan and northern China (*D. apposita* and *D. japonica*) have been tried in Europe and might have caught on if people had liked them. The yam *par excellence,* however, is tropical. The greater or Asiatic yam (*D. alata*), can grow to an enormous size, perhaps 90 lb (40 Kg), but that would be unusual. In any case, the smaller specimens are best to eat. This yam is grown in southern India, Southeast Asia, and the Caribbean. The white yam (*D. rotundata*) (*ratalu* in India) and the yellow yam (*D. cayenensis*) are also important, particularly in West Africa. There are very many others.

Elephant's foot or **suram** (*Amorphophallus campanulatus*) is a member of the anim family which is a native of India, where it is called *zamikand* and is very commonly grown. It is important because the tubers keep for a long time and so may be seen as an import in other countries. There are two types, one smooth-skinned, high-yielding, but very acrid (although this can be somewhat reduced by boiling) and the other much better to eat and free from acridity. The flesh is white or pale pink.

Dasheen, taro, eddo, colocasia, old cocoyam, elephant's ear, or *arvi* (*Colocasia* *antiquorum*) has been cultivated for so long and propagated vegetatively that it very rarely flowers. It is grown in damp places in the tropics and has leaves like those of the related arum lily but much larger. The leaves are much eaten in parts of India and are suitable for stuffing. Before they can be eaten, the corms (swollen underground stems) must be baked or boiled to destroy the acrid crystals of calcium oxalate which they may contain. From them is made the starchy paste called *poi,* a staple in the Pacific. To make this, the corms are boiled until they are soft and pounded in a mortar. Then water is added and the mass is allowed to ferment. Opinions of *poi* vary. It has been described as faintly acid and very palatable, but also as being like sour library paste. Dasheen and eddo are the Caribbean names; taro is the Pacific name. It is grown to some extent in the southern U.S.

Yautia, tannia, or **new cocoyam** (*Xanthosoma sagittifolium*), another member of the anim family, is much taller than dasheen and grows in slightly drier conditions, but is otherwise similar. It is commonly grown in the West Indies, especially in Puerto Rico, and in West Africa.

Yam beans are leguminous plants with swollen tuberous storage roots; the seeds and pods are also edible. The best-known yam bean, *Pachyrhizus tuberosus,* is native to tropical America but is also grown in West Africa, in India, where it is called *sankalu,* and in Malaysia as *bengkuang.* The plant is a strong creeper and is grown on ridges. The fully grown roots are tender and juicy, white and starchy. Only the young pods and seeds are cooked and eaten; they become poisonous as they grow older.

Oxalis tubers. *Oxalis* is a genus of some 500 species which includes wood sorrel (*O. acetosella*), of which the acid leaves may be eaten in moderation. The Bermuda buttercup or Cape sorrel (*O. pes-capres*), which carpets the orchards, orange groves, and almond fields around the Mediterranean in early spring, was brought in from South Africa at the end of the 18th century. As late as the beginning of this century, it was cultivated commercially on the Riviera, although the tubers, which are like very small, yellowish potatoes, are of no particular interest. Today the plant is a serious weed and its cultivation would be unthinkable.

Oka, occa or **oca** (*Oxalis tuberosa*) is a native of the South American Andes—Ecuador, Bolivia, and Peru. It is an important food tuber in South America with the typical shamrock-shaped leaf of the genus and whitish or brownish tubers. It grows quite well in the European climate and is said to have gone wild in parts of France. The tubers are acid when fresh, and in the Andes they are dried for several days in the sun before use to dissipate the acid. Although oka was introduced into England in 1829, it has never become popular. *Larousse Gastronomique* suggests parboiling and sautéing it in butter. Leaves and shoots can also be eaten in moderation, but like any *Oxalis* should be watched for oxalic acid.

Ysaño or **añu** (*Tropaeolum tuberosum*) is a South American tuber closely related to the nasturtium (*T. majus*). A perennial climber, it is widely grown as a decorative flower, but there are mixed opinions about the culinary value of its knobbly yellow tubers. In Bolivia, they are claimed to be a delicacy if they are frozen after boiling, but another view is that they are nasty.

Ulluco (*Ullucus tuberosus*) is another tuber from western South America. The plant is a half-hardy perennial which may be attractive to people who like uncommon vegetables. The small pink or yellow tubers are planted in the spring and lifted in the autumn after frost has killed the foliage.

PATRA (INDIA)

Pour boiling water over 4 oz (100 g) of tamarind, leave it to cool, and sieve the pulp from the seeds and fiber. Mix the pulp with 2 oz (50 g) of *gur* (brown sugar), 5 oz (150

g) of *besan flour, 1 teaspoon of powdered turmeric, 1 teaspoon of powdered coriander, 2 teaspoons of powdered chili (to taste), and 1 teaspoon of *garam masala. Add water to make a thick mixture of spreading consistency, and salt to taste. Cut out any thick stem and veins from 12 taro leaves (arvi), but otherwise keep them whole. Lay the first leaf glossy side down and spread a layer of the paste on the rough side. Put another leaf shiny side down on top and spread it. When you have a stack 6 leaves thick, interspersed with the besan spread, roll it like a jelly roll, and secure it with thread. Repeat with the remaining 6 leaves. Steam the rolls for 35–45 minutes (pierce them to see if they are tender), then remove the rolls, cover them with a cloth, and allow them to cool, but while they are still warm, cut them in slices ½ in. (1 cm) thick. Deep-fry the slices to a red-brown color and serve them garnished with 2 tablespoons of chopped green coriander leaves, 2 tablespoons of grated coconut, and wedges of lime or lemon. This is a well-known dish in Bombay—spicy, sweet-sour, and unusual.

CURRIED YAM (SURAM)

Peel 2 lb (1 Kg) of elephant's foot yam, cut it into cubes, and leave it to soak in salted water for 2 hours. Drain, dry, and fry it. In a separate pan, fry together 1 teaspoon each of coriander, cumin, and chili gently until they are brown (but not burned). Add the yam, give it a turn, and cool it with a dash of water. Add 1 oz (25 g) of tamarind pulp or yogurt when the yam is almost cooked. Sprinkle with chopped green coriander leaves before serving. Yam cubes may also be steamed, lightly browned in oil, then mixed with yogurt, chopped green chilies, and coriander leaves, seasoned with salt and a pinch of ground cumin seed, and served as a raïta with curry.

[Yam—French: igname; German: Jamwurzel; Italian: igname; Spanish: ñame]

YAM BEAN. See yam.

YARD-LONG BEAN. See cowpea.

YAUTIA. See yam (yautia).

YEAST. Men used yeast for thousands of years without knowing it was composed of a mass of living organisms. Yeasts are single-celled, microscopic fungi. They commonly multiply by budding off daughters—a few kinds simply split in two like bacteria—but they also go in for sexual acts occasionally, so can form hybrids. To resist adversity (such as drying or too much alcohol), they can form *spores for survival (not for multiplication). The atmosphere always has yeasts floating in it, and they are also introduced into the kitchen on fruit and vegetables. They drop into anything that is left uncovered.

Different species of yeast (and different strains within the same species) have individual characteristics. From a kitchen viewpoint, we can classify yeasts as wine yeasts, brewer's yeast, baker's yeast, wild yeasts, and others. Yeasts can multiply either with or without air, although air is usually excluded during fermentation (and is often excluded naturally by the carbon dioxide that is produced), because air would encourage the bacteria that turn alcohol into acetic acid. It is worth noting that because fermentation is caused by enzymes made by the yeasts, the process can go on even when the yeasts are dead, though treatment that kills yeast is likely also to destroy the enzymes. More heat than you can stand with your hand (about 120°F or 50°C) will quickly kill yeasts, even the spores, but they can stand being frozen, which is why yeast and bread dough can be kept for some time in the freezer. On the other hand, they need warmth to multiply—77°F (25°C) is about right—and they prefer an acid medium of pH 3.0–6.0; pH 5.3 is right for beermaking. Yeasts vary in their tolerance to alcohol (which they make themselves). It is no chance that man prizes yeasts that will thrive in a goodly amount of alcohol and calls the rest—the species which cannot hold their liquor—wild yeasts. Yeasts are inhibited by carbon dioxide gas under high pressure, a fact that is useful in the bulk storage of fruit juice in an unfermented state before filtration and bottling.

Baker's yeast (*Saccharomyces cerevisiae*) can be bought fresh, as a compressed, tan, claylike substance, or as dried active yeast granules. Fresh yeast is not a pure culture, but contains fully active vegetative cells which will start to multiply immediately when mixed with warm sugary water at about 100°F (37°C). It will store well in the refrigerator for 10–14 days. If frozen, it must be used as soon as it has defrosted, so it is most practical to package it for the freezer in ½-1-oz (15–30-g) lumps. Three-fourths oz (20 g) of yeast per 2¼ lb (1 Kg) of flour is sufficient for most bread, although for fast, light results, more can be used.

Active dry yeast has a considerable shelf life even at ordinary room temperature but, being in an inactive state, takes a little longer to get going. This yeast should be softened in warm water or milk at about 110°F (43°C), but if it proves stubborn about behaving as its packet says it should, add a bit of glucose or honey and a squeeze of lemon to the liquid. For baking, fresh yeast is replaced by half its weight of dried yeast.

Yeast cultures can be kept alive indefinitely by feeding them with sugar and starting up new bottles weekly with a bit of the old culture, as was once generally done and still is in out-of-the-way places. Such are the "hops" used by Australian drovers, and these yeast stocks usually produce *sourdough bread.

For some reason, many people fight shy of using yeast, but it is easy to handle. The usual reason for failure is getting the dough too hot and so killing the yeast, or keeping it too cold, in which case the yeast hardly has a chance to function. Keep the dough nicely warm, like a baby, and the yeast should work. One touch of perversity is that yeast, like people, may become sluggish in very hot weather. If bread is heavier than usual during a heat wave, add marginally more yeast than the recipe demands. And to test whether a yeast dough has finished its first rising, make a dent in the top of the dough with a fingertip. If the dent puffs back up, it should be left to rise further, until it does not spring back to the touch. Then it is ready to be punched down.

Brewer's yeast. There are two categories of brewer's yeast. One works mainly on the surface of the vat and is used for making most types of British beer; the other works more slowly and coolly on the bottom of the vat and is used to make lager and American beer. Serious home brewers must try to get the right type of yeast for the type of beer they wish to brew. Certainly never substitute ordinary baker's yeast if you can help it; the flavor will be very inferior.

Wine yeast (*Saccharomyces ellipsoideus*). Until fairly recently, winemakers relied on the yeasts that occurred naturally on their vines; strains of yeast were associated with different types of wine. Today with more scientific control, there is a tendency to introduce pure cultures of the strains required. Wine yeasts influence the taste of the wine (although a champagne yeast used on sugar and water will not make champagne). It is possible to buy suitable strains of yeast for various styles of wine from shops catering to home wine enthusiasts—you can even buy sherry yeasts which give the correct skin or *flor* on the surface of the vat. It is also possible to increase the alcoholic strength of the drink, since one of the important differences between wine yeasts and other types is their ability to tolerate alcohol. Under special laboratory conditions, they have produced a concentration of up to 20%, but 16% is more natural and 12–14% is the norm. Wine yeasts come in powdered, granulated, or tablet form, as well as in liquid yeast cultures.

Wild yeast (*Saccharomyces spiculatus*) and yeasts of the genera *Torula* and *Pichia*. The wild yeasts are a nuisance to winemakers because they create bad flavors. They are usually first off the mark with a vigorous fermentation, but luckily are sensitive to alcohol and stop multiplying when its concentration reaches 4%. They are much more sensitive to sulfur dioxide (*see* preservatives) than wine yeasts are, so even though the number of wild yeast cells on one grape is often around 10,000,000, as compared with 100,000 of the wine yeasts, they are easy to control—100 parts of sulfur dioxide per million is adequate. But this treatment of wine is frowned upon—there are legal limits in most countries. France allows up to 450 parts per million, but as little as 300 parts per million can be detected by taste in white wine. Another method of controlling wild yeasts is by alcohol. If the alcohol content of the must is brought up above the 4% mark by adding wine, then the wild yeasts will stop growing. Among other wild yeasts, some of the *Pichia* species are commonly seen growing on the surface of pickles, where they form a white skin or *flor* (as sherry yeasts form a *flor* on sherry). Though it is harmless, such a skin should be removed, because after a time it will create off-flavors in the pickles.

Yeasts in milk. There are usually yeasts in milk, and they are sometimes responsible for creating unpleasant yeasty tastes in cottage cheese and yogurt. They play a minor role in the microbiology of certain cheeses and are involved in the making of some sourmilk products. An example is a yeast called *Saccharomyces taete*, which is necessary in making Swedish *rångmjölk* or *täte*, a sourmilk product containing up to 0.5% alcohol. The correct souring of the milk depends on a bacterium called *Streptococcus lactis* which works in conjunction with the yeast, for the yeast will ferment milk sugar to alcohol only in the presence of lactic acid bacteria. Such symbiotic behavior makes it far from simple to understand what goes on in foods made by the action of microorganisms.

Health-food yeasts. During World War II, many inmates of prison camps managed to stay alive by growing yeast, which is very rich in protein, phosphorus, potassium, and some of the B vitamins. Health-food yeast is usually dried and dead (which it should be). It may be brewer's yeast or Torula yeast, which is even higher in nutrient value and more tolerable. Some yeasts are debittered to make them more palatable. It is usually recommended that yeast be taken in orange juice in the hope that this will mask the taste. Yeast tablets are fairly useless, since you can rarely take enough for them to be effective.

Yeast nutrient. Yeasts require small amounts of nitrogenous material and minerals for proper growth, so in some circumstances it is recommended to add a yeast nutrient to the culture. Yeast nutrient may be bought or it can be made up as follows:

Citric acid	130 g (57%)
Ammonium sulfate	60 g (28.3%)
Potassium phosphate	30 g (13.2%)
Magnesium sulfate	8 g (3.5%)

Use this at the rate of ¼–½ oz per gallon (3 g per liter).

[*Yeast:* French: *levure;* German: *Hefe, Bärme;* Italian: *lievito;* Spanish: *levadura*]

YEAST EXTRACT has been made since the turn of the century. It is not an extract in the usual sense of the word because it is not extracted from yeast itself but from what is formed after the proteins in the yeast cells have been broken down. The breaking down can be done either by chemical treatment or biologically by autolysis, in effect self-digestion by the yeast's own enzymes.

The simplest way of breaking down the yeast is by hydrolysis, which is brought about by warming it with dilute hydrochloric acid. A 1–5% solution is used at a temperature of 86–212°F (30–100°C) for anything from 30 minutes to 2 hours—various manufacturers use different combinations of time, temperature, and acid concentration. When hydrolysis of the proteins to amino acids is complete, the hydrochloric acid is neutralized with caustic soda to form common salt, but the mixture is left slightly acid because a slight sourness helps to mask the bitter taste of yeast. Careful filtration helps to take out even more of the yeasty bitterness. The clear liquid is concentrated by boiling it at 140°F (60°C) under reduced pressure until the extract will set to a paste on cooling. Flavorings such as celery are frequently included to make the result more palatable. A more modern chemical treatment, which modifies the proteins less, is to digest yeast with ammonia under pressure for some 7 hours. The ammonia is then allowed to evaporate.

The autolytic process is more complex and may involve adding sugar, blood, starch, gum arabic, phosphates, and other substances. These processes are usually trade secrets.

Yeast extracts contain useful amounts of vitamins B_1 and B_2, and a number of amino acids, plus choline and other essential food substances that are found in yeast, but they are not a complete protein food.

YERBA. *See* maté.

YOGURT. This sour-milk product has been introduced to almost the entire world in the last three decades. It may have originated in Central Asia but is now traditional over a large area of Asia and southeastern Europe, although for historical reasons Americans and Britons usually associate it with Bulgaria. Even the characteristic bacterium is called *Lactobacillus bulgaricus*. At the turn of this century, Elya Metchnikoff (1845–1916), the famous Russian microbiologist, proclaimed yogurt to be almost the elixir of life. His theory was based partly on the longevity of tough, yogurt-eating Bulgarians and partly on the scientific fact that the lactic acid in sour milk discourages putrefactive bacteria. Metchnikoff lived at a time when poisons from the putrefying contents of the human intestine were blamed for ill health, a process of auto-intoxication. As a result, Victorians helped nature with frequent and massive doses of castor oil and cascara, not to mention an occasional enema. As a result, survivors still suffer from constipation.

The yogurt bacterium does not survive in the human bowels (although that of acidophilus milk does better), and auto-intoxication seems to have been overrated as a source of illness. What is sure is that yogurt is much more rapidly and easily digested than raw milk, and its mild acidity falls kindly on the stomach. In an hour, only 32% of raw milk is ingested as against 91% of yogurt, and the lactic acid content helps in the assimilation of calcium phosphorus.

Yogurt is correctly made from whole sheep's, goat's or cow's milk, sometimes even from thin cream, but not, even in part, from reconstituted dried milk. It is a modern trick to add skim-milk powder to give more body to the yogurt. But then, the yogurt of the supermarket does not have much likeness to the good yogurt you can eat in Turkey. This is thick (it can be cut with a spoon) and never runny; it should be smooth, not grainy and with whey running out. It is even called "sweet," although by its very nature it must contain some lactic acid. It should certainly never be sour and bitter, although sour "old" yogurt is called for in some Indian recipes.

Making Yogurt
1. Apparatus. There are gadgets on the market, ranging from metal boxes lined with heat insulator and containing a set of pots (including a little one for the starter) to electric yogurt makers in which temperature is maintained by a heating coil and thermostat. All that is traditionally necessary is a pot or bowl, which should hold 1¾–3½ pt (1–2 lt) of milk, a plate (or a sheet of plastic wrap) big enough to cover it, and some wrapping to keep it warm. The wrapping may be a tin lined with cushions or (as I use myself) a styrofoam picnic chest. Wrapping in newspaper and then a blanket is a good makeshift. A vacuum flask is not recommended unless the yogurt is to be turned out into a cloth after it has clabbered.

2. The starter. It is not necessary to buy a starter. A little taken from any pot of plain yogurt will do as a starter, provided it contains live bacteria. Very little is needed—1 teaspoon of starter per 1¾ pt (1 lt) of milk— and too much starter makes sour yogurt. The starter should contain *Lactobacillus bulgaricus* and *Streptococcus thermophilus,* which both grow well at 104–113°F (40–45°C). This is more than the "lukewarm" that is usually recommended. The temperature should be measured with a thermometer (after stirring the milk to get the heat even). The classic, though much less reliable, way is to dip in the knuckle of your little finger. When you can dip it in and count to 10 slowly with some discomfort but without snatching it out with a scream, the temperature will be roughly right for yogurt.

3. The milk. Sheep's milk and goat's milk are normally used in the Middle East, which has comparatively few cows. The milk should be brought nearly to the boil before use or alternatively may be boiled for a while to concentrate it by reduction to a creamier state.

4. Method. Pour the boiling milk into the bowl or pot (which should first be scalded with boiling water). Leave it to cool until it reaches 113°F (45°C). Mix a tablespoonful or so smoothly with the starter, then pour it back into the milk and give a stir to distribute it evenly. Cover it with a plate and completely surround the pot with the insulation. Take a look after 5 hours and quickly wrap it up again if the milk has not clotted. Overnight is usually too long. When it has clotted, take it out of the wraps and put it in a cool place or, when it has cooled to room temperature, in the bottom of the refrigerator.

5. Thickening. If the yogurt is not thick enough, put it gently into a square of double cheesecloth and hang it up to drip until it is as you want it. (Long draining makes yogurt cheese or *labneh,* which is eaten with olive oil, Arab bread, and black olives.) An alternative is carefully to make a well in the surface with a ladle; after some time, the well fills with watery whey, which can be spooned out. If necessary, you can repeat the process until the yogurt is thick but it will still be almost undisturbed in the pot.

6. Troubles. There are three main reasons for failure. The first is failing to keep the pot warm enough. This happens if the insulation is insufficient or if you are trying to make yogurt in too small a quantity. Try better insulation or a hot-water bottle. The next is using a dud yogurt as a starter; it must contain living bacteria. Alternatively, you may have been killing the bacteria by putting them into milk that was too hot. Finally, you cannot use milk that contains antibiotics (which have been used to treat sick cows) or preservatives. Such things prevent the organisms from growing.

7. Cooking. Yogurt is much used in the cooking of the region from the Balkans to India. Yogurt made from goat's milk can be boiled (carefully) without its "breaking," but cow's-milk yogurt needs something to stabilize it. Add a teaspoon of cornstarch and the white of an egg to every 1¾ pt (1 lt) of yogurt. Boil it warily, and stir it smoothly in one direction. A teaspoon of salt per 1¾ pt (1 lt) is normally added as well.

DOOGH (IRAN)

This is one of the best refreshing drinks for hot weather. Beat 6 cups of yogurt with about 10 cups of water and salt it very well (you need salt to replace what you have lost in sweating)—about a heaping tablespoon is normal for this quantity, although it is added to taste. Chill thoroughly. I prefer to chill the yogurt and to dilute it with soda water. Bottled carbonated *doogh* can be bought in Iran. Lebanese *ayran* or *'ayraan* and Indian *lassi* are similar.

CURD CURRY (INDIA)

This is delicious served as a soup, with rice if you like. Mix 4 cups of yogurt with up to 8 cups of water (depending on how thick you like it) and beat in 1–2 tablespoons *besan flour. Chop and add a 1-in. (2½-cm) piece of fresh ginger and 4 green chilies (powdered ginger and chili powder can be used, but the taste is different). Put a tablespoonful of oil in a ladle, heat it, and add 6 cloves, 2 sticks of cinnamon about 2 in. (5 cm) long, about 10 curry leaves, ½ teaspoon of asafetida, and a teaspoon of black mustard seed. When the mustard seeds begin to splutter, immediately quench the whole ladle of goodies in the yogurt mixture, which is then put on the heat. Add 1 teaspoon *gur* or dark-brown sugar and salt to taste. Cook, stirring to begin with, until the soup is well thickened and the flavor has developed. Strain and serve garnished with chopped green coriander leaves if these are available. This is one of my favorite foods in hot weather. I use less water and the double quantity of *besan*, with a little powdered turmeric, which slightly alters the taste and gives color. Diced cucumber or okra can also be cooked in the soup.

AB DOOGH KHIAR (IRAN)

Finely chop 2 small cucumbers, 3 spring onions, and an herb mixture (say, 2 sprigs each of mint, basil, and savory). Also chop ½ cup of raisins and ¼ cup of walnuts. Mix with 4 cups of thick yogurt, season with salt, and chill in the refrigerator. This dish is correctly served as a kind of salad, but makes a healthful lunch in summer.

[*Yogurt*—French: *yaourt, yogourt;* German: *Joghurt;* Italian: *yog(h)urt;* Spanish: *yogur*]

YOUNGBERRY. *See* blackberry.

YSAÑO. *See* yam (*ysaño*).

YUCA. *See* cassava.

YUCCA. *See* beargrass.

Z

ZAMIKAND. *See* yam (elephant's foot).

ZAMPONE. A North Italian sausage for boiling. For this famous specialty, originally from around Modena, a boned pig's foot—correctly a forefoot—is stuffed with minced pork including some of the soft skin from the head and snout (as in *cotechino), which gives it the splendidly soft, gelatinous texture that it has when cooked. Zampone is flavored with salt, pepper, and garlic, but there are fancy varieties such as *zampone al cedro* (which contains candied citron peel and sweet white wine). In Emilia, pieces of pig skin are cut into convenient shapes—squares, ovals, rounds—and stuffed with the zampone mixture. They have names like *bombonetti, cappelletti, monchi,* and *vesici-chette. Zampone* needs to be simmered for about 2 hours (some soak it first) and is served, cut in thick slices like *cotechino,* with lentils or as part of a *bollito misto* with a piquant sauce such as *salsa verde. Zampone* is food for cold weather.

ZAPOTE. *See* sapodilla.

ZEDOARY. A spice, the dried rhizome of a plant (*Curcuma zedoaria*) related to turmeric and ginger, which is native to Southeast Asia. The taste is something like musty camphor, and it is used in Malay and Indonesian cooking. Zedoary can be obtained in dried bits in some shops that specialize in exotic ingredients. It is usually sold under its Dutch name, *kentjoer.*

[*Zedoary*—French: *zedoaire;* German: *Zitwerwurzel;* Italian: *zedoaria;* Spanish: *cedoaria*]

ZEST. Originally the outer tough skin of the walnut, but now used to denote the outer skin of citrus fruits, especially of lemon and orange, which contains the essential flavoring oils.

[*Zest*—French: *zeste;* German: *Stückchen; Zitronenschale;* Italian: *scarzetta;* Spanish: *luquete*]

ZIGEUNER SPECK. *See* bacon.

ZINC (Zn). An essential trace metal. It is thought that 10 mg a day is the usual human requirement. Rich sources are oysters (270–600 parts per million) and herrings (700–1200). Wheat germ and wheat bran are also rich in zinc, but it may not be absorbed efficiently from vegetable sources. Other sources are peanuts, liver, beef, mutton, cheese, cocoa, eggs, and pulses. Although zinc deficiency is not common, it occurs in some communities. Zinc is lost in sweat, which is one reason why deficiency is more likely to occur in hot countries. In quantity, zinc salts are emetic. Metallic zinc is used as coating for iron to stop rusting. This is known as galvanizing. Because zinc is very easily dissolved by acids, it is important not to put acid substances in galvanized boilers and buckets. Brass can be an alloy of zinc and copper.

[*Zinc*—French: *zinc;* German: *Zink;* Italian: *zinco;* Spanish: *zinc, cinc*]

ZITI. *See* pasta.

ZUCCHINI. *See* squash.